ADMIRALTY
AND
MARITIME LAW

VOLUME 2, SECOND EDITION

ADMIRALTY
AND
MARITIME LAW

Robert Force
Martin Davies

Volume 2, Second Edition

Beard Books
Washington, D.C.

CONTENTS

CHAPTER 1 — ADMIRALTY JURISDICTION AND PROCEDURE

A. Introduction

1. The Constitution of the United States

Article I

Section 1. All legislative Powers herein granted shall be vested in a Congress of the United States....

* * *

Section 8. The Congress shall have the Power ...
To regulate Commerce with foreign Nations, and among the several States, and with the Indian Tribes;

* * *

To constitute Tribunals inferior to the Supreme Court;
To define and punish Piracies and Felonies committed on the high Seas, and Offenses against the Law of Nations;
To declare War, grant Letters of Marque and Reprisal, and make Rules concerning Captures on Land and Water;

* * *

To make all Laws which shall be necessary and proper for carrying into Execution the foregoing Powers, and all other Powers vested by this Constitution in the Government of the Untied States, or in any Department or Officer thereof.

* * *

Article III

Section 1. The judicial Power of the United States, shall be vested in one supreme Court, and in such inferior Courts as the Congress may from time to time ordain and establish.*
Section 2. The judicial Power shall extend to ... all Cases of admiralty and maritime Jurisdiction.

---

* In *Oregon R. & Nav. Co. v. Balfour,* 179 U.S. 55, 21 S.Ct. 28, 45 L. Ed. 82 (1900), Mr. Chief Justice Fuller stated:

By the 2d section of article 3 of the Constitution, the judicial power extends "to all cases of admiralty and maritime jurisdiction," the word "maritime" having been added, out of abundant caution, to preclude a narrow interpretation of the word "admiralty."

Note: Implementation of Article III

The admiralty law of the United States has grown out of the statement in Article III, Section 2 of the Constitution. Article III, however, is not self-executing. It does not establish an admiralty judicial system; it just confers the judicial power. Congress had to implement Article III, which it did in the Judiciary Act of 1789, *infra*. The Supreme Court has interpreted this constitutional provision to contain three separate grants of power:

1) it empowered Congress to confer admiralty and maritime jurisdiction on the "Tribunals inferior to the Supreme Court" which were authorized by Art. I., Sect. 8, Cl. 9;

2) it empowered the federal courts in their exercise of admiralty and maritime jurisdiction which had been conferred to them, to draw on the substantive law "inherent in the admiralty and maritime jurisdiction and to continue the development of this law within constitutional limits; and

3) it empowered Congress to revise and supplement the maritime law within the limits of the Constitution.

---

2. The Judiciary Act of 1789

Chapter XX. An Act to Establish the Judicial Courts of the United States

1st Cong., 1st Sess., Sept. 24, 1789

1 Stat. 76

§ 9.   ... [T]he district courts shall have, exclusively of the courts of the several States, cognizance of all crimes and offenses that shall be cognizable under the authority of the United States, committed within their respective districts, or upon the high seas; ... and shall also have exclusive original cognizance of all civil causes of admiralty and Maritime jurisdiction, including all seizures under laws of impost, navigation or trade of the United States, where the seizures are made, on waters which are navigable from the sea by vessels of ten or more tons burthen, within their respective districts as well as upon the high seas; saving to suitors, in all cases, the right of a common law remedy, where the common law is competent to give it; and shall also have exclusive original cognizance of all seizures on land, or other waters than as aforesaid, made, and of all suits for penalties and forfeitures incurred, under the laws of the United States.... And the trial of issues in fact, in the district courts, in all causes except civil cases of admiralty and maritime jurisdiction, shall be by jury.

---

3. U.S.C. Title 28: Judiciary and Judicial Procedure

§ 1333. Admiralty, Maritime and Prize Cases

The district courts shall have original jurisdiction, exclusive of the courts of the States, of:

(1)   Any civil case of admiralty or maritime jurisdiction, saving to suitors in all cases all other remedies to which they are otherwise entitled.

(2)   Any prize brought into the United States and all proceedings for the condemnation of property taken as prize.

B. Navigable Waters: Evolution of the Requirement

1. The Basic Standard

Note: The Common Law Tradition

There are no comprehensive statutory criteria which can be used for determining when a case is within the admiralty and maritime jurisdiction of the federal courts, although there are some statutes such as the Admiralty Extension Act and the Death on the High Seas Act (DOHSA), which confer admiralty jurisdiction in specified circumstances. Unlike some countries, the United States does not have a comprehensive maritime code. There are numerous statutes that contain the substantive maritime law to be applied to certain transactions and events such as the Carriage of Goods by Sea Act (COGSA). However, these statutes are limited in scope. Therefore, much of the maritime law of the United States has been made by the courts in the tradition of the common law. This has occurred not only in regard to substantive rules but also with respect to the rules for determining jurisdiction. While, in 28 U.S.C. § 1333, Congress has declared in general terms that the federal courts may exercise jurisdiction in "admiralty" and "maritime" cases, it has, for the most part, been left to the courts to define the scope and meaning of those terms. In other words, the courts have had to formulate their own criteria for determining when a case comes within their admiralty and maritime jurisdiction.

The English courts give a rather narrow scope to their "admiralty" jurisdiction. The federal courts of the United States have, after a somewhat restrained beginning, interpreted the scope of admiralty and maritime jurisdiction in a much broader vein. In several cases decided in the mid-nineteenth century, the United States Supreme Court rejected the "tidal waters" and "within the county" rules which were applied in England and began to equate the scope of admiralty jurisdiction with "navigable waters."

It is also important to note that the early decisions on the scope of admiralty jurisdiction often bound up with a consideration of the scope of another constitutional provision: the power of Congress to regulate commerce under Article I, section 8 of the United States Constitution. The exercise of admiralty jurisdiction by federal courts was seen as going hand-in-hand with efforts by Congress to make the United States a national economic unit and to break down the barriers of State parochialism and protectionism. Water transportation was the major mode of interstate and foreign commerce, and played a crucial part in opening up and linking together the western territories and the Atlantic seaboard states.

JACKSON *et al* v. STEAMBOAT MAGNOLIA

61 U.S. (20 How.) 296, 15 L. Ed. 909 (1857)

Mr. Justice GRIER delivered the opinion of the court

The only question presented for our consideration on this appeal is, whether the court below had jurisdiction.

The libel purports to be in a cause of collision, civil and maritime. It alleges that the steamboat Wetumpka, a vessel of three hundred tons burden, was on a voyage from New Orleans to the city of Montgomery, in Alabama; that while ascending the Alabama river, she was run into and sunk by the steamboat Magnolia, which was descending the same.

The answer of the respondents, among other things, alleges "that the collision took place far above tide-water, on the Alabama river, in the county of Wilcox, in the State of Alabama, and therefore not within the jurisdiction of the District Court sitting in admiralty."

This plea was sustained by the court, and the libel dismissed. The record does not disclose the reasons on which this judgment was based. It is presumed, therefore, to be founded on the facts stated in the plea, viz:

1. That the collision was within the body of a county.
2. That it was above tide-water.

1. The Alabama river flows through the State of Alabama. It is a great public river, navigable from the sea for many miles above the ebb and flow of the tide. Vessels licensed for the coasting trade, and those engaged in foreign commerce, pass on its waters to ports of entry within the State. It is not, like the Mississippi, a boundary between coterminous States. Neither is it, like the Penobscot, (*see Veazie v. Moore*, 14 How., 568,) made subservient to the internal trade of the State by artificial means and dams constructed at its mouth, rendering it inaccessible to sea-going vessels. It differs from the Hudson, which rises in and passes through the State of New York, in the fact that it is navigable for ships and vessels of the largest class far above where its waters are affected by the tide.

Before the adoption of the present Constitution, each State, in the exercise of its sovereign power, had its own court of admiralty, having jurisdiction over the harbors, creeks, inlets, and public navigable waters, connected with the sea. This jurisdiction was exercised not only over rivers, creeks, and inlets, which were boundaries to or passed through other States, but also where they were wholly within the State. Such a distinction was unknown, nor (as it appears from the decision of this court in the case of *Waring v. Clark*, 5 How., 441) had these courts been driven from the exercise of jurisdiction over torts committed on navigable water within the body of a county, by the jealousy of the common-law courts.

When, therefore, the exercise, of admiralty and maritime jurisdiction over its public rivers, ports, and havens, was surrendered by each State to the Government of the United States, without an exception as to subjects or places, this court cannot interpolate one into the Constitution, or introduce an arbitrary distinction which has no foundation in reason or precedent.

The objection to jurisdiction stated in the plea, "that the collision was within the county of Wilcox, in the State of Alabama," can therefore have no greater force or effect from the fact alleged in the argument, that the Alabama river, so far as it is navigable, is wholly within the boundary of the State. It amounts only to a renewal of the old contest between courts of common law and courts of admiralty, as to their jurisdiction within the body of a county. This question has been finally adjudicated in this court, and the argument exhausted, in the case of *Waring v. Clark*. After an experience of ten years, we have not been called on by the bar to review its principles as founded in error, nor have we heard of any complaints by the people of wrongs suffered on account of its supposed infringement of the right of trial by jury. So far, therefore, as the solution of the question now before us is affected by the fact that the tort was committed within the body of a county, it must be considered as finally settled by the decision in that case.

2. The second ground of objection to the jurisdiction of the court is founded on the fact, that though the collision complained of occurred in a great navigable river, it was on a part of that river not affected by the flux and reflux of the tide, but "far above it."

This objection, also, is one which has heretofore been considered and decided by this court, after full argument and much deliberation. In the case of the *Genesee Chief* (12 How., 444,) we have decided, that though in England the flux and reflux of the tide was a sound and reasonable test of a navigable river, because on that island tide-water and navigable water were synonymous terms, yet that "there is certainly nothing in the ebb and flow of the tide that makes the waters peculiarly suitable for admiralty jurisdiction, nor anything in the absence of a tide that renders it unfit. If it is a public navigable water on which commerce is carried on between different States or nations, the reason for the jurisdiction is precisely the same. And if a distinction is made on that account, it is merely arbitrary, without any foundation in reason—and, indeed, contrary to it." The case of the *Thomas Jefferson* (10 Wheaton) and others, which had hastily adopted this arbitrary and (in this country) false test of navigable waters, were necessarily overruled.

Since the decision of these cases, the several district courts have taken jurisdiction of cases of collision on the great public navigable rivers. Some of these cases have been brought to this court by appeal, and in no instance has any objection been taken, either by the counsel or the court, to the jurisdiction, because the collision was within the body of a county, or above the tide. (*See Fritz v. Bull*, 12 How., 466; *Walsh v. Rogers*, 13 How., 283; *The Steamboat New World*, 16 How., 469; *Ure v. Kauffman*, 19 How., 56; *New York and Virginia S.B. Co. v. Calderwood*, 19 How., 245.)

In our opinion, therefore, neither of the facts alleged in the answer, nor both of them taken together, will constitute a sufficient exception to the jurisdiction of the District Court.

It is due however, to the learned counsel who has presented the argument for respondent in this case, to say, that he has not attempted to impugn the decision of this court in the case of *Waring v. Clark*, nor to question the sufficiency of the reasons given in the case of the *Genesee Chief* for overruling the case of the *Thomas Jefferson*; but he contends that the case of the *Genesee Chief* decided that the act of Congress of 1845, "extending the jurisdiction of the District Court to certain cases upon the lakes," &c., was not only constitutional, but also that it conferred a new jurisdiction, which the court did not possess before; and consequently, as that act was confined to the lakes, and "to vessels of twenty or more tons burden, licensed and employed in the business of commerce and navigation between ports and places in different States and Territories," it cannot authorize the District Courts in assuming jurisdiction over waters and subjects not included in the act, and more especially where the navigable portion of the river is wholly within the boundary of a single State. It is contended also that the case of *Fritz v. Bull*, and those which follow it, sustaining the jurisdiction of the court of admiralty over torts on the Mississippi river, cannot be reconciled with the points decided in the former case, as just stated, unless on the hypothesis that the act of 1845 be construed to include the Mississippi and other great rivers of the West; which it manifestly does not.

But it never has been asserted by this court, either in the case of *Fritz v. Bull*, or in any other case, that the admiralty jurisdiction exercised over the great navigable rivers of the West was claimed under the act of 1845, or by virtue of anything therein contained.

The Constitution, in defining the powers of the courts of the United States, extends them to "all cases of admiralty and maritime jurisdiction." It defines how much of the judicial power shall be exercised by the Supreme Court only; and it was left to Congress to ordain and establish other courts, and to fix the boundary and extent of their respective jurisdictions. Congress might give any of these courts the whole or so much of the admiralty jurisdiction as it saw fit. It might extend their jurisdiction over all navigable waters, and all ships and vessels thereon, or over some navigable waters, and vessels of a certain description only. Consequently, as Congress had never before 1845 conferred admiralty jurisdiction over the Northern fresh-water lakes *not* "navigable from the sea," the District Courts could not assume it by virtue of this clause in the Constitution. An act of Congress was therefore necessary to confer this jurisdiction on those waters, and was completely within the constitutional powers of Congress; unless, by some unbending law of nature, fresh-water lakes and rivers are necessarily within the category of those that are not "navigable," and which, consequently, could not be subjected to "admiralty jurisdiction," any more than canals or railroads.

When these States were colonies, and for a long time after the adoption of the Constitution of the United States, the shores of the great lakes of the North, above and beyond the ocean tides, were as yet almost uninhabited, except by savages. The necessities of commerce and the progress of steam navigation had not as yet called for the exercise of admiralty jurisdiction, except on the ocean border of the Atlantic States.

The judiciary act of 1789, in defining the several powers of the courts established by it, gives to the District Courts of the United States "exclusive original cognizance of all civil cases of admiralty and maritime jurisdiction, including all seizures. &c., when they are made on waters which are *navigable from the sea* by vessels of ten or more tons burden, *Sec.,* as well as upon the high seas."

So long as the commerce of the country was centered chiefly on the Eastern Atlantic ports, where the fresh-water rivers were seldom navigable above tide-water, no inconvenience arose from the adoption of the English insular test of "navigable waters." Hence it was followed by the courts without objection or inquiry.

But this act does not confine admiralty jurisdiction to tide-waters; and if the flux and reflux of the tide be abandoned, as an arbitrary and false test of a "navigable river," it required no further legislation of Congress to extend it to the Mississippi, Alabama, and other great rivers, "navigable from the sea." If the waters over which this jurisdiction is claimed by within this category, the act makes no distinction between them. It is not confined to rivers or waters which bound coterminous States, such as the Mississippi and Ohio, or to rivers passing through more than one State; nor does the act distinguish between them and rivers which rise in and pass through one State only, and are consequently "*infra corpus comitatus.*" The admiralty jurisdiction surrendered by the States to the Union had no such bounds as exercised by themselves, and is clogged with no such conditions in its surrender. The interpolation of such conditions by the courts would exclude many of the ports, harbors, creeks, and inlets, most frequented by ships and commerce, but which are wholly included within the boundaries of a State or the body of a county.

It seems to have been assumed, in the argument of this case, that because the District Courts had not exercised their admiralty jurisdiction above tide-water before the decision of this court of the case of the *Genesee Chief,* that such jurisdiction had been exercised by them as conferred by the act of 1845. It is upon this mistaken hypothesis that any difficulty is found in reconciling that case with the case of *Fritz v. Bull,* which immediately followed it.

The act of 1845 was the occasion and created the necessity for this court to review their former decisions.

It might be considered in fact as a declaratory act reversing the decision in the case of the Thomas Jefferson. We could no longer evade the question by a judicial notice of an occult tide without ebb or flow, as in the case of *Peyroux v. Howard,* (7 Pet., 343.) The court were placed in the position, that they must either declare the act of Congress void, and shock the common sense of the people by declaring the lakes not to be "navigable waters," or overrule previous decisions which had established an arbitrary distinction, which, when applied to our continent, had no foundation in reason.

In conclusion, we repeat what we then said, that "courts of admiralty have been found necessary in all commercial countries, not only for the safety and convenience of commerce, and a speedy decision of controversies where delay would be ruin, but also to administer the laws of nations in a season of war, and to determine the validity of captures and questions of prize or no prize in a judicial proceeding. And it would be contrary to the first principles on which this Union was formed, to confine these rights to the States bordering on the Atlantic, and to the tidewater rivers connected with it, and to deny them to the citizens who border on the lakes, and the great navigable streams of the Western States. Certainly, such was not the intent of the framers of the Constitution; and if such be the construction finally given to it by this court, it must necessarily produce great public inconvenience, and at the same time fail to accomplish one of the great objects of the framers of the Constitution; that is, perfect equality in the rights and privileges of the citizens of the different States, not only in the laws of the General Government, but in the mode of administering them."

The decree of the court below, dismissing the libel for want of jurisdiction, is therefore reversed, and it is ordered that the record be remitted, with directions to further proceed in the case as to law and justice may appertain.

Mr. Justice McLEAN delivered a separate opinion, and Mr. Justice CATRON, Mr. Justice DANIEL, and Mr. Justice CAMPBELL, dissented.

Mr. Justice CATRON concurred with Mr. Justice CAMPBELL in the opinion delivered by him.

Mr. Justice McLEAN:

I agree to the decision in this case; but as I wish to be on one or two points somewhat more explicit than the opinion of the court, I will concisely state my views.

The Constitution declares that the judicial power shall extend "to all cases of admiralty and maritime jurisdiction." The judiciary act of 1789 provides, "that the District Courts shall have exclusive original cognizance of all civil cases of admiralty and maritime jurisdiction."

The act of the 25th February, 1845, is entitled "An act to extend the jurisdiction of the District Courts to certain cases upon the lakes and navigable waters connecting with the same." This act was considered by Congress as extending the jurisdiction of the District Court; and it was so, very properly, treated by the court in the case of the *Genesee Chief.*

In the opinion, it was said this act was not passed under the commercial power, but under the admiralty and maritime jurisdiction given in the Constitution. No terms could be more complete than those used in the Constitution to confer this jurisdiction. In all cases of admiralty and maritime jurisdiction, such suits may be brought in the District Court.

The jurisdiction was limited in England to the ebb and flow of the tide, as their rivers were navigable only as far as the tide flowed. And as in this country the rivers falling into the Atlantic were not navigable above tide-water, the same rule was applied. And when the question of jurisdiction was first raised in regard to our Western rivers, the same rule was adopted, when there was no reason for its restriction to tide-water, as in the rivers of the Atlantic. And this shows that the most learned and able judges may, from the force of precedent, apply an established rule where the reason or necessity on which it was founded fails.

In England and in the Atlantic States, the ebb and flow of the tide marked the extent of the navigableness of rivers. But the navigability of our Western rivers in no instance depends upon the tide.

By the civil law, the maritime system extends over all navigable waters. The admiralty and maritime jurisdiction, like the common-law or chancery jurisdiction, embraces a system of procedure known and established for ages. It may be called a system of regulations embodied and matured by the most enlightened and commercial nations of the world. Its origin may be traced to the regulations of Wisbuy, of the Hanse Towns, the laws of Oleron, the ordinances of France, and the usages of other commercial countries, including the English admiralty.

It is, in fact, a regulation of commerce, as it comprehends the duties and powers of masters of vessels, the maritime liens of seamen, of those who furnish supplies to vessels, make advances, &c., and, in short, the knowledge and conduct required of pilots, seamen, masters, and everything pertaining to the sailing and management of a ship. As the terms import, these regulations apply to the water, and not to the land, and are commensurate with the jurisdiction conferred.

By the Constitution, "Congress have power to regulate commerce with foreign nations, and among the several States, and with the Indian tribes." The provision, "among the several States," limits the power of Congress in the regulation of commerce to two or more States; consequently, a State has power to regulate a commerce exclusively within its own limits; but beyond such limits the regulation belongs to Congress. The admiralty and maritime jurisdiction is essentially a commercial power, and it is necessarily limited to the exercise of that power by Congress.

Every voyage of a vessel between two or more States is subject to the admiralty jurisdiction, and not to any State regulation. A denial of this doctrine is a subversion of the commercial power of Congress, and throws us on the Confederation. It also subverts the admiralty and maritime jurisdiction of the Federal courts, given explicitly in the Constitution and in the judiciary act of 1789.

* * *

Antiquity has its charms, as it is rarely found in the common walks of professional life; but it may be doubted whether wisdom is not more frequently found in experience and the gradual progress of human affairs; and this is especially the case in all systems of jurisprudence which are matured by the progress of human knowledge. Whether it be common, chancery, or admiralty law, we should be more instructed by studying its present adaptations to human concerns, than to trace it back to its beginnings. Every one is more interested and delighted to look upon the majestic and flowing river, than by following its current upwards until it becomes lost in its mountain rivulets.

Mr. Justice DANIEL dissenting:

* * *

My convictions pledge me to an unyielding condemnation of pretensions once denominated, by a distinguished member of this court, "the silent and stealing progress of the admiralty in acquiring jurisdiction to which it has no pretensions;" and still more inflexibly of the fearful and tremendous assumptions of power now openly proclaimed for tribunals pronounced by the venerable Hale, by Coke, and by Blackstone, and by the authorities avouched for their opinions, to have been merely tolerated by, and always subordinate to, the authority of the common law—an usurpation licensed to overturn the most inveterate principles of that law; licensed in its exercise to invade the jurisdiction of sovereign communities, and to defy and abrogate the most vital immunities of their social or political organization. I cannot, without a sense of delinquency, omit any occasion of protesting against what to my mind is an abuse of the greatest magnitude, and one which, hopeless as at present the prospect of remedy may appear, it would seem could require nothing but attention to its character and tendencies to insure a corrective. It must of necessity be resisted in practice, as wholly irreconcilable with every guarantee of the rights of person or property, or with the power of internal police in the States.

* * *

The conclusion, then, from the eleventh section of the judiciary act, is inevitably this: that the power thereby vested with respect to *seizures*, is not an *admiralty* power—was never conferred by the investment of admiralty power in accordance with the Constitution; but is in its character distinct therefrom and is peculiar and limited in its extent. Such appears to have been the opinion of two distinguished commentators upon the admiralty jurisdiction of the courts of the United States, Chancellor Kent and Mr. Dane; the former of whom, in the 1st vol. of his Commentaries, p. 376, holds this language: "Congress had a right, in their discretion, to make all seizures and forfeitures cognizable in the District Courts; but it may be a question whether they had any right to declare them to be cases of admiralty jurisdiction, if they were not so by the law of the land when the Constitution was made. The Constitution secures to the citizen trial by jury in all criminal prosecutions, and in all civil suits at common law where the value in controversy exceeds twenty dollars. These prosecutions for forfeitures of large and valuable portions of property, under the revenue laws, are highly penal in their consequences; and the Government and its officers are always parties, and deeply concerned in the conviction and forfeiture. And if, by act of Congress or by judicial decisions, the prosecution can be turned over to the admiralty side of the District Court, as being neither a criminal prosecution nor a suit at common law, the trial of the cause is then transferred from a jury of the country to the breast of a single judge. It is probable, however, that the judiciary act did not intend to do more than to declare the jurisdiction of the District Courts over these cases; and that all the prosecutions for penalties and forfeitures upon seizures under laws of imposts, navigation, and trade, were not to be considered of admiralty jurisdiction when the case admitted of a prosecution at common law; for the act saves to *suitors in all cases* the right to a common-law remedy, where the common law was competent to give it. We have seen that it is competent to give it; because, under the vigorous system of the English law, such prosecutions *in rem* are in the exchequer, according to the course of the common law; and it may be doubted whether the case of *La Vengeance*, on which all subsequent decisions of the Supreme Court have rested, was sufficiently considered. The vice-admiralty courts in this country when we were colonies, and also in the West Indies, obtained jurisdiction in *revenue causes* to an extent totally unknown to the jurisdiction of the English admiralty, and with powers as enlarged as those claimed at the present day. But this extension, *by statute*, of the jurisdiction of the American vice-admiralty courts beyond their ancient limits to revenue cases and penalties, was much discussed and complained of at the commencement of the Revolution." Judge Conkling also, in his Treatise on the Admiralty, vol. 2, p. 391, says: "In England, all revenue seizures are cognizable *exclusively* in the *exchequer,* and such of them as are cognizable on the admiralty side of the District Courts of the United States are made so *only by force of a legislative act.*"

* * *

But the court, after having declared the correctness of the English rule and its adoption here, go on to say, nevertheless, "that a definition which would *at this day* limit public rivers to *tide-water rivers* is wholly inadmissible." And why? Because the Constitution, either by express language or by necessary implication, recognizes or looks to any change or enlargement in the principles or the extent of admiralty jurisdiction? Oh, no! For no such reason as this. "But we have *now* (say the court) thousands of miles of public navigable water, including lakes and rivers, in which there is no tide." Such is the argument of the court, and, correctly interpreted, it amounts to this: The Constitution, which at its adoption suited perfectly well the situation of the country, and which *then* was unquestionably of supreme authority, we now adjudge to have become unequal to the exigencies of the times; it must therefore be substituted by something more efficient; and as the people, and the States, and the Federal Legislature, are tardy or delinquent in making this substitution, the duty or the credit of this beneficent work must be devolved upon the judiciary. It is said by the court, that there is certainly no reason for admiralty power over a public tide-water, which does not apply with equal force to any other public waters used for commercial purposes.

Let this proposition be admitted literally, it would fall infinitely short of a demonstration, that because the Constitution, adequate to every exigency when created, did not comprise predicaments not then in existence or in contemplation, it can be stretched, by any application of judicial torture, to cover any such exigency, either real or supposed. This argument forcibly revives the recollection of the interpretation of the phrase *"necessary and proper,"* once ingeniously and strenuously wielded to prove that a bank, incorporated with every faculty and attribute of such an institution, was not in reality, nor was designed to be, a *bank*; but was essentially an agent, an indispensable agent, in the administration of the Federal Government. And with reference to this doctrine of necessity, or propriety, or convenience, it may here be remarked, that it is as gratuitous and as much out of place with respect to the admiralty jurisdiction, as it was with respect to the Bank of the United States—perhaps still more so; as it is certain, and obvious to every well-informed individual, that, with the exception of some of the lakes, there is not a watercourse in the country, situated above the ebb and flow of the tide, which is not bounded on one or on both its margins by some county. And in the case before us, it is alleged expressly in the pleading, and admitted throughout, that every fact in reference thereto transpired upon an inland water of the State of Alabama, two hundred miles above the tide, and within the county of Wilcox, in that State. And by adhering to what is an essential test of the admiralty jurisdiction in England, and formerly adopted and practiced upon in this country, there will be obtained a standard as to that jurisdiction, far more uniform and rational than that furnished by the tides. I allude to the rule which repels the pretensions of the admiralty whenever it attempts to intrude them *infra corpus comitatus*. This is the true rule as to jurisdiction, as it is susceptible of certainty, and concedes and secures to each system of jurisprudence, that of the admiralty and of the common law, its legitimate and appropriate powers. For this plain and rational test, this court now attempts to substitute one in its nature vague and arbitrary, and tending inevitably to confusion and conflict. It is now affirmed, that the jurisdiction and powers of the admiralty extend to all waters that are *navigable* within or without the territory of a State. In quest of certainty, under this new doctrine, the inquiry is naturally suggested, what are navigable waters? Will it be proper to adopt, in the interpretation of this phrase, an etymological derivation from *navis*, and to designate, as navigable waters, those only on whose bosoms ships and navies can be floated? Shall it embrace waters on which sloops and shallops, or what are generally termed river craft, can swim; or shall it be extended to any water on which a batteau or a pirogue can be floated? These are all, at any rate, *practicable* waters, navigable in a certain sense. If any point between the extremes just mentioned is to be taken, there is uncertainty, of contestation and expense. And if the last of these extremes be adopted, then there is scarcely an internal water-course, whether in its natural condition, or as improved under the authority and with the resources of the States, or a canal, or a mill-pond, some of which are known to cover many acres of land, (and, as this court can convert rivers without tides into *seas*, may be metamorphosed into small lakes,) which would not by this doctrine be brought within the grasp of the admiralty. Some of our canals are navigated by steam, and some of them by sails; some of them are adjuncts to rivers, and form continuous communications with the ocean; all of them are fed by, and therefore are made portions of, rivers. Under this new regime, the hand of Federal power may be thrust into everything, even into a vegetable or fruit basket; and there is no production of a farm, an orchard, or a garden, on the margin of these water-courses, which is not liable to be arrested on its way to the next market town by the *high admiralty power*, with all its parade of appendages; and the simple, plain, homely countryman, who imagined he had some comprehension of his rights, and their remedies under the cognizance of a justice of the peace, or of a county court, is now, through the instrumentality of some apt fomenter of trouble, metamorphosed and magnified from a country attorney into a proctor, to be confounded and put to silence by a learned display from Roccus de Navibus, Emerigon, or Pardessus, from the Mare Clausum, or from the Trinity Masters, or the Apostles.

* * *

Mr. Justice CAMPBELL dissenting:

I dissent from the judgment of the court in this cause, and from the opinion delivered by the judges composing a majority of the court.

* * *

It is my opinion that this court claims a power for the District Court not delegated to the Federal Government in the Constitution of the United States, and that Congress, in organizing the judiciary department, have not conferred upon any court of the United States. That this court has assumed a jurisdiction over a case only cognizable at the common law, and triable by a jury; and that its opinion and judgment contravene the authority and doctrine of a large number of decisions pronounced by this court, and by the Circuit Courts, after elaborate arguments and mature deliberation, and which for a long period have formed a rule of decision to the court, and of opinion to the legal profession; and that no other judgment of this court affords a sanction to this. (10 Wheat., 428; 7 Pet., 324; 11 Pet., 175; 12 Pet., 72; 5 How., 441; 6 How., 344; 4 Dall., 426; 2 Gal., 398; *The Anne*, 1 Mas., 109; 1 Bald., 544.)

* * *

The reign of Richard II was an epoch to be remembered with interest, and studied with care, by those concerned in administering the constitutional law of England or the United States. A formal complaint was made by the Commons of defects in the administration, as well about the Kings person and his household as in his courts of justice, and redress was demanded. Measures were taken for placing the judicial institutions of England upon a solid constitutional foundation, and to exclude from the realm the odious systems of the continent. The first of the enactments was directed against the usurpations of the great military officers, who administered justice by virtue of their seignoral powers—the Lords' Constable and the Earl Marshal. The acts of 8th and 13th Richard II provide that, "because the Commons do make a grievous complaint that the court of the Constable and Marshal have accroached to them, and do daily accroach, contracts, covenants, trespasses, debts, detinues, and many other actions pleadable at the common law, in great prejudice to the King, and to the great grievance and oppression of the people," therefore they were prohibited, and their jurisdiction confined "to contracts and deeds of arms without the realm," and "things that touch more within the realm which cannot be determined and discussed by the common law."

The Lord High Admiral received a similar rebuke. The preamble of the act of 13 Richard II recites, "that complaints had arisen because Admirals and their deputies hold their sessions within divers places of the realm, accroaching to them greater authority than belonged to their office, to the prejudice of the King, &c." It was declared that Admiral should not meddle with anything done within the realm, but only with things done upon the sea, as had been used in the time of Edward III. But this did not suffice to restrain the accroaching spirit of that feudal lord and his deputies.

Two years after, the Parliament enacted,

that the court of admiralty hath no manner of cognizance, power, nor jurisdiction of any manner of contract, plea, or quarrel, or of any other thing done or rising within the bodies of counties, either by land or water, and also with wreck of the sea; but all such manner of contracts, pleas, and quarrels, and all other things rising within the bodies of counties, as well by land as by water as aforesaid, and also wreck of the sea, shall be tried, termined, discussed, and remedied by the laws of the land, and not before, nor by the Admiral or his lieutenant, in no manner. Nevertheless, of the death of a man and of a mayhem done in great ships, being and hovering in the main stream of the great rivers, beneath the points of the same rivers, and in no other place of the same rivers, the Admiral shall have cognizance.

In the sixteenth year of the reign of Richard II, the rule of the Roman chancery, like that of the Lords Constable, Marshal, and Admiral, was banished from England. In that year it was enacted that, "Both those who shall pursue or cause to be pursued, in the court of Rome or elsewhere, any processes, or instruments, or other things whatsoever, which touch the King, against his crown and regality, or his realm, shall be outlawed and placed out of the Kings protection." In the following reign the accroaching spirit of the courts of admiralty received a further rebuke.

Upon the prayer of the Commons, the statutes of Richard II were confirmed, and a penalty was inflicted upon such as should maintain suits in the admiralty, contrary to their spirit.

This body of statute law served in a great degree to check the usurping tendencies of these anomalous jurisdictions, and to prevent in a measure the removal of suits triable at the common law *ad aliud examen*, and to be discussed *per aliam legem*. It placed upon an eminence the common law of the realm, and enabled the Commons to plead with authority against other encroachments and usurpations upon the general liberty. But, though a foreign law and despotism were not allowed to enter the kingdom through the courts martial, ecclesiastical, or admiral, the perversion of judiciary powers to purposes of oppression was not effectually prevented. The courts of the Star Chamber and of High Commission, originally limited to specific objects, "assumed power to intermeddle in civil causes and matters only of private interest between party and party, and adventured to determine the estates and liberties of the subject, contrary to the law of the land and the rights and privileges of the subject," and "had been by experience found to be an intolerable burden, and the means to introduce an arbitrary power and government." Among the cases of jurisdiction claimed by the Star Chamber were those between merchant strangers and Englishmen, or between strangers, and for the restitution of ships and goods unlawfully taken, or other deceits practiced on merchants.

* * *

But the statute did not terminate with this. The patriot leaders of that time, reviewing in the preamble to the act the various parliamentary enactments in regard to the legal institutions of England, and reciting those declarations of the public liberties which had extended over a period of four hundred years, proceeded to add another. It was solemnly enacted, "that neither his Majesty, nor his Privy Council, have, or ought to have, any jurisdiction, power, or authority, by English bill, petition, articles, libel, or any other arbitrary whatsoever, to examine or draw in question, determine, or dispose of the lands, tenements, hereditaments, goods, and chattels, of any of the subjects of this realm, but that the same ought to be tried and determined in the ordinary courts of justice, and by the ordinary course of the law."

This selection of a few sections from various English statutes, and the historical facts I have mentioned, is designed to illustrate the intensity and duration of the contest which resulted in placing the judiciary institutions of England on their existing foundation. In the midst of that contest, the settlements were formed in America in which those institutions were successfully planted.

They have been incorporated into the Constitution of the United States, and prevail from the Atlantic Ocean to the Pacific, and from the Lakes to the Gulf of Mexico. These statutes show how the courts martial, ecclesiastical, admiral, and courts proceeding from an arbitrary royal authority, were either limited or suppressed.

* * *

I proceed now to inquire of the admiralty jurisdiction as exercised by the courts of vice-admiralty in the colonies and in the United States before the adoption of the Constitution.

The jurisdiction included four subjects and a separate examination of each title of jurisdiction will shed light upon the discussion. These are—prize; breaches of the acts of navigation, revenue, and trade; crimes and misdemeanors on the high seas; and cases of civil and maritime jurisdiction.

* * *

There can be no room for doubt that the statesmen and jurists who composed the Congress of 1774 regarded the limits of the courts of admiralty as settled by the statutes of Richard II, Henry IV, Henry VIII, and the early acts of navigation and trade, and that the enlargement of this jurisdiction was such a wrong as to justify a resort to arms. Their declarations bear no other interpretation; and the admiralty system of the States before the Constitution was administered upon this opinion. (*Bee's Adm. R.*, 419, 433; 1 Dall., 33.)

* * *

That the framers of the Constitution designed to secure to the Federal Government a plenary control over all *maritime* questions arising in their intercourse with foreign nations, whether of peace or war, which assumed a juridical form through courts of its own appointment, is more than probable from the instrument and the contemporary expositions I have quoted. This was the primary and designed object of the authors of the Constitution in granting this jurisdiction. It is likewise probable that the jurisdiction which had been exercised from the infancy of the colonies to the reign of George III, by courts of admiralty, under laws of navigation, trade, and revenue, was considered as forming a legitimate branch of the admiralty jurisdiction. Such was the opinion of the First Congress under the Constitution, and it has been confirmed in this court. (3 Dall., 397; 2 Cr., 405; 4 Cr., 443; 2 H., 210.) If the instance jurisdiction of the court was at all remembered, the reminiscence was not of a nature to create alarm. The cases for its employment were few and defined. Those did not depend upon any purely municipal code, nor affect any question of public or political interest. They related for the most part to transactions at a distance, which did not involve the interests nor attract the observation of any considerable class of persons. No one could imagine that this jurisdiction, by the interpretation of those who were to exercise it, could penetrate wherever a vessel of ten tons might enter within any of the States.

The question arises, what are the power and jurisdiction claimed for the courts of the United States by this reversal of the judgment of the District Court of Alabama?

The Supreme Court requires that court to take cognizance of cases of admiralty and maritime jurisdiction that arise on lakes and on rivers, as if they were high seas. Dunlap, defining the constitutional jurisdiction in 1835, said, that 'it comprehends all maritime contracts, torts, and injuries. The latter branch is necessarily bounded by locality; the former extends over all contracts, whensoever they may be made and executed, or whatever may be the form of the stipulation which relates to the navigation, business, or commerce of the sea." (Dunlap's Pr., 43.)

This was the broad pretension for the admiralty set up by Mr. Justice Story, in *Delovio v. Boit*, in 1815, under which the legal profession and this court staggered for thirty years before being able to maintain it. The definition to be deduced from the present decision deprives that of any significance. That affords no description of the subject.

The definition under this decree, if carried to its logical extent, will run thus:

That the admiralty and maritime jurisdiction of the courts of the United States extends to all cases of contracts, torts, and injuries, which arise in or concern the navigation, commerce, or business of citizens of the United States, or persons commorant therein, on any of the navigable waters of the world.

* * *

The lakes are certainly not seas according to the signification of that word in the law of nations or the Admiral's commission. They are not common highways for all nations, open to the ships of all, and exempted from the municipal regulation and control of any. The sovereignty over them belongs to the riparian proprietors, in the same manner as over the Rhine or Rio Grande rivers; and the American States and British Queen have respectively courts to administer their laws within the limits of their several titles, to the middle of the lakes, against those who may offend against them. The jurisdiction of the court of admiralty cannot be supported upon the lakes as seas. But the lakes form an external maritime boundary of the United States, and are a commercial highway, which by treaty is common to the inhabitants of the two maritime and commercial countries whose possessions border them. The commerce of these countries is great and growing, and exposed to depredation; and in the absence of a navy, and without defined boundaries, the police of the States on this exposed frontier may be inefficient for the protection of the interests of the Union. I shall not inquire whether these considerations, or those among them which are applicable to the river Mississippi, authorized the decisions in the *Genesee Chief v. Fitzhugh*, 12 How.; and *Fritz v. Bull,* 12 How., 466; *Walsh v. Rogers*, 13 How., 283. I have yielded to the principle of *stare decisis*, and have applied the decisions as I found them when I came into this court. But not one of these considerations has any application to the case before this court. The Alabama river is not an inland Sea. Its navigation was not open to a single foreign vessel when this collision took place. No port had been established on it by the authority of Congress. The commerce that passes over it consists mainly of the products of the State, and the objects received in exchange, at the only seaport of the State. For its whole length it is subject to the same State Government, and its police does not involve a necessity for a navy.

The objection noticed in the opinion of the court in the *Genesee Chief* as opposed in the argument against the jurisdiction of the court, I have said does not meet the force of the adversary opinion. In France, the domain of the Admiral was limited to the sea, its coasts, ports, havens, and shores to the high-water mark, and his seignoral right to dispense justice was confined to his domain. The contest there was as to the extent of rival seignories. But in Great Britain the contest had a more profound significance than is to be found in a controversy merely between rival feudatories.

The Admiral's jurisdiction there had no relation to the saltness or freshness of the waters, nor whether the rivers were public or private, navigable or floatable. The question was, whether Englishmen should be governed by English laws, or "whether contracts, pleas, and quarrels, should be drawn *ad aliud examen*, and be sentenced *per aliam legem*." The English Commons abhorred the summary jurisdiction of the courts of civil law, their private examination of witnesses, their rejection of a jury of the vicinage, the discretion they allowed to the judge, and their foreign code. They erected a barrier of penal statutes to exclude them from the body of any county, either on land or water.

The people of the several States have retainned the popular element of the judicial administration of England, and the attachment of her people to the institutions of local self-government. In Alabama, the "trial by jury is preserved inviolate," that being regarded as "an essential principle of liberty and free government." In the court of admiralty the people have no place as jurors. A single judge, deriving his appointment from an independent Government, administers in that court a code which a Federal judge has described as "resting upon the general principles of maritime law, and that it is not competent to the States, by any local legislation, to enlarge, or limit, or narrow it." (2 STORY R., 456.)

If the principle of this decree is carried to its logical extent, all cases arising in the transportation of property or persons from the towns and landing-places of the different States, to other towns and landing-places, whether in or out of the State; all cases of tort or damage arising in the navigation of the internal waters, whether involving the security of persons or title to property, in either; all cases of supply to those engaged in the navigation, not to enumerate others, will be cognizable in the District Courts of the United States. If the dogma of judges in regard to the system of laws to be administered prevails, then this whole class of cases may be drawn *ad aliud examen,* and placed under the dominion of a foreign code, *whether they arise among citizens or others.* The States are deprived of the power to mould their own laws in respect of persons and things within their limits, and which are appropriately subject to their sovereignty. The right of the people to self-government is thus abridged—abridged to the precise extent, that a judge appointed by another Government may impose a law, not sanctioned by the representatives or agents of the people, upon the citizens of the State. Thus the contest here assumes the same significance as in Great Britain, and, in its last analysis, involves the question of the right of the people to determine their own laws and legal institutions. And surely this objection to the decree is independent of any consideration whether the river is subject to tides, or is navigable from the sea.

* * *

―――――――

2. *The Modern Standards*

Note: Interpretations of "Navigable Waters"

The admiralty jurisdiction of the federal courts extends not only to events on the high seas and territorial seas but to the inland waters of the United States so long as they satisfy the requirement of being "navigable waters". The interpretation of the term "navigable waters of the United States" has, itself, been the subject of a number of differing federal decisions. It refers to bodies of water that are navigable in fact, which means waters that are used or capable of being used as waterborne highways for commerce, *i.e.,* those presently sustaining or those capable of sustaining the transportation of goods or passengers by watercraft. Furthermore, in order to qualify as navigable waters of the Untied States, bodies of water must "form in their ordinary condition by themselves, or by uniting with other waters, a continued highway over which commerce is or may be carried on with other States or foreign countries in the customary modes in which such commerce is conducted by water." *The Daniel Ball,* 77 U.S. (10 Wall.) 557, 563, 19 L. Ed. 999 (1871).

Generally, inland water of the United States is "navigable" if: 1) it is capable of supporting maritime commerce; 2) it runs through two states or empties into the sea; and, 3) it is presently sustaining maritime commerce. Note that it is sufficient that the body of water be a *link* in the highway of interstate commerce. In other words, if a body of water (sustaining maritime commerce) runs into another body of water (sustaining maritime commerce) which runs between two states, admiralty jurisdiction applies.

―――――――

a. *"Contemporary Navigability in Fact" Test*

LeBLANC v. CLEVELAND

198 F.3d 353, 2000 AMC 609, (2d Cir. 1999)

PARKER, Circuit Judge:

Etoile LeBlanc and Stephen Ossen appeal from an order of the United States District Court for the Northern District of New York (Lawrence E. Kahn, Judge), entered October 1, 1997, dismissing their claims for lack of subject matter jurisdiction. The district court based the dismissal on its conclusion that the portion of the Hudson

River in which the accident giving rise to appellants' claims took place was not a navigable waterway for purposes of establishing federal admiralty jurisdiction.

We affirm.

I. Background

On July 4, 1994, Etoile LeBlanc and Stephen Ossen suffered personal injuries when the kayak they were paddling on the Hudson River was struck by a recreational motor boat operated by Terry Cleveland and owned by Robert Grant. LeBlanc and Ossen had rented their kayak from JRD Retailers, Ltd., d/b/a Syd & Dusty's Outfitters ("JRD"). The collision occurred approximately 29 miles upstream of Fort Edward, near Lake Luzerne.

On March 29, 1995, LeBlanc and Ossen sued Grant and Cleveland in the Southern District of New York, invoking federal admiralty jurisdiction. They alleged that Grant and Cleveland negligently caused the collision and their resulting injuries. On September 22, 1995, the action was transferred to the Northern District of New York. Cleveland and Grant then brought third-party complaints against JRD. Pursuant to Rule 14(c) of the FEDERAL RULES OF CIVIL PROCEDURE, these third-party complaints allowed the case to proceed as if LeBlanc and Ossen had sued JRD as well as Cleveland and Grant. FED. R. CIV. P. 14(c).

On July 22, 1997, JRD moved to dismiss the complaint filed by LeBlanc and Ossen for lack of subject matter jurisdiction. *See* FED. R. CIV. P. 12(b)(1). On October 1, 1997, the district court granted the motion, finding that the Hudson River is not "navigable in fact" at the location at which the accident took place and that, consequently, the court lacked admiralty jurisdiction over the lawsuit. The court acknowledged that the Hudson River below Fort Edward is a navigable waterway because it permits passage to the open sea. Nonetheless, the court found that the "part of the Hudson [where the accident took place] cannot ... be accessed from Fort Edward due to the presence of numerous areas of rapids, ... [nine] dams, and at least three major waterfalls of 30 feet or more in height." As a result, the court concluded that "[n]othing in the records suggests that the Hudson north of Fort Edward is now, or has ever been, an artery of maritime commerce" sufficient to support a finding of navigability necessary to the exercise of federal admiralty jurisdiction. LeBlanc and Ossen timely appealed.

II. Discussion

On appeal, LeBlanc and Ossen argue that the district court erred in finding that the Hudson River is unnavigable north of Fort Edward for purposes of establishing federal admiralty jurisdiction. In support of this argument, they contend, first, that the district court applied an incorrect standard when it found that navigability was precluded in part due to the existence of artificial dams. Appellants urge this Court to adopt a standard that focuses on the historic navigability of the river in its natural, unimproved state, rather than its present, improved state. Second, they assert that, whether the test focuses on historic or contemporary navigability, the Hudson is sufficiently navigable at the site of the accident to support federal admiralty jurisdiction over their claims. After setting forth the applicable standard of review, we address each argument in turn.

* * *

B. The Proper Standard for Determining Navigability

Appellants first contend that the district court applied an incorrect legal standard in finding admiralty jurisdiction lacking. Specifically, they argue for a jurisdictional test that focuses on the historic navigability of the waterway in question, without reference to present-day artificial obstructions, rather than on its contemporary navigability, including artificial dams. Under an historic navigability test, the argument continues, the district court erred in refusing to take into account the fact that, prior to 1951 and before the construction of several impassable dams, the logging industry regularly used the Hudson River upstream of Fort Edward to float logs to timber mills. For the reasons discussed below, appellants' argument fails.

* * *

The district court, like virtually every other court to consider the question of navigability for admiralty jurisdiction purposes, applied the definition of navigable waters first articulated in *The Daniel Ball*, 77 U.S. (10 Wall.) 557, 19 L.Ed. 999 (1870):

> Those rivers must be regarded as public navigable rivers in law which are navigable in fact. And they are navigable in fact when they are used, or are susceptible of being used, in their ordinary condition, as highways for commerce, over which trade and travel are or may be conducted in the customary modes of trade and travel on water. And they constitute navigable waters of the United States within the meaning of the acts of Congress, in contradistinction from the navigable waters of the States, when they form in their ordinary condition by themselves, or by uniting with other waters, a continued highway over which commerce is or may be carried on with other States or foreign countries in the customary modes in which such commerce is conducted by water.

Id. at 563; *see also Grubart*, 513 U.S. at 529-30, 115 S.Ct. 1043 (applying *The Daniel Ball* for purposes of determining admiralty jurisdiction); *In re Petition of Boyer*, 109 U.S. 629, 631-32, 3 S.Ct. 434, 27 L.Ed. 1056 (1884) (same). The district court found, and the parties did not dispute, that the Hudson River downstream of Fort Edward can be and is used as a continuous highway for interstate commerce because it permits passage beyond New York both to the south, where it empties into the Atlantic, and to the north, via the Champlain Canal (which begins near Fort Edward) and the St. Lawrence. However, the court found that the accident site is separated from Fort Edward, and therefore from any interstate or international waterway, by numerous impassable rapids, falls, and artificial dams.

Appellants do not dispute that *The Daniel Ball* sets forth the basic navigability test for purposes of admiralty jurisdiction. Instead, they first contend that by focusing on whether rivers are navigable "in their ordinary condition," the *Daniel Ball* test required the district court to measure navigability by reference to the river's historic, unimproved state, rather than its present, improved state.

This argument is foreclosed by subsequent Supreme Court caselaw. In *United States v. Appalachian Electric Power Co.*, 311 U.S. 377, 407, 61 S.Ct. 291, 85 L.Ed. 243 (1940), the Court found that "ordinary condition" as used in *The Daniel Ball* refers not to the absence of human interference with the course of the river, but "to volume of water, the gradients and the regularity of the flow" of the waterway. *Id.* at 407, 61 S.Ct. 291. Thus, under the *Daniel Ball* test, an otherwise unnavigable river may not be rendered navigable simply because, in extraordinary conditions, its waters rise high enough to support forms of transportation normally impossible. 1 STEVEN F. FRIEDELL, BENEDICT ON ADMIRALTY § 142, at 9-6 (7th ed. 1998) ("It is not enough that a fishing skiff or gunning canoe can be made to float at high water ... or that logs, poles and rafts are floated down in high waters."). But nothing in *The Daniel Ball* indicates that an historically navigable river remains navigable for admiralty jurisdiction purposes when it is made impassable by an artificial obstruction.

Perhaps recognizing that their interpretation of *The Daniel Ball* lacks legal support, appellant's next rely on *The Montello*, 87 U.S. (20 Wall.) 430, 22 L.Ed. 391 (1874), claiming that it "refined" the *Daniel Ball* test discussed above. In *The Montello*, the Supreme Court was called upon to determine whether Congress had the authority under the Commerce Clause to regulate steamships plying the waters of Wisconsin's Fox River. Congress's power to regulate activity on the Fox River turned on whether the river was navigable. Setting forth the standard of navigability applicable in this context, the Court wrote:

> The capability of use by the public for purposes of transportation and commerce affords the true criterion of the navigability of a river, rather than the extent and manner of that use. If it be capable in its natural state of being used for purposes of commerce, no matter in what mode the commerce may be conducted, it is navigable in fact, and becomes in law a public river or highway.

Id. at 441-42. Appellants contend that by referencing the "natural state" of the river in question, the *Montello* Court made clear that navigability should be judged without reference to artificial obstructions. Indeed, the Supreme Court has since specifically held that, for purposes of defining Congress's power to regulate under the Commerce Clause, an otherwise navigable river cannot be rendered unnavigable by the construction of artificial dams. *See, e.g., Economy Light & Power Co. v. United States*, 256 U.S. 113, 123, 41 S.Ct. 409, 65 L.Ed. 847 (1921).

Nonetheless, appellants' reliance on *The Montello* and its progeny is misplaced. As noted above, *The Montello* did not define navigable waters for purposes of establishing the limits of admiralty jurisdiction; instead, it defined navigable waters for the purpose of delimiting Congress's power to regulate under the Commerce Clause. The Supreme Court has recognized that the definition of navigable waters used in one context does not necessarily apply in another. *See Kaiser Aetna v. United States*, 444 U.S. 164, 170-72, 100 S.Ct. 383, 62 L.Ed.2d 332 (1979). Rather, "any reliance upon judicial precedent must be predicated upon careful appraisal of the purpose for which the concept of navigability' was invoked in a particular case." *Id.* at 171, 100 S.Ct. 383 (internal quotations omitted).

Careful appraisal of the purposes for which the *Montello* Court invoked the concept of navigability reveals that the same definition should not be used to determine the limits of the federal judicial power under Article III or 28 U.S.C. § 1331(1). As the Ninth Circuit put it:

> The definitions of navigability may vary because, as in the present case, the purposes served by the commerce clause and admiralty jurisdiction may vary. Congress' commerce power is designed in part to preserve and protect the nation's waterways which, in their natural condition, are navigable in interstate commerce. By virtue of this power, Congress may prevent or regulate obstruction of these waterways by the states through which they pass. The damming of a previously navigable waterway by a state cannot divest Congress of its control over a potentially useful artery of commerce, since such obstructions may always be removed. Hence the courts have reasonably held that a navigable river is not rendered non-navigable by artificial obstruction.
>
> However, if the damming of a waterway has the practical effect of eliminating commercial maritime activity, no federal interest is served by the exercise of admiralty jurisdiction over the events transpiring on that body of water, whether or not it was originally navigable. No purpose is served by application of a uniform body of federal law, on waters devoid of trade and commerce, to regulate the activities and resolve the disputes of pleasure boaters. Only the burdening of federal courts and the frustrating of the purposes of state tort law would be thereby served.

Adams v. Montana Power Co., 528 F.2d 437, 440-41 (9th Cir. 1975) (citations omitted); *see also Chapman v. United States*, 575 F.2d 147, 149-50 (7th Cir. 1978) *(en banc)* (quoting *Adams*).

Recognizing the distinction between legislative authority under the Commerce Clause and admiralty jurisdiction, every circuit court to confront the question has rejected the historic navigability jurisdictional test when determining admiralty jurisdiction. In *Adams,* the Ninth Circuit held that a dam that prevented a waterway from being used as an artery of interstate commerce also prevented federal courts from exercising admiralty jurisdiction over a recreational boating accident that occurred on the waterway. *Adams,* 528 F.2d at 440-41. Similarly, *in Livingston v. United States,* 627 F.2d 165 (8th Cir. 1980), the Eighth Circuit rejected a plaintiff's claim that because a river was navigable before the construction of an impassable dam, it remained navigable for all time:

> [T]he closing of waters to commercial shipping should likewise have the effect of eliminating admiralty jurisdiction over them. In other words, the concept of "navigability" in admiralty is properly limited to describing a present capability of the waters to sustain commercial shipping.

Id. at 169-70 (footnote omitted); *see also Three Buoys Houseboat Vacations USA Ltd. v. Morts,* 921 F.2d 775, 778 (8th Cir. 1990) ("the standard is one of contemporary navigability in fact' "). And in *Chapman,* the Seventh Circuit held that, even if a dammed river was navigable for purposes of the Commerce Clause, it was not navigable for admiralty jurisdiction purposes where it was not susceptible of commercial navigation "in [its] present [dammed] state." *Chapman,* 575 F.2d at 151. Those cases in which circuit courts have found dammed waterways navigable for jurisdictional purposes are easily distinguished by the fact that the waterway in question formed the border between two states, thereby rendering it capable of supporting interstate commerce despite the existence of artificial dams blocking downstream flow. *See, e.g., Mullenix v. United States,* 984 F.2d 101, 103-04 & n. 3 (4th Cir. 1993) (Potomac River navigable at point at which it forms the border of Maryland and West Virginia and supports ferry traffic between the two states); *Finneseth v. Carter,* 712 F.2d 1041, 1044 (6th Cir. 1983) (lake navigable where it straddled the border of Tennessee and Kentucky).

As their final argument in favor of an historic navigability standard, appellant's point us to *Adirondack League Club, Inc. v. Sierra Club,* 92 N.Y.2d 591, 684 N.Y.S.2d 168, 706 N.E.2d 1192 (1998). In *Adirondack League,* the New York Court of Appeals used an historic navigability standard for the purpose of identifying those "waterways [that] are of such practical utility that private ownership from the time of the original grant from the State or sovereign is subject to an easement for public travel." *Adirondack League,* 92 N.Y.2d at 601, 684 N.Y.S.2d at 170, 706 N.E.2d at 1194 (citation omitted). *Adirondack League,* of course, had nothing whatsoever to do with admiralty jurisdiction in the federal courts. Moreover, to state the purpose for which *Adirondack League* utilized the historic navigability standard is to distinguish it from the purpose admiralty jurisdiction serves. By its very nature, the process of determining which waterways are subject to public easements dating from a land grant by the State requires an historic navigability standard; under a contemporary navigability standard, the present-day owner of riparian rights could defeat a public easement merely by erecting an impassable obstacle in the waterway. This, of course, would defeat the purpose of the public easement doctrine. In contrast, and as discussed above, the purpose of federal admiralty jurisdiction is best served if the test for navigability is determined with reference to present-day artificial obstructions.

Thus, in light of the policies served by federal admiralty jurisdiction, we hold that a waterway at the situs in issue is navigable for jurisdictional purposes if it is presently used, or is presently capable of being used, as an interstate highway for commercial trade or travel in the customary modes of travel on water. Natural and artificial obstructions that effectively prohibit such commerce defeat admiralty jurisdiction.

C. The District Courts Application of the Legal Standard

Of course, under the contemporary navigability standard for purposes of determining admiralty jurisdiction, that we adopt today, it is immaterial that, prior to 1951 and before the construction of many of the nine dams, logs were floated down the Hudson near the accident site. Nonetheless, appellant's contend that even under the contemporary navigability standard, the district court had before it sufficient evidence of present-day navigability to support a finding of jurisdiction. But in the face of the district courts unchallenged factual findings, this argument necessarily fails.

As noted at the outset, the district court found that the Hudson River downstream of Fort Edward is capable of supporting interstate commerce. The court also found that "the presence of natural obstructions such as white water and falls as well as the presence of more recent man-made dams absolutely prevent continuous travel by any type of boat from the place of the accident to the waters below Fort Edward." Finally, the district court determined that the presence of dams between Fort Edward and the accident site would now impede any attempt to float timber on this stretch of the Hudson absent extraordinary river conditions. Appellants do not take issue with any of these findings on appeal. Nor could they: Each enjoys substantial support in the record and is not clearly erroneous.

Instead, appellant's contend only that the Hudson is navigable at the accident site because kayakers can portage around the dams separating the site from Fort Edward. But this argument lacks any legal support. Appellants cite, and we have found, no published decision holding that the possibility of recreational use assisted by multiple portages is, by itself, sufficient to render a waterway navigable for admiralty jurisdiction purposes. Navigability requires that the body of water be capable of supporting commercial maritime activity. It is irrelevant that the body of water is capable of supporting non-commercial maritime activity. "A waterway is navigable provided that it is used or susceptible of being used as an artery of commerce. Neither non-commercial fishing nor pleasure boating ... constitutes commerce. Commerce for the purpose of admiralty jurisdiction means activities related to shipping." *Adams,* 528 F.2d at 437; *see also Foremost,* 457 U.S. at 675, 102 S.Ct. 2654 (pleasure boating is "noncommercial maritime activity"). The possibility that the waterway is capable of supporting non-commercial maritime activity of the type suggested by appellant's does not render the waterway capable of supporting "commercial trade or travel in the customary modes of travel on water," as our holding today requires. As a result, the court did not err in finding that it lacked jurisdiction over appellants' claims.

III. Conclusion

For the foregoing reasons, the judgment of the district court is affirmed.

Note

Compare the principal case, *LeBlanc v. Cleveland* with *Complaint of Paradise Holdings, Inc.,* 795 F.2d 756, 1987 AMC 104 (9th Cir. 1986), indicating that the test for determining the navigability of inland waters was not applied to tidal water.

———————

Note: Different Definitions of "Navigability"

The Supreme Court has recently observed that precedent in this area must be evaluated carefully in light of "'the *purpose* for which the concept of "navigability" was invoked in a particular case.'" *Kaiser Aetna v. United States,* 444 U.S. 164, 171, 100 S.Ct. 383, 388, 62 L.Ed.2d 332 (1979) (quoting with approval from the district court opinion, 408 F. Supp. 42, 49 (emphasis in original)). The Court in that case identified four separate purposes underlying definitions of "navigability": to delimit the boundaries of the navigational servitude; to define the scope of Congress' regulatory authority under the commerce clause; to determine the extent of the authority of the Corps of Engineers under the Rivers and Harbors Act of 1899; and to establish the limits of federal admiralty jurisdiction. Each of these areas of the law might well require a different definition of "navigability."

Livingston v. United States, 627 F.2d 165, 169, 1982 AMC 1065 (8th Cir. 1980), *cert. denied,* 450 U.S. 914, 101 S.Ct. 1354, 67 L. Ed. 2d 338 (1981).

———————

b. Seasonal Navigability

WILDER v. PLACID OIL CO.

611 F. Supp. 841 (W.D. La. 1985), aff'd sub nom. Sanders v. Placid Oil Co.,

861 F.2d 1374, 1989 AMC 912 (5th Cir. 1988)

Ruling

LITTLE, District Judge

The issue pending before this Court is whether Catahoula Lake, a low lying portion of the Little River in the State of Louisiana, is navigable for purposes of admiralty jurisdiction. The matter has been briefed by the parties and presented by way of cross-motions for summary judgment.

* * *

Facts

These consolidated actions were instituted by Richard Sanders and James Michael Wilder against Placid Oil Company to recover damages for personal injuries and property loss allegedly sustained when Wilder's 15-foot outboard aluminum boat, in which both complainants were riding, struck a steel well-head casing pipe allegedly owned and maintained by Placid. According to the plaintiffs' pleadings, the pipe was submerged and was not marked. The actions were originally brought pursuant to the admiralty maritime jurisdiction of the Court, 28 U.S.C. § 1333 and designated under Fed. R. Civ. P. 9(h). Both plaintiff's subsequently filed amended complaints alleging diversity of citizenship pursuant to 28 U.S.C. § 1332 as an alternative basis of jurisdiction.

The uncontroverted material submitted by the parties indicates that the Little River is formed by the meeting of the Dudgdemona River and Bayou Castor just to the northeast of Rochelle, Louisiana. It flows in a more or less southerly direction into the lowlands which become Catahoula Lake in high water. From Catahoula Lake the water is discharged through several tributaries and distributaries until the tributaries finally rejoin into one channel at Archie, Louisiana. One such distributary is a diversion canal built by the U.S. Army Corps of Engineers and completed in May of 1972. This canal has a permanent dam structure across it which forecloses navigation except during flood stages. At Archie, the Corps has fabricated a weir across the span of the Little River. The weir, completed in June of 1973, is constructed out of concrete and crests at an elevation of 36 feet above sea level or 36 NGVD (National Geodetic Vertical Data). This keeps the water level at 36 NGVD from the outflow of the lake up to the structure itself. The water level of the lake is controlled by movable gates in the permanent dam in the diversion canal. Thus, when the water level of the Little River is higher than 36 NGVD, vessels may pass over the weir. The weir, while permanent, is not a total obstruction to navigation.

From Archie, Louisiana the water flows easterly to Jonesville and Trinity, Louisiana, where it joins the Ouachita and Tensas Rivers to form the Black River. The Black then runs into the Red River which in turn runs into either the Atchafalaya River, from which one may enter the Gulf Intracoastal Canal or the Lower Old River, which allows passage into the Mississippi River. A steady, if not substantial barge trade is conducted on the Atchafalaya, Black and Red Rivers, while the Mississippi River is a major maritime commercial artery. Accordingly, these waters form a continuous highway between states over which commerce may be conducted. In 1887, the Little River was navigated by steamboat from White Sulphur Springs, Louisiana above Catahoula Lake, to its end at Jonesville, Louisiana. *1887 Ann. Rep. of the Chief of Engineers,* Part II at 1499. The business on the river consisted of logging, fur trading and transportation of bales of cotton. *Id.*

The Little River, including Catahoula Lake, is a navigable waterway of the United States for the purposes of the Rivers and Harbors Appropriation Act of 1899, 33 U.S.C. § 401 *et. seq.* In 1932, the Corps listed the Little River as being navigable from its mouth at Jonesville to mile 82.8 at the Missouri-Pacific Railroad bridge. Currently the Corps limits its jurisdiction to mile 55.

By affidavit, Thomas William Coon testified that he piloted the MISS FLORENCE, a self-propelled barge measuring approximately 35 x 110 feet with a draft of 3 feet when empty, throughout Catahoula Lake from 1966 to 1979, and that on one occasion he piloted this vessel from Catahoula Lake through the system of waters described above to Orange, Texas. He also testified that he has been a passenger on crew boats as large as 40 feet in length which have passed into the Black River system from Catahoula Lake navigating over the weir at Archie, Louisiana, on several occasions.

Julian Wesley Thompson, age 46, has lived close to Catahoula Lake all his life. From 1957 through 1970 he operated the MISS FLORENCE and another self-propelled barge known as Barge No. 259 on the Little River and in Catahoula Lake. Barge No. 259 is approximately 40 x 200 feet. He personally piloted the MISS FLORENCE from Buffalo Bayou in the State of Mississippi to Catahoula Lake. He has also personally witnessed the passing of 40-foot crew boats over the weir at Archie, Louisiana. The last such crossing he witnessed was in May of 1985.

VernieA. Gibson, born in 1914, is a life-long resident of LaSalle Parish, Louisiana and has spent those years in close proximity to Catahoula Lake. He has worked portions of Catahoula Lake, Little River, Old River, Black River, Ouachita River, Atchafalaya River and the Mississippi River as a commercial fisherman and fur trapper since 1933.

He remembers the days of steamboat traffic from the Lake to the Black River. He has personally navigated vessels of 5 1/2 to 6 foot drafts over the weir at Archie, Louisiana, and has done so as recently as 1982.

For many years, including 1984 and 1985, Placid has operated crew boats, work boats, self-propelled barges and drilling barges on the Little River and in Catahoula Lake. The record is replete with photographs as recent as 1984 of those vessels in active navigation.

Navigation in Catahoula Lake and on Little River occurs all year round. Navigation over the weir is seasonal. Historically (1933 to 1967), the water level of the river has been above 36 NGVD from January through July with occasional instances in August, November and December. The highest level recorded was 59.41 NGVD on May 16, 1973. The lowest level was 20.89 NGVD on October 23, 1976. According to the record, navigation over the weir was possible during January-June of 1984; January–July and December of 1983; June and December of 1982; June of 1981; March–June of 1980; January–July of 1979; April–June of 1978; and March–May of 1977; 1981 and 1982 were drought years. Plaintiffs were injured in January of 1983. Navigation over the weir was possible at that time.

Law

Admiralty and maritime jurisdiction extends to all navigable waters within the United States. 28 U.S.C. § 1333; 46 U.S.C. §740; *see e.g., Southern S.S. Co. v. N.L.R.B.,* 316 U.S. 31, 41, 62 S.Ct. 886, 891-92, 86 L. Ed. 1246, 1256 (1942). Plaintiffs contend that because the Corps finds Little River a navigable water of the United States under the Rivers and Harbors Act, it is also a navigable water of the United States for purposes of admiralty jurisdiction.

In *Kaiser Aetna v. United States,* 444 U.S. 164, 100 S.Ct. 383, 62 L. Ed. 2d 332 (1979), the Supreme Court indicated that the term 'navigability', as used in past Supreme Court decisions has been used to define four separate and distinct concepts: to delineate the boundaries of navigational servitudes; to define the scope of Congress' regulatory authority under the Interstate Commerce Clause; to determine the extent of authority of the Army Corps of Engineers under the Rivers and Harbors Appropriation Act of 1899; and, to establish the limits of the jurisdiction of the federal courts conferred by Article 111, Section 2 of the United States Constitution over admiralty and maritime cases.

Finneseth v. Carter, 712 F.2d 1041, 1043 (6th Cir. 1983); *Kaiser Aetna v. United States,* 444 U.S. at 171-72, 100 S.Ct. at 388, 62 L. Ed. 2d at 340-41. Thus, the fact that the Little River is a navigable water for the purposes of the Rivers and Harbors Appropriation Act of 1899, 33 U.S.C. § 401, *et. seq.,* is not dispositive in this case since the requirement of navigability under that Act and navigability for admiralty jurisdiction are not the same. *Finneseth,* 712 F.2d at 1043 n.l; *see* discussion in *Kaiser-Aetna, supra.*

* * *

"Navigable water" subject to admiralty jurisdiction is defined as including waters that are navigable in fact. *The Propeller Genesee Chief v. Fitzhugh,* 12 How. 443, 13 L. Ed. 1058 (1852). *See also, e.g., The Belfast,* 7 Wall. 624, 19 L. Ed. 266 (1869). This includes man-made or artificial bodies of water. *Ex Parte Boyer,* 109 U.S. 629, 3 S.Ct. 434, 27 L. Ed. 1056 (1884); *The Robert W. Parsons,* 191 U.S. 17, 24 S.Ct.8, 48L.Ed. 73 (1903); *Marine Transit Corp. v. Dreyfus,* 284 U.S. 263, 52 S.Ct. 166, 76 L. Ed. 282 (1932).

At this juncture the Court is hard-pressed to find a definition of "navigable in fact" for purposes of admiralty jurisdiction. Legions of lower courts have cited the time-honored cases of *The Daniel Ball,* 77 U.S. (10 Wall.) 557, 19 L. Ed. 999 (1871) and *The Montello,* 87 U.S. (20 Wall.) 430, 22 L. Ed. 391 as including the Supreme Court's definition of this term for admiralty jurisdiction. Indeed, *Ex Parte Boyer* tells us that *The Daniel Ball* and *The Montello* "extended the salutary views of admiralty jurisdiction applied in *The Genesee Chief*"109 U.S. at 631-32, 27 L. Ed. at 1057. But in *Kaiser Aetna v. U.S.,* the Supreme Court cites those same cases for the definition of "navigable waters" within the boundaries of "Congress' regulatory authority under the Commerce Clause". 444 U.S. at 172,

100 S.Ct. 383, 62 L. Ed. 2d at 341. This is the Courts dilemma: How can we follow *Ex Parte Boyer* without doing harm to *Kaiser Aetna* since admiralty jurisdiction and jurisdiction under the Commerce Clause are separate and distinct?

In *The Genesee Chief*, the Supreme Court spoke repeatedly of the substantial amount of commerce conducted on the inland rivers and great lakes of this country and of how it was as rich as that conducted on the high seas. 12 How. at 457, 13 L. Ed. at 1064. It stands to reason that such commerce played an integral part in the courts extention of admiralty jurisdiction beyond the ebb and flow of the tide. Accordingly, in *The Steamboat Ad. Hine v. Trevor*, 71 U.S. (4 Wall.) 555, 18 L. Ed. 451 (1867), the Supreme Court stated that *The Genesee Chief* extended admiralty jurisdiction to "wherever ships float and navigation successfully aids commerce". 71 U.S. at 563, 18 L. Ed. at 453-54. Finally, in *Ex Parte Boyer*, it was held:

> Navigable water situated as this (Erie) canal is used for the purposes for which it is used, a highway for commerce between ports and places in different states, carried on by vessels such as those in question here (horse drawn barges), is public water of the United States, and within the legitimate scope of the admiralty jurisdiction conferred by the Constitution and statutes of the United States, even though the canal is wholly artificial, and is wholly within the body of a state, and subject to its ownership and control; and it makes no difference as to the jurisdiction of the district court that one or the other of the vessels was at the time of the collision on a voyage from one place in the state .to another place in that state.

109 U.S. at 632, 3 S.Ct. 434, 27 L. Ed. at 1057. *See, also, The Belfast*, 74 U.S. (7 Wall.) 624, 19 L. Ed. 266(1869). Thus, it appears that even if *The Daniel Ball* is a "separately distinct" Commerce Clause case, the cases cited above show that its definitions of "navigable waters" and waters "navigable in fact" are still appropriate for actions in admiralty:

> Those rivers must be regarded as public navigable rivers in law which are navigable in fact. And they are navigable in fact when they are used, or are susceptible of being used, in their ordinary condition, as highways for commerce, over which trade and travel are or may be conducted in the customary modes of trade and travel on water.

77 U.S. (10 Wall.) 557, 563, 19 L. Ed. 999, 1001 (1870). The Court can discern little difference between these definitions and the tenets extracted from *Ex Parte Boyer* above.

Placid Oil Company and at least one of its subdivisions explore for minerals in Catahoula Lake. According to the evidence, it has navigated crew boats over the weir at Archie, Louisiana to aid this exploration. The evidence also shows that at least one commercial fisherman has done the same in aid of his business. There is also evidence that part of this commerce has been conducted between states.

Defendant argues that if there is commerce on the Little River, it is not enough to support jurisdiction. Defendant does not deny its own transportation and drilling barge activities in that area. It has not rebutted Mr. Gibsons testimony. We think the amount of commerce is sufficient. *See, Respess v. U.S.*, 586 F. Supp. at 864 (commercial fishing); *Cf, Pippen v. Shell Oil Co.*, 661 F.2d 378, 384 (5th Cir. 1981) (offshore drilling is maritime commerce). *But see, Herb's Welding, Inc. v. Gray*, 470 U.S. 414, 105 S.Ct. 1421, 84 L. Ed. 2d 406 (1985) (welder working on fixed offshore oil-drilling platform held not engaged in maritime employment for purposes of the LHWCA, 33 U.S.C. §§ 901, *et. seq.*).

It is also relevant that the Army Corps of Engineers holds the Little River and Catahoula Lake as navigable waters of the United States, maintains structures throughout the system at issue in this case and deems it necessary that Placid obtain a permit which governs the placing of structures in those waters in order to conduct their exploration. These determinations are not controlling, *see, Kaiser Aetna v. U.S., supra*, but from an evidentiary point of view they are not without significance and may be taken into account. *Finneseth v. Carter*, 712 F.2d at 1045 n.4;

Hartman v. U.S., 522 F. Supp. 114, 117 (D. S.C. 1981); *Sawczyk v. U.S.C.G.,* 499 F. Supp. 1034, 1039 (W.D.N.Y. 1980); *see also, United States v. Oregon,* 295 U.S. 1, 23-24, 55 S.Ct. 610, 619, 79 L. Ed. 1267, 1278–79 (1935). The Court is also cognizant of the fact that Congress has declared that all the navigable rivers and waters in the former territories of Orleans and Louisiana shall be and forever remain public highways, 33 U.S.C. § 10, and accords that statement the weight it deserves.

Further, it is interesting to speculate that if the boat had caused injury in this case, plaintiff's might very well have petitioned this Court for limitation of liability. *See,* 46 U.S.C. § 188 (limitation applies to all vessels used on lakes or rivers or in inland navigation); *see generally,* Herman, *Limitation of Liability for Pleasure Craft,* 14 J. Mar. Law & Com. 417 (1983). In any event, the Court has no doubt that vessel navigation on the Little River is governed by the Inland Navigational Rules. 33 U.S.C. §§ 2001, *et. seq.* and both statutes are traditionally applied in admiralty. To draw the line for admiralty jurisdiction at the weir in Archie, as defendant would have us do, could only lead to confusion. The above statutes would then apply to boats downriver from the weir but not those upriver, even when the water is above 36 NGVD and conducive to through navigation. This we cannot do.

Defendant finally argues that the seasonal navigability over the weir renders the Little River above the weir and Catahoula Lake non-navigable. This argument also has no merit. Many rivers have portions of their waters which are impassable at certain times of the year. The upper Mississippi and the Saint Lawrence Seaway are examples of rivers that freeze during the winter months. Does this make those waters any less "navigable waters" for purposes of admiralty jurisdiction? We think not.

At this point, a quote from the appellate decision in *Foremost* is appropriate:

> We note additionally from the record that the place where the accident occurred (Amite River) is seldom, if ever, used for commercial activity. That does not cause us to vary from our holding. The waterway is not landlocked. It would be introducing another note of uncertainty to hold that admiralty jurisdiction extends only to a stretch of navigable water that presently functions as a commercial artery. Jurisdiction should be as readily ascertainable as courts can make it. If the waterway is capable of being used in commerce, that is a sufficient threshold to invoke admiralty jurisdiction.

Richardson v. Foremost Ins. Co., 641 F.2d 314, 316 (5th Cir. 1981), *aff'd. sub nom. Foremost Ins. Co. v. Richardson,* 457 U.S. 668, 102 S.Ct. 2654, 73 L. Ed. 2d 300, *rehearing denied,* 459 U.S. 899, 103 S.Ct. 198, 74 L. Ed. 2d 160 (1982). The Little River, including Catahoula Lake, is neither landlocked nor incapable of commerce. The Court finds the accident involved in this case is within its admiralty jurisdiction. The cases of *Adams v. Montana Power Co.,* 528 F.2d 437 (9th Cir. 1975) (completely obstructed portion of Missouri River); *Chapman v. U.S.,* 575 F.2d 147 (7th Cir. 1978) (Kankakee River found not usable for commerce); *Livingston v. U.S.,* 627 F.2d 165 (8th Cir. 1980) (Norfork River obstructed and incapable of commerce); *Edwards v. Hurtel,* 717 F.2d 1204 (8th Cir. 1983) (Table Rock Lake found not susceptible of use for commerce); *Land and Lake Tours, Inc. v. Lewis,* 738 F.2d 961 (8th Cir. 1984) (Lake Hamilton obstructed by two dams found non-navigable under admiralty jurisdiction); *Dunham v. DeMaine,* 559 F. Supp. 224 (E.D. Ark. 1983) (*Lake Hamilton, supra);* and *Smith v. Hustler, Inc.,* 514 F. Supp. 1265 (W.D. La. 1981) (Lake Bistineau obstructed by dam found incapable of commerce) are inapposite. Plaintiffs' motion is GRANTED.

---

c. Artificial Bodies of Water

Note

Does the fact that the body of water is man-made preclude it from being "navigable"?

The Illinois and Michigan Canal is an artificial navigable waterway connecting Lake Michigan and the Chicago river with the Illinois river and the Mississippi river.... We take judicial notice of this historical fact that the canal... is capable of being navigated by vessels, which a canal of such size will accommodate, and which can pass from Mississippi river to Lake Michigan and carry on interstate commerce, although the canal is wholly within the territorial bounds of the state of Illinois.

* * *

Navigable water situated as this [Erie] canal is used for the purposes for which it is used, a highway for commerce between ports and places in different states, carried on by vessels such as those in question here (horse drawn barges), is public water of the United States, and within the legitimate scope of the admiralty jurisdiction conferred by the Constitution and statutes of the United States, even though the canal is wholly artificial, and is wholly within the body of a state, and subject to its ownership and control; and it makes no difference as to the jurisdiction of the district court that one or the other of the vessels was at the time of the collision on a voyage from one place in the state to another place in that state.

Ex Parte Boyer, 109 U.S. 629, 631-632, 3 S.Ct. 434, 27 L. Ed. 105 (1884).

_____

d.   *The Commerce Clause: "Historical" Navigability Requirement*

For purposes of regulatory jurisdiction under the Commerce Clause, U.S. Const. art. I, § 8, cl. 3, it is sufficient to show historical navigability (i.e., that the waters in question were once navigable) rather than "contemporary navigability in fact", which is the requirement for adjudicatory jurisdiction (i.e. the jurisdiction of admiralty courts to hear and decide disputes). *Land and Lake Tours, Inc. v. Lewis,* 738 F.2d 961 (8th Cir.), *cert. denied,* 469 U.S. 1038, 105 S.Ct. 517, 83 L. Ed. 2d 406 (1984). In that case, the U.S. Court of Appeals for the Eighth Circuit held that the U.S. Coast Guard had jurisdiction to conduct safety inspections of amphibious vehicles operating on Lake Hamilton, Arkansas, a lake that was not "presently navigable in fact". The court said:

The case at bar did not involve the district courts article III admiralty jurisdiction, but instead Congress' article I power to regulate interstate commerce. As noted in *Kaiser Aetna v. United States,* 444 U.S. at 173-74, 100 S.Ct. at 389-90, Congress' article I power to regulate interstate commerce does not depend upon "navigability." Here, the federal government has an intense interest in the safety of passenger vessels, and the safety of passenger vessels has a substantial effect on interstate commerce. Undoubtedly Congress may require the inspection of passenger vessels, impose safety requirements, and "exercise its authority for such other reason as may seem to it in the interest of furthering navigation or commerce." *Id.* at 174, 100 S.Ct. at 390.

* * *

Thus, the vessel safety specifications and periodic safety inspection requirements represent an exercise of Congressional power under the commerce clause, which has been delegated to the Coast Guard.

_____

C. **Maritime Torts**

Note: *Jurisdiction in Tort*

In tort cases, a party seeking admiralty jurisdiction must allege that the tort occurred on navigable waters and that the tort bore some relationship to traditional maritime activity. The first requirement is referred to as the maritime location criterion and the second requirement is referred to as the maritime nexus criterion. Maritime location is satisfied by showing that the tort occurred on navigable waters. The maritime nexus criterion is of relatively recent origin and its meaning is still being developed. This criterion was created by the Supreme Court to restrict the scope of admiralty tort jurisdiction for various policy reasons, not the least of which were considerations of federalism and a desire to confine the exercise of admiralty jurisdiction to situations which implicate national interests.

_____

1. Maritime Location Criterion

Note

The locality requirement for admiralty tort jurisdiction was enunciated in *The Plymouth,* 70 U.S. (3 Wall.) 20, 18 L. Ed. 125 (1865), a case involving a fire aboard ship which had spread to and damaged a nearby wharf. There the Court stated:

> [T]he wrong and injury complained of must have been committed wholly upon the high seas or navigable waters, or, at least, the substance and consummation of the same must have taken place upon these waters to be within the admiralty jurisdiction....

* * *

> ... The jurisdiction of the admiralty over maritime torts does not depend upon the wrong having been committed on board the vessel, but upon its having been committed upon the high seas or other navigable waters.
>
> ... Every species of tort, however occurring, and whether on board a vessel or not, if upon the high seas or navigable waters, is of admiralty cognizance.

The locality test was a strictly applied as the Court stated further that:

> [T]he simple fact that [the fire originated] on navigable waters, but, the whole damage done upon the land, the cause of action not being complete on navigable waters, affords no ground for the exercise of the admiralty jurisdiction.

In most run of the mill maritime tort suits jurisdiction is beyond challenge. In typical situations involving collisions, or injury to persons or damage to property aboard a vessel in navigable waters, admiralty jurisdiction is evident.

This locality test, of course, was established and grew up in an era when it was difficult to conceive of a tortious occurrence on navigable waters other than in connection with a waterborne vessel. Indeed, for the traditional types of maritime torts, the traditional test has worked quite satisfactorily. As a leading admiralty text has put the matter:

> It should be stressed that the important cases in admiralty are not the borderline cases on jurisdiction; these may exercise a perverse fascination in the occasion they afford for elaborate casuistry, but the main business of the [admiralty] court involves claims for cargo damage, collision, seamen's injuries and the like—all well and comfortably within the circle, and far from the penumbra. G. Gilmore & C. Black, The Law of Admiralty 24 n.88 (1957).

Executive Jet Aviation, Inc. v. City of Cleveland, 409 U.S. 249, 93 S.Ct. 493, 34 L. Ed. 2d 454, 1973 AMC 1 (1972).

But as the *The Plymouth, supra,* shows, events which have their origin on the water may effect interests on land. Conversely, events which begin on land may impact on vessels in navigable waters. Thus, the strict locality rule has been modified both by Congress and the courts. In *The Blackheath,* 195 U.S. 361, 25 S.Ct. 46, 49 L. Ed. 236 (1904), the Supreme Court held that damage done by a vessel to fixed navigational aids, in this cases, a channel light, was within admiralty jurisdiction, despite the fact that the light was built on pilings and was not truly on "navigable waters. The Court continued to relax the rule in "borderline cases. *See, The Admiral Peoples,* 295 U.S. 649, 55 S.Ct. 885, 79 L. Ed. 1633 (1935), *infra.* In 1948, Congress extended tort jurisdiction to injuries and damage sustained on land with the enactment of the Admiralty Extension Act. *See,* Section 2, *infra.*

THE ADMIRAL PEOPLES

295 U.S. 649, 55 S.Ct. 885, 79 L. Ed. 1633 (1935)

Mr. Chief Justice HUGHES delivered the opinion of the Court

Petitioner was a passenger on the steamship "Admiral Peoples" on her voyage from Wilmington, Cal., to Portland, Or. While disembarking at Portland petitioner was injured by falling from a gangplank leading from the vessel to the dock. This libel *in rem* against the vessel alleged that respondent placed the gangplank so that it sloped from the ship toward the dock at an angle of from ten to fifteen degrees; that it was approximately two feet in width and eighteen feet in length and was equipped with the usual rope railings which terminated approximately three feet from each end; that the level of the plank at the shore end was about six inches above the level of the dock, thereby creating a step from the plank to the dock; that upon instructions from one of respondent's officers, libelant proceeded along the plank and as she reached its lower end, being unaware of the step and having no warning, she fell from the plank and was "violently and forcibly thrown forward upon the dock in such manner as to cause the injuries hereinafter set forth." Libelant alleged negligence in failing to provide a hand rope or railing extending along either side of the gangplank to the shore end, in failing to have the plank flush with the dock or taper off to the level of the dock, and in failing to give warning of the step.

Respondents exception to the libel, upon the ground that the case was not within the admiralty jurisdiction, was sustained by the District Court, and its judgment dismissing the libel was affirmed by the Circuit Court of Appeals. In view of an asserted conflict with other decisions of the federal courts, we granted a writ of certiorari. 294 U.S. 702, 55 S.Ct. 546, 79 L. Ed. —.

This is one of the border cases involving the close distinctions which from time to time are necessary in applying the principles governing the admiralty jurisdiction. That jurisdiction in cases of tort depends upon the locality of the injury. It does not extend to injuries caused by a vessel to persons or property on the land. Where the cause of action arises upon the land, the state law is applicable.

* * *

The basic fact in the instant case is that the gangplank was a part of the vessel. It was a part of the vessel's equipment which was placed in position to enable its passengers to reach the shore. It was no less a part of the vessel because in its extension to the dock it projected over the land. Thus, while the libelant was on the gangplank she had not yet left the vessel. This was still true as she proceeded to the shore end of the plank. If while on that part of the vessel she had been hit by a swinging crane and had been precipitated upon the dock, the admiralty would have had jurisdiction of her claim. *See Minnie v. Port Huron Terminal Company*, 295 U.S. 647, 55 S.Ct. 884, 79 L. Ed. —, decided this day. If instead of being struck in this way, the negligent handling of the vessel, as by a sudden movement, had caused her to fall from the gangplank, the cause of action would still have arisen on the vessel. We perceive no basis for a sound distinction because her fall was due to negligence in the construction or placing of the gangplank. By reason of that neglect, as the libel alleges, she fell from the plank and was violently thrown forward upon the dock. Neither the short distance that she fell nor the fact that she fell on the dock and not in the water, alters the nature of the cause of action which arose from the breach of duty owing to her while she was still on the ship and using its facility for disembarking.

This view is supported by the weight of authority in the federal courts. In *The Strabo* (D.C.) 90 F 110, *Id.* (C.C.A.) 98 F 998, libelant, who was working on a vessel lying at a dock, attempted to leave the vessel by means of a ladder which, by reason of the master's negligence, was not secured properly to the ship's rail and in consequence the ladder fell and the libelant was thrown to the dock and injured. The District Court, sustaining the admiralty jurisdiction, asked these pertinent questions (90 F 110, page 113): "If a passenger, standing at the gangway, for the purpose of alighting, were disturbed by some negligent act of the master, would the jurisdiction of this court depend upon the fact whether he fell on the dock, and remained there, or whether he was precipitated upon the dock in the first instance, or finally landed there after first falling on some part of the ship? If a seaman, by the masters neglect, should fall overboard, would this court entertain jurisdiction if the seaman fell in the water, and decline jurisdiction if he fell on the dock or other land? The inception of a cause of action is not usually defined by such a rule." The Circuit Court of Appeals of the Second Circuit, affirming the decision of the District Court (98 F 998, page 1000), thought it would be a too literal and an inadmissible interpretation of the language used in *The Plymouth, supra,* to say that "if a passenger on board a steamship should, through the negligence of the owner's, stumble on the ship upon a defective gangplank, and be precipitated upon the wharf, the injury would not be a maritime tort." "The language employed in the *Plymouth* decision," said the court, "and which was applicable to the circumstances of that case, does not justify such a conclusion." And, deciding the case before it, the Circuit Court of Appeals said: "The cause

---

*[70 U.S. (3 Wall.) 20, 18 L. Ed. 125 (1866) (admiralty does not provide a remedy for damage done to land structures by ships on navigable waters). Eds.]

of action originated and the injury had commenced on the ship, the consummation somewhere being inevitable. It is not of vital importance to the admiralty jurisdiction whether the injury culminated on the string piece of the wharf or in the water." *See, also, The Atna* (D.C.) 297 Fed. 673, 675, 676; *The Brand* (D.C.) 29 F. (2d) 792.

* * *

We think that the libel presented a case within the jurisdiction of admiralty. The decree of the Circuit Court of Appeals is reversed, and the cause is remanded for further proceedings in conformity with this opinion.

It is so ordered.

---

2. *The Admiralty Extension Act*

a. Text

46 U.S.C.A. § 30101 (2007)

§ 30101. Extension of jurisdiction to cases of damage or injury to land

(a) In General—The admiralty and maritime jurisdiction of the United States extends to and includes cases of injury or damage, to person or property, caused by a vessel on navigable waters, even though the injury or damage is done or consummated on land.

(b) Procedure—A civil action in a case under subsection (a) may be brought *in rem* or *in personam* according to the principles of law and the rules of practice applicable in cases where the injury or damage has been done and consummated on navigable waters.

46 U.S.C. § 740 (1948)

(Superseded Version)

The admiralty and maritime jurisdiction of the United States shall extend to and include all cases of damage or injury to person or property, caused by a vessel on navigable water, notwithstanding that such damage or injury be done or consummated on land.

In any such case suit may be brought *in rem* or *in personam* according to the principles of law and the rules of practice obtaining in cases where the injury or damage has been done and consummated on navigable water....[**]

Note: *The Purpose of the Admiralty Extension Act*

The legislative history of the Admiralty Extension Act describes its purposes, and the inequities which it was designed to correct:

> As a result of the denial of admiralty jurisdiction in cases where injury is done on land, when a vessel collides with a bridge through mutual fault and both are damaged, under existing law the owner of the bridge, being denied a remedy in admiralty, is barred by contributory negligence from any recovery in an action at law. But the owner of the vessel may bring a suit in admiralty recover half damages from the bridge, contributory negligence operating merely to reduce the recovery. Further, where a collision between a vessel and a land structure is caused by the fault of a compulsory pilot, the owner of the land structure is without remedies for his injuries since at law a compulsory pilot is not deemed the servant of the vessel's master or owner.... But if the vessel sheers off the land structure to collide with another vessel in the vicinity, the owner of the second vessel, by an in rem proceeding in admiralty, may recover full damages, for the wrong is viewed as that of

---

[**] The Act also provides as follows:

...Provided, That as to any suit against the United States for damage or injury done or consummated on land by a vessel on navigable waters, the Public Vessels Act or Suits in Admiralty Act, as appropriate, shall constitute the exclusive remedy for all causes of action arising after June 19, 1948, and for all causes of action where suit has not been hitherto filed under the Federal Tort Claims Act: Provided further, That no suit shall be filed against the United States until there shall have expired a period of six months after the claim has been presented in writing to the Federal agency owning or operating the vessel causing the injury or damage.

the vessel itself and compulsory pilotage is no defense.... [The Admiralty Extension Act] would correct these inequities as a result of providing that the admiralty courts shall take cognizance of all of them.

* * *

Adoption of the bill will not create new causes of action. It merely specifically directs the courts to exercise the admiralty and maritime jurisdiction of the United States already conferred by article III, section 2 of the Constitution and already authorized by the Judiciary acts.

U.S. Code Cong. Serv. 1898, 1899-1900 (1948).

This interpretation was confirmed in the Fifth Circuit in *Louisville & N.R. Co. v. M/V Bayou Lacombe*, 597 F.2d 469, 1980 AMC 2914 (5th Cir. 1979), in which a railroad company sought relief at admiralty for damage done by a vessel to the company's railroad bridge:

The [Admiralty extension Act] does not create new causes of action; it merely expands the locality rule of torts. As a result of the Act, a plaintiff is no longer precluded from suing in admiralty when a vessel collides with a land structure, such as a bridge.
597 F.2d 469, 472 (1979) (citations omitted).

* * *

Note: Application of the Admiralty Extension Act by the Supreme Court: Proximate Cause

In order for a plaintiff to invoke maritime jurisdiction under the Admiralty Extension Act, it must be alleged that the proximate cause of the plaintiff's injury on shore was negligence by the vessel or its defective appurtenances. This rule may be gleaned from two seminal Supreme Court decisions.

In *Gutierrez v. Waterman Steamship Corp.*, 373 U.S. 206, 83 S.Ct. 1185, 10 L. Ed. 2d 297 (1963), a longshoreman sued for injuries sustained when he slipped on beans that had become scattered about a dock during their unloading due to defective cargo containers.* The court found that:

The shipowner knew or should have known that injury was likely to result to persons who would have to work around the beans spilled from the defective bags, and it was negligent in allowing cargo so poorly stowed or laden to be unloaded. Petitioner fell on the beans and injured himself, and such injuries were proximately caused by the respondent's negligence and the unseaworthiness of its cargo or cargo containers. *Id.* at 207.

In determining that a claim had been properly raised under the Admiralty Extension Act, the Supreme Court stated:

* * *

I.

Respondent contends that it is not liable, at least in admiralty, because the impact of its alleged lack of care or unseaworthiness was felt on the pier rather than aboard ship. Whatever validity this proposition may have had until 1948, the passage of the Extension of Admiralty Jurisdiction Act, 62 Stat. 496, 46 U.S.C. § 740, swept it away when it made vessels on navigable water liable for damage or injury "notwithstanding that such damage or injury be done or consummated on land." Respondent and the carrier *amici curiae* would have the statute limited to injuries actually caused by the physical agency of the vessel or a particular part of it—such as when the ship rams a bridge or when its defective winch drops some cargo onto a longshoreman. *Cf. Strika v. Netherlands Ministry of Traffic*, 185 F.2d 555 (C.A. 2d Cir.); *Hagans v. Farrell Lines*, 237 F.2d 477 (C.A. 3d Cir.). Nothing in the legislative history supports so restrictive an interpretation of the statutory language. There is no distinction in admiralty between torts committed by the ship itself and by the ship's personnel while operating it, any more than there is between torts "committed" by a corporation and by its employees. And ships are libeled as readily for an unduly bellicose mate's assault on a crewman, *see Boudoin v. Lykes*

---

*[At one time, the Supreme Court recognized an action for unseaworthiness on behalf of longshoremen who qualified as "Sieracki seamen". This action was legislatively overruled by the 1972 Amendments to the Longshore Harbor Workers' Compensation Act. 33 U.S.C. § 905(b) (1982). Eds.]

Bros. Co., 348 U.S. 336, 339-340; *The Rolph,* 299 F. 52 (C.A. 9th Cir.), or for having an incompetent crew or master, *see Keen v. Overseas Tankship Corp.,* 194 F.2d 515, 517 (C.A. 2d Cir.), as for a collision. Various farfetched hypotheticals are raised, such as a suit in admiralty for an ordinary automobile accident involving a ship's officer on ship business in port, or for someone's slipping on beans that continue to leak from these bags in a warehouse in Denver. We think it sufficient for the needs of this occasion to hold that the case is within the maritime jurisdiction under 46 U.S.C. § 740 when, as here, it is alleged that the shipowner commits a tort while or before the ship is being unloaded, and the impact of which is felt ashore at a time and place not remote from the wrongful act. *Id.* at 209-10.

However, in *Victory Carriers, Inc. v. Law,* 404 U.S. 202, 92 S.Ct. 418, 30 L. Ed. 2d 383, 1972 AMC 1 (1971), the Court found that the Act did not encompass the injuries of a longshoreman which occurred during the loading process when the overhead protection rack of his fork lift, owned by the stevedoring company, came loose and fell on him. Confronted with the argument that the Act extended to the injury because the longshoreman had been engaged in the service of a vessel on navigable waters, the Court held:

* * *

The decision in *Gutierrez* turned, not on the "function" the stevedore was performing at the time of his injury, but, rather, upon the fact that his injury was caused by an appurtenance of a ship, the defective cargo containers, which the Court held to be an "injury, to person ... caused by a vessel on navigable water" which was consummated ashore under 46 U.S.C. § 740. The Court has never approved an unseaworthiness recovery for an injury sustained on land merely because the injured longshoreman was engaged in the process of "loading" or "unloading."[11] *Nacirema Operating Co. v. Johnson,* 396 U.S., at 223, a case decided several years after *Gutierrez,* makes this quite clear:

> There is much to be said for uniform treatment of longshoremen injured while loading or unloading a ship. But even construing the Extension Act to amend the Longshoremen's Act would not effect this result, since longshoremen injured on a pier by pier-based equipment would still remain outside the Act. Id. at 210-11, 92 S.Ct. at 424.

* * *

Consequently, the Supreme Court declined to "extend the reach" of the Act "to pier-side accidents caused by a stevedore's pier-based equipment." Id. at 204, 92 S.Ct. at 421.

---

b. Application of the Admiralty Extension Act: Cases and Notes

DULUTH SUPERIOR EXCURSIONS, INC. v. MAKELA

623 F.2d 1251, 1980 AMC 2518 (8th Cir. 1980)

BRIGHT, Circuit Judge

Duluth Superior Excursions, Inc. and Flamingo Excursions, Inc. (collectively, Excursions) brought this action in federal court seeking to limit their potential liability to Joseph Makela under the Shipowner's Limitation of Liability Act, 46 U.S.C. §§ 181-189 (1976). The district court dismissed the action, holding that Excursions had

---

[11] In *Gutierrez,* the Court concluded that "things about a ship, whether the hull, the decks, the machinery, the tools furnished, the stowage, or the cargo containers, must be reasonably fit for the purpose for which they are to be used." 373 U.S., at 213. In *Alaska S.S. Co. v. Petterson,* 347 U.S. 396 (1954), *aff'g 205* F.2d 478 (CA9 1953), and *Rogers v. United States Lines,* 347 U.S. 984 (1954), *rev'g* 205 F.2d 57 (CA3 1954), the Court decided without opinion that an unseaworthiness recovery would be possible to a longshoreman injured by equipment brought aboard ship by the stevedore company. In both these cases, the accident occurred on navigable water: both longshoremen were injured while in the hold of a ship by defective apparatus attached to the ship's gear.

failed to establish federal admiralty jurisdiction under 28 U.S.C. § 1333(1) (1976). For the reasons set forth below, we conclude that this determination was erroneous. Accordingly, we reverse.

I. Background

On the night of August 12, 1977, Joseph Makela was struck and seriously injured by a car while crossing Harbor Drive in Duluth, Minnesota. The driver of the car was allegedly intoxicated. Both Makela and the car's driver had just disembarked from the S.S. Flamingo after a three-hour privately chartered cruise around the Duluth-Superior harbor. The organizers of the charter cruise, having advertised it as a "booze cruise," had brought several kegs of beer on board. The Flamingo was owned by appellant Flamingo Excursions, Inc., and operated by appellant Duluth Superior Excursions, Inc.

In September 1977, Makelas attorney notified Excursions that a tort claim would be filed against them. Excursions responded by filing the present action in federal court on February 10, 1978, seeking to limit their potential liability to the value of the S.S. Flamingo, her equipment, and any pending freight as of August 12, 1977. *See* 46 U.S.C. § 183(a) (1976).[1] Excursions offered an ad interim stipulation for value in the sum of $51,000, alleging that this sum exceeded the aggregate value of their interest in the vessel.

In October 1978, Makela filed a tort action in Minnesota state court, naming as defendants the driver of the car that struck him, the driver's father, the cruise organizers, and Excursions.[2] Makelas claim against Excursions was that Excursions inadequately supervised the passengers aboard the Flamingo, who consequently became illegally intoxicated, and that Excursions failed to provide a safe means of exit for these passengers. The federal action brought by Excursions against Makela was dismissed for want of jurisdiction on November 8, 1979.

II. Analysis

In *Executive Jet Aviation v. City of Cleveland,* 409 U.S. 249, 93 S.Ct. 493, 34 L. Ed. 2d 454 (1972), the Supreme Court recounted the history of maritime tort jurisdiction. Traditionally, the test of jurisdiction was whether the tort was "located" on navigable waters. *E.g., The Plymouth,* 70 U.S. (3 Wall.) 20, 18 L. Ed. 125 (1866). Because this test has proven unsatisfactory in many cases, the Court in *Executive Jet* placed its imprimatur on the more modern test of whether the alleged wrong is related to traditional maritime activity. *See id.* at 261, 93 S.Ct. at 501.[3]

In the case at hand, there is little question that the wrongs allegedly committed by Excursions took place on navigable waters.[4] The district court held, however, that Excursions failed to show the requisite relationship between these wrongs and traditional maritime activities. The district court based this holding upon its conclusion that inadequate supervision, illegal intoxication, and failure to provide a safe exit are not traditional maritime acts.

The district court may well have been correct in this surmise. The question before the court, however, was whether these alleged acts were related to (*i.e.,* occurred in connection with) traditional maritime activities. Carrying passengers for hire is undoubtedly a traditional maritime activity, and suits in tort for personal injuries to passengers are clearly included in admiralty jurisdiction. *E.g., St. Hilaire Moye v. Henderson,* 496 F.2d 973 (8th Cir.), *cert. denied,* 419 U.S. 884, 95 S.Ct. 151, 42 L. Ed. 2d 125 (1974). *See* G. GILMORE AND C. BLACK, THE LAW OF ADMIRALTY 23 & 23 n.77 (2d ed. 1975). The nature of the allegedly negligent acts underlying Makelas claims against appellant's is largely irrelevant. It is sufficient for purposes of admiralty jurisdiction in this case that a passenger is suing for personal injuries allegedly due to the negligence of the vessels owner's and crew on navigable waters. *See Kermarec v. Compagnie Generale,* 358 U.S. 625, 79 S.Ct. 406, 3 L. Ed. 2d 550 (1959); *Gibboney v. Wright,* 517 F.2d 1054, 1059 (5th Cir. 1975).

---

[1] 46 U.S.C. § 183(a) provides in pertinent part as follows:

(a) The liability of the owner of any vessel, whether American or foreign, for any... act, matter, or thing, loss, damage, or forfeiture, done, occasioned, or incurred, without the privity or knowledge of such owner or owner's, shall not, except in the cases provided for in subsection (b) of this section, exceed the amount or value of the interest of such owner in such vessel, and her freight then pending. The district court did not reach the issue of whether this statute applies here; neither do we.

[2] The parties have informed us that this lawsuit has not yet gone to trial.

[3] At issue in *Executive Jet* was a claim for property damage to an airplane that crashed and sank in Lake Erie. The Court in that case held specifically that, absent either a showing of a significant relationship between the wrong and traditional maritime activity or legislation to the contrary, claims arising from airplane accidents over navigable waters are not cognizable in admiralty. *Id.* at 268, 93 S.Ct. at 504.

[4] It is true, as Makela notes, that the injury he suffered was consummated on dry land. That fact, however, does not change the locale of appellants' alleged wrongs, nor does it destroy admiralty jurisdiction in this case. *See* text at note 5 *infra*.

To be sure, the accident that injured Makela occurred on dry land. Under the terms of the Admiralty Extension Act, 46 U.S.C. § 740 (1976), however, this circumstance does not destroy admiralty jurisdiction over Makelas claims against the appellant's. The Admiralty Extension Act provides in pertinent part:

The admiralty and maritime jurisdiction of the United States shall extent to and include all cases of damage or injury, to person or property, caused by a vessel on navigable water, notwithstanding that such damage or injury be done or consummated on land.

In *Gutierrez v. Waterman* S.S. Corp., 373 U.S. 206, 210, 83 S.Ct. 1185, 1188, 10 L. Ed. 2d 297 (1963), the Supreme Court held that the Admiralty Extension Act applies not only to injuries caused by the impact of a vessel itself, but also to those due to alleged acts of negligence by a vessels crew. In that case, a longshoreman was injured when he slipped on loose beans that had been spilled on the dock from defective bags in the course of unloading. The defendant argued that the federal courts lacked jurisdiction to hear the longshoremans claims. The Court held, however, that admiralty jurisdiction is established when it is alleged that the shipowner commits a tort while or before the ship is being unloaded, and the impact of which is felt ashore at a time and place not remote from the wrongful act. [*Id.* at 210, 83 S.Ct. at 1188 (footnote omitted).] These conditions for admiralty jurisdiction are fully satisfied in the present case.[5] *Cf. Tullis v. Fidelity and Casualty Co. of New York*, 397 F.2d 22, 23-24 (5th Cir. 1968) (admiralty jurisdiction established by a crew boat passengers allegation that defendant boat owner failed to provide a reasonably safe means of debarking).[6]

* * *

Here, Mr. Makela, like the plaintiff in *Byrd*, was a passenger aboard a commercial vessel and the defendants are its owner's and operators. Their alleged negligence, unlike that of the defendant driver in *Peytavin*, involves their performance of maritime duties in caring for their passengers. *Cf St. Hilaire Moye v. Henderson*, supra (admiralty defendants found negligent in their operation of a pleasure boat). Finally, we note that the sequence of causal events alleged in this case started on board the vessel and ended on land, calling into play the Admiralty Extension Act. None of the cases cited by Makela shares this last critical feature. Nor do they address the duties of vessel owner's or operators to their passengers, a traditional maritime concern.

We conclude, then, that Makelas claim against Excursions comes within the admiralty jurisdiction of the federal courts. We reverse the decision of the district court dismissing the appellants' action, and remand the case for further proceedings consistent with this opinion.

---

[5] Although it might be argued that Makelas injury is remote from the wrongful act, the accident occurred some six minutes after the S.S. Flamingo docked on a street that adjoins the dock. In our view, this is not sufficiently remote in time and space to destroy admiralty jurisdiction. We intimate no view as to whether Makelas injury was remote in the sense of not having been proximately caused by the appellants' alleged acts of negligence. That issue remains for the trier of fact to decide. *But cf. Pryor v. American President Lines*, 520 F.2d 974 (4th Cir. 1975), cert. denied, 423 U.S. 1055, 96 S.Ct. 787, 46 L. Ed. 644 (1976), and cases there cited (requiring proximate cause to invoke the Admiralty Extension Act in cases where the only permissible inference is that the vessel did not proximately cause the injury).

[6] In *Gutierrez v. Waterman S.S. Corp.*, supra, the Supreme Court not only found admiralty jurisdiction, but also held that the defendant shipowner was negligent towards the plaintiff longshoreman and strictly liable for breach of its warranty of seaworthiness. The Court restricted the scope of this latter holding in *Victory Carriers, Inc. v. Law*, 404 U.S. 202, 92 S.Ct. 418, 30 L. Ed. 2d 383 (1971), another longshoreman suit for dockside injuries, this time caused by equipment owned and operated by the stevedore. After observing that "in *Gutierrez*, supra, federal admiralty jurisdiction was clearly present since the Admiralty Extension Act on its face reached the injury there involved [,]" the Court stated:

The decision in *Gutierrez* turned, not on the "function" the stevedore was performing at the time of his injury, but, rather, upon the fact that his injury was caused by an appurtenance of a ship, the defective cargo containers, which the Court held to be an "injury, to person . . . caused by a vessel on navigable water" which was consummated ashore under 46 U.S.C. § 740. The Court has never approved an unseaworthiness recovery for an injury sustained on land merely because the injured longshoreman was engaged in the process of "loading" or "unloading." [*Id.* at 210-11, 92 S.Ct. at 424 (footnote omitted).]

Since *Victory Carriers*, courts faced with onshore seaworthiness claims have typically attempted to ascertain whether the allegedly defective piece of equipment causing the injury was, at the time of the accident, an appurtenance of a vessel. *See, e.g., Kinsella v. Zim Israel Navigation Co., Ltd.*, 513 F.2d 701 (1st Cir. 1975). In the case at hand, however, this issue does not arise, as there is no claim of unseaworthiness. Makela Simply alleges that the appellant's were negligent in operating the S.S. Flamingo on navigable waters and in providing a safe means of exit for its passengers. *See generally* 7AMoore's Federal Practice P.325[4] (2d ed. 1979).

[7] Makela points out that his injuries, like those of the whiplash victim in *Peytavin*, show no particular maritime character. The same thing is true, however, of the fall on spilled beans suffered by the plaintiff longshoreman in *Gutierrez*, supra. *Cf. The Admiral Peoples*, 295 U.S. 649, 55 S.Ct. 885, 79 L. Ed. 1633 (1935) (admiralty plaintiff who fell off a step at the end of a gangplank onto the dock recovered damages). We do not consider the nature of the plaintiff's injury to be critical in determining the scope of admiralty jurisdiction.

Note

In *Young v. Players Lake Charles, L.L.C.*, 47 F.Supp.2d 1251, 1999 AMC 2529 (S.D.Tex. 1999), it was held that claims arising from a fatal car crash on Interstate 10 in Vinton, Louisiana, were within the court's admiralty jurisdiction. The crash was caused by the extreme intoxication of a driver who had been plied with free alcohol at a casino boat in Lake Charles, Louisiana, some 23 miles away. The operator of the casino boat sought to rely on a Louisiana statute that (remarkably) confers immunity on providers of alcohol from liability for the actions of those to whom they sell or serve alcohol: see La.Rev.Stat.Ann. § 9:2800.1. The court refused to apply the Louisiana statute. Because the case was within the court's admiralty jurisdiction, it was governed by general maritime law, not state law, and the court held that general maritime law imposes "dram shop" liability on providers of alcohol.

Question

Plaintiff is injured on land by bombs dropped during a training exercise by U.S. Navy aircraft from a U.S. Navy aircraft carrier. Does the case fall within admiralty jurisdiction by operation of the Admiralty Extension Act? See *Anderson v. U.S.*, 317 F.3d 1235, 2003 AMC 94 (11th Cir. 2003).

WHITTINGTON v. SEWER CONSTRUCTION COMPANY, INC.

541 F.2d 427, 1976 AMC 967 (4th Cir. 1976)

BOREMAN, Senior Circuit Judge

On motion of the defendant, Sewer Construction Company, Inc. (hereafter Company or defendant), the district court dismissed this suit for lack of asserted admiralty jurisdiction. From the judgment of dismissal the plaintiff, Lawrence Whittington (hereafter Whittington or plaintiff), prosecutes this appeal.

In his complaint, containing two counts, Whittington alleged that the jurisdiction of the district court arises under and by virtue of the admiralty and maritime jurisdiction of the district courts of the United States: that this is an admiralty or maritime claim within the meaning of Rule 9(h) of the Federal Rules of Civil Procedure; that the defendant had in its possession and under its control a certain barge which was in navigation on the inland waterways of the United States, that is, on the Elk River in Kanawha County, West Virginia; that at all times mentioned in the complaint the plaintiff was employed on said barge by the defendant, "performing the work of a deckhand and seaman"; that while the plaintiff was a member of the crew of said barge working on the Elk River, within the territorial jurisdiction of the district court as an "able-bodied seaman in connection with his assigned duties and tasks," the defendant was negligent in that the plaintiff was being lowered from an overhead bridge to said barge and, in being so lowered, the plaintiff fell into said barge and was thereby seriously injured. In the second count Whittington alleged that because of his injuries it became the duty of the defendant to furnish the plaintiff with prompt medical care, attention and medicine and "the expenses of his maintenances [*sic*] and cure."

* * *

At the time Whittington was injured he was 47 or 48 years old. His employer, the defendant, was engaged in the demolition of a bridge which spanned the Elk River in Kanawha County, West Virginia, and one section near the east bank of the river had partially collapsed. In that section a hole approximately twelve feet square had been cut in the bridge flooring and an open barge was moored in the water underneath the hole between a bridge pier and the river bank. As the bridge was dismantled some of the wood decking, steel, concrete, and portions of the bridge structure were loaded into the barge to be later towed away.

* * *

The sole question here is the very narrow one of the admiralty jurisdiction of the district court. The undisputed factual disclosures lead us to conclude that this controversy is not within the district court's admiralty jurisdiction. Consequently, we affirm the judgment dismissing the suit.

Turning to the discovery deposition of Whittington, we glean from the questions asked and his answers thereto certain facts which will be shown in the following four paragraphs.

At various times and for about twenty-one years of his adult life he had worked as an overhead crane operator for different manufacturing plants and he had labored at different jobs, including seasonal work for the West Virginia Highway Department.

When employed by the defendant he was hired "as a crane and backhoe operator" on a bridge demolition job. Whittington checked out a crane for approximately two hours when he first went to work for the defendant and then he was put to work operating a pick, shovel and a jack hammer tearing up the concrete on the bridge deck. The west end of the bridge was intact and the workmen gained access to the bridge from that end as it was possible to drive trucks out on the bridge to help carry away the debris. Referring to the hole in the bridge flooring Whittington stated "You could have dropped a truck down through it if you had backed it up."

There was a barge in the river underneath the hole in the bridge which was for the purpose of "hauling away" the dismantled portions. Stationed on the bridge was a motored winch equipped with a drum and a cable line, the line running from the drum through a pulley on the superstructure of the bridge which was used for lowering materials through the hole in the bridge into the barge. There was a hook on the end of the cable and on the day before the plaintiff was injured he and another workman were, in turn, lowered through the hole in the bridge into the barge by means of the cable so they could detach bridge materials from the cable hook. On that occasion Whittington thought he worked there as much as "a half of a day." On the following day the plaintiff was directed to go into the barge again by the same means, riding the cable down with a "choker on the end." As the plaintiff explained—"A choker is a steel cable with two eyes in the end, one in one end and one in the other; that would be two loops." The choker was a piece of steel cable about five feet long; and he stated that he put his foot in the lower loop of the choker, the upper loop being fastened to the hook on the end of the winch's cable, and he grasped the cable line above the hook, above the top end of the choker line. In preparing to be lowered he was standing at the east side of the hole in the bridge and a short distance underneath there was a steel beam with a flange on it which went across the bridge below the flooring. He had one foot on the flange of the beam and put his other foot in the eye of the choker which was swinging free, preparing to descend into the barge. He had descended about five feet when the hook on the end of the cable rubbed against a piece of steel. As Whittington described it, "Well as I was going down, trying to push myself off the flange of the bridge, the hook caught on the flange of the bridge and rubbed the choker off—rubbed the eye off that hook, that is all. I just fell the rest of the way." A workman was on top of the bridge to push the whipline out so that plaintiff could descend into the barge but apparently the line was not pushed out far enough to avoid the flange of the steel beam. Plaintiff was injured when he landed on the debris and dismantled materials which had already been placed in the barge.

Near the end of his deposition Whittington stated that when he was employed he was supposed to have been the only skilled craftsman on the bridge, an "operator," but he wound up, in effect, doing laborer work which was what most of the other men on the demolition job did. He was asked the question whether, at any time, he considered himself an able-bodied seaman. He was instructed by his counsel not to answer. He was asked further whether, at any time from the time he was hired until he was injured, he understood that he was to work on a boat as such, and his counsel again objected. His deposition concluded, however, with interrogation by his own counsel and answers to the questions. His counsel asked whether he understood on the day before he was injured and the day on which he was injured that he was to work on a barge and he answered "The day before—I will phrase it this way: On the day before I got hurt, Gary Backland come to me and said, 'Larry, they need a guy to work down on the barge.' I said, All right; I don't mind.'"

One who seeks to recover for injuries in a suit based upon admiralty jurisdiction must show (1) that his injuries occurred upon navigable waters and had a maritime nexus, or (2) that the injuries were caused by a vessel in navigable waters or an appurtenance of the vessel, or (3) that the person injured was a seaman, a member of a crew of a vessel, injured in the course of his employment. *See Swanson v. Marra Brothers, Inc.,* 328 U.S. 1, 4-5, 66 S.Ct. 869, 90 L. Ed. 1045 (1946); *Executive Jet Aviation, Inc. v. Cleveland,* 409 U.S. 249, 93 S.Ct. 493, 34 L. Ed. 2d 454 (1972); Admiralty Extension Act, 46 U.S.C. § 740; 7A J. MOORE, FEDERAL PRACTICE, 2nd Ed. 1972. ¶ 325[4] at p. 3575.

It is clear that Whittington's injuries do not qualify under the first ground of admiralty jurisdiction as injuries occurring upon navigable waters *and* having a maritime nexus. For jurisdictional purposes we must look to the place where the incident occurred which ultimately gave rise to the cause of action. *T. Smith & Son, Inc. v. Taylor,* 276 U.S. 179, 48 S.Ct. 228, 72 L. Ed. 520 (1928);[1] *Hastings v. Mann,* 340 F.2d 910 (4 Cir. 1965).[2] In the instant case the tortious act which caused the plaintiff's injuries occurred while he was suspended from the shore-based winch. There is no allegation of negligence with respect to the barge. The alleged tortious conduct involved the shore-based winch and its attached "choker." Since the accident was "initiated" while the plaintiff was upon an extension of the land[3] and involved only shore-based equipment and conduct, no admiralty jurisdiction exists. *See May v. Lease Service, Inc.,* 365 F. Supp. 1202 (E.D. La.), *aff'd per curiam,* 487 F.2d 915 (5 Cir. 1973).[4] The mere fortuitous circumstance that the winch line dropped Whittington onto the barge rather than onto the shore is insufficient to qualify his injuries as occurring upon navigable waters for jurisdictional purposes. *Bible v. Chevron Oil Co.,* 460 F.2d 1218 (5 Cir. 1972).[5] Since the alleged tort did not occur upon the navigable waters, it fails to meet the first of the above-stated conditions necessary to establish that ground of admiralty jurisdiction. We need not, therefore, consider whether the tort and the resultant injury had a maritime nexus.

It would seem equally clear that Whittington was not injured by a vessel in navigation or an appurtenance thereof. The winch from which Whittington fell was located on the bridge which was being demolished. It is well established that a bridge is not a vessel within admiralty jurisdiction. *Rodrigue v. Aetna Casualty & Surety Co.,* 395 U.S. 352, 360 (1969). Thus, the fact that the winch was attached to a bridge establishes that it was not an appurtenance of the vessel, even though it may customarily be utilized in loading operations. *Victory Carriers, Inc. v. Law,* 404 U.S. 202 (1971); *McCullum v. United International Corp.,* 493 F.2d 501 (9 Cir. 1974). We conclude, therefore, that Whittington was not injured by a vessel in navigation or an appurtenance thereof, and that admiralty jurisdiction cannot be invoked upon this ground.

* * *

We conclude that the judgment of the district court must be affirmed.
Affirmed.

---

[1] In *T. Smith & Son, Inc. v. Taylor,* 276 U.S. 179, 48 S.Ct. 228, 72 L. Ed. 520 (1928), the plaintiff's decedent, a stevedore, while unloading a ship was struck by the sling of a ship-based winch, which knocked him from the pier apron on which he was standing and dropped him into navigable waters where he drowned. Although the Court found the deceased was engaged in maritime work, it concluded that no admiralty jurisdiction existed since "[t]he substance and consummation of the occurrence which gave rise to the cause of action took place on land." *Id.* at 182, 48 S.Ct. at 229. The subsequent passage of the Admiralty Extension Act, 46 U.S.C. § 740, would appear to have modified the rule of that case where the injury is caused by an appurtenance of a vessel, but, where, as in the case now before us, the injury is caused by shore-based equipment the rule is unchanged that when the event which "gave rise to the cause of action" occurred while the injured party "was upon the land" and is the "sole, immediate and proximate" cause of the injury, no admiralty jurisdiction exists.

[2] The plaintiff in *Hastings v. Mann,* 340 F.2d 910 (4 Cir. 1965), was injured when he slipped and fell from the submerged end of a ramp designed for the launching of small boats. The plaintiff insisted that the accident gave rise to a cause of action in admiralty since he was standing at the submerged end of the ramp in navigable water when he slipped. We affirmed the district court's dismissal for lack of admiralty jurisdiction since the plaintiff had slipped from an extension of the land, the boat ramp. Judge Haynsworth, speaking for this court, observed, "The fact that the libelant's feet were awash, when he slipped and fell on the ramp, does not alter the nature and character of the ramp or enlarge Admiralty's jurisdiction to award damages for injuries occurring upon it." *Id.* at 912 (footnote omitted).

[3] Whittington had one foot in the loop of the "choker" of the shore-based winch when the accident occurred. For jurisdictional purposes, a shore-based winch is treated as an extension of the land and not as a part of the vessel which it services. *See McCullum v. United Int'l Corp.,* 493 F.2d 501 (9 Cir. 1974); *Snydor v. Villain & Fassio et Compania Int'l Di Genova Societa Reunite Di Naviagaione, S.P.A.,* 459 F.2d 365 (4 Cir. 1972).

[4] There is a remarkable similarity between the situation which confronted the court in *May v. Lease Service, Inc.,* 365 F. Supp. 1202 (E.D. La.), *aff'd per curiam,* 487 F.2d 915 (5 Cir. 1973), and the facts in the case now before us. In *May* the plaintiff was employed as a laborer on a "fixed platform" in the Gulf of Mexico. Plaintiff was using a makeshift crane which was permanently affixed to the platform to unload some equipment from a ship. The crane, which was powered by the ship's generators, malfunctioned, throwing plaintiff from the platform and onto the ship. The court dismissed the case for lack of admiralty jurisdiction, noting that the accident was "initiated" on the platform which was an extension of the land and the fact that plaintiff landed on the ship as a result of his fall was not relevant in determining jurisdiction.

[5] *Bible v. Chevron Oil Co.,* 460 F.2d 1218 (5th Cir. 1972), involved a plaintiff who was "pulled off the drilling platform by a defective winch apparatus, striking a platform support beam before falling several more feet into the sea." *Id.* at 1219. The court noted that "[since the substance and consummation of the occurrence giving rise to the injuries sustained took place on the drilling platform, the fact that Bible ultimately wound up in the drink does not transform this 'land based' injury into a maritime injury." *Id.* at 1219 (citations omitted). Although that case could be distinguished from the case now before us since the actual injuries there resulted from striking the platform support beam which is an extension of land, the Supreme Court rejected such distinctions as inconsequential in *T. Smith & Son, Inc. v. Taylor,* 276 U.S. 179, 48 S.Ct. 228, 72 L. Ed. 520 (1928). In *Smith* the Court refused, for jurisdictional purposes, to distinguish those injuries incurred upon the land from those incurred after the plaintiff fell into the water. 276 U.S. at 182, 48 S.Ct. at 228.

MARGIN v. SEA-LAND SERVICES, INC.

812 F.2d 973, 1988 AMC 1213 (5th Cir. 1987)

CLARK, Chief Judge:

A suit under 33 U.S.C. § 905(b) for injuries sustained by a welder while he was working on a dock was dismissed by the district court at the conclusion of the plaintiff's case on the ground that the court lacked subject matter jurisdiction. Finding that no maritime jurisdiction over the plaintiff's claims under the Admiralty Extension Act, 46 U.S.C. § 740, was properly alleged, we affirm.

I

Robert Margin was employed as a welder/fitter by the Boland Marine and Manufacturing Corporation, which does ship repair work in the New Orleans area. On July 5, 1983, he was assigned to do repair work at the Sea-Land dock in New Orleans. At that time cargo operations at the terminal were under the control of Cooper Stevedoring Company (Cooper), which was in charge of discharging containers and stacking frames and hatch covers. After Margin arrived at the dock, he was assigned to do repair work aboard the M/V BOSTON, a vessel owned and operated by Sea-Land Services, Inc. (Sea-Land). Later in that shift, he was assigned to the dock area to repair stacking frames that had been removed from the BOSTON.

Margin and a fellow employee, Augie Michele, were working ashore in the dock area, standing inside several stacking frames when a hatch cover from the BOSTON was lowered directly above them by a gantry crane located on the dock. Michele saw the hatch cover descending and warned Margin. In an effort to escape what he perceived to be imminent danger Margin attempted to scale the stacking frames but slipped and fell approximately eight feet to the ground, suffering a separated shoulder. He sued Sea-Land and its insurer, Travelers Insurance Company, for his injuries under § 905(b). After Sea-Land filed a third-party complaint against Cooper, Margin amended his complaint and made Cooper a defendant, alleging that Cooper was the owner and operator of the crane. In their answers, the defendants asserted various defenses and contended that the court lacked jurisdiction because the parties were not diverse in citizenship and because the injuries occurred on a wharf and, therefore, outside of maritime jurisdiction.

At the close of the plaintiff's case, the defendants moved for an involuntary dismissal pursuant to FED. R. CIV. P. 41(b) and dismissal for lack of subject matter jurisdiction under FED. R. CIV. P. 12(b)(1). The district court held that it lacked jurisdiction because the parties were not of diverse citizenship, and, since Margin had failed to establish vessel negligence, he did not fulfill the requirements to raise a maritime claim under § 905(b). The district court found that the only negligence in this case, if any existed, lay with Cooper because its employees off-loaded a hatch cover over the area where the plaintiff was welding on the stacking frames. The district court, therefore, dismissed Margins claims against all the defendants, including Cooper. In further support of its order, the court observed that any claim against Cooper under state law would be barred by the Louisiana one-year prescriptive period because suit was not filed against that company until sixteen month after the injury. Having found that it lacked jurisdiction, the district court did not expressly address the motion for involuntary dismissal on the ground that the plaintiff had shown no right to relief.

II

In ruling on the defendants motions to dismiss for lack of jurisdiction and for failure to show vessel negligence, the district court held that it lacked subject matter jurisdiction over Margins claims because he established no cause of action under § 905(b). Failure to prove a claim must be distinguished, however, from lack of jurisdiction. *See Daigle v. Opelousas Health Care, Inc.*, 774 F.2d 1344, 1346-48 (5th Cir. 1985). Although the distinction does not affect the outcome in this case, our jurisdictional limitations require that it be observed in the analysis of such matters.

A

By amending its complaint to add Cooper as a defendant, Margin destroyed diversity as a basis for subject matter jurisdiction. Jurisdiction could not rest on § 905(b), which only authorizes a cause of action when jurisdiction already exists. *See May v. Transworld Drilling Co.,* 786 F.2d 1261, 1263 (5th Cir.), *cert. denied,* — U.S. —, 479 U.S. 854, 107 S.Ct. 190, 93 L. Ed. 2d 123 (1986). Furthermore, Margin could not have invoked traditional maritime jurisdiction, because he did not allege a tort that occurred on navigable waters and thus failed to satisfy the locality rule. *See Executive Jet Aviation v. City of Cleveland,* 409 U.S. 249, 253, 93 S.Ct. 493, 497, 34 L. Ed. 2d 454 (1972).

Margin urges on appeal that the district court had maritime jurisdiction under the Admiralty Extension Act, 46 U.S.C. § 740. That Act extends admiralty jurisdiction to "all cases of damage or injury, to person and property, caused by a vessel on navigable water, notwithstanding that such damage or injury be done or consummated on land."

* * *

The rule that we derive from *Gutierrez* and *Victory Carriers* is that, to invoke maritime jurisdiction under the Admiralty Extension Act, a plaintiff injured on shore must allege that the injury was caused by a defective appurtenance of a ship on navigable waters. It is not enough that the plaintiff alleges he was engaged in stevedoring activities and the accident would not have occurred but for the presence of the ship alongside the dock. The vessel or its defective appurtenances must be the proximate cause of the accident. This court has refused to extend the reach of the Act absent proximate cause. *See Adams v. Harris County,* 452 F.2d 994, 996-97 (5th Cir. 1971), *cert. denied,* 406 U.S. 968, 92 S.Ct. 2414, 32 L. Ed. 2d 667 (1972) (vessel approaching draw bridge did not proximately cause motorcyclist's accident when bridge keeper negligently dropped barricade and opened bridge to allow passage); *Kent v. Shell Oil Co.,* 286 F.2d 746, 749-50 (5th Cir. 1961) (vessel did not cause injury sustained by truck driver when oil field pipe unexpectedly rolled off his truck bed onto him as he stood between truck and barge on which it was to be loaded). *See also Pryor v. American President Lines,* 520 F.2d 974, 979 (4th Cir. 1975), *cert. denied,* 423 U.S. 1055, 96 S.Ct. 787, 46 L. Ed. 2d 644 (1976) (agreeing "with the Fifth Circuit ... that a ship or its appurtenances must proximately cause an injury on shore to invoke the Admiralty Extension Act and the application of maritime law"). Accordingly, we must determine whether Margin alleged that a defective appurtenance of the BOSTON proximately caused his injury.

B

The district court is a court of limited jurisdiction and can only exercise that jurisdiction which is statutorily conferred upon it by Congress. The basis for federal subject matter jurisdiction must affirmatively appear in the pleading of the party seeking to invoke jurisdiction. *See* FED. R. CIV. P. 8(a); *Le Mieux Bros. v. Tremont Lumber Co.,* 140 F.2d 387, 389 (5th Cir. 1944). An attack on jurisdiction should seek to determine "some discreet jurisdictional requisite" without addressing the merits of the plaintiff's claim. *Green v. Ferrell,* 664 F.2d 1292, 1294 (5th Cir. 1982). If the defendant challenges the plaintiff's jurisdictional allegations, the plaintiff has the burden to prove jurisdiction. *Save Our Cemeteries, Inc., v. Archdiocese of New Orleans, Inc.,* 568 F.2d 1074, 1076 (5th Cir.), *cert. denied,* 439 U.S. 836, 99 S.Ct. 120, 58 L. Ed. 2d 133 (1978).

Neither Margins original complaint nor his amended complaint pled jurisdiction under the Admiralty Extension Act. If a complaint fails to cite the statute conferring jurisdiction, the omission will not defeat jurisdiction if the facts alleged satisfy jurisdictional requirements. *Hildebrand v. Honeywell, Inc.,* 622 F.2d 179, 181 (5th Cir. 1980). Margins amended complaint, however, fails to allege that his injury was caused by a defective appurtenance of the BOSTON. Margin alleges only that he was injured as a result of (1) defendants failure "to provided [him] with a safe place in which to work" and with "safe and competent supervisors, fellow servants and co-employees," (2) their failure to "take customary steps to protect [his] person," and (3) "the negligence of [defendants] agents and employees."

* * *

In ruling on the 12(b)(1) motion to dismiss for a lack of jurisdiction at the close of plaintiff's case, the district court mistakenly focused on whether Margin had proved a § 905(b) cause of action. It should have focused on the Admiralty Extension Act's requirement that the plaintiff allege an injury caused by a defective appurtenance of a vessel. In any event, the courts determination that § 905 vessel negligence did not cause Margins injury is akin to a finding under the Act that no vessel related acts proximately caused his injury and thus no maritime jurisdiction existed. The court's specific factual findings were:

> (12) Although Robert Margin allegedly slipped from the top of the stacking frames due to the presence of hydraulic fluids or grease, the Court finds no reasonable evidence or corroboration to support this allegation and concludes plaintiff simply fell in his attempt to avoid the hatchcover.
> (13) No mention was made of any hydraulic fluid or foreign substance on the stacking frames until plaintiff's deposition of February 1985, more than eighteen months after the accident.

The district court's finding that even the intimation of vessel negligence was an afterthought is equivalent to a determination that Margin failed to assert an injury caused by a defective appurtenance of a ship on navigable water.

Margins argument throughout the trial and appellate proceedings has stressed that the motion of the BOSTON'S hatch cover caused him to clamber over and slip and fall off the BOSTON'S stacking frames. These facts simply did not confer maritime jurisdiction under *Gutierrez* and *Victory Carriers*. The appurtenances themselves must be claimed to be defective extensions of the vessel. There was nothing wrong with the hatch cover. The BOSTON did not lower the hatch cover. Cooper was operating the land-based crane that had lifted the hatch cover. No action by the BOSTON caused Margin to scale the stacking frames or to fall to the ground. When he belatedly introduced the possible presence of oil or grease on the frames he did not connect it with the ship or with any act of vessel negligence. Margin wholly failed to allege that vessel negligence proximately caused his injury.

The liberality the district court extended to Margin in allowing factual development of the conclusory allegations in his pleadings cannot operate to confer subject matter jurisdiction where none was adequately alleged in the first instance. Had Margin alleged in his pleadings that his injury was caused by a defective appurtenance of a vessel—that the BOSTON caused the hatch cover to be lowered or that the BOSTON was responsible for allowing oil or grease to remain on the stacking frames—then we would be presented with a different case. However, Margin did not allege the discreet jurisdictional requirement that a defective appurtenance of a vessel caused his injury. This is further confirmed by the fact that he offered no proof at trial that would establish such negligence. Since Margin's cause of action asserts no more than a ship-side accident which was not proximately caused by the negligence of a vessel on navigable water there was no maritime jurisdiction over Margin's claims under the Admiralty Extension Act.

III

Our conclusion that the district court was correct in dismissing Margin's cause of action for a lack of subject mater jurisdiction makes it unnecessary for us to address the merits of the case. The district court's judgment is AFFIRMED.

Note: Liability of Shipbuilders Under the Act

In *Nissan Motor Corp. v. Maryland Shipbuilding, etc.*, 544 F. Supp. 1104, 1983 AMC 663 (D. Md. 1982), *aff'd,* 742 F.2d 1449 (4th Cir. 1984), the court applied the Admiralty Extension Act to a case involving a car manufacturer whose storage lot was located adjacent to a shipbuilding company. Nissan alleged its cars had been damaged as a result of the smoke and paint that emanated from the shipbuilder's activities. The court noted that the preliminary question was whether the case would be heard under Admiralty or Diversity jurisdiction. Finding that jurisdiction was properly invoked under the Admiralty Extension Act, the court held that the paint damage to Nissan's cars was caused by spray painting operations conducted from a barge or from the painting of vessels located on navigable waters. Further, the court ruled that the smoke damage was caused by emissions of soot and ash by vessels located on navigable waters or berthed at the defendant's piers.

Note: Vehicular Accidents

Two crew members sustained injury company when van in which they were riding was involved in an accident as it was transporting the men from the vessel where they had finished working their shift to the company office. The accident occurred approximately 45 minutes after they had left the vessel. The court found that neither the locus or nexus tests were satisfied. No activities on board the vessel caused or contributed to the accident. Limitation of liability was intended to protect shipowners against maritime disasters not automobile accidents at locations remote from the ship. The possible insolvency of a shipowner unable to limit is to remote from maritime commerce to satisfy nexus. *Complaint of Luhr,* 101 F. Supp. 2d 1156, 2000 AMC 2841 (E.D. Mo. 2000).

---

3. The Modern Criteria for Jurisdiction in Tort: Locality Plus Nexus

a.　Genesis of the Nexus Criterion: The Trilogy Cases

Notes

1. In *Executive Jet Aviation, Inc. v. City of Cleveland,* 409 U.S. 249, 93 S.Ct. 493, 34 L. Ed. 2d 454, 1973 AMC 1 (1972) the Supreme Court was faced with the question of whether or not the owner of a airplane which was damaged when it crashed into Lake Erie could bring a maritime tort action against the City which owned the airport. The plane was on a charter flight from Cleveland, Ohio to Portland, Maine and then on to White Plains, New York. As the plane was taking off, it flushed seagulls on the runway some of which were sucked into the plane's jet engine causing it to crash Plaintiff claimed that the damage occurred in Lake Erie, a navigable body of water and, therefore, the locality test had been satisfied. The Court stated that:

> It is far more consistent with the history and purpose of admiralty to require also that the wrong bear a significant relationship to traditional maritime activity. We hold that unless such a relationship exists, claims arising from airplane accidents are not cognizable in admiralty in the absence of legislation to the contrary.

Later it narrowed it by stating that: "in the absence of legislation to the contrary, there is no federal admiralty jurisdiction over aviation tort claims arising from flights by land-based aircraft between points within the continental United States."

In reaching its the decision the Court discussed some of the shortcomings of an all or nothing locality test as follows:

> Other serious difficulties with the locality test are illustrated by cases where the maritime locality of the tort is clear, but where the invocation of admiralty jurisdiction seems almost absurd. If a swimmer at a public beach is injured by another swimmer or by a submerged object on the bottom, or if a piece of machinery sustains water damage from being dropped into a harbor by a land-based crane, a literal application of the locality test invokes not only the jurisdiction of the federal courts, but the full panoply of the substantive admiralty law as well. In cases such as these, some courts have adhered to a mechanical application of the strict locality rule and have sustained admiralty jurisdiction despite the lack of any connection between the wrong and traditional forms of maritime commerce and navigation.[5] Other courts, however, have held in such situations that a maritime locality is not sufficient to bring the tort within federal admiralty jurisdiction, but that there must also be a maritime nexus—some relationship between the tort and traditional maritime activities, involving navigation or commerce on navigable waters. The Court of Appeals for the Sixth Circuit, for instance, in the *Chapman* case, where a swimmer at a public beach was injured, held that

> absent such a relationship, admiralty jurisdiction would depend entirely upon the fact that a tort occurred on navigable waters; a fact which in and of itself, in light of the historical justification for federal admiralty jurisdiction, is quite immaterial to any meaningful invocation of the jurisdiction of admiralty courts. 385 F.2d, at 966.[6]

---

[5] *Davis v. City of Jacksonville Beach,* 251 F. Supp. 327 (MD Fla. 1965) (injury to a swimmer by a surfboard); *King v. Tester man,* 214 F. Supp. 335, 336 (ED Tenn. 1963) (injuries to a water skier).

See also Horton v. J. &J. Aircraft, Inc., 257 F. Supp. 120, 121 (SD Fla. 1966). Cf. *Weinstein v. Eastern Airlines, Inc.,* 316 F.2d 758 (CA3 1963).

[6] In another injured-swimmer case, *McGuire v. City of New York,* 192 F. Supp. 866, 871-872 (SDNY 1961), the court stated:

> The proper scope of jurisdiction should include all matters relating to the business of the sea and the business conducted on navigable waters.

> The libel in this case does not relate to any tort which grows out of navigation. It alleges an ordinary tort, no different in substance because the injury occurred in shallow waters along the shore than if the injury had occurred on the sandy beach above the water line. Whether the City of New York should be held liable for the injury suffered by libellant is a question which can easily be determined in the courts of the locality. To endeavor to project such an action into the federal courts on the ground of admiralty jurisdiction is to misinterpret the nature of admiralty jurisdiction.

> Other cases holding that admiralty jurisdiction was not properly invoked because the tort, while having a maritime locality, lacked a significant relationship to maritime navigation and commerce, include: *Peytavin v. Government Employees Insurance Co.,* 453 F.2d 1121 (CA5 1972); *Gowdy v. United States,* 412 F.2d 525, 527-529 (CA6 1969); *Smith v. Guerrant,* 290 F. Supp. 111, 113-114 (SD Tex. 1968). *See also J. W. Petersen Coal & Oil Co. v. United States,* 323 F. Supp. 1198, 1201 (ND Ill. 1970); *O'Connor & Co. v. City of Pascagoula,* 304 F. Supp. 681, 683 (SD Miss. 1969); *Hastings v. Mann,* 226 F. Supp. 962, 964-965 (EDNC 1964), aff'd, 340 F.2d 910 (CA4 1965). A similar view is taken by the English courts. *Queen v. Judge of the City of London Court,* [1892] 1 Q.B. 273.

As early as 1850, admiralty scholars began to suggest that a traditional maritime activity, as well as a maritime locality, is necessary to invoke admiralty jurisdiction over torts. In that year, Judge Benedict expressed his "celebrated doubt"[7] as to whether such jurisdiction did not depend, in addition to a maritime locality, upon some "relation of the parties to a ship or vessel, embracing only those tortious violations of maritime right and duty which occur in vessels to which the Admiralty jurisdiction, in cases of contracts, applies." E. BENEDICT, THE AMERICAN ADMIRALTY 173 (1850). More recently, commentators have actively criticized the rule of locality as the sole criterion for admiralty jurisdiction, and have recommended adoption of a maritime relationship requirement as well. *See* 7A J. MOORE, FEDERAL PRACTICE, ADMIRALTY paras. .325 [3] and .325 [5] (2d ed. 1972); Black, *Admiralty Jurisdiction: Critique and Suggestions*, 50 COL. L. REV. 259, 264 (1950). In 1969, the American Law Institute's Study of the Division of Jurisdiction Between State and Federal Courts (ALI Study) also made that recommendation, stating (at 233):

It is hard to think of any reason why access to federal court should be allowed without regard to amount in controversy or citizenship of the parties merely because of the fortuity that a tort occurred on navigable waters, rather than on other waters or on land. The federal courts should not be burdened with every case of an injured swimmer.

* * *

Apart from the difficulties involved in trying to apply the locality rule as the sole test of admiralty tort jurisdiction, another indictment of that test is to be found in the number of times the federal courts and the Congress, in the interests of justice, have had to create exceptions to it in the converse situation—*i.e.*, when the tort has no maritime locality, but does bear a relationship to maritime service, commerce, or navigation. *See* 7A J. MOORE, FEDERAL PRACTICE, *Admiralty* para. .325 [4] (2d ed. 1972). For example, in *O'Donnell v. Great Lakes Dredge & Dock Co.*, 318 U.S. 36 (1943), the Court sustained the application of the Jones Act, 41 Stat. 1007, 46 U.S.C. § 688, to injuries to a seaman on land, because of the seaman's connection with maritime commerce. We relied in that case on an analogy to maintenance and cure:

[T]he maritime law, as recognized in the federal courts, has not in general allowed recovery for personal injuries occurring on land. But there is an important exception to this generalization in the case of maintenance and cure. From its dawn, the maritime law has recognized the seaman's right to maintenance and cure for injuries suffered in the course of his service to his vessel, whether occurring on sea or on land. *Id.*, at 41-42.

Similarly, the doctrine of unseaworthiness has been extended to permit a seaman or a longshoreman to recover from a shipowner for injuries sustained wholly on land, so long as those injuries were caused by defects in the ship or its gear. *Gutierrez v. Waterman S.S. Corp.*, 373 U.S. 206, 214-215 (1963). *See also Strika v. Netherlands Ministry of Traffic*, 185 F.2d 555 (CA2 1950).

Congress, too, has extended admiralty jurisdiction predicated on the relation of the wrong to maritime activities, regardless of the locality of the tort. In the Extension of Admiralty Jurisdiction Act, 62 Stat. 496, 46 U.S.C. § 740, enacted in 1948, Congress provided:

The admiralty and maritime jurisdiction of the United States shall extend to and include all cases of damage or injury, to person or property, caused by a vessel on navigable water, notwithstanding that such damage or injury be done or consummated on land.

This Act was passed specifically to overrule cases, such as *The Plymouth, supra*, holding that admiralty does not provide a remedy for damage done to land structures by ships on navigable waters. *Victory Carriers, Inc. v. Law*, 404 U.S., at 209 n.8; *Gutierrez v. Waterman S.S. Corp.*, 373 U.S., at 209-210.[8]

* * *

Just last Term, in *Victory Carriers, Inc. v. Law*, 404 U.S., at 212, we observed that in determining whether to expand admiralty jurisdiction, "we should proceed with caution...." Quoting from *Healy v. Ratta*, 292 U.S. 263, 270 (1934), we stated:

The power reserved to the states, under the Constitution, to provide for the determination of controversies in their courts may be restricted only by the action of Congress in conformity to the judiciary sections of the Constitution.... Due regard for the rightful independence of state governments, which should actuate federal courts, requires that they scrupulously confine their own jurisdiction to the precise limits which [a federal] statute has defined.

---

[7] *Hough, Admiralty Jurisdiction — Of Late Years*, 37 Harv. L. Rev. 529, 531 (1924).

[8] The Court has held, however, that there is no admiralty jurisdiction under the Extension of Admiralty Jurisdiction Act over suits brought by longshoremen injured while working on a pier, when such injuries were caused, not by ships, but by pier-based equipment. *Victory Carriers, Inc. v. Law, supra; Nacirema Co. v. Johnson*, 396 U.S. 212, 223 (1969). The Longshoremen's and Harbor Workers' Compensation Act, 33 U.S.C. § 901 *et seq.*, was amended in 1972 to cover employees working on those areas of the shore customarily used in loading, unloading, repairing, or building a vessel. Pub. L. No. 92-576, § 2, 86 Stat. 1251.

In the situation before us, which is only fortuitously and incidentally connected to navigable waters and which bears no relationship to traditional maritime activity, the Ohio courts could plainly exercise jurisdiction over the suit,[24] and could plainly apply familiar concepts of Ohio tort law without any effect on maritime endeavors.[25]

2. Subsequently, in *Foremost Insurance Co. v. Richardson*, 457 U.S. 668, 102 S.Ct. 2654, 73 L. Ed. 2d 300, 1982 AMC 2253 (1982), the court was asked to decide whether or not a collision between two pleasure boats on navigable waters was within admiralty tort jurisdiction. In concluding that it was, the Court extended its holding in *Executive Jet* to non-aviation maritime torts. The Court stated:

We recognize, as did the Court of Appeals, that the *Executive Jet* requirement that the wrong have a significant connection with traditional maritime activity is not limited to the aviation context. We also agree that there is no requirement that "the maritime activity be an exclusively commercial one." 641 F.2d, at 316. Because the "wrong" here involves the negligent operation of a vessel on navigable waters, we believe that it has a sufficient nexus to traditional maritime activity to sustain admiralty jurisdiction in the District Court.

We are not persuaded by petitioners' argument that a substantial relationship with commercial maritime activity is necessary because commercial shipping is at the heart of the traditional maritime activity sought to be protected by giving the federal courts exclusive jurisdiction over all admiralty suits. This argument is premised on the faulty assumption that, absent this relationship with *commercial* activity, the need for uniform rules to govern conduct and liability disappears, and "federalism" concerns dictate that these torts be litigated in the state courts.

Although the primary focus of admiralty jurisdiction is unquestionably the protection of maritime commerce, petitioner's take too narrow a view of the federal interest sought to be protected. The federal interest in protecting maritime commerce cannot be adequately served if admiralty jurisdiction is restricted to those individuals actually engaged in commercial maritime activity. This interest can be fully vindicated only if *all* operators of vessels on navigable waters are subject to uniform rules of conduct. The failure to recognize the breadth of this federal interest ignores the potential effect of noncommercial maritime activity on maritime commerce. For example, if these two boats collided at the mouth of the St. Lawrence Seaway, there would be a substantial effect on maritime commerce, without regard to whether either boat was actively, or had been previously, engaged in commercial activity. Furthermore, admiralty law has traditionally been concerned with the conduct alleged to have caused this collision by virtue of its "navigational rules—rules that govern the manner and direction those vessels may rightly move upon the waters." *Executive Jet*, 409 U.S., at 270. The potential disruptive impact of a collision between boats on navigable waters, when coupled with the traditional concern that admiralty law holds for navigation,[5] compels the conclusion that this collision between two pleasure boats on navigable waters has a significant relationship with maritime commerce.

* * *

Finally, our interpretation is consistent with congressional activity in this area. First, Congress defines the term "vessel," for the purpose of determining the scope of various shipping and maritime transportation laws, to include all types of waterborne vessels, without regard to whether they engage in commercial activity. *See, e.g.*, 1 U.S.C. § 3 ("Vessel' includes every description of watercraft or other artificial contrivance used, or capable of being used, as a means of transportation on water"). Second, the federal "Rules of the Road," designed for preventing collisions on navigable waters, *see, e.g.*, 94 Stat. 3415, 33 U.S.C. § 2001 *et seq.* (1976 ed., Supp. IV), apply to all vessels without regard to their commercial or noncommercial nature.[6] Third, when it extended admiralty jurisdiction to injuries on land caused by ships on navigable waters, Congress directed that "[t]he admiralty and maritime jurisdiction of the United States shall extend

---

[24] There is no diversity of citizenship between petitioner's and the City of Cleveland.

[25] The United States, respondent Dickens employer, can be sued, of course, only in federal district court under the Federal Tort Claims Act, 28 U.S.C. §§ 1346 (b) and 2674. Such an action has been filed by the petitioner's here, but even in that suit the federal court will apply the substantive tort law of Ohio. Thus, Ohio law will not be ousted in this case, and the pendency of the action under the Tort Claims Act has no relevance in determining whether the instant case should be heard in admiralty, with its federal substantive law.

The possibility that the petitioner's would have to litigate the same claim in two forums is the same possibility that would exist if their plane had stopped on the shore of the lake, instead of going into the water, and is the same possibility that exists every time a plane goes down on land, negligence of the federal air traffic controller is alleged, and there is no diversity of citizenship. This problem cannot be solved merely by upholding admiralty jurisdiction in cases where the plane happens to fall on navigable waters.

[5] Not every accident in navigable waters that might disrupt maritime commerce will support federal admiralty jurisdiction. In *Executive Jet*, for example, we concluded that the sinking of the plane in navigable waters did not give rise to a claim in admiralty even though an aircraft sinking in the water could create a hazard for the navigation of commercial vessels in the vicinity. However, when this kind of potential hazard to maritime commerce arises out of activity that bears a substantial relationship to traditional maritime activity, as does the navigation of the boats in this case, admiralty jurisdiction is appropriate.

[6] Petitioners argue that admiralty jurisdiction in the federal courts is unnecessary to ensure the uniform application of the Rules of the Road to boat navigation because state courts are bound by the construction federal courts give to statutes relating to navigation. Assuming that petitioner's are correct, this fact does not negate the importance that Congress has attached to the federal interest in having all vessels operating on navigable waters governed by uniform rules and obligations, which is furthered by consistent application of federal maritime legislation under federal admiralty jurisdiction.

[7] We refer to this language only to demonstrate that Congress did not require a commercial-activity nexus when it extended admiralty jurisdiction. We express no opinion on whether this Act could be construed to provide an independent basis for jurisdiction.

to and include all cases of damage or injury ... caused by a vessel on navigable water...." Extension of Admiralty Jurisdiction Act, 62 Stat. 496, 46 U.S.C. § 740.[7]

The dissent emphasized two factors, federalism and the historic relationship between the development of maritime law and commerce:

> No trend of decisions by this Court has been stronger—for two decades or more—than that toward expanding federal jurisdiction at the expense of state interests and state-court jurisdiction. Of course, Congress also has moved steadily and expansively to exercise its Commerce Clause and preemptive power to displace state and local authority. Often decisions of this Court and congressional enactments have been necessary in the national interest. The effect, nevertheless, has been the erosion of federalism—a basic principle of the Constitution and our federal Union.

* * *

> The absence of "commercial activity" on this waterway was held by the Court of Appeals to be immaterial. While recognizing that there was substantial authority to the contrary, the court held that federal admiralty law applied to this accident. This Court now affirms in a decision holding that "all operators of vessels on navigable waters are subject to uniform [federal] rules of conduct," conferring federal admiralty jurisdiction over *all* accidents. *Ante,* at 675 (emphasis deleted). In my view there is no substantial federal interest that justifies a rule extending admiralty jurisdiction to the edge of absurdity.

* * *

II

In an effort to rescue its logic, the Court refers to the "potential disruptive impact of a collision between boats on navigable waters...." *Ante,* at 675. Yet this reasoning is countered by *Executive Jet*—a decision that the Court acknowledges to be a key authority for this case. For if "potential disruptive impact" on traffic in navigable waters provides a sufficient connection with "traditional maritime activity," then the crash of an *airplane* "in the navigable waters of Lake Erie," 409 U.S., at 250, necessarily would support admiralty jurisdiction. The holding of *Executive Jet* is precisely to the contrary. The Court's reasoning in essence resurrects the locality rule that *Executive Jet* rejected, for *any* accident "located" on navigable waters has a "potential disruptive impact" on traffic there.

Oral argument in this case revealed the degree to which the Court's decision displaces state authority. The Court posed a hypothetical in which children, for their own amusement, used rowboats to net crawfish from a stream. Two of the boats collide and sink near the water's edge, forcing the children to wade ashore. Counsel for respondents replied that this accident *would* fall within the admiralty jurisdiction of the federal courts, provided that the waterway was navigable. Tr. of Oral Arg. 24. Today the Court agrees.

For me, however, this example illustrates the substantial—and *purposeless*—expansion of federal authority and federal-court jurisdiction accomplished by the Court's holding. In this respect I agree with Chief Judge Haynsworth:

> The admiralty jurisdiction in England and in this country was born of a felt need to protect the domestic shipping industry in its competition with foreign shipping, and to provide a uniform body of law for the governance of domestic and foreign shipping, engaged in the movement of commercial vessels from state to state and to and from foreign states. The operation of small pleasure craft on inland waters which happen to be navigable has no more apparent relationship to that kind of concern than the operation of the same kind of craft on artificial inland lakes which are not navigable waters. *Crosson v. Vance,* 484 F.2d 840 (CA4 1973).

---

[7] If a "potential disruptive effect" on interstate traffic in fact implicated a federal interest strong enough to support federal jurisdiction, then federal courts also should hear cases in which accidents disrupt similar land traffic. Cf. *71 Feared Dead as Plane Hits Bridge, Smashes Cars, Plunges Into Potomac,* Washington Post, Jan. 14, 1982, p. Al, col. 1.

According to the Court, the interest in expanding admiralty jurisdiction is supported by the difficulty of defining "pleasure boating." *Ante,* at 675-676. In view of the myriad of definitional tasks performed regularly by state and federal courts, determining in a particular case whether the boating at issue is essentially for pleasure rather than commerce rarely would present a difficult problem for any court.

The Court also states that its action "is consistent with congressional activity in this area," *ante,* at 676, *citing* a number of federal statutes. This point is of course wholly irrelevant to the *constitutional* extent of admiralty jurisdiction. Moreover, the only statute cited having any relation to jurisdictional matters is the Extension of Admiralty Jurisdiction Act, 62 Stat. 496, 46 U.S.C. § 740. This Act provides:

The admiralty and maritime jurisdiction of the United States shall extend to and include all cases of damage or injury, to person or property, caused by a vessel on navigable water, *notwithstanding that such damage or injury be done or consummated on land.*

In any such case suit may be brought *in rem* or *in personam* according to the principles of law and rules of practice obtaining in cases *where the injury or damage has been done and consummated on navigable water* (emphasis added).

As its text makes plain, "[t] his Act was passed specifically to overrule cases, such as *The Plymouth, supra,* holding that admiralty does not provide a remedy for damage done to land structures by ships on navigable waters." *Executive Jet,* 409 U.S., at 260. This purpose—and not any intent to expand or affect admiralty jurisdiction respecting pleasure boats— consistently appears in the Act's legislative history. See, e.g., S. Rep. No. 1593, 80th Cong., 2d Sess., 1-6 (1948); H.R. Rep. No. 1523, 80th Cong., 2d Sess., 1-6 (1948). *See also* Farnum, *Admiralty Jurisdiction and Amphibious Torts,* 43 Yale L.J. 34, 44-45 (1933); Note, 63 Harv. L. Rev. 861, 868 (1950); Note, *The Extension of Admiralty Jurisdiction to Include Amphibious Torts,* 37 Geo. L.J. 252 (1949); Note, *Effects of Recent Legislation Upon the Admiralty Law,* 17 Geo. Wash. L. Rev. 353 (1949). And this Court has never sustained the constitutionality of this Act.

With respect, the Court's statutory arguments must be regarded as makeweights.

3. *Sisson v. Ruby,* 497 U.S. 358, 110 S.Ct. 2892, 111 L. Ed. 2d 292, 1990 AMC 1801 (1990) refined the underlying policy and approach articulated in *Foremost Insurance Co. v. Richardson.* The Court held that admiralty jurisdiction may extend to a situation involving a vessel that was not being navigated but instead was docked at a Marina in Lake Michigan. A fire erupted in the vessel's washer/dryer unit and spread causing damage to neighboring boats and to the marina. The vessel owner brought an action in admiralty to limit his liability. The Court held that the tort was within admiralty jurisdiction. It referred to a footnote in *Foremost* and stated that:

> [n]ot every accident in navigable waters that might disrupt maritime commerce will support federal admiralty jurisdiction," *id.,* at 675, n.5 *(citing Executive Jet),* but that when a "potential hazard to maritime commerce arises out of activity that bears a substantial relationship to traditional maritime activity, as does the navigation of boats in this case, admiralty jurisdiction is appropriate." 457 U.S., at 675, n.5, 102 S.Ct. at 2658, n.5.

> This case involves a fire that began on a noncommercial vessel at a marina located on a navigable waterway. Certainly, such a fire has a potentially disruptive impact on maritime commerce, as it can spread to nearby commercial vessels or make the marina inaccessible to such vessels. Indeed, fire is one of the most significant hazards facing commercial vessels. *See, e.g., Southport Fisheries, Inc. v. Saskatchewan Govt. Ins. Office,* 161 F. Supp. 81, 83-84 (EDNC 1958).

> Respondents' only argument to the contrary is that the potential effect on maritime commerce in this case was minimal because no commercial vessels happened to be docked at the marina when the fire occurred. This argument misunderstands the nature of our inquiry. We determine the potential impact of a given type of incident by examining its general character. The jurisdictional inquiry does not turn on the actual effects on maritime commerce of the fire on Sisson's vessel; nor does it turn on the particular facts of the incident in this case, such as the source of the fire or the specific location of the yacht at the marina, that may have rendered the fire on the *Ultorian* more or less likely to disrupt commercial activity. Rather, a court must assess the general features of the type of incident involved to determine whether such an incident is likely to disrupt commercial activity. Here, the general features—a fire on a vessel docked at a marina on navigable waters—plainly satisfy the requirement of potential disruption to commercial maritime activity.

* * *

> We now turn to the second half of the *Foremost* test, under which the party seeking to invoke maritime jurisdiction must show a substantial relationship between the activity giving rise to the incident and traditional maritime activity. As a first step, we must define the relevant activity in this case. Our cases have made clear that the relevant "activity" is defined not by the particular circumstances of the incident, but by the general conduct from which the incident arose. In *Executive Jet,* for example, the relevant activity was not a plane sinking in Lake Erie, but air travel generally. 409 U.S., at 269-270, 93 S.Ct., at 505. *See also Foremost, supra,* at 675-677, 102 S.Ct., at 2658-2659 (relevant activity is navigation of vessels generally). This focus on the general character of the activity is, indeed, suggested by the nature of the jurisdictional inquiry. Were courts required to focus more particularly on the causes of the harm, they would have to decide to some extent the merits of the causation issue to answer the legally and analytically antecedent jurisdictional question. Thus, in this case, we need not ascertain the precise cause of the fire to determine what "activity" Sisson was engaged in; rather, the relevant activity was the storage and maintenance of a vessel at a marina on navigable waters.[3]

> Our final inquiry, then, is whether the storage and maintenance of a boat on a marina on navigable waters has a substantial relationship to a "traditional maritime activity" within the meaning of *Executive Jet* and *Foremost.*[4] Respondents would have us hold that, at least in the

---

[3] In this case, all of the instrumentalities involved in the incident were engaged in a similar activity. The *Ultorian* and the other craft damaged by the fire were docked at a marina, and the marina itself provided docking and related services. The facts of *Executive Jet* and *Foremost* also reveal that all the relevant entities were engaged in a common form of activity. *See Executive Jet Aviation, Inc. v. City of Cleveland,* 409 U.S. 249, 93 S.Ct. 493, 34 L. Ed. 2d 454 (1972) (entities involved in the incident were engaged in nonmaritime activity of facilitating air travel); *Foremost Ins. Co. v. Richardson,* 457 U.S. 668, 102 S.Ct. 2654, 73 L. Ed. 2d 300 (1982) (entities were both engaged in navigation). Different issues may be raised by a case in which one of the instrumentalities is engaged in a traditional maritime activity, but the other is not. Our resolution of such issues awaits a case that squarely raises them.

[4] The Circuits have interpreted this aspect of the jurisdictional inquiry variously. After *Executive Jet* but before *Foremost,* the Fifth Circuit adopted a four-factor test for deciding whether an activity is substantially related to traditional maritime activity. The factors are "the functions and roles of the parties; the types of vehicles and instrument alities involved; the causation and the type of injury; and traditional concepts of the role of admiralty law." *Kelly v. Smith,* 485 F.2d 520, 525 (1973). In other Circuits, this test has continued to dominate the landscape even in the wake of *Foremost. See, e.g., Drake v. Raymark Industries, Inc.,* 772 F.2d 1007, 1015 (CA1 1985); *Guidry v. Durkin,* 834 F.2d 1465, 1471 (CA9 1987); *Lewis Charters, Inc. v. Huckins Yacht Corp.,* 871 F.2d 1046, 1051 (CA11 1989). The Fourth Circuit appears to follow *Kelly* as well, although how closely is unclear. *Compare Oman v. Johns-Manville Corp.,* 764 F.2d 224, 230, and n.3 (CA4 1985) *(en banc)* (stating that "a thorough analysis of the nexus requirement should include a consideration of *at least* [the *Kelly* factors]") (emphasis added), with *Bub la v. Bradshaw,* 795 F. 2d 349, 351 (CA4 1986) (implicitly treating *Kelly* factors as exclusive). The precise state of the law in the Fifth Circuit after *Foremost* is also unclear. *Compare Mollett v. Penrod Drilling Co.,* 826 F.2d 1419, 1426 (CA5 1987) *(Mollett I)* (applying, in addition to *Kelly* factors, "(1) the impact of the event on maritime shipping and commerce (2) the desirability of a uniform national rule to apply to such matters and (3) the need for admiralty 'expertise' in the trial and decision of the case"), *with Mollett v. Penrod Drilling Co.,* 872 F.2d 1221, 1224-1226 (CA5 1989) *(Mollett II)* (applying the *Kelly* factors without explicit mention of the extra factors indentified in *Mollett I).*

Other Circuits have adopted different approaches. The Seventh Circuit in this case held that an activity must either be commercial or involve navigation to satisfy the "traditional maritime activity" standard. *In re Complaint of Sisson,* 867 F.2d 341, 345 (1989). The Second Circuit directly applies our language requiring a substantial relationship to traditional maritime activity without applying any additional factors. *See Keene Corp. v. United States,* 700 F.2d 836, 844 (1983); *Kelly v. United States,* 531 F.2d 1144, 1147-1148 (1976). Finally, the Sixth Circuit has criticized the Seventh Circuit's analysis in this case as "an indefensibly narrow reading of *Foremost Insurance,*" *In re Young,* 872 F.2d 176, 178-179, n. 4 (1989), but has not set forth in concrete terms the test it would apply, *cf. Petersen v. Chesapeake & Ohio R. Co.,* 784 F.2d 732, 736 (1986).

The parties and various *amici* suggest that we resolve this dispute by adopting one of the Circuits' tests (or some other test entirely). We believe that, at least in cases in which all of the relevant entities are engaged in similar types of activity (cf. n.3, *supra*), the formula initially suggested by *Executive Jet* and more fully refined in *Foremost* and in this case provides appropriate and sufficient guidance to the federal courts. We therefore decline the invitation to use this case to refine further the test we have developed.

context of noncommercial activity, only navigation can be characterized as substantially related to traditional maritime activity. We decline to do so. In *Foremost*, we identified navigation as an example, rather than as the sole instance, of conduct that is substantially related to traditional maritime activity. *See* 457 U.S., at 675, n.5, 102 S.Ct., at 2658, n.5. Indeed, had we intended to suggest that navigation is the only activity that is sufficient to confer jurisdiction, we could have stated the jurisdictional test much more clearly and economically by stating that maritime jurisdiction over torts is limited to torts in which the vessels are in "navigation." Moreover, a narrow focus on navigation would not serve the federal policies that underlie our jurisdictional test. The fundamental interest giving rise to maritime jurisdiction is "the protection of maritime commerce," *id.,* at 674, 102 S.Ct., at 2658, and we have said that that interest cannot be fully vindicated unless "all operators of vessels on navigable waters are subject to uniform rules of conduct," *id,* at 675, 102 S.Ct., at 2658. The need for uniform rules of maritime conduct and liability is not limited to navigation, but extends at least to any other activities traditionally undertaken by vessels, commercial or noncommercial.

The Court concluded that the activity satisfied this prong of the test. A concurring opinion questioned the need for so elaborate a test:

... In my view that test does not add any new substantive requirement for vessel-related torts, but merely explains *why all* vessel-related torts (which *ipso facto* have such a "significant relationship"), but only *some* non-vessel-related torts, come within § 1333. The Court's description of how one goes about determining whether a vessel-related tort meets the "significant relationship" test threatens to sow confusion in what had been, except at the margins, a settled area of the law.

* * *

The sensible rule to be drawn from our cases, including *Executive Jet* and *Foremost*, is that a tort occurring on a vessel conducting normal maritime activities in navigable waters—that is, as a practical matter, every tort occurring on a vessel in navigable waters—falls within the admiralty jurisdiction of the federal courts.

Note: Application of Executive Jet in the Lower Federal Courts

The *Executive Jet* decision did not make clear whether the nexus requirement was applicable only in aircraft cases or whether it supplemented the locality test in maritime tort cases generally. It also did not set forth the elements of the nexus criterion. Lower federal courts tried to fill this vacuum by adopting the nexus test as a supplement to the locality test. Some courts also tried to elaborate the elements of nexus. Prominent among these courts was the Court of Appeals for the Fifth Circuit. Prior to the Supreme Court decisions in *Foremost* and *Sisson*, the Fifth Circuit decided *Kelly v. Smith*, 485 F.2d 520, 1973 AMC 2478 (5th Cir. 1973), *cert. denied sub nom. Chicot Land Company, Inc. v. Kelly*, 416 U.S. 969, 94 S.Ct. 1991, 40 L. Ed. 2d 558 (1974). In the *Kelly* case, deer poachers surreptitiously slipped across the Mississippi River and landed on an island. Upon their discovery they fled the scene in their boat. While navigating in the Mississippi River they were fired upon by some people on the island and one of the poachers was wounded. The injured person brought suit. In determining whether the action was within admiralty jurisdiction, the court enumerated four factors which it deemed relevant to determine if the nexus requirement had been met, to wit: "the function and roles of the parties; the types of vehicles and instrumentalities involved; the causation and the type of injury; and traditional concepts of the role of admiralty law." Subsequent to the *Foremost*, but before *Sisson*, the Fifth Circuit in *Molett v. Penrod Drilling Co.*, 826 F.2d 1419, 1988 AMC 2112 (5th Cir. 1987), *cert. denied sub nom. Columbus McKinnon, Inc. v. Gearench*, 493 U.S. 1003, 110 S.Ct. 563, 107 L. Ed. 2d 558 (1989) added several factors namely, "(1) the impact of an event on maritime shipping and commerce (2)the desirability of a uniform rule to apply to such matters and (3) the need for admiralty expertise." Even after *Sisson* some courts continued to apply the *Kelly* factors, although *Sisson* cast some doubt on their continued viability. After the Supreme Court's decision in *Jerome B. Grubart, Inc. v. Great Lakes Dredge & Dock Company, infra,* it has become clear that the application of the *Kelly* factors was expressly rejected by the Supreme Court in *Grubart. Coats v. Penrod Drilling Corp.*, 61 F.3d 1113, 1996 AMC 1 (5th Cir. 1995).

---

b.   Interpretation of "Nexus"

JEROME B. GRUBART, INC. v. GREAT LAKES DREDGE & DOCK COMPANY

513 U.S. 527, 115 S.Ct. 1043, 130 L. Ed. 2d 1024, 1995 AMC 913 (1995)

Justice SOUTER delivered the opinion of the Court

On April 13, 1992, water from the Chicago River poured into a freight tunnel running under the river and thence into the basements of buildings in the downtown Chicago Loop. Allegedly, the flooding resulted from events several months earlier, when the respondent Great Lakes Dredge and Dock Company had used a crane, sitting on a barge in the river next to a bridge, to drive piles into the river bed above the tunnel. The issue before us is whether a court of the United States has admiralty jurisdiction to determine and limit the extent of Great Lakes's tort liability. We hold the case to be within federal admiralty jurisdiction.

I

The complaint, together with affidavits subject to no objection, alleges the following facts. In 1990, Great Lakes bid on a contract with the petitioner city of Chicago to replace wooden pilings clustered around the piers of several bridges spanning the Chicago River, a navigable waterway within the meaning of *The Daniel Ball*, 10 Wall. 557, 563, 19 L. Ed. 999 (1871). *See Escanaba Co. v. Chicago*, 107 U.S. 678, 683, 2 S.Ct. 185, 188-189, 27 L. Ed. 442 (1883). The pilings (called dolphins) keep ships from bumping into the piers and so protect both. After winning the contract, Great Lakes carried out the work with two barges towed by a tug. One barge carried pilings; the other carried a crane that pulled out old pilings and helped drive in new ones.

In August and September 1991, Great Lakes replaced the pilings around the piers projecting into the river and supporting the Kinzie Street Bridge. After towing the crane-carrying barge into position near one of the piers, Great Lakes's employees secured the barge to the river bed with spuds, or long metal legs that project down from the barge and anchor it. The workers then used the crane on the barge to pull up old pilings, stow them on the other barge, and drive new pilings into the river bed around the piers. About seven months later, an eddy formed in the river near the bridge as the collapsing walls or ceiling of a freight tunnel running under the river opened the tunnel to river water, which flowed through to flood buildings in the Loop.

After the flood, many of the victims brought actions in state court against Great Lakes and the city of Chicago, claiming that in the course of replacing the pilings Great Lakes had negligently weakened the tunnel structure, which Chicago (its owner) had not properly maintained. Great Lakes then brought this lawsuit in the United States District Court, invoking federal admiralty jurisdiction. Count I of the complaint seeks the protection of the Limitation of Vessel Owners Liability Act (Limitation Act), 46 U.S.C. app. § 181 *et seq.*, a statute that would, in effect, permit the admiralty court to decide whether Great Lakes committed a tort and, if so, to limit Great Lakes's liability to the value of the vessels (the tug and two barges) involved if the tort was committed "without the privity or knowledge" of the vessels' owner, 46 U.S.C. app. § 183(a). Counts II and III of Great Lakes's complaint ask for indemnity and contribution from the city for any resulting loss to Great Lakes.

The city, joined by petitioner Jerome B. Grubart, Inc., one of the state-court plaintiff's, filed a motion to dismiss this suit for lack of admiralty jurisdiction. FED. RULE CIV. PROC. 12(b)(1). The District Court granted the motion, the Seventh Circuit reversed, *Great Lakes Dredge & Dock Co. v. Chicago*, 3 F.3d 225 (1993), and we granted certiorari, 510 U.S. —, 114 S.Ct. 1047, 127 L. Ed. 2d 370 (1994). We now affirm.

II

* * *

A

A federal court's authority to hear cases in admiralty flows initially from the Constitution, which "extend [s]" federal judicial power "to all Cases of admiralty and maritime Jurisdiction." U.S. CONST., Art. III, § 2. Congress has embodied that power in a statute giving federal district courts "original jurisdiction ... of ... [a]ny civil case of admiralty or maritime jurisdiction...." 28 U.S.C. § 1333(1).

The traditional test for admiralty tort jurisdiction asked only whether the tort occurred on navigable waters. If it did, admiralty jurisdiction followed; if it did not, admiralty jurisdiction did not exist. *See, e.g., Thomas v. Lane*, 23 F. Cas. 957, 960 (No. 13902) (CC Me. 1813) (STORY, J., on Circuit). This ostensibly simple locality test was complicated by the rule that the injury had to be "wholly" sustained on navigable waters for the tort to be within admiralty. *The Plymouth*, 3 Wall. 20, 34, 18 L. Ed. 125 (1866) (no jurisdiction over tort action brought by the owner of warehouse destroyed in a fire that started on board a ship docked nearby). Thus, admiralty courts lacked jurisdiction over, say, a claim following a ship's collision with a pier insofar as it injured the pier, for admiralty law treated the pier as an extension of the land. *Martin v. West*, 222 U.S. 191, 197, 32 S.Ct. 42, 43, 56 L. Ed. 159 (1911); *Cleveland T. & V.R. Co. v. Cleveland S.S. Co., 208* U.S. 316, 319, 28 S.Ct. 414, 415, 52 L. Ed. 508 (1908).

This latter rule was changed in 1948, however, when Congress enacted the Extension of Admiralty Jurisdiction Act, 62 Stat. 496. The Act provided that "[t]he admiralty and maritime jurisdiction of the United States shall extend to and include all cases of damage or injury, to person or property, caused by a vessel on navigable water, notwithstanding that such damage or injury be done or consummated on land." 46 U.S.C. app. § 740. The purpose of the Act was to end concern over the sometimes confusing line between land and water, by investing admiralty with jurisdiction over "all cases" where the injury was caused by a ship or other vessel on navigable water, even if such injury occurred on land. *See, e.g., Gutierrez v. Waterman S.S. Corp.,* 373 U.S. 206, 209-210, 83 S.Ct. 1185, 1187-1188, 10 L. Ed. 2d 297 (1963); *Executive Jet Aviation, Inc. v. City of Cleveland,* 409 U.S. 249, 260, 93 S.Ct. 493, 500-501, 34 L. Ed. 2d 454 (1972).

After this congressional modification to gather the odd case into admiralty, the jurisdictional rule was qualified again in three decisions of this Court aimed at keeping a different class of odd cases out. In the first case, *Executive Jet, supra,* tort claims arose out of the wreck of an airplane that collided with a flock of birds just after take-off on a domestic flight and fell into the navigable waters of Lake Erie. We held that admiralty lacked jurisdiction to consider the claims. We wrote that "a purely mechanical application of the locality test" was not always "sensible" or "consonant with the purposes of maritime law," *id.,* at 261, 93 S.Ct., at 501, as when (for example) the literal and universal application of the locality rule would require admiralty courts to adjudicate tort disputes between colliding swimmers, *id.,* at 255, 93 S.Ct., at 498. We held that "claims arising from airplane accidents are not cognizable in admiralty" despite the location of the harm, unless "the wrong bear[s] a significant relationship to traditional maritime activity." *Id.,* at 268, 93 S.Ct., at 504.

The second decision, *Foremost Ins. Co. v. Richardson,* 457 U.S. 668, 102 S.Ct. 2654, 73 L. Ed. 2d 300 (1982), dealt with tort claims arising out of the collision of two pleasure boats in a navigable river estuary. We held that admiralty courts had jurisdiction, *id.,* at 677, 102 S.Ct., at 2659, even though jurisdiction existed only if "the wrong" had "a significant connection with traditional maritime activity," *id.,* at 674, 102 S.Ct., at 2658. We conceded that pleasure boats themselves had little to do with the maritime commerce lying at the heart of the admiralty court's basic work, *id.,* at 674-675, 102 S.Ct., at 2658-2659, but we nonetheless found the necessary relationship in "[t]he potential disruptive impact [upon maritime commerce] of a collision between boats on navigable waters, when coupled with the traditional concern that admiralty law holds for navigation...." *Id.,* at 675, 102 S.Ct., at 2658.

In the most recent of the trilogy, *Sisson v. Ruby,* 497 U.S. 358, 110 S.Ct. 2892, 111 L. Ed. 2d 292 (1990), we held that a federal admiralty court had jurisdiction over tort claims arising when a fire, caused by a defective washer/dryer aboard a pleasure boat docked at a marina, burned the boat, other boats docked nearby, and the marina itself. *Id.,* at 367, 110 S.Ct., at 2898. We elaborated on the enquiry exemplified in *Executive Jet* and *Foremost* by focusing on two points to determine the relationship of a claim to the objectives of admiralty jurisdiction. We noted, first, that the incident causing the harm, the burning of docked boats at a marina on navigable waters, was of a sort "likely to disrupt [maritime] commercial activity." *Id.,* 497 U.S., at 363, 110 S.Ct., at 2896. Second, we found a "substantial relationship" with "traditional maritime activity" in the kind of activity from which the incident arose, "the storage and maintenance of a vessel ... on navigable waters." *Id.,* at 365-367, 110 S.Ct., at 2897-2898.

After *Sisson,* then, a party seeking to invoke federal admiralty jurisdiction pursuant to 28 U.S.C. § 1333(1) over a tort claim must satisfy conditions both of location and of connection with maritime activity. A court applying the location test must determine whether the tort occurred on navigable water or whether injury suffered on land was caused by a vessel on navigable water. 46 U.S.C. app. § 740. The connection test raises two issues. A court, first, must "assess the general features of the type of incident involved," 497 U.S., at 363, 110 S.Ct., at 2896, to determine whether the incident has "a potentially disruptive impact on maritime commerce," *id.,* at 364, n.2, 110S. Ct., at 2896, n.2. Second, a court must determine whether "the general character" of the "activity giving rise to the incident" shows a "substantial relationship to traditional maritime activity." *Id.,* at 365, 364, and n.2, 110

S.Ct., at 2897, 2896, and n.2. We now apply the tests to the facts of this case.

B

The location test is, of course, readily satisfied. If Great Lakes caused the flood, it must have done so by weakening the structure of the tunnel while it drove in new pilings or removed old ones around the bridge piers. The weakening presumably took place as Great Lakes's workers lifted and replaced the pilings with a crane that sat on a barge stationed in the Chicago River. The place in the river where the barge sat, and from which workers directed the crane, is in the "navigable waters of the United States." Escanaba Co., 107 U.S., at 683, 2 S.Ct., at 188-89. Thus, if Great Lakes committed a tort, it must have done it while on navigable waters.

It must also have done it "by a vessel." Even though the barge was fastened to the river bottom and was in use as a work platform at the times in question, at other times it was used for transportation. *See* 3 F.3d, at 229. Petitioners do not here seriously dispute the conclusion of each court below that the Great Lakes barge is, for admiralty tort purposes, a "vessel." The fact that the pile-driving was done with a crane makes no difference under the location test, given the maritime law that ordinarily treats an "appurtenance" attached to a vessel in navigable waters as part of the vessel itself. *See, e.g., Victory Carriers, Inc. v. Law,* 404 U.S. 202, 210-211, 92 S.Ct. 418, 424-425, 30 L. Ed. 2d 383 (1971); *Gutierrez,* 373 U.S., at 209-210, 83 S.Ct., at 1187-1188.[1]

Because the injuries suffered by Grubart and the other flood victims were caused by a vessel on navigable water, the location enquiry would seem to be at an end, "notwithstanding that such damage or injury [have been] done or consummated on land." 46 U.S.C. app. § 740. Both Grubart and Chicago nonetheless ask us to subject the Extension Act to limitations not apparent from its text. While they concede that the Act refers to "all cases of damage or injury," they argue that "all" must not mean literally every such case, no matter how great the distance between the vessels tortious activity and the resulting harm. They contend that, to be within the Act, the damage must be close in time and space to the activity that caused it: that it must occur "reasonably contemporaneously" with the negligent conduct and no "farther from navigable waters than the reach of the vessel, its appurtenances and cargo." For authority, they point to this Courts statement in Gutierrez, *supra,* that jurisdiction is present when the "impact" of the tortious activity "is felt ashore at a time and place not remote from the wrongful act." *Id.,* at 210, 83 S.Ct., at 1188.[2]

The demerits of this argument lie not only in its want of textual support for its nonremoteness rule, but in its disregard of a less stringent but familiar proximity condition tied to the language of the statute. The Act uses the phrase "caused by," which more than one Court of Appeals has read as requiring what tort law has traditionally called "proximate causation." *See, e.g., Pryor v. American President Lines,* 520 F.2d 974, 979 (CA4 1975), *cert. denied,* 423 U.S. 1055, 96

S.Ct. 787, 46 L. Ed. 2d 644 (1976); *Adams v. Harris County,* 452 F.2d 994, 996-997 (CA5 1971), *cert. denied,* 406 U.S. 968, 92 S.Ct. 2414, 32 L. Ed. 2d 667 (1972). This classic tort notion normally eliminates the bizarre, *cf. Palsgrafv. Long Island R. Co.,* 248 N.Y. 339, 162 N.E. 99 (1928), and its use should obviate not only the complication but even the need for further temporal or spatial limitations. Nor is reliance on familiar proximate causation inconsistent with *Gutierrez,* which used its nonremote language, not to announce a special test, but simply to distinguish its own facts (the victim having slipped on beans spilling from cargo containers being unloaded from a ship) from what the Court called "[v]arious far-fetched hypotheticals," such as injury to someone slipping on beans that continue to leak from the containers after they had been shipped from Puerto Rico to a warehouse in Denver. 373 U.S., at 210, 83 S.Ct., at 1188. *See also Victory Carriers, supra,* 404 U.S., at 210-211, 92 S.Ct., at 424-425.

* * *

---

[1] Grubart argues, based on *Margin v. Sea-Land Services, Inc.,* 812 F.2d 973, 975 (CA5 1987), that an appurtenance is considered part of the vessel only when it is defective. *See* Brief for Petitioner in No. 93-762, pp. 34-35 (Grubart Brief). *Margin,* however, does not so hold. It dealt with a land-based crane that lowered a ship's hatch cover dangerously close to a welder working on a dock, and its result turned not on the condition of the hatch cover, the putative appurtenance, but on the fact that the plaintiff did not allege that "vessel negligence proximately caused his injury." 812 F.2d, at 977. Indeed, the argument that Congress intended admiralty jurisdiction to extend to injuries caused by defective appurtenances, but not to appurtenances in good condition when operated negligently, makes no sense. *See Gutierrez,* 373 U.S., at 210, 83 S.Ct., at 1188 ("There is no distinction in admiralty between torts committed by the ship itself and by the ship's personnel while operating it....").

[2] At oral argument, counsel for the city undercut this argument by conceding that admiralty jurisdiction would govern claims arising from an incident in which a ship on navigable waters slipped its moorings, drifted into a dam, and caused a breach in the dam that resulted in flooding of surrounding territory. Tr. of Oral Arg. 17.

C

We now turn to the maritime connection enquiries, the first being whether the incident involved was of a sort with the potential to disrupt maritime commerce. In *Sisson*, we described the features of the incident in general terms as "a fire on a vessel docked at a marina on navigable waters," *id.,* at 363, 110 S.Ct., at 2896, and determined that such an incident "plainly satisf[ied]" the first maritime connection requirement, *ibid.,* because the fire could have "spread to nearby commercial vessels or ma[d]e the marina inaccessible to such vessels" and therefore "[c]ertainly" had a "potentially disruptive impact on maritime commerce." *Id.,* at 362, 110 S.Ct., at 2896. We noted that this first prong went to potential effects, not to the "particular facts of the incident," noting that in both *Executive Jet* and *Foremost* we had focused not on the specific facts at hand but on whether the "general features" of the incident were "likely to disrupt commercial activity." 497 U.S., at 363, 110 S.Ct., at 2896.

The first *Sisson* test turns, then, on a description of the incident at an intermediate level of possible generality. To speak of the incident as "fire" would have been too general to differentiate cases; at the other extreme, to have described the fire as damaging nothing but pleasure boats and their tie-up facilities would have ignored, among other things, the capacity of pleasure boats to endanger commercial shipping that happened to be nearby. We rejected both extremes and instead asked whether the incident could be seen within a class of incidents that posed more than a fanciful risk to commercial shipping.

Following *Sisson*, the "general features" of the incident at issue here may be described as damage by a vessel in navigable water to an underwater structure. So characterized, there is little question that this is the kind of incident that has a "potentially disruptive impact on maritime commerce." As it actually turned out in this case, damaging a structure beneath the river bed could lead to a disruption in the water course itself, App. 33 (eddy formed above the leak); and, again as it actually happened, damaging a structure so situated could lead to restrictions on the navigational use of the waterway during required repairs. *See Pet. for Cert,* in No. 93-1094, p. 22a (District Court found that after the flood "[t]he river remained closed for over a month," "[r]iver traffic ceased, several commuter ferries were stranded, and many barges could not enter the river system ... because the river level was lowered to aid repair efforts"). *Cf. Pennzoil Producing Co. v. Offshore Express, Inc.,* 943 F.2d 1465 (CA5 1991) (admiralty suit when vessel struck and ruptured gas pipeline and gas exploded); *Marathon Pipe Line Co. v. Drilling Rig Rowan/Odessa,* 761 F.2d 229, 233 (CA5 1985) (admiralty jurisdiction when vessel struck pipeline, "a fixed structure on the seabed"); *Orange Beach Water, Sewer, and Fire Protection Authority v. M/V Alva,* 680 F.2d 1374 (CA11 1982) (admiralty suit when vessel struck underwater pipeline).

In the second *Sisson* enquiry, we look to whether the general character of the activity giving rise to the incident shows a substantial relationship to traditional maritime activity. We ask whether a tortfeasor's activity, commercial or noncommercial, on navigable waters is so closely related to activity traditionally subject to admiralty law that the reasons for applying special admiralty rules would apply in the case at hand. Navigation of boats in navigable waters clearly falls within the substantial relationship, *Foremost,* 457 U.S., at 675, 102 S.Ct., at 2658-2659; storing them at a marina on navigable waters is close enough, *Sisson, supra,* 497 U.S., at 367, 110 S.Ct., at 2898; whereas in flying an airplane over the water, *Executive Jet,* 409 U.S., at 270-271, 93 S.Ct., at 505-506, as in swimming, *id.,* at 255-256, 93 S.Ct., at 498-499, the relationship is too attenuated.

On like reasoning, the "activity giving rise to the incident" in this case, *Sisson, supra,* 497 U.S., at 364, 110 S.Ct., at 2897, should be characterized as repair or maintenance work on a navigable waterway performed from a vessel. Described in this way, there is no question that the activity is substantially related to traditional maritime activity, for barges and similar vessels have traditionally been engaged in repair work similar to what Great Lakes contracted to perform here. *See, e.g., Shea v. Rev-Lyn Contracting Co.,* 868 F.2d 515, 518 (CA1 1989) (bridge repair by crane-carrying barge); *Nelson v. United States,* 639 F.2d 469, 472 (CA9 1980) (KENNEDY, J.) (repair of wave suppressor from a barge); *In re New York Dock Co.,* 61 F.2d 777 (CA2 1932) (pile driving from crane-carrying barge in connection with the building of a dock); *In re P. Sanford Ross, Inc.,* 196 F. 921, 923-924 (EDNY 1912) (pile driving from crane-carrying barge close to waters edge), *rev'd on other grounds,* 204 F. 248 (CA2 1913); *cf. In re The V-14813,* 65 F.2d 789, 790 (CA5 1933) ("[t]here are many cases holding that a dredge, or a barge with a pile driver, employed on navigable waters, is subject to maritime jurisdiction"); *Lawrence v. Flatboat,* 84 F. 200 (SD Ala. 1897) (pile driving from crane-carrying barge in connection with the erection of bulkheads), *aff'd sub nom. Southern Log Cart & Supply Co. v. Lawrence,* 86 F. 907 (CA5 1898).

The city argues, to the contrary, that a proper application of the activity prong of *Sisson* would consider the city's own alleged failure at properly maintaining and operating the tunnel system that runs under the river. City Brief 48-49. If this asserted proximate cause of the flood victims' injuries were considered, the city submits, its failure to resemble any traditional maritime activity would take this case out of admiralty.

The city misreads *Sisson,* however, which did not consider the activities of the washer/dryer manufacturer, who was possibly an additional tortfeasor, and whose activities were hardly maritime; the activities of *Sisson,* the boat owner, supplied the necessary substantial relationship to traditional maritime activity. Likewise, in *Foremost,* we said that "[b]ecause the wrong here involves the negligent operation of a vessel on navigable waters, we believe that it has a sufficient nexus to traditional maritime activity to sustain admiralty jurisdiction...." 457 U.S., at 674, 102 S.Ct. at 2658. By using the word "involves," we made it clear that we need to look only to whether one of the arguably proximate causes of the incident originated in the maritime activity of a tortfeasor: as long as one of the putative tortfeasors was engaged in traditional maritime activity the allegedly wrongful activity will "involve" such traditional maritime activity and will meet the second nexus prong. Thus, even if we were to identify the "activity giving rise to the incident" as including the acts of the city as well as Great Lakes, admiralty jurisdiction would nevertheless attach. That result would be true to *Sissons* requirement of a "substantial relationship" between the "activity giving rise to the incident" and traditional maritime activity. *Sisson* did not require, as the city in effect asserts, that there be a complete identity between the two. The substantial relationship test is satisfied when at least one alleged tortfeasor was engaging in activity substantially related to traditional maritime activity and such activity is claimed to have been a proximate cause of the incident.

Petitioners also argue that we might get a different result simply by characterizing the "activity" in question at a different level of generality, perhaps as "repair and maintenance," or, as "pile driving near a bridge." The city is, of course, correct that a tortfeasor's activity can be described at a sufficiently high level of generality to eliminate any hint of maritime connection, and if that were properly done *Sisson* would bar assertion of admiralty jurisdiction. But to suggest that such hyper-generalization ought to be the rule would convert *Sisson* into a vehicle for eliminating admiralty jurisdiction. Although there is inevitably some play in the joints in selecting the right level of generality when applying the *Sisson* test, the inevitable imprecision is not an excuse for whimsy. The test turns on the comparison of traditional maritime activity to the arguably maritime character of the tortfeasor's activity in a given case; the comparison would merely be frustrated by eliminating the maritime aspect of the tortfeasor's activity from consideration.[4]

Grubart makes an additional claim that *Sisson* is being given too expansive a reading. If the activity at issue here is considered maritime-related, it argues, then virtually "every activity involving a vessel on navigable waters" would be "a traditional maritime activity sufficient to invoke maritime jurisdiction." Grubart Brief 6. But this is not fatal criticism. This Court has not proposed any radical alteration of the traditional criteria for invoking admiralty jurisdiction in tort cases, but has simply followed the lead of the lower federal courts in rejecting a location rule so rigid as to extend admiralty to a case involving an airplane, not a vessel, engaged in an activity far removed from anything traditionally maritime. *See Executive Jet,* 409 U.S., at 268-274, 93 S.Ct., at 504-506; *see also Peytavin v. Government Employees Ins. Co.,* 453 F.2d 1121, 1127 (CA5 1972) (no jurisdiction over claim for personal injury by motorist who was rear-ended while waiting for a ferry on a floating pontoon serving as the ferry's landing); *Chapman v. Grosse Pointe Farms,* 385 F.2d 962 (CA6 1967) (no admiralty jurisdiction over claim of swimmer who injured himself when diving off pier into shallow but navigable water). In the cases after *Executive Jet,* the Court stressed

---

[4] The city also proposes that we define the activity as "the operation of an underground tunnel connected to Loop buildings." City Brief 49-50. But doing this would eliminate the maritime tortfeasor's activity from consideration entirely. This (like the choice of a supreme level of generality, described in the text) would turn *Sisson v. Ruby,* 497 U.S. 358, 110 S.Ct. 2892, 111 L. Ed. 2d 292 (1990), on its head, from a test to weed out torts without a maritime connection into an arbitrary exercise for eliminating jurisdiction over even vessel-related torts connected to traditional maritime commerce.

the need for a maritime connection, but found one in the navigation or berthing of pleasure boats, despite the facts that the pleasure boat activity took place near shore, where States have a strong interest in applying their own tort law, or was not on all fours with the maritime shipping and commerce that has traditionally made up the business of most maritime courts. *Sisson*, 497 U.S., at 367, 110 S.Ct., at 2898; *Foremost*, 457 U.S., at 675, 102 S.Ct., at 2658-2659. Although we agree with petitioner's that these cases do not say that every tort involving a vessel on navigable waters falls within the scope of admiralty jurisdiction no matter what, they do show that ordinarily that will be so.[5]

Perhaps recognizing the difficulty of escaping the case law, petitioner's ask us to change it. In cases "involving land based parties and injuries," the city would have us adopt a condition of jurisdiction that "the totality of the circumstances reflects a federal interest in protecting maritime commerce sufficiently weighty to justify shifting what would otherwise be state-court litigation into federal court under the federal law of admiralty." City Brief 32. Grubart and the city say that the Fifth Circuit has applied a somewhat similar "four-factor test" looking to "the functions and roles of the parties; the types of vehicles and instrumentalities involved; the causation and the type of injury; and traditional concepts of the role of admiralty law." *Kelly v. Smith*, 485 F.2d 520, 525 (CA5 1973); *see also Molett v. Penrod Drilling Co.*, 826 F.2d 1419, 1426 (CA5 1987) (adding three more factors: the "impact of the event on maritime shipping and commerce"; "the desirability of a uniform national rule to apply to such matters"; and "the need for admiralty expertise in the trial and decision of the case"), *cert. denied sub nom. Columbus-McKinnon, Inc. v. Gearench, Inc.*, 493 U.S. 1003, 110 S.Ct. 563, 107 L. Ed. 2d 558 (1989). Although they point out that *Sisson* disapproved the use of four-factor or seven-factor tests "where all the relevant entities are engaged in similar types of activity," this rule implicitly left the matter open for cases like this one, where most of the victims, and one of the tortfeasors, are based on land. *See* 497 U.S., at 365, n.3, 110 S.Ct. at 2897 ("Different issues may be raised by a case in which one of the instrumentalities is engaged in a traditional maritime activity, but the other is not"). The city argues that there is a good reason why cases like this one should get different treatment. Since the basic rationale for federal admiralty jurisdiction is "protection of maritime commerce through uniform rules of decision," the proposed jurisdictional test would improve on *Sisson* in limiting the scope of admiralty jurisdiction more exactly to its rationale. A multiple factor test would minimize, if not eliminate, the awkward possibility that federal admiralty rules or procedures will govern a case, to the disadvantage of state law, when admiralty's purpose does not require it. *Cf. Foremost, supra,* at 677-686, 102 S.Ct., at 2659-2664 (POWELL, J., dissenting).

Although the arguments are not frivolous, they do not persuade. It is worth recalling that the *Sisson* tests are aimed at the same objectives invoked to support a new multifactor test, the elimination of admiralty jurisdiction where the rationale for the jurisdiction does not support it. If the tort produces no potential threat to maritime commerce or occurs during activity lacking a substantial relationship to traditional maritime activity, *Sisson* assumes that the objectives of admiralty jurisdiction probably do not require its exercise, even if the location test is satisfied. If, however, the *Sisson* tests are also satisfied, it is not apparent why the need for admiralty jurisdiction in aid of maritime commerce somehow becomes less acute merely because land-based parties happen to be involved. Certainly Congress did not think a land-based party necessarily diluted the need for admiralty jurisdiction or it would have kept its hands off the primitive location test.

Of course one could claim it to be odd that under *Sisson* a land-based party (or more than one) may be subject to admiralty jurisdiction, but it would appear no less odd under the city's test that a maritime tortfeasor in the most traditional mould might be subject to state common-law jurisdiction. Other things being equal, it is not evident why the first supposed anomaly is worse than the second. But other things are not even equal. As noted just above, Congress has already made the judgment, in the Extension Act, that a land-based victim may properly be subject to admiralty jurisdiction. Surely a land-based joint tortfeasor has no claim to supposedly more favorable treatment.

Nor are these the only objections to the city's position. Contrary to what the city suggests, City Brief 10, 14-15, 25-26, 30, exercise of federal admiralty jurisdiction does not result in automatic displacement of state law.

---

[5] Because we conclude that the tort alleged in Count I of Great Lakes's complaint satisfies both the location and connection tests necessary for admiralty jurisdiction under 28 U.S.C. § 1333(1), we need not consider respondent's alternative argument that the Extension of Admiralty Jurisdiction Act, 46 U.S.C. App. § 740, provides an independent basis of federal jurisdiction over the complaint.

It is true that, "[w]ith admiralty jurisdiction comes the application of substantive admiralty law." *East River S.S. Corp. v. Transamerica DeLaval Inc.,* 476 U.S. 858, 864, 106 S.Ct. 2295, 2298-2299, 90 L. Ed. 2d 865 (1986). But, to characterize that law, as the city apparently does, as "federal rules of decision," City Brief 15, is "a destructive oversimplification of the highly intricate interplay of the States and the National Government in their regulation of maritime commerce. It is true that state law must yield to the needs of a uniform federal maritime law when this Court finds inroads on a harmonious system. But this limitation still leaves the States a wide scope." *Romero v. International Terminal Operating Co.,* 358 U.S. 354, 373, 79 S.Ct. 468, 480-481, 3 L. Ed. 2d 368 (1959) (footnote omitted). *See East River, supra,* at 864-865, 106 S.Ct., at 2298-2299 ("Drawn from state and federal sources, the general maritime law is an amalgam of traditional common-law rules, modifications of those rules, and newly created rules" (footnote omitted)). Thus, the city's proposal to synchronize the jurisdictional enquiry with the test for determining the applicable substantive law would discard a fundamental feature of admiralty law, that federal admiralty courts sometimes do apply state law. *See, e.g., American Dredging Co. v. Miller,* 510 U.S. —, —, 114 S.Ct. 981, 987, 127 L. Ed. 2d 285 (1994); *see also* 1 S. Friedell, Benedict on Admiraeey § 112 p. 7-49 (7th ed. 1994).[6]

Finally, on top of these objections going to the city's premises there is added a most powerful one based on the practical consequences of adopting a multifactor test. Although the existing case law tempers the locality test with the added requirements looking to potential harm and traditional activity, it reflects customary practice in seeing jurisdiction as the norm when the tort originates with a vessel in navigable waters, and in treating departure from the locality principle as the exception. For better or worse, the case law has thus carved out the approximate shape of admiralty jurisdiction in a way that admiralty lawyers understand reasonably well. As against this approach, so familiar and relatively easy, the proposed four- or seven-factor test would be hard to apply, jettisoning relative predictability for the open-ended rough-and-tumble of factors, inviting complex argument in a trial court and a virtually inevitable appeal.

Consider, for example, just one of the factors under the city's test, requiring a district court at the beginning of every purported admiralty case to determine the source (state or federal) of the applicable substantive law. The difficulty of doing that was an important reason why this Court in *Romero, supra,* was unable to hold that maritime claims fell within the scope of the federal-question-jurisdiction statute, 28 U.S.C. § 1331. 358 U.S., at 375-376, 79 S.Ct., at 481-482 ("sound judicial policy does not encourage a situation which necessitates constant adjudication of the boundaries of state and federal competence"). That concern applies just as strongly to cases invoking a district court's admiralty jurisdiction under 28 U.S.C. § 1333, under which the jurisdictional enquiry for maritime torts has traditionally been quite uncomplicated.

Reasons of practice, then, are as weighty as reasons of theory for rejecting the city's call to adopt a multifactor test for admiralty jurisdiction for the benefit of land-based parties to a tort action.

Accordingly, we conclude that the Court of Appeals correctly held that the District Court had admiralty jurisdiction over the respondent's Limitation Act suit. The judgment of the Court of Appeals is

Affirmed.

Justice O'CONNOR, concurring.

I concur in the Court's judgment and opinion. The Court properly holds that, when a court is faced with a case involving multiple tortfeasors, some of whom may not be maritime actors, if one of the putative tortfeasors

---

[6] We will content ourselves simply with raising a question about another of the city's assumptions, which does not go to anything dispositive for us. It is true that this Court has said that "the primary focus of admiralty jurisdiction is unquestionably the protection of maritime commerce," *Foremost Ins. Co. v. Richardson,* 457 U.S. 668, 674, 102 S.Ct. 2654, 2658, 73 L. Ed. 2d 300 (1982); *see Sisson,* 497 U.S., at 367, 110 S.Ct., at 2898; *see id.,* at 364, n.2, 110 S.Ct., at 2896- 2897, n.2, a premise that recently has been questioned, *see* Casto, *The Origins of Federal Admiralty Jurisdiction in an Age of Privateers, Smugglers, and Pirates,* 37 Am. J. Legal Hist. 117 (1993). However that may be, this Court has never limited the interest in question to the "protection of maritime commerce through uniform rules of decision," as the city would have it. City Brief 19. Granted, whatever its precise purpose, it is likely that Congress thought of uniformity of substantive law as a subsidiary goal conducive to furthering that purpose. *See* Currie, *Federalism and the Admiralty: "The Devil's Own Mess,"* 1960 S.Ct. Rev. 158, 163 ("[A] uniform law was apparently one reason for the establishment of the admiralty jurisdiction in 1789" (footnote omitted)). But we are unwilling to rule out that the first Congress saw a value in federal admiralty courts beyond fostering uniformity of substantive law, stemming, say, from a concern with local bias similar to the presupposition for diversity jurisdiction. *See* The Federalist No. 80, p. 538 (J. Cooke ed. 1961) (A. Hamilton) ("maritime causes ... so commonly affect the rights of foreigners"); 1 M. Farrand, Records of the Federal Convention of 1787, p. 124 (1911); 2 *id.,* at 46; *see generally* D. Robertson, Admiralty and Federalism 95-103 (1970). After all, if uniformity of substantive law had been Congress's only concern, it could have left admiralty jurisdiction in the state courts subject to an appeal to a national tribunal (as it did with federal-question jurisdiction until 1875, and as the Articles of Federation had done with cases of prize and capture).

was engaged in traditional maritime activity alleged to have proximately caused the incident, then the supposedly wrongful activity "involves" traditional maritime activity. The possible involvement of other, nonmaritime parties does not affect the jurisdictional inquiry as to the maritime party. *Ante,* at 1051-1052. I do not, however, understand the Court's opinion to suggest that, having found admiralty jurisdiction over a particular claim against a particular party, a court must then exercise admiralty jurisdiction over all the claims and parties involved in the case. Rather, the court should engage in the usual supplemental jurisdiction and impleader inquiries. *See* 28 U.S.C. § 1367 (1988 ed., Supp. V); Fed. Rule Civ. Proc. 14; *see also ante,* at 1047. I find nothing in the Court's opinion to the contrary.

Justice THOMAS, with whom Justice SCALIA joins, concurring in the judgment.

I agree with the majority's conclusion that 28 U.S.C. § 1333(1) grants the District Court jurisdiction over the great Chicago flood of 1992. But I write separately because I cannot agree with the test the Court applies to determine the boundaries of admiralty and maritime jurisdiction. Instead of continuing our unquestioning allegiance to the multi-factor approach of *Sisson v. Ruby,* 497 U.S. 358, 110 S.Ct. 2892, 111 L. Ed. 2d 292 (1990), I would restore the jurisdictional inquiry to the simple question whether the tort occurred on a vessel on the navigable waters of the United States. If so, then admiralty jurisdiction exists. This clear, bright-line rule, which the Court applied until recently, ensures that judges and litigants will not waste their resources in determining the extent of federal subject-matter jurisdiction.

I

* * *

As recently as 1972, courts and parties experienced little difficulty in determining whether a case triggered admiralty jurisdiction, thanks to the simple "situs rule." *In The Plymouth,* 3 Wall. 20, 36, 18 L. Ed. 125 (1866), this Court articulated the situs rule thus: "[e]very species of tort, however occurring, and whether on board a vessel or not, if upon the high seas or navigable waters, is of admiralty cognizance." This simple, clear test, which Justice Story pronounced while riding circuit, *see Thomas v. Lane,* 23 F. Cas. 957, 960 (CC Me. 1813), did not require alteration until 1948, when Congress included within the admiralty jurisdiction torts caused on water, but whose effects were felt on land. *See* Extension of Admiralty Jurisdiction Act, 62 Stat. 496, 46 U.S.C. app. § 740.

The simplicity of this test was marred by modern cases that tested the boundaries of admiralty jurisdiction with ever more unusual facts. In *Executive Jet Aviation, Inc. v. City of Cleveland,* 409 U.S. 249, 93 S.Ct. 493, 34 L. Ed. 2d 454 (1972), we held that a plane crash in Lake Erie was not an admiralty case within the meaning of § 1333(1) because the tort did not "bear a significant relationship to traditional maritime activity." *Id.,* at 268, 93 S.Ct., at 504. What subsequent cases have failed to respect, however, is *Executive Jet's* clear limitation to torts involving aircraft. As we said: "One area in which locality as the exclusive test of admiralty tort jurisdiction has given rise to serious problems in application is that of aviation.... [W]e have concluded that maritime locality alone is not a sufficient predicate for admiralty jurisdiction in aviation tort cases." *Id.,* at 261, 93 S.Ct., at 501 (emphasis added). Our identification of the "significant relationship" factor occurred wholly in the context of a discussion of the difficulties that aircraft posed for maritime law. In fact, while we recognized the extensive criticism of the strict locality rule, we noted that "for the traditional types of maritime torts, the traditional test has worked quite satisfactorily." *Id.,* at 254, 93 S.Ct., at 497. Thus, *Executive Jet,* properly read, holds that if a tort occurred on board a vessel on the navigable waters, the situs test applies, but if the tort involved an airplane, then the "significant relationship" requirement is added.

Although it modified the strict locality test, *Executive Jet* still retained a clear rule that I could apply comfortably to the main business of the admiralty court. Nonetheless, the simplicity and clarity of this approach met its demise in *Foremost Ins. Co. v. Richardson,* 457 U.S. 668, 102 S.Ct. 2654, 73 L. Ed. 2d 300 (1982). That case involved the collision of two pleasure boats on the navigable waters, a tort that some commentators had argued did not fall within the admiralty jurisdiction because it did not implicate maritime commerce. *See, e.g.,* Stolz, *Pleasure Boating and Admiralty: Erie at Sea,* 51 Calif. L. Rev. 661 (1963). The Court could have resolved the case and found jurisdiction simply by applying the situs test. Instead, responding to the arguments that admiralty jurisdiction was limited to commercial maritime activity, the Court found that the tort's "significant connection with traditional maritime activity" and the accident's "potential disruptive impact" on maritime commerce prompted an exercise of federal jurisdiction. 457 U.S., at 674-675, 102 S.Ct., at 2658-2659.

It is clear that *Foremost* overextended *Executive Jet,* which had reserved the significant relationship inquiry for aviation torts. As Justice SCALIA noted in *Sisson, Executive Jet* is better "understood as resting on the quite simple ground that the tort did not involve a vessel, which had traditionally been thought required by the leading scholars in the field." 497 U.S., at 369-370, 110 S.Ct., at 2899 (opinion concurring in judgment). *Executive Jet* did not in the least seek to alter the strict locality test for torts involving waterborne vessels. *Foremost,* however, converted *Executive Jet's* exception into the rule. In addition to examining situs, *Foremost* required federal courts to ask whether the tort bore a significant relationship to maritime commerce, and whether the accident had a potential disruptive impact on maritime commerce. 457 U.S., at 673-675, 102 S.Ct., at 2657-2659. The lower courts adopted different approaches as they sought to apply *Foremost's* alteration of the *Executive Jet* test. *See Sisson, supra,* 497 U.S., at 365, n.4, 110 S.Ct., at 2897, n.4 (citing cases).

Sisson then affirmed the inherent vagueness of the *Foremost* test. *Sisson* involved a marina fire that was caused by a faulty washer-dryer unit on a pleasure yacht. The fire destroyed the yacht and damaged several vessels in addition to the marina. In finding admiralty jurisdiction, the Court held that the federal judicial power would extend to such cases only if: (1) in addition to situs, (2) the "incident" poses a potential hazard to maritime commerce, and (3) the "activity" giving rise to the incident bears a substantial relationship to traditional maritime activity. 497 U.S., at 362-364, 110 S.Ct., at 2895-2897. The traditional situs test also would have sustained a finding of jurisdiction because the fire started on board a vessel on the waterways. Thus, what was once a simple question—did the tort occur on the navigable waters—had become a complicated, multifactor analysis.

The disruption and confusion created by the *Foremost-Sisson* approach is evident from the post-*Sisson* decisions of the lower courts and from the majority opinion itself. Faced with the task of determining what is an "incident" or "activity" for *Sisson* purposes, the Fourth, Fifth, and Ninth Circuits simply reverted to the multi-factor test they had employed before *Sisson. See Price v. Price,* 929 F.2d 131, 135-136 (CA4 1991); *Coats v. Penrod Drilling Corp.,* 5 F.3d 877, 885-886 (CA5 1993); *Delta Country Ventures, Inc. v. Magana,* 986 F.2d 1260, 1263 (CA9 1993). The District Courts opinion in this case is typical: while nodding to *Sisson,* the court focused its entire attention on a totality-of-the-circumstances test, which includes factors such as "the functions and roles of the parties" and "[t]he traditional concepts of the role of admiralty law." *Pet. for Cert. of Chicago 32a.* Such considerations have no place in the *Sisson* test and should have no role in any jurisdictional inquiry. The dangers of a totality-of-the-circumstances approach to jurisdiction should be obvious. An undefined test requires courts and litigants to devote substantial resources to determine whether a federal court may hear a specific case. Such a test also introduces undesirable uncertainty into the affairs of private actors—even those involved in common maritime activities—who cannot predict whether or not their conduct may justify the exercise of admiralty jurisdiction.

Although the majority makes an admirable attempt to clarify what *Sisson* obscures, I am afraid that its analysis cannot mitigate the confusion of the *Sisson* test. Thus, faced with the "potential to disrupt maritime commerce" prong *ante,* at 1050, the majority must resort to "an intermediate level of possible generality" to determine the "'general features'" of the incident here, *id.,* at 1051. The majority does not explain the origins of "levels of generality," nor, to my knowledge, do we employ such a concept in other areas of jurisdiction. We do not use "levels of generality" to characterize residency or amount in controversy for diversity purposes, or to determine the presence of a federal question. Nor does the majority explain why an "intermediate" level of generality is appropriate. It is even unclear what an intermediate level of generality is, and we cannot expect that district courts will apply such a concept uniformly in similar cases. It is far from obvious how the undefined intermediate level of generality indicates that the "incident" for *Sisson* purposes is that of a vessel damaging an underwater structure.

The majority also applies levels of generality to the next prong of *Sisson*—whether the tortfeasor is engaged in "activity" that shows a "substantial relationship to traditional maritime activity." The majority decides that the activity is repair work by a vessel on a navigable waterway. But, as the petitioner's rightly argue, the "activity" very well could be bridge repair or pile driving. One simply cannot tell due to the ambiguities intrinsic to *Sisson* and to the uncertainty as to the meaning of levels of generality. The majority's response implicitly acknowledges the vagueness inherent in *Sisson:* "Although there is inevitably some play in the joints in selecting the right level of generality when applying the *Sisson* test, the inevitable imprecision is not an excuse for whimsy." *Ante,* at 1052. The Court cannot provide much guidance to district courts as to the correct level of generality; instead, it can only say that any level is probably sufficient so long as it does not lead to "whimsy." When it comes to these issues, I prefer a clearer rule, which this Court has demanded with respect to federal question or diversity jurisdiction. Indeed, the "play in the joints" and "imprecision" that the Court finds "inevitable" easily could be avoided by returning to the test that prevailed before *Foremost.* In its effort to create an elegant, general test that could include all maritime torts, *Sisson* has only disrupted what was once a simple inquiry.

II

* * *

In place of *Sisson* I would follow the test described at the outset. When determining whether maritime jurisdiction exists under § 1333(1), a federal district court should ask if the tort occurred on a vessel on the navigable waters. This approach won the approval of two Justices in *Sisson, see* 497 U.S., at 373, 110 S.Ct., at 2901 (SCALIA, J., joined by WHITE, J., concurring in judgment). Although Justice SCALIA's *Sisson* concurrence retained a "normal maritime activities" component, it recognized that anything a vessel does in the navigable waters would meet that requirement, and that "[i]t would be more straightforward to jettison the 'traditional maritime activity' analysis entirely." *Id.,* at 374, 110 S.Ct., at 2902. I wholly agree and have chosen the straightforward approach, which, for all of its simplicity, would have produced the same results the Court arrived at in *Executive Jet, Foremost, Sisson,* and this case. Although this approach "might leave within admiralty jurisdiction a few unusual actions," *ibid.,* such freakish cases will occur rarely. In any event, the resources needed to resolve them "will be saved many times over by a clear jurisdictional rule that makes it unnecessary to decide" what is a traditional maritime activity and what poses a threat to maritime commerce. *Id.,* at 374-375, 110 S.Ct., at 2901-2902.

* * *

Note: *Limits on Grubart*

The Court in *Grubart* suggests that practically any tort involving a vessel in navigation on navigable waters will satisfy the criteria for admiralty tort jurisdiction. Is that a fair reading of *Grubart?* If so, do you agree? Consider the following. Plaintiffs were injured by carbon monoxide fumes in a houseboat they rented from the appellant H_2O Houseboat Vacations (H_2O) at Lake Havasu in Arizona. At the time of the incident, the houseboat was tied to the shore of Lake Havasu which was a navigable waterway. Plaintiffs slept on the houseboat the night before they were to take it out on the lake the next day. As it was summertime they closed all of the windows in the sleeping area of the houseboat, turned on the air conditioning, and went to sleep. During the night, plaintiff's were seriously injured by carbon monoxide fumes within the houseboat which were probably the result of faulty equipment aboard the houseboat. H_2O filed its own action in the federal district court seeking to limit its liability under the Vessel Owner's Liability Act.

The Ninth Circuit in *H_2O Houseboat Vacations, Inc. v. Hernandez,* 103 F.3d 914, 1997 AMC 390 (9th Cir. 1996) used the following approach:

> The "connection" prong of the Grubart test has two subparts. The first subpart asks whether the general features of the incident causing the injury indicate the incident had a "potentially disruptive impact on maritime commerce." *Id.* To decide this question, we must first determine what was the incident that caused the injury. *See id.* at ____, ____, 115 S.Ct. at 1050-51.
>
> The Court told us how to do this in *Sisson v. Ruby,* 497 U.S. 358, 110 S.Ct. 2892, 111 L. Ed. 2d 292 (1990). There, a fire was caused by a defective washer/dryer aboard a pleasure boat docked at a marina on a navigable body of water. *Id.* at 360, 110 S.Ct. at 2894-95. The fire burned not only the boat itself but the marina and other boats docked nearby. *Id.* The Court did not describe the incident broadly as a "fire," nor narrowly as a "fire ... damaging nothing but pleasure boats." *Grubart,* 513 U.S. at ____, 115 S.Ct. at 1051. Rather, in *Sisson,* the Court described the incident at "an intermediate level of possible generality" as "'a fire on a vessel docked at a marina on navigable waters.'" *Grubart,* 513 U.S. at ___, ____, 115 S.Ct. at 1051, 1050 (quoting *Sisson,* 497 U.S. at 363, 110 S.Ct. at 2896). The question was whether that incident, so described, had a potential to disrupt maritime commerce. The court held it did.

Here, the incident that caused the injury was the emission of carbon monoxide fumes inside a contained space within a houseboat tied to the shore. This incident had no potential to disrupt maritime commerce. The carbon monoxide was dangerous only because it was contained in the sleeping area of the houseboat. The fumes would not be dangerous if they escaped. This is far different from the fire on the boat in *Sisson*. There, the fire had the potential of spreading to other boats and to the marina. Indeed, it did.

It is possible to speculate that the houseboat would have posed a hazard to maritime commerce if it had slipped its tie to the shore and had drifted onto Lake Havasu with the Hernandez family inside unconscious from carbon monoxide, or if the Hernandez family had taken the boat out on the lake and whoever was steering the boat had been overcome with carbon monoxide fumes and lost consciousness.

Such speculation, however, would require us to ignore the actual "incident" that caused injury to the Hernandez family. That incident was the emission of carbon monoxide fumes encapsulated within the houseboat tied to the shore. That incident, defined as required by *Sisson* and *Grubart*, did not have the potential to disrupt maritime commerce.

Is this a proper application of the *Grubart* criteria?

Notes:

1. Jurisdiction Over Aviation Torts

The Supreme Court in *Executive Jet* held that a crash into the navigable waters of the United States by a plane on a flight between places within the continental U.S. lacks a sufficient maritime nexus to support admiralty jurisdiction. 409 U.S. 249, 274 (1974). The Court, however, did not foreclose admiralty jurisdiction in all air crashes. To the contrary, it opined that admiralty jurisdiction *might* be appropriate where a plane engaged in an intercontinental flight crashes in navigable waters, inasmuch as such flights typically require the plane to fly over broad stretches of international waters and transportation over these bodies of water traditionally has been performed by vessels. 409 U.S. at 271. Subsequently, the Supreme Court in a case brought under the Death on the High Seas Act (DOHSA), 46 U.S.C.A. § 30302 (formerly 46 U.S.C. § 761), stemming from the crash of a helicopter in the Gulf of Mexico, held that DOHSA, in and of itself, is sufficient to confer admiralty jurisdiction. *Offshore Logistics, Inc. v. Tallentire*, 477 U.S. 207, 221, 106 S.Ct. 2485, 91 L. Ed. 2d 174, 1986 AMC 2113 (1986). Despite its conclusion that DOHSA confers admiralty jurisdiction, the Court also stated that:

> [notwithstanding] this statutory provision, admiralty jurisdiction is appropriately invoked here under traditional principles because the accident occurred on the high seas and in furtherance of an activity bearing a significant relationship to a traditional maritime activity. Although the decedents were killed while riding in a helicopter and not a more traditional maritime conveyance, that helicopter was engaged in a function traditionally performed by waterborne vessels: the ferrying of passengers from an "island" albeit an artificial one to the shore. (*Id.* 218 (citations omitted).

See also Miller v. U.S., 725 F.2d 1311, 1984 AMC 1169 (11th Cir.), *cert. denied*, 469 U.S. 821,105 S.Ct. 94, 83 L. Ed. 2d 40 (1984); *Roberts v. United States*, 498 F.2d 520, 524 (9th Cir.), *cert denied*, 419 U.S. 1070, 95 S.Ct. 656, 42 L. Ed. 2d 665, (1974); *Icelandic Coast Guard v. United Technologies Corp.*, 722 E Supp. 942 (D. Conn. 1989) (products liability). As a general proposition, aircraft have not been deemed to be vessels. *See Smith v. Pan Air Corp.*, 684 F.2d 1102, 1112, 1983 AMC 2836 (5th Cir. 1982) (a seaplane) and *Barger v. Petroleum Helicopters, Inc.*, 692 F.2d 337, 339, 1993 AMC 2854 (5th Cir. 1983) (a helicopter). That fact is not necessarily fatal to admiralty jurisdiction and depending on the circumstances does not preclude a finding of "nexus", as the *Tallentire* decision demonstrates. Suppose a helicopter is ferrying personnel from Louisiana to a fixed platform in the Gulf of Mexico, two miles off the Louisiana coast. Does the Courts finding of nexus in *Tallentire* independent of DOHSA, compel the conclusion that a crash in territorial waters likewise supports admiralty jurisdiction. If so, what law applies in a wrongful death action? *See Yamaha Motor Corp. v. Calhoun*, 516 U.S. 199, 116 S.Ct. 619, 133 L. Ed. 2d 578, 1996 AMC 305 (1996).

If a intercontinental flight, *e.g.*, London to New York, has crossed the Atlantic Ocean and crashes on land immediately after having crossed the U.S. coast, is there admiralty jurisdiction? Would such a situation fail the locality test. Cf. *Smith v. Pan Air Corp.*, 684 F.2d 1102, 1983 AMC 2836 (5th Cir. 1982). Suppose the pilot of a plane is negligent while the plane is over the high seas and this negligence results in a crash on land. Would there be admiralty jurisdiction? If a flight from one point in the continental United States to another point in the continental United States, *e.g.*, New Orleans to Miami, crashes in the Gulf of Mexico, which analysis prevails *Executive Jet* or *Tallentire*? *See Sullivan v. 43rd Aviation Flying Club, Inc.*, 16 Av. Cas. (CCH) ¶18, 260 (D. Conn. 1981).

2. Nexus v. Locus: Can Nexus Without Locus Ever be Sufficient?

Some commentators have suggested that the locality requirement be subsumed into the nexus requirement and not stand as an independent criterion. There are instances where the maritime interests are so strong that adherence to a strict locality rule would impede the fundamental purposes of admiralty jurisdiction:

Whether a tort occurs on the water should be one factor to be considered in determining whether the tort meets the nexus requirement. The admiralty extension Act has helped by including damage done on land by vessels in navigable waters, and the courts have made an exception for seamens claims arising out of their maritime status. As the courts are becoming accustomed to requiring a maritime nexus for tort claims as they have for contract claims, there seems to be no principled reason for excluding tort claims merely because they lack a maritime local. 1 BENEDICT ON ADMIRALTY § 171, p. 11-30–11-31 (7th ed. rev. by S. Friedel 1988) (citations omitted). *See also* Robert Force, *Determining Admiralty Tort Jurisdiction: An Alternative Analytical Framework,* 21 J. MAR. L. & COM. 1, 78-80 (1990).

The requirement of locality for admiralty jurisdiction has sometimes been dispensed with in torts involving seamen. For example, in a "blacklisting" case involving seamen suing marine protection and indemnity insurers for tortious interference with employment, the court found that the case was "so interwoven with present and potential maritime contractual relationships ... as to fall within that jurisdiction." *Carroll v. Protection Maritime Ins. Co.,* 512 F.2d 4, 8-9, 1975 AMC 1633 (1st Cir. 1975). The court found admiralty jurisdiction despite the fact that there was no direct connection to navigable waters, holding that the indirect connection, to employees on vessels in navigable waters, together with the potential impact on maritime contractual relationships, was sufficient.

However, in *LaMontagne v. Craig,* 817 F.2d 556, 1987 AMC 2477 (9th Cir. 1987), the Ninth Circuit denied jurisdiction in a case of alleged defamation of an officer on a merchant vessel by the vessel's chief engineer, through a letter sent to the shipping company. The alleged tort occurred on land and not navigable waters, and admiralty jurisdiction was therefore denied. But, in another case involving defamation, the same court reached the opposite conclusion where the tortious activity occurred aboard ship. In *Guidry v. Durkin,* 834 F.2d 1465, 1988 AMC 1979 (9th Cir. 1987), the Ninth Circuit found admiralty jurisdiction where the defendant-crew member wrote the alleged defamatory statement while on board his vessel, and gave it to the telex operator for transmission to shore. According to the court, the locality requirement was met because "all prima facie requirements for tortious libel were met at sea." (834 F.2d at 1470).

Torts committed against personnel engaged in oil or gas exploration or removal activities on fixed platforms satisfy neither the location nor nexus criteria. *Rodrigue v. Aetna Casualty & Surety Co.,* 395 U.S. 352, 89 S.Ct. 1835, 23 L. Ed. 2d 360 (1969). The Supreme Court there held that, generally, oil rigs are artificial islands, not vessels in navigation, and therefore "the accidents [in question] had no more connection with the ordinary stuff of admiralty than do accidents on piers." *Id.* at 360. The same reasoning was applied to an oil and gas worker who was *fortuitously* present on a vessel at the time of the accident. *In re Dearborn Marine Services, Inc.* 499 F.2d 263, 1975 AMC 1850 (5th Cir. 1974), *cert. dismissed,* 423 U.S. 886, 96 S.Ct. 163, 46 L. Ed. 2d 118 (1975).

The locality question is also raised where damages arise from torts occurring on a vessel during repairs. In *Sea Vessel, Inc. v. Reyes,* 23 F.3d 345, 1994 AMC 2736 (11th Cir. 1994), the court found that the locality test was satisfied where injuries resulted from a fire aboard a dry-docked vessel. Although the "water [had been] removed from about her," the vessel was not on "land," according to the court, any more "than would be such a vessel if fastened to a wharf in a dry harbor where, by the natural recession of the water by the ebbing tide, she for a time might be upon dry land." (23 F.3d at 348-49) "[T]he proposition that such repairs are made on land would practically deprive the admiralty courts of their largest and most important jurisdiction in connection with such repairs." *(Id.* at 348.)

4. Products Liability: Actions Based Upon Maritime Tort

EMPLOYERS INSURANCE OF WAUSAU v. SUWANNEE RIVER SPA LINES, INC.

866 F.2d 752, 1990 AMC 447 (5th Cir. 1989)

* * *

II.

A. The Effect of the East River Decision

1. Admiralty Jurisdiction

Defendants argue that in light of the Supreme Courts decision in *East River S.S. Corp. v. Transamerica Delaval, Inc.,* 476 U.S. 858, 106 S.Ct. 2295, 90 L. Ed. 2d 865 (1986), the federal courts have no admiralty jurisdiction over this case. In *East River,* the Supreme Court adopted the established rule of the Courts of Appeal that concepts of products liability, grounded in both negligence and strict liability, are a part of general maritime law. *Id.* at 865, 106 S.Ct. at 2299. The Court held, however, "that a manufacturer in a commercial relationship has no duty under either a negligence or strict products-liability theory to prevent a product from injuring itself." *Id.* at 871, 106 S.Ct. at 2302. "Thus, whether stated in negligence or strict liability, no products-liability claim lies in admiralty when the only injury claimed is economic loss." *Id.* at 876, 106 S.Ct. at 2304.

The defendants contend that because the plaintiffs' negligence claims, like those of the *East River* plaintiff's, allege only economic loss, those claims do not sound in maritime tort and therefore do not provide a basis for admiralty jurisdiction.[3]

The plaintiffs, however, note correctly that *East River's* holding has limited implications for the existence of admiralty jurisdiction. Whether a tort is maritime in nature, and therefore within the admiralty jurisdiction of the federal courts, turns on the application of the "situs" and "nexus" tests set forth in *Executive Jet Aviation, Inc. v. City of Cleveland,* 409 U.S. 249, 93 S.Ct. 493, 34 L. Ed. 2d 454 (1972). If those requirements are met, the court has jurisdiction. Whether the plaintiff may recover for those torts is not a question of admiralty jurisdiction but of substantive maritime law. In *East River* itself, the Supreme Court found that under the "locality" test the plaintiff's tort claims were within the admiralty jurisdiction.[4] Applying substantive maritime law, the Court then affirmed the granting of summary judgment in favor of defendants based on its conclusion that the negligence claims were not cognizable in maritime tort.

Although defendants argue here that plaintiff's have failed to state a claim on which relief can be granted, the Supreme Court made clear in *Bell v. Hood,* 327 U.S. 678, 66 S.Ct. 773, 90 L. Ed. 939 (1946), that whether the court lacks subject matter jurisdiction and whether the plaintiff fails to state a claim on which relief can be granted are distinct questions:

> Jurisdiction ... is not defeated ... by the possibility that the averments might fail to state a cause of action on which [the plaintiff] could actually recover. For it is well settled that the failure to state a proper cause of action calls for a judgment on the merits and not for a dismissal for want of jurisdiction. Whether the complaint states a cause of action on which relief could be granted is a question of law and just as issues of fact it must be decided after and not before the court has assumed jurisdiction over the controversy. If the court does later exercise its jurisdiction to determine that the allegations in the complaint do not state a ground for relief, then dismissal of the case would be on the merits, not for want of jurisdiction.

Id. at 682, 66 S.Ct. at 776. *Bell* recognized two exceptions to this rule. A suit may be dismissed for want of jurisdiction when (1) the allegations are clearly concocted for the sole purpose of obtaining federal jurisdiction, or (2) the claims are "wholly insubstantial and frivolous." *Id.*

Thus, the federal courts would lack subject matter jurisdiction over this suit only if the plaintiffs' tort claims are so clearly barred by the *East River* holding that they fall within one of the *Bell* exceptions. We do not think that the plaintiffs' negligence claims are "so patently without merit" as to deprive the federal courts of subject matter jurisdiction. *Id.* at 683, 66 S.Ct. at 776.

* * *

---

[3] Contracts relating to the construction of vessels are not considered maritime contracts. *Kossick v. United Fruit Co.,* 365 U.S. 731, 735, 81 S.Ct. 886, 889, 6 L. Ed. 2d 56 (1961); *Walter v. Marine Office of America,* 537 F.2d 89 (5th Cir. 1976). Consequently, claims for breach of such contracts are not within the admiralty jurisdiction. However, tort claims for negligent construction or design of a vessel will lie in admiralty if the negligence constitutes a maritime tort. *Jig the Third Corp. v. Puritan Marine Ins. Underwriters Corp.,* 519 F.2d 171, 174 (5 th Cir. 1975).

The district court correctly found that plaintiffs' negligence claims constituted maritime torts because (1) the harm allegedly caused by the tort occurred on the high seas—meeting the locality requirement for admiralty jurisdiction and (2) they occurred in the course of maritime commerce—satisfying the requirement that the tort bear a substantial relationship to traditional maritime activities. The district court also agreed to exercise pendent jurisdiction over the contract claims.

Because admiralty jurisdiction was premised in this case on plaintiffs' tort claims, defendants contend that if *East River* bars those claims, the grounds for admiralty jurisdiction are eliminated.

[4] The Supreme Court declined to decide whether the additional requirement of a "maritime nexus," necessary to establish admiralty jurisdiction over torts occurring on navigable waters within the United States, was also necessary to establish jurisdiction over torts occurring on the high seas. 476 U.S. at 864, 106 S.Ct. at 2298. Because the ships were engaged in maritime commerce, "a primary concern of admiralty law," the Court found that if there were a "maritime nexus" requirement it would have been met. *Id.* Similarly, there is a sufficient maritime nexus in this case to meet the second prong of the *Executive Jet* test.

SWOGGER v. WATERMAN STEAMSHIP CORP.

518 N.Y.S.2d 715, 1987 AMC 2679 (N.Y. Sup. Ct., New York County, 1987)

aff'd, 546 N.Y.S.2d 80 (N.Y.A.D. 1989)

MICHAEL J. DONTZIN, Justice

* * *

The underlying action, brought under the Jones Act (46 USC § 688) and General Maritime Law, was for personal injuries of David D. Swogger (Swogger) and his wrongful death due to malignant mesothelioma, allegedly caused by exposure to asbestos. The named defendants in the main action were shipowners of some 13 vessels upon which Swogger sailed as a marine engineer during his more than 35 years at sea.

The third-party action of Sealand seeks indemnity and/or contribution from various manufacturers and distributors of asbestos insulation products installed on ships on which Swogger sailed;[1] shipyards which installed these products,[2] and other shipowners[3] of ships upon which Swogger sailed. PRMMI's third-party action is against Todd Shipyards Corp. (Todd).

Swogger s action was settled as against all shipowners, and the third-party actions were severed.

Sealand s third-party complaint against the manufacturers and suppliers of asbestos products—alleges they failed to warn of the dangers and hazards of asbestos; negligently designed, tested, manufactured and distributed a dangerous product for marine use and breached various warranties with respect to fitness of asbestos for use aboard vessels; as against the shipyard defendants—alleges they negligently repaired and converted the vessel by installing asbestos products, and breached their warranty of safety and workmanlike services thereby creating the dangerous condition; as against the other shipowners—alleges they were negligent in failing to provide Swogger with a safe place to work and in failing to warn Swogger of the defective condition.

In short, Sealand claims that the acts of all third-party defendants created the unsafe condition aboard the vessels on which Swogger sailed; thereby causing his injuries and death.

PRMMIs third-party complaint against Todd substantially makes the same claims as does Sea-Land against the shipyards there involved.

The issues presented here are—whether this case is governed by Federal admiralty law; and whether, notwithstanding the General Obligations Law (if Federal admiralty law does not apply), are Sealand and PRMMI entitled to indemnification?

If there is admiralty jurisdiction, then substantive admiralty law applies since State courts must apply Federal law "to secure a single and uniform body of maritime law" (*Matter of Rederi* [*Dow Chemical*], 25 N.Y.2d 576, 581, *cert denied* 398 U.S. 939 [1970]; *Executive Jet Aviation v City of Cleveland*, 409 U.S. 249, 255 [1972]; *Lerner v Karageorgis Lines*, 66 N.Y.2d 479, 485 [1985]; *Larios v Victory Carriers*, 316 F.2d 63, 65 [2d Cir 1963]). Under Federal admiralty law, Sealand and PRMMI would not be barred from contribution or indemnification (*e.g.*, *The Ira M. Hedges*, 218 U.S. 264, 270 [1910]; *Garrett v Moore-McCormack Co.*, 317 U.S. 239, 245 [1942]; *Sealand Serv. v American Logging Tool Corp.*, 1986 AMC 1047, 1986 AMC 1047, 637 F. Supp. 240 (Wash. 1985) U.S. District Court, Wash. D.C.). If there is no admiralty jurisdiction here, Sealand and PRMMI concede that they have no right of contribution under the General Obligations Law, but are entitled to indemnification.

In order to come within the ambit of admiralty jurisdiction a tort claim must first satisfy the traditional "locality" requirement that the wrong occurred on the high seas or navigable waters within the United States (*The Plymouth*, 3 Wall 20, 35-36 (1866); *East River S.S. v Transamerica Delaval*, 476 U.S. 858, —, 90 L Ed 2d 865, 872

---

[1] The asbestos manufacturers/distributors that have submitted moving papers are Combustion Engineering, Inc., Raymark Industries, J.P. Stevens, A.W. Chesterton, Nicolet and John-Crane Houdaille. The members of the Asbestos Claims Facility, including 17 of the named third-party defendants (Fibreboard Corporation, Fibreboard Paper Products Corporation, Owens-Corning Fiberglass Corp., The Celotex Corporation, Philip Carey Manufacturing Co., Keene Corporation, Keene Building Products Corporation, Baldwin-Ehret Hill, Inc., H.K. Porter Co., Inc., Southern Textile Corporation, Pittsburgh Corning Corp., Rock Wool Manufacturing Company, Eagle-Picher Industries, Inc., Armstrong World Industries, Inc., National Gypsum Company, The Flintkote Company, and Thorpe Insulations, Inc.), GAF Corporation, Standard Asbestos Manufacturing & Insulation Company and U.S. Mineral Products.

[2] The third-party defendant shipyards that have submitted moving papers are Todd Shipyards, Kaiser Co., Inc. and Kaiser Steel Corp.

[3] The third-party defendant shipowners that have submitted moving papers are American Sugar Refining Co. and Amstar.

[1986]). Once having met the locality requirement there is the additional requirement of "maritime nexus"—the wrong must bear "a significant relationship to traditional maritime activity" *Executive Jet Aviation, Inc. v. City of Cleveland*, 409 U.S. at 268. (*Foremost Insurance Co. v. Richardson*, 457 U.S. 668 (1982); *East Riv. S.S. v Transamerica Delaval*, (*supra*)).

It should be noted that the Court in *East River* found it unnecessary to reach the question of whether the requirement of a maritime nexus must be established where a tort occurs on the high seas. However, the Court observed that if there "[w]ere such a requirement it clearly was met here, for these ships were engaged in maritime commerce, a primary concern of admiralty law" (*Id.*, 476 U.S., at —, 102 S.Ct. at 2298, 90 L. Ed. 2d, at 872-873). The relevancy of *East River* here is that the Supreme Court's observation that a manufacturer of an appurtenance on a ship may be held in strict products liability in admiralty, for an injury caused by a defective product while the ship was in navigation (*Id.*, 476 U.S., at —, 106 S.Ct. at 2299, 90 L. Ed. 2d, at 873). The argument that since the injuries to Swogger, a seaman, allegedly were caused by the wrongful acts of the third-party defendants on the high seas and therefore, the maritime nexus need not be established—is too simplistic to be dispositive of that issue here. The underlying legal concept to support that argument still awaits a definitive determination by the Supreme Court.

A review of the cases demonstrates that the determination of whether there is admiralty jurisdiction becomes a matter of focus—(*compare Keene Corp. v. United States*, 700 F2d 836 [2d Cir 1983], *cert denied* 464 U.S. 864 [1983]; and *Lingo v. Great Lakes Dredge & Dock Co.*, 638 F. Supp 30 [E.D.N.Y. 1986]; *with Austin v. Unarco Indus.*, 705 F2d 1 [1st Cir 1983], *Cert Petition dismissed*, 463 U.S. 1247 [1983] and *Sperry Rand Corp. v. RCA*, 618 F.2d 319 [5th Cir 1980]). In *Keene* and *Lingo* the Courts focus was on the activities of the defendants instead of the injured individuals activities, as was the case in *Austin* and *Sperry Rand*. *Keene* involved a suit for indemnity and contribution brought by an asbestos manufacturer, against the United States for designing and specifying asbestos insulation products and for failing to inspect the work place—which resulted in injuries to certain shipyard workers and those who had been exposed to asbestos aboard vessels at sea. The rationale of the Court in *Keene* in finding that there was no "maritime nexus" was that there was no independent connection between the asbestos products and traditional maritime activity. Specifically, the Court found that this asbestos insulation was not designed for maritime use and that the government activities in the role, design, and "specification of asbestos as a component of insulation [etc.] did not bear a significant relationship to traditional maritime activities" ... (*Id.*, at 844).

Similarly in *Lingo* the Court, relying on *Keene*, found that there was no admiralty jurisdiction on the ground, among others, that the complaint did not "allege that any of the [asbestos] manufacturers supplied products of a distinctly maritime nature" (*Id.* at 33).

In *Austin* the Court refused to accept the requirement of an independent connection between the manufacturers of a product and traditional maritime activity as a criteria of maritime nexus, but instead would extend it to the manufacturer of the product regardless of whether the manufacturer intended or knew that its products be used aboard ships (*Id.* at 9). In doing so the *Austin* Court, in part, relied upon *Sperry Rand* where the same rationale, of focusing on the injured party and surrounding circumstances, was employed in finding admiralty jurisdiction over a manufacturer of a component part of a marine gyropilot steering mechanism, even though that component was not specifically manufactured for marine use (*Id.* at 322), and upon situations where a cross claim in admiralty was allowed against the manufacturer of a component part of a ship's engine, despite the fact that there was no demonstration that the parts were designed for maritime use (*In re Queen/Corinthos*, 503 F. Supp. 361, 363 [E.D. Pa. 1980]).

It seems clear that the court's analysis in *Austin* and *Sperry Rand* was based on public policy considerations and the furthering of "important national interest in [establishing] uniformity of law and remedies for those facing the hazards of waterborne transportation" (*Kelly v. Smith*, 485 F.2d 520, 526 [5th Cir 1973]),[4] and to prevent

---

[4] A very amusing case arising from what the Circuit Court aptly characterized as a miniship-to-shore battle on the Mississippi River, between fleeing deer poachers (the Kellys) on a 15-foot outboard motorboat, and the rifle-firing caretakers of a private hunting island preserve ashore. The land detachment won the battle but lost the lawsuit, the Court holding that the tort claims of the Kellys, casualties aboard the boat, were within admiralty jurisdiction.

the undercutting of those interests, by refusing to distinguish between manufacturers according to whether they designed or intended their products for maritime use. (*Austin v. Unarco Industries, Inc., supra,* p. 10).

Turning to the case at hand, two points for consideration need little or no discussion. First, the "locality" requirement of admiralty jurisdiction is clearly met. The injuries complained of in the *Swogger* action, and the activities leading to those injuries, occurred at sea. Second, the products liability aspect of this case—whether founded on negligence or strict liability—is now clearly recognized as part of general maritime law (*East River S.S. v. Transamerica Delaval, supra,* 476 U.S. p. ____, 106 S.Ct. p. 2299, 90 L. Ed. 2d p. 873). What is debatable, is whether under the facts here, the "maritime nexus" requirement has been met. While third-party defendants urge that this court follow the rationale of *Keene* and *Lingo;* it seems that notwithstanding that those cases were decided in our local federal circuit, the rational in *Austin* and *Sperry Rand* is more compelling. The results achieved there are more consistent with the over-all purposes and designs of admiralty, to protect those men and women who go to sea from the hazards of that endeavor, over which they have little or no control, (*State of Maryland,* 85 F.2d 944, 945 [4th Cir. 1936]; *Seas Shipping Co. v. Sieracki,* 328 U.S. 85, 93 [1946]; *Waldron v. Moore-McCormack Lines,* 386 U.S. 724, 728 [1967]). Moreover, as previously stated, the results preserve the integrity of a uniform national law governing maritime cases.

Following the analysis which rejects the requirement of an independent connection between the offending product and traditional maritime activity, which to this court seems to be at best a mechanical test, but focusing instead on the activities of the injured party, in the context of the circumstances and locale of the injury—it is clear that there is a maritime nexus here. It should be noted that while the Court in *Austin* did not find that the plaintiff there was engaged in traditional seamans activities so as to create a maritime nexus, it was conceded that if the asbestos products there caused injury to a ship crewmember or passenger, admiralty jurisdiction would be established (*Id.* at p. 10).

Since asbestos was the offending product here, maritime jurisdiction should be extended to the manufacturers and installers of that product, as it was to manufacturers of other instrumentalities that caused unsafe and hazardous conditions aboard ship—even though the products originally may not have been specifically intended for maritime use (*See Sperry Rand Corp. v. RCA, supra; Jones v. Bender Welding & Machine Works, Inc.,* 581 F.2d 1331 [9th Cir. 1978]). In so holding, it assures that *all* of the demands made and arising out of the circumstances leading to injuries in the underlying action will be adjudicated in the same jurisdictional context. This is not only a desirable result but one that conforms with substantial justice; considering that Sealand and PRMMI, are held strictly liable for Swogger's injuries, where the claim is for unseaworthiness, despite that the conditions causing the injuries were created by others—allegedly the third-party defendants.

Other than a point of "focus" approach in assessing the relationship between the wrong and traditional maritime nexus, there is the four-factor analytical approach first enumerated in *Kelly (supra* p. 525). These are: "the functions and roles of the parties", "the types of vehicles and instrumentalities involved", "the causation and the type of injury", and "traditional concepts of the role of admiralty law".

Applying these factors to the situation here, while the first two factors may arguably favor admiralty jurisdiction—or weigh against it—the third and fourth factors weigh heavily in establishing a maritime nexus. During the some 30 years that Swogger served aboard ships as a marine engineer, he apparently was uniquely exposed to asbestos fiber whose release from the insulation in the engine room was commonplace. Indeed, the basis of his claim was that this very exposure to the asbestos in the engine room was the cause of his injuries and wrongful death.

As to the fourth factor—admiralty law has played a traditional and fundamental concerned role in protecting those exposed to the hazards of maritime service by furnishing remedies for those injured while at sea. (*State of Maryland, supra; Seas Shipping Co. v. Sieracki, supra; Waldron v. Moore-McCormack Lines, supra*)

It therefore follows, considering both of these factors, that if Swogger could have had a maritime remedy against the various manufacturers and distributors of asbestos insulation products, the shipyards which installed these products, as well as the other shipowners of ships upon which he sailed (the third party defendants here) then the third party complaints of Sealand and PRMMI are similarly within admiralty jurisdiction, even though they may be considered to be separate and distinct claims.

In view of the holding that Federal admiralty law governs here, it is unnecessary to formally consider whether Sealand and PRMMI would be entitled to indemnification under State law. However, this court is constrained to observe that under the circumstances here indemnification is not barred by § 15-108 of the General Obligations Law.

The right to indemnify, as distinguished from contribution ... "springs from a contract, express or implied, and full, not partial, reimbursement is sought"(*See, McFall v. Compagnie Marine Belge,* 304 N.Y. 314, 327-328 [1952]). Indemnification is designed to prevent unjust enrichment, and equity, the root source of indemnification, has developed a rule of fairness that provides "[w]here payment by one person is compelled, which another should have made ... a contract to reimburse or indemnify is implied by law". *Brown v. Rosenbaum,* 287 N.Y. 510, 518-519 [1942]. (*See also McDermott v. City of New York,* 50 N.Y.2d 211, 217 [1980]).

Given this conceptual background, one can readily understand the controlling rule of law in this State—that the limiting aspects of the General Obligations Law are applicable only to contribution rights and claims, and not to indemnification (*Reviello v. Waldron,* 47 N.Y.2d 297, 306 [1979]; *McDermott v. City of New York, supra,* at 219-220).

This Court takes cognizance of the great number of third party defendants against whom claims are made by Sealand. Whether these claims can be sustained when put to the test of proof is indeed an open question. However, for purposes of this proceeding, the allegations in the complaint must be deemed to be true. Moreover, the pleading is entitled to every favorable reference that may be drawn from it (*See Westhill Exports Ltd. v. Pope,* 12 N.Y.2d 491 [1963]). All that is required is that the complaint manifest a cause of action cognizable under law (*See Siegel, N.Y. Practice* § 265 p. 324), and for the reasons heretofore discussed, this Court finds that it does.

Accordingly, the motions and those proceedings misdesignated as cross motions are denied in all respects.

OMAN v. JOHNS-MANVILLE CORP.

764 F.2d 224, 1985 AMC 2317 (4th Cir. 1985) (en banc)

CHAPMAN, Circuit Judge

In this consolidated appeal we consider whether the federal courts may assert admiralty jurisdiction over manufacturers of products containing asbestos for injuries to land-based ship repair workers which injuries were allegedly caused by exposure to air-borne asbestos fibers. The parties argued this appeal before a three-judge panel on November 1, 1983. On June 6, 1984, this Court, *sua sponte,* called for an *en banc* hearing of this appeal to reconsider *White v. Johns-Manville Corporation,* 662 F.2d 234 (4th Cir. 1981) (White II). Today we overrule *White II,* adopt a four-part nexus test and hold, under the nexus test, that the federal courts may not exercise admiralty jurisdiction over damage claims by land-based ship repair or construction workers for employment-related, asbestos induced disease. In doing so we reverse the district court and remand the case for further proceedings consistent with this opinion.

I

This appeal grows out of four of the thousands of cases brought throughout this country against the manufacturers of asbestos containing products by workers who have contracted asbestosis and its related diseases. Plaintiffs, James T. Oman, Fred R. Walker, Hugh V. Reynolds, and Willie A. Gibbons, were land-based shipyard workers for Newport News Shipbuilding and Drydock Company. They claim to have contracted asbestosis after being exposed to asbestos fibers in the course of their employment.

In 1976 each plaintiff brought an action in federal court against the defendants, Johns-Manville Corp., Johns-Manville Sales Corporation, successor by merger with Johns-Manville Products Corporation; Raybestos-Manhattan, Inc.; The Celotex Corporation; Unarco Industries, Inc.; H. K. Porter Company; Southern Textile Corporation;

Eagle-Picher Industries, Inc.; Owens-Corning Fiberglas Corp. Generally, injured workers bring these types of actions in state court or in the federal courts under diversity jurisdiction. In either forum state substantive law governs. These plaintiff's, however, alleged that the district court could exercise its admiralty jurisdiction in their cases because of their employment in a shipyard. They claim to be in admiralty but they admittedly do not perform tasks traditionally done by sailors.

After consolidating these cases, the district court, in March 1978, issued an order declining to assert admiralty jurisdiction because the alleged injuries bore no reasonable relationship to traditional maritime activity. Throughout the entire history of these cases the defendants have objected to the exercise of admiralty jurisdiction.

After the trial of their cases plaintiff's appealed from the March 1978 order, as well as two others.[1] A three-judge panel of this court vacated the order of the district court. *White,* 662 F.2d at 238-40.

Since *White II* was decided five other courts of appeal[2] have considered this issue and for different reasons have rejected *White II* either in whole or in part. By different analyses, each circuit has concluded that admiralty jurisdiction does not extend to damage claims by land-based ship repair or construction workers for employment-related, asbestos-induced disease.

We now join these circuits. Before we conduct the analysis by which we reach this decision, we must discuss admiralty jurisdiction in general and our reasons for overruling *White II.*

* * *

III

We must review *White II* in light of the Supreme Court's reasoning in *Executive Jet* and *Foremost Insurance.* In *White II* this court first held that the location test had been met. We agree with *White II* that the plaintiffs' injuries satisfy the locality test.

> In the present case, the plaintiff employees alleged in their complaint that they had installed asbestos insulation materials during ship construction and repair in the course of their employment with Newport News. Their work was performed at both the shipyard and drydock areas as well as aboard the vessels while they were located on navigable waters. Thus, the allegations would meet the locality test of *Executive Jet.*

White II, 662 F.2d at 239; *Harville,* 731 F.2d at 783.

The court then held that the work done in the shipyards by the plaintiff's bore a significant relationship to traditional maritime activity because the installation of the asbestos products has a direct effect on marine navigation and commerce. *White II,* 662 F.2d at 239.

> [E]ach of these employees spent a significant part of his working career in the fabrication and replacement of various types of asbestos insulation materials for use on public and private ships. Without such shipyard efforts, these vessels would have been unable to perform their maritime role as carriers of people and cargo. Thus, installation of insulation materials, which by their very nature becomes an appurtenance, or integral part, of the ship, is clearly essential to the maritime industry. Therefore, the work done by these shipyards bears a "significant relationship to traditional maritime activity" because the installation of the asbestos products has a direct effect on marine navigation and commerce.

That second holding was then limited to the particular circumstances of the cases, "when the materials used by these shipyards workers were designed, advertised and marketed as maritime asbestos products...." *Id.* at 240.

---

[1] *See White II* for a complete procedural history of this case.

[2] *Myhran v. Johns-Manville Corp.,* 741 F.2d 1119 (9th Cir. 1984); *Harville v. Johns-Manville Products Corp.,* 731 F.2d 775 (11th Cir. 1984); *Lowe v. Ingalls Shipbuilding,* 723 F.2d 1173 (5th Cir. 1984); *Austin v. Unarco Industries, Inc.,* 705 F.2d 1 (1st Cir. 1983); *Keene Corp. v. United States,* 700 F.2d 836 (2d Cir. 1983); *Owens-Illinois v. United States District Court,* 698 F.2d 967 (9th Cir. 1983).

We are overruling *White II* for two reasons: (1) the analysis used to reach the holding that the nexus test had been met is flawed and (2) the cases relied on by the Court in *White II* are distinguishable. In discussing the nexus test and *Executive Jet*, the Court stated, "The opinion of the [Supreme] Court [in *Executive Jet*] gives no indication as to what actual activities would satisfy the maritime 'nexus' test." *Id.* at 239. The court overlooked the Supreme Court's discussion of the history and purpose of admiralty law, *see Executive Jet*, 409 U.S. at 269-70, which does give us guidance concerning the activities which satisfy the nexus test.

The Court, without the benefit of this guidance, then proceeded to analyze the facts in *White II* to determine if the nexus test had been met. In its analysis the Court focused almost exclusively on the function of the plaintiff's to reach its holding. "Hence, we must examine the function of these shipyard workers in fathoming their relationship to maritime commerce and navigation." *Id.* at 239. Although *White II* correctly discussed the importance to the maritime industry of the work done by these plaintiff's at the shipyards, nevertheless the Court reached the wrong conclusion because the Court failed to examine all the factors necessary for a complete analysis of the nexus relationship. By focusing exclusively on the plaintiff's and the work they performed, this Court overemphasized that factor and, in effect, created a mechanical test inconsistent with the Supreme Court's reasoning in *Executive Jet* and *Foremost Insurance*.

Also, in focusing on the plaintiff's activities the Court failed to consider that the activities of these plaintiff's were not the types of activities traditionally done by sailors.

Furthermore, the cases relied upon for support in *White II* are distinguishable. *White II* relied on *Pan-Alaska, Fisheries, Inc. v. Marine Construction*, 565 F.2d 1129 (9th Cir. 1977); *JIG the Third Corp. v. Puritan Marine Insurance Underwriters Corp.*, 519 F.2d 171 (5th Cir. 1975); *Jones v. Bender Welding & Machine Works, Inc.*, 581 F.2d 1331 (9th Cir. 1978); and *Sperry Rand Corp. v. Radio Corporation of America*, 618 F.2d 319 (5th Cir. 1980). In *Pan-Alaska* a ship caught fire and sank because of a defective fuel filter. In *JIG the Third Corp.* a ship sank because of a malfunctioning steel shaft. In *Jones* the ship's engine repeatedly failed because of manufacturer defects in the engine. In *Sperry Rand* the vessel grounded and was involved in a collision because of a defect in its gyro-pilot steering system. Unlike the present cases those four cases involved situations in which the defective products caused injuries to the ship which specifically implicated the maritime concerns discussed by the Supreme Court in *Executive Jet*.

The present cases involve injuries which do not implicate those maritime concerns and are not unique to seamen.

> The plaintiff's here were engaged in trades, such as pipefitting, welding, and insulating, linked more with the land than with the sea. Their skills and training are those of landsmen, not of sailors. The plaintiffs' "role and function", although related to maritime commerce do not call for the application of admiralty jurisdiction ... Nothing about the underlying claims would be different if the plaintiff's had been employed constructing or repairing buildings on land.... We can foresee no way in which a result in this case in favor of either the land-based shipyard workers or the asbestos manufacturing defendants will have any more than the most attenuated impact on maritime commerce. None of the issues that the Supreme Court listed in *Executive Jet* are involved. Rather, the issues that this litigation presents are identical to those presented in countless other asbestos suits; they involve questions of tort law traditionally committed to local resolution.

Harville, 731 F.2d at 785 and 786.

In this case the injury producing material was not the insulation but the asbestos fibers contained within the insulation. These naturally occurring fibers do not raise the same concerns as a gyro-pilot steering system; nor do the injuries produced by these fibers raise the same maritime concerns as the injuries caused by the malfunctioning steel shaft, the defects in the engine, or the defects in the fuel filter.

This would be a completely different case if these manufacturers were being sued because the asbestos was defective and, as a result, a fire spread throughout a ship causing it to sink. In such case the injury would be peculiar to admiralty and would invoke maritime concerns such as those mentioned by the Supreme Court in *Executive Jet. See Austin v. Unarco Industries, Inc.,* 705 F.2d 1, 10-11 (1st Cir. 1983).

Furthermore, the requirement in *White II* that the materials which caused the injuries be designed, advertised, and marketed as maritime products creates a mechanical analysis inconsistent with *Executive Jet* and *Foremost Insurance*. Under this requirement the nexus test would be met with some products whose use in maritime commerce is important but which do not raise the traditional maritime concerns discussed in *Executive Jet*. Other products which were not designed, advertised, and marketed as maritime products, but do invoke those maritime concerns, would not satisfy the nexus test. *See Austin,* 705 F.2d 9-11.

* * *

REVERSED AND REMANDED.

HALL and WIDENER, Circuit Judges, delivered dissenting opinions.

D. Maritime Contracts

Note: The Nature of a Maritime Contract

In general, a contract relating to a ship in its use as such, or to commerce or navigation on navigable waters, or to transportation by sea or to maritime employment is subject to maritime law and the case is one of admiralty jurisdiction, whether the contract is to be performed on land or water.

* * *

A contract is not considered maritime merely because the services to be performed under the contract have reference to a ship or to its business, or because the ship is the object of such services or that it has reference to navigable waters. In order to be considered maritime, there must be a direct and substantial link between the contract and the operation of the ship, its navigation, or its management afloat, taking into account the needs of the shipping industry, for the very basis of the constitutional grant of admiralty jurisdiction was to ensure a national uniformity of approach to world shipping.

* * *

1 BENEDICT ON ADMIRALTY 182, p. 12-4, 5, 6 (7th ed. rev. by S. Friedell 1988)

---

1. Types of Contracts Within the Cognizance of Admiralty

a. Marine Insurance Policies

INSURANCE COMPANY v. DUNHAM

78 U.S. (11 Wall.) 1, 20 L. Ed. 90 (1870)

Mr. Justice BRADLEY delivered the opinion of the court

* * *

The case, as thus brought before us, presents the question, whether the District Court for the District of Massachusetts, sitting in admiralty, has jurisdiction to entertain a libel *in personam* on a policy of marine insurance to recover for a loss.

This precise question has never been decided by this court. But, in our view, several decisions have been made which determine the principle on which the case depends. The general jurisdiction of the District Courts in admiralty and maritime cases has been heretofore so fully discussed that it is only necessary to refer to them very briefly on this occasion.

The Constitution declares that the judicial power of the United States shall extend "to all cases of admiralty and maritime jurisdiction," without defining the limits of that jurisdiction. Congress, by the Judiciary Act passed at its first session, 24th of September, 1789, established the District Courts, and conferred upon them, among other things, "exclusive original cognizance of all civil cases of admiralty and maritime jurisdiction."

As far as regards civil cases, therefore, the jurisdiction of these courts was thus made coextensive with the constitutional gift of judicial power on this subject.

Much controversy has arisen with regard to the extent of this jurisdiction. It is well known that in England great jealousy of the admiralty was long exhibited by the courts of common law.

The admiralty courts were originally established in that and other maritime countries of Europe for the protection of commerce and the administration of that venerable law of the sea which reaches back to sources long anterior even to those of the civil law itself; which Lord Mansfield says is not the law of any particular country, but the general law of nations; and which is founded on the broadest principles of equity and justice, deriving, however, much of its completeness and symmetry, as well as its modes of proceeding, from the civil law, and embracing, altogether, a system of regulations embodied and matured by the combined efforts of the most enlightened commercial nations of the world. Its system of procedure has been established for ages, and is essentially founded, as we have said, on the civil law; and this is probably one reason why so much hostility was exhibited against the admiralty by the courts of common law, and why its jurisdiction was so much more crippled and restricted in England than in any other state. In all other countries bordering on the Mediterranean or the Atlantic the marine courts, whether under the name of admiralty courts or otherwise, are generally invested with jurisdiction of all matters arising in marine commerce, as well as other marine matters of public concern, such as crimes committed on the sea, captures, and even naval affairs. But in England, partly under strained constructions of parliamentary enactments and partly from assumptions of public policy, the common law courts succeeded in establishing the general rule that the jurisdiction of the admiralty was confined to the *high* seas and entirely excluded from transactions arising on waters within the body of a county, such as rivers, inlets, and arms of the sea as far out as the naked eye could discern objects from shore to shore, as well as from transactions arising on the land, though relating to marine affairs.

With respect to contracts, this criterion of locality was carried so far that, with the exception of the cases of seamens wages and bottomry bonds, no contract was allowed to be prosecuted in the admiralty unless it was made upon the sea, and was to be executed upon the sea; and even then it must not be under seal.

Of course, under such a construction of the admiralty jurisdiction, a policy of insurance executed on land would be excluded from it.

But this narrow view has not prevailed here. This court has frequently declared and decided that the admiralty and maritime jurisdiction of the United States is not limited either by the restraining statutes or the judicial prohibitions of England, but is to be interpreted by a more enlarged view of its essential nature and objects, and with reference to analogous jurisdictions in other countries constituting the maritime commercial world, as well as to that of England. "Its boundary," says Chief Justice Taney,[1] "is to be ascertained by a reasonable and just construction of the words used in the Constitution, taken in connection with the whole instrument, and the purposes for which admiralty and maritime jurisdiction was granted to the Federal government." "Courts of admiralty," says the same judge in another case,[2] have been found necessary in all commercial countries, not only for the safety and convenience of commerce, and the speedy decision of controversies where delay would often be ruin, but also to administer the laws of nations in a season of war, and to determine the validity of captures and questions of prize or no prize in a judicial proceeding. And it would be contrary to the first principles on which the Union was formed to confine these rights to the States bordering on the Atlantic, and to the tide-water rivers connected with it, and to deny them to the citizens who border on the lakes and the great navigable streams which flow through the Western States."

---

[1] *The Steamer St. Lawrence, 1 Black, 527.*

[2] *The Genesee Chief, 12 Howard, 454.*

In accordance with this more enlarged view of the subject, several results have been arrived at widely differing from the long-established rules of the English courts.

* * *

Secondly, as to *contracts*, it has been equally well settled that the English rule which concedes jurisdiction, with a few exceptions, only to contracts made upon the sea and to be executed thereon (making *locality* the test) is entirely inadmissible, and that the true criterion is the nature and subject-matter of the contract, as whether it was a maritime contract, having reference to maritime service or maritime transactions. Even in England the courts felt compelled to rely on this criterion in order to sustain the admiralty jurisdiction over bottomry bonds, although it involved an inconsistency with their rules in almost every other case. In *Menetone v. Gibbons*,[3] Lord Kenyon makes this sensible remark:

> If the admiralty has jurisdiction over the subject-matter, to say that it is necessary for the parties to go upon the sea to execute the instrument, borders upon absurdity.

In that case there happened to be a seal on the bond, of which a strong point was made. Justice Buller answered it thus:

> The form of the bottomry bond does not vary the jurisdiction; the question whether the court of admiralty has or has not jurisdiction depends on *the subject-matter*.

Had these views actuated the common law courts at an earlier day it would have led to a much sounder rule as to the limits of admiralty jurisdiction than was adopted. In this court, in the case of *The New Jersey Navigation Company v. Merchants' Bank*,[4] which was a libel *in personam* against the company on a contract of affreightment to recover for the loss of specie by the burning of the steamer Lexington on Long Island Sound, Justice Nelson, delivering the opinion of the court, says:[5]

> If the cause is a maritime cause, subject to admiralty cognizance, jurisdiction is complete over the person as well as over the ship.... On looking into the several cases in admiralty which have come before this court, and in which its jurisdiction was involved, it will be found that the inquiry has been, not into the jurisdiction of the court of admiralty in England, but into the nature and subject-matter of the contract, whether it was a maritime contract, and the service a maritime service, to be performed upon the sea or upon waters within the ebb and flow of the tide.

[The last distinction based on tide, as we have seen, has since been abrogated.] Jurisdiction in that case was sustained by this court, as it had previously been in cases of suits by ship-carpenters and material-men on contracts for repairs, materials, and supplies, and by pilots for pilotage: in none of which would it have been allowed to the admiralty courts in England.[6] In the subsequent case of *Morewood v. Enequist*,[7] decided in 1859, which was a case of charter-party and affreightment, Justice Grier, who had dissented in the case of *The Lexington*, but who seems to have changed his views of the whole subject, delivered the opinion of the court, and, amongst other things, said: "Counsel have expended much learning and ingenuity in an attempt to demonstrate that a court of admiralty in this country, like those of England, has no jurisdiction over contracts of charter-party or affreightment. They do not seem to deny that these are maritime contracts, according to any correct definition of the terms, but rather require us to

---

[3] Term, 269.
[4] 6 Howard, 344.
[5] *Ib.* 392.
[6] *See* cases cited by Justice Nelson, 6 Howard, 390, 391.
[7] 23 Howard, 493.

abandon our whole course of decision on this subject and return to the fluctuating decisions of English common law judges, which, it has been truly said, 'are founded on no uniform principle, and exhibit illiberal jealousy and narrow prejudice.'" He adds that the court did not feel disposed to be again drawn into the discussion; that the subject had been thoroughly investigated in the case of *The Lexington*, and that they had then decided "that charter-parties and contracts of affreightment were 'maritime contracts,' within the true meaning and construction of the Constitution and act of Congress, and cognizable in courts of admiralty by process either *in rem* or *in personam*." The case of *The People's Ferry Co. v. Beers*,[8] being pressed upon the court, in which it had been adjudged that a contract for building a vessel was not within the admiralty jurisdiction, being a contract *made* on land and to be *performed* on land, Justice Grier remarked: "The court decided in that case that a contract to build a ship is not a maritime contract;" but he intimated that the opinion in that case must be construed in connection with the precise question before the court; in other words, that the effect of that decision was not to be extended by implication to other cases.

In the case of *The Moses Taylor*,[9] it was decided that a contract to carry passengers by sea as well as a contract to carry goods, was a maritime contract and cognizable in admiralty, although a small part of the transportation was by land, the principal portion being by water. In a late case of affreightment, that of *The Belfast*,[10] it was contended that admiralty jurisdiction did not attach, because the goods were to be transported only from one port to another in the same State, and were not the subject of interstate commerce. But as the transportation was on a navigable river, the court decided in favor of the jurisdiction, because it was a maritime transaction. Justice Clifford, delivering the opinion of the court, says:[11]

> Contracts, claims, or service, purely maritime, and touching rights and duties appertaining to commerce and navigation, are cognizable in the admiralty courts. Torts or injuries committed on navigable waters, of a civil nature, are also cognizable in the admiralty courts. Jurisdiction in the former case depends upon the nature of the contract, but in the latter it depends entirely upon the locality.

It thus appears that in each case the decision of the court and the reasoning on which it was founded have been based upon the fundamental inquiry whether the contract was or was not a *maritime contract*. If it was, the jurisdiction was asserted; if it was not, the jurisdiction was denied. And whether maritime or not maritime depended, not on the place where the contract was made, but on the *subject-matter* of the contract. If that was maritime the contract was maritime. This may be regarded as the established doctrine of the court.

The subject could be very copiously illustrated by reference to the decisions of the various District and Circuit Courts. But it is unnecessary. The authoritative decisions of this court have settled the general rule, and all that remains to be done is to apply the law to each case as it arises.

It only remains, then, to inquire whether the contract of marine insurance, as set forth in the present case, is or is not a maritime contract.

It is objected that it is not a maritime contract because it is made on the land and is to be performed (by payment of the loss) on the land, and is, therefore, entirely a common law transaction. This objection would equally apply to bottomry and respondentia loans, which are also usually made on the land and are to be paid on the land. But in both cases payment is made to depend on a maritime risk; in the one case upon the loss of the ship or goods, and in the other upon their safe arrival at their destination. So the contract of affreightment is also made on land, and is to be performed on the land by the delivery of the goods and payment of the freight. It is true that in the latter case a maritime service is to be performed in the transportation of the goods. But if we carefully analyze the contract of insurance we shall find that, in effect, it is a contract, or guaranty, on the part of the insurer, that the ship or goods shall pass safely over the sea, and through its storms and its many casualties, to the port of its destination; and if they

---

[8] 20 *Ib*. 401.
[9] 4 Wallace, 411.
[10] 7 Wallace, 624.
[11] 7 *Ib*. 637.

do not pass safely, but meet with disaster from any of the misadventures insured against, the insurer will pay the loss sustained. So in the contract of affreightment, the master guarantees that the goods shall be safely transported (dangers of the seas excepted) from the port of shipment to the port of delivery, and there delivered. The contract of the one guarantees against loss from the dangers of the sea, the contract of the other against loss from all other dangers. Of course these contracts do not always run precisely parallel to each other, as now stated; special terms are inserted in each at the option of the parties. But this statement shows the general nature of the two contracts. And how a fair mind can discern any substantial distinction between them on the question whether they are or are not, maritime contracts, is difficult to imagine. The object of the two contracts is, in the one case, maritime service, and in the other maritime casualties.

And then the contract of insurance, and the rights of the parties arising therefrom, are affected by and mixed up with all the questions that can arise in maritime commerce,—jettison, abandonment, average, salvage, capture, prize, bottomry, &c.

Perhaps the best criterion of the maritime character of a contract is the system of law from which it arises and by which it is governed. And it is well known that the contract of insurance sprang from the law maritime, and derives all its material rules and incidents therefrom. It was unknown to the common law; and the common law remedies, when applied to it, were so inadequate and clumsy that disputes arising out of the contract were generally left to arbitration, until the year A.D. 1601, when the statute of 43 Elizabeth was passed creating a special court, or commission, for hearing and determining causes arising on policies of insurance.

* * *

These facts go to show, demonstrably, that the contract of marine insurance is an exotic in the common law. And we know the fact, historically, that its first appearance in any code or system of laws was in the law maritime as promulgated by the various maritime states and cities of Europe. It undoubtedly grew out of the doctrine of contribution and general average, which is found in the maritime laws of the ancient Rhodians. By this law, if either ship, freight, or cargo was sacrificed to save the others, all had to contribute their proportionate share of the loss. This division of loss naturally suggested a previsional division of risk; first, amongst those engaged in the same enterprise; and, next, amongst associations of ship-owner's and shipping merchants. Hence it is found that the earliest form of the contract of insurance was that of mutual insurance, which, according to Pardessus, dates back to the tenth century, if not earlier, and in Italy and Portugal was made obligatory. By a regulation of the latter kingdom, made in the fourteenth century, every ship-owner and merchant in Lisbon and Oporto was bound to contribute two per cent. of the profits of each voyage to a common fund from which to pay losses whenever they should occur.[12] The next step in the system was that of insurance upon premium. Capitalists, familiar with the risks of navigation, were found willing to guaranty against them for a small consideration or premium paid. This, the final form of the contract, was in use as early as the beginning of the fourteenth century,[13] and the tradition is, that it was introduced into England in that century by the Lombard merchants who settled in London and brought with them the maritime usages of Venice and other Italian cities. Express regulations respecting the contract, however, do not appear in any code or compilation of laws earlier than the commencement of the fifteenth century. The earliest which Pardessus was able to find were those contained in the Ordinances of Barcelona, A.D. 1435; of Venice, A.D. 1468; of Florence, A.D. 1523; of Antwerp, A.D. 1537, &c.[14] Distinct traces of earlier regulations are found, but the ordinances themselves are not extant. In the more elaborate monuments of maritime law which appeared in the sixteenth and seventeenth centuries, the contract of insurance occupies a large space. *The Guidon de la Mer,* which appeared at Rouen at the close of the sixteenth century, was an elaborate treatise on the subject; but, in its discussion, the principles of every other maritime contract were explained. In the celebrated marine ordinance of

---

[12] 2 Pardessus, Lois Maritimes, 369; 6 *Id.* 303.

[13] *Id.* vol. 2, pp. 369, 370; vol. 4, p. 566; vol. 5, pp. 331, 493.

[14] *Id.* vol 5, pp. 493, 65; vol. 4, pp. 598, 37.

Louis XIV, issued in 1681, it forms the subject of one of the principal titles.[15] As is well known, it has always formed a part of the Scotch maritime law.

Suffice it to say, that in every maritime code of Europe, unless England is excepted, marine insurance constitutes one of the principal heads. It is treated in nearly every one of those collected by Pardessus, except the more ancient ones, which were compiled before the contract had assumed its place in written law. It is, in fact, a part of the general maritime law of the world; slightly modified, it is true, in each country, according to the circumstances or genius of the people. Can stronger proof be presented that the contract is a maritime contract?

But an additional argument is found in the fact that in all other countries, except England, even in Scotland, suits and controversies arising upon the contract of marine insurance are within the jurisdiction of the admiralty or other marine courts.[16]

* * *

The answer of the court, therefore, to the question propounded by the Circuit Court will be, that the District Court for the District of Massachusetts, sitting in admiralty, HAS JURISDICTION to entertain the libel in this case.

Answer accordingly.

---

b. Contract for Repairs

NORTH PACIFIC STEAMSHIP CO. v. HALL BROTHERS CO.

249 U.S. 119, 39 S.Ct. 221, 63 L. Ed. 310 (1919)

Mr. Justice PITNEY delivered the opinion of the court

This is a direct appeal under § 238, Judicial Code (Act of March, 1911, c. 31, 36 Stat. 1087, 1157), involving only the question whether the cause was within the admiralty jurisdiction of a District Court of the United States.

Both parties are corporations of the State of California. Appellee, which for convenience may be referred to as the "Shipbuilding Company," filed its libel *in personam* against appellant, which we may call the "Steamship Company," to recover a balance claimed to be due for certain work and labor done, services rendered, and materials furnished in and about the repairing of the steamship *Yucatan*. The Steamship Company filed an answer denying material averments of the libel, and a cross-libel setting up a claim for damages for delay in the making of the repairs. The cause having been heard upon the pleadings and proofs, there was a decree for a recovery in favor of the Shipbuilding Company and a dismissal of the cross-libel. After this the Steamship Company filed a motion to arrest and vacate the decree and to dismiss the cause for want of jurisdiction. The motion was submitted to the court upon the pleadings, the proofs taken upon the hearings of the merits, and some slight additional proof. It was denied, and the present appeal followed.

The facts were these: In the month of May, 1911, the Steamship Company was the owner of the American steamer *Yucatan*, which then lay moored or tied up at dock upon the waters of Puget Sound at Seattle, in the State of Washington. The vessel, which was of steel construction, was in need of extensive repairs. She had been wrecked, and had remained submerged for a long time; ice floes had torn away the upper decks, and some of her bottom plates also needed to be replaced. She was under charter for an Alaskan voyage, to be commenced as soon as the repairs could be completed. The Shipbuilding Company was the owner of a shipyard, marine railway, machine shops, and other equipment for building and repairing ships, situate upon and adjacent to the navigable waters of Puget Sound at Winslow, in the same State, and had in its employ numerous mechanics and laborers. Under these circumstances it was agreed between the parties that the Shipbuilding Company should tow the vessel from where

---

[15] *Lib.* 3, title 6.
[16] *See* Benedict's Admiralty, § 294, ed. 1870.

she lay to the shipyard, haul her out as required upon the marine railway to a position on dry land adjacent to the machine shop—the place being known as the "dry dock," and the hauling out being described as "docking"—and should furnish mechanics, laborers, and foremen as needed, who were to work with other men already in the employ of the Steamship Company, and under its superintendence; and the Shipbuilding Company was also to furnish plates and other materials needed in the repairs, and the use of air compressors, steam hammers, riveters, boring machines, lathes, blacksmith forge, and the usual and necessary tools for the use of such machines. At the time the contract was made, another vessel (the *Archer*) was upon the dry dock, and it was uncertain how soon she could be returned to the water. It was understood that the *Yucatan* should be hauled out as soon as the *Archer* came off, should remain upon the dry dock only during such part of the work as required her to be in that position, and at other times should be in the water alongside the plant. For the services to be performed and the materials and equipment to be furnished the Shipbuilding Company was to receive stated prices, thus: for labor of all classes, the actual rate of wages paid to the men plus 15 per cent.; for use of tug and scow, a stated sum per hour; for hauling out the vessel and the use of the marine railway, a stated sum for the first 24 hours, and a specified rate per day for 6 "lay days" immediately following the hauling out; for each working day thereafter, another rate; for vessel lying alongside the dock for repairs, no charge; for the running of air compressors, a certain charge per hour; for the use and operation of other machines, certain rates specified; and for materials supplied, invoice prices and cost of freight to plant, with 10 per cent additional.

The vessel was docked and repaired in the manner contemplated by the agreement; she was brought to the shipyard on the 27th of May, and lay in the water alongside of the dock there until the 17th of June, during which time upper decks and beams were put in and other work of a character that could be done as well while she was afloat as in the dry dock. On June 17 she was hauled out and remained in dry dock for about two weeks while her bottom plates were renewed. During the same period the propeller was removed to permit of an examination of the tail shaft, and as the shaft showed deterioration a new one was ordered to be supplied by a concern in San Francisco. Upon completion of the work upon the bottom plates, and on the 5th of July, the vessel was returned to the water and lay there for about two weeks awaiting arrival of the new tail shaft. When this arrived the vessel was again hauled out, the tail shaft and propeller were fitted, and the remaining repairs completed. Libelant's claim was for work and labor performed, services rendered, and materials furnished under the circumstances mentioned, and was based upon the agreed scale of compensation.

The question in dispute is whether a claim thus grounded is the subject of admiralty jurisdiction; appellant's contention being that the contract, or at least an essential part of it, was for the use by appellant of libelant's marine railway, shipyard, equipment, and laborers in such manner as appellant might choose to employ them, and that it called for the performance of no maritime service by libelant.

* * *

It must be taken to be the settled law of this court that while the civil jurisdiction of the admiralty in matters of tort depends upon locality—whether the act was committed upon navigable waters—in matter of contract it depends upon the subject-matter—the nature and character of the contract; and that the English rule, which conceded jurisdiction, with a few exceptions, only to contracts made and to be executed upon the navigable waters, is inadmissible, the true criterion being the nature of the contract, as to whether it have reference to maritime service or maritime transactions. *People's Ferry Co. v. Beers*, 20 How. 393, 401; *Philadelphia, Wilmington & Baltimore R.R. Co. v. Philadelphia, &c. Steam Towboat Co.*, 23 How. 209, 215; *Insurance Co. v. Dunham*, 11 Wall. 1, 26; *The Eclipse*, 135 U.S. 599, 608.

* * *

Neither in jurisdiction nor in the method of procedure are our admiralty courts dependent alone upon the theory of implied hypothecation; it being established that in a civil cause of maritime origin involving a personal responsibility the libelant may proceed *in personam* if the respondent is within reach of process.

* * *

That a materialman furnishing supplies or repairs may proceed in admiralty either against the ship *in rem* or against the master or owner *in personam* is recognized by the 12th Rule in Admiralty adopted in its present form in the year 1872 (13 Wall. xiv) after a long controversy that began with *The General Smith,* 4 Wheat. 438, and ended with *The Lottawanna,* 21 Wall. 558, 579, 581. *See The Glide,* 167 U.S. 606.

It is settled that a contract for building a ship or supplying materials for her construction is not a maritime contract. *People's Ferry Co. v. Beers,* 20 How. 393; *Roach v. Chapman,* 22 How. 129; *Edwards v. Elliott,* 21 Wall. 532, 553, 557; *The Winnebago,* 205 U.S. 354, 363. In the case in 20 Howard the court said (p. 402):

So far from the contract being purely maritime, and touching rights and duties appertaining to navigation (on the ocean or elsewhere), it was a contract made on land, to be performed on land.

But the true basis for the distinction between the construction and the repair of a ship, for purposes of the admiralty jurisdiction, is to be found in the fact that the structure does not become a ship, in the legal sense, until it is completed and launched. "A ship is born when she is launched, and lives so long as her identity is preserved. Prior to her launching she is a mere congeries of wood and iron—an ordinary piece of personal property—as distinctly a land structure as a house, and subject to mechanics' liens created by state law enforcible in the state courts. In the baptism of launching she receives her name, and from the moment her keel touches the water she is transformed, and becomes a subject of admiralty jurisdiction." *Tucker v. Alexandroff,* 183 U.S. 424, 438.

In *The Robert W. Parsons,* 191 U.S. 17, 33, 34, it was held that the admiralty jurisdiction extended to an action for repairs put upon a vessel while in dry dock; but the question whether this would apply to a vessel hauled up on land for repairs was reserved, the language of the court, by Mr. Justice Brown, being:

Had the vessel been hauled up by ways upon the land and there repaired, a different question might have been presented, as to which we express no opinion; but as all serious repairs upon the hulls of vessels are made in dry dock, the proposition that such repairs are made on land would practically deprive the admiralty courts of their largest and most important jurisdiction in connection with repairs.

In *The Steamship Jefferson,* 215 U.S. 130, it was held that the admiralty jurisdiction extends to a claim for salvage service rendered to a vessel while undergoing repairs in a dry dock.

What we have said sufficiently indicates the decision that should be reached in the case at bar. The contract as made contemplated the performance of services and the furnishing of the necessary materials for the repairs of the steamship *Yucatan.* It was an entire contract, intended to take the ship as she was and to discharge her only when completely repaired and fit for the Alaskan voyage. It did not contemplate, as is contended by appellant, either a lease, or a contract for use in the nature of a lease, of the libelant's marine railway and machine shop. The use of these was but incidental; the vessel being hauled out, when consistent with the progress of other work of the Shipbuilding Company, for the purpose of exposing the ships bottom to permit of the removal and replacement of the broken plates and the examination of the propeller and tail shaft. In *The Planter (Peyroux v. Howard),* 7 Pet. 324, 327, 341, the vessel, requiring repairs below the water line as well as above, was to be and in fact was hauled up out of the water; and it was held that the contract for materials furnished and work performed in repairing her under these circumstances was a maritime contract. We think the same rule must be applied to the case before us; that the doubt intimated in *The Robert W. Parsons,* 191 U.S. 17, 33, 34, must be laid aside; and that there is no difference in character as to repairs made upon the hull of a vessel dependent upon whether they are made while she is afloat, while in dry dock, or while hauled up by ways upon land. The nature of the service is identical in the several cases, and the admiralty jurisdiction extends to all.

This is recognized by the Act of Congress of June 23, 1910, c. 373, 36 Stat. 604, which declares that "Any person furnishing repairs, supplies, or other necessaries, including the use of dry dock or marine railway, to a vessel, whether foreign or domestic," upon the order of a proper person, shall have a maritime lien upon the vessel.

* * *

The principle was recognized long ago by Mr. Justice Nelson in a case decided at the circuit, *Wortman v. Griffith* (1856), 3 Blatchf. 528, 30 Fed. Cas. No. 18,057, which was a libel *in personam* to recover compensation for services rendered in repairing a steamboat. Libelant was the owner of a shipyard with apparatus consisting of a railway cradle and other fixtures and implements used for the purpose of hauling vessels out of the water and sustaining them while being repaired. Certain rates of compensation were charged for hauling the vessel upon the ways, and a per diem charge for the time occupied while she was under repair, in cases where the owner of the yard and apparatus was not employed to do the work but the repairs were made by other shipmasters, as was done in that case. The owner of the yard and apparatus, together with his employees, superintended and conducted the operation of raising and lowering the vessel and also of fixing her upon the ways preparatory to the repairs, a service requiring skill and experience and essential to the process of repair. Mr. Justice Nelson held there was no substantial distinction between such a case and the case where the shipmaster was employed to make the repairs; and that the admiralty jurisdiction must be sustained.

Nor is the present case to be distinguished upon the ground that the repairs in which libelant was to furnish work and materials and the use of a marine railway and other equipment were to be done under the superintendence of the Steamship Company. This affected the quantum of the services and the extent of the responsibility, but not the essential character of the services or the nature of the contract, which, in our opinion, were maritime.

Decree affirmed.

---

c. *Enforceability of Oral Contracts*

In *Kossick v. United Fruit Co.*, 365 U.S. 731, 81 S.Ct. 886, 6 L. Ed. 2d 56 (1961), the Supreme Court held that an oral contract was enforceable under general maritime law. General maritime law governed because the contract was a maritime one. The contract was enforceable even though it would have been struck down by the New York Statute of Frauds if state law had been applicable.

---

2. Preliminary, Collateral and Mixed Contracts

Note: Overview of Agreements

Agreements preliminary to maritime contracts, even though directly relevant to them, are not within the cognizance of admiralty. One example of such agreements is an agreement to make or procure a particular maritime insurance policy, although the policy itself is a maritime contract. *Angelina Casualty Co. v. Exxon Corp., U.S.A., Inc.*, 876 F.2d 40, 1989 AMC 2677 (3th Cir. 1989).

Agreements merely collateral to a maritime contract are not ordinarily cognizable in admiralty, either. For example, a bond securing the performance of a charter party. *Rhederi Actien Gesellschaft Oceana v. Clutha Shipping Co.*, 226 F. 339 (D. Md. 1915).

---

a. Executory Contracts

TERMINAL SHIPPING CO. v. HAMBERG

222 F. 1020 (D. Maryland, 1915)

ROSE, District Judge

This is a libel *in personam* with a clause of foreign attachment. It sets up a contract between the respondents and the libelant, by which the latter until December 31, 1915, was to do all stevedoring work required by the respondents' vessels at the port of Baltimore, except when some charter otherwise provided. It alleges that the Bertha arrived at this port, but that its master declined to permit the libelant to do the stevedoring work, although it tendered its services and had rigged up its gears and was ready and willing to perform. It is asserted that by such refusal the libelant lost $75, that being the amount of profit which it says it would have made, had it done the work under the contract and been paid the contract price.

To this libel the respondents have excepted, and on two grounds: First, that the cause of action is not within the jurisdiction of a court of admiralty; and, secondly, that the damages sought to be recovered are purely speculative.

There are cases in which recovery may be had for loss of profits. *Pennsylvania Steel Co. v. New York City Ry. Co.,* 198 Fed. 745, 117 C.C.A. 503. Under other circumstances they cannot be. *De Ford v. Maryland Steel Co.,* 113 Fed. 72, 51 C.C.A. 59. Whether in this case they can be will depend upon the facts as they may be shown in evidence. The question should not be determined on the face of the pleadings alone.

The second exception will therefore be overruled.

The breach of an executory contract does not, ordinarily, at least, give the injured party a maritime lien upon the ship, and therefore a libel filed *in rem* may not be filed to recover therefor. *Schooner Freeman v. Buckingham,* 18 How. 182, 15 L. Ed. 341; *Scott v. Ira Chaffee* (D.C.) 2 Fed. 401. It has also been decided that executory contracts to furnish all provisions that certain ships may require at a particular port, or all coal that they will need at that place, are not maritime contracts, and that admiralty has no jurisdiction, even *in personam,* to award damages for their breach. *Diefenthal v. Hamburg-Amerikanische Packetfahrt Actien-Gesellschaft* (D.C.) 46 Fed. 397; *Steamship Overdale Co., Ltd., v. Turner* (D.C.) 206 Fed. 339. In the case last cited it was pointed out that a contract to buy coal or provisions is not in its nature maritime, and does not become so until the coal or the stores are furnished to the ship.

The libelant in this case says that a contract to do stevedoring work on a ship calls for a service which can never be otherwise than maritime. Whatever may have been the original difference of opinion on the subject, it is now clearly settled that stevedoring services are maritime. *Atlantic Transport Co. of West Virginia v. Imbrovek,* 234 U.S. 52, 34 Sup. Ct. 733, 58 L. Ed. 1208, 51 L.R.A. (N.S.) 1157. Respondent replies that the contract is executory, and that for a breach of such a contract there is no remedy in the admiralty.

The reasoning, if not the express language, of Justice Story on circuit in *Andrews v. Essex Fire & Marine Ins. Co.,* 1 Fed. Cas. 889, goes far to justify this contention. In a number of cases in which a right of action *in rem* has been denied, doubt has been expressed as to whether there was any jurisdiction even *in personam. The Seven Sons* (D.C.) 69 Fed. 271. On the other hand, the jurisdiction *in personam* has been expressly sustained in a case on all fours with this. *The Allerton* (D.C.) 93 Fed. 219. The Circuit Court of Appeals for the Seventh Circuit has upheld such jurisdiction where the breach complained of was that of an executory contract for towing. *Boutin v. Rudd,* 82 Fed. 685, 27 C.C.A. 526.

The question seems to have been foreclosed in this circuit by the decision of the Circuit Court of Appeals in *Baltimore Steam Packet Co. v. Patterson,* 106 Fed. 736, 45 C.C.A. 575, 66 L.R.A. 193. It was there distinctly held that for the failure of a shipper to furnish cargo which he had bargained to ship recovery may be had in the admiralty upon a libel *in personam.*

It follows that the first exception must also be overruled.

———

b. General Agency Contracts

PERALTA SHIPPING CORPORATION v.
SMITH & JOHNSON (SHIPPING) CORP.

739 F.2d 798, 1985 AMC 989 (2d Cir. 1984), *cert. denied*, 470 U.S. 1031, 105 S.Ct. 1405, 84 L. Ed. 2d 791 (1985)

JON O. NEWMAN, Circuit Judge

Navigating the jurisdictional channels of the federal courts' admiralty jurisdiction sometimes presents a choice between observance of ancient landmarks and heeding the siren call of the commentators to venture out into uncharted waters. The choice is put to us squarely by this appeal in which we are asked to abandon the longstanding rule that suits upon general agency contracts are not within the jurisdiction of the silver oar. The request is made by plaintiff-appellant Peralta Shipping Corp. ("Peralta") in its appeal from a judgment of the District Court for the Southern District of New York (Vincent L. Broderick, Judge), dismissing for lack of subject matter jurisdiction Peralta's complaint against defendant-appellee Smith & Johnson (Shipping) Corp. ("S&J"). Though we find considerable merit in the arguments favoring classification of general agency and sub-agency agreements as "maritime contracts" cognizable in admiralty, we feel bound by controlling precedent of the Supreme Court and this Court to affirm the judgment of the District Court.

Facts

Peralta, a New York corporation, is the general agent in the United States, Mexico, and the Panama Canal Zone for the Bangladesh Shipping Corporation (also known as Bangladesh National Lines ("Bangladesh"), an operator of several ocean-going cargo vessels. On July 5, 1979, Peralta and S&J, also a New York corporation, executed an agreement entitled "Agency Agreement," whereby Peralta appointed S&J as "Gulf agents" responsible for arranging services for all Bangladesh vessels calling at ports between Brownsville, Texas, and Tampa, Florida.

S&J's principal obligations under the "Agency Agreement" were as follows:

> S&J shall act as ships' husbanding agents for [Bangladesh's] vessels at the [Gulf] ports and shall perform the services normally incident thereto, including arranging for entrance and clearance of vessels at the Custom House, execution of all Custom House documents incidental thereto, arranging for fuel, water, provisions, emergency repairs, port charges and other similar matter, and for stevedoring, storage and other cargo handling; arranging for tugs...; assisting in the procuring/repatriating necessary ship's personnel as requested by the Master; hospitalization of officers and other crew members; and shall issue bills of lading to shippers and passenger tickets to passengers as Agents as required; and shall use its best efforts in soliciting and securing cargoes in developing traffic and passengers for [Bangladesh's] vessels.
> [S&J shall appoint sub-agents] in all ports where S&J does not have its own offices....
> S&J will arrange for all services necessary for the prompt turnaround of vessels, including all matters of a ship husbanding nature, and will have qualified superintendents in attendance as necessary so as to at all times insure adequate supervision and the efficient working of the vessel, the cost of which is to be borne by S&J.

At a deposition Robert Johnson, President of S&J, summarized S&J's responsibilities more broadly—to handle [Bangladesh's] vessels at [the Gulf] ports, to shift cargo, enter and clear the vessels, supervise the loading of the vessels and account for the disbursements and expenditures and to collect and remit freights. "

Two years later, on September 10, 1981, Peralta commenced the present action. Although not specifically grounding jurisdiction on 28 U.S.C. § 1333 (1982), which grants the district courts jurisdiction over suits in admiralty, Peralta alleged the maritime nature of its suit: "This is an admiralty and maritime claim within the meaning of F. R. Civ. P. 9(h)." Peralta claimed that S&J had breached the "Agency Agreement" and sought an accounting and recovery of monies wrongfully retained by S&J—(i) freight collected on Bangladesh vessels in S&J's agency, and (ii) monies advanced by Peralta to pay Bangladesh's vessels' suppliers and vendors but improperly diverted by S&J. In its answer S&J contested admiralty jurisdiction, but the issue was not presented for a ruling by a motion to dismiss.

Peralta subsequently moved for summary judgment, alleging as undisputed S&J's debt in the amount of $112,831.27. S&J did not challenge the amount of the sum claimed, but maintained that it was entitled to summary judgment on the ground that its sister corporation, Smith & Johnson (Gulf), Inc., a bankrupt Louisiana corporation, had assumed, with Peralta's consent, sole responsibility for S&J's obligations under the Agency Agreement.

Judge Broderick initially granted Peralta's motion for summary judgment and found S&J liable in the amount of $112,831.27. The District Judge rejected S&J's contention that it had been relieved of its contractual obligations. Prior to the entry of final judgment, however, the District Court, on its own motion, questioned its jurisdiction over this action. After the parties briefed the issue, Judge Broderick concluded that the sub-agency contract under which S&J acted as local port agent for Bangladesh's vessels was not a maritime contract within the Court's admiralty jurisdiction. He relied upon our opinion in *CTI-Container Leasing Corp. v. Oceanic Operators Corp.*, 687 F.2d 377, 380 n.4 (2d Cir. 1982), and Judge Weinfeld's opinion in *P.D. Marchessini & Co. v. Pacific Marine Corp.*, 227 F. Supp. 17 (S.D.N.Y. 1964). Since S&J did not advance any other basis for federal jurisdiction, Judge Broderick dismissed the complaint pursuant to Fed. R. Civ. P. 12(h)(3). This appeal followed.

* * *

Discussion

As the Supreme Court has recognized, "[t]he boundaries of admiralty jurisdiction over contracts—as opposed to torts or crimes—being conceptual rather than spatial, have always been difficult to draw." *Kossick v. United Fruit Co.*, 365 U.S. 731, 735, 81 S.Ct. 886, 890, 6 L. Ed. 2d 56 (1961). Neither the Constitution nor applicable statutes lay down criteria for drawing the boundary between maritime and non-maritime jurisdiction. The framers of the Constitution did not undertake to mark the limits of admiralty jurisdiction; Article 3, Section 2 of the Constitution simply extends the judicial power of the United States "to all Cases of admiralty and maritime jurisdiction." And although Congress has expressly included certain transactions or events within admiralty, it has not sought to outline a general demarcation between maritime and non-maritime concerns.

In the absence of express guidance, courts and commentators have struggled to determine how to vindicate the purpose underlying the grant of jurisdiction—protecting the national interest in uniform judicial supervision of the concerns of maritime shipping. With respect to maritime contracts, courts' and commentators' competing jurisdictional "definitions" share a common focus—the relationship between the subject matter of the contract and the concerns of the maritime industry. Under Justice Story's formulation admiralty jurisdiction "extends over all contracts, (wheresoever they may be made or executed, or whatsoever may be the form of the stipulations,) which relate to the navigation, business or commerce of the sea." *De Lovio v. Boit*, 7 F Cas. 425, 444 (C.C.D. Mass. 1815) (No. 3,776). In *North Pacific S.S. Co. v. Hall Brothers Marine Ry. & S. Co.*, 249 U.S. 119, 125, 39 S.Ct. 221, 222, 63 L. Ed. 510 (1918), the Supreme Court described the inquiry as follows:

> in matters of contract it depends upon the subject-matter, the nature and character of the contract ... the true criterion being the nature of the contract, as to whether it have reference to maritime service or maritime transactions.

Kossick v. United Fruit Co., supra, 365 U.S. at 736, 81 S.Ct., at 890, adopted Benedict's approach: "'The only question is whether the transaction related to ships and vessels, masters and mariners as agents of commerce....'" (*quoting* 1 E. BENEDICT, THE LAW OF ADMIRALTY 131 (6th ed. 1940)). Other commentators define a maritime contract as one "for the furnishing of services, suppliers or facilities to vessels ... in maritime commerce or navigation," 7A J. MOORE, MOORE'S FEDERAL PRACTICE P.230[3] (2d ed. 1983), or "principally connected with maritime transportation," GILMORE & BLACK, THE LAW OF ADMIRALTY p. 31 (2d ed. 1975).

These broad guiding principles have proved difficult to apply. While the resulting conception of maritime jurisdiction "has been one of fairly complete coverage of the primary operational and service concerns of the shipping industry" some "anomalous exceptions" abound. *See* GILMORE & BLACK, THE LAW OF ADMIRALTY, *supra,* at 22. The lack of a clear line is not surprising. Obviously, not all contracts with any maritime connection warrant invocation of admiralty jurisdiction. Application of the broad verbal formulations cited above requires some limiting recognition "that the actual concerns of the shipping industry may reach as far as the last ranch that sends cattle to port, and, even without stretching the matter at all, maritime transactions are inseparably connected with and shade into the non-maritime," GILMORE & BLACK, THE LAW OF ADMIRALTY, *supra,* at 29.

The need for consistency and predictability in this area of law suggests that special deference be accorded to prior rulings. "Precedent and usage are helpful insofar as they exclude or include certain common types of contract," *Kossick v. United Fruit Co., supra,* 365 U.S. at 735, 81 S.Ct., at 890; "[i]n general we seek guidance from rulings in like or analogous situations in order to arrive at a reasoned decision in the circumstances at hand," *CTI-Container Leasing Corp. v. Oceanic Operations Co., supra,* 682 F.2d at 380; "[t]o the modern student ... the high-level concepts that have been suggested as keys to the definition, may be of interest, but he ought also to be aware that certain fields, without arguing the matter, may now be taken as settled within the jurisdiction, and others as equally certainly excluded from it." GILMORE &BLACK, THE LAW OF ADMIRALTY, *supra,* at 22.

A demarcation of ancient vintage, consistently recognized from the earliest days, is that agreements preliminary to a maritime contract are not cognizable in admiralty. An early defense of this rule has been of enduring influence.

> The distinction between preliminary services leading to a maritime contract and such contracts themselves have been affirmed in this country from the first, and not yet departed from. It furnishes a distinction capable of somewhat easy application. If it be broken down, I do not perceive any other dividing line for excluding from the admiralty many other sorts of claims which have a reference, more or less near or remote, to navigation and commerce. If the broker of a charter-party be admitted, the insurance broker must follow,—the drayman, the expressman, and all others who perform services having reference to a voyage either in contemplation or executed.

The Thames, 10 F. 848 (S.D.N.Y. 1881).

Under this rationale neither an agreement to procure insurance, *F.S. Royster Guano Co. v. W.E. Hedger Co.,* 48 F.2d 86 (2d Cir.), *cert. denied,* 283 U.S. 858, 51 S.Ct. 651, 75 L. Ed. 1464 (1931); *Marquardt v. French,* 53 F. 603 (S.D.N.Y. 1893), or crews, *Goumas v. K. Karras & Son,* 51 F. Supp. 145 (S.D.N.Y. 1943), *aff'd,* 140 F.2d 157 (2d Cir.), *cert. denied,* 332 U.S. 734, 64 S.Ct. 1047, 88 L. Ed. 1568 (1944), nor an undertaking to act as broker in securing cargo, The Harvey and Henry, 86 F. 656, 657 (2d Cir. 1898), or a charter party, *Christman v. Maristella Compania Naviera,* 349 F. Supp. 845, 848 (S.D.N.Y.), *aff'd,* 468 F.2d 620 (2d Cir. 1972); *Aktieselskabet Fido v. The Lloyd Braziliero,* 283 F.2d 62 (2d Cir.), *cert. denied,* 260 U.S. 737, 43 S.Ct. 97, 67 L. Ed. 489 (1922); *The Thames, supra,* have been cognizable in admiralty.

Nor has admiralty jurisdiction extended to general agency contracts that call for "husbanding" a vessel, *i.e.,* arranging for performance of a variety of services preliminary to maritime contracts, such as soliciting cargo or pasengers and procuring supplies, crews, stevedores, and tugboats. The Supreme Court so held in *Minturn v. Maynard,* 58 U.S. (17 How.) 477, 15 L. Ed. 235 (1854), where the Court affirmed the dismissal, for want of jurisdiction, of an action by a general agent or broker against its principal, the owner's of a steamship. "There is nothing in the nature of a maritime contract in the case.... The case is too plain for argument." *Id.*

This Court has faithfully adhered to the *Minturn* holding. Most prominent among our earlier cases are *Cory Brothers & Co. v. United States,* 51 F.2d 1010, 1011-12 (2d Cir. 1931) (SWAN, J.), and *Admiral Oriental Line v. United States,* 86 F.2d 201 (2d Cir. 1936) (HAND, J.), *modified in other respects sub nom. Admiral Oriental Line v. Atlantic Gulf & Oriental S.S. Co.,* 88 F.2d 26 (2d Cir. 1937). *Cory Brothers* involved an agreement to act as the vessel's local agent at Pernambuco, Brazil. Under the terms of the contract, the agent was required "not only to attend to the discharge of cargo at that port but also to book cargo for ports beyond." 51 F.2d at 1011. When the agent sued to recover expenses incurred in defending the steamship from an action for cargo damage brought by a shipper, the District Court dismissed the libel for want of admiralty jurisdiction. Although this Court sustained jurisdiction derived from the Tucker Act, it noted in dicta that "[i]t is difficult, if not impossible, to distinguish *Minturn v. Maynard* from the case at bar, and that decision would seem to be a controlling authority against admiralty jurisdiction of the present suit." *Id.* at 1012.

Admiral Oriental Line involved two agency agreements—(i) an operating contract, under which the United States, owner of the vessel, appointed Atlantic Gulf "'its Agent to Manage, operate and conduct the business of such vessel ... in accordance with the instructions'" of the United States and to ""man, equip, victual and supply"" the vessel, with compensation based on a percentage of gross receipts, and (ii) a sub-agency agreement under which Atlantic Gulf appointed Admiral Oriental Line "'General Freight Agents'" for its vessels in the Far East (the line assuming the obligation to appoint sub-agents at ports where it had no offices of its own)—and two lawsuits. 86 F.2d at 203. After successfully defending a shipper's suit against the vessel, the Line sued Atlantic Gulf to recover the litigation expenses. Atlantic Gulf in turn sued the United States for both any damages it might have to pay its subagent and its cost in defending against the Line's action. The Court found neither action "cognizable in admiralty; they are on all fours with *Minturn v. Maynard,* 17 How. 477, 15 L. Ed. 235, a case which the Supreme Court has never either overruled or even modified." *Admiral Oriental Line v. United States, supra,* 86 F.2d at 203. On reconsideration the Court explicitly stated that it would apply *Minturn's* holding to "managing operator" agreements: *Minturn* "still seems to us flat on point. The report is indeed very short, but it states that the libelant was a general ship's agent and broker, and we can see no material distinction between such an agent and a managing operator; if the case is to be overruled, only the Supreme Court should do it." *Admiral Oriental Line v. Atlantic Gulf & Oriental S.S. Co., supra,* 88 F.2d at 27.

Although these authorities have suffered some erosion in other circuits,[4] neither the Supreme Court[5] nor the courts of this Circuit have departed from their teachings. *See, e.g., P.D. Marchessini & Co. v. Pacific Marine Corp., supra,* 227 F. Supp. at 19 (performance of husbanding "within the preliminary or nonmaritime category under the authorities"). As the commentators recognize, *Minturn's* demarcation remains the general, well-settled rule—general agency contracts are not cognizable in admiralty. *See* 7A J. MOORE, MOORE'S FEDERAL PRACTICE P.250, p.3001 n.1 (2d ed. 1983) (majority rule that agency contracts not maritime contracts) (collecting cases); Gilmore & Black, *supra,* at 28; 1 E. BENEDICT, THE LAW OF ADMIRALTY 131 (6th ed. 1940).

Appellant invites us to distinguish these venerable authorities primarily on the ground that S&J's contractual obligations went beyond those of a traditional general agent and included supervising the performance of maritime contracts procured by it. We decline the invitation. We acknowledge that *Hinkins Steamship Agency v. Freighters, Inc.,*

---

[4] In *Hadjipateras v. Pacifica, S.A.,* 290 F.2d 697, 700, 703-04 (5th Cir. 1961), Judge Brown upheld jurisdiction over a vessel management contract not unlike that at issue in *Admiral Oriental Line, supra.* The Court concluded that the contract to operate the vessel, obtain freight and collect freight monies "is everything classically known as a maritime contract. It concerns a ship ... its very purpose is to effectuate the physical, economic operation and employment of a vesel." *Hadjipateras v. Pacifica, S.A., supra,* 290 F.2d at 703.

In *Hinkins Steamship Agency v. Freighters, Inc.,* 351 F. Supp. 373 (N.D. Cal. 1972), *aff'd,* 498 F.2d 411 (9th Cir. 1974), the Ninth Circuit upheld jurisdiction over a husbanding agreement. The Court questioned the continuing validity of *Minturn v. Maynard, supra,* and related precedent, and distinguished these authorities on the grounds that (i) the contract in *Hinkins* did not involve a continuing relationship between agent and principal but rather a voyage-specific contract, (ii) *Hinkins'* personnel did not merely procure but also supervised maritime services, and (iii) *Hinkins'* services were "necessary for the continuing voyage." *Id.* at 412. The latter distinctions are discussed in the text, *infra;* the first is properly criticized in Note, *Admiralty Jurisdiction Extends to Agent Who Actually Performs Essential Services for Vessel,* 4 J. Mar. L. Comm. 480, 490 (1973).

The distinction between "preliminary" and maritime contracts has also become somewhat blurred. *See, e.g., Stanley E. Scott & Co. v. Makah Development Corp.,* 496 F.2d 525, 526 (9th Cir.), *cert. denied,* 419 U.S. 837, 95 S.Ct. 66, 42 L. Ed. 2d 64 (1974) (contract to procure insurance within admiralty since it "arises out of a maritime contract"); *Bergen Shipping Co. v. Japan Marine Services, Ltd.,* 386 F. Supp. 430 (S.D.N.Y. 1974) (contract to procure crew cognizable in admiralty); *Interocean Steamship Corp. v. Amelco Engineers Co.,* 341 F. Supp. 995 (N.D. Cal. 1971) (contract to procure stevedoring services within admiralty since it "arises out" of maritime contract).

[5] Nothing in *Archawski v. Hanioti,* 350 U.S. 532, 76 S.Ct. 617, (1956), is inconsistent with *Minturn v. Maynard, supra. Archawski* held that an action on a maritime contract is not [sic] within admiralty even though the suit is in the nature of *indebitatus assumpsit.* The Court rejected the view that jurisdiction turns on the nature of relief sought rather than on the subject matter of the action. "[S]o long as the claim arises out of a maritime contract, the admiralty court has jurisdiction over it." *Id.* At 535. We disagree with those courts that have read the quoted sentence to mean that "preliminary" contracts are within admiralty on the theory that they arise out of a maritime relationship. *See, e.g., Stanley T. Scott & Co. v. Makah Development Corp., supra,* 396 F.2d at 526; *Interocean Steamship Corp. v. Amelco Engineers Co., supra,* 341 F. Supp. At 994. Such a board reading of *Archawski* would place virtually all "pre,iminary" contracts within admiralty. *See* lain *Stanley T. Scott & Co. v. Makah Development Corp., supra,* 496 F.2d at 526 (WALLACE, J., dissenting).

351 F. Supp. 373 (N.D. Cal. 1972), *aff'd,* 498 F.2d 411 (9th Cir. 1974), arguably carved such an exception to the general rule. In *Hinkins* the Ninth Circuit held that where a husbanding agent procures and supervises a variety of maritime services "necessary for the continuing voyage," the contractual arrangement is cognizable in admiralty. But we doubt the virtue of subdividing the category of general agency contracts based on the degree of importance of the services rendered by the agent or on the extent of supervision of performance. In the first place, almost every general agency agreement can be said to involve "necessary" services or some degree of supervision. To predicate jurisdiction on such hair-splitting distinctions would blur, if not obliterate, a rather clear admiralty demarcation. Moreover, as long as *Admiral Oriental Line* remains the law of our Circuit, the distinction espoused in *Hinkins* is unavailable here. In *Admiral Oriental Line,* this Court found no "material distinction," 88 F.2d at 27, between a "managing operator" contract, which required Atlantic Gulf "to manage, operate and conduct the business of such vessel as" the owner may assign and to "man, equip, victual and supply" the vessels, 86 F.2d at 203, and a contract for a ship's general agent. If Atlantic Gulf's "necessary" and "supervisory" services did not warrant admiralty jurisdiction, we would be hard-pressed to conclude that S&J's services do.

We find greater appeal in Peraltas suggestion that the entire class of general agency and sub-agency agreements should be brought into admiralty. We agree with the commentators that the jurisdictional boundaries should reflect the concerns underlying the grant of jurisdiction—the federal interest in promoting and protecting the maritime industry—and that "all those cases involving the enforcement, policing or adjustment of business arrangements as a practical matter primarily concerned with sea, lake and river transport," Black, *Admiralty Jurisdiction: Critique and Suggestions,* 50 Col. L. Rev. 259, 274-77 (1950), should be within the admiralty. A general agency relationship is intimately related with the shipping industry and would warrant inclusion with admiralty. *See* Gilmore & Black, The Law of Admiralty, *supra,* at 28 n.94b (criticizing *P.D. Marchessini & Co., supra,* as "of dubious defensibility. It is predicted that the Supreme Court, when the issue reaches it, will hold "general agency" and other vessel-management agreements within the jurisdiction—along with actions for accountings on them."); 7AJ. Moore, Moore's Federal Practice P.250 at 3006 (2d ed. 1983) ("Quite clearly, such agreements are an integral part of, and in furtherance of, maritime commerce, and consequently, should be cognizable within the admiralty jurisdiction of the district court.")

The prediction of Professors Gilmore and Black may be correct. However, we are not free to anticipate the Supreme Court's overruling of *Minturn v. Maynard,* though we would welcome it. Over forty years ago we indicated that if the rule precluding general agency contracts from admiralty is "to be overruled, only the Supreme Court should do it," *Admiral Oriental Line v. Atlantic Gulf & Oriental S.S. Co., supra,* 88 F.2d at 27. We continue to adhere to that position. The absence of subject matter jurisdiction required dismissal of the complaint.

* * *

Affirmed.

EXXON CORP. v. CENTRAL GULF LINES, INC.

500 U.S. 603, 111 S.Ct. 2071, 114 L. Ed. 2d 649, 1991 AMC 1817 (1991)

Justice MARSHALL, delivered the opinion of the Court

This case raises the question whether admiralty jurisdiction extends to claims arising from agency contracts. In *Minturn v. Maynard,* 17 How. 477 (1855), this Court held that an agent who had advanced funds for repairs and supplies necessary for a vessel could not bring a claim in admiralty against the vessel's owner's. *Minturn* has been interpreted by some lower courts as establishing a *per se* rule excluding agency contracts from admiralty. We now consider whether *Minturn* should be overruled.

This case arose over an unpaid bill for fuels acquired for the vessel, *Green Harbour ex William Hooper (Hooper)*. The *Hooper* is owned by respondent Central Gulf Lines, Inc. (Central Gulf) and was chartered by the Waterman Steamship Corporation (Waterman) for use in maritime commerce. Petitioner Exxon Corporation (Exxon) was Watermans exclusive worldwide supplier of gas and bunker fuel oil for some 40 years.

In 1983, Waterman and Exxon negotiated a marine fuel requirements contract. Under the terms of the contract, upon request, Exxon would supply Watermans vessels with marine fuels when the vessels called at ports where Exxon could supply the fuels directly. Alternatively, in ports where Exxon had to rely on local suppliers, Exxon would arrange for the local supplier to provide Waterman vessels with fuel. In such cases, Exxon would pay the local supplier for the fuel and then invoice Waterman. Thus, while Exxon's contractual obligation was to provide Waterman's vessels with fuel when Waterman placed an order, it met that obligation sometimes in the capacity of "seller" and other times in the capacity of "agent."

In the transaction at issue here, Exxon acted as Waterman's agent, procuring bunker fuel for the *Hooper* from Arabian Marine Operating Co. (Arabian Marine) of Jeddah, Saudi Arabia. In October 1983, Arabian Marine delivered over 4,000 tons of fuel to the *Hooper* in Jeddah and invoiced Exxon for the cost of the fuel. Exxon paid for the fuel and invoiced Waterman, in turn, for $763,644. Shortly thereafter, Waterman sought reorganization under Chapter 11 of the Bankruptcy Code; Waterman never paid the full amount of the fuel bill. During the reorganization proceedings, Central Gulf agreed to assume personal liability for the unpaid bill if a court were to hold the *Hooper* liable *in rem* for that cost.

Subsequently, Exxon commenced this litigation in federal district court against Central Gulf *in personam* and against the *Hooper in rem*. Exxon claimed to have a maritime lien on the *Hooper* under the Federal Maritime Lien Act, 46 U.S.C. § 971 (1982 ed.).[1] The District Court noted that "[a] prerequisite to the existence of a maritime lien based on a breach of contract is that the subject matter of the contract must fall within the admiralty jurisdiction." 707 F. Supp. 155, 158 (SDNY 1989). Relying on the Second Circuit's decision in *Peralta Shipping Corp. v. Smith & Johnson (Shipping) Corp.*, 739 F.2d 798 (CA2 1984), *cert. denied*, 470 U.S. 1031, 105 S.Ct. 1405, 84 L. Ed. 2d 791 (1985), the District Court concluded that it did not have admiralty jurisdiction over the claim. *See* 707F. Supp, at 159-161. In *Peralta*, the Second Circuit held that it was constrained by this Court's decision in *Minturn v. Maynard, supra,* and by those Second Circuit cases faithfully adhering to *Minturn,* to follow a *per se* rule excluding agency contracts from admiralty jurisdiction. *See Peralta, supra,* at 802-804. The District Court also rejected the argument that Exxon should be excepted from the *Minturn* rule because it had provided credit necessary for the Hooper to purchase the fuel and thus was more than a mere agent. To create such an exception, the District Court reasoned, "'would blur, if not obliterate, a rather clear admiralty distinction.'" 707 F. Supp., at 161, *quoting Peralta, supra,* at 804.[2]

The District Court denied Exxon's motion for reconsideration. The court first rejected Exxon's claim that in procuring fuel for Waterman it was acting as a seller rather than an agent. Additionally, the District Court declined Exxon's invitation to limit the *Minturn* rule to either general agency or preliminary service contracts.[3] Finally, the District Court determined that even if it were to limit *Minturn,* Exxon's contract with Waterman was both a general agency contract and a preliminary services contract and thus was excluded from admiralty jurisdiction under either exception. *See* 717 F. Supp. 1029, 1031-1037 (SDNY 1989).

---

[1] The relevant provision of the Federal Maritime Lien Act has been amended and recodified at 46 U.S.C. § 31342.

[2] In the same action, Exxon also claimed a maritime lien on the *Hooper* for a separate unpaid fuel bill for approximately 42 tons of gas oil Exxon had supplied directly to the *Hooper* in New York. The District Court held that because Exxon was the "supplier" rather than an agent with respect to the New York delivery, the claim for $13,242 fell within the court's admiralty jurisdiction. The court granted summary judgment in Exxon's favor on this claim. 707 F. Supp., at 161-162. This ruling is not at issue here.

[3] The preliminary contract rule, which excludes "preliminary services" from admiralty, was enunciated in the Second Circuit as early as 1881. *See The Thames,* 10 F. 848 (S.D.N.Y. 1881) ("The distinction between preliminary services leading to a maritime contract and such contracts themselves have [*sic*] been affirmed in this country from the first, and not yet departed from"). In the Second Circuit, the agency exception to admiralty jurisdiction—Ait *Minturn* rule—has been fused with the preliminary contract rule. *See Cory Bros. & Co. v. United States,* 51 F.2d 1010, 1012 (CA2 1931) (explaining *Minturn* as involving a preliminary services contract). In denying Exxon's motion for reconsideration, the District Court declined to "disentangle" the two rules, asserting that Circuit precedent had established the rule ok *Minturn* "as a subset of the preliminary contract rule." 717 F. Supp. 1029, 1036 (S.D.N.Y. 1989).

The Court of Appeals for the Second Circuit summarily affirmed the judgment of the District Court "substantially for the reasons given" in the District Courts two opinions. *App. to Pet. for Cert. A2*, judgt. order reported at 904 F.2d 33 (1990). We granted certiorari to resolve a conflict among the Circuits as to the scope of the *Minturn* decision[4] and to consider whether *Minturn* should be overruled. 498 U.S. —, 111 S.Ct. 750, 112 L. Ed. 2d 770 (1991). Today we are constrained to overrule *Minturn* and hold that there is no *per se* exception of agency contracts from admiralty jurisdiction.

II.

Section 1333(1) of Title 28 U.S.C. grants federal district courts jurisdiction over "any civil case of admiralty or maritime jurisdiction." In determining the boundaries of admiralty jurisdiction, we look to the purpose of the grant. *See Insurance Co. v. Dunham*, 11 Wall. 1, 24 (1871). As we recently reiterated, the "fundamental interest giving rise to maritime jurisdiction is 'the protection of maritime commerce.'" *Sisson v. Ruby*, 497 U.S. —, —, 110 S.Ct. 2892, 2897, 111 L. Ed. 2d 292 (1990), *quoting Foremost Ins. Co. v. Richardson*, 457 U.S. 668, 674, 102 S.Ct. 2654, 2658, 73 L. Ed. 2d 300 (1982). This case requires us to determine whether the limits set upon admiralty jurisdiction in *Minturn* are consistent with that interest.

The decision in *Minturn* has confounded many, and we think the character of that three-paragraph opinion is best appreciated when viewed in its entirety:

> The respondents were sued in admiralty, by process *in personam*. The libel charges that they are owner's of the steamboat Gold Hunter; that they had appointed the libellant their general agent or broker; and exhibits a bill, showing a balance of accounts due libellant for money paid, laid out, and expended for the use of respondents, in paying for supplies, repairs, and advertising of the steamboat, and numerous other charges, together with commissions on the disbursements, &c.
>
> The court below very properly dismissed the libel, for want of jurisdiction. There is nothing in the nature of a maritime contract in the case. The libel shows nothing but a demand for a balance of accounts between agent and principal, for which an action of *assumpsit*, in a common law court, is the proper remedy. That the money advanced and paid for respondents was, in whole or in part, to pay bills due by a steamboat for repairs or supplies, will not make the transaction maritime, or give the libellant a remedy in admiralty. Nor does the local law of California, which authorizes an attachment of vessels for supplies or repairs, extend to the balance of accounts between agent and principal, who have never dealt on the credit, pledge, or security of the vessel.
>
> The case is too plain for argument. 17 How. 477.

While disagreeing over what sorts of agency contracts fall within *Minturns* ambit, lower courts have uniformly agreed that *Minturn* states a *per se* rule barring at least some classes of agency contracts from admiralty. *See* n.4, *supra*[5]

Minturn appears to have rested on two rationales: (1) that the agent's claim was nothing more than a "demand for a balance of accounts" which could be remedied at common law through an action of *assumpsit*; and (2) that the agent had no contractual or legal right to advance monies "on the credit, pledge, or security of the vessel." The first rationale appears to be an application of the then-accepted rule that "the admiralty has no jurisdiction at all in matters of account between part owner's," The *Steamboat Orleans v. Phoebus*, 11 Pet. 175, 182 (1837), or in actions in *assumpsit* for the wrongful withholding of money, *see Archawski v. Hanioti*, 350 U.S. 532, 534, 76 S.Ct. 617, 620, 100 L. Ed. 676 (1956) ("A line of authorities emerged to the effect that admiralty had no jurisdiction to grant relief

---

[4] *Compare E. S. Binnings, Inc. v. M/V Saudi Riyadh*, 815 F.2d 660, 662-665, and n.4 (CA11 1987) (general agency contracts for performance of preliminary services excluded from admiralty jurisdiction); and *Peralta Shipping Corp. v. Smith & Johnson (Shipping) Corp.*, 739 F.2d 798 (CA2 1984) (all general agency contracts excluded), *cert. denied*, 470 U.S. 1031, 105 S.Ct. 1405, 84 L. Ed. 791 (1985) *with Hinkins Steamship Agency, Inc. v. Freighters, Inc.*, 498 F.2d 411, 411-412 (CA9 1974) *(per curiam)* (looking to the character of the work performed by a "husbanding agent" and concluding that the contract was maritime because the services performed were "necessary for the continuing voyage"); and *id.*, at 412 (arguably limiting *Minturn* to general agency as opposed to special agency contracts); and *Hadjipateras v. Pacifica, S.A.*, 290 F.2d 697, 703-704, and n.15 (CA5 1961) (holding an agency contract for management and operation of a vessel within admiralty jurisdiction and limiting *Minturn* to actions for "an accounting as such"). *See also Ameejee Valleejee & Sons v. M/V Victoria U.*, 661 F.2d 310, 312 (CA4 1981) (espousing a "general proposition of law" that a general agent may not invoke admiralty jurisdiction while a special agent can).

[5] As early as 1869, however, this Court narrowed the reach of *Minturn* and cast doubt on its validity. *See The Kalorama*, 10 Wall. 204, 217 (1869) (distinguishing *Minturn* and allowing agents who had advanced funds for repairs and supplies for a vessel to sue in admiralty where it was "expressly agreed that the advances should be furnished on the credit of the steamer").

in such cases"). The second rationale appears to be premised on the then-accepted rule that a contract would not be deemed maritime absent a "hypothecation" or a pledge by the vessel's owner of the vessel as security for debts created pursuant to the contract. In other words, to sue in admiralty on a contract, the claimant had to have some form of a lien interest in the vessel, even if the action was one *in personam*. *See e.g., Gardner v. The New Jersey*, 9 F. Cas. 1192, 1195 (No. 5233) (D. Pa. 1806); *see generally*, Note, 17 Conn. L. Rev. 595, 597-598 (1985).

Both of these rationales have since been discredited. In *Archawski, supra*, the Court held that an action cognizable as *assumpsit* would no longer be automatically excluded from admiralty. Rather, "admiralty has jurisdiction, even where the libel reads like *indebitatus assumpsit* at common law, provided the unjust enrichment arose as a result of the breach of a maritime contract." 350 U.S., at 536, 76 S.Ct., at 621. Only 15 years after *Minturn* was decided, the Court also cast considerable doubt on the "hypothecation requirement." In *Insurance Co. v. Dunham*, 11 Wall. 1 (1871), the Court explained that, in determining whether a contract falls within admiralty, "the true criterion is the nature and subject-matter of the contract, as whether it was a maritime contract, having reference to maritime service or maritime transactions." *Id.*, at 26. Several subsequent cases followed this edict of *Dunham* and rejected the relevance of the hypothecation requirement to establishing admiralty jurisdiction. *See North Pacific S.S. Co. v. Hall Bros. Marine Railway & Shipbuilding Co.,*249 U.S. 119,126, 39 S.Ct. 221,223, 63 L. Ed. 510(1919); *DetroitTrust Co. v. The Thomas Barium*, 293 U.S.21, 47-48, 55S.Ct. 31, 40, 79 L.Ed. 176 (1934).[6]

Thus, to the extent that *Minturn's* theoretical underpinnings can be discerned, those foundations are no longer the law of this Court. *Minturn's* approach to determining admiralty jurisdiction, moreover, is inconsistent with the principle that the "nature and subject-matter" of the contract at issue should be the crucial consideration in assessing admiralty jurisdiction. *Insurance Co. v. Dunham, supra*, at 26. While the *Minturn* Court viewed it as irrelevant "that the money advanced and paid for respondents was, in whole or in part, to pay bills due by a steamboat for repairs or supplies," the trend in modern admiralty case law, by contrast, is to focus the jurisdictional inquiry upon whether the nature of the transaction was maritime. *See e.g., Kossick v. United Fruit Co.*, 365 U.S. 731, 735-738, 81 S.Ct. 886, 890-92, 6 L. Ed. 2d 56 (1961).*See also Krauss Bros. Lumber Co. v. Dimon S.S. Corp.*, 290U.S. 117, 124,

54 S.Ct. 105, 107, 78 L. Ed. 216 (1933)("Admiralty is not concerned withthe form of the action, but with its substance").

Finally, the proposition for which *Minturn* stands—a *per se* bar of agency contracts from admiralty—ill serves the purpose of the grant of admiralty jurisdiction. As noted, the admiralty jurisdiction is designed to protect maritime commerce. *See supra*, at —. There is nothing in the nature of an agency relationship that necessarily excludes such relationships from the realm of maritime commerce. Rubrics such as "general agent" and "special agent" reveal nothing about whether the services actually performed pursuant to a contract are maritime in nature. It is inappropriate, therefore, to focus on the status of a claimant to determine whether admiralty jurisdiction exists. *Cf. Sisson*, 497 U.S., at —, n.2, 110 S.Ct., at 2896, n.2 ("the demand for tidy rules can go too far, and when that demand entirely divorces the jurisdictional inquiry from the purposes that support the exercise of jurisdiction, it *has* gone too far").

We conclude that *Minturn* is incompatible with current principles of admiralty jurisdiction over contracts and therefore should be overruled. We emphasize that our ruling is a narrow one. We remove only the precedent of *Minturn* from the body of rules that have developed over what types of contracts are maritime. Rather than apply a rule excluding all or certain agency contracts from the realm of admiralty, lower courts should look to the subject matter of the agency contract and determine whether the services performed under the contract are maritime in nature. *See generally Kossick, supra*, at 735-738 (analogizing the substance of the contract at issue to established types of "maritime" obligations and finding the contract within admiralty jurisdiction).

---

[6] These decisions were part of a larger trend started in the 19th century of eschewing the restrictive prohibitions on admiralty jurisdiction that prevailed in England. *See e.g., Waring v. Clarke*, 5 How. 441, 454-459 (1847) (holding that the constitutional grant of admiralty jurisdiction did not adopt the statutory and judicial rules limiting admiralty jurisdiction in England); *The Propeller Genesee Chief v. Fitzhugh*, 12 How. 443, 456-457 (1852) (rejecting the English tide-water doctrine that "measure[d] the jurisdiction of the admiralty by the tide"); *Insurance Co. v. Dunham*, 11 Wall., at 26 (rejecting the English locality rule on maritime contracts "which concedes [admiralty] jurisdiction, with a few exceptions, only to contracts made upon the sea and to be executed thereon").

III

There remains the question whether admiralty jurisdiction extends to Exxon's claim regarding the delivery of fuel in Jeddah. We conclude that it does. Like the District Court, we believe it is clear that when Exxon directly supplies marine fuels to Waterman's ships, the arrangement is maritime in nature. *See* 707 E Supp., at 161. *Cf. The Golden Gate,* 52 F.2d 397 (CA9 1931) (entertaining an action in admiralty for the value of fuel oil furnished to a vessel), *cert. denied sub nom. Knutsen v. Associated Oil Co.,* 284 U.S. 682, 52 S.Ct. 199, 76 L. Ed. 576 (1932). In this case, the only difference between the New York delivery over which the District Court asserted jurisdiction, *see* n.2, *supra,* and the Jeddah delivery was that, in *Jeddah,* Exxon bought the fuels from a third party and had the third party deliver them to the *Hooper.* The subject matter of the *Jeddah* claim, like the New York claim, is the value of the fuel received by the ship. Because the nature and subject matter of the two transactions are the same as they relate to maritime commerce, if admiralty jurisdiction extends to one, it must extend to the other. *Cf. North Pacific, supra,* at 128 ("There is no difference in character as to repairs made upon ... a vessel ... whether they are made while she is afloat, while in dry dock, or while hauled up [on] land. The nature of the service is identical in the several cases, and the admiralty jurisdiction extends to all").[7] We express no view on whether Exxon is entitled to a maritime lien under the Federal Maritime Lien Act. That issue is not before us, and we leave it to be decided on remand.

The judgment of the Court of Appeals is reversed, and the case is remanded for further proceedings consistent with this opinion.

It is so ordered.

---

c.   *Contracts to Lease Containers*

CTI-CONTAINER LEASING CORP. v. OCEANIC OPERATIONS

682 F.2d 377, 1982 AMC 2541 (2d Cir. 1982)

KEARSE, Circuit Judge:

Defendant-appellant Oceanic Operations Corporation ("Oceanic") appeals from so much of an order of the United States District Court for the Southern District of New York, Leonard B. Sand, *Judge,* as denied Oceanic's motion to dismiss the present action for want of admiralty jurisdiction and granted summary judgment against Oceanic on the issue of its liability to plaintiff-appellee CTI-Container Leasing Corporation ("CTI"). The principal issue on appeal concerns the scope of the federal courts' admiralty jurisdiction. Specifically, we must decide whether a contract for the lease of cargo shipping containers is sufficiently "maritime" that a suit for its breach is properly within our admiralty jurisdiction. In the circumstances of this case we agree with the district court that the lease agreement was a maritime contract and that partial summary judgment was appropriate.

Facts

The pertinent facts are not in dispute. CTI is in the business of leasing cargo shipping containers. Oceanic is an agent for several steamship lines. Neither party owns or operates ships. In November 1977, CTI and Oceanic entered into a written lease agreement pursuant to which CTI agreed to rent to Oceanic up to 170 forty-foot standard steel and aluminum containers. The containers were to be delivered by CTI in Norfolk, Virginia, and were to be returned to CTI by Oceanic in Manila, Philippines. Oceanic agreed to pay a per-container rental of $438 for the first 90 days plus $4.20 per day thereafter. Oceanic also agreed to pay $4,400 for any container lost or destroyed, and agreed to maintain the leased containers in good repair.

In accordance with the lease, CTI delivered 169 containers in Norfolk, Virginia in late 1977. In July 1978 the containers, loaded with cargo, arrived in Manila aboard the KARATACHI MARU, a ship owned by Ocean

---

[7] As noted, the District Court regarded the services performed by Exxon in the Jeddah transaction as "preliminary" and characterized the rule excluding agency contracts from admiralty as "a subset" of the preliminary contract doctrine. *See supra,* at 607, and n.3. This Court has never ruled on the validity of the preliminary contract doctrine, nor do we reach that question here. However, we emphasize that *Minturn* has been overruled and that courts should focus on the nature of the services performed by the agent in determining whether an agency contract is a maritime contract.

Transport Line Inc. ("Ocean Transport"). In Manila, however, the Philippine consignee failed to pay customs duties, and the cargo-laden containers were seized by the Philippine government. Nearly three years passed before the duty was paid and the shipment released, and the containers were eventually redelivered to CTI in Manila in April 1981. During the Philippine governments retention of the containers, Oceanic paid the agreed rental only until May 1980.

CTI commenced the present suit against Oceanic to recover unpaid rental for 1980 and 1981, plus repair charges resulting from Oceanics alleged failure to return the containers in undamaged condition. CTI premised jurisdiction on 28 U.S.C. § 1333 (1976), which grants the district courts jurisdiction over suits in admiralty.[1] Oceanic opposed the action principally on the grounds that the lease was not a maritime contract and the court therefore had no admiralty jurisdiction, and that in any event Oceanic had been acting solely as an agent for Ocean Transport and thus had no liability under the lease. CTI moved for summary judgment on its contract claim, contending that no material facts were genuinely in dispute, and Oceanic cross-moved for summary judgment dismissing the complaint for lack of subject matter jurisdiction. In an opinion dated October 30, 1981, reported unofficially at 1981 A.M.C. 2964, the district court denied Oceanics motion to dismiss,[2] granted partial summary judgment to CTI on the issue of liability, and referred the question of damages to a magistrate. This appeal followed.[3]

Discussion

On appeal, Oceanic renews its contention that the agreement sued upon is not a "maritime contract," and argues that there are disputed questions of material fact as to its liability. We find no merit in either contention.

A. Admiralty Jurisdiction

The precise categorization of the contracts that warrant invocation of the federal courts' admiralty jurisdiction has proven particularly elusive. "The boundaries of admiralty jurisdiction over contracts—as opposed to torts or crimes—being conceptual rather than spatial, have always been difficult to draw." *Kossick v. United Fruit Co.*, 365 U.S. 731, 735 (1961). If the contract is a "maritime contract," it is within the federal court's admiralty jurisdiction. *See id.* Traditional texts have defined a "maritime" contract as one that, for example, "relat[es] to a ship in its use as such, or to commerce or to navigation on navigable waters, or to transportation by sea or to maritime employment," 1 E. Benedict, Benedict on Admiralty § 183, 11-6 (7th ed. 1981), or as one "for the furnishing of services, supplies or facilities to vessels ... in maritime commerce or navigation." 7A J. Moore Federal Practice P.230[3], at 2773 (2d ed. 1948) (emphasis omitted). *See also Kossick v. United Fruit Co., supra*, 365 U.S. at 736 ("'The only question is whether the transaction relates to ships and vessels, masters and mariners, as the agents of commerce....'") (*quoting* 1 E. Benedict, The Law of American Admiralty 131 (6th ed. 1940)).

The definitions have proved easier to state than to apply, as seemingly incompatible results abound.[4] In general we seek guidance from rulings in like or analogous situations in order to arrive at a reasoned decision in the circumstances at hand. *See Kossick v. United Fruit Co., supra*, 365 U.S. at 735 ("Precedent and usage are helpful insofar as they exclude or include certain common types of contract...").

The question whether a contract for acquisition of cargo shipping containers is a maritime contract has apparently provoked little comment. The use of such containers, which are portable receptacles in which large numbers of smaller packages may be transported, is a relatively recent development that "enables the use of two or more modes of transportation, marine, motor, rail, or air, to transport goods on a door-to-door basis." Tombari, *Trends in Oceanborne*

---

[1] 28 U.S.C. § 1333 provides, in pertinent part, that "[t]he district courts shall have original jurisdiction ... of: (1) Any civil case of admiralty or maritime jurisdiction...." The parties agreethat admiralty isthe only possible basis for federal jurisdiction over the subject matter of the present case.

[2] The court also denied an alternative motion by Oceanic to amend its answer in order to assert a counterclaim, a matter that Oceanic has not pursued on appeal.

[3] 28 U.S.C. § 1292 (a) (3) (1976) permits appellate review of interlocutory orders that determine the rights and liabilities of the parties to admiralty suits in which appeals from finaldecrees are allowed.

[4] For example, it is well established that a contract to build a ship is not maritime, *The People's Ferry Co. v. Beers*, 61 U.S. (20 How.) 393 (1857), while a contract to repair a ship is, *New Bedford Dry Dock Co. v. Purdy*, 258 U.S. 96 (1922); 1 E. Benedict, *supra*, §§ 188, 189 11-34—11-40. A "general agency" agreement is outside admiralty jurisdiction, *P.D. Marchessini & Co. v. Pacific Marine Corp.*, 227 F. Supp. 17 (S.D.N.Y. 1964), while a contract for managing a ship is within it, *Hadjipateras v. Pacifica, S.A.*, 290 F.2d 697 (5th Cir. 1961). A contract to procure a policy of marine insurance is nonmaritime, *F.S. Royster Guano Co. v. W.E. Hedger Co.*, 48 F.2d 86 (2d Cir.), *cert. denied*, 283 U.S. 858 (1931), while a contract for marine insurance is maritime. *Wilburn Boat Co. v. Firemans Fund Insurance Co.*, 348 U.S. 310 (1955). A contract to purchase a vessel is outside admiralty jurisdiction, *Economou v. Bates*, 222 F. Supp. 988 (S.D.N.Y. 1963), while a contract to charter or hire a vessel is within it, *Fisser v. International Bank*, 175 F. Supp. 305 (S.D.N.Y. 1958).

Containerization and Its Implications for the U.S. Liner Industry, 10 J. Mar. L. & Com. 311, 311 (1979). Characterized by one commentator as "[o]ne of the most important technological developments in the transportation of goods by sea since steam replaced sail," Simon, *The Law of Shipping Containers*, 5 J. Mar. L. & Com. 507, 507 (1974), containerization has revolutionized maritime cargo-handling techniques. As the Supreme Court has described it,

> containerization permits the time-consuming work of stowage and unstowage to be performed on land in the absence of the vessel. The use of containerized ships has reduced the costly time the vessel must be in port and the amount of manpower required to get the cargo onto the vessel.

Northeast Marine Terminal Co. v. Caputo, 432 U.S. 249, 270 (1977) (footnote omitted).Consequently,in a varietyof contexts, the container has been characterized as "a modern substitute for the hold of the vessel," *id.*, and as ""functionally a part of the *ship*,"*Japan Line, Ltd. v. County of Los Angeles*, 441 U.S. 434, 443 (1979) (*quoting Leather's Best, Inc. v. S.S. Mormaclynx*, 451 F.2d 800, 815 (2d Cir. 1971).[5]

Given the function of the container and the growing dependence on the maritime industry on containerization, a shipowner's lease of containers has been held a maritime contract, *Integrated Container Service, Inc. v. Starlines Container Shipping, Ltd.*, 476 F. Supp. 119 (S.D.N.Y. 1979), much as other agreements for the acquisition of ship equipment have been viewed as maritime contracts, *e.g., Radiomarine Corp. v. Gulf Northern Co.*, 394 F. Supp. 381 (E.D. Mo. 1975) (radio and radar systems); *Houston-New Orleans, Inc. v. Page Engineering Co.*, 353 F. Supp. 890 (E.D. La. 1972) (control panel for crane mounted on ship). We concur in the view that a lease of cargo containers for use on a ship is a maritime contract.

The case before us focuses principally on the antecedent question of whether the agreement between CTI and Oceanic leased containers for use on a ship. Since containers may be used not only in ocean transport, but also in overland transport by truck or train or in overseas transport by freighter airplane, *see e.g.,* Schmeltzer & Peavy, *Prospects and Problems of the Container Revolution*, 1 J. Mar. L. & Com. 203, 204-06 (1970); Tombari, *Trends in Oceanborne Containerization and Its Implications for the U.S. Liner Industry, supra,* Oceanic argues that the containers leased here could have been used for purposes other than ocean transport, and that the lease has no necessarily maritime flavor.[6] Our review of the record persuades us that the district court properly viewed the lease between CTI and Oceanic as indicating that the containers would be transported by ship.

First, although the lease does not mention a ship or ships as such, it contains several provisions that point to shipping as the envisioned mode of use of CTI's containers. Since the containers were to be delivered by CTI in the United States and returned to CTI in the Philippines, overseas transport obviously was envisioned. Further, Clause 12 of the lease suggests that it was anticipated that transport to Manila would be by sea rather than by air, since that clause refers to the "point[s] or port[s]" of original delivery and redelivery, rather than to delivery at an air terminal. *See* Schmeltzer & Peavy, *Prospects and Problems of the Container Revolution, supra,* 1 J. Mar. L. & Com. at 206 ("the movement of a container consolidated at a port or air terminal and shipped to an overseas port or air terminal ... is termed a 'port-to-port' or 'air terminal-to-terminal' shipment.") In addition, Clause 8 of the lease, which required Oceanic to obtain insurance, refers to "Particular Average and General Averages," concepts of peculiar applicability to sea ventures. *See* Blacks Law Dictionary 172, 813 (4th ed. 1951). Further, it is undisputed that Oceanic at all relevant times was an agent for several steamship lines. Since there is no indication in the record that it acted as agent for airlines, railroads, or trucking companies, the nature of Oceanic's business also suggested that the containers were sought for ocean transport.

---

[5] None of these cases dealt with the maritime nature of a lease of containers, and each clearly arose in a maritime context. *See Japan Line, Ltd. v. County of Los Angeles, supra* (local tax on containers used on Japanese ships in commerce with United States); *Northeast Marine Terminal Co. v. Caputo, supra* (applicability of Longshoremens and Harbor Workers' Compensation Act, 33 U.S.C. § 901 *et seq.* (1976), to longshoremen injured while unloading containers that had been removed from ships); *Leather's Best, Inc. v. S.S. Mormaclynx, supra* (applicability of $500 package limitation in Carriage of Goods by Sea Act, 46 U.S.C. § 1304(5) (1970) to the container as a whole rather than to packages within).

[6] Oceanic also argues that the lease was partially nonmaritime because after the containers were seized by the Philippine government they were held on land. We find no merit in this or any of Oceanics other arguments.

Finally, we note that Oceanic has sought to escape liability in this action on the ground that it disclosed in the lease negotiations that the real lessee of the containers was to be Oceanic's principal, Ocean Transport, a commercial shipowner. While any such oral disclosures by Oceanic were not admissible to relieve it from liability on the lease, *see* part B, *infra*, we are not required to close our eyes to the light shed by Oceanics statements on the nature of the contract. Oceanic correctly concedes that a lease of the containers directly to Ocean Transport would have been a maritime contract. *See Integrated Container Service, Inc. v. Starlines Container Shipping, Ltd., supra.* We see no basis in logic to conclude that the present lease was not a maritime contract merely because Ocean Transport chose to acquire the containers through an agent. *Accord, Maryland Port Administration v. SS American Legend,* 453 F. Supp. 584, 589-90 (D. Md. 1978).

In the circumstances, we agree with the district court that the containers were leased for use in ocean transportation, and given the nature of such a container as the functional equivalent of the hold of the vessel, we must conclude that such a lease is a maritime contract. Accordingly, Oceanic's motion to dismiss for lack of admiralty jurisdiction was properly denied.

* * *

———————

d. Mixed Contracts

NORFOLK SOUTHERN RAILWAY CO. v. KIRBY

543 U.S. 14, 125 S.Ct. 385, 2004 AMC 2705 (2004)

Justice O'CONNOR delivered the opinion of the Court

This is a maritime case about a train wreck. A shipment of machinery from Australia was destined for Huntsville, Alabama. The intercontinental journey was uneventful, and the machinery reached the United States unharmed. But the train carrying the machinery on its final, inland leg derailed, causing extensive damage. The machinery's owner sued the railroad. The railroad seeks shelter in two liability limitations contained in contracts that upstream carriers negotiated for the machinery's delivery.

I

This controversy arises from two bills of lading (essentially, contracts) for the transportation of goods from Australia to Alabama. A bill of lading records that a carrier has received goods from the party that wishes to ship them, states the terms of carriage, and serves as evidence of the contract for carriage. *See* 2 T. Schoenbaum, Admiralty and Maritime Law 58-60 (3d ed.2001) (hereinafter Schoenbaum); Carriage of Goods by Sea Act (COGSA), 49 Stat. 1208, 46 U.S.C. App. § 1303. Respondent James N. Kirby, Pty Ltd. (Kirby), an Australian manufacturing company, sold 10 containers of machinery to the General Motors plant located outside Huntsville, Alabama. Kirby hired International Cargo Control (ICC), an Australian freight forwarding company, to arrange for delivery by "through" (i.e., end-to-end) transportation. (A freight forwarding company arranges for, coordinates, and facilitates cargo transport, but does not itself transport cargo.) To formalize their contract for carriage, ICC issued a bill of lading to Kirby (ICC bill). The bill designates Sydney, Australia, as the port of loading, Savannah, Georgia, as the port of discharge, and Huntsville as the ultimate destination for delivery.

In negotiating the ICC bill, Kirby had the opportunity to declare the full value of the machinery and to have ICC assume liability for that value. Cf. New York, N.H. & H.R. Co. v. Nothnagle, 346 U.S. 128, 135, 73 S.Ct. 986, 97 L.Ed. 1500 (1953) (a carrier must provide a shipper with a fair opportunity to declare value). Instead, and as is common in the industry, see Sturley, Carriage of Goods by Sea, 31 J. Mar. L. & Com. 241, 244 (2000), Kirby accepted a contractual liability limitation for ICC below the machinery's true value, resulting, presumably, in lower shipping rates. The ICC bill sets various liability limitations for the journey from Sydney to Huntsville. For the sea leg, the ICC bill invokes the default liability rule set forth in the Carriage of Goods by Sea Act. The COGSA "package limitation" provides:

"Neither the carrier nor the ship shall in any event be or become liable for any loss or damage to or in connection with the transportation of goods in an amount exceeding $500 per package lawful money of the United States ... unless the nature and value of such goods have been declared by the shipper before shipment and inserted into the bill of lading." 46 U.S.C. App. § 1304(5).

For the land leg, in turn, the bill limits the carrier's liability to a higher amount. So that other downstream parties expected to take part in the contract's execution could benefit from the liability limitations, the bill also contains a so-called "Himalaya Clause." It provides:

"These conditions [for limitations on liability] apply whenever claims relating to the performance of the contract evidenced by this [bill of lading] are made against any servant, agent or other person (including any independent contractor) whose services have been used in order to perform the contract."

Meanwhile, Kirby separately insured the cargo for its true value with its co-respondent in this case, Allianz Australia Insurance Ltd. (formerly MMI General Insurance, Ltd.).

Having been hired by Kirby, and because it does not itself actually transport cargo, ICC then hired Hamburg Südamerikanische Dampfschiflahrts-Gesellschaftt Eggert & Amsinck (Hamburg Süd), a German ocean shipping company, to transport the containers. To formalize their contract for carriage, Hamburg Süd issued its own bill of lading to ICC (Hamburg Süd bill). That bill designates Sydney as the port of loading, Savannah as the port of discharge, and Huntsville as the ultimate destination for delivery. It adopts COGSAs default rule in limiting the liability of Hamburg Süd, the bill's designated carrier, to $500 per package. See 46 U.S.C. App. § 1304(5). It also contains a clause extending that liability limitation beyond the "tackles"—that is, to potential damage on land as well as on sea. Finally, it too contains a Himalaya Clause extending the benefit of its liability limitation to "all agents ... (including inland) carriers ... and all independent contractors whatsoever."

Acting through a subsidiary, Hamburg Süd hired Petitioner Norfolk Southern Railroad (Norfolk) to transport the machinery from the Savannah port to Huntsville. Delivery failed. The Norfolk train carrying the machinery derailed en route, causing an alleged $1.5 million in damages. Kirbys insurance company reimbursed Kirby for the loss. Kirby and its insurer then sued Norfolk in the United States District Court for the Northern District of Georgia, asserting diversity jurisdiction and alleging tort and contract claims. In its answer, Norfolk argued, among other things, that Kirbys potential recovery could not exceed the amounts set forth in the liability limitations contained in the bills of lading for the machinery's carriage.

The District Court granted Norfolk's motion for partial summary judgment, holding that Norfolk's liability was limited to $500 per container. Upon a joint motion from Norfolk and Kirby, the District Court certified its decision for interlocutory review pursuant to 28 U.S.C. § 1292(b).

A divided panel of the Eleventh Circuit reversed. It held that Norfolk could not claim protection under the Himalaya Clause in the first contract, the ICC bill. It construed the language of the clause to exclude parties, like Norfolk, that had not been in privity with ICC when ICC issued the bill. 300 F.3d 1300, 1308-1309 (2002). The majority also suggested that "a special degree of linguistic specificity is required to extend the benefits of a Himalaya clause to an inland carrier." Id., at 1310. As for the Hamburg Süd bill, the court held that Kirby could be bound by the bill's liability limitation "only if ICC was acting as Kirby's agent when it received Hamburg Süd's bill." Id., at 1305. And, applying basic agency law principles, the Court of Appeals concluded that ICC had not been acting as Kirby's agent when it received the bill. Ibid. Based on its opinion that Norfolk was not entitled to benefit from the liability limitation in either bill of lading, the Eleventh Circuit reversed the District Court's grant of summary judgment for the railroad. We granted certiorari to decide whether Norfolk could take shelter in the liability limitations of either bill, 540 U.S. 1099, 124 S.Ct. 981, 157 L.Ed.2d 811 (2004), and now reverse.

II

The courts below appear to have decided this case on an assumption, shared by the parties, that federal rather than state law governs the interpretation of the two bills of lading. Respondents now object. They emphasize that, at bottom, this is a diversity case involving tort and contract claims arising out of a rail accident somewhere between Savannah and Huntsville. We think, however, borrowing from Justice Harlan, that "the situation presented here has a more genuinely salty flavor than that." *Kossick v. United Fruit Co.,* 365 U.S. 731, 742, 81 S.Ct. 886, 6 L.Ed.2d 56 (1961). When a contract is a maritime one, and the dispute is not inherently local, federal law controls the contract interpretation. *Id.,* at 735, 81 S.Ct. 886.

Our authority to make decisional law for the interpretation of maritime contracts stems from the Constitutions grant of admiralty jurisdiction to federal courts. *See* Art. III, § 2, cl. 1 (providing that the federal judicial power shall extend to "all Cases of admiralty and maritime Jurisdiction"). See 28 U.S.C. § 1333(1) (granting federal district courts original jurisdiction over "[a]ny civil case of admiralty or maritime jurisdiction"); R. Fallon, D. Meltzer, & D. Shapiro, Hart and Wechsler's The Federal Courts and the Federal System 733-738 (5th ed.2003). This suit was properly brought in diversity, but it could also be sustained under the admiralty jurisdiction by virtue of the maritime contracts involved. *See Pope & Talbot, Inc. v. Hawn,* 346 U.S. 406, 411, 74 S.Ct. 202, 98 L.Ed. 143 (1953) ("[S]ubstantial rights ... are not to be determined differently whether [a] case is labelled 'law side' or 'admiralty side' on a district courts docket"). Indeed, for federal common law to apply in these circumstances, this suit must also be sustainable under the admiralty jurisdiction. *See Stewart Organization, Inc. v. Ricoh Corp.,* 487 U.S. 22, 28, 108 S.Ct. 2239, 101 L.Ed.2d 22 (1988). Because the grant of admiralty jurisdiction and the power to make admiralty law are mutually dependent, the two are often intertwined in our cases.

Applying the two-step analysis from *Kossick,* we find that federal law governs this contract dispute. Our cases do not draw clean lines between maritime and non-maritime contracts. We have recognized that "[t]he boundaries of admiralty jurisdiction over contracts—as opposed to torts or crimes—being conceptual rather than spatial, have always been difficult to draw." 365 U.S., at 735, 81 S.Ct. 886. To ascertain whether a contract is a maritime one, we cannot look to whether a ship or other vessel was involved in the dispute, as we would in a putative maritime tort case. *Cf.* Admiralty Extension Act, 46 U.S.C.App. § 740 ("The admiralty and maritime jurisdiction of the United States shall extend to and include all cases of damage or injury ... caused by a vessel on navigable water, notwithstanding that such damage or injury be done or consummated on land"); R. Force & M. Norris, 1 The Law of Seamen § 1:15 (5th ed.2003). Nor can we simply look to the place of the contracts formation or performance. Instead, the answer "depends upon ... the nature and character of the contract," and the true criterion is whether it has "reference to maritime service or maritime transactions." *North Pacific S.S. Co. v. Hall Brothers Marine Railway & Shipbuilding Co.,* 249 U.S. 119, 125, 39 S.Ct. 221, 63 L.Ed. 510 (1919) (citing Insurance Co. v. Dunham, 11 Wall. 1, 26, 20 L.Ed. 90 (1871)). *See also Exxon Corp. v. Central Gulf Lines, Inc.,* 500 U.S. 603, 611, 111 S.Ct. 2071, 114 L.Ed.2d 649 (1991) ("[T]he trend in modern admiralty case law ... is to focus the jurisdictional inquiry upon whether the nature of the transaction was maritime").

The ICC and Hamburg Süd bills are maritime contracts because their primary objective is to accomplish the transportation of goods by sea from Australia to the eastern coast of the United States. See G. Gilmore & C. Black, Law of Admiralty 31 (2d ed.1975) ("Ideally, the [admiralty] jurisdiction [over contracts ought] to include those and only those things principally connected with maritime transportation" (emphasis deleted)). To be sure, the two bills call for some performance on land; the final leg of the machinery's journey to Huntsville was by rail. But under a conceptual rather than spatial approach, this fact does not alter the essentially maritime nature of the contracts.

In Kossick, for example, we held that a shipowner's promise to assume responsibility for any improper treatment his seaman might receive at a New York hospital was a maritime contract. The seaman had asked the shipowner to pay for treatment by a private physician, but the shipowner, preferring the cheaper public hospital, offered to cover the costs of any complications that might arise from treatment there. We characterized his promise as a "fringe benefit" to a shipowners duty in maritime law to provide "'maintenance and cure.'" 365 U.S., at 736-737, 81 S.Ct. 886. Because the promise was in furtherance of a "peculiarly maritime concer[n]," *id.,* at 738, 81 S.Ct. 886, it folded into federal maritime law. It did not matter that the site of the inadequate treatment—which gave rise to the contract dispute—was in a hospital on land. Likewise, Norfolk's rail journey from Savannah to Huntsville was a "fringe" portion of the intercontinental journey promised in the ICC and Hamburg Süd bills.

We have reiterated that the "'fundamental interest giving rise to maritime jurisdiction is "the protection of maritime commerce.'"" *Exxon, supra,* at 608, 111 S.Ct. 2071 (emphasis added) (quoting *Sisson v. Ruby,* 497 U.S. 358, 367, 110 S.Ct. 2892, 111 L.Ed.2d 292 (1990), in turn quoting *Foremost Ins. Co. v. Richardson,* 457 U.S. 668, 674, 102 S.Ct. 2654, 73 L.Ed.2d 300 (1982)). The conceptual approach vindicates that interest by focusing our inquiry on whether the principal objective of a contract is maritime commerce. While it may once have seemed natural to think that only contracts embodying commercial obligations between the "tackles" (*i.e.,* from port to port) have maritime objectives, the shore is now an artificial place to draw a line. Maritime commerce has evolved along with the nature of transportation and is often inseparable from some land-based obligations. The international transportation industry "clearly has moved into a new era—the age of multimodalism, door-to-door transport based on efficient use of all available modes of transportation by air, water, and land." 1 Schoenbaum 589 (4th ed. 2004). The cause is technological change: Because goods can now be packaged in standardized containers, cargo can move easily from one mode of transport to another. *Ibid. See also NLRB v. Longshoremen,* 447 U.S. 490, 494, 100 S.Ct. 2305, 65 L. Ed. 2d 289 (1980) ("'[C]ontainerization may be said to constitute the single most important innovation in ocean transport since the steamship displaced the schooner'" (citation omitted)); G. Muller, Intermodal Freight Transportation 15-24 (3d ed. 1995).

Contracts reflect the new technology, hence the popularity of "through" bills of lading, in which cargo owner's can contract for transportation across oceans and to inland destinations in a single transaction. See 1 Schoenbaum 595. Put simply, it is to Kirby's advantage to arrange for transport from Sydney to Huntsville in one bill of lading, rather than to negotiate a separate contract—and to find an American railroad itself—for the land leg. The popularity of that efficient choice, to assimilate land legs into international ocean bills of lading, should not render bills for ocean carriage nonmaritime contracts.

Some lower federal courts appear to have taken a spatial approach when deciding whether intermodal transportation contracts for intercontinental shipping are maritime in nature. They have held that admiralty jurisdiction does not extend to contracts which require maritime and nonmaritime transportation, unless the nonmaritime transportation is merely incidental—and that long-distance land travel is not incidental. *See, e.g., Hartford Fire Ins. Co. v. Orient Overseas Containers Lines,* 230 F.3d 549, 555-556 (C.A. 2 2000) ("[T]ransport by land under a bill of lading is not 'incidental' to transport by sea if the land segment involves great and substantial distances," and land transport of over 850 miles across four countries is more than incidental); *Sea-Land Serv., Inc. v. Danzig,* 211 F.3d 1373, 1378 (C.A. Fed. 2000) (holding that intermodal transport contracts were not maritime contracts because they called for "substantial transportation between inland locations and ports both in this country and the Middle East" that was not incidental to the transportation by sea); *Kuehne & Nagel (AG & Co.) v. Geosource, Inc.,* 874 F.2d 283, 290 (C.A.5 1989) (holding that a through bill of lading calling for land transportation up to 1,000 miles was not a traditional maritime contract because such "extensive land-based operations cannot be viewed as merely incidental to the maritime operations"). As a preliminary matter, it seems to us imprecise to describe the land carriage required by an intermodal transportation contract as "incidental"; realistically, each leg of the journey is essential to accomplishing the contract's purpose. In this case, for example, the bills of lading required delivery to Huntsville; the Savannah port would not do.

Furthermore, to the extent that these lower court decisions fashion a rule for identifying maritime contracts that depends solely on geography, they are inconsistent with the conceptual approach our precedent requires. *See Kossick,* 365 U.S., at 735, 81 S.Ct. 886. Conceptually, so long as a bill of lading requires substantial carriage of goods by sea, its purpose is to effectuate maritime commerce—and thus it is a maritime contract. Its character as a maritime contract is not defeated simply because it also provides for some land carriage. Geography, then, is useful in a conceptual inquiry only in a limited sense: If a bills sea components are insubstantial, then the bill is not a maritime contract.

Having established that the ICC and Hamburg Süd bills are maritime contracts, then, we must clear a second hurdle before applying federal law in their interpretation. Is this case inherently local? For not "every term in every maritime contract can only be controlled by some federally defined admiralty rule." *Wilburn Boat Co. v. Firemans Fund Ins. Co.*, 348 U.S. 310, 313, 75 S.Ct. 368, 99 L.Ed. 337 (1955) (applying state law to maritime contract for marine insurance because of state regulatory power over insurance industry). A maritime contracts interpretation may so implicate local interests as to beckon interpretation by state law. See Kossick, *supra*, at 735, 81 S.Ct. 886. Respondents have not articulated any specific Australian or state interest at stake, though some are surely implicated. But when state interests cannot be accommodated without defeating a federal interest, as is the case here, then federal substantive law should govern. *See Kossick, supra*, at 739, 81 S.Ct. 886 (the process of deciding whether federal law applies "is surely ... one of accommodation, entirely familiar in many areas of overlapping state and federal concern, or a process somewhat analogous to the normal conflict of laws situation where two sovereignties assert divergent interests in a transaction"); 2 Schoenbaum 61 ("Bills of lading issued outside the United States are governed by the general maritime law, considering relevant choice of law rules").

Here, our touchstone is a concern for the uniform meaning of maritime contracts like the ICC and Hamburg Süd bills. We have explained that Article III's grant of admiralty jurisdiction "'must have referred to a system of law coextensive with, and operating uniformly in, the whole country. It certainly could not have been the intention to place the rules and limits of maritime law under the disposal and regulation of the several States, as that would have defeated the uniformity and consistency at which the Constitution aimed on all subjects of a commercial character affecting the intercourse of the States with each other or with foreign states.'" *American Dredging Co. v. Miller*, 510 U.S. 443, 451, 114 S.Ct. 981, 127 L.Ed.2d 285 (1994) (quoting *The Lottawanna*, 21 Wall. 558, 575, 22 L.Ed. 654 (1875)). *See also Yamaha Motor Corp., U.S.A. v. Calhoun*, 516 U.S. 199, 210, 116 S.Ct. 619, 133 L.Ed.2d 578 (1996) ("[I]n several contexts, we have recognized that vindication of maritime policies demanded uniform adherence to a federal rule of decision" (citing *Kossick, supra*, at 742, 81 S.Ct. 886; *Pope & Talbot*, 346 U.S., at 409, 74 S.Ct. 202; *Garrett v. Moore-McCormack Co.*, 317 U.S. 239, 248-249, 63 S.Ct. 246, 87 L.Ed. 239 (1942))); *Romero v. International Terminal Operating Co.*, 358 U.S. 354, 373, 79 S.Ct. 468, 3 L.Ed.2d 368 (1959) ("[S]tate law must yield to the needs of a uniform federal maritime law when this Court finds inroads on a harmonious system [,] [b]ut this limitation still leaves the States a wide scope").

Applying state law to cases like this one would undermine the uniformity of general maritime law. The same liability limitation in a single bill of lading for international intermodal transportation often applies both to sea and to land, as is true of the Hamburg Süd bill. Such liability clauses are regularly executed around the world. See 1 Schoenbaum 595; Wood, Multimodal Transportation: An American Perspective on Carrier Liability and Bill of Lading Issues, 46 Am. J. Comp. L. 403, 407 (Supp. 1998). *See also* 46 U.S.C.App. § 1307 (permitting parties to extend the COGSA default liability limit to damage done "prior to the loading on and subsequent to the discharge from the ship"). Likewise, a single Himalaya Clause can cover both sea and land carriers downstream, as is true of the ICC bill. *See* Part III-A, infra. Confusion and inefficiency will inevitably result if more than one body of law governs a given contracts meaning. As we said in Kossick, when "a [maritime] contract ... may well have been made anywhere in the world," it "should be judged by one law wherever it was made." 365 U.S., at 741, 81 S.Ct. 886. Here, that one law is federal.

In protecting the uniformity of federal maritime law, we also reinforce the liability regime Congress established in COGSA. By its terms, COGSA governs bills of lading for the carriage of goods "from the time when the goods are loaded on to the time when they are discharged from the ship." 46 U.S.C.App. § 1301(e). For that period, COGSAs "package limitation" operates as a default rule. § 1304(5). But COGSA also gives the option of extending its rule by contract. See § 1307 ("Nothing contained in this chapter shall prevent a carrier or a shipper from entering into any agreement, stipulation, condition, reservation, or exemption as to the responsibility and liability of the carrier or the ship for the loss or damage to or in connection with the custody and care and handling of goods prior to the loading on and subsequent to the discharge from the ship on which the goods are carried by sea"). As COGSA permits, Hamburg Süd in its bill of lading chose to extend the default rule to the entire period in which the machinery would be under its responsibility, including the period of the inland transport. Hamburg Süd would not enjoy the efficiencies of the default rule if the liability limitation it chose did not apply equally to all legs of the journey for which it undertook responsibility. And the apparent purpose of COGSA, to facilitate efficient contracting in contracts for carriage by sea, would be defeated.

III

[On the merits of the case, the Court held that that Norfolk was entitled to rely on the COGSA limitation of liability, which was extended to it both by the Himalaya clause in the Hamburg Süd bill of lading and by the Himalaya clause in the ICC bill of lading. So far as the Himalaya clause in the ICC bill of lading was concerned, the Court held that there was no reason to read it restrictively so as to require some privity of contract between the carrier (ICC) and the person seeking protection under the clause (Norfolk). So far as the Hamburg Süd bill of lading was concerned, the Court held that Kirby was bound by its terms (including the Himalaya clause) because ICC was to be regarded as Kirbys agent "for a single, limited purpose: when ICC contracts with subsequent carriers for limitation on liability". These aspects of the case are considered in more detail in Vol. 1. Eds.]

IV

We hold that Norfolk is entitled to the protection of the liability limitations in the two bills of lading. Having undertaken this analysis, we recognize that our decision does no more than provide a legal backdrop against which future bills of lading will be negotiated. It is not, of course, this Court's task to structure the international shipping industry. Future parties remain free to adapt their contracts to the rules set forth here, only now with the benefit of greater predictability concerning the rules for which their contracts might compensate.

The judgment of the United States Court of Appeals for the Eleventh Circuit is reversed, and the case is remanded for further proceedings consistent with this opinion.

It is so ordered.

Notes:

1. *Commercial Union Ins. Co. v. Sea Harvest Seafood Co.*, 251 F.3d 1294, 2001 AMC 1990 (10th Cir. 2001) involved the issue as to whether suit on a Marine Open Cargo Policy for a warehouse to warehouse shipment came within the court admiralty jurisdiction. A shipment of frozen shrimp was transported from Bangkok, Thailand to Philadelphia, Pa. The cargo was unloaded from the vessel in California and sent by rail to Chicago and from there by rail to Philadelphia. In transferring the cargo from one train terminal to another, someone forgot to hook up the electrical generator that controlled the refrigeration system. Consequently, when the shipment arrived in Philadelphia the shrimp had spoiled. Notwithstanding the loss occurred on the land portion of the journey, the court characterized the land portion of the transport portion as "incidental to the overall maritime nature of the policy." *Compare Hartford Fire Ins. Co. v. Orient Overseas Container Lines (UK) Ltd.*, 230 F.3d 549, 2001 AMC 25 (2d Cir. 2000).

2. Short term storage in a land based facility after cargo has been discharged from a vessel does not preclude the exercise of admiralty jurisdiction. Long term storage, however, is not incident to the carriage of goods by sea. It is an end in and of itself. *Brosonic Co., Ltd. v. M/V "Mathilde Maersk"*, 120 F. Supp. 2d 372, 2001 AMC 506, (S.D.N.Y. 2000), *aff'd*, 270 F.3d 106 (2d Cir. 2001).

3. The decision in *Kirby*, however, is not the final word on the law applicable to liability in multimodal transport, because that case involved only the issue of whether federal or state law applied to the interpretation of a through bill of lading. There is also another question that has to be answered: which federal law, COGSA or the Carmack Amendment, applies to determine the liability of a carrier where goods shipped pursuant to a through bill of lading are lost or damaged during the overland leg of the transport? The Carmack Amendment was added to the Interstate Commerce Act, which is a comprehensive regulatory scheme applicable to transportation by truck and railroad, since modified to deregulate certain aspects of overland transport. Carmack prescribes the liability regime for loss or damage to goods during overland transport and imposes liability on carriers subject to the jurisdiction of the Surface Transportation Board (principally railroads and truckers), who transport goods in interstate and, to some extent, international commerce. This liability regime differs in some respects from COGSA in that it imposes virtually strict liability and,

as will be explained later, does not provide for limitation of liability as does COGSA. Although under certain circumstances a shipper and a carrier may limit the carrier's liability by contract, courts have been demanding as to what is required to achieve this result.

[T]he United States Court of Appeals for the Ninth *Circuit in Regal-Beloit Corp. v. Kawasaki Kisen Kaisha Ltd.*, 557 F.3d 984 (9th Cir. 2009) held that an ocean carrier and its agent that arranges for overland transport by rail have provided rail services and as such are subject the Carmack Amendment. In that case, the cargo was shipped aboard K-Line's vessel from China to the United States pursuant to a through bill of lading. K-Line's agent arranged by contract with a railroad to transport the goods to their destination in the Midwest. The cargo was damaged on the overland leg. The K-Line through bill of lading had a Tokyo forum selection clause. The clause would have been valid and enforceable under COGSA, but Carmack requires special measures for contracting out of that statute's venue provisions. The district court enforced the forum selection clause and dismissed the action. The Ninth Circuit reversed...

The Supreme Court granted certiorari in the *Regal-Beloit* case. On the merits, a majority of Justices found that the Carmack Amendment was not applicable and reversed the court of appeals. The Court unequivocally held "that the [Carmack] Amendment does not apply to a shipment originating overseas under a single through bill of lading. As in *Kirby*, the terms of the bill govern the parties' rights." ...

Carmack's statutory history supports the conclusion that it does not apply to a shipment originating overseas under a through bill. None of Carmack's legislative versions have applied to the inland domestic rail segment of an **import** shipment from overseas under a through bill.

Robert Force, "The *Regal – Beloit* Decision: What If Anything Would Happen To The Legal Regime For Multimodal Transport In The United States If It Adopted the Hamburg Rules?", 36 *Tul. Mar. L. J.* 685, 689-90, 693-694 (2012).

CHAPTER 2 — FEDERALISM AND ADMIRALTY JURISDICTION

A. Introduction: Concurrent Jurisdiction: "Saving to Suitors"

Admiralty jurisdiction in the United States is complicated because, under the federal system, it is possible to have concurrent state and federal jurisdiction over a claim. 28 U.S.C. § 1333 purports to give exclusive jurisdiction in admiralty and maritime cases to the federal courts, *"saving to suitors in all cases all other remedies to which they are entitled."* The "saving to suitors" clause is interpreted to reserve to suitors the right of non-admiralty remedy in all cases where the law is competent to give such a remedy. If you can find a state court that entertains a case of a particular class, that suit may be brought in state court, notwithstanding the fact that the case is also within the scope of admiralty jurisdiction. For example, ordinary maritime tort and contract cases may be brought in state court. Saving to suitors will also support bringing suit in federal court under diversity jurisdiction of a claim that is controlled by substantive maritime law.

B. Proceedings In Rem

THE HINE v. TREVOR

71 U.S. 555, 18 L. Ed. 451, 4 Wall. 555 (1866)

Mr. Justice MILLER delivered the opinion of the court

The record distinctly raises the question, how far the jurisdiction of the District Courts of the United States in admiralty causes, arising on the navigable inland waters of this country, is exclusive, and to what extent the State courts can exercise a concurrent jurisdiction?

Nearly all the States—perhaps all whose territories are penetrated or bounded by rivers capable of floating a steamboat—have statutes authorizing their courts, by proceedings *in rem*, to enforce contracts or redress torts, which, if they had the same relation to the sea that they have to the waters of those rivers, would be conceded to be the subjects of admiralty jurisdiction. These statutes have been acted upon for many years, and are the sources of powers exercised largely by the State courts at the present time. The question of their conflict with the constitutional legislation of Congress, on the same subject, is now for the first time presented to this court.

* * *

[T]he State courts have been in the habit of adjudicating causes, which in the nature of their subject-matter, are identical in every sense with causes which are acknowledged to be of admiralty and maritime cognizance; and they have in these causes administered remedies which differ in no essential respect from the remedies which have heretofore been considered as peculiar to admiralty courts. This authority has been exercised under State statutes, and not under any claim of a general common-law power in these courts to such a jurisdiction.[*]

---

[*] [Prior to the repudiation of the "tidal waters" and "within the county" restrictions on federal admiralty jurisdiction, litigation arising out of events and transactions involving inland waterways, in the absence of diversity jurisdiction, were often tried in state courts. As to matters cognizable in admiralty, state courts also exercised jurisdiction under the savings to suitors clause. Eds.]

It is a little singular that, at this term of the court, we should, for the first time, have the question of the right of the State courts to exercise this jurisdiction, raised by two writs of error to State courts, remote from each other, the one relating to a contract to be performed on the Pacific Ocean, and the other to a collision on the Mississippi River. The first of these cases, *The Moses Taylor*, had been decided before the present case was submitted to our consideration.

The main point ruled in that case is, that the jurisdiction conferred by the act of 1789, on the District Courts, in civil causes of admiralty and maritime jurisdiction, is exclusive by its express terms, and that this exclusion extends to the State courts. The language of the ninth section of the act admits of no other interpretation. It says, after describing the criminal jurisdiction conferred on the District Courts, that they "shall also have exclusive original cognizance of all civil causes of admiralty and maritime jurisdiction, including all seizures under laws of impost, navigation, or trade of the United States, when the seizures are made on waters which are navigable from the sea by vessels of ten or more tons burden." If the Congress of the United States has the right, in providing for the exercise of the admiralty powers, to which the Constitution declares the authority of the Federal judiciary shall extend, to make that jurisdiction exclusive, then, undoubtedly, it has done so by this act. This branch of the subject has been so fully discussed in the opinion of the court, in the case just referred to, that it is unnecessary to consider it further in this place.

It must be taken, therefore, as the settled law of this court, that wherever the District Courts of the United States have original cognizance of admiralty causes, by virtue of the act of 1789, that cognizance is exclusive, and no other court, state or national, can exercise it, with the exception always of such concurrent remedy as is given by the common law.

* * *

If the facts of the case before us in this record constitute a cause of admiralty cognizance, then the remedy, by a direct proceeding against the vessel, belonged to the Federal courts alone, and was excluded from the State tribunals.

It was a case of collision between two steamboats. The case of *The Magnolia*,** to which we have before referred, was a case of this character; and many others have been decided in this court since that time. That they were admiralty causes has never been doubted.

* * *

It is said that the statute of Iowa may be fairly construed as coming within the clause of the ninth section of the act of 1789, which "saves to suitors, in all cases, the right of a common-law remedy where the common law is competent to give it."

But the remedy pursued in the Iowa courts, in the case before us, is in no sense a common-law remedy. It is a remedy partaking of all the essential features of an admiralty proceeding *in rem*. The statute provides that the vessel may be sued and made defendant without any proceeding against the owner's, or even mentioning their names. That a writ may be issued and the vessel seized, on filing a petition similar in substance to a libel. That after a notice in the nature of a monition, the vessel may be condemned and an order made for her sale, if the liability is established for which she was sued. Such is the general character of the steamboat laws of the Western States.

While the proceeding differs thus from a common-law remedy, it is also essentially different from what are in the West called suits by attachment, and in some of the older States foreign attachments. In these cases there is a suit against a personal defendant by name, and because of inability to serve process on him on account of non-residence, or for some other reason mentioned in the various statutes allowing attachments to issue, the suit is commenced by a writ directing the proper officer to attach sufficient property of the defendant to answer any judgment which may be rendered against him. This proceeding may be had against an owner or part owner of a vessel, and his interest thus subjected to sale in a common-law court of the State.

Such actions may, also, be maintained *in personam* against a defendant in the common-law courts, as the common law gives; all in consistence with the grant of admiralty powers in the ninth section of the Judiciary Act.

** 20 Howard, 296.

But it could not have been the intention of Congress, by the exception in that section, to give the suitor all such remedies as might afterwards be enacted by State statutes, for this would have enabled the States to make the jurisdiction of their courts concurrent in all cases, by simply providing a statutory remedy for all cases. Thus the exclusive jurisdiction of the Federal courts would be defeated. In the act of 1845, where Congress does mean this, the language expresses it clearly; for after saving to the parties, in cases arising under that act, a right of trial by jury, and the right to a concurrent remedy at common law, where it is competent to give it, there is added, "any concurrent remedy which may be given by the State laws where such steamer or other vessel is employed."

THE JUDGMENT IS REVERSED, and the case is remanded to the Supreme Court of Iowa, with directions that it be

DISMISSED FOR WANT OF JURISDICTION.

C. Suits *In Personam*: Attachment

ROUNDS v. CLOVERPORT FOUNDRY AND MACHINE COMPANY

237 U.S. 303, 35 S. Ct. 596, 59 L. Ed. 966 (1915)

Mr. Justice HUGHES delivered the opinion of the court

The Cloverport Foundry and Machine Company, the defendant in error, brought this suit against F.T. Rounds and S.A. Jesse, of Owensboro, Kentucky, in the Breckinridge Circuit Court of that State, to recover the sum of $5,668.65 for work and materials furnished under a contract to repair and rebuild a steamboat formerly known as the *R.D. Kendall* and renamed the *Golden Girl*. The defendants were the owner's of the vessel. A specific attachment was issued under §§ 2480 to 2486 of the Kentucky Statutes which provided for a lien upon watercraft for work and supplies, etc., and the defendants procured a release of the boat by executing a forthcoming bond. By special demurrer, the defendants challenged the jurisdiction of the court to entertain the action upon the ground that the subject-matter was exclusively cognizable in the admiralty. The demurrer was overruled, and the defendants, reasserting the absence of authority in the court, answered denying the allegations of the petition and setting up a counter-claim for damages alleged to have been caused by defective work and by delay in completion. Upon the trial, the counter-claim was dismissed and the Company had judgment against the defendants for the amount demanded in its petition; it was further adjudged that, by virtue of the attachment and the applicable law, the plaintiff had a lien upon the vessel for the payment of the judgment and the vessel was ordered to be sold and the proceeds applied to the debt. The Court of Appeals of the State affirmed the judgment. 159 Kentucky, 414.

The question presented on this writ of error relates solely to the jurisdiction of the state court. It is contended by the plaintiff in error that the contract in suit was for repairs on the vessel and therefore was maritime in character; that the proceeding was *in rem* and beyond the competency of the local tribunal.

* * *

On the other hand, the defendant in error denies that the contract was maritime, contending that the old boat was dismantled, its identity destroyed, and a new boat built, and that the case in this aspect falls within the decisions relating to contracts for the original construction of a vessel.

* * *

Further, it is urged in support of the judgment that the proceeding was *in personam*, and not *in rem;* that the attachment and direction for sale were incidental to the suit against the owner's and for the purpose of securing satisfaction of the personal judgment. Accordingly, it is said, the proceeding was within the scope of the 'common law remedy saved to suitors by the Judiciary Act. 1 Stat. *77;* Rev. Stat., § 563; Judicial Code, § 24.

As the last point is plainly well taken, it is unnecessary to go further. It is well settled that in an action *in personam* the state court has jurisdiction to issue an auxiliary attachment against the vessel; and, whether or not the contract in suit be deemed to be of a maritime nature, it cannot be said that the state court transcended its authority. The proceeding *in rem* which is within the exclusive jurisdiction of admiralty is one essentially against the vessel itself as the debtor or offending thing,—in which the vessel is itself 'seized and impleaded as the defendant, and is judged and sentenced accordingly.' By virtue of dominion over the thing all persons interested in it are deemed to be parties to the suit; the decree binds all the world and under it the property itself passes and not merely the title or interest of a personal defendant.

* * *

Actions *in personam* with a concurrent attachment to afford security for the payment of a personal judgment are in a different category.

* * *

And this is so not only in the case of an attachment against the property of the defendant generally, but also where it runs specifically against the vessel under a state statute providing for a lien, if it be found that the attachment was auxiliary to the remedy *in personam*.

* * *

In the case of *Leon v. Galceran,** *supra*, the suit was *in personam*, in a court of the State of Louisiana, to recover mariners wages. Under a statute of the State the vessel was subject to a lien or privilege in favor of the mariner; and accordingly at the beginning of the suit, on the application of the plaintiff who asserted his lien, a writ of sequestration was issued and levied upon the vessel which was afterwards released upon the execution by the owner, the defendant in the suit, of a forthcoming bond, with surety. Judgment was recovered by the plaintiff for the amount claimed, and the vessel not being returned, suit was brought in the state court against the surety. Upon writ of error from this court to review the judgment in the latter action, it was contended, with respect to the issue and levy of the writ of sequestration, that the vessel had been seized under admiralty process in a proceeding *in rem* over which the state court had no jurisdiction *ratione materioe* and hence that the bond was void. The contention was overruled and the jurisdiction of the state court maintained. As this court said in *Johnson v. Chicago &c. Elevator Co.,* *supra*, in reviewing *Leon v. Galceran, supra*, it was held that 'the action *in personam* in the state court was a proper one, because it was a common law remedy, which the common law was competent to give, although the state law gave a lien on the vessel in the case, similar to a lien under the maritime law, and it was made enforceable by a writ of sequestration in advance, to hold the vessel as a security to respond to a judgment, if recovered against her owner, as a defendant; that the suit was not a proceeding *in rem*, nor was the writ of sequestration; that the bond given on the release of the vessel became the substitute for her; that the common law is as competent as the admiralty to give a remedy in all cases where the suit is *in personam* against the owner of the property; and that these views were not inconsistent, or in *The Belfast*.'

The result of the decisions is thus stated in *Knapp, Stout & Co. v. McCaffrey*, 177 U.S. 638, 646, 648. 'The true distinction between such proceedings as are and such as are not invasions of the exclusive admiralty jurisdiction is this: If the cause of action be one cognizable in admiralty, and the suit be *in rem* against the thing itself, though a monition be also issued to the owner, the proceeding is essentially one in admiralty. If, upon the other hand, the cause of action be not one of which a court of admiralty has jurisdiction, or if the suit be *in personam* against an individual defendant, with an auxiliary attachment against a particular thing, or against the property of the defendant in general, it is essentially a proceeding according to the course of the common law, and within the saving clause of the statute (§ 563) of a common law remedy.'

In the present case, as we have said, the suit was *in personam* and the attachment was in that suit. It had no other effect than to provide security for the payment of the personal judgment which was recovered, and it was for the purpose of satisfying this judgment that, in the same proceeding and by the terms of the judgment, the vessel

---

*[78 U.S. 185 (1870). Eds.]

was directed to be sold. It was within the scope of the common law remedy to sell the property of the judgment debtors to pay their debt. We are not able to find any encroachment upon the exclusive jurisdiction vested in the Federal court in admiralty.

Judgment affirmed.

Note: State Court Jurisdiction in Maritime Cases

Consider carefully the reasoning of the court in *The Hine*. Is the holding on exclusive jurisdiction based on the constitution or on statute? Is there not a logical flaw in the court's interpretation of the saving to suitors clause in the sense that the court assumes that saving common-law *remedies* is the same as saving concurrent state *jurisdiction?* Why didn't the court interpret the saving to suitors clause as preserving common-law remedies in federal (not state) court? Given the court's interpretation of the saving to suitors clause, can't almost all admiralty actions (except *in rem* actions) be brought in state court? Is this proper? Isn't the policy of the saving to suitors clause to preserve trial by jury rather than to preserve state court jurisdiction? This could be done by providing for a jury trial in federal court.

What is the essential difference between admiralty *in rem* actions and state law attachment proceedings? Is there really any distinction between the two? Suppose a state penal statute specifically allows sale and forfeiture—good against the world—of illegally used fishnets. Can such a forfeiture proceeding be brought in state court? *See CJ. Hendry v. Moore,* 318 U.S. 133, 63 S.Ct. 499, 87 L.Ed. 663 (1943) [forfeiture proceeding allowed in state courts because, as a matter of history, forfeiture proceedings could be brought at common law].

In 1948, the saving to suitors clause was revised to read as follows: "saving to suitors in all cases all other remedies to which they are otherwise entitled." 28 U.S.C. § 1333.

Is this 1948 formulation broader than its predecessor in that the limitation "common law remedies" is now gone? Robertson, after reviewing the cases, states as follows: "Thus, it appears that the '48 language has neither narrowed nor broadened the scope of common law jurisdiction saved, despite the fact that cases like *The Moses Taylor* and *Hendry* were based squarely and solely on the notion that the saving clause inquiry requires only that it be ascertained whether the state proceeding in question amounts to a common law remedy, and despite the fact that that language is altogether missing from the new saving clause." D. Robertson, Admiralty and Federalism 134 (1970).

Note: Statutory Proceedings

Practically any case which could be brought under 28 U.S.C. § 1333 may be brought in state court at the plaintiff's discretion. There are exceptions, such as where a statute expressly or impliedly confers exclusive jurisdiction in federal admiralty courts. Congress has provided for exclusive federal jurisdiction for several types of maritime actions by statute. Notable examples are the Limitation of Liability Act (46 U.S.C.A §§ 30501-30512 (formerly 46 U.S.C. § 183 *et seq.*)), the Ship Mortgage Act (46 U.S.C.A. §§ 31301-31343 (formerly 46 U.S.C. § 911 *et seq.*)), the Death on the High Seas Act (46 U.S.C.A. §§ 30301-30308 (formerly 46 U.S.C. § 761 *etseq.*)), the Suits in Admiralty Act (46 U.S.C.A. §§ 30901-30918 (formerly 46 U.S.C. § 741 *etseq.*)),and the Public Vessels Act (46 U.S.C.A. §§ 31101-31113 (formerly 46 U.S.C. § 781 *etseq.*)). However, the court may "read out" the term "exclusive" as the courts have done with the Death on the High Seas Act. *See Offshore Logistics, Inc. v. Tallentire,* 477 U.S. 207, 106 S.Ct. 2485, 91 L.Ed.2d 174, 1986 AMC 2113 (1986). Limitation of liability proceedings can only be brought in federal court under admiralty jurisdiction. However, there is concurrent jurisdiction of the state and federal courts over proceedings to determine liability on the underlying claims and to apportion the fund. The federal courts have exclusive jurisdiction over *in rem* proceedings to foreclose a preferred ship mortgage under the Ship Mortgage Act of 1920 (46 U.S.C.A. §§ 31301-31343 (formerly 46 U.S.C. §§ 911-984)).

Is federal court jurisdiction exclusive on the outer continental shelf, where the OCS Lands Act specifies "exclusive federal jurisdiction?" In *Gulf Offshore Oil Co. v. Mobil Oil Co.,* 453 U.S. 473, 101 S.Ct. 2870, 69 L.Ed.2d 784, 1981 AMC 2033 (1981), the court, in an action involving personal injuries to a worker on a fixed-platform drilling rig, held that "[n]othing inherent in exclusive federal sovereignty over a territory precludes a state court from entertaining a personal injury suit concerning events occurring in the territory and governed by federal law." 453 U.S. at 481. Are there sound reasons for this holding?

D. Sources of Law

SOUTHERN PACIFIC CO. v. JENSEN

244 U.S. 205, 37 S. Ct. 524, 61 L. Ed. 1086, 1996 AMC 2076 (1917)

Mr. Justice McREYNOLDS delivered the opinion of the court

Upon a claim regularly presented, the Workmens Compensation Commission of New York made the following findings of fact, rulings and award, October 9, 1914:

1. Christen Jensen, the deceased workman, was, on August 15, 1914, an employee of the Southern Pacific Company, a corporation of the State of Kentucky, where it has its principal office. It also has an office at Pier 49, North River, New York City. The Southern Pacific Company at said time was, and still is, a common carrier by railroad. It also owned and operated a steamship El Oriente, plying between the ports of New York and Galveston, Texas.

2. On August 15, 1914, said steamship was breathed for discharging and loading at Pier 49, North River, lying in navigable waters of the United States.

3. On said date Christen Jensen was operating a small electric freight truck. His work consisted in driving the truck into the steamship El Oriente where it was loaded with cargo, then driving the truck out of the vessel upon a gangway connecting the vessel with Pier 49, North River, and thence upon the pier, where the lumber was unloaded from the truck. The ship was about 10 feet distant from the pier. At about 10:15 A.M., after Jensen had been doing such work for about three hours that morning, he started out of the ship with his truck loaded with lumber, a part of the cargo of the steamship El Oriente, which was being transported from Galveston, Texas, to New York City. Jensen stood on the rear of the truck, the lumber coming about to his shoulder. In driving out of the port in the side of the vessel and upon the gangway, the truck became jammed against the guide pieces on the gangway. Jensen then reversed the direction of the truck and proceeded at third or full speed backward into the hatchway. He failed to lower his head and his head struck the ship at the top line, throwing his head forward and causing his chin to hit the lumber in front of him. His neck was broken and in this manner he met his death.

* * *

7. The injury was an accidental injury and arose out of and in the course of Jensens employment by the Southern Pacific Company and his death was due to such injury. The injury did not result solely from the intoxication of the injured employee while on duty, and was not occasioned by the wilful intention of the injured employee to bring about the injury or death of himself or another.

> This claim comes within the meaning of Chapter 67 of the Consolidated Laws as re-enacted and amended by Chapter 41 of the Laws of 1914, and as amended by Chapter 316 of the Laws of 1914.
>
> Award of compensation is hereby made to Marie Jensen, widow of the deceased, at the rate of $5.87 weekly during her widowhood with two years' compensation in one sum in case of her remarriage; to Harold Jensen, son of the deceased, at the rate of $1.96 per week and to Evelyn Jensen, daughter of the deceased, at the rate of $1.96 per week until the said Harold Jensen and Evelyn Jensen respectively shall arrive at the age of eighteen years, and there is further allowed the sum of One Hundred ($100) Dollars for funeral expenses.

In due time the Southern Pacific Company objected to the award

> upon the grounds that the Act does not apply because the workman was engaged in interstate commerce on board a vessel of a foreign corporation of the State of Kentucky which was engaged solely in interstate commerce; that the injury was one with respect to which Congress may establish, and has established, a rule of liability, and under the language of Section 114,[1] the Act has no application; on the ground that the Act

---

[1] *Section 114.* "The provisions of this chapter shall apply to employers and employees engaged in intrastate, and also in interstate or foreign commerce, for whom a rule of liability or method of compensation has been or may be established by the Congress of the United States, only to the extent that their mutual connection with intrastate work may and shall be clearly separable and distinguishable from interstate or foreign commerce, except that such employer and his employees working only in this state may, subject to the approval and in the manner provided by the commission and so far as not forbidden by any act of Congress, accept and become bound by the provisions of this chapter in like manner and with the same effect in all respects as provided herein for other employers and their employees."

includes only those engaged in the operation of vessels other than those of other states and countries in foreign and interstate commerce, while the work upon which the deceased workman was engaged at the time of his death was part of the operation of a vessel of another state engaged in interstate commerce, and hence does not come within the provisions of the Act; further, that the Act is unconstitutional,as it constitutes a regulation of and burden upon commerce among the several States in violation of Article I, Section 8, of the Constitution of the United States; in that it takes property without due process of law in violation of the 14th Amendment of the Constitution; in that it denies the Southern Pacific Company the equal protection of the laws in violation of the 14th Amendment of the Constitution because the Act does not afford an exclusive remedy, but leaves the employer and its vessels subject to suit in admiralty; also that the Act is unconstitutional in that it violates Article III, Section 2, of the Constitution conferring admiralty jurisdiction upon the courts of the United States.

Without opinion, the Appellate Division approved the award and the Court of Appeals affirmed this action (215 N.Y. 514, 519), holding that the Workmens Compensation Act applied to the employment in question and was not obnoxious to the Federal Constitution.

* * *

In *New York Central R.R. Co. v. White*, 243 U.S. 188, we held the statute valid in certain respects; and, considering what was there said, only two of the grounds relied on for reversal now demand special consideration. First. Plaintiff in error being an interstate common carrier by railroad is responsible for injuries received by employees while engaged therein under the Federal Employers' Liability Act of April 22, 1908, c. 149,35 Stat. 65, and no state statute can impose any other or different liability. Second. As here applied, the Workmen's Compensation Act conflicts with the general maritime law, which constitutes an integral part of the federal law under Art. Ill, § 2, of the Constitution, and to that extent is invalid.

* * *

Article III, § 2, of the Constitution, extends the judicial power of the United States "To all cases of admiralty and maritime jurisdiction;" and Article I, § 8, confers upon the Congress power "To make all laws which may be necessary and proper for carrying into execution the foregoing powers and all other powers vested by this Constitution in the government of the United States or in any department or officer thereof." Considering our former opinions, it must now be accepted as settled doctrine that in consequence of these provisions Congress has paramount power to fix and determine the maritime law which shall prevail throughout the country. *Butler v. Boston & Savannah Steamship Co.*, 130 U.S. 527; *In re Garnett*, 141 U.S. 1, 14. And further, that in the absence of some controlling statute the general maritime law as accepted by the federal courts constitutes part of our national law applicable to matters within the admiralty and maritime jurisdiction. *The Lottawanna*, 21 Wall. 558; *Butlerv. Boston & Savannah Steamship Co.*, 130 U.S. 527, 557; *Workman v. New York City*, 179 U.S. 552.
In *The Lottawanna*, Mr. Justice Bradley speaking for the court said:

That we have a maritime law of our own, operative throughout the United States, cannot be doubted. The general system of maritime law which was familiar to the lawyers and statesmen of the country when the Constitution was adopted, was most certainly intended and referred to when it was declared in that instrument that the judicial power of the United States shall extend 'to all cases of admiralty and maritime jurisdiction.'... One thing, however, is unquestionable; the Constitution must have referred to a system of law coextensive with, and operating uniformly in, the whole country. It certainly could not have been intended to place the rules and limits of maritime law under the disposal and regulation of the several States, as that would have defeated the uniformity and consistency at which the Constitution aimed on all subjects of a commercial character affecting the intercourse of the States with each other or with foreign states.

By § 9, Judiciary Act of 1789, 1 Stat. 76, 77, the District Courts of the United States were given "exclusive original cognizance of all civil causes of admiralty and maritime jurisdiction;... saving to suitors, in all cases, the right of a common law remedy, where the common law is competent to give it." And this grant has been continued. Judicial Code, §§ 24 and 256.

In view of these constitutional provisions and the federal act it would be difficult, if not impossible, to define with exactness just how far the general maritime law may be changed, modified, or affected by state legislation. That this may be done to some extent cannot be denied. A lien upon a vessel for repairs in her own port may be given by state statute, *The Lottawanna*, 21 Wall. 558, 579, 580; *The J.E. Rumbell*, 148 U.S. 1; pilotage fees fixed, *Cooley v. Board of Wardens*, 12 How. 299; *Ex parte McNiel, 13 Wall*. 236, 242; and the right given to recover in death cases, *The Hamilton*, 207 U.S. 398; *La Bourgogne*, 210 U.S. 95, 138. *See The City of Norwalk*, 55 Fed. Rep. 98, 106. Equally well established is the rule that state statutes may not contravene an applicable act of Congress or affect the general maritime law beyond certain limits. They cannot authorize proceedings *in rem* according to the course in admiralty, *The Moses Taylor*, 4 Wall. 411; *Steamboat Co. v. Chase*, 16 Wall. 522, 534; *The Glide*, 167 U.S. 606; nor create liens for materials used in repairing a foreign ship, *The Roanoke*, 189 U.S. 185. *See Workman v. New York City*, 179 U.S. 552. And plainly, we think, no such legislation is valid if it contravenes the essential purpose expressed by an act of Congress or works material prejudice to the characteristic features of the general maritime law or interferes with the proper harmony and uniformity of that law in its international and interstate relations. This limitation, at the least, is essential to the effective operation of the fundamental purpose for which such law was incorporated into our national laws by the Constitution itself. These purposes are forcefully indicated in the foregoing quotations from *The Lottawanna*.

A similar rule in respect to interstate commerce deduced from the grant to Congress of power to regulate it is now firmly established. "Where the subject is national in its character, and admits and requires uniformity of regulation, affecting alike all the States, such as transportation between the States, including the importation of goods from one State into another, Congress can alone act upon it and provide the needed regulations. The absence of any law of Congress on the subject is equivalent to its declaration that commerce in that matter shall be free." *Bowman v. Chicago & Northwestern Ry. Co.*, 125 U.S. 465, 507, 508; *Vance v. Vandercook Co.*, 170 U.S. 438, 444; *Clark Distilling Co. v. Western Maryland Ry. Co.*, 242 U.S. 311. And the same character of reasoning which supports this rule, we think, makes imperative the stated limitation upon the power of the States to interpose where maritime matters are involved.

The work of a stevedore in which the deceased was engaging is maritime in its nature; his employment was a maritime contract; the injuries which he received were likewise maritime; and the rights and liabilities of the parties in connection therewith were matters clearly within the admiralty jurisdiction. *Atlantic Transport Co. v. Imbrovek*, 234 U.S. 52, 59, 60.

If New York can subject foreign ships coming into her ports to such obligations as those imposed by her Compensation Statute, other States may do likewise. The necessary consequence would be destruction of the very uniformity in respect to maritime matters which the Constitution was designed to establish; and freedom of navigation between the States and with foreign countries would be seriously hampered and impeded. A far more serious injury would result to commerce than could have been inflicted by the Washington statute authorizing a materialman's lien condemned in *The Roanoke*. The legislature exceeded its authority in attempting to extend the statute under consideration to conditions like those here disclosed. So applied, it conflicts with the Constitution and to that extent is invalid.

Exclusive jurisdiction of all civil cases of admiralty and maritime jurisdiction is vested in the Federal District Courts, "saving to suitors, in all cases, the right of a common law remedy, where the common law is competent to give it." The remedy which the Compensation Statute attempts to give is of a character wholly unknown to the common law, incapable of enforcement by the ordinary processes of any court and is not saved to suitors from the grant of exclusive jurisdiction. *The Hine v. Trevor*, 4 Wall. 555, 571, 572; the *Belfast*, 7 Wall. 624, 644; *Steamboat Co. v. Chase*, 16 Wall. 522, 531, 533; *The Glide*, 167 U.S. 606, 623. And finally this remedy is not consistent with the policy of Congress to encourage investments in ships manifested in the Acts of 1851 and 1884 (Rev. Stats., §§ 4283-4285; § 18, Act of June 26, 1884, c. 121, 23 Stat. 57) which declare a limitation upon the liability of their owner's. *Richardson v. Harmon*, 222 U.S. 96, 104.

The judgment of the court below must be reversed and the cause remanded for further proceedings not inconsistent with this opinion.

Reversed.

Dissent: MR. JUSTICE HOLMES, dissenting

* * *

There is no doubt that the saving to suitors of the right of a common-law remedy leaves open the common-law jurisdiction of the state courts, and leaves some power of legislation at least, to the States. For the latter I need do no more than refer to state pilotage statutes, and to liens created by state laws in aid of maritime contracts. Nearer to the point, it is decided that a statutory remedy for causing death may be enforced by the state courts, although the death was due to a collision upon the high seas. *Steamboat Co. v. Chase*, 16 Wall. 522. *Sherlock v. Ailing*, 93 U.S. 99, 104. Knapp, *Stout & Co. v. McCaffrey*, 177 U.S. 638, 646. *Minnesota Rate Cases*, 230 U.S. 352, 409. The misgivings of Mr. Justice Bradley were adverted to in *The Hamilton*, 207 U.S. 398, and held at least insufficient to prevent the admiralty from recognizing such a state-created right in a proper case, if indeed they went to any such extent. *La Bourgogne*, 210 U.S. 95, 138.

The statute having been upheld in other respects, *New York Central R.R. Co. v. White*, 243 U.S. 188, I should have thought these authorities conclusive. The liability created by the New York act ends in a money judgment, and the mode in which the amount is ascertained, or is to be paid, being one that the State constitutionally might adopt, cannot matter to the question before us if any liability can be imposed that was not known to the maritime law. And as such a liability can be imposed where it was unknown not only to the maritime but to the common law, I can see no difference between one otherwise constitutionally created for death caused by accident and one for death due to fault. Neither can the statutes limiting the liability of owner's affect the case. Those statutes extend to non-maritime torts, which of course are the creation of state law. *Richardson v. Harmon*, 222 U.S. 96, 104. They are paramount to but not inconsistent with the new cause of action. However, as my opinion stands on grounds that equally would support a judgment for a maritime tort not ending in death, with which admiralty courts have begun to deal, I will state the reasons that satisfy my mind.

No doubt there sometimes has been an air of benevolent gratuity in the admiralty's attitude about enforcing state laws. But of course there is no gratuity about it. Courts cannot give or withhold at pleasure. If the claim is enforced or recognized it is because the claim is a right, and if a claim depending upon a state statute is enforced it is because the State had constitutional power to pass the law. Taking it as established that a State has constitutional power to pass laws giving rights and imposing liabilities for acts done upon the high seas when there were no such rights or liabilities before, what is there to hinder its doing so in the case of a maritime tort? Not the existence of an inconsistent law emanating from a superior source, that is, from the United States. There is no such law. The maritime law is not a *corpus juris*—it is a very limited body of customs and ordinances of the sea. The nearest to anything of the sort in question was the rule that a seaman was entitled to recover the expenses necessary for his cure when the master's negligence caused his hurt. The maritime law gave him no more. *The Osceola*, 189 U.S. 158, 175. One may affirm with the sanction of that case that it is an innovation to allow suits in the admiralty by seamen to recover damages for personal injuries caused by the negligence of the master and to apply the common-law principles of tort.

Now, however, common-law principles have been applied to sustain a libel by a stevedore *in personam* against the master for personal injuries suffered while loading a ship, *Atlantic Transport Co. v. Imbrovek*, 234 U.S. 52; and *The Osceola* recognizes that in some cases at least seamen may have similar relief. From what source do these new rights come? The earliest case relies upon "the analogies of the municipal law," *The Edith Godden*, 23 Fed. Rep. 43, 46,—sufficient evidence of the obvious pattern, but inadequate for the specific origin. I recognize without hesitation that judges do and must legislate, but they can do so only interstitially; they are confined from molar to molecular motions. A common-law judge could not say I think the doctrine of consideration a bit of historical nonsense and shall not enforce it in my court. No more could a judge exercising the limited jurisdiction of admiralty say I think well of the common-law rules of master and servant and propose to introduce them here *en bloc*. Certainly he could not in that way enlarge the exclusive jurisdiction of the District Courts and cut down the power of the States. If admiralty adopts common-law rules without an act of Congress it cannot extend the maritime law as understood by the Constitution. It must take the rights of the parties from a different authority, just as it does when it enforces a lien created by a State. The only authority available is the common law or statutes of a State. For from the often repeated statement that there is no common law of the United States, *Wheaton v. Peters*, 8 Pet. 591, 658; *Western Union Telegraph Co. v. Call Publishing Co.*, 181 U.S. 92, 101, and from the principles recognized in *Atlantic Transport Co. v. Imbrovek* having been unknown to the maritime law, the natural inference is that in the silence of Congress this court has believed the very limited law of the sea to be supplemented here as in England by the common law, and that here that means, by the common law of the State. *Sherlock v. Ailing*, 93 U.S. 99, 104. *Taylor v. Carryl*, 20 How. 583, 598. So far as I know, the state courts have made this assumption without criticism or attempt at revision from the beginning to this day; *e.g. Wilson v. MacKenzie*, 7 Hill (N.Y.), 95. *Gabrielson v. Way dell*, 135 N.Y. 1, 11. *Kalleck v. Deering*, 161 Massachusetts, 469. See *Ogle v. Barnes*, 8 T.R. 188. *Nicholson v. Mounsey*, 15 East, 384. Even where the admiralty has unquestioned jurisdiction the common law may have concurrent authority and the state courts concurrent power. *Schoonmaker v. Gilmore*, 102 U.S. 118. The invalidity of state attempts to create a remedy for maritime contracts or torts, parallel to that in the admiralty, that was established in such cases as *The Moses Taylor*, 4 Wall. 411, and *The Hine v. Trevor*, 4 Wall. 555, is immaterial to the present point.

The common law is not a brooding omnipresence in the sky but the articulate voice of some sovereign or quasi sovereign that can be identified; although some decisions with which I have disagreed seem to me to have forgotten the fact. It always is the law of some State, and if the District Courts adopt the common law of torts, as they have shown a tendency to do, they thereby assume that a law not of maritime origin and deriving its authority in that territory only from some particular State of this Union also governs maritime torts in that territory—and if the common law, the statute law has at least equal force, as the discussion in *The Osceola* assumes. On the other hand the refusal of the District Courts to give remedies coextensive with the common law would prove no more than that they regarded their jurisdiction as limited by the ancient lines—not that they doubted that the common law might and would be enforced in the courts of the States as it always has been. This court has recognized that in some cases different principles of liability would be applied as the suit should happen to be brought in a common-law or admiralty court. *Compare The Max Morris*, 137 U.S. 1, with *Belden v. Chase*, 150 U.S. 674, 691. But hitherto it has not been doubted authoritatively, so far as I know, that even when the admiralty had a rule of its own to which it adhered, as in *Workman v. New York City*, 179 U.S. 552, the state law, common or statute, would prevail in the courts of the State. Happily such conflicts are few.

It might be asked why, if the grant of jurisdiction to the courts of the United States imports a power in Congress to legislate, the saving of a common-law remedy, *i.e.*, in the state courts, did not import a like if subordinate power in the State. But leaving that question on one side, such cases as *Steamboat Co. v. Chase*, 16 Wall. 522, *The Hamilton*, 207 U.S. 398, and *Atlantic Transport Co. v. Imbrovek*, 234 U.S. 52, show that it is too late to say that the mere silence of Congress excludes the statute or common law of a State from supplementing the wholly inadequate maritime law of the time of the Constitution, in the regulation of personal rights, and I venture to say that it never has been supposed to do so, or had any such effect.

* * *

Mr. Justice PITNEY, dissenting

* * *

The argument is that even in the absence of any act of Congress prescribing the responsibility of a shipowner to his stevedore, the general maritime law, as accepted by the federal courts when acting in the exercise of their admiralty jurisdiction, must be adopted as the rule of decision by state courts of common law when passing upon any case that might have been brought in the admiralty; and that just as the absence of an act of Congress regulating interstate commerce in some cases is equivalent to a declaration by Congress that commerce in that respect shall be free, so non-action by Congress amounts to an imperative limitation upon the power of the States to interpose where maritime matters are involved.

This view is so entirely unsupported by precedent, and will have such novel and far-reaching consequences, that it ought not to be accepted without the most thorough consideration.

* * *

I have endeavored to show, from a consideration of the phraseology of the constitutional grant of jurisdiction and the act of the First Congress passed to give effect to it, from the history in the light of which the language of those instruments is to be interpreted, and from the uniform course of decision in this court from the earliest time until the present, these propositions: First, that the grant of jurisdiction to the admiralty was not intended to be exclusive of the concurrent jurisdiction of the common-law courts theretofore recognized; and, secondly, that neither the Constitution nor the Judiciary Act was intended to prescribe a system of substantive law to govern the several courts in the exercise of their jurisdiction, much less to make the rules of decision, prevalent in any one court, obligatory upon others, exercising a distinct jurisdiction, or binding upon the courts of the States when acting within the bounds of their respective jurisdictions. In fact, while courts of admiralty undoubtedly were expected to administer justice according to the law of nations and the customs of the sea, they were left at liberty to lay hold of common-law principles where these were suitable to their purpose, and even of applicable state statutes, just as courts of common law were at liberty to adopt the rules of maritime law as guides in the proper performance of their duties. This eclectic method had been practiced by the courts of each jurisdiction prior to the Constitution, and there is nothing in that instrument to constrain them to abandon it.

* * *

In the present case there is no question of lien, and, I repeat, no question concerning the jurisdiction of the state court; the crucial inquiry is, to what law was it bound to conform in rendering its decision? Or, rather, the question is the narrower one: Do the Constitution and laws of the United States prevent a state court of common law from applying the state statutes in an action *in personam* arising upon navigable water within the State, there being no act of Congress applicable to the controversy? I confess that until this case and kindred cases submitted at the same time were brought here, I never had supposed that it was open to the least doubt that the reservation to suitors of the right of a common-law remedy had the effect of reserving at the same time the right to have their common-law actions determined according to the rules of the common law, or state statutes modifying those rules. This court repeatedly has so declared, at the same time recognizing fully that the point involves the question of state power.

* * *

In the argument of the present case and companion cases, emphasis was laid upon the importance of uniformity in applying and enforcing the rules of admiralty and maritime law, because of their effect upon interstate and foreign commerce. This, in my judgment, is a matter to be determined by Congress. Concurrent jurisdiction and optional remedies in courts governed by different systems of law were familiar to the framers of the Constitution, as they were to English-speaking peoples generally. The judicial clause itself plainly contemplated a jurisdiction concurrent with that of the state courts in other controversies. In such a case, the option of choosing the jurisdiction is given primarily for the benefit of suitors, not of defendants. For extending it to defendants, removal proceedings are the appropriate means.

Certainly there is no greater need for uniformity of adjudication in cases such as the present than in cases arising on land and affecting the liability of interstate carriers to their employees. And, although the Constitution contains an express grant to Congress of the power to regulate interstate and foreign commerce, nevertheless, until Congress had acted, the responsibility of interstate carriers to their employees for injuries arising in interstate commerce was controlled by the laws of the States. This was because the subject was within the police power, and the divergent exercise of that power by the States did not regulate, but only incidentally affected, commerce among the States.

* * *

To what extent uniformity of decision should result from the grant of jurisdiction to the courts of the United States concurrent with that of the state courts, is a subject that repeatedly has been under consideration in this court, but it never has been held that the jurisdictional grant required state courts to conform their decisions to those of the United States courts. The doctrine clearly deducible from the cases is that in matters of commercial law and general jurisprudence, not subject to the authority of Congress or where Congress has not exercised its authority, and in the absence of state legislation, the federal courts will exercise an independent judgment and reach a conclusion upon considerations of right and justice generally applicable, the federal jurisdiction having been established for the very purpose of avoiding the influence of local opinion; but that where the State has legislated, its will thus declared is binding, even upon the federal courts, if it be not inconsistent with the expressed will of Congress respecting a matter that is within its constitutional power. The doctrine concedes as much independence to the courts of the States as it reserves for the courts of the Union.

* * *

I freely concede the authority of Congress to modify the rules of maritime law so far as they are administered in the federal courts, and to make them binding upon the courts of the States so far as they affect interstate or international relations, or regulate "commerce with foreign nations, and among the several States, and with the Indian tribes." What I contend is that the Constitution does not, *proprio vigore,* impose the maritime law upon the States except to the extent that the admiralty jurisdiction was exclusive of the courts of common law before the Constitution; that is to say, in the prize jurisdiction, and the peculiar maritime process *in rem;* and that as to civil actions *in personam* having a maritime origin, the courts of the States are left free, except as Congress by Legislation passed within its legitimate sphere of action may control them; and that Congress, so far from enacting legislation of this character, has from the beginning left the state courts at liberty to apply their own systems of law in those cases where prior to the Constitution they had concurrent jurisdiction with the admiralty, for the saving clause in the Judiciary Act necessarily has this effect.

* * *

The effect of the present decision cannot logically be confined to cases that arise in interstate or foreign commerce. It seems to be thought that the admiralty jurisdiction of the United States has limits coextensive with the authority of Congress to regulate commerce. But this is not true. The civil jurisdiction in admiralty in cases *ex contractu* is dependent upon the subject matter; in cases *ex delicto* it is dependent upon locality. In cases of the latter class, if the cause of action arise upon navigable waters of the United States, even though it be upon a vessel engaged in commerce wholly intrastate, or upon one not engaged in commerce at all, or (probably) not upon any vessel, the maritime courts have jurisdiction.

* * *

It results that if the constitutional grant of judicial power to the United States in cases of admiralty and maritime jurisdiction is held by inference to make the rules of decision that prevail in the courts of admiralty binding *proprio vigore* upon state courts exercising a concurrent jurisdiction in cases of maritime origin, the effect will be to deprive the several States of their police power over navigable waters lying wholly within their respective limits, and of their authority to regulate their intrastate commerce so far as it is carried upon navigable waters.

* * *

There is no doubt that, throughout the entire life of the nation under the Constitution, state courts not only have exercised concurrent jurisdiction with the courts of admiralty in actions *ex contractu* arising out of maritime transactions, and in actions *ex delicto* arising upon the navigable waters, but that in exercising such jurisdiction they have, without challenge until now, adopted as rules of decision their local laws and statutes, recognizing no obligation of a federal nature to apply the law maritime. State courts of last resort, in several recent cases, have had occasion to consider the precise contention now made by plaintiff in error, and upon full consideration have rejected it.

* * *

Mr. Justice BRANDEIS and Mr. Justice CLARKE concur in the dissent, both upon the grounds stated by Mr. Justice HOLMES and upon those stated by Mr. Justice PITNEY.

* * *

Note: Problems of Federalism: Choice of Law

The maritime law of the United States is *federal* law derived either from court decisions or from statute. The federal judiciary also enjoys the power to fashion substantive admiralty law rules and does so freely especially in cases of general maritime tort and contract. In *Southern Pacific v. Jensen* 244 US. 205, 214, 37 S. Ct. 524, 61 L. Ed. 1086, 1996 AMC 2076 (1917), the Supreme Court articulated the source of this federal power:

> Article III. sec. 2, of the Constitution, extends the judicial power of the United States "To all cases of admiralty and maritime jurisdiction;" and Article I. sec. 8, confers upon the Congress power "To make all laws which may be necessary and proper for carrying into execution the foregoing powers and all other powers vested by this Constitution in the government of the United State or in any department or officer thereof." Considering our former opinions, it must now be accepted as settled doctrine that in consequence of these provisions Congress has paramount power to fix an determine the maritime law which shall prevail throughout the country. *Butler v. Boston & Savannah Steamship Co.,* 130 U.S. 527 (1889); *In re Garnett,* 141 U.S. 1, 14). And further, that in the absence of some controlling statute the general maritime law as accepted by the federal courts constitutes part of our national law applicable to matters within the admiralty and maritime jurisdiction....

Note that this means that the power of Congress to enact legislation pertaining to maritime matters is independent of the Commerce Clause. Doesn't this also mean that the *federal* maritime law is applicable in state court actions under the saving clause as well as in federal court on grounds of diversity? In theory the choice of the forum is not supposed to influence the legal principles that are applicable. *See* D. ROBERTSON, ADMIRALTY AND FEDERALISM 242-46 (1970). Where federal maritime law is applied in state saving to suitor clause actions or in diversity cases, isn't it the reverse of the rule in *Erie v. Tompkins,* 304 U.S. 64, 58 S.Ct. 817, 82 L.Ed. 1188 (1938)?

Both admiralty tort and contract cases present situations which are within the federal judicial power and are also within state judicial power. However, as discussed above, an admiralty case is an admiralty case wherever it is brought. It must be governed generally by the same principles and rules of substantive maritime law regardless of whether it is brought in a state or federal court. When a case meets the criteria for admiralty jurisdiction, such as those that apply in tort cases, then the substantive rules of federal maritime tort law must be applied regardless of whether suit is brought in a federal court or in a state court. On the other hand, state law may be used to supplement federal law where it is not considered to be incompatible with federal law. In the absence of a federal statute or clearly established maritime law precedent, state law should be applied.

Introductory Note

The saving to suitors clause was part of the Judiciary Act of 1789, but it has its roots in America's colonial period. During that time, the High Court of Admiralty in England issued commissions to create the vice-admiralty courts in the colonies.[1] Their jurisdiction was significantly broader than the admiralty jurisdiction in England, which was a point of contention in the colonies.[2] The vice-admiralty courts heard cases without a jury and plaintiffs could choose to file suit there or in the common law courts.[3] In some colonies, admiralty jurisdiction was vested in the common law courts before the establishment of vice-admiralty courts. Once the vice-admiralty courts were established, the common law courts retained concurrent jurisdiction over maritime cases.[4] Thus, the Judiciary Act's grant of concurrent jurisdiction did not create "a novel jurisdictional system,

---

[1] BENEDICT ON ADMIRALTY § 61, at 5-1 to -2 (Steven F. Friedell, 7th ed. rev. 1992).

[2] *Id.* § 72, at 5-28 to -29 ("[I]t is undoubtedly true, that the extension of the admiralty jurisdiction beyond its ancient limits was . . . stated as one of the grievances of the colonies. . . . 'It was ordained,' says the old Congress in their list of grievances, 'that whenever offences should be committed in the colonies, against particular acts imposing duties and restrictions upon trade, the prosecutor might bring his action for the penalties in the Court of Admiralty.' These were in no sense admiralty and maritime cases . . . ."); *see also* STEVEN L. SNELL, COURTS OF ADMIRALTY AND THE COMMON LAW: ORIGINS OF THE AMERICAN EXPERIMENT IN CONCURRENT JURISDICTION 148 (2007); *Waring,* 46 U.S. at 456.

[3] SNELL, *supra,* at 143, 205 ("A potential plaintiff was able to weigh the alternatives, determining whether the opportunity to cross-examine witnesses in open court and availability of a jury mattered more than the speed of summary civil-law procedures . . . .").

[4] *Id.* at 131-36.

but rather merely codified an old one. In essence, the Saving-to-Suitors Clause merely preserved the status quo."[5] Before the American Revolution, the importance of the vice-admiralty courts waned as the number of cases filed there declined due to increased resentment toward the British Government in the colonies.[6]

There are no surviving records of any debate in Congress about the inclusion of the saving to suitors clause in the first Judiciary Act.[7] It is also not discussed in the early cases, which suggests that "both Congress and the courts accepted its meaning as self-explanatory and its purpose as self-evident."[8] As a practical matter, the clause allowed litigants to choose the forum that was most convenient for them.[9]

In *Dean v. Maritime Overseas Corp., 770 F. Supp. 309, 1993 AMC 2112 (E.D. La. 1991)*, the court stated:

* * *

1. The "Savings to Suitors" Clause

The United States Constitution provides that the judicial power of the federal courts extends to "all Cases of admiralty and maritime Jurisdiction." U.S. Const, art. III, § 2. Congress has codified this grant of federal jurisdiction in Title 28, United States Code, Section 1333, which provides in part:

> The district courts shall have original jurisdiction, exclusive of the courts of the States, of:
> (1) Any civil case of admiralty or maritime jurisdiction, saving to suitors in all cases all other remedies to which they are otherwise entitled.

28 U.S.C. § 1333 (Supp. 1989); *see* 14 C. Wright, A. Miller & E. Cooper, Federal Practice and Procedure § 3672 (1985 & Supp. 1991). The federal courts, therefore, have exclusive jurisdiction over all cases involving purely maritime matters. The "savings to suitors" clause, however, reserves the right of a plaintiff to pursue nonmaritime remedies in all other cases.

This clause, in general, provides for the application of common law remedies in all cases where such law is competent. One commentator has noted that,

> Since the common law is competent in all cases where the suit is *in personam*, a plaintiff in such causes may elect either to proceed in admiralty or to bring an ordinary civil action, either at law in state court or in a federal district court under federal diversity jurisdiction (or some other basis of federal jurisdiction). This rule is subject to two qualifications. There is exclusive admiralty jurisdiction over proceedings *in rem*, because the *in rem* action was not known to the common law....

T. Schoenbaum, Admiralty and Maritime Law § 3-13 (Prac. ed. 1987) (footnotes omitted); *see* G. Gilmore & C. Black, The Law of Admiralty § 1-13 (1975). The *in personam* suit, therefore, provides plaintiff's with a choice of forum either in state court or federal court, unless preempted by a federal statute. Moreover, the "savings to suitors" clause prohibits a defendant from removing a case from state court solely on the basis of maritime jurisdiction unless the suit falls under the federal courts' exclusive maritime jurisdiction.

The "savings to suitors" clause, however, does not preempt the application of federal maritime law where the claim arises under admiralty law—no matter whether the suit has been brought in federal court or state court. *See Atlantic & Gulf Stevedores, Inc. v. Ellerman Lines, Ltd.*, 369 U.S. 355, 359-60, 7 L. Ed. 2d 798, 82 S. Ct. 780 (1962); *Pope & Talbot, Inc. v. Hawn*, 346 U.S. 406, 409-11, 98 L. Ed. 143, 74 S. Ct. 202 (1953); *McCraine v. Hondo Boats, Inc.*, 399 So.2d 163, 165 (La. 1981), *cert. denied*, 458 U.S. 1105, 73 L. Ed. 2d 1366, 102 S. Ct. 3483 (1982). In fact, the United States Supreme Court in *Pope & Talbot* noted that, while state law may supplement federal maritime policies, federal maritime law controls rights of recovery rooted in admiralty. 346 U.S. at 409; *see Askew v. American Waterways Operators, Inc.*, 411 U.S. 325, 338, 36 L. Ed. 2d 280, 93 S. Ct. 1590 (1973). Further, the Supreme Court rejected the contention that a suit brought in diversity must be heard under state law. *Pope & Talbot, Inc.*, 346 U.S. at 411.

* * *

---

[5] *Id.* at 319. This statement is also supported by *New Jersey Steam Navigation Co. v. Merchant's Bank of Boston*, 47 U.S. (6 How.) 344, 390 (1848), where the Supreme Court stated, "The saving clause was inserted, probably, from abundant caution, lest the exclusive terms in which the power is conferred on the district courts might be deemed to have taken away the concurrent remedy which had before existed. This leaves the concurrent power where it stood at common law."

[6] Snell, *supra*, at 204.

[7] *Id.* at 307.

[8] *Id.* at 307-08.

[9] *Id.* at 308-11.

E. Application of State Law: Introductory Note

Despite the fact that maritime law is federal law regardless of the forum in which the case is heard, there are several theories under which state decisional law or legislation may be applied in maritime cases. First, the state or common-law rule may be "borrowed" and applied as the federal maritime law. For example, the law of general maritime torts applies common-law negligence, causation, and other state law tort rules. *See Watz v. Zapata Offshore Co.,* 431 F.2d 100, 1970 A.M.C. 2307 (5th Cir. 1970); *Petition of Kinsman Transit Co.,* 338 F.2d 708 (2d Cir. 1964). Second, under the doctrine of *Wilburn Boat,* discussed in the *Byrd* decision, *infra,* the law of the state will be applied where there is no settled admiralty rule and where the action involves a significant local interest (called "maritime but local"). Why was this rejected by the court in *Byrd?* Third, state statutory law that touches upon maritime matters may be upheld and followed if it is a valid exercise of the state's authority and does not interfere with the essential uniformity of maritime law. *See Askew v. American Waterways,* 411 U.S. 325, 1973 AMC 811 (1973). On the other hand, the application of a state law may be rejected, as in the case of *Carlson v. Palmer,* 472 F. Supp. 396, 398-99, 1980 AMC 1709 (D. Del. 1979) where the court stated:

Application of the Delaware statute governing expert witness fees in the instant case would directly contravene the federal statute governing taxation of witness fees as costs in maritime tort case. By enacting 28 U.S.C. § 1925, Congress indicated its intention to apply the provisions of Section 1821, among other federal statutes, to admiralty and maritime cases. Therefore, the provisions of Section 1821 constitute an element of federal maritime law and establish specific standards governing the taxation as costs of expert witness fees. Because the Delaware statute directly contravenes Section 1821, as construed to prevent expert witness fees from being taxed as costs, the provisions of the Delaware statute may not be applied in an admiralty court. Accordingly, defendant's motion to recover the costs of expert witness fees will be denied.

Compare *Madruga v. Superior Court,* 346 U.S. 556, 560, 74 S.Ct. 298, 98 L.Ed. 290 (1954), where the court held that California statutory law applied in an admiralty case for the sale of a vessel and partition of the proceeds:

Congress has passed detailed laws regulating the shipping industry with respect to ownership, sales, mortgages, and transfers of vessel.... But Congress has never seen fit to bar states from making such sales, or to adopt a national partition rule.... The scarcity of reported cases involving such partition ... indicates that ... a national partition rule is not of major importance to the shipping world....

A Texas court held that in a products liability claim by a seaman against the manufacturer of asbestos that Texas law allowing recovery for loss of consortium would apply notwithstanding the fact that the case is subject to admiralty jurisdiction. The court engages in choice of law analysis and finding that there was no statute or uniformly applied admiralty rule local interests predominated. The seaman was exposed to asbestos sometimes in state waters, the product was distributed on land, and the state remedy was supplemental. *Gaither v. Owens-Coming Fiberglass,* 1997 A.M.C. 76 (Tex. Dist. Ct. 1996).

Note: Application of State Law in Wrongful Death Actions

In *Yamaha Motor Corp. U.S.A. v. Calhoun,* 516 U.S. 199, 116 S. Ct. 619, 1996 AMC 305 (1996), a twelve yearoldgirl was killed will operating a jet ski in state territorial waters. Her parents filed suit under both diversity and admiralty in federal district court but based their claim on the state wrongful death statute in order to enhance the amount of damages that could be recovered. Defendants contended that as the general maritime law recognized a wrongful death action for deaths occurring in state territorial waters, the court should apply federal maritime law. The Supreme Court first determined that the case fell within admiralty jurisdiction. The Court then concluded that inasmuch as the decedent had not been a "seafarer" the federal interest in uniformity was not controlling. It also observed that there was no controlling federal statute. Finally, the court concluded "the damages available for the jet ski death of Natalie Calhoun are properly governed by state law. On remand, the Court of Appeals for the Fifth Circuit reviewing the decision of the district court after remand, ultimately held that the general maritime law controlled the issue as to whether or not the defendant was liable to plaintiff under the law of products liability or negligence. However, Pennsylvania state law, the law of plaintiff's and decedent's domicile determined the calculation wrongful death damages and Puerto Rican law, the law of the place of injury, controlled the issue of punitive damages. 216 F.3d 338, 2000 AMC 1865 (3d Cir.), *cert. denied,* 531 U.S. 1037, 121 S.Ct. 627 (2000). When the case was tried ultimately, the jury returned a verdict for defendants.

BYRD v. BYRD

657 F.2d 615, 1981 AMC 2563 (4th Cir. 1981)

MURNAGHAN, Circuit Judge

The question presented by the instant case—whether interspousal immunity applies within the federal admiralty jurisdiction to preclude a tort action by a wife against her husband for injuries sustained by her while on the husband's pleasure boat in navigable waters—is truly one of first impression. Authority, not only cases but comment by the treatise authors as well, appears to be nonexistent.[1]

The appeal arises out of a suit by appellant wife against her husband for injuries sustained by her on September 16, 1978, allegedly as a result of her husband's negligence in maintaining an unsafe boat. Appellant was injured, while on board her husband's pleasure craft in the navigable waters of the United States,[2] when the deck chair in which she was seated fell from the flying bridge where it had been placed. Appellant, seeking damages, sued her husband in admiralty in the Eastern District of Virginia. She claimed that her husband was negligent in failing either to affix the deck chair permanently to the deck of the flying bridge or to provide guard rails around the bridge.[3] Appellee admitted jurisdiction, denied liability, and raised, as an affirmative defense and by motion to dismiss, Virginias doctrine of interspousal immunity. The district court ruled that Virginia law controlled and that Virginia continued to recognize the doctrine of interspousal immunity and would apply it in this case. It, therefore, dismissed the suit, from which dismissal the wife appeals.

Both parties agree that the instant case falls within the Courts admiralty jurisdiction. This is clearly correct. *Richards v. Blake Builders Supply, Inc.*, 528 F.2d 745 (4th Cir. 1975) (HAYNSWORTFi, C.J.).[4] It does not, however, in and of itself, provide an answer to the question posed by the case. All cases involving a tort committed on navigable water, whether brought under federal admiralty jurisdiction, in state court under the saving-to-suitors clause, or in federal court under diversity jurisdiction, are governed by admiralty law. *Kermarec v. Compagnie Generale Transatlantique*, 358 U.S. 625, 628 (1959). But admiralty law, at times, looks to state law, either statutory or decisional, to supply the rule of decision where there is no admiralty rule on point. *E.g., Wilburn Boat Co. v. Fireman's Fund Insurance Co.*, 348 U.S. 310 (1955); *Bell v. Tug Shrike*, 332 F.2d 330 (4th Cir. 1964), *cert. denied*, 379 U.S. 844 (1964). The Supreme Court in *Wilburn Boat*, a case concerning a marine insurance contract, stated:

> Congress has not taken over the regulation of marine insurance contracts and has not dealt with the effect of marine insurance warranties at all; hence there is no possible question here of conflict between state law and any federal statute. But this does not answer the questions presented, since in the absence of controlling Acts of Congress this Court has fashioned a large part of the existing rules that govern admiralty. And States can no more override such judicial rules validly fashioned than they can override Acts of Congress. [Citation omitted.] Consequently the crucial questions in this case narrow down to these: (1) Is there a judicially established federal admiralty rule governing these warranties? (2) If not, should we fashion one? 348 U.S. at 314.

In the instant case, no federal statute speaks to the applicability of interspousal immunity in an admiralty case. Nor has either party, the district court or this Court been able to find any federal case which has even considered the question, much less established a federal admiralty rule determining it. The question in this case is, therefore,

---

[1] The California Supreme Court, in *Klein v. Klein*, 58 Cal. 2d 692, 26 Cal. Rptr. 102, 376 P.2d 70, 1963 A.M.C. 400 (1962), abolished interspousal immunity for negligent torts in California. Although the negligence there complained of occurred while husband and wife were on the husband's pleasure boat, there is no indication in the opinion that the injury arose on the navigable waters of the United States or, consequently, that there was any question of federal admiralty law. The opinion is grounded entirely in state law and does not consider whether there is any possibility that federal admiralty law might pertain or, if it did, what that law might be.

The Eastern District of Louisiana, in *Winter v. Eon Production, Ltd.*, 433 F. Supp. 742 (E.D. La. 1976) specifically noted that it was not required to resolve the question whether Louisiana's law on interspousal immunity would apply in a maritime collision case. 433 F. Supp. at 747 n.7.

[2] As the case was developed below, it apparently was assumed that the accident occurred while the boat was in Virginia waters. At argument, counsel for the appellant suggested that the occurrence took place at or near the border between Virginia and Maryland. Because of the result which we reach, this possible factual discrepancy is of no moment.

[3] She also claimed negligence in the alleged violation of the Federal Boat Safety Act of 1971, 46 U.S.C. § 1451 *et seq.*, and the Inland Navigation Rules, 33 U.S.C. § 151 *et seq.*

[4] This Court, in *Richards*, questioned the wisdom of invoking federal admiralty law to decide essentially local suits involving pleasure boats arising in the territorial waters of a state. Based on a reading of earlier Supreme Court cases, however, the Court concluded that such suits fell within federal admiralty jurisdiction until such time as Congress should specifically deal with jurisdiction over suits involving pleasure craft. Congress has not acted to change the law in the intervening six years and we, therefore, follow these earlier decisions and hold that admiralty law applies.

whether we should establish a federal admiralty rule governing interspousal immunity in maritime tort suits or whether we should look to applicable state law to provide the rule of decision.[5]

A state law, even though it does not contravene an established principle of admiralty law will, nevertheless, not be applied where its adoption would impair the uniformity and simplicity which is a basic principle of the federal admiralty law, *Moragne v. States Marine Lines, Inc.*, 398 U.S. 375, 402 (1970); *Kermarec, supra*, 358 U.S. at 631, or where its application would defeat an otherwise meritorious maritime cause of action. *St. Hilaire Moye v. Henderson*, 496 F.2d 973, 980 (8th Cir. 1974), *cert. denied*, 419 U.S. 884 (1974); *In re M/T Alva Cape*, 405 F.2d 962, 969-71 (2d Cir. 1969). *See Moore v. Hampton Roads Sanitation District Commission*, 557 F.2d 1030, 1035 (4th Cir. 1976), *reheard en banc and decided on other grounds*, 557 F.2d 1037 (4th Cir. 1977), *cert. denied*, 434 U.S. 1012 (1978). The state law involved here fails on both accounts.

Whereas at one time interspousal immunity in tort actions was, without significant exception, the law of all the states, presently, in whole or in part, thirty-two states have abrogated the doctrine.[6] On the other hand, eighteen states and the District of Columbia seem still to apply it generally.[7] Moreover, in those states where the doctrine has been abrogated, even greater disunity exists. Some states have abolished the doctrine entirely. Others have abolished it only in cases of intentional torts. Still others have abolished it only in cases arising out of automobile accidents, or only in cases of outrageous, intentional torts, or some other class of cases.[8] Clearly, reference to state law in deciding maritime tort suits between a husband and wife will not lead to uniform decisions.

Additionally, it is the standards of maritime law which measure rights and liabilities arising from conduct occurring on vessels on the navigable waters. Negligence in the operation of a boat creates a federal right of recovery in all who are injured by the negligence. *St. Hilaire Moye, supra*, 496 F.2d at 980-81. Therefore, application of a state's law on interspousal immunity, if that state does not permit suits between spouses arising out of negligent torts, as appellee husband contends that the law of Virginia did not, would operate to defeat a substantial admiralty right of recovery.[9] *See St. Hilaire Moye, supra*, 496 F.2d at 980-81 (Court refused to apply state boat guest statute because it would defeat federal right of recovery and disrupt uniformity of admiralty law). It is clear, therefore, that fashioning an admiralty rule dealing with interspousal immunity will further the goal of a uniform admiralty law. Additionally, since we decide that federal admiralty law will not recognize interspousal immunity, our refusal to apply Virginias law of interspousal immunity (assuming that, as defendant argues, the applicable state law would bar this suit) ensures that no federal right of recovery will be defeated by application of state law.[10]

There may, of course, be questions which, while arising in the context of an admiralty case, are so evidently local in nature and impact that a states local interest clearly outweighs the federal interest in national uniformity. *E.g., Tug Shrike, supra*, 332 F.2d 330 (beneficiary under Jones Act determined by looking to state law of domestic relations). Or, the area may be one where a declaration of preemption by federal rule would leave a complex area largely unregulated, despite complete regulation by the states. *E.g., Wilburn Boat, supra*, 348 U.S. at 316-20. This case is neither of these.

---

[5] That would require a determination of which state law governs, *see* n.2, *supra*, and beyond that, what the governing state's law is. Maryland still applies the doctrine of interspousal immunity in negligent tort cases although it has abrogated the rule in intentional tort cases. *Compare Arch v. Arch*, 11 Md. App. 395, 274 A.2d 646 (1971) *with Lusby v. Lusby*, 283 Md. 334, 390 A.2d 77 (1978). Virginia, at the time suit was brought, applied the doctrine generally except that it had abolished interspousal immunity in automobile cases and in wrongful death cases where one spouse has killed the other. *Counts v. Counts*, 221 Va. 151, 266 S.E.2d 895 (1980*); Korman v. Carpenter*, 216 Va. 86, 216 S.E.2d 195 (1973); *Surratt v. Thompson*, 212 Va. 191, 183 S.E.2d 200 (1971). Moreover, effective July 1, 1981, interspousal immunity in tort suits was abolished altogether in Virginia. Va. Code 8.01-220.1, Session Laws at S. 542, Ch. 451. Whether the old or the new law would apply to this case, and, if the old law applied, whether the instant case is sufficiently like an automobile accident case to warrant extending the exception announced in *Surratt, supra*, are questions we need not decide because of the result we reach.

[6] Alabama, Alaska, Arkansas, California, Colorado, Connecticut, Idaho, Indiana, Kentucky, Maryland, Massachusetts, Michigan, Minnesota, Nevada, New Hampshire, New Jersey, New Mexico, New York, North Carolina, North Dakota, Oklahoma, Oregon, Pennsylvania, Rhode Island, South Carolina, South Dakota, Texas, Vermont, Virginia, Washington, West Virginia, and Wisconsin. Annot., *Modern Status of Interspousal Tort Immunity in Personal Injury Actions and Wrongful Death Actions*, 92 A.L.R. 3d 901 (1979).

[7] Arizona, Delaware, District of Columbia, Florida, Georgia, Hawaii, Illinois, Iowa, Kansas, Louisiana, Maine, Mississippi, Missouri, Montana, Nebraska, Ohio, Tennessee, Utah, and Wyoming. However, a number of these jurisdictions permit suit for torts committed during the marriage in some situations where the marriage has terminated either by divorce or by the death of one of the spouses (victim or tort-feasor). Annot., *Modern Status of Interspousal Tort Immunity, supra*, 92 A.L.R. 3d901.

[8] *E.g., Surratt, supra*, 212 Va. 191, 183 S.E. 2d 200; *Lusby, supra*, 283 Md. 334, 390 A.2d 77. *See generally* Annot., *Modern Status of Interspousal Tort Immunity, supra*, 92 A.L.R. 3d901.

[9] This would be true, of course, only if, as we do, in fact, decide, admiralty law does not apply the doctrine of interspousal immunity. *See* discussion, *infra*.

[10] If we were to decide that federal admiralty law recognized immunity between spouses, and if the applicable state law also recognized such immunity we would have no need to reach the question presented by this case since, in either event, the result would be identical.

In *Wilburn Boat, supra,* the question presented to the Court was whether it should adopt a state rule relating to marine insurance contracts or fashion a federal one, there being no existing federal rule or policy dealing with the subject. The Court reviewed cases decided by it holding that the states could regulate all types of insurance, including marine, then reviewed the history of congressional action in the field ending with a discussion of the McCarran Act[11] in which it said:

> The measure Congress passed shortly there-after, known as the McCarran Act, was designed to assure that existing state power to regulate insurance would continue. Accordingly, the Act contains a broad declaration of congressional policy that the continued regulation of insurance by the States is in the public interest, and that silence on the part of Congress should not be construed to impose any barrier to continued regulation of insurance by the States.
>
> The hearings on the McCarran Act reveal the complexities and difficulties of an attempt to unify insurance law on a nationwide basis, even by Congress. Courts would find such a task far more difficult. Congress in passing laws is not limited to the narrow factual situation of a particular controversy as courts are in deciding lawsuits. And Congress could replace the presently functioning state regulations of marine insurance by one comprehensive Act. Courts, however, could only do it piecemeal, on a case-by-case basis. Such a creeping approach would result in leaving marine insurance largely unregulated for years to come. 348 U.S. at 319 (footnotes omitted). The Court

therefore determined that institution of a federal rule regarding marine insurance was better handled by Congress, which could regulate the whole field, than by the courts and held that admiralty should look to state law in that case.

In contrast, interspousal immunity is a common law doctrine, initiated by courts. *Counts, supra,* 266 S.E.2d at 898 (POFF, J., dissenting). Although there are statements in some cases that it should only be abolished by legislative action,[12] where, as here, there has been no previous consideration of the question of whether the doctrine applies at all in admiralty, this Court is as competent as any other within its respective jurisdiction to determine whether the doctrine is a wise one for establishment in the jurisdiction. Moreover, any decision which we make will establish an easily ascertainable and applied rule; it will not have the effect of leaving a complex field virtually unregulated.

Bell v. Tug Shrike, supra, 332 F.2d 330 also does not mandate the application of state law in the instant case. There, this Court was faced with the question whether a woman, "married" to a seaman in an invalid ceremony, qualified as a "surviving widow" for purposes of receiving benefits after the seamans death under the Jones Act.[13] The Court determined that there was no federal definition of "widow" either in the statute at issue or generally. In addition, the Court cited a number of cases involving other federal statutes where availability of some benefit turned on the familial status of the person claiming the benefit and noted that courts, including the Supreme Court, had repeatedly looked to state law to determine whether the claimant possessed the necessary status. The Court therefore held that it should apply state law rather than fashion a federal law of domestic relations, and, determining that the applicable state law did not recognize common law marriages, denied benefits. The Court "emphatically" rejected the argument that

> by applying the law of Virginia to interpret the term "surviving widow" in the Jones Act, a federal right is being defeated by the state. There can be no federal right unless the claimant can qualify as a beneficiary under the statute. Under the circumstances this can only be achieved through a lawful marriage as that term is interpreted in the only available domestic relations law—the law of the domicile.

---

[11] 15 U.S.C. § 1011, *et seq.*

[12] *See Counts, supra,* 266 S.E.2d at 896; *Lusby, supra,* 283 Md. at 343, 344, 346, 357, 390 A.2d at 81, 82, 88. *And see* cases cited in Annot., *Modern Status of Interspousal Tort Immunity, supra,* 92 A.L.R. 3d at 918-19.

[13] The Federal Employers Liability Act, 45 U.S.C. § 51 (1958), rendered a carrier liable to the decedent's "personal representative, for the benefit of the surviving widow ..." and other listed beneficiaries. The provision was specifically incorporated into the Jones Act, 46 U.S.C. § 688 (1958).

332 F.2d at 336-337.

Again, the instant case is distinguishable. Application of the state law contended for here by defendant will defeat a federal right which plaintiff otherwise already possesses. *See St. Hilaire Moye, supra,* 496 F.2d at 980-81 (negligence in operation of a boat creates a federal right of recovery in all who are injured by the negligence; state boat guest statute which would defeat the right should not be applied). In addition, domestic relations law, like insurance law, is a body of law where interrelated and sometimes intricate rules have developed over many years. Were the federal courts to declare those fields preempted by federal policy in the context of maritime actions, they would create a situation where no guidelines would exist in substantial areas of the law pending piecemeal and case-by-case structuring of a federal common law. *Wilburn Boat, supra,* 348 U.S. at 319. In contrast, the instant case involves a discrete rule of law, and establishment by this Court of a federal rule applicable in admiralty cases will not pull a thread so as to unravel an established, involved and interrelated body of law, leaving nothing in its place. Moreover, a person's familial status is a more or less permanent condition which is primarily pertinent in state law matters[14] and thus is of peculiarly local concern. On the other hand, the decision in the instant case may have national impact beyond that evident in a case involving pleasure craft. Because we must decide the case as a matter of admiralty law, *see Richards, supra,* 528 F.2d 745, the decision will affect not only private pleasure boats but commercial navigation as well, should appropriate facts arise there.

Finally, unlike the earlier pronouncements by the courts and Congress considered in *Wilburn Boat, supra,* and *Tug Shrike, supra,* the existing case law which is relevant here by analogy suggests that we should not apply state law. *Moore, supra,* 557 F.2d 1030 (Federal maritime law, which Court determines would not recognize municipal immunity from suit, applies, even though both parties are Virginia residents, rather than state law which might[15] hold municipality immune from suit and thus defeat federal admiralty claim); *St. Hilaire Moye, supra,* 496 F.2d 973 (state boat guest statute does not apply to defeat tort claim in federal admiralty case involving pleasure boat). *See Alva Cape, supra,* 405 F.2d 962 (district court should investigate whether the states law of municipal immunity was preempted by federal admiralty policy, the inquiry to "consider the need for preserving a uniform maritime rule, granting recovery for damage caused through negligence, against the varying exceptions created by the laws of the 50 states limiting the tort liability of cities". The Court specifically pointed to "adverse impact which might be caused by following state law in this area [which would] be especially evident in New York Harbor, since the laws of New Jersey and New York would create two different rules of recovery and the statutes governing the liability of the United States possibly a third" and to the Supreme Court's "solicitude toward maritime plaintiffs threatened with nonsuit under a local law"). We think, therefore, that it is appropriate here to determine a federal admiralty rule regarding interspousal immunity.

When we turn to the question of what the uniform admiralty rule should be, the answer seems plain. Interspousal immunity is a doctrine whose day has come and gone. One ancient foundation of the rule—that husband and wife are one flesh and that a wife cannot so separate herself from her husband s bodily corporation as to be capable of maintaining an action against him—"'cannot be seriously defended today'" *Surratt, supra,* 212 Va. at 194, 183 S.E.2d at 202 *quoting Immer v. Risko,* 56 N.J. 482, 488, 267 A.2d 481, 484 (1970). The other mainstay of the doctrine—that the prevention of suits between spouses encourages familial harmony—is, we surmise, inapplicable here. In suits involving the negligent operation of an automobile, the great probability of insurance and the consequent presence of an indemnitor to blunt and absorb the distress which a suit between spouses might otherwise be expected to generate, has been a primary justification for the abrogation of the doctrine of interspousal immunity in such cases. *E.g., Korman, supra,* 216 Va. 86, 216 S.E.2d 195; *Smith v. Kauffman,* 212 Va. 181, 183

---

[14] For example, the status of the claimant in *Tug Shrike* was relevant not only for determining eligibility for federal benefits but also for determining her right to participate in any estate which the deceased seaman may have left. The latter, of course, was clearly a matter of state concern.

[15] The Court indicated that it had doubts as to whether Virginia would extend immunity to the municipality in the circumstances of the case but found the question unnecessary to resolve because of its view that admiralty law governed. 557 F.2d at 1035.

S.E.2d 190 (1971); *Immer v. Risko, supra,* 56 N.J. at 489-90, 267 A.2d at 484-85.[16] For marine accidents involving pleasure boats, the insurance picture is likely to be similar. Virginia, where the parties are domiciled, does not have in force a compulsory insurance law for motor cars or for pleasure boats. Still the economic factors motivating both vehicle and boat owner's to take out casualty insurance are very strong.

Finally, we note that the general trend among the states is toward the abolition of interspousal immunity. *E.g.,* Va. Code 8.01-220.1, Session Laws at S. 542, Ch. 451, abolishing interspousal immunity effective July 1, 1981. It would be anomalous and, within the foreseeable future, creative of less rather than more harmony between state and federal law, to establish the doctrine of interspousal immunity as a living organism of the admiralty law at a time when the trend in the states is towards its abolition.

Accordingly, we hold that marriage between plaintiff and defendant does not create an immunity barring recovery for torts occurring within the federal admiralty jurisdiction. The judgment is reversed, and the case remanded for further proceedings.

REVERSED.

F. Forum Non Conveniens

AMERICAN DREDGING CO. v. MILLER

510 U.S. 443, 114 S. Ct. 981, 127 L. Ed. 2d 285, 1994 AMC 913 (1994)

Justice SCALIA delivered the opinion of the Court

This case presents the question whether, in admiralty cases filed in a state court under the Jones Act, 46 U.S.C. app. § 688, and the "saving to suitors clause," 28 U.S.C. § 1333(1), federal law pre-empts state law regarding the doctrine of *forum non conveniens.*

I

Respondent William Robert Miller, a resident of Mississippi, moved to Pennsylvania to seek employment in 1987. He was hired by petitioner American Dredging Company, a Pennsylvania corporation with its principal place of business in New Jersey, to work as a seaman aboard the M/V John R., a tug operating on the Delaware River. In the course of that employment respondent was injured. After receiving medical treatment in Pennsylvania and New York, he returned to Mississippi where he continued to be treated by local physicians.

On December 1, 1989, respondent filed this action in the Civil District Court for the Parish of Orleans, Louisiana. He sought relief under the Jones Act, which authorizes a seaman who suffers personal injury "in the course of his employment" to bring "an action for damages at law," 46 U.S.C. app. § 688(a), and over which state and federal courts have concurrent jurisdiction. *See Engel v. Davenport,* 271 U.S. 33, 37, 46 S. Ct. 410, 412, 70 L. Ed. 813 (1926). Respondent also requested relief under general maritime law for unseaworthiness, for wages, and for maintenance and cure. *See McAllister v. Magnolia Petroleum Co.,* 357 U.S. 221, 224, 78 S. Ct. 1201, 1203, 2 L. Ed. 2d 1272 (1958) (setting forth means of recovery available to injured seaman).

The trial court granted petitioner's motion to dismiss the action under the doctrine of *forum non conveniens,* holding that it was bound to apply that doctrine by federal maritime law. The Louisiana Court of Appeal for the Fourth District affirmed. 580 So. 2d 1091 (1991). The Supreme Court of Louisiana reversed, holding that Article 123(C) of the LOUISIANA CODE OF CIVIL PROCEDURE, which renders the doctrine of *forum non conveniens* unavailable in Jones Act and maritime law cases brought in Louisiana state courts, is not preempted by federal maritime law. 595 So. 2d 615 (1992). American Dredging Company filed a petition for a writ of certiorari, which we granted. 507 U.S. —, 113 S. Ct. 1840, 123 L. Ed. 2d 466 (1993).

---

[16] In fact, it is ironic that... [d]omestic harmony may be more threatened by denying a cause of action than by permitting one where there is insurance coverage. The cost of making the injured spouse whole would necessarily come out of the family coffers, yet a tortfeasor spouse surely anticipates that he will be covered in the event that his negligence causes his spouse injuries. This unexpected drain on the family's financial resources could likely lead to an interference with the normal family life. *Immer v. Risko, supra,* 56 N.J. at 489, 267 A.2d at 485.

II

The Constitution provides that the federal judicial power "shall extend ... to all Cases of admiralty and maritime Jurisdiction." U.S. Const. Art. III, § 2, cl. 1. Federal-court jurisdiction over such cases, however, has never been entirely exclusive. The Judiciary Act of 1789 provided:

That the district courts shall have, exclusively of the courts of the several States ... exclusive original cognizance of all civil causes of admiralty and maritime jurisdiction ... within their respective districts as well as upon the high seas; *saving to suitors, in all cases, the right of a common-law remedy, where the common law is competent to give it.* § 9, 1 Stat. 76-77 (emphasis added).

The emphasized language is known as the "saving to suitors clause." This provision has its modern expression at 28 U.S.C. § 1333(1), which reads (with emphasis added):

The district courts shall have original jurisdiction, exclusive of the courts of the States, of:

(1) Any civil case of admiralty or maritime jurisdiction, *saving to suitors in all cases all other remedies to which they are otherwise entitled.*

We have held it to be the consequence of exclusive federal jurisdiction that state courts "may not provide a remedy in rem for any cause of action within the admiralty jurisdiction." *Red Cross Line v. Atlantic Fruit Co.,* 264 U.S. 109, 124, 44 S. Ct. 274, 211, 68 L. Ed. 582 (1924). An *in rem* suit against a vessel is, we have said, distinctively an admiralty proceeding, and is hence within the exclusive province of the federal courts. *The Moses Taylor,* 4 Wall. 411, 431, 18 L. Ed. 397 (1867). In exercising *in personam* jurisdiction, however, a state court may "'adopt such remedies, and ... attach to them such incidents, as it sees fit' so long as it does not attempt to make changes in the 'substantive maritime law.'" *Madruga v. Superior Court of California,* 346 U.S. 556, 561, 74 S. Ct. 298, 301, 98 L. Ed. 290 (1954) (quoting *Red Cross Line, supra,* 264 U.S., at 124, 44 S. Ct., at 277). That proviso is violated when the state remedy "works material prejudice to the characteristic features of the general maritime law or interferes with the proper harmony and uniformity of that law in its international and interstate relations." *Southern Pacific Co. v. Jensen,* 244 U.S. 205, 216, 37 S. Ct. 524, 529, 61 L. Ed. 1086 (1917). The issue before us here is whether the doctrine of *forum non conveniens* is either a "characteristic feature" of admiralty or a doctrine whose uniform application is necessary to maintain the "proper harmony" of maritime law. We think it is neither.[1]

A

Under the federal doctrine of *forum non conveniens,* "when an alternative forum has jurisdiction to hear [a] case, and when trial in the chosen forum would establish ... oppressiveness and vexation to a defendant ... out of all proportion to plaintiff's convenience,' or when the chosen forum [is] inappropriate because of considerations affecting the court's own administrative and legal problems,' the court may, in the exercise of its sound discretion, dismiss the case," even if jurisdiction and proper venue are established. *Piper Aircraft Co. v. Reyno,* 454 U.S. 235, 241, 102 S. Ct. 252, 258, 70 L. Ed. 2d 419 (1981) (quoting *Koster v. (American) Lumbermens Mut. Casualty Co.,* 330 U.S. 518, 524, 67 S. Ct. 828, 831, 91 L. Ed. 1067 (1947)). In *Gulf Oil Corp. v. Gilbert,* 330 U.S. 501, 67 S. Ct. 839, 91 L. Ed. 1055 (1947), Justice Jackson described some of the multifarious factors relevant to the *forum non conveniens* determination:

---

[1] Justice STEVENS asserts that we should not test the Louisiana law against the standards of *Jensen,* a case which, though never explicitly overruled, is in his view as discredited as *Lochner v. New York,* 198 U.S. 45, 25 S. Ct. 539, 49 L. Ed. 937 (1905). *See post,* at 990-991. Petitioner's pre-emption argument was primarily based upon the principles established in Jensen, as repeated in the later cases (which Justice STEVENS also disparages, *see post,* at 991) of *Knickerbocker Ice Co. v. Stewart,* 253 U.S. 149, 40 S. Ct. 438, 64 L. Ed. 834 (1920), and *Washington v. W.C. Dawson & Co.,* 264 U.S. 219, 44 S. Ct. 302, 68 L. Ed. 646 (1924), *see* Brief for Petitioner 12-13. Respondent did not assert that those principles had been repudiated; nor did the Solicitor General, who, in support of respondent, discussed *Jensen* at length, *see* Brief for the United States as Amicus Curiae 5, 11-13, and n.12. Since we ultimately find that the Louisiana law meets the standards of *Jensen* anyway, we think it inappropriate to overrule *Jensen* in dictum, and without argument or even invitation.

An interest to be considered, and the one likely to be most pressed, is the private interest of the litigant. Important considerations are the relative ease of access to sources of proof; availability of compulsory process for attendance of unwilling, and the cost of obtaining attendance of willing, witnesses; possibility of view of premises, if view would be appropriate to the action; and all other practical problems that make trial of a case easy, expeditious and inexpensive. There may also be questions as to the enforcibility [sic] of a judgment if one is obtained....

Factors of public interest also have [a] place in applying the doctrine. Administrative difficulties follow for courts when litigation is piled up in congested centers instead of being handled at its origin. Jury duty is a burden that ought not to be imposed upon the people of a community which has no relation to the litigation. In cases which touch the affairs of many persons, there is reason for holding the trial in their view and reach rather than in remote parts of the country where they can learn of it by report only. There is a local interest in having localized controversies decided at home. There is an appropriateness, too, in having the trial of a diversity case in a forum that is at home with the state law that must govern the case, rather than having a court in some other forum untangle problems in conflict of laws, and in law foreign to itself." *Id.,* at 508-509, 67 S. Ct., at 843.[2]

Although the origins of the doctrine in Anglo-American law are murky, most authorities agree that *forum non conveniens* had its earliest expression not in admiralty but in Scottish estate cases. *See Macmaster v. Macmaster,* 11 Sess. Cas. 685, 687 (No. 280) (2d Div. Scot.) (1833); *McMorine v. Cowie,* 7 Sess. Cas. (2d ser.) 270, 272 (No. 48) (1st Div. Scot.) (1845); *La Société du Gaz de Paris v. La Société Anonyme de Navigation "Les Armateurs Français,"* [1926] Sess. Cas. (H.L.)13 (1925). *See generally* Speck, *Forum Non Conveniens and Choice of Law in Admiralty: Time for an Overhaul,* 18 J. Mar. Law & Com. 185, 187 (1987); Barrett, *The Doctrine of Forum Non Conveniens,* 35 Cal. L. Rev. 380, 386-387 (1947); Braucher, *The Inconvenient Federal Forum,* 60 Harv. L. Rev. 908, 909 (1947); *but see* Dainow, *The Inappropriate Forum,* 29 Ill. L. Rev. 867, 881, n.58 (1935) (doctrine in Scotland was "borrowed" from elsewhere before middle of 19th century).

Even within the United States alone, there is no basis for regarding *forum non conveniens* as a doctrine that originated in admiralty. To be sure, within federal courts it may have been given its earliest and most frequent expression in admiralty cases. *See The Maggie Hammond,* 9 Wall. 435, 457, 19 L. Ed. 772 (1870); *The Belgenland,* 114 U.S. 355, 365-366, 5 S. Ct. 860, 864-865, 29 L. Ed. 152 (1885). But the doctrine's application has not been unique to admiralty. When the Court held, in *Gilbert, supra,* that *forum non conveniens* applied to all federal diversity cases, Justice Black's dissent argued that the doctrine had been applied in maritime cases "[f]or reasons peculiar to the special problems of admiralty." *Id.,* 330 U.S., at 513, 67 S. Ct., at 845. The Court disagreed, reciting a long history of valid application of the doctrine by state courts, both at law and in equity. *Id.,* at 504-505, and n.4, 67 S. Ct., at 840-842, and n.4. It observed that the problem of plaintiffs' misusing venue to the inconvenience of defendants "is a very old one affecting the administration of the courts as well as the rights of litigants, and both in England and in this country the common law worked out techniques and criteria for dealing with it." *Id.,* at 507, 67 S. Ct., at 842. Our most recent opinion dealing with *forum non conveniens, Piper Aircraft Co. v. Reyno,* 454 U.S. 235, 102 S. Ct. 252, 70 L. Ed. 2d 419 (1981), recognized that the doctrine "originated in Scotland, and became part of the common law of many States," *id.,* at 248, n.13, 102 S. Ct., at 262, n.13 (citation omitted), and treated the *forum non conveniens* analysis of *Canada Malting Co. v. Paterson S. S., Ltd.,* 285 U.S. 413, 52 S. Ct. 413, 76 L. Ed. 837 (1932), an admiralty case, as binding precedent in the nonadmiralty context.

---

[2] *Gilbert* held that it was permissible to dismiss an action brought in a District Court in New York by a Virginia plaintiff against a defendant doing business in Virginia for a fire that occurred in Virginia. Such a dismissal would be improper today because of the federal venue transfer statute, 28 U.S.C. § 1404(a): "For the convenience of parties and witnesses, in the interest of justice, a district court may transfer any civil action to any other district or division where it might have been brought." By this statute, "[d]istrict courts were given more discretion to transfer ... than they had to dismiss on grounds of *forum non conveniens*." *Piper Aircraft Co. v. Reyno,* 454 U.S. 235, 253, 102 S. Ct. 252, 264, 70 L. Ed. 2d 419 (1981). As a consequence, the federal doctrine of *forum non conveniens* has continuing application only in cases where the alternative forum is abroad.

In sum, the doctrine of *forum non conveniens* neither originated in admiralty nor has exclusive application there. To the contrary, it is and has long been a doctrine of general application. Louisiana's refusal to apply *forum non conveniens* does not, therefore, work "material prejudice to [a] characteristic featur[e] of the general maritime law." *Southern Pacific Co. v. Jensen*, 244 U.S., at 216, 37 S. Ct., at 529.

B

Petitioner correctly points out that the decision here under review produces disuniformity. As the Fifth Circuit noted in *Ikospentakis v. Thalassic S. S. Agency*, 915 F.2d 176, 179 (1990), maritime defendants "have access to a *forum non conveniens* defense in federal court that is not presently recognized in Louisiana state courts." We must therefore consider whether Louisiana's rule "interferes with the proper harmony and uniformity" of maritime law, *Southern Pacific Co. v. Jensen, supra*, 244 U.S., at 216, 37 S. Ct., at 529.

In *The Lottawanna*, 21 Wall. 558, 575, 22 L. Ed. 654 (1875), Justice Bradley, writing for the Court, said of the Article III provision extending federal judicial power "to all Cases of admiralty and maritime Jurisdiction":

> One thing ... is unquestionable; the Constitution must have referred to a system of law coextensive with, and operating uniformly in, the whole country. It certainly could not have been the intention to place the rules and limits of maritime law under the disposal and regulation of the several States, as that would have defeated the uniformity and consistency at which the Constitution aimed on all subjects of a commercial character affecting the intercourse of the States with each other or with foreign states.

By reason of this principle, we disallowed in *Jensen* the application of state workers' compensation statutes to injuries covered by the admiralty jurisdiction. Later, in *Knickerbocker Ice Co. v. Stewart*, 253 U.S. 149, 163-164, 40 S. Ct. 438, 441, 64 L. Ed. 834 (1920), we held that not even Congress itself could permit such application and thereby sanction destruction of the constitutionally prescribed uniformity. We have also relied on the uniformity principle to hold that a State may not require that a maritime contract be in writing where admiralty law regards oral contracts as valid, *Kossick v. United Fruit Co.*, 365 U.S. 731, 81 S. Ct. 886, 6 L. Ed. 2d 56 (1961).

The requirement of uniformity is not, however, absolute. As *Jensen* itself recognized: "[I]t would be difficult, if not impossible, to define with exactness just how far the general maritime law may be changed, modified, or affected by state legislation. That this may be done to some extent cannot be denied." 244 U.S., at 216, 37 S. Ct., at 529. A later case describes to what breadth this "some extent" extends:

> It is true that state law must yield to the needs of a uniform federal maritime law when this Court finds inroads on a harmonious system[,] [b]ut this limitation still leaves the States a wide scope. State-created liens are enforced in admiralty. State remedies for wrongful death and state statutes providing for the survival of actions ... have been upheld when applied to maritime causes of action.... State rules for the partition and sale of ships, state laws governing the specific performance of arbitration agreements, state laws regulating the effect of a breach of warranty under contracts of maritime insurance—all these laws and others have been accepted as rules of decision in admiralty cases, even, at times, when they conflicted with a rule of maritime law which did not require uniformity. *Romero v. International Terminal Operating Co.*, 358 U.S. 354, 373-374, 79 S. Ct. 468, 480-481, 3 L. Ed. 2d 368 (1959) (footnotes omitted).

It would be idle to pretend that the line separating permissible from impermissible state regulation is readily discernible in our admiralty jurisprudence, or indeed is even entirely consistent within our admiralty jurisprudence. Compare *Kossick, supra* (state law cannot require provision of maritime contract to be in writing), with *Wilburn Boat Co. v. Firemans Fund Ins. Co.*, 348 U.S. 310, 75 S. Ct. 368, 99 L. Ed. 337 (1955) (state law can determine effect of breach of warranty in marine insurance policy).[3] Happily, it is unnecessary to wrestle with that difficulty today. Wherever the boundaries of permissible state regulation may lie, they do not invalidate state rejection of *forum non conveniens,* which is in two respects quite dissimilar from any other matter that our opinions have held to be governed by federal admiralty law: it is procedural rather than substantive, and it is most unlikely to produce uniform results.

As to the former point: At bottom, the doctrine of *forum non conveniens* is nothing more or less than a supervening venue provision, permitting displacement of the ordinary rules of venue when, in light of certain conditions, the trial court thinks that jurisdiction ought to be declined. But venue is a matter that goes to process rather than substantive rights—determining which among various competent courts will decide the case. Uniformity of process (beyond the rudimentary elements of procedural fairness) is assuredly not what the law of admiralty seeks to achieve, since it is supposed to apply in all the courts of the world. Just as state courts, in deciding admiralty cases, are not bound by the venue requirements set forth for federal courts in the United States Code, so also they are not bound by the federal common-law venue rule (so to speak) of *forum non conveniens.* Because the doctrine is one of procedure rather than substance, petitioner is wrong to claim support from our decision in *Pope & Talbot, Inc. v. Hawn,* 346 U.S. 406, 74 S. Ct. 202, 98 L. Ed. 143 (1953), which held that Pennsylvania courts must apply the admiralty rule that contributory negligence is no bar to recovery. The other case petitioner relies on, *Garrett v. Moore-McCormack Co.,* 317 U.S. 239, 248-249, 63 S. Ct. 246, 252-253, 87 L. Ed. 239 (1942), held that the traditional maritime rule placing the burden of proving the validity of a release upon the defendant pre-empts state law placing the burden of proving invalidity upon the plaintiff. In earlier times, burden of proof was regarded as "procedural" for choice-of-law purposes such as the one before us here, see, e.g., *Levy v. Steiger,* 233 Mass. 600, 124 N.E. 477 (1919); RESTATEMENT OF CONFLICT OF LAWS § 595 (1934). For many years, however, it has been viewed as a matter of substance, see *Cities Service Oil Co. v. Dunlap,* 308 U.S. 208, 212, 60 S. Ct. 201, 203, 84 L. Ed. 196 (1939)—which is unquestionably the the plaintiff to be free of the burden of proof "inhered in his cause of action," "was a part of the very substance of his claim and cannot be considered a mere incident of a form of procedure." 317 U.S., at 249, 63 S. Ct., at 253. Unlike burden of proof (which is a sort of default rule of liability) and affirmative defenses such as contributory negligence (which eliminate liability), *forum non conveniens* does not bear upon the substantive right to recover, and is not a rule upon which maritime actors rely in making decisions about primary conduct—how to manage their business and what precautions to take.

* * *

C

* * *

... Accordingly, we have held that the Jones Act adopts "the entire judicially developed doctrine of liability" under the Federal Employers' Liability Act (FELA), 35 Stat. 65, as amended, 45 U.S.C. §51 *et seq. Kernan v. American Dredging Co.,* 355 U.S. 426, 439, 78 S. Ct. 394, 401, 2 L. Ed. 2d 382 (1958). More particularly, we have held that the Jones Act adopts the "uniformity requirement" of the FELA, requiring state courts to apply a uniform federal law. *Garrett, supra,* 317 U.S., at 244, 63 S. Ct., at 250. And—to come to the point of this excursus— despite that uniformity requirement we held in *Missouri ex rel. Southern R. Co. v. Mayfield,* 340 U.S. 1, 5, 71 S. Ct. 1, 3,

---

[3] Whatever might be the unifying theme of this aspect of our admiralty jurisprudence, it assuredly is not what the dissent takes it to be, namely, the principle that the States may not impair maritime commerce, *see post,* at 994, 995. In *Firemans Fund,* for example, we did not inquire whether the breach-of-warranty rule Oklahoma imposed would help or harm maritime commerce, but simply whether the State had power to regulate the matter. The no-harm-to-commerce theme that the dissent plays is of course familiar to the ear—not from our admiralty repertoire, however, but from our "negative Commerce Clause" jurisprudence, *see Bendix Autolite Corp. v. Midwesco Enterprises, Inc.,* 486 U.S. 888, 891, 108 S. Ct. 2218, 2220, 100 L. Ed. 2d 896 (1988). No Commerce Clause challenge is presented in this case.

Similarly misdirected is the dissent's complaint that Article 123 of the Louisiana Code of Civil Procedure unfairly discriminates against maritime defendants because it permits application of *forum non conveniens* in nonmaritime cases, *see post,* at 993. The only issue raised and argued in this appeal, and the only issue we decide, is whether state courts must apply the federal rule of *forum non conveniens* in maritime actions. Whether they may accord discriminatory treatment to maritime actions by applying a state *forum non conveniens* rule in all except maritime cases is a question not remotely before us.

95 L. Ed. 3 (1950), that a state court presiding over an action pursuant to the FELA "should be freed to decide the availability of the principle of *forum non conveniens* in these suits according to its own local law." We declared *forum non conveniens* to be a matter of "local policy," *id.,* at 4, 71 S. Ct., at 2, a proposition well substantiated by the local nature of the "public factors" relevant to the *forum non conveniens* determination. *See Reyno, supra,* 454 U.S., at 241, and n.6, 102 S. Ct., at 25 and n.6 (quoting *Gilbert,* 330 U.S., at 509, 67 S. Ct., at 843).

* * *

Amicus the Solicitor General has urged that we limit our holding, that *forum non conveniens* is not part of the uniform law of admiralty, to cases involving domestic entities. We think it unnecessary to do that. Since the parties to this suit are domestic entities it is quite impossible for our holding to be any broader.

The judgment of the Supreme Court of Louisiana is
Affirmed.

* * *

Justice STEVENS, concurring in part and concurring in the judgment

It is common ground in the debate between the Court and Justice KENNEDY that language from the majority opinion in *Southern Pacific Co. v. Jensen,* 244 U.S. 205, 37 S. Ct. 524, 61 L. Ed. 1086 (1917), correctly defines this Court's power to forbid state tribunals from applying state laws in admiralty cases. *See ante,* at 985, *post,* at 993. In my view, Jensen is just as untrustworthy a guide in an admiralty case today as *Lochner v. New York,* 198 U.S. 45, 25 S. Ct. 539, 49 L. Ed. 937 (1905), would be in a case under the Due Process Clause.

In the *Jensen* case, five Members of this Court concluded that the State of New York did not have the authority to award compensation to an injured longshoreman because application of the state remedy would inter-fere with the "proper harmony and uniformity" of admiralty law. 244 U.S., at 216, 37 S. Ct., at 529. Justice Holmes' dissenting opinion in *Jensen,* no less eloquent than his famous dissent in *Lochner,* scarcely needs embellishment. *See id.,* at 218-223, 37 S. Ct., at 529-532.[1] Nonetheless, like *Lochner* itself, *Jensen* has never been formally overruled. Indeed, in *Knickerbocker Ice Co. v. Stewart,* 253 U.S. 149, 40 S. Ct. 438, 64 L. Ed. 834 (1920), the same majority that decided *Jensen* reached the truly remarkable conclusion that even Congress could not authorize the States to apply their workmen's compensation laws in accidents subject to admiralty jurisdiction. *See also Washington v. W.C. Dawson & Co.,* 264 U.S. 219, 44 S. Ct. 302, 68 L.Ed. 646 (1924).

As Justice Brandeis stated in dissent in *Washington,* it takes an extraordinarily long and tenuous "process of deduction" to find in a constitutional grant of judicial jurisdiction a strong federal pre-emption doctrine unwaivable even by Congress. *See id.,* at 230-231, 44 S. Ct., at 306-307. *Jensen* and its progeny represent an unwarranted assertion of judicial authority to strike down or confine state legislation—even state legislation approved by Act of Congress—without any firm grounding in constitutional text or principle. In my view, we should not rely upon and thereby breathe life into this dubious line of cases.

Jensen asks courts to determine whether the state law would materially impair "characteristic features" of federal maritime law. 244 U.S., at 216, 37 S. Ct., at 529. The unhelpful abstractness of those words leaves us without a reliable compass for navigating maritime pre-emption problems. As Justice KENNEDY demonstrates, the *forum non conveniens* doctrine may be classified as a "characteristic feature" of federal admiralty jurisprudence even though it did not *originate in,* nor is it *exclusive to,* the law of admiralty. *Compare ante,* at 985-987 *with post,* at 993-995. There is, however, no respectable judicial authority for the proposition that every "characteristic feature" of federal maritime law must prevail over state law.

---

[1] The central theme of Holmes' dissent was that nothing in the Constitution or in the Judiciary Act's grant of jurisdiction over admiralty cases to the district courts prevented New York from supplementing the "very limited body of customs and ordinances of the sea" with its statutory workers' compensation remedy. *Southern Pacific Co. v. Jensen,* 244 U.S. 205, 220, 37 S. Ct. 524, 531 (1917). Holmes *Jensen* dissent was the source of his famous observations that "judges do and must legislate, but they can do so only interstitially [,]" *id.,* at 221, 37 S.Ct., at 531, and that "[t]he common law is not a brooding omnipresence in the sky but the articulate voice of some sovereign or quasi-sovereign that can be identified [,]" *id,* at 222, 37 S.Ct., at 531.

As JUSTICE KENNEDY observes, *post,* at 993, it is not easy to discern a substantial policy justification for Louisiana's selective "open forum" statute, which exempts only federal maritime and Jones Act claims from the State's general *forum non conveniens* policy. The statute arguably implicates concerns about disruptive local restrictions on maritime commerce that help explain why admiralty has been a federal subject. I am not persuaded, however, that the answer to those concerns lies in an extension of the patchwork maritime pre-emption doctrine. If this Court's maritime pre-emption rulings can be arranged into any pattern, it is a most haphazard one. *See generally* Currie, *Federalism and the Admiralty: "The Devil's Own Mess,"* 1960 S. Ct. Rev. 158. Such a capricious doctrine is unlikely to aid the free flow of commerce, and threatens to have the opposite effect.

In order to decide this case, it is enough to observe that maritime pre-emption doctrine allows state courts to use their own procedures in Savings Clause and Jones Act cases, *see Offshore Logistics, Inc. v. Tallentine,* 477 U.S. 207, 222-223, 106 S. Ct. 2485, 2494-2495, 91 L. Ed. 2d 174 (1986), and that *forum non conveniens* is, as the Court observes, best classified as a kind of secondary venue rule. Equally significant is the fact that Congress, which has unquestioned power to decree uniformity in maritime matters, has declined to set forth a federal forum convenience standard for admiralty cases. *Ante,* at 989-990. It also appears to have withheld from Jones Act defendants the right of removal generally applicable to claims based on federal law. *See* 28 U.S.C. § 1445(a); 46 U.S.C. app. § 688(a); *In re Dutile,* 935 F.2d 61, 62 (CA5 1991). Congress may "determine whether uniformity of regulation is required or diversity is permissible," *Washington,* 264 U.S., at 234, 44 S. Ct., at 307 (BRANDEIS, J., dissenting). When relevant federal legislation indicates that Congress has opted to permit state "diversity" in admiralty matters, a finding of federal pre-emption is inappropriate. Just as in cases involving non-maritime subjects, *see, e.g., Cipollone v. Liggett Group, Inc.,* 505 U.S. —, —, 112 S. Ct. 2608, 2617, 120 L. Ed. 2d 407 (1992), we should not lightly conclude that the federal law of the sea trumps a duly enacted state statute. Instead, we should focus on whether the state provision in question conflicts with some particular substantive rule of federal statutory or common law, or, perhaps, whether federal maritime rules, while not directly inconsistent, so pervade the subject as to preclude application of state law. We should jettison *Jensen's* special maritime pre-emption doctrine and its abstract standards of "proper harmony" and "characteristic features."

The *Jensen* decision and its progeny all rested upon the view that a strong pre-emption doctrine was necessary to vindicate the purpose of the Admiralty Clause to protect maritime commerce from the "unnecessary burdens and disadvantages incident to discordant legislation[.]" *Knickerbocker Ice Co.,* 253 U.S., at 164, 40 S. Ct., at 441. *See also Washington,* 264 U.S., at 228, 44 S. Ct., at 305; *Jensen,* 244 U.S., at 217, 37 S. Ct., at 529. Whether or not this view of the Clause is accurate as a historical matter, *see* Castro, *The Origins of Federal Admiralty Jurisdiction in an Age of Privateers, Smugglers and Pirates,* 37 Am. J. Legal Hist. 117, 154 (1993) (original purpose of Clause was to ensure federal jurisdiction over prize, criminal and revenue cases; private maritime disputes were viewed as matters for state courts), protection of maritime commerce has been a central theme in our admiralty jurisprudence. While I do not propose that we abandon commerce as a guiding concern, we should recognize that, today, the federal interests in free trade and uniformity are amply protected by other means. Most importantly, we now recognize Congress' broad authority under the Commerce Clause to supplant state law with uniform federal statutes. Moreover, state laws that affect maritime commerce, interstate and foreign, are subject to judicial scrutiny under the Commerce Clause. And to the extent that the mere assertion of state judicial power may threaten maritime commerce, the Due Process Clause provides an important measure of protection for out-of-state defendants, especially foreigners. *See Asahi Metal Industry Co. v. Superior Court of California, Solano County,* 480 U.S. 102, 107 S. Ct. 1026, 94 L. Ed. 2d 92 (1987); *Helicopteros Nacionales de Colombia v. Hall,* 466 U.S. 408, 104 S. Ct. 1868, 80 L. Ed. 2d 404 (1984). [FN3] Extension of the ill-advised doctrine of *Jensen* is not the appropriate remedy for unreasonable state venue rules.

Accordingly, I concur in the judgment and in Part II-C of the opinion of the Court.

Justice KENNEDY, with whom Justice THOMAS joins, dissenting.

The Court gives a careful and comprehensive history of the *forum non conveniens* doctrine but, in my respectful view, draws the wrong conclusions from this account and from our precedents. Today's holding contradicts two just and well-accepted principles of admiralty law: uniformity and the elimination of unfair forum selection rules. When hearing cases governed by the federal admiralty and maritime law, the state courts, to be sure, have broad discretion to reject a *forum non conveniens* motion. They should not be permitted, however, to disregard the objection altogether. With due respect, I dissent.

Neither the Court nor respondent is well positioned in this case to contend that the State has some convincing reason to outlaw the *forum non conveniens* objection. For the fact is, though the Court seems unimpressed by the irony, the State of Louisiana commands its courts to entertain the *forum non conveniens* objection in all federal civil cases except for admiralty, the very context in which the rule is most prominent and makes most sense.... Louisiana's expressed interest is to reach out to keep maritime defendants, but not other types of defendants, within its borders, no matter how inconvenient the forum. This state interest is not the sort that should justify any disuniformity in our national admiralty law.

In all events, the Court misapprehends the question it should confront. The issue here is not whether *forum non conveniens* originated in admiralty law, or even whether it is unique to that subject, but instead whether it is an important feature of the uniformity and harmony to which admiralty aspires. *See Southern Pacific Co. v. Jensen*, 244 U.S. 205, 216, 37 S. Ct. 524, 529, 61 L. Ed. 1086 (1917). From the historical evidence, there seems little doubt to me that *forum non conveniens* is an essential and salutary feature of admiralty law. It gives ship owner's and operators a way to avoid vexatious litigation on a distant and unfamiliar shore. By denying this defense in all maritime cases, Louisiana upsets international and interstate comity and obstructs maritime trade. And by sanctioning Louisiana's law, a rule explicable only by some desire to disfavor maritime defendants, the Court condones the forum shopping and disuniformity that the admiralty jurisdiction is supposed to prevent.

In committing their ships to the general maritime trade, owner's and operators run an unusual risk of being sued in venues with little or no connection to the subject matter of the suit. A wage dispute between crewman and captain or an accident on board the vessel may erupt into litigation when the ship docks in a faraway port. Taking jurisdiction in these cases, instead of allowing them to be resolved when the ship returns home, disrupts the schedule of the ship and may aggravate relations with the state from which it hales. *See* Bickel, *The Doctrine of Forum Non Conveniens As Applied in the Federal Courts in Matters of Admiralty*, 35 Cornell L.Q. 12, 20-21 (1949) ("holding a ship and its crew in an American port, to which they may have come to do no more than refuel, may, in the eyes of the nation of the flag be deemed an undue interference with her commerce, and a violation of that comity and delicacy' which in the more courtly days of some of the earlier cases were considered normal among the nations" (footnote omitted)).

From the beginning, American admiralty courts have confronted this problem through the *forum non conveniens* doctrine. As early as 1801, a Pennsylvania District Court declined to take jurisdiction over a wage dispute between a captain and crewman of a Danish ship. *Willendson v. Forsoket*, 29 F. Cas. 1283 (No. 17,682) (Pa. 1801). "It has been my general rule," explained the court, "not to take cognizance of disputes between the masters and crews of foreign ships." *Id.*, at 1284. "Reciprocal policy, and the justice due from one friendly nation to another, calls for such conduct in the courts of either country." *Ibid.*

Dismissals for reasons of comity and *forum non conveniens* were commonplace in the 19th century. *See, e.g., The Infanta*, 13 F. Cas. 37, 39 (No. 7,030) (SDNY 1848) (dismissing claims for wages by two seamen from a British ship; "This court has repeatedly discountenanced actions by foreign seamen against foreign vessels not terminating their voyages at this port, as being calculated to embarrass commercial transactions and relations between this country and others in friendly relations with it");...

Long-time foreign trading partners also recognize the *forum non conveniens* doctrine. The Court notes the doctrine's roots in Scotland. *See La Société du Gaz de Paris v. La Société Anonyme de Navigation "Les Armateurs Français,"* [1926] Sess. Cas. 13 (H.L. 1925) (affirming dismissal of breach of contract claim brought by French manufacturer against French ship owner who had lost the manufacturer's cargo at sea). English courts have followed Scotland, although most often they stay the case rather than dismiss it. *See The Atlantic Star*, [1974] App. Cas. 436 (H.L. 1973) (staying action between a Dutch barge owner and a Dutch ship owner whose vessels had collided in

Belgian waters, pending the outcome of litigation in Antwerp); *The Po*, [1990] 1 Lloyd's Rep. 418 (Q.B. Adm. 1990) (refusing to stay action between Italian ship owner and American ship owner whose vessels had collided in Brazilian waters); *The Lakhta*, [1992] 2 Lloyds Rep. 269 (Q.B. Adm. 1992) (staying title dispute between Latvian plaintiff's and Russian defendant, so that plaintiff's could sue in Russian court). The Canadian Supreme Court has followed England and Scotland. *See Antares Shipping Corp. v. Delmar Shipping Ltd. (The Capricorn)*, [1977] 1 Lloyds Rep. 180, 185 (1976) (citing *Atlantic Star and Société du Gaz*).

From all of the above it should be clear that *forum non conveniens* is an established feature of the general maritime law. To the main point, it serves objectives that go to the vital center of the admiralty pre-emption doctrine. Comity with other nations and among the States was a primary aim of the Constitution. At the time of the framing, it was essential that our prospective foreign trading partners know that the United States would uphold its treaties, respect the general maritime law, and refrain from erecting barriers to commerce. The individual States needed similar assurances from each other. *See* THE FEDERALIST No. 22, pp. 143-145 (C. Rossiter ed. 1961) (Hamilton); MADISON, *Vices of the Political System of the United States*, 2 WRITINGS OF JAMES MADISON 62-363 (G. Hunt ed. 1901). Federal admiralty and maritime jurisdiction was the solution. *See* 2 J. STORY, COMMENTARIES ON THE CONSTITUTION OF THE UNITED STATES § 1672 (5th ed. 1833); The Federalist No. 80, *supra*, at 478 (Hamilton). And so, when the States were allowed to provide common law remedies for *in personam* maritime disputes through the saving to suitors clause, it did not follow that they were at liberty to set aside the fundamental features of admiralty law. "The confusion and difficulty, if vessels were compelled to comply with the local statutes at every port, are not difficult to see.... [T]he Union was formed with the very definite design of freeing maritime commerce from intolerable restrictions incident to such control." *Washington v. W.C. Dawson & Co.*, 264 U.S. 219, 228, 44 S. Ct. 302, 305, 68 L. Ed. 646 (1924). Accord, *The Lottawanna*, 21 Wall. 558, 575, 22 L. Ed. 558 (1875); *Jensen*, 244 U.S., at 215-217, 37 S. Ct., at 528-529.

Louisiana's open forum policy obstructs maritime commerce and runs the additional risk of impairing relations among the states and with our foreign trading partners. These realities cannot be obscured by characterizing the defense as procedural. *See ante*, at 988-989; *but see* Bickel, 35 Cornell L.Q., at 17 ("[T]he *forum non conveniens* problem ... is inescapably connected with the substantive rights of the parties in any given type of suit, rather than ... merely' an 'administrative' problem"). The reverse-*Erie* metaphor, while perhaps of use in other contexts, *see Offshore Logistics, Inc. v. Tallentire*, 477 U.S. 207, 222-223, 106 S. Ct. 2485, 2494-2495, 91 L. Ed. 2d 174 (1986), is not a sure guide for determining when a specific state law has displaced an essential feature of the general maritime law. *See Exxon Corp. v. Chick Kam Choo*, 817 F.2d 307, 319 (CA5 1987) ("drawing conclusions from metaphors is dangerous"). Procedural or substantive, the *forum non conveniens* defense promotes comity and trade. The States are not free to undermine these goals.

It is true that in *Missouri ex rel. Southern R. Co. v. Mayfield*, 340 U.S. 1, 71 S. Ct. 1, 95 L. Ed. 3 (1950), we held the state courts free to ignore *forum non conveniens* in FELA cases. But we did not consider the maritime context. Unlike FELA, a domestic statute controlling domestic markets, the admiralty law is international in its concern. A state court adjudicating a FELA dispute interposes no obstacle to our foreign relations. And while the Jones Act in turn makes FELA available to maritime claimants, that Act says nothing about *forum non conveniens*. *See* 46 U.S.C. app. § 688.

In any event, the Court's ruling extends well beyond the Jones Act; it covers the whole spectrum of maritime litigation. Courts have recognized the *forum non conveniens* defense in a broad range of admiralty disputes: breach of marine insurance contract, *Calavo Growers of Cal. v. Generali Belgium*, 632 F.2d 963 (CA2 1980); collision, *Ocean Shelf Trading, Inc. v. Flota Mercante Grancolumbiana S.A.*, 638 F. Supp. 249 (SDNY 1986); products liability, *Matson Navigation Co. v. Stal-Laval Turbin AB*, 609 F.Supp. 579 (ND Cal. 1985); cargo loss, *The Red Sea Ins. Co. v. S.S. Lucia Del Mar*, 1983 A.M.C. 1630 (SDNY 1982), *aff'd*, 729 F.2d 1443, 1983 A.M.C. 1631 (CA2 1983); and breach of contract for carriage, *Galban Lobo Trading Co. v. Canadian Leader Ltd.*, 1963 A.M.C. 988 (SDNY 1958), to name a few. *See* Brief for Maritime Law Association of the United States as *Amicus Curiae* 12. In all of these cases, federal district courts will now hear *forum non conveniens* motions in the shadow of state courts that refuse to consider it. Knowing that upon dismissal a maritime plaintiff may turn around and sue in one of these state courts, *see Chick Kam Choo v. Exxon Corp.,* 486 U.S. 140, 108 S. Ct. 1684, 100 L. Ed. 2d 127 (1988), a federal court is now in a most difficult position. May it overrule a *forum non conveniens* motion it otherwise would have granted, because the state forum is open? *See Ikospentakis v. Thalassic S.S. Agency,* 915 F.2d 176, 180 (CA5 1990) (reversing the grant of plaintiff's voluntary dismissal motion, because the *forum non conveniens* defense was not available to defendants in the Louisiana court where plaintiff had also sued; refusing "to insist that these foreign appellant's become guinea pigs in an effort to overturn Louisiana's erroneous rule"). Since the Court now makes *forum non conveniens* something of a derelict in maritime law, perhaps it is unconcerned that federal courts may now be retate in which they sit. Under federal maritime principles, I should have thought that the required accommodation was the other way around. The Supreme Court of Texas so understood the force of admiralty; it has ruled that its state courts must entertain a *forum non conveniens* objection despite a Texas statute mandating an open forum. *Exxon Corp. v. Chick Kam Choo,* No. D-1693, — S.W.2d — (Sup. Ct. Tex., Jan. 12, 1994).

The Court does seem to leave open the possibility for a different result if those who raise the *forum non conveniens* objection are of foreign nationality. The Court is entitled, I suppose, to so confine its holding, but no part in its reasoning gives hope for a different result in a case involving foreign parties. The Court's substance-procedure distinction takes no account of the identity of the litigants, nor does the statement that *forum non conveniens* remains "nothing more or less than a supervening venue provision," *ante,* at 988. The Court ought to face up to the consequences of its rule in this regard.

* * *

Notes: Maritime Law Preemption of State Law

1. In *Green v. Industrial Helicopters, Inc.,* 593 So.2d 634, 1992 AMC 1426 (La. 1992) a helicopter passenger brought action against a pilot and his employer to recover for injuries sustained when the helicopter made a crash landing on the high seas 150 miles off the coast of Louisiana. The Louisiana Supreme Court, found the state statute which imposed strict liability was not preempted by federal maritime law.

* * *

The narrow question presented in this case is whether Louisiana Civil Code article 2317,[1] which imposes strict liability for injury causing things in one's custody, is applicable in a case cognizable in admiralty but brought in a Louisiana state court pursuant to the "savings to suitors" clause of the Judiciary Act of 1789 as amended.

* * *

Generally, federal maritime jurisdiction is invoked whenever an accident occurs on the high seas and in furtherance of an activity bearing a significant relationship to a traditional maritime activity. *Offshore Logistics v. Tallentire,* 477 U.S. 207, 106 S. Ct. 2485, 91 L. Ed. 2d 174 (1986); *Executive Jet Aviation, Inc. v. City of Cleveland,* 409 U.S. 249, 93 S. Ct. 493, 34 L. Ed. 2d 454 (1972). The United States Supreme Court has stated that although a helicopter is not a "traditional maritime conveyance", when it is used to ferry passengers from an island to the shore or vice versa it is engaged in a function traditionally performed by waterborne vessels. *Tallentire* 477 U.S. at 217, 106 S. Ct. at 2492.

The United States Constitution grants to federal district courts jurisdiction in all "cases of admiralty and maritime jurisdiction." U.S. Const. art. III, section 2, *Rodrigue v. Legros,* 563 So.2d 248, 251 (La. 1990). State courts, however, have concurrent jurisdiction by virtue of the "savings to suitors" clause of the Judiciary Act of 1789. This case, although within the federal admiralty jurisdiction, is brought in state court pursuant to the savings clause.

It is well settled that by virtue of the savings clause "a state, 'having concurrent jurisdiction, is free to adopt such remedies, and to attach to them such incidents as it sees fit' so long as it does not attempt to make changes in the substantive maritime law." (citations omitted) *Tallentire* 477 U.S. at 221, 106 S. Ct. at 2494. As a general proposition, "[a] maritime claim brought in the common law state courts ... is governed by the same principles as govern actions brought in admiralty, *i.e.,* by federal maritime law." *Powell v. Offshore Navigation, Inc.,*

---

[1] La. C.C. art. 2317 states:

We are responsible, not only for the damage occasioned by our own act, but for that which is caused by the act of persons for whom we are answerable, or of the things which we have in our custody.

* * *

644 F.2d 1063, 1065 n.5 (5th Cir. 1981), *See also* T. Schoenbaum, Admiralty and Maritime Law § 4-1 at 123 (1987) [hereinafter, Schoenbaum]. Since the general maritime law is not a "complete or all inclusive system," a federal court may adopt state statutory law and common law principles as the federal admiralty rule. Schoenbaum, *supra*, § 4-1 at 123. State law and regulations may also supplement federal maritime law when "there is no conflict between the two systems of law, and the need for uniformity of decision does not bar state action". *Id.* at 123.

* * *

... The question whether La. C.C. art. 2317 applies under these circumstances is a *res nova* issue in this court. Nor has the U.S. Supreme Court directly addressed whether strict custodial liability may be part of the general maritime law, nor expressly authorized Louisiana's supplementation in that fashion for cases properly within Louisiana courts' jurisdiction and tried in those courts.

The process of determining the applicability of state law in cases within the admiralty jurisdiction has been described as:

one of accommodation entirely familiar in many areas of overlapping state and federal concern, or a process somewhat analogous to the normal conflict of laws situation where two sovereignties assert divergent interests in a transaction as to which both have some concern. *Kossick, supra at 738.*

Thus, state law may be applied where the state's interest in a matter is greater than the federal interest.

* * *

Louisiana has a strong interest in applying its own law in this case: Plaintiff is a Louisiana resident, Industrial a Louisiana corporation, the pilot a Louisiana resident, and the helicopter was stored in a Louisiana hangar. The contract of carriage between plaintiff's employer and defendants was confected in Louisiana. The mission started in Louisiana and was to end in Louisiana. Plaintiff and defendants, more likely than not, expected to be governed by Louisiana law.

Moreover, La. C.C. art. 2317 embodies a strong social policy to place liability with the owner or custodian of an injury causing thing. This type of liability is not imposed exclusively on helicopter or aircraft owner's. Article 2317 liability is imposed on owner's and custodians of any thing which, because of an unreasonably dangerous condition, causes injury to another. Also, in the personal injury area states have much freedom to provide redress for their citizens.

* * *

Accordingly, a Louisiana state court should respect Louisiana law unless there is some federal impediment to application of that law contained in federal legislation or a clearly applicable rule in the general maritime law. We have found no such impediment or contrary general maritime rule. Rather, the general maritime law authorizes application of state law as a supplement to the general maritime law.

* * *

Contrary to the implication of the court of appeal decision, finding an exact counterpart to strict custodial liability in the general maritime law is not a prerequisite for application of La. C.C. art. 2317. The proper inquiry is whether in this setting strict liability under Louisiana law thwarts the purpose of any specific Congressional pronouncement, or "work[s] material prejudice to the characteristic features of maritime law or interfere[s] with the proper harmony or uniformity of that law in its international and interstate relations". *Western Fuel Co. v. Garcia,* 257 U.S. 233, 42 S. Ct. 89, 66 L. Ed. 210 (1921); *Southern Pacific Co. v. Jensen,* 244 U.S. 205, 37 S. Ct. 524, 61 L. Ed. 1086 (1917).

* * *

The only federal legislation possibly applicable to this incident is Section 1333(a) of OCSLA, and that statute adopts state law as surrogate federal law. The relevant portions of that section state:

To the extent that they are applicable and not inconsistent with ... Federal laws and regulations ... the civil and criminal laws of each adjacent State are hereby declared to be the law of the United States for that portion of the subsoil and seabed of the outer Continental Shelf, and artificial islands and fixed structures erected thereon, (emphasis added) 43 U.S.C.A. 1333(a)2(A).

It appears that OCSLA is not applicable to accidents occurring near a structure located on the outer Continental Shelf. The U.S. Supreme Court has said as much in *Offshore Logistics v. Tallentire,* 477 U.S. 207, 106 S. Ct. 2485, 91 L. Ed. 2d 174 (1986), where the wives of two offshore drilling platform workers, who were killed when the helicopter carrying them from a platform to shore crashed on the high seas, contended that the more generous state law should apply rather than the Death on the High Seas Act (DOHSA). Specifically, the wives argued that state law applied via the state law extension clause of OCSLA because "OCSLA applies to traditionally maritime locales on the high seas, beyond the confines of the platform, when the decedent is a platform worker". *Id.* at 477 U.S. 218, 106 S. Ct. 2492. The U.S. Supreme Court dismissed this argument by stating:

The extension of OCSLA far beyond its intended locale to the accident in this case simply cannot be reconciled with either the narrowly circumscribed area defined by the statute or the statutory prescription that the Act not be construed to affect the high seas which cover the Continental Shelf. Nor can the extension of OCSLA to this case be reconciled with the operative assumption underlying the statute: that admiralty jurisdiction generally should not be extended to accidents in areas covered by OCSLA.

* * *

We do not interpret... 43 U.S.C. § 1333, to require or permit us to extend the coverage of the statute to the platform workers in this case who were killed miles away from the platform and on the high seas simply because they were platform workers. *Id.* 477 U.S. at 218, 106 S. Ct. at 2492....

Absent a clearly applicable act of Congress—and there is none here—we next look to the general maritime law to determine if application of La. C.C. art. 2317 would materially prejudice the "characteristic features of maritime law".

* * *

The U.S. Supreme Court has not addressed whether non-seamen passengers aboard a vessel have an action for unseaworthiness. Lower federal courts, however, have held that the basis of recovery of damages from a carrier for personal injury to a passenger is predicated on the theory of negligence. M. Norris, The Law of Maritime Personal Injuries 4th Ed. § 3:4 at 63 (1990) [hereinafter, Norris].

The latter are among the cases upon which the court of appeal in this case bases its conclusion, and Industrial relies, for its position that Article 2317 conflicts with the general maritime law. The argument is not without some appeal. However, it does not take into account that general maritime law distinctly authorizes application of supplementary state law in some situations. In our considered judgment, the general maritime law authorizes application of state law under the circumstances of this case.

Although the passenger-carrier cases referred to above are somewhat analogous there is this important difference. Those cases involved passengers aboard vessels. And the need for uniformity under the general maritime law is prompted primarily by concern regarding maritime shipping and commerce involving vessels. The U.S. Supreme Court has declared that helicopters and other aircraft are not vessels, and commentators have urged that aircraft should not be treated like vessels. *Offshore Logistics v. Tallentire, supra, Smith v. Pan Air Corp.,* 684 F.2d 1102 (5th Cir. 1982); *See also Schoenbaum, supra,* § 3-6 at 80; R. Greco, Aircraft. As Vessels Under the Jones Act and General Maritime Law, 22 S. Tex. L.J. 595 (1982); Comment, *Admiralty Jurisdiction: Airplanes and Wrongful Death in Territorial Waters,* 64 Columbia Law Review 1084, 1089 n.51-56 (1964). Aircraft are designed to cope with the perils of the air rather than the hazards of the sea. *Barger v. Petroleum Helicopters, Inc.,* 692 F.2d 337 (5th Cir. 1982), *rehearing denied* 698 F.2d 1216 (5th Cir. 1983). The U.S. Supreme Court in *Executive Jet Aviation, Inc. v. City of Cleveland, Ohio,* 409 U.S. 249, 93 S. Ct. 493, 34 L. Ed. 2d 454 (1972) "noted that substantive maritime law has developed to serve a specialized industry, the transportation of goods and persons by water. Although aviation has, to some extent, supplanted this traditional maritime activity, the ancient body of substantive law tailored to fit the needs of vessels and mariners was not suited to the problems of aircraft and aviation". J. Forney and M. Sydow, *Admiralty Jurisdiction Over Injuries to Offshore Workers: A Call for Reconsideration of Robison* 22 S. Tex. L.J. 461, 463 (1982). Had the helicopter crashed on land soon after taking off from Milton, Louisiana, without question a Louisiana court hearing the case could and should apply La. C.C. art. 2317.

Moreover, there is in the general maritime law no prohibition against strict liability. On the contrary, the general maritime law embraces strict liability in various forms. Most recently the U.S. Supreme Court has recognized "products liability, including strict liability, as part of the general maritime law." *East River S.S. Corp. v. Transamerica Delaval,* 476 U.S. 858, 106 S. Ct. 2295, 90 L. Ed. 2d 865 (1986). The rationale that "strict liability should be imposed on the party best able to protect persons from hazardous equipment" applies equally to strict products liability claims. *Id.* 476 U.S. at 866, 106 S. Ct. 2299. Another form of strict liability recognized in the general maritime law is the above discussed seaman's action for unseaworthiness. Given the lack of maritime rule clearly applicable to a helicopter crash on the high seas and the recognition of liability in the absence of fault in the general maritime law, strict custodial liability embodied in Louisiana Civil Code article 2317 cannot be said to "materially prejudice" characteristic features of the general maritime law

* * *

In summary we conclude that there is no applicable contrary federal legislation and that La. C.C. art. 2317 neither prejudices the characteristic features of the general maritime law nor interferes impermissibly with any required uniformity in such law.

WATSON, Justice, Concurring

In the field of personal injury, state law may supplement general maritime law. *Gulf Offshore Co. v. Mobil Oil Corp.,* 453 U.S. 473, 101 S. Ct. 2870, 69 L. Ed. 2d 784 (1981). Louisiana's law of strict liability applies to injuries on the outer continental shelf off the shores of Louisiana. *Olsen v. Shell Oil Company,* 365 So.2d 1285 (La. 1978). Only when there are deaths on the high seas does DOHSA preempt state law. *Tallentire; Smith v. Pan Air Corp.,* 684 F.2d 1102 (5th Cir. 1982).

I concur to note that the majority's analysis of OCSLA may err in drawing a bright line of demarcation between platform injuries and high sea injuries. In *Tallentire,* the platform workers were killed miles away from the platform. By its terms, OCSLA's scope is not limited to platforms. A platform worker who is injured in the water near a rig has maritime situs. *Executive Jet Aviation v. Cleveland,* 409 U.S. 249, 93 S. Ct. 493, 34 L. Ed. 2d 454 (1972). However, the worker may lack maritime status. *Rodrigue v. Aetna Casualty & Surety Co.,* 395 U.S. 352, 23 L. Ed. 2d 360, 89 S. Ct. 1835 (1969); *Herb's Welding, Inc. v. Gray,* 470 U.S. 414, 105 S. Ct. 1421, 84 L. Ed. 2d 406 (1985). Therefore, a platform worker's injuries in the water are not necessarily maritime and may be covered by OCSLA.

* * *

2. Offshore Conflicts

Oil and gas exploration and production activities in the Gulf of Mexico and in other areas give rise to situations where courts must determine whether federal or state law applies. *See, e.g., Demette v. Falcon Drilling Co., Inc.,* 280 F.3d 492, 2002 AMC 686 (5th Cir. 2002).

3. The United States Supreme Court has held that the savings clause in the Federal Boat Safety Act, 46 U.S.C. §§ 4301-4311 that saves state common law actions is not preempted by the Act or by the decision of the Coast Guard, which is given regulatory authority under the Act, not to promulgate a regulation requiring propeller guards on motorboats. *Sprietsma v. Mercury Marine,* 537 U.S. 51, 123 S.Ct. 518, 154 L.Ed.2d 466 (2002). In a wrongful death action in products liability and negligence based on an recreational boating accident on navigable waters, what is the source of the "common law action" that is saved, federal maritime law or state law?

G. Federal Judicial System

1. Admiralty Jurisdiction

ROMERO v. INTERNATIONAL TERMINAL OPERATING CO.

358 U.S. 354, 79 S. Ct. 468, 3 L. Ed. 2d 368 (1959)

Mr. Justice FRANKFURTER delivered the opinion of the Court

Petitioner Francisco Romero, a Spanish subject, signed on as a member of the crew of the *S.S. Guadalupe* for a voyage beginning about October 10, 1953. The *Guadalupe* was of Spanish registry, sailed under the Spanish flag and was owned by respondent Compania Trasatlantica (also known as Spanish Line), a Spanish corporation. At the completion of the voyage for which he signed, Romero continued uninterruptedly to work on the *Guadalupe.* Thereby, under the law of Spain, the terms and conditions of the original contract of hire remained in force. Subsequently the *S.S. Guadalupe* departed from the port of Bilbao in northern Spain, touched briefly at other Spanish ports, and sailed to the port of New York at Hoboken. From here the ship made a brief trip to the ports of Vera Cruz and Havana returning to Hoboken where, on May 12, 1954, Romero was seriously injured when struck by a cable on the deck of the *Guadalupe.* Thereupon petitioner filed suit on the law side of the District Court for the Southern District of New York.

The amended complaint claimed damages from four separate corporate defendants. Liability of Compania Trasatlantica and Garcia & Diaz, Inc., a New York corporation which acted as the husbanding agent for Compania's vessels while in the port of New York, was asserted under the Jones Act, 41 Stat. 1007, 46 U.S.C. § 688, and under the general maritime law of the United States for unseaworthiness of the ship, maintenance and cure[2] and a maritime tort. Liability for a maritime tort was alleged against respondents International Terminal Operating Co. and Quin Lumber Co. These two companies were working on board the *S.S. Guadalupe* at the time of the injury pursuant to oral contracts with Garcia & Diaz, Inc. Quin, a New York corporation, was engaged in carpentry work

---

[2] The claim for maintenance and cure under the general maritime law included an amount for wages to the end of the voyage. We have not before us an independent claim for wages due and therefore need express no opinion on such a claim by one in petitioner's position.

preparatory to the receipt of a cargo of grain. International Terminal, incorporated in Delaware, was employed as stevedore to load the cargo. The jurisdiction of the District Court was invoked under the Jones Act and §§ 1331[3] and 1332[4] of the Judicial Code, 28 U.S.C.

Following a pre-trial hearing the District Court dismissed the complaint. 142 F. Supp. 570.[5] The court held that the action under the Jones Act against Compania Trasatlantica must be dismissed for lack of jurisdiction since that Act provided no right of action for an alien seaman against a foreign shipowner under the circumstances detailed above. The claims under the general maritime law against Compania also were dismissed since the parties were not of diverse citizenship and 28 U.S.C. § 1331 did not confer jurisdiction on the federal law courts over claims rooted in federal maritime law. The District Court dismissed the Jones Act claim against Garcia & Diaz, Inc., pursuant to its finding that Garcia was not the employer of Romero nor, as a husbanding agent for Compania, did it have the operation and control of the vessel. The remaining claims, including those against the other respondents, were dismissed because of lack of the requisite complete diversity under the rule of *Strawbridge v. Curtiss*, 3 Cranch 267. Upon examination of the Spanish law the district judge also declined jurisdiction "even in admiralty as a matter of discretion." 142 F. Supp., at 574. The Spanish law provides Romero with a lifetime pension of 35% to 55% of his seamans wages which may be increased by one-half if the negligence of the shipowner is established; it also allows the recovery of the Spanish counterpart of maintenance and cure. These rights under the Spanish law may be enforced through the Spanish consul in New York.

The Court of Appeals affirmed the dismissal of the complaint, 244 F.2d 409. We granted certiorari, 355 U.S. 807, because of the conflict among Courts of Appeals as to the proper construction of the relevant provision of the Judiciary Act of 1875 (now 28 U.S.C. § 1331) and because of questions raised regarding the applicability of *Lauritzen v. Larsen*, 345 U.S. 571, to the situation before us. The case was argued during the last Term and restored to the calendar for reargument during the present Term. 356 U.S. 955.

I. Jurisdiction

(a) *Jurisdiction under the Jones Act.*— The District Court dismissed petitioner s Jones Act claims for lack of jurisdiction. "As frequently happens where jurisdiction depends on subject matter, the question whether jurisdiction exists has been confused with the question whether the complaint states a cause of action." *Montana-Dakota Utilities Co. v. Northwestern Public Service Co.*, 341 U.S. 246, 249. Petitioner asserts a substantial claim that the Jones Act affords him a right of recovery for the negligence of his employer. Such assertion alone is sufficient to empower the District Court to assume jurisdiction over the case and determine whether, in fact, the Act does provide the claimed rights. "A cause of action under our law was asserted here, and the court had power to determine whether it was or was not well founded in law and in fact." *Lauritzen v. Larsen*, 345 U.S. 571, 575.

(b) *Jurisdiction under 28 U.S.C. § 1331.*— Petitioner, a Spanish subject, asserts claims under the general maritime law against Compania Trasatlantica, a Spanish corporation. The jurisdiction of the Federal District Court, sitting as a court of law, was invoked under the provisions of the Judiciary Act of 1875 which granted jurisdiction to the lower federal courts "of all suits of a civil nature at common law or in equity, ... arising under the Constitution

---

[3] "The district courts shall have original jurisdiction of all civil actions wherein the matter in controversy ... arises under the Constitution, laws or treaties of the United States."

[4] "(a) The district courts shall have original jurisdiction of all civil actions where the matter in controversy ... is between:
* * *
"(2) Citizens of a State, and foreign state or citizens or subjects thereof;"

[5] Prior to the commencement of the trial respondents moved to dismiss the complaint on the ground that the District Court lacked "jurisdiction" over the subject matter. The answers of some of the respondents also contained motions to dismiss for failure to state a claim upon which relief can be granted. A pre-trial hearing on the issue of "jurisdiction" was held and the complaint was claim was stated upon which relief can be granted. Fed. Rules Civ. Proc., 12(d). Although the court considered evidence outside the pleadings, Federal Rule 12(c) allows such evidence to be admitted, requiring the court then to treat the motion as one for summary judgment under Rule 56. Summary judgment is proper if "there is no genuine issue as to any material fact and ... the moving party is entitled to a judgment as a matter of law." Fed. Rules Civ. Proc., 56(c). The determinations made by the District Court, in the course of its hearing on jurisdiction, insofar as they are relevant to our disposition, were within the properly conceived scope of Rule 56. Since all the requirements of Rule 12(c), relating to a hearing on a motion for judgment on the pleadings, were satisfied and the findings made were properly relevant to such a hearing, we need not restrict our disposition to the issue of "jurisdiction" merely because the proceedings below were inartistically labeled.

or laws of the United States,..." (now 28 U.S.C. § 1331).[6] Whether the Act of 1875 permits maritime claims rooted in federal law to be brought on the law side of the lower federal courts has recently been raised in litigation and has become the subject of conflicting decisions among Courts of Appeals.

* * *

Article III, § 2, cl. 1 (3d provision) of the Constitution and section 9 of he Act of September 24, 1789, have from the beginning been the sources of jurisdiction in litigation based upon federal maritime law. Article III impliedly contained three grants. (1) It empowered Congress to confer admiralty and maritime jurisdiction on the "Tribunals inferior to the Supreme Court" which were authorized by Art. I, § 8, cl 9. (2) It empowered the federal courts in their exercise of the admiralty and maritime jurisdiction which had been conferred on them, to draw on the substantive law "inherent in the admiralty and maritime jurisdiction," *Crowell v. Benson*, 285 U.S. 22, 55, and to continue the development of this law within constitutional limits. (3) It empowered Congress to revise and supplement the maritime law within the limits of the Constitution. *See Crowell v. Benson, supra,* at 55.

* * *

Section 9 not only established federal courts for the administration of maritime law; it recognized that some remedies in matters maritime had been traditionally administered by common-law courts of the original States.[12] This role of the States in the administration of maritime law was preserved in the famous "saving clause"—"saving to suitors, in all cases, the right of a common-law remedy, where the common law is competent to give it."[13] Since the original Judiciary Act also endowed the federal courts with diversity jurisdiction, common-law remedies for maritime causes could be enforced by the then Circuit Courts when the proper diversity of parties afforded access.

Up to the passage of the Judiciary Act of 1875[14] these jurisdictional bases provided the only claim for jurisdiction in the federal courts in maritime matters.[15] The District Courts, endowed with "exclusive original cognizance of all civil causes of admiralty and maritime jurisdiction," sat to enforce the comprehensive federal interest in the law of the sea which had been a major reason for their creation. This jurisdiction was exercised according to the historic procedure in admiralty, by a judge without a jury. In addition, common-law remedies were, under the saving clause, enforcible in the courts of the States and on the common-law side of the lower federal courts when the diverse citizenship of the parties permitted. Except in diversity cases, maritime litigation brought in state courts could not be removed to the federal courts.[16]

The Judiciary Act of 1875 effected an extensive enlargement of the jurisdiction of the lower federal courts. For the first time their doors were opened to "all suits of a civil nature at common law or in equity, ... arising under the Constitution or laws of the United States, or treaties made, or which shall be made, under their authority...."[17] From 1875 to 1950 there is not to be found a hint or suggestion to cast doubt on the conviction that the language of that statute was taken straight from Art. III, § 2, cl. 1, extending the judicial power of the United States "to all Cases, in Law and Equity, arising under this Constitution, the Laws of the United States, and Treaties made, or which shall be made, under their Authority." Indeed what little legislative history there is affirmatively indicates that this was the source.[18] Thus the Act of 1875 drew on the scope of this provision of Clause 1, just as the Judiciary Act of 1789 reflected the constitutional authorization of Clause 1 of Section 2, which extended the judicial power "to all Cases of admiralty and maritime Jurisdiction."

---

[6] Act of March 3, 1875, §1,18 Stat. 470. The modifications of language to be found in the present version of this Act, 28 U.S.C. § 1331, were not intended to change in anyway the meaning or content of the Act of 1875. *See* Reviser's Note to 28 U.S.C. § 1331. The recent amendments to this Act, 72 Stat. 415, affected only jurisdictional amount and are not relevant here. *See* 958 U.S. Code Cong. & Admin. News 2333, 85th Cong., 2d Sess.

[12] *See New Jersey Steam Navigation Co. v. Merchants' Bank of Boston,* 6 How. 344, 390; *The Hamilton,* 207 U.S. 398, 404; *2 Story, Commentaries on the Constitution of the United States,* § 1672. *See also Dodd, The New Doctrine of the Supremacy of Admiralty Over the Common Law,* 21 Col. L. Rev. 647 (1921); *Black, Admiralty Jurisdiction: Critique and Suggestions,* 50 Col. L. Rev. 259 (1950).

[13] *Act of Sept. 24, 1789,* § 9, 1 Stat. 76.

[14] Act of Mar. 3, 1875, 18 Stat. 470.

[15] *The Belfast,* 7 Wall. 624, 644; *Leon v. Galceran,* 11 Wall. 185, 188.

[16] The removal provisions of the original Judiciary Act of 1789, 1 Stat. 79, conferred a limited removal jurisdiction, not including cases of admiralty and maritime jurisdiction. In none of the statutes enacted since that time have saving-clause cases been made removable.

[17] Of course federal question jurisdiction was granted in the abortive Act of Feb. 13, 1801, § 11, 2 Stat. 92, repealed by Act of March 8, 1802, 2 Stat. 132.

[18] *See* 2 Cong. Rec. 4986-4987; Frankfurter and Landis, The Business of the Supreme Court (1928), 65-69.

These provisions of Article III are two of the nine separately enumerated classes of cases to which "judicial power" was extended by the Constitution and which thereby authorized grants by Congress of "judicial Power" to the "inferior" federal courts. The vast stream of litigation which has flowed through these courts from the beginning has done so on the assumption that, in dealing with a subject as technical as the jurisdiction of the courts, the Framers, predominantly lawyers, used precise, differentiating and not redundant language. This assumption, reflected in The Federalist Papers,[19] was authoritatively confirmed by Mr. Chief Justice Marshall in *American Ins. Co. v. Canter*, 1 Pet. 511, 544:

> We are therefore to inquire, whether cases in admiralty, and cases arising under the laws and Constitution of the United States, are identical.
>
> If we have recourse to that pure fountain from which all the jurisdiction of the Federal Courts is derived, we find language employed which cannot well be misunderstood. The Constitution declares, that 'the judicial power shall extend to all cases in law and equity, arising under this Constitution, the laws of the United States, and treaties made, or which shall be made, under their authority; to all cases affecting ambassadors, or other public ministers, and consuls; to all cases of admiralty and maritime jurisdiction.
>
> The Constitution certainly contemplates these as three distinct classes of cases; and if they are distinct, the grant of jurisdiction over one of them does not confer jurisdiction over either of the other two. The discrimination made between them, in the Constitution, is, we think, conclusive against their identity.

See also The Sarah, 8 Wheat. 391.

This lucid principle of constitutional construction, embodied in one of Marshall's frequently quoted opinions, was never brought into question until 1952.[20] It had been treated as black-letter law in leading treatises.[21] It was part of the realm of legal ideas in which the authors of the Act of 1875 moved. Certainly the accomplished lawyers who drafted the Act of 1875[22] drew on the language of the constitutional grant on the assumption that they were dealing with a distinct class of cases, that the language incorporated in their enactment precluded "identity" with any other class of cases contained in Article III. Thus the grant of jurisdiction over "suits of a civil nature at common law or in equity ... arising under the Constitution or laws of the United States...," in the Act of 1875, as derived from Article III, could not reasonably be thought of as comprehending an entirely separate and distinct class of cases— "Cases of admiralty and maritime Jurisdiction."[23]

---

[19] *See* The Federalist, No. 80 (Hamilton), note 8, *supra.*

[20] *See* treatises cited in Appendix, *post*, p. 385. Lack of clarity in Marshall's opinion was suggested in *Doucette v. Vincent*, 194 F.2d 834, 843-844, n.8.

[21] *E.g.*, Abbott in his treatise on the United States Courts and their Practice (3d ed. 1877), 60, discusses the Marshall formulation:

> The several cases to which the judicial power extends are to be regarded as independent, in the sense that any one clause is sufficient to sustain jurisdiction in a case to which it applies, and that it is neither restrained nor enlarged by the other clauses, with the exception of the restraint imposed by amendment XI....

The author then discusses the classes of cases in Article III, concluding

> The grant of jurisdiction over one of these classes does not confer jurisdiction over either of the others; the discrimination is conclusive against their identity. A case of admiralty and maritime jurisdiction is not to be regarded as one 'arising under the Constitution and laws of the United States,' merely because the exercise of judicial power in maritime cases is provided for in the Constitution and laws. (*Citing American Ins. Co. v. Canter.*)

See also Spear, The Law of the Federal Judiciary (1883), 46. Discussing the admiralty and maritime jurisdiction as granted by the Constitution, the author says:

> The cases coming within this jurisdiction, as referred to in the Constitution, are not identical with, or embraced in, the cases of law and equity referred to in the same instrument, as arising under the Constitution, laws, or treaties of the United States. They belong to a different category, and are provided for by a distinct and specific grant of judicial power.

He then quotes from Marshall's opinion in *Canter.*

[22] The provision of the Act of 1875 under scrutiny originated in the Senate. The bill was sponsored and managed by Senator Matthew Hale Carpenter of Wisconsin. Its authorship has been attributed to him. 7 Reports of the Wisconsin State Bar Association 155, 186. On his death the bar journal of his state wrote that "his love of and devotion to legal studies and pursuits— not as objects but as subjects—were the controlling passions of his life....

> ... Such, however, was the devotion of Mr. Carpenter to his profession that his election to the United States [S]enate seemed to be a matter of gratification principally for the broader field of professional labors which it enabled him to cultivate.... 1 Reports of Wisconsin State Bar Association 227.

[23] All suits involving maritime claims, regardless of the remedy sought, are cases of admiralty and maritime jurisdiction within the meaning of Article III whether they are asserted in the federal courts or, under the saving clause, in the state courts. Romero's claims for damages under the general maritime law are a case of admiralty and maritime jurisdiction. The substantive law on which these claims are based derives from the third provision of Art. III, § 2, cl. 1. Without that constitutional grant Romero would have no federal claim to assert. *Cf.* 2 Story, Commentaries on the Constitution of the United States, § 1672.

Of course all cases to which "judicial power" extends "arise," in a comprehensive, non-jurisdictional sense of the term, "under this Constitution." It is the Constitution that is the ultimate source of all "judicial Power"—defines grants and implies limits—and so "all Cases of admiralty and maritime Jurisdiction" arise under the Constitution in the sense that they have constitutional sanction. But they are not "Cases, in Law and Equity, arising under this Constitution, the Laws of the United States...."

Not only does language and construction point to the rejection of any infusion of general maritime jurisdiction into the Act of 1875, but history and reason powerfully support that rejection. The far-reaching extension of national power resulting from the victory of the North, and the concomitant utilization of federal courts for the vindication of that power in the Reconstruction Era, naturally led to enlarged jurisdiction of the federal courts over federal rights. But neither the aim of the Act of 1875 to provide a forum for the vindication of new federally created rights, nor the pressures which led to its enactment, suggest, even remotely, the inclusion of maritime claims within the scope of that statute. The provision of the Act of 1875 with which we are concerned was designed to give a new content of jurisdiction to the federal courts, not to reaffirm one long-established, smoothly functioning since 1789.[24] We have uncovered no basis for finding the additional design of changing the method by which federal courts had administered admiralty law from the beginning. The federal admiralty courts had been completely adequate to the task of protecting maritime rights rooted in federal law. There is not the slightest indication of any intention, or of any professional or lay demands for a change in the time-sanctioned mode of trying suits in admiralty without a jury, from which it can be inferred that by the new grant of jurisdiction of cases "arising under the Constitution or laws" a drastic innovation was impliedly introduced in admiralty procedure, whereby Congress changed the method by which federal courts had administered admiralty law for almost a century. To draw such an inference is to find that a revolutionary procedural change had undesignedly come to pass. If we are now to attribute such a result to Congress the sole remaining justification for the federal admiralty courts which have played such a vital role in our federal judicial system for 169 years will be to provide a federal forum for the small number of maritime claims which derive from state law, and to afford the ancient remedy of a libel *in rem* in those limited instances when an *in personam* judgment would not suffice to satisfy a claim.[25]

* * *

Petitioner now asks us to hold that no student of the jurisdiction of the federal courts or of admiralty, no judge, and none of the learned and alert members of the admiralty bar were able, for seventy-five years, to discern the drastic change now asserted to have been contrived in admiralty jurisdiction by the Act of 1875. In light of such impressive testimony from the past the claim of a sudden discovery of a hidden latent meaning in an old technical phrase is surely suspect.

The history of archeology is replete with the unearthing of riches buried for centuries. Our legal history does not, however, offer a single archeological discovery of new, revolutionary meaning in reading an old judiciary enactment.[27a] The presumption is powerful that such a far-reaching, dislocating construction as petitioner would now have us find in the Act of 1875 was not uncovered by judges, lawyers or scholars for seventy-five years because it is not there.

It is also significant that in the entire history of federal maritime legislation, whether before the passage of the Act of 1875 (*e.g.*, the Great Lakes Act—also a general jurisdictional statute and one often termed an anomaly in the maritime law because of its jury trial provision), or after (the Jones Act), Congress has not once left the availability

---

[24] *See* FRANKFURTER AND LANDIS, THE BUSINESS OF THE SUPREME COURT (1928), 64-65; Chadbourn and Levin, *Original Jurisdiction of Federal Questions*, 90 U. of Pa. L. Rev. 639, 644-645 (1942).

[25] Of course, in a few instances, Congress has provided the federal admiralty courts with a specific statutory jurisdiction. *E.g.*, Death on the High Seas Act, 41 Stat. 537 (1920), 46 U.S.C. §§ 761-767.

[27a] For reasons that would take us too far afield to discuss, *Erie R. Co. v. Tompkins*, 304 U.S. 64, is no exception.

of a trial on the law side to inference. It has made specific provision.[28] It is difficult to accept that in 1875, and in 1875 alone, a most far-reaching change was made subterraneously.

Not only would the infusion of general maritime jurisdiction into the Act of 1875 disregard the obvious construction of that statute. Important difficulties of judicial policy would flow from such an interpretation, an interpretation which would have a disruptive effect on the traditional allocation of power over maritime affairs in our federal system.

Thus the historic option of a maritime suitor pursuing a common-law remedy to select his forum, state or federal, would be taken away by an expanded view of § 1331,[29] since saving-clause actions would then be freely removable under § 1441 of Title 28.[30] The interpretation of the Act of 1875 contended for would have consequences more deeply felt than the elimination of a suitors traditional choice of forum. By making maritime cases removable to the federal courts it would make considerable inroads into the traditionally exercised concurrent jurisdiction of the state courts in admiralty matters—a jurisdiction which it was the unquestioned aim of the saving clause of 1789 to preserve. This disruption of principle is emphasized by the few cases actually involved.[31] This small number of cases is only important in that it negatives the pressure of any practical consideration for the subversion of a principle so long-established and so deeply rooted. The role of the States in the development of maritime law is a role whose significance is rooted in the Judiciary Act of 1789 and the decisions of this Court.[32] Recognition of the part the States have played from the beginning has a dual significance. It indicates the extent to which an expanded view of the Act of 1875 would eviscerate the postulates of the saving clause, and it undermines the theoretical basis for giving the Act of 1875 a brand new meaning.

Although the corpus of admiralty law is federal in the sense that it derives from the implications of Article III evolved by the courts, to claim that all enforced rights pertaining to matters maritime are rooted in federal law is a destructive oversimplification of the highly intricate interplay of the States and the National Government in their regulation of maritime commerce. It is true that state law must yield to the needs of a uniform federal maritime law when this Court finds inroads on a harmonious system.[33] But this limitation still leaves the States a wide scope. State-created liens are enforced in admiralty.[34] State remedies for wrongful death and state statutes providing for the survival of actions, both historically absent from the relief offered by the admiralty,[35] have been upheld when applied to maritime causes of action.[36] Federal courts have enforced these statutes.[37] State rules for the partition and sale of ships,[38] state laws governing the specific performance of arbitration agreements,[39] state laws regulating the effect of a breach of warranty under contracts of maritime insurance[40]—all these laws and others have been accepted as rules of decision in admiralty cases, even, at times, when they conflicted with a rule of maritime law which did not require uniformity. "In the field of maritime contracts," this Court has said, "as in that of maritime

---

[28] Such provisions are in the Jones Act, 41 Stat. 1007 (1920), 46 U.S.C. § 688, and in the Great Lakes Act, 5 Stat. 726 (1845), 28 U.S.C. § 1873. Neither the Suits in Admiralty Act of 1920, 41 Stat. 525, 46 U.S.C. § 741-752, nor the Death on the High Seas Act, 41 Stat. 537 (1920), 46 U.S.C. §§ 761-767, allows a jury trial in personal injury cases. When the Death on the High Seas Act was being debated it was stated that "That question was thrashed out and it was decided best not to incorporate into this bill a jury trial because of the difficulties in admiralty proceedings." Congressman Igoe, speaking for the Judiciary Committee, 59 Cong. Rec. 4482, 60th Cong., 2d Sess. (1920).

[29] The policy of unremovability of maritime claims brought in the state courts was incorporated by Congress into the Jones Act. *See Pate v. Standard Dredging Corp.,* 193 F.2d 498 (C.A. 5th Cir. 1952).

[30] 28 U.S.C. § 1441 (b): "Any civil action of which the district courts have original jurisdiction founded on a claim or right arising under the Constitution, treaties or laws of the United States shall be removable without regard to the citizenship or residence of the parties."

[31] *See* the compilation of state court cases in Seventh 5-Year Index-Digest of American Maritime Cases, 1953-1957 (1957), XLIII-XLVIII.

[32] *See, e.g., Madruga v. Superior Court of California,* 346 U.S. 556, 560-561: "[T] he jurisdictional act [the Act of 1789] does leave state courts 'competent' to adjudicate maritime causes of action in proceedings *In personam....* [T]his Court has said that a state, 'having concurrent jurisdiction, is free to adopt such remedies, and to attach to them such incidents, as it sees fit' so long as it does not attempt to make changes in the 'substantive maritime law.' *Red Cross Line v. Atlantic Fruit Co.,* 264 U.S. 109."

[33] *Southern Pacific Co. v. Jensen,* 244 U.S. 205; *Garrett v. Moore-McCormack Co.,* 317 U.S. 239; *Pope & Talbot, Inc., v. Hawn,* 346 U.S. 406. See *Maryland Casualty Co. v. Cushing,* 347 U.S. 409.

[34] *Vancouver S. S. Co., Ltd., v. Rice,* 288 U.S. 445; *Peyroux v. Howard,* 7 Pet. 324. See also *Edwards v. Elliott,* 21 Wall. 532.

[35] *The Harrisburg,* 119 U.S. 199. "Death is a composer of strife by the general law of the sea as it was for many centuries by the common law of the land." CARDOZO, J., in *Cortes v. Baltimore Insular Line, Inc.,* 287 U.S. 367, 371.

[36] *The Hamilton,* 207 U.S. 398; *Western Fuel Co. v. Garcia,* 257 U.S. 233; *Just v. Chambers,* 312 U.S. 383.

[37] *The Hamilton, supra,* *Just v. Chambers, supra,* *Western Fuel Co. v. Garcia, supra.*

[38] *Madruga v. Superior Court of California,* 346 U.S. 556.

[39] *Red Cross Line v. Atlantic Fruit Co.,* 264 U.S. 109.

[40] *Wilburn Boat Co. v. Firemans Fund Ins. Co.,* 348 U.S. 310.

torts, the National Government has left much regulatory power in the States."[41] Thus, if one thing is clear it is that the source of law in saving-clause actions cannot be described in absolute terms. Maritime law is not a monistic system. The State and Federal Government's jointly exert regulatory powers today as they have played joint roles in the development of maritime law throughout our history.[42] This sharing of competence in one aspect of our federalism has been traditionally embodied in the saving clause of the Act of 1789. Here, as is so often true in our federal system, allocations of jurisdiction have been carefully wrought to correspond to the realities of power and interest and national policy. To give a novel sweep to the Act would disrupt traditional maritime policies and quite gratuitously disturb a complementary, historic interacting federal-state relationship.

An infusion of general maritime jurisdiction into the "federal question" grant would not occasion merely an isolated change; it would generate many new complicated problems. If jurisdiction of maritime claims were allowed to be invoked under § 1331, it would become necessary for courts to decide whether the action "arises under federal law," and this jurisdictional decision would largely depend on whether the governing law is state or federal. Determinations of this nature are among the most difficult and subtle that federal courts are called upon to make.[43] Last Term's decision in *McAllister v. Magnolia Petroleum Co.*, 357 U.S. 221, illustrates the difficulties raised by the attempted application of a state statute of limitations to maritime personal injury actions. These problems result from the effort to fit state laws into the scheme of federal maritime law.

These difficulties, while nourishing academic speculation, have rarely confronted the courts. This Court has been able to wait until an actual conflict between state and federal standards has arisen, and only then proceed to resolve the problem of whether the State was free to regulate or federal law must govern. For example, if a State allowed the survival of a cause of action based on unseaworthiness as defined in the maritime law it was immaterial whether the standard was federal and governed by decisions of this Court, or was subject to state variations.[44] Thus we have been able to deal with such conceptual problems in the context of a specific conflict and a specific application of policy, as is so well illustrated by the *McAllister* case. However, such practical considerations for adjudication would be unavailable under an expanded view of § 1331. Federal courts would be forced to determine the respective spheres of state and federal legislative competence, the source of the governing law, as a preliminary question of jurisdiction; for only if the applicable law is "federal" law would jurisdiction be proper under § 1331. The necessity for jurisdictional determinations couched in terms of "state" or "federal law" would destroy that salutary flexibility which enables the courts to deal with source-of-law problems in light of the necessities illuminated by the particular question to be answered. Certainly sound judicial policy does not encourage a situation which necessitates constant adjudication of the boundaries of state and federal competence.

Typical also of the consequences that are implicit in this proposed modification of maritime jurisdiction, is the restriction of venue that would result from this novel interpretation of § 1331 of the Act of 1875. Litigants of

---

[41] *Id.,* at 313.

[42] "The grounds of objection to the admiralty jurisdiction in enforcing liability for wrongful death were similar to those urged here; that is, that the Constitution presupposes a body of maritime law, that this law, as a matter of interstate and international concern, requires harmony in its administration and cannot be subject to defeat or impairment by the diverse legislation of the States, and hence that Congress alone can make any needed changes in the general rules of the maritime law. But these contentions proved unavailing and the principle was maintained that a State, in the exercise of its police power, may establish rules applicable on land and water within its limits, even though these rules incidentally affect maritime affairs, provided that the state action 'does not contravene any acts of Congress, nor work any prejudice to the characteristic features of the maritime law, nor interfere with its proper harmony and uniformity in its international and interstate relations.' It was decided that the state legislation encountered none of these objections. The many instances in which state action had created new rights, recognized and enforced in admiralty, were set forth in *The City of Norwalk*, and reference was also made to the numerous local regulations under state authority concerning the navigation of rivers and harbors. There was the further pertinent observation that the maritime law was not a complete and perfect system and that in all maritime countries there is a considerable body of municipal law that underlies the maritime law as the basis of its administration. These views find abundant support in the history of the maritime law and in the decisions of this Court." *Just v. Chambers*, 312 U.S. 383, 389-390.

"It is a broad recognition of the authority of the States to create rights and liabilities with respect to conduct within their borders, when the state action does not run counter to federal laws or the essential features of an exclusive federal jurisdiction." *Id.,* at 391.

Thus Congress was careful to make the Death on the High Seas Act applicable only outside state territorial waters so as not to intrude on state legislative competence. 59 Cong. Rec. 4482-4486.

[43] *See, e.g., Caldarola v. Eckert, 332 U.S. 155.*

[44] Illustrative of this process is the recent case of *Allen v. Matson Navigation Co.*, 255 F.2d 273 (C. A. 9th Cir. 1958). The court remarked that "In discussing the question of the duty which the defendant owed to its passengers, all of the parties agreed that the law of California is to be applied. The trial court made a like assumption. We find it unnecessary to indicate any view as to whether in this the parties were correct for as we see it, no matter which law applies, the rule is the same, whether that of California, or that of the maritime law." *Id,* at 277.

diverse citizenship are now able to invoke the federal law forum for the trial of saving-clause cases. Such litigants are aided in their search for a federal forum by the liberality of the venue provisions applicable to actions based on diversity of citizenship. These provisions allow the action to be brought either "where all plaintiff's or all defendants reside."[45] If saving-clause actions were to be brought within the scope of § 1331, this choice could be no longer made. Plaintiffs would be subject to the rigid requirement that suit must be "brought only in the judicial district where all defendants reside...,"[46] and this would be so even where there is, in fact, diversity of citizenship.[47]

In the face of the consistent and compelling inferences to be drawn from history and policy against a break with a long past in the application of the Act of 1875, what justification is offered for this novel view of the statute? Support is ultimately reduced, one is compelled to say, to empty logic, reflecting a formal syllogism. The argument may thus be fairly summarized. It was not until recently, in a line of decision culminating in *Pope & Talbot, Inc., v. Hawn*, 346 U.S. 406, that it became apparent that the source of admiralty rights was a controlling body of federal admiralty law. This development led to a deepened consideration of the jurisdictional consequences of the federal source of maritime law. And so one turns to the Act of 1875. The Act of 1875 gave original jurisdiction to the federal courts over all cases arising under the Constitution and laws of the United States. Maritime law was federal law based on a constitutional grant of jurisdiction. Thus maritime cases arose under the Constitution or federal laws. By this mode of reasoning the words of the jurisdictional statute are found to "fit like a glove."[48]

Although it is true that the supremacy of federal maritime law over conflicting state law has recently been greatly extended, the federal nature of the maritime law administered in the federal courts has long been an accepted part of admiralty jurisprudence. The classic statement of Mr. Justice Holmes in *The Western Maid*, 257 U.S. 419, 432, summed up the accepted view that maritime law derived its force from the National Government and was part of the laws of the United States; and this was merely a restatement of a view which was clearly set forth in 1874 in *The Lottawanna*, 21 Wall. 558.[49] Thus the theory which underlies the effort to infuse general maritime jurisdiction into the Act of 1875 rests on no novel development in maritime law, but on premises as available in 1875 as they are today.

* * *

(c) *"Pendent" and Diversity Jurisdiction.*—Rejection of the proposed new reading of § 1331 does not preclude consideration of petitioner's claims under the general maritime law. These claims cannot, we have seen, be justified under § 1331. However, the District Court may have jurisdiction of them "pendent" to its jurisdiction under the Jones Act. Of course the considerations which call for the exercise of pendent jurisdiction of a state claim related to a pending federal cause of action within the appropriate scope of the doctrine of *Hum v. Oursler*, 289 U.S. 238, are not the same when, as here, what are involved are related claims based on the federal maritime law. We perceive no barrier to the exercise of "pendent jurisdiction" in the very limited circumstances before us. Here we merely decide that a district judge has jurisdiction to determine whether a cause of action has been stated if that jurisdiction has been invoked by a complaint at law rather than by a libel in admiralty, as long as the complaint also properly alleges a claim under the Jones Act. We are not called upon to decide whether the District Court may submit to the jury the "pendent" claims under the general maritime law in the event that a cause of action be found to exist.

Respondents Garcia & Diaz and Quin Lumber Company, New York corporations, and International Terminal Operating Company, a Delaware corporation, are of diverse citizenship from the petitioner, a Spanish subject. Since the Jones Act provides an independent basis of federal jurisdiction over the non-diverse respondent, Compania

---

[45] 28 U.S.C. § 1391(a).

[46] 28 U.S.C. § 1391(b).

[47] *Macon Grocery Co. v. Atlantic Coast Line R. Co.*, 215 U.S. 501. The more restrictive provisions apply in any action "wherein jurisdiction is not founded solely on diversity of citizenship...." 28 U.S.C. § 1391(b).

There may also well be situations in which the venue provisions prevent the joinder of defendants in a Federal District Court and the state court rules of procedure do not allow their joinder, thus precluding suit altogether.

[48] *Jenkins v. Roderick*, 156 F. Supp. 299, 301 (U.S.D.C. Mass. 1957).

[49] In *The Lottawanna*, the Court clearly recognized that maritime law was a body of uniform federal law drawing its authority from the Constitution and laws of the United States.

Trasatlantica, the rule of *Strawbridge v. Curtiss*, 3 Cranch 267, does not require dismissal of the claims against the diverse respondents. Accordingly, the dismissal of these claims for lack of jurisdiction was erroneous.

* * *

[The dissenting opinions of Justices Black and Brennan have been omitted. Eds.]

Note

As to the Outer Continental Shelf Lands Act as an independent basis for jurisdiction, *see Tennessee Gas Pipeline v. Houston Casualty Ins. Co.,* 87 F.3d 150, 1996 AMC 2296 (5th Cir. 1996), *infra.*

VODUSEK v. BAYLINER MARINE CORPORATION

71 F.3d 148, 1996 AMC 330 (4th Cir. 1995)

NIEMEYER, Circuit Judge

This personal injury case presents two questions of first impression in this circuit: (1) whether a jury may decide all issues in a case involving both admiralty and law claims, and (2) whether a district court may properly permit a jury to draw an adverse inference from a party's spoliation of relevant evidence. We resolve both questions affirmatively.

I

In June 1989, Donald Vodusek, Sr., fueled his 28-foot cabin cruiser by siphoning gas from several gas cans in preparation for a family boat ride from Pasadena, Maryland, where the boat was docked, to Baltimore's Inner Harbor. When he turned on the bilge pump roughly a half-hour later, the boat exploded and burned, causing Vodusek second and third degree burns over half of his body. Three months later, Vodusek died from burn-related complications.

Vodusek's boat was manufactured in 1978 by Bayliner Marine Corp. and sold to Stammer's Marine Center, Inc., a retail dealer. In 1984 Stammer's Marine performed a warranty repair for the boat's first owner, described on a warranty claim form: "Gas Tank Hose was kinked by Seat in Cabin. Remove Seat and Reroute Hose." Apparently, the repair was performed to the satisfaction of all parties involved. Four years later, Vodusek purchased the boat used from Stammer's Marine.

Following the death of her husband, Shirley Vodusek (hereinafter "Vodusek"), filed suit against Bayliner and Stammer's Marine contending that the fire resulted from a faulty bilge pump switch which sparked and ignited vapors from a leaking fuel system. In her complaint, she alleged an array of negligence and products liability claims for injuries sustained by her husband and for wrongful death. She sued Bayliner at law, relying on diversity jurisdiction, and Stammer's Marine in admiralty because the fire occurred on navigable waters.[1] The complaint included a demand for jury trial on all claims.

The district court submitted Vodusek's entire case to the jury, which returned a verdict in favor of the defendants. But, because the district court remained uncertain of whether this case should have been tried with or without a jury, it also rendered an independent decision on the merits as a court in admiralty. It, too, found in favor of the defendants. In arriving at its decision, the court disqualified Douglas Halsey, Vodusek's expert witness—even

---

[1] Vodusek alleged in her complaint:

[5] As to the defendant Stammer's only, this is an admiralty or maritime claim within the meaning of Rule 9(h) of the Federal Civil Judicial Procedure and Rules. This Court has admiralty jurisdiction over defendant Stammer's pursuant to 18[28] U.S.C. § 1333 and 46 U.S.C. [App.] § 740.

[6] This Court has diversity jurisdiction pursuant to 28 U.S.C. § 1332 as to defendant Bayliner. The citizenship of plaintiff and defendant Bayliner is diverse and the amount in controversy exceeds Fifty Thousand Dollars ($50,000.00), exclusive of interest and costs.

though his testimony had been considered by the jury—on the grounds that (1) Halsey's testimony was speculative and not based upon scientific principles; (2) Fialsey was not qualified to render an expert opinion on the design of the boat's fuel system; and (3) Halsey participated in the spoliation of relevant evidence. This appeal followed.

Vodusek contends that the entire case should have been tried exclusively to the jury and therefore that the bench trial was improper and unnecessary. In connection with the jury trial, she contends that the district court erred in (1) submitting to the jury the question of whether she engaged in the spoliation of evidence; (2) allowing cross-examination of her expert witness by depositions of experts who did not testify; and (3) interpreting 33 C.F.R. § 183.554, a federal regulation requiring access to fuel system components on boats, as not covering fuel vent hoses. In connection with the bench trial, if found permissible, Vodusek contends that the court erred in disqualifying her expert witness and disregarding his testimony.

According to Bayliner and Stammer's Marine, this is an admiralty case that was properly decided by the court without a jury. Because the jury trial was unnecessary, they argue that this court need not review any issue arising from it.

For the reasons that follow, we conclude that the district court properly submitted the entire case to the jury and therefore that the bench trial was superfluous. We also reject Vodusek's assignments of error regarding the jury trial. Accordingly, we affirm.

II

Because errors are assigned to both the jury and bench trials, we must first resolve whether all claims should have been submitted to a jury or some claims decided by the court without a jury.

In response to Vodusek's contention that this case was properly tried to the jury, Bayliner and Stammer's Marine contend that this case can be decided only in admiralty because the prerequisites of diversity jurisdiction, which formed the basis for allowing a jury trial, were not satisfied. Even though there was complete diversity between Vodusek and Bayliner to support the claims at law, Bayliner and Stammer's Marine argue that the court must consider the citizenship of all the parties to the action in deciding whether to submit a case to a jury, relying on *Powell v. Offshore Navigation*, 644 F.2d 1063 (5th Cir. Unit A. 1981) (holding that citizenship of defendant named in admiralty claim must be considered in determining diversity jurisdiction over law claims in which admiralty defendant was not named), *cert. denied*, 454 U.S. 972, 102 S. Ct. 521, 70 L. Ed. 2d 391 (1981). Because Stammer's Marine and Vodusek both have Maryland citizenship for diversity purposes, Bayliner and Stammer's Marine argue that complete diversity as required by *Strawbridge v. Curtiss*, 7 U.S. (3 Cranch) 267, 2 L.Ed. 435 (1806), does not exist. Without jurisdiction to maintain any claim at law, they argue, the court was not required to submit the case to the jury because admiralty cases are traditionally tried to the bench.

Federal courts are authorized, in one civil action, to exercise several types of subject matter jurisdiction historically exercised by separate courts, including courts of law, equity, and admiralty. As a result, a single federal court has at least three separate departments—law, equity, and admiralty—each of which has its own traditional procedures.[2] While the Seventh Amendment guarantees a jury trial in cases "at common law," no constitutional provision guarantees, or indeed prohibits, jury trials for cases tried in equity or in admiralty. Traditionally, however, admiralty courts and courts of equity did not rely on juries. *See generally Fitzgerald v. United States Lines Co.*, 374 U.S. 16, 83 S.Ct. 1646, 10 L. Ed. 2d 720 (1963).

When a civil action involves claims that historically would have been tried in different courts and a jury trial is demanded, the procedure for submitting part of the case to a jury can be complicated. *See, e.g., Ross v. Bernhard*, 396 U.S. 531, 90 S. Ct. 733, 24 L. Ed. 2d 729 (1970) ("[h]owever difficult it may have been to define with precision the line between actions at law dealing with legal rights and suits in equity dealing with equitable matters," the Seventh Amendment right to jury trial on legal claims must be preserved, even when complaint combines claims in equity

---

[2] Article III of the Constitution provides, "The judicial Power shall extend to all Cases, in Law and Equity, arising under this Constitution, the Laws of the United States, and [its] Treaties... [and] to all Cases of admiralty and maritime Jurisdiction." U.S. Const. art. 3, § 2. Federal Rule of Civil Procedure 1 implements the constitutional provision, and Federal Rule of Civil Procedure 2 provides for "one form of action" known as a "civil action."

with claims at law); *Dairy Queen, Inc. v. Wood,* 369 U.S. 469, 82 S. Ct. 894, 8 L. Ed. 2d 44 (1962) (holding that legal claims based on breach of contract must be determined by jury before final court determinations of equitable claims based on trademark infringement). While trials to different factfinders may be required in actions having law and equity components because of the jury's inability to fashion equitable remedies, that result is not compelled when claims at law and in admiralty, arising out of a single accident, are combined in a single complaint for damages. To render the trial process in that particular circumstance less cumbersome, confusing, and time-consuming, the Supreme Court has adopted the pragmatic procedural rule that both the admiralty claim and the law claim be decided by the jury so that "[o]nly one trier of fact [is] used for the trial of what is essentially one lawsuit to settle one claim split conceptually into separate parts because of historical developments." *Fitzgerald,* 374 U.S. at 21, 83 S. Ct. at 1650.

In *Fitzgerald,* an injured seaman sued his employer at law, alleging a claim for damages under the Jones Act, and in admiralty, alleging a claim for maintenance and cure. In ruling that both the admiralty and law claims should have been submitted to the jury, the Supreme Court focused on the confusion and complication that would result from trials before separate factfinders. The Court observed that the use of separate factfinders confounds the application of *res judicata* and collateral estoppel principles and unduly complicates damage calculations. With respect to the latter problem the Court explained:

> It is extremely difficult for a judge in trying a maintenance and cure claim to ascertain, even with the use of special interrogatories, exactly what went into the damages awarded by a jury—how loss of earning power was calculated, how much was allowed for medical expenses and pain and suffering, how much was allowed for actual lost wages, and how much, if any, each of the recoveries was reduced by contributory negligence. This raises needless problems of who has the burden of proving exactly what the jury did. And even if the judge can find out what elements of damage the jury's verdict actually represented, he must still try to solve the puzzling problem of the bearing the jury's verdict should have on recovery under the different standards of the maintenance and cure claim. In the absence of some statutory or constitutional obstacle, an end should be put to such an unfortunate, outdated, and wasteful manner of trying these cases. Fortunately, there is no such obstacle.

374 U.S. at 19-20, 83 S. Ct. at 1649-50 (footnotes omitted).

While we recognize that the circumstances in the case before us are somewhat different from those in *Fitzgerald,* we believe that the same pragmatic rule articulated in *Fitzgerald* should apply. In this case, the claims in admiralty and the claims at law name different defendants, each of whom is alleged to have contributed to liability through different conduct. Nevertheless, all of Vodusek's claims arise from the same boating accident and the same resulting injuries. Accordingly, the underlying reasons that motivated the Court's decision in *Fitzgerald* counsel us to extend the *Fitzgerald* rule to the circumstances here. Submitting both the admiralty and law claims to the jury better ensures that neither duplicative nor inadequate damages are awarded. Application of the *Fitzgerald* rule also avoids the substantial problems of applying principles of collateral estoppel when claims are tried separately. If, for example, the jury decided against Vodusek on her claims at law, determining the extent to which that verdict should bar aspects of her admiralty claims might require submitting detailed and therefore complicating interrogatories to the jury. We conclude that when the accident and injuries underlying the plaintiff's law and admiralty damage claims are the same, the considerations underlying the pragmatic rule of *Fitzgerald* dictate its application, even when the plaintiff has named different defendants in those claims.

Bayliner and Stammer's Marine argue that the *Fitzgerald* rule cannot apply here because the presence of Stammer's Marine destroys complete diversity and, along with it, the jurisdictional basis for the law claims. We reject this argument because it fails to recognize that the federal rules enable district courts to exercise their power in the three historically separate departments within a single case.

If Vodusek had filed separate suits against Bayliner at law and against Stammer's Marine in admiralty, she would have had a jurisdictional basis to proceed with each suit. Bayliner is a Delaware corporation with its principal place of business in Washington, and Vodusek is a Maryland citizen. Because the amount in controversy exceeds $50,000, Vodusek could have filed her claim at law against Bayliner in a federal court under the jurisdictional grant of 28 U.S.C. § 1332. Likewise, Vodusek's claim against Stammer's Marine could have been filed in admiralty under 28 U.S.C. App. § 1333 and 46 U.S.C. App. § 740 since the explosion and fire occurred on navigable waters. *See Sisson v. Ruby*, 497 U.S. 358, 110 S. Ct. 2892, 111 L. Ed. 2d 292 (1990); *Price v. Price*, 929 F.2d 131 (4th Cir. 1991). That both of Vodusek's claims are combined in one complaint does not by itself defeat the subject matter jurisdiction the court would have had over separate suits. The federal rules preserve the right to invoke jurisdiction in the historically separate departments of the district court in a single action. *See* FED. R. CIV. P. 1 (explaining that federal rules are applicable to all suits "whether cognizable as cases at law or in equity or in admiralty"); FED. R. CIV. P. 9(h) (authorizing invocation of admiralty jurisdiction when claim could be based on some other jurisdictional ground as well); Fed. R. Civ. P. 18(a) and 20(a) (permitting joinder of claims at law, in equity, and in admiralty and joinder of parties); Fed. R. Civ. P. 82 (explaining that "[t]hese rules shall not be construed to extend or limit the jurisdiction of the United States district courts"). Because Vodusek's claims in law and admiralty can be joined without affecting the court's jurisdiction over the defendants in each historical department, we must yield to Vodusek's explicit election in naming a different defendant in the claims filed in each department.

We reject the Fifth Circuit's approach in *Powell v. Offshore Navigation, Inc.*, 644 F.2d 1063 (1981) (holding that existence of non-diverse defendants, notwithstanding court's admiralty jurisdiction, destroyed plaintiff's right to jury trial). That decision, we believe, fails to recognize the facility provided by the federal rules for joining law and admiralty claims without destroying the jurisdictional and procedural distinctions between them. The decision also frustrates the choices preserved to litigants to invoke admiralty jurisdiction for one claim and to sue at law for another, electing a jury trial. *See* Barbara B. Woodhouse, Comment, *Powell v. Offshore Navigation, Inc.: Jurisdiction Over Maritime Claims and the Right to Trial by Jury*, 82 Colum. L.Rev. 784 (1982). *See also Fitzgerald*, 374 U.S. at 21, 83 S. Ct. at 1650; *Hassinger v. Tideland Elec. Membership Corp.*, 627 F. Supp. 65 (E.D.N.C. 1985), *aff'd only on related grounds*, 781 F.2d 1022 (4th Cir.), *cert. denied*, 478 U.S. 1004, 106 S. Ct. 3294, 92 L. Ed. 2d 709 (1986).

Because the district court properly submitted all claims to the jury, its decision rendered as a court in admiralty is superfluous, and any alleged error in the bench trial need not be reviewed.

* * *

AFFIRMED.

Note

Not all courts agree with *Vodusek, supra*, that a plaintiff may bring an *in rem* and an *in personam* claim together before a jury when the claims arise out of a single occurrence. In *T.N. T. Marine Service, Inc. v. Weaver Shipyards &Dry Dock, Inc.*, 702 F.2d 585, 1984 AMC 1341 (5th Cir. 1983), the U.S. Court of Appeals for the Fifth Circuit held that there was no right to a jury trial on a complaint that was designated as an admiralty and maritime claim, even though diversity jurisdiction existed and was alleged in the complaint as well.

Note: Plaintiff's Options

[A] plaintiff with *in personam* maritime claims has three choices. He may file suit in federal court under the federal court's admiralty jurisdiction, in federal court under diversity jurisdiction if the parties are diverse, or in state court. The difference between these choices is mostly procedural; of greatest significance is that there is no right to jury trial if general admiralty jurisdiction is invoked, while it is preserved for claims based on diversity or brought in state court. * * * The same substantive law pertains to the claim regardless of the forum, a type of "reverse-Erie" to ensure uniform application of admiralty law. *Ghotra v. Bandila Shipping, Inc.*, 113 F3d 1050, 1997 AMC 1936 (9th Cir. 1997), *cert. denied*, 522 U.S. 1107 (1998).

Although the statement above is correct as far as it goes, it is too narrow. A maritime claim may be brought in federal court under *any applicable basis for federal jurisdiction*, such as federal question jurisdiction such as Jones Act claims, etc. Likewise, the right to jury trial in federal court applies not only where diversity jurisdiction exists over a maritime claim, but whenever a maritime claim is brought in federal court on a basis of federal jurisdiction other than admiralty such as under federal question jurisdiction.

LUERA v. M/V ALBERTA

635 F.3d 181 (5th Cir. 2011)

KING, Circuit Judge:

Melinda Luera, a longshore worker, was injured while performing her job duties in the Port of Houston. Luera brought claims against two vessels, *in rem*, asserting admiralty jurisdiction. In the same complaint, Luera also brought claims against the owners and managers of those vessels, *in personam*, asserting diversity jurisdiction and demanding a jury trial. The district court, over the defendants' objection, ordered that all of Luera's claims, including her *in rem* admiralty claims, be tried together before a jury. The defendants appeal, arguing that Luera is not entitled to a jury trial because she has elected to proceed under the admiralty rules by virtue of the *in rem* claims in her complaint. We affirm the order of the district court.

* * *

II. Leave to Amend

The effect of Luera's amendment was to withdraw her Rule 9(h) election to proceed in admiralty, if there was any, with regard to her claims against the *in personam* defendants. A plaintiff's Rule 9(h) election is subject to the liberal standards for amending pleadings in Rule 15(a)(2), which provides that "[t]he court should freely give leave [to amend] when justice so requires." We have said that "Rule 9(h) is not a harsh rule," *T.N.T. Marine*, 702 F.2d at 588, and "[t]he pleader's identification of his claim as an admiralty or maritime claim or a failure to do so is not an irrevocable election," 5A CHARLES ALAN WRIGHT & ARTHUR R. MILLER, FEDERAL PRACTICE AND PROCEDURE § 1314 (3d ed.2004). Provided that there is no prejudice to the court or to the defendants, a plaintiff should be permitted to amend her complaint to change her Rule 9(h) election. *See Conti v. Sanko S.S. Co., Ltd.*, 912 F.2d 816, 818 (5th Cir. 1990).

Appellants argue that they were prejudiced by the amendment because Luera "exploited" admiralty procedures before the amendment. *See Brotherhood Shipping Co., Ltd. v. St. Paul Fire & Marine Ins. Co.*, 985 F.2d 323, 326 (7th Cir.1993) (doubting that leave to amend should be freely given where a plaintiff has already "used the distinctive procedures of admiralty" because the plaintiff should not be permitted to "have the best of both procedural worlds"). We disagree. Luera obtained the benefit of admiralty procedures with regard to her claims against the vessels by suing them in rem and obtaining letters of undertaking for both vessels. But she did not, and indeed she cannot, seek to change her Rule 9(h) election for those claims. *See T.N.T. Marine*, 702 F.2d at 588 ("[A]n action against a vessel in rem falls within the exclusive admiralty jurisdiction."). Rather, she sought to change only the election for her claims against the *in personam* defendants.

III. Jury Trial

Having decided that the district court did not err in permitting Luera to amend her complaint, we now consider whether a jury trial is unavailable in this case because Luera asserted *in rem* admiralty claims against two vessels in the same complaint as her *in personam* claims premised on diversity jurisdiction.

A. Rule 9(h) and the Admiralty Designation

We first provide some background regarding admiralty jurisdiction and procedures. The Constitution provides that the judicial power of the federal courts "shall extend ... to all Cases of admiralty and maritime Jurisdiction." U.S. CONST. art. III, § 2, cl. 1. Congress implemented this constitutional grant through 28 U.S.C. § 1333(1), which provides that the district courts have original jurisdiction over "[a]ny civil case of admiralty or maritime jurisdiction, saving to suitors in all cases all other remedies to which they are otherwise entitled." This statutory grant gives federal courts jurisdiction over all admiralty and maritime cases, regardless of the citizenship of the parties or the amount in controversy.

Under the "saving to suitors" clause in § 1333, a plaintiff whose claim does not fall within the exclusive admiralty jurisdiction of the federal courts may bring her claim "at law" in state court. The saving to suitors clause also allows a plaintiff to bring her claim "at law" under the federal court's diversity jurisdiction, provided the requirements for diversity and amount in controversy are met. *Atl. & Gulf Stevedores, Inc. v. Ellerman Lines, Ltd.*, 369 U.S. 355, 359–60, 82 S.Ct. 780, 7 L.Ed.2d 798 (1962); *see also* 14A CHARLES ALAN WRIGHT ET AL., FEDERAL PRACTICE AND PROCEDURE § 3672 (3d ed.1998) (noting that a plaintiff with a claim cognizable in admiralty and at law has three choices: she may bring her suit in federal court under admiralty jurisdiction, in federal court under diversity jurisdiction, or in state court).

When a plaintiff's claim is cognizable under admiralty jurisdiction and some other basis of federal jurisdiction, the Federal Rules of Civil Procedure allow the plaintiff to expressly designate her claim as being in admiralty. Rule 9(h) of the Federal Rules of Civil Procedure provides:

> If a claim for relief is within the admiralty or maritime jurisdiction and also within the court's subject-matter jurisdiction on some other ground, the pleading may designate the claim as an admiralty or maritime claim for purposes of Rules 14(c), 38(e), and 82, and the Supplemental Rules for Admiralty or Maritime Claims and Asset Forfeiture Actions. A claim cognizable only in the admiralty or maritime jurisdiction is an admiralty or maritime claim for those purposes, whether or not so designated.

"Numerous and important consequences" flow from a plaintiff's decision to file her claim under the federal court's admiralty jurisdiction or its diversity jurisdiction. *T.N.T. Marine*, 702 F.2d at 586. One of the most important consequences relates to the rules of procedure that will be applied to the case. If a claim is pleaded under diversity jurisdiction, the rules of civil procedure will apply, and the parties will be guaranteed, under the Seventh Amendment, a right to have the claim tried by a jury. *Atl. & Gulf Stevedores*, 369 U.S. at 360, 82 S.Ct. 780. If the claim is pleaded under admiralty jurisdiction, however, the plaintiff will invoke "those historical procedures traditionally attached to actions in admiralty." *Durden v. Exxon Corp.*, 803 F.2d 845, 849 n. 10 (5th Cir. 1986). One of the historical procedures unique to admiralty is that a suit in admiralty does not carry with it the right to a jury trial. *Waring v. Clarke*, 46 U.S. 441, 460, 5 How. 441, 12 L.Ed. 226 (1847); *see also Becker v. Tidewater, Inc.*, 405 F.3d 257, 259 (5th Cir.2005). Thus, "there is no right to a jury trial where the complaint contains a statement identifying the claim as an admiralty or maritime claim, even though diversity jurisdiction exists as well." *T.N.T. Marine*, 702 F.2d at 587.

By the plain terms of Rule 9(h), a claim cognizable only under admiralty jurisdiction does not require a Rule 9(h) election because admiralty procedures will automatically apply to that claim. Although Rule 9(h) appears to require an affirmative statement from the plaintiff to invoke the admiralty rules for claims cognizable under admiralty and some other basis of jurisdiction, we have held that the mere assertion of admiralty jurisdiction as a dual or an alternate basis of subject matter jurisdiction for a claim is sufficient to make a Rule 9(h) election to proceed in admiralty for that claim. *T.N.T. Marine*, 702 F.2d at 587–88. In *T.N.T. Marine*, the plaintiff brought an action against a vessel in rem and a dock *in personam*. Id. at 588. The complaint alleged both diversity and admiralty as alternate bases for the court's jurisdiction without specifying whether the plaintiff asserted a separate jurisdictional basis for each claim. *Id.* We held that by the "simple statement asserting admiralty or maritime claims" the plaintiff had elected to proceed under admiralty jurisdiction and procedures even without an explicit reference to Rule 9(h). Id.

Similarly, in *Durden v. Exxon Corp.*, the plaintiff, an injured seaman, filed an action against a vessel in rem and against its owners *in personam*, asserting that "the [c]ourt is vested with jurisdiction of this matter pursuant to the provisions of Title 28 Section 1332 of the United States Code *and/or* the General Maritime Law of the United States." 803 F.2d at 850 (emphasis added) (internal quotation marks omitted). The plaintiff later included a separate Jones Act claim against his employer, which carries a right to trial by jury. *Id.* at 847. The district court impaneled a jury to hear the case, but at the close of the plaintiff's evidence the court directed a verdict to the employer on the

Jones Act claim, dismissed the jury, and tried the remaining claims to the bench. *Id.* We held that the district court properly dismissed the jury because the non-Jones Act claims were brought under the court's admiralty jurisdiction with no right to a jury trial. Under the rule announced in *T.N.T. Marine*, the plaintiff's allegation of admiralty as an alternate basis of jurisdiction was sufficient to make a Rule 9(h)election to proceed in admiralty for all of his claims. *Id.*

Following these cases, in this circuit a plaintiff who asserts admiralty jurisdiction as a basis for the court's subject matter jurisdiction over a claim has automatically elected under Rule 9(h) to proceed under the admiralty rules, even if she states that her claim is also cognizable under diversity or some other basis of federal subject matter jurisdiction. However, we have not addressed the specific issue presented in this case, which is whether the plaintiff automatically makes a Rule 9(h) election to proceed under the admiralty rules when she specifically asserts only diversity jurisdiction for one claim in the same complaint as a separate claim cognizable only under admiralty jurisdiction.

B. Luera's Rule 9(h) Election

Appellants argue that this case is controlled by our prior decisions in *Durden* and *T.N.T. Marine*. According to appellants, these cases establish that when a plaintiff asserts alternative or dual bases of subject matter jurisdiction in a complaint, and one of those bases is admiralty jurisdiction, the plaintiff automatically makes a Rule 9(h) election to proceed in admiralty for the entire case. However, this case is readily distinguishable from *Durden* and *T.N.T. Marine*. In those cases, the plaintiffs had asserted both admiralty and diversity subject matter jurisdiction for *the same claim*. *Durden*, 803 F.2d at 849; *T.N.T. Marine*, 702 F.2d at 588. The plaintiffs in those cases, like Luera, could proceed against the vessels *in rem* only under admiralty jurisdiction, but, unlike Luera, the plaintiffs in *Durden* and *T.N.T. Marine* did not specifically assert diversity as the only basis for subject matter jurisdiction over their *in personam* claims. The rule flowing from *Durden* and *T.N.T. Marine*, therefore, is that a plaintiff who fails to choose between admiralty jurisdiction and some other basis of subject matter jurisdiction for a claim is presumed to have elected under Rule 9(h) to proceed under admiralty jurisdiction and the admiralty procedures *for that claim*. That presumption is not applicable here because Luera has not asserted alternate or dual bases of subject matter jurisdiction for her claims against the *in personam* defendants. Rather, she has definitively chosen to proceed under the district court's diversity jurisdiction for her *in personam* claims and is clear that she does not wish to elect admiralty procedures for those claims. Therefore, Luera cannot be said to have presumptively made a Rule 9(h) election for her *in personam* claims.

Appellants urge that the mere presence of *in rem* claim amounts to a 9(h) election for the remainder of her claims under *Durden* and *T.N.T. Marine*. However, by its plain language, Rule 9(h) applies to "claims" and not to entire cases. FED.R.CIV.P. 9(h)(1)("If a *claim* for relief is within the admiralty or maritime jurisdiction ..., the pleading may designate the *claim* as an admiralty or maritime *claim*." (emphases added)). Additionally, "[a] single case can include both admiralty or maritime claims and nonadmiralty claims or parties." *Id.*, Advisory Committee Note (1997 Amendment). Luera clearly expressed her intent that her claims against the *in personam* defendants are premised on the district court's diversity jurisdiction, rather than its admiralty jurisdiction, and we therefore hold that Luera did not make a Rule 9(h) election to proceed under the admiralty rules for those claims.

C. Consolidation and the Right to a Jury Trial

Although Luera did not make a Rule 9(h) election to proceed under the admiralty rules for her claims against the *in personam* defendants, the question remains whether her assertion of *in rem* admiralty claims in the same complaint nevertheless precludes a jury trial on her *in personam* claims. We conclude that the mere presence of admiralty claims in the same complaint as claims premised on diversity jurisdiction does not preclude a jury trial.

This case is instead controlled by the Supreme Court's decision in *Fitzgerald v. United States Lines Co.*, 374 U.S. 16, 83 S.Ct. 1646, 10 L.Ed.2d 720 (1963). In *Fitzgerald*, a seaman was injured while working aboard a ship. In his complaint, the plaintiff alleged three separate claims against his employer: a negligence claim based on the Jones Act, an unseaworthiness claim, and a maintenance and cure claim. *Id.* at 17, 83 S.Ct. 1646. The Jones Act claim carried a statutory right to a jury trial, but the unseaworthiness and maintenance and cure claims, brought under the court's admiralty jurisdiction, did not carry such a right. *Id.* The district court impaneled a jury to hear the Jones Act and unseaworthiness claims, and the jury found in favor of the employer on both claims. *Id.* The court then dismissed the jury and decided the maintenance and cure claim itself. *Id.* The plaintiff appealed, arguing that all of his claims should have been decided by the jury. *Id.*

The Supreme Court held that it was error for the district court to dismiss the jury because all of the claims ought to have been tried together to the same fact finder. *Id.* at 21, 83 S.Ct. 1646. The Court noted that the procedure used by the district court, trying a portion of the case to the jury and a portion to the bench, was commonly employed in Jones Act cases, but the Court concluded that separating the claims was an "outdated" and "wasteful" practice. *Id.* at 18–20, 83 S.Ct. 1646. Splitting the claims "unduly complicates and confuses a trial, creates difficulties in applying doctrines of res judicata and collateral estoppel, and can easily result in too much or too little recovery." *Id.* at 19, 83 S.Ct. 1646. The Court held that, because the claims arose out of one set of facts, "[o]nly one trier of fact should be used for the trial of what is essentially one lawsuit to settle one claim split conceptually into separate parts because of historical developments." *Id.* at 21, 83 S.Ct. 1646.

The Court's decision did not rest on any *right* of the plaintiff to have his admiralty claims tried by a jury:

> While this Court has held that the Seventh Amendment does not require jury trials in admiralty cases, neither that Amendment nor any other provision of the Constitution forbids them. Nor does any statute of Congress or Rule of Procedure, Civil or Admiralty, forbid jury trials in maritime cases.

Id. at 20, 83 S.Ct. 1646.

The Third and Fourth Circuits have also concluded that the presence of an admiralty claim does not defeat a plaintiff's properly preserved right to a jury trial. In *Vodusek v. Bayliner Marine Corp.*, 71 F.3d 148 (4th Cir.1995), the Fourth Circuit held that "when the accident and injuries underlying the plaintiff's law and admiralty damage claims are the same, the considerations underlying the pragmatic rule of *Fitzgerald* dictate its application, even when the plaintiff has named different defendants in those claims." *Id.* at 154. In *Blake v. Farrell Lines, Inc.*, 417 F.2d 264 (3d Cir.1969), the plaintiff, an injured longshoreman, filed a complaint alleging negligence against the shipowner under diversity jurisdiction and demanded a jury trial. *Id.* at 265. The shipowner then filed a separate suit in admiralty against the stevedoring company alleging indemnity. *Id.* The district court consolidated the two suits, trying the entire case to a jury. On appeal, the shipowners contended that the court should not have tried the issues in the admiralty suit to the jury. *Id.* Relying on *Fitzgerald*, the Third Circuit concluded that "if the circumstances justify such action, a district court exercising section 1333 jurisdiction over a maritime claim may require that the issues of fact be tried to a jury" in "closely related actions or claims" involving "common issues of fact." *Id.* at 266.

To be clear, we do not hold today that a plaintiff bringing an *in rem* admiralty claim, or any other claim brought under admiralty jurisdiction, has a *right* to a jury trial. No statute, rule, or constitutional provision confers such a right. But neither does any statute, rule, or constitutional provision provide Appellants with a right to a bench trial. The practice of trying admiralty claims to the bench is simply one of custom and tradition. That tradition cannot trump Luera's constitutional right to a jury trial for her non-admiralty claims, and "the non-jury component of admiralty jurisdiction must give way to the [S]eventh [A]mendment." *Ghotra*, 113 F.3d at 1057 (internal quotation omitted).

IV. Conclusion

For the forgoing reasons, we AFFIRM the order of the district court.

---

2. Ancillary and Pendent Jurisdiction—Textual Analysis

Pendent Jurisdiction

The doctrine of pendent jurisdiction was created by the federal courts to permit a court which unquestionably has jurisdiction over a "federal question" claim against a defendant also to entertain a claim against that same defendant based on state law even where there is no independent federal jurisdiction over the state claim. Thus, a plaintiff who alleges a claim against a defendant based on a federal statute may also assert a claim against that defendant based on state law even though both parties are citizens of the same state. For a state claim to be considered a pendent claim it must arise out of the same nucleus of operative facts as the federal question claim.[1] It would not make much sense to require plaintiff to split his cause of action by adjudicating the federal claim in federal court and the state claim in state court. Besides creating a risk of inconsistent verdicts or of double recovery, two separate proceedings would be wasteful of judicial resources and place a unnecessary burden on the parties and witnesses.

Ancillary Jurisdiction

The genesis of the doctrine of ancillary jurisdiction lies in other types of cases. Ancillary jurisdiction has been used to allow a federal court to entertain a claim over which the court has no independent ground of federal jurisdiction against a party to the action, such as in a compulsory counterclaim or a cross-claim situation or to entertain a claim over which the court has no jurisdiction by or against a person not an original party to the action such as in impleader and intervention as of right.[2] Although originally conceived as a tool to permit a person to protect his rights by intervening in litigation, the emphasis changed when courts began to use the doctrine of ancillary jurisdiction in situations where the claim which a person, party or not, sought assert in the case arose from the same nucleus of operative facts as the principal case. In other words the approach to ancillary jurisdiction began to resemble that used in pendent jurisdiction and judicial economy—the adjudication of the entire dispute in one lawsuit—became the important objective. The two doctrines had begun to merge into a single doctrine utilizing common criteria in its application.

Pendent Party Jurisdiction

The interplay between pendent and ancillary jurisdiction has been developed in various cases as a basis for constructing pendent party jurisdiction. These cases typically have involved situations where a *plaintiff* has attempted to assert in a federal action a state claim against a party over which the court had no independent federal jurisdiction simply on the ground that the state claim grew out of the same transaction or occurrence that was the subject matter of plaintiff's suit against a party as to which there was federal jurisdiction. The so-called "pendent party" doctrine had been recognized by some courts in various cases including admiralty cases. The admiralty cases sometimes have referred to the more liberal practice in admiralty proceedings.

Several decisions by the United States Supreme Court, however, had raised some questions as to use of ancillary and pendent jurisdiction in admiralty impleader practice.

Owen Equipment & Erection Co. v. Kroger

In *Owen Equipment & Erection Co. v. Kroger,*[3] plaintiff who had properly invoked diversity jurisdiction against the original defendant amended her complaint to also assert a claim directly against the non-diverse third-party

---

[1] As Justice Brennan said in *United Mine Workers v. Gibbs,* 383 U.S. 715, 725 (1966):

> Pendent jurisdiction, in the sense of judicial power, exists whenever there is a claim "arising under [the] Constitution, the laws of the United States, and treaties... under their authority ... and the relationship between that claim and the state claim permits the conclusion that the entire action before the court constitutes but one constitutional case.... The federal and state claims must derive from a common nucleus of operative fact.

[2] The Court in *Owen v. Kroger,* 437 U.S. at 375 n.18, indicated that this was the accepted view, although this statement was not necessary to the Court's holding.

[3] 437 U.S. 365, 98 S.Ct. 2396, 57 L.Ed.2d 274 (1978).

defendant who had been impleaded into the action by the defendant. Thereafter, the district court granted a motion for summary judgment in favor of the original defendant and dismissed it from the case. The case then proceeded to trial in plaintiff's action against the remaining defendant, that is the party who had originally been brought into the case as a third-party defendant. It was not until the third day of trial that the fact of lack of diversity was brought to the court's attention but the court continued with the trial. Plaintiff prevailed at trial and the court of appeals affirmed on the basis of ancillary jurisdiction.

The Supreme Court reversed. It refused to treat the third-party defendant as a "pendent party" to the original action against the defendant and held that the exercise of ancillary jurisdiction was inappropriate. The Court stated that jurisdiction over the plaintiff's claim against the original defendant was insufficient to confer jurisdiction over plaintiff's claim against the third-party defendant. Plaintiffs claim against a third-party defendant needed to be supported by independent grounds of federal jurisdiction to enable plaintiff to recover against the third-party defendant. The *Owen* case rejected the pendent party doctrine in the context of a diversity case. In refusing to apply ancillary jurisdiction to *plaintiff's* attempt to assert a claim against a non-diverse third-party defendant, the court contrasted that situation with the application of ancillary jurisdiction to support the assertion of a defendant's "claim over" in an impleader action. In *Owen* the court said that plaintiff's complaint against the third-party defendant "was entirely separate from her claim against ... [the original defendant] since ... [the third-party defendant's] liability to her depended not at all on whether ... [the original defendant] was also liable. Far from being an ancillary and dependent claim, it was a new and independent one." The court also noted that the state claim was asserted by the plaintiff who had the choice of selecting the forum and who could have sued both the defendant and the third-party defendant in state court. "[A]ncillary jurisdiction typically involves claims by a defending party haled into court against his will, or by another person whose rights might be irretrievably lost unless he could assert them in an ongoing action in federal court." The Court was unwilling to let plaintiff, by asserting a state claim against a third-party defendant, accomplish indirectly that which she could not accomplish directly, that is, sue a non-diverse party on a state claim in federal court. The fact that the state claim against the non-diverse party arose out of the same occurrence as the state claim against the diverse party was not a sufficient justification for undermining the complete diversity requirement. An important factor in *Owen* is that the case was a *diversity* case and the court made much of the fact that the policy of complete diversity requires strict construction. The bottom line is that "neither the convenience of the litigants nor considerations of judicial economy justify the extension of ancillary jurisdiction to *plaintiff's cause of action* against a citizen of the same State in a diversity case."

It should be noted, however, that by the Supplemental Jurisdiction Statute which now provides statutory authority for the jurisprudentially created doctrines of ancillary and pendent jurisdiction Congress has limited the application of this decision to diversity cases, this statute did not legislatively overrule the holding of the *Owen* case.

It should also be noted that in *Owen*, the Supreme Court observed that the lower federal courts had held that the doctrine of ancillary jurisdiction "to include cases that involve multi-party practice such as ... impleader,..." Resolution of "a third-party complaint depends at least in part upon the resolution of the primary lawsuit. Its relation to the original complaint is not a mere factual similarity but logical dependence."

Aldinger v. Howard

The case of *Aldinger v. Howard*[6] decided two years before Owen also had taken a restrictive view of pendent jurisdiction. The question decided by the Court was "whether pendent jurisdiction encompasses not merely the litigation of additional *claims* between parties with respect to which there is federal jurisdiction, but also the joining of additional *parties* with respect whom there is no independent basis of federal jurisdiction,..." In reviewing the

---

[4] Although one may suggest that the reach of the Court's holding should be limited by the fact that the diverse party was dismissed prior to trial and that ancillary jurisdiction should be exercised sparingly when there has been a pre-trial dismissal of the underlying claim, the Court spoke quite broadly in the case and did not purport to base its decision on that factor. Also the holding is compatible with the somewhat narrow approach the court has taken to the doctrines of ancillary and pendent jurisdiction, both of which will be discussed subsequently.
[5] 28 U.S.C.A. § 1367.
[6] 427 U.S. 1, 96 S.Ct. 2413, 49 L.Ed.2d 276 (1976).

cases on pendent jurisdiction the Court confined the scope of the doctrine to those cases in which the plaintiff has asserted a claim created by a federal statute (federal question jurisdiction) and also alleged another claim arising out of the same nucleus of facts based on state law. As to whether such a claim can be made against a party as to whom there is no federal question jurisdiction, the Court, as it subsequently did in *Owen*, refused to blend the doctrines of ancillary and pendent jurisdiction. Thus, it refused to adopt as a single, simple test for the application of pendent and ancillary jurisdiction the fact that both claims, the federal claim against one defendant and the state claim against another defendant, arose out of the same occurrence or transaction. To determine whether jurisdiction may be extended in these circumstances "whether by virtue of the statutory grant of subject matter jurisdiction, upon which ... [plaintiff's] principal claim against ... [one defendant] rests, Congress has addressed itself to the *party* as to whom jurisdiction pendent to the principal claim is sought." Here the principal claim against various government officers was based on the Federal Civil Rights Act and the claim against the governmental unit itself was based on state law. The Court found that Congress by not providing for a Civil Rights action against governmental units did not intend for such claims to be adjudicated in the federal courts, and it held that it would be contrary to that intent to allow a government unit to be joined as pendent parties in such actions against other persons.

In two situations not involved in *Owen* or *Aldinger* the lower courts continued to use pendent party doctrine. The first was in admiralty cases where Rule 14(c) was available, and the second was in cases in which the United States was a party defendant. In the latter situation, plaintiff may face a dilemma where there are joint tortfeasors. The United States may only be sued in federal court, and a suit against it in state court will invariably be removed to federal court. Where plaintiff has, for example, a tort claim against the United States and sues the United States in federal court, he cannot join as a co-defendant a person who is not of diverse citizenship. Suit against the joint tortfeasor may only be brought in state court. Under these circumstances even though there may have been only one casualty plaintiff must pursue two lawsuits. The United States can protect its interests by impleading the other tortfeasor under Rule 14(a), but the plaintiff does not have an independent jurisdictional basis for asserting a claim against the third-party defendant. It was thought by some that this situation makes a compelling need for pendent party jurisdiction. Unlike the circumstances in both *Aldinger* and *Owen*, a plaintiff who sues the United States has no choice of forum. Unlike the plaintiff's in those cases, the plaintiff with a claim against the Government and a non-diverse person cannot sue both parties in state court.

Finley v. United States

The Supreme Court in the third and most recent decision on the subject of pendent party jurisdiction held that the doctrine was likewise inapplicable. In *Finley v. United States*,[7] the Court was faced with the question of whether plaintiff who had filed suit under the Federal Tort Claims Act could also, under the pendent party doctrine, join a state claim against persons who were not of diverse citizenship. Since that possibility was alluded to in *Aldinger*, there was some belief that *Finley* would be the first Supreme Court case to legitimize the use of the pendent party doctrine. But this was not to happen. By a five to four vote the court held that an FTCA plaintiff may not append to its suit against the Government, a claim against a non-diverse party over which there is no independent federal jurisdiction. The reasoning of the Court represents its continued trend against permitting the exertion of federal jurisdiction against parties based on state claims where there is otherwise no independent ground for federal jurisdiction.

Unlike *Owen*, jurisdiction against the United States was based on a substantive right created by a federal statute; Finley was not a diversity case. Unlike *Aldinger*, there was no language in the FTCA or its legislative history from which it could be inferred that Congress intended to preclude the use of pendent or ancillary jurisdiction against a non-governmental defendant. In order to reach that result the Court, as pointed out in the dissent, had to substantially extend the holding of the prior cases. The court used a two-factor approach. First it examined the "posture" or "context" of the case. It found that the case involved claims against a party over whom the court had no independent jurisdiction. But this says very little because every pendent party case is cast in this "context" or

---

[7] 490 U.S. 545, 109 S.Ct. 2003, 104 L.Ed.2d 593, 1989 AMC 2112 (1989).

"posture". It is one of the characteristics of a "pendent party" claim. The second factor focuses on the "text of the jurisdictional statute at issue." "The FTCA ... confers jurisdiction over 'civil actions against the United States.'" Because the statute did not expressly refer to actions against parties other than the United States, let alone parties as to whom federal jurisdiction is lacking, and because the language of the statute does not support an inference that *Congress intended* by this statute to confer jurisdiction over any party other than the United States the use of pendent party jurisdiction was impermissible. The opinion of the majority read in the context of *Aldinger* and *Owen* sent a clear message to Congress. Although it grudgingly accepts the holding of the now classic *United Mine Workers v. Gibbs,*[8] a case that permitted a plaintiff to assert a state claim against a non-diverse defendant against whom it had also asserted a claim based on a federal question where both arose out of the same nucleus of operative facts, a majority of the present court appears to have simply drawn the bounds of pendent jurisdiction at that point. It has shown no inclination to follow the lead of some of the lower federal courts which have extended the doctrine of ancillary jurisdiction. It was in this context that Congress stepped in and accepted the Court's "invitation" to authorize a liberal scope to ancillary and pendent jurisdiction. This is precisely what Congress did in enacting the Supplemental Jurisdiction Act.[9] Despite the efforts of the Supreme Court to restrict the scope of ancillary and pendent jurisdiction, Congress, by enacting the Supplemental Jurisdiction Statute, has legislatively overruled the *Finley* decision and, perhaps, *Aldinger v. Howard* 28 U.S.C.A. § 1367 as well. Thus, the generally liberal approach to ancillary jurisdiction in admiralty cases has not received statutory authority.

---

3. *Supplemental Jurisdiction*

THE SUPPLEMENTAL JURISDICTION ACT

28 U.S.C. § 1367

§ 1367. Supplemental jurisdiction

(a) Except as provided in subsections (b) and (c) or as expressly provided otherwise by Federal statute, in any civil action of which the district courts have original jurisdiction, the district courts shall have supplemental jurisdiction over all other claims that are so related to claims in the action within such original jurisdiction that they form part of the same case or controversy under Article III of the United States Constitution. Such supplemental jurisdiction shall include claims that involve the joinder or intervention of additional parties.

(b) In any civil action of which the district courts have original jurisdiction founded solely on section 1332 of this title, the district courts shall not have supplemental jurisdiction under subsection (a) over claims by plaintiff's against person made parties under Rule 14, 19, 20, or 24 of the Federal Rules of Civil Procedure, or over claims by persons proposed to be joined as plaintiff's under Rule 19 of such rules, or seeking to intervene as plaintiff's under Rule 24 of such rules, when exercising supplemental jurisdiction over such claims would be inconsistent with the jurisdictional requirements of section 1332.

(c) The district courts may decline to exercise supplemental jurisdiction over a claim under subsection (a) if—

   (1) the claim raises a novel or complex issue of State law,
   (2) the claim substantially predominates over the claim or claims over which the district court has original jurisdiction,
   (3) the district court has dismissed all claims over which it has original jurisdiction, or
   (4) in exceptional circumstances, there are other compelling reasons for declining jurisdiction.

---

[8] 383 U.S. 715, 86 S.Ct. 1130, 16 L.Ed.2d 218 (1966).
[9] 28 U.S.C.A. § 1367.

(d) The period of limitations for any claim asserted under subsection (a), and for any other claim in the same action that is voluntarily dismissed at the same time as or after the dismissal of the claim under subsection (a), shall be tolled while the claim is pending and for a period of 30 days after it is dismissed unless State law provides fro a longer tolling period.

(e) As used in this section, the term "State" includes the District of Columbia, the Commonwealth of Puerto Rico, and any territory or possession of the United States.

(Added Pub. L. 101-650, Title III, § 310(a), Dec. 1, 1990, 104 Stat. 5113.)

JUDICIAL IMPROVEMENTS ACT

P.L. 101-650

Legislative History, HOUSE REPORT No. 101-734

Section 114. Supplemental Jurisdiction

This section implements a recommendation of the Federal Courts Study Committee found on pages 47 and 48 of its Report. The doctrines of pendent and ancillary jurisdiction, in this section jointly labeled supplemental jurisdiction, refer to the authority of the federal courts to adjudicate, without an independent basis of subject matter jurisdiction, claims that are so related to other claims within the district courts original jurisdiction that they form part of the same cases or controversy under Article III of the United States Constitution.

Supplemental jurisdiction has enabled federal courts and litigants to take advantage of the federal procedural rules on claim and party joinder to deal economically—in single rather than multiple litigation—with related maters, usually those arising form the same transaction, occurrence, or series of transactions or occurrences. Moreover, the district courts' exercise of supplemental jurisdiction, by making federal court a practical arena for the resolution of an entire controversy, has effectuated Congress's intent in the jurisdictional statutes to provide plaintiff's with a federal forum for litigating claims within original federal jurisdiction.

Recently, however, in *Finley v. United States*, 109 S. Ct. 2003[1] (1989), the Supreme Court cast substantial doubt on the authority of the federal courts to hear some claims within supplemental jurisdiction. In *Finley* the Court held that a district court, in a Federal Tort Claims Act suit against the United States, may not exercise supplemental jurisdiction over a related claim by the plaintiff against an additional, nondiverse defendant. The Court's rationale— that "with respect to the addition of parties, as opposed to the addition of only claims, we will not assume that the full constitutional power has been congressionally authorized, and will not read jurisdictional statutes broadly," 109 S. Ct. at 2007—threatens to eliminate other previously accepted forms of supplemental jurisdiction. Already, for example, some lower courts have interpreted *Finley* to prohibit the exercise of supplemental jurisdiction in formerly unquestioned circumstances.[14]

Legislation, therefore, is needed to provide the federal courts with statutory authority to hear supplemental claims. Indeed, the Supreme Court has virtually invited Congress to codify supplemental jurisdiction by commenting in *Finley*, "What ever we say regarding the scope of jurisdiction ... can of course be changed by Congress. What is of paramount importance is that Congress be able to legislate against a background of clear interpretive rules, so that it may know the effect of the language it adopts." *Finley*, 109 S. Ct. at 2007. This section would authorize jurisdiction in a case like *Finley*, as well as essentially restore the pre-*Finley* understandings of the authorization for and limits on other forms of supplemental jurisdiction. In federal question cases, it broadly authorizes the district courts to exercise supplemental jurisdiction over additional claims, including claims involving the joinder of additional

---

[1] 490 U.S. 545, 104 L. Ed. 2d 593.

[14] *See, e.g., Aetna Casualty & Surety Co. v. Spartan Mechanical Corp.*, 738 F. Supp. 664, 673-77 (E.D.N.Y 1990) (impleader) (reviewing conflicting court decisions)).

parties. In diversity cases, the district courts may exercise supplemental jurisdiction, except when doing so would be inconsistent with the jurisdictional requirements of the diversity statute. In both cases, the district courts, as under current law, would have discretion to decline supplemental jurisdiction in appropriate circumstances.

Subsection 114(a) generally authorized the district court to exercise jurisdiction over a supplemental claim whenever it forms part of the same constitutional case or controversy as the claim or claims that provide the basis of the district court's original jurisdiction.[15] In providing for supplemental jurisdiction over claims involving the addition of parities, subsection (a) explicitly fills the statutory gap noted in *Finley v. United States.*

Subsection 114(b) prohibits a district court in a case over which it has jurisdiction founded solely on the general diversity provision, 28 U.S.C. § 1332, form exercising supplemental jurisdiction in specified circumstances.[16] In diversity-only actions the district courts may not hear plaintiffs' supplemental claims when exercising supplemental jurisdiction would encourage plaintiff's to evade the jurisdictional requirement of 28 U.S.C. § 1332 by the simple expedient of naming initially only those defendants whose joinder satisfies section 1332's requirements and later adding claims not within original federal jurisdiction against other defendants who have intervened or been joined on a supplemental basis. In accord with case law, the subsection also prohibits the joinder or intervention of persons as plaintiff's if adding them is inconsistent with section 1332's requirements. The section is not intended to affect the jurisdictional requirements of 28 U.S.C. § 1332 in diversity-only class actions, as those requirements were interpreted prior to *Finley.*[17]

Subsection (b) makes one small change in pre-*Finley* practice. Anomalously, under current practice, the same party might intervene as of right under Federal Rule of Civil Procedure 23(a) and take advantage of supplemental jurisdiction, but not come within supplemental jurisdiction if parties already in the action sought to effect the joinder under Rule 19.[18] Subsection (b) would eliminate this anomaly, excluding Rule 23(a) plaintiff-intervenors to the same extent as those sought to be joined as plaintiffs under Rule 19.

If this exclusion threatened unavoidable prejudice to the interests of the prospective intervenor if the action proceeded in its absence, the district court should be more inclined not merely to deny the intervention but to dismiss the whole action for refiling in state court under the criteria of Rule 19(b).

Subsection 114(c) codifies the factors that the Supreme Court has recognized as providing legitimate bases upon which a district court may decline jurisdiction over a supplemental claim, even though it is empowered to hear the claim. Subsection (c)(l)-(3) codifies the factors recognized as relevant under current law. Subsection (c)(4) acknowledges that occasionally there may exist other compelling reasons for a district court to decline supplemental jurisdiction, which the subsection does not foreclose a court form considering in exceptional circumstances. As under current law, subsection (c) requires the district court, in exercising its discretion, to undertake a case-specific analysis.

If, pursuant to subsection (c), a district court dismisses a party's supplemental claim, a party may choose to refile that claim in state court. In that circumstance, the federal district court, in deciding the party's claims over which the court has retained jurisdiction, should accord no claim preclusive effect to a state court judgment on the supplemental claim. It is also possible that, if a supplemental claim is dismissed pursuant to this subsection, a party may move to dismiss without prejudice his or her other claims for the purpose of refiling the entire action in state court. Standards developed under Rule 41(a) of the Federal Rules of Civil Procedure govern whether the motion should granted.

Subsection 114(d) provides a period of tolling of statutes of limitations of any supplemental claim that is dismissed under this section and for any other claims in the same action voluntarily dismissed at the same time or after the supplemental claim is dismissed. The purpose is to prevent the loss of claims to statutes of limitations

---

[15] In so doing, subsection (a) codifies the scope of supplemental jurisdiction first articulated by the Supreme Court in *United Mine Workers v. Gibbs,* 383 U.S. 715 (1966).

[16] The net effect of subsection (b) is to implement the principal rationale of *Owen Equipment & Erection Co. v. Kroger,* 437 U.S. 365 (1978).

[17] *See Supreme Tribe of Ben Hur v. Cauble,* 255 U.S. 356, 41 S.Ct. 338, 65 L.Ed. 673 (1921); *Zahn v. International Paper Co.,* 414 U.S. 291, 94 S.Ct. 505, 38 L.Ed.2d 511 (1973).

[18] *See* 7AC. Wright, A. Miller, & M. Kane, Federal Practice and Procedure § 1917, at 472-81 (2d ed. 1986).

where state law might fail to toll the running of the period of limitations while a supplemental claim was pending in federal court. It also eliminates a possible disincentive form such a gap in tolling when a plaintiff might wish to seek voluntary dismissal of other claims in order to pursue an entire matter in state court when a federal court dismisses a supplemental claim.

Subsection 114(e) defines "State" in accordance with other sections of this title.

---

4. *Right to Trial by Jury: Joinder of Jones Act and Traditional Maritime Claims*

FITZGERALD v. UNITED STATES LINES CO.

374 U.S. 16, 83 S. Ct. 26, 11 L. Ed. 2d 99 (1963)

Mr. Justice BLACK delivered the opinion of the Court

Andres San Martin, a seaman, brought this action in the District Court for the Southern District of New York against the respondent United States Lines Company. His complaint alleged that he had twisted and strained his back while working for respondent on its ship. He claimed $75,000 damages based on the negligence of respondent and on the unseaworthiness of the ship and $10,000 based on respondents failure to provide him with medical attention, maintenance and cure, and wages as required by law.[1] Martins negligence claim invoked a remedy created by Congress in § 33 of the Jones Act, 46 U.S.C. § 688, which explicitly provides that a seaman can have a jury trial as of right; but the actions for unseaworthiness and for maintenance and cure are traditional admiralty remedies which in the absence of a statute do not ordinarily require trial by jury. The complainant here did demand a jury, however, for all the issues growing out of the single accident. The trial judge granted a jury trial for the Jones Act and the unseaworthiness issues but held the question of recovery under maintenance and cure in abeyance to try himself after jury trial of the other two issues. The jury returned a verdict for United States Lines on the negligence and unseaworthiness issues; the court then, after hearing testimony in addition to that presented to the jury, awarded Martin $224 for maintenance and cure. Sitting *en banc*, the Court of Appeals for the Second Circuit affirmed, four judges stating that it would be improper to submit a maintenance and cure claim to the jury, two believing it to be permissible but not required, and three maintaining that a seaman is entitled, as of right, to a jury trial of a maintenance and cure claim joined with a Jones Act claim. 306 F.2d 461. The lower courts are at odds on this issue.[2] We granted certiorari to decide it.[3] 371 U.S. 932.

For years it has been a common, although not uniform,[4] practice of District Courts to grant jury trials to plaintiff's who join in one complaint their Jones Act, unseaworthiness, and maintenance and cure claims when all the claims, as here, grow out of a single transaction or accident.[5] This practice of requiring issues arising out of a single accident to be tried by a single tribunal is by no means surprising. Although remedies for negligence, unseaworthiness, and maintenance and cure have different origins and may on occasion call for application of slightly different principles and procedures, they nevertheless, when based on one unitary set of circumstances, serve the same purpose of indemnifying a seaman for damages caused by injury, depend in large part upon the same evidence, and involve some identical elements of recovery. Requiring a seaman to split up his lawsuit, submitting part

---

[1] Martin died while his appeal was pending and a public administrator was substituted for him.

[2] *See* notes 4 and 5, *infra.*

[3] Because of our limited grant of certiorari, we do not consider petitioner's argument that the complaint and trial record show diversity of citizenship jurisdiction and that therefore plaintiff was entitled to a jury trial. *See Atlantic & Gulf Stevedores, Inc., v. Ellerman Lines,* 369 U.S. 355, 360 (1962). Nor do we find it necessary to reach petitioner's argument that we should reconsider that part of the holding of *Romero v. International Terminal Operating Co.,* 358 U.S. 354 (1959), which concluded that claims based upon general maritime law cannot be brought in federal courts under the federal question jurisdiction of 28 U.S.C. § 1331.

[4] *See, e.g., Jesonis v. Oliver J. Olson & Co.,* 238 F.2d 307 (C.A. 9th Cir. 1956); *Stendze v. The Boat Neptune, Inc.,* 135 F. Supp. 801 (D.C. Mass. 1955); *cf. Jordine v. Walling,* 185 F.2d 662 (C.A. 3d Cir. 1950).

[5] *See, e.g., Nolan v. General Seafoods Corp.,* 112 F.2d 515 (C.A. 1st Cir. 1940); *Lykes Bros. S.S. Co. v. Grubaugh,* 128 F.2d 387, *modified on rehearing,* 130 F.2d 25 (C.A. 5th Cir. 1942); *Bay State Dredging Contracting Co. v. Porter,* 153 F.2d 827 (C.A. 1st Cir. 1946); *Gonzales v. United Fruit Co.,* 193 F.2d 479 (C.A. 2d Cir. 1951); *Rosenquist v. Isthmian S.S. Co.,* 205 F.2d 486 (C.A. 2d Cir. 1953); *Mitchell v. Trawler Racer, Inc.,* 265 F.2d 426 (C.A. 1st Cir. 1959), *rev'd on other grounds,* 362 U.S. 539 (1960); *McDonald v. Cape Cod Trawling Corp.,* 71 F. Supp. 888, 891 (D.C. Mass. 1947); GILMORE AND BLACK, THE LAW OF ADMIRALTY (1957), 262.

of it to a jury and part to a judge, unduly complicates and confuses a trial, creates difficulties in applying doctrines of *res judicata* and collateral estoppel, and can easily result in too much or too little recovery.[6] The problems are particularly acute in determining the amount of damages. For example, all lost earnings and medical expenses are recoverable on a negligence count, but under the Jones Act they are subject to reduction by the jury if the seaman has been contributorily negligent. These same items are recoverable in part on the maintenance and cure count, but the damages are measured by different standards[7] and are not subject to reduction for any contributory negligence. It is extremely difficult for a judge in trying a maintenance and cure claim to ascertain, even with the use of special interrogatories, exactly what went into the damages awarded by a jury—how loss of earning power was calculated, how much was allowed for medical expenses and pain and suffering, how much was allowed for actual lost wages, and how much, if any, each of the recoveries was reduced by contributory negligence. This raises needless problems of who has the burden of proving exactly what the jury did. And even if the judge can find out what elements of damage the jury's verdict actually represented, he must still try to solve the puzzling problem of the bearing the jury's verdict should have on recovery under the different standards of the maintenance and cure claim. In the absence of some statutory or constitutional obstacle, an end should be put to such an unfortunate, outdated, and wasteful manner of trying these cases.[9] Fortunately, there is no such obstacle.

While this Court has held that the Seventh Amendment does not require jury trials in admiralty cases,[10] neither that Amendment nor any other provision of the Constitution forbids them.[11] Nor does any statute of Congress or Rule of Procedure, Civil or Admiralty, forbid jury trials in maritime cases. Article III of the Constitution vested in the federal courts jurisdiction over admiralty and maritime cases, and, since that time, the Congress has largely left to this Court the responsibility for fashioning the controlling rules of admiralty law. This Court has long recognized its power and responsibility in this area and has exercised that power where necessary to do so.[12] Where, as here, a particular mode of trial being used by many judges is so cumbersome, confusing, and time consuming that it places completely unnecessary obstacles in the paths of litigants seeking justice in our courts, we should not and do not hesitate to take action to correct the situation. Only one trier of fact should be used for the trial of what is essentially one lawsuit to settle one claim split conceptually into separate parts because of historical developments. And since Congress in the Jones Act has declared that the negligence part of the claim shall be tried by a jury, we would not be free, even if we wished, to require submission of all the claims to the judge alone. Therefore, the jury, a time-honored institution in our jurisprudence, is the only tribunal competent under the present congressional enactments to try all the claims. Accordingly, we hold that a maintenance and cure claim joined with a Jones Act claim must be submitted to the jury when both arise out of one set of facts. The seaman in this case was therefore entitled to a jury trial as of right on his maintenance and cure claim.

Judgment against the seaman on the Jones Act claim was affirmed by the Court of Appeals, and we declined to review it on certiorari. The shipowner points out that on remand the maintenance and cure claim would no longer be joined with a Jones Act claim and therefore, he argues, could be tried by a judge without a jury. We cannot agree.

---

[6] For an illuminating discussion of the practical problems, *see Jenkins v. Roderick*, 156 F. Supp. 299, 304-306 (D.C. Mass. 1957) (WYZANSKI, J.).

This Court has held that recovery of maintenance and cure does not bar a subsequent action under the Jones Act, *Pacific S.S. Co. v. Peterson*, 278 U.S. 130 (1928), but of course, where such closely related claims are submitted to different triers of fact, questions of *res judicata* and collateral estoppel necessarily arise, particularly in connection with efforts to avoid duplication of damages.

[7] Maintenance and cure allows recovery for wages only to the end of the voyage on which a seaman is injured or becomes ill. *The Osceola*, 189 U.S. 158, 175 (1903). Medical expenses need not be provided beyond the point at which a seaman becomes incurable. *Farrell v. United States*, 336 U.S. 511 (1949).

[8] *See, e.g., Bartholomew v. Universe Tankships, Inc.*, 279 F.2d 911, 915-916 (C.A. 2d Cir. 1960); *Stendze v. The Boat Neptune, Inc.*, 135 F. Supp. 801 (D.C. Mass. 1955). For another example of some of the difficulties involved in separate trials, compare *Claudio v. Sinclair Ref. Co.*, 160 F. Supp. 3 (D.C. E.D. N.Y. 1958), with *Lazarowitz v. American Export Lines*, 87 F. Supp. 197 (D.C. E.D. Pa. 1949).

[9] *See generally* Currie, *The Silver Oar and All That: A Study of the Romero Case*, 27 U. of Chi. L. Rev. 1 (1959); Kurland, *The Romero Case and Some Problems of Federal Jurisdiction*, 73 Harv. L. Rev. 817, 850 (1960); Note, 73 Harv. L. Rev. 138 (1959).

[10] *Waring v. Clarke*, 5 How. 441, 460 (1847).

[11] *The Genesee Chief v. Fitzhugh*, 12 How. 443, 459-460 (Dec. Term, 1851) (upholding constitutionality of jury trial provision in Great Lakes Act).

[12] *See, e.g., The John G. Stevens*, 170 U.S. 113 (1898); *Swift & Co. Packers v. Compania Colombiana Del Caribe, S.A.*, 339 U.S. 684, 690, 691 (1950); *Warren v. UnitedStates*, 340 U.S. 523, 527 (1951); *Wilburn Boat Co. v. Firemans Fund Ins. Co.*, 348 U.S. 310, 314 (1955); *Romero v. International Terminal Operating Co.*, 358 U.S. 354, 360-361 (1959); *The Tungus v.Skovgaard,358* U.S. 588, 597, 611 (1959) (opinion of BRENNAN, J., concurring in part and dissenting in part); *Mitchell v. Trawler Racer, Inc.*, 362 U.S. 539 (1960).

Our holding is that it was error to deprive the seaman of the jury trial he demanded, and he is entitled to relief from this error by having the kind of trial he would have had in the absence of error.

Reversed.

---

5. Right to Trial by Jury: Joinder of Jones Act and Maritime Claims In Rem

VODUSEK v. BAYLINER MARINE CORPORATION

71 F.3d 148, 1996 AMC 330 (4th Cir. 1995), *supra*

ZRNCEVICH v. BLUE HAWAII ENTERPRISES, INC.

738 F. Supp. 350, 1990 AMC 2450 (D. Haw. 1990)

FONG, Chief Judge

Introduction

The issue before this court is whether plaintiff has a right to a jury trial where the plaintiff has asserted admiralty and maritime claims *in rem* as well as a claim under the Jones Act, 46 U.S.C. app. § 688.

Background

On September 28, 1989, plaintiff Robert Zrncevich, a seaman, brought this action against defendants Blue Hawaii Enterprises, Inc. ("Blue Hawaii") *in personam* and the vessel F/V Haida, O.N. 605147, her engines, tackle, stores and equipment *in rem*, alleging personal injury aboard ship. Plaintiff accepted a Stipulation of Undertaking in the amount of $ 150,000 security as the *res* in lieu of arresting the vessel. Plaintiff had not made an effort to arrest the vessel.

Plaintiff Zrncevich was hired by defendant Blue Hawaii to perform tasks on board ship related to Blue Hawaii's commercial fishing operation. Plaintiff's primary task was the handling of lobster cages. Plaintiff alleges that he received injuries to his hands while working on board ship, with symptoms including pain, tingling, numbness, contractures and loss of strength in his hands. Plaintiff further alleges that defendant Blue Hawaii refused him care for these injuries both on board ship and after plaintiff returned to Honolulu. In his suit, plaintiff alleges negligence, unseaworthiness and maintenance and cure, unpaid wages and breach of contract.

Plaintiff designated his case as filed "In Admiralty." Plaintiff pled "admiralty and maritime claims within the meaning of Federal Rules of Civil Procedure 9(h)" and asserted jurisdiction under 28 U.S.C. § 1333 (federal jurisdiction for admiralty and maritime claims). Plaintiff also asserted federal jurisdiction under the Jones Act, 46 U.S.C. app. § 688, and included a Demand for a Jury Trial "on all issues triable herein."

On January 12, 1990 plaintiff moved for leave to file a first amended complaint to clarify his jurisdictional assertion under the Jones Act. Defendants objected and filed a cross-motion to strike plaintiff's jury demand. Defendants asserted that in spite of the statutory right to a jury trial on the Jones Act claim, plaintiff had no right to a jury trial because plaintiff elected to proceed *in rem* in admiralty. Magistrate Daral G. Conklin denied both motions in his March 6, 1990 order.

The Magistrate found that plaintiff's original complaint properly alleged a claim under the Jones Act and that accordingly, it was unnecessary for plaintiff to amend his complaint. The Magistrate held that the plaintiff has a right to try at least his Jones Act claim, and possibly other claims, to the jury. Accordingly, the Magistrate also denied defendant's motion to strike plaintiff's jury demand.

The parties here appeal from those parts of the Magistrate's order denying their respective motions.

Discussion

In their Motion to Strike Jury Demand, defendants assert that plaintiff has no right to a jury trial on his Jones Act claim because plaintiff affirmatively asserted admiralty claims and admiralty jurisdiction in his complaint. Plaintiff asserted admiralty and maritime jurisdiction by pleading claims within the meaning of F.R.C.P. 9(h), which states that

> A pleading or count setting forth a claim for relief within the admiralty and maritime jurisdiction that is also within the jurisdiction of the district court on some other ground may contain a statement identifying the claim as an admiralty or maritime claim for the purposes of Rules 14(c), 38(e), 82, and the Supplemental Rules for Certain Admiralty and Maritime Claims. F.R.C.P. 9(h).

Admiralty remedies such as actions for unseaworthiness and maintenance and cure do not ordinarily carry a right to trial by jury. While F.R.C.P. 38 generally preserves the Seventh Amendment right to a jury trial, Rule 38(e) provides that Rule 38 "shall not be construed to create a right to trial by jury of the issues in an admiralty or maritime claim within the meaning of Rule 9(h)...."

At the same time, the Jones Act specifically allows a seaman to bring his Jones Act claim before a jury. The Jones Act reads in relevant part:

> *Recovery for injury to or death of seaman.* Any seaman who shall suffer personal injury in the course of his employment may, at his election, maintain an action for damages at law, with the right of trial by jury.

46 U.S.C. app. § 688. Plaintiff here asserted Jones Act claims and elected trial by jury by including a Demand for a Jury Trial in his pleadings.

Defendants argue that the statutory construction of the Jones Act demands an irrevocable election between an action at law (with a right to trial by jury) or in admiralty (without a jury trial). Defendants argue that plaintiff has elected to place his case in admiralty by (1) designating his claim in admiralty, and (2) utilizing remedies *in rem.* Defendants assert that plaintiff secured his claims *in rem* by naming the vessel as a defendant *in rem* and by accepting a stipulation of undertaking substituted as the *res* in lieu of the arrest of the vessel.

Plaintiff argues that his right to a jury trial under the Jones Act is statutorily guaranteed by his Demand for Jury Trial in his pleadings, and is not precluded or waived in any way by his assertion of admiralty claims.

This court must resolve two issues: (1) whether a plaintiff who has asserted claims in admiralty along with his Jones Act claim has a right to bring all his claims in admiralty and the Jones Act before a jury or (2) whether proceeding *in rem* precludes the plaintiff from bringing *any* claim before the jury.

Right to a Jury Trial For Joined Claims

The Jones Act gives seamen a statutory right to a jury trial for claims of personal injury. 46 U.S.C. app. § 688. However, bringing a Jones Act claim does not preclude a seaman from also asserting the traditional admiralty claims of unseaworthiness and maintenance and cure. *Haskins v. Point Towing Co.,* 395 F.2d 737, 742 (3d Cir. 1968). It is a common practice for district courts to grant jury trials to plaintiff's who join their Jones Act, unseaworthiness, and maintenance and cure claims in one complaint, when all claims arise out of a single transaction or occurrence. *Fitzgerald v. United States Lines Co.,* 374 U.S. 16, 18, 10 L. Ed. 2d 720, 83 S. Ct. 1646 (1963). Accordingly, hybrid actions consisting of both law claims (such as Jones Act claims) and admiralty claims abound.

Courts have struggled to find the best procedural tack to take when traditional admiralty and law claims are consolidated. In *Romero v. International Terminal Operating Co.,* 358 U.S. 354, 3 L. Ed. 2d 368, 79 S. Ct. 468 (1959), the Supreme Court held that the district court has pendent jurisdiction over unseaworthiness and maintenance and cure claims when joined with a Jones Act claim. However, the Court left unanswered the question whether all three claims could be submitted to the jury. This question, however, was addressed by the Second Circuit later that year, which held that maritime claims joined with Jones Act claims may be tried before the jury. *Bartholomew v. Universe Tankships, Inc.,* 263 F.2d 437 (2d Cir. 1959). The *Bartholomew* court discussed at length the legal and legislative history enabling joined Jones Act and maritime claims, and discussed the problems of evidence, *res judicata,* and judicial economy that would arise if the plaintiff were required to split claims so factually intertwined and of "fundamental singleness." *Bartholomew* 263 F.2d at 444-446.

The *Bartholomew* court's decision foreshadowed the Supreme Court's decision in the seminal *Fitzgerald* case. *Fitzgerald,* 374 U.S. 16, 10 L. Ed. 2d 720, 83 S. Ct. 1646. In *Fitzgerald,* a seaman brought an action against a shipowner for damages stemming from an alleged shipboard injury. *Id.* at 17. The seaman brought claims under the Jones Act, as well as actions for unseaworthiness and for maintenance and cure, and demanded a jury trial for all issues growing out of the single accident. *Id.* In holding that a traditional maritime maintenance and cure claim joined with a Jones Act claim must be submitted to the jury when both arise out of one set of facts, the court reasoned that:

[r]equiring a seaman to split up his lawsuit, submitting part of it to a jury and part to a judge, unduly complicates and confuses a trial, creates difficulties in applying doctrines of *res judicata* and collateral estoppel, and can easily result in too much or too little recovery.

Id. at 18-19. The Court stated the principle, "Only one trier of fact should be used for the trial of what is essentially one lawsuit to settle one claim split conceptually into separate parts because of historical developments." *Id.* at 21.

The Court further stated that

since Congress in the Jones Act has declared that the negligence part of the claim shall be tried by a jury, we would not be free, even if we wished, to require submission of all the claims to the judge alone. *Id.*

Since *Fitzgerald* was decided, the majority of courts have held that traditional admiralty and maritime claims can be joined with claims having an independent basis of federal jurisdiction and brought together before the jury. In *Peace v. Fidalgo Island Packing Co.,* 419 F.2d 371 (9th Cir. 1969), the personal representative of a deceased seaman brought a claim for damages for negligence under the Jones Act and a claim for unseaworthiness under the Death On The High Seas Act, 46 U.S.C. app. § 761 *et seq. Citing Fitzgerald,* the Court of Appeals for the Ninth Circuit allowed plaintiff to join both claims and bring them before the jury. The appellate court held, "there is nothing in the Rules [of Civil Procedure] which prohibits a trial by jury on joined civil and admiralty claims." *Peace,* 419 F.2d at 371.

An appellate panel for the Ninth Circuit similarly held in *Owens-Illinois, Inc. v. U.S. District Court,* 698 F.2d 967 (9th Cir. 1983) that a jury trial is required where admiralty claims are joined with civil claims and common issues of fact are involved. The court would not allow defendants right to a jury trial under diversity jurisdiction to be precluded by plaintiff's assertion of admiralty jurisdiction, since "when admiralty claims are joined with civil claims and the issues cannot be segregated for separate trial, a jury trial if timely demanded is required." *Id.* at 972.

Defendant cites *Trentacosta v. Frontier Pacific Aircraft Indus.,* 813 F.2d 1553 (9th Cir. 1987), as supporting the proposition that plaintiff must elect to proceed either in admiralty or at law when plaintiff joins his maritime and admiralty claims with a Jones Act claim. The *Trentacosta* plaintiff, however, did not properly invoke admiralty jurisdiction for his maritime claims in his amended complaint. *Id.* at 1555. In fact, the appellate court noted that if plaintiff amended his complaint to invoke admiralty jurisdiction, those claims could be joined with his Jones Act claim and all tried before a jury. *Id.* at 1561 n.6.

It is the common rule in several districts that a seaman may bring unseaworthiness and maintenance and cure counts before the jury if joined with civil claims with independent federal jurisdictional basis, especially if the claims have arisen out of the same transaction or occurrence. *Duhon v. Koch Exploration Co.,* 628 F. Supp. 925 (W.D. La.

1986) (plaintiff's maritime claims may be joined with his Jones Act claim and tried to the jury and the maritime claims may still be governed according to the traditional rules of practice in admiralty); *Woosley v. Mike Hooks, Inc.,* 603 F. Supp. 1190 (W.D.La. 1985) (purely maritime claims "can and should" be tried to the jury when the Jones Act and maritime claims all arise out of the same transaction or occurrence); *Morrison v. United States Lines, Inc.,* 1983 A.M.C. 1769 (S.D.N.Y. 1983) (plaintiff seaman who withdrew his Jones Act claim no longer entitled to a jury trial on his maritime claim); *Red Star Towing & Transport Co. v. the Cargo Ship "Ming Giant",* 552 F. Supp. 367 (S.D.N.Y. 1982) (a litigant in admiralty is not entitled as a matter of right to a non-jury trial; claims may be joined and tried before the jury); *Drakatos v. R.B. Denison, Inc.,* 493 F. Supp. 942 (D. Conn. 1980) (admiralty claims may be tried to the jury when linked to a civil claim with an independent basis for federal jurisdiction); *Rok v. Continental Seafoods, Inc.,* 462 F. Supp. 894 (S.D. Ala. 1978) (where jurisdiction in a seamans action for personal injury was based, in part, on diversity of citizenship, plaintiff was entitled to trial by jury on both law claims and general maritime claims); *Mattes v. National Hellenic American Line, S.A.,* 427 F. Supp. 619 (S.D.N.Y. 1977) (where general maritime claims arise out of the same transaction as Jones Act claim, both may be tried to the jury although there is no diversity).

Accordingly, plaintiff is entitled to demand a jury trial on his joined Jones Act and admiralty and maritime claims.

In Rem Proceedings

Although bringing hybrid law and admiralty claims before the jury is common, courts are divided on how to proceed in hybrid actions when traditional admiralty actions have been invoked, such as *in rem* proceedings, or when a Rule 9(h) election to proceed in admiralty has been made.

Defendants in the instant case assert that either of these actions by a plaintiff affirmatively determines the election to proceed in admiralty, traditionally without the right to a jury trial. Defendants assert that plaintiff here has forfeited his ability to try any of his claims to the jury by positively asserting Rule 9(h) admiralty jurisdiction and proceeding *in rem*. Defendants rely on *T.N.T. Marine Services Inc. v. Weaver Shipyards and Dry Docks, Inc.,* 702 F.2d 585, 587-88 (5th Cir.), *cert. den.* 464 U.S. 847, 78 L. Ed. 2d 141, 104 S. Ct. 151 (1983) (*in rem* claims are cognizable only in admiralty notwithstanding allegations of diversity jurisdiction), *Romero v. Bethlehem Steel Corporation,* 515 F.2d 1249 (5th Cir. 1975) (plaintiff not entitled to jury trial under diversity jurisdiction where he refused to withdraw 9(h) designation) and *Truehart v. Blandon,* 685 F. Supp. 956 (E.D. La. 1988) (complaint and proceeding *in rem* designates plaintiff's claim as one in admiralty and disallows jury demand asserted under diversity jurisdiction). However, the *T.N.T., Romero,* and *Truehart* plaintiff's did not allege Jones Act claims. The Court in *Fitzgerald* specifically held that because of plaintiff's statutory right to a jury on the Jones Act claim, the Court is not free to take the joined claims away from the jury and try the case to the bench. *Fitzgerald,* 374 U.S. at 21.

Defendants also rely upon *Plamals v. the Pinar Del Rio,* 277 U.S. 151, 72 L. Ed. 827, 48 S. Ct. 457 (1927) which held that seamen may invoke remedies at law under the Jones Act or remedies in admiralty, but not both. In *Fernandes v. United Fruit Co.,* 303 F. Supp. 681 (D. Md. 1969), the district court followed *Plamals* in holding that plaintiff cannot utilize *in rem* proceedings when joining maritime and admiralty claims with Jones Act claims but must elect to place the whole case in either law or admiralty.

In contrast, several courts have held that the spirit of the Supreme Court's holding in Fitzgerald is best followed by allowing the plaintiff to bring the entire case to the jury regardless of the manner of assertion of claims in admiralty.

In *Haskins v. Point Towing Co.,* 395 F.2d 737 (3d Cir. 1968), the plaintiff seaman brought an action seeking recovery for personal injuries and asserted claims both *in rem* and *in personam*. *Id.* at 738. Notwithstanding the use of *in rem* proceedings, the *Haskins* court held that *Fitzgerald* gives a plaintiff, who demands a jury trial for his Jones Act claim, a right to join with it his claims under maritime law for unseaworthiness and maintenance and cure, and try them all before the jury. *Id.* at 743. The *Haskins* court stated further that *Fitzgerald* did not characterize the maritime claims as brought in law with the Jones Act claim, but specifically created a right to trial by jury for admiralty claims joined with a Jones Act claim. *Id.* at 741. The *Haskins* court also stated that the plaintiff should not have to bring the maritime claims at law just to secure the right to the jury trial:

> To require this would compel him to lose the advantages which inhere in the characteristic admiralty claims, such as *in rem* process, interlocutory appeals, admiralty attachment.... There is no reason to make relinquishment of the procedural advantages of these inherent admiralty claims for unseaworthiness and maintenance and cure the price for a jury trial.

Id. Although it did not mention *in rem* proceedings, the *Fitzgerald* opinion was not inapposite to the idea that maritime claims "may on occasion call for application of slightly different principles and procedures." *Fitzgerald, supra,* 374 U.S. at 18.

Similarly, in *Durden v. Exxon Corp.*, 803 F.2d 845 (5th Cir. 1986), plaintiff brought claims *in personam* and *in rem*. The court dismissed the plaintiff's Jones Act claim but noted that if it had not done so, *Fitzgerald* would have allowed plaintiff to bring maritime and admiralty claims to the jury along with his Jones Act claims. *Id.* at 848.

Neither is the Rule 9(h) assertion fatal to jury trial. In *Parfait v. Central Towing, Inc.*, 1979 A.M.C. 2485 (E.D. La. 1978), the court allowed the plaintiff to bring his maritime claims together with his Jones Act claim to the jury, even though plaintiff designated his unseaworthiness and maintenance and cure claims as admiralty claims pursuant to Rule 9(h) and also initiated an *in rem* seizure of the defendants boat. The court held that it was "more consonant with the spirit of *Fitzgerald* to allow a jury trial for all claims of a Jones Act plaintiff when he sues only his employer notwithstanding a 9(h) designation and the use of admiralty procedures." *Id.* at 2489.

These latter cases are more in keeping with the spirit of *Fitzgerald* and its progeny where a Jones Act plaintiff brings a hybrid cause of action. The reasoning of the *Fitzgerald* Court in joining the claims before the jury centers on judicial economy, especially on the logistical and fairness problems which would be created by trying one case before two triers of fact. *Fitzgerald* 374 U.S. at 19. The Court describes in particular the potential problems in the determination of damages by two triers of fact. *Id.* The Court also reasons that it is important to avoid the problems of *res judicata* and collateral estoppel created when what is essentially one lawsuit is split. *Id.*

Importantly, *Fitzgerald* emphasizes that there is no explicit prohibition against jury trials for admiralty claims:

> While this Court has held that the Seventh Amendment does not require jury trials in admiralty cases, neither that amendment nor any other provision of the Constitution forbids them. Nor does any statute of Congress or Rule of Procedure, Civil or Admiralty, forbid jury trials in maritime cases.

Id. at 20. (Footnotes omitted).

The Ninth Circuit agreed that there is nothing to prohibit a jury trial on joined admiralty and Jones Act claims. In a cause of action brought by the widow of a deceased seaman under the Jones Act and the Death On the High Seas Act, the court held that

> [t]here is nothing in the present rules of Civil Procedure which grants a trial by jury in an admiralty or maritime claim ... But there is nothing in the Rules which prohibits a trial by jury on joined civil and admiralty claims. Rule 9(h) ... which pertains to identifying claims, does not modify this result.

Peace v. Fidalgo, supra, at 371.

There is nothing inherently incongruous about bringing an *in rem* and an *in personam* claim together before the jury when the claims arise out of a single occurrence. *Continental Grain Co. v. Barge FBL-585*, 364 U.S. 19, 4 L. Ed.

2d 1540, 80 S. Ct. 1470 (1960), concerned the § 1404 transfer of a federal case in which plaintiff had brought both an *in rem* action against a ship and an *in personam* action against the owner, stemming from the same occurrence and issues. The Court held that while the *in rem* and *in personam* claims were two methods invoked to bring the owner into court, the substance of what had to be done to adjudicate the rights of the parties in an *in rem* and an *in personam* claim was not different at all. *Continental Grain* at 26.

The majority of cases, including *Fitzgerald,* which hold that the plaintiff is entitled to bring joined maritime and civil claims before the jury, generally do not address the procedural steps taken by plaintiff in asserting the admiralty claims. Most cases allowing the joined claims do not describe whether the plaintiff simply stated admiralty claims, made a specific Rule 9(h) election, or initiated proceedings *in rem. Fitzgerald* does not indicate that it was intended to apply only to admiralty claims asserted informally, where no Rule 9(h) election or *in rem* assertions were made. These actions would not lessen the concerns enumerated by the *Fitzgerald* Court for judicial economy and the fairness problems when a single case is split and tried to two triers of fact. Neither can such actions reasonably be construed to indicate that a plaintiff elects to waive his statutory right to a jury trial under the Jones Act, when a demand for a jury trial is properly included in the complaint.

Therefore, allowing the plaintiff to join his Jones Act claim and maritime claims before the jury serves the principles of judicial economy and fairness that result from bringing the joined claims before a single trier of fact when the claims arise out of a single transaction or occurrence. The Jones Act guarantees the plaintiff a jury trial if timely elected, and there is no prohibition against a jury trial for the admiralty claims. Therefore, at the election of the plaintiff the one trier of fact will be the jury.

Conclusion

The Jones Act gives plaintiff a right to a trial by jury if plaintiff so elects. Plaintiff here asserted the Jones Act and demanded a jury trial. *Fitzgerald* holds that the seaman can join the traditional admiralty claims for unseaworthiness, maintenance and cure with Jones Act claims before the jury. This court now finds that this right to a jury trial is not precluded even if plaintiff has made a specific assertion of admiralty claims and utilized proceedings *in rem.*

Accordingly, defendants' appeal from the Magistrate's order is DENIED. As it is unnecessary for plaintiff to amend his complaint to maintain his right to a jury trial, plaintiff's appeal from the Magistrate's order is also DENIED.

IT IS SO ORDERED.

Note

The Ghotras invoked the jurisdiction of two historically separate departments in a single action, combining claims at law under diversity jurisdiction with an *in rem* claim under admiralty jurisdiction. Under the Seventh Amendment, the Ghotras were entitled to a jury trial on the claims brought under the court's diversity jurisdiction. We find nothing inherently incongruous about bringing an *in rem* and an *in personam* claim together before the jury when the claims arise out of a single occurrence. Although the right to jury trial in the instant case derives from the savings to suitors clause rather than a statutory grant such as the Jones Act, the reasoning of *Fitzgerald* is equally persuasive and justifies a jury trial over all four claims, where the *in rem* claim arises out of the same factual circumstances as the other three claims. Contrary to the Vessel Interests' argument, such a holding would not "completely eliminate the election required under F.R.C.P. Rule 9(h)" or "nullify F.R.C.P. Rule 38(e) in all maritime cases in which a separate basis for subject matter jurisdiction could be articulated."

In light of the fact that the Ghotras could have brought two separate actions, one consisting of the *in personam* claims brought under diversity and one consisting solely of the in rem claim, which could then have been consolidated into one action under Federal Rule of Civil Procedure 42(a), we find no reason to penalize the Ghotras by ruling that the decision to combine the two into one single action constituted an election to proceed in admiralty alone without the right to jury trial. Such a holding would run contrary to the intent of the Federal Rules of Civil Procedure and result in a waste of judicial resources and duplication of testimony in parallel actions. Furthermore, because the Federal Rules contain provisions designed to prevent artificially constructed diversity actions that do not contain all necessary parties, we have not "opened the floodgates" to allow jury trials in all maritime cases. See Fed. R. Civ. P. 19. Finally, the Ghotras clearly asserted diversity as the jurisdictional basis for the *in personam* claims in each of their Complaints. This is not a case where the Ghotras changed their mind as to the jurisdictional basis in the midst of litigation. Nor is it a case where the Ghotras utilized the advantages of *in rem* procedures then turned around to use the same claim as the basis for diversity jurisdiction. *See Jose v. M/V Fir Grove,* 765 F.Supp. 1037, 1039 (D. Or. 1991). We conclude therefore that the Ghotras were entitled to a jury trial on their entire action.

Ghotra v. Bandila Shipping, Inc., 113 F.3d 1050, 1997 AMC 1936 (9th Cir. 1997), *cert. denied,* 522 U.S. 1107, 118 S.Ct. 1034 (1998).

---

6. Counterclaims

Note

Under Rule 13(b) of the Federal Rules of Civil Procedure, a permissive counterclaim can be brought in an admiralty proceeding. If the claim is within the court's admiralty jurisdiction and the parties are diverse, the counterclaimant may identify its claim as maritime or bring it under the "saving to suitors" clause.

---

a. Counterclaims: Right to Trial by Jury

WILMINGTON TRUST v. U.S. DISTRICT COURT FOR DISTRICT OF HAWAII

934 F.2d 1026, 1991 AMC 1849 (9th Cir. 1991)

SHUBB, District Judge

I

Procedural and Factual Background

Petitioners Wilmington Trust, as trustee for the International Organization of Masters, Mates and Pilots ("Union"), and the Union request this court to issue a writ of mandamus directing United States District Judge Samuel P. King to try the Union's claims before a jury. The court has jurisdiction to consider and issue the writ pursuant to 28 U.S.C. § 1651(a).[1]

The underlying action was initiated by Respondent Connecticut Bank & Trust Company ("Connecticut Bank"), solely as indenture trustee for Wartsila Marine Industries, Inc. ("Wartsila") a Finnish corporation. The complaint consists of an *in rem* claim to foreclose a First Preferred Ship Mortgage against the SS Monterey ("vessel"), and a related *in personam* claim against the owner of the vessel, the SS Monterey Limited Partnership ("Partnership").[2] The complaint also includes the assertion that "Plaintiff's claim is an Admiralty and Maritime Claim within the meaning of Rule 9(h) of the Federal Rules of Civil Procedure and the Ship Mortgage Act of 1920, 46 U.S.C. § 911 *et seq.*"[3]

The Union, though not a named defendant, answered the complaint and filed an *in rem* claim against the vessel to foreclose a Second Preferred Ship Mortgage and several other claims designated as "counterclaims" ("Counterclaims") against Wartsila. The Union demanded a jury trial. Those Counterclaims include both legal and equitable claims. Independent jurisdictional grounds are alleged for each claim and their joinder is not contested.

Wartsila's foreclosure action, and the Unions Counterclaims and foreclosure action, are factually interrelated and arise out of the following transactions. The Union exchanged its ownership interest in the vessel to the Partnership for a second preferred ship mortgage, an interest in the Partnership, and an agreement that the vessel would be

---

1. Section 1651(a) provides:

> The Supreme Court and all courts established by Act of Congress may issue all writs necessary or appropriate in aid of their respective jurisdictions and agreeable to the usages and principles of law.

[2] The parties concede that the claim against the Partnership is no longer part of the underlying action.
[3] The Ship Mortgage Act of 1920 was repealed effective January 1, 1989. Act of Nov. 23, 1988, Pub. L. 100-710, Title I, § 106(b)(2), 102 Stat. 4752.

staffed exclusively with Union members. One of the purposes of the exchange was to generate capital to refurbish the vessel. The Partnership contracted with Wartsila to refurbish the vessel and Wartsila extended credit to the Partnership in exchange for a first preferred ship mortgage.

The district court ordered the interlocutory sale of the vessel. Wartsila's indenture trustee, Connecticut Bank, is the named purchaser of the ship on behalf of Wartsila. According to undocumented assertions of counsel, Wartsila is involved in bankruptcy proceedings in Finland, and the Finnish Guaranty Board ("FGB"), a "foreign state" within the Foreign Sovereign Immunities Act, 28 U.S.C. §§ 1602-1611, extended a letter of credit to Connecticut Bank on behalf of Wartsila enabling the bank to purchase the vessel at the interlocutory sale.

On July 30, 1990, the district court entered an order striking the Unions timely jury demand for the "reasons set forth in the memoranda of the Plaintiff Connecticut Bank." Connecticut Bank had urged the district court to strike the Unions jury demand on two grounds: first, Wartsila's 9(h) election to proceed within the courts admiralty jurisdiction extinguished any right to a jury trial that the Union may have had; second, Wartsila has a right to a non-jury trial pursuant to the Foreign Sovereign Immunities Act. For the reasons discussed below, we order the writ to issue.

* * *

Wartsila's Rule 9(h)

Designation did not Extinguish the Unions Right to Jury Trial

The basis for admiralty jurisdiction is set forth in 28 U.S.C. § 1333, which states:

The district courts shall have original jurisdiction, exclusive of the courts of the States, of:

(1) Any civil case of admiralty or maritime jurisdiction, saving to suitors in all cases all other remedies to which they are otherwise entitled.

The "saving-to-suitors" clause establishes the right of a party to choose whether to proceed within the court's admiralty jurisdiction or general civil jurisdiction when both admiralty and non-admiralty federal jurisdiction exist. *See e.g., Atlantic & Gulf Stevedores, Inc. v. Ellerman Lines*, 369 U.S. 355, 359-60, 82 S. Ct. 780, 783-84, 7 L. Ed. 2d 798 (1962).

Prior to the 1966 merger of law and admiralty, a plaintiff exercised this option by filing a claim on the admiralty side or the civil side of the federal court. *Id.* With the merger of law and admiralty, the Federal Rules of Civil Procedure advisory committee recognized the need for a mechanism to inform the court of a claimant's election to proceed in admiralty on claims cognizable both in admiralty and the courts general civil jurisdiction. Consequently, the committee noted:

Many claims, however, are cognizable by the district courts whether asserted in admiralty or in a civil action, assuming the existence of a nonmaritime ground of jurisdiction. Thus at present the pleader has power to determine procedural consequences by the way in which he exercises the classic privilege given by the saving-to-suitors clause (28 U.S.C. § 1333) or by equivalent statutory provisions.

* * *

One of the important procedural consequences is that in the civil action either party may demand a jury trial, while in the suit in admiralty there is no right to jury trial except as provided by statute.

* * *

It is no part of the purpose of unification to inject a right to jury trial into those admiralty cases in which that right is not provided by statute…. The unified rules must therefore provide some device for preserving the present power of the pleader to determine whether these historically maritime procedures shall be applicable to his claim or not; the pleader must be afforded some means of designating his claim as the counterpart of the present suit in admiralty, where its character as such is not clear.

Fed. R. Civ. P 9(h) advisory committees notes to 1966 amendment.

Rule 9(h) provides the modern-day mechanism for invoking admiralty jurisdiction of claims that could also be brought within the courts general civil jurisdiction. Rule 9(h) provides in part:

> A pleading or count setting forth a claim for relief within the admiralty and maritime jurisdiction that is also within the jurisdiction of the district court on some other ground may contain a statement identifying the claims as an admiralty or maritime claim for the purposes of Rule 14(c), 38(e), 82 and the Supplemental Rules for Certain Admiralty and Maritime Claims. If the claim is cognizable only in admiralty, it is an admiralty or maritime claim for those purposes whether so identified or not.

A pleader may thus designate a claim as an "admiralty or maritime claim within the meaning of Rule 9(h)" to inform the court that the pleader has elected to proceed within the courts admiralty jurisdiction.

Although the Supreme Court has held that the Constitution does not require trial by jury in admiralty cases, it neither forbids trial by jury nor creates a right to a non-jury trial. *See Fitzgerald v. United States Lines Co.*, 374 U.S. 16, 20, 10 L. Ed. 2d 720, 83 S. Ct. 1646 (1963); *Beacon Theatres*, 359 U.S. at 510 ("no ... [constitutional] requirement protects trials by the court"). This general rule survived the merger; Rule 9(h) neither creates a right to a non-jury trial, nor compromises a party's right to a jury trial. *See* Fed. R. Civ. R 9(h) advisory committee's notes to 1966 amendment. "The right of trial by jury as declared by the Seventh Amendment to the Constitution or as given by a statute of the United States shall be preserved to the parties inviolate." Fed. R. Civ. P 38(a).

Wartsila argues that its Rule 9(h) designation attaches to all the claims in the case[4] and urges the court to adopt the reasoning of *Insurance Co. of North America v. Virgilio*, 574 F. Supp. 48, 50-51 (S.D. Cal. 1983) (holding that plaintiff's Rule 9(h) designation in an action for declaratory relief deprived defendant of a jury trial of defendant's legal counter-claims); *see also Harrison v. Flota Mercante Grancolombiana S.A.*, 577 F.2d 968, 987 (5th Cir. 1978) (holding that plaintiff's Rule 9(h) election prohibited jury trial of legal claims in third party complaint because "we refuse to permit a third-party defendant to emasculate the election given to the plaintiff by Rule 9(h) by exercising the simple expedient of bringing in a fourth-party defendant"); *Royal Ins. Co. of America v. Hansen*, 125 F.R.D. 5, 8-9 (D. Mass. 1988) (defendant not entitled to jury trial of counterclaims in face of plaintiff's 9(h) designation); *Arkwright-Boston Mfrs. Mut. Ins. Co. v. Bauer Dredging Co.*, 74 F.R.D. 461, 462 (S.D. Tex. 1977) (same).

In *Virgilio,* plaintiff insurance company filed an action against its insured requesting a declaration that the insurance contract would not cover any claim the insured might bring as a result of a boating accident. *Virgilio,* 574 F. Supp. at 49. Plaintiff designated its claim as a claim in admiralty pursuant to Fed. R. Civ. P. 9(h). *Id.* The defendant counterclaimed for breach of contract, breach of fiduciary duty, breach of the covenant of fair dealing and demanded a jury trial. *Id.* The court struck defendant's jury demand and distinguished *Fitzgerald*, 374 U.S. 16, 10 L. Ed. 2d 720, 83 S. Ct. 1646, *Blake v. Farrell Lines, Inc.,* 417 F.2d 264 (3rd Cir. 1969), and *Owens-Illinois,* 698 F.2d 967, because these cases did not involve "a plaintiff electing to proceed in admiralty under 9(h)." *Virgilio,* 574 F. Supp. at 51. The court also denied defendants request to try his claims to a jury separately from plaintiff's

---

[4] Because Wartsila's foreclosure action is a claim that can be brought only within the court's admiralty jurisdiction, a 9(h) designation was not necessary to apprise the district court that Wartsila had elected to proceed in admiralty. *See Emerson G.M. Diesel Inc. v. Alaskan Enter.,* 732 F.2d 1468, 1470 n. l (9th Cir. 1984) (ship lien foreclosure action cognizable exclusively in admiralty); Fed. R. Civ. P. 9(h).

claims. The court reasoned that to do so "would undercut the plaintiff's election under Rule 9(h)." *Id.* We reject the reasoning of *Virgilio*.[5]

Prior to the merger of law and admiralty, the Supreme Court recognized the right to a jury trial in admiralty notwithstanding the customary non-jury component of admiralty practice. *Fitzgerald,* 374 U.S. at 21. In *Fitzgerald,* plaintiff filed a complaint on the admiralty side of the court containing two claims; one claim was cognizable solely in admiralty, the other claim was triable to a jury under the Jones Act, 46 U.S.C. app. § 688. *Id.* at 17. The Supreme Court held that the plaintiff had a right to have all claims tried to a jury on the admiralty side of the court. *Id.* at 21; *see also Peace v. Fidalgo Island Packing Co.,* 419 F.2d 371, 371-72 (9th Cir. 1969) (right to jury trial as to Jones Act claim and to exclusive admiralty claim based on common facts); *Blake,* 417 F.2d at 266-67 (district court may require jury trial in case where legal claim is joined with exclusively maritime claim); and *Zrncevich v. Blue Haw. Enter. Inc.,* 738 F. Supp. 350, 354 (D. Haw. 1990) (Jones Act claim and non-jury admiralty claim tried to a jury in admiralty).

Since the election of the plaintiff in *Fitzgerald* to file a claim in admiralty did not deprive even the plaintiff of the right to a jury trial prior to 1966, then a plaintiff's post-merger election to proceed in admiralty via a Rule 9(h) designation does not affect another party's right to a jury.[6] *Cf. Emerson G.M. Diesel Inc. v. Alaskan Enter.,* 732 F.2d 1468, 1471 (9th Cir. 1984) (defendant in admiralty may designate third party claims in admiralty). Therefore, a defendant may also proceed within the court's general civil jurisdiction under the saving-to-suitors clause.

Regardless of whether a claim is cognizable in admiralty, the right to a jury trial on such claim is preserved despite plaintiff's election to proceed in admiralty. This court has acknowledged that the non-jury component of admiralty jurisdiction must give way to the seventh amendment. In Owens-Illinois, the court stated that:

Where plaintiff alleges both admiralty and diversity as bases for federal jurisdiction, pursuant to FED. R. CIV. P 9(h) he has the right to elect to have his admiralty claim adjudicated under admiralty procedures, including a bench trial, by identifying his claim as lying in admiralty. *As long as no conflict exists with a defendant's constitutional right to trial by jury, this election if properly made cannot be defeated by defendant's jury trial demand.*[7]

Owens-Illinois, 698 F.2d at 972 n.2 (emphasis added) (*citing Harrison,* 577 F.2d at 986-87). The United States Supreme Court has held that the right to a jury trial as provided by the seventh amendment overcomes another party's preference for a bench trial when those interests conflict. *See Beacon Theatres,* 359 U.S. at 510-511.

In *Beacon Theatres,* plaintiff brought suit for declaratory relief under the Sherman Antitrust Act ("Act") and defendant filed a counterclaim seeking treble damages under the Act. *Id.* at 502-03. Defendant demanded a jury trial pursuant to FED. R. CIV. P 38(b). The district court directed that the equitable issues be tried before the legal issues thereby "'limiting the petitioner's opportunity fully to try to a jury every issue which has a bearing upon its treble damage suit.'" *Id.* at 504 (*quoting Beacon Theatres, Inc. v. Westover,* 252 F.2d 864, 874 (9th Cir.), *cert. granted,* 356 U.S. 956 (1958), *rev'd,* 359 U.S. 500, 3 L. Ed. 2d 988, 79 S. Ct. 948 (1959)).

[T]he holding of the court below while granting ... [plaintiff] no additional protection unless the avoidance of jury trial be considered as such, would compel ... [defendant] to split his antitrust case, trying part to a judge and part to a jury. Such a result, which involves the postponement and subordination of ... [plaintiff's] own legal

---

[5] The result in *Virgilio* has been criticized for encouraging a race to the courthouse:

If the admiralty plaintiff wins, both claims will be tried to the bench. If the counterclaim claimant wins, his claim will be tried to a jury... [T]his result flies in the face of the Supreme Court's decision in *Beacon Theatres, Inc. v. Westover.* In that case, the Court held: "[I]f [the defendant] would have been entitled to a jury trial... against [the plaintiff] it cannot be deprived of that right merely because [the plaintiff] took advantage of the availability of declaratory relief to sue [the defendant] first." [*Beacon Theatres,* 359 U.S. at 504.]

Note, *The Jury on the Quarterdeck: The Effect of Pleading Admiralty Jurisdiction when a Proceeding Turns Hybrid,* 63 TEX. L. REV. 533, 562-63 (1984) (*citing* G. GILMORE & C. BLACK, THE LAW OF ADMIRALTY § 13, at 37 (2d ed. 1975)).

[6] The court in *Virgilio* mistakenly refused to consider *Fitzgerald* for the reason that it did not involve a 9(h) election. A 9(h) designation does nothing more than inform the court of the claimant's election to proceed in admiralty. A 9(h) designation today is equivalent to the earlier practice of filing a claim on the admiralty side of the court prior to the merger. The merger of law and admiralty does not diminish the authority of *Fitzgerald.*

[7] Any suggestion in *Owens-Illinois* that a plaintiff has the right to a non-jury trial except when defendant has a constitutional right to a jury trial is dictum. That court did not consider the conflict between a plaintiff's Rule 9(h) designation and a defendant's right to proceed under the saving-to-suitors clause on defendant's counterclaims.

claim for declaratory relief as well as of the counterclaim which ... [defendant] was compelled by the Federal Rules to bring, is not permissible.

Beacon Theatres, 359 U.S. at 508 (footnote omitted).

The Court further observed that the liberal joinder rules permit "legal and equitable causes to be brought and resolved in one civil action" and preserve any statutory or constitutional right to a jury trial. *Id.* at 509. The Court concluded that the "right to a jury trial of legal issues [cannot] be lost through prior determination of equitable claims." *Id.* at 511; *see also Dairy Queen*, 369 U.S. at 472-73 (both legal and equitable issues must be tried to the jury even if legal issues "incidental" to the equitable issues). The same concerns expressed by the Court in *Beacon Theatres* exist when parties join admiralty claims with claims to which a right to a jury trial attaches. The same conclusion is therefore warranted; Rule 38(a) of the Federal Rules of Civil Procedure provides that the right to a jury, whether statutory or constitutional, "shall be preserved inviolate."

If the Union's claims are cognizable in admiralty, then the Union's right to a jury trial is preserved by the saving-to-suitors clause, 28 U.S.C. § 1333(1), and FED. R. CIV. P. 38(a). We find that the Union has properly exercised its option under the saving-to-suitors clause: the Union's counterclaims include claims which carry the right to a jury trial and the Union has alleged independent bases of federal jurisdiction. If the Union's claims are not cognizable in admiralty, then the Union's right to demand a jury trial as provided by the constitution and FED. R. CIV. P 38(a) is preserved inviolate and the Union need not have alleged independent bases of jurisdiction.[8]

Therefore, we hold that Wartsila's election to proceed in admiralty does not deprive the Union of a jury trial on the Union's properly joined claims. We note that our holding may result in the entire case being tried before a jury. This result is likely to occur if all the claims are closely related factually. *See, e.g., Fitzgerald*, 374 U.S. at 21 (all claims must be submitted to jury when they "arise out of one set of facts"). If the claims are not related factually, then the district court may order separate trials in order to preserve the non-jury aspect of admiralty jurisdiction. *See, e.g. Koch Fuels, Inc. v. Cargo of 13,000 Barrels of No. 2 Oil*, 704 F.2d 1038, 1042 (8th Cir. 1983) (district court ordered a jury trial on defendant's counterclaim and tried admiralty claims separately; affirmed by court of appeals in absence of prejudice to defendant's right to jury trial).

Note: Jury Trial Issues

The Federal Rules by allowing a plaintiff to bring his claim as an admiralty claim forecloses the defendant's right to a jury trial where for instance there is both admiralty jurisdiction and diversity jurisdiction and plaintiff had made a Rule 9(h) election. If the defendant has no right to a jury trial why should a third-party defendant have any greater right? This approach has in fact been adopted in the Fifth Circuit. In *Harrison v. Flota Mercante Grancolombiana, S. A.*,[10] the third-party defendant[11] was impleaded under Rule 14(a) and the third-party impleader which was predicated on negligence and products liability could fall within diversity jurisdiction between third-party plaintiff and third-party defendant. The court referred to its earlier decision in *Romero v. Bethlehem Steel Corp.*,[12] In that case, the court stated:

"'The unification of the admiralty and civil rules in 1966 was intended to work no change in the general rule that admiralty claims are to be tried without a jury. Fed.R.Civ.P. 9(h), 38(e) and Advisory Committee Notes. See also Moore, Federal Practice, pars. *.59[3], 9.09, 38.35. *Fed.R.Civ. P. 9(h) serves only as a device by which the pleader may claim the special benefits of admiralty procedures and remedies, including a non-jury trial, when the pleadings show that both admiralty and some other basis of federal jurisdiction exist.* See Wright & Miller, Federal Practice and Procedure § 1313, at 454-55 (1969). Of course, an action for personal injury cognizable in admiralty may also be brought, assuming the existence of some independent jurisdictional base like diversity of citizenship, as a civil suit pursuant to the 'savings to suitors' clause of 28 U.S.C. § 1333 (emphasis added).'"

---

[8] The court therefore finds it unnecessary to determine whether the Union Counterclaims are cognizable in admiralty. *See, e.g., Executive Jet Aviation Inc. v. City of Cleveland*, 409 U.S. 249, 34 L. Ed. 2d 454, 93 S. Ct. 493 (1972).

[10] 577 F.2d 968 (5th Cir. 1978).

[11] This case actually involved a "fourth"-party defendant.

[12] 515 F.2d 1249, 1252 (5th Cir. 1975).

As one court has stated:

"*Romero* demonstrates that by electing to proceed under 9(h) rather than by invoking diversity jurisdiction, the plaintiff may preclude the defendant from invoking the right to trial by jury. The Advisory Committee's Notes to Rule 9(h) evince a similar conclusion and,... we feel the election made available to the pleader pursuant to Rule 9(h) is dispositive of the contention [jury trial demand] made by [third-party defendant]."[13]

The court refused third-party defendant's jury trial demand. It set forth several reasons for its conclusion.

"First, we refuse to permit a third-party defendant to emasculate the election given to the plaintiff by Rule 9(h) by exercising the simple expedient of bringing in a fourth-party defendant. Second, the fourth-party complaint is based upon the same set of operative facts which gave rise to the first complaint. That is, the facts which established admiralty jurisdiction for the plaintiff's original claim, injury upon navigable waters performing a task traditionally performed by seamen, also forms the basis for the fourth-party action. [citations omitted.] Third, the plaintiff amended his complaint to state a claim directly against [the fourth-party defendant]. In the amended complaint the plaintiff specified that the claim is brought pursuant to Rule 9(h). Furthermore, this case is clearly distinguishable from *McCrary v. Seatrain Lines, Inc.*, 469 F.2d 666 (9th Cir. 1972). In *McCrary* the court noted that the third-party claim was ancillary to the plaintiff's diversity claim and did not lie solely in admiralty. In the case at bar, the plaintiff has not alleged diversity as an alternative basis of jurisdiction."[14]

In *Hanjin Shipping Co. v. Jay*,[15] a carrier sued the shipper who impleaded the freight forwarder. Carrier's action was in admiralty and impleader originally was stated to be in admiralty. Defendant then attempted to change his admiralty impleader to a law claim based on diversity of citizenship and moved for a bifurcation of proceedings so that he could have a jury trial on the third-party claim. The court rejected the approach taken by the Fifth Circuit in *Harrison v. Flota Mercante Grancolombiana*, S.A., supra. Following the reasoning in the Wilmington Trust case, the court in *Hanjin* held that defendant was entitled to a jury trial on the claims raised in his third-party complaint.[16]

One court has held that when a third-party defendant is tendered to the plaintiff, the third-party defendant should be treated as a defendant.[17] Therefore if the plaintiff claims against the third-party defendant would ordinarily give that defendant a right to jury trial, then it is entitled to a jury trial. The court analyzed the situation:

Commentators have noted that when a third party is tendered to the plaintiff under Rule 14(c), the Court must inquire as to the basis for the court's jurisdiction over the plaintiff's cause of action against the third party defendant. See Dane S. Ciolino & Gary R. Roberts, *The Missing Direct–Tender Option in Federal Third–Party Practice: A Procedural and Jurisdictional Analysis*, 68 N.C. L.Rev. 423, 445–47 (1990). The authors of this article base their claim on the very wording of Rule 14(c), which provides "the action shall proceed as if the plaintiff had commenced it against the third-party defendant as well as the third-party plaintiff." FED. R. CIV. P. 14(c). "In short, for jurisdictional purposes, courts should treat the tendered defendant as a newly joined defendant—not as a traditional third party." Ciolino & Roberts, *supra*

---

[13] Harrison v. Flota Mercante Grancolombiana, S.A., 577 F.2d 968, 986 (5th Cir. 1978).

[14] *Id.* at 987. Other courts have held that that third-party and fourth-party defendants are not entitled to a jury trial when plaintiff invokes the admiralty jurisdiction of a federal court. *See, e.g.*, Cantey v. Flensburger Dampfercompagnie Harald Schuldt & Co., 55 F.R.D. 127 (E.D.N.C. 1971).

[15] 1991 A.M.C. 2596 (C.D. Cal. 1991).

[16] The Hanjin court based its conclusions on several factors:

"(1) The rationale of Wilmington Trust supports the jury right

In rejecting the reasoning of *Virgilio*, the Ninth Circuit focused on the result of depriving a defendant of a right to a jury trial of legal counter-claims in cases where the plaintiff has elected to proceed in admiralty. Such a rule is inefficient in that it encourages a race to the courthouse by potential defendants anxious to preserve their right to a jury. This is true regardless of whether the potential defendant is an original party or brought in as a third-party. In order to avoid a race to the courthouse by defendants who suspect they may be impleaded under Rule 14(c), the saving-to-suitors exception must be available for their non-admiralty claims.

"(2) *The election given to plaintiffs by Rule 9(h) is not protected*

If a defendant who is sued in admiralty and who can counterclaim only in admiralty is permitted to defeat plaintiff's election to proceed without a jury simply by bringing pendent, non-admiralty claims against a third party defendant, plaintiff's 9(h) election is rendered largely meaningless. Although some courts have refused to permit this result, the Ninth Circuit finds it unobjectionable. See *Wilmington Trust, supra*, criticizing, *Harrison v. Flota Mercante Grancolombiana S.A.*, 1979 AMC 824, 577 F.2d 968 (5 Cir. 1978) (holding that a plaintiff's Rule 9(h) election prohibited the jury trial of legal claims in third party complaint because 'we refuse to permit a third party defendant to emasculate the election given to the plaintiff by Rule 9(h) by exercising the simple expedient of bringing in a fourth-party defendant.'); *Royal Ins. Co. of America v. Hansen*, 125 F.R.D. 5, 8-9 (D.Mass. 1988) (defendant not entitled to jury trial of counterclaims in face of plaintiff's 9(h) designation); and *Arkwright-Bosion Mfrs. Mut. Ins. Co. v. Bauer Dredging Co.*, 74 F.R.D. 461, 462 (S.D. Tex. 1977) (same).

"To the contrary, the Ninth Circuit expressly noted that the holding of *Wilmington Trust* may result in the entire case being tried before a jury, especially where all the claims are closely related factually. *Wilmington Trust, supra*, 1991 AMC at 1855, 934 F.2d at 1032, *citing Fitzgerald*, 374 U.S. at 21, 1963 AMC at 1097, (all claims must be submitted to jury when they 'arise out of one set of facts')." *Hanjin*, 1991 A.M.C. at 2601-02.

[17] Cascio v. TMA Marine, 2003 U.S. Dist. LEXIS 5245, 2003 WL 1751371 (E.D. La. 2003).

at 447. Another commentator, in considering Rule 14(c) tenders and the right to a jury trial, has noted that "courts will afford jury trials on the pendent non-maritime claims if such claims would have been entitled to jury trials in the state courts." Billy Coe Dyer, *The Jury on the Quarterdeck: The Effect of Pleading Admiralty Jurisdiction When a Proceeding Turns Hybrid*, 63 Tex. L.Rev. 533, 545 (1984). As noted above, the plaintiff's claim against Flag Container sounds in diversity jurisdiction, not admiralty jurisdiction. Thus, if Flag Container were joined as a defendant, it would be entitled to a jury demand under the Seventh Amendment. Accordingly, Flag Container is entitled to a jury trial. The Court must now reconcile that issue with the plaintiff's desire to proceed with a bench trial under Rule 9(h).[18]

The court concluded that it would empanel a jury to act as an advisory jury on plaintiff's maritime claims and to decide the liabilities of the third party defendants. In a similar but slightly different situation, plaintiff's filed suit under the Jones Act and the general maritime law and demanded a jury trial. Defendant impleaded the third-party defendant who also demanded a jury trial. The third-party complaint did not assert that it was a claim in admiralty. The court concluded that it had ancillary jurisdiction over the third-party complaint and that the third-party defendant was entitled to a jury trial.[19]

* * *

GAUTHIER v. CROSBY MARINE SERVICE, INC.

87 F.R.D. 353, 1981 AMC 1179 (E.D. La. 1980)

CASSIBRY, District Judge

Motion to Dismiss Cross-Claim

The main action is a suit by plaintiff, Leonard Gauthier, against Crosby Marine Service, Inc. ("Crosby"), Dixie Oil Tools, Inc. ("Dixie"), and other defendants for personal injuries he sustained while serving on the M/V Ricky III. Plaintiff's employer, Crosby, was hired to transport some oilwell fishing tools from a dock to a workover rig. Plaintiff fell asleep on the dock while awaiting the arrival of the tools, which were being transported to the dock by Dixie. The tools were delivered while plaintiff was asleep. When plaintiff awoke and attempted to lift the tools, he allegedly injured himself.

Plaintiff sued Crosby for negligence under the Jones Act and for unseaworthiness and maintenance and cure under the general maritime law. Plaintiff also sued Dixie and other defendants[1] under the general maritime law. Crosby thereupon cross-claimed against Dixie seeking contribution and indemnity and offering Dixie as a substitute defendant. *See* FED. R. CIV. P 14(c).

Dixie then moved to have the plaintiff's main demand against it dismissed for lack of maritime jurisdiction. Conceding that maritime jurisdiction was lacking, plaintiff did not oppose the motion, and plaintiff's claim against Dixie was dismissed.

Dixie now seeks to have the cross-claim filed by Crosby dismissed for lack of subject matter jurisdiction. The parties agree that the cross-claim lacks independent grounds of jurisdiction. It therefore may be maintained only, if at all, as a third-party demand, since the plaintiff's main demand has been dismissed. *Picou v. Rimrock Tidelands, Inc.,* 29 F.R.D. 188 (E.D. La. 1962). In *Picou*, the court recognized the rule that a cross-claim is ordinarily dismissed when the original claim to which it is connected is dismissed for lack of subject matter jurisdiction, unless the cross-claim is supported by independent jurisdictional grounds. 29 F.R.D. at 189 *quoting Pierce v. Perlite Aggregates,* 110 F. Supp. 684 (N.D. Cal. 1952) and 3 MOORE'S FEDERAL PRACTICE § 13.36 (2d ed.). The *Picou* court nevertheless denied a motion to dismiss—to avoid delay and additional expense—since the intended cross-defendant could properly have been impleaded as a third-party defendant under Federal Rule 14(a).

If the main action in the instant case were an ordinary civil action, third-party impleader would likewise be proper under Rule 14(a) because the third-party demand arises out of the same claim as the main action. A third-

---

[18] *Id.* at *2.
[19] Fawcett v. Pac. Far E. Lines, Inc. 76 F.R.D. 519, 521 (N.D. Cal. 1977).
[1] The other defendants include the owner of the dock and the owner of the workover rig.

party claim may be maintained in federal court under the doctrine of ancillary jurisdiction even if it does not have independent grounds of jurisdiction, as long as it involves the same set of operative facts giving rise to the main cause of action. *See United States v. Joe Grasso & Son, Inc.,* 380 F.2d 749 (5th Cir. 1967); *Dery v. Wyer,* 265 F.2d 804 (2d Cir. 1959); 6 C. Wright & A. Miller, Federal Practice and Procedure § 1444, at 219-222 (1971). The main cause of action in this case, however, is an admiralty case within the meaning of Federal Rule 9(H). The law is far from settled whether ancillary jurisdiction can apply to an impleader under the provisions of Rule 14(c), which governs third-party practice in maritime suits. *Compare Leather's Best, Inc. v. S.S. Mormalynx,* 451 F.2d 800, 810 n.12 (2d Cir. 1971) and *Spearing v. Manhattan Oil Transportation Corp.,* 375 F. Supp. 764 (S.D.N.Y. 1974) *with McCann v. Falgout Boat Co.,* 44 F.R.D. 34 (S.D. Tex. 1968). The Fifth Circuit has expressly recognized the problem, but it has withheld resolution because in the cases under consideration, it did find independent grounds of jurisdiction to support the cross-claims. *In re Motorship Carrier,* 489 F.2d 152 (5th Cir. 1974); *Watz v. Zapata,* 431 F.2d 100 (5th Cir. 1970).

Judge Noel argues strenuously against the use of ancillary jurisdiction with Rule 14(c) impleader. *McCann v. Falgout Boat Co.,* 44 F.R.D. 34 (S.D. Tex. 1968), *followed, Stinson v. S.S. Kenneth McKay,* 360 F. Supp. 674 (S.D. Tex. 1973). On the other hand, the *McCann* opinion has been roundly criticized. ALI Study of the Division of Jurisdiction Between State and Federal Courts 228 (1969); 3 Moore's Federal Practice J 14.36 (2d ed. 1979); 6 C. Wright & A. Miller, Federal Practice and Procedure § 1465, at 348-50 (1971); Lander, *By Sleight of Rule: Admiralty Unification and Ancillary and Pendent Jurisdiction,* 51 Tex. L. Rev. 50, 63 n.55 (1972); Comment, Davidson, L., *Impleader of Nonmaritime Claims Under Rule 14(c),* 47 Tex. L. Rev. 120 (1968); Comment, *Admiralty Practice After Unification: Barnacles on the Procedural Hull,* 81 Yale L.J. 1154 (1972) (hereafter "Barnacles"). I feel compelled to add my weight to the growing body off judicial authority[2] allowing a cause of action lacking independent grounds of jurisdiction to be appended under Rule 14(c) to an admiralty claim, as long as it passes the traditional "same claim" test used for ancillary jurisdiction under Rule 14(a) impleader.[3]

The major argument in favor of ancillary jurisdiction in the admiralty context, as in the civil context, is judicial economy. The arguments against ancillary jurisdiction are history, impermissible enlargement of federal jurisdiction, and possible denial of the third-party plaintiff's right to a jury trial. Judge Friendly found that the historical reason's preventing ancillary jurisdiction in the admiralty context have been ameliorated by the merger of the admiralty rules with the civil rules. *Leather's Best, Inc. v. S.S. Mormalynx,* 451 F.2d 800, 810 n.12 (2d Cir. 1971); *see Barnacles,* 81 Yale at 1173-76. The other objections voiced in *McCann* are adequately answered by the other authorities cited above. I also note that in this case, the jury trial objection is irrelevant because the case includes a claim under the Jones Act, 46 U.S.C. § 688 (1976), and will be tried to a jury on all claims. *Fitzgerald v. United States Lines, Co.,* 374 U.S. 16(1963). The interest in judicial economy, then, remaining, I think the intent of the merger of the admiralty with the civil rules was to allow ancillary jurisdiction in admiralty impleader under Rule 14(c), preserving the substitute defendant practice unique to admiralty.

Because Crosby's cross-claim arises out of the same core of operative facts as plaintiff's main demand, it may be maintained notwithstanding it does not have independent grounds of jurisdiction. Dixie's motion to dismiss is therefore denied.

McCANN v. FALGOUT BOAT COMPANY

44 F.R.D. 34 (S.D. Tex. 1968)

NOEL, District Judge

---

[2] *Fawcett v. Pacific Far Lines, Inc.,* 76 F.R.D. 519 (N.D. Cal. 1977); *Morse Electro Products Corp. v. S.S. Great Peace,* 437 F. Supp. 474 (D. N.J. 1977); *Spearing v. Manhattan Oil Transportation Corp.,* 375 F. Supp. 764 (S.D.N.Y. 1974); *see Leather's Best, Inc. v. S.S. Mormalynx,* 451 F.2d 800, 810 n.12 (2d Cir. 1971) (*dicta*). *Contra, Young v. United States,* 272 F. Supp. 738 (D. S.C. 1967) (based on cases pre-dating the merger between the civil and admiralty rules).

[3] For a discussion of the "same claim" test in the Fifth Circuit *see United States v. Joe Grasso & Son, Inc.,* 380 F.2d 749 (5th Cir. 1967). *See* 6 C. Wright & A. Miller, Federal Practice and Procedure § 1444, at 219-222 (1971).

In 1966, Plaintiff, a resident of Texas and employed as a seaman aboard the vessel Campeche Seal, is alleged to have sustained injuries caused by the negligence of the defendant, its masters, agents, servants and employees, and/or the unseaworthiness of the Campeche Seal. Plaintiff instituted suit in this court against Falgout Boat Company, the operator of the Campeche Seal, asserting a claim for damages arising from the alleged injuries and within the admiralty jurisdiction of the court, 28 U.S.C. § 1333, and identified as such under Federal Rule 9(h).[1] Defendant filed a third-party complaint (impleader) under Federal Rules of Civil Procedure, Rule 14(c) against Dr. Wesley R. T. Metzner, alleging that he is liable to the plaintiff for the damages complained of or is liable to the defendant in indemnity and/or contribution for any damages awarded plaintiff against defendant. Defendant has not alleged any basis of independent jurisdiction over Dr. Metzner or the subject matter of the third-party complaint, but urges that the third-party action should be treated as being ancillary to the main claim.

Plaintiff contends that he sustained a fracture to his right hand on October 16, 1966, while aboard the vessel Campeche Seal. At the time of the alleged injury the Campeche Seal was in a Japanese port, and the following day plaintiff was treated by a Japanese physician at Kushiro, Japan.

On October 20, 1966, plaintiff returned to the United States and his home in San Antonio, Texas. He received additional medical treatment to the injured hand from a San Antonio physician, Dr. Wesley R. T. Metzner. The treatment continued through April 15, 1967; however, plaintiff complains that he still suffers and will continue to suffer great physical pain and mental anguish, and that as a result of the injury his earning capacity has been impaired. Defendant contends that Dr. Metzner's treatment was improper, and that had plaintiff received proper medical treatment the fracture would have healed properly and without any residual disability. Defendant also alleges that plaintiff's extended period of recuperation and disability is due to the negligence and malpractice of third-party defendant.

The third-party defendant, Dr. Metzner, has moved to have the third-party complaint dismissed on the ground that the subject matter—medical malpractice—is not within the courts admiralty and maritime jurisdiction and that the court does not otherwise have jurisdiction over the subject matter or the person of Dr. Metzner. I agree, and the third-party complaint must be dismissed.

Federal Rule 14(c) governs the third-party practice in a case of admiralty jurisdiction. It provides as follows:

Admiralty and Maritime Claims. When a plaintiff asserts an admiralty claim within the meaning of Rule 9(h), the defendant or claimant, as a third-party plaintiff, may bring in a third-party defendant who may be wholly or partly liable, either to the plaintiff or to the third-party plaintiff, by way or remedy over, contribution, or otherwise on account of the same transaction, occurrence, or series of transactions or occurrences. In such a case the third-party plaintiff may also demand judgment against the third-party defendant in favor of the plaintiff, in which event the third-party defendant shall make his defense to the claim of the plaintiff as well as that of the third-party plaintiff....[2]

Rules 9(h) and 14(c) were amended to the Federal Rules of Civil Procedure as a part of the unification of the Admiralty and Civil Rules.[3] Prior to the amendments, the third-party practice in an admiralty case was governed by Admiralty Rule 56, after which Rule 14(c), in substance, was patterned.[4]

---

[1] Rule 9(h) sets forth the procedure for identifying a claim for relief as being one within the admiralty or maritime jurisdiction where there is also some other basis for jurisdiction in the district court. "If the claim is cognizable only in admiralty it is an admiralty or maritime claim for those purposes whether so identified or not." Rule 9(h).

[2] An impleaded party stands as one charged with fault by the original petition, although in fact it did not so charge and is not amended. The cause is treated as if the petition had been filed against both the defendant and third-party defendant. *See* 2 Benedict, Admiralty § 351 (6th ed. 1940).

[3] Amended on February 28, 1966 and effective as of July 1, 1966.

[4] Admiralty Rule 56 read as follows:

> Right to bring in party jointly liable in any suit, whether *in rem* or *in personam*, the claimant or respondent (as the case may be) shall be entitled to bring in any other vessel or person (individual or corporation) who may be partly or wholly liable either to the libellant or to such claimant or respondent by way of remedy over, contribution or otherwise, growing out of the same matter. This shall be done by petition, on oath, presented before or at the time of answering the libel, or at any later time during the progress of the cause that the court may allow. Such petition shall contain suitable allegations showing such liability, and the particulars thereof, and such other vessel, or person ought to be proceeded against in the same suit for such damage, and shall pray that process be issued against such vessel or person to that end. Thereupon such process shall issue, and if duly served, such suit shall proceed as if such vessel or person had been originally proceeded against; the other parties in the suit shall answer the petition; the claimant of such vessel or such new party shall answer the libel; and such further proceedings shall be had and decree rendered by the court in the suit as to law and justice shall appertain. But every such petitioner shall, upon filing his petition, give a stipulation, with sufficient sureties, or an approved corporate surety, to pay the libellant and to any claimant or any new party brought in by virtue of such process, all such costs, damages, and expenses as shall be awarded against the petitioner by the court on the final decree, whether rendered in the original or appellate court; and any such claimant or new party shall give the same bonds or stipulations which are required in the like cases from parties brought in under process issued on the prayer of a libellant.

The great majority of the courts had construed Admiralty Rule 56 not to allow the admiralty court to bring before it a third-party whose alleged obligation was non-maritime in character. *Aktieselskabet Fido v. Lloyd Braziliero,* 283 F. 62, 72 (2d Cir.), *cert. denied,* 260 U.S. 737, 43 S. Ct. 97, 67 L. Ed. 489 (1922); *David Crystal, Inc. v. Cunard Steamship Co.,* 223 F. Supp. 273, 291-292 (S.D.N.Y. 1963), *aff'd on other grounds,* 339 F.2d 295 (2d Cir. 1964), *cert. denied, John T. Clark and Son v. Cunard Steamship Co.,* 380 U.S. 976, 85 S. Ct. 1339, 14 L. Ed. 2d 271 (1965); *Capital Transp. Corp. v. Thelning,* 167 F. Supp. 379, 380 (E.D. S.C. 1958); *Mangone v. Moore-McCormack Lines, Inc.,* 152 F. Supp. 848 (E.D.N.Y. 1957); *Warner v. The Gas Boat Bear,* 126 F. Supp. 529, 15 Alaska 370 (D. Alaska 1955); *The S.S. Samovar,* 72 F. Supp. 54, 582 (N.D. Calif. 1947). *See also* 3 Moore, Federal Procedure para. 14.20, at 669 (1966), and cases cited therein. The courts reasoned that when jurisdiction was based solely upon the admiralty nature of the cause of action, Rule 56 could not be read to enlarge the Federal courts jurisdiction to include a matter respecting which it would otherwise have no jurisdiction; the issues to be resolved all had to be of a maritime character. Another serious obstacle, pronounced by the Second Circuit, was the fact that in an admiralty case there is no right to a jury;[5] yet, if a party could be impleaded on a non-maritime matter, he, in effect, would be denied his right to have a jury pass upon that matter—raising grave Seventh Amendment constitutional problems. *Aktieselskabet Fido v. Lloyd Braziliero, supra.*

A cry for unification of the Admiralty and Civil Rules and the recognized need for modernization of the Admiralty Rules led to the drafting of proposed rules by the Advisory Committee on Admiralty Rules, and the subsequent adoption of the unified rules by the United States Supreme Court.[6] This resulted in the evolution of one body of Federal Rules to cover both civil and admiralty proceedings; as of July 1, 1966, the former Admiralty Rules were rescinded. As will be seen, however, complete procedural unification was not achieved.

Prior to unification, Rule 14 uniformly had been construed to follow liberal impleading of parties and issues so as to avoid multiplicity of suits. *See Pennsylvania R.R. Co. v. Erie Avenue Warehouse Co.,* 302 F.2d 843, 845 (3d Cir. 1962); *Dery v. Wyer,* 265 F.2d 804, 806-807 (2d Cir. 1959). The courts implemented this policy by treating a third-party claim as one ancillary to the main claim, upon which the court's jurisdiction had been based.[7] The 1966 amendments to Rule 14(a) neither extended nor limited the courts ancillary jurisdiction in cases of civil (non-maritime) jurisdiction.[8] Thus, as always, if the court has diversity jurisdiction over the main suit, no independent jurisdiction is required to implead a third party if the requirements of Rule 14(a) are otherwise met. *H.L. Peterson Co. v. Applewhite,* 383 F.2d 430, 433 (5th Cir. 1967); *Thompson v. United Artists Theatre Circuit, Inc.* 43 F.R.D. 197 (S.D.N.Y. 1967). Admiralty courts had taken a more discriminating position with respect to third-party practice under Admiralty Rule 56; for, as previously indicated, non-maritime impleading was not permitted. The practice under Rule 14 and Admiralty Rule 56 differed in another important respect. While traditionally there has been no right to a trial by jury in an admiralty case, a party impleaded under Rule 14(a) or (b) was and still is entitled to demand a jury trial on the issues raised in the third-party complaint or answer (of any issue so triable). Fed. R. Civ. P. Rule 38(b). *See* 2B Barron and Holtzoff, Federal Practice and Procedure § 893 (1961).

What effect, if any, did the unification of Civil Rule 14 and Admiralty Rule 56 have upon the third-party practice in a case of admiralty and maritime jurisdiction, within the meaning of Rule 9(h), where the alleged obligation of the third party is nonmaritime in nature, and, in any event, upon the right of a third party to a jury trial? Prefatory to resolving these matters, a brief examination will be made of the origin and development of admiralty jurisdiction in the federal courts.

---

[5] *See Waring v. Clarke,* 46 U.S. (5 How.) 441, 460-462, 12 L. Ed. 226 (1847), Gilmore and Black, Admiralty 9 (1957). There are statutory exceptions for specific cases under 28 U.S.C. § 1873 and for a person accused of a maritime criminal offense, 18 U.S.C. § 7, 5 Moore, Federal Practice para. 38.35 (1966).

[6] The history of the Admiralty Rules and the unification process is surveyed in Bradley, *Admiralty Aspects of the Civil Rules,* 41 F.R.D. 257 (1967), and in Colby, *Admiralty Unification,* 54 Geo. L.J. 1258 (1966).

[7] This policy is not without its limitations. *See* 3 Moore, Federal Practice para. 14.25 (1966); *Mazzella v. Pan Oceanica A/S Panama,* 232 F. Supp. 29 (S.D.N.Y. 1964). See further discussion in note 12, *infra.*

[8] The only change in Rule 14(a) relates to a third-party complaint which is within the admiralty and maritime jurisdiction. The portion added provides: "The third-party complaint, if within the admiralty and maritime jurisdiction, may be *in rem* against a vessel, cargo, or other property subject to admiralty or maritime process *in rem,* in which case references in this rule to the summons include the warrant of arrest, and references to the third-party plaintiff or defendant include, where appropriate, the claimant of the property arrested."

Article III, section 2 of the United States Constitution states that the judicial power of the United States courts shall extend "to all cases of admiralty and maritime Jurisdiction...." Section 9 of the Judiciary Act of 1789 implemented this constitutional grant by giving the district courts "exclusive original cognizance of all civil causes of admiralty and maritime jurisdiction ... saving to suitors, in all cases, the right of a common law remedy, where the common law is competent to give it...." Judiciary Act of 1789, Ch. 20, §1,1 Stat. 76-77. The Judiciary Act of 1789 was later revised, and substantially the identical language is contained in 28 U.S.C. Section 1333.[9]

Congress cannot confer upon the inferior courts of the United States jurisdiction over cases and controversies that are not within the judicial power of the United States (*i.e.,* beyond the limits of the Constitution). *Hodgson v. Bowerbank,* 5 Cranch 303, 3 L. Ed. 108 (1809). Federal courts, unlike state courts, have jurisdiction limited to those matters enumerated in the Constitution, such as Article III, section 2, and over those matters Congress has granted them by valid statute.[10] 1 MOORE, FEDERAL PRACTICE para. 0.60 [3] (1964). However, supplementing such grants of jurisdiction, federal courts have ancillary, auxiliary or pendent jurisdiction over such matters as, for example, would arise under Federal Rule 14 (third-party practice).

The district courts have jurisdiction over admiralty and maritime matters pursuant to 28 U.S.C. Section 1333, a carry-over of the Judiciary Act of 1789, *supra. See generally Romero v. International Terminal Operating Co.,* 358 U.S. 354, 79 S. Ct. 468, 3 L. Ed. 2d 368 (1959). This jurisdiction is exclusive unless the claim is one within the "saving to suitors" clause of the Judiciary Act of 1789 (now 28 U.S.C. § 1333); if it does fall within the latter clause, the suitor may elect to bring suit in state court or in federal court either on the admiralty side or on the law side, provided that in the latter instance there is some basis for jurisdiction other than the admiralty or maritime nature of the claim. The reason for the exclusive jurisdiction in admiralty matters is to allow the formulation and preservation of "the uniformity and consistency at which the Constitution aimed on all subjects of a commercial character affecting the intercourse of the States with each other or with foreign States." *Rodd v. Heartt, (Lottawanna)* 88 U.S.(21 Wall.) 558, 575, 22 L. Ed. 654(1874). *See also Southern Pacific Co. v. Jensen,*244 U.S. 205,37 S. Ct.524, 61 L. Ed. 1086 (1917).

Admiralty jurisdiction depends upon the maritime nature of the event out of which the claim arises. In the case of a tort, such jurisdiction depends upon the locality of the injury. *The Admiral Peoples,* 295 U.S. 649, 651, 55 S. Ct. 885, 79 L. Ed. 1633 (1935). In the case at hand, the injury complained of by plaintiff occurred aboard a seagoing vessel. The complaint filed by plaintiff designates the suit as "a cause of action in Admiralty as defined by Section 9(h)," and none of the parties has questioned the fact that the court has admiralty and maritime jurisdiction of this case. Clearly it is maritime in nature. *Igneri v. Cie. de Transports Oceaniques,* 323 F.2d 257, 259 (2d Cir., *cert. denied,* 376 U.S. 949, 84 S. Ct. 965, 11 L. Ed. 2d 969 (1964). Whether there could be some other basis for jurisdiction in the federal court has not been raised;but, as plaintiff has expressly designated this as a Rule9 (h) cause of action, the inquiry has become academic. The third-party complaint has been attacked as being nonmaritime in nature. The issue now is whether this court, ancillary to its admiralty jurisdiction over the main cause of action, has jurisdiction over a non-maritime third-party complaint filed pursuant to Rule 14(c). This, so far as I am able to discern, is a case of first impression.[11]

It has been demonstrated that Rule 14(c) follows the language of rescinded Admiralty Rule 56. In drafting proposed Rule 14(c), the Advisory Committee must have been aware that Admiralty Rule 56 had been construed to require independent, and perhaps admiralty, jurisdiction over a third-party complaint. If the Committee wished

---

[9] *See Note* 17, *infra.* The coordination between section 1333 and the 1789 version is analyzed in Black, *Admiralty Jurisdiction: Critique and Suggestions,* 50 Colum. L. Rev. 259 (1950).

[10] District courts are vested with jurisdiction over (a) federal crimes, (b) admiralty, (c) bankruptcy, (d) variety of civil actions where jurisdiction rests upon diversity of citizenship and amount in controversy, (e) matters under a special grant of federal jurisdiction, or (f) general federal questions. But district courts do not have exclusive jurisdiction over all these matters. I Moore, Federal Practice, para. 0.2 [2], at 14 (1964).

[11] The issue was raised but not resolved in *Williams v. United States,* 42 F.R.D. 609, 614 (S.D.N.Y. 1967). The question was also raised in *Young v. United States,* 272 F. Supp. 728 (D. S.C. 1967). *Young* was pending at the time the Admiralty and Federal Rules were unified. Rule 86(e) provided that the new amendments would govern all suits brought after July 1, 1966 and all actions then pending, except where the court was of the opinion that in cases then pending application of the new rules would not be feasible or would work an injustice. Reasoning that the government's position that the third party had waived the right to jury would raise constitutional objections (right to trial by jury), the court concluded that denial of a jury trial would violate the spirit of Rule 86(e). 272 F. Supp. at 742-743. Therefore, the impleading petition was dismissed.

to change that interpretation, a desire to do so was not expressed. The implication is that the practice under Admiralty Rule 56 (disallowing non-maritime impleaded where sole basis of jurisdiction lay in admiralty) was to be retained. This follows for several reasons. First, the Supreme Court, which adopted Rule 14(c), has said on numerous occasions that, as an aide to construction, a prior interpretation of a statute must be deemed to have received legislative approval by the reenactment of the statutory provision without material change. *See*, for example, *United States v. Dakota-Montana Oil Co.*, 288 U.S. 459, 466, 53 S. Ct. 435, 77 L. Ed. 893 (1933). I am confident that the Supreme Court would not apply a different standard in the construction of a Federal rule. Secondly, while the Advisory Committees Note to Rule 14(c) does not cover specifically the problem of jurisdiction over a non-maritime third-party complaint, it did say: "Retention of the admiralty practice in those cases that will be counter-parts of a suit in admiralty is clearly desirable." Thirdly, allowing a non-maritime impleader in an admiralty case would be an extension of the court's jurisdiction which had not been permitted under Admiralty Rule 56. Rule 82, however, states: "These rules shall not be construed to extend or limit the jurisdiction of the United States district court...." Fourthly, and a matter which will be discussed later in some detail, Rule 38(e) did not remove one of the serious objects to a non-maritime third-party complaint—the right of the third party to a trial by jury.

I construe Rule 14(c) to mean that, like its predecessor Admiralty Rule 56, there can be no non-maritime impleader in an action where the jurisdiction of the district court is based exclusively upon the maritime nature of the plaintiff's claim for relief—absent independent, and perhaps admiralty, jurisdiction over the third party or the subject matter of the third-party complaint. Unification did not automatically extend the liberal third-party practice permitted under Rule 14(a) and (b), where independent jurisdiction normally is not required, to Rule 14(c). In fact, Rule 14(c), unlike Rule 14(a) and (b), relates specifically and exclusively to the third-party practice in cases of admiralty and maritime jurisdiction. If a defendant were allowed to implead a party under Rule 14(c) who might be liable to the original plaintiff but whose alleged obligation is non-maritime in character and over whom the court has no independent jurisdiction, the result would be to permit an extension of the federal court's jurisdiction contrary to the mandate of Rule 82 and beyond that traditionally accorded under the more liberal, jurisdiction-wise, Rule 14(a).[12] *See*, for example, *Friend v. Middle Atlantic Transp. Co.*, 153 F.2d 778 (2d Cir.), *cert. denied*, 328 U.S. 865, 66 S. Ct. 1370, 90 L. Ed. 1635 (1946).

Rule 14(c) permits such an impleader of a third party "who may be wholly or partly liable, either to the plaintiff or to the third-party plaintiff, by way of remedy over, contribution or otherwise on account of the *same transaction, occurrence, or series of transactions or occurrences*." (Emphasis added.) Taking into account the fact that United States district courts are courts of limited jurisdiction, the traditional philosophy of admiralty jurisdiction as expressed in the courts' interpretations of rescinded Admiralty Rule 56,[13] and the rules of construction applicable to Rule 14(c), relief sought against the third-party defendants must arise out of the same *maritime* transaction, occurrence, or series of transactions or occurrences. This construction applies to a case, such as the one at hand, where no independent ground for federal jurisdiction has been asserted. The claim against Dr. Metzner is reduced, therefore, to an entirely separate and independent action which cannot be maintained against a third party under Rule 14. *Joe Grasso & Son, Inc. v. United States*, 42 F.R.D. 329 (S.D. Tex. 1966), *aff'd*, 380 F.2d 749 (5th Cir. 1967).[14]

The situs of a tort (*i.e.* locality of the injury) determines whether or not it is maritime in nature—it must occur upon the high seas or upon navigable waters. *The Admirals Peoples*, 295 U.S. 649, 55 S. Ct. 885 (1935); *Forgione v. United States*, 202 F.2d 249, 252-253 (3d Cir.), *cert. denied*, 345 U.S. 966, 73 S. Ct. 950, 97 L. Ed. 1384 (1953).

---

[12] Pursuant to Rule 14(c), a defendant may bring in a third party who may be liable either to the plaintiff or to the defendant by way of remedy over, contribution, or otherwise on account of the same transaction or occurrences or series of transactions or occurrences. Prior to 1946, a defendant in a civil action could implead a third party who might be liable to either plaintiff or defendant. But Rule 14 was amended in 1946 to allow a defendant only to bring in a person who may be liable to the defendant for plaintiffs' claim against him. This philosophy has been brought forward in Rule 14(a). *See* 3 Moore, Federal Practice para. 14.26, at 701; *Railey v. Southern Ry. Co.*, 31 F.R.D. 519 (E.D. S.C. 1963). Thus, if jurisdiction exists between plaintiff and defendant, it is not necessary that independent jurisdiction exist between defendant and third-party defendant in order for the defendant to recover a judgment against the third-party defendant. *Huggins v. Graves*, 337 F.2d 486, 488 (6th Cir. 1964). On the other hand, a defendant may not cause a third party to be brought in to a federal action under Rule 14(a) to answer the plaintiff's claim if plaintiff and third party are citizens of the same state and federal jurisdiction does not otherwise appear. *Friend v. Middle Atlantic Transp. Co.*, 153 F.2d 778 (2d Cir.), *cert. denied*, 328 U.S. 856, 66 S. Ct. 1370 (1946). Established boundaries of federal jurisdiction must be observed. *Ibid.*

[13] *Compare Petition of Klarman*, 270 F. Supp. 1001, 1003 (D. Conn. 1967), where the court refused to construe Rule 14(c) in a manner which would conflict with the interpretation given Admiralty Rule 56.

[14] In this regard, it is worth noting that "claim" is defined as "a group of operative facts giving occasion for judicial action." 380 F.2d at 751.

The medical malpractice tort alleged in the third-party complaint against Dr. Metzner arose in San Antonio, Texas, and by no stretch of the imagination occurred upon the high seas or upon navigable waters, the third-party action, being non-maritime in nature, cannot be brought under Rule 14(c). But, there is yet another reason why the third-party complaint must be dismissed.

The Advisory Committee must have been cognizant of the courts' most serious objection to allowing a nonmaritime impleader in an admiralty suit—denial of the third party's constitutional right to trial by jury under the Seventh Amendment. Had the Committee wished to speak on this matter, it would have done so in the amendment to Rule 38, Rule 38(e). If the committee did speak, it was in the negative, for Rule 38(e) provides: "Admiralty and Maritime Claims. These rules shall not be construed to create a right to trial by jury of the issues in an admiralty or maritime claim within the meaning of Rule 9(h)." Rule 38(e) thereby preserves for admiralty and maritime cases the plaintiff's right to foreclose a demand by defendant for trial and creates no new right of a third party to trial by jury. This is made certain in the Committee's Note to Rule 9(h), where it says: "It is no part of the purpose of unification to inject a right to jury trial into those admiralty cases in which that right is not provided by statute."[15] 7A MOORE, *supra* at 387; Rule 9, 28 U.S.C.A. at 143 (1967 Supp.). This position is expressed somewhat more strongly in 2B BARRON AND HOLTZOFF, FEDERAL PRACTICE AND PROCEDURE § 871 (1967 Supp.):

The merger of civil and admiralty procedure in 1966 does not affect the right to jury trial. If the only basis for jurisdiction is that the case is an admiralty case, there is no right to a jury. If jurisdiction can alternatively be based on a federal question, or on diversity and the necessary jurisdictional amount, either party may demand a jury trial unless plaintiff has chosen to identify the claim as an admiralty or maritime claim, as permitted by Rule 9(h). If he exercises that option Rule 38(e) provides that there is no right to a trial by jury.

See also 2B BARRON AND HOLTZOFF, *op. cit. supra* § 872, and 1A BARRON AND HOLTZOFF § 309 (1967 Supp.). This important aspect of impleaded jurisdiction merits further examination.

The Seventh Amendment to the United States Constitution was proposed by the First Congress on September 25, 1789, and ratified by the states on December 15, 1791. It provides: "In Suits at common law, where the value in controversy shall exceed twenty dollars, the right of the trial by jury shall be preserved, and no fact tried by a jury, shall be otherwise reexamined in any Court of the United States, than according to the rules of the common law."[16] However, on September 24, 1789, Congress had passed the Judiciary Act of 1789, which provided that "the trial of issues in fact, in the district courts, in all cases except civil causes of admiralty and maritime jurisdiction, shall be by jury." Judiciary Act of 1789, ch. 20, § 9, 1 Stat. 73, 77. Trial by jury is not available in the admiralty suits because Congress felt that jurisdiction of transactions so peculiar as those of the sea should be exercised by judges schooled to understand its unique character. 2 BENEDICT, ADMIRALTY § 224 (1940). This section of the Judiciary Act of 1789 was repealed in 1940, and subsequent thereto the Supreme Court, reflecting upon *Waring v. Clarke, supra,* in 1963 held that while the Seventh Amendment does not require jury trials in admiralty cases, neither the Seventh Amendment nor any other provision in the Constitution, nor any statute of Congress or civil or admiralty

---

[15] 28 U.S.C. § 1873 expressly gives the right to trial by jury upon demand by either party in cases of admiralty and maritime jurisdiction relating to matters of contract or tort arising out of or concerning certain vessels operating upon the Great Lakes. This is an exception to the general rule. *See Texas Menhaden Co. v. Palermo,* 329 F.2d 579, 580 (5th Cir. 1964) (*Per curiam*).

[16] The historical significance is explored, in a narrow context, in a recent article. Henderson, *The Background of the Seventh Amendment,* 80 Har. L. Rev. 289 (1966).

[17] In *Fitzgerald,* the court was faced with the situation of a seaman bringing suit against his employer for negligence under the Jones Act, 46 U.S.C. § 688, on the "law" side rather than the admiralty side of the federal court (*i.e.,* some basis for jurisdiction other than admiralty) in order to have a jury hear his case, but who also sought recovery for maintenance and cure and unseaworthiness which traditionally are within the court's admiralty and maritime jurisdiction. The Court held that he was entitled to a jury trial on all issues. Section 1333(1), 28 U.S.C., popularly called the "Saving to Suitors" clause, provides that the district courts shall have jurisdiction exclusive of the state courts of "Any civil case of admiralty or maritime jurisdiciton, saving to suitors in all cases all other remedies to which they are otherwise entitled." This section allows a person to pursue a cause of action *in personam* arising out of an admiralty or maritime transaction in the state court or on the civil ("law") side of the federal court, provided he seeks a remedy which the common law was capable of giving him prior to the passage of the Judiciary Act of 1789. This procedure is outlined in 7A MOORE, FEDERAL PRACTICE para. 59 [3] (1967). *See Atlantic and Gulf Stevedores, Inc. v. Ellerman Lines, Ltd.,* 369 U.S. 355, 82 S. Ct. 780, 7 L. Ed. 2d 798 (1962). Under the savings to suitors clause, seemingly there would be nothing to prevent a plaintiff from bringing a maritime-type suit on the law side of the federal court if there were diversity of citizenship and jurisdictional amount. In such a case, a party like Dr. Metzner could be impleaded under Rule 14(a). *See* Currie, *The Silver Oar and All That: A Study of the Romero Case,* 27 U. Chi. L. Rev. 1, 5-6 (1959).

rule of procedure forbids jury trials in maritime cases. *Fitzgerald v. United States Lines Co.* 374 U.S. 16,20, 83 S. Ct. 1646, 10 L. Ed. 2d 720 (1963).[17] Nonetheless, with or without Congressional or Supreme Court sanction, the courts have followed the tradition of disallowing a demand for a jury in admiralty cases, except under the specific authorization of 28 U.S.C. § 1873. *See Texas Menhaden Co. v. Palermo,* 329 F.2d 579, 580 (5th Cir. 1964) (*Per curiam).* In *Fitzgerald,* the Court noted that Congress has left to the Supreme Court the responsibility of fashioning the controlling rules of admiralty law,[18] 374 U.S. at 20, 83 S. Ct. 1646; but when the Court adopted the proposed amendments to the Federal Rules (unification of Admiralty and Civil Rules) in 1966, no specific provision was included to allow a jury trial in a maritime action. It would appear, therefore, that the Supreme Court acquiesced to the tradition of not allowing a jury trial if the federal courts jurisdiction is founded upon the admiralty and maritime nature of the suit.

The right of a party to a trial by jury, where permitted, is sacrosanct. If there is a question as to whether trial by jury is permitted or not, it would appear that any doubt should be resolved in favor of permitting a jury trial, if timely demanded. In *Dimick v. Schiedt,* 293 U.S. 474, 486, 55 S. Ct. 296, 301, 79 L. Ed. 603 (1935), the Supreme Court was moved to say: "Maintenance of the jury as a fact-finding body is of such importance and occupies so firm a place in our history and jurisprudence that any seeming curtailment of the right to a jury trial should be scrutinized with the utmost care." *See also Beacon Theatres, Inc. v. Westover,* 359 U.S. 500, 79 S. Ct. 948, 3 L. Ed. 2d 988 (1959), which the Fifth Circuit construed to hold "that where the presence of legal and equitable causes in the same case requires the selection between a jury and a non-jury determination of certain common issues, the discretion of the trial court is Very narrowly limited and must, wherever possible, be exercised to preserve jury trial.'" *Thermo-Stitch, Inc. v. Chemi-Cord Processing Corp.,* 294 F.2d 486, 490 (5th Cir. 1961).[19] These pronouncements are in keeping with 28 U.S.C. Section 2072, which provides: "Such rules [prescribed by the Supreme Court] shall ... preserve the right of trial by jury as at common law and as declared by the Seventh Amendment to the Constitution."

I construe Rule 38(e) to mean that if a third party is impleaded pursuant to Rule 14(c), the third party does not have a right to a jury trial either on the issues raised in the third-party complaint on those he raises by way of his answer. Under this construction, if in an admiralty-jurisdiction suit a defendant could implead a person under a non-maritime, third-party complaint, the third party would be denied the right to demand a jury trial. This would raise a serious constitutional question, and the Rules should be construed so as to avoid even a doubt as to their constitutionality. *See Schneider v. Smith,* 390 U.S. 17, 88 S. Ct. 682, 19 L. Ed.2d 799 (Jan. 16,1968); *United States v. Harriss,* 347 U.S. 612, 618 n.6, 74 S. Ct. 808, 98 L. Ed. 989 (1954); *NLRB v. Jones & Laughlin Steel Corp.,* 301 U.S. 1, 30, 57 S. Ct. 615, 81 L. Ed. 893 (1937), and cases cited therein. And if there are two possible constructions of the rules, one which would raise a constitutional question and one which would not, the Rules should be construed in a way that will avoid the constitutional issue. *Compare NLRB v. Fruit and Vegetable Packers and Warehousemen, Local 760,* 377 U.S. 58, 63, 84 S. Ct. 1063, 12 L. Ed. 2d 129 (1964); *Ashwander v. T.V.A.,* 297 U.S. 288, 56 S. Ct. 466, 80 L. Ed. 688 (1936). Both as a matter of constitutional and practical construction, Rule 14(c) does not permit a person to be impleaded in an admiralty suit without an independent basis of federal, and perhaps admiralty, jurisdiction.

Now, therefore, it is hereby ordered

(a) that the third-party complaint filed against Wesley R. T. Metznerbe,and the same is, dismissed;

(b) that each party shall bear and pay its costs incurred herein.

————————

[18] See 28 U.S.C. § 2072.

[19] In a Jones Act case brought on the "law" side, the Fifth Circuit concluded that the district court had substituted its judgment for that of the jury's. The court said: "That it is violative of the Seventh Amendment to the Constitution of the United States for a court to so invade the province of a jury is so fundamental that it need not be supported by citation." *Korbut v. Keystone Shipping Co.,* 380 F.2d 352, 354 (5th Cir. 1967).

Note: Ancillary Jurisdiction Over F.R.C.P. 14(c) Impleader

HARCREST INTERNATIONAL, LTD. v. M/V ZIM KEELUNG

681 F. Supp. 354 (E.D. La. 1988)

* * *

In *Joiner v. Diamond M. Drilling Co.*, 677 F.2d 1035 (5th Cir. 1982), the Fifth Circuit apparently removed any impediments to ancillary jurisdiction over 14(c) impleaders. In *Joiner*, a seamans widow filed an admiralty action against her late husband's employer, who impleaded a third-party with a non-admiralty cause of action. The main admiralty action was subsequently settled. The Fifth Circuit held that it would not retain ancillary jurisdiction over the non-maritime impleader which remained pending after the settlement of the principal action. However, *Joiner* addressed the issue of whether ancillary jurisdiction is applicable to a 14(c) impleader. The *Joiner* court specifically stated that because the rules of admiralty and civil procedure have merged, there is no impediment to the exercise of ancillary jurisdiction over state law claims appended to admiralty claims. *Id.* at 1040. It further "held" that a "third-party claim lacking independent grounds of jurisdiction may be appended to an admiralty action and is cognizable in federal court under the doctrine of ancillary jurisdiction as long as the ancillary claim arises out of the same core of operative facts as the main admiralty action." *Id.* at 1041.

* * *

Note: Admiralty Actions and Impleaders: Right to Jury Trial

In *Hanjin Shipping v. Jay*, 1991 AMC 2596 (C.D. Cal. 1991), the court, following *Wilmington Trust v. U.S. Dist. Court for the Dist. of Hawaii*, 934 F.2d 1026, 1991 AMC 1849, held that:

* * *

A defendant in an admiralty action who impleads a third party pursuant to FRCP 14(c) is entitled to a jury trial of his non-maritime claims in that complaint, provided that an independent basis of jurisdiction, such as diversity of citizenship, is pleaded.

* * *

8. Joinder of Parties Prior to the Supplemental Jurisdiction Act

Prior to the Supplemental Jurisdiction Act, 28 U.S.C. § 1367, federal courts could only hear disputes that would have fallen outside their usual jurisdiction if the claims in question fell within the court's pendent or ancillary jurisdiction. Pendent jurisdiction permitted the court sitting in admiralty to hear a state law claim that arose out of the same underlying facts as a federal admiralty claim, even if the state law claim was against a different defendant. See, e.g., *Leather's Best, Inc. v. S.S. Mormaclynx*, 451 F.2d 800, 1971 AMC 2383 (2nd Cir. 1971), where a federal admiralty court held that it had jurisdiction to hear a state tort law claim against a subsidiary of a shipowner who was a defendant to a federal admiralty proceeding, because the facts underlying the two claims were identical. See also *Roco Carriers Ltd v. M/V Nurnberg Express*, 899 F.2d 1292, 1990 AMC 913 (2nd Cir. 1990), where it was held that pendent jurisdiction was available in relation to a state law claim against a warehouse operator arising out of the same facts as two claims brought in admiralty against an ocean carrier and its ship. The court held that pendent party jurisdiction arose in admiralty cases where the state law claim against an additional party arose out of a common nucleus of operative facts with the admiralty claim and the resolution of the factually connected claims in a single proceeding would further the interests of conserving judicial resources and fairness to the parties.

9. Removal

Note: Overview of Removal

Where the plaintiff has brought suit in a state court, the defendant may, under specified circumstances, have the power to affect that choice by "removing" the suit to a federal court under 28 U.S.C. § 1441. Generally, a suit may be removed from a state court to a federal court only where it could have been commenced initially in a federal court; that is, where a federal court would have had original jurisdiction to entertain it. When a suit has been properly removed from a state court to a federal court, it will be resolved in the federal court as though it had been brought in the federal court from the very beginning.

As with most rules, there are exceptions to the removal rule, and there are circumstances where, even though federal jurisdiction is present, a defendant is not permitted to remove a case that has been brought in a state court. The right of a plaintiff under the "saving to suitors" clause to elect to bring his claim in a non-admiralty forum such as a state court has been deemed to be a clear expression of Congressional intent which may not be defeated by removal. This means that, when a plaintiff has brought such a claim in a state court, the defendant may not remove it to a federal court even though initially it could have been commenced by the plaintiff in a federal court as an admiralty case under 28 U.S.C. § 1333. In other words, suits brought in a state court under the "saving to suitors" clause are exceptions to the right to remove. (*See Romero v. International Terminal Operating Co.*, 358 U.S. 354, 79 S. Ct. 468, 3 L.Ed.2d 368 (1959), *supra.*)

As further complication, however, if there is an alternative basis for federal jurisdiction, such as diversity of citizenship, then removal is permitted. The advantage of the state remedy is that a plaintiff may have his case tried to a jury. In a federal court, matters that proceed under admiralty jurisdiction are tried by the court alone without a jury. (An exception to this is actions brought under the Jones Act, which provides for trial by jury, or actions combined with a Jones Act count.) However, if the plaintiff and defendant are of diverse citizenship, instead of suing in a state court or suing in a federal court under its admiralty jurisdiction, the plaintiff may bring suit in a federal court by invoking the courts diversity of citizenship jurisdiction. In this situation, the plaintiff would also be able to have the matter resolved by a jury. Removal of a case in which there is a diversity of citizenship does not deprive a plaintiff of his right to a jury trial and does not undermine the "saving to suitors" provisions.

If there is diversity jurisdiction allowing the suit to be removed, will it be an admiralty action within Rule 9(h)? In *Scurlock v. American President Lines*, 162 F. Supp. 78 (N.D. Cal. 1958, the defendant was successful, because of diversity, in removing the case to admiralty. The court, however, granted that plaintiff's motion to transfer the case to the law side of the court where the plaintiff could have a jury trial. Doesn't present law merely allow forum shopping by the plaintiff? *See generally* Morse, *Removal of Saving Clause Suits as Civil Actions Within the Original Jurisdiction of the District Courts*, 4 MAR. LAW. 197 (1979).

By statute (28 U.S.C. § 1445(a)), Congress has provided that civil actions against a railroad under the Federal Employees' Liability Act (FELA) are not removable. This has been held to apply to actions by seamen under the Jones Act, which incorporates the provisions of the FELA. *Pate v. Standard Dredging Corp.*, 193 F.2d 498, 1952 A.M.C. 287 (5th Cir. 1952). Thus, Jones Act claims are not removable even where there is diversity jurisdiction. But suppose a Jones Act claim is joined with general maritime claims for unseaworthiness and maintenance and cure. If there is no diversity, the Romero rule would prevent removal. If there is diversity, however, would the entire case be removable under § 1441(c), or at least the unseaworthiness and maintenance and cure claims? In *Pate*, the court stated that the unseaworthiness claim was not independent of the Jones Act claim for purposes of § 1441(c). The court further stated that although the maintenance and cure claim was independent, the jurisdictional amount prerequisite for diversity jurisdiction was not met so there could be no removal. But what if there is sufficient jurisdictional amount on the maintenance and cure claim? *Compare Sawyer v. Federal Barge Lines*, 510 F. Supp. 39, 1981 AMC. 2688 (S.D. 111. 1981) with *Consalves v. Amoco Shipping Co.*, 1982 AMC 1399 (S.D.N.Y. 1982), *reversed*, 733 F.2d 1020, 1984 AMC 2665 (2d Cir. 1984).

SUPERIOR FISH CO., INC. v. ROYAL GLOBE INSURANCE CO.

521 F. Supp. 437, 1982 AMC 710 (E.D. Pa. 1981)

LUONGO, District Judge

Plaintiff, Superior Fish Co., Inc. (Superior Fish), initially brought this removed action in the Philadelphia Court of Common Pleas seeking to recover damages for the value of a shipment of eels which spoiled while being transported from Glassboro, New Jersey, to Trieste, Italy. Named as defendants are Royal Globe Insurance Company (Royal Globe), which issued an insurance policy to plaintiff allegedly covering this loss; Jugolinija, the Yugoslav organization which operates the ship that transported the eels to Trieste; and Insurance Company of North America (INA), the insurer of Burgmeyer Brothers, Inc., the firm that transported the eels from Glassboro to Baltimore, Maryland, where they were loaded upon ship. Plaintiff proceeded directly against INA because Burgmeyer is currently involved in bankruptcy proceedings and cannot be sued because of the automatic stay provision of the Bankruptcy Code, 11 U.S.C. § 362.

INA has filed a motion to dismiss for failure to state a claim upon which relief can be granted, F. R. Civ. P. 12(b)(6), on the ground that plaintiff does not have a right of direct action against it as a matter of law. Upon initial consideration of that motion I noted that there appeared to be no independent grounds of subject matter jurisdiction over plaintiff's claim against INA and that, therefore, there were serious questions as to whether there was removal jurisdiction in this case. 28 U.S.C. § 1441. After an informal in-chambers conference the parties submitted memoranda of law on the related issues of removal and subject matter jurisdiction. After consideration of these memoranda I conclude that there is no removal jurisdiction in this court and the entire case will be remanded to the Philadelphia Court of Common Pleas. 28 U.S.C. § 1447.

The jurisdictional problems in this case are caused by the fact that INA and plaintiff are both citizens of Pennsylvania and plaintiff's claim against INA is a state law claim based either on Pennsylvania's direct action statute, 40 P.S. § 117, or on a theory that it is a third-party beneficiary of the insurance contract between INA and Burgmeyer. Accordingly, no independent grounds of original subject matter jurisdiction over the claims against INA are present. The parties supporting jurisdiction in this case, Jugolinija and Royal Globe, assert that, despite the absence of independent grounds of jurisdiction over the claims against INA, jurisdiction is proper because the provisions of the general removal statute, 28 U.S.C. § 1441, have been satisfied.

The removal statute provides:

(a) Except as otherwise expressly provided by Act of Congress, any civil action brought in a State court of which the district courts of the United States have original jurisdiction, may be removed by the defendant or the defendants, to the district court of the United States for the district and division embracing the place where such action is pending.

(b) Any civil action of which the district courts have original jurisdiction founded on a claim or right arising under the Constitution, treaties or laws of the United States shall be removable without regard to the citizenship or residence of the parties. Any other such action shall be removable only if none of the parties in interest properly joined and served as defendants is a citizen of the State in which such action is brought.

(c) Whenever a separate and independent claim or cause of action, which would be removable if sued upon alone, is joined with one or more otherwise non-removable claims or causes of action, the entire case may be removed and the district court may determine all issues therein, or, in its discretion, may remand all matters not otherwise within its original jurisdiction.

The removal petition filed by Jugolinija and Royal Globe states that removal of this case is pursuant to § 1441(b). Specifically, they assert that "(p)laintiff's complaint sets forth a claim or cause of action against the petitioner's of which this Court has original jurisdiction founded on a claim or right arising under the Constitution, treaties, or laws of the United States within the meaning of 28 U.S.C. § 1441(b), in that the allegations of the Complaint constitute an Admiralty and Maritime claim under the meaning of Rule 9(h) of the Federal Rules of Civil Procedure and are within the Admiralty and Maritime jurisdiction of the United States and of this Honorable Court." (Petition for Removal P 3). Apparently the removing defendants contend that plaintiff's claims against them are maritime because they stem from the ocean transport of the eels. Although not stated in their petition, Royal Globe and Jugolinija now also contend that the claims against Royal Globe and Jugolinija are separate and independent from the claim against INA and that, therefore, removal is also proper under § 1441(c).

I. § 1441(b)

It is now well settled that maritime claims, as such, are not claims that arise under the "Constitution, treaties or laws of the United States." *Romero v. International Terminal Operating Company*, 358 U.S. 354, 79 S. Ct. 468, 3 L. Ed. 2d 368 (1958).

* * *

Review of the complaint fails to reveal an independent ground of federal jurisdiction which would allow removal of the entire case under § 1441(b). Although there is diversity of citizenship between plaintiff, Royal Globe and Jugolinija, the entire case is not removable on diversity grounds. The absence of complete diversity, occasioned by the presence of INA, makes this case fall outside the original diversity jurisdiction of the federal courts, 28 U.S.C. § 1332, and accordingly, the case does not meet the original jurisdiction prerequisite of § 1441(b). Nor are there any other independent jurisdictional grounds supporting § 1441(b) removal.[6]

II. § 1441(c)

Although not stated in the removal petition, Royal Globe and Jugolinija also contend that removal of the entire case is proper under § 1441(c), which allows removal of the entire case when a separate and independent claim which would be removable if sued on alone, is joined with a non-removable claim. In the instant case, if Royal Globe and Jugolinija had been sued alone there would be no removal problem as there would be original jurisdiction on the basis of diversity. It must be determined, therefore, whether the claims against either of these parties are separate and independent from the claims against INA.

The separate and independent claim language of § 1441(c) was analyzed by the Supreme Court in *American Fire & Casualty Company v. Finn*, 341 U.S. 6, 71 S. Ct. 534, 95 L. Ed. 702 (1951). In *Finn*, a case removed to federal court under § 1441(c), plaintiff brought suit against two insurance companies, which were of diverse citizenship, and the companies' non-diverse mutual agent, seeking damages for loss of property due to a fire. The Supreme Court reversed the judgment rendered in plaintiff's favor on the grounds that the case was not properly removed under § 1441(c) because the claims made were not separate and independent. The court stated "that where there is a single wrong to plaintiff, for which relief is sought, arising from an interlocked series of transactions, there is no separate and independent cause of action under § 1441(c)." 341 U.S. at 14, 71 S. Ct. at 540 (footnote omitted).

A review of plaintiff's complaint establishes that the claims against Royal Globe and Jugolinija are not separate and independent from the claim against INA and, therefore, the entire case is not removable under § 1441(c). Although it has stated five separate counts, plaintiff essentially seeks recovery for a single injury, the loss of its eels. It names different defendants because, at this point, it is simply unable to ascertain how the damage occurred. Plaintiff's claims against INA and Jugolinija (counts III, IV and V) allege that the injury to the eels was caused either by Jugolinija, or INA (through Burgmeyer), or both. The fact that INA's liability is predicated on the truck transport of the eels by land and Jugolinija's on the ship transport, does not make these separate and independent claims since they are clearly related factually and stem from the same transaction—the shipment of the eels. Indeed, the relationship between the claims against INA and Jugolinija is illustrated by the fact that in count V of the complaint plaintiff alleges that these parties are jointly and severally liable for its injury, an allegation which dictates a finding that the claims are not separate and independent.

* * *

Accordingly, in the instant case, where plaintiff is suing for a single injury arising out of a series of interlocked transactions, removal is improper under § 1441(c). Because removal is similarly improper under § 1441(b), the entire case will be remanded.

---

[6] Royal Globe also asserts that although not specifically mentioned in the complaint, plaintiff's claims against Jugolinija implicate both the Carriage of Goods by Sea Act, 46 U.S.C. § 1300, *et seq.*, and/or the Harter Act, 46 U.S.C. § 190, *etseq.* Assuming that the complaint states such claims, the problems created by the lack of subject matter jurisdiction over INA are not cured and removal is still not proper under 28 U.S.C. § 1441(b).

A number of courts have permitted removal of statutory maritime claims on the grounds that they are acts regulating commerce, and fall within the original jurisdictional grant of 28 U.S.C. § 1337. Accordingly, these claims are deemed to have an independent ground of federal jurisdiction. *See, e.g., Puerto Rico v. Sea-Land Service, Inc.*, 349 R Supp. 964, 973- 75 (D.P.R. 1970); *Crispin Company v. Lykes Brothers Steamship Co.*, 134 F. Supp. 704 (S.D. Tex. 1955). The validity of these holdings, however, are suspect in light of *Romero's* strong policy against the evisceration of the "savings to suitors" clause through a liberal approach to removal. The holding in *Romero*, that maritime claims do not arise under the laws of the United States, is equally applicable to federal statutory maritime claims as well as "common-law" claims. *See Eastern Steel & Metal Co. v. Hartford Fire Insurance Co., supra*, 376 F. Supp. at 765. Accordingly, the use of 28 U.S.C. § 1337 to avoid the reach of *Romero* has been questioned. *See Pacific Agencies, Inc. v. Colen & Villalon, Inc.*, 372 F. Supp. 62, 64 (D.P.R. 1973).

Note:

> *See The Tokio Marine and Fire Ins. Co., Ltd. v. American President Lines, Ltd.,*1999 WL 356308 and cases cited therein.

TENNESSEE GAS PIPELINE v. HOUSTON CASUALTY INS. CO.

87 F.3d 150, 1996 AMC 2296 (5th Cir. 1996)

REAVLEY, Circuit Judge:

An ocean-going vessel, in the tow of a tug whose helmsman was reading a novel, allided with a platform secured to the outer continental shelf some 35 miles off the coast of Louisiana. The platform owner filed suit in state court against a non-diverse insurer of the tug, contending both that the allision gave rise to a federal maritime claim that was "saved to suitors" under 28 U.S.C. § 1333, and that the Louisiana direct action statute gave it the right to proceed against the insurer directly. The insurer removed the case, asserting that the federal courts had federal question jurisdiction because the suit arose under the Outer Continental Shelf Lands Act (OCSLA).[1] The platform owner's moved for remand. The district court denied remand, but, finding it a close case, certified the question for interlocutory appeal.[2] We permitted appeal, and we now affirm.

Tennessee Gas Pipeline Company (Tennessee Gas or appellant), a citizen of Texas, owned and operated a fixed platform in West Cameron Block 192, on the outer continental shelf approximately 35 miles off the coast of Louisiana. On September 23, 1992, the barge Iron Mike, in the tow of the tug M/V Gulf Miss, allided with the platform, substantially damaging it and disrupting its operation for a considerable length of time. Houston Casualty Company (HCC or appellee), also a citizen of Texas, is an insurer of the several entities which owned, operated, or chartered the M/V Gulf Miss (collectively Tidewater).

Following the allision, Tennessee Gas sued HCC in the state direct action suit at issue in this appeal. Tennessee Gas admits forthrightly that it attempted to craft its lawsuit to avoid federal removal jurisdiction. First, in order to defeat diversity jurisdiction, and as allowed under Louisiana law, Tennessee Gas sued only HCC, even though HCC underwrote only 4% of the risk covered under Tidewater's insurance policy. And second, Tennessee Gas tried to defeat federal question jurisdiction by asserting only a general maritime claim saved to suitors under 28 U.S.C. § 1333,[3] purposely choosing not to assert a claim under OCSLA.

But even assuming that Tennessee Gas has defeated diversity jurisdiction and that its well-pleaded complaint asserts a maritime claim that is saved to suitors, we nevertheless have removal jurisdiction.

A. Anchored Law

HCC, the removing party, bears the burden of demonstrating the propriety of removal[4] under the statute, 28 U.S.C. § 1441, which reads:

(a) Except as otherwise expressly provided by Act of Congress, any civil action brought in a State court of which the district courts of the United States have original jurisdiction, may be removed by the defendant or the defendants, to the district court of the United States for the district and division embracing the place where such action is pending....

(b) Any civil action of which the district courts have original jurisdiction founded on a claim or right arising under the Constitution, treaties or laws of the United States, shall be removable without regard to the citizenship

---

[1] 43 U.S.C. § 1331, *et seq.*

[2] *See* 28 U.S.C. § 1292(b).

[3] 28 U.S.C. § 1333 states:

> The district courts shall have original jurisdiction, exclusive of the courts of the States, of: (1) Any civil case of admiralty or maritime jurisdiction, saving to suitors in all cases all other remedies to which they are otherwise entitled....

[4] *Gaitor v. Peninsular & Occidental Steamship Co., 287 F.2d 252, 253-54 (5th Cir. 1961).*

or residence of the parties. Any other such action shall be removable only if none of the parties in interest properly joined and served as defendants is a citizen of the State in which such action is brought.

It is well-established that maritime claims do not "aris[e] under the Constitution, treaties or laws of the United States" for purposes of federal question and removal jurisdiction.[5] Tennessee Gas's maritime claim is not removable under the first sentence of 28 U.S.C. § 1441(b) by falling within the admiralty jurisdiction of the federal courts. But it is also well-established that the saving clause does not prevent the removal of maritime claims when original jurisdiction is based on something other than admiralty.[6] As we have stated:

The "saving to suitors" clause does no more than preserve the right of maritime suitors to pursue nonmaritime remedies. It does not guarantee them a nonfederal forum, or limit the right of defendants to remove such actions to federal court where there exists some basis for federal jurisdiction other than admiralty.[7] In this case OCSLA provides an alternative basis for original jurisdiction.

B. OCSLA Original Jurisdiction

OCSLA declares that "the subsoil and seabed of the outer Continental Shelf appertain to the United States and are subject to its jurisdiction, control, and power of disposition...."[8] OCSLA also declares that "the outer Continental Shelf is a vital national resource reserve held by the Federal Government for the public...."[9] In order to provide expeditious but environmentally safe development of the resources on the OCS, OCSLA explicitly prevents individual states from authorizing mineral leases covering the OCS.[10] Thus OCSLA is an assertion of national authority over the OCS at the expense of both foreign governments and the governments of the individual states.

One purpose of OCSLA was to define the law applicable to the seabed, subsoil, and fixed structures on the OCS.[11] Section 4 of OCSLA[12] makes federal law exclusive in its regulation of the OCS, but in order to fill the substantial gaps in the coverage of federal law, OCSLA adopts the "applicable and not inconsistent" laws of the adjacent states as surrogate federal law.[13] State law was adopted as federal law because Congress knew that federal law, including maritime law, was inadequate to meet the full range of disputes that would arise on the OCS.[14]

While OCSLA was intended to apply to the full range of disputes that might occur on the OCS, it was not intended to displace general maritime law. This is clear from both the statute itself and holdings of this court. According to the statute, "this subchapter shall be construed in such a manner that the character of the waters above the outer Continental Shelf as high seas and the right to navigation and fishing therein shall not be affected."[15] Furthermore, 43 U.S.C. § 1333(f) makes clear that the applicability of OCSLA law under 43 U.S.C. § 1333(a) shall not give rise to any inference that other provisions of law (such as general maritime law), do not also apply.[16]

---

[5] *Romero v. International Terminal Operating Co.*, 358 U.S. 354, 377-79, 79 S. Ct. 468,483,3 L. Ed. 2d 368 (1959) (holding, *inter alia,* that federal courts do not have federal question jurisdiction over general maritime claims because such claims do not "arise under the Constitution, treaties, or laws of the United States" within the meaning of 28 U.S.C. § 1331); *In re Dutile,* 935 F.2d 61, 63 (5th Cir. 1991) (holding that saving clause claims cannot be removed under 28 U.S.C. § 1441 (b) on the sole basis that the maritime claim presents a federal question).

[6] *See, e.g., Poirrier v. Nicklos Drilling Co.*, 648 F.2d 1063, 1066 (5th Cir.1981) (permitting removal of a maritime claim where diversity jurisdiction exists); *Williams v. M/V Sonora*, 985 F.2d 808 (5th Cir. 1993) (permitting removal of a maritime claim where jurisdiction is proper under the Federal Sovereign Immunities Act).

[7] *Poirrier,* 648 F.2d at 1066.

[8] 43 U.S.C. § 1332(1).

[9] 43 U.S.C. § 1332(3).

[10] 43 U.S.C. § 1333(a) (1) (providing that mineral leases on the outer continental shelf shall be maintained or issued only under the provisions of OCSLA).

[11] *Rodrigue v. Aetna Cas. And Sur. Co.*, 395 U.S. 352, 355-56, 89 S. Ct. 1835, 1837, 23 L. Ed. 2d 360 (1969).

[12] 43 U.S.C. § 1333.

[13] *Gulf Offshore Co. v. Mobil Oil Corp.*, 453 U.S. 473, 479-81, 101 S. Ct. 2870, 2876, 69 L. Ed. 2d 784 (1981); 43 U.S.C. § 1333(a)(2).

[14] *Rodrigue,* 395 U.S. at 357-58, 360-66, 89 S. Ct. at 1838, 1840-42.

[15] 43 U.S.C. § 1332(2).

[16] 43 U.S.C. § 1333(f) is entitled "Provisions as nonexclusive," and states:

The specific application by this section of certain provisions of law to the subsoil and seabed of the outer Continental Shelf and the artificial islands, installations, and other devices referred to in subsection (a) of this section or to acts or offenses occurring on committed thereon shall not give rise to any inference that the application to such islands and structures, acts, or offenses of any other provision of law is not intended.

It is not surprising, therefore, that this court has declared that where OCSLA and general maritime law both could apply, the case is to be governed by maritime law.[17]

OCSLA not only defines the law applicable to the OCS, but also grants federal courts jurisdiction over disputes occurring there. The jurisdictional grant, contained in 43 U.S.C. § 1349(b)(1), is very broad. With exceptions not relevant here, the statute provides that

> the district courts of the United States shall have jurisdiction of cases and controversies arising out of, or in connection with (A) any operation conducted on the outer Continental Shelf which involves exploration, development, or production of the minerals, of the subsoil and seabed of the outer Continental Shelf, or which involves rights to such minerals, or (B) the cancellation, suspension, or termination of a lease or permit under this subchapter.

We have no difficulty in deciding that § 1349 grants original jurisdiction in federal court over Tennessee Gas's claim. The statute does not define the term "operation." However, this court has defined "operation" to be "the doing of some physical act." In our case, Tennessee Gas alleged that its platform was affixed to the OCS and was used to extract and transport minerals from the OCS. This was clearly enough physical activity on the OCS to constitute an operation. In *EP Operating Ltd. Partnership v. Placid Oil Co.,*[19] this court considered whether it had jurisdiction under § 1349 over a partition action brought to determine ownership of an offshore platform not then being used. The defendants argued that there was no operation because use of the platform had ceased. We disagreed, noting that construction of the platform and pipes to transport minerals was sufficient physical activity to constitute an operation under § 1349.[20]

It is clear that the operation involves "exploration, development, or production" of minerals on the OCS. These terms denote respectively the processes involved in searching for minerals on the OCS;[21] preparing to extract them by, *inter alia*, drilling wells and constructing platforms;[22] and removing the minerals and transferring them to shore.[23] Tennessee Gass platform was constructed to aid in the "development" of minerals on the OCS, and Tennessee Gas's allegations that the accident caused losses due to the inability to extract minerals implicates the "production" of minerals on the OCS.

But did the accident "arise out of, or in connection with" Tennessee Gas's operation on the OCS? In *Recar v. CNG Producing Co.*, we applied a "but for" test under § 1349 to resolve whether a dispute "arises out of, or in connection with" an operation, thus granting the federal courts subject matter jurisdiction.[24] Use of the but-for test implies a broad jurisdictional grant under § 1349, but we have concluded that "a broad, not a narrow, reading of this grant is supported by the clear exertion of federal sovereignty'" over the OCS.[25]

In our case it is clear there would have been no accident but for Tennessee Gas's operation on the OCS. Tennessee Gas argues that the dispute "arose out of" a navigational error, and not an operation on the OCS. But there would have been no navigational error but for the existence of the platform and Tennessee Gas's extractive activities. Tennessee Gas also argues that the platform itself did nothing to cause the accident, so that the controversy is not connected with any physical act constituting an operation. This contention is meritless. The undeniable fact

---

[17] *See, e.g., Smith v. Penrod Drilling Corp.*, 960 F.2d 456 (5th Cir. 1992) (for OCSLA to apply, federal maritime law must not apply of its own force); *Laredo Offshore Constructros, Inc. v. Hunt Oil Co.*, 754 F.2d 1223, 1229 (5th Cir. 1985) ("[W]here admiralty and OCSLA jurisdiction overlap, the case is governed by maritime law."); *Smith v. Pan Air Corp.*, 684 F.2d 1102, 1110 n.26 (5th Cir. 1982) (assuming that admiralty jurisdiction is lacking if the substantive law applicable is OCSLA-imposed state law).

[18] *Amoco Production Co. v. Sea Robin Pipeline Co.*, 844 F.2d 1202, 1207 (5th Cir. 1988).

[19] 26 F.3d 563 (5th Cir. 1994).

[20] *Id* at 567-68.

[21] 43 U.S.C § 1331(k).

[22] 43 U.S.C §1331(l).

[23] 43 U.S.C. §1331(m).

[24] 853 F.2d 367, 369 (5th Cir. 1988) (adopting under § 1349 the but-for test this court has applied under § 1333(b)(2) to determine whether the death of an employee occurred "as the result of operations conducted on the outer Continental Shelf for the purpose of exploring for, developing, removing or transporting" the natural resources of the OCS).

[25] *EP Operating*, 26 F.3d at 569 (quoting *Fluor Ocean Servs., Inc. v. Rucker Co.*, 341 F. Supp. *151*, 760 (E.D. La. 1972)).

is that there would not have been an accident had Tennessee Gas not built its platform to extract minerals from the OCS. Jurisdiction therefore exists under OCSLA.

Our conclusion that OCSLA confers original jurisdiction over this suit is unaffected by the maritime nature of the underlying claim. In Recar we considered whether OCSLA conferred subject matter jurisdiction over the plaintiff's action to recover damages for injuries sustained on the OCS. The plaintiff argued that OCSLA did not confer jurisdiction because of the maritime nature of the case. We held that the district court may have both admiralty and OCSLA jurisdiction.[26]

C. Removal of Maritime Claims Under OCSLA

Our conclusion that OCSLA vests the federal courts with original subject matter jurisdiction over this case establishes that removal is proper under 28 U.S.C. § 1441(a). We go to § 1441(b) and encounter a problem in deciding whether we have removal jurisdiction under the first sentence.

The question under the first sentence of § 1441(b) is whether the district court has "original jurisdiction founded on a claim or right arising under the Constitution, treaties or laws of the United States."[27] There is an argument it does not. We have decided original jurisdiction because of OCSLA, but does Tennessee Gas's claim "arise under the Constitution, treaties or laws of the United States?" A maritime claim does not present federal question jurisdiction.

Two of our cases may be read to support removal of general maritime claims under the first sentence of § 1441(b) when original jurisdiction is conferred by OCSLA. The first is Sea Robin. In that case, Amoco filed suit against Sea Robin in Louisiana state court, alleging that Sea Robin breached a take-or-pay contract to buy natural gas Amoco produced on the OCS. Sea Robin removed, and we held that removal was proper because "this controversy is within federal jurisdiction under OCSLA."[28] The opinion contains almost no discussion of § 1441(b) and does not mention the citizenship of the parties.

The second case is Recar, which concerned the court's original, not removal, jurisdiction. In that case, we held that we had original jurisdiction under OCSLA (43 U.S.C. § 1349) over a personal injury claim, even if maritime law eventually provided the substantive law in the case.[29] In the opinion we stated that "[t]he district court may well have both admiralty jurisdiction under the general maritime law and federal question jurisdiction by virtue of OCSLA."[30] However, nowhere in the opinion does the court address 28 U.S.C. § 1331, and we do not believe the court meant to say that federal question jurisdiction exists by virtue of jurisdiction under 43 U.S.C. § 1349.

Two district court cases are on point. In *Walsh v. Seagull Energy Corp.*[31] and *Fogleman v. Tidewater Barges, Inc.*,[32] the courts considered removal of general maritime claims when OCSLA provided original jurisdiction. In each case, the court concluded that removal could not be based on the first sentence of § 1441(b) (because maritime claims do not arise under federal law),[33] and denied removal under the second sentence of § 1441(b) because the defendant was a citizen of the state in which suit was brought.[34]

In our case, unlike in Walsh and Fogleman, removal is consistent with the second sentence of § 1441(b)—HCC is a citizen of the state of Texas, but suit was brought in Louisiana. We recognize that it may be a distortion of the legal scheme to decide this case on the citizenship of HCC. Given the national interests that prompted Congress to pass OCSLA and grant broad jurisdiction under 43 U.S.C. § 1349, Congress arguably intended to vest the federal courts with the power to hear any case involving the OCS, even on removal, without regard to citizenship.

---

[26] *Recar*, 853 F.2d at 369.
[27] 28 U.S.C. § 1441(b).
[28] *Sea Robin*, 844 F.2d at 1210.
[29] *Recar*, 853 F.2d at 369.
[30] *Id.* (emphasis added).
[31] 836 F Supp. 411 (S.D. Tex. 1993).
[32] 747 F Supp. 348 (E.D. La. 1990).
[33] *See Walsh*, 836 F Supp. at 417-18; *Fogleman*, 747 F Supp. at 355-56.
[34] *See Walsh*, 836 F Supp. at 417; *Fogleman*, 747 F Supp. at 350, 356.

Perhaps congressional intent under OCSLA may have supported removal under the first sentence of § 1441(b), though the language of that sentence might not carry the intent; while the language of the second sentence supports removal, though the purpose of the sentence (diversity) is arguably irrelevant to our case. We need not resolve this conundrum, however, for removal is consistent with the second sentence of § 1441(b), if not the first.

For the foregoing reasons, we AFFIRM the judgment of the district court denying remand to state court, and remand the case to the district court for further proceedings.

AFFIRMED.

E. GRADY JOLLY, Circuit Judge, specially concurring:

I concur, but in doing so I simply observe that the majority's discussion of the applicability of the first sentence of 28 U.S.C. § 1441(b) to claims over which we have original jurisdiction under 43 U.S.C. § 1349, Slip Op., at 4202-4203, is unnecessary to decide this case, and thus constitutes only dicta.

---

a. Non-Removability

SANDERS v. CAMBRIAN CONSULTANTS (CC) AMERICA, INC.

132 F.Supp.3d 853 (S.D. Tex., 2015)

GRAY H. MILLER, District Judge.

Pending before the court is plaintiff Samantha Sanders' motion to remand. Having considered the motion, response, reply, and applicable law, the court is of the opinion that the motion should be GRANTED and this case should be REMANDED to the 215th District Court of Harris County, Texas.

I. Background

Sanders filed a petition in the 215th District Court of Harris County, Texas, against RPS Group, PLC, WesternGeco AS, WesternGeco, LLC, Schlumberger, Ltd., and Volstad Maritime AS, asserting various claims associated with the alleged sexual assault against Sanders by the captain of the seismic vessel M/V "Geco Tau" while Sanders was working aboard the vessel….[O]n March 13, 2015, defendant Volstad Maritime AS ("Volstad") removed the case to this court, arguing that Sanders is asserting a general maritime claim removable under 28 U.S.C. § 1441(a) and that Sanders is not a seaman as a matter of law because she served as a marine mammal observer while aboard the M/V "Geco Tau." Sanders now moves for remand, asserting that (1) general maritime cases are not removable; and (2) Volstad cannot show that Sanders is not a seaman.

ANALYSIS

While admiralty claims traditionally are not removable, this court has held that amendments to the removal statute in 2011, when read in conjunction with binding caselaw from the Fifth Circuit, rendered previously unremovable admiralty claims removable. See *Ryan v. Hercules Offshore, Inc.*, 945 F.Supp.2d 772 (S.D. Tex. 2013). Sanders asks that this court reconsider its decision in *Ryan* in light of several cases that have rejected Ryan. The Fifth Circuit has yet to address the issue. In addition to her maritime claim, Sanders asserts a Jones Act claim. Volstad concedes that Jones Act claims are not removable per 28 U.S.C. § 1445(a), which is incorporated into the Jones Act. Volstad contends, however, that the Jones Act claim does not bar removal in this case because Sanders's Jones Act claim is fraudulently pleaded. Sanders contends that she was a seaman and that Volstad cannot meet the heavy burden of proving otherwise. Sanders additionally argues that even if Volstad could offer evidence that Sanders was not a seaman while aboard the M/V "Geco Tau," the issue of determining seaman status is ordinarily left to the jury.

[The court first concluded that Sanders was a seaman and that her claim to seaman status had not been fraudulently pleaded.]

B. Removability of Maritime Claims

Since the Jones Act claim does not prohibit removal, the court must consider, for the second time, whether the new removal statute permits removal of general maritime claims. The court starts this analysis by noting that *Ryan* was properly decided on the facts and arguments presented in that case. Several courts considering similar facts and arguments have followed *Ryan*. Several others have elected not to follow *Ryan*. In the absence of binding authority and given the dramatic change to admiralty law associated with the court's reading of the amended statute, disagreement amongst the district courts was not unexpected. Disagreement alone does not cause the court to waiver in its confidence in its decision in the *Ryan* case. That being said, the court is charged with ensuring justice is done, and it is thus willing to reconsider previous decisions when new arguments or facts merit taking a second look.

Here, Sanders has presented a sophisticated argument that was not raised in the *Ryan* case. When the court was considering *Ryan*, there had been no development of caselaw or legal commentary on how the amendment to the removal statute impacted admiralty claims in light of historical precedent and the Savings to Suitors clause. While the Fifth Circuit has not had the opportunity to address the amended statute since the *Ryan* case, numerous legal scholars have considered the issue. The best example of scholarly work on the issue, in the court's opinion, can be found in *Gregoire v. Enterprise* Marine Services, LLC, 38 F.Supp.3d 749 (E.D.La. 2014) (Duval, J.). While *Gregoire* is an opinion, not a law review article, it thoroughly explores the history of the law as it relates to admiralty jurisdiction and removal of admiralty cases. It then provides a convincing argument why the amendments to the removal statute do not impact the historical bar on removal of maritime claims filed at law in state court. Specifically, when a maritime claim is filed in state court under the Savings to Suitors Clause, it is transformed into a case at law, as opposed to admiralty. The federal district courts thus do not have original jurisdiction under the Savings to Suitors Clause, which provides original jurisdiction over "[a]ny civil case of admiralty or maritime jurisdiction, saving to suitors in all cases all other remedies to which they are otherwise entitled." 28 U.S.C. § 1333 (emphasis added); *Gregoire*, 38 F.Supp.3d at 759–62. Sanders, unlike the plaintiff in *Ryan*, raised this argument. The court holds, pursuant to the reasoning set forth in *Gregoire*, that it does not have jurisdiction over the claim Sanders filed in state court pursuant to the Savings to Suitors Clause. Sanders's motion to remand is therefore granted.

Also, add the following at the end of the case extract:

Note

For a better understanding of removal and admiralty cases, see R. Force, "Understanding the Nonremovability of Maritime Cases: Lessons Learned from 'Original Intent'," 89 *Tul. L. Rev.* 1019 (2014-15).

CHAPTER 3 — ADMIRALTY REMEDIES

Introductory Note on Maritime Remedies

An action that arises from an admiralty claim may be based on the *in personam* liability of the defendant or, under the "personification" doctrine, based on the *in rem* liability of maritime property. An *in personam* claim may be commenced in a federal district court by serving process on the defendant as authorized by Rule 4 of the Federal Rules of Civil Procedure and for actions filed in state courts under the "saving to suitors clause", by serving process in the manner authorized by the state for instituting *in personam* actions in that state.

With the unification of the Federal Rules of Civil Procedure in 1966, those rules now apply in admiralty actions. However, Supplemental Rules A through F of the Federal Rules of Civil Procedure maintain certain traditional maritime remedies. The action *in rem* is specifically preserved in the Supplemental Rules. The action *in rem* may be brought to enforce a maritime lien and it may be brought together with an *in personam* action against the owner of the res. This is provided for in Rule C(1). Supplemental Rules B and E of the Federal Rules of Civil Procedure also prescribe a method for instituting an action in a federal court based on the *in personam* liability of a defendant by "attaching" (seizing) the defendant's property within the federal district in which the court is located. Supplemental Rule B also permits an admiralty action to be commenced in federal court by utilizing state attachment procedures.

Supplemental Rules C and E provide a method for instituting an action *in rem* against maritime property. Under the personification doctrine[20] maritime property such as a ship is liable for torts committed by personnel in control of the property. Thus, if a ship is involved in a collision because of the negligence of its crew, not only is the owner of the ship liable for damages *in personam* based on *respondeat superior*, but the ship, itself, is liable *in rem* for damage or injury that resulted from the collision. The personification doctrine applies in contract cases as well. For example, if "necessaries" are furnished to a ship, not only is the person who contracted to obtain the necessaries for the ship liable *in personam* to pay for the necessaries, but the ship can be sued *in rem* to recover the amount due on the contract. Thus, in a real sense, a ship can be held liable for "its" torts and contracts. Of course the personification doctrine is a legal fiction, but one that has been found to be useful in maritime cases. The true ownership of a vessel might not always be easy to ascertain and locating the whereabouts of the owner may be equally difficult. Thus, recourse against the vessel, from a practical perspective, may be a plaintiff's only real remedy.[21] In order for an action to be commenced *in rem*, the property that is the subject of the dispute must be seized by the court, actually or constructively in the district where the property is located.[22] The seizure accomplishes two objectives: (1) it provides the court with jurisdiction over the property and (2) it provides security to the plaintiff in the event he is successful. It is important to note that in U.S. maritime law, the action is against the property that has been seized is not against the owner of the property; it is a true action *in rem*. This distinguishes the U.S. view of "arrest" from the law of many countries[23] such as England[24] where the "seizure" of maritime property sometimes denominated as an "arrest" or "attachment", proceeds on a procedural theory, the object of which is to have the owner appear

---

[20] *Tucker v. Alexandroff*, 183 U.S. 424, (1902); *United States v. The Little Charles*, 26 Fed. Cas. 979, 981-82 (C.C.D. Va. 1818) (No. 15, 612); *Salazar v. The "Atlantic Sun"*, 881 F.2d 73, 1989 AMC 2594 (3d Cir. 1989).

[21] Martin Davies, *In defense of Unpopular Virtues: Personification and Ratification*, 75 Tul. L. Rev. 337 (2000).

[22] *Carry Marine, Inc. v. The Motorvessel Papillon*, 872 F.2d 751, 1990 AMC 828 (6th Cir. 1989).

[23] *Belcher Co. of Alabama, Inc. v. M/V Maratha Mariner*, 724 F.2d 1161, 1984 AMC 1697 (5th Cir. 1984).

[24] *Trinidad Foundry and Fabricating, Ltd. v. M/V K.A.S. Camilla*, 966 F.2d 613, 1992 AMC 2636 (11th Cir. 1992).

and subject himself to *in personam* jurisdiction.[25] The law of the United States differentiates between a seizure of property by means of a judicial process called an "arrest" and a seizure of property by means of a judicial process called an "attachment". The arrest process is used to commence an *in rem* action against the property itself based on the liability of the property. Many countries do not personify property and do not authorize an action based on the liability of property as does U.S. law.

The attachment proceeding in the U.S. is used to commence an action "*quasi-in-rem*" against the owner of the property based on the personal liability of the owner. One common factor shared by Supplemental Rules B and C other than they are commenced by the seizure of property is that the underlying claim must be a maritime claim, that is, the action must satisfy the criteria for admiralty jurisdiction.

"While the mode of proceeding in the admiralty courts of the United States was required by the Practice Act of 1789 to be according to the course of the civil law, the process of attachment to compel the appearance of an absent defendant had the sanction of that system of jurisprudence. It has the sanction of the act of 1792, because it is according to the principles, rules, and usages which belong to courts of admiralty. It has also the sanction of the act of 1842. Under that act this court, at the December Term, 1844, prescribed "rules of practice for the courts of the United States in admiralty and maritime jurisdiction on the instance side." The second of those rules is as follows: "In suits *in personam* the mesne process may be by a simple warrant of arrest of the person of the defendant in the nature of a capias, or by a warrant of arrest of the person of the defendant, with a clause therein that if he cannot be found to attach his goods and chattels to the amount sued for; or, if such property cannot be found, to attach his credits and effects to the amount sued for in the hands of the garnishees named therein, or by a simple monition in the nature of a summons, to appear and answer to the suit, as the libellant shall in his information pray for or elect."

Atkins v. The Disintegrating Co., 88 U.S.271 (1873).

A. Textual Analysis: Enforcement of Maritime Claims, Liens and Mortgages in the United States

1. In Rem *Actions*

An action *in rem* is commenced by arresting property, typically a vessel, under Supplemental Rules C and E of the Federal Rules of Civil Procedure. The mere fact that the procedural device for instituting an *in rem* action is called an "arrest" does not mean that an *in rem* action in the United States is the same type of action which in other countries is commenced by an "arrest" procedure. An *in rem* action in the United States is an action against the named property itself. It need *not* be based on the personal liability of the owner of the property. It is *not* a means for obtaining *in personam* jurisdiction over a non-resident property owner. The law of the United States differentiates between a seizure of property by means of a judicial process called an "arrest" and a seizure of property by means of a judicial process called an "attachment". The arrest process is used to commence an *in rem* action. The attachment process, sometimes referred to as a "*quasi-in-rem*" proceeding, is used to commence an action *in personam*.

When Available—Maritime Liens

An *in rem* action may be brought to enforce maritime liens under the Federal Maritime Lien Act, to enforce other maritime liens created under the general maritime law, and as authorized by statute such as under the Federal Ship Mortgage Act.[2] Generally actions for breach of maritime contracts and actions based on maritime torts give rise to maritime liens which may be enforced through an action *in rem*. Also statutes have conferred liens status in certain situations.

---

[25] *Salazar v. The "Atlantic Sun"*, 881 F.2d 73, 1989 AMC 2594 (3d Cir. 1989).
[1] 46 U.S.C §§31341 - 31343 (1989 Supp.).
[2] 46 U.S.C §§31231 - 31330 (1989 Supp.).

The following give rise to maritime liens.
1. Seamen's claim for wages
2. Master's claims for wages[3]
3. Salvage claims
4. Maritime torts including collision and personal injury claims
5. General Average claims
6. Preferred ship mortgage[4]
7. Supply and repair claims
8. Towage, wharfage, pilotage, stevedoring, etc. claims
9. Cargo damage caused by improper loading, stowage, custody, etc.
10. Ship's claim against cargo for unpaid freight
11. Breach of charter party

Arrest Procedures

When an *In Rem* Proceeding May be Brought

Supplemental Rule C of the Federal Rules of Civil Procedure[5] specifies the rules applicable in *in rem* proceedings. It provides that an action *in rem* may be brought to enforce a maritime lien or whenever a federal statute provides for a maritime action *in rem*. Furthermore, an action *in rem* may be brought against the United States when authorized by statute, but the vessel in question may not actually be physically seized. Generally, a party who elects to proceed *in rem* also may proceed *in personam* against any party who may be liable.

The Complaint

In an *in rem* action plaintiff must file a "complaint" that describes the property that is subject to the action and states that it is in or will be in the judicial district during the pendency of the action. If the property is not within the district where the action is commenced and there is no prospect of it being so, an *in rem* action will not lie.[6]

Judicial Review—Notice

The complaint along with supporting papers must be reviewed by the court, and, if the conditions for an action *in rem* appear to exist, the court shall issue an order authorizing a warrant for the arrest of the vessel or other property that is the subject to the action. No notice other than execution is required. But if the property is not released within ten days, the plaintiff must give public notice of the action and the arrest in a newspaper of general circulation. This notice must specify the time within which the answer is required to be filed.

Claimant's Response

A claimant of property that is the subject of an action *in rem* must file its claim of a right of possession or ownership interest within ten days after process has been executed unless the court allows additional time. It must file its answer within twenty days after filing its claim. There are additional procedural matters applicable to actions *in rem* contained in Supplemental Rule E, but as they are equally applicable to "attachments" they will be discussed later.

Execution of Process

For an action *in rem* to be commenced the property that is the subject matter of the action must be subjected "physically" to the jurisdiction of the court.[7] It is not enough that the property is present in the judicial district

---

[3] 46 U.S.C § 11112 (1989 Supp.), master of a documented vessel.

[4] As will be discussed later, preferred mortgages have been given a lien, may be enforced in an *in rem* proceeding, and are given priority over certain other claims.

[5] Unless stated otherwise or unless apparent from the context, the procedures referred to herein are prescribed in Supplemental Rule C of the Federal Rules of Civil Procedure.

[6] *But see infra,* Necessity for Seizure & Retention - Exceptions.

[7] *But see infra,* Necessity for Seizure & Retention - Exceptions.

where the court is located. A court officer, the United States Marshal, must physically seize the property, actually or figuratively, and take it into custody, if possible. In the case of an arrest of a vessel, however, service of the arrest papers on the master and placing a "keeper" on the vessel will suffice. In an *in rem* action jurisdiction over the property is required to give the court jurisdiction over the action, but as will be discussed this requirement has been weakened to some extent. Subject to the qualifications discussed below, seizure of the property is essential to give the court jurisdiction over the property.

---

2. Admiralty Attachments and Garnishments

There is an alternative method for obtaining *in personam* jurisdiction other than by service of process on the defendant or its agents authorized to receive process either in fact or by law. This procedure is sometimes referred to as *quasi-in-rem* jurisdiction and is accomplished by an attachment of defendant's property within a state. The presence of defendant's property within a state may be sufficient to constitute the "minimum contacts" required under the Due Process Clause. The seizure of the property may be sufficient to satisfy the service of process requirement. The nature and extent of the property, its use in the state, and the relationship, if any, between the property and the events that have given rise to the claim may assure that the due process fairness requirements have been satisfied.

Supplemental Rule B of the Federal Rules of Civil Procedure makes special provisions for bringing a maritime claim in federal court by commencing an *in personam* action by seizing property of the defendant by attachment or garnishment.

Attachment Procedures[8]

When Available—Complaint

A plaintiff who has asserted an admiralty or maritime claim *in personam* may include in its verified complaint a request for process to attach the defendant's goods and chattels, or credits and effects in the hands of garnishees named in the process up to the amount sued for. Rule B is available only where plaintiff has asserted a maritime or admiralty claim. The property plaintiff seeks to attach or garnish must be within the geographic boundaries of the federal judicial district wherein the action is brought.

Defendant "Not Found Within the District"

Attachment and garnishment are permissible under the Rule only "if the defendant shall not be found within the district." Note the use of the term "district". Most states because of their size or population have been divided by Congress into several federal judicial districts in order to facilitate the operation of the federal district courts. For example, the state of Louisiana contains three federal judicial districts, the Eastern District of Louisiana, the Middle District and the Western District, each with its own geographic boundaries.

Plaintiff must submit an affidavit to the effect that defendant cannot be found within the district where suit is brought. Usually plaintiff will set forth the steps it or its attorney took which support the allegation that defendant is not present within the district. An allegation that defendant cannot be found within the district has two dimensions:

1. defendant is not present for jurisdictional purposes;
2. defendant is not present for service of process.

To defeat an attachment and secure the release of property defendant must show that it is present in the district *both* in the jurisdictional sense (minimum contacts) and that it is amenable to service of process personally or through an agent authorized to accept service of process. The fact that defendant is present within the *state* is

---

[8] Unless stated otherwise or unless apparent from the context, the procedures referred to herein are prescribed in Supplemental Rule B of the Federal Rules of Civil Procedure.

insufficient to bar a Rule B action if defendant is not present within the geographic area comprising the federal judicial district in which the action has been commenced.

Judicial Review—Notice

The procedures under Rule B are similar in many respects to the procedures required by Rule C. A court must review the complaint and affidavit and if it appears that plaintiff is entitled to have process issued, the court will so order. Notice is given to the garnishee or person in possession of the property when process, the attachment, is served on that person in order to secure physical control of the property by the court. Rule B provides that no default shall be taken unless there is proof that the plaintiff or the garnishee gave notice to the defendant. Notice may be given by mail with return receipt, or by actual service of process. Notice is not required if plaintiff or garnishee has been unable to give it despite diligent efforts to do so.

Answer

The garnishee has twenty days from service of process to file an answer. Plaintiff may serve interrogatories on the garnishee. The defendant has thirty days after process has been executed to file its answer.

Attachment and Arrest Distinguished

Rule B attachment differs from Rule C arrest in several respects. First, Rule C arrest may be used even though defendant can be found within the district.

Secondly, to invoke Rule C the property arrested must be related to the claim. The *in rem* action which is implemented by an arrest must be based on a maritime lien or be authorized by statute. By contrast Rule B attachment applies to *any* property of the defendant that is present within the district even though it is totally unrelated to the events giving rise to the claim. Unlike the rule of some countries a "sister ship" may not be arrested in the United States, *i.e.,* may not be the defendant in an *in rem* proceeding. Nevertheless, the "sister ship" doctrine would be applicable in a Rule B attachment as would any property of the defendant. Furthermore, an attachment need only be based on a maritime claim regardless of whether or not the claim gave rise to a maritime lien.

Third, in a Rule C *in rem* proceeding plaintiff's claim is predicated on the liability of the property itself. In rule B attachment, liability is always predicated on the personal liability of the defendant. If under the applicable substantive rules, a defendant is not personally liable, its property may not be attached. In an *in rem* proceeding, judgment is entered against the property which may be sold to satisfy the judgment against it. In such proceedings the purchaser takes free and clear of all maritime liens. In attachment proceedings judgment is entered against the owner of the property. The property may be sold to satisfy the judgment against the owner, but this does not necessarily affect the rights of other persons such as those who have maritime liens or a preferred ship mortgage on the property.

Rule B, however, specifically authorizes the plaintiff to use state provisions for attachment and garnishment in addition to or in the alternative to maritime attachment under the Rule, but the provisions of the Supplemental Rules are not applicable to such state actions. An action under a state attachment or garnishment procedure may also be brought in state court. Note, however, an admiralty action *in rem* may only be brought in federal court. A state court may not order the arrest of property in a case in which admiralty and maritime law is applicable.

---

3. Additional Provisions Applicable to Arrest and Attachment

Supplemental Rule E contains additional procedural provisions that are applicable to both maritime arrest and attachment proceedings.[9]

---

[9] Unless stated otherwise or unless apparent from the context, the procedures referred to herein are prescribed in Supplemental Rule E of the Federal Rules of Civil Procedure.

The Complaint

A complaint filed by a plaintiff under Rules B and C must state the circumstances under which the claim arose with such particularity that the defendant or claimant, without requesting additional information, will be able to begin investigating the facts and prepare a responsive pleading. The Federal Rules of Civil Procedure generally are not very demanding in regard to the facts pleaded as the basis for a complaint because they authorize parties to engage in extensive pre-trial discovery practices. Thus, the requirement of Supplemental Rule E that the facts be stated with sufficient particularity for the defendant to begin its investigation of the incident on which the arrest or attachment is based is a more demanding standard. It should be noted that arrest warrants and writs of attachment are issued *ex parte* after the court has reviewed only the documents presented by the plaintiff. These documents must adequately inform the court that it should order process to be issued.

Security for Costs

The Rule also authorizes the court to require any party to post security for costs and expenses that may be awarded against him.

Property Not Within The District

Even where the property that is to be seized is not within the geographic bounds of the federal district court, the plaintiff may still apply for the issuance of process for its seizure. Plaintiff may then request that execution of process be delayed until the property is brought within the courts territorial jurisdiction or until some arrangement by way of stipulation may be agreed upon by the parties. Property may not be seized under Supplemental Rules B, C, and E unless it is within the district because process authorizing its seizure may only be served within the district.

Seizure and Retention—General Rule

Until recently it was thought that jurisdiction *in rem* or *quasi-in-rem* which was obtained by virtue of a seizure of property could be maintained only as long as the court had custody of the property unless the property had been released upon giving proper security, the parties stipulated the jurisdiction of the court or defendant waived any objection to the exercise of jurisdiction by the court. As stated previously, if process issues but is not executed the court will not have jurisdiction. Once the property has been seized, however, the court will not lose jurisdiction if the property is subsequently released even where there is no proper security, stipulation or waiver. Where a court no longer retains the property or security it does have some discretion to dismiss a case where a judgment entered by the court could not be enforced.

Necessity for Seizure & Retention—Exceptions

Under certain circumstances an action may proceed *in rem* or *quasi-in-rem* without an actual physical seizure or retention of the property in question. Supplemental Rule E states that where process of arrest or attachment and garnishment has issued "such process shall be stayed, or the property released, on the giving of security, to be approved by the court or clerk, or by stipulation of the parties, conditional to answer the judgment of the court...."

Under this provision, if property is seized, it may be released upon posting of a sufficient bond. In regard to the property that has been arrested, plaintiff's maritime lien is transferred from that property to the bond that has been given by way of security. Plaintiff no longer has a maritime lien on the property. Even where the property has not been seized the parties (plaintiff and defendant) may enter into a stipulation that:

1. the property will not be seized;
2. the matter may proceed *in rem* or *quasi-in-rem* as the case may be;
3. defendant undertakes to honor any judgment;
4. defendant consents to the court's continuing with the action;

In reality this means that the parties may confer *in rem* or *quasi-in-rem* jurisdiction upon the court by express agreement. *In rem* or *quasi-in-rem* jurisdiction may be conferred by waiver as well. Even where no property has been seized, a defendant who makes a general appearance and responds to the substance of plaintiff's complaint without clearly reserving an objection to the courts' jurisdiction will be considered to have waived the jurisdictional defect. At the extreme point, this means that an action may proceed *in rem* notwithstanding the fact that the property was never seized within the court's jurisdiction or was never within the court's jurisdiction where the parties so agree such as by stipulation or where defendant waives the right to object to the court's jurisdiction such as by failure to promptly and properly make the objection.

Service of Process

Supplemental Rule E (4) specifies the method of serving process on both tangible and intangible property.

Expenses of Seizing and Keeping Property

The expenses of seizing and keeping property are provided for by federal statute.[10]

Post Arrest/Post Attachment Hearing

Supplemental Rule E (4) (f) confers upon a person whose property has been arrested or attached and garnished the right to a prompt judicial hearing at which hearing the plaintiff has the burden of proving that the arrest or attachment was authorized and lawful.

Release of Property—Security

The nature and amount of security to release property that has been seized or to stay execution of process prior to seizure may be fixed by agreement of the parties. Where the parties fail to agree the court will fix the security at an amount sufficient to cover "the plaintiff's claim fairly stated with accrued interest and costs."[11] This amount of security may not exceed twice the amount of the plaintiff's claim or the value of the property as determined by appraisal. The bond or stipulation offered as security must provide for the payment of the principal sum and interest of 6% per year.

The owner of a vessel may file a general bond or stipulation, with sufficient surety, which undertakes to satisfy any judgment of that court in all actions which may be brought in that court subsequently in which the vessel is attached or arrested. Where such a bond is filed, execution of process shall be stayed as long as the amount secured by the bond or stipulation is at least double the aggregate amount claimed by all plaintiff's in actions begun and pending in which arrest or attachment process against the vessel has been issued.

Property attached and garnished or arrested shall be released by the marshal upon acceptance and approval of a stipulation, bond or other security, signed by the party in whose behalf the property is detained or its attorney which expressly authorizes its release. However, all costs and charges of the court and its officers, including the marshal, must first have been paid. The marshal may not release the property in any other circumstance except upon order of the court. However, the clerk of the court, upon the giving of approved security as provided by law and the Supplemental Rules may enter an order as of course releasing the property. Likewise where an action is dismissed or discontinued the clerk may enter an order as of course releasing the property. Notwithstanding that Federal Rule of Civil Procedure 62 provides for an automatic stay in situations where a court has dismissed an action, it has been held that this does not override the provision of Supplemental Rule E which authorizes the clerk to release property "as of course" when an action has been dismissed. In case of a dismissal the plaintiff should specifically request the court to order a stay of the release of the detained property.

Increase or Decrease of Security; Counter-Security

Supplemental Rule E provides for certain practical contingencies. Thus, the court may order either a reduction of or an increase in security where it is appropriate to do so. Furthermore, where a counterclaim, including a claim

---

[10] 28 U.S.C § 1921 (1987 P.P.).
[11] FEDERAL RULES OF CIVIL PROCEDURE, Supplemental Rule E5(a).

for wrongful seizure, arising out of the same transaction or occurrence is asserted by the defendant who has provided security on the original claim, the court may order the plaintiff to give security on the counterclaim.

Restricted Appearance

Sometimes a party whose property has been attached and garnished or arrested faces a dilemma because it may want to defend against that claim without submitting generally to the jurisdiction of the court in respect to other claims for which arrest and attachment and garnishment are not available. Supplemental Rule E specifically authorizes such a restricted appearance, but the restrictive nature of the appearance must be expressly stated.

Sale of Property

All sales of property shall be made by the marshal and the proceeds paid into the registry of the court, where they will be dispersed according to law.

---

4. Actions in State Courts

Under Title 28 of the United States Code § 1333 a plaintiff who has a maritime claim is authorized by the "saving to suitors" provision to seek a state remedy in a state court where the law of a state makes such remedy available. Thus, an ordinary breach of maritime contract case or maritime tort case may be brought in state court. In such cases the procedures described in Supplemental Rules, B, C and E are not applicable. Instead state procedures for the enforcement of claims will be followed. Generally, state law, unlike federal law, makes no special provision for the enforcement of maritime claims. The usual state procedures applicable to *in personam* civil proceedings would be followed and remedies in such proceedings would be granted.

The United States Supreme Court has determined that except in extraordinary situations where important state interests are implicated such as forfeiture proceedings, a plaintiff who seeks to enforce a maritime claim in an *in rem* proceeding may do so only in a federal court. A state court may not entertain a maritime claim in an *in rem* proceeding. However, a plaintiff may use the full range of *in personam* procedures including the attachment and garnishment procedures in an action *quasi-in-rem* to the extent they are available under the law of the particular state in which suit is brought.

---

5. Further reading

For a more detailed overview of admiralty remedies, *see* S. Friedell and N.J. Healy, *An Introduction to In Rem Jurisdiction and Procedure in the United States*, 20 J. Mar. L. & Com. 55 (1989).

B. Arrest—Supplemental Rule C—Federal Rules of Civil Procedure

Rule C. In Rem Actions: Special Provisions

(1) When Available. An action *in rem* may be brought:
(a) To enforce any maritime lien;
(b) Whenever a statute of the United States provides for a maritime action *in rem* or a proceeding analogous thereto. Except as otherwise provided by law a party who may proceed *in rem* may also, or in the alternative, proceed *in personam* against any person who may be liable.
Statutory provisions exempting vessels or other property owned or possessed by or operated by or for the United States from arrest or seizure are not affected by this rule. When a statute so provides, an action against the United States or an instrumentality thereof may proceed on *in rem* principles.

(2) Complaint. In an action *in rem* the complaint must:

(a) be verified;

(b) describe with reasonable particularity the property that is the subject of the action; and

(c) state that the property is within the district or will be within the district while the action is pending.

(3) Judicial Authorization and Process.

(a) Arrest Warrant.

(i) The court must review the complaint and any supporting papers. If the conditions for an *in rem* action appear to exist, the court must issue an order directing the clerk to issue a warrant for the arrest of the vessel or other property that is the subject of the action.

(ii) If the plaintiff or the plaintiff's attorney certifies that exigent circumstances make court review impracticable, the clerk must promptly issue a summons and a warrant for the arrest of the vessel or other property that is the subject of the action. The plaintiff has the burden in any post-arrest hearing under Rule E(4)(f) to show that exigent circumstances existed.

(b) Service.

(i) If the property that is the subject of the action is a vessel or tangible property on board a vessel, the warrant and any supplemental process must be delivered to the marshal for service.

(ii) If the property that is the subject of the action is other property, tangible or intangible, the warrant and any supplemental process must be delivered to a person or organization authorized to enforce it, who may be: (A) a marshal; (B) someone under contract with the United States; (C) someone specially appointed by the court for that purpose; or, (D) in an action brought by the United States, any officer or employee of the United States.

(c) Deposit in Court. If the property that is the subject of the action consists in whole or in part of freight, the proceeds of property sold, or other intangible property, the clerk must issue--in addition to the warrant--a summons directing any person controlling the property to show cause why it should not be deposited in court to abide the judgment.

(d) Supplemental Process. The clerk may upon application issue supplemental process to enforce the court's order without further court order.

(4) Notice. No notice other than execution of process is required when the property that is the subject of the action has been released under Rule E(5). If the property is not released within 14 days after execution, the plaintiff must promptly--or within the time that the court allows--give public notice of the action and arrest in a newspaper designated by court order and having general circulation in the district, but publication may be terminated if the property is released before publication is completed. The notice must specify the time under Rule C(6) to file a statement of interest in or right against the seized property and to answer. This rule does not affect the notice requirements in an action to foreclose a preferred ship mortgage under 46 U.S.C. §§ 31301 et seq., as amended.

(5) Ancillary Process. In any action *in rem* in which process has been served as provided by this rule, if any part of the property that is the subject of the action has not been brought within the control of the court because it has been removed or sold, or because it is intangible property in the hands of a person who has not been served with process, the court may, on motion, order any person having possession or control of such property or its proceeds to show cause why it should not be delivered into the custody of the marshal or other person or organization having a warrant for the arrest of the property, or paid into court to abide the judgment; and, after hearing, the court may enter such judgment as law and justice may require.

(6) Responsive Pleading; Interrogatories.

(a) Statement of Interest; Answer. In an action *in rem*:

(i) a person who asserts a right of possession or any ownership interest in the property that is the subject of the action must file a verified statement of right or interest:

(A) within 14 days after the execution of process, or

(B) within the time that the court allows;

(ii) the statement of right or interest must describe the interest in the property that supports the person's demand for its restitution or right to defend the action;

(iii) an agent, bailee, or attorney must state the authority to file a statement of right or interest on behalf of another; and

(iv) a person who asserts a right of possession or any ownership interest must serve an answer within 21 days after filing the statement of interest or right.

(b) Interrogatories. Interrogatories may be served with the complaint in an *in rem* action without leave of court. Answers to the interrogatories must be served with the answer to the complaint.

C. Supplemental Rule E—Federal Rules of Civil Procedure

Rule E. Actions *In rem* and *Quasi In rem*: General Provisions

(1) Applicability. Except as otherwise provided, this rule applies to actions *in personam* with process of maritime attachment and garnishment, actions *in rem*, and petitory, possessory, and partition actions, supplementing Rules B, C, and D.

(2) Complaint; Security.

(a) *Complaint.* In actions to which this rule is applicable the complaint shall state the circumstances from which the claim arises with such particularity that the defendant or claimant will be able, without moving for a more definite statement, to commence an investigation of the facts and to frame a responsive pleading.

(b) *Security for Costs.* Subject to the provisions of Rule 54(d) and of relevant statutes, the court may, on the filing of the complaint or on the appearance of any defendant, claimant, or any other party, or at any later time, require the plaintiff, defendant, claimant, or other party to give security, or additional security, in such sum as the court shall direct to pay all costs and expenses that shall be awarded against the party by any interlocutory order or by the final judgment, or on appeal by any appellate court.

(3) Process.

(a) *Territorial Limits of Effective Service.* Process *in rem* and of maritime attachment and garnishment shall be served only within the district.

(b) *Issuance and Delivery.* Issuance and delivery of process *in rem*, or of maritime attachment and garnishment, shall be held in abeyance if the plaintiff so requests.

(4) Execution of Process; Marshal's Return; Custody of Property; Procedures for Release.

(a) *In General.* Upon issuance and delivery of the process, or, in the case of summons with process of attachment and garnishment, when it appears that the defendant cannot be found within the district, the marshal shall forthwith execute the process in accordance with this subdivision (4), making due and prompt return.

(b) *Tangible Property.* If tangible property is to be attached or arrested, the marshal shall take it into the marshals possession for safe custody. If the character or situation of the property is such that the taking of actual possession is impracticable, the marshal shall execute the process by affixing a copy thereof to the property in a conspicuous place and by leaving a copy of the complaint and process with the person having possession or the persons agent. In furtherance of the marshals custody of any vessel the marshal is authorized to make a written request to the collector of customs not to grant clearance to such vessel until notified by the marshal or a deputy marshal or by the clerk that the vessel has been released in accordance with these rules.

(c) *Intangible Property.* If intangible property is to be attached or arrested the marshal shall execute the process by leaving with the garnishee or other obligor a copy of the complaint and process requiring the garnishee or other obligor to answer as provided in Rules B(3)(a) and C(6); or the marshal may accept for payment into the registry of the court the amount owed to the extent of the amount claimed by the plaintiff with interest and costs, in which event the garnishee or other obligor shall not be required to answer unless alias process shall be served.

(d) *Directions with Respect to Property in Custody.* The marshal may at any time apply to the court for directions with respect to property that has been attached or arrested, and shall give notice of such application to any or all of the parties as the court may direct.

(e) *Expenses of Seizing and Keeping Property; Deposit.* These rules do not alter the provisions of Title 28, U.S.C., § 1921, as amended, relative to the expenses of seizing and keeping property attached or arrested and to the requirement of deposits to cover such expenses.

(f) *Procedure for Release from Arrest or Attachment.* Whenever property is arrested or attached, any person claiming an interest in it shall be entitled to a prompt hearing at which the plaintiff shall be required to show why the arrest or attachment should not be vacated or other relief granted consistent with these rules. This subdivision shall have no application to suits for seamen's wages when process is issued upon a certification of sufficient cause filed pursuant to Title 46, U.S.C. §§ 603 and 604 or to actions by the United States for forfeitures for violation of any statute of the United States.

(5) Release of Property.

(a) *Special Bond.* Except in cases of seizures for forfeiture under any law of the United States, whenever process of maritime attachment and garnishment or process *in rem* is issued the execution of such process shall be stayed, or the property released, on the giving of security, to be approved by the court or clerk, or by stipulation of the parties, conditioned to answer the judgment of the court or of any appellate court. The parties may stipulate the amount and nature of such security. In the event of the inability or refusal of the parties so to stipulate the court shall fix the principal sum of the bond or stipulation at an amount sufficient to cover the amount of the plaintiff's claim fairly stated with accrued interest and costs; but the principal sum shall in no event exceed (i) twice the amount of the plaintiff's claim or (ii) the value of the property on due appraisement, whichever is smaller. The bond or stipulation shall be conditioned for the payment of the principal sum and interest thereon at 6 per cent per annum.

(b) *General Bond.* The owner of any vessel may file a general bond or stipulation, with sufficient surety, to be approved by the court, conditioned to answer the judgment of such court in all or any actions that may be brought thereafter in such court in which the vessel is attached or arrested. Thereupon the execution of all such process against such vessel shall be stayed so long as the amount secured by such bond or stipulation is at least double the aggregate amount claimed by plaintiff's in all actions begun and pending in which such vessel has been attached or arrested. Judgments and remedies may be had on such bond or stipulation as if a special bond or stipulation had been filed in each of such actions. The district court may make necessary orders to carry this rule into effect, particularly as to the giving of proper notice of any action against or attachment of a vessel for which a general bond has been filed. Such bond or stipulation shall be indorsed by the clerk with a minute of the actions wherein process is so stayed. Future security may be required by the court at any time.

If a special bond or stipulation is given in a particular case, the liability on the general bond or stipulation shall cease as to that case.

(c) *Release by Consent or Stipulation; Order of Court or Clerk; Costs.* Any vessel, cargo, or other property in the custody of the marshal or other person or organization having the warrant may be released forthwith upon the marshals acceptance and approval of a stipulation, bond, or other security, signed by the party on whose behalf the property is detained or the party's attorney and expressly authorizing such release, if all costs and charges of the court and its officers shall have first been paid. Otherwise no property in the custody of the marshal, other person or organization having the warrant, or other officer of the court shall be released without an order of the court; but such order may be entered as of course by the clerk, upon the giving of approved security as provided by law and these rules, or upon the dismissal or discontinuance of the action; but the marshal or other person or organization having the warrant shall not deliver any property so released until the costs and charges of the officers of the court shall first have been paid.

(d) *Possessory, Petitory, and Partition Actions.* The foregoing provisions of this subdivision (5) do not apply to petitory, possessory, and partition actions. In such cases the property arrested shall be released only by order of the court, on such terms and conditions and on the giving of such security as the court may require.

(6)   Reduction or Impairment of Security.

(a) *In General.* Whenever security is taken the court may, on motion and hearing, for good cause shown, reduce the amount of any security given; and if the surety shall be or become insufficient, new or additional sureties may be required on motion and hearing.

(b) *Multiple Claims.* Should an incident or occurrence give rise to multiple claims *in rem* against a vessel in excess of its value and the vessel is attached or arrested, security shall be reduced to an amount as hereinafter set forth provided the owner, demise charterer or operator of the vessel shall enter a general appearance whereby such person shall become liable for any deficiency in excess of security filed. Upon such entry of appearance and the posting of a security equal to the value of the vessel plus pending freight, together with such sum as the court may fix to provide for the costs of the proceeding, conditioned to answer the judgment of the court or any appellate court with respect to all actions arising out of such incident or occurrence in which process for the attachment or arrest of the vessel has been or may thereafter be issued, such vessel shall be released. The filing of such security shall be deemed in the nature of an interpleader for the value of the vessel and the execution of further process against the vessel arising out of such incident or occurrence shall be stayed. Such stay shall not affect the right of a claimant to file an action *in personam* against any person with respect to such incident or occurrence in any forum in a jurisdiction in which he may be found or the right of any person to seek removal or transfer of any action under applicable rule or law.

(c) *Absent Claimants.* In an action under Rule E(6)(b), venue shall be the district the Vessel within which the Vessel is located. Where any lien claimant cannot be served within the State, or does not voluntarily appear, the court may order the absent claimant to appear and plead by a day certain. Such order, together with the stay issued under E(6)(B), shall be served on the absent claimant personally if practicable, wherever found. Where personal service is not practicable, the order and stay shall be published as the court may direct, not less than once a week for six consecutive weeks. If any absent claimant does not appear or plead within the time allowed, the court may proceed as if the absent claimant had been served with process within the State, but any adjudication shall, as regards the absent claimant without appearance, affect only his interest in the Vessel as a lien claimant in the action. Any defendant, not so personally notified may intervene at any time prior to final judgment.

(7)   Security on Counterclaim. Whenever there is asserted a counterclaim arising out of the same transaction or occurrence with respect to which the action was originally filed, and the defendant or claimant in the original action has given security to respond in damages, any plaintiff for whose benefit such security has been given shall give security in the usual amount and form to respond in damages to the claims set forth in such counterclaim, unless the court, for cause shown, shall otherwise direct; and proceedings on the original claim shall be stayed until such security is given, unless the court otherwise directs. When the United States or a corporate instrumentality thereof as defendant is relieved by law of the requirement of giving security to respond in damages it shall nevertheless be treated for the purposes of this subdivision E(7) as if it had given such security if a private person so situated would have been required to give it.

(8)   Restricted Appearance. An appearance to defend against an admiralty and maritime claim with respect to which there has issued process *in rem*, or process of attachment and garnishment whether pursuant to these Supplemental Rules or to Rule 4(e), may be expressly restricted to the defense of such claim, and in that event shall not constitute an appearance for the purposes of any other claim with respect to which such process is not available or has not been served.

(9)   Disposition of Property; Sales.

(a) *Actions for Forfeitures.* In any action *in rem* to enforce a forfeiture for violation of a statute of the United States the property shall be disposed of as provided by statute.

———————————

D. *In rem* Jurisdiction: Cases

1. *Arrest Procedures*

SALAZAR v. THE "ATLANTIC SUN"

881 F.2d 73, 1989 AMC 2394 (3d Cir. 1989)

WEIS, Circuit Judge

* * *

Before docking at the port of Salem, New Jersey, a dispute had arisen between the captain and seamen aboard The Atlantic Sun and the ship's owner over alleged unpaid wages and the crew's failure to pick up cargo at a Brazilian port. After the vessel arrived at Salem, negotiations took place, but were unsuccessful.

At the instance of the captain, the district court ordered the ship arrested and ultimately set bond at $75,000. Apparently unable to secure a bond, the owner filed a petition in bankruptcy under Chapter 11. After a hearing, the bankruptcy judge lifted the automatic stay, and the district court scheduled a marshal's sale.

On the day set for sale, the owner presented a bond for $75,000, which the district court found defective in form and inadequate in amount because of increased charges resulting from the lapse of time. After the marshal's auction, the court set the time for a confirmation hearing. Near the conclusion of that hearing, the owner asked for a delay of two weeks to post a bond in the amount of $140,000, the high bid at the auction. The court denied the request, and instead confirmed the sale. When the owner did not present a supersedeas bond on the morning of the following day, the court refused a stay of confirmation. A panel of this Court denied a twenty-four hour stay.

On appeal, the owner argues that the sale should be set aside and the vessel returned. The owner asserts that the district court's failure to conduct an adversarial post-arrest hearing resolving challenges to the plaintiffs' claims amounts to a denial of due process and a violation of the Federal Rules of Civil Procedure. The owner also argues that the district judge denied it a reasonable opportunity to post a bond at the conclusion of the confirmation hearing.

* * *

Arrest of a vessel is an *in rem* procedure in admiralty law having an ancient lineage. Utilized even before the Elizabethan era, it had become a dominating feature of admiralty practice by the nineteenth century. *See generally* F. Wiswall, The Development of Admiralty Jurisdiction and Practice Since 1800 155-208 (1970), noted in *Merchants Nat'l Bank v. The Dredge Gen. G.L. Gillespie*, 663 F.2d 1338, 1342 n.8 (5th Cir. Unit A Dec. 1981), *cert. dismissed*, 456 U.S. 966, 102 S. Ct. 2263, 72 L. Ed. 2d 865 (1982).

Seizure of a vessel by court officials at the instance of a complainant serves the dual purpose of securing jurisdiction and providing a source for the satisfaction of a maritime lien. In the English view—the so-called "procedural" theory—the arrest of a vessel is intended to force the owner to appear so as to give the court *in personam* jurisdiction. American courts, by and large, adopted a "personification" theory in which the vessel itself is a party and judgments are entered against her without the necessity of securing jurisdiction over the owner.

The Supreme Court in *Tucker v. Alexandroff*, 183 U.S. 424, 438, 22 S. Ct. 195, 201, 46 L. Ed. 264 (1902), described the personification theory in modern admiralty practice. *See also United States v. The Little Charles*, 26 F. Cas. 979, 981-82 (C.C.D. Va. 1818) (No. 15,612) (MARSHALL, C.J., sitting as Circuit Justice). Although subjected to academic criticism, *e.g.*, G. Gilmore & C. Black, The Law of Admiralty § 9-3 (2d ed. 1975), the personification theory has provided a useful jurisprudential concept in formulating procedures for the arrest process where maritime liens are in existence.

In 1844, the Supreme Court adopted the Rules of Practice in Causes of Admiralty and Maritime Jurisdiction, codifying *in rem* procedures then in practice. 44 U.S. (3 How.) iii-xiv (1844). The Court revised the rules in later years, and in 1966 admiralty practice was unified through amendments to the Federal Rules of Civil Procedure.

Rules A–F of the Supplemental Rules for Certain Admiralty and Maritime Claims ("Supplemental Admiralty Rules") addressed the unique admiralty *in rem* action.

A few years later, common law *in rem* proceedings attracted the concern of the Supreme Court. In a series of decisions beginning with *Sniadach v. Family Fin. Corp.*, 395 U.S. 337, 89 S. Ct. 1820, 23 L. Ed. 2d 349 (1969), the Court outlined procedural due process requirements in attachment and garnishment, emphasizing particularly the need for a pre- or post-seizure hearing. *See Fuentes v. Shevin*, 407 U.S. 67, 92 S. Ct. 1983, 32 L. Ed. 2d 556 (1972); *Mitchell v. W.T. Grant Co.*, 416 U.S. 600, 94 S. Ct. 1895, 40 L. Ed. 2d 406 (1974); *North Georgia Finishing, Inc. v. Di-Chem Inc.*, 419 U.S. 601, 95 S. Ct. 719, 42 L. Ed. 2d 751 (1975). In another opinion affecting traditional *in rem* procedures, the Court insisted on the presence of a defendants minimum contacts with the forum, *Shaffer v. Heitner*, 433 U.S. 186, 97 S. Ct. 2569, 53 L. Ed. 2d 683 (1977), a matter not at issue here.

None of these decisions by the Supreme Court arose in the admiralty context, and some federal courts reasoned that the unique historical and constitutional foundations of admiralty law may place maritime claims beyond the sweep of common law *in rem* cases. *See, e.g., Merchants Nat'l Bank*, 663 F.2d at 1345-46; *Amstar Corp. v. S/S Alexandros T,* 664 F.2d 904, 911-12 (4th Cir. 1981). At least two district courts, however, considered procedures under the Supplemental Admiralty Rules to be suspect. *Alyeska Pipeline Serv. Co. v. The Vessel Bay Ridge*, 509 F. Supp. 1115, 1120 (D. Alaska 1981), *appeal dismissed*, 703 F.2d 381 (9th Cir. 1983), *cert. dismissed*, 467 U.S. 1247, 104 S. Ct. 3526, 82 L. Ed. 2d 852 (1984); *Karl Senner Inc. v. M/V Acadian Valor*, 485 F. Supp. 287, 295 (E.D. La. 1980).

In *Merchants National Bank*, the Court of Appeals commented that local rules making a prompt post-seizure hearing available on request would cure any alleged constitutional defects in the arrest procedure. Where no such local rules exist, the Court declared that "every Admiralty Court has the inherent power to assure the protections contemplated." *Merchants Nat'l Bank,* 663 F.2d at 1344.

Despite the existence of local rules in many districts, the Maritime Law Association, concerned about the uncertainty over due process in attachment and arrest cases, presented to the Advisory Committee on Civil Rules proposals to amend Supplemental Admiralty Rules B, C, D, and E of the Federal Rules of Civil Procedure. These suggestions resulted in the 1985 adoption of amendments to the admiralty rules, providing for pre- and postseizure procedures. In addition to these rules, many district courts, including New Jersey, have adopted complementary local rules.

We narrow our discussion to the Rules specifically addressing arrest procedures—Supplemental Admiralty Rules C and E and New Jersey Local Admiralty Rule (e). Supplemental Admiralty Rule C(3) provides that a complaint seeking the arrest of a vessel is to be reviewed by the court before a warrant is issued. Rule E(4)(f) states, with exceptions not pertinent here, that after an arrest, "any person claiming an interest in [the ship] shall be entitled to a prompt hearing at which the plaintiff shall be required to show why the arrest ... should not be vacated or other relief granted." In the District of New Jersey, Local Admiralty Rule (e)(8) ensures that "[a]n adversary hearing following arrest ... be conducted by the Court within three (3) court days after a request for such hearing, unless otherwise ordered."

Supplemental Admiralty Rule E(5)(a) permits the owner to secure the release of its vessel by posting a bond in an amount stipulated by the parties, or if they are unable to agree, in an amount fixed by the court that is "sufficient to cover the amount of the plaintiff's claim fairly stated with accrued interest and costs." The Supplemental Rules authorize the court to direct an interlocutory sale if the vessel is subject to deterioration, the expense of keeping her is disproportionate, or "if there is unreasonable delay in securing [her] release." Fed. R. Civ. P. Supp. Adm. R. E(9)(b).

Not specifically mentioned in the rules, but frequently used, is the plaintiff's agreement to the release of a vessel on the promise of the owner or its counsel to deliver a so-called Letter of Undertaking. This document is an agreement that the owner will enter an appearance, acknowledge ownership, and, whether the vessel be lost or not, pay any final decree entered against the ship. *See Continental Grain Co. v. Barge FBL-585*, 364 U.S. 19, 29, 80 S. Ct. 1470, 4 L. Ed. 2d 1540 (1960) (WHITTAKER, J., dissenting); McCreary, *Going for the Jugular Vein: Arrests and Attachments in Admiralty,* 28 Ohio St. L.J. 19, 31 (1967).

With this general review of arrest procedures as background, we then come to the owner's assertion that the district court in this case did not conduct a post-arrest hearing.

* * *

The owner's argument on this appeal that the district court disposed of the case without a hearing or consideration of the necessary facts is a departure from its previous statements made in appeals to this Court. In its September 7, 1988 Emergency Petition for a Writ of Prohibition, the owner complained that the district judge did not explain the basis on which he set bond at $75,000. The owner speculated: "Presumably, [the district court] either rejected compelling proofs that the arrest had been improvident and the underlying claims specious, or it acted in the ... erroneous view that it ... must specially favor wards of admiralty...." Emergency Petition of Atlantic Sun, Ltd., for a Writ of Prohibition at 3. Thus, the owner itself confesses that evidence it considered at least "compelling" had been submitted to the district court.

Also in the petition, the owner acknowledged that from July 14 to August 24 the parties had attempted to agree on a bond amount, and that "[t]he district court was kept advised of the total lack of progress in these negotiations." *Id.* at 14 n.14. It is remarkable, too, that in light of the owner's present emphasis on the lack of a post-arrest hearing, not one word referring to such an alleged deprivation was included in the Petition for a Writ of Prohibition, although all other bases were covered.

The district court record contains no entry showing that the owner requested a prompt post-arrest hearing—other than the August 5 proceeding—in which to submit other matters to the court. Supplemental Admiralty Rule E(4)(f) and Local Admiralty Rule(e)(8) state that the person claiming an interest is entitled to a hearing, but do not relieve the individual from asking for one. No such request appears in the record here.

To summarize, the owner had notice of the suit against the vessel on July 1, 1988, and filed a detailed defense on July 28, before counsel appeared in a court proceeding on August 5. Thereafter, counsel for both parties submitted memoranda before the district court fixed the bond amount on August 24.

It is pertinent that the owner has failed to present any evidence that the August 5, 1988 proceeding did not constitute a post-arrest hearing. What transpired that day could have been documented by the owner, which as appellant has the responsibility for presenting the full record on appeal. *See* Fed. R. App. P. 10(b)(1) ("the appellant shall order from the reporter a transcript of such parts of the proceedings not already on file as the appellant deems necessary").

Where no transcript of a hearing is prepared, Fed. R. App. P. 10(c) allows the appellant to "prepare a statement of the ... proceeding[ ] from the best available means, including the appellant's recollection." The owner has not done so here. Moreover, we deem it significant that the owner's original counsel who were before the court on August 5, 1988 have not filed an affidavit or any other document asserting that the proceedings were not considered a post-arrest hearing or a satisfactory equivalent. *Cf. Bilmar Drilling, Inc. v. IFG Leasing Co.,* 795 F.2d 1194, 1200 (5th Cir. 1986) (mere recital by counsel of what happened during pre-trial conference is not enough).

The Supplemental Admiralty Rules do not specify what form the post-arrest hearing must follow. Consequently, the type of proceeding is left to the discretion of the district court. Whether a full adversary hearing with testimony and cross-examination of witnesses in open court is necessary depends on the nature of the issues in controversy.

The post-arrest hearing is not intended to resolve definitively the dispute between the parties, but only to make a preliminary determination whether there were reasonable grounds for issuing the arrest warrant, and if so, to fix an appropriate bond. Generally speaking, an exhaustive adversarial hearing is not necessary for resolution of those issues. Thus, in many instances we would expect that an informal proceeding, perhaps in the nature of a conference before the district court, supplemented by affidavits and legal memoranda as directed by the court might be sufficient.

It should be obvious at this point that a record should be made of whatever post-arrest hearing the district court may deem necessary under the circumstances. Where there is no record of a hearing or a summary of the necessary facts or evidence that the parties stipulated to certain facts, the appellate court is severely hampered in its review.

We are persuaded that the owner has not demonstrated that it was deprived of a post-arrest hearing. First, the owner failed to produce record evidence that the August 5 proceeding was not in fact an appropriate hearing. Second, although admitting that it had presented compelling proofs to the district court, the owner has not brought to our attention what other evidence it would have presented there, and thus has not demonstrated that injury has occurred. Finally, the owner did not comply with the Supplemental and Local Admiralty Rules by requesting another hearing, if in its view, the August 5 proceeding did not meet the requirement of the post-arrest hearing to which it was entitled. We also note that the district court reviewed the request for arrest before directing the clerk to issue a warrant. *See Mitchell,* 416 U.S. at 616-17.

Consequently, we reject the owner's claim of denial of due process.

* * *

The owner's second argument on appeal is that "[t]he owner of property seized *in rem* must be given a reasonable opportunity to obtain and post a release bond." Appellants Brief at 28. As stated, the point might well be sustained. As the facts demonstrate, however, what is urged here is that after an auction has been held, an owner has the absolute right to possession of its vessel upon posting a bond equal to the amount of the highest bid. The owner cites no controlling authority for that proposition, but instead relies on two district court decisions that are not on point—*Gerard Constr. Co. v. Motor Vessel Virginia,* 480 F. Supp. 488 (W.D. Pa. 1979), and *Fair Ocean Co. v. Cargo of the Permina Samudra XII,* 423 F. Supp. 1037 (D. Guam 1976).

In effect, the owner is asking this Court to import into admiralty *in rem* proceedings a maritime version of the right of redemption familiar in the area of residential mortgage law. In the abstract, the idea is not without appeal. The central purpose of the arrest procedure, after all, is to provide the plaintiff with a means for satisfying his maritime lien. But penalizing the shipowner by wresting resources beyond those needed to meet a plaintiff's claim is neither helpful to commerce nor consistent with equitable considerations that influence admiralty jurisprudence.

Determining the shipowner's right to possession of its vessel by providing security for satisfaction of the plaintiff's lien, but yet giving due consideration to the bidder's position, is a task squarely within the discretionary powers of the court sitting in admiralty. Buoying up this point, Judge Brown wrote, "The Chancellor is no longer fixed to the woolsack. He may stride the quarter-deck of maritime jurisprudence and, in the role of admiralty judge, dispense, as would his landlocked brother, that which equity and good conscience impels." *Compania Anonima Venezolana de Navegacion v. A.J. Perez Export Co.,* 303 F.2d 692, 699 (5th Cir.), *cert. denied,* 371 U.S. 942, 83 S. Ct. 321, 9 L. Ed. 2d 276 (1962).

Generally speaking, a ship at auction will bring less than its actual value and less than replacement costs. Consequently, in many instances, the shipowner may emerge from a judicial sale with losses substantially in excess of the amount needed to satisfy the maritime lien. The party profiting in that situation is not the plaintiff who receives no more than his due, but the successful bidder at the auction who receives the vessel at a bargain price.

That is not to say that the successful bidder's interests are not worthy of consideration. As the Court of Appeals remarked in *Munro Drydock, Inc. v. M/V Heron,* 585 F.2d 13, 14 (1st Cir. 1978), "The policy of inspiring confidence in sales under the supervision of the court favors confirmation of a sale made to the highest bidder at a fairly conducted public auction." Recognizing that the purpose of a judicial sale is to benefit both creditors and debtors, courts must heed the aphorism that "[a]uctions should not be empty exercises." *First Nat'l Bank v. M/V Lightning Power,* 776 F.2d 1258, 1261 (5th Cir. 1985).

Nevertheless, the bidder at a sale is merely an offeror and has no rights to possession of the ship until the court's acceptance through the confirmation process. *Puget Sound Prod. Credit Ass'n v. Oil Screw Johnny A.,* 819 F.2d 242, 246 (9th Cir. 1987) (*quoting The East Hampton,* 48 F.2d 542, 544 (2d Cir. 1931)). Giving the owner the opportunity to match the successful bid might well dampen the enthusiasm of prospective bidders, but is not likely to pose a formidable barrier to successful auctions. The history of mortgage redemption procedures would seem to provide adequate assurances on that score.

We do not overlook the fact that on two occasions, the owner failed to post a bond within the time set by court orders, and may thereby have waived its right to release of the vessel. We, however, choose not to steer that course here.

Having concluded that the owner's theory of a quasi right of redemption theory may have some merit, we assume, but only *arguendo,* its legitimacy. We next consider whether in the circumstances present here, such a right should be enforced. As noted before, the successful bidder at a judicial auction is in the position of an offeror, but becomes the owner of the vessel when the bid is accepted at confirmation. If the sale is held valid, the previous owner has no further interest in the property and the claims are transferred to the fund created. The sale price thus substitutes for the vessel as the *res.*

It follows that if the owner wishes to redeem the vessel, that action must take place, at the very latest, before confirmation of the sale. Because the owner's redemption would prevent—and is thus an obstacle to—confirmation, the intent to exercise any such right must be made known to the court in the form of an objection in advance, as is true with other challenges to the regularity of the sale.

Some elaboration of the facts is helpful at this point. After the court set bond at $75,000 in its August 24, 1988 order, plaintiff's asked, on September 1, that the amount be increased to $200,000. The district court did not act on this request. In rejecting the owner's offer to post $75,000 on November 9, 1988, the date set for the auction, the district court explained that "the passage of time and the play of events had rendered what may always have been an inadequate bond now hopelessly insufficient to cover plaintiffs' claims." Specifically, the court concluded that the plaintiffs' claim for penalty wages, although hotly contested, was "not as a matter of law foreclosed," and that administrative fees occasioned by the vessel's *in custodia legis* status had increased substantially. On November 10, 1988, the day following the auction, plaintiffs moved for an order to show cause why the bond should not be increased to $356,000.

Local Admiralty Rule (e)(12)(e) requires an interested person objecting to a sale to file a writing within three days following the sale and to deposit with the marshal an amount sufficient to pay the vessel's custodial expenses for at least one week. The owner here failed to do so, and thus the district judge held that it had no standing to contest confirmation. A disappointed bidder, however, did file an objection and the court scheduled a hearing. The judge then allowed testimony on alleged defects in the bidding procedure asserted by the disappointed bidder. After hearing the evidence, the district court rejected the objection and confirmed the sale.

During the same hearing on November 17, 1988, the court, acting on the plaintiffs' motion, decided that the bond should be raised to $140,000. This amount, the highest bid at the sale, represented the best record evidence of the value of the vessel. When the court inquired of the plaintiffs' counsel why it requested an increase of the bond after the auction, counsel explained that the purpose was to prevent the owner from making a claim for proceeds of the sale in excess of the $75,000 bond.

Toward the conclusion of the hearing, the owner asked for two weeks in which to raise the bond. The court denied this request, as well as one for a shorter period. The court instead stated that it would confirm the sale, but granted the owner until noon the following day to post a bond as a condition for a stay of confirmation pending appeal. When on the following morning the owner requested a further extension until 4:00 p.m. that day to post a bond—not as a supersedeas—but for the release of the vessel, the court refused. The court explained, "Vindication of the legitimate rights of the successful bidder on the vessel and of the legitimacy of a properly conducted judicial sale, coupled with the Court's familiarity with the long history of delays in this case, informed our denial of defendant's request."

Although in most cases one could expect the court to give an owner some time to post a bond, circumstances here were not of the usual nature. Granting the owner the right to post a release bond after confirmation would be, in effect, an abrogation of the confirmation proceeding. Because it had filed no objection, the owner had no standing at the time of the hearing to post a bond, and consequently, properly was not given time to do so.

The order raising the bond at that stage was probably unnecessary. The same result could have been more appropriately effected by the plaintiffs' requesting the court to deny any withdrawals from proceeds of the sale in the court's registry pending further examination of the actual amounts of the claims in controversy. The court had already decided that the $75,000 amount was inadequate; plaintiff's, therefore, need not have feared that the court would release to the owner any sums in excess of that amount without additional review. The situation here was quite unlike the instance where, absent fraud in appraisement or posting of a bond, a court loses the power to increase the bond on a vessel once it has been released on providing security. *See The Haytian Republic*, 154 U.S. 118, 126, 14 S. Ct. 992, 38 L. Ed. 930 (1894); *United States v. Ames*, 99 U.S. 35, 41-42, 25 L. Ed. 295 (1878).

Because we conclude that the owner had waived its right to release of the vessel upon posting of a bond, we find no error in the district court's decision to confirm the sale rather than to grant additional time to the owner.

The judgment of the district court will be affirmed.

TRANSORIENT NAVIGATORS CO., S.A. v. M/S SOUTHWIND

788 F.2d 288 (5th Cir. 1986)

THORNBERRY, Circuit Judge

This admiralty case arises from the collision of two ships near a U.S. Army Corps of Engineers dredging site in the Mississippi River-Gulf Outlet (MR-GO). Westwind Africa Line appeals the district court's allocation of fault between Westwind's ship, the SOUTHWIND, and the United States. Westwind also contend that the district court erred in awarding the United States contribution against the SOUTHWIND and in computing the interest owed by Westwind to Transorient Navigator Co., owner of the ASTROS, the second ship involved in the collision. Transorient cross-appeals, arguing that the district court erred in refusing to permit it to recover from Westwind the interest on its damages that by statute it cannot recover from the United States. We affirm in part, reverse in part, and remand.

I. Background

The M/S SOUTHWIND and the M/V ASTROS collided in the MR-GO on June 17, 1977 when the SOUTHWIND sheered across the center line. The sheer was the result of hydrodynamic forces caused by the underwater configuration of a borrow pit left by the U.S. Army Corps of Engineers. The SOUTHWIND was carrying a cargo owned by Flour Mills of Nigeria, Ltd. Both ships and the cargo suffered damage in the collision.[1] Transorient sued Westwind *in personam* and the SOUTHWIND *in rem*. Transorient later sued the United States. Westwind sued Transorient *in personam* and the ASTROS *in rem*. Westwind also sued the United States, alleging that the Corps of Engineers was negligent in digging the borrow pit and in failing to warn pilots of the pit's configuration. Flour Mills sued Transorient *in personam*, the ASTROS *in rem*, and the United States for damage to its cargo. The district court consolidated these actions. At trial the district court found that the entire fault for the collision rested with the SOUTHWIND's compulsory pilot, Mark Delesdernier. *Transorient Navigators Co. S/A v. M/S Southwind* 524 F. Supp. 373, 380-81 (E.D. La. 1981).

On appeal, this Court found that the district court had clearly erred in absolving the United States of all fault in the collision. The Court concluded that the Army Corps of Engineers' failure to publish information concerning the configuration of the borrow pit constituted a failure to use due care and further held that the Corps' breach of duty was a proximate cause of the collision. *Transorient Navigators Co., S.A. v. M/S Southwind*, 714 F.2d 1358, 1367, 1370 (5th Cir. 1983). The Court also held that the district court had clearly erred in finding that Pilot Delesdernier knew of the borrow pit's underwater contours; rather, we concluded that the pilot should have known of the pit's characteristics and that he breached his duty to inform himself of them. *Id.* at 1369. We remanded the case to the district court for allocation of liability on the basis of comparative fault under the rule of *United States v. Reliable Transfer Co.*, 421 U.S. 397, 95 S. Ct. 1708, 44 L. Ed. 2d 251 (1975).

On remand the district court allocated 80% of the fault for the collision to Pilot Delesdernier and 20% to the United States. *Transorient Navigators Co. S/A v. M/S Southwind*, 609 F. Supp. 634, 636 (E.D. La. 1985). The court awarded Transorient $516,576.98 against the SOUTHWIND and $129,144.25 against the United States. The

---

[1] For a complete account of the facts in this case, see our earlier opinion, *Transorient Navigators Co., S.A. v. M/S Southwind*, 714 F.2d 1358 (5th Cir. 1983).

court assessed interest against the SOUTHWIND in accordance with LA. CIV. CODE ANN>. art. 2924 (West Supp. 1985), compounded daily. The court assessed interest against the United States at the 4% simple rate provided by 46 U.S.C. § 743, 745 (1982). The court rejected Transorient's argument that it was entitled to recover from the SOUTHWIND the portion of interest for which the United States was not liable by virtue of § 743 and 745. 609 F. Supp. at 637.

The district court's finding of liability against the United States revived the claims of Flour Mills and Westwind. The court concluded that both Flour Mills and Westwind could recover their full damages against the United States.[2] The court held further that the United States could recover from the SOUTHWIND 80% of the damages paid by the government to Flour Mills and Westwind. *Id.* at 638-39.

Westwind appeals the district court's judgment. Transorient cross-appeals.

II. Discussion

A. Appeal by Westwind

Westwind contends that the district court erred in apportioning fault between Pilot Delesdernier and the United States. It also argues that the court erred in awarding the United States contribution against the SOUTHWIND and in assessing interest against the SOUTHWIND for the damages it owes Transorient. We consider these points in turn.

1. *Allocation of Fault.* The district court apportioned 80% of the fault for the collision to Pilot Delesdernier and 20% to the Army Corps of Engineers. We review the court's apportionment of fault under the "clearly erroneous" standard. *See Canal Barge Co. v. China Ocean Shipping Co.,* 770 F.2d 1357, 1362 (5th Cir. 1985); Fed. R. Civ. P. 52(a). We have carefully reviewed the record on this appeal, as we did on the first appeal in this case. Although we might have apportioned fault differently in the first instance, the district court's 80%-20% division is well supported by the record. Nothing in our earlier opinion is to the contrary.

2. *Contribution Against the SOUTHWIND.* The district court permitted the United States to recover from the SOUTHWIND 80% of the damages that the government was ordered to pay Flour Mills and Westwind. Westwind contends that the court erred in awarding contribution.

The district court properly held that because Delesdernier was a compulsory pilot, his negligence could be imputed to the SOUTHWIND, but not to Westwind. *See Homer Ramsdell Transportation Co. v. La Compagnie Generale Transatalantique,* 182 U.S. 406, 182 U.S. 406, 416-17, 21 S. Ct. 831, 835-36, 45 L. Ed. 1155 (1901); *The Steamship China v. Walsh,* 74 U.S. (7 Wall.) 53, 67-69, 19 L. Ed. 67 (1869); 2 S. BELLMAN, A. JENNER, B. CHASE & J. LOO, BENEDICT ON ADMIRALTY § 9 (7th ed. 1985). Thus, Westwind was without fault in the collision. If the United States is to receive contribution, it must do so against the SOUTHWIND *in rem.*

Westwind argues that the United States cannot recover contribution against the SOUTHWIND for two reasons: (1) an action against a ship *in rem* will lie only if the plaintiff has a maritime lien against the ship, and the United States has no lien against the SOUTHWIND; (2) even if the United States had a maritime lien against the SOUTHWIND, it never arrested the ship, a necessary prerequisite for an action *in rem.* The United States responds that neither a maritime lien nor seizure of the ship is necessary for contribution *in rem* when the issue of the ship's liability has been fully litigated. Because we resolve the second point against the United States, we do not address the first.

Rule C of the Supplemental Rules for Certain Admiralty and Maritime Claims prescribes the procedure for obtaining jurisdiction *in rem* in admiralty cases. Rule C(2) requires the filing of a verified complaint stating that the property which is the subject of the action "is within the district or will be during the pendency of the action." Rule C(3) provides for issuance of a warrant for the arrest of the vessel or other property that constitutes the *res* of the action. The United States did not follow the procedures specified in Rule C. It filed no cross-claim for contribution against the SOUTHWIND, and it did not procure a warrant for the vessel's arrest.

---

[2] Flour Mills is barred from recovering against the SOUTHWIND by the Carriage of Goods by Sea Act § 4(2)(a), 46 U.S.C. § 1304(2)(a) (1982), which provides that "[n]either the carrier nor the ship shall be responsible for loss or damage arising or resulting from ... [a]ct, neglect, or default of the ... pilot ... in the navigation or in the management of the ship."

The United States contends that the district court had jurisdiction over the SOUTHWIND *in rem* notwithstanding the governments failure to observe Rule C's procedures because the SOUTHWIND had already been brought before the court to respond to Transorient' s action *in rem*, and Westwind had posted a bond for its release. But this argument overlooks the distinction between a special bond and a general bond. Rule E(5)(a) permits *in rem* process to be stayed or the property released "on the giving of security, to be approved by the court or clerk, or by stipulation of the parties, conditioned to answer the judgment of the court or of any appellate court." This form of security, the special bond, permits the shipowner to restrict his appearance to the action for which the bond has been posted. *See Overstreet v. Water Vessel "Norkong," 706*F.2d 641,644 (5th Cir. 1983). By contrast, a shipowner may post a general bond, "conditioned to answer the judgment of such court in all or any actions that may be brought thereafter in such court in which the vessel is attached or arrested." Rule E(5)(b).

The bond posted by Westwind to secure the SOUTHWIND s release states:

KNOW ALL MEN BY THESE PRESENTS, that Transorient Navigators Company S/A had brought suit *in rem* against the M/S SOUTHWIND in the United States District Court for the Eastern District of Louisiana, bearing Civil Action No. 77-2107 "E" and effected seizure of the vessel....

* * *

NOW, THEREFORE, we, Westwind Africa Line, Ltd., as principal, and Insurance Company of North America, as surety, are held and firmly bound unto Transorient Navigators Company S/A in the sum of ONE MILLION TOW [*sic*] HUNDRED FIFTY-THOUSAND AND NO/100 ($1,250,000.00) DOLLARS, lawful money of the United States for the payment whereof to the said Transorient Navigators Company S/A, its successors or assigns, we jointly and severally bind ourselves, our heirs, executors and administrators, firmly by these presents.

NOW, the condition of the above obligation is such that if said principal and surety abide by all orders, interlocutory or final, of the Court and pay said Transorient Navigators company S/A, upon presentation of a certified copy of final decree, the amount awarded by the final decree rendered in the Court to which process is returnable, or in any appellate court, then the foregoing obligation is to be void, but otherwise shall remain in full force and effect.

This language makes clear that the bond posted by Westwind is a special bond, conditioned solely on payment of a judgment in favor of Transorient. The bond does not run in favor of any other party to the litigation. This bond brings the SOUTHWIND before the court for the sole purpose of answering Transorient's claim. *See Overstreet,* 706 F.2d at 644; 7A J. Moore & A. Pelaez, Moore's Federal Practice ¶ E.13[2], at 620 (2d Ed. 1983). If the United States wished to file a cross-claim for contribution against the SOUTHWIND, it should have had the vessel arrested in accordance with the procedures specified in Rule C. Because it did not, we hold that the district court lacked jurisdiction to award the United States contribution against the SOUTHWIND *in rem. See Pacific Employers Insurance Co. M/V Gloria,* 767 F.2d 229, 234 (5th Cir. 1985) (district court erred in entering judgment against vessel *in rem* where no *in rem* process was issued, the vessel was not arrested, no answer was filed on the vessel's behalf, and the vessel owner did not waive attachment); *Associated Metals & Minerals Corp. v. SS Portoria,* 484 F.2d 460, 461-62 (5th Cir. 1973) (same).[4]

---

[3] We note that the "*Reliable Transfer* contribution shortcut," *Edmonds v. Compagnie Generate Transatlantique,* 443 U.S. 256, 271 n.30, 99 S. Ct. 2753, 2762 n.30, 61 L. Ed. 2d 521 (1979), does not apply here. In *United States v. Reliable Transfer,* 421 U.S. 397, 95 S. Ct. 1708, 44 L. Ed. 2d 251 (1975), the Court abandoned the divided damages rule in maritime collision cases in favor of apportionment of liability on the basis of fault. *See id.* at 411. In *Edmonds* the Court stated:

> [T]he general rule is that a person whose negligence is a substantial factor in the plaintiff's indivisible injury is entirely liable even if other factors concurred in causing the injury. Normally, the chosen tortfeasor may seek contribution from another concurrent tortfeasor. If both are already before the court-for example, when the plaintiff himself is the concurrent tortfeasor or when the two tortfeasors are suing each other as in a collision case like *Reliable Transfer-2,* separate contribution action is unnecessary, and damages are simply allocated accordingly.

443 U.S. at 271 n.30, 99 S. Ct. at 2762 n.30. Here the SOUTHWIND was not "before the court" for any purpose other than responding to Transorient's action.

[4] As noted above, we do not address either the need for a maritime lien to obtain contribution from a vessel *in rem* or the related question whether a maritime lien for contribution arises against a vessel tortfeasor in favor of a nonvessel joint tortfeasor that was not itself injured by the vessel's tortious conduct. Nor do we address Westwind's assertion that the United States is now barred by laches from bringing a contribution action against the SOUTHWIND.

3. *Interest Against the SOUTHWIND.* The district court ordered the SOUTHWIND to pay interest to Transorient for the vessel's 80% share of damage to the ASTROS at the rate prescribed by LA. CIV. STAT. ANN. ART. 2924 (West Supp. 1985): 7% from the date of the collision through September 11, 1980; 10% from September 12, 1980 through September 11, 1981; and 12% from September 12, 1981 until the judgment is paid. The court ordered that the interest be compounded daily. *See Transorient,* 609 F. Supp. at 638. Westwind contends that the district court abused its discretion in ordering that the interest be compounded daily.

In *Todd Shipyards Corp. v. Auto Transportation, S/A,* 763 F.2d 745 (1985), this Court considered and rejected an almost identical contention. That litigation began in 1975. The district court entered judgment in 1984. The court assessed interest according to art. 2924, compounded daily. This court "perceive[d] no abuse of discretion either in this methodology or in the resulting award." *Id.* at 753. Westwind attempts to distinguish Todd on the ground that there evidence of the high interest rates prevailing during the litigation was presented to the district court, while in this case Transorient offered no such evidence. This argument is meritless. The district court may properly take judicial notice of prevailing interest rates. *See* FED. R. EVID. 201(b) (permitting judicial notice of adjudicative facts that are "generally known within the territorial jurisdiction of the trial court"). We hold that the district court did not abuse its discretion in ordering that the interest against the SOUTHWIND be compounded daily.

* * *

---

2. Intervention

OVERSTREET v. THE WATER VESSEL "NORKONG"

706 F.2d 641, 1987 AMC 818 (3th Cir. 1983)

ALVIN B. RUBIN, Circuit Judge

We are urged to expand an ancient remedy to accommodate a new right. A seaman libelled a foreign vessel for injuries allegedly sustained while he was employed aboard the vessel. The owner supplied a release bond and the vessel was released from seizure. Over a year later the seaman's estranged wife sought to intervene in the suit on her own behalf and on behalf of the children of the marriage to assert the cause of action for loss of consortium first recognized by this court in 1981, on the thesis that the surety bond covered not only the seaman's claim but theirs. The district court, 538 F. Supp. 53, denied the intervention in reliance on an 1895 Supreme Court decision, *The Oregon,* 158 U.S. 186, 15 S. Ct. 804, 39 L. Ed. 943 (1895). Finding that, in principle, *The Oregon's* wake still controls our course, we affirm.

The seaman, Norman P. Overstreet, was injured while working aboard the M/V NORKONG, as a member of its crew, on February 16, 1980. Overstreet sued the NORKONG *in rem* under general maritime law on grounds of unseaworthiness.[1] He also sued her owner, Asiatic Drilling Company (Asiatic), and his employer, Scan Drilling Company (Scan), *in personam,* under the Jones Act, 46 U.S.C. § 688 (1976), for negligence. On the day Overstreet filed his complaint, the district court issued a warrant for the arrest of the NORKONG to answer to both the *in rem* and *in personam* claims. The warrant was executed, and the vessel brought to Pascagoula, Mississippi. Asiatic provided a bond issued by Insurance Company of North America (INA) in the amount of $750,000, the condition of which was that Asiatic and INA would "pay the said plaintiff the amount awarded by the final decree rendered in" the proceeding. The vessel was thereupon released and sailed away, never, perhaps, to return. After a hearing, the district court dismissed Overstreet's complaint against Asiatic and Scan for lack of personal jurisdiction. The district court also granted the NORKONG's motion to strike from the complaint Overstreet's allegations of negligence under the Jones Act. *Plamalsv. The Pinar Del Rio,* 277 U.S. 151, 48 S. Ct. 457, 72 L. Ed. 827 (1928) (Jones Act

---

[1] *The Osceola,* 189 U.S. 158, 175, 23 S. Ct. 483, 487, 47 L. Ed. 760, 764 (1903) (vessel and her owner are liable for injuries to seaman inconsequence of unseaworthiness).

claim based on negligence is solely *in personam* and may not be asserted against vessel).The bond must now answer only to Overstreet's unseaworthiness claim against the vessel.

Mrs. Overstreet, appearing individually and for her four minor children, seeks to assert an *in rem* claim under the same bond for what she indiscriminately describes as "loss of consortium, society and services" arising from her husbands injuries. She contends that she has a right to intervene under Fed. R. Civ. P. 24(a)(2). It is a prerequisite of her intervention that she claim "an interest relating to the property or transaction which is the subject of the action," so we examine first whether she has such an interest in the sole property that is within the court's jurisdiction, the INA bond that stands in the place of the vessel.[2]

In 1981 we held that the spouse of an injured seaman has a cause of action for loss of the seaman's society separate from the seamans claim for his injuries, and that the spouses claim need not be asserted in the same proceeding as the seamans claim.[3] Because the spouses claim turns on the same facts and involves the same issues, presentation of both claims in the same action, when practicable, is desirable.[4] But the claim is not the seaman's. It is not a "latent development of [his] damages," as Mrs. Overstreet contends. It is a separate claim asserted by a separate party, for separate damages.

In *The Oregon*, after a libel had been filed against the vessel, the surety gave a stipulation for its release. The court refused to allow additional claimants to intervene, saying, "We know of no authority which permits the liability of sureties upon such a stipulation to be enlarged by the inclusion of claims other than the ones which the stipulators agree to pay."[5] It continued, explaining why it found the district court in error, "But if, after the stipulation is given, and the vessel is discharged from custody, other libels are filed, a new warrant of arrest must be issued, and the vessel again taken into custody."[6]

The rationale of *The Oregon* was in part that permitting the intervention might prejudice the original libellant if the sureties were unable to respond to the full amount of their stipulation, or to an amount sufficient to pay all the claims.[7] Mrs. Overstreet seeks to obviate the problem by conceding priority to her husband's claims. She has, therefore, persuaded us that this reason for the decision in *The Oregon* is not applicable here.

A second reason for refusing intervention in *The Oregon* was that "[t]he stipulators may be so well satisfied that the [owner of the vessel] has a defense to the original libel as to be willing to take upon themselves the contingency of a decree requiring its payment, but they may neither know, nor be able to conjecture, what other demands may be made against the property."[8] Mrs. Overstreet correctly points out that her claim stands or falls with her husband's and, if he fails, so does she. But this does not mean that INA should reasonably have anticipated, when it negotiated the bond, the interjection of her consortium claim and those of her four children into Overstreet's personal injury action, or that INA could estimate the amount that she and her children might claim. In all likelihood, INA was not apprised of Overstreets family relationships, nor able to conjecture the degree to which his accident might impair those relationships, when it agreed to post bond for a certain permium. While neither the probability of losing the case nor INA's maximum exposure would be increased by the intervention of Mrs. Overstreet and her children, the amount of the possible award, up to the bond's maximum, would be enlarged. The evidence gives us no way to determine whether this would have affected INA's willingness to supply the bond on the fee charged.

The Supplemental Rules for Certain Admiralty and Maritime Claims of the Federal Rules of Civil Procedure provide for release of an arrested vessel on the giving of either a "special bond" [Rule E(5)(a)] or a "general bond" [Rule E(5)(b)]. The special bond is given for libels that have already issued. It the parties do not agree on an amount, it is to be "an amount sufficient to cover the amount of the plaintiff's claim fairly stated with accrued interest and

---

[2] Once a vessel is released from arrest by a bond, the vessel itself can no longer be held to answer for the claims the bond is designed to meet. The bond is the claimant's sole source of recovery. *See The Oregon* (stipulation deemed substitute for vessel itself); G. Gilmore& C. Black, The Law of Admiralty §9-89(1975);Harmon,*Discharge and Waiver or Maritime Liens,*47 Tulane L. R. 786, 795 (1973) ("The effect of the filing of a bond to release a vessel from seizure is to transfer the lien from the ship to the fund represented by the bond or stipulation.").

[3] *Cruz v. Hendy Int'l Co.,* 638 F.2d 719, 725-26 (5th Cir. 1981).

[4] *Kotsiris v. Ling,* 451 S.W. 2d 411 (Ky. 1970) (joinder not required, although it is desirable and will probably occur in most cases).

[5] *The Oregon,* 158 U.S. at 206, 15 S. Ct. at 812, 39 L.Ed. at 952.

[6] *Id.* at 210, 15 S. Ct. at 814, 39 L. Ed. at 954.

[7] *Id.* at 210, 15 S. Ct. at 814, 39 L. Ed. at 954.

[8] *Id.* at 206, 15 S. Ct. at 812, 39 L. Ed. at 952.

costs." On the other hand, a general bond is given for actions that may subsequently be brought in which the vessel may be attached or arrested.[9] The bond given here was a special bond, and its effect is prescribed by the Rule. When a shipowner secures the release of a vessel seized pursuant to process *in rem*, the Supplemental Rules permit the shipowner to restrict, expressly, his appearance to the defense of that claim and that appearance does not constitute an appearance for the purpose of any other claim with respect to which process is not available or has not been served. FED. R. CIV. P. Supp. R. E(5). Whatever the reason for the rule, it is explicit and categorical.

If a special bond is not obtained to secure the release of an arrested vessel, and the vessel is sold to meet the resulting judgment, the proceeds of the sale are deposited in the registry of the court. Third persons who claim an interest in the proceeds may then intervene.[10] This, however, is not an intervention in the suit leading to sale. It simply permits all those who did not participate in that proceeding, but who have claims against the vessel that were obliterated by the sale, to assert their claims against the fund into which the vessel has been converted. The proceeds remaining after the libel has been satisfied represent the vessel.[11] The surety bond provides no such residual fund for other claimants. It is posted to assure the payment of a single claim, not to stand in place of the vessel for all claims that might be asserted against her.

Mrs. Overstreet contends that the bond should be read in accordance with the intent of the court and that, because the magistrate who fixed the amount of the bond also held that her claim could be asserted against it, we should divine that it was his intention to require the bond to protect against her claims. There are several insurmountable obstacles to this conclusion. The first is that the bond is not ambiguous. The second is that the magistrate did not dictate the terms of the bond, only its amount. And the final one is that he has never suggested that this was his original intention.

We are unable to distinguish *The Oregon* on the basis that it involved a stipulation rather than a bond.[12]

Finally, Mrs. Overstreet argues that we are not bound by *The Oregon* in determining her right of intervention because the cause of action for loss of consortium did not exist when *The Oregon* was decided. She urges us to follow the example of the Supreme Court in *Moragne v. State Marine Lines, Inc.,* 398 U.S. 375, 90 S. Ct. 1772, 26 L. Ed. 2d 339 (1970), in which that Court concluded that the principles underlying the doctrine of *stare decisis* did not counsel against overruling a prior decision. The power to overrule the Supreme Court's decision lies in that court, not in us. While there may be occasional situations when subsequent Supreme Court opinions erode the authority of an earlier Supreme Court case without explicitly overruling it so that we may follow the Courts later lead,[13] no such change has occurred with regard to the posting of bonds to secure the release of vessels. While the few cases reported since 1895 involving the issue did not involve loss of consortium, *The Oregon* has been followed. *The Willamette,* 70 F. 874 (D.C. Ill. 1892); *Norker v. The S/T Sister Katingo,* 201 F. Supp. 223 (D. Conn. 1962). Indeed the Supplemental Rules, adopted in 1966, appear to confirm, not to undermine, *The Oregon.* The genesis of additional claims by new decisions does not alter the reading of the bond.

---

[9] 7 A J. MOORE & A. PELAEZ, FEDERAL PRACTICE: ADMIRALTY ¶ E.13[1] & n.7 (1982).

[10] *Jackson v. Inland Oil and Transport Co.,* 318 F.2d 802 (5th Cir. 1963); *Crabtree v. The S.S. Julia,* 290 F.2d 478 (5th Cir. 1961). *See* Fed. R. Civ. P. Supp. R. E. (9)(c) (proceeds of sale to be paid into registry and disposed of according to law).

[11] *The Oregon,* 158 U.S. at 211, 15 S. Ct. at 814, 39 L. Ed. at 954.

[12] 7 A. J. MOORE & A. PELAEX, FEDERAL PRACTICE: ADMIRALTY ¶ E. 13 [1] & n.17 (1982) ("[T]he terms "bond" and "stipulation" are used interchangeably in the admiralty...."). The distinction that once existed is explained by Gilmore and Black, The Law of Admiralty 796-97 (2d ed. 1975) (footnote omitted):

> The release of ships from arrest has been governed both by a statutory provision (which is now 28 U.S.C.A. § 2464) and by the former Admiralty Rules. The statute provided for the posting of bonds with the United States Marshal in specified amounts. The Rules provided for release on a stipulation for value entered into by the parties with the amount of the stipulation and the security therefor to be determined by the district judge if the parties could not agree. The stipulation for value was the procedure usually followed for the excellent reason (from the shipowner's point of view) that the release value under stipulation was less than the bonds requied under § 2464.

> The authors then explain that, "The matter is currently covered by Supplemental Rule E(5) (F.R.C.P.) which, according to the Advisory Committee's Note, restates the substance of the former Admiralty Rules and also incorporates 28 U.S.C.A. § 2464 'with changes of terminology, and with a substantial change as to the amount of the bond.' " "*Id.* They characterize the consolidation a a "light-hearted approach to § 2464." *Id.* Gilmore and Black state, "Bonds under § 2464 and stipulations for value under the former Admiralty Rules seem always to have been treated as indentical in their legal effect. Presumably, bonds under subsection (a) and (b) of Rule E(5) will continue to be treated as having the same legal effect as stipulations under subsection (c)." *Id.* At 798.

[13] *Rowe v. Peyton,* 383 F.2d 709, 714 (4th Cir. 1967), *aff'd,* 391 U.S. 54, 88 S. Ct. 1549, 20 L. Ed. 2d 426 (1968).

In view of the result we have reached, we do not decide whether the claims of a spouse and child for "loss of consortium and society and services" occasioned by a seaman's injury are supported by a maritime lien[14] or whether the Overstreet children, like their mother, have a cognizable claim separate from that of their father.

For these reasons, the judgment is AFFIRMED.

---

3. *Waiver: verified statement of right or interest*

CACTUS PIPE & SUPPLY CO., INC. v. M/V MONTMARTRE

756 F.2d 1103, 1985 AMC 2150 (5th Cir. 1985)

JOHN R. BROWN, Circuit Judge

This appeal arises from claims for damage to a cargo of steel tubing shipped aboard the M/V MONTMARTRE in July, 1979. Because we find that *in rem* jurisdiction was established in one case of this consolidated action, we reverse. We also reverse and remand for a determination of whether the vessel was liable *in rem*. We affirm the trial court's finding that appellee, vessel owner, was not liable as the carrier of cargo because there was no evidence that the vessel owner authorized issuance of the bills of lading either by actual or apparent authority.

How It All Began

Appellant, Cactus Pipe & Supply Co., Inc. (Cactus), contracted with Corinth Pipeworks, S.A. (Corinth) to purchase steel tubing. Under this agreement, the trial court found that Corinth was to arrange for shipment from Corinth, Greece to Houston, Texas. The cargo was shipped aboard the M/V MONTMARTRE owned by appellee Orient Leasing Co., Ltd. (Orient).

Before the carriage of cargo in issue, Orient bareboat chartered the MONTMARTRE to Eternity Navigation Co., S.A. (Eternity), in September, 1976. Eternity, as bareboat charter owner, time chartered the vessel to Iino Kaiun Kaisha, Ltd. (Iino). Iino in turn time chartered the MONTMARTRE to Canadian Forest Navigation Co., Ltd. (Canadian) in June, 1979. In July, 1979, Canadian voyage chartered the MONTMARTRE to Seanav International Co. (Seanav). Seanav in turn voyage chartered the vessel to Corinth.

Nine bills of lading covering the cargo were issued on July 14, 1979, signed by Delpa Shipping and Transportation Co., Ltd. (Delpa) "For The Master." The vessel arrived in Houston in August, 1979, and surveyors observed damage in the hold before unloading. In addition to damage, appellant Cactus contends that portions of the cargo were never delivered.

Cactus, consignee of the cargo of steel tubing, instituted two causes of action seeking recovery of its damages. The First action (District Court No. H-80-1721) was brought in Cactus' name by its subrogated underwriter against the MONTMARTRE, Orient and Corinth. The Second action (District Court No. H-80-1769) was instituted by Cactus seeking recovery of the unisured portion of its loss (approximately $10,000) against the vessel and against Orient, the vessel owner. The MONTMARTRE was never arrested. However, a claim of owner was filed by Orient in both actions.* Subsequently the two cases were consolidated pending trial.

On July 6, 1983, the district court, after a bench trial, entered its opinion finding that the cargo was damaged and short upon delivery in Houston, Texas. It also found that Corinth, the voyage charterer and shipper, was liable as a carrier of the cargo and that Orient, the vessel owner, was not liable because it was not the COGSA carrier. The trial court found that the MONTMARTRE, although the carrying vessel, was not liable to Cactus because it was not liable for the acts or omissions of the charterer/shipper, Corinth. The district court entered judgment in favor

---

[14] Most maritime claims give rise to liens, but, *e.g.*, a seaman's statutory action for personal injury under the Jones Act, 46 U.S.C. § 688 (1976), does not. *See* G. GILMORE & C. BLACK, THE LAW OF ADMIRALTY § 9-20 & nn. 86, 95b (1975) (Jones Act claims based on shipowner's negligence do not give rise to liens, but on principle maritime torts should create liens).

* *Editors' note:* In 2000, Supplemental Admiralty Rule C(6)(b)(i) was amended to read: "A person who asserts a right of possession or any ownership interest in the property that is the subject of the action must file a verified statement of right or interest..." Since 2000, the expression "verified statement of right or interest" has replaced the earlier terminology of "claim of owner".

of Cactus and against Corinth for $28,673.51 plus interest. On August 11, 1983, the trial court issued amended conclusions of law determining that *in rem* jurisdiction over the vessel did not exist because the vessel was never arrested nor had any bond or letter of undertaking been filed in the court by the owner of the vessel. The court held that the claims of owner filed by the vessel owner, Orient, manifested only the vessel owner's interest in the vessel and did not establish *in rem* jurisdiction. The district court also determined that, although a voyage charterer such as Corinth may be liable as a carrier, the evidence was insufficient to hold Corinth liable as a carrier under the facts of this case. Accordingly, Cactus was awarded nothing.

The MONTMARTRE—*In Rem* Jurisdiction

Cactus disputes the district court's conclusion that there was no *in rem* jurisdiction established over the MONTMARTRE. Specifically, Cactus urges that the claims of owner filed by Orient constituted an appearance on the part of the vessel thereby establishing *in rem* jurisdiction.

Generally, the power of the court to exercise jurisdiction over a vessel depends upon the arrest of the vessel within the courts territorial jurisdiction. *Reed v. The YAKA*, 307 F.2d 203, 204, 1962 A.M.C. 1226, 1228 (3d Cir. 1962), *rev'd on other grounds*, 373 U.S. 410, 83 S. Ct. 1349, 10 L. Ed. 2d 448, 1963 A.M.C. 1373 (1963); *see also* Rule C, Supplemental Rules for Admiralty and Maritime Claims. A claimant, however, can waive the necessity of *in rem* seizure and consent to jurisdiction so far as its interest in the vessel is concerned. *The YAKA*, 307 F.2d at 204, 1962 A.M.C. at 1228. Thus in *Continental Grain Co. v. Federal Barge Lines, Inc.*, 268 F.2d 240, 1959 A.M.C. 2158 (5th Cir. 1959), *aff'd sub nom. Continental Grain Co. v. Barge FBL-585*, 364 U.S. 19, 80 S. Ct. 1470, 4 L. Ed. 2d 1540, 1961 A.M.C. 1 (1960), we dealt with the issue of whether an *in rem* proceeding upon application of a willing claimant could be transferred under 28 U.S.C. 1404(a) to a district in which the *res* was not located. However, we initially determined that the issuance of a letter of undertaking on behalf of the vessel and a Non-Waiver of Rights Clause in the letter perfected the *in rem* jurisdiction of the court. On the filing of the action *in rem* and *in personam* for damage to a cargo of soybeans, the barge FBL-585 was not seized. We pointed out that in accordance with the practice in major seaports, a letter of undertaking was given by the vessel owner providing that in consideration of the barge not being seized and released on bond, the vessel owner would "file claim to Barge FBL-585, ... and that, vessel lost or not lost would pay any final decree which may be rendered against said vessel in said proceedings." 268 F.2d at 243, 1959 A.M.C. at 2160. We determined that the letter of undertaking, and particularly the Non-Waiver of Rights Clause, required that "we treat it as though, upon the libel being filed, the vessel had actually been seized, a Claim filed, a stipulation to abide decree with sureties executed and filed by Claimant, and the vessel formally released." *Id.* Essentially, the underlying rationale for all of this was the necessity of avoiding "needless costs, time, and inconvenience to litigants, counsel, ships, Clerks, Marshal's, Keepers and court personnel...." *Id.* In *Associated Metals & Minerals Corp. v. S.S. PORTORIA*, 484 F.2d 460, 1973 A.M.C. 2095 (5th Cir. 1973), no *in rem* process was issued, the vessel was not arrested, and the owner did not waive attachment of the vessel. We thus determined on those grounds that the district court erred in entering judgment against the vessel *in rem*.

In other contexts, a party can waive an objection to *in personam* jurisdiction. *See* F. R. Civ. P. 12. Rule 12(h)(1) provides that the defense of lack of jurisdiction over the person is waived (i) if omitted from a motion under 12(g), or (ii) if it is neither made by motion under Rule 12 nor included in a responsive pleading or an amendment. *See Golden v. Cox Furniture Mfg. Co.*, 683 F.2d 115 (5th Cir. 1982) (objection to personal jurisdiction waived when answer and amended answer filed without raising *in personam* jurisdiction objection); *Jackson v. Hayakawa*, 682 F.2d 1344, 1347 (9th Cir. 1982) (jurisdiction attaches if a defendant makes a voluntary general appearance, as by filing an answer through an attorney); *Familia De Boom v. Arosa Mercantil, S.A.*, 629 F.2d 1134, 1140, 1981 A.M.C. 2937, 2944 (5th Cir. 1980), *cert. denied*, 451 U.S. 1008, 101 S. Ct. 2345, 68 L. Ed. 2d 861, 1981 A.M.C. 2100 (1981) (service of process and personal jurisdiction may be waived by a party); *United States v. Fishing Vessel MARY ANN*, 466 F.2d 63, 1972 A.M.C. 2652 (5th Cir. 1972), *cert. denied sub nom. Walter v. United States*, 410 U.S. 929, 93 S. Ct. 1365, 35 L. Ed. 2d 590 (1973) (action to foreclose preferred ship mortgage—two defendants not served with process but answered asserting defenses on the merits).

Generally, an appearance in an action involves some presentation or submission to the court. *Port-Wide Container Co. v. Interstate Maintenance Corp.*, 440 F.2d 1195, 1196 (3rd Cir. 1971) (no appearance found). An appearance may result from the filing of an answer without raising jurisdictional defects. An appearance may also arise by implication "from a defendant's seeking, taking, or agreeing to some step or proceeding in the cause beneficial to himself or detrimental to plaintiff other than one contesting only the jurisdiction or by reason of some act or proceedings recognizing the case as in court." 6 C.J.S. *Appearances* § 18 at 22 (1975); *see also Grammenos v. Lemos*, 457 F.2d 1067, 1070 (2d Cir. 1972) (if a party enters a case and fails to object to jurisdiction, and requests the court to do some affirmative act on its behalf in some substantive way, the party will be held to have waived further objection).

In this case we must decide whether the filing of a claim of owner in a proceeding characterized expressly in the complaint as both *in rem* and *in personam* with the traditional prayer for issuance of process *in rem* against the vessel is sufficient to obtain *in rem* jurisdiction over the vessel. We hold that it does.

Some procedural background in this case is necessary to our analysis of *in rem* jurisdiction. In the First suit (District Court No. H-80-1721), the subrogated underwriter brought suit in the name of its assured, Cactus, against the vessel owner, vessel and charterer, Corinth. Cactus' prayer requested:

> that process in due form of law according to the practice of this Honorable Court in causes of admiralty and maritime jurisdiction may issue against the M/V MONTMARTRE, *citing* all persons having any interest in said vessel to appear and answer on oath all and singular the matters aforesaid.... That the said M/V MONTMARTRE may be condemned and sold to pay the damages, with interest, costs and disbursements.

There was also a prayer for process against Orient and Corinth, and in fact, process was issued only as to Orient and Corinth. Orient answered for itself and there was no mention of an *in rem* jurisdiction challenge. Orient also filed several third party complaints and pursued discovery against all parties. On September 16, 1981, Orient filed its Claim of Owner to the MONTMARTRE and a motion for consolidation of the two pending cases.

In Second suit (District Court No. H-80-1769) the complaint was filed by Cactus against the MONTMARTRE and Orient for $10,000 on August 6, 1980 (recovery of the uninsured portion of its loss). Cactus' complaint prayed:

> that process in due form of law according to the practices of this Honorable Court in causes of admiralty and maritime jurisdiction may issue against M/V MONTMARTRE, her engines, boilers, tackle, etc., and that all persons having any right, title and interest therein be cited to appear and answer on oath all and singular the matters aforesaid, and that the said M/V MONTMARTRE may be condemned and sold to pay the damages of the aforesaid, with interest and cost.

No *in rem* process was issued by the Clerk. The only process issued was against Orient.

The Second case proceeded as a separate suit in a different district court. In November, 1980, an order of dismissal was entered by the trial judge for failure to prosecute. The judge later granted reinstatement of the case. Cactus moved for entry of a default judgment which the trial court later granted. The default judgment recites that both the vessel and vessel owner were defendants, were properly served, and they failed to appear and answer. Two months later on August 12, 1981, Orient and the MONTMARTRE filed in the Second suit a motion to vacate and set aside the default judgment. Apparently the complaint was sent to Orient in Japan and there was some confusion with the First suit already on file. It is important to point out that in this motion, an objection to *in rem* jurisdiction was raised on the ground that the vessel was not arrested. The trial judge set aside the default judgment on September 8, 1981. On September 16, 1981, Orient filed its answer—only as to itself—and expressly asserted an objection to *in rem* jurisdiction. Orient also filed interrogatories and a third party complaint each raising the jurisdiction objection. On the same day, Orient filed its claim of owner specifically preserving its objection to the jurisdiction of the court.

On September 22, 1981, both trial judges in the two pending suits entered an order consolidating the cases "for all purposes." After the consolidation, on October 6, 1981, Orient as defendant and claimant and the

MONTMARTRE as defendant moved for summary judgment on the merits and on the ground that there was no *in rem* jurisdiction. Thereafter, the trial judge entered his memorandum and order denying the motion for summary judgment. The trial court did state, however, that there was a colorable challenge to the *in rem* jurisdiction of the court. Since neither party had adequately briefed this issue, the defendant was permitted to resubmit a motion to dismiss for lack of *in rem* jurisdiction. The consolidated cases were tried before the judge, and he entered his findings in July, 1983, and amended conclusions of law in August, 1983. Initially the trial court determined that Corinth, the voyage charterer, was liable as the carrier but Orient and the MONTMARTRE were exonerated.

The trial court issued amended conclusions of law holding that there was no *in rem* jurisdiction over the vessel and the evidence was insufficient to hold Corinth responsible for the damage to the cargo.

Rule C(6), Supplemental Rules for Admiralty and Maritime Claims clearly defines the purpose of filing a claim of owner. The claimant must state his interest in the vessel by *virtue* of which the claimant demands *restitution* of the vessel and *the right to defend* it. The vessel owner's right to file an answer is predicated upon the filing of the claim of owner pursuant to Supplemental Rule C(6). "The right of answering in denial or avoidance of the libel, and all of it, in a suit *in rem* in the admiralty, depends upon the right to claim.... [T]he claimant in admiralty may defend *in rem*, because he demands the redelivery to him of the arrested vessel." *The CARTONA*, 297 F. 827, 828, 1924 A.M.C. 771, 772 (2d Cir. 1924). We thus agree with the trial court that claim of owner manifests the owner's interest in the vessel. We must disagree with the trial court's determination that an unconditional claim does not give rise to *in rem* jurisdiction. When the vessel owner lays claim to the vessel he has appeared on its behalf.

In The ROSALIE M, 12 F.2d 970, 1927 A.M.C. 999 (5th Cir. 1926) a warrant of seizure was issued in a forfeiture proceeding and the vessel was seized. Appellant filed an answer and *claimed* the vessel as agent for the owner. On appeal, the appellant contended that (i) the seizure of the vessel was unlawful because it was made beyond the territorial jurisdiction of the United States since the Volstead Act (a cargo of liquor was seized) had no effect beyond three miles from the shore and (ii) the Coast Guard had no authority outside the twelve mile limit under the Tariff Act of 1922.

We determined that, conceding that the Volstead Act was not in operation at the point where the vessel was initially seized, the vessel was nevertheless subject to seizure because she was engaged in an unlawful enterprise. We further conceded, without deciding, that the Coast Guard cutter was not authorized to operate outside the twelve mile limit. We reasoned that it did not necessarily follow that the judgment was illegal and that the objection to the authority of the Coast Guard to make the seizure was purely technical and without merit. We stated that "after a ship is brought into the custody of the marshal through proper admiralty process, any irregularity in the initial seizure is immaterial, and is *waived by* filing *a claim* or answer." 12 F.2d at 971, 1927 A.M.C. at 1002 (emphasis supplied). The Supreme Court similarly ruled in *The MERINO*, 22 U.S. (9 Wheat.) 391, 400, 6 L. Ed. 118, 120 (1824), in which the vessel owner questioned irregularities in the *in rem* process. The Court reasoned that all objections to the irregularities were waived by the appearance of the parties interested in the property seized and filing their claims to the *res. Id.*

In this case there were two claims of owner filed. In the First suit (District Court No. H-80-1721 suit brought by subrogated underwriter) the claim of owner stated: "Now appears Orient ... and makes claim to the [MONTMARTRE] ... and said claimant avers that it was ... owner ... wherefore it prays to defend accordingly." In the Second suit (District Court No. H-80-1769) the claim of owner was the same as that filed in the other case except it stated "... without waiving its defense that it is not subject to the jurisdiction of this Honorable Court."

We are persuaded that the claim of owner filed in the First suit (District Court No. H-80-1721) perfected the *in rem* jurisdiction of the district court. By the filing of this claim without any jurisdictional objection—and without any prior objection in the pleadings—the MONTMARTRE has appeared. The Claim of Owner does more than state the vessel owner's interest. The Claim specifically demands the return of the vessel—a substantive request that is detrimental to the plaintiff. The filing of the claim of owner also bears many of the earmarks of the filing of a claim of owner with a letter of undertaking in *Continental Grain*, 268 F.2d at 243, 1959 A.M.C. at 2160, and was effective under the circumstances of this case.

In the Second suit (District Court No. H-80-1769), however, the vessel owner adequately preserved its challenge to *in rem* jurisdiction. From Orients and the MONTMARTRE's initial motion to vacate the default judgment through the consolidation of the cases, the objection to *in rem* jurisdiction was adequately raised and preserved. *See Aetna Business Credit, Inc. v. Universal Decor & Interior Design, Inc.*, 635 F.2d 434 (5th Cir. 1981) (objections to adequacy of service of process preserved).

We hold therefore that the trial court incorrectly determined that there was no *in rem* jurisdiction over the vessel in the consolidated action insofar as that action relates to the allegations in the First suit (District Court No. H-80-1721). However, the action asserted by Cactus against the vessel and vessel owner in the Second suit (District Court No. H-80-1769) was correctly dismissed for lack of *in rem* jurisdiction.

* * *

Patrick E. HIGGINBOTHAM, Circuit Judge, dissenting:

The majority has concluded that the filing of a Claim of Owner alone subjects a vessel to the *in rem* jurisdiction of the court. In my view, *in rem* jurisdiction over the vessel existed only if the owner intended to waive its arrest or if a waiver of arrest was the necessary legal consequence of the filing of a Claim of Owner. The owner did not intend to concede *in rem* jurisdiction, and nothing in the applicable rules of procedure contemplates the found waiver of arrest. There is, then, no legal basis for the implication of *in rem* jurisdiction, and I dissent.

I

The record leaves no doubt but that the vessel owner did not intend to concede *in rem* jurisdiction. As pointed out by the majority, there were two suits consolidated before the same judge. Claims of Owner were filed in both suits. The claims of ownership were identical except that in the second suit, the Claim of Owner stated "... without waiving its defense that it is not subject to the jurisdiction of this honorable court." The owner has always contested the absence of *in rem* jurisdiction. Yet, the majority concludes that the omission of the "without waiving its defense" qualifying language gave the court *in rem* jurisdiction in the first case. Even if an intent to waive arrest could be inferred from this plain inadvertence, it ought not be; certainly the district court was not required to do so. An admiralty court has the "power" to "withdraw from the extremes to which the general appearance rule ha[s] been pushed and to find no waiver when there [is] no *intentional* abandonment of the jurisdictional objection." *Giannakouros v. Oriental Tanker Corp.*, 338 F.2d 649, 650 (4th Cir. 1964), *cert denied*, 380 U.S. 979, 85 S. Ct. 1343, 14 L. Ed. 2d 272 (1965) (emphasis added). *See also Untersinger v. United States*, 172 F.2d 298, 301 (2d Cir. 1949) (no waiver where objection to venue in admiralty action made in answer that also pleaded to merits).

II

If waiver of arrest here cannot rest upon a conclusion that the owner intended to concede *in rem* jurisdiction, the majority's opinion then must rest upon a reading of the rules that the filing of a Claim of Owner necessarily subjects the vessel to *in rem* jurisdiction. I find nothing to support that reading.

It is true that the Supplemental Rules of Admiralty are only *supplemental*. Actions *in rem* are governed by the general Rules of Civil Procedure, "except to the extent that they are inconsistent with [the] Supplemental Rules." FED. R. CIV. P. A, Supplemental Rules for Certain Admiralty and Maritime Claims. But it does not follow, as the majority urges, that a Claim of Owner, as a responsive pleading, is analogous to a Rule 12 motion or an answer in which jurisdictional objection must be made or be held waived. The civil rules explicitly provide for waiver. The admiralty rule has not such requirement.

Admiralty Rule C sets the procedural scheme for bringing and responding to an *in rem* claim. After outlining notice and arrest procedures, the Rule addresses the *necessary* initial response to such action. Rule C(6) provides in part:

(6) Claim and Answer; Interrogatories. The claimant of property that is the subject of an action *in rem* shall file his claim within 10 days after process has been executed, or within such additional time as may be allowed by the court,

and shall serve his answer within 20 days after the filing of the claim. *The claim* shall be verified on oath or solemn affirmation, and *shall state the interest in the property by virtue of which the claimant demands its restitution and the right to defend the action.* If the claim is made on behalf of the person entitled to possession by an agent, bailee, or attorney, it shall state that he is duly authorized to make the claim.... (emphasis added).

The claim may be filed by any person asserting either an ownership or a possessory interest in a vessel subject to *in rem* arrest or service of process. 7A J. MOORE, MOORE'S FEDERAL PRACTICE ¶ C.16 at 700.13. "The filing of a claim is a *prerequisite* to the right to file an answer and defending on the merits." *Id.* at 700.14 (emphasis added). *See also United States v. Fourteen (14) Handguns,* 524 F. Supp. 395, 397 (S.D. Tex. 1981). The Advisory Committee Notes, while not addressing this issue, state that the purpose of Rule C(6) was to provide a uniform rule "so that any claimant or defendant can readily determine when he is required to file or serve a claim or answer," and to require "claimants to come forward and identify themselves at an early stage of the proceedings—*before they could fairly be required to answer.*" (emphasis added). *See also Bank of New Orleans & Trust Co. v. Marine Credit Corp.,* 583 F.2d 1063, 1068 n.7 (8th Cir. 1978) (Rule C(6) "provides an appropriate method by which to assert ... claim"). Apparently, then, the Claim simply confers the standing necessary to answer a libel against a vessel. *See United States v. $4,255,625.39,* 528 F. Supp. 969, 971 (S.D. Fla. 1981).

Rule C(6) requires all claimants to demand "restitution and the right to defend the action." A vessel owner, then, makes no substantive demand beyond that required by the Rules when he demands return of the vessel. Moreover, in the Claim held here to constitute an appearance, Orient made claim to the MONTMARTRE as its owner and asked only "to defend accordingly." Although the majority suggests otherwise, Orient did not specifically demand the vessel's return in its initial Claim.

A Claim of Owner lacks "many of the earmarks" of the inherently consensual letter of undertaking. Admiralty courts have traditionally waived strict adherence to the jurisdictional requirement of arrest, and allowed release of a vessel from custody upon the posting of a bond or a stipulation for value. Such a bond confers jurisdiction even in the absence of arrest. G. GILMORE & C. BLACK, THE LAW OF ADMIRALTY, § 9-89, at 796-801 (2d ed. 1975). In effect, the ship's owner *consents* to the court's *in rem* jurisdiction to avoid the attendant delays and economic costs associated with attachment. *See United States v. Marunaka Maru No. 88,* 559 F. Supp. 1365, 1368-69 (D. Alaska 1983). As the majority points out, admiralty courts have also recently permitted private letters of undertaking between the owner and claimant to take the place of bond or stipulation. *See* G. GILMORE & C. BLACK, *supra,* at 800-01. In *Continental Grain Co. v. Federal Barge Lines, Inc.,* 268 F.2d 240, 243 n.3, 1959 A.M.C. 2158 (5h Cir. 1959), *aff'd sub nom. Continental Grain Co. v. Barge FBL-585,* 364 U.S. 19, 80 S. Ct. 1470, 4 L. Ed. 2d 1540 (1960), for example, the undertaking expressly stated that the parties' rights would be treated as if the vessel had, in fact, been arrested. The court thus treated the letter "as though, upon the libel being filed, the vessel had actually been seized, a Claim filed, a stipulation to abide decree with sureties executed and filed by Claimant, and the vessel formally released." *Id.* at 243. The bond, stipulation for value, and letter of undertaking, then, become jurisdictional substitutes for the vessel itself, the *res* upon which the court may act. *See Continental Grain Company,* 364 U.S. at 38, 80 S. Ct. at 1481 (WHITTAKER, J., dissenting) ("This Court has from an early day consistently held that a bond, given to prevent the arrest or procure the release of the vessel, is substituted for and stands as the vessel in the custody of the court"); *J.K. Welding Co., Inc. v. Gotham Marine Corp.,* 47 F.2d 332, 335 (S.D.N.Y. 1931) ("The stipulation for value is a complete substitute for the *res,* and the stipulation for value *alone* is sufficient to give jurisdiction to a court because its legal effect is the same as the presence of the *res* in the courts custody....") (emphasis added). *See also Alyeska Pipeline Service Co. v. Vessel Bay Ridge,* 703 F.2d 381, 384 (9th Cir. 1983), *cert. denied,* 467 U.S. 1247, 104 S. Ct. 3526, 82 L. Ed. 2d 852 (1984); *American Bank of Wage Claims v. Registry of District Court of Guam,* 431 F.2d 1215, 1218 (9th Cir. 1970). The Claim of Owner then, is an unlikely substitute for the arrested vessel, for it provides no affirmative "undertaking" from which an *in rem* judgment could be satisfied.

The majority relies upon *Reed v. YAKA,* 307 F.2d 203, 204, 1962 A.M.C. 1226, 1228 (3d Cir. 1962), *rev'd on other grounds,* 373 U.S. 410, 83 S. Ct. 1349, 10 L. Ed. 2d 448 (1963). There, the vessel was outside the courts territorial jurisdiction, was never arrested, and no bond or stipulation for value was ever filed. The owner answered on the merits, averring that "it voluntarily appeared as claimant to avoid attachment and delay of the vessel if it should subsequently be present" within the territory. *Id.* He failed to raise the lack of *in rem* jurisdiction until appeal. The court held the owner's "voluntary appearance" was equivalent to a letter of undertaking, waiving arrest and consenting to jurisdiction so far as "its interest in the ship." *Id.* at 205. Unlike *Orient* here, the owner in *Reed* made a general appearance, answered on the merits, and never raised a jurisdictional objection until after trial and on appeal. *The ROSALIE M,* 12 F.2d 970, 1927 A.M.C. 999 (5th Cir. 1926), dealt with waiver of irregularities in arrest "[a]fter a ship is brought into the custody of the marshal through proper admiralty process." *Id.* at 971 (emphasis added). *The MERINO,* 22 U.S. (9 Wheat.) 391, 401, 6 L. Ed. 118 (1824), dealt with irregularities in service of process, which the Supreme Court held had "nothing to do with the question of jurisdiction." The Court expressly stated that the property at issue was within the territorial jurisdiction of the district court. *Id.*

I find no basis to quarrel with the district court's ruling. I must dissent, respectfully.

Note: *Letter of undertaking with a non-waiver of rights clause*

The following is an example of a non-waiver of rights clause:

> It is the intent of this undertaking and guarantee that the rights of the parties shall be precisely the same as they would have been had the MV GREEN WAVE been arrested under the process issued out of the United States District court, and had been released upon the filing of a corporate surety bond in the foregoing amount, reserving on behalf of the respective vessels, their owner's, operators, and underwriters, all other objections and defenses otherwise available, including the denial of all liability for the damages claimed.

> This letter of undertaking is written entirely without prejudice as to any rights or defenses which the MV GREEN WAVE or her owner's may have under any contracts, laws or statutes in effect, none of which is to be regarded as waived.

---

4. *Waiver: Request for Relief*

GABARICK v. LAURIN MARITIME (AMERICA), INC.

54 F.Supp.3d 602 (E.D. La 2014)

IVAN L.R. LEMELLE, District Judge.

Before the Court is Laurin Maritime (America) Inc., Laurin Maritime AB, Whitefin Shipping Co. Ltd., and Anglo–Atlantic Steamship Limited's (collectively the "Tintomara Interests") "Motion for Summary Judgment Against National Liability and Fire Insurance Company."

* * *

FACTS OF THE CASE AND PROCEDURAL HISTORY

The facts underlying this consolidated matter are well-known to the Court and the Parties, and they need not be set forth with any detail here. These matters arise out of the July 23, 2008 collision between barge DM–932, which was under tow by the M/V MEL OLIVER, and the M/V TINTOMARA. ACL owned both the MEL OLIVER and barge DM–932, although both were operated by D.R.D. Towing Company, LLC ("DRD") under a demise charter at the time of the collision. The collision split the barge into pieces and released its load, over 300,000 gallons of oil, into the Mississippi River.

That event spawned a number of suits in this Court. Most pertinent here, each of DRD, ACL, and the Tintomara Interests filed limitation actions and, separately, DRD's liability insurers filed an interpleader action, in which they ultimately deposited $9,000,000.00, DRD's policy limit. Each of these actions was consolidated with the instant matter.

In November of 2008, the Tintomara Interests filed a verified claim in ACL's consolidated limitation action, seeking judgment against the MEL OLIVER, *in rem*, and against ACL *in personam* for damages incurred by TINTOMARA as a result of the collision.

After a lengthy bench trial, the Court, by written opinion, found DRD and the MEL OLIVER to be solely at fault for the incident and entered Judgment that "D.R.D. Towing Company, LLC, *in personam* and the M/V MEL OLIVER, *in rem*, are liable to and shall pay ... [the Tintomara Interests and ACL] ... their respective stipulated recoverable damages, plus interest and costs, as set forth in" the aforementioned stipulation.[26] While appeal on such judgment was pending, the Court granted both (i) the Tintomara Interests' motion for disbursement of $750,000 (the amount of their principal damages) and (ii) ACL's motion for disbursement of $7,100,000 in partial satisfaction of that party's principal damages.. In each instance, the funds were drawn from the $9,000,000 in DRD's insurer-initiated interpleader action. The Court's judgment has since been affirmed in a one-paragraph per curiam opinion.*

CONTENTIONS OF THE TINTOMARA INTERESTS

The Tintomara Interests move this Court to grant summary judgment awarding pre- and post-judgment costs and interests, for which the MEL OLIVER has been held liable *in rem*, by having that judgment enforced against the LOU furnished by ACL's underwriter in ACL's original limitation action, National Liability. The Tintomara Interests' argument is premised upon the notion that the LOU furnished by National Liability was effectively substituted in the place of the MEL OLIVER as a *res* against which an *in rem* judgment is enforceable to the same extent that such judgment would be enforceable against the vessel itself. The movants characterize an action for limitation of liability in the admiralty context as one premised on both *in personam* and *in rem* liability. Thus, as security furnished in ACL's limitation of liability action, the fact that ACL was exonerated from *in personam* liability is immaterial in light of the residual *in rem* liability of the MEL OLIVER, which was also covered by the LOU as security in that action.

CONTENTIONS OF ACL

For purposes of enforcement of the *in rem* judgment against the LOU, ACL argues that limitation of liability is a personal defense and that the LOU was furnished as security only for successful claims in ACL's limitation action. Because ACL was exonerated from liability, ACL contends there are no "successful claims" in that limitation action which can be enforced against the LOU, to the extent that it only secures ACL's potential *in personam* liability as owner of the MEL OLIVER.

* * *

BACKGROUND LAW

The Personification of the Vessel and Bareboat Chartering

Central to the present issue is the concept of the personification of the vessel, whereby a claim may be enforced against a vessel for which the vessel's owner is not liable at the time of suit. This concept is of particular relevance in the contractual context where, as here, the vessel is operated pursuant to a bareboat or demise charter. Under such an agreement, the charterer (here, DRD) takes complete control of the vessel, mans it with its own crew, and is treated by law as its legal owner. This form of charter amounts to the transfer of full possession and control of the vessel for the period covered by the contract. Importantly, the charterer:

as owner *pro hac vice* is also potentially liable for collision, personal injuries to the master, crew, and third parties, pollution damages, and for loss or damage to the chartered vessel. The owner normally has no personal liability, but the vessel may be liable *in rem*. The charterer, however, has an obligation to indemnify the vessel owner if the damage was incurred through the charterer's negligence or fault.

---

[26] The parties had stipulated their various damages. (Eds.).

This result arises by virtue of the fact that a vessel may become encumbered by a maritime lien through the actions of anyone lawfully in possession of the vessel at the time of the casualty.

* * *

The Limitation of Liability Action

A full understanding of the issues before the Court also implicates the procedural device of the limitation action. The Limitation of Shipowners' Liability Act creates a procedure whereby the shipowner may limit its liability for claims arising out of a casualty to the value of his interest in the vessel. 46 U.S.C. § 181 et seq.; Fed.R.Civ.P. Supp. Rule F. It also provides a single forum for resolving the questions of the liability of the shipowner as well as the merits of competing claims in an action arising out of a particular casualty. Of essential importance to the instant action, "[l]imitation extends both *in personam* to the shipowner as well as *in rem* " to the ship. A shipowner who anticipates that claims arising out of a casualty might exceed the value of the vessel will file the limitation action, where applicable, either as a defense to a complaint for damages or as an independent complaint in admiralty. As a condition to the filing of the limitation action, the vessel owner must either transfer his interest in the vessel and pending freight to a trustee or deposit with the court the amount or value of his interest in the vessel and pending freight, or approved security therefor. Once the shipowner has complied with the requirements for the limitation action, the Court will stay all proceedings against the owner arising out of the incident in question and set a "monition" period during which all prospective claimants must file their claims in the same concursus action under pain of default.

Security Substituted as a Res

An important aspect of the modern limitation action is the opportunity for the vessel owner to furnish security in lieu of attachment of the vessel itself. Recognizing that general economic efficiency and productivity were best served by returning a ship as promptly as possible to commerce, admiralty courts began to approve various security devices as substitutes for the vessel itself. Under these arrangements "[a]special bond or letter of undertaking effectively replaces the arrested property for purposes of the *in rem* action, allowing the owner to continue to use the property, while providing the plaintiff with security for any judgment it may obtain against the vessel." It is within the foregoing legal framework that this Court must ascertain the enforceability of the *in rem* judgment in this case.

APPLICATION

* * *

Enforceability as a Matter of Law

* * *

Before the Court is the situation where the vessel owner has been exonerated from liability, while the vessel itself has been found liable *in rem* and the demise charterer liable *in personam*. Despite ACL's contentions to the contrary, the substitution for the vessel in its limitation action for the LOU furnished by National Liability does not serve to depart from the outcome that would have occurred had there been no substitution in the first place. As examined more fully above, the LOU operates as a substitute res, in place of the vessel, against which the Court's judgment is enforceable to the same extent that it would be were the vessel actually in the custody of the Court or a designated trustee. To this end, it is clear that in the absence of any substituted fund, upon the Court's entry of judgment against the MEL OLIVER, *in rem*, the practical consequence would be the Tintomara Interests' entitlement to seizure and sale of the MEL OLIVER. This would obviously operate to the financial detriment of ACL, despite that entity's theoretical exoneration from liability. This, however unfortunate, is a symptom of reality that cannot be overcome by the legal fiction of a personified vessel distinct from its owner for purposes of liability. There is no practical distinction between the foregoing scenario and one in which the owner has substituted the vessel itself for posted security. Indeed, in such circumstances, the owner receives the benefit of freeing the vessel to return to commerce during the pendency of the action.

* * *

The Terms of the Letter of Undertaking

In its opposition, ACL further attempts to confuse the issues by arguing that the terms of the letter of undertaking fail to cover the present scenario. The cited provisions read as follows:

> For [ACL] to file an action for exoneration from or limitation of liability pursuant to the [Limitation Act] … the undersigned, [National Liability], hereby agrees to the following undertaking:
>
> > 1. To cause to be filed an action by [ACL], as owner of the M/V MEL OLIVER, seeking exoneration from or limitation of liability in the United States District Court for the Eastern District of Louisiana, New Orleans Division.
> > 2. In the event a final decree (after appeal, if any) may be entered in favor of any claimant in the action described in paragraph 1, then the undersigned party agrees to pay and satisfy up to … the sum of [\$780,000].

Based on these provisions, ACL argues that the LOU was furnished only to cover an action against ACL in its capacity "as owner of the M/V MEL OLIVER" (i.e., *in personam*). It further argues that the exoneration of ACL from *in personam* liability in its limitation action, therefore, means that there can be no judgment "rendered in favor of any claimant in the action described in paragraph 1," because the action described in paragraph 1 relates only to the *in personam* limitation action of ACL. This argument fails in two respects.

First, the language ACL cites is not supportive of its contention on this issue. To be sure, the action referred to in the first paragraph is indeed ACL's limitation action brought as owner of the M/V MEL OLIVER. However, a limitation action necessarily extends both to the *in personam* liability of the owner as well as the *in rem* liability of the ship. The mere fact that the LOU refers to ACL "as the owner of the M/V MEL OLIVER" is insufficient to constrain the action referred to in paragraph 1 to the point of excluding an *in rem* judgment against the M/V MEL OLIVER. This conclusion is further supported by the language of ACL's original petition for limitation, which states: "… Petitioner shows that in the event *it or the* M/V MEL OLIVER should be held responsible to any party by reason of the matters set forth above, Petitioner claims the benefit of the limitation of liability provided in [the Limitation Act]." Thus, "the action" referred to in paragraph 2 is the limitation action extending both to the *in personam* liability of ACL and the *in rem* liability of the MEL OLIVER; the present claim is covered by the terms of the LOU itself.

Second, ACL has entirely overlooked paragraph 3 of the LOU which states: "This letter is to be binding whether the M/V MEL OLIVER is lost or not lost, in port or not in port, and *is given without prejudice to all rights or defenses which ACL or others at interest may have, none of which is to be regarded as waived.*" In *Continental Grain Co.*, 364 U.S. at 29, 80 S.Ct. 1470, a letter of undertaking including this species of "no-waiver of rights" clause was found to amount to a substitute res in place of the vessel. Granted, the clause at issue in that case contained express language to the effect that "the rights of the claimant-respondent [were] precisely the same as they would have been had the vessel been taken into custody." *Id.* Nonetheless, there is no question that to deprive the Tintomara Interests in this instance of the opportunity to enforce an *in rem* judgment against the LOU (when they otherwise would have been so entitled were the vessel whose freedom that letter secured in the custody of the Court) would be to "prejudice a right" of the Tintomara Interests in direct contravention of the language of paragraph 3 of that instrument.

Finally, it should be noted that the position taken by ACL on this issue is a dangerous one in light of the "long history of trust in the shipping industry concerning the wording of forms commonly used by marine insurance companies." *Michael Marks Cohen, Restoring the Luster to the P & I Letter of Undertaking, 42 J. Mar. L. & Com.*

255, 260 (2011). In a prior era, maritime insurers took a very long time to issue marine insurance policies, often waiting until well after an insured event to issue a policy, with entire lawsuits proceeding on the basis of a broker's cover note and neither the parties nor the court even sighting the actual policy until the conclusion of litigation. *See id.* In order that the expectations of the parties not be frustrated by eventual discrepancies between the cover notes and ultimately-issued policies, parties relied upon an atmosphere of trust wherein it was rare for one party to attempt to deny coverage that was previously contemplated based on formalistic arguments relating to the terms of marine policies. "This climate of trust was extended to LOUs. So it was not unusual, when an LOU was offered by a club, that often the first time the plaintiff's lawyer would see the wording would be when he was given the signed document by the club's lawyer." *Id.* The advantage provided by this trust is to prevent the parties and courts from becoming waylaid at the outset litigating which particular aspects of liability or events are to be covered by the relevant instrument before the liabilities of the various parties have been determined. It is also the basis upon which a court is willing to accept approved security in return for the expedient release of a vessel that would otherwise be subject to attachment in a limitation action. In this light:

> The LOU is an unusually creative and valuable document: it is cheap and mutually advantageous since it can be quickly provided anywhere, as well as easily adapted to even the most unusual circumstances, in connection with a threatened or actual ship arrest. But the extraordinary usefulness of the LOU to the shipping industry can be impaired by efforts to reduce the obligations the clubs assume when issuing them. The high regard originally accorded to LOUs should be carefully protected. *This can be accomplished only if the security which the clubs offer in an LOU is 'as substantial, risk free and available as either the arrested vessel tied to the dock and ready for execution, or a bail bond.'"*

In accordance with the foregoing, IT IS ORDERED that the Tintomara Interests' Motion for Summary Judgment is GRANTED and judgment be entered in favor of the same and against National Liability in the amount of $387,215.41, plus costs and and interest.* * *

* * *

5. Jurisdiction to Review In rem Judgments

FARWEST STEEL CORP. v. BARGE SEA-SPAN 241

769 F.2d 620, 1987 AMC 926 (9th Cir. 1985)

FARRIS, Circuit Judge

* * *

Farwest commenced an action *in rem* against the Barge in the district court. Farwest also brought an action *in personam* against West Coast, the Barges owner; S.A. DeSantis, principal of West Coast; Lakeview Charters, the predecessor owner of the Barge; and Nichols, the repair contractor. West Coast made a general appearance and counterclaimed against Farwest for wrongful arrest of the Barge. In preliminary rulings, the district court quashed the arrest of the Barge, and dismissed the claims against DeSantis and Lakeview.

In remaining actions against Nichols and West Coast, the district courts held that it had admiralty jurisdiction based on the existence of a maritime contract. 28 U.S.C. § 1333. The court also held that it continued to have *in rem* jurisdiction to decide Farwest's lien claim, despite the quashing of the arrest and the subsequent sale of the Barge by West Coast to a nonparty, The Carnation Company. The court then ruled that Farwest and intervenor corporations did not have a lien under either the Maritime Lien Act, 46 U.S.C. §§ 971-975, or the Washington Vessel lien law. RCW 60.36.010. It dismissed the claims against the Barge and West Coasts counterclaim for wrongful arrest. Farwest timely appeals.

Farwest also brought suit in the Superior Court of Clark County, Washington, to enforce state chattel and vessel liens against West Coast. That court, upheld by the Washington Supreme Court, *see Farwest Steel Corp. v DeSantis*, 102 Wash. 2d 487, 687 P.2d 207 (1984), *cert. denied*, 471 U.S. 1018, 105 S. Ct. 2024, 85 L. Ed. 2d 305 (1985), dismissed Farwest s claim because federal maritime law had preempted the state liens.

I. Subject Matter Jurisdiction

The district court had admiralty jurisdiction if it was adjudicating either a maritime lien, *see Alyeska Pipeline Service Co. v. Vessel Bay Ridge*, 703 F.2d 381, 384 (9th Cir. 1983), *cert. dismissed*, 467 U.S. 1247, 104 S. Ct. 3526, 82 L. Ed. 2d 852 (1984), or a contract relating to the repair of an already constructed vessel. *Owens-Illinois, Inc. v. United States District Court*, 698 F.2d 967, 970 (9th Cir. 1983); 28 U.S.C. § 1333. Thus, even if we find that Farwest did not have a maritime lien on the Barge, the underlying contractual claim will support the district court's admiralty jurisdiction. *See Aktieselskabet Fido v. Lloyd Braziliero*, 283 F.62, 73-74 (2d Cir.), *cert. denied*, 260 U.S. 737-38, 43 S. Ct. 97, 67 L. Ed. 489 (1922); *Reichert Towing Line, Inc. v. Long Island Machine & Marine Constr. Co.*, 287 F. 269 (E.D.N.Y 1922) (subcontractor providing supplies directly to vessel would "no doubt" have a maritime contract); 1 Benedict on Admiralty § 106, at 7-17, 18 (1983) (admiralty jurisdiction can arise from either a claim to enforce a maritime lien or "any claim in respect of the furnishing of repairs, supplies ... or other necessaries to a vessel."). We therefore have jurisdiction over the timely filed appeal from the district court. 28 U.S.C. § 1291.

II. The *In Rem* Jurisdiction of the District Court

Before considering the merits of Farwest's lien claim, we must determine whether the district court retained jurisdiction over the Barge even after it quashed the vessels arrest and permitted the Barge to be removed from the courts territorial waters.

Under the prevailing rule, the release or removal of the *res* from the control of the court will terminate jurisdiction, unless the *res* is released accidentally, fraudulently, or improperly. *United States v. $57,480.05 United States Currency and Other Coins*, 722 F.2d 1457, 1458 (9th Cir. 1984); *United States v. Vertol H21C Reg. No. N8540*, 545 F.2d 648, 650 (9th Cir. 1976). Because the Barge began plying the waters between Washington and Hawaii shortly after it was sold to The Carnation Company on April 23, 1982, and there is no allegation that it was released improperly, under this rule the district court would have been deprived of jurisdiction midway through its proceedings. The courts ensuing judgment that Farwest was not entitled to a lien would therefore be without jurisdictional base, and we would only have appellate jurisdiction to review the dismissal of Farwest s *in personam* claim. *See Alyeska Pipeline*, 703 F.2d at 384; *American Bank of Wage Claims v. Registry of District Court of Guam*, 431 F.2d 1215, 1218 & n.3 (9th Cir. 1970).

The rule that the vessel be present in order to preserve *in rem* jurisdiction is founded on "a long-standing admiralty fiction that a vessel may be assumed to be a person for the purpose of filing a lawsuit and enforcing a judgment." *See Continental Grain Co. v. Barge FBL-585*, 364 U.S. 19, 22-23, 4 L. Ed. 2d 1540, 80 S. Ct. 1470, 1473 (1960). This fiction, however, has been referred to as "archaic", "an animistic survival from remote times," "irrational", and "atavistic", 364 U.S. at 23, 80 S. Ct. at 1473; and in several cases where vessels have been removed from their territorial reach, courts have "refused to myopically apply this fiction" of *in rem* jurisdiction. *Treasure Salvors v. Unidentified Wrecked and Abandoned Sailing Vessel*, 569 F.2d 330, 334 (5th Cir. 1978); *see Continental Grain*, 364 U.S. 19, 80 S. Ct. 1470, 4 L. Ed. 2d 1540 (permitting transfer of a claim on an *in rem* admiralty action to a district in which the *res* was not present); *Inland Credit Corp. v. M/T Bow Egret*, 552 F.2d 1148, 1152, *reh'g denied*, 556 F.2d 756 (5th Cir. 1977); *Reed v. Steamship Yaka*, 307 F.2d 203 (3d Cir. 1962), *rev'd on other grounds*, 373 U.S. 410, 10 L. Ed. 2d 448, 83 S. Ct. 1349 (1963).

These courts have derived jurisdiction to review an *in rem* decision from the existence of either consent or *in personam* jurisdiction over a shipowner whose other contacts with the forum satisfied "traditional notions of fair play and substantial justice," *International Shoe Co. v. Washington*, 326 U.S. 310, 316, 90 L. Ed. 95, 66 S. Ct. 154, 158 (1945). When a claimant has consented to, or is otherwise subject to the courts *in personam* jurisdiction, these court have suggested that due process is not violated by also finding *in rem* jurisdiction. *Continental Grain,* 364 U.S. at 22-23; *Reed,* 307 F.2d at 204-05; *The Willamette,* 70 E 874 (9th Cir. 1895).

In all these cases, of course, the *res,* while beyond the courts territorial jurisdiction, was owned by a party actually before this court, over whom the court already held *in personam* jurisdiction. In this case, both Farwest and West Coast would have us appropriate a *res* not only from a location beyond the court's territorial realm, but from a nonparty over whom the district court never had personal jurisdiction. We need not resolve this question since counsel at oral argument indicated that he had authority to speak for Carnation Company, the nonparty owner, and that Carnation had actual knowledge of the lien claim and had consented to *in rem* jurisdiction over the Barge. Alex L. Parks is an attorney at law. Parks approved and endorsed a pretrial order which says, in part:

> On or about April 23, 1982 West Coast Charters sold the barge CERES to The Carnation Company. There will be no claim that the sale to The Carnation Company was a sale to a purchaser without notice. The Carnation Company took the barge CERES subject to the claims of liens, if any, asserted herein and West Coast Charters has agreed to indemnify and hold the Carnation Company harmless from all claims of liens, if any. This case will be tried as if the barge had not been sold to The Carnation Company. *If the Court enters a judgment in rem against the barge Ceres in favor of the plaintiff* and plaintiff-intervenors and the judgment is not paid, *the Court may enter an order for seizure of the barge CERES and foreclosures of the liens.*

(Emphasis added). Parks endorsed the pretrial order on behalf of defendants, Barge Sea Span 241, aka Barge CERES, her tackle, gear and furnishings, *in rem;,* West Coast Charters, Inc.; and Nichols Boat & Barge Builders, Inc.

The consent to *in rem* jurisdiction troubled us because Carnation was not a party to the proceedings. When combined with the fact that during oral argument Parks acknowledged actual notice of the lien—thus removing any due process concerns about notice—we find from the record that Carnation consented to *in rem* jurisdiction. The district court retained jurisdiction over the Barge throughout its proceedings, and we have jurisdiction to review its *in rem* judgment.

* * *

REPUBLIC NATIONAL BANK OF MIAMI v. U.S.

306 U.S. 80, 113 S. Ct. 554, 121 L. Ed. 2d 474, 1993 AMC 2010 (1992)

Justice BLACKMUN announced the judgment of the Court and delivered the opinion of the Court with respect to Parts I, II, and IV, and an opinion with respect to Part III in which Justice STEVENS and Justice O'CONNOR joined.

The issue in this case is whether the Court of Appeals may continue to exercise jurisdiction in an *in rem* civil forfeiture proceeding after the res, then in the form of cash, was removed by the United States Marshal from the judicial district and deposited in the United States Treasury.

I

In February 1988, the Government instituted an action in the United States District Court for the Southern District of Florida seeking forfeiture of a specified single-family residence in Coral Gables. The complaint alleged that Indalecio Iglesias was the true owner of the property; that he had purchased it with proceeds of narcotics trafficking; and that the property was subject to forfeiture to the United States pursuant to § 511(a)(6) of the Comprehensive Drug Abuse Prevention and Control Act of 1970, as amended, 92 Stat. 3777, 21 U.S.C. § 881(a)(6). A warrant for the arrest of the property was issued, and the United States Marshal seized it.

In response to the complaint, Thule Holding Corporation, a Panama corporation, filed a claim asserting that it was the owner of the *res* in question. Petitioner Republic National Bank of Miami filed a claim asserting a lien interest of $800,000 in the property under a mortgage recorded in 1987. Thule subsequently withdrew its claim. At the request of the Government, petitioner Bank agreed to a sale of the property. With court approval, the residence was sold for $1,050,000. The sale proceeds were retained by the Marshal pending disposition of the case.

After a trial on the merits, the District Court entered judgment denying the Banks claim with prejudice and forfeiting the sale proceeds to the United States pursuant to § 881(a)(6). App. 25. The court found probable cause to believe that Iglesias had purchased the property and completed the construction of the residence thereon with drug profits. It went on to reject the Banks innocent-owner defense to forfeiture. *United States v. One Single Family Residence*, 731 F. Supp. 1563 (SD Fla. 1990). Petitioner Bank filed a timely notice of appeal, but did not post a supersedeas bond or seek to stay the execution of the judgment.

Thereafter, at the request of the Government, the United States Marshal transferred the proceeds of the sale to the Assets Forfeiture Fund of the United States Treasury. The Government then moved to dismiss the appeal for want of jurisdiction.

The Court of Appeals granted the motion. 932 F.2d 1433 (CA11 1991). Relying on its 6 to 5 en banc decision in *United States v. One Lear Jet Aircraft*, 836 F.2d 1571, cert. denied, 487 U.S. 1204, 108 S. Ct. 2844, 101 L. Ed. 2d 881 (1988), the court held that the removal of the proceeds of the sale of the residence terminated the District Courts *in rem* jurisdiction. 932 F.2d, at 1435-1436. The court also rejected petitioner Bank's argument that the District Court had personal jurisdiction because the Government had served petitioner with the complaint of forfeiture. *Id.*, at 1436-1437. Finally, the court ruled that the Government was not estopped from contesting the jurisdiction of the Court of Appeals because of its agreement that the United States Marshal would retain the sale proceeds pending order of the District Court. *Id.*, at 1437.

In view of inconsistency and apparent uncertainty among the Courts of Appeals, we granted certiorari. — U.S. —, 112 S. Ct. 1159, 117 L. Ed. 2d 406 (1992).

II

A civil forfeiture proceeding under § 881 is an action *in rem*, "which shall conform as near as may be to proceedings in admiralty." 28 U.S.C. § 2461(b). In arguing that the transfer of the res from the judicial district deprived the Court of Appeals of jurisdiction, the Government relies on what it describes as a settled admiralty principle: that jurisdiction over an *in rem* forfeiture proceeding depends upon continued control of the res. We, however, find no such established rule in our cases. Certainly, it long has been understood that a valid seizure of the res is a prerequisite to the *initiation* of an *in rem* civil forfeiture proceeding. *United States v. One Assortment of 89 Firearms*, 465 U.S. 354, 363, 104 S. Ct. 1099, 1105, 79 L. Ed. 2d 361 (1984); *Taylor v. Carryl*, 61 U.S. (20 How.) 583, 599, 15 L. Ed. 1028 (1858); 1 S. Friedell, Benedict on Admiralty § 222, p. 14-39 (7th ed. 1992); H. Hawes, The Law Relating to the Subject of Jurisdiction of Courts § 92 (1886). *See also* Supplemental Rules for Certain Admiralty and Maritime Claims C(2) and C(3). The bulk of the Government's cases stands merely for this unexceptionable proposition, which comports with the fact that, in admiralty, the "seizure of the RES, and the publication of the monition or invitation to appear, is regarded as equivalent to the particular service of process in law and equity." *Taylor v. Carryl*, 61 U.S. (20 How.), at 599.

To the extent that there actually is a discernible rule on the need for continued presence of the res, we find it expressed in cases such as *The Rio Grande*, 90 U.S. (23 Wall.) 458, 23 L. Ed. 158 (1875), and *United States v. The Little Charles*, 26 F. Cas. 979 (CC Va. 1818). In the latter case, Chief Justice Marshall, sitting as Circuit Justice, explained that "continuance of possession" was not necessary to maintain jurisdiction over an *in rem* forfeiture action, citing the "general principle, that jurisdiction, once vested, is not divested, although a state of things should arrive in which original jurisdiction could not be exercised." *Id.*, at 982. The Chief Justice noted that in some cases there might be an exception to the rule, where the release of the property would render the judgment "useless" because "the thing could neither be delivered to the libellants, nor restored to the claimants." *Ibid.* He explained, however, that this exception "will not apply to any case where the judgment will have any effect whatever." *Ibid.* Similarly, in *The Rio Grande*, this Court held that improper release of a ship by a marshal did not divest the Circuit Court of jurisdiction. "We do not understand the law to be that an actual and continuous possession of the *res* is required to sustain the jurisdiction of the court. When the vessel was seized by the order of the court and brought within its control the jurisdiction was complete." 90 U.S. (23 Wall.), at 463. The Court there emphasized the impropriety of the ship's release. The Government now suggests that the case merely announced an "injustice" exception to the requirement of continuous control. But the question is one of jurisdiction, and we do not see why the means of the res' removal should make a difference.[3]

Only once, in *The Brig Ann,* 13 U.S. (9 Cranch) 289, 290, 3 L. Ed. 734 (1815), has this Court found that events subsequent to the initial seizure destroyed jurisdiction in an *in rem* forfeiture action. In that case, a brig was seized in Long Island Sound and brought into the port of New Haven, where the collector took possession of it as forfeited to the United States. Several days later, the collector gave written orders for the release of the brig and its cargo from the seizure. Before the ship could leave, however, the District Court issued an information, and the brig and cargo were taken by the Marshal into his possession. This Court held that, because the attachment was voluntarily released before the libel was filed and allowed, the District Court had no jurisdiction. Writing for the Court, Justice Story explained that judicial cognizance of a forfeiture *in rem* requires

> a good subsisting seizure *at the time when the libel or information is filed and allowed.* If a seizure be completely and explicitly abandoned, and the property restored by the voluntary act of the party who has made the seizure, all rights under it are gone. Although judicial jurisdiction once attached, it is divested by the subsequent proceedings; and it can be revived only by a new seizure. It is, in this respect, like a case of capture, which, although well made, gives no authority to the prize Court to proceed to adjudication, if it be voluntarily abandoned *before judicial proceedings are instituted. Id.,* at 291 (emphasis added).

Fairly read, *The Brig Ann* simply restates the rule that the court must have actual or constructive control of the res when an *in rem* forfeiture suit is initiated. If the seizing party abandons the attachment prior to filing an action, it, in effect, has renounced its claim. The result is "to purge away all the prior rights acquired by the seizure," *ibid.,* and, unless a new seizure is made, the case may not commence. *The Brig Ann* stands for nothing more than this.

The rule invoked by the Government thus does not exist, and we see no reason why it should. The fictions of *in rem* forfeiture were developed primarily to expand the reach of the courts and to furnish remedies for aggrieved parties, *see Continental Grain Co. v. Barge FBL-585,* 364 U.S. 19, 23, 80 S. Ct. 1470, 1473, 4 L. Ed. 2d 1540 (1960); *United States v. Brig Malek Adhel,* 43 U.S. (2 How.) 210, 233, 11 L. Ed. 239 (1844), not to provide a prevailing party with a means of defeating its adversary's claim for redress. Of course, if a "defendant ship stealthily absconds from port and leaves the plaintiff with no res from which to collect," *One Lear Jet,* 836 F.2d, at 1579 (VANCE, J., dissenting), a court might determine that a judgment would be "useless." *Cf. The Little Charles,* 26 F. Cas., at 982. So, too, if the plaintiff abandons a seizure, a court will not proceed to adjudicate the case. These exceptions, however, are closely related to the traditional, theoretical concerns of jurisdiction: enforceability of judgments, and fairness of notice to parties. *See* R. Casad, Jurisdiction in Civil Actions § 1.02, pp. 1-13 to 1-14 (2d ed. 1991); *cf. Miller v. United States,* 78 U.S. (11 Wall.) 268, 294-295, 20 L. Ed. 135 (1870) ("Confessedly the object of the writ was to bring the property under the control of the court and keep it there, as well as to give notice to the world. These objects would have been fully accomplished if its direction had been nothing more than to hold the property

---

[3] *See also The Bolina,* 3 F. Cas. 811, 813-814 (CC Mass. 1812) (STORY, J., as Circuit Justice) ("[O]nce a vessel is libelled, then she is considered as in the custody of the law, and at the disposal of the court, and monitions may be issued to persons having the actual custody, to obey the injunctions of the court.... The district court of the United States derives its jurisdiction, not from any supposed possession of its officers, but from the act and place of seizure for the forfeiture.... And when once it has acquired a regular jurisdiction, I do not perceive how any subsequent irregularity would avoid it. It may render the ultimate decree ineffectual in certain events, but the regular results of the adjudication must remain."); 1 J. Wells, A Treatise on the Jurisdiction of Courts 275 (1880) (actual or constructive seizure provides jurisdiction in admiralty forfeiture action. "And, having once acquired regular jurisdiction, no subsequent irregularity can defeat it; or accident, as, for example, an accidental fire.").

subject to the order of the court, and to give notice."). Neither interest depends absolutely upon the continuous presence of the res in the district.

Stasis is not a general prerequisite to the maintenance of jurisdiction. Jurisdiction over the person survives a change in circumstances, *Leman v. Krentler-Arnold Co.*, 284 U.S. 448, 454, 52 S. Ct. 238, 241, 76 L. Ed. 389 (1932) ("[A]fter a final decree a party cannot defeat the jurisdiction of the appellate tribunal by removing from the jurisdiction, as the proceedings on appeal are part of the cause," citing *Nations v. Johnson*, 65 U.S.C. (24 How.) 195, 16 L. Ed. 628 (1860)), as does jurisdiction over the subject-matter, *Louisville, N.A. & C.R. Co. v. Louisville Trust Co.*, 174 U.S. 552, 566, 19 S. Ct. 817, 822, 43 L. Ed. 1081 (1899) (mid-suit change in the citizenship of a party does not destroy diversity jurisdiction); *St. Paul Mercury Indemnity Co. v. Red Cab Co.*, 303 U.S. 283, 289-290, 58S. Ct. 586, 590-591, 82 L. Ed. 845 (1938) (jurisdiction survives reduction of amount in controversy). Nothing in the nature of *in rem* jurisdiction suggests a reason to treat it differently.

If the conjured rule were genuine, we would have to decide whether it had outlived its usefulness, and whether, in any event, it could ever be used by a plaintiff—the instigator of the *in rem* action—to contest the appellate court's jurisdiction. The rules illusory nature obviates the need for such inquiries, however, and a lack of justification undermines any argument for its creation. We agree with the late Judge Vances remark in *One Lear Jet*, 836 F.2d, at 1577: "although in some circumstances the law may require courts to depart from what seems to be fairness and common sense, such a departure in this case is unjustified and unsupported by the law of forfeiture and admiralty." We have no cause to override common sense and fairness here. We hold that, in an *in rem* forfeiture action, the Court of Appeals is not divested of jurisdiction by the prevailing party's transfer of the res from the District.[4]

* * *

The judgment of the Court of Appeals is reversed, and the case is remanded for further proceedings consistent with this opinion.

It is so ordered.

Note: Applicability of Republic National Bank of Miami to Admiralty Arrest and Attachment

The Ninth Circuit has applied the rule of *Republic National Bank of Miami* to both admiralty arrest and attachment cases. *Stevedoring Services of America v. Ancora Transport*, 941 F.2d 1378, 1992 A.M.C. 883 (9th Cir. 1991), *cert. granted and judgment vacated by,* 506 U.S. 1043, 113 S. Ct. 955, 122 L. Ed. 2d 112 (1993), *on remand to,* 59 F.3d 879, 1995 A.M.C. 2688 (9th Cir. 1995) (attachment); *Edlin v. M/V Truthseeker*, 69 F.3d 392, 1996 AMC 1216 (9th Cir. 1994). In *Newpark Shipbuildng & Repair, Inc.,* 2 F.3d 572, 1994 AMC 133 (5th Cir. 1993), the Fifth Circuit, recognizing that rule formulated in Republic National bank was applicable to admiralty cases, invoked the "useless judgment" exception to that rule, and dismissed the appeal.

Note: Equitable Exceptions to the Traditional Rule

Even before the *Republic National Bank of Miami* case, the rule of continuous control was not absolute. In *The Rio Grande*, 90 U.S. (23 Wall.) 458, 465, 23 L. Ed. 158 (1874), the Court stated:

> We hold the rule to be that valid seizure and actual control of the *res* by the marshal gives jurisdiction of the subject matter, and that an accidental or fraudulent or improper removal of it from his custody, or a delivery to the party upon security, does not destroy jurisdiction.

---

[4] We note that on October 28, 1992, the President signed the Housing and Community Development Act of 1992, 106 Stat. 3672. Section 1521 of that Act (part of Title XV, entitled the Annunzio-Wylie Anti-Money Laundering Act) significantly amended 28 U.S.C. § 1355 to provide, among other things:

> In any case in which a final order disposing of property in a civil forfeiture action or proceeding is appealed, removal of the property by the prevailing party shall not deprive the court of jurisdiction. Upon motion of the appealing party, the district court or the court of appeals shall issue any order necessary to preserve the right of the appealing party to the full value of the property at issue, including a stay of the judgment of the district court pending appeal or requiring the prevailing party to post an appeal bond.

106 Stat., at ___. Needless to say, we do not now interpret that statute or determine the issue of its retroactive application to the present case.

6. *Pleading Requirements: Heightened Particularity*

Supplemental Rule E(2)(a) requires the complaint to "state the circumstances from which the claim arises with such particularity that the defendant or claimant will be able, without moving for a more definite statement, to commence an investigation of the facts and to frame a responsive pleading". This standard of particularity is higher than under the general Federal Rules of Civil Procedure. In *Riverway Co. v. Spivey Marine & Harbor Service Co.*, 598 F. Supp. 909, 912-13 (S.D. Ill. 1984), the court said:

> The construction placed upon Rule 9(b) of the Federal Rules of Civil Procedure requiring the circumstances of an action for fraud be stated with particularity, is helpful in determining the meaning of Supplemental Rule E(2)(a)...The purposes served by the heightened particularity in pleading requirements for an *in rem* maritime claim counsel for a similar reading of Supplemental Rule E(2)(a). The complaint should state the date, time, place, nature of the damaging incident, and the alleged wrongful action. Those usual requirements are, of course, always subject to the general standard that the complaint sufficiently notify the defendant of the incident in dispute and afford a reasonable belief that the claim has merit. The nature of an admiralty suit *in rem* compels such a standard. An admiralty action *in rem* involves arrest and seizure of the offending vessel simply upon filing a verified complaint. Supplemental Rule C(3). The drastic measure of seizing the vessel is demanded by the nature of maritime commerce, where the plaintiff's only security for his loss may at any time up anchor and sail for friendlier waters and less convenient forums, demands this drastic measure. Seizure of the *res*, therefore, has long been a necessary element of admiralty remedies. *See Manro v. Almeida*, 23 U.S. (10 Wheat.) 473 (1825). Inland riverway tugs do not usually steam to foreign ports, but the concern to maintain the plaintiff's security within the court's jurisdiction remains. The defendants, in turn, are entitled to freedom from the threat of seizure of their livelihood upon conclusory allegations and dubious circumstances. Their fifth amendment rights protect them from arbitrary deprivation of property. Pleading specific circumstances is one part of the process which guards against the improper use of admiralty seizure proceedings. When the complaint posits sufficient facts so that the defendants may begin an investigation and prepare a responsive pleading, their interests are adequately protected.

---

7. *Security on Counterclaims*

INCAS AND MONTEREY PRINTING AND PACKAGING, LTD. v. M/V *SANG JIN*

747 F.2d 958, 1985 AMC 968 (5th Cir. 1984)

JOHN R. BROWN, Circuit Judge

This is an appeal from an order of the district court in an admiralty case requiring plaintiff's to post counter security under Supplemental Admiralty Rule E(7), on pain of loss of its security for its original claim, which would likely destroy the *in rem* jurisdiction of the district court. We review the claims, vacate the district court order and remand.

In the Beginning

The controversy spawning this legal action began in 1982, when plaintiffs arranged for the carriage of two consignments of paper aboard the M/V SANG JIN.[2] Although the vessel was to proceed to East Africa, it instead made an unexpected stop in Pensacola, Florida, where plaintiffs' cargo was discharged. Plaintiffs demanded possession of their cargo from defendants, Van Weelde Bros., the time charterers, and Joong Ang Shipping, the owner's of the vessel. Defendants, however, refused delivery, claiming a lien on the cargo for the expense of discharging it in Florida.[3] Plaintiffs, seeking recovery of their cargo and damages for breach of contract of carriage, filed a complaint and had the M/V SANG JIN judicially arrested in Galveston on September 3, 1982 pursuant to Supplemental Admiralty Rule C.[4] One week later, the district court entered an order requiring that security of $1,600,000 be posted for release of the vessel, and that plaintiffs post security of $125,000 for release of their cargo, in light of defendants' lien for discharge expenses.

---

[2] One consignment was taken on board in Savannah, Georgia, and the other in St. John, New Brunswick.

[3] Although the vessel sailed without issuing bills of lading, a third defendant, Grundvig Chartering, Inc., subsequently issued bills of lading as subcharterer. Defendant Van Weelde alleges that these bills of lading were fraudulently issued. Grundvig Chartering, named as a defendant in plaintiffs' complaint, has yet to appear in this action.

[4] In its complaint, Incas invoked F. R. Civ. P. 9(h) to obtain the benefit of the Supplemental Rules for Admiralty.

On September 17, 1982, defendant Van Weelde filed its answer to plaintiffs' complaint, including counterclaims seeking $2,960,000 in damages. Van Weelde, the time charterer, alleged that plaintiff's had wrongfully seized the M/V SANG JIN with resultant commercial losses, including loss to its business reputation.[5] On the same day, Van Weelde moved that plaintiff's be required to post counter-security for these counterclaims, as provided for in Supplemental Admiralty rule E(7).[6]

On September 24, 1982, the parties reached an agreement whereby plaintiffs' cargo in Pensacola would be released without the posting of the $125,000 security required by the court's order, on condition that plaintiff's agree to accept security for the vessel for $125,000 less than the $1,600,000 previously ordered by the court, and with plaintiffs' agreement not to use the release of the cargo as an additional defense to Van Weelde's lien against the cargo. On the same day, the court ordered that, defendants having posted security of $1,475,000 in the form of $375,000 deposited in the court registry and a letter of undertaking from the vessel owner's Protection and Indemnity Club in the amount of $1,100,000, plaintiff's would be required to post equivalent counter-security for defendants' counterclaims.

Plaintiffs having failed to post counter-security, defendants moved on October 4, 1982 that the court impose sanctions in the form of a release of the security posted by the vessel interests. Plaintiffs responded by requesting the court to reconsider its order requiring counter-security, a request which was denied by the court on March 16, 1983.[7] On September 13, 1983,[8] the district court repeated its order of September 24, 1982 that plaintiffs post counter-security in the amount of $1,475,000. The court also ordered that the security posted by the vessel interests be released if counter-security was not posted within 10 days. On September 20, 1983, plaintiffs filed notice of appeal of the September 13, 1983 order. On September 22, 1983, this court granted a stay of the district court's order, pending "further orders of the court." Plaintiffs thereafter sought alternate relief from the district court's order in the form of a petition for writ of mandamus. Ultimately, this court ordered the petition for writ of mandamus carried with the case pending determination of the appealability of the district court order of September 13, 1983.

Finally, the Merits

This brings us to plaintiffs' contention that Van Weelde's counterclaims are not the type for which countersecurity may be required under Admiralty Rule E(7).[15]

Defendant Van Weelde's counterclaim asserts that plaintiffs (1) wrongfully seized the SANG JIN, (2) requested grossly excessive security, resulting in (3) interference with Van Weelde's contractual obligations, and

---

[5] Defendant Joong Ang, who filed a Claim as Owner of the M/V SANG JIN, has made no counterclaims.

[6] Supplemental Admiralty Rule E(7) provides as follows:

> (7) Security on counterclaim. Whenever there is asserted a counterclaim arising out of the same transaction or occurrence with respect to which the action was originally filed, and the defendant or claimant in the original action has given security to respond in damages, any plaintiff for whose benefit such security has been given shall give security in the usual amount and form to respond in damages to the claims set forth in such counterclaim, unless the court, for cause shown, shall otherwise direct; and proceedings on the original claim shall be stayed until such security is given, unless the court otherwise directs....

Thus, a counterclaim arising "out of the same transaction or occurrence" as the original claim is a prerequisite to the posting of counter-security under Rule E(7).

[7] Plaintiffs moved the court to amend its denial of reconsideration to permit an interlocutory appeal pursuant to 28 U.S.C. § 1292(b). On September 13, 1983, the court denied plaintiffs' motion to so certify the order.

[8] The parties were not idle in the intervening months. During this time period, the court considered numerous discovery motions, as well as repeated motions by defendants to require plaintiffs to post security.

[13] Our decision that the order is appealable under this section renders unnecessary any determination whether, as plaintiffs assert, it is appealable under 28 U.S.C. § 1292(a)(3), providing for appeal of certain orders in admiralty cases. We also need not consider plaintiffs' petition for writ of mandamus to decide this question.

[14] In *Firestone Tire and Rubber Co. v. Risjord*, 449 U.S. 368, 101 S. Ct. 669, 66 L. Ed. 2d 571 (1981), the Supreme Court stressed that even if an order meets all the other criteria for the *Cohen* doctrine, it is not appealable under § 1291 unless it would "be effectively unreviewable on appeal from a final judgment." *Id.* at 376, 101 S. Ct. at 674, 66 L. Ed. 2d at 580.

[15] Defendants also argue that even if the September 13, 1983 order is appealable, our review may only encompass the district court's decision to release defendants' security, and that we cannot address the propriety of the court's decision to order counter-security in the first place. They maintain that since counter-security was first required by the order of September 24, 1982, any appeal of that decision is time-barred. *See* F. R. App. P. 4(a)(1). This argument ignores the fact that the very order from which plaintiffs' appeal expressly repeats the directive that plaintiffs post counter-security for defendants' counterclaim. *See, supra* note 9. The requirement that plaintiffs post counter-security being part of the September 13, 1983 order, it is properly before us for review. 28 U.S.C. § 2106.

Nor is the fact that plaintiffs' Notice of Appeal refers only to the sanctions section of the September 13 order fatal to our jurisdiction. The requirement of F. R. App. P. 3(c) that a notice of appeal designate the judgment from which it is taken is not to be so strictly construed as to defeat an appeal where appellant's overriding intent to appeal is clear. *Foman v. Davis*, 371 U.S. 178, 83 S. Ct. 227, 9 L. Ed. 2d 222 (1962); *see Comfort Trane Air Conditioning v. Trane Company*, 592 F.2d 1373, 1390 at n.15 (5th Cir. 1979); *U.S. v. Stromberg*, 227 F.2d 903, 904 (5th Cir. 1955).

(4) disparagement of Van Weelde's name in the business community.[16] The cornerstone of these allegations is that plaintiff's had no right to employ the admiralty rules to arrest the SANG JIN in the first place. Since the admiralty is not concerned with common law labels as to theories of recovery, or causes of action, *See Kermarec v. Compagnie Generale Transatlantique*, 358 U.S. 625, 79 S. Ct. 406, 3 L. Ed. 2d 550, 1957 AMC 597 (1959), we are entitled to treat this broadly as a claim for wrongful seizure, whether denominated as such or as one for abuse of process, malicious prosecution, or all three.

In *Frontera Fruit Co. v. Dowling*, 91 F.2d 293, 1937 AMC 1259 (5th Cir. 1937), we held that the right to recover damages for wrongful seizure of a vessel is based on a showing of bad faith, malice or gross negligence on the part of the libellant. *Id.* at 297, 1937 AMC at 1266. Since that time, we have had occasion to decide, on the basis of *Frontera*, whether such bad faith existed as to warrant the award of damages for a wrongful seizure in admiralty. *See e.g., Cardinal Shipping Corp. v. M/S SEISHO MARU*, 744 F.2d 461 (5th Cir. 1984); *TTT Stevedores of Texas, Inc. v. M/V JAGAT VIJETA*, 696 F.2d 1135 (5th Cir. 1983); *Tampa Ship Repair & Dry Dock Co. v. Esso Export Corp.* 237 F.2d 506, 1956 AMC 217 (5th Cir. 1956). In none of these cases, however, were we required to decide the precise issue presented to us on this appeal: whether a counterclaim for wrongful seizure is an appropriate basis for requiring counter-security to be posted under Admiralty Rule E(7), or its predecessor, former Admiralty Rule 50.[17] Upon examination of the intent of the Rule, we are of the opinion that counter-security should not be ordered for such a claim.

Under the terms of Rule E(7), counter-security may be required when a counterclaim is asserted which arises "out of the same transaction or occurrence" as the original libel. This language is identical to that defining compulsory counterclaims under F. R. Civ. P. 13(a). Thus, as Professor Moore has suggested, we can draw guidance on the proper scope of Rule E(7) by examining the test for counterclaims under F. R. Civ. P. 13(a). 7A J. Moore & A Pelaez, Moore's Federal Practice, E-727 (2d ed. 1983).

Under the broad test for Rule 13(a) adopted by this Circuit, a counterclaim is compulsory when there is any "logical relationship" between the claim and the counterclaim. *Plant v. Blazer Financial Services*, 598 F.2d 1357 (5th Cir. 1979). *See also 6* C. Wright & A. Miller, Federal Practice & Procedure § 1410 (1971) (indicating breadth of this test). However, even under this liberal standard, it is clear that an action in the nature of wrongful seizure or malicious prosecution does not lie as a compulsory counterclaim under F.R. Civ. P. 13(a). *See, e.g., Olsen v. Puntervold*, 338 F.2d 21 (5th Cir. 1964) (malicious prosecution); *U.S. General, Inc. v. City of Joliet*, 598 F.2d 1050 (7th Cir. 1979) (malicious prosecution). *See generally 3* J. Moore, Moore's Federal Practice ¶ 13.13, 13-78, n.26 (2d ed. 1984).

---

[16] The pertinent portions of defendants' counterclaim are as follows:

> Count XXI

> For further cause defendant, Van Weelde Bros. Shipping, Ltd., would show that Plaintiffs lack any standing to assert an *in rem* claim against the vessel. No rights or title to goods have accrued to Plaintiff since the bills of lading were fraudulently issued. Moreover, Plaintiffs derive their contract of carriage, if any exists, by virtue of unauthorized acts of a third party not through any actions of the owner of the vessel or his employees. The bills of lading in question bear neither the signature of the Master nor anyone authorized by him. Thus, Plaintiffs may have a claim against the wrongdoing party who issued the fraudulent bills but does not have a cause of action against those who neither knew of the fraud nor participated in it, neither have they any *in rem* action against the property of such innocent parties. Accordingly, Plaintiffs are liable for the wrongful seizure of the M/V SANG JIN and all damages arising or a result of Plaintiffs's wrongful seizure....

> Count XXIII

> For further cause Defendant, Van Weelde Bros. Shipping, Ltd., would show that the plaintiffs' grossly excessive and improper demand for security has subjected Defendant, to unnecessary and unwarranted expenses. Accordingly, plaintiffs are liable for all of Defendant's damages resulting from plaintiffs' grossly excessive and improper demand for security....

[17] Admiralty Rule 50:

> Whenever a cross-libel is filed upon any counterclaim arising out of the same contract or cause of action for which the original libel suit was filed, and the respondent or claimant in the original suit shall have given security to respond in damages, the respondent in the cross-libel shall give security in the usual amount the form to respond in damages to the claims set forth in said cross-libel, unless the court, for cause shown, shall otherwise direct; and all proceedings on the original libel shall be stayed until such security be given, unless the court otherwise directs.

Such a counterclaim not "arising out of the same transaction or occurrence" as the original action for purposes of federal practice, and there being neither history nor practice in the admiralty suggesting any difference, we see no justification for applying Rule E(7) to a broader class of counterclaims than that permitted under F. R. Civ. P. 13(a).[18] This is especially appropriate in light of the 1966 Unification of Admiralty and Civil Practice. We therefore conclude that, whether or not an action for wrongful seizure, abuse of process or malicious prosecution may be asserted as a counter claim in admiralty practice, counter-security under Rule E(7) may not be required for such a claim.

This holding is supported by the decisions of the federal courts which have considered this precise question. In *Amerada Hess Corp. v. S.S. ATHENA*, 1984 AMC 130 (D. Md. 1984), the court denied defendant's request for counter-security based on counterclaims alleging abuse of process and wrongful use of civil proceedings. In denying counter-security, the court reasoned that, since such a counterclaim would not be permitted under F. R. Civ. P. 13(a), it could not be the basis for requiring counter-security under Admiralty Rule E(7). *Id.* at 132.

A similar conclusion was made under former Admiralty Rule 50 in *Solomon v. Bruchhausen*, 305 F.2d 941, 1963 AMC 210 (2d Cir. 1962), *cert. denied sub nom Isbrandtsen v. Maximo*, 371 U.S. 951, 83 S. Ct. 506, 9 L. Ed. 2d 499, 1963 AMC 1646 (1963). There, the district court had ordered libellants to post counter-security for respondent's cross-claim of abuse of process in the arrest of respondent's vessels. The Second Circuit dismissed the cross-claim stating that an action for abuse of process could not be considered to have arisen out of the original action.[19]

We thus decide that the district court improperly ordered the posting of security for defendants' counterclaims. Having found appellate jurisdiction to decide this issue, plaintiffs' petition for Writ of Mandamus in No. 83-2627 is mooted, and is therefore dismissed.

For the foregoing reasons, the district court's order requiring appellant to post counter-security is vacated, and the cause remanded for further proceedings.

Vacated and Remanded.

Note: Appeals in Admiralty Cases

As interpreted by the courts, 28 U.S.C. § 1291, which provides for appeals from a district court to a court of appeals, an appeal will not lie until after final judgment has been entered. This is known as the "final judgment rule". There are exceptions to that rule. 28 U.S.C. § 1292(b) allows for an interlocutory appeal where a district court certifies an order as dispositive and certifies that it involves an issue of "a controlling question of law as to which there is a substantial ground for difference of opinion and that an immediate appeal from the order may materially advance the ultimate determination of the litigation." This provision applies to all cases including admiralty cases. However, the exercise of appellate jurisdiction in such cases lies in the discretion of the court of appeals. There is also a special interlocutory appeals provision that applies to admiralty cases. 28 U.S.C. § 1292(a) provides: (a) Except as provided in subsections (c) and (d) of this section, the courts of appeals shall have jurisdiction of appeals from***: (3) Interlocutory decrees of such district courts or the judges thereof determining the rights and liabilities of the parties to admiralty cases in which appeals from final decrees are allowed." In applying this rule some circuits are more restrictive than others. See, Robert Force, 4A BENEDICT ON ADMIRALTY, Chapter 5 (Seventh Revised Edition (Mathew Bender 2016).

---

[18] As the Supreme Court has stated,

> Traditionally, admiralty has narrowly circumscribed the filing of unrelated cross-libels and defenses.... [V]arious reasons have been offered for refusal to entertain unrelated defenses: protection of the seaman's wage claims; preservation of relatively simple proceedings not affecting third-party rights; and the recognition that allowing cross-libels might deprive litigants of jury trials to which they would otherwise be entitled if the cross-libel were pressed in an independent proceeding. *United States v. Isthmanian SS Co.*, 359 U.S. 314, 320, 79 S. Ct. 857, 860-61, 3 L. Ed. 2d 845, 849-50, 1959 AMC 1332, 1337 (1959).

Given this traditional narrow construction, the court concluded:

> The law on this point in admiralty has been settled beyond doubt in the lower courts for many years and an Admiralty Rule of this Court recognizes this case law. We think that if the law is to change it should be by rulemaking or legislation and not by decision. Id. at 323, 79 S. Ct. at 862, 3 L. Ed. 2d at 851.

[19] While the Solomon court held that a claim of wrongful seizure would not lie at *all* as a cross-claim in admiralty, 305 F.2d at 943, we do not decide that question. We merely hold that countersecurity may not be required under Rule E(7) for such a claim. We observe, however, that other courts have reached the same conclusion as the court in *Solomon. See, Maritime Terminals v. M/S JAN*, 1978 AMC 1236 (N.D. 111. 1978) (claim of wrongful arrest does not lie as cross-claim in admiralty); *United States v. M/V PITCAIRN*, 272 F.Supp. 518 (E.D. La. 1967) (wrongful seizure claim does not arise out of the same cause of action as the original libel).

TITAN NAVIGATION, INC. v. TIMSCO, INC.

808 F.2d 400, 1987 AMC 1396 (5th Cir. 1987)

POLITZ, Circuit Judge

This appeal involves the interpretation and application of Rule E(7) of the Supplemental Rules for Admiralty, in an instance in which a complainant possessed of a maritime lien secured the posting of security and, in turn, was ordered to post counter-security for the defendant's counterclaim. For the reasons assigned, and with the caveats noted, we affirm.

Background

In late 1982 Timsco, Inc. contracted to furnish computer hardware and software for vessels owned by Titan Navigation, Inc. Titan preferred not to purchase the system outright, but opted to enter into a lease agreement with Marine Leasing, Inc., a corporation organized for the specific purpose of purchasing the systems and leasing them to vessels.

In July 1984, Titan and related corporations sued Timsco and Marine Leasing for rescission of the contract and damages, contending that the computers were faulty. Timsco and Marine Leasing counterclaimed, seeking enforcement of the contract. Exercising its maritime lien rights, Marine Leasing arrested, or initiated an action to arrest vessels belonging to Titan. Titan secured the release of these vessels by posting the requisite security. Thereafter, Titan and its vessels counterclaimed, ultimately alleging breach of contract, misrepresentation, violation of the Texas Deceptive Trade Practices Act, breach of warranty, breach of indemnity, and violations of the Texas Uniform Commercial Code. Titan also requested that Timsco and Marine Leasing be ordered to post countersecurity under Rule E(7) of the Supplemental Rules for Admiralty.

The trial court ordered Timsco and Marine Leasing to either post countersecurity or release the security given in lieu of the arrest of Titans vessels. Marine Leasing appealed and presented issues not brought to the attention of the district court. We remanded for reconsideration. After further discovery and proceedings, the district court again ordered the posting of countersecurity. Marine Leasing noticed the present appeal.

Analysis

At the threshold we confirm appellate jurisdiction. Under our holding in *Incas and Monterey Printing and Packaging, Ltd. v. M/V SANG JIN*, 747 F.2d 958 (5th Cir. 1984), the countersecurity order is appealable. We address the merits of appellant's claims.

This appeal turns on the language of Rule E(7), in light of its historical development. The pertinent language of this section is straightforward:

> 7) Security on Counterclaim. Whenever there is asserted a counterclaim arising out of the same transaction or occurrence with respect to which the action was originally filed, and the defendant or claimant in the original action has given security to respond in damages, any plaintiff for whose benefit such security has been given shall give security in the usual amount and form to respond in damages to the claims set forth in such counterclaim, unless the court, for cause shown, shall otherwise direct;...

Marine Leasing first contends that the countersecurity provisions of the rule apply only to counterclaims in admiralty. In that regard it points out that Titans counterclaim invokes only diversity and federal question jurisdiction. In support of this contention appellant relies on *United States v. Isthmian Steamship Co.*, 359 U.S. 314, 79 S. Ct. 857, 3 L. Ed. 2d 845 (1959). We find that reliance misplaced. Isthmian simply holds that the cross-libel referred to in Admirality Rule 50 (the predecessor to Rule E(7)), included only those claims which related to the original libel. In the case at bar, all of the claims arise out of the same transaction and are at least within the pendent jurisdiction of the district court sitting in admiralty. In this resolution we are guided, as was the district court, by the scholarly opinion of Judge Friendly in *leather's Best, Inc. v. S.S. MORMACLYNX*, 451 F.2d 800 (2d Cir. 1971).

Titan was entitled to invoke the countersecurity provisions of Rule E(7) despite the fact that the counterclaim was not based in admiralty.

The more serious and difficult question posed by this appeal involves the ordering of the posting of countersecurity by one who possesses and has exercised an admiralty lien. The answer to that question requires a brief review of the historicity of this provision.

The concept of countersecurity is found in the first promulgation of rules in American admiralty courts, and it has continued to date with little substantive change.[2] With the merger of law and admiralty in 1966, admiralty's classic and ancient phraseology of libels and cross-libels was replaced with the more mundane terminology of claims and counterclaims, but Rule E(7) retained the essence of Admiralty Rule 50. *See* Advisory Committee's Note, *Proposed Supplemental Rules for Certain Admiralty and Maritime Claims, reprinted in* 39 F.R.D. 146, 160 (1966).

The rule is straightforward. When the defendant posts security to guarantee payment of an adverse judgment—typically the posting of a bond to secure release of a vessel—the complainant may be required to furnish security for the satisfaction of a counterclaim. Although the language of the rule is automatic it is not absolute, for the original seizing complainant may be excused by the court "for cause shown." Absent this relief by the court, the intent of the rule is manifest; it is "to place the parties on an equality as regards security." *Washington-Southern Navigation Co. v. Baltimore & Philadelphia Steamboat Co.*, 263 U.S. 629, 638-39, 44 S. Ct. 220, 223-24, 68 L. Ed. 480 (1924).[3]

The determination of "for cause shown" is relegated to the sound discretion of the district court. The extent of that discretion is critical to the resolution of this and similar appeals. We are persuaded that the discretion, although broad, is significantly cabined in some cases.

A survey of the jurisprudence reflects instances in which demands for countersecurity were carefully weighed and charily granted. Courts have recognized that seamen should not be forced to post countersecurity when they act to enforce their privileged position. *Washington-Southern Navigation Co. v. Baltimore & Philadelphia Steamboat Co.; Zubrod v. Associated Metals & Minerals Trade Co.*, 243 F. Supp. 340 (E.D. Pa. 1965); *Cudworth v. The St. Cuthbert*, 146 F. Supp. 857, 858 (E.D. Va. 1957) (action by seamen on salvage liens, holding seamen not required to post countersecurity because "to hold otherwise, salvage claims instituted by seamen could be effectively foreclosed.") The rationale for excusing seamen from posting security comes from their traditional role as wards of the court and the fact that Congress has long permitted them to prosecute civil actions without posting security. 28 U.S.C. § 1916.

Similarly, when a party is financially unable to post countersecurity, courts often dispense with the requirement of the rule, although the cases are not unanimous. The leading case on this point, with which we agree, remains *The Beaumont*, 8 F.2d 599 (4th Cir. 1925):

> The rule never contemplated, ... that, where the parties to the original libel had established their rights and obtained security, this should be lost to them, because of their inability, arising from insolvency or other good reason, to procure a bond to respond to a large claim asserted in the cross-libel, and that as a result their libel should be dismissed. This would not only be unjust, but would in effect negative and nullify the provision of the rule giving to the trial court full discretion to act upon the very subject involved.

---

[2] The first countersecurity rule in admiralty was Admiralty Rule 54, adopted at 7 Wall, v (1868), which provided:

> Whenever a cross-libel if filed upon any counter claim arising out of the same cause of action for which the original libel was filed, the respondents in the cross-libel shall give security in the usual amount and form, to respond in damages as claimed in said cross-libel, unless the court on cause shown, shall otherwise direct; and all proceedings upon the original libel shall be stayed until such security shall be given.

The same rule was re-adopted as Admiralty Rule 53 at 210 U.S. 562 (1907). In 1920 the provision became Admiralty Rule 50, 254 U.S. at 24 (Appendix), providing:

> Whenever a cross-libel is filed upon any counterclaim arising out of the same contract or cause of action for which the original libel was filed, and the respondent or claimant in the original suit shall have given security to respond in damages, the respondent in the cross-libel shall give security in the usual amount and form to respond in damages to the claims set forth in said cross-libel, unless the court, for cause shown, shall otherwise direct; and all proceedings on the original libel shall be stayed until such security be given unless the court otherwise directs.

[3] *See, e.g., Seaboard & Caribbean Transp. Corp. v. Hafen-Dampfschiffahrt A.G.*, 329 F.2d 538 (5th Cir. 1964); *Spriggs v. Hoffstot*, 240 F.2d 76 (4th Cir. 1957); *Expert Diesel, Inc. v. Yacht "Fishin Fool"*, 627 F. Supp. 432 (S.D. Fla. 1986); *Williamett Transp., Inc. v. Cia. Anonima Venezolana de Navegacion*, 491 F. Supp. 442 (E.D. La. 1980); *Empresa Maritima a Vapor v. North & South American Steam Nav. Co.*, 16 F. 502 (S.D.N.Y. 1883).

8 F.2d at 601. *See also Spriggs v. Hoffstot*, 240 F.2d 76 (4th Cir. 1957) (finding no abuse of discretion in trial court's decision not to require countersecurity); *Whitney-Fidalgo Seafoods v. Miss Tammy*, 542 F. Supp. 1302 (W.D. Wash. 1982) (refusing counterclaimants argument that the defendant on the counterclaim might be unable to pay a judgment and should therefore be required to post security); *cf. Flota Maritima Browning de Cuba v. M/V Ciudad de la Habana*, 245 F. Supp. 205 (D. Md. 1965); *Geotas Compania de Vapores v. S.S. Arie H.*, 237 F. Supp. 908 (E.D. Pa. 1964) (considering financial statements of cross libellant, requiring reduced countersecurity). We have recognized the pertinency of this consideration by concluding that financial difficulties would not automatically excuse the countersecurity requirement. *Seaboard & Caribbean Transp. Corp. v. Hafen-Dampfschiffahrt*, 329 F.2d 538 (5th Cir. 1964).

Finally, the court should not require countersecurity where the counterclaim is frivolous or so lacking in merit that the court can only conclude that the counterclaim was advanced solely to secure a negotiating advantage over the complainant.

In summary, we conclude that the exercise of the trial court's discretion to order countersecurity is to be guided by the essential and equitable purposes of the rule. In doing so, the court must weigh the importance of the security interest giving rise to the initial seizure, and the burden of posting countersecurity, against the potential injustice of requiring the defendant-counterclaimant to post security without affording reciprocal protection.

We believe the guidon for this analysis is the courts obligation to preserve the integrity of maritime liens. These vintage security devices endure and are protected because of their commercial usefulness. Despite the advent of instant communications, and the availability of sophisticated international financing, the ability of a ships master to bind his vessel *in rem* continues to facilitate the prompt supply of goods and services. Similarly, liens under the law of general average permit the ships master to make expeditious decisions regarding imperiled cargo; salvage liens encourage sailors to save property which would otherwise be lost; and liens arising out of collisions and other torts give innocent parties a source of financial responsibility, even though ultimate responsibility may lie with a distant and unreachable individual or corporation.

The considerable deference to be given maritime liens where countersecurity is requested was explained by Mr. Justice Brandeis in *Washington-Southern Navigation Co. v. Baltimore & Philadelphia Steamboat Co.*, where he discussed at length the history of Rule 50 and its predecessors, and rejected a rigid construction under which "a libellant may be automatically barred from prosecuting his suit, merely because he is unable or unwilling to give security to satisfy the claim made in the cross-libel." 263 U.S. at 632, 44 S. Ct. at 221. Justice Brandeis reasoned that such a rigid construction of the rule would impair the rights of litigants to proceed in admiralty and would result in wasteful machinations on the part of litigants, concluding:

An intention to introduce a practice so capricious is not to be lightly imputed.

To ascertain the true meaning of the rule, it must be read, also, in the light of the established admiralty jurisdiction, of the general principles of maritime law, and of the appropriate function of rules of court.

263 U.S. at 632, 44 S. Ct. at 221.

* * *

The construction given to Rule 50 by the district court would, by imposing an impossible or onerous condition, deprive many litigants of the right to prosecute their claims in admiralty. Among others, it would, if applied generally, deny this right to seamen, upon whom, regardless of their means or nationality, Congress, shortly before the adoption of Rule 50, had conferred the right to prosecute their claims, in both trial and appellate courts, without giving security even for costs. It would likewise deny to poor citizens of the United States the right to proceed in admiralty.... Obviously, it was not the intention of this Court, in adopting the rule, to disregard the right of seamen, of poor persons or of others to prosecute suits in admiralty.[4]

---

[4] Significantly, Justice Brandeis spoke for a unanimous court shortly after its promulgation of Admiralty Rule 50. Although at that time Rule 50 could result in dismissal of the libellant's *only* right of action, while modern litigants may proceed against a defendant *in personam*, countersecurity requirements may still work a hardship on parties, and the argument retains its force. *See* Pelaez, *supra*, 17 Duq. L. Rev. at 268-69.

263 U.S. at 634-35, 44 S. Ct. at 221-22 (citations omitted).

Justice Brandeis's blazings guide today's interpretation and application of Rule E(7). We can readily contemplate instances when permitting one party to enjoy security without requiring countersecurity could result in injustice. For example, when no maritime lien or statutory right is involved, as in an action commenced *quasi in rem* under Rule B, there usually would be little or no reason to permit a complainant to enjoy unilateral security rights, absent strong justification—or in the terms of Rule E(7), "cause shown." On the other hand, the court should not lightly order countersecurity if to do so would diminish the utility of the maritime liens established by Congress or long-standing precedents. The circumstances of each case must govern the propriety of the ordering of countersecurity.

It is against this backdrop that we examine the propriety of the countersecurity order in the case at bar.

In its analysis the trial court questioned whether Marine Leasing would be able to post the countersecurity. If it failed to do so it would lose the advantage of the security posted by Titan for release of the arrested vessels. Should this materialize, the effect of the trial court's order would be to force a lien-holder to relinquish a privileged position because of a financial inability to post countersecurity.

The trial court was persuaded that in the event the failure to post the countersecurity caused Marine Leasing to forfeit its secured position, its rights would be adequately protected by its *in personam* action against Titan. Implicit in this is a finding that Titan could respond in damages should it be cast in judgment. While we are reluctant to approve an *in personam* remedy as a substitute for a lien against a *res in custodia legis*, we cannot conclude that in this specific instance the district court abused its discretion.

We conclude that the ordering of countersecurity, under the particular facts presented, does no substantial harm to the sanctity or efficaciousness of maritime liens. In this case, the contract which gave rise to the lien was the result of careful negotiation between officials of the corporate parties. There is no indication whatsoever that Marine Leasing relied on the credit of any of the seized vessels in deciding to enter into the mesne contract between Timsco and Titan. We thus perceive no impairment of the fundamental utility of maritime liens, *i.e.*, as an inducer of credit for a ship's needed goods and services. Therefore, although we are loathe to approve what may develop to be a discharge of a maritime lien because of the lienholder's financial limitations, under the specific and narrowly defined facts of this particular case, we are not prepared to say that the trial court abused its discretion in ordering countersecurity.

The order requiring the posting of countersecurity is AFFIRMED.

---

8. *Res Judicata*

CENTRAL HUDSON GAS & ELECTRIC CORP. v. EMPRESA NAVIERA SANTA S.A.

56 F.3d 359, 1996 AMC 163 (2d Cir. 1995)

MESKILL, Circuit Judge

This appeal involves the interplay of the doctrines of *res judicata* and collateral estoppel within the confines of admiralty jurisdiction. Empresa Naviera Santa S.A. (Empresa) appeals the decision of the United States District Court for the Southern District of New York, Broderick, J., entering summary judgment against Empresa *in personam* following a judgment *in rem* against a vessel chartered by Empresa. As we find that *res judicata* does not bar the claims asserted, and that Empresa is collaterally estopped from contesting the district court's prior determinations, we affirm.

Background

This case arose on January 16, 1988 when the M/V LUNAMAR II (the Vessel), a motor tanker flying the Panamanian flag, dragged an anchor on a voyage up the Hudson River, thereby damaging an electrical cable pipeline owned by Central Hudson Gas & Electric Corporation (Central Hudson). Central Hudson filed suit against the Vessel *in rem* and Seiriki One (Panama) S.A. (Seiriki), the Vessel's registered owner, three days later (the *in rem* action). On January 21, 1988 the Vessel's underwriters delivered a $3 million letter of undertaking to Central Hudson to avoid the arrest of the Vessel. The letter, moreover, constituted only an estimate of the damage to the cable pipeline, given that the portion of the river where the accident occurred was frozen and a more accurate estimate could not be obtained immediately.

Although the Vessel's crew had stated that they were employed by Empresa, a foreign corporation operating the Vessel as bareboat charterparty, the letter of undertaking was executed on behalf of Seiriki as registered owner and did not expressly include any charterparties. Central Hudson thereafter sought to determine the party or parties in control of the Vessel by filing an interrogatory during discovery requesting the names of all of its charterparties. The defendants in the *in rem* action did not respond to this interrogatory, even after having been ordered to do so by a magistrate judge on May 2, 1989. On July 3, 1990, however, shortly before trial of the *in rem* action, Seiriki and Empresa filed restricted appearances as the Vessels registered owner and owner "pro hac vice," respectively, pursuant to Rule E(8) of the Supplemental Rules for Certain Admiralty and Maritime Claims of the Federal Rules of Civil Procedure (Supplemental Rules). In filing the restricted appearance Empresa confirmed its relationship to the Vessel for the first time.

A bench trial of the *in rem* action then commenced on July 31, 1990. Seiriki and Empresa participated in the defense of the Vessel in their representative capacities. On October 3, 1990, following the conclusion of the trial but prior to the entry of the district court's decision, Central Hudson filed a quasi *in rem* action in Louisiana to attach the SANTA ROSA de LIMA (SANTA ROSA), another ship operated by Empresa. Additionally on that date Central Hudson filed an *in personam* suit against Empresa in the Southern District of New York. Both actions alleged that Empresa was personally liable for the damage to the cable pipeline. The two actions were consolidated in the Southern District before Judge Broderick and were placed in abeyance pending his decision in the *in rem* action. The district court issued its findings in the *in rem* action on April 7, 1992, dismissing the *in personam* claim against Seiriki for lack of service and finding the Vessel liable on the *in rem* claim. On September 9, 1992 the court entered judgment in the amount of $4,477,584.15, constituting approximately $3.37 million in damages and $1.1 million in prejudgment interest, together with costs. We affirmed that decision. *See Central Hudson Gas & Elec. Corp. v. M/V LUNAMAR II*, 797 F. Supp. 1244 (S.D.N.Y. 1992) (LUNAMAR II), *aff'd mem.*, 993 F.2d 1534 (2d Cir. 1993). The judgment was only partially satisfied through the $3 million letter of undertaking, and an amount of $1,486,134.44 remained unsatisfied.

Judge Broderick then activated the consolidated *in personam* and quasi *in rem* cases. Empresa moved to dismiss both cases and to vacate the attachment of the SANTA ROSA, arguing that under the doctrine of *res judicata* the *in rem* judgment against the Vessel barred the subsequent lawsuits. Central Hudson cross-moved for summary judgment, arguing that Empresa was collaterally estopped from relitigating the issues of liability and damages. Judge Broderick denied Empresa's motions and entered summary judgment in favor of Central Hudson, concluding that the consolidated action was, in essence, simply composed of lawsuits filed to collect on the unpaid portion of the *in rem* judgment. Judge Broderick also rejected Empresa's argument that Central Hudson could not pursue both *in rem* and *in personam* claims for the same injury. The district court then awarded prejudgment interest of $364,761.39 on the $1,486,134.44 remaining unpaid from the *in rem* judgment, and entered judgment against Empresa for the total of $1,850,895.83. Empresa now appeals.

Discussion

***

I. Jurisdiction

Empresa initially contends that in the prior action the district court possessed jurisdiction only to the extent of the value of the *res* or the amount of any bond substituted therefor, and thus lacked jurisdiction to enter a judgment in excess of the value of the $3 million letter of undertaking. Indeed, Empresa points to the rule that "an *in rem* action is an action against the arrested *res* itself and any judgment is thus limited to the value thereof or the value of the bond or stipulation substituted for the *res* to obtain its release." 7A JAMES WM. MOORE, MOORE'S FEDERAL PRACTICE ¶ E.16[2] at E-779 (2d ed. 1995) (footnote omitted; emphasis added).

While this rule generally governs *in rem* actions, it is axiomatic that a district court sitting in admiralty exercises "powers akin to those of a court of equity." *The MINNETONKA*, 146 F. 509, 515 (2d Cir.), *cert. denied*, 203 U.S. 589, 27 S. Ct. 777, 51 L.Ed. 330 (1906). By virtue of those powers, a court possesses jurisdiction to enter judgment in excess of the value of an arrested res. Indeed, as we explained in *MINNETONKA*, "[a] court of admiralty ... should not be hampered in its efforts to reach ... substantial justice." *Id.; see also Mosher v. Tate*, 182 F.2d 475, 479 (9th Cir. 1950) ("[W]e think that under all of the circumstances of this case and in order to achieve substantial justice the trial court has power to enter a personal decree against appellees without any additional service of process or supplemental libel."); *The FAIRISLE*, 76 F. Supp. 27, 32 (D. Md. 1947) (holding "no principle of admiralty law ... prohibits this Court from rendering a decree against claimant for the total amount of the award," even where award exceeds amount of bond posted as security), *aff'd sub nom. Waterman S.S. Corp. v. Dean*, 171 F.2d 408 (4th Cir. 1948); *see generally* 7A MOORE'S FEDERAL PRACTICE ¶ E.16[2] at E-780 ("[I]n some instances the owner or claimant who procures the release of the *res* or who enters a restricted appearance to defend the *res* may be held personally accountable for damages in excess of the value of the arrested *res* or the substitute bond or stipulation provided to obtain its release.").[1] We find, under the circumstances of this case, that the district court properly exercised its authority as an admiralty court to enter a judgment in excess of the value of the letter of undertaking.

In essence, *Empresa's* argument rests on a confusion between damages and liability. The district court's decision in *LUNAMAR II* determined that the damage to Central Hudson's cable pipeline was caused by the Vessel, and calculated the value of this damage at $4,477,584.15. This factual finding became final when we affirmed that judgment. *See In re PCH Assocs.*, 949 F.2d 585, 593 (2d Cir. 1991) (where district court determined issue in earlier case and where appellate court did not disapprove, it was law of the case). Thus, the amount of Central Hudson's damages is not at issue here.

The question, rather, is whether Central Hudson can collect on the unrecovered portion of the *in rem* judgment from Empresa in this *in personam* action. Central Hudson cannot, of course, simply execute on the *in rem* judgment against a defendant not yet found to be liable. *See Cooper v. Reynolds*, 77 U.S. (10 Wall.) 308, 318, 19 L.Ed. 931 (1870) ("[T]he judgment of the court, though in form a personal judgment against the defendant, has no effect beyond the property attached in that suit. No general execution can be issued for any balance unpaid after the attached property is exhausted."). Therefore, Empresa must be found liable *in personam* before it can be held responsible for the uncollected portion of the *in rem* judgment. This requirement, however, is legally distinct from the issue of whether the district court possessed the authority to enter judgment in excess of the value of the res. We thus turn to the proper question raised by this appeal: whether Empresa can be held liable *in personam* for the uncollected portion of the *in rem* judgment.

II. Can Central Hudson Bring This *in personam* Action?

A. Whether an *in rem* Judgment Bars Subsequent *in personam* Suits

Empresa next asserts that since the prior judgment was entered against the Vessel *in rem*, that judgment bars any subsequent *in personam* claim. Empresa bases this argument on the distinction between *in rem* and *in personam* jurisdiction in admiralty law. Central Hudson argued below, and the district court agreed, that the 1966 Amendments to the Admiralty Rules specifically permit separate *in rem* and *in personam* actions. We concur.

Empresa relies on three prior decisions in this Circuit to support its argument that a litigant cannot pursue separate *in rem* and *in personam* claims regarding the same injury in sequential suits: *Burns Bros. v. Central Railroad,*

---

[1] The cases on which Empresa relies actually support this general proposition. For example, *Empresa* cites *Industria NacionaldelPapel, C.A. v. M/V "ALBERTF"* 730 F.2d622 (11th Cir.), *cert. denied*, 469 U.S. 1037, 105 S. Ct. 515, 83 L. Ed. 2d 404 (1984), in support of its argument that a judgment on an *in rem* claim must be limited to the value of the *res. Industria Nacional,* however, concerned a claimant who sought an order compelling a vessel owner to post additional security. The Eleventh Circuit simply held that the claimant could not obtain an *in personam* judgment against the vessel owner for the additional amount because the district court had no independent basis on which to exercise personal jurisdiction over the owner. *See id.* at 627. Likewise, *Maritima Antares, S.A. v. Vessel ESSI CAMILLA*, 633 F. Supp. 694 (E.D. Va. 1986), also cited by *Empresa* for the same proposition, similarly fails. *Maritima Antares* concerned the issue of whether the security posted for a vessel's release became a complete substitute for that vessel where the letter of undertaking included an agreement not to rearrest the vessel. The court reached the unassailable conclusion that a vessel cannot be held liable twice *in rem* for the same claim. *See id.* at 697.

This appeal also can be distinguished from those cases in which claimants seek duplicative damages, a matter not at issue here. *See, e.g., Beck v. Levering*, 947 F.2d 639, 642 (2d Cir. 1991) (*per curiam*) (no *res judicata* issue where subsequent suit did not create duplicative award but merely decreased second judgment by amount awarded in prior suit), *cert. denied*, 504 U.S. 909, 112 S.Ct. 1937, 118 L.Ed.2d 544 (1992).

202 F.2d 910 (2d Cir. 1953); *Sullivan v. Nitrate Producers' S.S. Co.*, 262 F. 371 (2d Cir. 1919); and *Bailey v. Sundberg*, 49 F. 583 (2d Cir. 1892), *cert. denied*, 154 U.S. 494, 14 S. Ct. 1142, 38 L.Ed. 1078 (1894). *Burns Bros.* involved a plaintiff who lost a previous decision *in personam* against the owner of a carfloat (although the plaintiff won against the co-defendant carfloat operator) following a collision between the carfloat and the plaintiff's barge, and who subsequently filed an action *in rem* against the carfloat. Judge Learned Hand, after reviewing the Sullivan and Bailey decisions, concluded that "a decree *in rem* is a bar to a suit in personam, and we cannot see why the rule should not work both ways." *Burns Bros.*, 202 F.2d at 913. The Court then found:

> When the plaintiff has two alternative remedies available to him upon the same "cause of action," he may not reserve one and sue upon the other, and a judgment for the defendant upon one will be a bar to a later suit upon the other; but obviously this rule ought not to apply when at the time of the first action only one of the two remedies was available to the plaintiff.... If we regard the "cause of action" at bar as the same as that in the first suit, as we must, the present libel *in rem* was an alternative remedy to the libel in personam, so that this appeal comes down to whether a libel *in rem* was "available" to Burns Bros, in the first suit, since, if it was, it could have been joined with the libel *in personam* under the 14th Admiralty Rule [now Rule C(l)(b) of the Supplemental Rules].

Id.

Judge Hand's discussion raises several points pertinent to the instant appeal. We note initially that Burns Bros, did not concern a suit filed to collect damages established by a prior judgment, but involved a suit to establish liability and damages anew. Burns Bros, thus does not govern a suit essentially seeking collection of an unpaid portion of a judgment against a joint tortfeasor. *See generally* Grant Gilmore & Charles L. Black, Jr., The Law of Admiralty § 9-17, at 614 n.73 (2d ed. 1975) ("A plaintiff who has recovered a judgment in an *in rem* action which remains in part unsatisfied may proceed against the owner *in personam* to recover the deficiency.").

Second, as the district court in the instant case noted, the Supplemental Rules do not require a party to bring *in rem* and *in personam* claims in the same action. Rule C(1)(b) of the Supplemental Rules specifically provides that "a party who may proceed *in rem* may also, or in the alternative, proceed *in personam* against any person who may be liable." (emphasis added). Thus Central Hudson is barred from bringing its *in personam* claim against Empresa, if a tall, by the doctrine of *res judicata* and not by the Admiralty Rules, a conclusion supported by Judge Hand's holding in *Burns Bros. See* 202 F.2d at 912-13. Indeed, while Central Hudson and the district court both read Rule C(l)(b) to "abrogate" the prior doctrine set forth in *Burns Bros.*, we decline to do so. Instead, *Burns Bros,* and its predecessors should be read simply to apply *res judicata* principles to successive *in rem* and *in personam* actions, a holding with which Rule C(l)(b) is not inconsistent.[2]

Finally, the 1966 Amendments to the Admiralty Rules did not affect the previously existing right of plaintiff's to file separate or successive *in rem* and *in personam* actions. As reflected in the Advisory Committee Notes to the 1966 Amendments, the Amendments were not intended to change prior law:

> The main concern of Admiralty Rules 13-18 [now Supplemental Rule E] was with the question whether certain actions might be brought *in rem* or also, or in the alternative, in personam. Essentially, therefore, these rules deal with questions of substantive law, for in general an action *in rem* may be brought to enforce any maritime lien, and no action *in personam* may be brought when the substantive law imposes no personal liability.

The dissenting opinion relies on *The B & B NO. 10*, 121 F. 2d 704 (2d Cir. 1941), in support of the argument that the doctrine of *res judicata* bars successive *in rem* and *in personam* actions. *B &B No. 10*, however, involved a claimant that split its cause of action, attempting to rely on a prior judgment of liability for damages to two of its barges in a subsequent action seeking damages to a third. *See id. B &B No. 10*, therefore, involved an action to recover additional damages, not an action to collect damages established in a prior action, and thus the holding is inapplicable here.

Supplemental Rule C(1) advisory committee's note (emphasis added). The fact that the 1966 Amendments did not affect *in rem* and *in personam* filings is further reflected in the case law. *Compare United States v. Matson Nav. Co.,* 201 F.2d 610, 618 (9th Cir. 1933) (pre-Amendment case holding that where causes of action arose from single collision, claimant could proceed *in rem* against ship and *in personam* against owner's and masters), *with Belcher Co. v. M/V MARATHA MARINER,* 724 F.2d 1161, 1163 (5th Cir. 1984) (post-Amendment case holding that "[u]nder the admiralty law of the United States, *in personam* and *in rem* actions may arise from the same claim, and may be brought separately or in the same suit"). Accordingly, we find that this *in personam* action is barred by the *in rem* judgment, if at all, only by the doctrine of *res* judicata, to which we now turn.

B. *Res Judicata*

The doctrine of *res judicata,* or claim preclusion, holds that following entry of a valid final judgment, "the parties to the suit and their privies are thereafter bound 'not only as to every matter which was offered and received to sustain or defeat the claim or demand, but as to any other admissible matter which might have been offered for that purpose.'" *C.I.R. v. Sunnen,* 333 U.S. 591, 597, 68 S. Ct. 715, 719, 92 L.Ed. 898 (1948) (quoting *Cromwell v. County of Sac,* 94 U.S. 351, 352, 24 L.Ed. 195 (1876)); *In re Teltronics Servs.,* 762 F.2d 185, 190 (2d Cir. 1985).[3] Empresa contends that *res judicata* bars this action because Central Fiudson could have sued Empresa in its *in personam* capacity during the *in rem* action, but failed to do so. In particular, Empresa asserts that Central Fiudson knew of its status as the Vessel's bareboat charterparty as early as August 1988, from depositions taken of the Vessel's crew, and that it was amenable to the district court's jurisdiction because it maintained a shipping agent in New York. It is undisputed that Central Fiudson knew of Empresa's relationship to the Vessel one month prior to trial, and did not move to amend its complaint to add an *in personam* claim. Central Fiudson contends, however, that it did not have sufficient knowledge to name Empresa as a defendant because Empresa concealed its interests in the Vessel as part owner and bareboat charterparty, despite a discovery order by a magistrate judge. Central Fiudson argues that Empresa should not now be rewarded by the barring of this action for this obstruction of discovery.

Such allegations may be considered by this Court in assessing the availability of a claim for *res judicata* purposes. *See La Societe Anonyme des Parfums Le Galion v. Jean Patou, Inc.,* 495 F.2d 1265, 1276 (2d Cir. 1974). While the district court noted that Empresa's specific interest in the Vessel was "lurking in the background" of the *in rem* action, however, the court did not address directly the issue of Empresa's availability. We need not do so either, as we find Central Fiudson's claim would not be barred by *res judicata* even if Empresa had been available.

Notably, Central Fiudson did not seek duplicative or additional damages in this action, and the essence of its claim was that Empresa, as the operator of the Vessel, was also liable as a joint tortfeasor for the damage to its cable pipeline. When a litigant files consecutive lawsuits against separate parties for the same injury, the entry of a judgment in the prior action does not bar the claims against other potentially liable parties. *See United States v. Lacey,* 982 F.2d 410, 412 (10th Cir. 1992); *White v. Kelsey,* 935 F.2d 968, 970 (8th Cir. 1991); *Gill & Dujfus Servs. v. A.M. Nural Islam,* 675 F.2d 404, 406-07 (D.C. Cir. 1982) *(per curiam); McClelland v. Facteau,* 610 F.2d 693, 695 n.l (10th Cir. 1979); *see generally* RESTATEMENT (SECOND) OF JUDGMENTS § 49 cmt. a (1982) (For preclusion purposes, "the claim against others who are liable for the same harm is regarded as separate."); 18 CHARLES A. WRIGHT, ARTHUR R. MILLER & EDWARD H.COOPER, FEDERAL PRACTICE AND PROCEDURE § 4407, at 52-53 ("A single plaintiff ... has as many causes of action as there are defendants to pursue."). Since Central Hudson's *in personam* claim against Empresa is distinct from its claim against the Vessel in rem, and since the *in personam* claim has not been adjudicated, *res judicata* does not bar this action. *See Montana v. United States,* 440 U.S. 147, 154, 99 S. Ct. 970, 974, 59 L. Ed. 2d 210 (1979) ("A cause of action which a non-party has vicariously asserted differs by definition from that which he subsequently seeks to litigate in his own right."); *Gargiul v. Tompkins,* 790 F.2d 265, 272-73 (2d Cir. 1986).

---

[3] As a preliminary matter, since both parties attempt to employ the preclusive effects of the judgment in the *in rem* action, this appeal appears to raise issues traditionally considered under the rule of mutuality. This rule conferred the positive preclusive effects of a judgment only on those parties who also would have been bound by any unfavorable preclusive effects of that judgment. *See* 18 Charles A. Wright, Arthur R. Miller & Edward H. Cooper, Federal Practice and Procedure § 4463, at 559 (1981). Following the Supreme Court's decision in *Nevada v. United States,* 463 U.S. 110, 143-44, 103 S.Ct. 2906, 2924-25, 77 L.Ed.2d 509 (1983), however, this Circuit generally no longer considers mutuality for preclusion purposes. *See Amalgamated Sugar Co. v. NL Indus.,* 825 F.2d 634, 640 (2d Cir.), *cert, denied,* 484 U.S. 992, 108 S.Ct. 511, 98 L. Ed. 2d 511 (1987); *Cahill v. Arthur Andersen & Co.,* 659 F. Supp. 1115, 1120-21 (S.D.N.Y. 1986), *aff'd,* 822 F.2d 14 (2d Cir. 1987) *(per curiam).* We thus need not consider the preclusive effects of a different result in the *in rem* action when reviewing the arguments of either party.

This assumes, of course, that Empresa was not in privity with the Vessel, despite its assistance in the defense of the *in rem* action. Privity traditionally has denoted a "successive relationship to the same rights of property." *Bailey,* 49 F. at 585. In its modern form, the principle of privity bars relitigation of the same cause of action against a new defendant known by a plaintiff at the time of the first suit where the new defendant has a sufficiently close relationship to the original defendant to justify preclusion. *See Amalgamated Sugar Co. v. NL Indus.,* 825 F.2d 634, 640 (2d Cir.), *cert. denied,* 484 U.S. 992, 108 S. Ct. 511, 98 L. Ed. 2d 511 (1987). This determination often requires a court to inquire whether a party "control[led] or substantially participate[d] in the control of the presentation on behalf of a party" to the prior action. *National Fuel Gas Distribution Corp. v. TGX Corp.,* 950 F.2d 829, 839 (2d Cir. 1991) (quotation omitted); *see also Alpert's Newspaper Delivery v. New York Times Co.,* 876 F.2d 266, 270 (2d Cir. 1989).

Undoubtedly, Empresa participated in and shared control of the defense of the Vessel in the *in rem* action. Empresa did so, however, in a representative capacity. Its interests in the Vessel therefore were not identical to the interests it defended in an action alleging *in personam* liability. *Cf. United States v. International Bhd. of Teamsters,* 964 F.2d 180, 184 (2d Cir. 1992) (concluding privity requires coinciding interests to third parties). Because the *res judicata* effects of the *in rem* judgment affect Empresa only in its representative capacity, we find that Empresa was not in privity with the Vessel. *See Hurt v. Pullman, Inc.,* 764 F.2d 1443, 1448 (11th Cir. 1985); *cf.* Restatement (Second) of Judgments § 39 cmt. e (1982) ("[A] trustee who takes control of litigation involving another in order to protect the trust is not on that account bound in a subsequent action in which he appears in his individual capacity.").

* * *

Accordingly, we find that the *in rem* judgment does not bar this action.

Finding that neither the Admiralty Rules nor *res judicata* bar this *in personam* action, we next address Empresas contention that the district court incorrectly made a finding of *in personam* liability by applying the doctrine of collateral estoppel. Collateral estoppel, or issue preclusion, bars the relitigation of issues actually litigated and decided in the prior proceeding, as long as that determination was essential to that judgment. *See Beck v. Levering,* 947 F.2d 639, 642 (2d Cir. 1991) *(per curiam), cert. denied sub nom., Levy v. Martin,* 504 U.S. 909, 112 S. Ct. 1937, 118 L. Ed. 2d 544 (1992). Four elements must be met for collateral estoppel to apply: (1) the issues of both proceedings must be identical, (2) the relevant issues were actually litigated and decided in the prior proceeding, (3) there must have been "full and fair opportunity" for the litigation of the issues in the prior proceeding, and (4) the issues were necessary to support a valid and final judgment on the merits. *See Gelb v. Royal Globe Ins. Co.,* 798 F.2d 38, 44 (2d Cir. 1986) (setting forth four-part test), *cert. denied,* 480 U.S. 948, 107 S. Ct. 1608, 94 L. Ed. 2d 794 (1987). If these requirements were met, the district court properly estopped Empresa from relitigating the issue of liability for the damage to the cable pipeline. *See Beck,* 947 F.2d at 642 (applying *Gelb* test to offensive collateral estoppel).

Empresa does not contend that the district court improperly estopped it from litigating the issue of Central Hudsons quantum of damages, and contests only the district court's finding of liability. Specifically, Empresa argues that (1) it had no "full and fair opportunity" to litigate its liability in the *in rem* action, (2) its liability was neither litigated nor decided in that action, and (3) since Central Hudson had the opportunity to join Empresa as a defendant in the *in rem* action and failed to do so, collateral estoppel does not apply. We reject each of these arguments.

Given its control of and participation in the litigation, Empresa cannot seriously contend that it had no "full and fair opportunity" to litigate all issues decided in the *in rem* trial. *Cf. Sherman v. Kirshman,* 369 F.2d 886 (2d Cir. 1966) (refusing to enforce judgment entered against defendants in another federal district court where the prior judgment was *in rem* and where defendants neither appeared nor litigated action). We thus turn to the central issue: whether Empresa's liability was fully litigated and decided in the *in rem* action.

Empresa first contends that its liability was not determined in the *in rem* action because the district court never distinguished whether the Vessels crew, or the pilots Empresa was required to hire to steer the Vessel up the Hudson River, were responsible for the damage to the cable pipeline. Empresa offered the possible negligence of the compulsory pilots as an affirmative defense in the instant action. Empresa thus bore the burden of establishing the pilots' exclusive negligence. *See Avondale Indus, v. International Marine Carriers*, 15 E3d 489, 492-93 (5th Cir. 1994) (discussing negligence standards governing relationship of vessel master to compulsory pilot). Empresa failed to provide any evidence of this defense, much less enough to establish a genuine issue of material fact for trial. *See* Fed. R. Civ. P. 56(e); *Matsushita Elec. Indus, v. Zenith Radio Corp.*, 475 U.S. 574, 586-87, 106 S. Ct. 1348, 1355-56, 89 L. Ed. 2d 538 (1986). Further, neither *Empresa* nor *Seiriki* even raised this defense in the *in rem* trial, nor did Empresa seek to implead the pilots as co-defendants during either action. *See The CHINA*, 74 U.S. (7 Wall.) 53, 64, 19 L.Ed. 67 (1868) (party asserting compulsory pilot defense must show "affirmatively that the pilot was in fault, and that there was no fault on the part of the officers or crew, which might have been in any degree conducive to the damage") (quotation omitted). Empresa's compulsory pilot defense, in short, has no bearing here.

Empresa also contends that the district court's liability determination in the *in rem* action was limited solely to the Vessel, and that it made no finding of Empresa's liability due to the negligence of its officers and crew. The parties entered into a stipulation during the *in rem* trial, however, in which they agreed that the Vessel's officers and crew were negligent if the court determined that the Vessel's anchor caused the damage to the pipeline:[4]

> It has been stipulated by counsel for Central Hudson and counsel for the defendant that if the Court finds the LUNAMAR II dragged her starboard anchor on the Hudson River, then the LUNAMAR II stipulates that relevant statutory regulations and proper navigational precautions and practices were not followed by the crew and officers of the LUNAMAR II.

The district court then explicitly found that the damage to Central Hudson's pipeline was caused by the dragging of the Vessel's anchor, thereby also determining the negligence of the Vessel's officers and crew. Moreover, as the bareboat charterparty, Empresa was considered the owner of the Vessel pro hac vice. *See Reed v. Steamship YAKA*, 373 U.S. 410, 83 S. Ct. 1349, 10 L. Ed. 2d 448 (1963); *Bergan v. International Freighting Corp.*, 254 F.2d 231, 232 (2d Cir. 1958). Thus, Empresa was clearly liable under the principle of respondeat superior for the negligence of the Vessel's officers and crew, who were in fact Empresa's employees. *See The BARNSTABLE*, 181 U.S. 464, 468, 21 S. Ct. 684, 686, 45 L.Ed. 954 (1901) ("As the charterers hired the Barnstable for a definite period, and agreed to select their own officers and crew, ... the charterers would be liable for the consequences of negligence in her navigation."); *Uni-Petrol Gesellschaft Fur Mineraloel Produkte M.B.H. v. M/T LOTUS MARU*, 615 F. Supp. 78, 80-81 (S.D.N.Y. 1985). The district court's determination that the Vessel caused the damage to the pipeline therefore entailed a finding of Empresa's liability, and that issue was both necessary to the *in rem* judgment and fully litigated by the parties.

Finally, Empresa argues that it was available as a defendant in the *in rem* action, and asserts that Central Hudson's failure to join it as a defendant precludes its reliance on the collateral estoppel doctrine. Empresa relies on dicta in *Parklane Hosiery Co. v. Shore*, 439 U.S. 322, 99 S. Ct. 645, 58 L. Ed. 2d 552 (1979), as support for its argument. There, the Supreme Court stated the "general rule" that offensive collateral estoppel should not apply "in cases where a plaintiff could easily have joined in the earlier action or where ... the application of offensive collateral estoppel would be unfair to a defendant." *Id.* at 331, 99 S. Ct. at 652. *Parklane Hosiery* concerned a plaintiff, filing suit on behalf of a class of stockholders, who failed to join an earlier action filed against the same defendants on

---

[4] *Empresa* argues that because the parties did not manifest an intent to be bound by this stipulation in a subsequent action, the issue of the negligence of the officers and crew was not "actually litigated" for estoppel purposes in the *in rem* action. *See Red Lake Band v. United States*, 607 F.2d 930, 934, 221 Ct. Cl. 325 (Ct. Cl. 1979). Because a finding of negligence on the part of the Vessel's officers and crew was essential to the district court's determination of liability, we find that the parties intended the stipulation to be binding. While it is true, as the dissenting opinion appears to argue, that not every stipulation necessary to a finding of liability sufficiently manifests the parties' intent to be bound in subsequent litigation, as the district court held the facts established in the *in rem* action are sufficient to support such a finding here. We therefore reject this argument.

the same cause of action by the Securities and Exchange Commission (SEC). The Supreme Court did not apply the general rule to the class action, finding that the stockholders probably could not have joined in the action filed by the SEC. *See id.* at 331-33, 99 S. Ct. at 651-53. These facts do not suggest the inapplicability of collateral estoppel to successive cases involving the same plaintiff and separate defendants, and in any case the *Parklane Hosiery* Court noted the "preferable approach ... [is] to grant trial courts broad discretion" in determining when collateral estoppel should apply. *Id.* at 331, 99 S. Ct. at 651. We agree with the district court that the facts of this case amply support the application of collateral estoppel. *See, e.g., Beck,* 947 F.2d at 642 (affirming use of offensive collateral estoppel against defendants who were not defendants in prior action). Moreover, none of the fairness concerns recognized by the Supreme Court in Parklane Hosiery are present here, as the *in rem* action did not involve small or nominal damages and the *in personam* action afforded Empresa no procedural opportunities previously unavailable to it. *See Parklane Hosiery,* 439 U.S. at 330-31, 99 S. Ct. at 651-52. The district court therefore properly found Empresa collaterally estopped from contesting its liability for the unrecovered portion of the *in rem* judgment.

* * *

For the reasons stated above, we affirm the judgment of the district court in all respects.

* * *

The dissenting opinion of Judge Jacobs is omitted (eds.).

E. Maritime Attachment

Introductory Note: The Process of Foreign Attachment: Historical Background and Purpose

In *Trans-Asiatic Oil Ltd., S.A. v. Apex Oil Co.,* 604 F. Supp. 4, 1984 AMC 2741 (D.FR. 1983), *aff'd,* 804 F.2d 773, 1987 AMC 1115 (1st Cir. 1986), the history and purpose of maritime attachment was considered by the district court which stated the following:

* * *

The process of foreign attachment which plaintiff used in this case has been recognized to be of ancient origin and preceding the founding of this Republic. As stated in *Manro v. Almeida,* 23 U.S. (10 Wheat.) 206, 6 L. Ed. 369 (1825):

> Thus, this process has the clearest sanction in the practice of the civil law, and during the three years that the admiralty courts of these states were referred to the practice of the civil law for their "forms and modes of proceeding," there could have been no question that this process was legalized. Nor is there anything in the different phraseology adopted in the act of 1792, that could preclude its use. That it is agreeable to the "principles, rules and usages, which belong to courts of admiralty," is established, not only by its being resorted to in one at least of the courts of the United States, but by the explicit declaration of a book of respectable authority, and remote origin, in which it is laid down thus: "If the defendant has concealed himself, or has absconded from the kingdom, so that he cannot be arrested, if he have *[sic*any goods, merchandise, ship or vessel, on the sea, or within the ebb or flow of the sea, and within the jurisdiction of the Lord High Admiral, a warrant is to be impetrated to this effect, *viz.,* to attach such goods or ship of D., the defendant, in whose hands soever they may be; and to cite the said D. specially as the owner, and all others who claim any right to title to them, to be and appear on a certain day to answer unto P., in a civil and maritime cause.

The process of foreign attachment, developed to meet the necessities of those engaged in the multiple aspects of martime commerce has two purposes as established in *Swift & Co. v. Compania Colombiana,* 339 U.S. 684, 70 S. Ct. 861, 94 L. Ed. 1206 (1949): (1) to secure the appearance of the respondents and (2) to secure satisfaction in case the suit is successful. *See also San Rafael Compania Naviera, S.A. v. American Smelting & Refining Co.,* 327 F.2d 581, 589 (9th Cir. 1964). It should be noted that foreign attachment was originally found in Rule 2 of the former Rules of Admiralty which, after the unification of those rules with the F.R.C.P. in 1966, became Supplemental Rule B.

* * *

Rule B. In Personam Actions: Attachment and Garnishment

(1) When Available; Complaint, Affidavit, Judicial Authorization, and Process.

In an in personam action:

(a) If a defendant is not found within the district when a verified complaint praying for attachment and the affidavit required by Rule B(1)(b) are filed, a verified complaint may contain a prayer for process to attach the defendant's tangible or intangible personal property--up to the amount sued for--in the hands of garnishees named in the process.

(b) The plaintiff or the plaintiff's attorney must sign and file with the complaint an affidavit stating that, to the affiant's knowledge, or on information and belief, the defendant cannot be found within the district. The court must review the complaint and affidavit and, if the conditions of this Rule B appear to exist, enter an order so stating and authorizing process of attachment and garnishment. The clerk may issue supplemental process enforcing the court's order upon application without further court order.

(c) If the plaintiff or the plaintiff's attorney certifies that exigent circumstances make court review impracticable, the clerk must issue the summons and process of attachment and garnishment. The plaintiff has the burden in any post-attachment hearing under Rule E(4)(f) to show that exigent circumstances existed.

(d)(i) If the property is a vessel or tangible property on board a vessel, the summons, process, and any supplemental process must be delivered to the marshal for service.

(ii) If the property is other tangible or intangible property, the summons, process, and any supplemental process must be delivered to a person or organization authorized to serve it, who may be (A) a marshal; (B) someone under contract with the United States; (C) someone specially appointed by the court for that purpose; or, (D) in an action brought by the United States, any officer or employee of the United States.

(e) The plaintiff may invoke state-law remedies under Rule 64 for seizure of person or property for the purpose of securing satisfaction of the judgment.

(2) Notice to Defendant.
No default judgment may be entered except upon proof--which may be by affidavit--that:

(a) the complaint, summons, and process of attachment or garnishment have been served on the defendant in a manner authorized by Rule 4;

(b) the plaintiff or the garnishee has mailed to the defendant the complaint, summons, and process of attachment or garnishment, using any form of mail requiring a return receipt; or

(c) the plaintiff or the garnishee has tried diligently to give notice of the action to the defendant but could not do so.

(3) Answer.

(a) By Garnishee. The garnishee shall serve an answer, together with answers to any interrogatories served with the complaint, within 21 days after service of process upon the garnishee. Interrogatories to the garnishee may be served with the complaint without leave of court. If the garnishee refuses or neglects to answer on oath as to the debts, credits, or effects of the defendant in the garnishee's hands, or any interrogatories concerning such debts, credits, and effects that may be propounded by the plaintiff, the court may award compulsory process against the garnishee. If the garnishee admits any debts, credits, or effects, they shall be held in the garnishee's hands or paid into the registry of the court, and shall be held in either case subject to the further order of the court.

(b) By Defendant. The defendant shall serve an answer within 30 days after process has been executed, whether by attachment of property or service on the garnishee.

CREDIT(S)

(Added Feb. 28, 1966, eff. July 1, 1966, and amended Apr. 29, 1985, eff. Aug. 1, 1985; Mar. 2, 1987, eff. Aug. 1, 1987; Apr. 17, 2000, eff. Dec. 1, 2000.)

Note

For an overview of maritime attachment procedure under Rule B, see *Jarvis, An Introduction to Maritime Attachment Practice Under Rule B,* 20 J. MAR. L. & COM. 521 (1989).

---

2. Cases and Notes: *The Nature of Rule B Jurisdiction*

a. Quasi In Rem *Proceedings*

EAST ASIATIC CO., LTD. v. INDOMAR, LTD.

422 F. Supp. 1335, 1976 AMC 2039 (S.D.N.Y. 1976)

ENNEY, District Judge

Indomar, Ltd. ("Indomar"), a Bahamian corporation, moves pursuant to Rule 60(b)(1) of the Federal Rules of Civil Procedure ("Rules") for an order correcting and amending a default judgment entered against it as defendant in an admiralty proceeding. The original action arose in connection with an alleged breach of a charter party between Indomar and East Asiatic Co., Ltd. ("East Asiatic"), the plaintiff's in the prior action and the current opponents to the motion to amend. Indomar defaulted, and judgment was had against it for $1,149,577.77, the entire amount claimed in East Asiatics complaint, plus costs. Indomar moves to reduce that figure to $16,883.76, asserting that the lesser sum represents the maximum liability exposed to the Courts jurisdiction in the original proceedings. East Asiatic contends that the Court properly possessed jurisdiction to award the sum contained in the judgment and pleads that it be permitted to stand. For the reasons stated below, Indomar's motion to correct and amend the judgment is granted.

I

East Asiatic began its action against Indomar by process of maritime attachment levied against $16,883.76 of defendant's assets located within the Southern District of New York. Since the unification of admiralty and civil procedure, see Order of Supreme Court of United States, 383 U.S. 1031 (1966), maritime attachment procedure has been governed by Rule B of the Supplemental Rules for Certain Admiralty and Maritime Claims of the Federal Rules of Civil Procedure ("Supplemental Rules").[1] Maritime attachment is, however, a traditional remedy whose "origin is to be found in the remotest history, as well of the civil as of the common law." *Manro v. Almeida,* 23 U.S. (10 Wheat.) 473, 490, 6 L. Ed. 369 (1825). The remedy has "a dual purpose: (1) to obtain jurisdiction of the respondent *in personam* through his property and (2) to assure satisfaction of any decree in libelants favor." *Seawind Compania, S.A. v. Crescent Line, Inc.,* 320 F.2d 580 (2d Cir. 1963) (*Seawind)*'*; see Swift & Company Packers v. Compania Columbiana Del Caribe, S.A.,* 339 U.S. 684, 70 S. Ct. 861, 94 L. Ed. 1206 (1950); *Chilean Line Inc. v. United States,* 344 F.2d 757, 760 (2d Cir. 1965); 2 E. BENEDICT, ADMIRALTY, § 288 (6th ed. A. Knauth 1940) (BENEDICT). The historic rule, which is followed in this Circuit, is that "[t]he two purposes may not be separated ... for security cannot be obtained except as an adjunct to obtaining jurisdiction." *Seawind, supra,* 320 F.2d at 582; 2 BENEDICT, *supra,* § 288.

---

[1] Supplemental Rule B reads in pertinent part:

Attachment and Garnishment: Special Provisions

(1) When Available; Complaint, Affidavit, and Process. With respect to any admiralty or maritime claim *in personam* a verified complaint may contain a prayer for process to attach the defendant's goods and chattels, or credits and effects in the hands of garnishees named in the complaint to the amount sued for, if the defendant shall not be found within the district. Such a complaint shall be accompanied by an affidavit signed by the plaintiff or his attorney that, to the affiant's knowledge, or to the best of his information and belief, the defendant cannot be found within the district. When a verified complaint is supported by such an affidavit the clerk shall forthwith issue a summons and process of attachment and garnishment. In addition, or in the alternative, the plaintiff may, pursuant to Rule 4(e), invoke the remedies provided by state law for attachment and garnishment or similar seizure of the defendant's property. Except for Rule E(8) these Supplemental Rules do not apply to state remedies so invoked.

(2) Notice to Defendant. No judgment by default shall be entered except upon proof, which may be by affidavit, (a) that the plaintiff or the garnishee has given notice of the action to the defendant by mailing to him a copy of the complaint, summons, and process of attachment or garnishment, using any from of mail requiring a return receipt, or (b) that the complaint, summons, and process of attachment or garnishment have been served on the defendant in a manner authorized by Rule 4(d) or (i), or (c) that the plaintiff or the garnishee has made diligent efforts to give notice of the action to the defendant and has been unable to do so.

East Asiatic overlooks this rule, however, and in substance contends that use of the maritime attachment process under Supplemental Rule B does not preclude the simultaneous assertion of pure *in personam* jurisdiction over defendant. Thus, East Asiatic alleges that this Court had in personam jurisdiction[2] over Indomar not only by virtue of the maritime attachment but also through compliance with the standard requirements for *in personam* jurisdiction, *i.e.,* that Indomar had sufficient contacts with the forum and that substituted service of process was made in accordance with Rule 4. Making this assertion, however, East Asiatic misapprehends the nature of maritime attachment and the relationship of Supplemental Rule B to the main body of the Federal Rules of Civil Procedure. Unification of admiralty and civil procedure has not abrogated the traditional jurisdictional function of maritime attachment, and compliance with Supplemental Rule B does not constitute service of process under Rule 4.

In admiralty, as in civil law, the courts direct *in personam* jurisdiction over defendant depends upon the latter's contacts with the forum and the correct service of process. *Ivanhoe Trading Co. v. M/S Bornholm,* 160 F. Supp. 900 (S.D.N.Y. 1957); *Arpad Szabo v. Smedvig Tankrederi A.S.,* 95 F. Supp. 519 (S.D.N.Y. 1951); *Belgian Mission for Economic Cooperation v. Zarati Steamship Co., Ltd.,* 90 F. Supp. 741 (S.D.N.Y. 1950). Maritime attachment, on the other hand, is available to the plaintiff only when the defendant is not "found" within the district. Supplemental Rule B(l). To determine whether defendant is "found" within the district "a two-pronged inquiry [is made]: first, whether [defendant] can be found within the district in terms of jurisdiction, and second, if so, whether it can be found for service of process." *United States v. Cia. Naviera Continental S.A.,* 178 F. Supp. 561, 563 (S.D.N.Y. 1959); *see Chilean Line Inc. v. United States,* 344 F.2d 757, 760 (2d Cir. 1965); *Seawind, supra,* 320 F.2d at 582. If either inquiry produces a negative answer, attachment is permitted.[3] This two-pronged test results in a small group of cases where, in theory, plaintiff could acquire *in personam* jurisdiction either by traditional means or through maritime attachment. 2 BENEDICT, *supra,* §288; 7A MOORE'S FEDERAL PRACTICE ¶ B.03. For example, a defendant having an agent in the district and doing business within the state—but not within the district—would be subject either to maritime attachment jurisdiction or to pure *in personam* jurisdiction. However, there is no case cited to this Court wherein both methods of acquiring *in personam* jurisdiction were simultaneously employed. Nor can there logically be such a case, for such a holding would reduce maritime attachment to nothing more than a security lien. This cannot be done, for "[i]t is crystal clear that the historical purpose of the writ of foreign attachment is to compel the respondent's appearance. Although an incidental purpose thereof is to supply the libelant with security, this objective can only be obtained as an adjunct to jurisdiction." *D/S A/S Flint v. Sabre Shipping Corp.,* 228 F. Supp. 384, 388 (E.D.N.Y. 1964), *aff'd sub nom. Det Bergenske Dampskibesselskab v. Sabre Shipping Corp.,* 341 F.2d 50 (2d Cir. 1965) (*"Flint v. Sabre"*).

Unification of admiralty and civil procedure has done nothing to distort this basic principle, although East Asiatic apparently interprets the Notes of Advisory Committee on Supplemental Rule B ("Advisory Notes") as permitting the simultaneous acquisition of *in personam* jurisdiction by conventional process and by maritime attachment. This Court does not agree. The text in question reads as follows:

---

[2] All suits in admiralty are denominated either *"in personam* or *"in rem."* The *in rem* proceeding, which does not concern us here, is against the thing itself and operates after plaintiff has acquired a lien against the property "The lien and the proceedings *in rem* are, therefore, correlative—where one exists, the other can be taken, and not otherwise." *The Rock Island Bridge,* 73 U.S. (6 Wall.) 213, 215, 18 L. Ed. 753 (1867); *see* Supplemental Rule C. Suits *in personam,* like the one at bar, are against an individual and do not depend upon the acquisition of a maritime lien. Benedict states that

[m]ost actions may be maintained either *in rem* (if there is a maritime lien on a *res* in the jurisdiction) or *in personam* (if the defendant or respondent can be personally served with process or reached by means of an attachment proceeding), or both *in rem* and *in personam.* Benedict, *supra,* § 226.

[3] Because maritime attachment operates on a defendant by tying up his property prior to the determination of his liability, *Thyssen Steel Corp. v. Federal Commerce & Navigation Co.,* 274 F. Supp. 18 (S.D.N.Y. 1967), litigation in this area has largely turned on whether defendant could defeat an often onerous attachment by demonstrating that he is "found" within the district. The theory behind the typical maritime attachment controversy was expressed in *Federazione Italiana Dei Consorzi Agrariv. Mandask Compania De Vapores, S.A.,* 158 F. Supp. 107, 111 (S.D.N.Y. 1957):

In the usual case it is the libelant who asserts that the respondent's activities in the district are sufficient to make it amenable to service, and the respondent in turn denies that it was doing business in the district in this sense. Here the reverse is true for it appears to the advantage of the libelant to claim that the respondent is not doing business within the district so that it may be free to attach the very substantial funds standing to respondent's credit here, whereas the respondent affirmatively asserts that it is doing business here, and that it could have been served had the libelant been so minded.

See Antco Shipping Company v. Yukon Compania Naviera, S.A., 318 F. Supp. 626 (S.D.N.Y. 1970) (attempted attachment of defendant's ship); McCreary, *Going for the Jugular Vein: Arrests and Attachments in Admiralty,* 28 Ohio St. L.J. 19 (1967).

The case at bar presents the unusual situation where plaintiff opts to commence proceedings by attaching a mere fraction of the claim asserted, and defendant chooses not to protect theses assets either by special appearance to dispute the attachment, Supplemental Rule E(8), or by general appearance to defend against the complaint.

A change in the context of the practice is brought about by Rule 4(f), which will enable summons to be served throughout the state instead of, as heretofore, only within the district. The Advisory Committee considered whether the rule on attachment and garnishment should be correspondingly changed to permit those remedies only when the defendant cannot be found within the state and concluded that the remedy should not be so limited.

The effect is to enlarge the class of cases in which the plaintiff may proceed by attachment or garnishment although jurisdiction of the person may be independently obtained. This is possible at the present time where, for example, a corporate defendant has appointed an agent within the district to accept service of process but is not carrying on activities there sufficient to subject it to jurisdiction ... or where, though the foreign corporations activities in the district are sufficient to subject it personally to the jurisdiction, there is in the district no officer on whom process can be served. (Citations omitted).

The enlargement of which the Advisory Notes speak refers to a situation which prevailed prior to the unification of admiralty and civil procedure in 1966. At that time an admiralty defendant doing sufficient business in the district but subject to service only beyond its borders, although within the state, could be subjected to the in personam jurisdiction of the court solely through process of maritime attachment. This class of defendants is now amenable to traditional *in personam* jurisdiction through the statewide service permitted by Rule 4(f). However, the Advisory Notes make it plain that these defendants remain vulnerable to attachment, and thus a plaintiff may proceed against them either by Rule 4(f) process or by maritime attachment. At the same time, Supplemental Rule B continues to permit attachment by a plaintiff proceeding against a foreign corporation which, although "present" in the district through its activities, can be reached for service only through extraterritorial process under Rule 4(e) or 4(i). In other words, the Advisory Notes recognize that attachment continues to be an option in certain cases where pure *in personam* jurisdiction might be alternatively achieved over the same defendants. But plaintiff cannot compel the defendants appearance through Rule 4 and, at the same time, attach its property through Supplemental Rule B. Compelling defendants appearance through extra-district process obviates the need to compel that appearance through maritime attachment. This Court cannot conclude that in widening a class of cases in which plaintiff may choose his approach, the Advisory Committee intended to undermine the venerable jurisdictional rationale of maritime attachment.

Moreover, even if it is assumed that use of maritime attachment does not preclude the simultaneous use of Rule 4 process to achieve pure *in personam* jurisdiction over the defendant, East Asiatic has not accomplished service upon Indomar as mandated by Rule 4. East Asiatic argues that in complying with the notice provisions of Supplemental Rule B(2) it satisfied the service requirements of Rule 4 and cites the various references to Rule 4 in Supplemental Rule B to support its contention that Supplemental Rule B is "a statute of the United States ... [which] provides for service of a summons ... upon a party not an inhabitant of or found within the state in which the district court is held," as provided for in Rule 4. Plaintiff overlooks the fact that Supplemental Rule B in no way concerns service of process, which, indeed, is not required to effect maritime attachment under Supplemental Rule The Rule is by its own terms a form of process, and its operation confers jurisdiction on the court. Supplemental Rule B does not even direct that notice be given to defendant until such time as default judgment is to be entered. And notice is then given purely on the ground of "fairness," since "none is required by the principles of due process." Advisory Notes, Subdivision (2). The method of communicating this default notice is governed internally by Supplemental Rule B(2).

Although East Asiatic did comply with Supplemental Rule B(2) in notifying Indomar before default was entered, this notification was no more than that necessary to permit execution thereafter on the property attached, and bears no significance with respect to service of process under Rule 4. Nor may East Asiatic state that it has conformed to any of the other provisions of Rule 4. It has not complied with the Rule 4(e) alternative which permits service as provided by "any statute or rule of the court of the state in which the district court is held." It has not satisfied the requirements of New York Business Corporation Law §307 (McKinney Supp. 1975), which, in conjunction with

New York CPLR §302 (McKinney Supp. 1975), permits service upon a non-domiciliary corporation transacting business within the state if service is made upon the Secretary of State. Finally, East Asiatic has not met any of the terms of Rule 4(i) relating to service in a foreign country, and it is not proceeding against an in state defendant within the contemplation of Rule 4(d)(3) and Rule 4(f).

II.

Having determined that East Asiatic had but one base of *in personam* jurisdiction against Indomar, *i.e.,* that which it acquired through maritime attachment, it remains only to determine the effect of a default judgment in these circumstances. Although the jurisdiction achieved through maritime attachment is denominated *in personam,* it is clear that, absent an appearance by defendant, the judgment had is in the nature of *quasi in rem.* Indeed, the term "*quasi in rem*" is used in the title of Supplemental Rule E, which concerns actions commenced by maritime attachment. *See* Supplemental Rule E. The United States Court of Appeals for the Second Circuit has referred to Supplemental Rule B(1) as "a *quasi in rem* proceeding." *Maryland Tuna Corp. v. MS Benares,* 429 F.2d 307, 311 (2d Cir. 1970); *see Societe Commerciale de Transports Transatlantiques (S.C.T.T.) v. S.S. "African Mercury",* 366 F. Supp. 1347 (S.D.N.Y. 1973).

Although attachment may issue against property held for the defendant in the district up to the amount sued for, *see* Supplemental Rule B(1), "execution in proceedings commenced by maritime *in personam* attachments in which defendant has not been personally served or appeared cannot exceed the value of the attached property." 7A Moore's Federal Practice ¶ B.03 n.6 (2d ed. 1972); *see* 2 Benedict, *supra,* § 288. The same proposition is well established outside admiralty. In *Cooper v. Reynolds,* 10 Wall. 308, 19 L. Ed. 931 (1870), the Supreme Court discussed the limits of a judgment based on jurisdiction over the *res* rather than over the persona. "[T]he judgment of the court, though in form a personal judgment against the defendant, has no effect beyond the property attached in that suit. No general execution can be issued for any balance unpaid after the attached property is exhausted." *Id.* at 318-19, 19 L. Ed. 931; *see Freeman v. Alderson,* 119 U.S. 185, 7 S. Ct. 165, 30 L. Ed. 372 (1886); *Pennoyer v. Neff,* 95 U.S. 714, 24 L. Ed. 565 (1878). The judgment in such a case is not entitled to full faith and credit in another district. *See Sherman v. Kirshman,* 369 F.2d 886, 889 (2d Cir. 1966).

Although it is possible that East Asiatic could have achieved pure *in personam* jurisdiction over Indomar in this Court through the defendant's contacts with the forum and receipt of perfected service, it elected to proceed by means of a Supplemental Rule B attachment, which then represented the sole basis of the Court's jurisdiction over Indomar. Since Indomar did not appear to perfect the Court's *in personam* jurisdiction, *see Atkins v. Fibre Disintegrating Co.,* 85 U.S. (18 Wall.) 272, 21 L. Ed. 841 (1873),[4] East Asiatic's recovery is limited according to the principles of *quasi in rem* jurisdiction. In order to avoid possible harassment of the defendant through improper registration of an unenforceable judgment in another district, *see* 28 U.S.C. § 1963,[5] the judgment against Indomar must be reduced to $16,883.76, the extent of the property subjected to the process of maritime attachment.

Submit amended judgment in conformity herewith.

So ordered.

---

[4] In a case commenced by maritime attachment, defendants made a general appearance. The court noted that "[t] his made their position just what it would have been if they had been brought in regularly by the service of process. In this aspect of the case all defects were cured and the jurisdiction of the court over their persons became complete. This warranted the decree *in personam* for the amount adjudged to the libellants." *Atkins v. Fibre Disintegrating Co., supra,* 85 U.S. at 298.

Section 1963 reads as follows:

§ 1963. Registration in Other Districts

A judgment in an action for the recovery of money or property now or hereafter entered in any district court which has become final by appeal or expiration of time for appeal may be registered in any other district by filing therein a certified copy of such judgment. A judgment so registered shall have the same effect as a judgment of the district court of the district where registered and may be enforced in like manner.

A certified copy of the satisfaction of any judgment in whole or in part may be registered in like manner in any district in which the judgment is a lien.

Notes

1. *But see, Stevedoring Services of America v. Ancora Transport,* 941 F.2d 1378, 1992 AMC 883 (9th Cir. 1991), *cert. granted and judgment vacated by,* 506 U.S. 1043, 113 S. Ct. 955, 122 L. Ed. 2d 112 (1993), *on remand to,* 59 E3d 879, 1995 AMC 2688 (9th Cir. 1995), where the court intimated that it is possible for a plaintiff to invoke both *quasi in rem* (via attachment) and *in personam* (via service of process) jurisdiction in the same proceeding:

> While it is true that SSA was free to assert both *quasi in rem* and *in personam* jurisdiction by serving the defendants not in that district but in the state, SSA alleged no facts in its complaint asserting appellees were subject to personal jurisdiction of the court, nor did they properly serve them to obtain personal jurisdiction.

2. The Nature of an Attachment Action

In *Teyseer Cement Company v. Halla Maritime Corporation,* 794 F.2d 472, 476-77, 1986 AMC 2705 (9th Cir. 1986), the court said:

> A cause of action for damages because of the loss of cargo is normally *in personam* in the sense that the amount of damages to be awarded is not limited to the value of a particular asset if personal jurisdiction over the defendant exists. If personal jurisdiction cannot be obtained, however, and the personal appearance of a defendant is secured only by the arrest of his assets, the *in personam* character of the cause of action is largely meaningless. To our knowledge, all courts and commentators that have squarely addressed the question have stated that the nature of the jurisdiction the court acquires by a Rule B attachment is properly denominated "*quasi in rem*"because any judgment rendered is limited to the value of the attached property. *E.g., Belcher Co. v. M/V Maratha Mariner,* 724 F.2d 1161, 1164 (5th Cir. 1984) (characterizing as "*quasi in rem*"actions that are begun by attachment when the court has no jurisdiction over the defendant's person but has jurisdiction over the thing belonging to the defendant); *Maryland Tuna Corp. v. MS Benares,* 429 F.2d 307, 311 (2d Cir. 1970) (proceeding begun under Rule B(1) is "*quasi in rem*" in nature); *Engineering Equipment Co. v. S.S. Selene,* 446 E Supp. 706, 709 n.9 (S.D.N.Y. 1978) ("Although the jurisdiction achieved through maritime attachment is sometimes denominated *in personam,* there is no doubt that any judgment rendered is *quasi in rem* in nature and is limited to the value of the attached property."); *East Asiatic Co. v. Indomar, Ltd.,* 422 E Supp. 1335, 1341-42 (S.D.N.Y. 1976) (same); 7A J. Moore & A. Pelaez, Moore's Federal Practice ¶ B.02, at B-103 n.6 (2d ed. 1983) (hereinafter Moore's) ("[Execution in proceedings commenced by maritime *in personam* attachments in which the defendant has not been personally served or appeared cannot exceed the value of the attached property."); Comment, *The Use of Maritime Attachment as a Jurisdictional Device,* 12 Cornell Int'l L. J. 329, 332-33 (1979) (citation omitted) ("It should be emphasized that, despite the language in Rule B limiting its scope to claims brought "*in personam J* the Rule is in fact a classic example of *quasi in rem* jurisdiction....").

* * *

> Thus, Teyseer's argument that its action is *in personam,* and that the release of the security is irrelevant, misses the mark. The filing of a purely *in personam* action does not determine jurisdiction over the defendant. Limited jurisdiction over the defendant may be acquired by the seizure of his assets. In that event, the *in personam* action takes on characteristics of an action *in rem,* and with respect to the consequences of a release of the security, is guided by *in rem* precedents.

Halla had argued that release of the security deprived the court of jurisdiction. In *Republic National Bank of Miami v. U.S.,* 506 U.S. 80, 113 S. Ct. 554, 121 L. Ed. 2d 474, 1993 AMC 2010 (1992), the Supreme Court held that the court is not divested of jurisdiction by removal of the *res.*

———————

TEYSEER CEMENT CO. v. HALLA MARITIME CORP.

794 F.2d 472, 1986 AMC 2705 (9th Cir. 1986)

WIGGINS, Circuit Judge

Teyseer Cement Company and Qatar General Insurance and Reinsurance Company (collectively referred to as Teyseer) appeal the district courts orders dismissing for improper venue Teyseers admiralty action and affirming the dismissal upon reconsideration. We agree with the contention of appellee Halla Maritime Corporation (Halla) that the appeal is moot and accordingly dismiss it.

Background

Teyseer, a resident of Qatar, contracted with Halla, a resident of South Korea, for the shipment of raw cement from South Korea to Qatar aboard the M/V RHODIAN SAILOR, a vessel under time charter to Halla. Halla issued a bill of lading that contained a foreign court selection clause providing that any disputes would be litigated in South Korea "to the exclusion of the jurisdiction of the courts of any other country."

The ship sank enroute to Qatar, and the cement was lost. In March 1983, Teyseer filed a complaint in admiralty in the United States District Court for the Western District of Washington to recover damages for the loss of the cement. Pursuant to Rule B(1) of the Federal Rules of Civil Procedure Supplemental Rules for Certain Admiralty and Maritime Claims and Local Rule 115(c) of the Western District of Washington, the district court clerk issued a summons and process of attachment, causing the United States Marshal to attach the ATLAS CHALLENGER, a ship owned by Halla and then docked in the Western District of Washington. The only jurisdiction asserted by Teyseer over Halla or its assets was that which may have been acquired by reason of the attachment of the ATLAS CHALLENGER.

Halla obtained the release of the ATLAS CHALLENGER by submitting a letter of undertaking to Teyseer in which Halla agreed that it would enter an appearance in the district court, without prejudice to its right to assert any defenses, including improper forum. *See* FED. R. CIV. P. Supp. Rules for Certain Admir. and Maritime Claims Rule E(5). Halla also stated in the letter that: (1) "the value of the security given as represented by this letter shall be the value of the vessel ATLAS CHALLENGER, ... or U.S. $1,800,000 whichever is less"; and (2) "this letter ... shall stand with the same force and effect as if the ATLAS CHALLENGER had remained attached under process and had been thereafter duly released upon a release bond to respond to your complaint." In October 1983, the district court entered an order establishing the value of the ATLAS CHALLENGER as $855,250 and limiting the security to that amount.

Halla then entered a restricted appearance under Rule E(8) of the Federal Rules of Civil Procedure Supplemental Rules for Certain Admiralty and Maritime Claims. Rule E(8) provides:

An appearance to defend against an admiralty and maritime claim with respect to which there has issued ... process of attachment and garnishment ... may be expressly restricted to the defense of such claim, and in that event shall not constitute an appearance for the purposes of any other claim with respect to which such process is not available or has not been served.

Halla moved to dismiss the action for improper venue, relying on the clause in the bill of lading requiring that all actions be brought in South Korea. Halla also counterclaimed for damages, alleging that attachment in the United States breached this clause. Teyseer opposed the motion and requested alternatively that the district court at least maintain the security represented by the letter of undertaking to ensure satisfaction of a judgment of the courts of Qatar, where it had filed an action against Halla. The district court enforced the foreign court selection clause, dismissed the action, and released the security that the letter represented. The district court stated that no authority permitted it to attach Halla's property for the sole purpose of acquiring security for enforcement of a judgment obtained in another forum. Halla later dismissed its counterclaim voluntarily.

Teyseer filed a timely motion under FED. R. CIV. P. 59(e) to alter or amend the judgment of dismissal and a motion for reconsideration. It sought reconsideration of that part of the district court's dismissal order denying Teyseer's request that the court maintain the security for the enforcement of a future Qatar judgment. Upon reconsideration, the district court withdrew its previous ruling that it was powerless to maintain the security for execution of a foreign judgment. *Teyseer Cement Co. v. Halla Maritime Corp.,* 583 F. Supp. 1268, 1270 (W.D. Wash. 1984). It recognized that under *Polar Shipping, Ltd. v. Oriental Shipping Corp.,* 680 F.2d 627, 632 (9th Cir. 1982), it had discretion to maintain the security. *Teyseer,* 583 F. Supp. at 1270. It held, however, that the language of the foreign court selection clause deprived it of "jurisdiction" to maintain the security. *Id.* at 1271. It did not withdraw its order releasing the security represented by the letter of undertaking.

* * *

Teyseer filed this timely appeal. It neither sought a stay of the order releasing the security nor filed a supersedeas bond. It has informed this court in its reply brief that on March 12, 1985, it obtained a default judgment in a Qatar court against Halla in the amount of $1,149,260.

Analysis

* * *

Effect of Halla's Appearance

[To meet Halla's assertion that the matter had become moot because the release of the security had deprived the appellate court of jurisdiction, Tyseer contended that Halla's appearance constituted a general appearance which conferred *in personam* jurisdiction. Halla's argument that release of the *res* deprived the court of jurisdiction could not have been made after *Republic National Bank of Miami v. U.S.,* 506 U.S. 80, 113 S. Ct. 554, 121 L. Ed. 2d 474, 1993 AMC 2010 (1992), where the Supreme Court held that the court is not divested of jurisdiction by removal of the *res.* Eds.]

Teyseer also argues that by appearing, asserting the forum selection clause as a defense, and by defending the judgment on this appeal, Halla in effect generally appeared, subjecting itself to *in personam* jurisdiction. This argument is unpersuasive. Although a defendant may waive any objections to personal jurisdiction or venue by consent or conduct, *Hoffman v. Blaski,* 363 U.S. 335, 343, 80 S. Ct. 1084, 1089, 4 L. Ed. 2d 1254 (1960), we are unable to conclude that Halla did or said anything in this case to waive its objections to jurisdiction or venue.

Halla expressly entered a "restricted appearance" under Rule E(8). As noted earlier, the language of that Rule permits a defendant to restrict its appearance to the defense of the claim as to which there has issued process of attachment and garnishment. *See* Moore's ¶ E.16, at E-767. We have no reason to question the validity of restricted appearances, which have long been a part of admiralty proceedings. *See* Currie, *Attachment and Garnishment in the Federal Courts.* 59 Mich. L. Rev. 337, 379 n.178 (1961). "It is clear that a defendant or owner entering a restricted appearance to an *in rem* or *quasi in rem* maritime proceeding can vigorously defend the merits of the claim against him without converting his restricted appearance into a general appearance." Moore's ¶ E.16[1], at E-772. Rule E(8) permits a defendant whose appearance is obtained by attachment to avoid the dilemma of either defending the attached property by generally appearing and thus risking a loss greater than the value of the property, or letting it go by default. *Id.* at E-768.

Although not raised by Teyseer, we note that Halla in its amended answer asserted a counterclaim, alleging breach of the forum selection clause in its contract with Teyseer. Assertion of a counterclaim may result in a waiver of objection to *in personam* jurisdiction depending on whether the counterclaim is permissive or compulsory and upon when the counterclaim is raised. *See Gates Learjet Corp. v. Jensen,* 743 F.2d 1325, 1330 n.1 (9th Cir. 1984), *cert. denied,* 471 U.S. 1066, 105 S. Ct. 2143, 85 L. Ed. 2d 500 (1985). In *Gates Learjet* we noted that assertion of a compulsory counterclaim does not constitute waiver of jurisdictional defenses. We observed that this court had not decided whether assertion of a permissive counterclaim constitutes a waiver but held that a permissive counterclaim asserted after a motion to dismiss for lack of personal jurisdiction or in the same pleading that raises lack of personal jurisdiction as a defense does not waive jurisdictional defenses. *Id.*

In this case there is no need to determine whether Halla's counterclaim is permissive or compulsory in order to resolve the question of whether the counterclaim waived any objection to personal jurisdiction. Halla did not move for dismissal based on lack of personal jurisdiction, but it had no reason to do so. Halla entered a restricted appearance below to allow it to appear and protect its interest in the *res* that had been attached. Halla's restricted appearance indicated that it did not consent to personal jurisdiction. We hold that by entering a restricted appearance Halla objected to *in personam* jurisdiction as effectively as it could have through a motion to dismiss on that ground, and that its subsequent assertion of a counterclaim did not result in a waiver of that objection. *See Gates Learjet,* 743 F.2d at 1330 n.1.

* * *

Note: Waiver of Jurisdictional Defenses

In *Trans-Asiatic Oil Ltd., S. A. v. Apex Oil Co.,* 804 F.2d 773, 1987 AMC 1115 (1st Cir. 1986), the First Circuit confronted the same basic issue addressed by the Teyseer court: namely, that dissolution of the attachment is immaterial where the defendant has consented to *in personam* jurisdiction. However, the court in the instant case found the following:

* * *

Although both *Teyseer* and the matter before us involve the identical legal issue of whether dissolution of a B(1) attachment renders moot any subsequent appeal, the two cases differ with respect to one key factor. The defendant-appellee in *Teyseer* only entered a limited appearance. Halla never appeared generally nor was there a trial on the merits. In the instant case, appellee Apex initially entered a limited appearance to challenge the constitutionality of the B(1) attachment proceeding. After this court upheld the constitutionality of the B(1) procedure, a pretrial order was issued by the court below stating that "there is no dispute between the parties that the Court has jurisdiction over the parties and the subject matter of this action." Apex acquiesced to this language in the pretrial order without jurisdictional reservation, appeared generally, and defended the claim fully on the merits. Thus, while appellees initial entry of a restricted appearance manifested its lack of consent to personal jurisdiction, Apex's actions after remand constituted a waiver of its jurisdictional defenses. We do not hold that Apex's general appearance automatically nullified its jurisdictional defenses. We hold only that Apex's consent to the language in the pretrial order amounted to a waiver of its jurisdictional reservation.

We note also that the underlying purpose of the Rule B attachment procedure is to facilitate the adjudication of admiralty claims. The Fifth Circuit has held, in the course of resolving a Rule C action, that "when a legal fiction which exists solely to effectuate the adjudication of disputes is invoked for the opposite purpose, we have no hesitation in declining to employ it." *United States v. An Article of Drug Consisting of 4,680 Pails,* 725 F.2d 976, 983 (5th Cir. 1984); *Treasure Salvors, Inc. v. Unidentified Wrecked and Abandoned Sailing Vessel,* 569 F.2d 330, 334 (5th Cir. 1978). Thus, in some *in rem* actions where the underlying *res* was outside the jurisdiction of the court, the Fifth Circuit has dispensed with the fiction that its jurisdiction over the matter wholly depended on the location of the *res.* Instead, the Fifth Circuit has held that "owner's who appeared in an *in rem* action to contest plaintiff's claims may equitably be treated as if they had been brought into court by personal process." *United States v. An Article of Drug,* 725 F.2d at 983. The treatise writers also have recognized that a court's jurisdiction in a maritime attachment proceeding may not be wholly circumscribed by the presence and amount of the attachment:

> Attachment, unlike *in rem* arrest, serves the function of providing the court with a type of *in personam* jurisdiction over the absent defendant. Since the insulation afforded by the restricted appearance applies to "other claims" that may be asserted against that defendant, it could well be argued that the defendant's appearance to defend that already asserted claim should subject him to the full potential consequences of that suit—including a duty to pay any portion of the *in personam* judgment that exceeds the value of the property attached by the suit.

7A J. Moore & A. Pelaez, Moore's Federal Practice ¶ E16[2] at E-790 (2d ed. 1986). We have no intention of eroding the boundaries between *in rem* and *in personam* jurisdiction, or *quasi in rem* and *in personam* jurisdiction. Because of Apex's consent to the language in the pretrial order, and because of our hesitancy to construe Rule B(1) in a hypertechnical manner that would frustrate its adjudicative purpose, we hold that this court does have jurisdiction to hear this matter and that Trans-Asiatic's appeal is not moot.

* * *

Note: Attachment: Time of "Execution"

In *Narada Shipping Ltd. v. North Atlantic Oil, Ltd.,* 398 F. Supp. 95 (S.D. Ala. 1975), the court, addressing the issue of when a writ of maritime attachment has been properly executed, found the following:

* * *

This cause came on for hearing on June 6, 1975, on defendant North Atlantic Oil Ltd.'s motion to vacate a writ of maritime attachment.

On May 12, 1975, the plaintiff's in this action filed a complaint seeking damages against the defendant for breach of four time charter contracts and also requesting the issuance of a writ of maritime attachment pursuant to the provisions of Supplemental Rule B(1) of the Federal Rules of Civil Procedure. The subjects of the requested maritime attachment were several parcels of real property owned by the defendant and located within this district. On May 13, 1975, this Court issued to the Marshal for the Southern District of Alabama a Monition and Writ of Foreign Attachment concerning the real property specified in the plaintiffs' complaint. Prior to any action being taken by the Marshal to execute the writ, the defendant filed an answer on May 27, 1975, thereby making a general appearance in this action and submitting to the *in personam* jurisdiction of this Court.

The issue presently before this Court is whether or not the defendant's appearance occurred prior to the execution of the attachment and thereby making any attachment under Supplemental Rule B(1) improper. *Cocotos S.S. of Panama S. A. v. Sociedad Maritima Victoria S. A. Panama,* 146 F. Supp. 540, 542 (S.D.N.Y. 1956). In opposition to the motion to vacate the writ, the plaintiff's asserted in their brief that the attachment was executed prior to the defendant's appearance.

The contention that their appearance defeats the writ of maritime attachment is like-wise vitiated, for the attachment was fully executed upon its issuance to the Marshal's office and upon the knowledge, actual or constructive, that the defendant could not be found within the district. Such knowledge was evidenced by the affidavit attached to the complaint to be delivered to the Marshal's office with the writ of attachment. It therefore follows that the appearance made by the defendant was made subsequent to the full execution of the attachment, although the attachment may not have in fact been carried through to the point of posting the writ of attachment or notice thereof on some tree or stanchion of the defendant's property. (Plaintiffs' Brief)

The Court does not agree with the plaintiffs' conclusion. Alabama law, whether statutory or common, does not clearly specify what actions must be taken by the executing officer before an attachment on real property can be said to have been "executed". However, the Court is of the opinion that the officer must, at the least, have [assumed] dominion and control of it by some notorious acts." Landers v. Moore, 21 Ala. App. 12, 13, 106 So. 223,224 (1925). This conclusion is further supported by the provisions of Sections 531, 852 and 861 of Title 7 of the Code of Alabama.

Under the facts presently before the Court, no such actions by the Marshal had occurred prior to the defendant's general appearance on May 27, 1975. Accordingly, the Court is of the opinion that the attachment sought by the plaintiff's had not been executed prior to the defendant's general appearance and that the defendant's motion to vacate the writ of maritime attachment should therefore be granted. The Court further notes, without deciding the issue, that there is considerable doubt whether real property within the district is subject to successful attachment under Supplemental Rule B(l). 7A Moore's Federal Practice, ¶ B.04.

Therefore, it is ordered, adjudged and decreed that the defendant's motion to vacate the writ of maritime attachment is granted and that the Monition and Writ of Foreign Attachment issued in the present action by this Court on May 13, 1975, is hereby vacated.

---

b. "Found Within the District": A Two-Prong Test

SEAWIND COMPANIA, S.A. v. CRESCENT LINE, INC.

320 F.2d 580 (2d Cir. 1963)

WATERMAN, Circuit Judge

Seawind Compania, S.A., appeals from an order of the United States District Court for the Southern District of New York, BONSAL, J., sitting in the admiralty, by which the attachment of credits and effects of respondent-appellee, Crescent Lines, Inc., now known as Falcon Shipping Corp., was vacated. The attachment had been made pursuant to Rule 2 of the Rules of Practice in Admiralty and Maritime Cases promulgated by the United States Supreme Court. We affirm the order below.[1]

By its libel filed March 20, 1962, Seawind sought recovery of damages from Crescent Line and others for the alleged breach of a maritime agreement. The same day a citation *in personam* with a clause of foreign attachment in the usual form was issued to the United States Marshal for the Southern District of New York. The Marshal was directed to cite Crescent Line "if [it] shall be found in your District," and "if the said Respondent cannot be found," to attach its credits and effects in the hands of named garnishees. On March 21, 1962, a Deputy Marshal served the citation with clause of foreign attachment upon the named garnishees, and at the same time effected personal service upon the other respondents in the case. Although the Marshal's return certified that he was unable to find Crescent Line, Inc. "after due and diligent search," it is conceded that libelant did not inform the Marshal where Crescent Line, Inc., might be found and no attempt was made by him to locate or to serve this respondent.

By order to show cause dated March 29, 1962, Crescent Line moved pursuant to Rule 21 of the Admiralty Rules of the District Court for an order vacating the attachment. Appellee contended that it had been present and doing business in the Southern District of New York for several years, as Seawind well knew, and that the attachment

---

[1] Our jurisdiction rests upon 28 U.S.C. § 1291; *Swift & Co. Packers v. Compania Columbiana Del Caribe, S.A.,* 339 U.S. 684, 689, 70 S. Ct. 861, 94 L. Ed. 1206 (1950).

was, therefore, illegally and improperly made. After a hearing, Judge Bonsai granted the motion and vacated the attachment on April 9, 1962. Reargument of the motion was held on April 17, 1962, and on the same day Judge Bonsais Memorandum Decision was entered adhering to his original determination. This appeal followed.

An attachment under Rule 2 of the Admiralty Rules, customarily referred to as a foreign attachment, has a dual purpose: (1) to obtain jurisdiction of the respondent *in personam* through his property, and (2) to assure satisfaction of any decree in libelants favor. 2 BENEDICT, ADMIRALTY § 288 (6th ed. 1940); *Swift & Company Packers v. Compania Columbiana Del Caribe, S.A.*, 339 U.S. 684, 70 S. Ct. 861, 94 L. Ed. 1206 (1950). The two purposes may not be separated, however, for security cannot be obtained except as an adjunct to obtaining jurisdiction.

Rule 2 provides, in pertinent part:

> In suits *in personam* the mesne process shall be by a simple monition in the nature of a summons to appear and answer to the suit, or by a simple warrant of arrest of the person of the respondent in the nature of a capias, as the libellant may, in his libel or information pray for or elect; in either case with a clause therein to attach his goods and chattels, or credits and effects in the hands of the garnishees named in the libel to the amount sued for, *if said respondent shall not be found within the district....* (Emphasis supplied.)

Thus, on motions to vacate foreign attachments, the essential issue before the district court is whether respondent could have been found within the district. We must affirm Judge Bonsais determination that respondent-appellee could have been so found unless he applied an erroneous legal standard or his determination of subsidiary facts was clearly erroneous. *McAllister v. United States*, 348 U.S. 19, 75 S. Ct. 6, 99 L. Ed. 20 (1954); *cf.* Rule 52(a), FED. R. CIV. P.

The Admiralty Rules do not define the expression "found within the district." In the cases construing Rule 2, however, the requirement is said to present "a two-pronged inquiry: first, whether [the respondent] can be found within the district in terms of jurisdiction, and second, if so, whether it can be found for service of process." *United States v. Cia Naviera Continental S.A.*, 178 F. Supp. 561, 563 (S.D.N.Y. 1959); *see American Potato Corp. v. Boca Grande S.S. Co.*, 233 F. 542 (E.D. Pa. 1916); *Insurance Co. of North America v. Canadian American Navigation Co. (The Melmay)*, 1933 A.M.C. 1057.

Considering the second question first, there is no doubt, we believe, that Crescent Line, Inc. (Falcon Shipping Corp.) could be found within the Southern District of New York on March 21, 1962, for service of process. In Admiralty, as under Rule 4(d) of the Federal Rules of Civil Procedure, service upon a corporation may properly be effected by service upon "an officer, a managing or general agent, or ... any other agent authorized by appointment or by law to receive service of process." *Ashcraft-Wilkinson Co. v. Compania De Navegacion Geamar, S.R.L.*, 117 Supp. 162, 164 (S.D.N.Y. 1953); *Patel Cotton Co. v. Steel Traveler*, 107 F. Supp. 191, 193 (S.D.N.Y. 1952); 2 BENEDICT, ADMIRALTY § 280 (6th ed. 1940).

Here, appellant does not deny that during the relevant period of time Crescent Line had a managing agent within the district, James W. Elwell & Co., Inc., with offices at 17 State Street in New York City; that the Elwell office was in the charge of David W. Swanson, president of both Elwell and Crescent Line (Falcon Shipping Corp.), who was present in his office at 17 State Street during normal business hours on March 21, 1962; and that the Secretary and proctor for both Crescent Line and Elwell was Henry P. Molloy, Jr., Esq., with offices at 26 Broadway in New York City.

Moreover, the district court could properly conclude that appellant knew, or ought to have known, the above facts, for both Swanson and Molloy signed the contract in suit, as President and Secretary of Crescent Line respectively; James W. Elwell & Co., Inc. was referred to in the contract as the Managing Agent of the respondent; and on February 19 and February 26, 1960, appellant, through its President, directed correspondence to "Crescent Line, Inc., James W. Elwell & Co., Inc., Agent, 17 State Street, New York 4, New York, Attention: Mr. David Swanson, President."

Appellant argues that because Crescent Line, on or about February 26, 1960, changed its corporate name to Falcon Shipping Corp., and sold its former name and good will, appellant no longer knew whether Swanson, Molloy, and James W. Elwell & Co., Inc. continued to serve as officers and agents of respondent-appellee. On March 16, 1960, however, invoices bearing the names of both Crescent Line and James W. Elwell & Co., Inc., were sent to appellant's attorney; and on April 7 and July 27, 1960, Henry P. Molloy, signing his name as "Secretary" of Falcon Shipping Corp., corresponded with appellant's attorney concerning Seawind Compania.

Even if appellant was ignorant, however, of the continuing relationships of Swanson, Molloy, and James W. Elwell & Co., Inc., to Falcon Shipping Corp., we must assume that appropriate inquires would have revealed these facts. No such inquiries were made. Judge Bonsai was clearly correct in ruling, therefore, that libelant failed to make a bona fide effort to locate respondent in the district, as we hold it was required to do. *Federazione Italiana Dei Consorzi Agrari v. Mandask Compania De Vapores, S.A.,* 158 F. Supp. 107, 111 (S.D.N.Y. 1957); *Birdsall v. Germain Co.,* 227 F. 953 (S.D.N.Y. 1915).

We turn, thus, to the question whether respondent-appellee was to be "found within" the Southern District of New York for the purpose of being subject to *in personam* jurisdiction in the court below. If foreign attachment in admiralty is permitted only as a means of enabling the libelant's suit to proceed, it might be supposed that the known presence of an agent authorized to accept process would suffice to preclude such an attachment under Rule 2. The cases, however, suggest an additional requirement, namely, that the respondent be engaged in sufficient activity in the district to subject it to jurisdiction even in the absence of a resident agent expressly authorized to accept process. *American Potato Corp. v. Boca Grande S.S. Co.,* 233 F. 542, 543 (E.D. Pa. 1916); *Insurance Co. of North America v. Canadian American Navigation Co. (The Melmay),* 1933 A.M.C. 1057; *see Federazione Italiana D. C.A. v. Mandask Compania D. V., supra', United States v. Cia Naviera Continental S.A., supra; Sociedad Transoceanica Canopus, S.A. v. Interamerican Refining Corp.,* 185 F. Supp. 294 (D. N.J. 1960). *But see The Valmar,* 38 F. Supp. 615 (E.D. Pa. 1941).

Here, the minimum conditions necessary to a foreign corporations being "found within the district" under Rule 2 need not be determined, for we believe that the district court's ruling was not clearly erroneous even under the rigorous standard suggested by the cases cited above.

Respondent-appellee is a Liberian corporation which, during 1962, was in the process of dissolution. Its major, and perhaps sole, business during that year was in the processing of cargo claims. Despite the fact that the corporate minutes and stock transfer books were kept in New York, and all of the corporations officers were present in the district, this volume of activity would possibly not, by itself, qualify as "doing business" under ordinary tests *See Hanson v. Denckla,* 357 U.S. 235, 78 S. Ct. 1228, 2 L. Ed. 2d 1283 (1958); *Blount v. Peerless Chemicals, Inc.,* 316 F.2d 695 (2 Cir. 1963); and *see generally* Kurland, *The Supreme Court, the Due Process Clause and In personam Jurisdiction of State Courts,* 25 U. CHI. L. REV. 569 (1958); Note, *Jurisdiction over Foreign Corporations—an Analysis of Due Process,* 104 U. PA. L. REV. 381 (1955).

What respondent-appellee's volume of business may lack under ordinary tests, however, appellant supplies by the nature of its claim. The contract in suit was made and allegedly breached by Crescent Lines in New York. For such activities respondent-appellee could clearly be made subject to suit in New York, even in the absence of a resident agent expressly authorized to accept process. *See McGee v. International Life Ins. Co.,* 355 U.S. 220, 78 S. Ct. 199, 2 L. Ed. 2d 223 (1957); *Travelers Health Ass'n v. Com. of Virginia,* 339 U.S. 643, 70 S. Ct. 927, 94 L. Ed. 1154 (1950); *International Shoe Co. v. Washington,* 326 U.S. 310, 66 S. Ct. 154, 90 L. Ed. 95 (1945).

Under these circumstances, we cannot say that Judge Bonsais determination that Crescent Line could be found within the district was clearly erroneous.

The order of the district court vacating the attachment of appellees credits and effects is affirmed, and the cause is remanded for further proceedings in the district court.

———

NIKKO SHIPPING CO. v. M/V SEA WIND

941 F. Supp. 587, 1997 AMC 399 (D. Md. 1996)

JOSEPH H. YOUNG, *Senior District Judge*

This action results from an attempt by Nikko Shipping Company, Inc. ("Nikko") to attach or arrest the M/V SEA WIND, which is an ocean-going cargo vessel registered under the laws of Liberia and owned by Kite Maritime, Inc. ("Kite"). The Court permitted the M/V SEA WIND to leave Baltimore after Kite agreed to post security in the event the Court determined that the attachment or arrest was proper.

I. Facts

Kite and Nikko entered into a charter party involving the M/V SEA WIND on November 15, 1994. The charter of the M/V SEA WIND continued from December 4, 1994 until February 26, 1996. A dispute arose between Kite and Nikko related to the charter party. Nikko claims Kite owes it $179,957.50 and Kite, in turn, claims Nikko owes it $74,575.74. Pursuant to the terms of the charter party, as understood by the parties, Nikko and Kite submitted their dispute to arbitration in London in March 1996.

After an unsuccessful attempt to obtain security from Kite through London counsel in anticipation of a favorable arbitration award, on August 30, 1996, Nikko filed a Verified Complaint for Arrest and Attachment against the M/V SEA WIND *in rem* and Kite *in personam* pursuant to Rules B and C of the Supplemental Rules for Certain Admiralty and Maritime Claims of the Federal Rules of Civil Procedure while the M/V SEA WIND was discharging cargo in the Port of Baltimore and had appointed a local ship's agent. Counsel for Kite filed a General Appearance on behalf of Kite before Nikko could serve any process attaching or arresting the M/V SEA WIND. The Court permitted the M/V SEA WIND to sail from Baltimore after Kite agreed to post security in the event the Court determined the attachment or arrest was proper. The parties have fully briefed the issues and a hearing was held.

II. *In Personam* Attachment (Rule B)

Rule B of the Supplemental Rules for Certain Admiralty and Maritime Claims of the Federal Rules of Civil Procedure authorizes attachment of the assets of a defendant in admiralty and maritime cases as a means of obtaining jurisdiction over the defendant provided the defendant "shall not be found within" the federal district in which the assets are sought to be attached. Supp. R. Fed. R. Civ. P. B(1). In determining whether Kite is "found within" the District of Maryland, the Court applies a three-part test: "[A] defendant's property ... within a district will be subject to attachment ... unless (1) personal jurisdiction can be obtained therein; and (2) he can, with due diligence, be served with process therein; and (3) at least where the defendant is a foreign corporation, it does sufficient business within the district to otherwise subject it to the jurisdiction of the court." 7A JAMES W. MOORE ET AL., MOORE FEDERAL PRACTICE ¶ B.06, at B-252 (2d ed. 1996), cited w/approval in, *Rea B Shipping Corp. v. Uiterwyk Lines*, 1983 A.M.C. 544, 546 (D. Md. 1982).

By filing a General Appearance, Kite attempted to make itself subject to personal jurisdiction and available for service of process. Kite, however, has not introduced sufficient evidence of "minimum contacts" with the District of Maryland. The only apparent contact between Kite and the District of Maryland is the M/V SEA WIND's lone call at the Port of Baltimore on August 30, 1996, which included the appointment of a local ship's agent. Kite does not suggest any other contacts with Maryland in the past nor does it assert that there will be any future contacts with Maryland. *See Grevas v. M/V Olympic Pegasus*, 557 F.2d 65, 68 (4th Cir. 1977) (holding that a single eight-day call in Norfolk for loading a cargo of soybeans could not establish the requisite contacts to permit the exercise of *in personam* jurisdiction over a foreign corporation), *cert. denied*, 434 U.S. 969, 98 S. Ct. 515, 54 L. Ed. 2d 456 (1977); *Morewitz v. S/S Alexandros B.*, 1978 A.M.C. 1509, 1512-13 (E.D. Va. 1977) (holding that three visits to Virginia over six and one-half years did not establish sufficiently substantial contacts to authorize exercise of personal jurisdiction over nonresident defendants); *Pappas v. S/S ARISTIDIS,* 1965 A.M.C. 2148, 2150-51 (E.D. Va. 1965) (ruling that two visits to Virginia by defendants vessels over five years were insufficient to serve as predicate for exercise of personal jurisdiction); *Skarpelis v. M/T ARTHUR P.,* 1969 A.M.C. 299, 300-01 (E.D. Va. 1969) (holding that "two visits totaling thirty hours over a period of several years" were not sufficient to vest personal jurisdiction over nonresident defendants).

Kite's General Appearance alone, absent significant contacts with the District of Maryland, is not sufficient to conclude that Kite was "found within" the district. *See Construction Exporting Enter., Uneca v. Nikki Maritime Ltd.,* 558 F. Supp. 1372, 1375 (S.D.N.Y. 1983) ("The right to the attachment is not defeated by the filing of a general appearance. But for the security of an attachment, because there is no real presence here, the appearance will be of no assistance to plaintiff in enforcing its rights, and is not equivalent to being found within the district."), *appeal dismissed,* 742 F.2d 1432 (2d Cir. 1983); *Navieros Inter-Americanos, S.A. v. M/V Vasilia Express,* 930 F. Supp. 699, 708 (D.P.R. 1996) ("Service of process will not be effective to establish jurisdiction, unless the corporation also is doing business so as to be amendable to service and the assertion of jurisdiction in the state. The title of agent has no particular significance, unless it is linked to a bona-fide corporate presence within a district, which is not the case here."); *Iran Express Lines v. Sumatrop, A.G.,* 563 F.2d 648, 652 (4th Cir. 1977) (HALL, J. concurring) (stating that "carefully arranged timing and connivance [should not be allowed] to skirt equity and to defeat the attachment."). Accordingly, Nikko was entitled to attach the M/V SEA WIND pursuant to Rule B, and Kite will be ordered to post security.

Order

In accordance with the attached Memorandum, it is this 22nd day of October, 1996, by the United States District Court for the District of Maryland, ORDERED:

1. That Plaintiff's Verified Complaint seeking to attach and arrest the M/V SEA WIND BE, and the same IS, hereby GRANTED; and
2. That Defendant, Kite Maritime, Inc., POST security in the amount of two hundred fifty thousand dollars ($250,000) on or before the 29th day of October, 1996, subject to further proceedings in this Court.

Notes:

1. "Jurisdictional Presence"

In the context of Supplemental Admiralty Rule B, it is well established that a defendant is "found within the district", only if the defendant is able to accept process and engaged in sufficient activity in the district. Moreover, previous engagement in business activities in the district is not sufficient activity in the district for purpose of this maritime attachment rule. In *V.T.T. Vulcan Petroleum, S. A. v. Langham-Hill Petroleum, Inc.,* 684 F. Supp. 389, 1989 AMC 1301 (S.D.N.Y. 1988), the court held that the prior activity in the district, though constituting past general jurisdiction, was not sufficient to preclude attachment under this special maritime rule. The court stated:

* * *

Past general jurisdictional contacts, unrelated to the subject matter of the litigation, provide no security to a plaintiff who wants to ensure that any judgment in its favor might be satisfied. Unlike specific jurisdictional contacts which do not terminate when a defendant physically leaves the forum state, general jurisdictional contacts do terminate when the defendant physically ends all continuous and systematic contact with the forum. Although past general jurisdictional contacts might satisfy due process concerns in other contexts, such past general jurisdictional contacts cannot satisfy the "jurisdictional presence" prong of the test for vacating a maritime attachment.

In the present case, there is no contract—nor any other subject of the litigation—which was made, performed, or breached in New York. Under these circumstances, Langham-Hill's contacts with New York prior to March 22, 1988, are insufficient to provide the showing of "jurisdiction presence" necessary to allow this Court to vacate the attachment here. *See Seawind,* 320 F.2d at 583.

* * *

2. *Service of Process Via Agent*

The issue of whether service upon a local port agent constitutes valid service on a foreign shipowner was addressed in *Cobelfret-CIE Beige v. Samick Lines Co., Ltd.*, 542 F. Supp. 29, 1983 AMC 547 (W.D. Wash. 1982). The court determined the following:

* * *

The test's second prong, whether Samick could be found for service of process within the district, is sharply contested. Defendant contends it was amenable to service of process through its local port agent, Olympic Steamship Company. Generally, in order to serve a party through its subagent, an agent's actions must be substantial, continual and on more than just a ship-to-ship basis. *Marvirason Compania Naviera, S.A. v. H.J. Baker &Bro., 1979 A.M.C.* 625, 628 (S.D.N.Y. 1978). Although some courts have found that service upon a local port agent providing ordinary husbanding services on a ship-to-ship basis is valid service on a foreign shipowner, *see, e.g., Murphy v. Arrow Steamship*, 124 F. Supp. 199, 1954 A.M.C. 1423 (E.D. Pa. 1954), the majority of courts have held that subagents or husbanding agents are not authorized to accept service of process which will bind the vessel's owner. *See Serpe v. Eagle Ocean Transport Agency Co.*, 53 F.R.D. 21, 1971 A.M.C. 748 (E.D. Wis. 1971); *Amicale Industries, Inc. v. The S.S. Rantum*, 259 F. Supp. 534, 1967 A.M.C. 96 (D. S.C. 1966).

Having reviewed the file and the briefs herein, I find that the defendant could not be found with reasonable diligence within the district for service. *Tug GO GETTER* at 398 F.2d 874. Before the SAMICK ATLANTIC was attached, plaintiff's counsel checked the following in an unsuccessful attempt to locate the defendant in the district: (1) the 1981 List of Active Corporations in the State of Washington, (2) the 1980 Coast Marine Transportation Directory, (3) the 1979-80 Pacific Coast Maritime Directory, (4) Pacific Northwest Bell telephone book and the Information operators, (5) Pacific Marine Directory, (6) Shipping News Directory, (7) Lloyd's Shipping Directory, (8) Northwest Shipping Directory, and (9) the Seattle City Directory. Counsel also contacted the Corporate Records Division of Washington's Secretary of State and was advised that Samick Lines was not qualified to do business in Washington and had not appointed a registered agent to receive process.

Finally, neither the Affidavit of Gordon Cleverdon, Olympic Steamship's Vice President, nor his deposition and the exhibits attached indicated that Olympic had specific authority, express or implied, to receive service of process. *See generally* 2 MOORE'S FEDERAL PRACTICE P 4.22(1) (2d ed. 1982).

* * *

3. *Service of Process on Official Agent*

Many jurisdictions have a rule permitting service of process on a state official (often the Secretary of State) as the defendant's "appointed" representative when a non-resident defendant is not present in the jurisdiction for purposes of service. In such a jurisdiction, the second prong of the "found within the district" test is satisfied only if suit is brought in the district where service on the state official can be accomplished. See, e.g., *LaBanca v. Ostermunchner*, 664 F.2d 65, 1982 AMC 205 (5th Cir. 1981), where Rule B attachment in the Middle District of Florida was permitted despite plaintiff's ability to serve process on the Florida Secretary of State as defendant's agent, because service on the Secretary of State had to be made at the State Capitol, which was in the Northern District of Florida.

---

c. The Distinction Between Proceedings: Attachment and Actions *In Rem*

BELCHER COMPANY OF ALABAMA, INC. v. M/V MARATHA MARINER

724 F.2d 1161, 1984 AMC 1679 (5th Cir. 1984)

Alvin B. RUBIN, Circuit Judge

This *in rem* libel against a vessel to recover for fuel bunkers supplied to it was dismissed on the ground that a pending action in the Netherlands, in which jurisdiction had been obtained by attachment of the vessel, was the equivalent of an *in rem* action and hence was *lis alibis pendens*. Because the Netherlands permits no *in rem* actions, and, therefore, the suit pending there is *in personam*, and because the ultimate issues in the two suits are different, we reverse the judgment of dismissal.

Belcher Company of Alabama, Inc. (Belcher), filed an *in rem* libel against the vessel M/V Maratha Mariner of Bombay, India, and against all persons having or claiming any interest in the vessel, alleging that Belcher had supplied fuel bunkers to the vessel and had not been paid the amount due it, $99,344. The vessel had been chartered from its owner, Chowgule Steamship Company, Ltd. (Chowgule), by Armada Bulk Carriers of Denmark (Armada). Armadas broker had ordered fuel from Baymar, a California broker, and Baymar had, in turn, contracted with

Belcher, which supplied the fuel to the vessel in Mobile, Alabama. Chowgule asserts that Armada paid Baymar for the fuel and that Baymar, in turn, made partial payment to Belcher and subsequently went out of business before paying the balance.

In 1979, Belcher had the vessel attached in the Netherlands to satisfy the alleged outstanding debt. Chowgule secured the release of the vessel by posting 275,000 Dutch guilders ($138,000 in U.S. dollars) in the form of a letter of undertaking, as security for its claim. That litigation is still pending in Rotterdam, the Netherlands. The vessel was later arrested in Houston, Texas, three years later, and this libel was initiated in the Southern District of Texas.

The Federal Maritime Lien Act provides, "[a]ny person furnishing ... necessaries, to any vessel, whether foreign or domestic, upon the order of the owner of such vessel, or of a person authorized by the owner, shall have a maritime lien on the vessel, which may be enforced by suit *in rem*..." 46 U.S.C. § 971. This lien attaches when necessaries are ordered by and supplied to a charterer,[1] unless the supplier has notice that the person who orders the necessaries lacked authority to do so.[2] Thus, when Belcher supplied fuel to the M/V Maratha Mariner, a maritime lien may have arisen by operation of law, and, if such a lien did arise, its enforceability may be subject to any defenses that may be available to the vessel owner, such as laches. The owner of the vessel is not itself liable for payment, however, unless it has entered into the contract for the supply of necessaries. It has no personal obligation even though a lien attaches to its vessel.[3]

Under the admiralty law of the United States, *in personam* and *in rem* actions may arise from the same claim, and may be brought separately or in the same suit. Supplemental Admiralty Rule C(1)(b). As its name implies, the *in personam* action is filed against the owner personally. An *in rem* action, on the other hand, is filed against the *res*, the vessel; and a maritime lien on the vessel is a prerequisite to an action *in rem*.[4] There is a third category of claims sometimes known as actions *quasi in rem*. Supplemental Admiralty Rule E. These are actions based on a claim for money begun by attachment or other seizure of property when the court has no jurisdiction over the person of the defendant, but has jurisdiction over a thing belonging to him or over a person who is indebted to, or owes a duty to the defendant.[5] A state has jurisdiction by an action *quasi in rem* to enforce a personal claim against a defendant to the extent of applying the property seized to the satisfaction of the claim.[6]

If American law had been applicable when the vessel was attached in the Netherlands, the supplier of fuel would have had a lien on the vessel and an action *in rem* could have been brought to enforce the maritime lien. The Netherlands action was, however, based on contract principles because Dutch law does not recognize the concept of maritime lien and, therefore, provides no mechanism by which such a lien can be enforced. The fact that an *in rem* action could not be brought in the Netherlands does not convert the attachment there filed into an *in rem* proceeding.

Chowgule contends that Belcher has admitted the foreign action to be in effect *in rem* because Belcher has asserted in the course of that action that, despite the difference in the two legal systems, "the position of the owner of the vessel is not essentially enhanced or changed [under Dutch law]. In the present [Netherlands] case the vessel was attached, whereupon by the law of the U.S.A. a lien could have been served. In order to withdraw this attachment, a guarantee was obtained. Possible judgment against Chowgule and possible non-compliance therewith will lead to compensation under guarantee and therewith indirectly on that item of property which by the law of the U.S.A. would be the debtor."

This is not, however, an admission that the foreign attachment is a libel *in rem*. As Belcher's pleading in the Netherlands case further states:

---

[1] 46 U.S.C. § 973, as amended by Pub. L. No. 92-79, 85 Stat. 285 (1971); *Dampskibsselskzabet Dannebrog v. Signal Oil and Gas Company*, 310 U.S. 268, 60 S. Ct. 937, 84 L. Ed. 1197 (1939); G. GILMORE & C. BLACK, THE LAW OF ADMIRALTY 685 (2d ed. 1975) and cases cited therein.

[2] 46 U.S.C. §§ 972 & 973; G. Gilmore & C. Black, *supra* 685 *etseq.*

[3] *See generally* G. Gilmore & C. Black, *supra*, § 9-19; *but see infra* note 8.

[4] G. Gilmore & C. Black, § 1-12 at 35; *see, e.g., The Rock Island Bridge*, 73 U.S. (6 Wall.) 213, 215, 18 L. Ed. 753, 754 (1862) (*cited in* G. Gilmore & C. Black at *id.*); *The Resolute*, 168 U.S. 437, 440, 18 S. Ct. 112, 113, 42 L. Ed. 533, 535 (1897); *Rainbow Line, Inv. v. M/V Tequila*, 480 F.2d 1024, 1028 (2d Cir. 1973).

[5] RESTATEMENT (Second) of Judgments (1982) § 8; James, Civil Procedure 613 (1965).

[6] RESTATEMENT (Second) of Judgments (1982) § 9.

By Dutch law of procedure which in effect does not provide for the action *in rem*, an action *in personam* must be brought therefore, whereby be it so, the owner of the vessel becomes debtor of the claim under section 321 paragraph 1 Wvk, whereas by the law of the U.S.A. the case itself, in the present instance the vessel, is the debtor.

Therein the true difference lies. In the *in rem* action, the issues are whether: (1) Belcher delivered the claimed quantity of fuel to the M/V Maratha Mariner; (2) the fuel delivered to the bunkers was a necessary within the meaning of the Maritime Lien Act, 46 U.S.C. § 971; (3) the charges claimed are reasonable in amount; and (4) the person who placed the order had authority to do so, either real, apparent, or statutorily presumed. In the attachment action, the sole question is whether Chowgule became liable to Belcher contractually. While it is necessary to resolve a number of questions to determine that issue, the reasonableness of the charges and the status of the fuel as necessaries are irrelevant, and the methods of proving the authority of the person who placed the order differ.

The distinction between these types of proceedings is made clear by the Supplemental Rules. Attachment issues "with respect to any admiralty or maritime claim *in personam*" and its purpose is to "attach the defendant's goods and chattels" or other assets if the defendant shall not be found in the jurisdiction. Rule B. Attachment may be used for any debt. An action *in rem* on the other hand, is available only to enforce a maritime lien or when authorized by statute. Rule C. The arrest warrant extends only to the vessel "or other property that is the subject of the action." Rule C(3).

The Fourth Circuit has held that the judicial sale of a vessel in a Mexican bankruptcy action was sufficiently similar in substance to an American *in rem* action to remove an *in rem* lien on the vessel. *Gulf and Southern Terminal Corp. v. The SS President Roxas*, 701 F.2d 1110 (4th Cir.), *cert. denied*, 462 U.S. 1133, 103 S. Ct. 3115, 77 L. Ed. 2d 1369 (1983). In that case, the Mexican bankruptcy court had possession of the vessel, and sold it "free of encumbrances." The sale erased the lien despite the fact that Mexican law does not provide explicitly for an *in rem* proceeding both because the procedures employed were "virtually identical to those which are denominated as an *in rem* proceeding under American law" and because "the vessel was an asset of the bankrupt, under the control and proper jurisdiction of the Mexican court." *Id.* 701 F.2d at 1112. A bankruptcy court that has possession of any property has the power to sell the property free and clear of liens.[7]

Attachment does in many respects resemble arrest. In each proceeding the vessel is seized and it may later be sold to satisfy a judgment. In each, the vessel itself may be released and other security substituted. Nevertheless, not only do the issues in the two actions differ; the basic theory on which each is brought is different. In the *in rem* proceeding the owner bears no personal liability. The vessel is sold solely to satisfy the lien. If the proceeds of the sale are inadequate, there is no liability on the owner's part for the residue. Indeed the admiralty court will not render a personal judgment against the owner in excess of the amount of the release bond.[8] Only a personal action against the owner can establish such liability. In the attachment action, the object of the action is a personal judgment for the full sum due. The vessel is seized only to compel the owner's appearance by subjecting to the courts control property within its territorial jurisdiction. If the proceeds of sale of the vessel do not satisfy the judgment, the owner remains liable for the balance of the debt.

Chowgule asserts that, when it provided security to release the vessel from attachment, this discharged the lien. With respect to the lien sought to be enforced, the release does transfer the lien from the vessel to the fund represented by the bond or letter of undertaking.[9] This does not imply that release from an attachment likewise clears the lien. An execution sale in an *in rem* proceeding clears the vessel of all liens. An execution sale pursuant to a writ of attachment is not, however, the equivalent of a judicial sale in admiralty. The ship is not sold free of all liens; instead only the owner's interest, whatever it may be, is adjudicated.[11] Indeed, it could not do so, for the attachment bond does not substitute for a lien but only for the owner's personal liability.

---

[7] *Matter of Buchman*, 600 F.2d 160, 165 (8th Cir. 1979).

[8] *The Susana*, 2 F.2d 410, 412-13 (4th Cir. 1924); *Red Star Towing & Transp. Co.*, 5 F. Supp. 502 (E.D.N.Y. 1933); G. Gilmore & C. Black, *supra*, at 802.

[9] *Gray v. Hopkins-Carter Hardware Co. (The Lois)*, 32 F.2d 876, 878 (5th Cir. 1929); G. Gilmore & C. Black, *supra*, at 799.

[10] *The Trenton*, 4 F. 657 (E.D. Mich. 1880); *Zimmern Coal Co. v. Coal Trading Association of Rotterdam (The Totilax Harold)*, 30 F.2d 933 (5th Cir. 1929); G. Gilmore & C. Black, *supra*, at 787, et seq.

[11] G. Gilmore & C. Black, *supra*, at 802.

In its analysis of the *lis alibis pendens* argument, the district court correctly stated the applicable rule: a court having jurisdiction should exercise it unless a compelling reason not to do so is demonstrated.[12] It found compelling reason, however, in the supposed hardship on Chowgule of defending two actions and in the possibility of double recovery. Both of these can readily be averted without the damage to Belcher that dismissal occasions. The Netherlands action has been tried and is awaiting decision. Staying proceedings in this action would avoid repetitive litigation of the issues there involved. If Belcher prevails, its judgment will be satisfied out of the security posted in that court. Thus both the expense of the second litigation and the possibility of double liability will be averted. If Chowgule prevails in the Netherlands action, its undertaking will be released and only those issues unique to the *in rem* action need be determined in the United States court. If, on the other hand, this action is dismissed and Belcher fails to prevail in the Netherlands action, it will be deprived of an opportunity to prove its claim *in rem*. No hardship is imposed on Chowgule by continuing the action, for the same undertaking posted in the Netherlands stands as security for the *in rem* action.

For these reasons the judgment is REVERSED and the case is REMANDED for further proceedings consistent with this opinion.

DAY v. TEMPLE DRILLING CO.

613 F. Supp. 194 (S.D. Miss. 1985)

BARBOUR, District Judge

This matter is before the Court upon the Motion of Defendant, Temple Drilling Company ("Temple"), to Dismiss and to Quash the Writs of Attachment and Garnishment against Garnishee/Defendants, Chevron U.S.A., Inc., Gulf Oil Corporation and Shell Oil Company.

Facts

On April 26, 1985, Plaintiff, ChristoperA. Day ("Day"), sued Temple, his employer, and requested that writs of garnishment be issued against Chevron, Gulf and Shell pursuant to Rule B of the Supplemental Rules for Certain Admiralty and Maritime Claims of the Federal Rules of Civil Procedure. According to the Complaint, Day, a Mississippi resident, was employed by Temple as a "maintenance roustabout" on an offshore drilling rig known as the "Cheyenne." Day alleges that in January 1984, while engaged in the scope of his employment, he slipped and fell down a greasy and rain-covered stairway leading to the motor room of the rig. As a result of this fall, Day claims he sustained severe and permanent injuries attributable to the negligence of Temple for which he is entitled to recover.

Since Temple is not subject to the personal jurisdiction of this Court, Day requested that Chevron, Gulf and Shell be personally served with writs of garnishment pursuant to Rule B(1) of the Supplemental Rules of Certain Admiralty and Maritime Claims. Rule B(1) provides in pertinent part:

> With respect to any admiralty or maritime claim *in personam* a verified complaint may contain a prayer for process to attach the defendants goods and chattels, or credits and effects in the hands of garnishees ..., if the defendant shall not be found within the district.

Gulf answered the writ of garnishment, admitting a debt owed to Temple in the amount of $1,010,000.00. Gulf also answered interrogatories served with the writ of garnishment, stating that the debt owed Temple arose out of billings from Temple for services performed by Temple pursuant to a contract between it and Gulf. Gulf further states that the contract was not executed in Mississippi nor were the services performed by Temple in Mississippi or its territorial waters.

---

[12] See *Gulf Oil Corp. v. Gilbert*, 330 U.S. 501, 67 S. Ct. 839, 91 L. Ed. 1055 (1947); *The Belgenland*, 114 U.S. 355, 5 S. Ct. 860, 29 L. Ed. 152 (1885); *Chiazorv. Transworld Drilling Co. Ltd.*, 648 F.2d 1015, 1019 (5th Cir. 1981); *Poseidon Schiffahrt, G.M.B.H. v. The M/S Netuno*, 474 F.2d 203, 204 (5th Cir. 1973); *Perusahaan Umum Listrik Negara Pusat v. M/V Tel Aviv*, 711 F.2d 1231 (5th Cir. 1983) (upholding conditional dismissal on forum non conveniens grounds because only connection with U.S. forum was in rem action and adequate alternative forum was substantially more convenient; conditional dismissal preserved plaintiff's rights and remedies).

Shell has also responded to garnishment interrogatories, stating that one of its subsidiaries has entered into a contract with Temple for services to be performed by Temple in Louisiana with payment for the services to be made by the Shell subsidiary from Texas. Chevron has not answered at this time.

Temple moves to dismiss and to quash the writs of garnishment for the following reasons:

(1) No property or *res* belonging to Temple is present within the district to support personal jurisdiction over Temple;

(2) No "minimum contacts" exist in Mississippi to support jurisdiction over Temple.

* * *

The Existence of a Res in Mississippi

Temple argues that this Court does not have jurisdiction over it pursuant to Rule B because Day has not attached or garnished property of Temple located within the district. In essence, Temple argues that the situs of a debt does not follow the debtor so that jurisdiction over the garnishee/defendants does not grant jurisdiction over the debts.

* * *

In this case, the garnishee/defendants have been personally served with the writs of garnishment. Gulf has answered, admitting owing Temple a sizeable indebtedness. Shell has admitted a debt may be owed by its subsidiary to Temple. Chevron has not answered. As such, a *"res"* exists in Mississippi such that jurisdiction over Temple is proper.

Although no cases have been found considering the situs of the debt in *quasi in rem* admiralty actions, this Court is persuaded by the decision of the Fifth Circuit in *Belcher Company of Alabama, Inc. v. M/V Maratha Mariner*, 724 F.2d 1161 (5th Cir. 1984) such that if the court has jurisdiction over the garnishee/defendant, it has jurisdiction over the *"res"*.

Belcher involved an *in rem* libel action against a vessel to recover for fuel bunkers furnished the vessel. Jurisdiction was obtained by attachment of the vessel. The Court noted that under the admiralty law of the United States there are three categories of claims: (1) an *in personam* action filed against the owner of the vessel personally; (2) an *in rem* action filed against the vessel; and (3) a *quasi in rem* action based on a claim for money begun by attachment or other seizure of property

> *... when the court has no jurisdiction over the person of the defendant, but has jurisdiction over a thing belonging to him or over a person who is indebted to, or owes a duty to the defendant.* 724 F.2d at 1164. [*Emphasis added*].

The Court further noted that attachment issues

> with respect to any admiralty or maritime claim *in personam* and its purpose is to attach the defendant's goods or chattels' or other assets if the defendant shall not be found in the jurisdiction. Rule B. *Attachment may be used for any debt.*

Id. [*Emphasis added*]. Consequently, it appears that the Fifth Circuit would hold that in *quasi in rem* actions, if the court has jurisdiction over the garnishee-defendant, it has jurisdiction over the debt.

Likewise, in *Engineering Equipment Company v. S/F Selene*, 446 F. Supp. 706 (S.D.N.Y. 1978), the plaintiff sought leave to file a Rule B(1) complaint attaching the property of certain foreign defendants to obtain *quasi in rem* jurisdiction. The defendants suggested that the debts the plaintiff sought to garnish had no local situs and, therefore, the court had no jurisdiction. The court found:

> ... this contention is without merit. Since the Holt defendants (the garnishees) are subject to our *in personam* jurisdiction, the debts are deemed to have their situs within the district. Thus, there is no doubt that the requirements of Rule B(1) have been satisfied in this case.

446 F. Supp. at 708-09.

In so ruling, the court deferred to state law to ascertain whether jurisdiction over the garnishee-defendant was synonymous with jurisdiction over the debt. 446 F. Supp. at 709 n.5. Mississippi law also holds that jurisdiction over the garnishee-defendant is synonymous with jurisdiction over the debt. *See, e.g., Keathley v. Hancock,* 53 So.2d 29 (Miss. 1951).

This Court concludes that since it has personal jurisdiction over the garnishee/defendants, Gulf, Shell and Chevron, it also has jurisdiction over any indebtedness owed by the garnishee/defendants to Temple. This issue appears to be a matter of first impression. The Court recognizes that its decision has a considerable ef-fect on parties like Temple. However, the ruling of this Court is not inconsistent with the purpose of Rule B.

[B]y preserving maritime attachment and garnishment, a claimant is enabled to obtain jurisdiction over credits and effects of the defendant in any number of places where these may be attacked or garnished, although the defendant's residence or place of business may be half-way around the world and the occurrence underlying the suit took place in some other district, or the high seas, or in a foreign country. The practical importance to plaintiff's in preserving this remedy, which antedates the formulation of a comparable common law remedy, is readily apparent. 7A Moore's Federal Practice ¶ 90 at 493.

Necessity of Minimum Contacts

Temple next argues that Rule B(l) violates the substantive due process clause of the Fifth Amendment because it permits the Court to exercise jurisdiction despite the absence of minimum contacts as required by *Shaffer v. Heitner,* 433 U.S. 186 (1977).

This contention is without merit. In *Grand Bahama Petroleum Company, Ltd. v. Canadian Transportation Agencies, Ltd.,* 450 F. Supp. 447, 453 (W.D. Wash. 1978), the court considered at length the applicability of *Shaffer v. Heitner* to Rule B, and concluded that:

... maritime attachment is part and parcel of admiralty jurisprudence and has its justification in the maritime context. The history of maritime attachment itself indicates as well that the common law principles enunciated in *Shaffer* do not necessarily apply to it.

Since admiralty deals with circumstances generally different from those of the common law, this Court is of the opinion that dismissal of this action based upon *Shaffer v. Heitner* would be improper. *See also, Trans-Asiatic Oil Limited S.A. v. Apex Oil Company,* 743 F.2d 956, 959 (1st Cir. 1984).

* * *

Note on Property Subject to Attachment: the Electronic Funds Transfer (EFT)

The Court of Appeals for the Second Circuit in *Winter Storm Shipping, Ltd. v. TPI,*[27] held that electronic funds transfers (EFTs) were property subject to Rule B attachment. EFTs are generated by a bank in one country (the initiating bank), pass electronically through a bank in a second country (the intermediary bank) where they are converted into the currency of the second country and then are electronically deposited to the account of a beneficiary, in a bank in a third country (the destination bank). *Winter Storm* was overruled by The Shipping Corporation of India Ltd. v. Jaldhi Overseas Pte Ltd.[28] The court in *Jaldhi* enumerated the consequences of *Winter Storm*:

---

[27] 310 F.3d 263, 2002 AMC 2705 (2d Cir. 2002).
[28] 585 F.3d 58, 2009 AMC 2409 (2d Cir. 2009).

"The unforeseen consequences of *Winter Storm* have been significant. According to *amicus curiae* The Clearing House Association L.L.C.—whose members are ABN AMRO Bank N.V.; Bank of America, National Association; The Bank of New York Mellon; Citibank, National Association; Deutsche Bank Trust Company Americas; HSBC Bank USA, National Association; JPMorgan Chase Bank, National Association; UBS AG; U.S. Bank National Association; and Wells Fargo Bank, National Association—from October 1, 2008 to January 31, 2009 alone "maritime plaintiffs filed 962 lawsuits seeking to attach a total of $1.35 billion. These lawsuits constituted 33% of all lawsuits filed in the Southern District, and the resulting maritime writs only add to the burden of 800 to 900 writs already served daily on the District's banks." Amicus Br. 3–4. Judge Scheindlin recently outlined the effect of *Winter Storm* on international banks located in New York:

> This Court was recently informed that, currently, leading New York banks receive numerous new attachment orders and over 700 supplemental services of existing orders *each day*. This is confirmed by the striking surge in maritime attachment requests in this district, which now comprise approximately one third of all cases filed in the Southern District of New York. As a consequence, New York banks have hired additional staff, and suffer considerable expenses, to process the attachments. The sheer volume ... leads to many false "hits" of funds subject to attachment, which has allegedly introduced significant uncertainty into the international funds transfer process."

Cala Rosa Marine Co. Ltd. v. Sucres et Deneres Group, 613 F.Supp.2d 426, 431–32 n. 7 (S.D.N.Y.2009) (citation omitted).

Our holding in *Winter Storm* not only introduced "uncertainty into the international funds transfer process," id., but also undermined the efficiency of New York's international funds transfer business. As the Federal Reserve Bank of New York noted in its *amicus curiae* brief in support of the motion for rehearing en banc by the defendant in *Winter Storm*, "efficiency is fostered by protecting the intermediary banks; justice is fostered by expressly telling litigants where the process should be served.... [*Winter Storm*] disrupt[ed] this balance and threaten[ed] the efficiency of funds transfer systems, perhaps including Fedwire." Amicus Br. of Federal Reserve Bank of New York 9, *Winter Storm*, 310 F.3d 263 (No. 02–7078). Undermining the efficiency and certainty of fund transfers in New York could, if left uncorrected, discourage dollar-denominated transactions and damage New York's standing as an international financial center. *See, e.g.*, PEB Commentary 6 n. 4 ("*Winter Storm* and its progeny have had a far greater, and damaging, potential impact on U.S. and foreign banks located in New York than might have been anticipated."); Newman & Zaslowsky, 241 N.Y. L.J. at 3.[29]

Previously, the federal courts in New York contrived various devices to deal with the deluge of Rule B actions. The Second Circuit held that registering as a domestic corporation with the New York Secretary of State meant that the corporation could "found" within the district. A district judge held that service of process would not be deemed continuous and that the garnishee bank would have to possess the defendant's property when the process was served. Another judge required a "plausible showing" that defendant's property was present in the district. Courts expressed concern that plaintiffs would post process servers at banks in order to be ready to serve process at the moment the EFT enters a bank's system.

The court in *Jaldhi* overruled itself for two reasons. First it found that it improperly relied on a non-Rule B seizure case. That case did not hold that EFTs were "property", but only that the U.S could forfeit funds that could be traced to illegal activity. The second basis for overruling *Winter Storm* was a mistaken conclusion that EFTs in the momentary hands of an intermediary bank were "property". Clearly funds in an originating bank are property before they are sent to an intermediary bank. Likewise, once they are deposited at the destination bank, they are

---

[29] *The Shipping Corporation of India Ltd. v. Jaldhi Overseas Pte Ltd.*, 585 F.3d 58, 62, 2009 AMC 2409, 2412-14 (2d Cir. 2009).

property. EFTs, however, are not property under New York Law, and the Uniform Commercial Code makes it clear that a beneficiary had no property interest in an EFT until the transfer has been completed by acceptance by the beneficiary's bank on his behalf. Simply stated when received by an intermediary bank, an EFT is not property.

---

e.   Questions of Constitutionality

1.   Due Process Requirements in a Maritime Context

Note

Litigation of the procedural due process issues (prior notice and hearing) challenging Rules B and C also occurred during the late 1960s through the 1980s. These challenges have abated and have not emerged in the twenty first century. One reason for this is that various federal courts of appeals have rejected the constitutional challenges to the Supplemental Rules. One of the strongest rejections is contained in the case of *Schiffahartsgesellschaft Leonhardt & Co. v. A Bottacchi S.A. De Navegacion*,[30] a case that involve an attack on attachment procedures. Also see *Polar Shipping Ltd. v. Oriental Shipping Corp.*,[31]

Attacks based on the alleged unconstitutionality of Rule C on procedural due process claims have also been rejected on grounds similar to those discussed above. In *The Merchants National Bank of Mobile v. The Dredge G.L. Gillespie*,[32] the Court of Appeals for the Fifth Circuit upheld the validity of Rule C. Several of the grounds of attack would not be relevant today under the amended Rules, namely that the writ issues without judicial sanction and the lack of the right to a post arrest hearing since both are now provided in the amended Rules. The court refers to the unique needs of the arrest procedure in the maritime context.

The other constitutional issue stems from the Court's decision in *Shaffer v. Heitner*[33] in which it held that the quasi-in-rem procedure as used in that case violated the minimum contacts requirement of due process. In *The Merchants National Bank of Mobile v. The Dredge G.L. Gillespie*,[34] the court specifically addresses a challenge based on Shaffer and rejects it. The court reviews that long history of the arrest procedure and its role in maritime law. It also points to the unique nature of the maritime lien as the predicate for arrest. In this case the arrest was based on a preferred ship mortgage which bestows a maritime lien on mortgagees and confers the remedy of arrest. The lienor has an "interest" in the property which the law permits to be perfected through the seizure of the property.

The Court of Appeals for the First Circuit in *Trans-Asiatic Oil Ltd. S.A. v. Apex Oil Co.*,[35] held that Rule B does not violate the Supreme Court's decision in *Shaffer*.

2.   *In Personam* Jurisdiction: Long Arm Statutes—Requisite Minimum Contacts

Note: Federal Rules of Civil Procedure

Rule 4

(k) Territorial Limits of Effective Service.
(1) *In General.* Serving a summons or filing a waiver of service establishes personal jurisdiction over a defendant:

> **(A)** who is subject to the jurisdiction of a court of general jurisdiction in the state where the district court is located;
> **(B)** who is a party joined under Rule 14 or 19 and is served within a judicial district of the United States and not more than 100 miles from where the summons was issued; or
> **(C)** when authorized by a federal statute.

(2) *Federal Claim Outside State-Court Jurisdiction.* For a claim that arises under federal law, serving a summons or filing a waiver of service establishes personal jurisdiction over a defendant if:

> **(A)** the defendant is not subject to jurisdiction in any state's courts of general jurisdiction; and
> **(B)** exercising jurisdiction is consistent with the United States Constitution and laws.

---

[30] 773 F.2d 1528, 1986 AMC 1 (11th Cir. 1985).
[31] 680 F.2d 627, 1982 AMC 2330 (9th Cir. 1982).
[32] 663 F.2d 1338, 1982 AMC 1 (5th Cir. 1981).
[33] 433 U.S. 186 (1977).
[34] 663 F. 2d 1338, 1982 AMC 1 (5th Cir. 1981).
[35] 743 F.2d 956, 1985 AMC 1 (1st Cir. 1984).

WORLD TANKER CARRIERS CORP. v. M/V YA MAWLAYA

99 F.3d 717, 1997 AMC 305 (5th Cir. 1996)

DUHE, Circuit Judge

Plaintiff-Appellant World Tanker Carriers Corp. appeals the district court's dismissal of its maritime law claim against Defendants-Appellees M/V Ya Mawlaya, et al. for want of personal jurisdiction. The court held that Appellant could not assert personal jurisdiction over Appellees pursuant to either the Louisiana long-arm statute or FED. R. CIV. P. 4(k)(2). Because we conclude that the district court erred in its interpretation of Rule 4(k)(2), we reverse and remand.

I. Factual Background

Two vessels, the M/V Ya Mawlaya ("Ya Mawlaya") and the M/V New World ("New World"), collided in international waters off the coast of Portugal. The New World, an ocean-going tanker registered under the laws of Hong Kong and owned by Appellant World Tanker Carriers Corp. ("World Tanker") of Liberia, was proceeding from Gabon to France. The Ya Mawlaya, an ocean-going bulk carrier registered under the laws of Cyprus, was proceeding to Italy with a cargo of soybeans, owned by Cereol Italia Srl. and loaded in Destrehan, Louisiana, within the port of New Orleans. The ownership of the Ya Mawlaya is unclear; World Tanker alleges that the ship's registered owner is Kara Mara Shipping Company, Ltd., of Cyprus, while Appellees claim that the owner is Vestman Shipping Company, Ltd., also of Cyprus. Both have been named as defendants along with others, as individuals and as companies, all foreign, who allegedly have ownership or management interests in the Ya Mawlaya, Vestman Shipping Company, Ltd., and/or Kara Mara Shipping Company, Ltd.

The collision caused an explosion and fire, resulting in the deaths of eight crew members, personal injury to others, and property damage to the vessels and their cargoes. Several lawsuits were filed as a result:... All suits were consolidated.

Appellees moved to dismiss all proceedings against them, asserting as a defense lack of personal jurisdiction. World Tanker, the lead plaintiff, opposed this motion, advancing two jurisdictional theories. First, World Tanker asserts that Appellees are subject to jurisdiction in the Eastern District of Louisiana under the Louisiana long-arm statute; this claim depends on the extent of Appellees "minimum contacts" with Louisiana. Second, World Tanker argues that even if the court finds that minimum contacts have not been established, Appellees are nonetheless subject to the long-arm jurisdiction of the district court pursuant to FED. R. CIV. P. 4(k)(2) based on their contacts with the nation as a whole.

The district court disagreed, granting Appellees' motion to dismiss and holding that neither the state long-arm statute nor Rule 4(k)(2) provides a basis for personal jurisdiction over Appellees. The court first found that World Tanker failed to establish a prima facie case of jurisdiction demonstrating Appellees' minimum contacts with Louisiana sufficient to satisfy the due process requirements of the state long-arm statute. The court then dismissed the case for lack of jurisdiction on the theory that it could not order the requested additional jurisdictional discovery under Rule 4(k)(2) because the consolidated cases did not present a claim "arising under federal law," the jurisdictional predicate of Rule 4(k)(2). The court interpreted this phrase as a reference to "federal question cases" and therefore found the rule inapposite insofar as World Tanker had not raised a federal question claim against Kara Mara. Because we disagree with the court's interpretation of Rule 4(k)(2), we cannot today hold that World Tanker cannot establish a prima facie showing of personal jurisdiction. We therefore reverse and remand for additional jurisdictional discovery pursuant to Rule 4(k)(2).[4]

* * *

---

[4] Because we remand for further proceedings consistent with this opinion, we need not reach the merits of World Tanker's claim under the Louisiana long-arm statute.

III. Discussion

A. National Contacts Pursuant to Rule 4(k)(2)

1. Scope of Rule 4(k)(2)

Fed. R. Civ. P. 4(k)(2) provides:

> If the exercise of jurisdiction is consistent with the Constitution and laws of the United States, serving a summons or filing a waiver of service is also effective, with respect to claims arising under federal law, to establish personal jurisdiction over the person of any defendant who is not subject to the jurisdiction of the courts of general jurisdiction of any state.

Rule 4(k)(2) thus sanctions personal jurisdiction over foreign defendants for claims arising under federal law when the defendant has sufficient contacts with the nation as a whole to justify the imposition of United States' law but without sufficient contacts to satisfy the due process concerns of the long-arm statute of any particular state. *See Pacific Employers Ins. Co. v. M/T Iver Champion et al*, No. 91-0911, 1995 WL 295293, at *5 (E.D.La. May 11, 1995); 4 Charles A. Wright & Arthur R. Miller, Federal Practice & Procedure § 1069 (Supp. 1996).

At the core of this case is whether admiralty actions arise under federal law, an issue of first impression for this Court. Before we determine whether admiralty claims fall under Rule 4(k)(2), we must first consider the meaning of "arising under federal law." World Tanker argues that the district court improperly reads the jurisdictional predicate of Fed. R. Civ. P. 4(k)(2) narrowly as to circumscribe solely federal question cases. Several arguments rooted in text and legislative history support World Tanker's proposition.

The text of Rule 4(k)(2) does not, by its terms, limit itself solely to federal question cases. Instead, the rule states that it applies to "claims arising under federal law," the plain meaning of which incorporates all substantive federal law claims. The Advisory Committee Notes following Rule 4(k)(2) buttress this argument. Throughout its discussion of the Rule, the Advisory Committee refers to federal law broadly as substantive law, not narrowly as a jurisdictional requirement pursuant to 28 U.S.C. § 1331. For example, the Advisory Committee states that Rule 4(k)(2) "authorizes the exercise of territorial jurisdiction over the person of any defendant against whom is made a claim arising under any federal law if that person is subject to personal jurisdiction in no state." (emphasis added). The use of the word "any" to qualify "federal law" strongly suggests that the Advisory Committee intended Rule 4(k)(2) to reach not just federal question cases under § 1331 but all claims arising under substantive federal law. As the court in *United Trading Company S.A. v. M. V Sakura Reefer et al.* points out, had the Advisory Committee meant to limit the scope of Rule 4(k)(2) to federal question claims, it clearly could have done so. No. 95-2846, 1996 WL 374154, at *4 (S.D.N.Y. July 2, 1996) (holding that Rule 4(k)(2) does apply to admiralty cases). Instead, it chose to describe the rule with the phrase "any federal law."

The Advisory Committee concludes its discussion by distinguishing federal law as substantive law distinct from state law, stating that "[t]his narrow extension of the federal reach applies only if a claim is made against the defendant under federal law. It does not establish personal jurisdiction if the only claims are those arising under state law or the law of another country...." Had the Advisory Committee intended to narrowly define "federal law" to refer only to subject matter jurisdiction pursuant to § 1331, it would have compared "arising under" jurisdiction to diversity jurisdiction, the other basis for federal court subject matter jurisdiction. Instead, it chose to compare federal law with state law, suggesting that "federal law" is meant to be used in its broader, substantive law sense.[5]

---

[5] In their discussion of Rule 4, commentators Wright and Miller define "federal question" as follows:

> The subject matter jurisdiction of the federal courts ordinarily is divided into jurisdiction based on diversity of citizenship, as set out in 28 U.S.C.A. § 1331 [sic], and federal question jurisdiction, which encompasses 28 U.S.C.A. §§ 1332-1364 [sic]. The term "federal question jurisdiction" sometimes is used more narrowly to refer only to subject matter jurisdiction based on a claim arising under the Constitution, laws, or treaties of the United States as provided in 28 U.S.C.A. § 1332 [sic]. The term is used in this section for its broader meaning.

4 Charles A. Wright and Arthur R. Miller, Federal Practice and Procedure § 1067.1 n.8 (1987 and Supp. 1996) (incorporating this explanation in their discussion of Rule 4(k)(2)). References to "federal question jurisdiction" are thus to be used interchangeably with descriptions of non-diversity federal claims.

The Rule's legislative history lends support to this argument. Rule 4(k)(2) was adopted not as an adjunct to §1331 but to correct an anomaly in the federal courts' *in personam* jurisdiction of alien defendants. The Advisory Committee explained the purpose of the Rule:

Under the former rule, a problem was presented when the defendant was a non-resident of the United States having contacts with the United States sufficient to justify the application of United States law and to satisfy federal standards of forum selection, but having insufficient contact with any single state to support jurisdiction under state long-arm legislation or meet the requirements of the Fourteenth Amendment limitation on state court territorial jurisdiction.

Thus, there was a gap in the courts' jurisdiction: while a defendant may have sufficient contacts with the United States as a whole to satisfy due process concerns, if she had insufficient contacts with any single state, she would not be amenable to service by a federal court sitting in that state. Although the Supreme Court recognized this problem in Omni Capital International v. Rudolf Wolff & Co., it declined to correct it by decisional rule. "In Omni Capital, the Court determined that the jurisdiction of a federal court, even in federal question cases, in the absence of a statutory provision for service, was limited by the forum state's long-arm statute as a result of the incorporation by Rule 4(e), and not by the Due Process Clause." 4 CHARLES A. WRIGHT & ARTHUR R. MILLER, FEDERAL PRACTICE AND PROCEDURE § 1069, at 88 (Supp. 1996). Rule 4(k)(2) was adopted in response to this problem of a gap in the courts' jurisdiction; there is no suggestion in the Notes discussing Rule 4(k)(2) that the Rule was meant as a companion to 28 U.S.C.A. § 1331. For these reasons, we hold, for purposes of Rule 4(k)(2), "arising under federal law" refers not only to federal question cases as understood in § 1331 but to all substantive federal law claims.

2. Applicability of Rule 4(k)(2) to Admiralty Cases

Concluding that Rule 4(k)(2) does indeed encompass claims arising under federal law, the issue becomes whether federal law incorporates admiralty law. In reaching its conclusion, the district court may have relied erroneously on the Supreme Court's opinion in *Romero v. International Terminal Operating Co.,* 358 U.S. 354, 79 S. Ct. 468, 3 L. Ed. 2d 368 (1959), in which the Court rejected the argument that all cases arising under the admiralty "common law" necessarily arise under the federal question jurisdiction of federal courts under § 1331. The *Romero* principle has had procedural importance in the context of removal jurisdiction, *see e.g., In re Dutile,* 935 F.2d 61, 63 (5th Cir. 1991) (citing *Romero* to explain that cases of admiralty and general maritime claims are not removable under § 1441(a)), and the right to jury trial, *see e.g., Rachal v. Ingram Corp.,* 795 F.2d 1210, 1216 (5th Cir. 1986) (citing *Romero* for proposition that admiralty jurisdiction does not give right to jury trial). But even Justice Frankfurter's opinion in *Romero,* referring repeatedly to "federal maritime law," accepted uncritically the idea that the general maritime law constitutes our national law. In fact, the Supreme Court has long recognized the federal nature of maritime law. *See Southern Pacific Co. v. Jensen,* 244 U.S. 205, 215, 37 S. Ct. 524, 528-29, 61 L.Ed. 1086 (1917).

Article III, § 2, cl. 3 of the United States Constitution extends the judicial power of the federal sovereign to "all Cases of admiralty and maritime Jurisdiction." Congress first conferred the judicial power upon federal courts to hear maritime cases in the Judiciary Act of 1789. Today, that allocation of judicial competence over maritime claims is contained in 28 U.S.C. § 1333, which provides in part:

The district courts shall have original jurisdiction, exclusive of the courts of the States, of: (1) Any civil case of admiralty or maritime jurisdiction, saving to suitors in all cases all other remedies to which they are otherwise entitled.

The first clause thus allocates to federal courts the power to hear any matter which is in admiralty, regardless of the existence of a federal statute creating the maritime right, diversity of citizenship, or the minimum amount in controversy. *See* FRANK L. MARAIST, ADMIRALTY 10 (3d ed. 1996). The second clause grants state courts subject matter jurisdiction, concurrent with federal courts, over most maritime matters. *See id.* at 10-11. Significantly, the second clause does not "grant[ ] states the right to apply their own substantive law to maritime matters pending in their courts...." *Id.* at 11. Application of the substantive law of that state with the most significant relationship to the controversy is appropriate only when the "maritime but local" doctrine applies; that is, when the matter is maritime in nature but there is neither an applicable federal statute governing the claim nor a perceived need for uniformity of maritime law. *See id.* at 12; *see also* 14 CHARLES A. WRIGHT, ARTHUR R. MILLER & EDWARD H. COOPER, FEDERAL PRACTICE AND PROCEDURE § 3671 (1985).

The substantive maritime law of the United States is thus federal law, except in the limited circumstances where the "maritime but local" doctrine applies. Policy concerns support a federal admiralty law. The Supreme Court has long recognized the necessity of a uniform national maritime law. *See Southern Pacific*, 244 U.S. at 217, 37 S. Ct. at 529 (stating that Constitution was designed to establish uniformity in maritime matters). This maritime law encompasses numerous statutes and a substantial body of judge-made law. *See* MARAIST, *supra*, at 6 ("[T]he federal judiciary, fashioning a 'federal admiralty common law.' has provided much of the substantive law of admiralty."); *see also* 14 CHARLES A. WRIGHT, ARTHUR R. MILLER & EDWARD H. COOPER, FEDERAL PRACTICE AND PROCEDURE § 3671, at 419 (1985) (stating that constitutional grant of federal court jurisdiction over admiralty cases "has assumed the existence of a uniform body of substantive maritime law applicable throughout the country.").

Indeed, courts have observed repeatedly that maritime law is federal law. *See e.g. Yamaha Motor Corp., U.S.A. v. Calhoun*, 516 U.S. 199, 210 n.8, 116 S. Ct. 619, 626 n.8, 133 L. Ed. 2d 578 (1996) (referring to "[t]he federal cast of admiralty law"); *Tullier v. Halliburton Geophysical Svcs., Inc. et al.*, 81 F.3d 552, 553 n.l (5th Cir. 1996) (referring to "federal maritime law"); *Guevara v. Maritime Overseas Corp.*, 59 F.3d 1496, 1513 (5th Cir. 1995) (referring to need for uniformity within "federal admiralty law"). Moreover, since the enactment of Rule 4(k)(2), several district courts have recognized its applicability to admiralty cases. *See e.g. United Trading Co.*, 1996 WL 374154, at *3-*4 (holding that claims arising under admiralty law do fall within Rule 4(k)(2) rubric and criticizing district court in World Tanker for its narrow reading of Rule 4(k)(2)); *Nissho Iwai Corp. v. M/V Star Sapphire et al.*, No. 94-1599, 1995 WL 847172, at *3 (S.D.Tex. Aug. 24, 1995) (applying Rule 4(k)(2) to admiralty claim); *Eskofiot A/S v. E.I. Du Pont De Nemours & Co. et al.*, 872 F. Supp. 81, 87 (S.D.N.Y. 1995) (same). For the reasons stated above, we conclude that federal law includes admiralty cases for the purposes of Rule 4(k)(2).

3. Jurisdictional Analysis Under Rule 4(k)(2)

Concluding that Rule 4(k)(2) applies to cases of admiralty, we have satisfied the first prerequisite to its employment. We must now consider whether the Rule provides a basis for personal jurisdiction over Appellees in the instant case. That is, we must determine whether Appellees have contacts with the nation as a whole sufficient to satisfy due process concerns. The now familiar minimum contacts analysis is used to determine whether the assertion of personal jurisdiction would offend "traditional notions of fair play and substantial justice." *Eskofiot A/S*, 872 F. Supp. at 87, *citing Asahi Metal Indus. Co., Ltd. v. Superior Ct.*, 480 U.S. 102, 113, 107 S. Ct. 1026, 1032-33, 94 L. Ed. 2d 92 (1987); *see also Felch v. Transportes Lar-Mex Sa De CV et al.*, 92 F.3d 320, 323-24 (5th Cir. 1996); *Pacific Employers Ins. Co. v. M/T Iver Champion et al.*, No. 91-0911, 1995 WL 295293, at *5 (E.D.La. May 11, 1995). The burden of persuasion remains with the plaintiff to make a prima facie showing of defendants nationwide minimum contacts. *See Ham v. La Cienega Music Co. et al.*, 4 F.3d 413, 415 (5th Cir. 1993).

Based on the record before us, we conclude that World Tanker has not carried its burden. We are persuaded by World Tanker's argument, however, that the district court foreclosed World Tanker's ability to make its prima facie showing when it dismissed the jurisdictional claim. The courts finding was premised on its conclusion that Rule 4(k)(2) did not apply to admiralty cases, and thus, an analysis of Appellees' nationwide contacts would be irrelevant. We determine that this conclusion is erroneous. Accordingly, we reverse and remand this case to the district court for additional jurisdictional discovery as to Appellees' nationwide contacts and further proceedings consistent with this opinion.

***

IV. Conclusion

For the foregoing reasons, we REVERSE AND REMAND.

Note: Venue in Admiralty Cases

In ordinary admiralty *in personam* cases, unlike civil cases, venue is not statutorily prescribed. Rule 82 of the Federal Rules of Civil Procedure states:

> These rules shall not be construed to extend or limit the jurisdiction of the United States district courts or the venue of actions therein. An admiralty or maritime claim within the meaning of Rule 9(h) shall not be treated as a civil action for the purposes of Title 28, U.S.C. §§ 1391-93. [Venue provisions for civil cases.]

Thus, in ordinary *in personam* admiralty actions, venue lies in any place where defendant may be properly served. In rem actions and actions commenced by attachment may be brought in any place where defendants property may be seized. As the Supreme Court stated in *In re Louisville Underwriters*, 134 U.S. 488, 10 S. Ct. 387, 33 L. Ed. 991 (1890):

> By the ancient and settled practice of courts of admiralty, a libel *in personam* may be maintained for any cause of action within their jurisdiction, whenever a monition can be served on the libelee, or an attachment made of any personal property or credits of his;...

The United States Supreme Court in *BNSF Ry. Co. v. Tyrrell*, 137 S. Ct. 1549 (2017) held that § 56 of the Federal Employers Liability Act, which allows an FELA suit to be brought in any place "in which the defendant shall be doing business at the time of commencing of the action," is a statute that deals with venue, not personal jurisdiction. Notwithstanding the fact that the railroad had 2,000 miles of track in Montana and employed over 2,000 workers in Montana, this was not sufficient to make the corporation "at home" there. Merely doing business in the state can be insufficient to confer jurisdiction. The employee was not injured in Montana and was not a citizen of Montana, therefore, there was no basis for exercising specific jurisdiction, and the claim for general jurisdiction also failed. Thus, the court's holdings in *Goodyear Dunlop Tires Operations, S.A. v. Brown*, 564 U.S. 915 (2011) and *Daimler A.G. v. Bauman*, 134 S. Ct. 746 (2014) are being applied across the board. This makes questionable the decision of the District Court for the Eastern District of Louisiana in *O'Berry v. Ensco Intern'l, LLC.* 2017 WL 1048029 (E.D. La. 2017). In that case, the court found that there was no basis for general jurisdiction following the lead of the Supreme Court and inasmuch as the incident did not occur in the state, there was no basis for specific jurisdiction. Instead, the court upheld jurisdiction under § 4(k)(2) of the Federal Rules of Civil Procedure. The Supreme Court's recent decisions cast doubt as to whether or not § 4(k)(2) can satisfy the due process clause. It should be noted, however, that in the *Tyrrell* case suit was brought in a state court not a federal court. One may argue the Section 4(k)(2) confers jurisdiction in United States District Court. Therefore, the issue is different because the question is whether the United States District may exercise personal jurisdiction. The focus shifts from whether the defendant is at home in a particular state to whether the defendant is at home in the United States.

28 U.S.C. § 1404 permits a court in which suit has been properly brought to transfer the case to another court where it could have been commenced for the convenience of the parties or in the interest of justice. This statute has been used in admiralty cases and seems to apply even where the action is brought *in rem*. *Continental Grain Co v. The FBL-585 and Federal Barge Lines, Inc.*, 364 U.S. 19, 80 S. Ct. 1470, 4 L. Ed. 2d 1450 (1960).

CHAPTER 4 — MARITIME LIENS

A. The Nature of Maritime Liens

Note: Definition and Enforcement of Maritime Liens

A maritime lien is a secured right peculiar to maritime law. A lien is a charge on property for the payment of a debt, and a maritime lien is a special property right in a vessel given to a creditor by law as security for a debt or claim arising from some service rendered to the ship to facilitate her use in navigation or from an injury caused by the vessel in navigable waters.

Most maritime claims deriving from tort, contract, or from a peculiarly maritime operation, such as salvage, give rise to maritime liens. Exceptions may be established by precedents or by statute. For example, a seaman's claim for personal injuries under the Jones Act is not supported by a lien. *Plamals v. Steamship Pinar Del Rio*, 277 U.S. 151, 48 S.Ct. 457, 72 L. Ed. 827, 1928 AMC 932 (1928). Historically, the premiums that are due under a contract of marine insurance were not supported by a lien. *In re Insurance Co. of Pennsylvania*, 22 F. 109 (N.D.N.Y. 1884), *aff'd*, 24 F. 559 (C.N.D.N.Y. 1885). However, in *Equilease Corp. v. The Sampson*, 793 F.2d 598, 1986 AMC 1826 (5th Cir.) *(en banc), cert. denied sub nom. Fred S. James &Co. of Texas, Inc. v. Equilease Corp.*, 479 U.S. 984, 107 S.Ct. 570, 93 L. Ed. 2d 575, 1987 AMC 2406 (1986), the Fifth Circuit held that unpaid insurance premiums did give rise to a maritime lien.

Other maritime claims that give rise to maritime liens include the following: seamens claims for wages; salvage; claims under the general law of maritime tort; general average; the preferred ship mortgage; supplies, repairs, and other necessaries; towage, wharfage, pilotage, stevedoring; cargo damage caused by the fault of the carrier; ships claims for unpaid freight; and breach of charter parties.

A maritime claim may be enforced by an action *in personam* in a federal district court or in a state court under the "saving to suitors" clause. Such an action presupposes that the court has subject-matter jurisdiction and that the defendant is properly before the court. A judgment in an *in personam* action may be enforced by the seizure and sale of the entire property of the judgment—debtor; his liability is unlimited unless jurisdiction was based on an attachment of defendant's property and the defendant made a limited appearance. In such a case, the judgment may be enforced only against the property that was attached.

Most maritime claims also may be enforced by an action *in rem*. Such an action must be brought in a federal district court in admiralty; state courts do not have concurrent jurisdiction under the "saving to suitors" clause. An *in rem* action presupposes the presence of the *res* before the court, and a judgment ordinarily may be enforced only against the *res*. Under the circumstances, the liability of the defendant is limited to the value of the *res*.

An action *in rem* is available for the enforcement of a *maritime lien*. All maritime liens may be "executed", that is, foreclosed, by an action *in rem*. A person entitled to a maritime lien is not necessarily limited to an action *in rem*; he may also have an action *in personam*. In such a case, he may proceed both *in rem* and *in personam* if the prerequisites for each action are met. Exceptionally, however, a maritime claim may be enforceable only by an action *in personam* or only by an action *in rem*.

An *in rem* action is theoretically addressed against the *res*, which in the framework of maritime law may be a vessel, its cargo, or earned freight. In this way, the *res* is personified. This fiction pervades nineteenth-century American jurisprudence, but its applications are questionable in modern law. *See Continental Grain Co. v. Barge FBL-585*, 364 U.S. 19, 80 S.Ct. 1470, 4 L. Ed. 2d 1540, 1961 AMC 1 (1960).

The question has arisen whether new forms of maritime liens may be created. Despite its decision in *Equilease, supra*, the Fifth Circuit has declared:

> But admiralty law has long ceased to create new liens. The only liens recognized today are those created by statute and those historically recognized by maritime law. There are no liens by analogy, and maritime liens ... cannot be conferred on the theory of unjust enrichment or subrogation. This principle is summed up in the dictum that the maritime lien is *stricti juris* and will not be extended by construction, analogy or inference.

In re Admiralty Lines, Ltd., 280 F. Supp. 601 (E.D. La. 1968), *aff'd A*10 F.2d 398 (5th Cir. 1969).
See also Nadlev. M/V Tequila, 1973 AMC 909 (S.D.N.Y. 1973); *Kane v. Motor Vessel Leda*, 355 F. Supp. 796, 1972 AMC 2094, 1973 AMC 2296 (E.D. La. 1972), *aff'd*, 491 F.2d 899, 1974 AMC 425 (5th Cir. 1974). In *Kane* the court declared:

Admiralty will entertain a claim for unjust enrichment, or as it is sometimes called, quasi-contract.... This claim does not however give rise to a lien. It is purely *in personam*.

---

1. *The Law of Maritime Liens: Nineteenth Century Jurisprudence*

THE BRIG NESTOR

18 F. Cas. 9 (C.C.D. Maine, 1831)

STORY, J.

* * *

Now a lien by the maritime law is not strictly a Roman hypothecation, though it resembles it, and is often called a tacit hypothecation. It also somewhat resembles what is called a privilege in that law, that is, a right of priority of satisfaction out of the proceeds of the thing in a concurrence of creditors. Emerigon says, that this privilege was strictly personal, and gave only a preference upon simple contract creditors, and had no effect against those, who were secured by express hypothecations; and that this personal privilege given by the Roman law is unknown in the French jurisprudence; for by the law of France every privilege carries with it a tacit and privileged hypothecation, at least as to the thing which is the subject of it.

* * *

Lord Tenterden has remarked, that a contract of hypothecation made by the master does not transfer the property of the ship; but only gives the creditor a privilege or claim upon it, to be carried into effect by legal process. And this is equally true, whether the hypothecation be express or tacit.

THE BOLD BUCCLEUGH

13 Eng. Rep. 884 [7 Moo. P.C. 267] (1851)

A maritime lien does not include or require possession. The word is used in Maritime Law not in the strict legal sense in which we understand it in Courts of Common Law, in which case there could be no lien where there was no possession, actual or constructive; but to express, as if by analogy, the nature of claims which neither presuppose nor originate in possession. This was well understood in the Civil Law, by which there might be a pledge with possession, and a hypothecation without possession, and by which in either case the right traveled with the thing into whosoever possession it came. Having its origin in this rule of the Civil Law, a maritime lien is well defined by Lord Tenterden, to mean a claim or privilege upon a thing to be carried into effect by legal process; and Mr. Justice Story (1 Sumner, 78) explains that process to be a proceeding *in rem*, and adds, that wherever a lien or claim is given upon the thing, then the Admiralty enforces it by a proceeding *in rem*, and indeed is the only Court competent to enforce it. A maritime lien is the foundation of the proceeding *in rem*, a process to make perfect a right inchoate from the moment the lien attaches: and whilst it must be admitted that where such a lien exists, a proceeding *in rem* may be had, it will be found to be equally true, that in all cases where a proceeding *in rem* is the proper course, there a maritime lien exists, which gives a privilege or claim upon the thing, to be carried into effect by legal process. This claim or privilege travels with the thing, into whosoever possession it may come. It is inchoate from the moment the claim or privilege attaches, and when carried into effect by legal process, by a proceeding *in rem*, relates back to the period when it first attached.

* * *

This rule, which is simple and intelligible, is, in our opinion applicable to all cases. It is not necessary to say that the lien is indelible, and may not be lost by negligence or delay where the rights of third parties may be compromised; but where reasonable diligence is used, and the proceedings are had in good faith, the lien may be enforced, into whosoever possession the thing may come.

THE BRIG MALEK ADHEL

43 U.S. (2 How.) 210, 11 L. Ed. 239 (1844)

Mr. Justice STORY delivered the opinion of the court

This is an appeal from a decree of the Circuit Court of the United States for the district of Maryland, sitting in admiralty, and affirming a decree of the District Court rendered upon an information *in rem*, upon a seizure brought for a supposed violation of the act of the 3d of March, 1819, ch. 75, (ch. 200,) to protect the commerce of the United States, and to punish the crime of piracy. The information originally contained five counts, each asserting a piratical aggression and restraint on the high seas upon a different vessel.

* * *

It was fully admitted in the court below, that the owner's of the brig and cargo never contemplated or authorized the acts complained of; that the brig was bound on an innocent commercial voyage from New York to Guayamas, in California; and that the equipments on board were the usual equipments for such a voyage. It appears from the evidence that the brig sailed from the port of New York on the 30th of June, 1840, under the command of one Joseph Nunez, armed with a cannon and ammunition, and with pistols and daggers on board. The acts of aggression complained of, were committed at different times under false pretenses, and wantonly and willfully without provocation or justification, between the 6th of July, 1840, and the 20th of August, 1840, when the brig arrived at Bahia; where, in consequence of the information given to the American consul by the crew, the brig was seized by the United States ship Enterprize, then at that port, and carried to Rio Janeiro, and from thence brought to the United States.

* * *

The next question is, whether the innocence of the owner's can withdraw the ship from the penalty of confiscation under the act of Congress. Here, again, it may be remarked that the act makes no exception whatsoever, whether the aggression be with or without the co-operation of the owner's. The vessel which commits the aggression is treated as the offender, as the guilty instrument or thing to which the forfeiture attaches, without any reference whatsoever to the character or conduct of the owner. The vessel or boat (says the act of Congress) from which such piratical aggression, &c., shall have been first attempted or made shall be condemned. Nor is there any thing new in a provision of this sort. It is not an uncommon course in the admiralty, acting under the law of nations, to treat the vessel in which or by which, or by the master or crew thereof, a wrong or offense has been done as the offender, without any regard whatsoever to the personal misconduct or responsibility of the owner thereof. And this is done from the necessity of the case, as the only adequate means of suppressing the offense or wrong, or insuring an indemnity to the injured party. The doctrine also is familiarly applied to cases of smuggling and other misconduct under our revenue laws; and has been applied to other kindred cases, such as cases arising on embargo and nonintercourse acts. In short, the acts of the master and crew, in cases of this sort, bind the interest of the owner of the ship, whether he be innocent or guilty; and he impliedly submits to whatever the law denounces as a forfeiture attached to the ship by reason of their unlawful or wanton wrongs. In the case of the *United States v. The Schooner Little Charles*, 1 Brock. Rep. 347, 354, a case arising under the embargo laws, the same argument which has been addressed to us, was upon that occasion addressed to Mr. Chief Justice Marshall. The learned judge, in reply, said: "This is not a proceedings against the owner; it is a proceeding against the vessel for an offense committed by the vessel; which is not the less an offense, and does not the less subject her to forfeiture because it was committed without the authority and against the will of the owner. It is true that inanimate matter can commit no offense. But this body is animated and put in action by the crew, who are guided by the master. The vessel acts and speaks by the master. She reports herself by the master. It is therefore not unreasonable that the vessel should be affected by this report." The same doctrine was held by this court in the case of the *Palmyra*, 12 Wheat. R. 1, 14, where referring to seizures in revenue causes, it was said: "The thing is here primarily considered as the offender, or rather the offense is primarily attached to the thing; and this whether the offense be *malum prohibitum* or *malum in re*. The same thing applies to proceeding *in rem* or seizures in the Admiralty."

* * *

The ship is also by the general maritime law held responsible for the torts and misconduct of the master and crew thereof, whether arising from negligence or a willful disregard of duty; as for example, in cases of collision and other wrongs done upon the high seas or elsewhere within the admiralty and maritime jurisdiction, upon the general policy of that law, which looks to the instrument itself, used as the means of the mischief, as the best and surest pledge for the compensation and indemnity to the injured party.

* * *

The remaining question is, whether the cargo is involved in the same fate as the ship. In respect to the forfeiture under the act of 1819, it is plain that the cargo stands upon a very different ground from that of the ship. Nothing is said in relation to the condemnation of the cargo in the fourth section of the act; and in the silence of any expression of the legislature, in the case of provisions confessedly penal, it ought not to be presumed that their intention exceeded their language. We have no right to presume that the policy of the act reached beyond the condemnation of the offending vessel.

* * *

The present case seems to us fairly to fall within the general principle of exempting the cargo. The owner's are confessedly innocent of all intentional or meditated wrong. They are free from any imputation of guilt, and every suspicion of connivance with the master in his hostile acts and wanton misconduct. Unless, then, there were some stubborn rule, which, upon clear grounds of public policy, required the penalty of confiscation to extend to the cargo, we should be unwilling to enforce it. We know of no such rule. On the contrary, the act of Congress, pointing out, as it does, in this very case, a limitation of the penalty of confiscation to the vessel alone, satisfies our minds that the public policy of our government in cases of this nature is not intended to embrace the cargo. It is satisfied by attaching the penalty to the offending vessel, as all that public justice and a just regard to private rights require. For these reasons, we are of opinion that the decrees condemning the vessel and restoring the cargo, rendered in both the courts below, ought to be affirmed.

* * *

Note: Functional Characteristics

In the United States, the law of maritime liens is largely the product of nineteenth-century jurisprudence. A maritime lien has been said to be a *jus in re* (rather than *ad rem*), that is, a *real* rather than a *personal* right. *The John G. Stevens*, 170 U.S. 113, 18 S.Ct. 544, 42 L. Ed. 969 (1898). In civil law terms, such a right confers direct and immediate authority over a thing, and may be asserted against subsequent acquirers of the thing, whether they are in good or in bad faith. *See* A. Yiannopoulos, Civil Law Property §§ 144-146 (2d ed. 1980). In order to explain the priority of liens of the same rank, admiralty courts have declared that a maritime lien is a "proprietary" interest and that the lienor is a part owner. However, in order to explain the ranking of maritime liens, courts have resorted to different rationalizations. *See* section on priority of liens, *infra*.

The best way to determine the nature of maritime liens is to focus attention on their function. A maritime lien is a nonpossessory security device that is created by operation of law. *The Bold Buccleugh, supra.* Parties do not enjoy contractual freedom to create new forms of maritime liens or to exclude the creation of certain forms of maritime liens *(e.g.,* liens for torts, wages, or salvage). The lienor has the right to follow the *res* and is entitled to preferential treatment from the proceeds of the sale of the *res* or from a release bond that is a substitute for the *res*.

A maritime lien is enforceable by process against the *res*. Thus, jurisdictional requirements are satisfied by the presence of the *res* before the court. Jurisdiction over the person of the defendant is not required.

A maritime lien also serves as a device for limitation of liability. In cases in which there is liability *in rem* though no liability *in personam,* the liability of the defendant is ordinarily limited to the value of the *res. See The China,* 74 U.S. (7 Wall.) 53, 19 L. Ed. 67 (1868).

---

2. Comparative Law

Note: Comparison: Civil and Common Law Jurisdictions

The law of maritime liens has developed along different lines in England and in civil law jurisdictions. All countries recognize that the vessel may be the object of security rights. The creditor of a shipowner may have a privilege against the proceeds of the sale of a ship for preferential satisfaction of his claim, whether the claim is based on tort, contract, or some other source of obligations. *See* John M. Kriz, *Ship Mortgages, Maritime Liens, and Their Enforcement: The Brussels Conventions of 1926 and 1952,* 1964 DUKE L.J. 70 (1964).

According to the prevailing view on the continent, however, a privilege is not a real right as distinguished from a personal right; it is merely a cause of preference attached to a real or personal right. A privileged creditor cannot proceed against the vessel, an inanimate object. Legal process is always directed against a natural person or a legal entity, such as a partnership or a corporation. A ship, like any other thing that belongs to the debtor, may be seized by the creditor in order to compel the appearance of the owner before the court or in order to secure the execution and preferential satisfaction of a judgment. In this sense, the seizure of a vessel under continental law may be compared to a foreign attachment under American admiralty practice. However, the analogy would be misleading for a number of reasons.

In most continental countries, the mere seizure of a vessel does not establish jurisdiction for the adjudication of the merits of a claim. Exceptionally, legislation in certain countries establishes a *forum arresti,* and courts may adjudicate the merits of a claim for which the vessel was arrested. In the majority of countries, however, the seizure is a conservatory measure and if the court has no jurisdiction, the seizure will be lifted.

Also in contrast with American law, a judgment rendered by a continental court may be satisfied from the entire property of the defendant. The seizure does not result in a judgment that may be satisfied only from the proceeds of the thing seized.

Note: International Conventions

In spite of its great commercial importance, the matter of maritime liens and mortgages is characterized by a high degree of international uncertainty. National laws differ widely with respect to the creation and enforcement of maritime liens. In order to harmonize these uncertainties, the Comite Maritime International drafted and the Brussels Diplomatic Conference adopted three international conventions to establish a standard list of maritime liens and a common method of their enforcement. The first effort was the International Convention for the Unification of Certain Rules of Law Relating to Maritime Liens and Mortgages (Brussels, April 10, 1926). Enforcement problems were dealt with in the International Convention Relating to the Arrest of Seagoing Ships (Brussels, May 10, 1952). In 1967, a convention to replace the 1926 Convention was adopted by the Brussels Diplomatic Conference, but this has not gained widespread international acceptance. The principal innovation of the 1967 Convention was the elimination of the maritime lien for masters' contracts. *See generally,* Jan M. Sandström, *The Changing International Concept of the Maritime Lien as a Security Right,* 47 TUL. L. REV. 681 (1973).

Neither the 1926 Liens Convention nor the 1952 Arrest Convention nor the 1967 Liens Convention achieved widespread international acceptance. In response, the International Maritime Organization (an arm of the United Nations) has made further efforts to produce international uniformity of the law of maritime liens and mortgages. In 1993, yet another liens convention was made, the International Convention on Maritime Liens and Mortgages (Geneva, May 6, 1993). The 1993 Liens Convention entered into force internationally on September 5th, 2004, six months after 11 countries became party to it (Ecuador, Estonia, Monaco, Nigeria, Russia, St Vincent and the Grenadines, Spain, Syria, Tunisia, Ukraine and Vanuatu). Enforcement problems raised by the 1952 Arrest Convention were addressed in 1999, in the International Convention on Arrest of Ships (Geneva, March 12, 1999), which has not yet come into force internationally (it needs 10 parties to do so; it presently has seven).

The United States has not ratified any of the five conventions. There is no indication that it is likely to do so.

B. Vessels to Which Maritime Liens Attach

Note on the Stewart and Lozman Cases

The United States Supreme Court has provided a definition of the term "vessel" at least for purposes of applying the Jones Act and the Longshore and Harbor Workers' Compensation Act. In *Stewart v. Dutra Const. Co.,*[17] the Court framed the issue: "The question in this case is whether a dredge is a 'vessel' under the Longshore and Harbor Workers' Compensation Act. We hold that it is." The dredge was used to scoop out

---

[17] Stewart v. Dutra Const. Co., 543 U.S. 481, 125 S. Ct. 1118, 160 L. Ed. 2d 932, 2005 A.M.C. 609 (2005).

Boston Harbor in the "Big Dig" construction project. The court of appeals had held that the dredge was not a vessel because its primary purpose was not navigation or commerce and also because it was not in "actual transit" at the time plaintiff was injured. The Supreme Court rejected these criteria for determining vessel status. The Court looked to the statutory scheme provided by Congress with respect to the Jones Act and the LHWCA. At the time both the Jones Act and the LHWCA were enacted, the Revised Statutes of 1873 provided: "In determining the meaning of the revised statutes or of any act or resolution of Congress passed subsequent to February twenty-fifth, eighteen hundred and seventy-one ... [t]he word 'vessel' includes every description of water-craft or other artificial contrivance used, or capable of being used, as a means of transportation on water." That definition is now contained in 1 U.S.C.A. App. §3. In footnote 1 to the Court'/s opinion, the Court stated that: "the Shipping Act of 1916 defines the term 'vessel' for purposes of the Jones Act. See 46 U.S.C.A. App. §801." That statute is substantially similar to the language of 1 U.S.C.A. App. §3.

As has been previously stated, the Court found that the Revised Statute provided the "definition of the term 'vessel'" in the LHWCA. The definition of the term "vessel" contained in the statutes reflected the development of that term under the general maritime law. For example, historically dredges were treated as "vessels" in the case law. An exception to the broad statutory definition was developed by the courts with regard to structures that had become fixed structures, that is, attached to the land under circumstances that rendered them "not practically capable of being used as a means of transportation." The Court observed that "applying §3 brings within the purview of the Jones Act the sorts of water craft considered vessels at the time Congress passed the Act." By including special-purpose vessels like dredges, §3 sweeps broadly, but the other prerequisites to qualifying for seaman status under the Jones Act such as the employee's role on the vessel and his relationship with it provide some limits, notwithstanding §3's breadth.

In rejecting the approach of the court of appeals, the Court held: "Section 3 requires only that a watercraft be 'used or capable of being used as a means of transportation on water' to qualify as a vessel. It does not require that a watercraft be used *primarily* for that purpose." The Court noted that in this case, not only was the dredge capable but also it did in fact transport equipment and workers over water. The Court unequivocally stated, "a watercraft need not be in motion to qualify as a vessel under §3." The "'in navigation' requirement is an element of the vessel status of a watercraft. It is relevant to whether the craft is 'used or capable of being used' for maritime transportation." In previous decisions, the Court had indicated that under certain circumstances a structure that would otherwise qualify as a "vessel" may not satisfy the Jones Act requirement if it has been withdrawn from navigation. The Court states, "The question remains in all cases whether the watercraft's use 'as a means of transportation on water' is a practical possibility or merely a theoretical one." Thus, the term "vessel" for determining Jones Act status and the remedy available to workers covered under §905(b) of the LHWCA is the same.

The United States Supreme Court in *Lozman v. City of Riviera Beach, Fla.*,[36] has further muddied the waters in determining what qualifies as a vessel. In this case, the issue was whether or not a particular houseboat was a vessel. The structure was not used for transportation at all. It was used exclusively as the residence of the owner. It had only been moved four times in a seven year period, and there was no intention to engage in any transportation function. The Court stated:

> Not every floating structure is a "vessel." To state the obvious, a wooden washtub, a plastic dishpan, a swimming platform on pontoons, a large fishing net, a door taken off its hinges, or Pinocchio (when inside the whale) are not "vessels," even if they are 'artificial contrivance[s]' capable of floating, moving under tow, and incidentally carrying even a fair-sized item or two when they do so.

The Court stressed the transportation part of the definition of vessel in the statute. It points out the difference between the structure in the case before it and the structure involved in *Stewart* as follows: "The basic difference, we believe, is that the dredge was regularly, but not primarily, used (and designed in part to be used) to transport workers and equipment over water." The court added to the *Stewart* test the following:

> [A] structure does not fall within the scope of the statutory phrase unless a reasonable observer, looking to the home's physical characteristics and activities, would consider it designed to a practical degree for carrying people or things over water.

The Court, also stated that the test should not rest on "evidence of the subjective intent" although it qualifies statement by saying that intent is not necessarily a totally irrelevant consideration. How will this new test be applied? The dissent questioned whether the new test adds anything to *Stewart* and suggested it will cause confusion. Do we merely look at the structure itself? Do we look at the environment in which the structure is placed? Do we look at how it is being used or how it once was used or how it may be used in the future? If we are to use an objective test, then it is submitted that we look not only to the structure itself but also to its surrounding environment and its use or potential use. Courts recognize that many structures today that are used to transport people, cargo or equipment do not in the least physically resemble bulk cargo vessels, oil tankers, cruise ships, etc. There is a whole range of "special purpose" structures that have long been accorded vessel status and it is doubtful the court means to alter this view.

---

[36] 568 U.S. 115; 133 S. Ct. 735, 184 L. Ed. 2d 604, 2013 A.M.C. 1 (2013).

Note: Component Parts and Accessories of a Vessel

Contracts to construct a vessel or to supply materials for the construction of vessels are not maritime contracts and do not create maritime liens. Likewise, only a "vessel" can be the subject of a "preferred ship mortgage" and the lien afforded thereby. *Chase Manhattan Fin. Serv., Inc. v. McMillian*, 896 F.2d 452, 1990 AMC 1702 (10th Cir. 1990).

A vessel "is considered to consist of the hull, tackle, apparel and furniture." *The Joseph Warner*, 32 F. Supp. 532, 1940 AMC 217 (D. Mass. 1939). Thus as a general rule, when a maritime lien attaches to a vessel it also attaches to its component parts and accessories.

The *component parts* of a vessel are things attached to the vessel so as to become "an integral part" of it. A maritime lien on the vessel reaches these things even if they belong to a person other than the owner of the vessel, such as a charterer, a lessor, or a vendor under a conditional sale. *See The Steamship Tropic Breeze*, 456 F.2d 137, 1972 AMC 1622 (1st Cir. 1972):

> The traditional admiralty rule is that the vessel itself and all equipment which is "an integral part of the vessel and [is] essential to its navigation and operation," are subject to preferred maritime liens on the vessel.
>
> The cement equipment involved in this case is clearly of the type that is subject of such claims. The Tropic Breeze became, with the installation of the equipment, a bulk cement carrier. The equipment was essential to its operation as such a carrier. It could not be removed without substantial cost, and the value of the ship would be substantially less without it. The fact that the equipment was owned by Tropical, a time charterer, does not change the result.

Id. at 141. (citations omitted).

For other cases in which things attached to a vessel were held to be an integral part of it, *see Turner v. United States*, 27 F.2d 134, 1928 AMC 1089 (2d Cir. 1928) [refrigeration equipment]; *The Witch Queen*, F. Cas. 396 (D.C. Cal. 1874) (No. 17,916) [diving bell and air pump]; *The Hope*, 191 F. 243 (D. Mass. 1911) [net lifter and motor for its operation]; *The Paraiso*, 226 F. 966 (W.D. Wash. 1915) [oil tanks]; *First Suffolk National Bank v. The Air Brant*, 125 F. Supp. 709, 1955 AMC 2130 (E.D.N.Y. 1954) [fish pumps, block, and fish boat davits].

Accessories are things that are placed on a vessel for its completion or ornamentation, but are not attached so as to become an integral part of it. When accessories belong to the owner of the vessel, they are clearly subject to the maritime liens that attach to the vessel. *See United States v. Fishing Vessel Zarco*, 187 F. Supp. 371, 1961 AMC 78 (S.D. Cal. 1960) [generator armature]. However, difficult questions arise when accessories belong to a person other than the shipowner. In these circumstances, admiralty courts tend to apply the rules that common-law courts have developed with respect to Fixtures. *See First National Bank & Trust Co. of Escanaba v. Oil Screw Oliver L. Moore & Barge Wiltranco I*, 379 F. Supp. 1382, 1976 AMC 657 (W.D. Mich. 1973), *aff'd*, 521 F.2d 1401 (6th Cir. 1975); *The Joseph Warner*, 32 F. Supp. 532, 1940 AMC 217 (D. Mass. 1939).

In a number of cases, courts have held that maritime liens do not attach to leased thing. *See San Diego Trust & Savings Bank v. Oil Screw Linda Lee*, 1949 AMC 324 (S.D. Cal. 1947) [radio equipment]; *C.I.T. Corp. v. Oil Screw Peggy*, 424 F.2d 767, 1970 AMC 1550 (5th Cir. 1970) [radar equipment]; *United States v. F/V Golden Dawn*, 222 F. Supp. 186, 1964 AMC 691 (E.D.N.Y. 1963) [fishfinder]; *W.R. Grace & Co. v. Charleston Lighterage & Transfer Co.*, 193 F.2d 539, 1952 AMC 689 (4th Cir. 1952) ["equipment"]. *But see United States v. F/V Sylvester F. Whalen*, 217 F. Supp. 916, 1963 AMC 2389 (D. Me. 1963) [fathometer and radar equipment]; *The Augusta*, 15 F.2d 727 (E.D. La. 1920) [wireless equipment].

In *First National Bank & Trust Co. of Escanada v. Oil Screw Olive L. Moore, supra*, the court held that leased equipment does not become subject to the lien of a preferred ship mortgage even if it could become subject to traditional maritime liens. *See also United States v. F/V Golden Dawn, supra; but see First Suffolk National Bank v. The Air Brant, supra; United States v. The Sylvester F. Whalen, supra*.

It has been held that accessories belonging to a vendor under a conditional sale are reached by maritime liens on the vessel. *See The Hope, supra*, and *The Showboat*, 47 F.2d 286, 1931 AMC 19 (D. Mass. 1930). In the latter case, the court held that furnishings provided under a conditional sale agreement for the operation of a vessel as a restaurant and dance hall were not subject to a maritime lien that attached on the vessel; however, portable fire extinguishers provided under a similar agreement were held to be subject to a maritime lien. What is the difference between the two types of equipment?

Prepaid freight is not a part of the vessel. *Galban Lobo Trading Co. S.A. v. The Diponegaro*, 103 F. Supp. 452, 1952 AMC 181 (S.D.N.Y. 1951). Likewise, cargo carried on a vessel is not a component part of the vessel, even if it belongs to the owner of the vessel. Thus, a maritime lien on the vessel does not extend to its cargo. *See Vlavianos v. The Cypress*, 171 F.2d 435, 1949 AMC 9 (4th Cir. 1948), *cert. denied*, 337 U.S. 924, 69 S.Ct. 1168, 93 L. Ed. 1732 (1949). Unpaid seamen, however, may have a lien for wages on earned freight. *Id.*

Does the case law governing accessories defy rational analysis? Does the distinction between things that are essential or necessary for the operation of a vessel and those that are not furnish a rational criterion? *Compare The Hope, supra*; *United States v. The Sylvester F. Whalen, supra*; *The Augusta, supra*, with *W.R. Grace & Co. v. Charleston L. &T. Co., supra*; *First Nat! Bank & Trust Co. v. Oil Screw Olive L. Moore, supra*. Should the existence of a written agreement control the outcome? *See The Linda Lee, supra*. How about a process of "balancing equities" as under the common law of fixtures? Should the creditor under a preferred ship mortgage be given protection at the expense of a lessor or a conditional vendor of movable equipment?

2. *Time of Attachment*

ARQUESSHIPYARDS v. THE S.S. CHARLESVAN DAMME

175 F. Supp. 871 (N.D. Cal. 1959)

WOLLENBERG, District Judge

This libel *in rem* alleges a maritime lien (45 U.S.C.A. § 971) for "wharfage, berthage, dockage facilities, towing and materials to be used in and upon said vessel."

* * *

The affidavit in support of the exceptions states that on December 1, 1957, the respondent vessel was towed to Jack London Square, Oakland, California, where it was opened for business as a restaurant. The affidavit then sets forth facts showing that said vessel was permanently connected to the mainland.

However, it seems clear that admiralty jurisdiction does not depend on respondents classification when in use as a restaurant, but rather on (1) whether the materials furnished and the services performed were capable of giving rise to a maritime lien, or (2) the respondent's status at such time.

* * *

Libelant's affidavit states that the maritime lien is based on materials and services furnished prior to December 1,1957. If this is so,then such period is the crucial time for testing admiralty jurisdiction. The question of respondent's status when in use asa restaurant would be immaterial except in so far as the nature of the services and materials related to such use. If a maritime lien arose at the time such services and materials were furnished it seems clear that a Court of Admiralty could not be ousted from jurisdiction by subsequent changes in the character of the respondent S.S. Charles Van Damme.

* * *

Therefore, in accordance with the above opinion, the exceptions to the libel are hereby overruled.

Note: The "DeadShip"Doctrine

Maritime liens may attach to "vessels". As a general rule, if a structure is a vessel for purposes of admiralty jurisdiction, it is also susceptible of maritime liens.

Under the "dead ship" doctrine, however, a vessel withdrawn from navigation, though still a vessel for purposes of admiralty jurisdiction, is not susceptible of maritime liens. Thus, persons rendering services to a vessel withdrawn from navigation are not entitled to maritime liens for wages. See *Slavin v. Port Service Corp.*, 138 F.2d 386, 1944 AMC 687 (3d Cir. 1943); *Hayford v. Doussony*, 32 F.2d 605, 1929 AMC 849 (5th Cir. 1929), *aff'd*, 42 F.2d 439 (5th Cir. 1930). Moreover, the contract of employment under which services are rendered may not be a maritime contract. See *The Sirius*, 65 F. 226 (N.D. Cal. 1895).

The determination of whether a vessel has been withdrawn from navigation is not always an easy matter. In *In re The Queen, Ltd.*, 1973 AMC 646 (Bankr. E.D. Pa. 1973), *aff'd*, 361 F. Supp. 1009, 1973 AMC 2510 (E.D. Pa. 1973), the court questioned the viability of the "dead ship" doctrine and seemingly held that as long as a floating structure is a vessel, it is susceptible of maritime liens. The court found that the S.S. Queen Elizabeth was a vessel to which maritime liens could attach, although it had been tied to the dock and not removed form its berth; it was not used for transportation or any maritime purpose; and it was actually used as a restaurant and hotel. In the course of its opinion, the court declared:

There is a line of court decisions, known as "The Showboat" cases, in which ships were used as restaurants, dance halls, or the like, in which the courts have held that the mere restructuring of the watercraft for such purposes did not change their characters as "vessels", unless the structure was permanently attached to the land: *Ark* (D.C., Fla.), 17 F.2d 444, 1927 AMC 38; *Showboat* (D.C., Mass.), 47 F.2d 286, 1931 AMC 19; *Club Royale* (D.C., N.J.), 13 F. Supp. 123, 1936 AMC 441. In *Miami River Boat Yard, Inc. v. 60'Houseboat* (5th Cir.), 390 F.2d 596, 1968 AMC 336, the Court held that, although the watercraft "has no motive power and must, as would the most lowly of dumb barges, be towed, does not deprive her of the status of a "vessel"". And, in the same circuit, in the case of *M/V Marifax v. McCrory* (5 th Cir.), 391 F.2d 909, 1968 AMC 965, the court held that a landing craft which had been in mothballs for 15 years, was still a "vessel" because it was not "navigably impotent."

In *Johnson v. Oil Transport Co.*, 440 F.2d 109, 1971 AMC 1038 (3th Cir.), *cert. denied*, 404 U. S. 868, 92 S.Ct. 109, 30 L. Ed. 2d 111 (1971), the court held that a vessel undergoing general overhaul in a dry dock is withdrawn from navigation. Thus, a person injured aboard such a vessel is not entitled to a maritime tort lien. Is there a lien for repairs?

---

2. Vessels in Custodia Legis: *Expenses of Justice*

NEW YORK DOCK CO. v. S.S. POZNAN

274 U.S. 117, 47 S.Ct. 482, 71 L. Ed. 933 (1927)

Mr. Justice STONE delivered the opinion of the Court

This case involves the right of a wharf owner to preferential payment from the proceeds of a vessel, for wharfage furnished the vessel while in the custody of a United States marshal under a warrant of arrest in admiralty The owner of the S.S. Poznan entered into a contract with petitioner, the owner of a private pier in New York harbor, for the use of the pier for discharging cargo from December 1, 1920 until completion. The rate agreed upon was $250 per day, plus certain incidental charges not now material. On December 2, 1920, the Poznan was made fast to the pier. Later in the day, she was arrested by the United States marshal for the district upon libels, afterward consolidated into a single cause, for non-delivery of the vessels cargo and for damages for breach of contracts of affreightment. The marshal allowed the vessel to remain at the pier. Later, on application of one of the libelling cargo owners, the district court ordered the delivery of a part of the cargo which that libellant had shipped, and made the order applicable to all other libellants who should make a like claim. The discharge of the cargo was then begun and deliveries were made to the several libellants in the consolidated cause, including respondent, the John B. Harris Co.

After the cargo had been about one-half discharged, the charterer applied to the district court for leave to move the vessel to another pier where the cargo could be removed more expeditiously. But, on request of some of the libellants and a committee representing the shippers, the application was denied on January 5, 1921. The vessel was unloaded by February 18, 1921. Delivery of the cargo from the pier was completed March 1, 1921, but the vessel remained fast to the pier to and including March 11, 1921, when she was removed.

Meanwhile, the marshal having declined to pay the bill for wharfage without an order of the court, petitioner, in April, 1921, filed its libel against the vessel for the balance of wharfage charges unpaid, aggregating $17,462. By order of the district court, the libellants in the consolidated cause were permitted to intervene. Respondent, the John B. Harris Co., served notice of intervention, and filed its answer denying the allegations in the libel and praying that it be dismissed on the ground, among others, that the wharfage was furnished while the vessel was in the custody of the marshal, and hence no maritime lien could arise. Respondent has since prosecuted the defense in behalf of all the other libellants in the consolidated cause.

The vessel was later sold under an order in the consolidated cause and the proceeds, which were not enough to satisfy the libellants, paid into the registry of the court. The libellants in the consolidated suit have made common cause by stipulation that the recovery under the final decree should be paid to trustees and distributed in accordance with the instructions of a committee representing all of them. The committee found the total claims of the libellants to exceed the amount of the proceeds of the ship. A pro rata distribution has been made to the claimants and an adequate amount reserved to pay the demand of the petitioner, if allowed in this suit. The marshal, although refusing petitioner's request for payment of the wharfage charge, nevertheless included it in his bill of costs and expenses in the consolidated cause and charged his commission on this amount. The court disallowed these items but "without prejudice to any rights of the New York Dock Company to have recourse against the proceeds of the vessel...."

The district court, in the present libel, allowed as a preferential payment from the proceeds of the ship, the reasonable value of the benefits resulting to the consolidated libellants from the wharfage and incidental service furnished by petitioner, to be determined by a special master. This was found by the master and held by the district court to be the reasonable value of the wharfage. A decree for this amount, less certain payments on account made by the owner of the ship, pursuant to the original contract of wharfage, 297 Fed. 345, was reversed by the circuit court of appeals for the second circuit. 9 F.2d 838. This Court granted certiorari. 269 U.S. 547.

The court below held that as the wharfage was furnished after the arrest of the ship, and while it was in the custody of the law, no maritime lien could attach, and that a preferential payment could not be supported upon any other theory applicable to the facts of this case.

A question much argued, both here and below, was whether the case could be considered an exception to the general rule that there can be no maritime lien for services furnished a vessel while in *custodia legis. Cf. The Young America*, 30 Fed. 789; *The Nisseqogue*, 280 Fed. 174; *Paxson v. Cunningham*, 63 Fed. 132; *The Willamette Valley*, 66 Fed. 565. But, in the view we take, the case does not turn upon possible exceptions to that rule, as we think petitioner's right of recovery depends, as the district court ruled, not upon the existence of a maritime lien, but upon principles of general application which should govern whenever a court undertakes the administration of property or a fund brought into its custody for the benefit of suitors.

The libellants in the consolidated cause were not only concerned as owners in securing delivery of the cargo, but as lienors they were interested in the ship and, as eventually appeared, in the whole of her proceeds. Service rendered to the ship after arrest, in aid of the discharge of cargo, and afterward pending the sale, necessarily inured to their benefit, for it contributed to the creation of the fund now available to them. The most elementary notion of justice would seem to require that services or property furnished upon the authority of the court or its officer, acting within his authority, for the common benefit of those interested in a fund administered by the court, should be paid from the fund as an "expense of justice." *The Phebe*, 1 Ware 354, 359, Fed. Cases 11065. This is the familiar rule of courts of equity when administering a trust fund or property in the hands of receivers. The rule is extended, in making disposition of the earnings of the property in the hands of the receiver, to require payment of sums due for supplies furnished before the receivership, where their use by the debtor or receiver in the operation of the property has produced the earnings.

* * *

Such preferential payments are mere incidents to the judicial administration of a fund. They are not to be explained in terms of equitable liens in the technical sense, as is the case with agreements that particular property shall be applied as security for the satisfaction of particular obligations or vendors' liens and the like, which are enforced by plenary suits in equity. They result rather from the self-imposed duty of the court, in the exercise of its accustomed jurisdiction, to require that expenses which have contributed either to the preservation or creation of the fund in its custody shall be paid before a general distribution among those entitled to receive it.

* * *

Such a preferential payment from the proceeds of the ship, for wharfage furnished to her while in custody, was allowed by the court below in *The St. Paul*, 271 Fed. 265. But in the present case, that court thought that *The St. Paul* case was to be distinguished on the ground that there the wharfage service was furnished and the obligation incurred in accordance with an order made by the court and with the consent of the libellants. But here the court denied a motion to remove the ship from petitioner's wharf with the consent of some of the libellants and with full knowledge of all concerned that the wharfage was then being furnished. The libellants in the consolidated cause, who are united in interest with respondent in the present case, thus appear to have acquiesced in this determination. We are unable to perceive any basis for a distinction between action of the court in authorizing the ship to proceed to the wharf to enable it to discharge its cargo in the one case, and authorizing it to remain there for a like purpose in the other. It is enough if the court approves the service rendered or permits it to be rendered, and it inures to the benefit of the property or funds in its custody.

* * *

Note: Vessels in Custodia Legis

In accord with *Poznan, supra,* maritime liens do not arise when the admiralty court permits a consent-keeper to operate the arrested vessel. *See Roy v. M/VKateri Tek,* 238 F. Supp. 813, 1966 AMC 1830 (E.D. La. 1963). In such a case, however, supplymen are entitled to priority payment as an expense of justice. The same rule applies when a person makes advances for the maintenance of the vessel with the approval of the court or of the marshal. *See* 46 U.S.C.A. § 31326(b)(1) (formerly 46 U.S.C. § 953(B)(2)), which provides that a preferred ship mortgage shall be subordinated to "expenses and fees allowed costs taxed...." *Challenger, Inc. v. Durno,* 245 F.2d 815, 1958 AMC 125 (5th Cir. 1957); *United States v. The Audrey II,* 185 F. Supp. *Ill,* 1960 AMC 1977 (N.D. Cal. 1960). As will be discussed, *infra,* 46 U.S.C. § 953(b)(2) has been recodified at 46 U.S.C. § 31326(b)(1) which continues to provide that a preferred ship mortgage is subordinate to "expenses and fees allowed by the court, costs imposed by the court...."

Expenses contracted in *custodia legis* must be based upon the credit of the vessel. Otherwise, all or part of such expenses may be denied. *See Larsen v. New York Dry Dock,* 166 F.2d 687, 1948 AMC 756 (2d Cir. 1948). It is preferable to obtain a court order prior to contracting expenses to ensure that the expenses will be given priority over earlier claims, including maritime liens and mortgages. *See The Audrey II,* 185 F. Supp. *Ill,* 1960 AMC 1977 (N.D. Cal. 1960). However, *THE POZNAN* decision is authority for the position that reasonable expenses incurred for the common benefit of all creditors made without prior court order should nonetheless be given priority.

After a vessel has been arrested, other persons with lien claims may be permitted to intervene in the action and rearrest the vessel. The court may require intervenors to share in the expenses *custodia legis. Beauregard, Inc. v. Sword Services LLC,* 107 F.3d 351, 1997 AMC 1788 (5th Cir. 1997).

Maritime liens may arise, however, when a vessel is attached under state law. *See City of Erie Port Commission v. Steamship North American,* 267 F. Supp. 875, 1968 AMC 500 (W.C. Pa. 1967); *The Pacific Hemlock,* 3 F. Supp. 305, 1933 AMC 298 (W.D. Wash. 1932); *but compare United States v. Oil Screws Ken Jr., Linda Sue,* 275 F. Supp. 792 (E.D. La. 1967).

* * *

Note: Vessels Owned or Operated by a Sovereign

There is normally no reason to assert a maritime lien against a vessel operated by a sovereign because of the recognized availability of *in personam* relief against all levels of government. Furthermore, such vessels are normally immune from *in rem* process. Yet the issue may arise whether a lien can be asserted against such a vessel after it is sold or reverts to private ownership. In a well-known opinion by Justice Holmes, the Supreme Court answered no to this question. *See The Western Maid,* 257 U.S. 419, 42 S.Ct. 159, 66 L. Ed. 299 (1922). For further discussion of this issue see the chapter on Governmental Immunities.

C. Tort Liens

1. Marine Pollution

STATE OF CALIFORNIA, DEPT. OF FISH AND GAME v. S.S. BOURNEMOUTH

307 F. Supp. 922, 1970 AMC 642 (C.D. Cal. 1969)

FERGUSON, District Judge

The plaintiff, State of California, by and through its Department of Fish and Game, filed a complaint *in rem* against the vessel S.S. Bournemouth to recover damages incurred by discharging a quantity of bunker oil into the navigable waters of the State of California and of the United States.

The complaint alleges that the S.S. Bournemouth (hereinafter called "Bournemouth") is a ship of the Liberian Flag, Lloyds Registry Identification Number 516-2504, Official Number 720, owned and operated by Bournemouth Shipping Company, Monrovia, Liberia, and presently under charter to States Marine Lines, Inc., a Delaware corporation.

The acts complained of allegedly occurred on or about October 3, 1969, while the Bournemouth was moored in the navigable waters at Long Beach, California, Berth 10, Pier A, to discharge cargo. Plaintiff seeks relief in the form of damages to compensate for injury to property arising out of pollution to the water and for costs of abatement.

The Bournemouth, while lying at anchor at Berth 10, Pier A, Long Beach, California, was seized, arrested and taken into possession October 5, 1969, by the United States Marshal for the Central District of California subject to a warrant for arrest in an action *in rem*. A bond was posted, and the Bournemouth was permitted to leave the United States.

The defendant made a restricted appearance under Admiralty and Maritime Claims Rule E(8) and moved to dismiss for lack of jurisdiction....

Plaintiff ... urges that injury caused by oil pollution to its navigable waters states a maritime cause of action giving rise to a maritime lien and a suit *in rem* in admiralty independent of any statute. Defendant, on the other hand, contends that not every maritime tort results in a maritime lien, which lien both parties agree is a condition precedent to an action *in rem*. Defendant takes the position that only two types of maritime torts create maritime liens: collision claims and personal injury claims.

The issue before the court in ruling on defendant's motion to dismiss is therefore a narrow one. Stated simply, the issue is whether the tort of injury to plaintiff's property (navigable waters and marine life) will give rise to a maritime lien and thereby support an admiralty action *in rem* against the Bournemouth.

The court finds no merit in defendant's position and is of the opinion ... that a maritime lien against the Bournemouth arises in favor of the plaintiff which will support an admiralty action *in rem*, as a matter of general maritime law without the aid or necessity of a statutory lien.

* * *

The court acknowledges the fact that the great bulk of maritime tort litigation involving suits *in rem* which hold that a maritime lien arises against the vessel falls within the two broad categories: collision claims and personal injury claims, suggested by defendant. The cases do not, however, support the view that these categories are all inclusive or that the tort liability of a vessel for its unlawful acts should be so limited. Nor can the court find support in any public policy or set of reasons advanced by defendant for so limiting maritime liens.

* * *

It is the view of this court that the general maritime law has consistently provided *in rem* relief to the owner of property tortiously damaged by conversion while such property is upon the navigable waters. While here the alleged injury was to the water itself, and possibly the marine life also, efforts to distinguish between various types of injury which may occur to various types of property would serve no useful purpose....

* * *

In the instant case it is admitted by defendant's counsel that the owner's of the Bournemouth are not present and subject to personal service of process. It is further admitted that the vessels present schedule does not call for her to return to the United States. The injury to property alleged to have been caused by defendant in discharging bunker oil into the navigable waters of the State of California is the basis for a claim of the same general merit as any conversion of property historically recognized by the general maritime law and is protected by the creation of a maritime lien.

Oil pollution of the nations navigable waters by seagoing vessels both foreign and domestic is a serious and growing problem. The cost to the public, both directly in terms of damage to the water and indirectly of abatement is considerable. In cases where it can be proven that such damage to property does in fact occur, the governmental agencies charged with protecting the public interest have a right of recourse *in rem* against the offending vessel for damages to compensate for the loss.

* * *

2. Liability of the Vessel: Personification of the Res

THE CHINA

74 U.S. (7 Wall.) 53, 19 L. Ed. 67 (1868)

Mr. Justice SWAYNE delivered the opinion of the court

This is a case arising out of a collision between the steamship China, a British vessel, then leaving the port of New York for Liverpool, and the brig Kentucky, then on a voyage from Cardenas to New York. The facts are few and undisputed. The collision occurred on the 15th of July, 1863, a short distance outside of Sandy Hook. The brig was sunk. The steamship was wholly in fault. It was not alleged, in the argument here for the appellants, that there was either fault or error on the part of the brig. The case turns upon the effect to be given to the statute of New York, of the 3d of April, 1857. At the time of the collision the steamship was within the pilot waters of the port of New York, and was in charge of a pilot, licensed under this act, and taken by the master pursuant to its provisions. The pilot's orders were obeyed, and the catastrophe was entirely the result of his gross and culpable mismanagement. No question was made in the argument, upon the subject; the evidence is too clear to admit of any. These are all the facts material to be considered.

The questions with which we have to deal, are questions of law. No others arise in the case.

It is insisted by the appellant's that the statute referred to compelled the master of the steamship to take the pilot, and that they are therefore not liable for the results of his misconduct.

* * *

1. Was the steamship *compelled* to take the pilot?

* * *

In this connection it is proper to consider the particular provisions of the New York statute. It enacts that the master "*shall* take a licensed pilot;" that in case of refusal, pilotage shall be paid, and that it shall be paid to the first pilot offering his services. Any person not holding a license under this act, or the law of New Jersey, who shall pilot or offer to pilot any vessel to or from the port of New York, by way of Sandy Hook, except such as are exempt by virtue of this act; or any master on board a steamtug who shall tow such vessel without a licensed pilot on board, shall be punished by a fine not exceeding one hundred dollars, or imprisonment not exceeding sixty days; and all persons employing a person not licensed under this act, or the laws of New Jersey, are subjected to a penalty of one hundred dollars.

It was contended by the counsel for the appellee, that if the master had chosen to proceed without a pilot, he would have been liable only to the payment of pilotage; and that none of the other penal provisions of the statute, according to its true meaning, apply in such a case. We have not found it necessary to examine this subject. Giving to the statute either construction, it seems to us clear, in the light of both reason and authority, that the pilot was taken by the steamship upon compulsion.

2. This brings us to the examination of the second proposition. Does the fact that the law compelled the master to take the pilot, exonerate the vessel from liability?

* * *

The New York statute creates a system of pilotage regulations. It does not attempt, in terms, to give immunity to a wrongdoing vessel. Such a provision in a State law would present an important question, which, in this case, it is not necessary to consider.

The argument for the appellant's proceeds upon the general legal principle that one shall not be liable for the tort of another imposed upon him by the law, and who is, therefore, not his servant or agent.

The reasoning by which the application of this principle to the case before us is attempted to be maintained, is specious rather than solid. It is necessary that both outward and inward bound vessels, of the classes designated in the statute, should have pilots possessing full knowledge of the pilot grounds over which they are to be conducted. The statute seeks to supply this want, and to prevent, as far as possible, the evils likely to follow from ignorance or mistake as to the qualifications of those to be employed, by providing a body of trained and skilful seamen, at all times ready for the service, holding out to them sufficient inducements to prepare themselves for the discharge of their duties, and to pursue a business attended with so much of peril and hardship. The services of the pilot are as much for the benefit of the vessel and cargo as those of the captain and crew. His compensation comes from the same source as theirs. Like them he serves the owner and is paid by the owner. If there be any default on his part, the owner has the same remedies against him as against other delinquents on board. The difference between his relations and those of the master is one rather of form than substance. It is the duty of the master to interfere in cases of the pilot's intoxication or manifest incapacity, in cases of danger which he does not foresee, and in all cases of great necessity. The master has the same power to displace the pilot that he has to remove any subordinate officer of the vessel. He may exercise it or not, according to his discretion.

The maritime law as to the position and powers of the master, and the responsibility of the vessel, is not derived from the civil law of master and servant, nor from the common law. It had its source in the commercial usages and jurisprudence of the middle ages. Originally, the primary liability was upon the vessel, and that of the owner was not personal, but merely incidental to his ownership, from which he was discharged either by the loss of the vessel or by abandoning it to the creditors. But while the law limited the creditor to this part of the owner's property, it gave him a lien or privilege against it in preference to other creditors.

The maxim of the civil law—*sic utere tuo ut non loedas alienum*—may, however, be fitly applied in such cases as the one before us. The remedy of the damaged vessel, if confined to the culpable pilot, would frequently be a mere delusion. He would often be unable to respond by payment—especially if the amount recovered were large. Thus, where the injury was the greatest, there would be the greatest danger of a failure of justice. According to the admiralty law, the collision impresses upon the wrongdoing vessel a maritime lien. This the vessel carries with it into whosesoever hands it may come. It is inchoate at the moment of the wrong, and must be perfected by subsequent proceedings. Unlike a common-law lien, possession is not necessary to its validity. It is rather in the nature of the hypothecation of the civil law. It is not indelible, but may be lost by laches or other circumstances.

The proposition of the appellants would blot out this important feature of the maritime code, and greatly impair the efficacy of the system. The appellees are seeking the fruit of their lien.

All port regulations are compulsory. The provisions of the statute of New York are a part of the series within that category. A damaging vessel is no more excused because she was compelled to obey one than another. The only question in all such cases is, was she in fault? The appellant's were bound to know the law. They cannot plead ignorance. The law of the place makes them liable. This ship was brought voluntarily within the sphere of its operation, and they cannot complain because it throws the loss upon them rather than upon the owners of the innocent vessel. We think the rule which works this result is a wise and salutary one, and we feel no disposition to disturb it.

* * *

Note: Shipowner's Liability for Acts of Compulsory/Noncompulsory Pilots

The rule of *The China* is still in force. *See* Vol. 1, Chapter 4, pp. [1-8 to 1-9], for consideration of vicarious liability for the negligence of pilots.

---

3. Liability of the Vessel: Negligence of Charterer

THE BARNSTABLE

181 U.S. 464, 21 S.Ct. 684, 45 L. Ed. 954 (1901)

Mr. Justice BROWN, after stating the case, delivered the opinion of the court

The question involved in this case is, whether the owner's of a vessel, who have let it out upon charter party and agreed to pay "for the insurance on the vessel," are liable, as between themselves and the charterers, for damage done to another vessel by a collision resulting from the negligence of the officers and crew, who are appointed and paid by the charterers.

* * *

Whatever may be the English rule with respect to the liability of a vessel for damages occasioned by the neglect of the charterer, ... the law in this country is entirely well settled, that the ship itself is to be treated in some sense as a principal, and as personally liable for the negligence of any one who is lawfully in possession of her, whether as owner or charterer.

* * *

As the charterers hired the Barnstable for a definite period, and agreed to select their own officers and crew, and pay all the running current expenses of the vessel, including the expense of loading and discharging cargoes—the owner's only assuming to deliver the vessel to the charterers in good order and condition, and to maintain her in an efficient state during the existence of the charter party, there can be no doubt that, irrespective of any special provision to the contrary, the charterers would be liable for the consequences of negligence in her navigation, and would be bound to return the steamer to her owner's free from any lien of their own contracting, or caused by their own fault....

* * *

If, then, the owners be liable for the negligence of the charterers, such liability must arise from the particular stipulation in the charter party that "the owners shall pay for the insurance on the vessel." The language of the clause is peculiar and significant. It is not an agreement to insure, or to procure or provide insurance, but to pay for such insurance as the owner should see fit to take out—and perhaps inferentially to apply such insurance toward the extinguishment of any liability of the charterers for losses covered by the policy.

* * *

But, whatever be the obligation as between the insured and his underwriters, this clause in the charter party should be construed in consonance with its other provisions, and with the obvious intention of the parties that the duty of the owner is discharged by keeping the vessel in good order and condition, and that the charterers assumed and agreed to pay all her running expenses. Conceding that damages done to another vessel are neither the one nor the other, they are incident rather to the navigation than to the preservation of the vessel, although the cost of the premiums may be referable to the preservation of the ship, inasmuch as the owner obtains the benefit of them in case of damages or loss, for which, as between him and the charterer, he is chargeable. If the responsibility for an extraordinary class of damages that is done to another vessel be thus shifted from the charterer, by whose agents the damage is done, and to whom its reimbursement properly belongs, to the owner's, it should be evidenced by some definite undertaking to that effect, and not be inferred from an obscure provision of the charter party, which seems to have been designed for a different purpose. It is scarcely credible that the owner's could have intended to assume a liability for the acts of men not chosen by themselves and entirely beyond their control, which in this case equalled the hire of the ship for eight months, and might, had the Fortuna been of greater value, have exceeded the whole amount of rent payable by the charterers.

* * *

In conclusion, we are of opinion that, if anything more were intended by the insurance clause than to impose on the owners the duty of paying the premiums, it was fully satisfied by an ordinary policy of insurance against perils of the sea; that such policy would not cover damage done to another vessel by a collision with the vessel insured, and that the primary liability for such damage rested upon the charterers and not upon the owners. We express no opinion as to the effect of any payment that may have been actually made by the underwriters upon this loss.

* * *

Note: Liability in Rem Without Liability in Personam

Dicta in *The Barnstable* continues to decide cases. A vessel may be arrested and judgment may be rendered *in rem* for torts committed by one lawfully in possession, such as a bareboat charterer. Typically, however, when the fault is attributed to the charterer only, the shipowner is entitled to full indemnity. *See Demsey & Associates, Inc. v. Steamship Sea Star,* 461 F.2d 1009, 1972 AMC 1440 (2d Cir. 1972); *United Nations Childrens Fund v. Steamship Nordstern,* 251 F. Supp. 833 (S.D.N.Y. 1965); *British West Indies Produce, Inc. v. Steamship Atlantic Clipper,* 353 F. Supp. 548, 1973 AMC 163 (S.D.N.Y. 1973).

The question whether there can be liability *in rem* without liability *in personam* may arise in a variety of contexts. *See Grillea v. United States,* 232 F.2d 919, 1956 AMC 1009 (2d Cir. 1956) [suit by injured longshoreman against the vessel *in rem* and against the bareboat charterer *in personam*]. The United States Supreme Court avoided determination of the issue in *Guzman v. Pichirlo,* 369 U.S. 698, 82 S.Ct. 1095, 8 L. Ed. 2d 205, 1962 AMC 1142 (1962) by finding no demise and in *Reed v. The Yaka,* 373 U.S. 410, 83 S.Ct. 1349, 10 L. Ed. 2d 448, 1963 AMC 1373 (1963) by finding that the bareboat charterer was personally liable. In *Baker v. Raymond International, Inc.,* 656 F.2d 173, 1982 AMC 2752 (5th Cir. 1981), *cert. denied,* 456 U.S. 983, 102 S.Ct. 2256, 72 L. Ed. 2d 861 (1982), the court held that an injured seaman may sue the bareboat charterer, his employer, *in personam* and the shipowner both *in rem* and *in personam* for injuries occasioned by the unseaworthiness of the vessel. The court declared:

> We make explicit what was implicit in *The Barnstable*: a seaman may have recourse *in personam* against the owner of an unseaworthy vessel, without regard to whether owner or bareboat charterer is responsible for the vessel's condition. This personal liability is not, of course, unlimited. It is subject to the ceiling established by the Limitation Act, 46 U.S.C. sec. 183(a). If the vessels unseaworthiness is not the result of the owner's knowledge or privity, his total actual exposure may be limited to the value of the vessel.

Effect of in rem judgment. Ordinarily, an *in rem* judgment may not exceed the value of the bond given for the release of the vessel. Under exceptional circumstances, however, a decree *in rem* may exceed the value of a bond fixed by the court. *See The Fairisle,* 76 F. Supp. 27 (D. Md. 1947), *aff'd, Waterman Steamship Corp. v. Dean,* 171 F.2d 408, 1948 AMC 794 (4th Cir. 1948), *cert. denied,* 337 U.S. 924, 69 S.Ct. 1168, 93 L. Ed. 1732 (1949). After a vessel is released on bond, there can be no new seizure *in rem* on the same cause of action. *The Cleveland,* 98 F. 631 (N.D. Wash. 1899). The Rule is otherwise when a vessel is attached and released on bond in an *in personam* action.

Note: Res Judicata

If an *in rem* action is dismissed, the decree is a bar to a subsequent action *in personam* on the same cause of action. *Bailey v. Sundberg,* 49 F. 583 (2d Cir. 1892). Likewise, if an *in personam* action is dismissed, the decree is ordinarily a bar to a subsequent action *in rem* on the same cause of action. *See Burns Brothers v. Central Railroad,* 202 F.2d 910, 1953 AMC 718 (2d Cir. 1953). In this case, the court stated that a vessel is not a different party from its owner and declared:

> Disputes arise between human beings, not inanimate things; and it would be absurd to give the beaten party another chance because on second trial he appear as the claimant of a vessel that is, and can be nothing but the measure of his stake in the controversy.

Id. at 913.

However, on account of extraordinary circumstances, the court allowed plaintiff to proceed *in rem*. *See* G. Gilmore & C. Black, The Law of Admiralty, § 9-17 at 613-14 (2d ed. 1975).

In contrast, it was held in *Central Hudson Gas &Elec. Corp. v. Empresa Naviera Santa, S. A.,* 56 F.3d 359, 1996 AMC 163 (2d Cir. 1995) that judgment *in rem* against the ship did not preclude plaintiff from suing the demise charterer *in personam.*

When a judgment *in personam* remains unsatisfied, it has been held that the creditor may bring a new suit *in rem* on the same cause of action. *The Eastern Shore,* 24F.2d443, 1928 AMC 327 (D. Md. 1928)', *see also, Pratt v. United States,* 340 F. 2d 174 (1st Cir. 1964). In such a case, the decree *in personam* is not *res judicata. Baun v. The Ethel G.,* 125 F. Supp. 835, 1955 AMC 374 (D. Alaska 1954). It is the same when a judgment *in rem* remains unsatisfied; the creditor may proceed *in personam* on the same cause of action and the previous decree ought not to have the effect of *res judicata. See* G. GILMORE & C. BLACK, THE LAW OF ADMIRALTY § 9-90 at 801-805 (2ded. 1975); *Central Hudson Gas & Elec. Corp. v. Empresa Naviera Santa, S.A.,* 56 F.3d 359, 1996 AMC 163 (2d Cir. 1995).

D. Contract Liens

Note: The Creation of Contract Liens

The law of maritime liens in the United States consists largely of rules developed by federal courts in order to meet the demands of the shipping industry. State courts did not have concurrent jurisdiction for the enforcement of maritime liens because an action *in rem* was not a remedy known to common law. States also did not have concurrent legislative jurisdiction to establish maritime liens except under the "home port" doctrine. State created maritime liens were enforceable only in admiralty and were accorded a low priority.

Dissatisfaction with the law governing service liens led to the enactment of the Federal Maritime Lien Act in 1910. Furthermore, the need for effective means of ship financing at the end of the First World War led to the enactment of the Federal Ship Mortgage Act in 1920. The Lien Act was amended in 1920 and reenacted as a part of the Ship Mortgage Act.

The Maritime Lien Act superseded all state statutes that established maritime liens for necessaries. Today, such statutes are either moribund or dead. *See* G. GILMORE & C. BLACK, THE LAW OF ADMIRALTY § 9-35 at 659 (2d ed. 1975). However, state created contract liens that are not for necessaries may be still enforceable in Admiralty. *See Burdine v. Walden,* 91 F.2d 321, 1937 AMC 1149 (5th Cir. 1937) [master's lien for wages]; *Grow v. The Steel Gas Screw Loraine K,* 310 F.2d 547, 1963 AMC 2044 (6th Cir. 1962) [maritime insurance premium]. For liens for shipbuilding, a non-maritime contract, *see Armstrong v. United States,* 364 U.S. 40, 80 S.Ct. 1563, 4 L. Ed. 2d 1554, 1961 AMC 17 (1960).

Contract liens for necessaries are essentially statutory. The broad application given to the Federal Maritime Lien Act in this area has rendered nineteenth-century precedents obsolete. Other contract liens, however, are still governed by the general maritime law as altered by the federal statutes. Thus, to assume that statutes are "the sole repository of contract liens" is to disregard the long history of maritime jurisprudence. *Rainbow Line, Inc. v. M/VTequila,* 341 F. Supp. 459, 1972 AMC 1540 (S.D.N.Y. 1974), *aff'd,* 480 F.2d 1024, 1973 AMC 1431 (2d Cir. 1973).

In this century, admiralty courts have been expanding the scope of their jurisdiction in matters of contract. *See Hinkins Steamship Agency, Inc. v. Freighters, Inc.,* 351 F. Supp. 373, 1973 AMC 348 (N.D. Cal. 1972), *aff'd* A98 F.2d 411, 1974 AMC 1397 (9th Cir. 1974) [procuration of husbanding services]; *Bergen Shipping Co. Ltd. v. Japan Marine Services, Ltd.,* 386 F. Supp. 430, 1975 AMC 490 (S.D.N.Y. 1974) [agreement to procure crew]; *Ocean Science & Engineering v. International Geomarine Corp.,* 312 F. Supp. 825, 1971 AMC 143 (D. Del. 1970) [oceanographic survey]. This development, however, has not led to the recognition of new forms of contract liens.

1. Executory Contracts/Partial Execution

OSAKA SHOSEN KAISHA v. PACIFIC EXPORT LUMBER CO.

260 U.S. 490, 43 S.Ct. 172, 67 L. Ed. 364 (1923)

Mr. Justice McREYNOLDS delivered the opinion of the Court

March 19, 1917, through its agent at Tacoma, Wash., Osaka Shosen Kaisha, incorporated under the laws of Japan and owner of the Japanese steamer "Saigon Maru," then at Singapore, chartered the whole of that vessel, including her deck, to respondent Lumber Company to carry a full cargo of lumber from the Columbia or Willamette River to Bombay. In May, 1917, the vessel began to load at Portland, Ore. Fiaving taken on a full under-deck cargo and 241,559 feet upon the deck, the captain refused to accept more. After insisting that the vessel was not loaded to capacity and ineffectively demanding that she receive an additional 508,441 feet, respondent libeled her, setting up the charter party and the captains refusal, and claimed substantial damages. The owner gave bond; the vessel departed and safely delivered her cargo.

The Lumber Company maintains that it suffered material loss by the ship's refusal to accept a full load; that she is liable therefor under the general admiralty law.

* * *

Petitioner excepted to the libel upon the ground that the facts alleged showed no lien or right to proceed *in rem*.

* * *

Both courts below acted upon the view that while the ship is not liable *in rem* for breaches of an affreightment contract so long as it remains wholly executory, she becomes liable therefor whenever she partly executes it, as by taking on board some part of the cargo. In support of this view, it is said: Early decisions of our circuit and district courts held that under maritime law the ship is liable *in rem* for any breach of a contract of affreightment with owner or master. That *The Freeman* (1856), 18 How. 182, 188, and *The Yankee Blade* (1857), 19 How. 82, 89, 90, 91, modified this doctrine by denying such liability where the contract remains purely executory, but left it in full force where the vessel has partly performed the agreement, as by accepting part of the indicated cargo.

* * *

We think the argument is unsound.

* * *

The Freeman and *The Yankee Blade* distinctly rejected the theory of the earlier opinions. They are inconsistent with the doctrine that partial performance may create a privilege or lien upon the vessel. And in so far as the lower courts express approval of this doctrine in their more recent opinions, they fail properly to interpret what has been said here.

While, perhaps, not essential to the decision, this Court, through Mr. Justice Curtis, said in *The Freeman*:

Under the maritime law of the United States the vessel is bound to the cargo, and the cargo to the vessel, for the performance of a contract of affreightment; but the law creates no lien on a vessel as a security for the performance of a contract to transport cargo, until some lawful contract of affreightment is made, and a cargo shipped under it.

In *The Yankee Blade*, Mr. Justice Grier, speaking for the Court, declared:

The maritime privilege' or lien is adopted from the civil law, and imports a tacit hypothecation of the subject of it. It is a *jus in re*,' without actual possession or any right of possession. It accompanies the property into the hands of a bona fide purchaser. It can be executed and divested only by a proceeding *in rem*. This sort of proceeding against personal property is unknown to the common law, and is peculiar to the process of courts of admiralty. The foreign and other attachments of property in the State courts, though by analogy loosely termed proceedings *in rem*, are evidently not within the category. But this privilege or lien, though adhering to the vessel, is secret one; it may operate to the prejudice of general creditors and purchasers without notice; it is therefore 'stricti juris,' and cannot be extended by construction, analogy, or inference. 'Analogy,' says Pardessus, (Droit Civ., vol. 3, 597,) 'cannot afford a decisive argument, because privileges are of strict right. They are an exception to the rule by which all creditors have equal rights in the property of their debtor, and an exception should be declared and described in express words; we cannot arrive at it by reasoning from one case to another.'

Now, it is a doctrine not to be found in any treatise on maritime law, that every contract by the owner or master of a vessel, for the future employment of it, hypothecates the vessel for its performance. This lien or privilege is founded on the rule of maritime law as stated by Cleirac, (597:) 'Le batel est obligee a la marchandise et la marchandise au batel.' The obligation is mutual and reciprocal. The merchandise is bound or hypothecated to the vessel for freight and charges, (unless released by the covenants of the charter-party,) and the vessel to the cargo. The bill of lading usually sets forth the terms of the contract, and shows the duty assumed by the vessel. Where there is a charter-party, its covenants will define the duties imposed on the ship. Hence it is said, (1 VALIN, ORDON. DE MAR., b. 3, tit. 1, art 11,) that 'the ship, with her tackle, the freight, and the cargo, are respectively bound (affectee) by the covenants of the charter-party.' But this duty of the vessel, to the performance of which the law binds her by hypothecation, is to deliver the cargo at the time and place stipulated in the bill of lading or charter-party, without injury or deterioration. If the cargo be not placed on board, it is not bound to the vessel, and the vessel cannot be in default for the non-delivery, in good order, of goods never received on board. Consequently, if the master or owner refuses to perform his contract, or for any other reason the ship does not receive cargo and depart on her voyage according to contract, the charterer has no privilege or maritime lien on the ship for such breach of the contract by the owner's, but must resort to his personal action for damages, as in other cases....

* * *

Later opinions approve the same general rule.

> The doctrine that the obligation between ship and cargo is mutual and reciprocal, and does not attach until the cargo is on board, or in the custody of the master, has been so often discussed and so long settled, that it would be useless labor to restate it, or the principles which lie at its foundation. The case of the *Schooner Freeman v. Buckingham*, decided by this court, is decisive of this case. *The Lady Franklin*, 8 Wall. 325, 329.

* * *

The maritime privilege or lien, though adhering to the vessel, is a secret one which may operate to the prejudice of general creditors and purchasers without notice and is therefore *stricti juris* and cannot be extended by construction, analogy or inference. *The Yankee Blade, supra.* The contract of affreightment itself creates no lien, and this Court has consistently declared that the obligation between ship and cargo is mutual and reciprocal and does not attach until the cargo is on board or in the master's custody. We think the lien created by the law must be mutual and reciprocal; the lien of the cargo owner upon the ship is limited by the corresponding and reciprocal rights of the ship owner upon the cargo. *See The Thomas P. Sheldon*, 113 Fed. 779, 782, 783.

The theory that partial acceptance of the designated cargo under a contract of affreightment creates a privilege or lien upon the ship for damages resulting from failure to take all, is inconsistent with the opinions of this Court and, we think, without support of adequate authority. In *The S.L. Watson*, 118 Fed. 945, 952, the court well said:

> The rule of admiralty, as always stated, is that the cargo is bound to the ship and the ship to the cargo. Whatever cases may have been decided otherwise disregarded the universal fact that no lien arises in admiralty except in connection with some visible occurrence relating to the vessel or cargo or to a person injured. This is necessary in order that innocent parties dealing with vessels may not be the losers by secret liens, the existence of which they have no possibility of detecting by any relation to any visible fact. It is in harmony with this rule that no lien lies in behalf of a vessel against her cargo for dead freight, or against a vessel for supplies contracted for, but not actually put aboard. *The Kiersage*, 2 Curt. 421, Fed. Cas. No. 7,762; *Pars. Ship. & Adm.* (1869), 142, 143. It follows out the same principle that Mr. Justice Curtis states in *The Kiersage*, 2 Curt. 424, Fed. Cas. No. 7,762, that admiralty liens are *stricti juris,* and that they cannot be extended argumentatively, or by analogy or inference. He says, 'They must be given by the law itself, and the case must be found described in the law'

Reversed.

_____

Note: Breach of Executory Contract

A maritime lien does not attach for breach of an executory contract. May a time-charterer maintain an action *in rem* for prospective lost profits in connection with the breach of the charter party by the shipowner? In *Interocean Shipping Co. v. M/V Lygaria*, 512 F. Supp. 960, 1981 AMC 2244 (D. Md. 1981), the court held that the time charterer was not entitled to a lien for prospective lost profits because the cargo to be carried was never loaded on the vessel. *But see, E.A.S. T, Inc. of Stamford Conn. v. M/V Alea*, 673 F. Supp. 796, 1988 AMC 1396, (E.D. La.) *aff'd*, 876 F.2d 1168, 1989 AMC 2024 (5th Cir. 1987) (action for breach of warranty of seaworthiness—Charterer had paid charter hire, advanced money to agent to pay port charges and had cargo on dock ready for shipment).

In *Krauss Brothers Lumber Co. v. Dimon Steamship Corp. (The Pacific Cedar)*, 290 U.S. 117, 54 S.Ct. 105, 78 L. Ed. 216 (1933), the Court considered whether a maritime lien attached to a claim by a shipper for the difference between the freight paid and the freight earned at the agreed rate. The Court stated as follows:

We see no distinction, either in principle or with respect to the practical operation or convenience of maritime commerce, between the lien asserted here for overpayment of freight by mistake and those for overpayments similarly made but induced by other means. Here, as there, the overpayment, made as the cargo was unloaded, occurred while the union of ship and cargo continued, and the liability asserted was determined by events contemporaneous with that union. The circumstances which called the lien into being do not differ in point of notoriety from those giving rise to other affreightment liens upon the vessel. While it is true that the maritime lien is secret, hence is *stricti juris* and not to be extended by implication, this does not mean that the right to the lien is not to be recognized and upheld, when within accepted supporting principles, merely because the circumstances which call for its recognition are unusual or infrequent.

Is this case consistent with the decision in *Osaka Shosen Kaisha v. Lumber Co?*.

---

2. Contracts of Passage

ACKER v. THE CITY OF ATHENS

177 F.2d 961 (4th Cir. 1949)

PER CURIAM

Certain passenger-claimants seek an order from this court staying, without bond, the distribution of a fund of $400,000 derived from the sale of the steamship, City of Athens, now on deposit in the Registry of the District Court.... The claims are based upon a prepayment of passage money for a voyage which the ship failed to make. Hence the passengers did not board the ship nor was their baggage placed on board for the purposes of the voyage. When the claims were rejected in the District Court the passengers noted an appeal and prayed that the distribution of the fund to other claimants be stayed pending the action of this court,...

The contentions of the passenger-claimants are: (1) that the failure of the ship to perform her obligations to them as a common carrier amounted to a tort which gave rise to a maritime lien in their favor; and (2) that they acquired a maritime lien by way of subrogation to the extent that the passenger monies were used to secure supplies for the ship and to pay the wages of the crew. Arguments have been made and briefs have been filed on behalf of the passengers and other lien claimants opposing the motion and have been considered by the court, and we have reached the conclusion upon the merits, for the reasons given in the opinion of the District Judge, *Todd Shipyards Corp. v. City of Athens*, D.C., 83 F. Supp. 67, that the claims of the passengers to a maritime lien cannot be sustained under the established rules of Admiralty law, and hence it would serve no good purpose to postpone further the distribution of the fund, already long delayed, to the claimants entitled thereto.

Note: Carriage of Passengers

Would a lien exist if the passengers on The City of Athens had gone on board the vessel before the voyage was cancelled? Does *in personam* liability exist?

---

3. Seamens Liens for "Wages"

WEST WINDS, INC. v. M.V. RESOLUTE

720 F.2d 1097, 1984 AMC 319 (9th Cir. 1983)

REINHARDT, Circuit Judge

Appellants are 23 seamen and the trustees of their union's trust funds whose motion to intervene of right under FED. R. CIV. P. 24(a)(2) was denied by the district court. The sole issue on appeal is whether contributions to trust funds created for the benefit of the employees are "wages of the crew" that may serve as the basis for a preferred maritime lien under 46 U.S.C. § 953 (1976). We are compelled by precedent in this circuit to hold that they are not, at least in the absence of a loss of benefits. Accordingly, we affirm the district court's denial of the motion to intervene.

West Winds, Inc., Nautical Electric, Inc., and Schou-Gallis Co., Ltd., filed an admiralty complaint against the M/V RESOLUTE, *in rem*, and Coast Line Associates, the owner and operator of the vessel, *in personam*, under 46 U.S.C. § 971 (1976), to recover the costs of repairs, supplies, and other necessaries furnished to the vessel. The 23 seamen appellant's were employed by Coast Line Associates between January and June 1982. Under the provisions of its collective bargaining agreement with the International Organization of Masters, Mates and Pilots, Coast Line was required to contribute to trust funds that provide health, retirement, pension, training, vacation, and similar benefits to the seamen. Coast Line failed to make the contributions for the 23 seamen as required by the collective bargaining agreement. To protect their interest in procuring the payment of the delinquent trust fund contributions, the trustees and the seamen sought to intervene of right in the underlying action under FED. R. CIV. P. 24(a)(2).

Appellants claim that the delinquencies give rise to a preferred maritime lien as "wages of the crew" under the Ship Mortgage Act of 1920, section 30, subsection M, 46 U.S.C. § 953 (1976). Under the Act, "a lien for ... wages of the crew of the vessel" is a "preferred maritime lien" that has priority over all other claims and may be asserted in any *in rem* proceeding brought against a vessel. *Id.* Appellants maintain that, because contributions to the trust funds are a form of compensation, they should be treated as "wages of the crew." They do not allege, however, that the failure to make contributions has caused or will cause any loss of benefits.

The district court issued a memorandum and order denying appellants' motion to intervene. Relying upon *Long Island Tankers Corp. v. S.S. Kaimana*, 265 F. Supp. 723 (N.D. Cal. 1967), the district court held that the delinquent trust fund contributions were not "wages of the crew" for purposes of section 953 and that therefore there was no basis for the assertion of a preferred maritime lien. Accordingly, the district court held that the applicants-in-intervention did not allege "an interest relating to the property or transaction which is the subject of the action" as required for intervention of right under FED. R. CIV. P. 24(a)(2).

* * *

II.

As appellees argue, there is Ninth Circuit precedent directly on point in this case. In *Cross v. S.S. Kaimana*, 401 F.2d 182 (9th Cir. 1968) *(per curiam)*, *cert. denied*, 393 U.S. 1095, 89 S.Ct. 879, 21 L. Ed. 2d 785 (1969), in a one sentence opinion, we adopted the reasoning of the district court and held that contributions of employers to trust funds created pursuant to collective bargaining agreements to provide vacation, pension, and welfare benefits to seamen do not constitute "wages of the crew" under 46 U.S.C. § 953. The district court decision, *Long Island Tankers Corp. v. S.S. Kaimana*, 265 F. Supp. 723 (N.D. Cal. 1967), affirmed in *Cross*, addressed a factual situation strikingly similar to the one before us. In that case, as here, the employers were required to make contributions to the trust funds based upon the number of days and type of work performed by their employees. In *Long Island Tankers*, after several employers failed to make contributions the trustees of the funds brought an action seeking to assert preferred maritime liens to recover the contributions as "wages of the crew" under 46 U.S.C. § 953. The district court dismissed the action and held that the contributions were not "wages of the crew" that could serve as the basis for the trustees' assertion of preferred maritime liens. *See* 265 F. Supp. at 726-27.

Appellants contend that we should distinguish *Long Island Tankers* because seamen, as well as trustees of the trust funds, seek to assert the lien here. We decline to do so. Appellants correctly assert that *Long Island Tankers* reserved a question regarding the right of seamen to assert a preferred maritime lien. The question reserved, however, was only whether seamen could assert a preferred maritime lien for a *loss of benefits* caused by an employer's failure to make trust fund contributions. 265 F. Supp. at 727-28. The court did not reserve the question whether seamen could assert a preferred maritime lien for a failure to make contributions when no accompanying loss of benefits was claimed. In reserving the question it did, the court expressly relied on the distinction between contributions that merely serve to fund benefits and the benefits themselves. *Id.* at 727-29. Because the seamen here do not allege any loss of benefits due to Coast Line's failure to make the trust fund contributions, we hold that they fall within the rule established in *Long Island Tankers*. However, like the court in that case, we reserve to another day the question whether seamen may assert a preferred maritime lien for a loss of benefits caused by an employer's failure to make contributions.

Appellants challenge the present-day validity of the reasoning of *Long Island Tankers*. In *Long Island Tankers* the court relied heavily upon the Supreme Court's decision in *United States v. Embassy Restaurant, Inc.*, 359 U.S. 29, 79 S.Ct. 554, 3 L. Ed. 2d 601 (1959). *Embassy Restaurant* held that employer contributions to trust funds were not entitled to priority over other debts as "wages ... due to workmen" under the Bankruptcy Act. *See* 359 U.S. at 35, 79 S.Ct. at 558. Claiming that *Embassy Restaurant* was "overruled" by Congress in the Bankruptcy Reform Act, Pub. L. No. 95-598 § 507, 92 Stat. 2549, 2583-85 (1978), appellant's argue that Long Island Tankers is no longer good law. We disagree.

In the Bankruptcy Reform Act, Congress placed "contributions to employee benefit plans" immediately below "wages, salaries, or commissions" on the hierarchy of debt priorities in bankruptcy proceedings. *See* 11 U.S.C. § 507(a)(3), (4).... In *Embassy Restaurant,* the Court declined to treat contributions as wages; when Congress adopted the Bankruptcy Reform Act, it, too, refused to treat contributions as wages. Instead, it created a completely new category, with a lesser priority than wages, for such claims. Under the Bankruptcy Reform Act, if there are insufficient funds to pay both wages and contributions, the wages are paid and the contributions are not. This type of lesser priority for contributions was not considered by the *Embassy* Court.

* * *

Although the Bankruptcy Reform Act changed the priority afforded to claimants like those in *Embassy,* Congress did not "overrule" *Embassy* or even reject its reasoning. *Long Island Tankers* therefore survives as precedent that is binding upon us.

Cross' affirmance of *Long Island Tankers* does not stand alone. Other courts addressing the issue have held that employer contributions to trust funds created to benefit employees are not "wages of the crew" under 46 U.S.C. § 953. *Barnouw v. S.S. Ozark,* 304 F.2d 717, 719-20 (5th Cir. 1962); *Brandon v. S.S. Denton,* 302 F.2d 404, 415-16 (5th Cir. 1962); *Irving Trust Co. v. The Golden Sail,* 197 F. Supp. 777, 778-79 (D. Or. 1961). Moreover, a recent Supreme Court decision defining "wages" under another maritime statute suggests the vitality of the holding in *Long Island Tankers.*

In *Morrison-Knudsen Construction Co. v. Director, Office of Workers' Compensation Programs,* 461 U.S. 624, 103 S.Ct. 2045, 2049, 76 L. Ed. 2d 194 (1983), the Supreme Court held that employer contributions to union health, welfare, pensions, and training trust funds are not "wages" for the purpose of computing compensation benefits under section 2(13) of the Longshoremen's and Harbor Workers' Compensation Act, 33 U.S.C. § 902(13) (1976). The Court emphasized that, because contributions are not "benefits with a present value that can be readily converted into a cash equivalent on the basis of their market values," they should not be treated as "wages." 103 S.Ct. at 2049. Rather than constituting benefits convertible to a cash equivalent, contributions generally accumulate in trust funds, which, after investment, finance future benefits that are non-convertible, and may vary according to an employee's needs. *See id.*; *Long Island Tankers,* 265 F. Supp. at 727.

Despite *Morrison-Knudsen,*appellants argue that, because contributions to trust funds are increasingly given by employers to employees as a form of compensation, "wages of the crew" should be read to include such contributions. Appellants point out that some courts interpreting other statutes have held that "wages" includes contributions because they are, in fact, part of the total compensation for employment. *See, e.g., W.W. Cross & Co. v. NLRB,* 174 F.2d 875, 877-78 (1st Cir. 1949); *Inland Steel Co. v. NLRB,* 170 F.2d 247, 251 (7th Cir. 1948), *cert. denied,* 336 U.S. 960, 69 S.Ct. 887, 93 L. Ed. 1112 (1949); *Dunlop v. Tremayne,* 62 Cal.2d 427, 431, 398 P.2d 774, 777, 42 Cal. Rptr. 438, 441 (1965). Although we are sympathetic to appellants' argument, we are not free to accept it here. Part of the reason lies in certain limits that we perceive to exist with respect to the function of statutory interpretation.

It has long been recognized that:

> increasingly as a statute gains in age ... its language is called upon to deal with circumstances utterly uncontemplated at the time of its passage. Here the quest is not properly for the sense originally intended by the statute, for the sense sought originally to be put into it, but rather for the sense which can be *quarried out of it* in the light of the new situation.

Llewellyn, *Remarks on the Theory of Appellate Decision and the Rules or Canons about How Statutes are to be Construed,* 3 VAND. L. REV. 395, 400 (1950) (emphasis in original); *see* H. HART & A. SACKS, THE LEGAL PROCESS 1410-11 (tent, ed. 1958) (unpublished manuscript). For this reason, generally, a court interpreting a statute should:

> ask itself not only what the legislation means abstractly, or even on the basis of legislative history, but also what it ought to mean in terms of the needs and goals of our present day society. This approach is required by the insuperable difficulties of readjusting old legislation by the legislative process and by the fact that it is obviously impossible to secure an omniscient legislature.

Phelps, *Factors Influencing Judges in Interpreting Statutes,* 3 VAND. L. REV. 456, 469 (1950); *see In re Grand Jury Subpoena of Persico,* 522 F.2d 41, 64-65 (2d Cir. 1975); *see also* G. CALABRESI, A COMMON LAW IN THE AGE OF STATUTES 163-66 (1982) (suggesting that courts explicitly turn to common law principles to update statutes); Note, *Intent, Clear Statements, and the Common Law: Statutory Interpretation in the Supreme Court,* 95 HARV. L. REV. 892, 913 (1982) (proposing a "common law model of statutory interpretation" that would allow courts to "view statutes as statements of consensually agreed upon principles").

Despite the general validity of this approach to statutory interpretation, the judiciary is not the proper branch of government to update complex statutes when legislative decisionmaking is necessary. For example, in the case of the Bankruptcy Reform Act's creation of a new intermediate level of debt priorities covering contributions, Congress was the only branch of government capable of making the necessary change; courts could only decide whether "wages" includes contributions and could not create a new, separate, and lesser priority category. *See* G. CALABRESI, *supra,* at 158-62 (recognizing inherent difficulties in courts' updating of detailed and technical statutes); G. GILMORE, THE AGES OF AMERICAN LAW 96 (1977) ("[T]he more tightly a statute was drafted originally, the more difficult it becomes to adjust the statute to changing conditions without legislative revision." (footnote omitted)). Here, as with the bankruptcy laws, in order to bring the Ship Mortgage Act up to date, it may be necessary to create a new, separate, and lesser priority category for contributions. That, as we have already said, we cannot do.

We must reject appellants' argument for another reason, as well. The Supreme Court recently refused to define "wages" as including contributions in another maritime act despite its recognition of the changes that have occurred in the methods of paying compensation. *See Morrison-Knudsen,* 103 S.Ct. at 2051-53. It did so partly because the legislative history and administrative practice under the Longshoremen's and Harbor Workers' Compensation Act did not reflect an intention to include contributions. *See id.* at 2050-51. In light of this reasoning, we do not believe that we are free to ignore the judicial history of the Ship Mortgage Act and *Long Island Tankers* simply because of those same changes.

In conclusion, Ninth Circuit precedent and other persuasive authority, as well as the complexities implicated by a judicial restructuring of lien priorities, compel the conclusion that contributions, at least in the absence of any actual loss of benefits, are not "wages of the crew" under 46 U.S.C. § 953 and therefore cannot serve as the basis for the assertion of a preferred maritime lien.

III.

Although we are not free to afford appellant's the relief they seek, they have offered compelling reasons why employer contributions to trust funds should be afforded some form of priority treatment for maritime lien purposes. Demands for contributions to trust funds providing benefits to employees increasingly serve as a substitute for wage demands in collective bargaining negotiations. *See* S. Rep. No. 989, 95th Cong., 2d Sess. 69 (1978), *reprinted in* 1978 U.S. Code Cong. & Ad. News 5787, 5855; H. Rep. No. 533, 93d Cong., 2nd Sess. 2-3 (1974), *reprinted in* 1974 U.S. Code Cong. & Ad. News 4639, 4640-41; *see also* Employee Retirement Income Security Act, Pub. L. No. 93-406, 88 Stat. 829 (1974) (extensively regulating the increasing number of trust funds created pursuant to collective bargaining agreements). For this reason alone, contributions to seamens trust funds would warrant some form of priority treatment similar to that afforded "wages of the crew." Moreover, affording priority treatment to trust fund contributions would further the purpose of the preferred maritime lien—to protect the compensation given seamen. *See* S. Rep. No. 573, 66th Cong., 2nd Sess. 9 (1920). Finally, there is somewhat of an anomaly in the fact that money given by an employer directly to an employee to spend on benefits is treated as "wages," but the same funds, if given to a trust fund that bestows identical benefits upon the employee, are not. *See Duncanson-Harrelson Co. v. Director, Office of Workers' Compensation Programs*, 686 F.2d 1336, 1345 (9th Cir. 1982), *vacated and remanded*, 462 U.S. 1101, 103 S.Ct. 2446, 77 L. Ed. 2d 1329 (1983).

As these arguments strongly suggest, Congress may, as it did in enacting the Bankruptcy Reform Act, wish to "recognize [ ] the realities of labor contract negotiations, where fringe benefits may be substituted for wage demands." S. Rep. No. 989, 95th Cong., 2d Sess. 69 (1978), *reprinted in* 1978 U.S. Code Cong. & Ad. News 5787, 5855. Significant changes in economic conditions suggest the inadequacies of the present debt priorities in the Ship Mortgage Act—priorities that have not been changed since the Act was originally adopted in 1920. Amending 46 U.S.C. § 953 to bring the lien priorities in line with modern economic reality would further the purpose of the section and avoid anomalous results.

IV.

We conclude that, at least absent any loss of benefits, seamen may not assert a preferred maritime lien for "wages of the crew" under 46 U.S.C. § 953 based on an employers failure to make contributions to trust funds. Therefore, the district court's denial of appellant's motion to intervene of right is

Affirmed.

Note: Seamen's Wages

Seamen's wage claims are traditionally the most sacrosanct of transactions giving rise to maritime liens, 46 U.S.C. § 31301(5)(D). Under 46 U.S.C. § 11112 a wage lien is provided for masters of U.S. documented vessels as well. Nevertheless, troublesome questions arise. Are shares in the catch of a fishing vessel "wages"? *See Harison v. The Beverly Lynn*, 172 F. Supp. 719, 1960 AMC 921 (D.P.R. 1959). Would seamen have a lien for unpaid withholding taxes and F.I.C.A. payments? *See P.C. Pfeiffer Co. v. The Pacific Star*, 183 F. Supp. 932, 1960 AMC 1666 (E.D. Va. 1960). Should income tax on wages be paid ahead of maritime liens? *See Marine Midland Trust Co. of New York v. United States*, 299 F.2d 724 (4th Cir. 1962).

---

4. Contract for Sale vs. Contract to Charter Vessel

Question

Breach of a contract to sell a vessel does not give rise to a maritime lien because a contract to sell a ship is not a maritime contract. S.C. Loveland, Inc. v. East West Towing, Inc., 608 F.2d 160, 164, 1980 AMC 2947 (5th Cir. 1979), cert. denied sub nom. St. Paul Mercury Ins. Co. v. East West Towing, Inc., 446 U.S. 918, 100 S.Ct. 1852, 64 L. Ed. 2d 272 (1980). Breach of a charterparty contract to hire a vessel does give rise to a maritime lien because a charterparty contract is a maritime contract. Natasha, Inc. v. Evita Marine Charters, Inc., 763 F.2d 468, 470, 1986 AMC 490 (1st Cir. 1985). Should there be a maritime lien for breach of a sale contract disguised as a charterparty contract? See, e.g., Cary Marine, Inc. v. Motorvessel Papillon, 872 F.2d 751, 1990 AMC 828 (6th Cir. 1989) (arrangement including bareboat charter with option to purchase held to be for sale rather than charter).

---

5. The Preferred Ship Mortgage

Note: The Ship Mortgage Act, 1920

In *Bogart v. The Steamboat John Jay,* 58 U.S. (17 How.) 399, 15 L. Ed. 95 (1854), the court held that admiralty did not have jurisdiction for the foreclosure of a ship mortgage. *See also McCorkle v. First Pennsylvania Banking & Trust Co.,* 459 F.2d 243, 1972 AMC 1596 (4th Cir. 1972). Such a mortgage could be established under state law and could be foreclosed in a state court, but not in an *in rem* action. If a vessel was arrested by a person having a maritime lien, a mortgage creditor could appear before the admiralty court to claim sums remaining after the satisfaction of maritime liens. In such a case, the mortgage creditor was in competition with other persons who did not enjoy the status of a lienor under the maritime law and, for all practical purposes, the security of the mortgage was worthless. In order to encourage investments in the shipping industry and to allow the United States to effectively dispose of the fleet of vessels that it had acquired in the war years, Congress enacted the Ship Mortgage Act in 1920, 46 U.S.C. §§ 911-916.

The constitutionality of the Ship Mortgage act was upheld in *Detroit Trust Co. v. The Thomas Barium,* 293 U.S. 21, 55 S.Ct. 31, 79 L. Ed. 176, 1934 AMC 1417 (1934). In the same case, the court established the proposition that a preferred ship mortgage need not secure a maritime claim. Thus, a preferred ship mortgage may be created for the construction of a vessel. *See State of Israel v. M/V Nili,* 435 F.2d 242, 1971 AMC 428 (5th Cir. 1970), *cert. denied,* 401 U.S. 994, 91 S.Ct. 1232, 28 L. Ed. 2d 532, 1971 AMC 1325 (1971).

By virtue of a 1954 amendment to 46 U.S.C. § 951 (recodified as 46 U.S.C.A. § 31325), a preferred ship mortgage established in a foreign country may be foreclosed in the United States in the same way as a similar mortgage created under the laws of the United States; however, a mortgage on a foreign vessel is subordinated to claims for necessaries furnished in the United States. An anti-lien clause in the mortgage cannot circumvent this provision. *State of Israel v. M/V Nili,* 435 F.2d 242, 1971 AMC 428 (5th Cir. 1970).

The Ship Mortgage Act, 1920 has been amended and recodified at 46 U.S.C. §§ 31301 *et seq.* which became effective January 1, 1989.

TITLE 46 UNITED STATES CODE

46 U.S.C. §§31301 *et seq.*

Chapter 313—Commercial Instruments and Maritime Liens

Subchapter I—General

Sec.

31301. Definitions.

31302. Availability of instruments, copies, and information.

31303. Certain civil actions not authorized.

31304. Liability for noncompliance.

31305. Waiver of lien rights.

31306. Declaration of citizenship.

31307. State statutes superseded.

31308. Secretary of Commerce or Transportation as mortgagee.

31309. General civil penalty.

SUBCHAPTER I—GENERAL

§ 31301. Definitions

In this chapter—

    (1) "acknowledge" means making—

        (A) an acknowledgment ornotarization before a notary public or other official authorized by a law of the United States or a State to take acknowledgments of deeds; or

        (B) a certificate issued under the Hague Convention Abolishing the Requirement of Legalisation for Foreign Public Documents, 1961;

    (2) [omitted eds.]

    (3) "mortgagee" means—

        (A) a person to whom property is mortgaged; or

        (B) when a mortgage on a vessel involves a trust, the trustee that is designated in the trust agreement;

    (4) "necessaries" includes repairs, supplies, towage, and the use of a dry dock or marine railway;

    (5) "preferred maritime lien" means a maritime lien on a vessel—

        (A) arising before a preferred mortgage was filed under section 31321 of this title;

        (B) for damage arising out of maritimetort;

        (C) for wages of a stevedore when employed directly by a person listed in section 31341 of this title;

        (D) for wages of the crew of the vessel;

        (E) for general average; or

        (F) for salvage, including contract salvage; and

    (6) "preferred mortgage"—

        (A) means a mortgage that is a preferred mortgage under section 31322 of this title; and

        (B) also means in sections 31325 and 31326 of this title, a mortgage, hypothecation, or similar charge that is established as a security on a foreign vessel if the mortgage, hypothecation, or similar charge was executed under the laws of the foreign country under whose laws the ownership of the vessel is documented and has been registered under those laws in a public register at the port of registry of the vessel or at a central office.

§ 31302. Availability of instruments, copies, and information

The Secretary of Transportation shall—

    (1) make any instrument filed or recorded with the Secretary under this chapter available for public inspection;

(2) on request, provide a copy, including a certified copy, of any instrument made available for public inspection under this chapter; and

(3) on request, provide a certificate containing information included in an instrument filed or recorded under this chapter.

§ 31303. Certain civil actions not authorized

If a mortgage covers a vessel and additional property that is not a vessel, this chapter does not authorize a civil action *in rem* to enforce the rights of the mortgagee under the mortgage against the additional property.

§ 31305. Waiver of lien rights

This chapter does not prevent a mortgagee or other lien holder from waiving or subordinating at any time by agreement or otherwise the lien holders right to a lien, the priority or, if a preferred mortgage lien, the preferred status of the lien.

§ 31307. State statutes superseded

This chapter supersedes any State statute conferring a lien on a vessel to the extent the statute establishes a claim to be enforced by a civil action *in rem* against the vessel for necessaries.

SUBCHAPTER II—COMMERCIAL INSTRUMENTS

§ 31321. Filing, recording, and discharge

(a) (1) A bill of sale, conveyance, mortgage, assignment, or related instrument, whenever made, that includes any part of a documented vessel or a vessel for which an application for documentation is filed, must be filed with the Secretary of Transportation to be valid, to the extent the vessel is involved, against any person except—

(A) the grantor, mortgagor, or assignor;

(B) the heir or devisee of the grantor, mortgagor, or assignor; and

(C) a person having actual notice of the sale, conveyance, mortgage, assignment, or related instrument.

(2) Each bill of sale, conveyance, mortgage, assignment, or related instrument that is filed in substantial compliance with this section is valid against any person from the time it is filed with the Secretary.

(3) The parties to an instrument or an application for documentation shall use diligence to ensure that the parts of the instrument or application for which they are responsible are in substantial compliance with the filing and documentation requirements.

(b)   To be filed, a bill of sale, conveyance, mortgage, assignment, or related instrument must—

(1) identify the vessel;

(2) state the name and address of each party to the instrument;

(3) state, if a mortgage, the amount of the direct or contingent obligations (in one or more units of account as agreed to by the parties) that is or may become secured by the mortgage, excluding interest, expenses, and fees;

(4) state the interest of the grantor, mortgagor, or assignor in the vessel;

(5) state the interest sold, conveyed, mortgaged, or assigned; and

(6) be signed and acknowledged.

(e)   The Secretary shall—

(1) record the bills of sale, conveyances, mortgages, assignments, and related instruments of a documented vessel complying with subsection (b) of this section in the order they are filed; and

(2) maintain appropriate indexes, for use by the public, of instruments filed or recorded, or both.

(f)   On full and final discharge of the indebtedness under a mortgage recorded under subsection (e)(1) of this section, a mortgagee, on request of the Secretary or mortgagor, shall provide the Secretary with an acknowledged certificate of discharge of the indebtedness in a form prescribed by the Secretary The Secretary shall record the certificate.

* * *

(h) On full and final discharge of the indebtedness under a mortgage deemed to be a preferred mortgage under section 31322(d) of this title, a mortgagee, on request of the Secretary, a State, or mortgagor, shall provide the Secretary or the State, as appropriate, with an acknowledged certificate of discharge of the indebtedness in a form prescribed by the Secretary or the State, as applicable. If filed with the Secretary, the Secretary shall enter that information in the vessel identification system under chapter 125 of this title.

§ 31322. Preferred mortgages

(a)   (1) A preferred mortgage is a mortgage, whenever made, that—
    (A) includes the whole of a vessel;
    (B) is filed in substantial compliance with section 31321 of this title;
    (C) (i) covers a documented vessel; or
        (ii) covers a vessel for which an application for documentation is filed that is in substantial compliance with the requirements of chapter 121 of this title and the regulations prescribed under that chapter; and
    (D) has as the mortgagee—
        (i) a State;
        (ii) the United States Government;
        (iii) a federally insured depository institution, unless disapproved by the Secretary;
        (iv) an individual who is a citizen of the United States;
        (v) a person qualifying as a citizen of the United States under section 2 of the Shipping Act, 1916 (46 App. U.S.C. 802); or
        (vi) a person approved by the Secretary of Transportation.
    (2) Paragraph (1)(D) of this subsection does not apply to a vessel operated only as a fishing vessel, fish processing vessel, or a fish tender vessel (as defined in section 2101 of this title) or to a vessel operated only for pleasure.
(b) A preferred mortgage filed or recorded under this chapter may have any rate of interest that the parties to the mortgage agree to.
(c)   (1) If a preferred mortgage includes more than one vessel or property that is not a vessel, the mortgage may provide for the separate discharge of each vessel and all property not a vessel by the payment of a part of the mortgage indebtedness.
(d)   (1) A mortgage or instrument granting a security interest perfected under State law covering the whole of a vessel titled in a State is deemed to be a preferred mortgage if—
    (A) the Secretary certifies that the State titling system complies with the Secretary's guidelines for a titling system under section 13106(b)(8) of this title; and
    (B)   information on the vessel covered by the mortgage or instrument is made available to the Secretary under chapter 125 of this title.
    (2) This subsection applies to mortgages or instruments covering vessels titled in a State after—
    (A) the Secretary's certification under paragraph (1)(A) of this subsection; and
    (B)   the State begins making information available to the Secretary under chapter 125 of this title.
    (3) A preferred mortgage under this subsection continues to be a preferred mortgage if the vessel is no longer titled in the State where the mortgage was made.

(e) If a vessel is already covered by a preferred mortgage when an application for titling or documentation is filed—

(1) the status of the preferred mortgage covering the vessel to be titled in the State is determined by the law of the jurisdiction where the vessel is currently titled or documented; and

(2) the status of the preferred mortgage covering the vessel to be documented under chapter 121 is determined by subsection (a) of this section.

§ 31323. Disclosing and incurring obligations before executing preferred mortgages

(a) On request of the mortgagee and before executing a preferred mortgage, the mortgagor shall disclose in writing to the mortgagee the existence of any obligation known to the mortgagor on the vessel to be mortgaged.

(b) After executing a preferred mortgage and before the mortgagee has had a reasonable time to file the mortgage, the mortgagor may not incur, without the consent of the mortgagee, any contractual obligation establishing a lien on the vessel except a lien for—

(1) wages of a stevedore when employed directly by a person listed in section 31341 of this title;

(2) wages for the crew of the vessel;

(3) general average; or

(4) salvage, including contract salvage.

§ 31324. Retention and examination of mortgages of vessels covered by preferred mortgages

(a) On request, the owner, master, or individual in charge of a vessel covered by a preferred mortgage shall permit a person to examine the mortgage if the person has business with the vessel that may give rise to a maritime lien or the sale, conveyance, mortgage, or assignment of a mortgage of the vessel.

(b) A mortgagor of a preferred mortgage covering a self-propelled vessel shall use diligence in keeping a certified copy of the mortgage on the vessel.

(Added Pub. L. 100-710, Title I, § 102(c), Nov. 23, 1988, 102 Stat. 4744.)

§ 31325. Preferred mortgage liens and enforcement

(a)   A preferred mortgage is a lien on the mortgaged vessel in the amount of the outstanding mortgage indebtedness secured by the vessel.

(b)   On default of any term of the preferred mortgage, the mortgagee may enforce the preferred mortgage lien in—

(1) a civil action *in rem* for a documented vessel, a vessel to be documented under chapter 121 of this title; or a foreign vessel and;

(2) a civil action *in personam* in admiralty against the mortgagor, comaker, or guarantor for the amount of the outstanding indebtedness secured by the mortgaged vessel or any deficiency in full payment of that indebtedness; and

(3) a civil action against the mortgagor, comaker, or guarantor for the amount of the outstanding in debtedness secured by the mortgaged vessel or any deficiency in full payment of that indebtedness.

(c)   The district courts have original jurisdiction of a civil action brought under subsection (b)(1) or (2) of this section. However, for a documented vessel, a vessel to be documented under chapter 121 of this title, or a foreign vessel, this jurisdiction is exclusive of the courts of the States for a civil action brought under subsection (b)(1) of this section.

(d)(1) Actual notice of a civil action brought under subsection (b)(1) of this section, or to enforce a maritime lien, must be given in the manner directed by the court to—

(A) the master or individual in charge of the vessel;

(B) any person that recorded under section 31343(a) or (d) of this title a notice of a claim of an undischarged lien on the vessel; and

(C) a mortgagee of a mortgage filed or recorded under section 31321 of this title that is an undischarged mortgage on the vessel.

(2) Notice under paragraph (1) of this subsection is not required if, after search satisfactory to the court, the person entitled to the notice has not been found in the United States.

(3) Failure to give notice required by this subsection does not affect the jurisdiction of the court in which the civil action is brought. However, unless notice is not required under paragraph (2) of this subsection, the party required to give notice is liable to the person not notified for damages in the amount of that persons interest in the vessel terminated by the action brought under subsection (b)(1) of this section. A civil action may be brought to recover the amount of the terminated interest. The district courts have original jurisdiction of the action, regardless of the amount in controversy or the citizenship of the parties. If the plaintiff prevails, the court may award costs and attorney fees to the plaintiff.

(e) In a civil action brought under subsection (b)(1) of this section—

(1) the court may appoint a receiver and authorize the receiver to operate the mortgaged vessel and shall retain *in rem* jurisdiction over the vessel even if the receiver operates the vessel outside the district in which the court is located; and

(2) when directed by the court, a United States marshal may take possession of a mortgaged vessel even if the vessel is in the possession or under the control of a person claiming a possessory common law lien.

§ 31326. Court sales to enforce preferred mortgage liens and maritime liens and priority of claims

(a) When a vessel is sold by order of a district court in a civil action *in rem* brought to enforce a preferred mortgage lien or a maritime lien, any claim in the vessel existing on the date of sale is terminated, including a possessory common law lien of which a person is deprived under section 31325(e)(2) of this title, and the vessel is sold free of all those claims.

(b) Each of the claims terminated under subsection (a) of this section attaches, in the same amount and in accordance with their priorities to the proceeds of the sale, except that—

(1) the preferred mortgage lien has priority overall claims against the vessel (except for expenses and fees allowed by the court, costs imposed by the court,and preferred maritime liens); and

(2) for a foreign vessel, the preferred mortgage lien is subordinate to a maritime lien for necessaries provided in the United States.

§ 31327. Forfeiture of Mortgagee Interest

[omitted eds.]

§ 31328. Limitations on Parties Serving as Trustees of Mortgaged Vessel Interests

[omitted eds.]

§ 31329. Court Sales of Documented Vessels

(a) A documented vessel may be sold by order of a district court only to—

(1) a person eligible to own a documented vessel under section 12102 of this title; or

(2) a mortgagee of that vessel.

(b) When a vessel is sold to a mortgagee not eligible to own a documented vessel—

(1) the vessel must be held by the mortgagee for resale;

(2) the vessel held by the mortgagee is subject to section 902 of the Merchant Marine Act, 1936 (46 App. U.S.C. 1242); and

(3) the sale of the vessel to the mortgagee is not a sale foreign within the terms of the first proviso of section 27 of the Merchant Marine Act, 1920 (46 App. U.S.C. 883).

(c) Unless waived by the Secretary of Transportation, a person purchasing a vessel by court order under subsection (a)(1) of this section or from a mortgagee under subsection (a)(2) of this section must document the vessel under chapter 121 of this title.

(d) The vessel may be operated by the mortgagee not eligible to own a documented vessel only with the approval of the Secretary.

(e) A sale of a vessel contrary to this section is void.

(Added Pub. L. 100-710, Title I, § 102(c), Nov. 23, 1988, 102 Stat. 4747.)

§ 31330. Penalties

[omitted Eds.]

SUBCHAPTER III—MARITIME LIENS

[These provisions are found in Section 6 *infra*, Liens for Necessaries]

---

6. Liens for Necessaries

Note: The "Home Port" Doctrine and the Enactment of the Maritime Lien Act

Early admiralty decisions established the proposition that one who furnishes supplies or materials to a vessel in a foreign port acquires a maritime lien under the general maritime law. In *The General Smith*, 17 U.S. (4 Wheat.) 438, 4 L. Ed. 609 (1819), however, the United Sates Supreme Court established the converse proposition that there is no maritime lien under the general maritime law for the furnishing of supplies or repairs at the home port of a vessel. The court reasoned that in the home port suppliers and materialmen are presumed to rely on the credit of the owner of the vessel rather than on that of the vessel.

Under the "home port" doctrine, states had legislative jurisdiction to enact statutes establishing maritime liens for services furnished to vessels at the home port. In the course of the nineteenth century, many states enacted statutes designed to fill the lacuna in the general maritime law created by *The General Smith*. Such liens, however, could only be executed in federal district courts in admiralty, and their priority was low.

Determination of the home port of a vessel also proved to be a difficult matter and incongruous results were reached in practice. *See The St. Jago de Cuba,* 22 U.S. (9 Wheat.) 409, 6 L. Ed. 122 (1824). In *The Lottawanna,* 88 U.S. (21 Wall.) 558, 22 L. Ed. 654, 1996 AMC 2372 (1874), interested parties asked the United States Supreme Court to overrule *The General Smith*. In a celebrated opinion by Justice Bradley, the court decided to stay the course. According to the court, the general maritime law of the United States did not recognize a maritime lien for services in the home port of a vessel, and a change in the law was a matter that had to be addressed to the Congress.

Yielding to mounting pressures, Congress enacted the Maritime Lien Act in 1910. Ten years later, the act was amended and reenacted as a part of the Ship Mortgage Act of 1920. The purpose of the amendment was to broaden the scope of the lien act by expansion of the notion of "necessaries." As previously discussed, the Ship Mortgage Act has been amended and recodified. *See* 46 U.S.C. §§ 31301, *etseq., infra*. It is important, however, to be familiar with the Maritime Lien Act since caselaw relying upon its provisions serves as the basis for interpreting the current statutory law regarding maritime liens.

THE FEDERAL MARITIME LIEN ACT

46 U.S.C. §971 *etseq.*

(superseded version)

§971. Persons Entitled to Lien

Any person furnishing repairs, supplies, towage, use of dry dock or marine railway, or other necessaries, to any vessel, whether foreign or domestic, upon the order of the owner of such vessel, or of a person authorized by the owner, shall have a maritime lien on the vessel, which may be enforced by suit *in rem*, and it shall not be necessary to allege or prove that credit was given to the vessel.

§ 972. Persons Authorized to Procure Repairs, Supplies, and Necessaries

The following persons shall be presumed to have authority from the owner to procure repairs, supplies, towage, use of dry dock or marine railway, and other necessaries for the vessel: The managing owner, ship's husband, master, or any person to whom the management of the vessel at the port of supply is intrusted. No person tortiously or unlawfully in possession or charge of a vessel shall have authority to bind the vessel.

§ 973. Notice to Persons Furnishing Repairs, Supplies, and Necessaries

The officers and agents of a vessel specified in section 972 of this title shall be taken to include such officers and agents when appointed by a charterer, by an owner *pro hac vice*, or by an agreed purchaser in possession of the vessel.

§ 974. Waiver of Right to Lien

Nothing in this chapter shall be construed to prevent the furnisher of repairs, supplies, towage, use of dry dock or marine railway, or other necessaries, or the mortgagee, from waiving his right to a lien, or in the case of a preferred mortgage lien, to the preferred status of such lien, at any time by agreement or otherwise; and this chapter shall not be construed to affect the rules of law existing on June 5, 1920, in regard to (1) the right to proceed against the vessel for advances, (2) laches in the enforcement of liens upon vessels, (3) the right to proceed *in personam*, (4) the rank of preferred maritime liens among themselves, or (5) priorities between maritime liens and mortgages, other than preferred mortgage, upon vessels of the United States.

§ 975. State Statutes Superseded

This chapter shall supersede the provisions of all State statutes conferring liens on vessels, insofar as such statutes purport to create rights of action to be enforced by suits *in rem* in admiralty against vessels for repairs, supplies, towage, use of dry dock or marine railway, and other necessaries.

---

a. Current Statutory Provisions Relating to Maritime Liens

Commercial Instruments and Maritime Liens

46 U.S.C. § 31301, *etseq.*

§ 31301. Definitions

(4) "Necessaries" includes repairs supplies, towage and the use of a dry dock or marine railway.

§ 31305. Waiver of Lien Rights

This chapter does not prevent a mortgagee or other lien holder from waiving or subordinating at any time by agreement or otherwise the lien holders right to a lien, the priority or, if a preferred mortgage lien, the preferred status of the lien.

§ 31307. State Statutes Superseded

This chapter supersedes any State statute conferring a lien on a vessel to the extent the statute establishes a claim to be enforced by a civil action *in rem* against the vessel for necessaries.

SUBCHAPTER III—MARITIME LIENS

§ 31341. Persons presumed to have authority to procure necessaries

(a) The following persons are presumed to have authority to procure necessaries for a vessel:
   (1) the owner;
   (2) the master;
   (3) a person entrusted with the management of the vessel at the port of supply; or
   (4) an officer or agent appointed by—
      (A) the owner;
      (B) a charterer;

(C) an owner *pro hac vice*; or

(D) an agreed buyer in possession of the vessel.

(b) A person tortiously or unlawfully in possession or charge of a vessel has no authority to procure necessaries for the vessel.

§ 31342. Establishing Maritime Liens

(a) Except as provided in subsection (b) of this section, a person providing necessaries to a vessel on the order of the owner or a person authorized by the owner —

(1) has a maritime lien on the vessel;

(2) may bring a civil action in rem to enforce the lien; and

(3) is not required to allege or prove in the action that credit was given to the vessel.

(b) This section does not apply to a public vessel.

§ 31343. Recording and Discharging Liens on Preferred Mortgage Vessels

(a) Except as provided under subsection (d) of this section, a person claiming a lien on a vessel covered by a preferred mortgage filed or recorded under this chapter may record with the Secretary of Transportation a notice of that persons lien claim on the vessel. To be recordable, the notice must—

(1) state the nature of the lien;

(2) state the date the lien was established;

(3) state the amount of the lien;

(4) state the name and address of the person; and

(5) be signed and acknowledged.

(b) The Secretary shall record a notice complying with subsection (a) of this section.

(c) On full and final discharge of the indebtedness that is the basis for a claim recorded under subsection(b)of this section, on request of the Secretary or owner, the person having the claim shall provide the Secretary with an acknowledged certificate of discharge of the indebtedness. The Secretary shall record the certificate.

(d) A person claiming a lien on a vessel covered by a preferred mortgage under section 31322(d) of this title must record and discharge the lien as provided by the law of the Sate in which the vessel is titled.

---

b. Interpretation of Current Statutory Provisions: Relevant Decisions Based Upon the Federal Maritime Lien Act

i. 46 U.S.C. § 31342: "A Person Providing Necessaries to a Vessel...."

PIEDMONT COAL CO. v. SEABOARD FISHERIES CO.

254 U.S. 1, 41 S.Ct. 1, 65 L. Ed. 97 (1920)

Mr. Justice BRANDEIS delivered the opinion of the court

The Atlantic Phosphate and Oil Corporation owned a fleet of nineteen fishing steamers. It owned also factories at Promised Land, Long Island, and Tiverton, Rhode Island, to which the fish caught were delivered and at which its vessels coaled. When the fishing season of 1914 opened the company was financially embarrassed. Its steamers and factories had been mortgaged to secure an issue of bonds. Bills for supplies theretofore furnished remained unpaid. The company had neither money nor credit. It could not enter upon the seasons operations unless some arrangement should be made to supply its vessels and factories with coal. After some negotiations, the Piedmont and Georges Creek Coal Company, then a creditor for coal delivered during the year 1913, agreed to furnish the Oil Corporation such coal as it would require during the season of 1914—the understanding of the parties being that the coal to be delivered would be used by the factories as well as by the vessels, that the greater part would be used by the vessels, that the law would afford a lien on the vessels for the purchase price of the coal and that the Coal Company would thus have security. Shipments of coal were made under this agreement from time to time during the spring and summer as ordered by the Oil Corporation. In the autumn receivers for the corporation were appointed by the District Court of the United States for the District of Rhode Island, and later a suit was brought to foreclose the mortgage upon the vessels and factories. At the time the receivers were appointed five cargoes of coal shipped under the above agreement had not been paid for. The Coal Company libeled twelve of the steamers asserting maritime liens for the price and value of either all the coal or of such parts as had been used by the libeled vessels respectively. Meanwhile, the vessels were sold under the decree of foreclosure. The Seaboard Fisheries Company became the purchaser and, intervening as claimant in the lien proceedings, denied liability. The District Court held that the Coal Company had a maritime lien on each vessel for the coal received by it. *The William B. Murray*, 240 Fed. Rep. 147. The Circuit Court of Appeals reversed these decrees with costs and directed that the libels be dismissed. *The Walter Adams*, 253 Fed. Rep. 20. Then this court granted the Coal Company's petition for a writ of certiorari. 248 U.S. 556.

As to the facts proved there is no disagreement between the two lower courts. The substantial question presented is whether these facts constitute a furnishing of supplies by the Coal Company to the vessels upon order of the owner within the provisions of the Act of June 23, 1910, c. 373, § 1, 36 Stat. 604. That coal was furnished to the vessels to the extent to which they severally received it on board, is clear. The precise question, therefore, is: Was the coal furnished by the libelant, the Coal Company, or was it furnished by the Oil Corporation, the owner of the fleet? In determining this question additional facts must be considered:

No coal was delivered by the Coal Company directly to any vessel; and it had no dealings of any kind concerning the coal directly with the officers of any vessel. All the coal was billed by the Coal Company to the Oil Corporation and there was no reference on any invoice, or on its books, either to the fleet or to any vessel. There was no understanding between the companies when the agreement to supply the coal was made or when the coal was delivered that any part of it was specifically for any one of the several vessels libeled, or that it was for any particular vessel of the fleet, or even for the vessels then composing the fleet. Indeed, the first shipment was stated on the invoice to be "coal for factory." The negotiations of the Oil Corporation with the Coal Company did not relate to coal required at that time by the particular vessels subsequently libeled as distinguished from other vessels of the fleet.

The coal was sold f.o.b. at the Coal Company's piers which were at St. George, Staten Island, and Port Reading, New Jersey. At these piers it was loaded on barges which were towed either to the Oil Corporation's plant at Promised Land or to that at Tiverton. Some of these barges were supplied by the Oil Corporation, some by the Coal Company. If supplied by the latter, trimming and towing charges were added to the agreed price of the coal. Upon arrival of the coal at the factories it was placed in the Oil Corporation's bins. At Promised Land—which received four of the five shipments—the bins already contained other coal (1068 tons) which had been theretofore purchased by the Oil Corporation and had been paid for. With this coal on hand that delivered by libelant was commingled. At each plant both the vessels and the factory were from time to time supplied with coal from the same bins; but the greater part of the coal supplied from each plant was used by the vessels. Weeks, and in some instances months, elapsed between placing the coal in the bins and the delivery of it by the Corporation to the several vessels. When it made such deliveries it furnished coal to the vessels, as it did to the factories, not under direction of the Coal Company but in its discretion as owner of the coal and of the business.

The quantity of coal delivered to each vessel was proved; but to what extent the coal supplied to the several vessels which bunkered at Promised Land came from the 1068 tons previously purchased, and to what extent it came from the lots purchased from the Coal Company, it was impossible to determine. In making the computations which formed the basis of the decrees in the District Court, it was assumed that, of the coal supplied to the several vessels which bunkered at Promised Land, a proportionate part of that received by each had come from the coal purchased from libelant.

The Coal Company contends on these facts that it furnished necessary supplies to the several vessels within the meaning of § 1 of the Act of June 23, 1910. But the facts show that no coal was furnished by that company to any vessel "upon the order of the owner." The tide to the coal had passed to the Oil Corporation when it was loaded on board the barges at the Coal Company's piers. It was delivered to Promised Land and Tiverton as the Oil Corporations coal and placed in its bins. As its coal the later distribution was made in its discretion to vessels and factories. A large part of the coal so acquired by the Oil Corporation for use in its business was subsequently appropriated by it specifically to the use of the several vessels of the fleet and this use of the coal by vessels of the fleet was a use which had been contemplated by the parties when it was purchased. But the fact that such a use had been contemplated does not render the subsequent appropriation by the owner a furnishing by the coal dealer to the several vessels.

To hold that a lien for the unpaid purchase price of supplies arises in favor of the seller merely because the purchaser, who is the owner of a vessel, subsequently appropriates the supplies to her use would involve abandonment of the principle upon which maritime liens rest and the substitution therefor of the very different principle which underlies mechanics' and materialmen's liens on houses and other structures. The former had its origin in desire to protect the ship; the latter mainly in desire to protect those who furnish work and materials. The maritime lien developed as a necessary incident of the operation of vessels. The ship's function is to move from place to place. She is peculiarly subject to vicissitudes which would compel abandonment of vessel or voyage, unless repairs and supplies were promptly furnished. Since she is usually absent from the home port, remote from the residence of her owner's and without any large amount of money, it is essential that she should be self-reliant—that she should be able to obtain upon her own account needed repairs and supplies. The recognition by the law of such inherent power did not involve any new legal conception, since the ship had been treated in other connections as an entity capable of entering into relations with others, of acting independently and of becoming responsible for her acts. Because the ship's need was the source of the maritime lien it could arise only if the repairs or supplies were necessary; if the pledge of her credit was necessary to the obtaining of them; if they were actually obtained; and if they were furnished upon her credit. The mechanic's and materialman's lien, on the other hand, attaches ordinarily although the labor and material cannot be said to have been necessary; although at the time they were furnished there was no thought of obtaining security upon the building; and although the credit of the owner or of others had in fact been relied upon. The principle upon which the mechanic's lien rests is, in a sense, that of unjust enrichment. Ordinarily, it is the equity arising from assumed enhancement in value resulting from work or materials expended upon the property without payment therefor which is laid hold of to protect workmen and others who, it is assumed, are especially deserving, would ordinarily fail to provide by agreement for their own protection and would often be unable to do so.

* * *

In the case at bar there was no understanding when the contract was made, or when the coal was delivered by the libelant, that any part of it was for any particular vessel or even for the vessels then composing the fleet. And it was clearly understood that the purchasing corporation would apply part of the coal to a nonmaritime use. The difficulty here (unlike that presented in *The Vigilancia*, 58 Fed. Rep. 698; *The Cimbria*, 156 Fed. Rep. 378, 382; and *The Curtin*, 165 Fed. Rep. 271) is not in failure to show that the coal was furnished to the vessels but in failure to prove that it was furnished by the libelant.

* * *

Affirmed.

_____

FOSS LAUNCH & TUG CO. v. CHAR CHING SHIPPING U.S.A.

808 F.2d 697, 1987 AMC 913 (9th Cir. 1987)

GOODWIN, Circuit Judge

The only substantial question in this appeal is whether a lessor of container boxes to a company that operates a fleet of container ships can assert a maritime lien against a vessel pursuant to 46 U.S.C. §§ 971-975. The district court granted summary judgment for the lien claimant. We reverse.

The essential facts are not in dispute. Appellees leased containers to CC Line under a series of separate lease agreements. The containers were to be used by CC Line in connection with its transpacific shipping service between various ports in Asia and the United States. Under the lease agreements, containers were delivered to CC Line at different times in a variety of locations. The containers are substantially uniform in design and construction, and are treated by carriers as fungible. Some deliveries under the Flexivan agreements were apparently made to CC Lines own container yards that service its transpacific operations. The Transamerica, Nautilus, Genstar, and Itel leasing contracts, however, provided for the delivery of containers to CC Line at container manufacturing plants and at the lessor's own container depots. Once the CC Line took possession of the containers, CC Line had unrestricted authority to designate which containers would be placed aboard the particular vessels operating in its transpacific service.[1] The lease agreements likewise did not restrict the use of the leased containers to exclusive use in maritime transportation. These boxes are designed for intermodal transportation.

The vessel "C.C. San Francisco" entered CC Lines transpacific service in 1983. It was specially designed for carrying cargo packed in containers. One or more of each lessor's containers was actually used aboard the "C.C. San Francisco" for the transport of ocean cargo.

In late August, 1984, the vessel "C.C. San Francisco" was arrested in Los Angeles in an *in rem* maritime action by appellees. The registered owner of the vessel, "Char Yigh Marine (Panama) S.A.," thereafter appeared in district court and sought a post-seizure hearing to have plaintiffs-appellees justify their maritime lien claims. Cross-motions for summary judgment were filed with the district court and on August 20, 1985, the district court ruled in favor of plaintiffs' liens. The district court held:

(1) that the plaintiffs' container leases with "CC Line" are maritime contracts; (2) that plaintiffs' containers served as the functional equivalent of the hold of the "CC San Francisco" and are therefore "necessaries" within the meaning of 46 U.S.C. § 971; (3) that plaintiff's "furnished" containers to the "CC San Francisco" within the meaning of 46 U.S.C. § 971; (4) that plaintiffs have valid maritime liens for necessaries against the vessel "CC San Francisco" for all containers carried aboard that vessel; and (5), that the maritime lien encompasses all periods plaintiffs' containers served as the functional equivalent of the hold of the "CC San Francisco," including incidental land use.

Flexivan Leasing, Inc. v. M/V C.C. San Francisco, 628 F. Supp. 1077, 1080 (C.D. Cal. 1985).

* * *

We have no difficulty in following the cases which have found similar container leases to be sufficiently related to maritime transportation to support the extension of federal admiralty jurisdiction. *CTI-Container Leasing Corp. v. Oceanic Operations Corp.,* 682 F.2d 377, 380-81 (2d Cir. 1982); *American President Lines, Ltd. v. Green Transfer & Storage, Inc.,* 568 F. Supp. 58, 60 (D. Or. 1983); *Integrated Container Service, Inc. v. Starlines Container Shipping, Ltd.,* 476 F. Supp. 119, 125 (S.D.N.Y. 1979).[2]

Of the remaining issues raised on appeal, each turns on an interpretation of the governing federal maritime lien statute, 46 U.S.C. § 971. That statute provides as follows:

---

[1] This practice is apparently consistent with the current industry practice with respect to containerization. Containers are leased in bulk lots so that they can be employed interchangably or sequentially in the conveyance of freight by means of various modes of transport including ships, airplanes, railroads, and trucks.

[2] We express no opinion on the effect of "incidental land uses" of containers employed in "inter-modal" freight conveyance, originating on maritime vessels, upon the proper boundaries of admiralty jurisdiction. We need not decide whether a creditor could permit maritime attachment of containers located far in the interior of the country even though they may have been subject to the preference accorded maritime liens while aboard ship.

Any person furnishing repairs, supplies, towage, use of dry dock or marine railway, or other necessaries, to any vessel, whether foreign or domestic, upon the order of the owner of such vessel, or of a person authorized by the owner, shall have a maritime lien on the vessel, which may be enforced by suit *in rem*, and it shall not be necessary to allege or prove that credit was given to the vessel.

46 U.S.C. § 971 (1982).

A recent decision of this court, *Farwest Steel Corp. v. Barge Sea-Span*, 241, 769 F.2d 620, 623 (9th Cir. 1985), instructs that there are three requirements for the grant of a maritime lien under 46 U.S.C. § 971. A person lien claimant must have: (1) furnish[ed] repairs, supplies, or other necessaries, (2) to any vessel, (3) "upon the order of the owner of such vessel, or of a person authorized by the owner." 46 U.S.C. § 971.

* * *

The second requirement, that the lien claimant be a person "furnishing ... to any vessel," presents a closer question. Its resolution turns on the intent of Congress in drafting a form of the verb "to furnish" into the text of 46 U.S.C. § 971. There is no doubt that containers furnished by the lien claimant were carried on one of a group of vessels intended to carry such containers. The question is whether the lien claimant furnished the attached containers "to" that vessel under the Act. In other words, is it a condition precedent to a lien that containers which have been leased to managers of a fleet of container vessels also must have been specifically set apart for use on the particular vessel against which a lien is asserted?

The "furnishing" question has recently been faced in two other circuits. Apparently in an effort to accommodate the professed expectations and needs of the shipping industry, each court applied a broad construction of "furnishing." In the most recent decision, the Fifth Circuit noted the closeness of the question but nevertheless concluded: "We find no persuasive reason to read the term 'furnishing ... narrowly.... The statute was intended to encourage private investment in the maritime industry. We will not begin now to defeat the purpose of the Act by layering technicalities onto its interpretation." *Equilease*, 793 F.2d at 603. Similarly, a Florida district court noted that "for purposes of creating a valid maritime lien, it may not be essential, and indeed may not be desirable, that the container be delivered directly to the vessel, be sold rather than leased, or be earmarked for a particular vessel." *Transamerica ICS*, 1984 A.M.C. at 490.

We respect the reasoning of these courts. But we are reluctant to subject the heretofore relatively certain law of maritime liens to the uncertainty and flux of developing shipping industry practices when the controlling precedents governing interpretation of the Act favor a narrow construction of the "furnishing" requirement.

We begin with the plain meaning of 46 U.S.C. § 971. Stripped to its essentials, the statute states that "[a]ny person furnishing ... necessaries ... to any vessel...." We note initially that the verb "to furnish" as found in the statute appears in the form of the active and not the passive voice. For example, the statute could have been drafted to state that "necessaries that *are furnished* to any vessel" can support a maritime lien. In such circumstance, it would have been possible for even the fortuitous application or use of necessaries by a vessel to create a valid maritime lien against a vessel. In creating a preferred class of secured creditors, Congress chose not to draft the Act in the passive voice and we think the correct inference is that Congress intended "furnishing" to require active forethought or advance identification of particular vessels in relation to "necessaries" supplied.

This inference is consistent with the historical vessel-specific character of a maritime lien. Under the law of maritime liens, a vessel is considered to be a distinct entity responsible only for its own debts. *Riffe Petroleum Co. v. Cibro Sales Corp.*, 601 F.2d 1385, 1389 (10th Cir. 1979). As a consequence, maritime liens are enforced through *in rem* proceedings, *see* Rule C, Supplemental Rules for Certain Admiralty and Maritime Claims, Fed. R. Civ. P., and jurisdiction lies only in the district where the vessel is located.

Our restrictive interpretation of "furnishing" is supported by longstanding precedents interpreting 46 U.S.C. § 971. *Piedmont & Georges Creek Coal Co. v. Seaboard Fisheries Co.*, 254 U.S. 1, 41 S.Ct. 1, 65 L. Ed. 97 (1920), and its progeny are particularly apposite to this action. In *Piedmont*, the Supreme Court denied maritime liens sought against vessels that had received coal which had been sold to the vessels' owner on credit. The defect was not "in failure to show that the coal was furnished to the vessels but in failure to prove that it was furnished *by* the libelant." *Piedmont,* 254 U.S. at 13, 41 S.Ct. at 5.

Appellees contend that *Piedmont* represents a case driven by a simple failure of proof as to the amounts of coal actually received by each vessel in a group of vessels supplied with coal. However, it is clear that *Piedmont* has not been interpreted in such a limited fashion. In *Bankers Trust Co. v. Hudson River Day Line,* 93 F.2d 457 (2d. Cir. 1937), maritime liens were denied a supplier of oil who had delivered oil to a buyer's barges under a single bulk supply contract. In denying the lien, the *Bankers Trust* court understood the holding of Piedmont on the "furnishing" question to require that "supplies, though delivered in mass to the owner of the fleet under a single contract, [must be] expressly ordered by the owner and delivered to him by the supplyman for the use of *named vessels in specified portions.*" *Id.* at 458 (emphasis supplied by Second Circuit) (*quoting The American Eagle,* 30 F.2d 293, 295 (D. Del. 1929)).

In *Dampskibsselskabet Dannebrog v. Signal Oil & Gas Co.,* 310 U.S. 268 (1940), the Supreme Court decided to grant a maritime lien only after distinguishing *Piedmont* in the following manner: "In the instant case, the oil was supplied exclusively for the vessels in question, was delivered directly to the vessels and was so invoiced; and there was nothing in the general contract to the effect that the supplies were to be furnished [to some degree] upon the credit of the vessels." *Id.* at 277. Thus, the holding of *Dampskibsselskabet* should be read to encompass only those cases in which a materialman has taken care, in an ascertainable manner, to designate the items or services he contracts to provide for use on the particular vessel against which a lien is subsequently sought. *See also The Everosa,* 93 F.2d 732, 735 (1st Cir. 1937) (lien granted) ("In the present case, the master of a particular vessel requisitioned for coal to the coal company; it was sent to a particular vessel, loaded on her by the coal company's representative and paid for by her master"); *Carr v. George E. Warren Corp.,* 2 F.2d 333, 334 (4th Cir. 1924) (lien granted) ("In this case, the coal was actually purchased on the credit of the steamers, billed to the steamers, and used by them.")

Piedmont was also responsible for the incorporation of the *stricti juris* principle, long a feature of the law of maritime liens, *see Vandewater v. Mills,* 60 U.S. 82, 19 How. 82, 89, 15 L. Ed. 554 (1857), into the law governing the interpretation of maritime liens under the Act. *Piedmont,* 254 U.S. at 12, 41 S.Ct. at 4. Because the maritime lien under 46 U.S.C. § 971 is secret and may operate to the prejudice of prior mortgagees and other creditors without notice, it will not be "extended by construction, analogy or inference." *Ida, See also W.A. Marshall & Co. v. S.S. "President Arthur",* 279 U.S. 564, 568, 49 S.Ct. 420, 421, 73 L. Ed. 846 (1929); *Bankers Trust Co.,* 93 F.2d at 459; *Bellingham Nat. Bank,* 587 F. Supp. at 28-29.

The facts and posture of the instant action parallel those found in Piedmont. In each case a materialman provided bulk supplies—coal in *Piedmont,* containers here—in circumstances where the final allocation of supplies, to any vessel of the group intended to be supplied, was left to the discretion of the procuring authority. Although, in both cases, it was understood that the supplies provided would predominantly be put to maritime use, in neither case was there any evident attempt to designate any individual vessel to receive any identifiable component of the supplies.

Appellees vainly attempt to distinguish *Piedmont.* First, they contend that their ability to identify precisely which containers were carried on board the "C.C. San Francisco" at which time adequately answers the concern in Piedmont over the grant of equally proportional liens against each of the vessels in the group that received coal. However, this is simply not a distinguishing characteristic. The *Piedmont* holding was not made contingent on the district court's inability to establish the exact amount of coal used by a particular vessel in the group. Rather, the defect was in the unstructured character of the contractual arrangements for the supply of coal to the *Piedmont* vessel group. *Piedmont,* 254 U.S. at 13, 41 S.Ct. at 4.

Second, appellees argue that the fact that the coal supplied in *Piedmont* was found to have been partially consumed in the owner's dockside factory instead of in vessels potentially subject to maritime liens is a distinguishing characteristic. While the Supreme Court did note that it was concerned about the potential for nonmaritime use of coal supplied to the owner's dock, *see Piedmont,* 254 U.S. at 13, 41 S.Ct. at 4, a similar problem is presented here by the potential for "inter-modal" use of containers. In an attempt to cure this deficiency the district court granted maritime liens only to the extent that containers were the "functional equivalent of the hold" of the "C.C. San Francisco." However, under the leasing agreements entered into with CC Line, none of the appellees restricted the "inter-modal" use of their leased containers to exclusively maritime conveyance. Thus, despite the district court's holding below, it cannot be gainsaid that nonmaritime use analogous to that in *Piedmont*, was permitted under the container leasing agreements in issue here.

Finally, it is particularly instructive to compare the similarity in the reasoning supporting the holdings of both the district court in *Piedmont* and the district court in this action. The *Piedmont* district court, in its attempt to justify a broad interpretation of the "furnishing" requirement, stated:

> As supplies for fleets of vessels under a common ownership and management in the ordinary course of business are contracted for in view of the general requirements of the entire fleet, as supply men will thus be called upon to furnish supplies in advance of the arrival of the vessels, as at the time supplies are ordered there may be uncertainty as to which vessel may require them and use them, *the statute should receive a construction which will make it applicable to and consistent with modern business conditions.* A supply man who furnished supplies ready for any vessel of a fleet that may call for it should not be deprived of the same right to a lien as a supply man who is told the name of the vessel which is to require the supplies.

240 F. 147, 153 (D. R.I. 1917) (emphasis added). The district court in this action similarly stated that

> In light of today's shipping practices [the bulk leasing of containers], defendants contention that a container need be furnished to a specific vessel, rather than to a fleet of vessels, in order for a valid maritime lien to exist, is highly impractical.

Flexivan, 628 F. Supp at 1079 (emphasis added).

Like the Supreme Court in *Piedmont*, we are not persuaded that "modern business conditions" in the shipping industry are sufficient justification to expand the "furnishing to any vessel" requirement of 46 U.S.C. § 971.[4] Accordingly, we hold that cargo containers leased in bulk to a time-charterer of a group of vessels for unrestricted use on board the vessels in that group, are not furnished to any particular vessel of the group, on which they subsequently happen to be employed, within the meaning of 46 U.S.C. § 971.

We reverse the order of the district court with respect to the establishment of maritime liens under the Federal Maritime Lien Act, 46 U.S.C. § 971. This cause is remanded to the district court for further proceedings as may be necessary to discharge the lien.

Reversed and remanded.

J. BLAINE ANDERSON, Circuit Judge, concurring in part and dissenting in part:

* * *

With respect to the holding that the containers were not furnished to the vessel "C.C. San Francisco" in particular, however, I disagree with the majority. In my view, the containers were "furnished" to the vessel under 46 U.S.C. § 971 in a manner sufficient to attach a lien. The majority finds a restrictive reading of the "furnishing ... to any vessel" requirement is supported by inferential Congressional intent and prior cases interpreting section 971. For me, these two bases are not persuasive. The active and not passive language used in the statute is not a distinction which supports the inference that Congress intended a restrictive reading when viewed against the purpose of the Act. Also, previous cases interpreting section 971 support a broader interpretation of the furnishing requirement.

---

[4] Appellees' contention that there is no substantive difference between a container company leasing 10 containers to steamship company A, pre-allocating them only for use on a group of 5 specified vessels, and that company leasing 10 other containers to steamship company B, without pre-allocation but where the containers actually were carried aboard five vessels, misses the mark. We are presented with a question of interpretation of the statute and under a narrow interpretation of "furnishing," in neither case would a maritime lien likely attach. The relevant comparison is between companies A & B and a company C which leases an identified set of containers specifically for use on a named vessel.

The purpose behind the Act, as amended in 1971, was as a matter of equity to protect suppliers who in good faith furnish necessaries to a vessel. *See,* H.R. REP. No. 92-340, 92nd Cong., 1st Sess. 1, *reprinted in* 1971 U.S. CODE CONG. & AD. NEWS 1363-1365; *Equilease Corp. v. M/V Sampson,* 793 F.2d 598, 603 (5th Cir. 1986) (*en banc*) ("The statute [46 U.S.C. § 971] was intended to encourage private investment in the maritime industry. We will not begin now to defeat the purpose of the Act by layering technicalities onto its interpretation"). If the purpose of the Act is to be fulfilled, the construction of the "furnishing ... to any vessel" requirement should not be a restrictive one. The majority's restrictive interpretation is contrary to the purpose Congress expressed when it amended the Act. In this, the majority places reliance for its holding upon the fact that the verb "to furnish" is active and not passive. I find this distinction to be of little weight. While use of the active voice may create an inference of Congressional intent, such an inference should be decidedly subordinate to Congress' stated purpose. *See Gulf Trading and Transportation Co. v. M/V Tento,* 694 F.2d 1191, 1194 (9th Cir. 1983).

I also find the cases cited by the majority to be inapposite. The question presented is: "Is it a condition precedent to a lien that containers which have been leased to managers of a fleet of container vessels also must have been specifically set apart for use on the particular vessel against which a lien is asserted?" The answer has already been provided and the answer is "no." In *Piedmont & George's Creek Coal Co. v. Seaboard Fisheries Co.,* 254 U.S. 1, 41 S.Ct. 1, 65 L. Ed. 97 (1920), the Court stated:

[T]he fact that the coal which was supplied to the several vessels had been purchased under a single contract presents no difficulty. For while one vessel of a fleet cannot be made liable under the statute for supplies furnished to the others, even if the supplies are furnished to all upon orders of the owner under a single contract ... each vessel so receiving supplies may be made liable for the supplies furnished to it.

Id. at 10-11, 41 S.Ct. at 4 (citations omitted). The majority's reliance on *Piedmont* is misplaced. In *Piedmont,* delivery was not made to the vessels but to another location, the owner's factory. The parties understood that the owner would be dividing the supplies (coal) between the factory and the vessels. Title to the supplies passed to the factory as an entity before the supplies were divided for vessel and non-vessel usage. *Piedmont* is therefore clearly distinguishable on this ground.

Here, there is no question the lessor presented the containers to CC Line for use by the vessels. The containers were not diverted, after the passing of title to another entity, for non-vessel use. That the CC Line had the authority to interchange the containers between particular vessels is of no consequence since "each vessel so receiving supplies may be made liable for the supplies furnished to it." *Piedmont* at 11, 41 S.Ct. at 4.

Later, in *Dampskibsselskabet Dannebrog v. Signal Oil & Gas Co.,* 310 U.S. 268, 60 S.Ct. 937, 84 L. Ed. 1197 (1940), the Court interpreted Piedmont as permitting a lien to attach, in that the supplies were "furnished," where delivery was made to a number of vessels since the supplies were presented exclusively for the vessels in question. *Dampskibsselskabet* at 277, 60 S.Ct. at 94. From this it is clear that a contract for delivery of supplies to a number of vessels without designation of particular vessels will not cause a maritime lien to fail under section 971 for want of "furnishing ... to any vessel" as long as there is no diversion of title to an intermediate entity.

The additional cases cited by the majority err for the same reason the majority opinion does. They read *Piedmont* too narrowly. The controlling feature of *Piedmont* is not the result reached but the principle stated. *Piedmont* and its progeny allow a lien to attach to a particular vessel, even though the supplies were not delivered to a prespecified vessel, if the vessel in fact received the supplies furnished.

Note

  In *Freret Marine Supply v. Harris Trust & Savings Bank*, 73 Fed. Appx. 698 (5th Cir. 2003), a bank that had processed credit card transactions for a cruise ship operator sued two cruise ships *in rem* to recover sums that it had had to repay to credit card companies on behalf of the cruise ship operator when the cruise ship operator went bankrupt and ceased operations. The U.S. Court of Appeals for the Fifth Circuit held that the bank did not have a maritime lien over the cruise ships. The court held that the contract between the bank and the cruise ship operator was not a maritime contract, but even if it had been, the banks services were provided to the cruise ship operator itself, not to the individual ships.

---

ii. 46 U.S.C. § 31301(4): "'Necessaries' Includes Repairs, Supplies, Towage, and the Use of a Dry Dock or Marine Railway...."

CLUBB OIL TOOLS, INC. v. M/V GEORGE VERGOTTIS

460 F. Supp. 835, 1980 AMC 556 (S.D. Tex. 1978)

Carl O. BUE, Jr., District Judge

* * *

  Plaintiff contends, and the Court concludes, that the rental of the pipe to Trefalcon [the time charterer] creates a lien in its favor against the GEORGE VERGOTTIS pursuant to 46 U.S.C.A. § 971.

* * *

  Defendant Franconia Sea Transport urges the applicability of *J. Ray McDermott & Co. v. The Off-Shore Menhaden Company*, 262 F.2d 523 (5th Cir. 1959), wherein Chief Judge John R. Brown held that a lien was not created in favor of the claimant for the cost of dredging a slip for use as a permanent berth. The capital nature of the facility led the court to conclude that it should not come within the purview of the Lien Act, for to do so would open the door to claims that the costs of constructing wharves, docks, warehouse sheds and other permanent capital improvements may also be the subject of maritime liens.

* * *

  While plaintiff concedes the absence of case authority directly on point, it urges that the prevailing broad meaning given the phrase "other necessaries" and the reasoning behind the act combine to compel the conclusion that a lien exists in the instant case. In support of this position, plaintiff urges that the pipe rental is analogous to stevedoring services which may form the basis for a maritime lien. *Nacirema Operating Co., Inc. v. S.S. Al Kulsum*, 407 F. Supp. 1222 (S.D.N.Y. 1975). After analyzing the briefs submitted by the parties and the relevant treatises and case authority, the Court concludes that the rental of oil pipe in the present case does come within the meaning of the term "other necessaries" and may give rise to a maritime lien.

  While the Lien Act has in the past been strictly construed so as to avoid the creation of a lien, "the present state of the law is not far from the point where any service which is "convenient, useful and at times necessary may qualify as a lien under the Lien Act." G. GILMORE & C. BLACK, THE LAW OF ADMIRALTY 658 (2nd ed. 1975). Thus, "other necessaries" has been defined to include "those items or services which a prudent owner or master would deem to be reasonably required to facilitate the use of the ship, save her from danger and enable her to perform those acts currently demanded of her.... (T)he furnished goals and services must be reasonably needed for the venture in which the ship is engaged." 2 I. HALL, A. SANN & S. BELLMAN, BENEDICT ON ADMIRALTY 3-27 (7th ed. 1975).

  Application of this definition to the facts of the present case indicates that the furnishing of oil pipe was reasonably required to facilitate the vessel's mission. The unrebutted testimony at trial revealed that the only feasible means of loading the oil was through the use of a pipeline. Thus, the creation of a lien to cover the cost of the renting of the pipe to defendant Trefalcon is consistent with the purpose of the Lien Act "to keep the ship active, thereby facilitating the flow of commerce and protecting the interests of the owner's and secured parties".

* * *

This Court concludes that the facts of this case are clearly distinguishable from *J. Ray McDermott & Co. v. The Off-Shore Menhaden Company* in that the pipe rental in the instant case was not in the nature of a permanent capital improvement as was the permanent slip dredged in *J. Ray McDermott*. The short duration of the rental agreement coupled with the temporary manner in which the pipeline was strung indicate that the clear intent of all the parties was a short-term rental designed to effectuate the loading of the vessel on this one-time basis. Thus, the fear expressed by Chief Judge John R. Brown that the allowance of a lien in *J. Ray McDermott* might set a dangerous precedent for the creation of liens in a multitude of situations where capital improvements are made to ports is not applicable to the instant case, which instead fits the category of cases in which the proper application of the Lien Act leads "to the allowance of maritime liens to new and infrequent situations".

* * *

Note: Liens for "Other Necessaries"

46 U.S.C. § 31301(4) defines "necessaries" furnished to a vessel as including certain specific services or supplies. The Federal Maritime Lien Act not only contained identical language but also the phrase "other necessaries". *See* 46 U.S.C. § 971, *supra*. Courts have given a broad application to § 971 (recodified as 46 U.S.C.A. § 31342) and have held various sorts of services and supplies to be "necessaries." It has been said: "The present state of the law is not far from the point where any service that is 'convenient, useful and at times necessary' may qualify as a lien under the Lien Act." G. GILMORE & C. BLACK, THE LAW OF ADMIRALTY 543 (2d ed. 1975).

In *Blair v. M/V Blue Spruce*, 315 F. Supp. 555, 1970 AMC 1298 (D. Mass. 1970), it was held that pilotage services were a "necessary" for the purposes of the Federal Maritime Lien Act, thus entitling the pilot to a maritime lien, even though the ship had refused the pilot's services. In addition to addressing the issue of whether services were "furnished" to the vessel, the Court also had to determine whether pilotage which was tendered but refused was "necessary" within the meaning of the federal statute. In resolving this issue the Court stated:

> To effectuate the purposes of the statute, courts have held that the phrase "other necessaries" should be broadly interpreted. *See J. Ray McDermott & Co. v. The Off-Shore Menhaden Co.*, 1959, 5 Cir., 262 F.2d 523, *rehearing denied* Feb. 11, 1959; *City of Erie v. S.S. North American*, 1967, W.D. Pa., 267 F. Supp. 875; *Layton Industries, Inc. v. The Sport Fishing Cruiser Gladiator*, 1967, D. Mass., 263 F. Supp. 356 (FORD, J.); *Allen v. The M/V Contessa*, 1961, S.D. Tex., 196 F. Supp. 649. One recent case from this district has phrased the test as whether the services are reasonably needed in the ship's business. *See Layton Industries, Inc. v. The Sport Fishing Cruiser Gladiator*, 1967, D. Mass., 263 F. Supp. 356 (FORD, J.). Under this statute a variety of items have been found by courts to be "other necessaries." A sampling of the more unusual items includes *Colonial Press of Miami, Inc. v. The BMV Allen's Cay*, 1960, 5 Cir., 277 F.2d 540 (printing materials); *The Susquehanna*, 1923, D. Mass., 3 F.2d 1014 (fumigation of passengers' baggage); *In re Burton S.S. Co.*, 1925, D. Mass., 3 F.2d 1015 (Cape Cod Canal charges); *City of Erie v. S.S. North American*, 1967, W.D. Pa., 267 F. Supp. 875 (wharfage); *Allen v. The M/V Contessa*, 1961, S.D. Tex., 196 F. Supp. 649 (cigarettes). One item of personal service, fairly similar to piloting, which has been held to be an "other [necessary]" is stevedoring. *See In re North Atlantic and Gulf Steamship Co.*, 1962, S.D.N.Y., 204 F. Supp. 899, 907, *aff'd sub nom. Schilling v. Dannebrog*, 1963, 2 Cir., 320 F.2d 628; *The Little Charley*, 1929, D. Md., 31 F.2d 120; *United States v. Certain Sub freights Due S.S. Neponset*, 1924, D. Mass., 300 F. 981, *rev'd on other grounds, United States v. Robins Dry Dock and Repair Co.*, 1926, 13 F.2d 808; *The Henry S. Grove*, 1922, W.D. Wash., 285 F. 60; *International Terminal Operating Co., Inc. v. S.S. Valmas*, 1967, 4 Cir., 375 F.2d 586 [dictum].
>
> Although there is a dearth of cases squarely facing whether pilotage is an "other [necessary]," the cited instances of "necessaries" tend to support the view that pilotage is a necessary. Furthermore, the only references to the issue imply that pilotage services create a lien either under general maritime law, *The Alligator*, 1908, 3 Cir., 161 F. 37 [dictum], or under the Federal Maritime Lien Act, G. GILMORE & C. BLACK, THE LAW OF ADMIRALTY, p. 516 (1957).

* * *

Other services which have been held to be a "necessary" giving rise to a maritime lien include those of a marine architect who drew plans for the installation of new engines in a vessel although the installation did not take place. *Tug Miki Miki*, 1970 AMC 1828 (N.D. Cal. 1969). Advertising expense for a cruise ship is a necessary. *Stem, Hays &Lang, Inc. v. M/V Nili*, 407 F.2d 549, 1969 AMC 13 (5th Cir. 1969). *See also Atlantic Steamer Supply Co. v. The Steamship Tradewind*, 153 F. Supp. 354, 1957 AMC 2169 (D. Md. 1957). An expense incurred by a travel agency for the transportation of crew members to or from the vessel is also a necessary. *See Carl Enterprises v. Barge Hudson Handler*, 475 F. Supp. 42, 1980 AMC 1759 (S.D. Ala. 1979). However, in *J.H. Westerbeke Corp. v. The Golden Fleece*, 1970 AMC 1740 (D. Mass. 1970), the court held that the purchase of a generator was not necessary because the vessel already had two functional generators either of which was sufficient for its navigation. Likewise, in *McDermott & Co. v. The Off-Shore Menhaden Co.*, 262 F.2d 523, 1959 AMC 527 (5th Cir. 1959), the court held that the dredging out of a special slip for use as permanent berth of a vessel was not a necessary.

Are the services of the master of a vessel a "necessary"? An American citizen who serves as master of a vessel has a lien for wages under 46 U.S.C. § 11112. A foreign citizen, however, does not have a lien for masters wages; he may have a contract lien under 46 U.S.C. § 31301, § 31342. In *Medina v. Marvirazon Compania Naviera, S.A.,* 533 F. Supp. 1279, 1287, 1983 AMC 2116 (D. Mass. 1982), the court declared that "[s]urely a captain's services are necessary." *But see Vlavianos v. The Cypress,* 171 F.2d435, 1949 AMC 9 (4th Cir. 1948), *cert. denied,* 337 U.S. 924, 69 S.Ct. 1168, 93 L. Ed. 1732 (1949). A passenger on the Cypress who had paid $300 in advance for his passage was so impatient at the failure of the vessel to sail on schedule that he had Captain Vlavianos arrested in order to secure the return of his money. A crewmember of the Cypress incurred a taxi bill of $5 to go to the Central Police Station in Baltimore where the captain was confined, and he also advanced the captain $300 with which to purchase his freedom. Subsequently, the crewmember claimed a lien on the ship for $305, asserting that the captain was necessary to a ship, basing his claim on 46 U.S.C. § 971. The court held: "It is obvious that the statute has no application to this situation," and denied the lien.

The issue of whether cargo containers are "necessaries" under the Federal Maritime Lien Act was addressed by the court in *Foss Launch & Tug Company v. Char Ching Shipping U.S.A. Ltd., supra.* Although the court concluded that the containers at issue were not furnished to the vessel, the Ninth Circuit had no difficulty in determining that the term "necessaries" included cargo containers. The court stated:

* * *

The term, in modern interpretations, has been expanded to encompass any item which is "reasonably needed for the venture in which the ship is engaged." 2 S. Friedell, S. Bellman, A. Jenner & J. Loo, Benedict on Admiralty § 37 at 3-27 (7th ed. 1986). *See also Farwest Steel Corp.,* 769 F.2d at 623 ("[t]he term necessaries' under section 971 refers to supplies which are necessary to keep the ship going' ").

The wide range of items that can be characterized as "necessaries" under the Act is exemplified by the result in *Equilease Corp. v. M/V Sampson,* 793 F.2d 598, (5th Cir. 1986) *(en banc).* In *Equilease,* the court stated:

The term necessary' under the FMLA [Act] includes most goods or services that are useful to the vessel, keep her out of danger, and enable her to perform her particular function.... What is a necessary' is to be determined relative to the requirements of the ship." *Equilease,* 793 F.2d at 603 (citations omitted). The court's resulting conclusion was that "because insurance is essential to keep a vessel in commerce, insurance is a necessary' under 46 U.S.C. § 971. 793 F.2d at 604.

During all relevant periods of the operations of the "C.C. San Francisco," cargo containers of the type leased by appellees were more than reasonably necessary to the successful operation of the vessel. Although theoretically it might have been possible to convert the "C.C. San Francisco" from a container carrier to another type of cargo vessel, such transformation or modification was not attempted here. The vessel entered service in 1983 designed to transport cargo containers of the type supplied by appellees. It was engaged in container shipping throughout its time-charter period of operation by CC Line. We therefore hold that containers provided to the "C.C. San Francisco" under the leasing agreements were "necessaries" within the meaning of 46 U.S.C. § 971. *Accord Transamerica ICS, Inc. v. M/V Panatlantic,* 1984 A.M.C. 489, 490 (S.D. Fla. 1983) ("the Court is convinced that containers are necessaries' within the meaning of 46 U.S.C., sec. 971"); *Nautilus Leasing Services, Inc. v. M/V Cosmos, et al.,* 1983 A.M.C. 1483 (S.D.N.Y. 1983) ("we have no difficulty holding that the containers in the instant case are necessaries' within 46 U.S.C., sec. 971").

* * *

_____

Note: Absence of Maritime Contract

Suppose a supplier of necessaries would qualify for a maritime lien because it literally satisfies the requirements of the Lien Act, would the lien be defeated if the underlying contract between the vessel owner and the supplier does not qualify as a "maritime contract"? *See Ventura Packers, Inc. v. F/V Jeanine Kathleen,* 305 F.3d 913, 2002 AMC 2248 (9th Cir. 2002).

_____

iii. 46 U.S.C. § 31341: "Persons ... Presumed to Have Authority to Procure Necessaries for a Vessel...."

Note: "Presumed... Authority" and "Authorized by the Owner"

Under the Federal Maritime Lien Act the owner of a vessel or a person authorized by the owner could establish maritime liens for necessaries. *See* 46 U.S.C. § 971. The persons presumed "to have authority from the owner to procure" necessaries "for the vessel" under § 972 were "the managing owner, ship's husband, master, or any person to whom the management of the vessel at the port of supply [was] intrusted." Section 973 further stated that "[t]he officers and agents of a vessel specified in § 972 ... include[d] such officers and agents when appointed by a charterer, by an owner *pro hac vice,* or by an agreed purchaser in possession of the vessel." In interpreting this statutory language, courts faced a myriad of issues. It was not always easy to determine whether the person who ordered the supplies or repairs was the owner of the vessel. *See The Josephine Lanasa (Findley v. Lanasa),* 276 F.2d 907, 1960 AMC 1444 (5th Cir. 1960). Was the "economic owner" of a vessel or a person having an equitable title "owner" within the meaning of § 971? *See Diaz v. The Steamship Seathunder,* 191 F. Supp. 807, 1961 AMC 561 (D. Md. 1961). What about a prospective owner? *See Freedom Line, Inc. v. Glenrock,* 268 F. Supp. 7, 1968 AMC 507 (S.D. Fla. 1967). Were these persons presumed "to have authority from the owner" under section 972?

It has been held that for the determination of the question whether one was "a person authorized by the owner" under section 971, ordinary principles of agency, ratification, and estoppel were applicable. *See Esso International, Inc. v. Steamship Captain John,* 322 F. Supp. 314, 1970 AMC 2086 (S.D. Tex. 1970), *aff'd,* 443 F.2d 1144, 1971 AMC 2285 (5th Cir. 1971).

Under 46 U.S.C. § 31341 the persons presumed to have authority to procure necessaries are: "(1) the owner, (2) the master, (3) a person entrusted with the management of the vessel at the port of supply; or an officer or agent appointed by (A) the owner; (B) a charterer; (C) an owner *pro hac vice;* or (D) an agreed buyer in possession of the vessel." Under § 31342 a maritime lien arises in favor of "a person providing necessaries to a vessel... on order of a person listed in section 31341 ... or a person authorized by the owner...." Though the wording of sections 31341-2 and the applicable provisions of the Federal Maritime Lien Act differs, many of the issues addressed in interpreting the language of the Federal Maritime Lien Act are equally relevant when considering the current statutory provisions.

EPSTEIN v. CORPORACION PERUANA DE VAPORES

325 F. Supp. 535, 1971 AMC 1259 (S.D.N.Y., 1971)

CROAKE, District Judge

Memorandum

This is a suit in admiralty brought by the plaintiff, Stratford International Tobacco Company, against the Corporacion Peruana de Vapores to recover a balance of $7,206.50 due on a $13,436.50 purchase of cigarettes and liquor made on May 6, 1965. The facts of the case are as follows.

I.

Plaintiff is a corporation engaged in the sale of tax-free cigarettes and liquor to vessels in the Port of New York (Transcript page 11, line 15). Alfred Parodi is a salesman in plaintiff's employ. On May 4, 1965 and May 5, 1965, Parodi had conversations with Luis E. Saavedra, the Captain of the S.S. NAPO (one of defendants ships). On May 6, 1965, pursuant to these conversations, Saavedra agreed to purchase 2,270,000 cigarettes totalling $12,251.50 and 40 cases of liquor totalling $1,185.00 from plaintiff. Broken down, the cigarette sales consisted of 1,000,000 Salem cigarettes, 500,000 Kents, 300,000 Lucky Strikes, 200,000 Chesterfield Regulars, 100,000 Camels, 100,00 Half 'n Halfs and 70,000 Montclairs (plaintiff's exhibit #1). The liquor consisted of ten cases of Chivas Regal, ten cases of Old Parr, ten cases of Ye Monks Flagons, five cases of White Fiorse, two cases of Black & White, two cases of Drambuie and one case of B & B.

These goods were delivered to the S.S. NAPO on May 6, 1965, and copies of the invoices for them given to the captain. However, contrary to its usual practice of cash payment at the time of delivery, plaintiff reluctantly consented to a sale on partial credit as the result of Saavedra's simply not having enough cash to pay for the cigarettes and liquor he had ordered. As Parodi himself later testified, "We were more or less forced into granting credit.... I was not aware that credit would occur until the last moment when the captain did not receive the money that he was supposed to have received."

Following delivery of the goods, plaintiff made repeated demands of Saavedra for the $7,206.50 still due on the sale. However, these demands were met only by promises that the money would be forthcoming. When these promises were not met, copies of the original invoices were forwarded to defendant's home office in Peru with a demand for payment. Defendant received these invoices on November 2, 1965. Disclaiming all knowledge of the transaction, it refused to pay, and began an investigation into the conduct of Saavedra. On December 1, 1965, the captain was discharged by the company. Fie died shortly thereafter.

It is not disputed by either party that the master of a vessel possesses full authority to make purchases binding upon the vessel's owner for "necessaries" to be used on board his own ship unless the contrary is clearly stated to all concerned.* In describing the origins of this authority, BENEDICT's THE LAW OF AMERICAN ADMIRALTY states—

---

* 46 U.S.C. § 972 then provided that: "The following persons shall be presumed to have authority from the owner to procure.. .necessaries for the vessel: The.. .master.." The equivalent provision is now 46 U.S.C. § 31341(a)(2).

A ship is, of necessity, a wanderer. She visits shores where her owner's are not known or are inaccessible. The master is the fully authorized agent of the distant owner's, but is not usually of sufficient pecuniary ability to respond to unforeseen demands of the voyage. These and other kindred characteristics of maritime commerce underlie the practice...." Benedict, The Law of American Admiralty, 6th Edition (1940), volume 1, pp. 19-20.

Also, it should be noted that cigarettes have been held to be "necessaries" within the meaning of maritime law. *Allen v. The M/V Contessa*, 196 F. Supp. 649 (S.D. Texas 1961).

However, the amount of cigarettes and liquor purchased by Captain Saavedra makes it clear that these supplies were not purchased for consumption by the S.S. NAPO alone. Indeed, plaintiff itself concedes that, in March of 1965 (some six weeks before the transaction in question), the same captain of the same vessel purchased 1,500,000 cigarettes, admittedly "more than what was necessary for the use of the ship."

However, while admitting that the sale in question did not constitute "necessaries" for the S.S. NAPO itself, plaintiff contends that the supplies were purchased by the captain as "necessaries" for other ships owned by the defendant corporation. These cigarettes and liquor, it is claimed, were to be carried by the S.S. NAPO to a home port in Peru where they were to be redistributed to other vessels which had no access to United States ports. Accordingly, it is argued, the captain had authority to make the purchase and defendant should be bound thereby.

Defendant, in turn, denies any knowledge of or authorization for the captain's conduct. It maintains that the captain was never authorized to purchase the supplies in question for his own or any other ship in defendant's fleet, and speculates that the real motive behind the purchase was the captain's participation in a scheme to smuggle tax-free, contraband cigarettes and liquor totally outside the scope of his duties as ship's captain. Accordingly, defendant refuses to be bound by the obligation owing from the captain to the plaintiff, and will not pay the balance due unless so ordered by this court. This court rules as follows.

II.

The key question before the court in the instant matter is whether or not the captain of the S.S. NAPO had any kind of authority to purchase the cigarettes and liquor in question and bind the defendant thereby. Clearly, the owner of a vessel is liable for contractual obligations incurred by its master where such obligations were incurred pursuant to either express, apparent, or implied authority. But whether such authority existed in the case at bar is not an easy matter for resolution.

It is the judgment of this court that the captain of the S.S. NAPO was clearly without express authority to make the purchases in question. Express authority is that authority which a principal intentionally confers upon his agent by manifestations to him. In the instant case, not only were such overt manifestations lacking; the captain was specifically forbidden to make purchases such as the one in question by the internal regulations of defendant company (*See* Appendix for English language translations of these regulations— defendants exhibits A and B). This prohibition was furthered bolstered by defendant's policy of not supplying the captains of its ships with American cash except for that supplied by Hansen & Tidemann (its American agent) for payroll purposes.

The absence of express authority, of course, does not rule out the possibility of apparent or implied authority. Apparent authority is that authority which a principal holds his agent out as possessing or which he permits the agent to represent that he possesses. However, in the instant case, one is hard-pressed to find any such conduct on the part of defendant.

Defendant did nothing to encourage the idea that the captain had authority to purchase the supplies in question. Indeed, the testimony of plaintiff's sole witness, Alfred Parodi, reveals that plaintiff never received any requisition forms directly from the defendant corporation nor did it receive purchasing requests from Hansen & Tidemann. Rather, it always dealt directly with the ship's master.

To counter this, plaintiff argues that past transactions of a similar nature established a pattern of apparent authority in the captain to make these purchases. But the evidence fails to link these transactions to the defendant company itself. In most instances, payment was by cash and, in those few cases where payment was by check, the check was not drawn on the account of defendant, but rather by a bank in Peru upon the Chase Manhattan Bank in New York. Thus the court finds apparent authority in the captain also lacking.

Plaintiff also claims that the captain of the S.S. NAPO had implied authority to bind defendant to the purchases in question. Implied authority is that authority which comes in conformity either with law or the general business customs of a particular trade.

Where conformity with law is concerned, the captain of a vessel has, as previously noted, implied authority to bind the owner thereof to the purchase of "necessaries" for the use of his ship. However, in the instant case, the court is concerned not with the purchase of necessaries for the captains own vessel, but with the purchase of necessaries for other ships. Thus, the crucial question becomes one of whether or not a captain has implied authority to purchase "necessaries" for a ship other than his own.

This court holds that he does not. A captain is master of his own ship, not of any other. And no definition of "necesaries" dating back one hundred years that this court has been able to uncover holds to the contrary....

Thus, plaintiff is left with the contention that the captain had implied authority to purchase the supplies in question because said purchase was in conformity with general business customs. This proposition must also fail.

Plaintiff's witness, Alfred Parodi, testified to the custom of captains purchasing more than their own ships' necessary requirements of cigarettes and liquor and distributing them to other vessels which do not reach the United States. But there is little else before this court to support the proposition that such a custom actually exists—a proposition which this court declines to accept in view of its earlier finding that a captain does not have implied authority to purchase necessaries for ships other than his own as a matter of case or statute law. And, even if such a custom did exist, one must doubt its applicability to the case at bar. For there is little to show that plaintiff sold the cigarettes and liquor in question to Saavedra in the belief that they would be transferred to other ships belonging to defendant. Indeed, the evidence is to the contrary. Parodi himself testified that, once the goods were cleared with customs and tax agents, his job was at an end and he was "not concerned" with the fate of the goods.

It is the conclusion of this court then, that the captain of the S.S. NAPO was without authority—express, apparent, or implied—to bind defendant to the purchase in question. The record supports the belief that, whatever the purpose of Captain Saavedra in making these purchases, it was outside the scope of his employment by defendant, and plaintiff had no reason to think otherwise....

(a) Authority to Lien a Vessel Under the General Maritime Law

Under the general maritime law, a necessaries supplier did not acquire a maritime lien if it could by reasonable diligence have ascertained that the person ordering the necessaries did not have authority to lien the vessel.

Under what circumstances, if under any, a charterer who has control and possession of a vessel under a charter party requiring him, at his own cost, to provide for necessary supplies and repairs, may pledge the credit of the vessel, it is not necessary now to determine. We mean only to decide, at this time, that one furnishing supplies or making repairs on the order simply of a person or corporation acquiring the control and possession of a vessel under such a charter party cannot acquire a maritime lien if the circumstances attending the transaction put him on inquiry as to the existence and terms of such charter party, but he failed to make inquiry, and chose to act on a mere belief that the vessel would be liable for his claim.

The Valencia v. Ziegler, 165 U.S. 264, 272-73, 17 S.Ct. 323, 326, 41 L. Ed. 710 (1897).

(b) Authority to Lien a Vessel Under the Federal Maritime Lien Act: Pre-1971

Before the Federal Maritime Lien Act (now the Commercial Instruments and Maritime Liens Act) was amended in 1971, the Act contained language that barred the attachment of a maritime lien where the necessaries provider "knew, *or by reasonable diligence could have ascertained*, that because of the terms of the charter party" (emphasis added) the person ordering the materials "was without authority to bind the vessel therefor."

This version of the legislation imposed on the necessaries provider an obligation to inquire into the authority of the person ordering necessaries for the ship. This focused attention on the terms of the charterparty, and the scope of authority it conferred on the charterer. In The South Coast, 251 U.S. 519, 40 S.Ct. 233 (1920), the Supreme Court held that because the terms of the charterparty provided that the owner might demand redelivery of the chartered ship if any liens were not discharged within 30 days, it impliedly recognized the authority of the charterer to lien the ship. In contrast, in *United States v. Carver*, 260 U.S. 482, 43 S.Ct. 181 (1923), the Supreme Court distinguished *The South Coast*, despite the presence of very similar words in the charterparty, on the ground that the *Carver* charterparty specifically provided that "the charterers will not suffer nor permit to be continued any lien." If the necessaries provider had made inquiries with "reasonable diligence," as the statute then required it to do, it would have discovered that the charterer ordering the necessaries did not have authority to bind the ship.

In *Dampskibsselkabet Dannebrog v. Signal Oil & Gas Co. of California (The Stjerneborg)*, 310 U.S. 268, 60 S.Ct. 937 (1940), the charterparty contained no express provision prohibiting the charterer from creating liens for necessary supplies, and so the necessaries provider was held to be entitled to a maritime lien for necessaries ordered by the charterer. The Supreme Court reconciled its two previous decisions in The South Coast and Carver by saying (310 U.S. at 275; 60 S.Ct. at 941):

> "We think that the fair import of our decision in *The South Coast* is that when the charterer has the direction and control of the vessel and it is his business to provide necessary supplies, and the charter party does not prohibit the creation of a maritime lien therefor, the material-man is entitled to furnish the supplies upon the credit of the vessel as well as upon that of the charterer and the lien is not defeated by the fact that the charterer has promised the owner to pay. When, however, the charter party, with knowledge of which the material-man is charged, prohibits the creation of a lien for supplies ordered by the charterer or the charterer's representative, no lien will attach. This was decided in *United States v. Carver...*"

(c) The Effect of the 1971 Amendment: No-Lien Clauses

Note: The 1971 Amendment

In 1971 Congress deleted the language from 46 U.S.C. § 973 that barred the attachment of a maritime lien where the materialman "knew, or by the exercise of reasonable diligence could have ascertained that because of the terms of the charter party" the person ordering the materials had no authority "to bind the vessel therefor."

In G. Gilmore & C. Black, The Law of Admiralty 687 (2d ed. 1975), the authors state that "the principal (and desirable) effect of the 1971 amendment will prove [to be] the abrogation of the absolute duty to make inquiry established in *Carver* and affirmed in *Signal Oil* and a return toward the general maritime theory announced in *The Kate* and *The Valencia*. That is, a materialman who neither knows nor has reason to know that he is dealing with a chartered ship will be entitled to rely on the presumption of authority established by § 972. If, under all the circumstances, he has reason to know that the she is chartered, and makes no further inquiry, the prohibition of lien clause in the charter should be effective against him."

In *Lake Union Dry Dock Co. v. M/V Polar Viking*, 446 F. Supp. 1286, 1978 AMC 1477 (W.D. Wash. 1978), Judge Beeks handed down the following opinion:

> In this case plaintiffs Lake Union Drydock Company (Lake Union) and Duwamish Shipyard, Inc. (Duwamish) seek to foreclose maritime liens against the M/V Polar Viking pursuant to the Maritime Lien Act. Plaintiffs supplied materials and/or rendered services to the vessel while she was under a sub-demise charter to Northland Marine Lines (NML) from her owner *pro hac vice* Red Circle Transport (Red Circle), claimant herein.

On December 10, 1975 Red Circle subchartered the Polar Viking to NML for a period of one year. Between January 17 and February 18, 1976 Duwamish fabricated a stern roller with hydraulic actuated pins for the Polar Viking at the request of NML for $14,153.53. Duwamish did not install the stern roller on the vessel nor was the vessel in Duwamish's yard. Red Circle alleges, and Duwamish does not dispute, that Duwamish knew that NML utilized chartered vessels prior to commencing such work.

In June and again in August, 1976 Lake Union performed certain repairs on the Polar Viking at the request of NML. The first services were invoiced on July 20 in the amount of $10,614.73. The August repairs were invoiced on September 24, 1976 at $3,481.23. According to the deposition of Mr. Stebbins, manager of Lake Union's drydock facility, NML generally hired Lake Union to perform emergency repairs only, as were those performed on the Polar Viking.

While the Polar Viking was in drydock, Lake Union learned that the vessel was under charter. Lake Union then attempted to discover the ownership of the vessel through listings in Dun & Bradstreet, which led to an interior design firm. (The vessel was apparently listed under its former name, Ocean Gulf). Its requests to see NML's charter and a financial statement were refused, but it was assured that NML was negotiating to purchase the vessel at that time and that the account would be paid in a matter of days.

* * *

The primary question, which arises from the undisputed fact that the charter agreement between Red Circle and NML contained a no-lien clause, is whether § 973 of the Maritime Lien Act, as amended in 1971, precludes the assertion of such clause against the plaintiffs, thus barring their maritime lien claims. This is a question of first impression.

Claimant adopts the contention of Professors Gilmore and Black that the amended statute merely reinstates the prestatutory general maritime law enunciated in *The Kate* and *The Valencia*. This argument discerns the materialman's general maritime duty of inquiry pursuant to *The Kate* and *The Valencia* to be perceptibly different form his pre-71 statutory duty as developed under *U.S. v. Carver.*

I find no such difference, however, and if there be one it is too ethereal for application. The materialmen on the *The Valencia* and those who supplied the vessel Clio in *U.S. v. Carver* possessed the same quantum of knowledge; neither had knowledge that the vessels were chartered. However, the Supreme Court imputed to them constructive knowledge of the charter and its terms. The Court found that the materialmen had a duty to inquire with "reasonable diligence," and that such inquiry would have revealed a lack of authority by the party requesting the services to bind the vessel. Thus, the materialman's duty to inquire under general maritime law was identical to his duty under the statute prior to amendment in 1971. The former duty provision of § 973 merely incorporated and codified the general maritime law.

Claimant essentially argues that the amended statute, which deleted a duty of reasonably diligent inquiry, requires a duty of reasonably diligent inquiry. It is clear, then, that Red Circle's argument cannot be accepted for it would render useless the Congressional intendment in amending the statute. Statutory amendments are usually intended to alter the law and I believe this to be such an amendment. The statement found in the legislative history that the amendment makes no change in the law of maritime liens is merely an attempt by Congress to serve notice that the effect of the amendment is limited. It is not intended to affect the law of maritime liens generally, but merely to enlarge the right of a materialman to assert a lien against a vessel when he has no knowledge that the person requesting necessaries is without authority to do so.

The meaning of § 973 cannot be determined solely on its face because Congress has unfortunately failed to clearly express itself. Rather, three factors must be evaluated to discern the meaning of the statute: language, history, and the relationship of the provision of the entire statutory scheme. The statute on its face demonstrates that the duty of inquiry has been eliminated. The legislative history indicates that a lien will be barred if the materialman has knowledge of the no-lien clause. In harmonizing these two factors, the statute must be construed to entitle a materialman to a maritime lien for necessaries furnished to a vessel unless he has actual knowledge that the vessel is operating under a charter which contains a no-lien provision. In other words, the assertion of a lien will be barred only if the materialman has actual knowledge of the no-lien clause. Since actual knowledge will bar the assertion of a lien, plaintiffs' contention that a materialman's lien vests absolutely is erroneous.

This interpretation is in harmony with the presumption of authority provisions of §§ 972 and 973. The owner of a vessel must now establish that the materialman had actual knowledge of a no-lien clause if he is to overcome the materialman's statutory presumption. The imposition of this burden is supported by the legislative history. Congress intended to place the greater burden upon the vessel owner: "As a practical matter, the owner can more easily protect himself contractually by bonds or otherwise at the time he charters the vessel, than can the American materialman who furnishes necessaries to a vessel under great economic pressure to put back to sea."

I believe that § 973, as here construed, will achieve the purpose desired by Congress. It recognized that an innocent materialman required greater protection than the pre-amendment statute provided. It also recognized that a materialman with actual knowledge needed no further protection; he could protect himself by refusing to service a vessel, by arranging for payment, or he could merely assume a known risk.

Claimant also contends that the intent of Congress was to deal solely with itinerant foreign flag vessels. While Congress certainly had this problem in mind when the statute was enacted, it did not so limit its application. Another motivation for favoring the materialman was to relieve him of the time pressures inherent in the requirement of reasonably diligent inquiry. "Granting the materialman a lien encourages the prompt furnishing of necessaries to vessels so that they can be speedily turned around and put to sea. This is especially significant today when the emphasis on vessel performance is reduced port time and increased speed." Surely itinerant foreign flag vessels have no monopoly on concern for vessel performance.

In light of the above, it is clear that the no-lien clause of the charter under which NML operated the Polar Viking is not binding upon plaintiffs. Neither had actual knowledge thereof.

Even if there is no lien, may the owner of the vessel be liable *in personam* on an unjust enrichment theory?

BELCHER OIL CO. v. M/V GARDENIA

766 F.2d 1508, 1986 AMC 1745 (11th Cir. 1985)

Daniel Holcombe THOMAS, District Judge

Appellants Belcher Oil Company and Belcher Towing Company (collectively "Belcher") brought an action *in rem* against the M/V GARDENIA pursuant to the Federal Maritime Lien Act, 46 U.S.C. § 971, *et seq.*, to recover for necessaries furnished to the M/V GARDENIA. Specifically, Belcher sought to recover that value of towage and bunkering services provided to the vessel upon the charterer's insolvency. Appellee M/V GARDENIA, through its owner, N.V. Stoomvaart Maatschappij Oostzee (hereinafter the "owner"), defended the action and asserted as affirmative defenses (1) that at all times material to Belchers claim, Belcher had knowledge that Pan Atlantic Lines, the vessels time-charterer, and Chester, Blackburn & Roeder ("CB&R"), its agent, lacked the authority to bind the vessel; (2) that at all times material to Belcher's claim, Belcher had knowledge of the prohibition of lien clause contained in the charter party for the M/V GARDENIA; and (3) assuming maritime liens against the vessel were created, Belcher waived those liens by their conduct indicating that they intended to rely exclusively on the credit of the time charterer Pan Atlantic Lines or its agent CB&R.

The action was tried without a jury on July 3, 1984. The owner's did not contest that Belcher provided the necessaries. It was stipulated that Belcher had a *prima facie* case and that the M/V GARDENIA would present its defenses to rebut the statutory presumptions enjoyed by Belcher pursuant to 46 U.S.C. § 971, *et seq.* Final Judgment and written Findings of Fact and Conclusions of Law were entered in favor of the M/V GARDENIA on all three defenses. This appeal follows and we affirm.

In January 1983, the M/V GARDENIA was operating out of the Port of Miami, under time charter to Pan Atlantic Lines. CB&R acted as Pan Atlantic Lines' agent in the Port of Miami to handle Pan Atlantic Lines' accounts for the procurement of, and payment for, service and supplies required by its chartered vessel. During the time the M/V GARDENIA was operating in the Port of Miami, Belcher provided towage and bunkering services to the vessel.

Under the terms of the chapter party Pan Atlantic Lines, as charterers, were responsible for the various ports of the M/V GARDENIA. The charter party also contained a "prohibition of lien" clause which prohibited the charterer from incurring any maritime liens against the vessel and/or her owner's for supplies or necessaries.

The facts, as found by the district court, are paraphrased below.

At all material times Pan Atlantic Lines was the time charterer of the M/V GARDENIA and CB&R was the agent for Pan Atlantic Lines. Belcher had a long-standing business relationship with both CB&R and Pan Atlantic Lines and was familiar with the intricacies of the operation of CB&R and Pan Atlantic Lines.

Upon the orders of Pan Atlantic Lines' agent, CB&R, Belcher provided fuel bunkers to the M/V GARDENIA on May 25, 1983, and towing services on March 5 and June 5, 1983. Prior to the time these "necessaries" were furnished, Belcher had knowledge that CB&R was an agent for Pan Atlantic Lines and that CB&R had no authority other than to act on behalf of Pan Atlantic Lines.

Belcher was advised by the manager of CB&R's Accounts Payable Department, prior to delivery of the services at issue, that Pan Atlantic Lines was the time charterer of the M/V GARDENIA and that the charter party prohibited Belcher from looking to the vessel and/or her owner's for payment of these services. Therefore, Belcher knew that CB&R and Pan Atlantic Lines had no authority to bind the vessel or its owner's and could only look to Pan Atlantic Lines for payment.

Belcher was further advised by the manager of CB&R's Accounts Payable Department that there was, in fact, a prohibition of lien clause contained in the charter party. Therefore, Belcher knew or certainly should have known that the charter party contained such a clause. The court further found that Belcher had actual knowledge of the prohibition of lien clause. The court's conclusion that Belcher had actual knowledge of the prohibition of lien clause was found to be corroborated by the fact that several of Belcher's previous bunkering certificates for the M/V GARDENIA, while time-chartered to Pan Atlantic Lines, contained the disclaimer language "for and/or in behalf of time-charterers without recourse to myself and/or Owners of the Vessel."

On May 25, 1983, a dispute arose on board the M/V GARDENIA among representatives of CB&R, Belcher and the officers of the vessel with respect to the execution of Belcher's bunkering certificates for the fuel bunkers delivered by Belcher on that day. The Master of the vessel informed CB&R's fuel coordinator that he would not sign the bunkering certificate without a disclaimer stamp. The district court found that, at this time, Belcher was again informed that the charter party contained a prohibition of lien clause which prohibited the vessel from being liened. Belcher subsequently consented to accepting the signature of CB&R's representative after being informed of the provisions of the charter party agreement.

The court further found, assuming *arguendo* that a lien had been created, Belcher waived any such lien by failing to withdraw the bunkers. Instead, Belcher elected to accept the signature of CB&R's representative in order to facilitate the sale of the bunkers, thereby waiving any lien it may have had against the vessel.

The Dispositive Issue

On appeal, Belcher enumerates six assignments of error. However, we need only address the question of whether actual knowledge of a prohibition of lien clause contained in a charter party is the only manner in which a vessel and/or her owner's can establish a charterers lack of authority to bind the vessel so as to defeat a maritime lien afforded the supplier pursuant to 46 U.S.C. § 971, *et seq.*

The Federal Maritime Lien Act

Section 971 of the Federal Maritime Lien Act provides:

> Any person furnishing repairs, supplies, towage, use of dry dock or marine railway, or other necessaries, to any vessel, whether foreign or domestic, *upon the order of the owner* of such vessel, *or of a person authorized by the owner*, shall have a maritime lien on the vessel, which may be enforced by suit *in rem*, and it shall not be necessary to allege or prove that the credit was given to the vessel. 46 U.S.C. § 971. (emphasis added).

Section 972 of the Act provides:

> The following persons shall be presumed to have authority from the owner to procure repairs, supplies, towage, use of dry dock or marine railway, and other necessaries for the vessel: The managing owner, ship's husband, master, or any person to whom the management of the vessel at the port of supply is intrusted. No person tortiously or unlawfully in possession or charge of a vessel shall have authority to bind the vessel. 46 U.S.C. § 972.

Section 973 of the Act was amended in 1971. Prior to 1971, this section provided:

> The officers and agents of a vessel specified in section 972 of this title shall be taken to include such officers and agents when appointed by a charterer, by an owner *pro hac vice*, or by an agreed purchaser in possession of the vessel; but nothing in this chapter shall be construed to confer a lien when the furnisher knew, or by exercise of reasonable diligence could have ascertained, that because of the terms of a charter party, agreement for sale of the vessel, or for any other reason, the person ordering the repairs, supplies, or other necessaries was without authority to bind the vessel. 46 U.S.C. § 973 (pre-1971).

The duty of inquiry imposed by 46 U.S.C. § 973, prior to 1971, eventually became a substantial obstacle for those persons furnishing supplies and other necessaries to maritime vessels. In virtually every instance the supplier was under a duty to ascertain the authority of the individual ordering supplies for a ship to incur liens on the vessel. *See United States v. Carver*, 260 U.S. 482, 43 S.Ct. 181, 67 L. Ed. 361 (1923); *Dampskibsselskabet Dannebrog v. Signal Oil & Gas Co.*, 310 U.S. 268, 60 S.Ct. 937, 84 L. Ed. 1197 (1940). Such a duty of inquiry became quite impractical in light of the various chartering and subchartering practices of foreign and domestic vessels. Furthermore, vessel owner's and charterers engaged in sub-chartering activities began to insert "prohibition of lien" or "no lien" provisions in charter parties. This practice effectively shifted the risk of loss to the supplier since a reasonably diligent inquiry would almost certainly yield information which would effectively bar any lien.

In response to this problem, Congress amended 46 U.S.C. § 973 in 1971[1] by deleting the language imposing a duty of inquiry on the materialman. The 1971 amendment to the Federal Maritime Lien Act, 46 U.S.C. § 973, deleted the words "but nothing in this chapter shall be construed to confer a lien when the furnisher knew, or by exercise of reasonable diligence could have ascertained, that because of the terms of the charter party ... the person ordering the repairs, supplies, or other necessaries was without authority to bind the vessel."[2]

The primary concern of the legislators supporting the 1971 amendment was that suppliers were frequently unable to either ascertain the existence of a charter and determine if the charter party contained a prohibition of lien clause or to perform an adequate check on the entity ordering the supplies. *See* H.R. 92-340, 92 Cong., 1st Sess., *reprinted in* 1971 U.S. Code Cong. & Ad. News 1363; 177 Cong. Rec. 25,762 (1971); *Id.* at 25,763; *Id.* at 25,764.

Knowledge of Lack of Authority v. Knowledge of Prohibition of Lien Clause

As noted above, the district court held, *inter alia*, that the presumption of a lien will be defeated if the vessel and/or her owner's establish either that the supplier had actual knowledge that the person ordering the supplier or other necessaries lacked the authority to bind the vessel, or that the supplier had actual knowledge of a prohibition of lien clause in the charter party.

Belcher maintains that these two findings are inconsistent with the decided cases and defeat the intent of the 1971 amendment. Belcher contends that nothing short of *actual knowledge of a prohibition lien clause* will defeat the lien afforded under 46 U.S.C. § 71. (emphasis added). We disagree.

Section 971 of the Federal Maritime Lien Act clearly states that a maritime lien will arise in favor of one furnishing necessaries to a vessel when those necessaries are ordered by the owner or a *person authorized by the owner* to bind the vessel. (emphasis added) Section 972 of the Act provides that a charterer is *presumed* to have authority to bind the vessel. (emphasis added). The statute is clear that a lien will not arise when necessaries are ordered by one without authority to bind the vessel. Although a charterer is presumed to have authority to bind the vessel, the lien does not vest absolutely as a matter of law, but rather, "the burden is upon the owner to show that the supplier of necessaries had actual knowledge of the existence of any lack of authority relied upon as a defense." *Jan C. Uiterwhy Co., Inc. v. M/V MARE ARABICO*, 459 F. Supp. 1325, 1331 (D. Md. 1978). This was made even clearer in the case of *Belcher Co. of Alabama, Inc. v. M/V MARTHA MARINER*, 724 F.2d 1161 (5th Cir. 1984) in which it is stated, "This lien [46 U.S.C. § 971] attaches when necessaries are ordered by and supplied to the charterer, unless the supplier has notice that the person who orders the necessaries lacked authority to do so."

Gilmore & Black, in the 2nd Edition of THE LAW OF ADMIRALTY at page 685, give a very interesting discussion on the effect of the 1971 amendment to § 973. Among other things, Gilmore & Black state, "If the person who orders the services is not authorized by the owner to create liens and if the furnisher of the services has notice of the lack of authority, it is entirely clear that no lien will arise."

---

[1] 46 U.S.C. § 973 now provides:

The officers and agents of a vessel specified in Section 972 of this title shall be taken to include such officers and agents when appointed by a charterer, by an owner, *pro hac vice*, or by an agreed purchaser in possession of the vessel.

[2] Due to the nature of the shipping business, materialmen furnishing supplies and other necessaries to a vessel rarely have sufficient time in which to ascertain whether a vessel is under charter or to review complicated charter provisions prior to entering into contracts for the furnishing of necessaries to a vessel which may be in port for only a brief period.

Belcher's emphasis upon the supplier obtaining actual knowledge of prohibition of lien clauses is misplaced. If a supplier has actual knowledge of prohibition of lien clause in a charter party then he certainly has actual knowledge of the charterer's lack of authority to bind the vessel. Actual knowledge of a prohibition of lien clause is merely one way of obtaining actual knowledge of one's lack of authority to bind the vessel.

The cases relied upon by Belcher do not support such a requirement. TTT Stevedores of Texas, Inc. v. M/V JAGAT VIJETA, 696 F.2d 1135 (5th Cir. 1983); *Gulf Oil Trading Co. v. M/V CARBIE MAR*,757 F.2d 743 (5th Cir. 1985); *Jan C. Uiterwyk Co., Inc. v. M/V MARE ARABICO, supra; Lake Union Drydock Co. v. M/V POLAR VIKING,446 F. Supp. 1286 (W.D. Wash. 1978).*

Belcher relies primarily upon *TTT Stevedores of Texas, Inc., v. M/V JAGAT VIJETA, supra.* In that case the Fifth Circuit Court of Appeals recognized that actual knowledge of a prohibition of lien clause would bar the lien. 696 F.2d at 1138. It must be noted, however, that the court did not hold that actual knowledge of a prohibition of lien clause is the only manner in which it can be established that the charterer lacked authority to bind the vessel. The court in *TTT Stevedores of Texas Inc. v. M/V JAGAT VIJETA, supra,* merely held that a lien would be barred if the supplier had actual knowledge of a prohibition of lien clause in a charter party prior to furnishing necessaries to the vessel.

A careful reading of the cases cited by Belcher on this issue reveals that in no case were the suppliers presented with the question as to the authority of the one ordering the supplies. In each of those cases the supplies were ordered either by one having authority, or presumed authority (§ 972) which was never questioned. Thus, the courts in each of those cases did not address the issue herein.

We therefore hold that a maritime lien, created pursuant to 46 U.S.C. § 971, may be defeated when the vessel and/or her owner's establish that the supplier of necessaries either had actual knowledge that the person ordering the supplies lacked the authority to bind the vessel or had knowledge of a prohibition of lien clause in the charter.

Our holding is not, in any way, to be construed so as to either limit the supplier's ability to rely on the presumptions afforded him or to impose a duty of inquiry. However, a supplier should not be allowed to rely on such beneficial presumptions when he has actual knowledge to the contrary. Suppliers of necessaries are afforded the protection of a lien when they have no knowledge of a prohibition of lien clause and no knowledge that the person ordering the supplies has no authority to do so. These concerns are, of course, moot when a supplier has actual knowledge of the buyer's lack of authority to bind the vessel—be it by knowledge of a prohibition of lien clause or otherwise. The supplier who has such knowledge is then in a position to make an informed business decision and may refuse to supply the vessel, make other arrangements for payment, or assume the risk.

In the instant case, the record clearly supports a finding that Belcher had sufficient knowledge that Pan Atlantic Lines and CB & R lacked the authority to bind the vessel. In any event, were we to accept Belcher's contention that only actual knowledge of the prohibition of lien clause would defeat the lien, we find that the record sufficiently supports the district court's finding that Belcher had actual knowledge of the prohibition of lien clause contained in Pan Atlantic Lines charter agreement.

In light of our disposition of the above issue we do not reach Belcher's remaining contentions. Based on the foregoing, WE AFFIRM.

MARINE FUEL SUPPLY & TOWING, INC. v. M/V KEN LUCKY

859 F.2d 1405, 1989 AMC 390 (9th Cir. 1988) *opinion amended and superseded by* 869 F.2d 473 (9th Cir. 1988)

NELSON, Circuit Judge

Marine Fuel Supply & Towing, Inc. ("Marine Fuel") appeals the district court's refusal to grant Marine Fuel a maritime lien on the M/V KEN LUCKY ("Ken Lucky") pursuant to 46 U.S.C. §§ 971-75 (1982). The district court exercised jurisdiction pursuant to 28 U.S.C. § 1333 and we have jurisdiction pursuant to 28 U.S.C. § 1291. We reverse and remand.

Background

Ken Hieng Navigation Company S.A. ("Ken Hieng") owns the Ken Lucky. During the time Marine Fuel alleges the lien arose, Ken Hieng had time chartered the vessel to Compaigne Continental Paris ("Continental Grain"). A time charter entails a division of responsibilities between the owner and charterer. *Dampskibsselskabet Dannebrog v. Signal Oil & Gas Co.,* 310 U.S. 268, 278, 84 L. Ed. 1197, 60 S.Ct. 937 (1940) *("Signal Oil").* Continental Grain in turn subchartered the vessel to Bulkferts, Inc. ("Bulkferts"). Both charter agreements contained "no lien" clauses, which prohibited maritime liens asserted by suppliers against the vessel.

When the Ken Lucky reached Tampa, Florida, in September 1984, it needed bunker fuel. To arrange for the supplies, Bulkferts' managing agent, Eurostem Maritime Limited ("Eurostem"), contacted Brook Oil Ltd. ("Brook"). Brook then instructed Gray Bunkering Services ("Gray") to place the order for the Ken Lucky's supplies with Marine Fuel. Marine Fuel asked Gray for assurances about payment before delivery of the bunkers. In response, Gray sent a telex on September 3, 1984 notifying Marine Fuel that it had been "nominated by the owner" of the Ken Lucky to supply the vessel. Ken Lucky's local (husbanding) agent arranged for delivery of the supplies. On September 6, 1984, Marine Fuel supplied the Ken Lucky with bunkers worth $223,480.10. The master of the Ken Lucky, appointed by the owner, approved the acceptance of the supplies by the vessel's chief engineer. Marine Fuel billed Gray for the bunkers, referencing Brooks account. Marine Fuel unsuccessfully sought payment from Brook, which was forced into receivership in October of 1984.

Marine Fuel arrested the Ken Lucky in Portland, Oregon. Ken Lucky posted cash as security for Marine Fuel's claim, which counsel for the parties deposited in a Portland bank. The district court refused to grant Marine Fuel a maritime lien. The cross appeal has been dismissed. Marine Fuel timely appealed.

* * *

Discussion

I. Authorization of the Supply Order

Marine Fuel contends that Brook, the bunker broker, had presumed authority under the Federal Maritime Lien Act (the Act) from Bulkferts and Eurostem, the subcharterer and its managing agent, to incur a lien on behalf of the Ken Lucky. The district court found that because no agency relationship existed between Bulkferts and Brook, no presumed authority under the Act was established. Marine Fuel contends that Brook had implied authority from Bulkferts or the ship's owner to incur the lien. Alternatively, Marine Fuel argues that Bulkferts, as a person authorized under section 971 or 972 had presumed authority under the Act to order fuel and to incur a lien against the vessel. The district court concluded that the charter agreements' no lien clauses prevented Brook from acting pursuant to implied authority to incur a lien.

* * *

A. The Federal Maritime Lien Act

"The federal Maritime Lien Act grants a maritime lien to any person 1) furnishing repairs, supplies, or other necessaries 2) to any vessel 3) upon the order of the owner of such vessel, or of a person authorized by the owner.'"*Farwest I,* 769 F.2d at 623 (*quoting* 46 U.S.C. § 971). The parties agree that Marine Fuel furnished necessaries to the Ken Lucky. Ken Lucky admits that Bulkferts was in possession and control of the vessel during the time it docked in Tampa. Thus, Bulkferts qualifies as an authorized person under section 972 because it was the"person to whom the management of the vessel at the port of supply [was] intrusted."[3]

---

[3] *The Susana,* 2 F.2d 410, 412-13 (4th Cir. 1924); *Red Star Towing & Transp. Co.,* 5 F. Supp. 502 (E.D.N.Y. 1933); G. Gilmore & C. Black, *supra,* at 802.

In a few cases, however, owners appearing in an *in rem* action to contest the libelants' claims have been "treated as if they had been brought into court by personal process" and held personally liable for judgment in excess of the security. *The Fairisle,* 76 F. Supp. 27,34 (D. Md. 1947), *aff'd subnom. Waterman S.S. Corp. v. Dean,* 171 F.2d408 (4th Cir. 1948) (*quoted in Treasure Salvors v. The Unidentified Wrecked and Abandoned Sailing Vessel,* 569 F.2d 330, 335 (5th Cir. 1978)); *see also Mosher v. Tate,* 182 F.2d 475, 479-80 (9th Cir. 1950); G. Gilmore & C. Black, *supra,* at 802-02.

The district court based its refusal to find an agency relationship between Bulkferts and Brook on two propositions: 1) that Brook was an independent corporation; and 2) that Brook was a back-to-back trader. Marine Fuel argues that Brook can be an independent corporation and still have acted as Bulkferts' agent in the disputed transaction. *See Protective Ins. Co. v. Coleman,* 144 Ill. App. 3d 682, 494 N.E.2d 1241, 1250, 98 Ill. Dec. 914 (1986); RESTATEMENT (SECOND) AGENCY § 14 (1958). We look to principles of agency to interpret the Act's references to agents. *Cactus Pipe & Supply Co. v. M/V Montmartre,* 756 F.2d 1103, 1111 (5th Cir. 1985). We examine the roles of the parties in the transactions at issue to determine if a person has presumed authority under the Act. *See, e.g., Farwest I,* 769 F.2d at 623-24; *Farwest Steel Corp. v. Barge Sea-Span,* 828 F.2d 522, 525-26 (9th Cir. 1987), *cert. denied,* 485 U.S. 1034, 108 S.Ct. 1594, 99 L. Ed. 2d 909 (1988) *("Farwest II").*

The parties agree that the order originated from Bulkferts. Thus, we need not reach the question whether the district court's conclusion that Brook was not *Bulkfert's* agent is erroneous because appellees have already admitted that the fuel and bunkers were sold to *Bulkferts.* We conclude that Marine Fuel need not establish agency between Brook and Bulkferts to fall within the scope of one entitled to a maritime lien under the Act.

Ken Lucky concedes that Bulkferts was authorized to bind the vessel. It is clear that Eurostem, as managing agent for Bulkferts, did order the fuel and it is also clear that Marine Fuel delivered the fuel *to the vessel.* Section 971 states that any person furnishing supplies or other necessaries *to a vessel* "upon" the order of a person authorized to bind the vessel shall be entitled to lien. It is clear that Eurostem, as managing agent for Bulkferts, ordered the fuel, and it is also clear that Marine Fuel delivered the fuel *to the vessel.* Bulkferts had statutory authority to order the fuel under section 972 and it did so. Marine Fuel delivered the fuel to the vessel after Bulkferts ordered it. Thus, this case can be easily distinguished from the situation present in *Farwest II.*

In *Farwest II,* we affirmed the district courts finding that the general contractor did not qualify as an "authorized person" to bind the vessel under § 972. *Id.* at 525-26. We distinguished between the general contractor's responsibility for vessel repairs and one who has broad management powers to qualify as a person "intrusted" with management of the vessel under § 972, relying on a line of cases in which courts "have uniformly held that the general repair contractor was not endowed with sufficient 'management' authority to support a section 971 lien." *Id.* at 526. However, no restrictive repair contract line of cases governs the issue here. Further, no specific instruction was given in *Farwest,* as Bulkferts gave here, authorizing Eurostem to order the bunkers through Brook.

In *Farwest,* the steel was ordered by a contractor repairing the vessel. No one with authority to lien the vessel originated the order. Here Bulkferts, which clearly possessed the statutory authority to bind the vessel, ordered and received the bunkers and fuel. Thus, we are not confronted with a *Farwest II* situation, where a person who never had authority originated the order.

B. Statutory Authority to Bind the Vessel Under Section 972

Ken Lucky also concedes that the master of the Ken Lucky, appointed by the owner, accepted the supplies. Ken Lucky contends that the master had no authority to accept the supplies and incur a lien against the vessel because of the no lien clauses in the charter agreements. However, such reasoning contradicts the language of § 972, which states that a ship's master has presumed authority to incur a lien. *See Atlantic & Gulf Stevedores, Inc. v. M/V Grand Loyalty,* 608 F.2d 197, 200 (5th Cir. 1979) (chief officer who ordered services possessed management powers envisioned by Act and thus had presumed authority as well as actual authority to incur lien).

A claimant's dealings with an intermediary at the port rather than a charterer or owner does not preclude the existence of a lien. *Reinholm Crane & Rigging Co., Inc. v. M/V Ocean Crown,* 484 F. Supp. 935, 936 (W.D. Wash. 1979). The parties agree that the order originated from Bulkferts. Eurostem, Bulkferts' managing agent, placed the order with Brook. Marine Fuel received a telex from Gray confirming that the owner authorized the order, identifying Fillette as Ken Lucky's local (husbanding) agent. Before delivering the bunkers, Marine Fuel notified Fillette of the order and Fillette arranged for delivery of the bunkers. Fillette received a telex from Bulkferts' domestic agent, WKM Ship Management Services, stating that WKM was arranging for a purchase of bunkers in the same amount for the ship. Ken Lucky's chief engineer accepted the bunkers, acknowledging receipt, with the approval of the master. The ship's master also had presumed authority to incur a lien under the Act. The vessel certainly benefited from the bunker supply.

We conclude that this sequence of events is sufficient to establish implied authority to incur a lien against the vessel for fuel. *See Yacht, MARY JANE v. Broward Marine, Inc.,* 313 F.2d 516, 517 (5th Cir. 1963) (implied authority existed because the "real" captain failed to object although he was aware of work being done for vessel); *Reinholm,* 484 F. Supp. at 936 (no objections from vessel's master, owner or charterer to obvious and prolonged services precluded summary judgment because material issue of fact remained as to the existence of implied authority); *Jan C. Uiterwyk Co. v. M/V MARE ARABICO,* 459 F. Supp. 1325, 1330-31 (D. Md. 1978) (subcharterer was held to have had implied authority from the time charterer to procure the services because masters of the vessels who ordered the services were held to be agents of persons with apparent authority to bind the vessels, the time charterer and owner).

Moreover, the district court's reliance on the no lien clause to deny the lien thwarts the purpose of the statute by charging Marine Fuel with the onerous duty of resolving the ambiguities in the Sipra-Bulkferts-Eurostem-Brook relationship. *Cf. Signal Oil,* 310 U.S. at 280 (purpose of lien act thwarted if courts compel the "material-man furnishing supplies to the vessel to resolve the ambiguities which may be found in [the charter agreements]"). We recently noted, construing a lien under the Preferred Ship Mortgage Act, that "one of the purposes of the Maritime Liens Act, 46 U.S.C. §§ 971-75 ... is to create liens in favor of those who furnish necessaries for the vessel's operation. Permitting [a] contrived financial scheme to prevail effectively destroys the liens of suppliers and subverts the purposes of the Maritime Liens Act." *Wardley Int'l Bank, Inc. v. Nasipit Bay Vessel,* 841 F.2d 259, 264 (9th Cir. 1988) (citation omitted).

* * *

C. Effect of the No Lien Clauses

Ken Lucky admits that the purpose of the Act is to help suppliers determine who has authority to incur a lien. The Act's presumption in favor of granting liens to suppliers "was enhanced in 1971 when Congress deleted the requirement that materialmen inquire about the existence of any no-lien clauses before furnishing supplies." *Farwest I,* 769 F.2d at 623; *see Foss Launch,* 808 F.2d at 700 (one purpose of amendment was "to ensure that any party to whom the management of the vessel is entrusted will be presumed to have authority to procure necessaries and supplies which may give rise to maritime liens"); *Gulf Trading & Transp. Co. v. M/V Tento,* 694 F.2d 1191, 1194 (9th Cir. 1982), *cert. denied,* 461 U.S. 929, 77 L. Ed. 2d 301, 103 S.Ct. 2091 (1983). Congress was concerned that the duty of inquiry had become a "substantial obstacle" for persons furnishing supplies. H. REP. No. 340, 92d Cong., 1st Sess., *reprinted in* 1971 U.S. CODE CONG. & ADMIN. NEWS 1363, 1364-65. *See Belcher Oil,* 766 F.2d at 1511; *Lake Union Drydock Co. v. M/V Polar Viking,* 446 F. Supp. 1286, 1289-91 (W.D. Wash. 1978); *Ryan-Walsh Stevedoring Co., Inc. v. M/V Khalij Star,* 507 F. Supp. 36, 38 (W.D. Wash. 1980).

> [The] duty of inquiry became quite impractical in light of the various chartering and sub-chartering practices of foreign and domestic vessels. Furthermore, vessel owner's and charterers engaged in sub-chartering activities began to insert "prohibition of lien" or "no lien" provisions in charter parties. This practice effectively shifted the risk of loss to the supplier....

Belcher Oil, 766 F.2d at 1511; *see Atlantic,* 608 F.2d at 201 & n.7 (no lien provisions a primary concern of the amendments).

The 1971 amendment obviously was directed at reducing the force of owners' and charterers' prohibition of lien clauses. GILMORE & BLACK, THE LAW OF ADMIRALTY § 9-39, at 669-70 (2d ed. 1975). However, Congress did not explicitly prohibit no lien clauses and the effectiveness of prohibition of lien clauses after the amendment has not been settled. *See id.* § 9-46a, at 685-86. This presents an issue of first impression in this circuit. Several courts have held that a no lien clause is not effective to rebut a statutory presumption of authority without proof of the supplier's actual knowledge of the clause. *See, e.g., Ramsay Scarlett & Co.y Inc. v. S.S. Koh Eun,* 462 F. Supp. 277, 284-85 (E.D. Va. 1978); *lake Union Drydock,* 446 F. Supp. at 1291. We agree. Even though a no lien clause is present, we conclude that the purposes of the Act, in light of the 1971 amendment, would be thwarted if the actual knowledge inquiry were not undertaken.

The record below reveals that the issue of notice was before the trial court. The defendant Ken Lucky had an opportunity to present evidence that Marine Fuel had knowledge of the no lien clause, but defendant offered no such evidence. Therefore, the no lien clause is not effective to rebut a statutory presumption of authority. *Belcher Oil,* 766 F.2d at 1512 (*quoting Jan C. Uiterwyk Co.,* 459 F. Supp. at 1331). "[T]he Act now requires that the owner take affirmative action to notify the supplier of necessaries that the master of a vessel or the charterer is *not* authorized to order services, the performance of which will result in the creation of liens." *Jan C. Uiterwyk,* 459 F. Supp. at 1331. Knowledge that the charterer is mere "time charterer" does not amount to actual knowledge of the time charterer's lack of authority to incur a lien for necessaries. *Ramsay Scarlett,* 462 F. Supp. at 284-85. II.

* * *

REVERSED.

Notes

1. Compare the *Ken Lucky* case with *Galehead, Inc. v. M/V Anglia,* 183 F.3d 1242, 1999 AMC 2952 (11th Cir. 1999). In *Anglia,* Genesis, the charterer of the vessel, contacted Polygon to obtain bunkers for the ANGLIA. Polygon contacted Assamar to supply the fuel. Assamar, in turn, contracted with Coastal, which actually supplied the fuel. The bunker confirmation prepared by Polygon listed Coastal as the supplier and Assamar as the seller. Assamar paid Coastal and, when Genesis failed to pay Assamar, the vessel was arrested. The court held that, although Assamar provided necessaries to the ANGLIA, it did not do so "on the order of the owner or agent," and, thus, had no maritime lien. In other words, the bunkers were not supplied "on the order of the owner or a person authorized by the owner." Assamar provided the bunkers on the order of Polygon and Polygon was not a "person presumed to have authority to procure necessaries." The court observed that there was no evidence that Polygon acted as Genesis' agent as opposed to one merely under a contract to supply Genesis with fuel.

2. In *Lake Charles Stevedores, Inc. v. M/V Professor Vladimir Popov,* 199 F.3d 220, 2000 AMC 2273 (5th Cir. 1999), a stevedore that had been hired by the shipper of a cargo of rice claimed to have a maritime lien over the ship for the cost of its stevedoring services. The U.S. Court of Appeals for the Fifth Circuit rejected the stevedore's claim, holding that a stevedore hired by a shipper would not have a maritime lien absent evidence that the shipper had actual or apparent authority to employ stevedores on behalf of the vessel, rather than on its own behalf.

Note: Subcontractors

1. Where a general contractor which has entered into a contract with a person authorized to procure necessaries, subcontracts some of the work, does the subcontractor have a maritime lien? *Compare Turecamo of Savannah, Inc. v. U.S.,* 36 F.3d 1083, 1996 AMC 2003 (11th Cir. 1994), *cert. denied,* 516 U.S. 1028, 116 S.Ct. 673, 133 L. Ed. 2d 522 and *Marine Coatings of Alabama, Inc. v. U.S.,* 932 F.2d 1370, 1991 AMC 2487 (11th Cir. 1991) with *Crescent City Marine, Inc. v. M/V NUNKI,* 20 F. 3d 665, 1994 AMC 2195 (5 th Cir. 1994) and *Bonanni Ship Supply, Inc. v. U.S.,* 959 F. 2d 1558, 1992 AMC 2165 (11th Cir. 1992).

2. Yang Ming, an ocean shipping company, operated a number of vessels. It contacted OW Bunker Far East to negotiate terms for the delivery of fuel to Yang Ming's ships in Russia. Yang Ming subsequently contacted OW Far East to supply fuel to its ship the *YM Success.* The sales confirmation listed OW Far East as the seller and Transbunker as the supplier. Far East then engaged Bunker Holdings to supply the fuel. On two occasions fuel was supplied to the YM Success but it was actually supplied by Baltic Tanker Co. Ltd. pursuant to an agreement with Bunker Holdings. The issue was whether Bunker Holdings had a maritime lien on the vessel.

"The question therefore becomes whether OW Far East was authorized by Yang Ming to bind the YM Success. As other courts have recognized, there are two lines of cases that provide a framework for answering this question: the general contractor/subcontractor line, *see, e.g., Port of Portland v. M/V Paralla,* 892 F.2d 825 (9th Cir. 1989), and the principal/agent, or middleman, line, *see, e.g., Marine Fuel Supply & Towing, Inc. v. M/V Ken Lucky,* 869 F.2d 473 (9th Cir. 1989).

Under the general contractor line of cases, "[i]t is the general rule that a general contractor does not have the authority to bind a vessel." *Port of Portland,* 892 F.2d at 828. Consequently, a subcontractor will normally not be entitled to a maritime lien. *Id.* "The sole exception to the rule against the subcontractor lien will occur where the subcontractor has been engaged by a general contractor in circumstances where the general contractor was acting as an agent at the direction of the owner to engage specific subcontractors...." *Farwest Steel Corp. v. Barge Sea-Span 241*, 828 F.2d 522, 526 (9th Cir. 1987). Meanwhile, under the middleman line of cases, "courts hold that physical suppliers in a line of agency relationships can assert a lien against vessels, even though there are numerous intermediaries between supplier and vessel." *O'Rourke Marine Servs. L.P., L.L.P. v. MV COSCO Haifa*, ___ F. Supp. 3d ____, 2016 WL 1544742, at *4 (S.D.N.Y. Apr. 8, 2016); *see also Lake Charles Stevedores, Inc. v. PROFESSOR VLADIMIR POPOV MV*, 199 F.3d 220, 229 (5th Cir. 1999).

Simply put, to obtain a maritime lien against the *YM Success*, Bunker Holdings must demonstrate that either (1) OW Far East was acting as an agent for Yang Ming, or (2) Yang Ming directed OW Far East to engage Bunker Holdings as the specific subcontractor to supply the Nakhodka fuel.

With respect to the former, Bunker Holdings has failed to show that OW Far East and Yang Ming had an agency relationship. At the outset, Bunker Holdings has not submitted any evidence that Yang Ming expressly appointed OW Far East as its agent. Although Bunker Holdings contends that OW Far East had implied authority, Bunker Holdings has not pointed to representations from Yang Ming to Bunker Holdings about OW Far East's authority. *See Port of Portland*, 892 F.2d at 829. Indeed, the record is devoid of any communications between Yang Ming and Bunker Holdings until the November 2014 demand letter ("Prior to receipt of Bunker

Holdings' demand letter... Yang Ming had not had any communication with Bunker Holdings Ltd. regarding the Nakhodka Fuel Deliveries....").

As for the latter, Bunker Holdings argues that Yang Ming and OW Far East contemplated and understood that OW Far East would engage Bunker Holdings to provide the fuel for the Nakhodka deliveries. To support this argument, Bunker Holdings points to the email exchanges between Yang Ming and OW Far East. In two emails, OW Far East informs Yang Ming that its "local managers in Vladivostok will take good care of the deliveries and planning.." In another email, Yang Ming asks OW Far East to "[p]lease arrange our order"…

Bunker Holdings has failed to support the inferences that follow from these statements with evidence. There is no evidence in the record that Yang Ming directed, authorized, or was even involved in the selection of Bunker Holdings as the supplier for the Nakhodka fuel deliveries. Indeed, the evidence in the record shows otherwise.("[Yang Ming] was unaware of any orders or agreements between Bunker Holdings Ltd. and OW Bunker Far East relating to [the Nakhodka fuel] deliveries," Yang Ming did not direct OW Bunker Far East to contract with Bunker Holdings for the Nakhodka Fuel Deliveries for the YM Success and did not approve of any such contract.")

Bunker Holdings v. M/V YM Success, 2016 AMC 1723 (W.D. Wash. 2016).

Note: Additional Persons to Whom the Vessel is "Entrusted"

Is a watchman a person to whom the vessel is "entrusted"? In *The E.S. Loop*, 63 F. Supp. 105, 1946 AMC 467 (S.D. Cal. 1945), the court found the following:

Under the allegations of the libel, the gasoline and supplies, for which claim is made, were allegedly furnished at the request of the owner. When one who claims to be the agent of the owner furnishes such supplies, no maritime lien arises. Furthermore, I do not think that a watchman can be called a "person to whom the management of the vessel at the port of supply is entrusted." These words imply a broader direction and control of the vessel than is implied in the mere act of watching a vessel out of commission.

A part owner and prospective purchaser of a vessel is a person entrusted with the vessel under 46 U.S.C.A. § 31341 (formerly 46 U.S.C. § 972) and presumed to have the authority of the owner. *Hercules Co. v. The Brigadier General Absolom Baird*, 214 F.2d 66, 1954 AMC 1201 (3d Cir. 1954). What would be the effect of an anti-lien clause in a conditional sale agreement? *See Kane v. M/V Leda*, 355 F. Supp. 796, 1972 AMC 2094 (E.D. La. 1972). In this case, the court held that the purchaser of a vessel under a conditional sale was not a person authorized by the owner to create liens for necessaries under 46 U.S.C. § 972. Provisions of state law according to which the purchaser was "owner" were held to be immaterial. At any rate, the conditional sale agreement contained an anti-lien clause of which the repairman had notice.

Is a person who assumes the position of a master "entrusted with the vessel?" In *Findley v. Red Top Super Markets*, 188 F.2d 834, 1951 AMC 1113 (5th Cir. 1951), supplies were ordered by a person who purported to be the master of the vessel. The court dismissed a libel on the ground that ordinary care would have shown that the impostor did not have the authority of the owner. Should the solution be the same after the 1971 amendment? Under the current provisions of Chapter 313—Commercial Instruments and Maritime Liens?

Is a time charterer presumed to have authority from the owner under 46 U.S.C. § 972? *See Clubb Oil Tools, Inc. v. M/V George Vergottis*, 460 F. Supp. 835, 1980 AMC 556 (S.D. Tex. 1978). The court held that the time charterer was liable for breach of contract (rental of pipeline equipment for the loading of the vessel) and that the liability of the shipowner on the maritime lien was joint and several with the liability of the time charterer on the breach of contract claim. There was no anti-lien clause in the charter party.

Note: Authority of "an Agreed Buyer"

Under 46 U.S.C. § 973 "an agreed purchaser in possession of the vessel" was presumed to have authority to lien a vessel. In *First National Bank & Trust Co. of Vicksburg, Mississippi v. The Towboat Seneca*, 179 F. Supp. 847, 1960 AMC 766 (E.D. La. 1960), repairs were ordered by one Flowers who had exercised an option to purchase the vessel and was in possession of it in his capacity as master. At the time, the vessel was under a charter that contained an anti-lien clause. After the repairs were done, the contract of sale was executed and preferred ship mortgage was granted and recorded. Upon default of payment, the mortgage creditor sought foreclosure and the repairman claimed a preferred maritime lien for repairs. The court denied the lien. It reasoned:

It is true that Flowers was the master of the Seneca and that ordinarily a shipyard may rely on that officer's presumed authority to lien the vessel. But such presumption does not relieve the shipyard of its statutory duty to use reasonable diligence to determine whether or not such authority does in fact exist. Where it is shown that the shipyard, by reasonable diligence, could have ascertained the truth, the presumption of authority in the master of the vessel disappears. Here, admittedly, a simple request to see the ship's papers, after Flowers' representation that that was acting for her owner, would have disclosed the true facts. It would have disclosed (a) that Flowers was neither the owner nor its representative, (b) that the charterer was prohibited from liening the vessel, and (c) that a maritime mortgage to the Merchants Bank existed, which mortgage, incidentally, was retired with the money raised through the mortgage in suit.

Further inquiry would also have disclosed that DeSoto had exercised its option of purchase the vessel. But such disclosure would not justify the shipyard in accepting Flowers' interpretation of the legal effect of that exercise. True such disclosure would have advised the shipyard that DeSoto was "an agreed purchaser in possession of the vessel." However, as the statute specifically provides, the duty of the shipyard to use reasonable diligence to determine whether such "agreed purchaser" has authority to bind the vessel still persists. Actually, as the record demonstrates, shipyard intervenor was not concerned with binding the vessel. Flowers, as master of the Seneca, had a course of dealings with intervenor for many months. The shipyard's bills were always addressed to and paid by the charterer. The disclosure that the charterer might not be the owner of the vessel would have been of little interest to intervenor, at least insofar as payment of its bills was concerned, particularly in view of the then outstanding maritime mortgage.

The history of the Ship Mortgage Act shows that Congress was interested in encouraging the investment of capital in the American Merchant Marine. Before the passage of the Act, because a mortgage on a vessel was not a maritime contract, such mortgage was primed by all maritime liens, whenever attached. Under the Act, the maritime ship mortgage, with certain exceptions, protects the investor against all maritime liens subsequently attached. The Act goes further, however. It protects the maritime ship mortgage against prior obligations resulting from repairs or supplies to the vessel unless those repairs or supplies were authorized by her owner. The Act provides the means by which an owner may charter his vessel and prohibit the attachment of liens by the charterer. In this way an investor requiring a ship mortgage may accept with assurance the owner's certificate that no prior maritime liens have attached, at least during the pendency of the charter. Consequently, if an investor is to be given the protection intended by Congress, he should be allowed to proceed with confidence on the recorded ship's documents. He should not be required to guess who the equitable owner of the vessel may be. He should be able to rely, as to ownership at least, on the title which is recorded with the Collector of Customs as required by law.

Here, the bank did just that. It had the title to the Seneca examined in the proper offices. It received the certificate of her recorded owner that no prior maritime liens existed. It studied the charter party prohibiting the charterer from liening the vessel. Under the circumstances, its investment should be protected against putative owner's of the vessel who, having had the vessel repaired prior to the execution of the warranty deed and ship mortgage, failed to disclose to the title owner and the bank that the bill for such repairs remained unpaid, or even that it had ever been incurred. It is true that the shipyard here may also have been victimized by these putative owner's. But if the shipyard had used the reasonable diligence required by the Act, it would have learned, in advance of the repairs, that the vessel would not be bound therefor.

Decree accordingly.

Would the court have reached the same conclusion even in the absence of a preferred ship mortgage? How would this case be decided after the 1971 amendment to 46 U.S.C § 973? After the enactment of 46 U.S.C. § 31341 ("an agreed buyer in possession of the vessel" is presumed to have authority to procure necessaries)?

E. Persons Who May Acquire Maritime Liens

YAMAMOTO v. M/V LUTA

2017 WL 586361 (D.N. Mariana Islands 2016)

FRANCES M. TYDINGCO–GATEWOOD, Designated Judge

I. INTRODUCTION

On February 10, 2017, this matter came on for a post-arrest hearing pursuant to Rule E(4)(f) of the Supplemental Rules for Admiralty or Maritime Claims and Asset Forfeiture Actions to determine whether the arrest of In Rem Defendant M/V LUTA, O.N. 635750 ("Vessel") should not be vacated. After hearing argument from the parties and having considered the briefing papers and exhibits submitted, the Court found that probable cause for the arrest of the Vessel did not exist and ordered the Vessel released as soon as the fees of Substitute Custodian National Maritime Services, Inc. ("NMS") are paid. This memorandum decision sets forth the reasons for that ruling.

II. BACKGROUND

On October 25, 2016, Plaintiff Takahisa Yamamoto filed an *in rem* action against the Vessel to recover funds advanced or loaned to purchase goods and services and asserting a maritime lien against the Vessel under Supplemental Rule C. He moved for a warrant to arrest the Vessel and for an order appointing NMS as substitute custodian for the United States Marshal The Court granted both motions. Subsequently, three other plaintiffs were permitted to intervene and arrest the Vessel

On January 9, 2017, on motion of Plaintiff Yamamoto, the Court ordered an interlocutory sale of the Vessel. In opposition to the motion, Defendants had asserted that Yamamoto did not have a maritime lien because he was a joint venturer and/or co-owner and not a stranger to the Vessel. Because the intervenors clearly had maritime liens and had joined in seeking an interlocutory sale, the Court granted the motion.

By the end of January, all the intervenors had settled their claims with Defendants, no longer favored an interlocutory sale, and released the Vessel from their warrants. At a hearing on January 31, Defendants requested a post-arrest hearing to put Yamamoto to his burden of showing probable cause existed to keep the Vessel under arrest to testify.

III. DISCUSSION

At a post-arrest hearing in an *in rem* action to enforce a maritime lien, the validity of the arrest of a vessel may be challenged. "To establish a sufficient interest in the vessel to justify its arrest, [plaintiff] must prove prima facie entitlement to a maritime lien."…The court applies a reasonable grounds/probable cause standard, which "translates roughly to requiring that plaintiff show entitlement to a maritime lien."…"In the post-seizure hearing, the plaintiff has the burden of showing why the arrest should not be vacated." 4–II Benedict on Admiralty § 2.19. *See Vitol, S.A. v. Primerose Shipping Co. Ltd.*, 708 F.3d 527, 547 (4th Cir. 2013) (noting that Supplemental Rule E(4)(f) places burden on plaintiff).

It is well settled that a joint venturer/co-owner may not assert a valid maritime lien. Because "a joint venturer does not rely on the credit of the vessel(s), but only on the credit of the co-venturer[,]" joint venturers cannot hold a maritime lien. *Fulcher's Point Pride Seafood, Inc. v. M/V Theodora Maria*, 935 F.2d 208 (11th Cir. 1991): *see Security Pacific Nat. Bank v. OL.s. Pacific Pride*, O/N 621200, 549 F. Supp. 53 (W.D. Wash. 1982) ("the law is clear that owners, part owners, joint venturers and stockholders cannot have a valid maritime lien on any vessel in which they own an interest").

To determine whether a joint venture existed, the court "look[s] to the whole relationship" between the plaintiff and the owner. *Fulcher's Point*, 935 F.2d at 211. Factors include (1) whether the plaintiff exerted significant control over the vessel beyond what a creditor might have had, (2) whether the parties had a joint propriety interest in the vessel, (3) whether they had agreed to share in the profits and losses, and (4) whether they had intended to create a joint venture. Id. at 212 (citing *Sasportes v. M/V Sol de Copacabana*, 581 F.2d 1204. 1208 (5th Cir. 1978)). "Perhaps the best example of a joint venture would be a party whose prospective gains resemble the owner's, who has the owner's prerogatives, and who might otherwise appear to investigating creditors to be a part owner. Such a party may, of course have an In personam contract claim against the true owner. But when the seas get rough one who looks, thinks, acts and profits like an owner cannot retreat to the relatively safe harbor of a maritime lienor, who of course has a claim against the ship itself." *Sasportes*, 581 F.2d at 1208–9.

The following evidence reflects that the whole relationship between Yamamoto and the Mendiolas was one of a joint venture in accordance with the *Fulcher's Point* factors. E-mails exchanged between Yamamoto and various Defendants substantiate this relationship. On January 19, 2016, Yamamoto wrote to Defendant Robert Toelkes asking to help "make a good agreement about our business" with Defendant Fidel Mendiola. "My basic intention," wrote Yamamoto, "is as follows: Fidel's family and my family are having fifty-fifty relationship about the business when we work together". Yamamoto asked for an accounting from the Vessel's owner, Luta Mermaid, LLC: "I would love to get accounting transaction from last October about Luta Mermaid LLC".

On March 27, 2016, Yamamoto wrote to Abelina Mendiola expressly proposing "our agreement about Luta Mermaid LLC based on fifty-fifty relationship between your family and my family". Yamamoto proposed that the Mendiolas would hold 51 percent of the shares and "Yamamoto family hold 25% stocks (voting stocks) ... 24% stocks (non voting stocks)". Yamamoto expressly proposed a profit-sharing arrangement ("2. How we share the profit") and "3. Accounting rules" (*id.*). Yamamoto was not loaning Luta Mermaid money: he was investing: "The reason why I try to tell you about this issue [profit sharing] is I don't want to be arrogant investor" (*id.*). Yamamoto was involved in all aspects of Luta Mermaid's purchase and operation of the Vessel: "I would like to study as follows (1) safety rules and regulations for this business[;] ... (3) Port rules: (4) Labor law: (5) repair and maintain the vessel".

In a local newspaper, the *Marianas Variety* (May 30, 2016), Yamamoto was quoted as saying he "covered the cost to buy the vessel" and gave Luta Mermaid, LLC business advice and financial support In an e-mail to Abelina Mendiola on June 4, he apologized for talking to a reporter about the Vessel but reiterated that "Mv Luta is joint venture between your family and my family".

* * *

IV. CONCLUSION

From the beginning, Plaintiff Takahisa Yamamoto intended to be involved and was intimately involved in a joint business venture to purchase a commercial shipping vessel to help out the people of Rota, with the prospect of making a respectable profit for himself as a co-owner. He took active part in the structuring of the business and exerted control beyond what a creditor would exert in an arm's length transaction. His whole relationship with Defendants demonstrates he was a joint venturer. Plaintiff has failed to carry his burden to show probable cause that he has a maritime lien on the Vessel.

This is not to say Plaintiff was not harmed by Defendants, that he has no cause to complain about their conduct, or that he cannot prosecute an *in personam* action against them. But his arrest of the Vessel cannot stand. For these reasons, the Court ORDERS as follows:

(1) The arrest of the Vessel is VACATED and all warrants for arrest of the Vessel are QUASHED.

(2) The January 9, 2017 order for the interlocutory sale of the Vessel (ECF No. 70) is VACATED.

Note: Owners, Stockholders, and Agents

Owners, part-owner's, and general agents may not acquire maritime liens. This may seem an application of the civil law principle of confusion of rights: one may not have a partial right in a thing owned because ownership is an all-inclusive right. However, the rule is better explained in the light of policy considerations. Since most maritime liens are secret, an owner should not be allowed to establish such equities for his benefit to the prejudice of creditors.

The question whether one is "owner" of a vessel is not always easy to determine. *Cf. Diaz v. The Steamship Seathunder*, 191 F. Supp. 807, 1961 AMC 561 (D. Md. 1961); *The Josephine Lanasa (Findley v. Lanasa)*, 276 F.2d 907, 1960 AMC 1444 (5th Cir. 1960).

A part owner occupies the same position as a full owner; he may not assert a maritime lien on the ship she owns in indivision. *See The Lena Mowbray,* 71 F. 720 (S.D. Ala. 1895); *The Morning Star,* 1 F.2d 410, 1924 AMC 1571 (W.D. Wash. 1924). However, a joint venturer for the purchase of a vessel who incurs expenses for outfitting may have a lien for necessaries. *See Compagnia Maritima La Empresa v. Pickard,* 320 F.2d 829, 1964 AMC 109 (5th Cir. 1963); *The Odysseus III,* 77 F. Supp. 297, 1948 AMC 608 (S.D. Fla. 1948).

When advances are made by a stockholder, a lien may or may not arise depending on the circumstances. A stockholder has to overcome the presumption that the advances were made on general credit. *See The Cimbria,* 214 F. 131 (D.N.J. 1914). If he overcomes this presumption, a lien may arise if other creditors are not unfairly prejudiced. *See The Puritan,* 258 F. 271 (D. Mass. 1919); *The Murphy Tugs,* 28 F. 429 (E.D. Mich. 1886).

A "general agent" represents the owner and occupies the same position as a part owner. He is presumed to rely on the credit of the owner for any advances he makes. *See Savas v. Maria Trading Co.,* 285 F.2d 336, 1961 AMC 260 (4th Cir. 1960). For rebuttal of the presumption, *see Compagnia Maritime La Empresa S.A. v. Pickard, supra.*

Note: Advances and Assignment of Liens

A maritime lien may be assigned, and the assignee is subrogated to the rights of the assignor, unless, of course, the assignee is a person who may not acquire a maritime lien. One who advances sums for the discharge of a maritime lien occupies the position of an assignee. He acquires a lien of the same class and rank as the lien that has been discharged. *Sasportes v. M/V Sol de Copacabana,* 581 F.2d 1204, 1980 AMC 791 (5th Cir. 1978).

The lien discharged by an advance of money need not be in existence at the time of the advance. Thus one who advances money for necessaries acquires a lien under 46 U.S.C.A. § 31342 (formerly 46 U.S.C. § 971). *See Crustacean Transportation Corp. v. Atlanta Trading Corp.,* 1967 AMC 362 (5th Cir. 1966).

F. Priorities of Liens

Introductory Note

The sale of a vessel in an *in rem* proceeding generates a fund in the registry of an admiralty court. When this fund, or comparable security posted by the shipowner to secure the vessels release, is insufficient to satisfy all valid liens and claims, the priority of the different categories of claims becomes of paramount importance.

There is no authoritative scheme of priorities among maritime liens. No statute has created it and, although a number of judicial decisions give an order of ranking, in each case it is incomplete. Consequently, the issue of ranking competing maritime liens and claims has been left to legal scholars and to the federal courts. *See* W. Tetley, Maritime Liens and Claims, 392-304 (2d ed. 1989); George L. Varian, *Rank and Priority of Maritime Liens,* 47 Tul. L. Rev. 751 (1973); G. Gilmore & C. Black, The Law of Admiralty §§ 9-58-76 (2d ed. 1975); *Rayon Y Celanese Peruano, S.A. v. Ml VPHGH,* 471 F. Supp. 1363 (S.D. Ala. 1979). However, the ranking of maritime lien claims by the district and circuit courts in conjunction with the priority rules codified in 46 U.S.C. §§ 31301 (5)-(6), 31326(b)(l)-(2) has resulted in allowing the following rules of ranking to be generally observed:

1. expenses of justice during *custodia legis* (*see* 46 U.S.C. § 31326(b)(1));
2. the following preferred maritime liens (*see* 46 U.S.C. § 31301(5)(A)-(F)):

    (a) wages of the crew; maintenance and cure; as to masters' wages, *see* 46 U.S.C. § 11112; wages of stevedore when directly employed by the shipowner or his agent (*see* 46 U.S.C. § 31341);

    (b) salvage, including contract salvage, and general average;

    (c) maritime torts, including personal injury, property damage and cargo tort liens;

3. All maritime contract liens *which arise before the filing of a preferred ship mortgage* (U.S. flag vessel) (*see* 46 U.S.C. § 31301(5)(A)). These include liens for "necessaries", such as repairs, supplies, towage, and the use of a dry dock or marine railway (*see 46* U.S.C. § 31301 (4)), as well as cargo contract damage liens and contract charterer's liens;
4. preferred ship mortgages (U.S. flag vessels);
5. other maritime contract liens which accrue *after* the filing of a preferred ship mortgage (U.S. flag vessels) and *prior* to a foreign preferred ship mortgage. *However.* all necessaries provided in the United States have priority over foreign preferred ship mortgages irrespective of the time they arose. (*See 46* U.S.C. § 31326(b)(2));
6. foreign preferred ship mortgages;

7. maritime contract liens, excluding those for necessaries provided in the U.S., accruing *after* foreign preferred ship mortgages such as contract cargo damage liens and contract charterer's liens;
8. state-created liens of a maritime nature;
9. maritime liens for penalties and forfeitures for violation of federal statutes;
10. perfected non-maritime claims, including tax liens;
11. attaching liens in causes of action within the admiralty and maritime jurisdiction (foreign attachment);
12. maritime liens in bankruptcy;
13. all other general creditors/claimants.

According to the above ranking scheme, competing liens are initially ranked as to superiority by class. The top priority liens will of course be paid first. If, however, the funds in the registry of the admiralty court are insufficient to fully pay all of the claims within a particular class, the issue of priority of claims within the class itself must be resolved. There are various rules of ranking claims within the same class which are generally agreed upon. "The basic general rule is the *inverse order* rule that claims of the same class are given priority amongst themselves according to the inverse order of their accrual. In other words the last lien given will supercede the preceeding'." TETLEY, *supra*, at 399 *(citing The St. Jago de Cuba,* 22 U.S. (9 Wheat) 409, 416, 6 L. Ed. 122 (1824); *The John G. Stevens,* 170 U.S. 113, 119, 18 S.Ct. 544, 42 L. Ed. 969 (1898)). Though the inverse order rule is the basic general rule for the ranking of claims within a class, for practical reasons the rule has been "subjected to a series of special rules which in effect have largely displaced it." GILMORE & BLACK, *supra,* § 9-62 at 744.

1. Priority of Wage Claims

In *The Cf. Saxe,* 145 F. 749 (S.D.N.Y. 1906), the court held that a claim for wages ranks higher than a claim for damages for collision. This holding remains unchallenged. In *Fredelos v. Merritt-Chapman & Scott (The Padre Island),* 447 F.2d 435, 1971 AMC 2192 (5th Cir. 1971), the court held that a claim for maintenance and cure has the same priority as a wage claim and ranks higher than a claim for salvage. One court has stated that 46 U.S.C. § 10313 affords seamen a "super priority" for unpaid wages. *Isbrandtsen Marine Services, Inc. v. M/V Inagua Tania,* 93 F.3d 728, 1997 AMC 912 (11th Cir. 1996).

2. Tort vs. Contract Liens

A maritime tort lien takes priority over a maritime contract lien. In *The John G. Stevens,* 170 U.S. 113, 122, 18 S.Ct. 544, 548, 42 L. Ed. 969 (1898), the Court said:

That the maritime lien upon a vessel, for damages caused by her fault to another vessel, takes precedence of a maritime lien for supplies previously furnished to the offending vessel, is a reasonable inference, if not a necessary conclusion, from the decisions of this court, above referred to, the effect of which may be summed up as follows:

The collision, as soon as it takes place, creates, as security for the damages, a maritime lien or privilege, *jus in re,* a proprietary interest in the offending ship, and which, when enforced by admiralty process *in rem,* relates back to the time of the collision. The offending ship is considered as herself the wrongdoer and as herself bound to make compensation for the wrong done. The owner of the injured vessel is entitled to proceed *in rem* against the offender, without regard to the question who may be her owner's, or to the division, the nature or the extent of their interests in her. With the relations of the owner's of those interests, as among themselves, the owner of the injured vessel has no concern. All the interests, existing at the time of the collision, in the offending vessel, whether by way of part-ownership, of mortgage, of bottomry bond or of other maritime lien for repairs or supplies, arising out of contract with the owner's or agents of the vessel, are parts of the vessel herself, and as such are bound by and responsible for her wrongful acts...

The Court went on to conclude that "a suit by the owner of a tow against her tug, to recover for an injury to the tow by the negligence on the part of the tug, is a suit *ex delicto* and not *ex contractu*". 170 U.S. 113, 125, 18 S.Ct. 544, 549.

3. Claims for Negligent Towage

In *The Interstate No. 1,* 290 F. 926, 1923 AMC 1118 (2d Cir.), *cert. denied,* 262 U.S. 753, 43 S.Ct. 701, 67 L. Ed. 1216 (1923), liens for negligent towage were subordinated to liens for supplies furnished in the same voyage, apparently on the theory that such claims arise out of contract rather than tort.

When a tug with a flotilla of barges collides with a third vessel due to the fault of the tug, the owner of the third vessel has a lien against the tug only. *See Sturgis v. Boyer,* 65 U.S. (24 How.) 110, 16 L. Ed. 591 (1860); *Walker v. Tug Diane,* 350 F. Supp. 1388, 1974 AMC 1567 (D.V.I. 1972). In the last case, the court held that the tow is not liable *in rem* when it is not manned at the time of the collision. *But see The Sif,* 266 F. 166 (2d Cir. 1920); *S.C. Loveland Co. v. United States,* 207 F. Supp. 450, 1963 AMC 260 (E.D. Pa. 1962) [barges liable for general average contribution]. The tow has a lien against the tug. *See The Steamer Webb,* 81 U.S. (14 Wall.) 406, 20 L. Ed. 774 (1872).

1. Ranking of Liens of the Same Class: the "Inverse Order" Rule

Introductory Note: The Inverse Order Rule

In *The William Leishear,* 21 F.2d 862, 863 (D. Md. 1927), the court described the "inverse order" rule in the following way:

There is the general rule that maritime liens rank in an order inverse to the order of their creation *(The St. Jago de Cuba,* 9 Wheaton, 409, 6 L. Ed. 122), a principle contrary to what is common in other branches of the law. Without going at any length into the ancient historical reasons for this anomaly, suffice it to say that in this country two theories exist as the basis of this admiralty doctrine. They are, first, that each person acquires a *jus in re,* and becomes a sort of coproprietor in the *res,* and therefore subjects his claim to the next similar lien which attaches; and, second, that the last beneficial service is the one that continues the activity of the ship as long as possible, and therefore should be preferred, provided that what is produced or contributed to by the service is a voyage. *The Glen Island* (D.C.) 194 F. 744. Under the second theory, there is the consideration that beneficial additions subsequent to earlier liens add to the value of the ship, and that, therefore, to prefer such additions will not deprive the earlier lienors of any interest which they would have had, if no such services had been rendered.

Generally speaking, the law of maritime liens may be said to be made up of exceptions to the above doctrine, which gives priority to the lien latest in point of time, so that to-day it is possible to deduce, from the decisions, the following order of priority, existing irrespective of time, which represents the weight of authority: (1) Seamen's wages; (2) salvage; (3) tort and collision liens; (4) repairs, supplies, towage, wharfage, pilotage, and other necessaries; (5) bottomry bonds in inverse order of application; (6) nonmaritime claims. This, however, is no more than a very general statement, since any summary is subject to further exceptions of more or less narrow application.

In *The Frank G. Fowler,* 17 F. 653 (S.D.N.Y. 1883), the court reasoned that the inverse order rule applies to successive service liens because each incumbrance "is actually benefited by reason of the successive incumbrance." Since this rationale is inapplicable to successive tort liens, the court held that the sufferer of the first tort of collision "ought not to lose the benefit of his lien arising out of the first tort or collision." This decision was criticized in *The America,* 168 F. 424 (D.N.J. 1909) as follows:

Judge Blatchford's reasoning was in effect that, since the second collision did not benefit the vessel, it was not entitled to priority over the lien created by the first collision, thereby seemingly adopting the rule that a subsequent lien is entitled to priority only when it has benefited or increased the value of the vessel out of which all liens are to be satisfied. It is manifest, however, that priorities between collision liens cannot be determined on the theory of benefit to the offending vessel. No collision, be it the first, the second, or the third, can or does benefit the vessel. *The John G. Stevens, supra,* moreover, expressly held that a tort lien, although it did not benefit the vessel, nevertheless had priority over an earlier lien for supplies, which presumably did. There is no apparent reason why the rule in cases of collision should be different than it is in the matter of successive liens for repairs or supplies, which are ordinarily paid in their inverse order. The proprietary interest created in the vessel in favor of the party injured by the first collision is subject, like all other proprietary interests in her, to subsequent marine perils, including collisions. That a maritime lien created by collision gives a proprietary interest in the *res* to the injured party is laid down in many cases, among them *The John G. Steven, supra.*

The "proprietary interest" rationale may adequately explain the inverse order rule; however, it fails to explain the postponement of contract liens to tort liens or the postponement of salvage and tort liens to liens for wages. What is the rationale for these rules?

---

1. Maritime Contract Liens

The inverse order rule has the benefit of forcing the claimant to act quickly but it could also incite a supplier of necessaries to arrest the vessel on the same day as the necessaries were supplied in order to remain ahead of future suppliers. Such a practice would contradict the basic purpose of the maritime lien which is to provide security for a claim whilst permitting the ship to proceed on her way in order to earn the freight or hire necessary to pay of the claim. In consequence, various special time rules—voyage, season and calendar year— have been devised, whereby liens of a class accruing during a specific period are ranked *pari passu* [without preference]. TETLEY, *supra* at 399-400.

The oldest special time rule, the voyage rule, results in all contract and service liens from the same voyage having an equal priority and sharing *pro rata.* However, these liens will be primed by all contract and service liens "which accrue in connection with the next voyage." George L. Varian, *Rank and Priority of Maritime Liens,* 47 TUL. L. REV. 751, 760 (1973). For a discussion of additional special time rules *see Todd Shipyards Corp. v. The City of Athens, infra.*

2. Other Maritime Liens

Outside the service lien field the inverse order rule is simple, easy to apply and causes no great difficulty or discussion. With respect to wage claims, the issue never arises: these claims have an over-riding priority and are paid in full, without regard to when they were earned, before any other liens share in the distribution. If the proceeds were not enough even to pay all wages, the decision whether all wage claimants should prorate or whether the claims for more recent wages should have priority would undoubtedly lie within the discretion of the trial judge. In the salvage field, it is rare that more than one set of salvage liens is in issue: if two or more salvage operations had been performed on distinct occasions, the more recent liens would have priority as a matter of course. The same is true for collision tort liens: successive collisions are rare but they do happen; when they happen, the inverse order rule applies, even as to collisions that take place on the same voyage. The problem of successive personal injury liens is seldom raised. If several such liens arise on a single occasion—collision or fire, and the ship lost—they share equally, both in the value of the ship and in the [$420] per ton set up for their benefit by the Limitation of Liability Act. If the liens arise on "distinct occasions" the Limitation Act requires the setting up of separate [$420] per ton funds for each occasion, so that the question of priorities between the groups of liens arising on each "occasion" could arise only if the [$420] per ton funds were insufficient.

GILMORE & BLACK, *supra*, § 9-62 at 743.

3. Maritime Contract Liens — Time of Attachment

Barge owner exercised its option to extend a charter of a towboat for an additional year. Thereafter the owner sold the towboat. The purchaser (new owner) obtained a preferred ship mortgage to finance the transaction. After the mortgage had been obtained, the new owner breached the charter party by failing to deliver the vessel or an equivalent vessel to the charterer. A question arose as to when lien for the breach of the charter party arose, at the time that the contract was entered into or at the time of the breach. The Court of Appeals for the Fifth Circuit relying on venerable authorities held that a "maritime lien attaches at the commencement of the undertaking and any subsequent breach perfecting the lien relates back to that time." The court found that the executory contract doctrine was not applicable inasmuch as this was time charter party and not a contract of affreightment. Pursuant to the charter party, prior to extension of its term, the vessel had been delivered to the charterer and had made several voyages. *Bank One, Louisiana N.A., v. Mr. Dean M/V*, 293 F.3d 830, 2002 AMC 1617 (5th Cir. 2002).

4. No Inverse Order Rule for Attachments

The inverse order rule applies only to maritime liens, which can be enforced by an action *in rem* under Rule C. It does not apply to successive attachments under Rule B, where the usual "first in time, first in right" rule applies. In *A. Coker & Co. Ltd v. National Shipping Agency Corp.*, 2000 AMC 489 (E.D. La. 1999), the court said:

> Bisso argues that the theory behind the inverse-order rule applies equally to Rule B attachment liens as to Rule C maritime liens. The Court disagrees. The rationale underlying this rule is that "the vessel must get on" and that the most recent lienholders perform services that keep the vessel in operation so that revenue can be generated to satisfy the earlier claims. *See* GILMORE & BLACK, *supra*, 9-62, at 742-43 (*citing The St. Jago de Cuba*, 22 U.S. 409, 416 (1824)). As stated above, this case does not involve a seized vessel but simply cash held in an agent's account. That Bisso may have provided necessary services to a vessel owned by NSAC does not benefit Coker. Accordingly, the Court finds no exception to the rule set forth in *Triton*, that competing attachment lien claims have priority according to the first-in-time rule.

---

2. Special Time Rules

TODD SHIPYARDS CORPORATION v. THE CITY OF ATHENS

83 F. Supp. 67 (D. Md. 1949)

CHESNUT, District Judge

The SS "City of Athens", a trans-Atlantic passenger-cargo ship, was libelled in the Port of Baltimore on July 12, 1947 by the Todd Shipyards Corporation of New York, for the balance due for repairs and reconstruction of the ship in the total amount of $491,077. Many intervening libels and other claims against the ship were filed; and in due course the ship was sold by the Marshal of the court on August 13, 1947 to the Panamanian Lines, Inc., for $400,000, which sum (together with the sum of $1837.71 representing earned freight) less certain expenses of administration, represents the total sum available for lien claims in the amount of $775,457.82. On August 14, 1947 the case was referred to Mr. L. Vernon Miller, a member of the Baltimore Bar thoroughly experienced in admiralty matters, as Commissioner, "to take evidence therein and to report to the Court his findings of law and fact therein with all convenient speed", and the clerk was directed to give notice by publication that all claims against the proceeds of the ship should be filed within a specified time. The Commissioner s report was filed October 7, 1948.

* * *

Schedule X (the last page of the report) lists in summary all claims allowed as liens. They embrace basic wages of the crew in the amount of $24,733.74; additional wages for the crew at $15,141.54; one extra months pay for certain members of the crew $2,033; repatriation claims $945; additional wages to skeleton crew July 12 to July 22, 1947, $1,375.66; maintenance and cure $236.25; personal injury claims $4,000, and unclassified crew claims in the amount of $8,422.25; head tax claims of $1,624, and cargo claims $1,074.57. The total of such claims was $59,586.01. Other claims for supplies or "necessaries" to the ship on various voyages allowed as liens aggregated $715,871.81. Of this latter amount those accruing in the calendar year 1947 amounting to $291,921.68 were determined to be paid in full as having priority, and the remainder, $423,950.13, a large amount of which was allowed to the Todd Shipyards Corporation arising in 1946, was to be deferred to the prior payment claims. The estimated net fund available for distribution after deducting certain expenses of administration including the Commissioner's fee, will be about $380,000. The total claims allowed priority in payment and thus to be paid in full, aggregate $351,507.69. As the deferred claims aggregate $423,950.13, and the remainder of the fund available for distribution is only about $30,000 it appears that the claims deferred in payment by the Commissioner's report will receive a dividend of less than 10%.

* * *

The ship was built in 1920 at Hog Island, Pennsylvania, and named "The American Banker". She was of 7430 gross tonnage, 436.9 feet in length and 58.2 foot beam. Later she was renamed the "Ville D'Anviers" and under that name acquired in 1946 by the Sociedad Naviera Trans-Atlantica S.A. a Panamanian corporation, and registered under the Honduras flag. The corporation seems to have had little or no assets other than the ownership of the ship, but the stock of the corporation was owned by Basil Hanioti, of Greek extraction but a citizen of the United States. He also owned directly or indirectly at the time one or more other ships. It is said that Hanioti paid $430,000 for the ship which he purchased for the special purpose of passenger and cargo transportation between New York and Mediterranean ports. The ship had previously been used as troop transport. To adapt her to the new and anticipated large passenger traffic, it was deemed essential to make extensive repairs and for that purpose the Todd Shipyards, a New York corporation, was employed. Todd began work on the ship in October 1946. It was evidently a rush job because Hanioti was insistent upon early completion to take advantage of anticipated large passenger business. It appears that the work was done night and day with much overtime and possibly without adequate detailed supervision in the interests of the owner. But the Commissioner found no satisfactory evidence to contradict the reasonableness of the itemized invoices and accounts rendered by Todd in support of its claim. By November 12, 1946 Todd had done work as per invoices in the amount of $646,105. The ship made her first voyage to Europe leaving New York in November 1946. In due course she returned to New York about January 1, 1947 and thereafter during 1947 made three additional round-trips, the last one terminating at Baltimore in early July 1947. During 1947 Todd performed additional repair and construction work on the ship making its aggregate charges $758,010, with total cash and credits paid or allowed in the amount of $266,933, with balance now claimed to be due in the amount of $491,077, of which amount the Commissioner by schedule D (page 157) has allowed $104,972 as ranking in 1947; and allowed a balance of $386,105 ranked in 1946 for deferred payment.

It appears from the report that the cost of repair of the ship by Todd was very greatly in excess of what Hanioti had anticipated, and that his insufficient capital resources finally resulted in the libelling of the ship. After the ship was libelled in Baltimore Hanioti was unable to pay the wages due to the crew not only for the last voyage but for some preceding voyages. During each of the ship's voyages it became necessary to obtain for her, frequently in foreign ports, supplies and "other necessaries". Claims for these have been filed in these proceedings and practically all have been allowed by the Commissioner as maritime liens, all those arising from the last three voyages of the ship in 1947 to be paid in full and those incidental to the first voyage in 1946 were also allowed but defered as to payment.

* * *

The second question of general importance arising on the exceptions relates to the *marshalling of maritime liens.* The applicable law is to be found in judicial decisions, and is not controlled by any federal statute. With respect to the ranking of liens of different classes, the judicial decisions, while not entirely uniform, are substantially in accord. The law was conveniently summarized in this court by Judge Coleman twenty years ago in the case of *The William Leishear*, D.C., 21 F.2d 862, 863.... In the instant case there are several classes of liens including seamens wages, a tort claim, and liens for repairs, supplies and other necessaries; but as the case presents no controversy with respect to the preferred payment of seamens wages and the tort claim, the only question of priority of payment arising with respect to the claims for repairs, supplies and other necessaries, all of which are claims of the same class and rank. But, as the fund for distribution is insufficient to pay all of them in full, there is necessarily involved here the question where the line is to be drawn between those claims of this latter class.

On this point it has sometimes been said that the judicial decisions are in confusion; but an examination of very many cases leads to the conclusion that this statement is correct only insofar as it is applicable to other than ocean voyages of ships. The rule originally developed in admiralty law and still the basic rule is that maritime liens of the same class are entitled to priority of payment in the inverse order of the time of accrual and that therefore liens arising in connection with the last voyage of the ship have priority of payment over liens accruing on a prior voyage. The rule was thus expressed by Judge Brown in the well-known case of *The Proceeds of the Gratitude*, D.C.N.Y. 1890, 42 F. 299, at page 300—

The general maritime law adjusts all liens by the voyage.... By the general rule ... the priority of liens continues only till the next voyage. The liens connected with every new voyage start with a priority over all former ones after the ship has sailed, if there has previously been opportunity to enforce them.

* * *

Cases which have departed from the "voyage" rule will be found, without exception I think, to have related to ships engaged in other than ocean voyages, as for instance, harbor tugs, coastwise vessels, transportation on the Great Lakes, and comparatively small craft plying local waters. The voyage rule contemplates that at the end of each voyage liens that have arisen during its course should be promptly enforced before the ship departs on another voyage, if there is opportunity to the claimant to so enforce it by libel. As indicated in the opinion of Judge Smith for the Court of Appeals for the Fourth Circuit in the case above cited, the application of the voyage rule presupposes that the voyages are separated "by an appreciable length of time". While this is necessarily still true with respect to transatlantic or other similar ocean voyages, it is obviously not so with respect to the much shorter and more frequent voyages of harbor craft and merely coastwise vessels or other comparatively local transportation. To meet the necessities of such particular local conditions and to accord with the customary business practice locally prevailing it has been found necessary to substitute a rule of priorities other than the voyage rule, and the tendency seems to have been to adopt, as the period allowed prior to the filing of the libel for preferential claims arising therein, a period which can be regarded as a reasonable time for the extension of credit. Thus for New York harbor craft, that period has been fixed at 40 days, and in Puget Sound at 90 days; while on the Great Lakes, where the rigor of winter generally interrupts navigation, the period has been fixed as the navigating season, and thus claims arising during such a particular season are preferred over those of a prior season. More recently, apparently by analogy to this so-called season rule, a rule of priority has been applied by which liens arising in a particular calendar year are given priority over those arising in a prior year; and in a number of cases this latter rule, the so-called "calendar" year rule, has been applied to vessels engaged in coastwise commerce. *The Interstate No. 1, supra*, 290 F. at page 934. About twenty years ago, in a series of three cases in this court, Judge Coleman applied this latter calendar year rule to small craft locally engaged. While there seems to be no case in the Supreme Court dealing with this particular subject, it seems clearly established in the First Circuit (*The Interstate No. 1, supra,* 290 F. at page 934) that the voyage rule still applies with respect to "vessels engaged in commerce on the ocean." And it is, I think, likewise, the rule announced in this Fourth Circuit in the case of the *Steam Dredge A,* 204 F. 262, 264, although on what appears to have been a factually unsatisfactory record, the rule actually applied in the case of a ship apparently engaged in coastwise trade was the so called calendar year rule.

In the instant case the Commissioner's report expresses his preference for the *voyage* rule but actually applied the *calendar year* rule. It is important, however, to note that in doing so he found that in effect both the voyage rule and the calendar year rule would produce the same actual result with respect to payment of the liens. This was true because the ship made four voyages, one in the latter months of 1946 and the remaining three in 1947; and the fund for distribution was sufficient to pay in full all the allowed lien claims arising in 1947, leaving a balance for a percentage distribution of less than 10% to the lien claims arising in connection with the first voyage in 1946. It was, therefore, unnecessary in applying the voyage rule, to distinguish between claims arising on the second, third and fourth voyages as to respective priority. In particular figures the Commissioner thus allowed for prior payment claims for supplies and other necessaries arising on the last three voyages in the aggregate amount of $291,921.68, all to be paid in full from the fund, while those arising in 1946 and to be deferred to the former amounted to $423,950.13, of which the balance due Todd Shipyards represents nearly 90%.

Counsel for Todd and the few other claimants whose liens arose in connection with the first voyage, vigorously protest the correctness of the classification made by the Commissioner. In the first place they point out that in the cases applying the so-called calendar year rule the expression sometimes used by the court is the "year" rule and that, therefore, the period of time referred to should be considered a twelve-month period preceding the date of the libel; but as to this an examination of most if not all of the cases referred to shows from the facts involved that claims allowed (with only trivial exceptions, if any) were those which arose during the calendar year in which the libel was filed; and I have found no case which establishes a twelve month period for the classification of preferred and deferred lien claims.

The next argument advanced is that by reason of changed conditions with respect to ocean voyages which are now generally of much shorter duration than when the voyage rule was established, and since means of communication between the owner and the master of the ship, possibly in a foreign port, are more rapid because of the facilities of cable and radio, the voyage rule should be regarded as obsolete and a different new rule substituted therefor.

In support of this contention particular reference is made to the view expressed by Robinson on ADMIRALTY p. 427, in which that generally excellent author, after referring to the season rule prevailing with regard to shipping on the Great Lakes, and the 90-day rule for credit in navigation in Puget Sound said:

> It is questionable how much further the application of this principle can be carried and to what jurisdictions it extends. But it is sufficient here to point out that for short trips the voyage rule is no longer a test and has given place to rules in which there are local variances. Even where the longer voyages of ocean steamers are concerned, the courts have ceased to apply a technical interpretation of the term 'voyage' and talk in terms of years.

> The year is considered representative of the voyage. This shows a tendency, even in the case of larger vessels, to apply a time measured by *a reasonable period of credit* rather than voyage. Passenger liners today make the transatlantic run in less than a week so that the larger steamship companies in a certain measure are beset with the same problem which faced harbor craft at an earlier date. Judge Brown in *The Gratitude ante,* note 181, remarked of the 40 day rule: 'It accords in some degree with the period of modern (1890) voyages.' (Italics supplied)

However, an examination of the four cases mentioned in the note documenting this view fails to show that any of them related to transatlantic or other ocean voyages. Two of the cases were among those decided some twenty years ago by Judge Coleman and which have been above referred to. They related to small craft locally navigating the Chesapeake Bay.

While counsel for the particular exceptants concede that there is no definite judicial authority in support of their contention they urge that, as the decided cases present such variable rules for determining priorities, some new and definite rule should now be established, and further urge that the new rule to be adopted should be the year rule as they contend it should be understood, that is, that all liens arising in a period of one year prior to the libel should rank *pari passu;* or, in other words, that the period of a year as "a reasonable period of credit" should be established as the test rather than that of the voyage.

My conclusion of law is that the voyage rule still prevails despite greater rapidity of transportation and communication. The reasons which originally gave rise to the voyage rule still exist even though their importance in some respects may have been lessened. Many ocean voyages are still of several months' duration and there is still at times the most imperative need that a ship in a port far distant from the owner should have the ability to obtain repairs and supplies on the credit of the ship itself. This ability to obtain such credit would obviously be much impaired if a long prior claim originating in connection with a previous voyage, as in this case, and amounting to a sum much larger than the sale value of the ship, were to rate equally with the supplies or repairs on the last voyage, imperatively needed to keep the ship a "going concern", and to enable it to return to its home.

* * *

With regard to the argument that the court should establish a new rule with respect to priorities and lien claimants, it is sufficient to say that I would not feel warranted in doing so where, as I find, the voyage rule is still the established one for ocean voyages. Nor do I think this case presents in its factual situation a proper one for the establishment of the new twelve-months rule which is advocated. I will add that while I have concluded that the voyage rule must be observed here, I do not think, apart from it, the facts of the case would justify the application of the calendar year rule. If we were to disregard the voyage rule and accept in lieu thereof as a test, a reasonable period of credit, the facts of the particular case do not furnish an adequate basis for determining what this period should be. Should it be forty days as a possible inference from what Judge Brown said in the case of *The Gratitude* above quoted, or two months for a transatlantic liner, or six months as the calendar year rule has in effect been applied by the Commissioner's report, or a year or at least eight months as contended for by the exceptants? While the calendar year rule, analogized to the season rule, may be fairly applicable to the smaller craft navigating locally only, the court is not in possession of sufficient information in this case with respect to conditions in general affecting transatlantic or ocean voyages to say what period of time should be regarded as reasonable. Change in the law in this respect and in the establishment of such a definite period, if to be made at all, should be made only after the fullest possible information of all relevant conditions which ordinarily could be brought to the attention of a legislative body with full powers of investigation. While it may be entirely appropriate and desirable for a court dealing with a particular local situation, as for instance affecting the New York harbor or Puget Sound or the Great Lakes or the Chesapeake Bay, to lay down a general rule that is locally applicable, it is a far more difficult and wider question to determine such a rule for ocean voyages which, in many cases, may involve navigation extending around the globe.

* * *

Note: *Periods of Priority: Service Liens*

For another application of the voyage rule, *see Rayon y Celanese Peruana, S.A. v. M/V Phgh*, 471 F. Supp. 1363, 1974 AMC 2682 (S.D. Ala. 1979). A "season rule" applies in the Great Lakes. *See The City of Tawas*, 3 F. 170 (E.D. Mich. 1880). There is a forty-day priority period in the New York harbor. *See Proceeds of the Gratitude*, 42 F. 299 (S.D.N.Y. 1890); *The Samuel Little*, 221 F. 308 (2d Cir. 1915). In *The Interstate No. 1,290* F. 926, 1923 AMC 1118 (2d Cir.), *cert. denied*, 262 U.S. 753, 43 S.Ct. 701, 67 L. Ed. 1216 (1923), the Second Circuit held that the forty-day period in the New York harbor is a single priority period. All other liens of the same rank dating more than forty days share in the proceeds *pro rata*. A ninety-day rule applies in Seattle Harbor and the Puget Sound. *See The Edith*, 217 F. 300 (W.D. Wash. 1914). In certain parts of the United States a calendar year rule applies.

---

3. *"Preferred" Maritime Liens*

Prior to the enactment of the Ship Mortgage Act in 1920, ship mortgages were subordinate to maritime liens. However, as a result of the Act, common law rules regulating competing maritime liens were altered with the statutory creation of "preferred" maritime liens. This term was defined in 46 U.S.C. § 953 (recodified as 46 U.S.C.A. § 31343(5)).

THE SHIP MORTGAGE ACT

46 U.S.C. § 953

(superseded version)

§ 953. Preferred Maritime Lien; Priorities; Other Liens

(a) When used hereinafter in this chapter, the term "preferred maritime lien" means (1) a lien arising prior in time to the recording and indorsement of a preferred mortgage in accordance with the provisions of this chapter; or (2) a lien for damages arising out of tort, for wages of a stevedore when employed directly by the owner, operator, master, ship's husband, or agent of the vessel, for wages of the crew of the vessel, for general average, and for salvage, including contract salvage.

(b) Upon the sale of any mortgaged vessel by order of a district court of the United States in any suit *in rem* in admiralty for the enforcement of a preferred mortgage lien thereon, all preexisting claims in the vessel, including any possessory common-law lien of which a lienor is deprived under the provisions of section 952 of this title, shall be held terminated and shall thereafter attach, in like amount and in accordance with their respective priorities, to the proceeds of the sale; except that the preferred mortgage lien shall have priority over all claims against the vessel, except (1) preferred maritime liens, and (2) expenses and fees allowed and costs taxed, by the court.

Unless a lien met the requirements set forth in section 953, it did not have preferred status and was therefore primed by a preferred ship mortgage (U.S. flag vessel). The Ship Mortgage Act has been amended and recodified at 46 U.S.C. § 31301, *et seq.* The current statutory provisions relating to preferred maritime liens and their ranking, which make no substantive change in the law, are as follows:

Commercial Instruments and Maritime Liens

46 U.S.C. §§ 31301, *et seq.*

§ 31301

(5) "preferred maritime lien" means a maritime lien on a vessel—

(A) arising before a preferred mortgage was filed under section 31321 of this title;

(B) for damage arising out of maritime tort;

(C) for wages of a stevedore when employed directly by a person listed in section 31341 of this title;

(D) for wages of the crew of the vessel;

(E) for general average; or

(F) for salvage, including contract salvage; and

§ 31326. Court sales to enforce preferred mortgage liens and maritime liens and priority of claims

(a) When a vessel is sold by order of a district court in a civil action *in rem* brought to enforce a preferred mortgage lien or a maritime lien, any claim in the vessel existing on the date of sale is terminated, including a possessory common law lien of which a person is deprived under section 31325(e)(2) of this title, and the vessel is sold free of all those claims.

(b) Each of the claims terminated under subsection (a) of this section attaches, in the same amount and in accordance with their priorities to the proceeds of the sale, except that—

    (1) the preferred mortgage lien has priority over all claims against the vessel (except for expenses and fees allowed by the court, costs imposed by the court, and preferred maritime liens); and

    (2) for a foreign vessel, the preferred mortgage lien is subordinate to a maritime lien for necessaries provided in the United States.

(Added Pub. L. 100-710, Title I, § 102(c), Nov. 23, 1988, 102 Stat. 4746.)

---

a. Priority Determination

THE HOME

65 F. Supp. 94 (W.D. Wash. 1946)

BOWEN, District Judge

The libelant Bank filed this libel *in rem* against the respondent vessel seeking judgment on a promissory note and to foreclose a preferred ship mortgage securing its payment recorded April 28, 1944. Intervening libelant, Sunde & d'Evers Co., has intervened with its claim for debt and maritime liens for ship's supplies, some of which were furnished to the vessel in 1944 prior to the recording of the mortgage and some of which were furnished subsequent to the recording of the mortgage in 1944 and 1945. The other intervening libelants assert similar claims for ship's supplies and work and repairs furnished to the vessel subsequent to the recording of the mortgage in 1944 and 1945.

The money items sued for by libelant include the principal and interest now due on the promissory note, the costs of suit and also a reasonable sum to be allowed as libelants attorneys fees under the provisions of the promissory note and the mortgage securing the note. Libelant further asks to have all of these sums paid out of the proceeds of the foreclosure sale of the vessel and her equipment before any portion of any of the claims of intervenors are paid, with the possible exception of that portion of the Sunde & d'Evers claim comprising a preferred maritime lien which covers supplies furnished to the vessel prior to the recording of the mortgage.

As to the amount of such preferred maritime lien claim, however, there is some dispute because Sunde & d'Evers did not, until a few days before the trial, undertake to allocate as between new and old items of the account certain part payments. Then that creditor did attempt to allocate such part payments to the items of the account furnished subsequent to the recording of the mortgage in order thereby to leave a larger amount protected by the preferred maritime lien covering the items supplied before the recording of the mortgage. It is contended by some of the parties that allocation of such part payments to the oldest items of the account is to be presumed in the absence of proof of intention to the contrary formed on the part of the creditor or debtor before the action was commenced.

But that contention cannot prevail here. Unlike the situation where only unsecured claims are involved, the law presumes that a creditor, like Sunde & d'Evers, having two claims, one secured by a first rank security and the other by a lower rank security, intends to allocate such part payments as are received to the payment of the claim with the lower rank security, in the absence of proof of a contrary intention. RESTATEMENT OF THE LAW, CONTRACTS, Sec. 394(1)(b)(ii), Page 743, and Illustration 5, Page 746; *Washington Grocery Co. v. Citizens' Bank,* 132 Wash. 244, 231 P. 780; *Field v. Holland,* 6 Cranch 8, 10 U.S. 8, 3 L. Ed. 136.

Sunde & d'Evers Co. will, therefore, be paid $270.47, the full amount of its preferred maritime lien for all items supplied prior to the recording of the mortgage. As to the balance of its account, it will be on the same basis as other lien claimants subsequent to the mortgage.

Another question is whether the Ship Mortgage Act, 46 U.S.C.A. §§ 911, 921 *et seq.,* permits maritime liens inferior to the lien of the mortgage to participate in a fund set aside from the sale proceeds to meet a preferred maritime lien. In this connection it is contended by some of the intervenors that before the enactment of the Ship Mortgage Act a lien later in time was prior in rank and that, unless the Ship Mortgage Act is to be regarded as changing that rule, the liens here arising subsequent to the mortgage should in their bids for prior payment displace the earlier statutory superior lien claim of the preferred maritime lien, once the fund is set aside from the proceeds of the sale of the vessel to meet the preferred maritime lien.

Respecting that contention, lien relationship before the Ship Mortgage Act does not compare with such relationship after the Act because in respect to the statutory mortgage and preferred maritime lien those relationships are not alike. It would seem clear that to allow lien claims arising later than the mortgage to participate in any fund taken out of the sale proceeds ahead of the mortgage for satisfying the preferred maritime lien would defeat the very purpose and provisions of the statute which expressly protects the preferred maritime lien. If the preferred maritime lien should not be paid ahead of the mortgage out of the proceeds of the sale, no matter for what reason, the provision of the statute intending that result would not be carried out and the statute would be violated. The Court, therefore, denies the right of other lien claimants to participate in any fund realized for the payment of the preferred maritime lien of Sunde & d'Evers Co. for items of supplies furnished to the vessel prior to the recording of the mortgage.

It has also been questioned whether under this ship mortgage the indebtedness secured thereby is to include a reasonable sum to be fixed by the Court as an attorney's fee for libelant's proctor. Upon this question counsel cite only one case, namely, *The John Jay,* D.C., 15 F. Supp. 937, which decided that, as between the mortgagee and the mortgagor, the mortgage lien secured the contingent amount of attorney's fees as a part of the mortgage indebtedness where the mortgage securing the indebtedness was evidenced by a promissory note containing a provision for the payment of reasonable attorney's fees to be fixed by the Court in case of mortgage foreclosure. No cases were cited where junior incumbrancers objected to attorney's fees, undetermined before the Court's decision, becoming a part of the senior mortgage indebtedness; but in this state, mortgages on land securing indebtedness evidenced by notes which in turn in language similar to that here provide for the payment of reasonable attorney's fees to be fixed by the Court are usually held to include such attorney's fee obligation within the mortgage debt protection of the mortgage lien. *Cutler v. Keller,* 88 Wash. 334, 153 P. 15, L.R.A. 1917C, 1116. No reason appears why the same rule should not apply in the case of preferred ship mortgages with attorney's fee and costs provisions like those in the mortgage and note here. An attorney's fee for libelant in the sum of $350 is reasonable and will be allowed and shall have the same lien rank as the principal mortgage indebtedness.

It is agreed by the parties that in this case maritime liens for supplies arising in a later year shall take priority over those created in an earlier year, and that all of such liens of any one year shall have the same rank and be paid pro rata out of any funds applicable to liens of their respective class. This agreement of course does not apply to the statutory preferred maritime lien of Sunde & d'Evers for supplies furnished prior to the recording of the mortgage.

* * *

---

b. Single/Severable Contracts

REDWOOD, ETC., ASS'N v. FISHING VESSEL OWNERS, ETC.

530 F. Supp. 75 (W.D. Wash. 1981)

BEEKS, Senior District Judge

Upon motion for judgment on the pleadings by intervening plaintiff, Fishing Vessel Owners Marine Ways (FVOMW), this court, on July 10, 1981, ordered that judgment in favor of FVOMW be entered *in rem* against the O/S ANCIENT MARINER, and *in personam* against Olivia Elaine Mouser/Viken (Mouser/Viken) in both her individual and representative capacities. FVOMW also sought a declaration of lien priority over the preferred ship mortgage on the vessel held by plaintiff Redwood Empire Production Credit Association (REPCA). Notwithstanding the court's ruling above-stated, a factual issue remained as to whether the work done after the date of the recordation and endorsement of the mortgage was pursuant to a severable contract, or whether it was pursuant to a single repair contract commenced before the mortgage lien attached. The court held the priority determination in abeyance pending a further factual showing, which was accomplished by a stipulation of the parties filed on September 30, 1981.

It appears that on or about November 15, 1976, pursuant to an oral agreement between FVOMW and Mouser/Viken, FVOMW began large scale repairs including the removal of after fuel tanks, removal and reinstallation of an auxiliary engine, repair of after bait tanks, installation of new decking and deck beams, caulking of the afterdeck and foredeck, refinishing the fo'c'sle with paneling, bunks, electric stove, and sink, and replacing old plastic pipe in the engine room with steel piping, all of which were completed in October, 1977. In accordance with the established policy of FVOMW, the agreement was verbal and FVOMW was to perform it on a time and material basis with payments to be made each time the account balance reached $5,000.00.

The intervening complaint of FVOMW alleged that at the special instance and request of Mouser/Viken extensive repairs were performed and new equipment and fittings were installed; that the reasonable and agreed value of the repairs was $47,063.91, and that a balance of $7,860.96 had not been paid and was due and owing, all of which has been admitted by Mouser/Viken.

The primary criterion for determining whether an agreement is a single contract or a number of severable contracts is the intention of the parties as determined by a fair construction of the agreement, by the subject matter to which it has reference, and by the circumstances of the particular transaction giving rise to the question. 17 Am.Jur.2d Contracts § 325 (1964). Accord, *Saletic v. Stamnes*, 51 Wash.2d 696, 321 P.2d 547 (1958). The parties to the contract, FVOMW and Mouser/Viken, agree that the contract was a single agreement covering the period from November of 1976 to October of 1977, inclusive. The only party to this litigation claiming the contract to be severable is REPCA, not a party to the contract.

All matters considered, the court finds that the parties entered into a single contract to make the vessel seaworthy, which involved continuous performance of the work described herein, for which FVOMW has a maritime lien prior and superior to the preferred ship mortgage lien of REPCA.

Hence, in accordance with previous orders of this court, REPCA shall pay "in cash" to FVOMW the sum of $7,860.96, plus its costs and interest, both prejudgment and postjudgment, at the rate of 10% per annum calculated from October 18, 1977 until paid. 28 U.S.C. § 1961 (1970); R.C.W. 4.56.110(2) (West Supp. 1980); Local Admiralty Rule 155, W.D. Wash.

It Is So Ordered.

---

c. Liens for Cargo Damage: Contract or Tort?

ALL ALASKAN SEAFOODS, INC. v. M/V SEA PRODUCER

882 F.2d 425, 1989 AMC 2935 (9th Cir. 1989)

DAVID R. THOMPSON, Circuit Judge

All Alaskan Seafoods Inc. ("All Alaskan"), a shipper and the plaintiff in this admiralty case, appeals the district courts partial summary judgment. The district court held that All Alaskans maritime lien on a vessel was subordinate to a mortgagees ship's mortgage. The district court determined that under the Ship Mortgage Act, All Alaskans claim for cargo damage could only arise under contract law, not under tort law; therefore the claim was not entitled to priority as a maritime lien under 46 U.S.C. § 953(a)(2). We reverse and remand.

Facts

In October 1986, All Alaskan commenced an action for cargo damage against the vessel M/V Sea Producer and against Express Marine Transportation Co. ("Express Marine"), the vessel's operator. In its complaint, All Alaskan alleged that it suffered losses of approximately $1.5 million when its shipment of frozen king crab thawed while in transit from Molar, Alaska to Seattle, Washington, and was contaminated by a refrigerant leakage in the hold of the Sea Producer. All Alaskan further alleged that the losses it suffered were caused by the negligence of Express Marine.

In April 1987, People's National Bank of Washington ("People's") intervened in the action to foreclose a preferred maritime mortgage on the Sea Producer.

Before discovery commenced, All Alaskan and People's filed cross-motions for partial summary judgment on the issue of the priority of their respective liens against the Sea Producer. The district court denied All Alaskans motion and granted partial summary judgment for People's Bank, holding that All Alaskans claim sounded only in contract, not in tort, and thus was inferior to the lien created by People's preferred mortgage. All Alaskan appeals that judgment.

* * *

B. Merits

All Alaskan contends that the district court erred in ruling that, under the Ship Mortgage Act, a claim for cargo damage could sound only in contract, not in tort, and thus that All Alaskan's lien was subordinate to People's mortgage. We review de novo the district court's grant of partial summary judgment. *See Ashton v. Cory*, 780 F.2d 816, 818 (9th Cir. 1986).

The Ship Mortgage Act (the "Act"), gives lien status and relatively high priority to a mortgage which complies with the Act. 46 U.S.C. § 953. The statutory mortgage, sometimes referred to as a preferred ship mortgage, was created to encourage investment in the shipping industry. *See Seattle First Nat'l Bank v. Bluewater Partnership*, 772 F.2d 565, 569 (9th Cir. 1985). Under the Act, a preferred ship mortgage lien has priority over most claims against a vessel, including contract claims, but is subordinate to preferred maritime liens. Subsection 953(a)(2) defines "preferred maritime liens" to include "a lien for damages arising out of tort...."

In its motion for summary judgment on the issue of lien priority, All Alaskan alleged that damage to its shipment of king crab resulted from the negligent operation of the vessel Sea Producer as a common carrier. Thus, All Alaskan argued, its cargo damage claim gave rise to a tort lien which was superior, under the Ship Mortgage Act, to People's mortgage. The district court acknowledged that liens against a ship for cargo damage are "hard to rank with precision," and have been viewed by courts as both "breaches of the contract of affreightment or as breaches of a duty imposed by law and, therefore tort." The district court was concerned however, that allowing All Alaskan to plead its cargo damage claim in tort, and thus secure priority over the bank's preferred ship mortgage, would undercut the purpose of the Ship Mortgage Act, that of encouraging investment in shipping. Thus, without determining what duty of care Express Marine owed to All Alaskan under common law or maritime statutory law, the district court ruled that All Alaskan's claim for cargo damage could sound only in contract. As a result, it was not entitled to priority under 46 U.S.C. 953(a)(2).

In ruling as it did, the district court considered the contractual relationship between All Alaskan and Express Marine to preclude a maritime lien for damages premised on tort liability. We disagree with this premise. In *The John G. Stevens*, 170 U.S. 113, 42 L. Ed. 969, 18 S.Ct. 544 (1898), the Supreme Court held that a claim for damage to a tow sounded in tort independent of any contract made, and was thus superior as a maritime lien to other purely contractual liens. In the course of its opinion, the Court rejected the argument that the tug's liability was analogous to that of a common carrier for loss of goods carried and thus could sound only in contract. The Court stated:

> But even an action by a passenger, or by an owner of goods against a carrier, for neglect to carry and deliver in safety, is an action for the breach of a duty imposed by the law, independently of contract or of consideration, and is therefore founded in tort.

Id. at 124-25. Although this statement may be read as dictum, it has served as a basis for classifying claims for cargo damage as torts and for giving such claims tort priority. *See, e.g., Oriente Com'l v. American Flag Vessel M/V Floridian*,

529 F.2d 221, 222 (4th Cir. 1975); *The Henry Breyer*, 17 F.2d 423, 429 (D. Md. 1927); *Morrisey v. S.S.A. & J. Faith*, 252 F. Supp. 54, 59 (N.D. Ohio 1965).

The proposition that the existence of a contractual relationship between the parties does not limit claims between them to contract actions was reaffirmed by the Supreme Court in *Stevens v. The White City*, 285 U.S. 195, 201, 76 L. Ed. 699, 52 S.Ct. 347 (1932), and in *Cortes v. Baltimore Insular Line*, 387 U.S. 367, 372 (1932). In *Cortes*, the Court held that a seaman who fell ill aboard a ship and died ashore after his ship reached home port had a remedy in tort against the owner of the vessel for breach of the Jones Act duty of maintenance and cure. Judge Cardozo, writing for the Court, rejected the argument that the only duty owed the seaman was a contract duty incident to the seamans contract of employment:

> We think the origin of the duty is consistent with the remedy in tort, since the wrong if a violation of the contract, is also something more. The duty, as already pointed out, is one annexed by law to a relation, annexed as an inseparable incident without heed, to any expression of the will of the contracting parties. For breach of a duty thus imposed, the remedy upon the contract does not exclude an alternative remedy built upon the tort.

Cortes, 287 U.S. at 372 (emphasis added).

Applying these principles, the Fourth Circuit in a case similar to the one now before us held that a claim for cargo damage against a ship as a common carrier was a claim for damages arising out of tort and thus a preferred maritime lien under 46 U.S.C. § 953(a). *Oriente Com'l v. American Flag Vessel, M/V Floridian*, 529 F.2d 221, 223 (4th Cir. 1975). In *Oriente*, the shipper, Oriente Commercial, Inc. ("Oriente") was one of many *in rem* claimants against the M/V Floridian which was arrested and sold. The United States held two valid preferred ship mortgages on the vessel. Oriente took a default judgment on its claim that a shipment of meat had been negligently damaged in transit. The various liens asserted against the vessel exceeded the proceeds from its sale. Litigation over priority of the liens ensued.

The district court in *Oriente*, guided by the same policy concerns that informed the district court decision at issue here, reasoned that because cargo claims should be subordinated to preferred mortgages such claims should sound only in contract as a matter of law. The Fourth Circuit reversed. After reviewing the Supreme Court's decision in *John Stevens* as well as a number of lower court decisions which recognized that cargo damage claims may give rise to tort liability, the Fourth Circuit observed that the:

> [Ship Mortgage Act] draws no distinction between cargo claims that sound in tort, the so-called hybrid liens, and any other type of claim for damages arising out of tort. While Congress might have been well advised to subordinate cargo claims, it flatly granted priority to all claims arising out of tort. The result reached by the district court and pressed by the United States would carve out an exception to the statute unwarranted by its language. Whatever Congress meant, it stated that all tort liens are prior to preferred mortgage liens. In light of cases decided both before and after enactment of the Ship Mortgage Act, holding that cargo claims such as those in the instant case sound in tort, we cannot say that Congress intended something else.

Id. at 223.

We find the Fourth Circuit's analysis cogent and follow it in this case. Although the district court here was guided by important policy considerations, neither the weight of authority nor the language of the Ship Mortgage Act justifies the district court's decision. If Express Marine breached its duty of care with respect to All Alaskan then that breach of duty can give rise to tort liability irrespective of contract obligations between the parties. *See*

Oriente, 529 F.2d at 222-23. Accordingly, we hold it was error for the district court to rule, as a matter of law, that All Alaskans cargo claims could not sound in tort.

* * *

Conclusion

The district court's partial summary judgment is reversed. This case is remanded to the district court. On remand the district court should determine the merits of All Alaskan's claim, and resolve the dispute as to whether the Sea Producer was a common carrier in its carriage of All Alaskan's goods, or whether the parties contracted that the duties of a common carrier would be owed to All Alaskan regardless of whether the Sea Producer was a common carrier.

REVERSED AND REMANDED.

Note: *Priority of Preferred Liens: Expiration*

Liens for supplies and repairs attaching after the creation of a maritime mortgage (U.S. flag vessels) are maritime liens, though subordinated to the mortgage. *Morse Dry Dock & Repair Co. v. Steamship Northern Star*, 271 U.S. 552, 46 S.Ct. 589, 70 L. Ed. 1082, 1926 AMC 977 (1926). However, the priority of the lien of a preferred ship mortgage does not expire on the date of the maturity of the mortgage; thus, supplies furnished after the date of maturity are subordinated to the preferred mortgage. *The Favorite*, 120 F.2d 899 (2d Cir. 1941). The court left open the question whether the priority of the lien of a preferred mortgage may be lost by laches by a finding that the mortgage creditor was not guilty of a delay in the pursuit of his claim.

The priority of a preferred lien for necessaries may be lost when the conduct of the lienor is tainted by deception and concealment. *See Florida Bahamas Lines, Ltd. v. Steel Barge Star 800 of Nassau*, 433 F.2d 1243, 1970 AMC 2189 (5 th Cir. 1970).

Note: *Conflicts of Law*

According to choice of law rules developed by federal courts, a maritime lien may arise under the law of a foreign country in which a contract was made or in which services or supplies were furnished. Parties may thus plead and prove foreign law. In the absence of proof, foreign law may be presumed to be the same as United States law. *See Symonette Shipyards, Ltd. v. Clark*, 365 F.2d 464, 1966 AMC 2383 (5th Cir. 1966), *cert. denied*, 387 U.S. 908, 87 S.Ct. 1690, 18 L. Ed. 2d 625 (1967); *Rayony Celanese Peruana, S.A. v. M/V Phgh*, 471 F. Supp. 1363, 1979 AMC 2682 (S.D. Ala. 1979).

U.S. courts will apply American law to protect an American supplier of fuel to a foreign vessel in a U.S. port even if the supply contract was made in a foreign jurisdiction. *See Gulf Trading & Transportation Co. v. Vessel Hoegh Shield*, 658 F.2d 363, 1982 AMC 1138 (5th Cir. 1981). In *Gulf Trading & Transportation Co. v. M/V Tento*, 694 F.2d 1191, 1983 AMC 872 (9th Cir. 1982), the Ninth Circuit addressed the issue of choice of law in maritime lien cases.

In the *M/V Tento*, liens were filed against the vessel when it docked in California. The underlying claims arose from two separate transactions. The Norwegian owner of the vessel placed it under a time charter to a U.S. company, which subchartered the vessel to another U.S. company. The owner's charter provided that U.S. law would govern certain aspects of the agreement and that the charterer was responsible for obtaining the vessel's fuel oil. On the voyage giving rise to these claims, the vessel embarked from the U.S. for the Suez Canal.

While en route the subcharterer decided to refuel in Italy, where the transaction with Gulf occurred. Gulf, a Delaware corporation, used an Italian company to deliver the fuel oil in Italy. Gulf paid the Italian company and charged the vessel. Neither the subcharterer nor the owner had paid the invoice.

The second transaction was with Permal, a New York corporation. Permal advanced approximately $40,000 for the vessel's Suez Canal transit. Permal's invoice has not been paid. The court stated:

> Gulf and Permal initiated these *in rem* actions against the vessel. The owner contends that Italian and Egyptian law govern the transactions, and that under those laws the owner's vessel is not subject to liens for expenses incurred by a subcharterer. It argues that the correct choice of law is determined by a single point of contact for the separate transactions—namely, the country where supplies were obtained.

In *Lauritzen v. Larsen,* 345 U.S. 571 (1953), the U.S. Supreme Court resolved a choice of law question in a maritime tort suit under the Jones Act. It adopted an approach similar to the RESTATEMENT (SECOND) OF CONFLICT OF LAWS, setting forth the points of contact between the transaction and various jurisdictions and weighing them. Its review included the place of the wrongful act, the flag of the ship, allegiance or domicile of the injured seaman allegiance of the shipowner, place of signing the employment contract accessibility of a foreign court, and the law of the forum.

The Second Circuit has already discredited the notion that choice of law in maritime lien cases should be made by looking solely to the law of the place of supply. *Rainbow Line, Inc. v. M/V Tequila,* 480 F.2d 1024 (1973). Instead, the court required consideration of all points of contact with the various nations.

To hold that the choice of law in maritime lien cases is controlled by the significance of multiple contacts is consistent with this court's previous holdings, both in maritime cases involving other types of disputes and in non-maritime contract choice of law cases. A single contact approach would run counter to an important principle—the desirability, even the necessity, of accommodating the legitimate interests of separate sovereigns in vindicating their own legal policies. This court concludes that all relevant contacts must be considered in maritime lien cases.

* * *

A shipowner can protect itself by bonding the charterer or by dealing only with reliable charterers. It is not, moreover, inequitable to require shipowners whose charters make orders on a multinational level to know the law of the nation in which their charterers have extensive contacts.

A test giving dominance to the location where supplies were delivered does not even have the advantage of simplicity to recommend it. Where the place of furnishing supplies to provide the law for resolving each contractual dispute involving a ship that stops at many ports, courts would be required to embark upon an odyssey in foreign law that both they and the law would soon regret. Judicial efficiency is a relevant factor in choice of law analysis, and it is not served by the place of supply rule advocated here.

In short, choice of law questions involving maritime liens are to be resolved by weighing and evaluating the points of contact between the transaction and the sovereign legal systems touched and affected by it. The substantial contacts between the U.S. and the Gulf and Permal transactions point towards U.S. law as the most appropriate for resolving this litigation.

In *Ocean Ship Supply Ltd v. M/V Leah,* 729 F.2d 971, 1984 AMC 2089 (**4th** Cir. 1984), the court undertook a "points of contact" choice of law inquiry before holding that Canadian law governed the question whether a necessaries supplier acquired a maritime lien for the supply of necessaries in Canada. The supplier's claim to have a maritime lien failed, because Canadian law gave no maritime lien.

In *Liverpool and London S.S. Protection and Indemnity Assn v. M/V Queen of Leman,* 296 F.3d 350, 2002 AMC 1521 (5th Cir. 2002), the court held that U.S. law governed the question whether a U.K.-based P. & I. Club had a maritime lien for unpaid calls (i.e., insurance premiums). The court did not apply U.S. law as the law of the forum (*lex fori*) but because the contract in question (the P. & I. Club Rules) provided that it was to be governed by English law but enforcement was to be "in accordance with local law". Although English law would not give the Club a maritime lien for its unpaid calls, U.S. law did, and it was applicable for enforcement purposes as the relevant "local law".

Several courts have held that a clause in a necessaries supplier's contract choosing U.S. maritime law as the governing law of the contract is sufficient to give the necessaries supplier a maritime lien enforceable in the United States, whether or not the necessaries were supplied in the United States by a U.S. necessaries supplier. *Trans-Tec Asia v. M/V Harmony Container,* 518 F.3d 1120, 2008 AMC 684 (9th Cir. 2008); *Triton Marine Fuels Ltd, S.A. v. MV Pacific Chukotka,* 575 F.3d 409, 2009 AMC 1885 (4th Cir. 2009); *World Fuel Services Trading, D.M.C.C. v. Hebei Prince Shipping Co. Ltd,* 783 F.3d 507, 2015 AMC 929 (4th Cir. 2015); *World Fuel Services Singapore Pte Ltd v. Bulk Juliana MV,* 822 F.3d 766, 2016 AMC 2722 (5th Cir. 2016). For a diametrically opposed point of view in a different circuit, see *A/S Dan-Bunkering Ltd v. MV Centrans Demeter,* 633 Fed. Appx. 755, 2016 AMC 1117 (11th Cir. 2015). These decisions seem to be flatly inconsistent with the fundamental notion that maritime liens are created by operation of law, not by agreement of the parties: see Martin Davies, "Choice of Law and U.S. Maritime Liens," 83 *Tul. L. Rev.* 1435 (2009).

Note: Ranking of Liens: Law of the Forum

The ranking of all liens is determined under the law of the forum. Thus, a lien created under the law of a foreign country will be given the priority of a corresponding lien under the laws of the United States. *See Potash Co. of Canada, Limited v. M/V Raleigh,* 361 F. Supp. 120, 1973 AMC 2658 (D.D.C. Zone 1973); *Rayony Celanese Peruana S.A. v. M/VPhgh, supra. See also Rainbow Line, Inc. v. M/V Tequila,* 341 F. Supp. 459, 1972 AMC 1540 (S.D.N.Y. 1972), *aff'd,* 480 F.2d 1024, 1973 AMC 1431 (2d Cir. 1973).

G. Extinction of Maritime Liens

1. *Laches*

BERMUDA EXP., N.V. v. M/V LITSA (Ex. LAURIE U)

872 F.2d 554, 1989 AMC 1537 (3d Cir. 1989)

Opinion of the Court

SLOVITER, Circuit Judge

I.

Issues

The appellant vessel in an *in rem* action appeals from the district courts final adjudication and judgment awarding three stevedoring companies the full amount of their claims based on maritime liens for unpaid invoices for stevedoring services provided to the vessel before it was sold to its present owner. The principal issue on appeal is whether the claims of the stevedore lienors were barred by the equitable doctrine of laches. The conflicting interests involve, on one hand, those of maritime lienors whose services are essential for the smooth functioning of maritime commerce and, on the other hand, those of bona fide purchasers in good faith of vessels which may be subject to such liens....

* * *

II.

Facts

Most of the facts relevant to this appeal are not in dispute. Appellees, Port Stevedoring, Inc. (Port), Ryan-Walsh Stevedoring Company (Ryan-Walsh), and Southeastern Maritime Company (Semco), are in the business of supplying stevedoring services to vessels at various ports in the southern portion of the United States. In 1982, Uiterwyk Corporation (Uiterwyk), the general agent for Uiterwyk Lines, Ltd. which owned the vessel, contracted with appellees to provide stevedoring services for vessels nominated by Uiterwyk. This contract covered the vessel involved in this litigation, then known as the M/V LAURIE U, which sailed under Liberian registry. The contracts all called for payment of 80% of the amount due for services rendered upon completion of such services for each vessel and presentation of an invoice. Under the Port and Semco contracts, the balance became due a reasonable time after presentation of duly documented bills, while under the Ryan-Walsh contract final payment was due within sixty days after the presentation of such bills.

Semco provided services to the M/V LAURIE U on May 27 and 28, 1982 in Charleston, giving rise to a claim of $22,184.87. Ryan-Walsh provided services to the M/V LAURIE U on July 26-August 6, 1982 in New Orleans, giving rise to a claim for $25,404.21. Port provided services to the M/V LAURIE U in Houston on three occasions in 1982, May 13-23, August 11-14, and October 14-20, giving rise to claims for $112,994.71, $46,692.26, and $71,873.97 respectively.

On October 21, the M/V LAURIE U left United States waters and did not return until April 2, 1983. In the interim, two significant events took place. On December 8, 1982, Uiterwyk Lines, Ltd. sold the M/V LAURIE U to Star Warrant Shipping Corp. (Star), a shipping company operating out of Piraeus, Greece. In the contract of sale, Uiterwyk Lines, Ltd. warranted to Star that there were no maritime liens against the vessel, and Star's search of the Liberian registry in New York revealed that no claims had been filed against the ship. Star renamed the vessel M/V LITSA. Shortly after the sale, on January 27, 1983, Uiterwyk, the general agent, filed a petition in bankruptcy in the Middle District of Florida.

Upon learning of the bankruptcy, appellees filed individual claims in the bankruptcy court and contacted Lloyds Watch of London to determine the status of Uiterwyk vessels which they had serviced. Lloyds informed appellees of the purchase of the M/V LAURIE U and the name change, and continued to track the vessel's movements until it returned to United States waters on April 2, 1983. Bermuda Express, another claimant who has since settled with Star, arrested the M/V LITSA in the Port of Philadelphia on April 6, 1983. The district court had jurisdiction over this suit in admiralty under 28 U.S.C. § 1333 (1982).

Appellees intervened as plaintiff's and proceeded to trial against the M/V LITSA on their claims. After a bench trial, the district court determined that all three appellees had acted with the extraordinary degree of diligence required to preserve their maritime liens, and that neither their participation in the bankruptcy proceedings nor their failure to file notice of their maritime liens waived their right to assert those liens....

* * *

III.

Legal Principles

A.

* * *

In *The Bold Buccleugh*, 7 MOORE, P.C. 267 (1852), the English Privy Council case which serves as the original authority on the issue, G. Gilmore & C. Black at 595, the court enforced a maritime lien against the ship although it had since been sold; the court, however, noted that the lien may be lost "by negligence or delay where the rights of third parties may be compromised." *Id.* at 285.

Shortly thereafter, the United States Supreme Court enunciated a similar principle. In *The Key City*, 81 U.S. (14 Wall.) 653, 660, 20 L. Ed. 896 (1872), the Court stated that "laches or delay in the judicial enforcement of maritime liens will, under proper circumstances, constitute a valid defence;" that there is no "arbitrary or fixed period of time" for its operation but that the determination that a lienor was guilty of laches would "depend on the peculiar equitable circumstances of that case;" and that "where the lien is to be enforced to the detriment of a purchaser for value, without notice of the lien, the defence will be held valid under shorter time, and a more rigid scrutiny of the circumstances of the delay, than when the [party claiming laches] is the owner at the time the lien accrued."

The parties dispute whether a maritime lienor must exercise "extraordinary diligence" in order to preserve a claim against a bona fide purchaser ... or whether "reasonable diligence" is sufficient ... we believe that the lienor should be held to a "reasonable diligence" standard. *See Merchants & Marine Bank v. The T.E. Welles*, 289 F.2d 188, 190 (5th Cir. 1961) (applying a reasonable diligence test). The lienor must take such steps as are appropriate under the circumstances. The district court used the standard most favorable to the vessel and found nonetheless that the lienors exercised the "extraordinary high degree of diligence" required to preserve and enforce the liens.... If we conclude that there is the requisite support for a conclusion of reasonable diligence, we are bound to affirm.

B.

Appellant argues that in considering the diligence of the lienors in this case, we need look no further than the analysis used by the courts in the two *Everosa* cases decided half a century ago. In the first *Everosa* case, *The Everosa (Southern Coal & Coke Co. v. Kugniecibas)*, 93 F.2d 732 (1st Cir. 1937), the libelant, Southern Coal & Coke Company, had provided coal to the vessel at issue on November 22, 1933 and May 8, 1934 for which it had received only partial payment. Shortly after the second coaling, the ship sailed for foreign waters and did not return until November 1934, at which time Southern libeled the ship. *Id.* at 733-35. While it had been in foreign waters, it was sold to a bona fide purchaser.

* * *

The appellate court ... considered the ships laches defense, apparently as a matter of first impression, and held that laches did not bar enforcement of the lien for the second coaling because the ship left the United States nine days after the coaling and "[a]bsence of the vessel from the country operates to relieve the lienor to some extent from the imputation of laches." *Id.* at 735. Although the court noted that there was evidence that the ship had returned to this country before the voyage on which she was libeled, *id.*, it nonetheless held "there was clearly no laches." *Id.*

The question of the enforceability of the lien for the first coaling was, the court noted, "very close." *Id.* It concluded that that lien was barred by laches because the ship had "called at various gulf ports of this country half a dozen times between the first coaling and the second," and thus the lienor "unquestionably" had "a reasonable opportunity to enforce the lien." *Id.* The court also noted that the lienor "knew or could easily have discovered" that the vessel at the time of the coalings was held by the party receiving the coal under charter and not as owner, "and that rights of third persons might be affected." *Id.* at 735-36.

The second *Everosa* case, *The Everosa (Swan & Sons v. Kugniecibas)*, 20 F. Supp. 8 (E.D.N.Y. 1937), involved claims filed by companies which had supplied the vessel in Norfolk, Virginia, in February 1934 and in New Orleans in April 1934 before it sailed for foreign waters in May 1934. In this case, however, the lienors did not file their libels until 1937, although the ship had returned to United States waters twice in the interim. The court held that inasmuch as the company supplying the vessel at Norfolk had an opportunity to enforce its lien when the vessel returned to Norfolk in May 1934 before it sailed abroad, and that the creditors (including the libelant) were notified of the bankruptcy proceeding of the operator which was initiated in June 1934, *see id.* at 11, both of which events were prior to the transfer of title of the ship in August 1934, the balance of equities required dismissal of the libel. On the other hand, the court held that the second lienor was not barred by laches because the ship sailed abroad within a month of its supply services, and, although the ship returned to the United States at various times, it did not return to New Orleans during those visits. It held that failure to take advantage of those opportunities for affirmative action "does not fatally portray lack of diligence." *Id.* at 13.

Appellant urges that the *Everosa* cases mandate a finding that Semco, Ryan-Walsh, and Port did not exercise the requisite diligence in enforcing their liens. Although some of the facts in the *Everosa* cases are analogous to the M/V LAURIE U situation, all of the cases stress that the question of due diligence is one peculiar to the facts of each case. For this reason, it is not particularly useful to review the facts of the many other cases referred to by appellant and the distinguishing factors pointed out by appellees. We accept the legal principles from the *Everosa* cases that lienors are not required to attempt to enforce their liens in foreign waters and that the existence of a reasonable opportunity for the lienor to arrest the vessel before the purchase is an important factor in the laches analysis.

However, the fact that it would have been possible or even feasible to locate and arrest the vessel at a port in the United States is not dispositive of the question of whether or when the appellees in this case should have done so. The custom of the shipping industry, for example, must also inform the analysis of what constitutes diligence under the circumstances of a given case.

The arrest of a vessel is a remedy of last resort, and one which has the potential to seriously disrupt the flow of maritime commerce. Therefore, we decline to establish a firm rule which would require a maritime lienor to arrest a vessel, particularly if there are available other reasonable methods, consistent with industry custom, to secure payment. The relevant consideration instead is what would have been the commercially reasonable practice. Components of diligence thus include industry custom, the amount of the lien, the pattern of dealing between the parties, and whether the lienor had information that the interests of a third party would likely be adversely affected by its failure to act.

Appellant argues that we should also consider whether the lienors filed their claims on the ship's register. It claims that the lienors' failure to file claims of their liens on the Liberian Registry in New York, a relatively simple and inexpensive means of giving notice, evinces a failure of the lienors to exercise the requisite degree of diligence.

Several cases have treated failure to record a claim of lien as a relevant factor in assessing the equities of a laches defense. *See, e.g., Tagaropulos, S.A. v. S.S. Santa Paula*, 502 F.2d 1171, 1172 (9th Cir. 1974); *John W. Stone Oil Distributor, Lnc. v. M/V Miss Bern*, 663 F. Supp. 773, 780 (S.D. Ala. 1987); *Dixie Machine Welding and Metal*

Works, Inc. v. M/V Andino, 1983 A.M.C. 1166, 1168 (S.D. Fla. 1982); *Waterways Marine, Lnc. v. Brooks Liquid Transport, Inc.,* 291 F. Supp. 703 (N.D. 111. 1968). Each case, however, has its own set of facts and no situation directly parallels the one before us.

All parties agree that there is no statutory requirement that a maritime lien be filed in order to be valid. At the time Congress enacted the Maritime Liens Act, it could have but failed to require filing. It has made no attempt to change the statute in this respect since then. The district court thus concluded that the lienors here did not lack diligence "merely because the claims were not filed with the Liberian Ship Registry in New York." App. at 376 (emphasis added). Obviously, however, the ability to have filed the lien is a consideration that cannot be completely ignored in the relevant balancing. It is significant whether it was a custom of the industry to record liens for necessaries.

Poised against the diligence or lack thereof of the lienor is the action of the purchaser of the vessel. A balancing of the equities requires consideration not only of the bona fides of the purchaser, *i.e.,* its lack of actual knowledge of unpaid liens and its search of the ship's registry, but also of its efforts to ascertain whether, in light of the absence of any legal requirement of filing liens, there are in fact liens outstanding. *See Tagaropulos S.A. v. S.S. Santa Paula,* 502 F.2d 1171, 1172 (9th Cir. 1974) (Purchaser "made every effort to unearth all claims against the ship." It checked both the home port and ship's log for liens; although no liens were entered in the log, purchaser discovered entries for repairs, contacted shipyards and learned of outstanding unpaid bills).

Finally, we note that it is for the district court in the first instance to perform the equitable balancing of all the relevant factors. Our review will be facilitated if the district courts fully discuss the factors considered on the issue of diligence and make explicit their balancing of the equities in reaching a decision on laches. We thus proceed to examine the record to discern the factors which explicitly or implicitly informed the district court's judgment in this case.

C.

* * *

The initial inquiry relevant to appellees' diligence is thus whether they had a reasonable opportunity to enforce their liens between the time each lien arose and October 21, 1982, when the ship left United States waters.

Patently, Port could not have taken any action in United States waters to enforce its third lien, that based on the services it provided between October 14-20, 1982, because the vessel left the United States immediately thereafter. Semco and Ryan-Walsh, on the other hand, had provided their services earlier. However, throughout the entire period following the services provided by Semco in Charleston (May 27 and 28) and by Ryan-Walsh in New Orleans (July 26—August 6), the vessel was out of the country except for two Houston stops (August 9-14 and October 14-21) and one stop at Port Arthur, Texas (October 9-14). If we look to the vessel's return to the particular port where the stevedoring company provided the services, which was the dispositive factor leading the court to determine that laches did not bar one of the claims in the second *Everosa* case, 20 F. Supp. at 13, we note that the vessel did not return to Charleston or New Orleans following the provision of services by Semco and Ryan-Walsh at these ports.

We are aware, as appellant argues, that modern technology associated with the shipping industry has made it easier than in the *Everosa* period for lienors to track ships, thus increasing opportunities to arrest vessels and enforce liens. Nonetheless, we cannot rule on the record developed by the appellant here that the stevedore companies had the obligation to track the vessel, which primarily served foreign ports throughout this entire period, to the Texas ports and arrest the ship on one of the three occasions when it would have been possible to do so.

It is true, as appellant argues, that these companies could have easily filed their liens on the ship's registry and thereby given notice to a prospective purchaser. However, we have pointed out that there is no legal requirement for such an action and, significantly, there was no evidence of an industry custom to do so.

* * *

Appellees' failure to enforce the liens was consistent with their past practice in dealing with Uiterwyk, which was a slow payer. Previously, their demands for payment and threats to arrest vessels were sufficient to procure payment, albeit belatedly. Appellant has not shown it was commercially unreasonable of appellees to wait for payment. In light of these circumstances, we find no basis to question the district court's conclusion that these lienors exercised the requisite diligence with respect to their liens and that Port exercised such diligence with respect to its October lien.

It is more difficult to evaluate Port's diligence in the case of its two earlier liens, that arising from its May services and that arising from its August services. Port clearly had the opportunity to take action against the ship because it returned to Houston where Port provided additional services notwithstanding the unpaid bills. In both instances Port extended further credit for new services.

However, Port's liens were only five months and two months old at the time the ship left United States waters. In many of the relevant cases the liens had been outstanding for substantially over a year before the lienor sought enforcement. *See Tagaropulos, S.A. v. S.S. Santa Paula,* 502 F.2d 1171, 1172 (9th Cir. 1974) (two years); *Phelps v. The Cecelia Ann,* 199 F.2d 627, 628 (4th Cir. 1952) (more than two years); *The John Cadwalader,* 99 F.2d 678, 679 (3d Cir. 1938) (five to nine years); *Dixie Machine Welding and Metal Works, Inc. v. M/V Andino,* 1983 A.M.C. 1166 (S.D. Fla. 1982) (two and one-half years).

Appellant has shown little that Port could have done short of the draconian measure of arresting the ship, with the exception of filing the lien which we have noted is not required as a matter of law. Appellant introduced no evidence of other commercially reasonable practice available to Port. Port's Vice-President testified that it was not customary for Port or any other stevedoring company to require advance payment before it rendered services.... Moreover, Port was receiving payments from Uiterwyk through 1982. While it did not receive any payment which was applied to the invoices for this particular vessel, it did receive $100,000 from Uiterwyk on November 10, 1982 which was applied to older bills ... thus giving it reason to believe that it would eventually be paid. Therefore, we cannot conclude that Port was guilty of a lack of diligence that would deprive it of its maritime lien.

Under these circumstances, we need not consider whether there were some steps that Star, a sophisticated shipowner which purchased over 70 vessels, could have taken to protect itself which it failed to take, such as the inquiry of the general agent or of the port agents and suppliers in the ports that the vessel had visited. *See Tagaropulos,* 502 F.2d at 1172.

* * *

VI.

Conclusion

We recognize that it may appear inequitable to permit enforcement of maritime liens against a purchaser without notice of those liens, particularly when giving notice through registration of the liens is a simple matter. However, whether such registration should be imposed as a requirement for the ability to satisfy liens against a ship when it has been acquired by a subsequent purchaser is a policy decision that is more appropriately made by Congress than by the courts. The judicial decision on a laches defense must be made without interposition of our view as to what the law should be. In this case, we cannot say that the outstanding liens were so long overdue that, in the circumstances here, the district court was obliged to hold that they could not be enforced.

LEOPARD MARINE & TRADING, LTD. v. EASY STREET LTD

2016 AMC 1141 (S.D.N.Y. 2016)

JED S. RAKOFF, District Judge

Plaintiff Leopard Marine & Trading, Ltd. ("Leopard") brought this action seeking a declaratory judgment that defendant Easy Street Ltd. ("Easy Street") is barred from enforcing its maritime lien against Leopard's vessel, the

M/V *Densa Leopard* (the "Vessel"), under the doctrine of laches. The parties cross-moved for summary judgment. For the following reasons, the Court grants plaintiff's motion, denies defendant's motion, and enters final judgment declaring enforcement of Easy Street's lien barred by laches.

The key facts of this case are not in dispute…Leopard owns the Vessel and chartered her to third party Allied Maritime, Inc. ("Allied"). Under the written charter agreement, Allied was to fuel the Vessel and agreed not to suffer liens with priority over Leopard"s title. Leopard had a lien on cargoes for any amount due under the charter agreement. Allied took delivery of the Vessel on June 30, 2011.

On August 23, 2011, Allied purchased $848,847.60 worth of fuel for the Vessel from defendant Easy Street, creating a maritime lien against the Vessel. The invoice for this fuel fell due on September 26, 2011. Allied never paid the invoice.

Allied redelivered the Vessel on November 4, 2011. At re-delivery, the Vessel contained 593.99 metric tons of bunker fuel. Leopard credited Allied $409,853.10 for the remaining fuel. Allied paid Leopard the final hire payment of $23,885.15, which took into account this credit, on December 2, 2011.

On March 16, 2012, Allied gave Easy Street a written assurance that it would pay the fuel invoice by April 17, 2012…On April 20, 2012, Allied again made a written assurance that it would pay within a month. *Id.* Ex. 7. On November 6, 2012, Allied was declared bankrupt by a court in Greece. Easy Street made no attempt to arrest the Vessel to recover on the unpaid fuel invoice prior to November 6, 2012, and never considered suing Allied.

The parties dispute when exactly Leopard learned that Allied had not paid for the fuel. Leopard claims it did not learn of Allied's failure to pay until March 30, 2015…Easy Street claims that it sent two emails to Leopard on October 10, 2013, and October 24, 2013, informing Leopard of Allied's non-payment…Regardless of when Leopard first learned of Easy Street's claim, Easy Street sent it an email on March 30, 2015, demanding payment for the bunkers in the amount of $1,394,807.76, the cost of the unpaid fuel plus interest and legal fees.

On April 19, 2015, Easy Street arrested the Vessel in Panama, exercising its lien for the unpaid fuel. On April 20, 2015, Leopard commenced the present action, seeking declaratory relief that Easy Street's lien was barred by laches, and also seeking attorneys' fees and costs. After discovery, the parties filed the present cross-motions for summary judgment. There is only one pertinent issue raised on these motions: whether laches bars enforcement of Easy Street's lien.

When considering laches in a case at admiralty, federal courts look to the analogous state statute of limitations, but it does not necessarily control the outcome. Judge Friendly explained the inquiry to determine if laches bars a claim at admiralty as follows:

> [w]hen the suit has been brought after the expiration of the state limitation period, a court applying maritime law asks why the case should be allowed to proceed; when the suit, although perhaps long delayed, has nevertheless been brought within the state limitation period, the court asks why it should not be…When a plaintiff who asserts a maritime claim after the state statute has run, presents evidence tending to excuse his delay, the court must weigh the legitimacy of his excuse, the inference to be drawn from the expiration of the state statute, and the length of the delay, along with evidence as to prejudice if the defendant comes forward with any.

Larios v. Victory Carriers, Inc., 316 F.2d 63, 66-67, 1963 AMC 1704, 1707-8 (2d Cir 1963) (Friendly, Ct.J.).

The first question for the Court, then, is whether the analogous state statute of limitations has run.

The analogous state statute of limitations is New York's statute of limitations controlling liens on vessels. *See* N.Y. Lien Laws 83. Leopardargues that this statute of limitations is most analogous because this case concerns a lien on a vessel. Easy Street objects that New York's lien law expressly excludes maritime liens and requires that a lien on a vessel be contracted within New York. See N.Y. Lien Laws 80. Although Easy Street's arguments demonstrate that New York's lien law does not apply outright, that is not the question here. Instead, the Court is merely looking for the most analogous state statute. Even if it does not apply of its own accord, a state statute concerning liens on vessels is the most analogous statute for a case concerning a lien on a vessel.

The analogous state statute of limitations has not run on Easy Street's lien. N.Y. Lien Laws 83 provides the following statute of limitations provision:

[e]very lien for a debt shall cease at the expiration of twelve months after the debt was contracted. If, upon the expiration of the time herein limited .., such vessel shall be absent from the port at which the debt was contracted, the lien shall continue until the expiration of thirty days after the return of such vessel to such port.

Allied purchased the fuel bunkers in Mejillones, Chile and has not returned to that port since. Accordingly, under the plain language of N.Y. Lien Laws 83, the statute of limitations on Easy Street's lien has not run. Leopards counsel conceded as much at oral argument...

But the state statute of limitations is only a "rule-of-thumb." *Larios v. Victory Carriers, Inc.*, 316 F.2d 63, 66, 1963 AMC 1704, 1707 (2d Cir 1963). While the fact that it has not run weighs against Leopard, the Court must still ask whether there are good reasons for the suit not to proceed. In particular, the Court asks whether Easy Street inexcusably delayed and Leopard suffered prejudice. *See Oroz v. Am. President Lines, Ltd.*, 259 F.2d 636, 639, 1958 AMC 2342, 2345 (2d Cir. 1958). Both inexcusable delay and prejudice are present in this case.

First, Easy Street inexcusably delayed enforcing its lien against the Vessel. It made no attempt to arrest the Vessel prior to November 6, 2012, when Allied was declared bankrupt and more than a year after Allied's bill became due...Easy Street argues that it delayed because it received written assurances from Allied that Allied would pay the debt. The parties dispute whether Leopard's [sic] reliance on Allied's [sic] assurances was reasonable. Leopard argues that Allied had failed to pay Easy Street for fifteen other invoices and that the relationship between Easy Street and Allied was not arms-length...Easy Street responds that Allied was a good customer, otherwise settling a large volume of transactions on time...This dispute is immaterial. Regardless of whether Easy Street's reliance on Allied's assurances was reasonable, its *in personam* dealings with Allied constituted a choice not to pursue *in rem* remedies against the Vessel. Easy Street must bear the consequences of this choice. *See The Mendotta II*, 13 F.Supp. 1019, 1020, 1936 AMC 68, 70 (E.D.N.Y. 1935) ("Where the libellant ... instead of proceeding with reasonable diligence to arrest the vessel, preferred to collect *in personam*, such delay, occasioned by such choice, cannot be overlooked if months after the year has elapsed libelant now seeks to proceed *in rem*.").

Easy Street also argues that its delay was excusable because of legal barriers to enforcing maritime liens for necessities in foreign ports. In particular, at oral argument, Easy Street's counsel suggested that the lien could only be enforced in the United States, France, and Panama...The Court received supplementary briefing on this question. It is true that the laws of relatively few countries create maritime liens for necessities, and "outside the U.S. the general rule obtains that a foreign maritime claim should be enforced as a maritime lien only if there is a maritime lien under both foreign law and the law of the forum." Thomas J. Schoenbaum, *Admiralty and Maritime Law* 738 (5th ed. 2012); *see Trans-Tec Asia v. M/V Harmony Container*, 518 F.3d 1120, 1123 n.4, 2008 AMC 684, 687 (9 Cir. 2008) ("Fewer than thirty countries recognize [a maritime lien for necessities.]").

However, exceptions to this general rule are relevant in this case. *See* Thomas J. Schoenbaum, *Admiralty and Maritime Law* 738 (5th ed. 2012) ("[S]ome jurisdictions .. will recognize and enforce a U.S. lien which would not have lien status under domestic law."). To begin with, "a foreign maritime lien for necessaries ... arising under the proper law of the contract will be recognized as enforceable in Canada although the contract if made in Canada would not give rise to a maritime lien." *Marlex Petroleum v. The Har Rai*, 1984 AMC 1649, 1652, [1984] 2 F.C. 345 (Can.). Furthermore, defendant concedes that a U.S. maritime lien can be enforced in Panama – after all, defendant arrested the Vessel in Panama....The Vessel was located in Canada from March 17, 2012, to March 22, 2012, and in Panama from April 4, 2012, to April 5, 2012....

Moreover, Easy Street has arrested vessels in South Korea, Brazil, and Nigeria because of unpaid invoices... The Vessel called at ports in South Korea, Nigeria, and Brazil in October and November 2011, December 2011, and June 2012, respectively...Accordingly, Easy Street had several opportunities to arrest the Vessel during the year it chose to pursue *in personam* dealings with Allied and cannot rely on general legal barriers to the enforcement of maritime liens as an excuse for its delay.

Second, Leopard was prejudiced in several ways by Easy Street's delay. Leopard paid Allied for the substantial portion of the fuel that remained aboard the Vessel upon re-delivery. Moreover, Leopard argues that, had it known of Allied's unpaid bill, it would have exercised its rights under the charter agreement by liening the Vessel's cargoes and bringing an arbitration action against Allied…However, because Easy Street waited until after Allied was declared bankrupt to pursue the lien, Leopard would have had to pursue an arbitration in London against an entity in Greek bankruptcy proceedings or assert a claim in the bankruptcy proceedings. The parties agree that asserting a claim in the bankruptcy proceedings would be futile…

Easy Street argues that there was no prejudice to Leopard because the Greek court retroactively declared Allied bankrupt beginning on January 1, 2012. Thus, if Easy Street had arrested the vessel anytime after January 1, 2012, Leopard would still be in its current position: with its Vessel arrested and no practical recourse against Allied. But the relevant inquiry here is not whether Leopard was harmed by Easy Street's delay before or after a certain time. The question is whether Leopard was harmed, at any time, in ways that could have been prevented by Easy Street taking action. If harms had occurred but Easy Street still timely brought its claim, then Leopard would bear the costs of the harms. But if a lienholder waits for too long with no excuse, it must bear the prejudicial costs.

Because Leopard has adequately demonstrated both inexcusable delay by Easy Street and prejudice to Leopard, and there are no material facts in dispute, the Court concludes that enforcement of Easy Street's lien is barred by laches, grants Leopard's motion for summary judgment, and denies Easy Street's motion for summary judgment.

Note: Private Sale and Laches

The private sale of a vessel to a bona fide purchaser without notice or knowledge of pre-existing liens does not result in the extinction of the liens. However, in appropriate circumstances, a court may conclude that the lien sought to be enforced against the purchaser has been extinguished by laches. *See The Dredge Gloucester (McLaughlin v. The Dredge Gloucester)*, 230 F. Supp. 623, 1964 AMC 2123 (D.N.J. 1964):

> Where a maritime lien is to be enforced to the detriment of a bona fide purchaser without notice, the libellant must act with extraordinary diligence. As against such a purchaser such lien will be lost in equity after the lapse of a much shorter period of time under the doctrine of laches, than under analogous limitation statutes.

* * *

In *Robert Gaskin*, 9 F. 62 (E.D. Mich. 1881), where the libellant let 6 years elapse before filing his libel, the vessel having been within the jurisdiction several times and further, the vessel having been sold to a bona fide purchaser having no knowledge of the claim, it was held that libellant could not recover even though the libel had been filed before the sale, but process not effected until 3 months thereafter. In *The Lauretta*, 9 F. 622 (D. N.J. 1881), at page 624, the following is aptly stated:

> There is no explanation of the delay in the present case. The alleged liability of the vessel was incurred in August 1876. Nearly two years elapsed before the libel was filed. In the meantime the vessel was transferred to the claimant, without notice of the lien. She was within reach of the process of the courts (Philadelphia oyster rader in Delaware River and Bay), if the libellant had made nay effort to hold her. I am clearly of the opinion that he ought no now be allowed to collect his claim out of the property of an innocent purchaser, and that the libel must be dismissed.' (Parenthesis supplied.)

---

2. Comparison: Foreign Attachment and Actions in Rem

BELCHER CO. OF ALABAMA, INC. v. M/V MARATHA MARINER

724 F.2d 1161, 1984 AMC 1679 (5th Cir. 1984)

Alvin B. RUBIN, Circuit Judge [The facts are stated *supra*.]

* * *

The Fourth Circuit has held that the judicial sale of a vessel in a Mexican bankruptcy action was sufficiently similar in substance to an American *in rem* action to remove an *in rem* lien on the vessel. *Gulf and Southern Terminal Corp. v. The SS President Roxas*, 701 F.2d 1110 (4th Cir.), *cert. denied*, 462 U.S. 1133, 103 S.Ct. 3115, 77 L. Ed. 2d 1369 (1983). In that case, the Mexican bankruptcy court had possession of the vessel, and sold it "free of encumbrances." The sale erased the lien despite the fact that Mexican law does not provide explicitly for an *in rem* proceeding both because the procedures employed were "virtually identical to those which are denominated as an *in rem* proceeding under American law" and because "the vessel was an asset of the bankrupt, under the control and proper jurisdiction of the Mexican court." *Id.* 701 F.2d at 112. A bankruptcy court that has possession of any property has the power to sell the property free and clear of liens.[7]

Attachment does in many respects resemble arrest. In each proceeding the vessel is seized and it may later be sold to satisfy a judgment. In each, the vessel itself may be released and other security substituted. Nevertheless, not only do the issues in the two actions differ; the basic theory on which each is brought is different. In the in *rem* proceeding the owner bears no personal liability. The vessel is sold solely to satisfy the lien. If the proceeds of the sale are inadequate, there is no liability on the owner's part for the residue. Indeed the admiralty court will not render a personal judgment against the owner in excess of the amount of the release bond.[8] Only a personal action against the owner can establish such liability. In the attachment action, the object of the action is a personal judgment for the full sum due. The vessel is seized only to compel the owner's appearance by subjecting to the courts control property within its territorial jurisdiction. If the proceeds of sale of the vessel do not satisfy the judgment, the owner remains liable for the balance of the debt.

Chowgule asserts that, when it provided security to release the vessel from attachment, this discharged the lien. With respect to the lien sought to be enforced, the release does transfer the lien from the vessel to the fund represented by the bond or letter of undertaking.[9] This does not imply that release from an attachment likewise clears the lien. An execution sale in an in *rem* proceeding clears the vessel of all liens.[10] An execution sale pursuant to a writ of attachment is not, however, the equivalent of a judicial sale in admiralty. The ship is not sold free of all liens; instead only the owner's interest, whatever it may be, is adjudicated.[11] Indeed, it could not do so, for the attachment bond does not substitute for a lien but only for the owner's personal liability.

In its analysis of the *lis alibis pendens* argument, the district court correctly stated the applicable rule: a court having jurisdiction should exercise it unless a compelling reason not to do so is demonstrated. It found compelling reason, however, in the supposed hardship on Chowgule of defending two actions and in the possibility of double recovery. Both of these can readily be averted without the damage to Belcher that dismissal occasions. The Netherlands action has been tried and is awaiting decision. Staying proceedings in this action would avoid repetitive litigation of the issues there involved. If Belcher prevails, its judgment will be satisfied out of the security posted in that court. Thus both the expense of the second litigation and the possibility of double liability will be averted. If Chowgule prevails in the Netherlands action, its undertaking will be released and only those issues unique to the in *rem* action need be determined in the United States court. If, on the other hand, this action is dismissed and Belcher fails to prevail in the Netherlands action, it will be deprived of an opportunity to prove its claim in *rem*. No hardship is imposed on Chowgule by continuing the action, for the same undertaking posted in the Netherlands stands as security for the in *rem* action.

---

[7] *Matter of Buchman*, 600 F.2d 160, 165 (8th Cir. 1979).

[8] *The Susana*, 2 F.2d 410, 412-13 (4th Cir. 1924); *Red Star Towing & Transp. Co.*, 5 F. Supp. 502 (E.D.N.Y. 1933); G. GILMORE & C. BLACK, *supra*, at 802.

In a few cases, however, owners appearing in an *in rem* action to contest the libelants' claims have been "treated as if they had been brought into court by personal process" and held personally liable for judgment in excess of the security. *The Fairisle*, 76 F. Supp. 27,34 (D. Md. 1947), *aff'd subnom. Waterman S.S. Corp. v. Dean*, 171 F.2d408 (4th Cir. 1948) (quoted in *Treasure Salvors v. The Unidentified Wrecked and Abandoned Sailing Vessel*, 569 F.2d 330, 335 (5th Cir. 1978)); *see also Mosher v. Tate*, 182 F.2d 475, 479-80 (9th Cir. 1950); G. Gilmore & C. Black, *supra*, at 802-02.

[9] *Gray v. Hopkins-Carter Hardware Co. (The Lois)*, 32 F.2d 876, 878 (5th Cir. 1929); G. GILMORE & C. BLACK, *supra*, at 799.

[10] *The Trenton*, 4 F. 657 (E.D. Mich. 1880); *Zimmern Coal Co. v. Coal Trading Association of Rotterdam (The Totilax Harold)*, 30 F.2d 933 (5th Cir. 1929); *G. Gilmore & C. Black*, *supra*, at 787, *et seq.*

[11] G. GILMORE & C. BLACK, *supra*, at 802.

For these reasons the judgment is REVERSED and the case is REMANDED for further proceedings consistent with this opinion.

Note: Judicial Sale

Ever since the decision in *The Trenton*, 4 F. 657 (E.D. Mich. 1880), it has been assumed that the judicial sale of a ship by a foreign court of competent jurisdiction discharges all maritime liens. In this case, the court declared that a foreign judgment may be impeached by the owner or other person interested by showing:

(1) that the court or officer making the sale had no jurisdiction of the subject-matter by actual seizure and custody of the thing sold. Whether it be not also essential that there should have been proper judicial proceedings upon which to found the decree, and personal or public notice of the pendency of such proceedings, it is unnecessary here to determine, since it appears that sworn petitions were filed, and notice of the pendency of the proceedings given through the newspapers, pursuant to the practice of the maritime court. (2) That the sale was made by fraudulent collusion, to which the purchaser at such sale was a party. (3) That the sale was contrary to natural justice. In case of sale by a master, the court will inquire into the circumstances and see whether it was necessary and for the interest of all concerned; but the effect of such sale to discharge liens is the same. *The Amelie*, 73 U.S. (6 Wall.) 18, 18 L. Ed. 806 (1867).

Should constitutional limitations of due process, applicable to arrests and attachments of vessels in the United States, be also applicable to proceedings before foreign courts? *See* Chapter on Admiralty Jurisdiction and Procedure.

A vessel may be attached and sold by a state court in the same way as any other things that belong to a debtor. Such a sale, however, does not extinguish maritime liens. *See The Winnebago*, 205 U.S. 354, 27 S.Ct. 509, 51 L. Ed. 836 (1907); *The Gazelle*, 10 Fed. Cas. 127, No. 5, 289 (D. Mass. 1858). Likewise, a sale under a state forfeiture statute does not extinguish maritime liens. *See Bard v. The Silver Wave*, 98 F. Supp. 271, 1951 AMC 1079 (D. Md. 1951).

---

3. Effect of Sale by Foreign Court of Competent Jurisdiction

ATLANTIC SHIP SUPPLY, INC. v. M/V LUCY

392 F. Supp. 179 (M.D. Fla. 1975)

KRENTZMAN, District Judge

* * *

The primary issue which this Court was called upon to resolve was the effect of the sale of a Costa Rican flag vessel by a Costa Rican Court with respect to maritime liens (46 USCA § 941) existing in favor of American suppliers which antedated such sale. For the reasons hereinafter stated, this Court holds that the maritime liens asserted by plaintiff and intervening plaintiff's were extinguished by the sale of the vessel by the Second Civil Court of San Jose, Costa Rica. Having heard the evidence without a jury, the Court makes the following findings of fact:

The plaintiff, Atlantic Ship Supply, Inc., is a Florida corporation and brings this action to foreclose its maritime lien against the M/V LUCY (formerly the M/V EL CENTROAMERICANO) for supplies and necessaries furnished to that vessel in the Port of Tampa, Florida, between January 16 and January 24, 1973 in the total amount of $8,242.63.

Intervening plaintiff, Metro Stevedores, Inc., is a Florida corporation and brings this action to foreclose its maritime lien against the M/V LUCY for stevedoring services supplied to that vessel at the Port of Tampa, Florida, between January 17 and January 24, 1973, in the total amount of $8,886.00.

Intervening plaintiff, Central Oil Company, Inc., is a Florida corporation and brings this action to foreclose its maritime lien against the M/V LUCY for diesel oil and intermediate fuel oil supplied to that vessel at the Port of Tampa, Florida, on or about January 1, 1973, in the total amount of $6,348.03.

Claimant, Hercules Trading Company, S.A. Panama, is a Panamanian corporation and is the present owner of the M/V LUCY and derives its title to such vessel from a Mr. George Lymberopoulos, who was the successful bidder at a public auction of that vessel which was held in Costa Rica on July 27, 1973, pursuant to Court order.

On or about the 27th day of March, 1974, the M/V LUCY (formerly the EL CENTROAMERICANO) was arrested in Tampa, Florida, by the United States Marshal pursuant to process issued out of this Court pursuant to Supplemental Admiralty and Maritime Rule C, and was at all times relevant to this lawsuit properly within the jurisdiction of this Court.

Claimant, Hercules Trading Co., S.A. Panama, after the arrest of said vessel in Tampa, Florida, made claim to that vessel and appeared in this action to defend its interests,and upon the consent of all the parties to this action,said vessel was released from arrest by order of this Court, it appearing that satisfactory security had been posted to secure the liens of the plaintiff and the intervening plaintiff's herein.

* * *

The M/V LUCY (formerly the EL CENTROAMERICANO) was at the time of the services provided by the plaintiff and intervening plaintiff's, a vessel of Costa Rican Registry engaged in general commerce. On the 5th day of March, 1973, an action was commenced in the Second Civil Court of San Jose, Costa Rica, by Citizens & Southern International Bank, an American banking corporation, to foreclose a first preferred ship's mortgage on the M/V LUCY which was duly recorded in accordance with Costa Rican law.

Pursuant to said action, the Second Civil Court of San Jose, Costa Rica, ordered that the M/V LUCY be"embargoed" which in our parlance is equivalent to arrest. On March 10, 1973, the M/V LUCY was duly arrested while she lay in territorial waters of Costa Rica at the Port of Puerto Limon, Costa Rica.

Plaintiff and intervening plaintiff's argue that:

1. The sale of the vessel did not comply with the formalities of Costa Rican law in that notice of the proceedings was never published in the Judicial Bulletin in conformity with Article 579 of the Commercial Code of 1964 and that therefore, such proceedings were void;

2. Even if such proceedings were not void under Costa Rican law by reason of failure to publish notice thereof in the Judicial Bulletin, the failure to publish offends our traditional Constitutional protections of notice and an opportunity to be heard, and therefore, this Court should not give its judgment full faith and credit or comity; and,The proceedings in Costa Rica were analogous to our common law mortgage foreclosure proceedings and are therefore only binding on the parties before the Court and not strangers to such proceedings who were neither present and who did not have actual notice thereof.

Costa Rican Law

Article 579 of the Costa Rican Commercial Code of 1964, upon which plaintiffs rely to support their contention that Costa Rican law requires publication of notice of proceedings, only requires such publication when a known person cannot be located by the Court. It does not require publication of notice of the proceedings to the world at large. (*Compare* Supplemental Admiralty and Maritime Rule C(4)). This interpretation is supported by a reading of the relevant Article an the testimony of claimant's expert witness, Fernando Fournier, who fully explained the relevant Article and its interpretation in Costa Rica.

Notice and an Opportunity to be Heard

Plaintiffs' argument that they were denied our Constitutional protection of notice and an opportunity to be heard has been decided by the Fifth Circuit Court of Appeals in *Zimmern Coal v. Coal Trading Association of Rotterdam*, 30 F.2d 933 (5th Cir. 1929).

In that case a supplier of coal arrested a vessel to enforce a maritime lien after the vessel had been sold at a judicial sale in Holland. Its lien, like the ones at bar, *ante-dated* the sale. Dutch law, like Costa Rican law, did not require publication of notice of the proceedings, and the Court held that the failure to publish did not affect the validity of the sale.

It is not publication of notice of the proceedings which is the notice required by law. Seizure of the thing itself is the constructive notice which makes the decree of an admiralty court in an *in rem* proceeding binding on the entire world. A person having an interest in the *res* has constructive notice of its seizure. 2 Benedict on Admiralty § 231 (6th Ed.)

The evidence at trial was clear that the plaintiffs could have intervened in Costa Rica to protect their lien interests. Others did so. The fact that they may not have had actual notice of the proceedings is not controlling because they did have constructive notice.

The Nature of the Costa Rican Proceedings

Plaintiffs argue that the Costa Rican proceedings were not *in rem* but were *in personam* and were analogous to our common law mortgage foreclosure proceedings.

It must first be stated that it is a recognized principle of admiralty that the sale of a vessel by a court with admiralty jurisdiction gives title to the purchaser good against the entire world:

> That the sale of a vessel made pursuant to the decree of a foreign court of admiralty will be held valid in every other country, and will vest a clear and indefeasible title in the purchaser, is entirely settled, both in England and America.... (cites omitted) *The Trenton*, 4 Fed. 657, 659 (E.D. Mich. 1880)

* * *

This Court is of the ... opinion that the Costa Rican proceedings were truly *in rem:* The *res* was in the jurisdiction and under the control of a Court having the power to adjudicate its disposition. The Courts decree or Edict specified that the vessel was sold "free of encumbrances". And the proceedings were directed at the *res* because under Costa Rican law the litigants had to first exhaust their remedies against the property before they could look to any satisfaction *in personam*. For the foregoing reasons the Court makes the following additional findings of fact:

The Second Civil Court of San Jose does have admiralty and maritime jurisdiction, and this jurisdiction derives from Book III of the Costa Rican Commercial Code of 1853.

The Commercial Code of 1853 provides in pertinent part that if a vessel is sold through judicial intervention that the purchaser at the sale of that vessel receives title to it free and clear of all liens and encumbrances.

Under Costa Rican law a first preferred mortgage on a vessel such as the one in favor of the Citizens & Southern International Bank creates a maritime lien on that vessel, and foreclosure of such lien, under Costa Rican law, renders to the purchaser at a public auction title free and clear of all liens and encumbrances.

The Second Civil Court of San Jose exercised its maritime jurisdiction with respect to the M/V LUCY.

All the procedural requirements of Costa Rican law were complied with in this instance, and the M/V LUCY was duly sold by Court order at public auction on July 27, 1973, and the purchaser at that sale, Mr. George Lymberopoulos, received title to the M/V LUCY free and clear of all maritime liens and encumbrances, including those of the plaintiff and intervening plaintiff's in this cause.

The Court further finds that under Costa Rican law a foreign judgment or decree is entitled to full faith and credit and that this Court should give equal treatment to the judgment and decree of the Court of Costa Rica which had subject matter jurisdiction and properly exercised that jurisdiction in this instance.

---

4. Admiralty and Bankruptcy

Notes

1. *Jurisdiction*

A petition in bankruptcy does not extinguish maritime liens. The automatic stay of all other proceedings mandated by the Bankruptcy Code, 11 U.S.C. § 362(a), applies to admiralty proceedings *in rem*. *In re Louisiana Ship Management, Inc.*, 761 F.2d 1025, 1985 AMC 2667 (5ᵗʰ Cir. 1985). Upon filing of a bankruptcy petition, the bankruptcy court has exclusive jurisdiction over the debtor's property, including any vessels that have been subject to arrest pursuant to *in rem* proceedings. *U.S. v. Le Bouf Bros. Towing Co., Inc.*, 45 B.R. 887, 1985 AMC 1956 (E.D. La. 1985). It is possible for concurrent jurisdiction in admiralty and bankruptcy to exist if *in rem* proceedings in admiralty are brought while the vessel is subject to the exclusive jurisdiction of the bankruptcy court. *Peter Pan Seafoods, Inc. v. M/V Polar Viking*, 446 F. Supp. 1283, 1978 AMC 2606 (W.D. Wash. 1977). *See generally* Frank R. Kennedy, *Jurisdictional Problems Between Admiralty and Bankruptcy Courts*, 59 Tul. L. Rev. 1182, 1182-1211 (1985).

2. *Bankruptcy and Reorganization*

Neither bankruptcy nor reorganization results in extinction of maritime liens. *See In re Sterling Navigation Co. Ltd. (The Regal Sword)*, 31 B.R. 619, 1983 AMC 2240 (S.D.N.Y. 1983). A maritime lien on subfreights for breach of charter party is not subject to Article 9 of the Uniform Commercial Code and has priority over the trustee without need to file.

One bankruptcy court has held that the automatic stay bars a lienholder from seizing a vessel in which the debtor has any legal or equitable interest, including a vessel under time charter to the debtor. *In re American Trading & Shipping, Inc.*, 24 B.R. 32 (Bankr. S.D. Fla. 1982).

Is the "pragmatic" approach to the conflict of bankruptcy and admiralty workable? In the 1978 legislation Congress apparently intended that bankruptcy courts consider not only matters directly related to the debtor's reorganization and bankruptcy but also any litigation to which the debtor is a party. 28 U.S.C. §§ 1471 and 1481. This means that splintered jurisdiction between admiralty and bankruptcy was eliminated and that *in rem* actions to enforce maritime liens must either be halted or continued in the bankruptcy court upon the filing of the debtor's bankruptcy petition. However, this broadening of jurisdiction of the bankruptcy courts was thrown into doubt by *Northern Pipeline Construction Co. v. Marathon Pipeline Co.*, 458 U.S. 50, 102 S.Ct. 2858, 73 L. Ed. 2d 598 (1982), which held that the bankruptcy courts could not constitutionally entertain Article III litigation because the judges were not granted life tenure. It is expected that curative legislation will remove this problem and that bankruptcy courts will in the future be able to assume complete jurisdiction over a vessel and will be able to enjoin proceedings against a vessel in any other forum.

---

5. *Waiver*

THE FEDERAL MARITIME LIEN ACT

46 U.S.C. § 971, *et seq.*

(Superseded Version)

§ 974. Waiver of Right to Lien

Nothing in this chapter shall be construed to prevent the furnisher of repairs, supplies, towage, use of dry dock or marine railway, or other necessaries, or the mortgagee, from waiving his right to a lien, or in the case of a preferred mortgage lien, to the preferred status of such lien, at any time by agreement or otherwise; and this chapter shall not be construed to affect the rules of law existing on June 5, 1920, in regard to (1) the right to proceed against the vessel for advances, (2) laches in the enforcement of liens upon vessels, (3) the right to proceed *in personam*, (4) the rank of preferred maritime liens among themselves, or (5) priorities between maritime liens and mortgages, other than preferred mortgage, upon vessels of the United States. *a. Current Statutory Provisions Relating to Maritime Liens*

Commercial Instruments and Maritime Liens

46 U.S.C. § 31301, *et seq.*

§ 31305. Waiver of Lien Rights

This chapter does not prevent a mortgagee or other lien holder from waiving or subordinating at any time by agreement or otherwise the lien holder s right to a lien, the priority or, if a preferred mortgage lien, the preferred status of the lien.

MARITREND, INC. v. SERAC & CO. (SHIPPING) LTD

348 F.3d 469, 2003 AMC 2743 (5th Cir. 2003)

DENNIS, Circuit Judge

Maritrend, Inc., appeals the district courts ruling that it waived its maritime lien on a vessel to which it had provided stevedoring services. We reverse and remand this case for the entry of judgment in favor of Maritrend on its *in rem* claim against the vessel.

I. BACKGROUND

In July 2000, Maritrend contracted with Serac & Company (Shipping) Ltd. ("Serac"), the agent for an undisclosed charterer, to provide stevedoring services to the M/V SEVILLA WAVE in the Port of New Orleans. After providing those services, Maritrend sent invoices to Serac but never received payment.

Seeking to recover the value of its services, Maritrend filed an *in personam* action against Serac in the United States District Court for the Eastern District of Louisiana. Maritrend later amended its complaint to add an *in rem* claim against the SEVILLA WAVE, which it simultaneously seized. Pimpernel Shipping Company, Ltd. ("Pimpernel"), claimed ownership of the vessel and filed an answer to the amended complaint.

After a full bench trial, the district court found Serac liable *in personam* to Maritrend for the claimed amount, $73,104.80, plus interest. But the court rejected Maritrend s *in rem* claim against the SEVILLA WAVE, concluding that Maritrend had relied solely on Serac's credit for payment for its stevedoring services and had therefore waived its maritime lien against the vessel. Maritrend timely appealed.

II. ANALYSIS

* * *

B. Creation and Waiver of Federal Maritime Liens

Congress enacted the Federal Maritime Lien Act ("FMLA") in 1910 to bring uniformity to the law governing maritime liens. Although Congress recodified the FMLA in 1988 as part of the Commercial Instruments and Maritime Liens Act ("CIMLA"), it did not make any substantive changes to the law. Section 31342(a) of the current codification provides that a person providing necessaries to a vessel on the order of the owner or a person authorized by the owner—(1) has a maritime lien on the vessel; (2) may bring a civil action in rem to enforce the lien; and (3) is not required to allege or prove in the action that credit was given to the vessel.

"Necessaries" include stevedoring services, and there is no dispute here that Maritrend provided such services to the SEVILLA WAVE. It is likewise undisputed that Serac had the authority to procure necessaries, including stevedoring services, for the SEVILLA WAVE. The only question before us is whether Maritrend relied on the credit of the SEVILLA WAVE for payment for its services.

Prior to the initial passage of the FMLA, "the law was settled that a federal maritime lien could arise only for necessaries furnished in reliance upon the credit of the vessel. Credit to the ship, as distinguished from credit to the owner, was essential to the existence of a maritime lien." *Equilease Corp. v. M/V SAMPSON,* 793 F.2d 598, 605 (5th Cir. 1986) (en banc). Although § 31342(a)(3) of the CIMLA, like former § 971 of the FMLA, provides that the supplier "is not required to allege or prove ... that credit was given to the vessel," the Supreme Court has held that this language "serve[s] only to remove from the creditor the burden of proving that he had relied on the credit of the vessel." *Id.* (discussing *Piedmont & George's Creek Coal Co. v. Seaboard Fisheries Co.,* 254 U.S. 1, 41 S.Ct. 1, 65 L.Ed. 97 (1920)). We have therefore recognized that "the idea of credit to the vessel being a prerequisite to a lien, and the concomitant principle that credit to the owner negates the lien, are still very much with us today." *Equilease,* 793 F.2d at 605. Thus, under § 31342(a), "a presumption arises that one furnishing supplies to a vessel acquires a maritime lien, and the party attacking this presumption has the burden of establishing that the personal credit of the owner or charterer was solely relied upon." *Id.* "To meet this burden, evidence must be produced that would permit the inference that the supplier purposefully intended to forego the lien." *Id.* at 606.

Because the statutory presumption in favor of a maritime lien is a strong one, we are usually reluctant to conclude that a supplier has waived its lien. We have held that the supplier's primary reliance on the personal credit of a charterer is insufficient to rebut the statutory presumption. For example, in *Gulf Trading & Transportation Co. v. The Vessel HOEGH SHIELD ("HOEGH SHIELD")*658 F.2d 363, 364-65 (5th Cir. Unit A Oct. 1981), the plaintiff brought an *in rem* action against a vessel to which it had supplied fuel within the territorial jurisdiction of the United States pursuant to a contract with the vessels English charterer. After delivering the fuel, the plaintiff sent an invoice to the charterer in London, but the charterer never made payment. In the action against the vessel, the vessels owner argued that the plaintiff had waived its maritime lien because: (1) according to the deposition testimony of the plaintiff's credit agent, the fuel was supplied on the charterer's credit; (2) there had been no conversations between the plaintiff and the vessels owner; (3) the plaintiff never sent an invoice to the vessels owner; and (4) the plaintiff took no action against the vessel until the charterer became insolvent. Although these facts clearly indicated that the plaintiff was relying on the charterer's credit when it supplied the fuel, we held that they were insufficient to establish sole reliance on that credit or to permit an inference that the plaintiff purposefully intended to forgo its lien on the vessel.

Similarly, we concluded in *Gulf Oil Trading Co. v. M/V CARLBE MAR* 658 F.2d 363, 364-65 (5th Cir. Unit A Oct.1981), that sole reliance on personal credit, as opposed to the credit of the vessel, was not established even though the creditor had a long-term business relationship with the charterer, had extended large amounts of credit to the charterer in the past, and was aware of the prohibition of lien clause in the contract. Thus, "the simple existence of a business relationship and credit arrangements could hardly be realistically construed as an intent or purpose by [the creditor] to waive its lien on the vessel." *Id.*

Despite our prior caselaw reiterating the difficulty of proving that a creditor has waived its lien, two cases subsequent to *Hoegh Shield* and *Gulf Oil Trading Co.* identify the circumstances that support a finding of waiver. In *Equilease Corp. v. M/V SAMPSON,* this court determined that sufficient evidence exists to find that a creditor waives its right to a federal maritime lien when a creditor's testimony that he relied solely on entities besides the vessel for credit is combined with unambiguous statements in the creditor's original brief indicating the credit relied on was not the vessel's. The fact that the creditor also testified that "[t]here was no intent for us to give up anything" did not disturb the district court's finding that any federal maritime lien that existed was waived because the bulk of the evidence and testimony showed that creditor did not rely on the credit of the vessel.

In *Racal Survey U.S.A., Inc. v. M/V COUNT FLEET,* 231 F.3d 183, 189 this court found that a creditor had clearly indicated its intent to forgo a federal maritime lien based on the testimony of the creditor company's president. When asked whether the creditor was relying on the credit of the ship, the creditor's president testified that there was no reliance because the customer was a stevedoring company, not the vessel or the vessels' owner, and thus he had no contract or dealings with the ship. In finding waiver, this court stated that "[a]lmost nothing is more conclusive than such testimony" on the critical issue of the reliance necessary to preserve the lien. *Id.* at 190.

Taken together, *Equilease* and *Racal Survey* stand for the proposition that testimony regarding which party a creditor relied on can be determinative of whether the maritime lien was waived. But those decisions did not weaken the heavy burden placed on the party attacking the presumption. If the evidence shows that the claimant relied on the credit of the vessel *to some extent,* we will not find a waiver of the maritime lien.

C. The Evidence at Trial and Review of the District Court's Decision

A bench trial in this case was held on January 14, 2002. At trial, the district court heard testimony and was presented exhibits on behalf of both parties. Maritrend president William Bergeron ("Bergeron") testified that Maritrend "initially reil[ies] upon the contract that we have with the party, but we always rely on a maritime lien right," as a "fallback position." Indeed, in his testimony, Bergeron attests to this belief at least five times. Bergeron also indicated that he thought Serac owned the vessel to which Maritrend was providing stevedoring services. Similarly, Donald Broussard, an employee at Maritrend, testified that "the first course of action" was always to recover payment from Serac, but if it failed to pay, the company "implemented vessel seizure procedures." Finally, Petra Smith, Maritrend's vice president, testified that it was her responsibility to collect delinquent and overdue invoices for stevedoring services and that she only contacted Serac, as opposed to the owner's or managers of the SEVILLA WAVE, for payment.

Among the exhibits offered at trial were the tariff document and copies of invoices. The tariff document, which was part of the stevedoring services contract, was prepared by Maritrend and placed on file with the Board of Commissioners of the Port of New Orleans. The tariff document does not explicitly state that the SEVILLA WAVE was responsible for stevedoring services, however, as the district court noted, there was no indication in the tariff document or any of the record evidence that Maritrend intended to waive its federal maritime lien. While the invoices were not sent directly to the SEVILLA WAVE, they indicated on their face that the charges contained therein were made "FOR THE ACCOUNT OF THE OWNER(S)/AGENT(S) AND/OR CHARTERER(S) OF THE M/V SEVILLA WAVE." There is no language on the invoices that indicates any intent to waive a maritime lien.

In holding for Pimpernel, the district court found that the trial testimony established that "Maritrend relied solely on the credit of Serac, its customer, for payment of [the stevedoring] services." It rested its decision on the both testimonial and documentary evidence. The principal testimony that the district court relied on was the testimony that Maritrend failed to seek payment from the vessel until several months after non-payment by Serac and that Maritrend expected its customer, Serac, to pay the invoices. The district court also noted that the documentary evidence supported its conclusion because Maritrend's invoices were only addressed and sent to Serac and the tariff document was silent as to whether the vessel was responsible for stevedoring charges.

The district court also stated that in light of our decisions in *Racal Survey* and *Equilease*, it was bound to rule against Maritrend. It decided this despite the fact that it found Bergerons testimony that Maritrend always relied on the credit of the vessel as a fallback position when providing stevedoring services was "completely credible," and "the record evidence did not suggest any reason that Maritrend would relinquish its right to a lien."

After reviewing the record and applicable case law, we find that there was insufficient evidence adduced at trial to overcome the presumption that Maritrend relied on the credit of the SEVILLA WAVE with respect to the stevedoring services it provided in order to preserve a federal maritime lien. This court has repeatedly indicated the strength of the maritime lien presumption, especially in traditional areas such as stevedoring. *See Atlantic & Gulf Stevedores, Inc. v. M/V GRAND LOYALTY*, 608 F.2d 197, 201 (5th Cir. 1979). Such a strong presumption in favor of a lien places a "heavy burden" on parties seeking to show a waiver of the lien, forcing them to show that a creditor "*deliberately intended* to forego the valuable privilege which the law accords and look solely to the owner's personal credit." *Gulf Oil Trading Co.*, 757 F.2d at 750 (emphasis in original) (citations and internal quotation marks omitted). Neither *Equilease Corp.* nor *Racal Survey* weakens this presumption or the burden placed on the party attacking the presumption.

In applying this standard, this court has found testimonial evidence sufficient to defeat this presumption only in cases where testimony *"clearly indicate[d]* that [the creditor] did not rely on the credit of the vessels," *Racal Survey*, 231 F.3d at 190 (emphasis added) and there was no other evidence, testimonial or otherwise, supporting the creditors reliance on the vessel. Furthermore, this court has found evidence such as only invoicing the charterer or a long-standing business relationship with the charterer to be inadequate to show that a creditor relied solely on such charterer. *Gulf Oil Trading Co.*, 757 F.2d at 750.

Here, neither testimonial nor documentary evidence supports the conclusion that Maritrend "solely relied" on the credit of Serac. First, although the testimony as a whole shows that Maritrend relied on Serac for payment, it also shows that Maritrend did not rely solely on Serac because it was aware of and generally relied upon its maritime lien rights against the SEVILLA WAVE. Bergeron, who the district court found "completely credible," testified that Maritrend always intended to rely on the credit of the vessel as a "fallback" position. This testimony was further supported by Broussard's statement that Maritrend's practice was to implement ship seizure procedures when invoices for stevedoring services were not timely paid. Therefore, this situation is unlike the cases in *Equilease* and *Racal Survey*, where there was clear testimonial evidence by the party seeking to impose a federal maritime lien that it did not rely on the credit of the vessel.

Second, the documents presented to the district court provide no evidence that Maritrend did not rely on the credit of the vessel. As discussed above, invoicing only the charterer is not dispositive because it only shows that a party attempted to receive the payment from the charterer first, not that it never intended to rely on the credit of the vessel. It is true that the tariff document expressly identifies certain charges to be applied to the vessel and that this list does not include stevedoring services. Again, this only shows that Serac, the charterer, was initially responsible for the stevedoring payments. Nothing in the tariff document shows that Maritrend did not intend to seek payment from the vessel in the event that Serac failed to pay. Therefore, these documents are insufficient to overcome the strong presumption that a federal maritime lien exists when necessaries, such as stevedoring services, are provided to a vessel.

In sum, we disagree that our decisions in *Equilease* and *Racal Survey* compelled the district court to rule against Maritrend based on these case facts. As the district court observed, Maritrend's resorting to its lien only after Serac defaulted is "typical of what is done in the normal course of business." If a supplier of necessaries forfeits his lien on the vessel by conducting his business in accordance with this prevailing practice, then the lien would be available only to suppliers who do not need it. Neither the CIMLA nor our cases interpreting its provisions supports such a result. The implied maritime lien is a security device, and its purpose is "to enable a vessel to obtain supplies or repairs necessary to her continued operation by giving a temporary underlying pledge of the vessel which will hold until payment can be made or more formal security given." *PROFESSOR VLADIMIR POPOV,* 199 F.3d at 223 (quoting *S. Coal & Coke Co. v. F. Grauds Kugniecibas ("The Everosa"),* 93 F.2d 732, 735 (1st Cir. 1937)). We would frustrate this purpose if we prohibited enforcement of the lien whenever the suppliers efforts to collect from the person who ordered the necessaries were unsuccessful.

Although Maritrend expected Serac to pay for the stevedoring services, and its conduct reflected that reasonable expectation, Bergerons trial testimony established that Maritrend relied on the credit of the SEVILLA WAVE as a "fallback position," which is exactly what the law contemplates. Because Pimpernel offered no evidence to rebut that testimony, and the district court did not find that testimony incredible, it could not meet its burden of proving that Maritrend relied solely on Serac's credit. We therefore hold that the district court's finding that Maritrend waived its lien on the SEVILLA WAVE was erroneous as a matter of law.

III. CONCLUSION

For the foregoing reasons, we reverse the district courts ruling that Maritrend waived its maritime lien on the SEVILLA WAVE and remand this case for the entry of judgment in favor of Maritrend on its *in rem* claim against the vessel for the value of the stevedoring services it provided.

REVERSED AND REMANDED WITH INSTRUCTIONS.

Note: Destruction and Release of the Res

A maritime lien may be extinguished by the permanent and total destruction of the *res* or by the release of the *res* on bond which is a substitute for the *res.*

For extinction of liens as a result of the destruction of the *res, see Walsh v. Tadlock,* 104 F.2d 131, 1939 AMC 1278 (9th Cir. 1939):

With the total destruction of the vessel the liens thereon were of necessity extinguished. 38 C.J.S. 1247. These liens did not attach to the proceeds of the insurance, nor did appellants' lien on the boat per se entitle them to participate in the division of the insurance money.... Their right to do that was dependent on the contract of insurance.

When the destruction of the *res* is only partial, maritime liens continue to burden the part that remains. *See Chapman v. Engines of Greenpoint,* 38 F. 671 (S.D.N.Y. 1889). Likewise, when a vessel is dismantled and reassembled, maritime liens persist. *See Dann v. Dredge Sandpiper,* 222 F. Supp. 838 (D. Del. 1963). In such a case, the destruction of the *res* is not permanent.

For release of a vessel on bond, *see Hawgood & Avery Transit Co. v. Dingman,* 94 F. 1011 (8th Cir. 1899):

When a ship which has been arrested under a libel is released upon an appraisal and a deposit, or a bond, or a stipulation, not given under the limited liability act, the deposit or bond or stipulation is substituted for the vessel as to all those who have then filed their libels and become parties to the proceedings but as to no other parties. The proceeds of the deposit, bond, or stipulation inure to the benefit of those who were parties to the proceeding when the release was made. But they inure to the benefit of no others. The vessel is discharged from the liens of these parties, and upon their liens only. Lienholders who have not filed their libels, and have not become parties to the proceeding when the ship is discharged, may not be permitted to share in the proceeds of the deposit or bond or stipulation, and their liens are neither detached nor affected by the release. The vessel returns to the claimant subject to the maritime liens of all who were not parties to the proceeding before the discharge was made, and they may libel and arrest her to enforce their liens to the same extent and with the same effect as though she had never been seized before.

For the effect that a judgment *in personam* may have on maritime liens, *see Pratt v. United States,* 340 F.2d 174, 1967 AMC 1302 (4th Cir. 1964).

Note: *Res judicata*

In *Marine Oil Trading Ltd v. M/V Sea Charm,* 2003 AMC 882 (E.D. La, 2003), plaintiff proceeded *in rem* in the U.S. District Court for the Eastern District of Louisiana against the *Sea Charm* and *in personam* against its owner, to recover a debt arising from the supply of bunkers to the ship in Montevideo, Uruguay. Plaintiff had previously proceeded against the ship *in rem* in Panama. The Panamanian Maritime Court held, and the Panamanian Supreme Court affirmed on appeal, that plaintiff had no right *in rem* against the ship because the bunker supply contract was governed by English law, which does not recognize a maritime lien for the supply of necessaries. The district court granted summary judgment for the defendants, holding that the Panamanian courts' decisions made the matter *res judicata.*

CHAPTER 5 — LIMITATION OF LIABILITY

Introductory Note

Shipowners have long been granted the privilege of being able to obtain from a court a decree granting limitation of liability with respect to marine casualties. Although the origin of this practice has been traced to the medieval sea laws, the modern law dates from 1734 in England and from 1851 in the United States. Despite increased criticism in recent years, limitation of liability remains an important part of maritime law. This section covers the process and standards contained in the basic law in the United States, The Limitation of Shipowner's Liability Act. Limitation with regard to liability for cargo damage claims and fire damage is considered in the chapter on Carriage of Goods.

A review of the law in this area can be found in the *Admiralty Law Institute Symposium on Limitation of Liability,* 53 Tul. L. Rev. 999 (1979).

A. Practice and Procedure

1. The Federal Limitation of Shipowner's Liability Act

Federal Limitation of Shipowner s Liability Act
46 U.S.C.A. §§ 30501-30512

§ 30501. Definition

In this chapter, the term "owner" includes a charterer that mans, supplies, and navigates a vessel at the charterer's own expense or by the charterer's own procurement.

§ 30502. Application

Except as otherwise provided, this chapter (except section 30503) applies to seagoing vessels and vessels used on lakes or rivers or in inland navigation, including canal boats, barges, and lighters.

§ 30503. Declaration of nature and value of goods

(a) In General—If a shipper of an item named in subsection (b), contained in a parcel, package, or trunk, loads the item as freight or baggage on a vessel, without at the time of loading giving to the person receiving the item a written notice of the true character and value of the item and having that information entered on the bill of lading, the owner and master of the vessel are not liable as carriers. The owner and master are not liable beyond the value entered on the bill of lading.

(b) Items—The items referred to in subsection (a) are precious metals, gold or silver plated articles, precious stones, jewelry, trinkets, watches, clocks, glass, china, coins, bills, securities, printings, engravings, pictures, stamps, maps, paper, silks, furs, lace, and similar items of high value and small size.

§ 30504. Loss by fire

The owner of a vessel is not liable for loss or damage to merchandise on the vessel caused by a fire on the vessel unless the fire resulted from the design or neglect of the owner.

§ 30505. General limit of liability

(a) In General—Except as provided in section 30506 of this title, the liability of the owner of a vessel for any claim, debt, or liability described in subsection (b) shall not exceed the value of the vessel and pending freight. If the vessel has more than one owner, the proportionate share of the liability of any one owner shall not exceed that owner's proportionate interest in the vessel and pending freight.

(b) Claims subject to limitation—Unless otherwise excluded by law, claims, debts, and liabilities subject to limitation under subsection (a) are those arising from any embezzlement, loss, or destruction of any property, goods, or merchandise shipped or put on board the vessel, any loss, damage, or injury by collision, or any act, matter, or thing, loss, damage, or forfeiture, done, occasioned, or incurred, without the privity or knowledge of the owner.

(c) Wages—Subsection (a) does not apply to a claim for wages.

§ 30506. Limit of liability for personal injury or death

(a) Application—This section applies only to seagoing vessels, but does not apply to pleasure yachts, tugs, towboats, towing vessels, tank vessels, fishing vessels, fish tender vessels, canal boats, scows, car floats, barges, lighters, or nondescript vessels.

(b) Minimum liability—If the amount of the vessel owner's liability determined under section 30505 of this title is insufficient to pay all losses in full, and the portion available to pay claims for personal injury or death is less than $420 times the tonnage of the vessel, that portion shall be increased to $420 times the tonnage of the vessel. That portion may be used only to pay claims for personal injury or death.

(c) Calculation of tonnage—Under subsection (b), the tonnage of a self-propellled vessel is the gross tonnage without the deduction for engine room, and the tonnage of a sailing vessel is the tonnage for documentation. However, space for the use of seamen is excluded.

(d) Claims arising on distinct occasions—Separate limits of liability apply to claims for personal injury or death arising on distinct occasions.

(e) Privity or knowledge—In a claim for personal injury or death, the privity or knowledge of the master or the owner's superintendent or managing agent, at or before the beginning of each voyage, is imputed to the owner.

§ 30507. Apportionment of losses

If the amounts determined under sections 30505 and 30506 of this title are insufficient to pay all claims—

(1) all claimants shall be paid in proportion to their respective losses out of the amount determined under section 30505 of this title; and

(2) personal injury and death claimants, if any, shall be paid an additional amount in proportion to their respective losses out of the additional amount determined under section 30506(b) of this title.

§ 30508. Provisions requiring notice of claim or limiting time for bringing action

(a) Application—This section applies only to seagoing vessels, but does not apply to pleasure yachts, tugs, towboats, towing vessels, tank vessels, fishing vessels, fish tender vessels, canal boats, scows, car floats, barges, lighters, or nondescript vessels.

(b) Minimum time limits—The owner, master, manager, or agent of a vessel transporting passengers or property between ports in the United States, or between a port in the United States and a port in a foreign country, may not limit by regulation, contract, or otherwise the period for—

(1) giving notice of, or filing a claim for, personal injury or death to less than 6 months after the date of the injury or death; or

(2) bringing a civil action for personal injury or death to less than one year after the date of the injury or death.

(d) Effect of failure to give notice—When notice of a claim for personal injury or death is required by a contract, the failure to give the notice is not a bar to recovery if—

(1) the court finds that the owner, master, or agent of the vessel had knowledge of the injury or death and the owner has not been prejudiced by the failure;

(2) the court finds there was a satisfactory reason why the notice could not have been given; or

(3) the owner of the vessel fails to object to the failure to give the notice.

(e) Tolling of period to give notice—If a claimant is a minor or mental incompetent, or if a claim is for wrongful death, any period provided by a contract for giving notice of the claim is tolled until the earlier of—

(1) the date a legal representative is appointed for the minor, incompetent, or decedents estate; or

(2) 3 years after the injury or death.

§ 30509. Provisions limiting liability for personal injury or death

(a) Prohibition—

(1) In general—The owner, master, manager, or agent of a vessel transporting passengers between ports in the United States, or between a port in the United States and a port in a foreign country, may not include in a regulation or contract a provision limiting—

(A) the liability of the owner, master, or agent for personal injury or death caused by the negligence or fault of the owner or the owner's employees or agents; or

(B) the right of a claimant for personal injury or death to a trial by court of competent jurisdiction.

(2) Voidness—A provision described in paragraph (1) is void.

(b) Emotional distress, mental suffering, and psychological injury—

(1) In general—Subsection (a) does not prohibit a provision in a contract or in ticket conditions of carriage with a passenger that relieves an owner, master, manager, agent, operator, or crewmember of a vessel from liability for infliction of emotional distress, mental suffering, or psychological injury so long as the provision does not limit such liability when the emotional distress, mental suffering, or psychological injury is—

(A) the result of physical injury to the claimant caused by the negligence or fault of a crewmember or the owner, master, manager, agent, or operator;

(B) the result of the claimant having been at actual risk of physical injury, and the risk was caused by the negligence or fault of a crewmember or the owner, master, manager, agent, or operator; or

(C) intentionally inflicted by a crewmember or the owner, master, manager, agent or operator.

(2) Sexual offenses—This subsection does not limit the liability of a crewmember or the owner, master, manager, agent, or operator of a vessel in a case involving sexual harassment, sexual assault, or rape.

§ 30510. Vicarious liability for medical malpractice with regard to crew

In a civil action by any person in which the owner or operator of a vessel or employer of a crewmember is claimed to have vicarious liability for medical malpractice with regard to a crewmember occurring at a shoreside facility, and to the extent the damages resulted from the conduct of any shoreside doctor, hospital, medical facility, or other health care provider, the owner, operator, or employer is entitled to rely on any statutory limitations of liability applicable to the doctor, hospital, medical facility, or other health care provider in the State of the United States in which the shoreside medical care was provided.

§ 30511. Action by owner for limitation

(a) Ingeneral—The owner of a vessel may bring a civil action in a district court of the United States for limitation of liability under this chapter. The action must be brought within 6 months after a claimant gives the owner written notice of a claim.

(b) Creation of Fund—When the action is brought, the owner (at the owner s option) shall—

(1) deposit with the court, for the benefit of claimants—

(A) an amount equal to the value of the owner s interest in the vessel and pending freight, or approved security; and

(B) an amount, or approved security, that the court may fix from time to time as necessary to carry out this chapter; or

(2) transfer to a trustee appointed by the court, for the benefit of claimants—

(A) the owner s interest in the vessel and pending freight; and

(B) an amount, or approved security, that the court may fix from time to time as necessary to carry out this chapter.

(c) Cessation of other actions—When an action has been brought under this section and the owner has complied with subsection (b), all claims and proceedings against the owner related to the matter in question shall cease.

§ 30512. Liability as master, officer, or seaman not affected

This chapter does not affect the liability of an individual as a master, officer, or seaman, even though the individual is also an owner of the vessel.

Federal Limitation of Shipowner's Liability Act

(Superseded Version)

46 app. U.S.C. §§ 181-189

§ 181. Liability of masters as carriers

If any shipper of platina, gold, gold dust, silver, bullion, or other precious metals, coins, jewelry, bills of any bank or public body, diamonds or other precious stones, or any gold or silver in a manufactured or unmanufactured state, watches, clocks, or timepieces of any description, trinkets, orders, notes, or securities for payment of money, stamps, maps, writings, title deeds, printings, engravings, pictures, gold or silver plate or plated articles, glass, china, silks in a manufactured or unmanufactured state, and whether wrought up or not wrought up with any other material, furs, or lace, or any of them, contained in any parcel, or package, or trunk, shall lade the same as freight or baggage, on any vessel, without at the time of such lading giving to the master, clerk, agent, or owner of such vessel receiving the same a written notice of the true character and value thereof, and having the same entered on the bill of lading therefor, the master and owner of such vessel shall not be liable as carriers thereof in any form or manner; nor shall any such master or owner be liable for any such goods beyond the value and according to the character thereof so notified and entered.

* * *

[§ 182, which deals with loss by fire, is considered in the chapter on Carriage of Goods.]

§ 183. Amount of liability: loss of life or bodily injury; privity imputed to owner; "seagoing vessel"

(a) The liability of the owner of any vessel, whether American or foreign, for any embezzlement, loss, or destruction by any person of any property, goods, or merchandise shipped or put on board of such vessel, or for any loss, damage, or injury by collision, or for any act, matter, or thing, loss, damage, or forfeiture, done, occasioned, or incurred, without the privity or knowledge of such owner or owner's, shall not, except in the cases provided for in subsection (b) of this section, exceed the amount or value of the interest of such owner in such vessel, and her freight then pending.

(b) In the case of any seagoing vessel, if the amount of the owner's liability as limited under subsection (a) of this section is insufficient to pay all losses in full, and the portion of such amount applicable to the payment of losses in respect of loss of life or bodily injury is less than $420 per ton of such vessel's tonnage, such portion shall be increased to an amount equal to $420 per ton, to be available only for the payment of losses in respect of loss of life or bodily injury. If such portion so increased is insufficient to pay such losses in full, they shall be paid therefrom in proportion to their respective amounts.

(c) For the purposes of this section the tonnage of a seagoing steam or motor vessel shall be her gross tonnage without deduction on account of engine room, and the tonnage of a seagoing sailing vessel shall be her registered tonnage: *Provided*, That there shall not be included in such tonnage any space occupied by seamen or apprentices and appropriated to their use.

(d) The owner of any such seagoing vessel shall be liable in respect of loss of life or bodily injury arising on distinct occasions to the same extent as if no other loss of life or bodily injury had arisen.

(e) In respect of loss of life or bodily injury the privity or knowledge of the master of a seagoing vessel or of the superintendent or managing agent of the owner thereof, at or prior to the commencement of each voyage, shall be deemed conclusively the privity or knowledge of the owner of such vessel.

(f) As used in subsections (b), (c), (d) and (e) of this section and in section 183b of this title, the term "seagoing vessel" shall not include pleasure yachts, tugs, towboats, towing vessels, tank vessels, fishing vessels or their tenders, self-propelled lighters, nondescript self-propelled vessels, canal boats, scows, car floats, barges, lighters, or nondescript non-self-propelled vessels, even though the same may be seagoing vessels within the meaning of such term as used in section 188 of this title.

[Former § 183a was repealed in 1936—Eds.]

§ 183b. Stipulations limiting time for filing claims and commencing suit

(a) It shall be unlawful for the manager, agent, master, or owner of any sea-going vessel (other than tugs, barges, fishing vessels and their tenders) transporting passengers or merchandise or property from or between ports of the United States and foreign ports to provide by rule, contract, regulation, or otherwise a shorter period for giving notice of, or filing claims for loss of life, or bodily injury, than six months, and for the institution of suits on such claims, than one year, such period for institution of suits to be computed from the day when the death or injury occurred.

(b) Failure to give such notice, where lawfully prescribed in such contract, shall not bar any such claim—

(1) If the owner or master of the vessel or his agent had knowledge of the injury, damage, or loss and the court determines that the owner has not been prejudiced by the failure to give such notice; nor

(2) If the court excuses such failure on the ground that for some satisfactory reason such notice could not be given; nor

(3) Unless objection to such failure is raised by the owner.

(c) If a person who is entitled to recover on any such claim is mentally incompetent or a minor, or if the action is one for wrongful death, any lawful limitation of time prescribed in such contract shall not be applicable so long as no legal representative has been appointed for such incompetent, minor, or decedents estate, but shall be applicable form the date of the appointment of such legal representative: *Provided, however*, That such appointment be made within three years after the date of such death or injury.

§ 183c. Stipulations limiting liability for negligence invalid

(a) Negligence

It shall be unlawful for the manager, agent, master, or owner of any vessel transporting passengers between ports of the United States or between any such port and a foreign port to insert in any rule, regulation, contract, or agreement any provision or limitation (1) purporting, in the event of loss of life or bodily injury arising from the negligence or fault of such owner or his servants, to relieve such owner, master, or agent from liability, or from liability beyond any stipulated amount, for such loss or injury, or (2) purporting in such event to lessen, weaken, or avoid the right of any claimant to a trial by court of competent jurisdiction on the question of liability for such loss or injury, or the measure of damages therefor. All such provisions or limitations contained in any such rule, regulation, contract, or agreement are declared to be against public policy and shall be null and void and of no effect.

(b) Infliction of emotional distress, mental suffering, or psychological injury

(1) Subsection (a) of this section shall not prohibit provisions or limitations in contracts, agreements, or ticket conditions of carriage with passengers which relieve a crewmember, manager, agent, master, owner, or operator of a vessel from liability for infliction of emotional distress, mental suffering, or psychological injury so long as such provisions or limitations do not limit such liability if the emotional distress, mental suffering, or psychological injury was—

(A) the result of physical injury to the claimant caused by the negligence or fault of a crewmember or the manager, agent, master, owner, or operator;

(B) the result of the claimant having been at actual risk of physical injury, and suchriskwas causedby the negligence or fault of a crewmember or the manager, agent, master, owner, or operator; or

(C) intentionally inflicted by a crewmember or the manager, agent, master, owner, or operator.

(2) Nothing in this subsection is intended to limit the liability of a crewmember or the manager, agent, master, owner, or operator of a vessel in a case involving sexual harassment, sexual assault, or rape.

§ 184. Apportionment of compensation

Whenever any such embezzlement, loss, or destruction is suffered by several freighters or owners of goods, wares, merchandise, or any property whatever, on the same voyage, and the whole value of the vessel, and her freight for the voyage, is not sufficient to make compensation to each of them, they shall receive compensation from the owner of the vessel in proportion to their respective losses; and for that purpose the freighters and owner's of the property, and the owner of the vessel, or any of them, may take the appropriate proceedings in any court, for the purpose of apportioning the sum for which the owner of the vessel may be liable among the parties entitled thereto.

§ 185. Petition for limitation of liability; deposit of value of interest in court; transfer of interest to trustee

The vessel owner, within six months after a claimant shall have given to or filed with such owner written notice of claim, may petition a district court of the United States of competent jurisdiction for limitation of liability within the provisions of this chapter and the owner (a) shall deposit with the court, for the benefit of claimants, a sum equal to the amount or value of the interest of such owner in the vessel and freight, or approved security therefor, and in addition such sums, or approved security therefor, as the court may from time to time fix as necessary to carry out the provisions of section 183 of this title, or (b) at his option shall transfer, for the benefit of claimants, to a trustee to be appointed by the court his interest in the vessel and freight, together with such sums, or approved security therefor, as the court may from time to time fix as necessary to carry out the provisions of section 183 of this title. Upon compliance with the requirements of this section all claims and proceedings against the owner with respect to the matter in question shall cease.

§ 186. Charterer may be deemed owner

The charterer of any vessel, in case he shall man, victual, and navigate such vessel at his own expense, or by his own procurement, shall be deemed the owner of such vessel within the meaning of the provisions of this chapter relating to the limitation of the liability of the owners of vessels; and such vessel, when so chartered, shall be liable in the same manner as if navigated by the owner thereof.

§ 187. Remedies reserved

Nothing in sections 182, 183, 184, 185 and 186 of this title shall be construed to take away or affect the remedy to which any party may be entitled, against the master, officers, or seamen, for or on account of any embezzlement, injury, loss, or destruction of merchandise, or property, put on board any vessel, or on account of any negligence, fraud, or other malversation of such master, officers, or seamen, respectively, nor to lessen or take away any responsibility to which any master or seaman of any vessel may by law be liable, notwithstanding such master or seaman may be an owner or part owner of the vessel.

§ 188. Limitation of liability of owner's applied to all vessels

Except as otherwise specifically provided therein, the provisions of sections 182, 183, 183b-187, and 189 of this title shall apply to all seagoing vessels, and also to all vessels used on lakes or rivers or in inland navigation, including canal boats, barges, and lighters.

§ 189. Limitation of liability of owner's of vessels for debts

The individual liability of a shipowner shall be limited to the proportion of any or all debts and liabilities that his individual share of the vessel bears to the whole; and the aggregate liabilities of all the owner's of a vessel on account of the same shall not exceed the value of such vessels and freight pending: *Provided*, That this provision shall not prevent any claimant from joining all the owner's in one action; nor shall the same apply to wages due to persons employed by said shipowners.

---

2. Federal Rules of Civil Procedure, Supplemental Rule F

Supplemental Admiralty Rule F of the Federal Rules of Civil Procedure, which follows, should be studied carefully to determine the procedure and content of the pleadings in a limitation action.

Rule F - Limitation of Liability

(1) *Time for Filing Complaint: Security.* Not later than six months after his receipt of a claim in writing, any vessel owner may file a complaint in the appropriate district court, as provided in subdivision (9) of this rule, for limitation of liability pursuant to statute. The owner (a) shall deposit with the court, for the benefit of claimants, a sum equal to the amount or value of his interest in the vessel and pending freight, or approved security therefor, and in addition such sums, or approved security therefor, as the court may from time to time fix as necessary to carry out the provisions of the statutes as amended; or (b) at his option shall transfer to a trustee to be appointed by the court, for the benefit of claimants, his interest in the vessel and pending freight, together with such sums, or approved security therefor, as the court may from time to time fix as necessary to carry out the provisions of the statutes as amended. The plaintiff shall also give security for costs and, if he elects to give security, for interest at the rate of 6 per cent annum from the date of the security.

(2) *Complaint.* The complaint shall set forth the facts on the basis of which the right to limit liability is asserted, and all facts necessary to enable the court to determine the amount to which the owner's liability shall be limited. The complaint my demand exoneration from as well as limitation of liability. It shall state the voyage, if any, on which the demands sought to be limited arose, with the date and place of its termination; the amount of all demands including all unsatisfied liens or claims of lien, in contract or in tort or otherwise, arising on that voyage, so far as known to the plaintiff, and what actions and proceedings, if any, are pending thereon; whether the vessel was damaged, lost, or abandoned, and, if so, when and where; the value of the vessel at the close of the voyage or, in case of wreck, the value of her wreckage, strippings, or proceeds, if any, and where and in whose possession they are; and the amount of any pending freight recovered or recoverable. If the plaintiff elects to transfer his interest in the vessel to a trustee, the complaint must further show any prior paramount liens thereon, and what voyages or trips, if any, she has made since the voyage or trip on which the claims sought to be limited arose, and any existing liens arising upon any such subsequent voyage or trip, with the amounts and causes thereof, and the names and addresses of the lienors, so far as known; and whether the vessel sustained any injury upon or by reason of such subsequent voyage or trip.

(3) *Claims Against Owner: Injunction.* Upon compliance by the owner with the requirements of subdivision (1) of this rule all claims and proceedings against the owner or his property with respect to the matter in question shall (4) cease. On application of the plaintiff the court shall enjoin the further prosecution of any action or proceeding against the plaintiff or his property with respect to any claim subject to limitation in the action.

(5) *Notice to Claimants.* Upon the owner's compliance with subdivision (1) of this rule the court shall issue a notice to all persons asserting claims with respect to which the complaint seeks limitation, admonishing them to file their respective claims with the clerk of the court and to serve on the attorneys for the plaintiff a copy thereof on or before a date to be named in the notice. For cause shown, the court may enlarge the time within which claims may be filed. The notice shall be published in such newspaper or newspapers as the court may direct once a week for four successive weeks prior to the date fixed for the filing of claims. The plaintiff not later than the day of second publication shall also mail a copy of the notice to every person known to have made any claim against the vessel or the plaintiff arising out of the voyage or trip on which the claims sought to be limited arose. In cases involving death a copy of such notice shall be mailed to the decedent at his last known address, and also to any person who shall be known to have made any claim on account of such death.

(6) *Claims and Answer.* Claims shall be filed and served on or before the date specified in the notice provided for in subdivision (4) of this rule. Each claim shall specify the facts upon which the claimant relies in support of his claim, the items thereof, and the dates on which the same accrued. If a claimant desires to contest either the right to exoneration from or the right to limitation of liability he shall file and serve an answer to the complaint unless his claim has included an answer.

(7) *Information to be Given Claimants.* Within 30 days after the date specified in the notice for filing claims, or within such time as the court thereafter may allow, the plaintiff shall mail to the attorney for each claimant (or if the claimant has no attorney to the claimant himself) a list setting forth (a) the name of each claimant, (b) the name and address of his attorney (if he is known to have one), (c) the nature of his claim, *i.e.,* whether property loss, property damage, death, personal injury, etc., and (d) the amount thereof.

(8) *Insufficiency of Fund or Security.* Any claimant may by motion demand that the funds deposited in court or the security given by the plaintiff be increased on the ground that they are less than the value of the plaintiff's interest in the vessel and pending freight. Thereupon the court shall cause due appraisement to be made of the value of the plaintiff's interest in the vessel and pending freight; and if the court finds that the deposit or security is either insufficient or excessive it shall order its increase or reduction. In like manner any claimant may demand that the deposit or security be increased on the ground that it is insufficient to carry out the provisions of the statutes relating to claims in respect of loss of life or bodily injury; and, after notice and hearing, the court may similarly order that the deposit or security be increased or reduced.

(9) *Objections to Claims: Distribution of Fund.* Any interested party may question or controvert any claim without filing an objection thereto. Upon determination of liability the fund deposited or secured, or the proceeds of the vessel and pending freight, shall be divided pro rata, subject to all relevant provisions of law, among the several claimants in proportion to the amounts of their respective claims, duly proved, saving, however, to all parties any priority to which they may be legally entitled.

(10) *Venue; Transfer.* The complaint shall be filed in any district in which the vessel has been attached or arrested to answer for any claim with respect to which the plaintiff seeks to limit liability; or, if the vessel has not been attached or arrested, then in any district in which the owner has been sued with respect to any such claim. When the vessel has not been attached or arrested to answer the matters aforesaid, and suit has not been commenced against the owner, the proceedings may be had in the district in which the vessel may be, but if the vessel is not within any district and no siut has been commenced in any district, then the complaint may be filed in any district. For the convenience of parties and witnesses, in the interest of justice, the court may transfer the action to any district; if venue is wrongly laid the court shall dismiss or, if it be in the interest of justice, transfer the action to any district in which it could have been brought. If the vessel shall have been sold, the proceeds shall represent the vessel for the purposes of these rules.

COMPLAINT OF CARIBBEAN SEA TRANSPORT, LTD.

748 F.2d 622, 1985 AMC 1995 (11th Cir. 1984)

James C. HILL, Circuit Judge

This admiralty appeal challenges the district court's order requiring the plaintiff/appellant shipowner to post security pursuant to sections 183(a) and 183(b) of the Limitation of Liability Act, 46 U.S.C. § 183 *et seq*. We affirm in part, but remand for a more complete hearing as to whether security need be posted pursuant to section 183(b).

This admiralty case arises from a collision between the M/V ANTILLES SUN (ANTILLES), a steel cargo carrier, and the CORAIN II (CORAIN). After leaving Miami on February 11, 1982, and discharging cargo at several Caribbean ports, the ANTILLES was on its way back to Miami from Kingston, Jamaica, when the collision occurred in waters off Cuba on February 24, 1982. The ANTILLES sank in deep waters where salvage was impossible. Appellee-claimant Francisco Russo, the second mate on the CORAIN, apparently suffered a back injury as a result of the collision.

On July 27, 1982, plaintiff-appellant Caribbean Sea Transport, Ltd, the owner of the ANTILLES, filed a petition for exoneration from or limitation of liability in the district court, pursuant to 46 U.S.C. § 183 *et seq*. and Rule F of the Supplemental Rules for Certain Admiralty and Maritime Claims (Admiralty Rules). Claims against the ANTILLES were then filed by cargo shippers, the owner's of the CORAIN, and Russo.

On October 6, 1983, claimant Russo brought a motion pursuant to Admiralty Rule F(7) to require appellant to post security required by 46 U.S.C. § 183 and Admiralty Rule F(l). Following a non-evidentiary hearing on November 4, 1983, the district court ordered that the appellant post security in the amount of $112,000 plus interest: $82,000 pursuant to section 183(a) and $30,000 pursuant to section 183(b). Appellants, who still have not posted the amount, appealed.

Discussion

A. Background on Limitation of Liability in Admiralty

The Limitation of Liability Act (Limitation Act), 46 U.S.C. § 183 *et seq.,* is intended to limit the liability of shipowners following maritime accidents. The Limitation Act provides that the liability of the shipowner for any maritime injury or loss shall be limited (to all but personal injury claimants, who may be entitled to a greater, but still limited, amount) to the extent of the shipowner's investment in and earnings from the voyage, provided that the injury or loss involves no privity or knowledge on the owner's part. Admiralty Rule F sets up the procedural provisions for limitation of liability actions.

* * *

The Limitation Act's protection is typically triggered when the shipowner files a complaint seeking limitation of liability pursuant to section 185 and Admiralty Rule F(1). Rule F(1) also provides that as a condition to filing the complaint, the shipowner

> shall deposit with the court, for the benefit of claimants, a sum equal to the amount or value of his interest in the vessel and pending freight, or approved security therefor, and in addition such sums, or approved security therefor, as the court may from time to time fix as necessary to carry out the provisions of the statutes as amended;

or, in the alternative, shall transfer his interest in the vessel and pending freight to a trustee. Admiralty Rule F(1). The posting of security must include six percent yearly interest. *Ld.* If a claimant is at any time concerned that the amount of security posted is insufficient, Admiralty Rule F(7) provides that

> [a]ny claimant may by motion demand that the funds deposited in court or the security given by the plaintiff be increased on the ground that they are less than the value of the plaintiff's interest in the vessel and pending

freight. Thereupon the court shall cause due appraisement to be made of the value of the plaintiff's interest in the vessel and pending freight; and if the court finds that the deposit or security is either insufficient or excessive it shall order its increase or reduction. In like manner any claimant may demand that the deposit or security be increased on the ground that it is insufficient to carry out the provisions of the statutes relating to claims in respect of loss of life or bodily injury; and, after notice and hearing, the court may similarly order that the deposit or security be increased or reduced.

Once an action is filed and security posted, the court proceeds to determine if the owner should be exonerated from liability or if he is entitled to limitation of liability. An owner will be exonerated from liability when he, his vessel, and crew are found to be completely free from fault. *Tittle v. Aldacosta*, 544 F.2d 752, 755 (5th Cir. 1977). To limit his liability to the amounts calculated under section 183, the shipowner must merely show that he had no privity to or knowledge of the negligence or unseaworthiness which caused injuries. *Ld.* at 756. If the owner is not exonerated but prevails in his plea for limitation, the section 183 security fund is distributed on a pro rata basis to claimants and the owner's liability is at an end. Admiralty Rule F(8). Therefore, a determination of the amount of security that need be posted under section 183 constitutes a determination of the maximum amount of liability that the shipowner will be subject to under the Limitation Act.

* * *

[The remainder of the courts opinion deals with issues relating to the Limitation Fund and is discussed *infra*. Eds.]

---

3. Concursus of Claims

LEWIS v. LEWIS & CLARK MARINE, INC.

531 U.S. 438, 121 S. Ct. 993, 148 L. Ed. 2d 931, 2001 AMC 913 (2001)

Justice O'CONNOR delivered the opinion of the Court.

This case concerns a seaman's ability to sue a vessel owner in state court for personal injuries sustained aboard a vessel. Federal courts have exclusive jurisdiction over admiralty and maritime claims, but the jurisdictional statute "sav[es] to suitors in all cases all other remedies to which they are otherwise entitled." 28 U.S.C. § 1333(1). Another statute grants vessel owner's the right to seek limited liability in federal court for claims of damage aboard their vessels. 46 U.S.C. App. § 181 *et seq.* In this case, the District Court, after conducting proceedings to preserve the vessel owner's right to seek limited liability, dissolved the injunction that prevented the seaman from litigating his personal injury claims in state court. The Eighth Circuit Court of Appeals reversed, concluding that the vessel owner had a right to contest liability in federal court, and that the seaman did not have a saved remedy in state court. The question presented is whether the District Court abused its discretion in dissolving the injunction.

I

Petitioner, James F. Lewis, worked as a deckhand aboard the M/V *Karen Michelle*, owned by respondent, Lewis & Clark Marine, Inc. Petitioner claims that on March 17, 1998, he was injured aboard the M/V *Karen Michelle* when he tripped over a wire and hurt his back. App. 12. In April 1998, petitioner sued respondent in the Circuit Court of Madison County, Illinois.... Petitioner did not demand a jury trial in state court.

In anticipation of petitioner's suit, respondent had filed a complaint for exoneration from, or limitation of, liability in the United States District Court for the Eastern District of Missouri pursuant to the Limitation of Liability Act (Limitation Act or Act), 46 U.S.C.App. § 181 *et seq.* The District Court followed the procedure for a limitation action provided in Supplemental Admiralty and Maritime Claims Rule F. The court entered an order approving a surety bond of $450,000, representing respondent's interest in the vessel. The court ordered that any person with a claim for the events of March 17, 1998, file a claim with the court within a specified period. The court then enjoined the filing or prosecution of any suits against respondent related to the incident on March 17, 1998. App. 30-33.

Petitioner filed an answer to respondent's complaint, a claim for damages for injury, and a motion to dissolve the restraining order. Petitioner averred that he was the sole claimant concerning the events of March 17, 1998. He waived any claim of res judicata concerning limited liability based on a state court judgment; he stipulated that respondent could relitigate issues relating to the limitation of liability in District Court. *Id.*, at 72. Petitioner later stipulated that the value of his claim was less than the value of the limitation fund, *id.*, at 102, recanting his earlier allegation that his claim exceeded the vessels value.

The District Court dissolved the restraining order that prevented petitioner from proceeding with his cause of action in state court. *In re Complaint of Lewis & Clark Marine, Inc.,* 31 F. Supp. 2d 1164 (E.D. Mo. 1998). The court recognized that federal courts have exclusive jurisdiction to determine whether a vessel owner is entitled to limited liability. The court also noted, however, that the statute that confers exclusive jurisdiction over admiralty and maritime claims to federal courts contains a clause that saves to suitors "all other remedies to which they are otherwise entitled." 28 U.S.C. § 1333(1). The court reasoned that "a tension exists between the exclusive jurisdiction vested in the admiralty courts to determine a vessel owner's right to limited liability and the savings to suitors clause." 31 F. Supp. 2d, at 1168.

The District Court found two exceptions to exclusive federal jurisdiction under which a claimant is allowed to litigate his claim in state court. The first is where the value of the limitation fund exceeds the total value of all claims asserted against the vessel owner. The second is where a single claimant brings an action against the vessel owner seeking damages in excess of the value of the vessel. The court concluded that it should dissolve the injunction in this case because petitioner met the limited fund exception and probably met the single claimant exception as well. *Id.*, at 1169, and n. 3. The court decided to retain jurisdiction over the limitation action to protect the vessel owner's right to limitation in the event that the state proceedings necessitated further proceedings in federal court.

The Eighth Circuit Court of Appeals held that the District Court abused its discretion in dissolving the injunction. 196 F.3d 900 (1999). The Court of Appeals, like the District Court, recognized potential tension between the saving to suitors clause in the jurisdictional statute and the Limitation Act. The Court of Appeals, however, perceived no conflict between those provisions in the instant case. The Court of Appeals explained that a court must consider whether the vessel owner has the right to remain in federal court and whether the claimant is seeking a saved remedy in another forum. The court concluded that respondent had a right to seek exoneration from liability, not merely limitation of liability, in federal court. The court also concluded that because petitioner did not request a trial by jury, he had not sought a saved remedy in state court. The court determined that there was no substantive difference between the remedies afforded petitioner in state court and federal court. For these reasons, the court held that there was no basis for dissolving the injunction.

* * *

II

A

* * *

Thus, the saving to suitors clause preserves remedies and the concurrent jurisdiction of state courts over some admiralty and maritime claims. *See also Madruga v. Superior Court of Cal., County of San Diego,* 346 U.S. 556, 560-561, 74 S.Ct. 298, 98 L.Ed. 290 (1954); *American_Steamboat Co. v. Chase,* 83 U.S. [16 Wall.] 522, 533-534, 21 L.Ed. 369 (1872).

B

Admiralty and maritime law includes a host of special rights, duties, rules, and procedures. *See, e.g.,* 46 U.S.C. App. § 721 *et seq.* (wrecks and salvage); § 741 *et seq.* (suits in admiralty by or against vessels or cargoes of the United States); 46 U.S.C. § 10101 *et seq.* (merchant seamen protection and relief). Among these provisions is the Limitation Act, 46 U.S.C. App. § 181 *et seq.* The Act allows a vessel owner to limit liability for damage or injury, occasioned without the owner's privity or knowledge, to the value of the vessel or the owner's interest in the vessel. The central provision of the Act provides:

> The liability of the owner of any vessel, whether American or foreign, for any embezzlement, loss, or destruction by any person of any property, goods, or merchandise shipped or put on board of such vessel, or for any loss, damage, or injury by collision, or for any act, matter, or thing, loss, damage, or forfeiture, done, occasioned, or incurred, without the privity or knowledge of such owner or owner's, shall not, except in the cases provided for in subsection (b) of this section, exceed the amount or value of the interest of such owner in such vessel, and her freight then pending. § 183(a).

See also § 183(b) (requiring supplemental fund for some vessels for personal injury and death claimants).

Congress passed the Limitation Act in 1851 "to encourage ship-building and to induce capitalists to invest money in this branch of industry." *Norwich & N.Y. Transp. Co. v. Wright,* 13 Wall. 104, 121, 20 L.Ed. 585 (1871). *See also British Transport Commn v. United States,* 354 U.S. 129, 133-135, 77 S.Ct. 1103, 1 L.Ed.2d 1234 (1957); *Just v. Chambers,* 312 U.S. 383, 385, 61 S.Ct. 687, 85 L.Ed. 903 (1941). The Act also had the purpose of "putting American shipping upon an equality with that of other maritime nations" that had their own limitation acts. *The Main v. Williams,* 152 U.S. 122, 128, 14 S.Ct. 486, 38 L.Ed. 381 (1894). *See also Norwich Co., supra,* at 116-119 (discussing history of limitation acts in England, France, and the States that led to the passage of the Limitation Act).

The Act is not a model of clarity. *See* 2 T. SCHOENBAUM, ADMIRALTY AND MARITIME LAW 299 (2d ed. 1994) ("Th[e] 1851 Act, badly drafted even by the standards of the time, continues in effect today"). Having created a right to seek limited liability, Congress did not provide procedures for determining the entitlement. This Court did not have an opportunity to review the Act in detail until 20 years after its enactment. *See Norwich Co., supra.* Deeming the Act "incapable of execution" without further instructions to courts, *id.,* at 123, we designed the procedures that govern a limitation action, and promulgated them the same Term, *see* Supplementary Rules of Practice in Admiralty, 13 Wall. xii-xiv. We later explained that the scheme "was sketched in outline" by the Act, and "the regulation of details as to the form and modes of proceeding was left to be prescribed by judicial authority." *Providence & New York S.S. Co. v. Hill Mfg. Co.,* 109 U.S. 578, 590, 3 S.Ct. 379, 27 L.Ed. 1038 (1883).

The 1872 rules were "intended to facilitate the proceedings of the owner's of vessels for claiming the limitation of liability secured by the statute." *The Benefactor,* 103 U.S. 239, 244, 26 L.Ed. 351 (1880). Under the rules, a vessel owner seeking limitation of liability had to file a petition. The district court would obtain an appraisal of the vessel's value or the owner's interest in the vessel, and ensure that payment or some guarantee of payment was deposited with the court. The court would then order all claimants to appear. Supplemental Rule of Practice in Admiralty 54, 13 Wall, at xii-xiii. In the process of seeking limited liability, the owner was permitted to contest the fact of liability. Rule 56, 13 Wall., at xiii. The ability to contest liability relieved vessel owners of the "very onerous" English rule, which required vessel owner's to confess liability in order to seek the benefit of limitation. *The "Benefactor," supra,* at 243 ("[T]his court, in preparing the rules of procedure for a limitation of liability, deemed it proper to allow a party seeking such limitation to contest any liability whatever"). The claimants would then contest the vessel owner's claims for exoneration and limitation of liability. Rule 56, 13 Wall., at xiii. If the owner succeeded in its effort to limit liability, but was not exonerated, the court was responsible for distributing the fund deposited in the court among the claimants. Rule 55, 13 Wall., at xiii.

The procedure for a limitation action is now found in Supplemental Admiralty and Maritime Claims Rule F. Much like its predecessor provisions, Rule F sets forth the process for filing a complaint seeking exoneration from, or limitation of, liability The district court secures the value of the vessel or owner's interest, marshals claims, and enjoins the prosecution of other actions with respect to the claims. In these proceedings, the court, sitting without a jury, adjudicates the claims. The court determines whether the vessel owner is liable and whether the owner may limit liability. The court then determines the validity of the claims, and if liability is limited, distributes the limited fund among the claimants.

C

Some tension exists between the saving to suitors clause and the Limitation Act. One statute gives suitors the right to a choice of remedies, and the other statute gives vessel owner's the right to seek limitation of liability in federal court. We confronted this tension in *Langnes v. Green*, 282 U.S. 531, 51 S.Ct. 243, 75 L.Ed. 520 (1931). The respondent in *Langnes* was employed on the petitioner's vessel. The employee sued the vessel owner in state court for $25,000 for personal injuries suffered aboard the vessel. The vessel owner later filed a petition for limitation of liability in Federal District Court. The District Court enjoined any further proceedings in state court and issued a notice that all claimants appear. The employee filed his claim in District Court. The parties stipulated that the vessel was worth no more than $5,000.

The employee sought dissolution of the injunction. He argued that the state court had jurisdiction over his claim, that he was the only possible claimant, that there was only one vessel owner, and therefore the vessel owner could claim the benefit of the Limitation Act by proper pleading in state court. The District Court denied the motion and proceeded to decide the merits, concluding that the vessel owner was not liable. The Court of Appeals reversed on the issue of limitation.

On review, this Court concluded that both courts erred in failing to recognize that the state court was competent to hear the employee's personal injury claim and the vessel owner's claim for limitation. In our view, the choice before the District Court was whether it should retain the limitation action and preserve the right of the vessel owner but destroy the right of the employee in state court to a common law remedy, or allow the action in state court to proceed and preserve the rights of both parties. We concluded that the latter course was just. We decided that the District Court should have dissolved the injunction and allowed the employee to proceed with his claim in state court, and retained jurisdiction over the petition for limitation of liability in the event that the state proceedings necessitated further proceedings in federal court. We explained that the District Courts decision is "one of discretion in every case," and remanded for further proceedings. *Id.*, at 544, 51 S.Ct. 243.

After our decision, the employee was permitted to pursue his claim in state court. *See Ex parte Green,* 286 U.S. 437, 52 S.Ct. 602, 76 L.Ed. 1212 (1932). In those proceedings, notwithstanding this Court's recognition of the vessel owner's right to seek limitation of liability in federal court, the employee sought to litigate that issue in state court. We approved of the District Court's decision to enjoin any further proceedings in state court until the employee agreed to withdraw his submission on the issue of limited liability. *Id.,* at 440, 52 S.Ct. 602.

We have also considered the conflict between the saving to suitors clause and the Limitation Act in a case where several claimants attempted to sue a vessel owner in state court. *Lake Tankers Corp. v. Henn,* 354 U.S. 147, 77 S.Ct. 1269, 1 L.Ed.2d 1246 (1957). A pleasure yacht, the *Blackstone,* capsized after a collision with a tug that was push-towing a barge, injuring several persons and killing one. Claimants sued the owner of the tug and barge in state court actions. The owner filed a petition for exoneration from, or limitation of, liability in federal court. The owner also filed a bond for the tug in the amount of approximately $119,000 and a bond for the barge in the amount of $165,000. The District Court enjoined other proceedings concerning the collision. Thereafter, the claimants made their demands for damages; the total claims were less than the amount of the two bonds. All claimants relinquished any right to damages in excess of that set forth in their claims. They further waived any claim of res judicata relating to the issue of the vessel owner's ability to limit liability. The District Court decided to dissolve the injunction because the total limitation fund exceeded the amount of the claims. The Court of Appeals affirmed.

We affirmed the Court of Appeals' decision. In examining the Limitation Act and its history, we found it "crystal clear that the operation of the Act is directed at misfortunes at sea where the losses incurred exceed the value of the vessel and the pending freight." *Id.*, at 151, 77 S.Ct. 1269. Where the value of the vessel and the pending freight exceed the claims, however, there is no necessity for the maintenance of the action in federal court. *Id.*, at 152, 77 S.Ct. 1269. The stipulations, in addition to other restrictions on the state court proceedings, ensured "beyond doubt that [the owner's] right of limitation under the Act was fully protected." *Ibid.* We explained that to expand the scope of exclusive jurisdiction to prevent the state court actions

would transform the Act from a protective instrument to an offensive weapon by which the shipowner could deprive suitors of their common-law rights, even where the limitation fund is known to be more than adequate to satisfy all demands upon it. The shipowner's right to limit liability is not so boundless. The Act is not one of immunity from liability but of limitation of it and we read no other privilege for the shipowner into its language over and above that granting him limited liability. In fact, the Congress not only created the limitation procedure for the primary purpose of apportioning the limitation fund among the claimants where that fund was inadequate to pay the claims in full, but it reserved to such suitors their common-law remedies. *Id.*, at 152-153, 77 S.Ct. 1269.

Since these decisions, the Courts of Appeals have generally permitted claimants to proceed with their claims in state court where there is only a single claimant, as in *Langnes,* or where the total claims do not exceed the value of the limitation fund, as in *Lake Tankers.* See, *e.g., Beiswenger Enterprises Corp. v. Carletta,* 86 F.3d 1032 (C.A. 11 1996); *Linton v. Great Lakes Dredge & Dock Co.,* 964 F.2d 1480 (C.A.5 1992). *See also Kreta Shipping S.A. v. Preussag International Steel Corp.,* 192 F.3d 41 (C.A.2 1999) (foreign forum).

III

In the instant case, we believe that the District Court properly exercised its discretion in dissolving the injunction that prevented petitioner from pursuing his claims in state court. The District Court, guided by our prior cases, attempted to reconcile petitioner's right to his remedy under the saving to suitors clause with respondent's right to seek limited liability under the Limitation Act. The court dissolved the injunction against the state court proceedings after it concluded that respondent's right to seek limitation of liability would be adequately protected. Respondent's rights were protected by petitioner's stipulation that his claim did not exceed the limitation fund, petitioner's waiver of any defense of res judicata with respect to limitation of liability, and the District Court's decision to stay the Limitation Act proceedings pending state court proceedings.

The Eighth Circuit held that the District Court should not have dissolved the injunction without first "finding ... actual statutory conflict between the Limitation Act and the 'saving to suitors' clause in the case at bar." 196 F.3d, at 906. The Court of Appeals concluded that there was no conflict here because respondent had a right to seek exoneration from liability in federal court, and petitioner did not have a saved remedy under the saving to suitors clause. That reasoning misapprehends this Court's prior decisions.

In this case, there was a conflict between the saving to suitors clause and the Limitation Act. Petitioner sued respondent in state court; under the saving to suitors clause, that court had jurisdiction to hear his claims. Respondent sought limited liability for petitioner's claims in federal court; the Limitation Act granted the federal court jurisdiction over that action. Both parties selected legitimate forums for their claims, and therein lies the conflict. Had petitioner sought to institute *in rem* proceedings against respondent in state court, that court would have lacked jurisdiction because the saving to suitors clause does not reach actions *in rem.* Similarly, had respondent sought limited liability for payment of wages in federal court, that court would not have had jurisdiction under the Limitation Act because claims for wages due employees are not covered. 46 U.S.C.App. § 189. *See also In re East River Towing Co.,* 266 U.S. 355, 367, 45 S.Ct. 114, 69 L.Ed. 324 (1924). Here, however, there appears to have been no obstacle to each party pursuing its claim in the forum of its choice, except the competing action.

In deciding that the case should proceed in federal court, the Court of Appeals relied on two flawed premises: that the Limitation Act grants vessel owners a right to obtain exoneration from liability in federal court where limitation of liability is not at issue, and that the saving to suitors clause reserves to claimants only the right to receive a jury trial.

By its own terms, the Limitation Act protects the right of vessel owners to limit their liability to the value of the vessel, provided that the events or circumstances giving rise to the damage occurred without the vessel owner's privity or knowledge. The Act was designed to encourage investment and protect vessel owners from unlimited exposure to liability. We have also made clear, however, that the scope of exclusive federal jurisdiction is proportional to the federal interest in protecting the vessel owner's right to seek limitation of liability. *See Lake Tankers,* 354 U.S., at 153, 77 S.Ct. 1269. We have explained that "[t]he Act is not one of immunity from liability but of limitation of it." *Id.,* at 152, 77 S.Ct. 1269. We see no reason to revisit that conclusion and decline respondents invitation to expand the scope of the Act.

In construing the Limitation Act, this Court long ago determined that vessel owners may contest liability in the process of seeking limited liability, and we promulgated rules to that effect pursuant to our "power to regulate ... proceedings." *The Benefactor,* 103 U.S., at 244; Supplemental Rule of Practice in Admiralty 56, 13 Wall., at xiii; Supplemental Admiralty and Maritime Claims Rule F(2). Thus, we agree with respondent that a vessel owner need not confess liability in order to seek limitation under the Act. The Act and the rules of practice, however, do not create a freestanding right to exoneration from liability in circumstances where limitation of liability is not at issue. In this case, petitioner stipulated that his claim for damages would not exceed the value of the vessel and waived any claim of res judicata from the state court action concerning issues bearing on the limitation of liability. The District Court concluded that these stipulations would protect the vessel owner's right to seek limited liability in federal court. Then, out of an "abundance of caution," the court stayed the limitation proceedings so that it could act if the state court proceedings jeopardized the vessel owner's rights under the Limitation Act. 31 F.Supp.2d, at 1170-1171. We believe nothing more was required to protect respondent's right to seek a limitation of liability.

The district courts have jurisdiction over actions arising under the Limitation Act, and they have discretion to stay or dismiss Limitation Act proceedings to allow a suitor to pursue his claims in state court. If the district court concludes that the vessel owner's right to limitation will not be adequately protected—where for example a group of claimants cannot agree on appropriate stipulations or there is uncertainty concerning the adequacy of the fund or the number of claims—the court may proceed to adjudicate the merits, deciding the issues of liability and limitation. *See, e.g., Lake Tankers, supra,* at 152, 77 S. Ct. 1269; *Port Arthur Towing Co. v. John W. Towing, Inc.,* 42 F.3d 312, 314 (C.A.5 1995). But where, as here, the District Court satisfies itself that a vessel owner's right to seek limitation will be protected, the decision to dissolve the injunction is well within the courts discretion.

The Court of Appeals reasoned that the District Court also erred in dissolving the injunction because petitioner had no saved remedy in state court. The Court of Appeals apparently treated as dispositive petitioner's failure to demand a jury trial in state court. The jurisdictional statute, however, reserves to suitors "all other remedies to which they are otherwise entitled." 28 U.S.C. § 1333(1). Tracing the development of the clause since the Judiciary Act of 1789, it appears that the clause was designed to protect remedies available at common law. *See, e.g., The Hine v. Trevor,* 4 Wall. 555, 18 L.Ed. 451 (1866). We later explained that the clause extends to "all means other than proceedings in admiralty which may be employed to enforce the right or to redress the injury involved." *Red Cross Line,* 264 U.S., at 124, 44 S. Ct. 274. Trial by jury is an obvious, but not exclusive, example of the remedies available to suitors. *See Lake Tankers, supra,* at 153, 77 S. Ct. 1269; *Red Cross Line, supra,* at 123-125, 44 S. Ct. 274.

The Court of Appeals concluded that forum choice could not be a saved remedy under the saving to suitors clause because a claimant does not have the ability to control the forum in which his claim will be heard. 192 F.3d, at 909. The prospect that a vessel owner may remove a state court action to federal court, however, does not limit a claimant's forum choice under the saving to suitors clause any more than other litigants' forum choices may be limited. We have previously refused to hold that admiralty claims, such as a limitation claim, fall within the scope of federal question jurisdiction out of concern that saving to suitors actions in state court would be removed to federal court and undermine the claimant's choice of forum. *Romero v. International Terminal Operating Co.*, 358 U.S. 354, 371-372, 79 S.Ct. 468, 3 L.Ed.2d 368 (1959). We explained that to define admiralty jurisdiction as federal question jurisdiction would be a "destructive oversimplification of the highly intricate interplay of the States and the National Government in their regulation of maritime commerce." *Id.*, at 373, 79 S.Ct. 468. Moreover, in this case respondent raised a Jones Act claim, which is not subject to removal to federal court even in the event of diversity of the parties. *See* 28 U.S.C. § 1445(a) (incorporated by reference into the Jones Act, 46 U.S.C.App. § 688(a)). Respondent's arguments to limit and enumerate the saved remedies under the saving to suitors clause must fail in view of the consistent recognition by Congress and this Court that both state and federal courts may be proper forums for adjudicating claims such as petitioner's.

In sum, this Court's case law makes clear that state courts, with all of their remedies, may adjudicate claims like petitioner's against vessel owners so long as the vessel owner's right to seek limitation of liability is protected. Respondent seeks to invert that rule, making run of the mill personal injury actions involving vessels a matter of exclusive federal jurisdiction except where the claimant happens to seek a jury trial. We reject that proposal and hold that the Court of Appeals erred in reversing the District Court's decision to dissolve the injunction.

The judgment of the United States Court of Appeals for the Eighth Circuit is therefore reversed, and the case is remanded for further proceedings consistent with this opinion.

It is so ordered.

Notes

1. *Sufficiency of Stipulations*

A court may lift an injunction and allow plaintiffs to proceed in state court even though there are multiple plaintiffs so long as their stipulations either by subordinating claims, prioritizing claims or by statements that they would seek only a pro rata share of the limitation fund adequately protects the shipowner. The court also held that the plaintiff did not have to limit their claim to a stated amount which the defendant alleged was the limitation fund so long as they agree not to enforce any state judgment they receive in excess of the limitation fund until the owner's right to limitation has been determined in admiralty.

In *In re Aramark Sports & Entertainment Services*, LLC, 2010 WL 4791443 (D. Utah 2010), the court noted that the circuits are divided on whether a party who may seek indemnity or contribution from a shipowner must be a party to any stipulation that would allow a district court to stay the limitation action. It cites cases in the Sixth and Eighth Circuit that do not require potential third-party claimant's to enter into a stipulation before the potential claimants could proceed in state court, whereas the Second and Third Circuits do. The court in this case followed the approach of the Second and Third Circuits.

2. *Trial by Jury*

There is no right to a jury trial in limitation proceeding. If, however, a party is entitled to a jury determination as to a liability issue, the court may impanel a jury for this purpose. *See McKeithen v. Steamship Frosta*, 75 F.R.D. 7, 1978 AMC 12 (E.D. La. 1977). Where the exceptions to the concursus rule are not applicable and plaintiffs are enjoined from bringing their common law claims in state court, should their request for a jury trial on the merits of their claims be granted. *See Complaint Poling Transp. Corp.*, 776 F. Supp. 779, 1992 AMC 1075 (S.D.N.Y. 1991).

3. *Joinder of Parties and Claims*

Liberal rules of joinder are applied in a limitation proceeding, allowing the court to adjudicate the claims and cross-claims of all vessel interests. *See British Transport Commission v. United States*, 354 U.S. 129, 77 S. Ct. 1103, 1 L. Ed. 2d 1234, 1957 AMC 1151(1957).

What is the procedure if limitation is denied? *Compare Harford Accident & Indemnity Co. v. Southern Pacific Co.*, 273 U.S.207, 47 S.Ct.357, 71 L.Ed. 612, 1927 AMC 402 (1927) and *In re Petition of Wood*, 230 F.2d 197, 1956 AMC 547 (2d Cir. 1956).

The Six-Month Rule

In re ECKSTEIN MARINE SERVICE, L.L.C.

672 F.3d 310, 2012 AMC 305 (5th Cir. 2012)

PATRICK E. HIGGINBOTHAM Circuit Judge

Plaintiff-appellant Marquette Transportation Company Gulf–Inland LLC challenges the district court's dismissal of its limitation action as untimely. Finding no error, we affirm.

I.

Claimant-appellee Lorne Jackson was a crew member of the M/V ST. ANDREW, a 65–foot tug owned and operated by appellant Marquette. While on deck on February 28, 2009, Jackson became entangled in a line and was pulled into a mooring bit, seriously injuring his left leg at the femur, fibula, tibia, knee and ankle, including fractures, soft tissue damage and ligament injuries. Jackson was immediately transported to a hospital and remained there for the next two weeks.

On April 28, 2009 Jackson served Marquette with a Texas state court complaint alleging the February 28 accident was caused by the unseaworthiness of the M/V ST. ANDREW and by the negligence of Marquette and its employees. Jackson claimed his injuries permanently and substantially impaired him and requested damages including past loss of earnings, future loss of earning capacity, past and future disability, past and future disfigurement, past and future medical and hospital expenses, past and future pain and mental anguish, and maintenance and care. The petition alleged the amount sought was in excess of jurisdictional amounts but did not specify a sum. Marquette filed an answer on June 10.

Following discovery, Jackson made a settlement demand for $3 million on December 2. Marquette refused. On January 18, 2010 Marquette filed an action for exoneration from or limitation of liability in federal district court to cap its liability at $750,000, the value of the M/V ST. ANDREW and its pending freight at the time of the accident. Jackson responded with a motion to dismiss, which the district court denied without prejudice. In July, Jackson renewed his motion, and the district court granted it. In the state court trial that followed, Jackson won a judgment in excess of $750,000. Marquette filed this appeal.

* * *

III.

The Limitation of Shipowners' Liability Act allows a vessel owner to limit its liability in certain actions for damages to the value of the vessel (and pending freight) on which the incident giving rise to the litigation occurred. To obtain this statutory protection, the owner must "bring a civil action in a district court ... within 6 months after a claimant gives the owner written notice of a claim." If the action is not filed within that six-month period, it is dismissed as untimely. The district court found that Marquette received written notice of Jackson's claim when it was served with his state court complaint on April 28, 2009. Because Marquette did not file its limitation of liability action until January 18, 2010—eight and a half months later—it failed to meet the statute's timeliness requirement. The district court therefore dismissed Marquette's complaint for lack of subject matter jurisdiction.

A.

Marquette first challenges the district court's treatment of Jackson's motion to dismiss as an attack on subject matter jurisdiction under Fed.R.Civ.P. 12(b)(1). His argument is two-fold: (1) timeliness is not a jurisdictional issue, and (2) Marquette did not have notice that Jackson was disputing the court's jurisdiction.

This circuit, like several other courts, has held that a party alleging a limitation petition was not timely filed challenges the district court's subject matter jurisdiction over that petition. Marquette contends we are not bound to follow this precedent because filing deadlines are never jurisdictional. This is simply inaccurate. While many statutory filing deadlines are not jurisdictional, we have long recognized that some are. The Limitation Act's six-month filing requirement is one of these.

* * *

Finally, Jackson's pleadings gave adequate notice to Marquette that he was mounting a challenge to the district court's jurisdiction based on the untimely filing of Marquette's limitation action, even though they did not actually cite to Fed.R.Civ.P. 12(b)(1). The motion's primary argument for dismissal was that Marquette had missed the six-month filing deadline. The first paragraph of Jackson's renewed motion to dismiss declared that "[t]he six-month time limit is jurisdictional and this matter is time-barred." Jackson also made the jurisdictional argument explicit in his answer to the limitation complaint. The original answer stated that "Claimant admits the admiralty and maritime jurisdiction of this Honorable Court, but denies the Petitioner's right to claim limitation or exoneration from liability in this case." Following a hearing on his motion, however, Jackson obtained leave to amend his answer. The only change in the amended version was to this paragraph, which now read: "Claimant denies the admiralty and maritime jurisdiction of this Honorable Court because this limitations action was not filed within six months from the time limitation plaintiff received notice of claim."

* * *

IV.

The judgment of the district court is AFFIRMED.

---

4. Interplay of State and Federal Proceedings: Raising Limitation Defensively

VATICAN SHRIMP CO., INC. v. SOLIS

820 F.2d 674, 1987 AMC 2426 (5th Cir. 1987)

E. GRADY JOLLY, Circuit Judge

* * *

The appellee, Gabriel Solis, was a crew member on the F/V VATICAN when, in April 1983, an anchor line struck and injured his wrist, later treated for a contusion with no fracture. Approximately sixteen months after the accident, on October 12, 1984, Solis filed a Jones Act claim in Texas state court, alleging negligence and unseaworthiness on the part of the vessel and its owner's and seeking $700,000 in damages. In its state court answer, Vatican Shrimp raised the defense of exoneration from or limitation of liability to the value of the F/V VATICAN and its pending freight, which Vatican Shrimp assessed at $200,331.83. On April 17, 1986, one and one-half years after the suit was filed, Vatican Shrimp petitioned the federal district court for limitation of liability under 46 U.S.C. § 185 and for restraint of the state court trial. The district court temporarily restrained the state court proceedings, but it later dismissed Vatican Shrimps section 185 petition as untimely. Vatican Shrimp appealed.

* * *

On May 15, 1986, Vatican Shrimp removed the case from state to federal court under 28 U.S.C. § 1441. Because it had previously ruled that Vatican Shrimp could not limit its liability in the federal courts, the district court, on the plaintiff's motion, entered an order remanding the case to state court.... [Vatican Shrimp then filed a petition for writ of mandamus challenging the order of remand.]

* * *

II

This court has not previously addressed the first question that Vatican Shrimp raises; that is, under what circumstances does a federal court have jurisdiction to adjudicate a contested claim for limitation of liability when the shipowner has pled limitation defensively in a properly filed state court answer. To date, this question has only been addressed by the Sixth Circuit which held that defensive pleading in a state court answer alone was not an adequate procedural method for attaining federal adjudication of the limitation claim. In the Sixth Circuit, a shipowner, who faces litigation in state court, "acts at his peril" if he does not file a petition for limitation in a federal court under 46 U.S.C. § 185 within six months of receiving written notice of the claim. *Cincinnati Gas & Elec. Co. v. Abel,* 533 F.2d 1001, 1005 (6th Cir. 1976).

We hold that on the facts of the case now before us, Vatican Shrimp's section 185 petition was untimely, and Vatican Shrimp's defensive pleading in the state court answer did not provide the federal court with jurisdiction to hear the shipowner's limitation claim.

A.

In reaching our holding, in addition to the case law, we have reviewed the background of the Limitation of Liability Act of 1851, 46 U.S.C. §§ 181-96 (1982) (amended 1936)....

* * *

The Act provides shipowners with two procedural methods for limiting their liability. *Signal Oil & Gas Co. v. Barge W-701,* 654 F.2d 1164, 1172 (5th Cir. 1981). Under 46 U.S.C. § 185, a shipowner may file a limitation petition in federal district court. Congress amended this section in 1936 by adding a time bar that requires a vessel owner to file its petition in federal court within six months of receiving "written notice of claim."

The second method has its source in 46 U.S.C. § 183, which, unlike section 185, imposes no time bar. Section 183, which has remained virtually unchanged since its enactment in 1851, sets forth generally the Act's substantive provisions that permit a vessel owner, in the absence of privity or knowledge, to limit liability to the owner's interest in the vessel and its pending freight. A shipowner can "set up [limitation] as a defense" by pleading the general substantive provisions of section 183 in an answer filed in any court, including a state court. *Langnes v. Green,* 282 U.S. 531, 543, 51 S. Ct. 243, 247-48, 75 L. Ed. 2d 520 (1931). However, once the shipowner's right to limit liability is contested, only a federal court may exercise jurisdiction of the matter because the cause becomes cognizable only in admiralty. *Id.*

* * *

In the "Green Cases," decided before the six-month filing period was added to section 185, the Supreme Court established the proper procedure that a shipowner should follow to limit liability in a single claimant case that is originally filed in state court. *Id.; Ex Parte Green,* 286 U.S. 437, 52 S. Ct. 602, 76 L. Ed. 2d 1212 (1932). In *Langnes v. Green,* a crew member sued the vessel owner in state court to recover for personal injuries. The parties stipulated to the value of the vessel, and the vessel owner's right to limit liability was not contested. Nevertheless, two days before the state trial was scheduled to begin, the vessel owner petitioned a federal district court to limit his liability under section 185. The district court enjoined the state court proceedings and tried the case on the merits. The Supreme Court, addressing the issue of the crew member's right to pursue a common law remedy in state court, ordered the district court to remand the case, holding that under the saving to suitors clause, 28 U.S.C. § 1333(1), the state court had jurisdiction to decide the crew member's claim. The Court made it clear, however, that if a vessel owner's right to limit liability were contested (which it had not been), a federal court would have "exclusive cognizance of such a question." *Langnes,* 282 U.S. at 543, 51 S. Ct. at 248. As a precautionary measure, the Court instructed the district court to retain the section 185 petition in the event that limited liability should become a contested issue in the state court action. *Id.* at 541-43, 51 S. Ct. at 247-48.

Following remand to the state court, the crew member did, in fact, challenge the vessel owner's right to limit liability. *Ex Parte Green,* 286 U.S. at 440, 52 S. Ct. at 603. The district court once again granted the vessel owner's motion to restrain the state court proceedings. On appeal, the Supreme Court held that because the owner's right to limited liability had been put into issue, "the cause became cognizable only in admiralty," and the district court, having retained the vessel owner's section 185 petition, was "authorized to resume jurisdiction and dispose of the whole case." *Id.*

B.

We apply the procedure prescribed in *Langnes* but modify it to reflect the 1936 amendment to section 185. That is, we recognize that shipowners may choose to set up the defense of limitation of liability under either method: by pleading the substantive provisions of section 183 in a properly filed answer in any court, or by filing a section 185 petition in a federal district court. However, if a shipowner is sued in state court, the owner's failure to file a section 185 petition in a federal district court within six months after receiving written notice of the claim will result in forfeiture of the right to limit liability should the claimant contest the limitation defense. This is so because solely filing in the state court an answer in which limitation is pled obviously does not provide a federal court with jurisdiction to act. In contrast, defensive pleading under section 183 in a federal district court answer does not present the same jurisdictional problems. The district court, having jurisdiction to hear the entire case initially filed with it, can adjudicate and rule on a limited liability issue that is raised in a properly filed answer.

In sum, once written notice of a claim is received, unless that notice is a complaint filed in federal court, the prudent shipowner would file a timely section 185 petition in district court and move to stay the federal proceedings on the limitation petition until such time as limited liability is contested. This practice will ensure that a federal court may exercise its exclusive jurisdiction to hear the limitation issue even if the claimant eventually files suit in a state court and contests limitation more than six months after giving written notice of the claim.

C.

Applying the modified *Langnes* procedure to the facts in this case, we have determined that Vatican Shrimp had notice of the claim at the very latest upon the service of the state court complaint in October 1984, thus commencing the six-month time period in section 185, which inarguably begins to run from the shipowners receipt of written notice of the claim. Vatican Shrimp, however, failed to file its section 185 petition until April 18, 1986, approximately one and one-half years after its receipt of written notice. There is no question that Vatican Shrimp failed to comply with the six-month time limit. Its defensive pleading of limitation in the state court answer did not toll the six-month filing period under section 185; nor did the state court answer provide the federal court with jurisdiction to hear the limitation claim. *See* Volk & Cobbs, *supra* at 976 (assertion of the defense of limitation in a state court suit will not extend the section 185 six-month time period). The district court therefore correctly dismissed the section 185 petition as untimely.

III

On petition for writ of mandamus, Vatican Shrimp argues that the district court abused its discretion in remanding the case to state court. The reason the district court gave for remanding the case was that, in dismissing the section 185 petition, it had previously decided that the federal court could not adjudicate the limitation issue. Vatican Shrimp contends that the prior dismissal does not control the propriety of its petition for removal. It argues, and Solis agrees, that the timeliness of removal is governed by 28 U.S.C. § 1446(b), which provides that a petition for removal must be filed within thirty days of the date on which the case became removable. Both parties contend that the case became removable when limited liability was contested, because such a claim is exclusively cognizable in federal court. Vatican Shrimp claims that Solis first contested limitation on April 15, 1986, when he denied certain admissions of fact regarding limited liability. The shipowner argues that the petition for removal, filed on May 15, 1986, was therefore timely. Solis counters that the initial complaint, filed on October 12, 1984, was removable because it was clear that Solis sought damages exceeding the value of the vessel and that contested limitation rights were at issue. Under Solis' theory, the case should have been removed within thirty days of the filing of the complaint. We need not reach the parties' arguments.

Remand to the state court is required "[i]f at any time before a final judgment it appears that the case was removed improvidently and without jurisdiction...." 28 U.S.C. § 1447(c). In its memorandum opinion filed with the order of remand, the district court stated, "Defendant's contention that there is an exclusive federal question in this case is unfounded.... The court finds that there is no exclusive federal question and that this case was improvidently removed." Based on this statement, it is clear that the district court predicated the remand under 28 U.S.C. § 1447(c). An order remanding a case to the state court from which it was removed is not reviewable on appeal or otherwise, except in certain civil rights cases. 28 U.S.C. § 1447(d); *Thermtron Products, Inc. v. Hermansdorfer*, 423 U.S. 336, 96 S. Ct. 584, 46 L. Ed. 2d 542 (1976); *Spencer v. New Orleans Levee Bd.*, 737 F.2d 435, 438 (5th Cir. 1984). The only vehicle for relief from an order of remand is to petition for a writ of mandamus. *New Orleans Public Service, Inc. v. Majoue*, 802 F.2d 166, 167 (5th Cir. 1986). The writ will be granted only if the district court "has affirmatively stated and relied upon a non-1447(c) ground for remand." *Royal v. State Farm Fire & Casualty Co.*, 685 F.2d 124, 126 (5th Cir. 1982); *see also Gravitt v. Southwestern Bell Telephone Co.*, 430 U.S. 723, 97 S. Ct. 1439, 52 L. Ed. 2d 1 (1977). The district court stated and relied upon section 1447(c) as its ground for remand, and, accordingly, the writ of mandamus cannot be granted.

* * *

V

In conclusion, we hold that the district court correctly dismissed as untimely Vatican Shrimp's section 185 petition to limit liability, we deny Vatican Shrimp's petition for writ of mandamus,...

E. GRADY JOLLY, Circuit Judge:

In its petition for rehearing en banc, Vatican Shrimp argues that the panel's opinion has effectively "modified out of existence the shipowner's right to raise limitation in state court." Vatican Shrimp claims that because this court has held that a vessel owner may raise the limitation defense in an answer filed in federal court without regard to the six-month time limit in section 185, *Signal Oil and Gas v. Barge W-701*, 654 F.2d 1164, 1173 (5th Cir. 1981), a vessel owner should therefore be able to raise the limitation defense in an answer filed in state court and then litigate the issue in federal court without regard to the six-month time restriction. Vatican Shrimp gives three reasons in support of its argument: (1) the 1936 amendments to the Limitation of Liability Act, 46 U.S.C. §§ 181-96 (1982) ("the Act"), do not indicate that Congress intended to take away the right of the vessel owner to raise limitation in an answer filed more than six months after receipt of notice of the claim; (2) Congress did not amend section 183 to include a time restraint similar to that now present in section 185; and (3) the purpose of adding the six-month time limitation to section 185 was to require the shipowner to act promptly, which is not contravened when limitation is pleaded in an answer to the plaintiff's complaint. As a policy matter, Vatican Shrimp emphasizes that a severe economic burden will be placed on fishing boat owners and small workboat owners who will be forced to incur the expense of filing federal limitation actions in conjunction with their state court claims.

As we noted in our opinion, *Vatican Shrimp Co., Inc. v. Solis*, 820 F.2d at 678 n.4 (5th Cir. 1987), we are not insensitive to the economic burdens that will be placed on small-vessel owners. Notwithstanding our concern over these added economic burdens, we are unable to reach a different legal conclusion without violating the precedent of many years that control us. First, we are unable to find any precedent holding that state courts have jurisdiction to adjudicate a contested limitation-of-liability defense; nor does any authority indicate that state courts ever had such jurisdiction; nor is there any authority that the 1936 amendments granted such jurisdiction to state courts; nor have any courts since the 1936 amendments suggested that state courts do have such jurisdiction. Moreover, the United States Supreme Court has expressly held in the *Green* cases, *Langnes v. Green*, 282 U.S. 531, 51 S. Ct. 243, 75 L.Ed. 520 (1931); *Ex Parte Green*, 286 U.S. 437, 52 S. Ct. 602, 76 L.Ed. 1212 (1932), albeit decided before the 1936 amendments to the Act, that once the vessel owner's right to limit liability is contested, the cause becomes exclusively cognizable in a federal court of admiralty.

Finally, apart from a section 185 petition or proper removal from the state court to the federal district court, there exists *no* mechanism for getting the matter before a federal court. In this case, it is clear that a section 185 petition was of no avail to Vatican Shrimp because the vessel owner failed to comply with the six-month time limitation. Also, the district court held that removal was improper and remanded the case to state court. The order of remand is nonreviewable on appeal, 28 U.S.C. § 1447(d), which leaves Vatican Shrimp with no possible avenue for reaching federal court.

We are mindful that prior to the 1936 amendments, a vessel owner could delay filing a section 185 petition in federal court until the eve of the state court trial. In response to the problems this practice caused, particularly in complex multiple-claimant litigation such as that arising from the MORRO CASTLE disaster, Congress amended the Act in 1936 by adding a six-month time limitation to section 185 that forced the vessel owner to act more promptly. *See* G. Gilmore and C. Black, *The Law of Admiralty,* § 10-14 & n.57 (1975). Since the passage of the 1936 MORRO CASTLE amendments, Congress has not changed section 185 to provide that the six-month time limitation is tolled by pleading limitation as a defense in a state court answer. We are not a legislature and are therefore powerless to add such a provision to the statute; nor can we interpret the unambiguous language of sections 185 or 183 to contemplate such a tolling of the six-month time period. Despite the serious consequences to small vessel owners, this may simply be an unfortunate result that has slipped through the statutory cracks.

The only way that we could provide a remedy to the petitioner would be either to bend the removal rules or to overrule United States Supreme Court precedent holding that a contested issue of limited liability is subject to the exclusive jurisdiction of the federal admiralty courts. This panel lacks the sanguinity to do so, and, treating the suggestion for rehearing en banc as a petition for panel rehearing, the petition for panel rehearing is DENIED.

No member of the panel nor judge in regular active service of this court having requested that the court be polled on rehearing en banc (Federal Rules of Appellate Procedure and Local Rule 35), the suggestion for rehearing en banc is DENIED.

Note: State Court Proceedings

Several courts have held that the limitation of liability statute may be raised in a state court even though no concursus limitation proceeding had been filed in federal court. *Mapco Petroleum, Inc. v. Memphis Barge Line, Inc.,* 849 S.W.2d 312, 1993 AMC 2113 (Tenn.), *cert. denied,* 510 U.S. 815, 114 S. Ct. 64, 126 L. Ed. 2d 33 (1993); *Howell v. American Casualty Co.,* 691 So. 2d 715, 1997 AMC 1739 (La. App. 4 Cir. 1997).

Note: Federal Court Proceedings in Diversity

In *Hellweg v. Baja Boats, Inc.,* 818 F. Supp. 1022, 1993 AMC 2122 (E.D. Mich. 1992), the court disagreed with the *obiter* view expressed by the *Vatican Shrimp* court that:

[D]efensive pleading under section 183 in a federal district court answer does not present the same jurisdictional problems. The district court, having jurisdiction to hear the entire case initially filed with it, can adjudicate and rule on a limited liability issue that is raised in a properly filed answer.

The *Hellweg* court held that this might be true if the federal district court had jurisdiction over the filed claim in admiralty, but it was not true if the basis of the district court's jurisdiction was diversity. The court said:

As previously stated, a case present before the district court as a civil action over which the court has jurisdiction solely due to the diversity of the parties, must be treated as would the same action filed in state court. This treatment includes the realization that the court in diversity cannot adjudicate matters only cognizable before a court exercising its admiralty jurisdiction. This disposition does not deny shipowners their admiralty rights to limit their liability pursuant to 46 U.S.C.App. §§ 183 and 185. Section 183 can be raised as a defense to an *in personam* action filed in any court. If contested, however, the issue can only be adjudicated by a district court presiding over the case as filed in admiralty. This is so because § 183 provides a defense to admiralty actions that are not filed *in rem* and, therefore, are not otherwise limited to the value of the vessel. The relief provided by the procedures of § 185 is available to any shipowner sued in any court so long as the procedures are followed. Defendants did not comply with the procedures of § 185, and this Court will not allow them to circumvent these procedures and now petition the Court to exercise its admiralty jurisdiction through § 183. Defendants can raise the defense, but that does not confer jurisdiction where it does not already lie. Defendants failed to petition the Court under § 185 at their own peril, and now they must accept the consequences.

Hellweg, 818 F. Supp. at 1028-29.

B. The Limitation Fund

COMPLAINT OF CARIBBEAN SEA TRANSPORT, LTD.

748 F.2d 622, 1985 AMC 1995 (11th Cir.1984)

[The facts and first part of the court's opinion are provided *supra*,Eds.]

* * *

B. Section 183(a) and Pending Freight

As mentioned above, a condition to bringing a limitation action is that the shipowner deposit with the court as security as um equal to the value of the vessel and pending freight, unless the owner transfers his interest in the vessel and freight to a trustee. The law is well established that the valuation of the vessel is its value at the termination of the voyage. *Norwich Co. v. Wright*, 13 Wall. (80 U.S.) 104, 20 L. Ed. 585 (1872). "Freight," as used in the Limitation Act, refers to the compensation received for carriage of goods, and not the goods themselves. "Pending freight" is the total earnings for the voyage, both prepaid and uncollected. *The Main v. Williams*, 152 U.S. 122, 131, 14 S. Ct. 486, 488, 38 L. Ed. 381 (1894); *The William J. Riddle*, 111 F. Supp. 657, 658 (S.D.N.Y. 1953).

[On Petition for rehearing, *Complaint of Caribbean Sea Transport, Ltd.,* 753 F.2d 948, 949 (11th Cir. 1985) the following paragraph was substituted for deleted language:]

Freight is generally not "earned," and thus is not pending," until the cargo is carried to and delivered at the place of destination. *Pacific Coast Co. v. Reynolds,* 114 F. 877, 881-82 (9th Cir.), *cert. denied,* 187 U.S. 640, 23 S. Ct. 841, 47 L. Ed. 345 (1902); *see* G. GILMORE & C. BLACK, JR., THE LAW OF ADMIRALTY § 10-32 (2d Ed. 1975). However, pending freight includes "prepaid freight which under the terms of [the shipowner's] agreement with his shippers is not to be returned in case the voyage is not completed." 3 Benedict on Admiralty § 65 (7th Ed. 1983); *see In re LaBourgogne,* 210 U.S. 95, 136, 28 S. Ct. 664, 679, 52 L. Ed. 973 (1908).

In our present case it is undisputed that the vessel is lying at the bottom of the sea and has no value whatsoever. However, appellant raises a number of attacks on the courts $82,000 valuation of "freight pending on the voyage." Peeling away the appellant's various arguments, the bone of contention on this issue boils down to the factual question of what constitutes "the voyage" in this case. Appellant asserts that "the voyage" was merely the ship's return trip from Kingston to Miami. The appellee contends that "the voyage" encompasses the entire round trip of the ship from Miami back to Miami.

What constitutes a voyage is a question of fact, which depends on the circumstances of the situation. *The William J. Riddle,* 111 F. Supp. at 658. Where an accident occurs on the return of a round-trip voyage, it may be that only the freight on the return voyage is "pending." For instance, in *In re La Bourgogne,* 210 U.S. 95, 28 S. Ct. 664, 52 L. Ed. 973 (1908), a vessel made trips between France and New York without any intermediate stops, discharging freight and picking up new freight at each end of the journey. The vessel collided with another ship on one of its trips from New York to France. The court held that each of these trips between France and New York or vice-versa was a separate voyage, so that the owner did not need to surrender freight earned in the ship's prior sailing from France to New York. *Id.*

However, if a round-trip voyage is equivalent to a "single adventure," earned freight *for the round trip* must be surrendered even if the collision occurs on the return leg of the trip after delivery of all cargo to various points. For example, in *The San Simeon,* 63 F.2d 798 (2d Cir.), *cert. denied,* 290 U.S. 643, 54 S. Ct. 61, 78 L. Ed. 558 (1933), the ship was on a voyage from the Pacific Coast to New York and Philadelphia. She had delivered cargo in New York, thus necessarily earning freight on it, and she was sailing up the Delaware River with the remainder of her cargo when she collided. The Second Circuit determined that "the voyage" encompassed the entire trip from the West Coast to Philadelphia; and that "pending freight" thus included freight already earned on cargo that was delivered in New York. Likewise, in *The William J. Riddle,* 111 F. Supp. 657, the court held that the round trip constituted the voyage. There, a steamship carrying a cargo of animals to foreign ports delivered the animals to the ports and returned to the United States empty except for the animal handlers. The following evidence indicated that "the voyage" encompassed the round trip: there was no expectation of return cargo; the ship's accountant carried the round trip on his logs as a single voyage; and the bill of lading and manifest of the ship provided for the round trip of the animal handlers. *Id.* at 658. *La Bourgogne* was distinguished as a situation where each east or west-bound trip had no connection whatsoever in purpose with the preceding trip in the other direction. *Id.*

The facts of this case fall under the holdings of *The William J. Riddle* and *The San Simeon.* Evidence indicated that the ANTILLES was running a typical "liner" service in which it would pick up cargo in Miami, make a circle of deliveries, and come back to the originating port in Miami, normally with an empty cargo hold. The cargo manifests of the ANTILLES, kept in the ordinary course of business, classified as a single voyage the entire trip leaving from Miami on February 11th to deliver cargo in Aruba, Curacao, and Antigua. From this evidence in the record, the district judge properly determined that the entire trip constituted "the voyage."[2] Thus, all freight earned on the deliveries of cargo prior to the collision should be posted as security pursuant to section 183.

[On Petition for rehearing, *Complaint of Caribbean Sea Transport, Ltd.* 753 F.2d 948, 949-50 (11th Cir. 1985) the following language was substituted for deleted language:]

The cargo manifests of the ANTILLES indicate that the appellant earned freight on the voyage in the amount of $74,558.71 by the completed delivery of cargo prior to the collision. This is pending freight that must be posted as security pursuant to section 183(a). However, it appears that when the ship sank it still contained cargo which was to have been delivered to Antigua, for which freight was prepaid in the amount of $7,900. The record on appeal does not indicate whether the shipping agreement underlying this carriage of goods permits the shipper to recover the amount of prepaid freight in the event the goods are not delivered because the voyage cannot be completed. Therefore, we affirm the district courts order as far as it requires the posting of $74,558.71 as security pursuant to section 183(a). This amount, plus 6% interest running from July 27, 1982 (the date this limitation proceeding was commenced), must be immediately posted to enable appellant to continue these limitation proceedings. We vacate the portion of the district court's order requiring the posting of security under section 183(a) over the amount of $74,558.71, and remand for further proceedings to determine whether an additional $7,900 should be posted under that section. If, under the terms of the shipping agreement, the prepaid freight can and will be recovered by the shipper because the goods were not delivered, then the appellant need not post the $7,900 amount. *Pacific Coast,* 114 F. at 882. If the shipping agreement does not permit the shipper to recover this prepaid freight, the $7,900 is completely earned, constitutes "pending freight," and must be posted as security. *LaBourgone,* 210 U.S. at 136, 28 S. Ct. at 679; *The Steel Inventor,* 36 F.2d399, 400 (S.D.N.Y. 1929).

C. Section 183(b) and the Personal Injury Claim

Section 183(b) was passed to protect claimants who have suffered bodily injury or loss of life, and provides that when the section 183(a) limitation fund "is insufficient to pay all losses in full," then the shipowner will be required to meet the claims for personal injuries up to an amount equal to $60* per ton of the vessels tonnage. Appellant contends that the district court improperly granted the $30,000 of additional security under this subsection, arguing that additional security should be required only when the section 183(a) limitation fund is rendered insufficient to meet all the claims: that is, only once the limitation proceeding is concluded and the personal injury claims are liquidated; or in the alternative, only upon a clear showing that the section 183(a) fund will be insufficient to cover all the personal injury claims.

---

[2] Appellant distorts the *Le Bourgogne* holding, arguing that the concept of "voyage" in admiralty practice is equivalent to each trip from one port to another. However, under our present facts each trip from one port to another was merely a leg of the voyage. As the district judge realized, appellant's interpretation would mean that a ship would never have "pending freight" in the situation of an open sea collision, because the ship could not have earned any freight between the time it left its last port and the time of the collision. The only time there would then be "pending freight" is when the ship arrives at a port, delivers its cargo, and right after delivery sinks before it can leave port.

*[Subsequently increased to $420 per ton. Eds.]

The law is not clear as to when, how, and under what conditions the court can order additional security posted under section 183(b). As Gilmore states;

> [a]ssume that death and injury claims have been filed against a shipowner who petitions for limitation, alleging that the value of the ship (which has been lost) is zero. Could the court with which the limitation petition is filed require the owner, as a condition of limitation, to post bond in an amount sufficient (up to the statutory ceiling) to satisfy his maximum liability under the claims (which are still unliquidated); or should the court first determine the basic questions of liability and right to limitation before requiring the owner to provide funds or sureties to satisfy the judgments? The first alternative would be more satisfactory to claimants who would be protected against supervening insolvency of the shipowner or dissipation of assets during possible protracted judicial proceedings; the second alternative would be more to the shipowner's liking. The statute offers no sure guide to solution, although, on a purely verbal level of statutory construction, the statement that the $60 per ton fund comes into operation only "if the amount of the owner's liability as limited under subsection (a) is insufficient" might be read to suggest that the questions of liability and limitation under section 183(a) must be first settled before the additional fund is set up. However in two recent cases where the aggregate of the death and injury claims was many times in excess of the section 183(a) fund, the trial judges sensibly ordered that section 183(b) funds be set up at the outset of the proceedings.

G.GILMORE & C.BLACK, JR., THE LAW OF ADMIRALTY, § 10-34 (2d Ed. 1975). Gilmore also notes that the provision in Admiralty Rule F(7), that "any claimant may demand that the deposit or security be increased on the ground that it is insufficient to carry out the provision of the statutes relating to claims in respect of loss of life or bodily injury," should presumably be taken to increase the limitation courts discretion in granting such "demands." *Id.* at n.l38a.

The two recent cases cited by Gilmore are *In Re Pan Oceanic Tankers Corp.,* 332 F. Supp. 313 (S.D.N.Y. 1971), and *In Re Alva Steamship Company,* 262 F. Supp. 328 (S.D.N.Y. 1966), which were both mass disaster cases where the district courts required the posting of additional security pursuant to section 183(b) when the dollar amount of personal injury and loss of life claims was much greater than the section 183(a) limitation fund.[4] These cases indicate that a district judge does have discretion to augment the security fund pursuant to section 183(b) prior to the conclusion of the limitation proceedings and the liquidation of personal injury claims.

However, section 183(b) does provide that the owner's liabiity to personal injury claimants will be increased only if the section 183(a) fund "is insufficient to pay all losses in full." Thus we think that personal injury claimants must make a clear, preliminary showing that the section 183(a) fund will be insufficient to cover all personal injury claims before a court should augment that fund under section 183(b). We hold that in order to augment the security fund pursuant to section 183(b), the district court must make preliminary determinations of the nature and extent of personal injury claims and the likelihood of recovery based on those claims, concluding that there is a likelihood that the section 183(a) fund will be insufficient to pay those claims in full. This will usually require some sort of evidentiary hearing. We emphasize that the product of such a hearing does not represent a final adjudication of liability and damages, but merely represents a preliminary appraisal of the shipowner's exposure to damages.

In our present case, the district court required the posting of section 183(b) security after a cursory hearing in which no evidence was taken. It does appear that evidence as to Russo's injury was available in the form of medical reports and Russo's deposition; but none of this evidence is present in the record of this case. At the hearing, Russo's counsel alleged that as a result of the collision Russo was knocked unconscious and hospitalized with a fractured vertebra; but there is no indication of the seriousness of this injury. Russo is the only claimant alleging personal injury in this case, so this is certainly not a mass disaster situation with huge potential liability. A remand would

---

[4] In *Pan Oceanic,* the section 183(a) fund was $100.00, compared to unliquidated claims for loss of life or bodily injury totalling $28,500,000.00. Thus the court considered it appropriate to increase the fund pursuant to section 183(b). 332 F. Supp. at 314-15. In *Alva Steamship,* the shipowner was faced with approximately $30,000,000.00 in personal injury claims. Although he had already posted section 183(a) security, the court required the owner to post bond under section 183(b) equivalent to $60.00 per ton of his vessel. 262 F. Supp. at 330.

be unnecessary if Russos counsel had presented any evidence regarding the nature and extent of injury; but under the circumstances of this case, we must vacate that portion of the district court's order requiring the posting of $30,000 security pursuant to section 183(b), and remand to the district court for a hearing and preliminary factual determination under the aforementioned standards.[5]

Therefore, the district court's opinion is AFFIRMED in part, and VACATED and REMANDED in part for further proceedings not inconsistent with this opinion.

Note: Prior Encumbrances

Supplemental Rule F does not require a shipowner to pay or secure all pre-existing encumbrances against the vessel before filing a limitation proceeding. The pleader must simply "show in his complaint the prior paramount liens and any existing liens that arose upon subsequent voyages." *In the Matter of Rodco Marine Services v. Migliaccio*, 651 F.2d 1101, 1985 AMC 605 (5th Cir. 1981). In *Rodco Marine Services*, the court held that a ship mortgage affecting the vessel is not a prior encumbrance that bars the owner from filing a proceeding to limit his liability and that "salvage claims are not prior encumbrances but instead are part of the claims arising from the voyage during which the casualty occurred and probably become a part of the limitation proceeding." The court stated that:

[T]here is no condition precedent to an owner of a vessel filing a petition for limitation of his liability. The petitioner must offer to surrender title of the vessel to a trustee to be appointed by the court or alternatively offer to pay into court a sum equal to the value of the vessel. If a trustee is appointed the vessel must be sold and the proceeds paid into the registry of the court. The court then determines the priority of the liens against the fund. If the entire fund is not available to voyage claimants, distribution should be made to the proper lienors and the owner denied exoneration.

Note: Computation of the Limitation Fund

Under American law the fund is equal to the value of the vessel after the casualty plus the pending freight. *Norwich & New York Transportation Co. v. Wright*, 80 U.S. (13 Wall.) 104, 20 L. Ed. 585 (1871). Compare the following provisions of the 1976 Convention on the Limitation of Maritime Claims, as amended by the 1996 Protocol:

Article 6 - The General Limits

1. The limits of liability for claims other than those mentioned in Article 7, arising on any distinct occasion, shall be calculated as follows:
(a) in respect of claims for loss of life or personal injury,
(i) 2 million Units of Account for a ship with a tonnage not exceeding 2,000 tons,
(ii) for a ship with a tonnage in excess thereof, the following amount in addition to that mentioned in (i): for each ton from 2,001 to 30,000 tons, 800 Units of Account; for each ton from 30,001 to 70,000 tons, 600 Units of Account; and for each ton in excess of 70,000 tons, 400 Units of Account,
(b) in respect of any other claims,
(i) 1 million Units of Account for a ship with a tonnage not exceeding 2,000 tons,
(ii) for a ship with a tonnage in excess thereof, the following amount in addition to that mentioned in (i): for each ton from 2,001 to 30,000 tons, 400 Units of Account; for each ton from 30,001 to 70,000 tons, 300 Units of Account; and for each ton in excess of 70,000 tons, 200 Units of Account.
2. Where the amount calculated in accordance with paragraph 1 (a) is insufficient to pay the claims mentioned therein in full, the amount calculated in accordance with paragraph 1 (b) shall be available for payment of the unpaid balance of claims under paragraph 1 (a) and such unpaid balance shall rank ratably with claims mentioned under paragraph 1(b).
3. However, without prejudice to the right of claims for loss of life or personal injury according to paragraph 2, a State Party may provide in its national law that claims in respect of damage to harbor works, basins and waterways and aids to navigation shall have such priority over other claims under paragraph 1 (b) as is provided by that law.
4. The limits of liability for any salvor not operating from any ship or for any salvor operating solely on the ship to, or in respect of which he is rendering salvage services, shall be calculated according to a tonnage of 1,500 tons.
5. For the purpose of this Convention the ship's tonnage shall be the gross tonnage calculated in accordance with the tonnage measurement rules contained in Annex I of the International Convention on Tonnage Measurement of Ships, 1969.

---

[5] At this hearing, the appellant shipowner may also present evidence as to the space occupied by seamen on the ANTILLES, which is excluded from the gross tonnage of the ship to reach the "tonnage" figure which is multiplied by $60 to obtain the amount of the section 183(b) fund. *See* 46 U.S.C. § 183(b), (c). We think that the shipowner properly has the burden of proof on the calculation of "tonnage" under section 183(c).

Article 7 - The Limits for Passenger Claims

1. In respect of claims arising on any distinct occasion for loss of life or personal injury to passengers of a ship, the limit of liability of the shipowner thereof shall be an amount of 175,000 Units of Account multiplied by the number of passengers which the ship is authorized to carry according to the ship's certificate.

2. For the purpose of this Article "claims for loss of life or personal injury to passengers of a ship" shall mean any such claims brought by or on behalf of any person carried in that ship:

    (a) under a contract of passenger carriage, or
    (b) who, with the consent of the carrier, is accompanying a vehicle or live animals which are covered by a contract for the carriage of goods.

Article 8 - Unit of Account

1. The Unit of Account referred to in Articles 6 and 7 is the Special Drawing Right as defined by the International Monetary Fund. The amounts mentioned in Articles 6 and 7 shall be converted into the national currency of the State in which limitation is sought, according to the value of that currency at the date the limitation fund shall have been constituted, payment is made, or security is given which under the law of that State is equivalent to such payment. The value of a national currency in terms of the Special Drawing Right, of a State Party which is a member of the International Monetary Fund, shall be calculated in accordance with the method of valuation applied by the International Monetary Fund in effect at the date in question of its operations and transactions. The value of a national currency in terms of the Special Drawing Right, of a State Party which is not a member of the International Monetary Fund, shall be calculated in a manner determined by that State Party.

[NB: The International Monetary Fund publishes exchange rates for the Special Drawing Right to various international currencies. They can be found at http://www.imf.org/external/np/tre/sdr/db/rms_five.cfm. On December 21st, 2004, the exchange rate of the S.D.R. to the U.S. dollar was 1 to F539620. At that exchange rate, the 2 million S.D.R. limit in the first step of the scale for loss of life or personal injury would be worth US$3,079,240. The limit for subsequent steps would be correspondingly higher. Eds.]

Note: The "Flotilla" Rule

In *Liverpool, Brazil and River Plate Steam Navigation Co. v. Brooklyn Eastern District Terminal,* 251 U.S. 48, 40 S. Ct. 66, 64 L. Ed. 130 (1919), the court held that where two or more vessels under common ownership are involved in the same accident, only the vessel actively at fault (the tug) must be valued or surrendered for purposes of the limitation fund. In *Sacramento Navigation Co. v. Salz,* 273 U.S. 326, 47 S. Ct. 368, 71 L. Ed. 663, 1927 AMC 397 (1927), the court, in a Harter Act case not involving the limitation act, stated that a tug and barge were considered one vessel. In dicta, the court distinguished *Liverpool* as involving "pure tort, not a contract of affreightment". This spawned the "flotilla" rule based on a contractual obligation theory that all vessels engaged in a marine venture must be included in the limitation fund. *Standard Dredging Co. v. Kristiansen,* 67 F.2d 548, 1933 AMC 1621 (2d Cir. 1933).

In *South Carolina State Highway Department v. Jacksonville Shipyards, Inc.,* 1976 AMC 456 (S.D. Ga. 1975), the court, in a case in which the master of a tug negligently allowed a barge to hit a bridge, included only the value of the tug and her freight in the limitation proceeding. The court explained:

> Lower courts have reluctantly followed *Liverpool* in pure tort situations…. In [one] case the district court said that it is "at least doubtful whether the *Liverpool* doctrine is responsive to the realities of the situation."
>
> The rigidity of the "pure tort" concept has been relaxed by distinct courts able to find that the barge itself was an "offending vessel" independently of the propelling tug to which it was attached or temporarily detached. A distinction has been drawn where a tow breaks away from a tug and "the independent act of the barge breaking its mooring … resulted in damage to the pier." A similar result was reached [in another case where] barges had been moored by a tug that temporarily detached itself and in the interim they had broken loose from their mooring damaging a lock an dam on the Ohio River.
>
>   * * *
>
> The doctrinal treatment by federal courts of limitation of liability in flotilla type situations is illogical when the result is (a) that a tug and attached barge are considered as two separate vessels if the damage to a third party amounts to a *tort* and the tug is the offending instrumentality, but (b) where a *contractual* element is involved, the same tug and barge constitute a single vessel when damage to a contracting party occurs through fault of the tow.
>
> The collision with the Hilton Head bridge was by the barge and not the tug. It would not have occurred except for the presence of the former alongside *JaxI* which considerably increased the total beam of the flotilla. The barge was pushed into the fenders by the

tug which was the offending vessel. The barge was merely a passive, well-less component of the rig. In short, the instant case simply cannot be distinguished from the fact background that underlay the 56-year old decision in *Liverpool.*

The able, always interesting and occasionally crusading authors of THE LAW OF ADMIRALTY [GILMORE AND BLACK] (who predict it to be most unlikely that the Supreme Court "will ever agree to hear another flotilla case") challenge "some daring federal judge" to come forward and give the *Liverpool* decision that "cavalier treatment" which the federal courts have accorded to it in the case of the exception where a flotilla is used in performance of a contract. The worst that can happen to such a judge is that he will be reversed....

Several comments are appropriate in respect to this ringing call to district court judges. First, the Congress enacted the legislation out of which grew the controversial interpretation thereof in Liverpool. The legislative branch can change the law when it desires. Secondly (and relatedly), the question of flotilla liability is subsumed by the imperious issue of continued existence of the limitation theory. Should it be scuttled as an archaic vestige of the days of merchant sailing ships and coal-burning steamships? Finally, district courts are bound by decisions of the Supreme Court and the law is settled by *Liverpool....*

All that can be hoped of in this case, assuming an appeal and affirmance, is that the Supreme Court will see fit to grant certiorari and agree to reappraise its 1919 decision which so effectively and regrettably forecloses a contrary ruling below.

Some courts have been more adventurous. Notwithstanding the *Liverpool, Brazil and River Plate* decision by the Supreme Court, several lower courts have required that the limitation fund equal the value of several vessels engaged in a common project, even when the claims are made in tort. *In re United States Dredging Corp.,* 264 F.2d 339 (2d Cir. 1959); *Brown & Root Marine Operators, Inc. v. Zapata Off-Shore Co.,* 377 F.2d 724, 727 (5th Cir. 1967), *Cenac Towing Co. v. Terra Resources, Inc.,* 734 F.2d251 (5th Cir. 1984), *Complaint of Tom-Mac, Inc.,* 76 F.3d678, 684, 1996 AMC 1244 (5th Cir. 1996), *In re Offshore Specialty Fabricators, Inc.,* 2002 AMC 2055 (E.D. La. 2002).

Note: Distribution of the Fund

Rule F (8) governs the distribution of the limitation fund. In distributing the fund, courts apply lien priority rules as principles of equitable subordination to give preference to personal injury and cargo claimants over a negligent vessel's claim for collision damages. *The CATSKILL,* 95 F. 700 (S.D.N.Y. 1899).

In collision cases the balance of damages must be struck before limitation. *The North Star,* 106 U.S. 17, 26-29, 1 S. Ct. 41, 27 L. Ed. 91 (1882).

Are personal injury claimants restricted to the 46 U.S.C.A. § 30508 tonnage fund? *See Oliver J. Olsen & Co. v. American Steamship Marine Leopard,* 356 F.2d 728, 1966 AMC 1064 (9th Cir. 1966).

C. Parties and Vessels Entitled to Limit

1. Demise vs. Time Charterer

Note: Bareboat Charterers

In *Complaint of Cook Transp. System, Inc.* 431 F. Supp. 437 (W.D. Tenn. 1976), a petition for limitation of liability was filed by charterers of a barge and grew out of an incident on a barge when its cargo of soybeans exploded while it were being unloaded injuring many workmen.

"Complainants CTS, Cook and UMTC allege in the action under consideration that the accident and damage in question was occasioned due to no fault on their part, and that it occurred without privity or knowledge on their part. The barge was a steel-hulled river barge with no independent means of power. It is also alleged that C.T.S. and Cook were "demise charterers" of this Barge.

The barge charter agreement . . . was between [the owner of the barge] UMTC, and C.T.S. [It provided that] UMTC, for valuable consideration, was to deliver the barge to C.T.S. free from lien and in a seaworthy condition. "Delivery" and "possession" were made over to C.T.S., which was obligated to return in "as good running order . . . ordinary wear and tear excepted" with a qualified marine surveyor to inspect at the beginning and end of the approximate four (4) year term. C.T.S. was to maintain hull insurance to a minimum value of $40,000 naming C.T.S. and UMTC as their interests may appear, but C.T.S. was to indemnify UMTC from "any and all loss or damage of or to the barge . . . excluding liability at law of UMTC . . . as a tower." "All necessary maintenance and cleaning for the barges during the Charter term shall be arranged by UMTC for the account of Cook, provided that UMTC shall be responsible for one-half the cost of all ordinary maintenance, excluding cleaning. Cook shall be solely responsible for keeping the barges in a clean and safe condition, including the cleaning of meal or other commodities off the decks which are detrimental to the life of the barge or the safety of crews."

Cook was further under the charter to be responsible for pollution damage, but "UMTC *shall have the exclusive right to tow all barges covered by this Agreement.*" (emphasis added by eds.) Cook guaranteed "unconditionally and absolutely" the "agreements" and "obligations" of C.T.S. "as if (it) were an original party."

Other characteristics of a demise arrangement, however, were present here. The owner furnished a vessel in seaworthy state at the outset, and C.T.S. was to return it in good condition, except for normal wear and tear; survey was provided for. Responsibility for providing insurance was also covered as in a typical demise situation. Some indicia of a kind of title transfer, moreover, was made on the barge letters were changed from "UM 388" to "CKI-388" "for the convenience of the parties," the costs being equally divided. Though a vessel, the barge itself would be manned by very limited personnel, so it would not be expected that much thought would have been given to "manning" or "victualing" the barge, *but there was some at least indirect reference to "navigating". That reference was to the exclusive right of UMTC in towing the barge; thus, UMTC could direct the navigation even though for the account of and under the general instruction of C.T.S.* (emphasis added by eds). While so towing, C.T.S.'s indemnification liability would not apply. Also, UMTC retained the right to arrange for all necessary maintenance and cleaning for the barge during the term, the cost of maintenance to be borne one-half (1/2) by each. This would indicate a continuing recognition of its interest in and indirect control over maintenance (and cleaning) by the owner at least to some degree, since it would bear one-half (1/2) the cost thereof.

Since the burden is upon each complainant to establish its right to exoneration and/or limitation, (and no provision of the towing agreement between C.T.S. and UMTC that would indicate an outright transfer or a complete and exclusive relinquishment of control has been called to our attention), this Court holds that C.T.S., as a charter party, has failed to carry its burden of showing that it is entitled to the extraordinary maritime relief applicable to a demise charterer. Cook, as an unconditional guarantor, stands in a somewhat different position than C.T.S., but it can claim no better position as to limitation than its subsidiary, C.T.S....

This Court is mindful that circumstances pertaining to a barge without an independent power source may differ from that of a vessel with its own means of propulsion. Some courts have indicated that charter of a barge without power is, in fact, a demise See R. Lenahan, 48 F.2d 110 (2nd Cir., 1931); *Ira S. Bushey & Sons v. Hedger & Co.*, 40 F.2d 417 (2nd Cir., 1930) *The Nat E. Sutton*, 42 F.2d 229 (E.D.N.Y., 1930); *Moran Towing v. City of New York*, 36 F.2d 417 (S.D.N.Y., 1929); *Dailey v. Carroll*, 248 F. 466 (2nd Cir., 1917); *The Daniel Burns*, 52 F. 159 (S.D.N.Y., 1892). These cases and their holdings are noted in The Doyle, 105 F.2d 113, 114 (3rd Cir., 1939), but in the latter case which held a barge charterer to become the "owner pro hac vice", it was important that the charterer was a towing company with the right of and in the exercise of navigation of the barge, which caused damage to its cargo. *R. D. Wood Co. v. Phoenix Steel Corp.*, 211 F.Supp. 924, 927 (E.D.Pa., 1962) also comments on the latter aspect of Doyle, observing that "... the towing company had clearly taken over complete control of the vessel and was, therefore, correctly treated as the owner."

2. Shipowner's Insurer

Note: Insurance

In Louisiana and Puerto Rico, by statute, direct actions against the insurer are allowed, but insurance carriers are denied the benefit of limitation of liability because this privilege is personal to the shipowner. In *Maryland Casualty Co. v. Cushing.*, 347 U.S. 409, 74 S. Ct. 608, 98 L. Ed. 806, 1954 AMC 837 (1954), in a 4-1-4 split opinion, a majority of the justices nevertheless agreed that any conflict between a direct action statute and the Limitation Act could be resolved by staying the direct action suit until completion of the limitation proceeding. Thus, in these jurisdictions, if insurance policy amounts are sufficient to cover all claims, the limitation proceeding is moot. If, however, the insurance is insufficient, the shipowner who is granted limitation will receive credit for the insurance recovery. The maximum sum available to pay claims is then the greater of either the insurance fund or the limitation fund. *See in re Independent Towing Co.*, 242 F. Supp. 950, 1965 AMC 818 (E.D. La. 1965).

How does this differ from jurisdictions with no direct action statute?

CROWN ZELLERBACH CORP. v. INGRAM INDUSTRIES, INC.

783 F.2d 1296, 1986 AMC 1471 (5th Cir. 1986) *(en banc)*

JOHN R. BROWN, Circuit Judge:

The sole remaining issue for en banc determination is the validity of the provision of a marine protection and indemnity (P. & I.) policy fixing the underwriter's maximum liability to that of the assured shipowner's judicially declared limitation of liability. Stated obversely, the question is whether the P & I underwriter is liable in excess of the assured shipowner's admitted limited liability. Along the way we will determine the continued vitality of our earlier *Nebel Towing* decision [FN2. *Olympic Towing Corp. v. Nebel Towing Co.*, 419 F.2d 230, 1969 AMC 1571 (5th

Cir. 1969)—Eds] on which the trial court and the panel majority relied. We hold that the underwriter is not liable for the excess and in doing so overrule *Nebel Towing*.

I.

This appeal grows out of an allision on the Mississippi River between the tow in tow of the tug F.R. BIGELOW and Crown Zellerbach's (CZ) water intake structure. Involved also was the tug's (and owners') maritime limitation of liability proceeding in which CZ brought a Louisiana direct action against prime and excess P & I underwriters of the vessel owner/operator. After trial, the District Court held that Ingram Industries, Inc. (Ingram), the tug owner/operator, was liable, but was entitled to limit its liability to the value of the vessel and the pending freight. The excess P. & I. underwriter was held liable for nearly $2,000,000 of the portion of CZ's damages that exceeded the limited liability of the vessel owner. We approved the trial court's holding of (i) no "privity or knowledge" by the tug owner, (ii) the valuation of the vessel, (iii) the computation of CZ's damages, and (iv) the award of prejudgment interest calculated from a date later than the accident. However, the Court by divided vote determined that the District Court was free of error in holding the tug owner's underwriter liable beyond the dollar limits fixed, or ascertainable, in the P. & I. policy.

How it All Happened

On February 3, 1979, the tugboat F.R BIGELOW owned (or bareboat chartered) by Ingram, while pushing 15 loaded barges down the Mississippi River in heavy fog and rain, caused its forward lead barge to collide with and damage CZ's water intake structure, located above Baton Rouge, Louisiana. Shortly after this incident, CZ began to repair the structure, but these repairs were interrupted on May 18, 1979, when another tugboat collided with the structure and damaged the remaining portion. The structure was not rebuilt in kind, but was rebuilt in a different form.

CZ filed suit against the tugboat F.R. BIGELOW, and Ingram, her bareboat charterer, in April of 1979. Subsequently, it amended its complaint to include Cherokee Insurance Company (Cherokee), the prime P & I insurer of Ingram, with a policy limit of $1,000,000, and London Steam-Ship Owners' Mutual Insurance Association (London Steam-Ship), excess P & I insurers of Ingram, with a deductible franchise of $1,000,000.

In its answer to the suit based upon the accident of February 3, 1979, Ingram, the charterer-owner/operator of the F.R. BIGELOW, sought limitation of its liability to the value of the vessel plus freight then pending. *See* 46 U.S.C. § 183. Ingram stipulated liability for striking the intake structure, and the issues of damages and limitation of liability were tried. Following trial, the District Court entered judgment for CZ in the "total sum" of $3,948,210.31 with prejudgment interest calculated from December 11, 1980. The District Court granted Ingram's prayer for limitation of liability, valued the vessel at $2,134,918.88, and limited the owner's liability to that amount. Since Cherokee's prime P & I policy was for $1,000,000, the District Court decreed the total sum of CZ's judgment as follows:

Table 1

(a)	Total Damages to CZ		$3,948,210.31
(b)	Payable by Owner and Cherokee Prime P & I	$1,025,000.00	
(c)	Payable by Owner and London Steam Excess P & I	$1,109,918.88	
(d)	Owner's Limited Liability		$2,134,918.88
(e)	Balance by London Steam Excess P & I		$1,813,291.44

Following the entry of judgment, Ingram and its two P. & I. underwriters made payments up to Ingram's limited liability ($2,134,918.88).

London Steam-Ship challenged the portion of the District Courts judgment holding that underwriter liable for the amount ($1,813,291.44) of CZ's claim over and above Ingrams fixed limited liability ($2,134,918.88). The panel, by divided vote, affirmed that holding.

The P. & I. Coverage

For its protection against claims for damage to piers and other fixed (non-vessel) structures, Ingram, as chartered owner of the tug BIGELOW, had two P & I covers. The prime cover was with Cherokee, with the amount of insurance being specified as $1,000,000. London Steam-Ship, through A. Bilbrough and Company as managers, dove-tailing Cherokee's cover with a deductible franchise of $1,000,000, supplied an excess P & I cover in accordance with its Rules.

Louisiana Enters the Fray

In what at one time was thought to be the tranquil waters of *Jensen* [*See Southern Pac. Co. v. Jensen*, 244 U.S. 205, 37 S. Ct. 524, 61 L. Ed. 1086, 1996 AMC 2076 (1917) - Eds] with its jealous guard of admiralty uniformity unsettled by *Wilburn Boat* [*Wilburn Boat Co. v. Fireman's Fund Ins. Co.*, 348 U.S. 310, 75 S. Ct. 368, 99 L. Ed. 337 (1955) — Eds] and the intrusion of state laws into these sacred waters, our problem comes about by the Louisiana Direct Action statute, La.R.S. 22:655.

This statute, as its name implies, allows a direct action against a liability insurer for Louisiana-incurred damages. But the statute does not create new Louisiana liabilities. On the contrary, by its own terms, reinforced by Louisiana judicial decisions, the statute imposes liability on the insurer subject "to all of the lawful conditions of the policy or contract and the defenses which could be urged by the insurer to a direct action brought by the insured, provided the terms and conditions of such policy or contract are not in violation of the laws of this State."

II.

In our much discussed decision of *Olympic Towing Corp. v. Nebel Towing Co.*, 419 F.2d 230, 1969 A.M.C. 1571, *rehearing denied*, 419 F.2d 238 (5th Cir.1969) (en banc), *cert. denied*, 397 U.S. 989, 90 S.Ct. 1120, 25 L.Ed.2d 396 (1970), the Court relied in part on the Louisiana Direct Action Statute to affirm the District Courts award of judgment in excess of the limitation value against the underwriter of the vessel at fault.

The P. & I. policy in *Nebel Towing* did not by its terms limit the insurer's liability to the vessel owner's limited liability. That meant that the P. & I. underwriter, in its effort to limit its liability, had to contend that as the insurer it had the right to claim the vessel owner's *statutory* right to limit its liability.

In holding the statutory limitation right unavailable to the insurer, the *Nebel Towing* court reasoned as follows: the enigmatic but undeniable *Cushing* decision [FN6. *Maryland Casualty Co. v. Cushing*, 347 U.S. 409, 74 S. Ct. 608, 98 L. Ed. 806, 1954 AMC 837 (1954) - Eds] declined to hold the Louisiana statute to be preempted by the paramount federal maritime power. Therefore, the Court tested the insurers claim of entitlement to the shipowner's statutory right to limit liability according to the law of Louisiana.

> The insurer attempted to rely on a clause in its policy limiting its liability to "such sums as the assured * * * shall have become legally liable to pay and shall have paid on account." This no-action clause, however, directly ran afoul of the Louisiana Direct Action Statute.

> The statute simply voids any policy clause which conditions the right of the injured person to enforce against the insurer its contractual obligation to pay the insured s debt upon, as prerequisite, the obtaining by the injured person of a judgment against the insured.

Hidalgo v. Dupuy, 122 So.2d 639, 644-45 (La.App.1960), *quoted in Nebel Towing*, 419 F.2d at 237.

The *Nebel Towing* court also held that the limitation of liability defense was a defense "personal" to the shipowner and could not be availed of by the insurer. *See* LA.CIV.CODE ANN. art. 1801 (West 1985). As we discuss below, this holding was the result of a flawed analogy to Louisiana immunity law and was wholly unnecessary to the *Nebel Towing* decision.

III.

Out of the Fog of Nebel Towing

It is here that we must part ways with *Nebel Towing* In a nutshell, the distinction between this case and *Nebel Towing* is a simple one. *Nebel Towing* dealt solely with the contention that the P. & I. underwriter was entitled to the shipowner's *statutory* right to limit liability. Here the claim is quite different: the P. & I. underwriter is claiming only that, as prescribed by the Louisiana Direct Action Statute, the terms of its own insurance policy limits maximum liability to the dollar amount for which the shipowner-assured would be liable upon successfully maintaining the right to limit its liability. The P. & I. underwriter is not claiming the *statutory* right of the assured. To the contrary, it is here claiming only the limitation of the insurance policy defense itself. As we explain below, this policy limitation cannot be contrary to Louisiana law nor to the public policy of the state.

London Steam-Ship Coverage

London Steam-Ship (known in the parlance as a "P. & I .Club")[7] promulgated rules which defined its liabilities and defenses.

The uncontradicted record traces the history of London Steam-Ship Rules from 1881-82, when liability was fixed at 30 per entered ton with a limit of 3000 tons, to 1952-53, when the maximum of 3000 entered tons was deleted. The Club realized that, in this day and time of almost unlimited, astronomical liabilities with aggravated uncertainties as to the shipowner's ability successfully to maintain the statutory right to limit liability and the practical demands of its shipowner members, it was faced with the problem of determining in what manner its total liability exposure could be expressed. Beginning in 1955—long before *Nebel Towing* was decided—this was handled by Rule 8(i):

When a Member for whose account a ship is entered in this Class, is entitled to limit his liability, the liabilityof the Class shall not exceed the amount of such limitation....

In sharp contrast to the situation in *Nebel Towing* in which the P. & I. claimed only the right to a *statutory* defense, London Steam-Ship s excess P. & I. policy by Rule 8(i) has a policy term which limits its liability to that of the owner's limited liability. This is a *policy* not a *statutory* defense. The P & I insurer is not claiming the owner's *statutory* right to a shipowner's limited liability, but merely the right to assert its *policy defense*.

Since there can be no question that Rule 8(i) is one of the "... lawful conditions of the policy or contract," it brings us face to face with the critical provision of the Louisiana Direct Action Statute that "any action brought hereunder shall be subject to ... the *defenses which could be urged by the insurer to a direct action brought by the insured....*"

Direct Action

We start with our decisions which today are still very much intact. For example, *see Degelos v. Fidelity & Casualty Co.,* 313 F.2d 809 (5th Cir. 1963) and *Tokio Marine & Fire Insurance Co. v. Aetna Casualty Co.,* 322 F.2d 113, 1964 A.M.C. 308 (5th Cir. 1963).

---

[7] By the deposition of John Hawkes, director of Bilbrough, it is uncontradicted that London Steam-Ship, the "Club," is an association composed of a number of members, all of whom are shipowners, who "severally and individually, not jointly nor in partnership, nor the one for the other of them, but each only in his own name" agree to protect and indemnify *each other* in respect of the vessel entered for protection and indemnity risk in accordance with the Rules of the association.

The decisions of the Louisiana courts have been as unambiguous as the language of the Direct Action Statute itself: there must be a legal liability on part of the assured for the insurer to have a direct action liability. In *Burke v. Massachusetts Bonding & Insurance Co.*, 209 La. 495, 24 So.2d 875 (1946), the question was whether under the law of Mississippi a wife had a right of action against her husband's Louisiana liability insurer for a tort that her husband committed against her in Mississippi. The Louisiana Supreme Court stated:

> The statute does not give plaintiff any more rights than she has under the law of Mississippi. It only furnishes her with a method to enforce in Louisiana whatever rights she has in Mississippi. Since she has no cause of action under the law of Mississippi, necessarily Act No. 55 of 1930 confers upon her no cause of action in Louisiana. The mere fact that under the statute plaintiff was able to obtain jurisdiction against her husband's liability insurer in a direct action in this State does not create, as against her husband, *or as against her insurer,* a substantive cause of action that does not exist under the law of the State where the wrongful act occurred.

24 So.2d at 877 (emphasis added).

> *See also Ruiz v. Clancy,* 182 La. 935, 162 So. 734, 735-36 (1935):
> The statute does not purport to interfere with the right of an insurance company to limit the so-called coverage, "in any policy against liability," to "liability imposed upon him [the assured] by law," as this policy provides. *An insurance company therefore, may*—as the company did in this instance—*limit the coverage, or liability of the company, to pay only such sums as the insured shall become obligated to pay by reason of the liability imposed upon him by law.* The attorney for the insurance company contends that the statute would interfere with the freedom of parties to enter into contracts, and would be therefore unconstitutional, if it forbade insurers to limit their so-called coverage in liability insurance policies, so as to cover only the legal liability of the insured. The statute does not purport to do that, by merely giving an injured person a right of action against the insurer, and by compelling the insurer to respond—*within the limits of the policy*—to the obligation of the insured.

(Emphasis added).

In the face of these strong precedents, from both Louisiana and this Court, the contrary result reached in *Nebel Towing* cannot stand. The policy provision 8(i) is not couched as a claim to the shipowner's *statutory* right to limit liability. What—and all—it says is that we, the P. & I. underwriters, will pay up to but not beyond the assured's legal liability. Whatever the assured is liable for we will pay, 100% in full with no discount, but no more.

In the face of such a wholesome economic principle there is nothing in *Nebel Towing* that could lead this Court to say—as did the panel and concurring opinion, 745 F.2d 998,—that this is contrary to public policy or, in the words of § 655 "in violation of the laws of [the] state." From the standpoint of Louisiana's concern—reflected in § 655—about the injured victims of a tort, how could an insurance policy be more fair than to say: whatever your (the assured's) liability, we will pay 100% in full without reduction?

And what, from the standpoint of fairness and Louisiana's public policy could be unfair about the P. & I. policies expressing the insurer's maximum liability, not in terms of dollars, but rather in words which are plain and readily ascertainable; not in terms of contentions or hopes, but in words of a realized permanent judicial decision?

IV.

Related to the concept of personal defense which serves as an additional ground for our decision is the fact that Rule 8(i) is a defense that is personal to London Steam-Ship. The defense asserted by London Steam-Ship is not a defense of Ingram, its assured. Indeed, London Steam-Ship is not asserting any defense of Ingram, the owner.

As a policy clause, Rule 8(i) is a defense personal to London Steam-Ship, the underwriter as a solidary obligor. Article 2098 allows a debtor to raise all defenses that "are personal to himself," as this policy defense certainly is. *See supra* note 15. London Steam-Ship may raise this defense without regard to whether Ingram's right to limit liability is a defense personal to it.

> [I]nsurers may assert defenses which result from the nature of the obligation—contributory negligence, assumption of risk, confusion, collateral estoppel and res judicata, for example, as well as those common to all co-debtors.... Additionally, *insurers enjoy and frequently assert defenses personal to themselves, such as coverage, policy limits,* and procurement by misstatement of material facts in the application.

Alcoa Steamship Co. v. Charles Ferran, Inc., 251 F. Supp. 823, 831 (E.D.La.1966), *aff'd,* 383 F.2d 46 (5th Cir.1967), *cert. denied,* 393 U.S. 836, 89 S.Ct. 111, 21 L.Ed.2d 107 (1968) (emphasis added).

This result makes it unnecessary for us to decide whether, in view of the Supreme Court's enigmatic 4-1-4 decision for that day and time only in *Cushing v. Maryland Casualty Co.,* 347 U.S. 409, 74 S.Ct. 608, 98 L.Ed.2d 806, 1954 A.M.C. 837 (1954), there is yet a final decision on the constitutionality of the Louisiana Direct Action Statute *vis-a-vis* the federal shipowner's limitation of liability statute, 46 U.S.C. § 183 *et seq.*

Conclusion

Nebel Towing is overruled and the District Court is reversed with respect to the liability of London Steam-Ship for amounts in excess of Ingram's limited liability. In all other respects the District Court is affirmed.

REVERSED IN PART, AFFIRMED IN PART.

THORNBERRY, Circuit Judge, specially concurred in an opinion that is not reproduced here.

TATE, Circuit Judge, wrote a dissenting opinion, in which ALVIN B. RUBIN, POLITZ, JOHNSON and JERRE S. WILLIAMS, Circuit Judges, joined. It, too, is not reproduced here.

Notes

1. *Direct Actions Against Insurers: The Limitation of Liability Defense*

For discussion of the Crown Zellerbach decision, see Gordon P. Gates, *Crown Zellerbach Dethrones Nebel Towing: Shipowner's Limitation of Liability Is Available To Insurers,* 62 TUL. L. REV. 615, 615-23 (1988).

A limiting term in a marine insurance policy thus gives rise to a valid defense, and a direct-action plaintiff may not successfully challenge such a policy term on the grounds that the term contravenes either the Louisiana law or federal maritime law. *In the Matter of Magnolia Marine Transportation Co. v. Laplace Towing Corporation,* 964 F.2d 1571, 1994 AMC 303 (5th Cir. 1992). The interpretation of a limiting term in a marine insurance policy does not fall within the exclusive jurisdiction of the limitation forum; state courts have concurrent jurisdiction under the "saving to suitors" clause. *Id.*

2. *Persons Entitled to Limit Liability*

Who is the "owner" of a vessel for purposes of asserting limitation? *See Caulkins v. Graham,* 667 F.2d 1292, 1982 AMC 2433 (9th Cir. 1982). Does limitation apply in favor of the United States? *See Dick v. United States,* 671 F.2d 724, 1982 AMC 913 (2d Cir. 1982).

Should the right to limit be extended to include time charterers and insurers? What about the master, the crew, salvors, or an independent contractor like a shipyard? Consider the following provision of the Convention on the Limitation of Maritime Claims, 1976:

Article 1. Persons Entitled to Limit Liability

1. Shipowners and salvors, as hereinafter defined, may limit their liability in accordance with the rules of this Convention for claims set out in Article 2. [claims subject to limitation].

2. The term shipowner shall mean the owner, charterer, manager and operator of a seagoing ship.

3. Salvor shall mean any person rendering services in direct connection with salvage operations. Salvage operations shall also include operations referred to in Article 2, paragraph 1 (d), (e) and (f) [raising, removal or destruction of the ship or cargo].

4. If any claims set out in Article 2 are made against any person or whose act, neglect or default the shipowner or salvor is responsible, such person shall be entitled to avail himself of the limitation of liability provided for in this Convention.

5. In this Convention the liability of a shipowner shall include liability in an action brought against the vessel herself.

6. An insurer of liability for claims subject to limitation in accordance with the rules of this Convention shall be entitled to the benefits of this Convention to the same extent as the assured himself.

7. The act of invoking limitation of liability shall not constitute an admission of liability.

3. Vessels Subject to Limitation

Pleasure boats are, generally, vessels for purposes of admiralty jurisdiction. *See Sisson v. Ruby,* 497 U.S. 358, 110 S. Ct. 2892, 111 L. Ed. 2d 292, 1990 AMC 1801 (1990). Are pleasure boats also vessels for purposes of the Limitation of Liability Act? *See* Rodriguez and Jaffe, *An Overview of U.S. Law of Shipowners Limitation of Liability,* MLA REPORT 9621, 9625-9628 (October 31, 1991):

The application of the Act to pleasure vessels has been more problematic, and this issue has generated considerable litigation in the last several years. Since 1975, eight federal courts of appeal have taken up the question. Seven of these courts have concluded that the Act is applicable to pleasure craft. However, in 1989, the Seventh Circuit decided to "go it alone" in the *Sisson* case by holding that limitation was unavailable to a private pleasure craft. This holding was reversed by the U.S. Supreme Court, but the Court did not specifically address the issue of the Act's general applicability to pleasure craft.

Those courts which have held that the Act applies to pleasure craft have noted that, as originally enacted, the Limitation Act expressly stated that it did not apply to "any canal boat, barge, or lighter, or to any vessel of any description whatsoever, used in rivers or inland navigation." In 1886, Congress amended that Act to extend it to include "... all vessels used on lakes or rivers or in inland navigation." Thereafter, the Act was applied to pleasure craft as early as 1927; yet when the Act was amended in 1935, 1936, and 1984, no attempt was made to exclude pleasure craft from its ambit. Therefore, these courts have determined that, although application of the Act to pleasure craft might be illogical, the working of the Act and its legislative history dictate such a result.

The circuit court in *Sisson* and those district courts which have refused to permit application of the Act to pleasure craft have adopted a quite different approach, relying on jurisdictional arguments to deny limitation. In particular, these courts have held that where there is no admiralty jurisdiction over the underlying tort, the Limitation Act does not provide a separate basis for admiralty jurisdiction. Under this analysis, the court would be without subject matter jurisdiction to decide limitation. It also has been held that the Limitation Act does not confer upon the federal court either Federal Question jurisdiction or Commerce Clause jurisdiction.

In *Sisson,* a pleasure yacht docked at a marina on Lake Michigan caught fire. The fire destroyed the yacht and caused extensive damage to the marina and several other boats. The Seventh Circuit held that, although the fire at the marina satisfied the locality test of admiralty jurisdiction, it did not meet the Nexus test as the tort did not bear a significant relationship to "traditional maritime activity." The circuit court, therefore, held that there was no admiralty jurisdiction. Additionally, the court rejected the argument that the Limitation Act provides a separate basis of admiralty jurisdiction notwithstanding a 1911 Supreme Court decision which held the Act to be applicable both to non-maritime and maritime torts. The court of appeals refuse to follow the 1911 decision because 1) the need that inspired that decision no longer exists and 2) the decision predated the new, more restrictive tests for admiralty jurisdiction.

The Supreme Court decision in the *Sisson* case reversed that of the Seventh Circuit and remanded the case for further proceedings. The court held that a fire in a marina does meet the admiralty nexus test and therefore that admiralty jurisdiction existed. Additionally, the Supreme Court left open the question of whether the Limitation Act itself provides an independent basis for admiralty jurisdiction where the facts of a case do not meet the "nexus" test of admiralty jurisdiction. Interestingly, even though the Supreme Court had requested the parties to brief the continuing validity of that case even though it has been strongly questioned and expressly not followed by the Seventh Circuit.

By limiting its ruling solely to the admiralty tort jurisdiction test, and by expressing this test in broad terms, the Supreme Court has left open many potential challenges to application of the Limitation Act to pleasure craft. Therefore, it is likely that, notwithstanding the appellate decisions holding that the Act does apply to pleasure craft, the considerable amount of litigation on this point will continue.

One of the most dramatic examples of the application of the Limitation Act to pleasure craft is a decision holding that the Act applies to limit the liability of the owner of a jet-ski. *Keys Jet Ski Inc. v. Kays,* 893 F.2d 1225, 1990 AMC 609 (11th Cir. 1990).

Are airplanes, seaplanes, and helicopters "vessels" for purposes of limitation of liability? *See Hubschman v. Antilles Airboats,* 440 F. Supp. 828 (D. V. I. 1977); *Noakes v. Imperial Airways,* 29 F. Supp. 412 (S.D.N.Y. 1939).

Is a wharfboat a vessel for purposes of limitation of liability? *See Evansville & Bowling Green Packet Co. v. Chero Cola Bottling Co.,* 271 U.S. 19, 46 S. Ct. 379, 70 L. Ed. 805 (1926).

Are offshore structures "vessels"? *See Texas Co. v. Savoie,* 240 F.2d 674, 1957 AMC 747 (5th Cir. 1957) and *In re United States Air Force Texas Tower No. 4,* 203 F. Supp. 215 (S.D.N.Y. 1962).

D. Grounds for Denying Limitation: Privity or Knowledge

WATERMAN STEAMSHIP CORPORATION v. GAY COTTONS

414 F.2d 724 (9th Cir. 1969)

DUNIWAY, Circuit Judge

On February 7, 1962, the S.S. CHICKASAW ran aground on Santa Rosa Island, off the coast of Southern California. The island is 40 miles long and 400 feet high. The ship had left Yokohama for Los Angeles on January 27, 1962. No celestial fixes had been obtained after noon on February 5, because of stormy weather. The crew took several fixes with the radio direction finder, which had no recent compensation card, but obtained "wildly divergent" results. The vessel's mechanical sounding device had been pried off the deck in Japan and sold for scrap. The fathometer was not used because Third Mate Jensen thought it was inoperative. He had last tried to use it while the ship was on Japans Inland Sea on December 25, 1961, when he obtained red flashes all around the dial. He had told the master, Capt. Patronas, that the fathometer was inoperable, but the master did not have it checked at the next port. And the radar was broken, having stopped operating just before the ship's arrival in Japan. It had not been fixed because the repair company in Yokohama could not obtain the necessary part in Japan.

The stranding resulted in total loss of the vessel and substantial loss of cargo. Waterman Steamship Corp., her owner, petitioned for complete exoneration of liability under the Carriage of Goods by Sea Act (COGSA), 46 U.S.C. § 1300 *et seq.* or alternatively, for limitation of liability to the amount of its limitation fund, about $250,000, under the Limitation of Liability Act, 46 U.S.C. § 183(a). The cargo is claimed to be worth about two million dollars. Determination of the actual damages has been deferred until the question of liability has been resolved.

* * *

The District Court entered findings of fact and conclusions of law denying both exoneration and limitation. The court also filed a memorandum opinion which is reported at 265 F. Supp. 595, 1966 A.M.C. 2219. Waterman has appealed pursuant to 28 U.S.C. § 1292(a) (3). *See Republic of France v. United States*, 5 Cir., 1961, 290 F.2d 395, 397. We affirm.

Although there was substantial evidence that the vessel was unseaworthy because much of its navigational equipment was in poor shape and had not been inspected recently, the District Court rested its denial of exoneration and limitation solely on the ground that Capt. Patronas was negligent in failing to check the fathometer after Jensen had told him it was inoperative, and that Capt. Patronas' negligence was imputed to Waterman because he had been delegated entire managerial responsibility over repairs to the vessel in the Far East. The court specifically rejected findings proposed by appellees[3] which would have found "direct fault" by Waterman because of its failure to inspect and maintain the equipment, on the ground that such findings were beyond the scope of its memorandum decision.

Limitation of Liability—Negligence of the Captain

Under COGSA, 46 U.S.C. § 1304, the lack of due diligence of any employee which occurs before or at the beginning of a voyage and results in unseaworthiness is sufficient to preclude complete exoneration of liability. Under the Limitation of Liability Act, 46 U.S.C. § 183 (a), however, a shipowner is permitted to limit its liability to the value of its ship, plus freight charges, if it can prove that the lack of due diligence to make seaworthy was not within its "privity or knowledge."

But appellees contend that, because the owner's duty to make a vessel seaworthy is nondelegable, any negligence which results in unseaworthiness is presumed as a matter of law to be within the privity and knowledge of the owner. They rely on statements to that effect in *Federazione Italiana Dei Corsorzi Agrari v. Mandask Compania de Vapores, S.A. (THE PERAMA)*, 2 Cir., 1968, 388 F.2d 434, 439-440, in *States S.S. Co. v. United States (THE PENNSYLVANIA)*, 9 Cir., 1958, 259 F.2d 458, 474, and in GILMORE & BLACK, ADMIRALTY 696, 701-02 (2d

---

[3] Appellees are claimants whose cargo was lost or damaged in the standing: Gay Cottons, Inc., Shalom Baby Wear, and the United States.

ed. 1957). The *Perama* language, however, is dictum. The court had found that the lack of due diligence was attributable to employees who were "sufficiently high in the managerial hierarchy of the appellant so that their general and detailed knowledge and their close privity to the repair project was imputed to the corporation." 388 F.2d at 439 n.6. The *Perama* court cited GILMORE &BLACK, *States S.S. Co., supra,* and *W.R. Grace & Co. v. Charleston Lighterage & Transfer Co. (THE ONE LIGHTER),* 4 Cir., 1952, 193 F.2d 539. The latter case involved an old rotting barge which had not been repaired or properly inspected for a number of years. The court in *Perama* ignored several of its own recent cases which recognize that COGSA has different standards from those applicable under the Limitation Act.[12]

The *States Steamship* language was also dictum. The court had found that the negligence was attributable to one Vallet, a "port engineer" who was in charge of maintenance and repair of all the owner's vessels. On a petition for rehearing, we emphasized that we were denying limitation because the lack of due diligence was charged to managing officers of the corporation. We said that we were not holding that "in any case where the Steamship Company fails to use due diligence to make the vessel seaworthy at the inception of her voyage, limitation must be denied." 259 F.2d at 471-472. *See Avera v. Florida Towing Co. (THE EILEEN ROSS),* 5 Cir., 1963, 322 F.2d 155, 163 n.13, where the court, in discussing this circuit's opinion in *Admiral Towing Co. v. Woolen (THE COMPANION),* 9 Cir., 1961, 290 F.2d 641, 646-649, said "The 9th Circuit was especially careful not to adopt the broad view suggested in GILMORE & BLACK, ADMIRALTY, § 10-24, pp. 701-704 (1957), that privity and knowledge for a corporate shipowner is equated with nondelegable duties. *See* 290 F.2d 641 at 648, and note 6, p. 649."

Notwithstanding the conclusion of Gilmore & Black, we have found no case which has denied limitation of liability because of the negligence of a non-managerial employee. On the contrary, all cases denying limitation of liability to a corporate shipowner have emphasized that the negligence or lack of due diligence to make seaworthy was attributable to managerial personnel. Many cases have granted limitation of liability because the corporate owner proved that none of its managerial personnel were negligent or had notice of any negligence.

We conclude that standards under the Limitation Act are different from those under COGSA. The Shipowner is entitled to limitation of liability if it can show that the lack of due diligence is not within its "privity or knowledge." As to corporate owner's, this has been interpreted to mean that the negligence must be that of a "managing officer" or, more properly, a "supervisory employee."

> While the cases generally speak of the knowledge of managing officers as being the knowledge of the corporation, the real test is not as to their being officers in a strict sense but as to the largeness of their authority. *In re P. Sanford Ross, Inc.,* 2 Cir., 1913, 204 F. 248, 251.
>
> [A managing officer is] any one to whom the corporation has committed the general management or general superintendence of the whole or a particular part of its business. *The Marguerite,*7 Cir., 1944, 140 F.2d 491, 494. *Petition of United States (THE EDMUND FANNING), supra,* 105 F. Supp. at 371. *See also Coryell v. Phipps (THE SEMINOLE),* 1943, 317 U.S. 406, 410-411, 63 S. Ct. 291, 87 L. Ed. 363.

The District Court recognized that the negligence of a master is normally not imputed to the owner, but concluded that, because "entire managerial responsibility" had been delegated to Capt. Patronas to oversee repairs in the Far East, he was a "managing officer" with respect to decisions made within that delegation of authority. Consequently, his failure to check the fathometer after Jensen had said it was inoperative was within the "privity

---

[12] In *Petition of Kinsman Transit Co. (THE MacGILVRAYSHIRAS),* 2 Cir., 1964, 338 F.2d 708, 714-716, limitation was granted where a non-managerial employee negligently moored a steamer in Buffalo. The company was headquartered in Cleveland, but at that time had four of its five vessels moored in Buffalo. In *Moore-McCormack Lines, Lnc. v. Armco Steel Co.(THE MORMACKLTE),* 2 Cir., 1959, 272 F.2d 873, 876-877, limitation was granted where the corporate owner's managing officers had no notice of the improper stowage of ore in South American ports in violation of the company's own rules. "As was obviously necessary in foreign ports, it was left to those in charge to follow these directions, and if they failed, their failure did not charge the owners with 'privity or knowledge.'"

and knowledge" of Waterman.[17] Waterman does not contest the finding that its "entire managerial responsibility as respects repairs" had been delegated to Patronas. Instead, it only contests the conclusion that such delegation is sufficient to deny limitation of liability.

Although Capt. Patronas was the master of the S.S. CHICKASAW, his negligence, as found by the court, did not arise out of his authority over the vessel on the high seas. Instead, the finding rests on his failure to have the fathometer checked in the next port after Jensen had told him that it was inoperative. Certainly there is language in some of the cases which would indicate that limitation might be denied under such circumstances. Thus, in *Spencer Kellogg & Sons, Lnc. v. Hicks (THE LINSEED KING),* 1932, 285 U.S. 502, 511-512, 52 S. Ct. 450, 453, 76 L. Ed. 903, the Supreme Court distinguished *La Bourgogne,* 1908, 210 U.S. 95, 28 S. Ct. 664, 52 L. Ed. 973, as involving the master's failure to obey rules on the high seas, and said:

> There is no analogy between such a situation and that presented in the cited cases where the emergency must be met by the master alone. In these there is no opportunity of consultation or cooperation or of bringing the proposed action of the master to the owner's knowledge. The latter must rely upon the master's obeying rules and using reasonable judgment.

In *Admiral Towing Co. v. Woolen (THE COMPANION),* 9 Cir., 1961, 290 F.2d 641, 648, limitation was denied where the individual owner of a tugboat knew that the master was going to hire a crewman, but made no attempt to insure that the crewman was competent. In dictum, we said that limitation would be granted even where the master has been given unlimited authority but his negligence was "instantaneous negligence ... over which the shipowner could not possibly exercise control." In *The Argent,* S.D.N.Y., 1915, 1940 A.M.C. 508, 509, Judge Hough said:

> The philosophy of shipowners' limitation seems to me this: There are so many things which shipowners must do by deputy, and must have done at great distances and under circumstances where human fallibility is peculiarly prone to produce error, that they long have been saved by statute from the consequences of their agents' acts.

Yet it is clear that an owner cannot close its eyes to what prudent inspections would disclose. An owner must avail itself of whatever means of knowledge are reasonably necessary to prevent conditions likely to cause losses. "If lack of actual knowledge were enough, imbecility, real or assumed, on the part of owners would be at a premium." *The Argent, supra,* 1940 A.M.C. at 509.

However, we must be careful to avoid indiscriminately transferring to the case at bar the broad language of other cases with vastly different fact situations. The great majority of the cases denying limitation of liability have involved old barges, tugs, and other vessels obviously more capable of control by the home office than a freighter thousands of miles away. And most of these cases involved either a long-standing practice of failing adequately to inspect the vessel, or otherwise to exercise control over activities in the home port.

In contrast, limitation of liability has been granted much more often where the vessel involved was a large ship and the negligence did not occur in the home port or in a drydock. Limitation has been denied in large ship cases under a variety of circumstances, but we have found no case which has attributed the negligence of the master to the corporate owner.

---

[17] *See* Finding of Fact 6:

It was the Waterman Steamship Corporations obligation to exercise due diligence to make the S.S. CHICKASAW seaworthy at the commencement of the voyage from the Far East. This included an obligation that the ship's navigational equipment be put in a suitable state of repair before going to sea.... As to repairs, Waterman placed all authority, including authority to decide whether repairs should be made at all, with the master, and had in the Far East no supervisory or managerial personnel to carry out its obligation to exercise due diligence to make the vessel seaworthy. Waterman therefore had delegated to the master its entire managerial responsibility as respects such repairs at the commencement of this voyage and therefore Waterman had knowledge, privity, and is at fault for the decision not to repair the fathometer....

[The] more restricted the operation in which a vessel is engaged, the greater will be the degree of control which the corporate owner will be required to exercise over master, crew and subordinate shoreside employees.... [The] duty to control increases along with the possibility of control.... GILMORE & BLACK, ADMIRALTY (2d ed. 1957) 704, *quoted in Avera v. Florida Towing Co. (THE EILEEN ROSS),* 5 Cir., 1963, 322 F.2d 155, 165.

The District Court's conclusion that Waterman had privity and knowledge of Capt. Patronas' failure to have the fathometer checked in Japan because he had sole authority over repairs in the Far East would be a substantial extension from prior cases. Indeed, it would be inconsistent with the recent cases of *Petition of Kinsman Transit Co. (THE MacGILVRAY SHIRAS)* and *Moore-McCormack Lines, Ltd. v. Armco Steel Co. (THE MORMACKITE), supra* note 12. We do not believe that such an extension is warranted. Although modern communication and transportation facilities make all acts performed in any foreign port within the potential control of the shipowner, we believe that an extension of the requirement of privity or knowledge to cover all such acts should only come from Congress. We are unwilling to impose on all shipowners the burden of maintaining at every port of call an agent with authority over maintenance and repair. We are equally unwilling to transmute the master into such an agent whenever the ship calls at a foreign port in which the owner does not have such an agent. The statute applies to both small and large carriers; many small ones may be unable to meet the burden of such requirements.

We conclude that Capt. Patronas' failure to have the fathometer checked at the next port after Jensen told him that it was inoperative does not support the denial of limitation of liability.

Limitation of Liability—Defective equipment

Appellees contend that the denial of limitation of liability can be affirmed on other grounds. Although they filed no cross-appeals, they argue that certain of the District Court's findings of fact were clearly erroneous.

The District Court found that:

> The S.S. CHICKASAW was equipped with a radio direction finder, which instruments often have deviational errors which vary depending upon the bearing of the stations and which may change from time to time. It is normal and good practice for a vessel to have available for use with a radio direction finder a card or chart so that its readings may be corrected and that such a card be checked for accuracy at least once a year. No such card had been prepared for the S.S. CHICKASAW in recent years, and while this stranding took place in 1962, the card posted dated back to 1957....

This finding is fully supported by the record.

> Failure to have on board an up-to-date correction card or chart was not merely contrary to good practice; it was a violation of a statutory duty.
> Under 47 U.S.C. § 351(a) (2), (1964), it was unlawful for the CHICKASAW
>
> to be navigated ... in the open sea, or ... to leave any harbor or port of the United States for a voyage in the open sea, unless ... equipped with an efficient radio direction finding apparatus (radio compass) properly adjusted in operating condition as hereinafter provided, which apparatus is approved by the [Federal Communications] Commission....

*   *   *

The District Court, however, found that the condition of the radio direction finder did not cause or contribute to the stranding.

The court did not specifically consider the burden of proof. But because there was a statutory violation, the Pennsylvania Rule *(The Pennsylvania*, 1873, 86 U.S. (19 Wall.) 125, 136, 22 L. Ed. 148) places a very heavy burden of proof on Waterman:

But when, as in this case, a ship at the time of a collision is in actual violation of a statutory rule intended to prevent collisions, it is no more than a reasonable presumption that the fault, if not the sole cause, was at least a contributory cause of the disaster. In such a case the burden rests upon the ship of showing not merely that her fault might not have been one of the causes, or that it probably was not, but that it could not have been. Such a rule is necessary to enforce obedience to the mandate of the statute.

* * *

We hold that the court's finding that the stranding was not caused by the ship's failure to have an efficient radio direction finder, is, in the light of the Pennsylvania Rule, clearly erroneous.

Finally, it is urged that the court did not find that the defective condition of the R.D.F. that we have described was with the privity and knowledge of Waterman, and that, absent such privity and knowledge, limitation cannot be denied. It is true that the court made no such finding; it was unnecessary for it to do so, because as we have seen, it found lack of causation. Because we hold that that finding was clearly erroneous, we must consider the privity and knowledge of Waterman.

* * *

The question then is, would the record support a finding that the defect was without the privity or knowledge of Waterman? If the evidence is such that a finding either way would be supported, we should remand for a finding on this question. On the other hand, if the record requires a finding of privity and knowledge, so that a contrary finding would be clearly erroneous, such a remand would be futile, particularly in this case. This action was filed on July 30, 1962. The question was fully explored. If the action can be properly terminated now, that is what should be done. We think that it can properly be done.

Waterman's Port Captain, Frank Murdock, testified that Waterman had no program for insuring that a recent table of corrections is kept on board. It relied on the annual check by the FCC and on RCA, which it hired to check the R.D.F. According to Murdock, the last time a cam was cut to adjust the functioning of the R.D.F. was in 1952. He had no knowledge of the last time that the ship was swung to test the accuracy of the R.D.F. He knew of no entry in the CHICKASAW's log showing that this had been done, as company rules require, within 90 days before the annual FCC check. Waterman had no program for finding out whether the R.D.F. needed repairs; it relied solely on the Master, the chief mate of the deck department or the FCC to recommend that repairs be made. He knew of no piece of paper handed to the FCC or RCA men showing that the R.D.F. had been checked. Waterman left it to the master to check and to furnish a certificate to the FCC; it considered that the FCC provided an automatic check. He knew that the FCC would accept up to 5 degrees error in R.D.F. bearings, and that there should be a table that the crew could use to correct R.D.F. readings. He never had any check made on board ship to see that there was such a table on board. The company had no system or program for doing so. The second mate and the captain have the most to do with the navigational equipment. The chief mate may be bucking for master and therefore also be extremely interested in that equipment. He could recall no conversation with any of those officers about the R.D.F. before the ship was grounded. He was on board the CHICKASAW several times, but could not remember noting the tables of radio direction finder error that the captain had posted in the ship.

Captain Patronas was given no instruction to check the R.D.F. against visual bearings. The second mate, Filippone, knew of no time that this had been done since 1958. Jensen, the third mate gave similar testimony, as did English, the first mate. And neither Patronas nor Filippone knew whether the 1957 table, the only one on board, was accurate. As Waterman's expert, Capt. Slack said: "Q. ... it really isn't possible, sir, to use this instrument for accurate navigation unless you know what this error is, is it? A. That is correct."

* * *

As we have previously pointed out, an owner cannot close its eyes to what prudent inspection would disclose. *See also States Steamship Co. v. United States, (THE PENNSYLVANIA), supra,* 259 F.2d at 466. That is just what Waterman did in this case. We conclude that a finding of lack of privity or knowledge on Waterman's part would be clearly erroneous.

AFFIRMED.

Note: Privity or Knowledge of Corporate Shipowners

When the shipowner is a corporation (as is often the case), it is necessary to determine whether "privity or knowledge" of an employee should be attributed to the corporation. Generally speaking, the employee must be relatively senior in the corporate hierarchy before her or his "privity or knowledge" is regarded as being that of the corporation. S *American Dredging Co. v. Lambert,* 81 F.3d 127, 130, 1996 AMC 2929 (11th Cir. 1996) ("[W]hen the shipowner is a corporation, privity or knowledge means the privity or knowledge of a managing agent, officer, or supervisory employee"). See, however, *McNeil v. Lehigh Valley R. Co.,* 387 F.2d 623, 624 (2d Cir. 1967) ("The evidence showed that appellant's General Marine Inspector inspected the barge at least once every three weeks. Adequate inspection would have disclosed the hole in the planking. Negligent failure to discover constitutes privity and knowledge within the meaning of the statute").

Note: Breaking the Assertion of Limitation

The Convention of Limitation of Liability for Maritime Claims, 1976 provides as follows:

Article 4 — Conduct Barring Limitation

A person liable shall not be entitled to limit his liability if it is proved that the loss resulted from his personal act or omission, committed with the intent to cause such loss, or recklessly and with knowledge that such loss would probably result.

How would this change the present American rule?

For a more recent case applying the American rule, *see Complaint of Bankers Trust Co.,* 651 F.2d 160, 1981 AMC 1497 (3d Cir. 1981).

E. Claims Subject to Limitation

SIGNAL OIL & GAS CO. v. BARGE W-701

654 F.2d 1164, 1982 AMC 2603 (5th Cir. 1981)

GEE, Circuit Judge

* * *

Signal Oil & Gas Company, Louisiana Land & Exploration Company, Amerada Hess Corporation, and Marathon Oil Company ("SLAM") jointly operated an oil production rig in the Gulf of Mexico off the coast of Louisiana. The SLAM pipeline was the conduit for production from the SLAM platform to shore. Sun Oil Company ("Sun") operated a platform nearby but did not enjoy a similar access to shore. SLAM and Sun negotiated an agreement allowing Sun to hook up to the SLAM pipeline. Sun agreed to indemnify SLAM for any losses it might suffer thereby. Sun contracted with J. Ray McDermott ("McDermott") to handle this construction. McDermott, in turn agreed to indemnify Sun for any losses incident to the construction. McDermott contracted with Williams-McWilliams ("Williams"), the vessel owner, for the use of a barge and crew in aid of its construction activities. McDermott and Williams did not enter into any indemnity agreement.

While operating near the SLAM platform, the Williams barge fouled anchor on an obstruction—the SLAM pipeline, as was shortly seen. Meeting resistance in his efforts to retrieve the anchor and change positions, the barge superintendent, Southon, ordered a "dogging" technique to free it. In "dogging," the anchor line is drawn tight and secured while the barge is in a trough; when the barge is lifted by the next swell, the power of the sea itself is used to dislodge the anchor. Unfortunately for all concerned, this retrieval also "dislodged" a chunk of SLAM pipeline. SLAM production operations were interrupted and substantial repairs required.

A round robin of claims were consolidated for trial. In the liability phase of this bifurcated trial, the judge arrived at the following conclusions: (1) the negligence of the barge superintendent, for which Williams bore full responsibility, was the sole proximate cause of the accident; (2) Williams was consequently liable to SLAM in tort; (3) Sun was liable to SLAM on its contract of indemnity; (4) McDermott was liable on its indemnity agreement to Sun; and (5) Williams was liable for tort indemnity to Sun and McDermott. These findings were affirmed on appeal in an opinion of this court dated November 29, 1976, and are not before us on this appeal.

The tidy circle above, in which the negligent party was to bear the loss, was broken by the judge's more recent decision on damages that prompts this appeal. The district court found SLAM entitled to full recovery of its loss—$1,116,234.62. The tortfeasor Williams, however, pursuant to 46 U.S.C. § 181 *et seq.,* was entitled to limit its legal liability to the value of the barge, subsequently found by the district judge to be $450,000. The insurance carried by Williams in excess of its first $500,000 of coverage was held not subject to the Louisiana direct action statute. [This conclusion was based on the fact that the excess insurance, which was taken out by Williams's parent corporation, Zapata Norness, was not written or delivered within Louisiana and the accident took place outside the boundaries of the state.—Eds.] The combined effect of Williams' resort to the limitations statute and the inaccessibility to suit of its excess insurance coverage produced a maximum recovery, extractable from Williams and its insurers, of $500,000. Plaintiff SLAM consequently turned to indemnitor Sun for relief and Sun to McDermott. McDermott, left holding the bag with instructions to fill it, is the chief appellant here. It maintains that the district court erred ... in allowing Williams to limit its liability for the results of this accident.

* * *

McDermott does not dispute that the nature of the accident and the parties makes this incident generally the kind in which the vessel owner may move to limit its liability. Rather, the argument that this limitation defense should have been denied Williams relies on McDermott's allegations that by its actions Williams has incurred liability that traditionally escapes the statute's protective sweep. McDermott argues that Williams' actual liability should exceed the limitation amount under the "Personal Contract Doctrine."

* * *

Before further considering its application to this case, we examine briefly the nature of the Personal Contract Doctrine. ... As noted by G. GILMORE & C. BLACK, THE LAW OF ADMIRALTY § 10-26, at 899 (2d ed. 1975) (hereinafter GILMORE & BLACK), subsequent cases have rendered such a reading of the doctrine improper. "It is by no means clear exactly what a personal contract' is, but it is clear that not all contracts are personal', even though entered into personally by the shipowner." *Id.* Analysis of the cases delineating the types of contracts that fall within the designation "personal" is of scant assistance to our inquiry. For example, bills of lading have been held not to be personal contracts, *Earle & Stoddart, Inc. v. Ellermans Wilson Line, Ltd.,* 287 U.S. 420, 53 S. Ct. 200, 77 L. Ed. 403 (1932); GILMORE & BLACK, § 10-26 at 899. Charter parties, on the other hand, have been four times treated as personal contracts by the Supreme Court in denying limitation to vessel owner's. GILMORE & BLACK, *id.* The parties have not directed our attention to, nor have we found, any case discussing the proper characterization of this contract for the services of a workover barge in offshore oil production.

The initial characterization, moreover, does not necessarily dispose of the question whether liability resulting from a vessel owner's contractual relationships is properly subject to limitation under the statute: "To call a given type of contract personal' does not automatically lead to the conclusion that the shipowner will under all circumstances be denied the right to limit against the claims of his promisee." GILMORE & BLACK, § 10-27 at 904. Learned Hand, sitting as a district judge in *The Soerstad,* 257 F. 130 (S.D.N.Y. 1919), suggested a narrow reading of the personal contract doctrine, restricting its application to situations in which the breach, as well as the execution, of the contract could be said to be "personal" to the vessel owner. His approach in *The Soerstad* has gathered support in subsequent cases, including dicta considered supportive by GILMORE AND BLACK, *see* § 10-27 at 904-05, in *Cullen Fuel Co. v. WE. Hedger, Inc.,* 290 U.S. 82, 88-89, 54 S. Ct. 10, 11, 78 L. Ed. 189 (1933). There is no more recent or more certain authority. This case, however, does not require us to fill that gap. Whether *The Soerstad's* narrowing of the personal contract doctrine is correct or appropriate need not concern us here; McDermott, the party seeking application of the doctrine, presents its grounds for Williams' liability in post-*Soerstad* terms: breaches of warranties of seaworthiness, performance in a workmanlike manner, and provision of "effectual" insurance coverage. McDermott makes no claim that Williams should be denied limitation simply because it personally agreed to provide the vessel in aid of the construction operation. We leave, then, further consideration of the scope of the personal contract doctrine to scholarly commentators and to judges directly confronting the issue.

* * *

Even if the first two warranties were made and could theoretically form the basis of a recovery beyond the limitation fund, they were not here breached. McDermott's seaworthiness and workmanlike performance arguments would impose on Williams a responsibility more direct than *respondeat superior* for the barge superintendent's negligent act. In loosing on an unsuspecting world an inadequately trained and poorly schooled master of the vessel, the argument runs, Williams has incurred a liability that should penetrate the statute's protective cover; it must answer for its "own fault, neglect, and contracts." Whether the law might support McDermott's contentions need not concern us, since the facts clearly do not. The trial judge found that "the on-the-job training which was provided to him [Southon, the barge superintendent] created an obviously capable man with an excellent reputation...." 468 F. Supp. at 815. In ten years as a barge superintendent Southon had suffered only one similar incident. He was an experienced, able captain with a good safety record. As the district court found, "it is clear that Captain Southon was not incompetent but merely negligent." 468 F. Supp. at 814. Furthermore, despite McDermotts vigorous argument to the contrary, we find that Williams violated no duty in failing to promulgate formal written procedures for freeing anchors and unfouling lines. Its reliance on the skill and judgment of its superintendents does not become negligently misplaced merely because of this accident. The attempt to bootstrap the negligence of Southon into a breach of warranties of seaworthiness and workmanlike performance is insupportable in fact. From the results of its employees' negligence, Williams is entitled to the full benefit of the limitation statute.

The third claim of breach of warranty, that Williams failed to secure its promised insurance coverage, ... was simply not breached here. Williams purchased all the coverage indicated in its notices of insurance to McDermott. That insurance was in effect and available to satisfy appropriate claims. Unfortunately for McDermott, a statute embodying the congressional policy of encouraging the mid-nineteenth century American shipping industry allowed Williams and its insurers to cut the losses they otherwise would have suffered. Under these circumstances, the trial court's decision that the umbrella insurance policy held by Williams' parent corporation could not be reached directly ... does make this coverage in some sense "ineffectual," as leaving McDermott liable for an unanticipated loss. McDermott's quarrel, however, is with Congress and the Louisiana legislature, not with Williams. In this instance, McDermott stands exactly where it would in any one of the 48 states that allow no direct action against insurers. Insurance in those states is clearly not "ineffectual" merely because tortfeasors alone, and not their carriers, may be sued.

* * *

After review of the arguments raised to avoid application of the limitation statute here, we arrive at the same conclusion reached by the district judge: Williams is entitled to limit its liability to the value of the barge W-701 at the time of the accident.

* * *

Note: *Excluded Claims*

The personal contract doctrine was applied in the leading case of *Cullen Fuel Oil v. W.E. Hedger, Inc.,* 290 U.S. 82, 54 S. Ct. 10, 78 L. Ed. 189 (1933) [charter parties]. 46 U.S.C.A. § 30505 specifically excludes wages of seamen from limitation, and claims for maintenance and cure are said to be rights arising from a seaman's employment contract and therefore not subject to limitation. *See Hugney v. Consolidation Coal Co.,* 345 F. Supp. 1079, 1973 AMC 534 (W.D. Pa. 1971). Contracts for supplies and repairs have also been excluded. *Richardson v. Harmon,* 222 U.S. 96, 32 S. Ct. 27, 56 L. Ed. 110 (1911).

Is liability for wreck removal under the Wreck Act [33 U.S.C. § 409] subject to limitation? *See Wyandotte Transportation Co. v. United States,* 389 U.S. 191, 88 S. Ct. 379, 19 L. Ed. 2d 407 (1967) and *Inre Pacific Far East Line,* 314 F. Supp. 1339, 1970 AMC 1592 (N.D. Cal. 1970), *aff'd,* 472 F.2d 1382 (9th Cir. 1973).

Is liability for pollution under state law subject to limitation? *See Askew v. American Waterways, Inc.,* 411 U.S. 325, 93 S. Ct. 1590, 36 L. Ed. 2d 280, 1973 AMC 811 (1973). Liability for pollution damages under federal law is generally not subject to limitation under 46 U.S.C.A. § 30505-30506; other concepts of limitation of liability apply.

In contrast to the American law, the 1976 Convention on Limitation of Maritime Claims provides as follows:

Article 2 — Claims Subject to Limitation

1. Subject to Articles 3 and 4 the following claims, whatever the basis of liability may be, shall be subject to limitation of liability:

> (a) claims in respect of loss of life or personal injury or loss of or damage to property (including damage to harbour works, basins and waterways and aids to navigation), occurring on board or in direct connection with the operation of the ship or with salvage operations, an consequential loss resulting therefrom;
> (b) claims in respect of loss resulting from delay in the carriage by sea of cargo, passengers or their luggage;
> (c) claims in respect of other loss resulting from infringement of rights other than contractual rights, occurring in direct connection with the operation of the ship or salvage operations;
> (d) claims in respect of the raising, removal, destruction or the rendering harmless of a ship which is sunk, wrecked, stranded or abandoned, including anything that is or has been on board such ship;
> (e) claims in respect of the removal, destruction or the rendering harmless of the cargo of the ship;
> (f) claims of a person other than the person liable in respect of measures taken in order to avert or minimize loss for which the person liable may limit his liability in accordance with this Convention, and further loss caused by such measures.

2. Claims set out in paragraph 1 shall be subject to limitation of liability even if brought by way of recourse or for indemnity under a contract or otherwise. However, claims set out under paragraphs 1(d), (e) and (f) shall not be subject to limitation of liability to the extent that they relate to remuneration under a contract with the person liable.

Article 3 — Claims Excepted From Limitation

The rules of this Convention shall not apply to:

> (a) claims for salvage or contribution in general average;
> (b) claims for oil pollution damage within the meaning of the International Convention on Civil Liability for Oil Pollution Damage, dated 29 November 1969 or of any amendment or Protocol thereto which is in force;
> (c) claims subject to any international convention or national legislation governing or prohibiting limitation of liability for nuclear damage;
> (d) claims against the shipowner of a nuclear ship or nuclear damage;
> (e) claims by servants of the shipowner or salvor whose duties are connected with the ship or the salvage operations, including claims of their heirs, dependents or other persons entitled to make such claims, if under the law governing the contract of service between the shipowner or salvor and such servants the shipowner or salvor is not entitled to limit his liability in respect of such claims, or if he is by such law only permitted to limit his liability to an amount greater than that provided for in Article 6.

F. Choice of Law

1. *The Nature of Limitation Law: Substantive or Procedural*

MATTER OF BETHLEHEM STEEL CORP.

631 F.2d 441, 1980 AMC 2122 (6th Cir. 1980)

LIVELY, Circuit Judge

This admiralty case presents several issues related to limitation of liability which have not been decided previously by this court.

I.

The Steelton, a Great Lakes steamship owned by the plaintiff Bethlehem, collided with highway bridge which spanned the Welland Canal. The Welland Canal lies wholly within the territorial boundaries of Canada. The bridge, owned by the St. Lawrence Seaway Authority, was extensively damaged and the canal was completely blocked for approximately two weeks. A number of ships were required to interrupt their voyages and stand by until the canal was cleared. Shortly after the collision Bethlehem filed an action in the Federal Court of Canada for limitation of liability under Canadian law, naming as defendants the Seaway Authority "and all other persons having claims against the plaintiff, its ship 'Steelton or the fund hereby to be created." The Canadian court entered an order limiting liability to $671,489 (Canadian), plus interest to date of deposit. Bethlehem deposited with the Canadian court $680,733, including interest ($691,761 (U.S.)). The Canadian court stayed all further proceedings arising out of the collision and entered a notice with provision for publication, requiring all persons who claimed damage from the collision to file their claims which that court.

A number of actions asserting claims arising out of the Steelton incident were filed against Bethlehem in the United States District Court for the Northern District of Ohio. Thereafter Bethlehem filed the present action in that court petitioning for limitation of liability under 46 U.S.C. § 185 while claiming the benefit of the lesser limitation provided by the Canada Shipping Act. The district court then ordered all persons claiming damage from the Steelton incident to file claims with it, and enjoined the institution and prosecution of any actions arising from the incident, except the instant proceeding and the one already pending in the Federal Court of Canada. The total claims filed in the two actions were far in excess of the amount available for their satisfaction under the limitation provisions of either Canadian law or 46 U.S.C. § 183.

II.

A.

The district court recognized the general rule that the right to recover for a tort is governed by the law of the place where the tort occurred. At the same time, the court recognized that the law of the forum determines procedural matters. Thus, the district court convened a hearing to determine whether the Canadian limitation law is substantive or procedural. Both Bethlehem and the claimants produced expert witnesses, Canadian attorneys, who agreed that there are no Canadian cases which define the nature of the limitation law. However, the experts disagreed in their opinions on the nature of the law, Bethlehem's witness proclaiming it substantive and the claimants' witness labeling it procedural.

After considering the expert testimony and several English decisions, the district court concluded that "the limitation of liability provisions of the Canada Shipping Act are procedural and do not attach to the rights created by that Act." Thus, the court held that 46 U.S.C. § 183, the law of the forum, determines the maximum limitation of the fund created in this action. The effect of this ruling was to set Bethlehem's potential liability at $850,000 rather than $691,000. This is the holding from which Bethlehem has filed its cross-appeal.

* * *

III.

In *Ocean Steam Navigation Co. v. Mellor (The Titanic)*, 233 U.S. 718 (1914), the primary question was whether the owner of a foreign ship may limit its liability for losses on the high seas by resort to the courts of the United States. The Supreme Court held that when a foreign ship is sued in the courts of this country it may invoke limitation under U.S. law. This is so even though the foundation for recovery is a British tort and under the circumstances of the case the ship is not subject to the substantive law of the United States.

Lower court decisions following *Titanic* have concluded that limitation of liability statutes relate to remedy rather than to liability or the right to recover. *E.g., Royal Mail Steam Packet Co. v. Companhia de Navegaco Lloyd Brasileiro*, 31 F.2d 757 (E.D.N.Y. 1928), *aff'd*, 55 F.2d 1082 (2d Cir.), *cert. denied*, 287 U.S. 607 (1932); *The Mando*, 102 F.2d 459 (2d Cir. 1939). The Supreme Court cast some doubt on the accepted rule of *The Titanic* in *Black Diamond Steamship Corp. v. Robert Stewart & Sons, Ltd. (Norwalk Victory)*, 336 U.S. 386 (1949). In that case the only issue decided was the amount of bond required to be posted in the United States district court by the shipowner seeking to limit its liability for losses which occurred in foreign waters. The plaintiff sought limitation under the Brussels Convention and tendered a bond which would have satisfied the requirements of the Convention. The district court dismissed the action for failure to post the larger bond required by the American limitation statute. The Supreme Court reversed and remanded with directions to set aside the dismissal and make a determination of which limitation provision to apply. The Court also required the plaintiff to post the larger American bond to preserve the *status quo* pending appeal from the district court's ultimate decision. *Norwalk Victory* recognizes that the limitation statute of the forum does not always apply—contrary to the assumption of a number of courts following *The Titanic*. In looking at "the question whether there are any circumstances under which the Belgian limitation would be enforceable by our courts," the Supreme Court stated, "... if, indeed, the Belgian limitation attaches to the right, then nothing in *The Titanic*, 233 U.S. 718, stands in the way of observing that limitation." 336 U.S. at 395.

In *Norwalk Victory*, Justice Frankfurter did not disagree with the rule of *The Titanic*. He noted that the Court was dealing in that case with "a liability assumed already to exist on other grounds." *Id*. On the other hand, the district court in *Norwalk Victory* dismissed on the assumption that the law of the forum controlled because limitation laws are always procedural. Upon remand the district court was to determine "if it is the law of Belguim that the wrong creates no greater liability than that recognized by the Convention...." *Id*. In other words, an American court may not assume that a foreign limitation of liability act is procedural. It must make a determination whether an independent basis of liability exists or whether under that nation's law "the wrong creates no greater liability than that recognized...." by the limitation act. If the right to recover is coextensive with the limitation on amount of recovery, then a limitation act is substantive and must be enforced by the forum. Viewed in this light *Norwalk Victory* does not represent a departure from the doctrine of *The Titanic*. Rather, it commands an inquiry into the nature of a foreign limitation act where it may not be assumed that liability already exists on other grounds.

In *Kloeckner Reederei Und Kohlenhandel G.M.B.H. v. A/S Hakedal (The Western Farmer)*, 210 F.2d 754, 757 (2d Cir. 1954), Judge Learned Hand wrote, "*The Titanic* ... finally settled it for us that such statutes [limitation acts] are part of the remedy, and that the law of the forum applies." He found nothing in *Norwalk Victory* which qualified this rule. Implicit in the holding is the assumption that liability for the tort existed on other grounds.

In *Petition of Chadade Steamship Co. (The Yarmouth Castle)*, 266 F. Supp. 517 (S.D. Fla. 1967), the Panamanian owner of a cruise ship which burned and sank on the high seas petitioned a United States court for limitation of liability. The district court followed the procedure directed by the Court in *Norwalk Victory* and received expert testimony on the nature of the Panamanian limitation law. The court stated its conclusion as follows:

> The limitation of liability contained in the Panamanian law is substantive rather than procedural and attaches specifically to the right.

266 F. Supp. at 522.

Perceiving no overriding public policy of the United States which precludes doing so, the court applied the limitation provision of the law of Panama. The court in *Complaint of Ta Chi Navigation (Panama) Corp. S.A.*, 416 F. Supp. 371 (S.D.N.Y. 1976), refused to follow *The Yarmouth Castle*, applied the limitations provision of the United States rather than the Panamanian limitation provision, and held that the decision in *The Titanic* "still is the controlling law in the instant case." *Id.* at 377.

It is not surprising that the cases have produced different results. *The Titanic* concerned a disaster on the high seas. *Norwalk Victory*, on the other hand, dealt with a collision in Belgian territorial waters. One case involved great loss of life, the other only property damage. In some cases the parties seeking to limit their liability have been insurers rather than shipowners. *See Complaint of Ta Chi Navigation, supra*, 416 F. Supp. at 379. In a field as complex as maritime tort law the choice-of-law problems are difficult, and the circumstances of each case determine the ultimate choices which the courts make. *See* M. HANCOCK, TORTS IN THE CONFLICT OF LAWS, Ch. IX (1942).

The district judge in the present case followed the command of the Court in *Norwalk Victory*. Judge Krupansky received the testimony of Canadian lawyers and found the expert witness of the claimants the more persuasive. This witness stated his opinion that "the fixing of the amount or value of the Steelton's owner's limitation of liability is a matter of procedure and not a matter of substance." He stated that the Canadian limitation act provides for a "quantification" of damages, that it merely provides a procedural remedy for scaling down claims to the proportionate share of a limited fund. The witness supported his testimony with references to several English and Canadian decisions dealing with damages.

This court accepts the district court's conclusion that the Canadian limitation statute is procedural. This conclusion is supported by competent testimony. Furthermore, it represents a desirable choice-of-laws decision. The Steelton is an American ship. The parties who will be affected by this limitation decision chose to sue the Steelton's owner in a court of the United States rather than a court of Canada. Though the collision occurred in Canadian waters, insofar as the limitation between the present parties is concerned, the interest of the United States in applying its own legislatively determined concept of limitation is stronger than that of Canada. This appears to be a proper case for application of the law of the forum.

* * *

AFFIRMED.

Note: The Choice of Law Problem

Most commentators have agreed with Gilmore and Black's view (*see* THE LAW OF ADMIRALTY, § 10-44 at 944) that Judge Mehrtens in the *Yarmouth Castle* came perilously close to "overruling a ... decision of the Supreme Court." *See* George E. Duncan, *Limitation of Shipowner's Liability: Parties Entitled to Limit; the Vessel; the Fund*, 53 TUL. L. REV. 1046, 1051-52 (1979). *See also* Judge Tennys opinion in *InRe Ta Chi Navigation*, 416 E Supp. 371 (S.D.N.Y. 1976).

---

2. *The Brussels Convention: Procedural in Nature*

COMPLAINT OF COMPANIA GIJONESA DE NAVEGACION, S.A.
590 F. Supp. 241, 1985 AMC 1469 (S.D.N.Y. 1984)

CANNELLA, District Judge

Wah Yuen Shipping, Inc.'s ["Wah Yuen"] motion to increase the security fund is granted. FED. R. CIV. P., Supp. R. F(7) for Admiralty & Maritime Claims ["Rule F(7)"].

Background

On July 6, 1983, Compania Gijonesa De Navegacion, S.A. ["Gijonesa"] commenced this action claiming exoneration from liability from a vessel collision and seeking the application of liability limitations pursuant to the Limitation of the Liability of Owners of Sea-Going Ships (1957) ["Brussels Convention"] and 46 U.S.C. § 183. This action arises out of a collision in Spain on January 11, 1983 of its Spanish vessel, the M/V Cimadevilla ["Cimadevilla"] with the M/V Crusader, a Panamanian vessel owned by the claimant Wah Yuen. As a result of the collision, Wah Yuen presented its damages claim of $607,644.10 to Gijonesa and thereafter, Gijonesa instituted this action and asserted that its interest in the Cimadevilla was $98,110.77. It then deposited that amount as security with the court for the benefit of claimants, permitting them to challenge the amount.

As a claimant Wah Yuen objected to the amount of security and challenges the law employed by Gijonesa in calculating the limited fund. Wah Yuen asserts that the security should be increased to total $1,784,800, representing Gujonesa's $1,715,000 interest in the Cimadevilla at the end of the voyage plus $34,800, the value of the freight. In addition, Wah Yuen timely filed a claim in this Court for $607,644.10.

Wah Yuen argues that the Brussels Convention is a matter of procedural rather than substantive law and that a Spanish court would not apply the official rate of exchange of gold for conversion of pesatas into poincare francs. Wah Yuen's expert on Spanish law opines that a Spanish court would apply Article 837 of Spain's Commercial Code which provides that the limitation fund equals the value of the vessel plus the value of pending freight. This is also the valuation specified in Rule F(7) and 46 U.S.C. § 183(a). With respect to the instant dispute, Wah Yuen argues that the court, as the forum court should apply the federal liability limitation.

Gijonesa alleges that generally 46 U.S.C. § 183 and the Federal Rules of Civil Procedure limit liability *unless* the foreign substantive law which limits the right provides a different and lower limitation, as Spanish law does in the instant action. Thus, Gijonesa argues that the Brussels Convention is substantive and applies to the limitation of liability issue because it attaches to a right and limits it. Gijonesa argues that Spanish law mandates the limitation value used herein because of its domestic enactment of the Brussels Convention.

With respect to the valuation of the poincare franc, Gijonesa argues that Spanish courts would use the official rate for the value of gold in converting poincare francs, based on the opinion of its expert. The official rate of gold was the only rate at the time of the formulation of the Brussels Convention.

Discussion

Generally, "in the absence of some overriding domestic policy translated into law, the right to recover for a tort depends upon and is measured by the law of the place where the tort occurred." *Black Diamond S.S. Corporation v. Robert Stewart & Sons (Norway Victory),* 336 U.S. 386, 396 (1949) ["Black Diamond"] (citations omitted). Because the collision occurred in the territorial waters of Spain, the rights and liabilities of the parties are governed by Spanish substantive law.

With respect to procedural rules, it is well-settled that the law of the forum controls. *See Bournias v. Atlantic Maritime Co.,* 220 F.2d 152, 154 (2d Cir. 1955). Gijonesa, when it deposited the $98,110.77 with the court, claimed that Spanish law provides that this is the monetary limit pursuant to the Brussels Convention. Gijonesa contends that the Brussels Convention is a substantive rather than procedural part of the laws of Spain. Wah Yuen contends that while the substantive rights involved are governed by Spanish law, it claims that the calculation of the liability limitation is a matter of procedure governed by the forums laws.

Wah Yuen further argues, in the alternative, that if Spanish substantive laws were to apply, its Commercial Code would control rather than the Brussels Convention. The Spanish Commercial Code provides that the limitation of liability is the value of the vessel plus pending freight. This valuation is identical to that of the laws of the United States. Calculating liability is further complicated by the fact that the "official" rate has been eliminated in Spain and no other rate has been adopted.

Wah Yuen also argues that even if the Brussels Convention applied, Article 4 directs:
Without prejudice to the provisions of Article 3, §2, of this Convention,the rules relating to the constitution and distribution of the limitation fund, if any,and the rules of procedures hall be governed by the national law of the State in which the fund is constituted.

Thus, Wah Yuen argues that even the Brussels Convention's laws mandate that limiting the fund is a matter of procedural law governed by United States law.

The Supreme Court determined that the procedural rules of the forum would control the amount of the security to be posted in limitation proceedings. *Oceanic Steam Navigation Co. v. Mellor (Titanic)*, 233 U.S. 718 (1914) ["The Titanic"]. Thereafter, the Supreme Court although not overruling *The Titanic*, determined that if the substantive rights of the parties are controlled by foreign law and if the foreign limitation "attaches" to such rights, then the foreign limitation governs rather than the forum state's limitation laws. *See Black Diamond, supra*, 336 U.S. at 395-396; *See also Matter of Bowoon Sangsa Co.*,720F.2d 595, 599 & n.5(9th Cir. 1983). In*Black Diamond,supra*, the Supreme Court further stated in dictathatif foreign law merelyprovides "procedural machinery" toalready existing claims, the forum's procedural laws would apply. 336 U.S. at 396. Thus, pursuant to the Supreme Court's directive, the Court must determine whether Spains limitation of liability is a matter of substantive or procedural law. *See Matter of Bethlehem Steel Corp.*, 435 F. Supp. 944, 947 (N.D. Ohio 1976), *aff'd*, 631 F.2d 441 (3d Cir. 1980), *cert. denied*, 450 U.S. 921 (1981).

The parties have submitted affidavits of Spanish lawyers, knowledgeable in Spanish law, which indicate disagreement on the issue of whether the Brussels Convention is a matter of substantive or procedural law. Wah Yuen's witness, Manuel Gonzalez Rodriguez, contends that the Brussels Convention is considered procedural in Spain. He further states that a Spanish Court would apply its Commercial Code to the instant dispute. He contends that the right to recover monetary damages caused by a collision was created statutorily by Article 826 of the commercial Code of 1885. The Brussels Convention was not enacted until much later. Thus, he concludes that the limitation of liability provision of the Brussels Convention merely modifies a pre-existing right and, therefore, is procedural. Recognizing that the official rate of gold was eliminated as the basis of the international monetary system by the International Monetary Fund ["IMF"] in 1975, *see Trans World Airlines v. Franklin Mint Corp.*, 466 U.S. 243, 104 S.Ct. 1776, 80 L. Ed. 2d 273 (1984), which Gijonesa's witness Jose Maria Alcántara concedes, Mr. Rodriguez contends that the official conversion rate is not used in Spain.

Mr. Alcantara contends that the Brussels Convention is a matter of substantive law in Spain, claiming that it "qualifies the right of limitation itself in a substantive manner." He further opines that the Commercial Code was substantively amended by the Brussels Convention and that a Spanish Court would apply the Brussels Convention and the official conversion rate when calculating the limitation fund.

Initially, the Court notes that there is no Spanish or Second Circuit case that is dispositive on the issues involved in this action. Following the analysis of *Black Diamond*, it appears that the foreign limitation of liability is procedural. *First*, the limitation of liability provision of the Brussels Convention does not attach to the right of recovery resulting from a collision because it is a pre-existing right by virtue of the Spanish Commercial Code. *See Matter of Bethlehem Steel Corp., supra*, 435 F. Supp. at 948. The right to recovery existed as early as 1810 and continues to exist pursuant to the Commercial Code. The subsequent enactment of the Brussels Convention in Spain, does not alter this fact. *Second*, limitation of liability which determines the amount to be posted for claimants, defines the remedy, and is a matter of procedure. *See Kloeckner, Reederei und Kohlenhandel v. A/S Hakedal, (The Western Farmer)*, 210 F.2d 754, 756 (2d Cir. 1954), *appeal dismissed*, 348 U.S. 801 (1955). The limitation of liability simply measures damages and does not attach to a pre-existing right. It merely provides a limited fund for all claimants. *See Black Diamond, supra*, 336 U.S. at 395-96.

Because the limitation of liability provision at issue is procedural, the Court applies the laws of the forum—United States law. Mindful that such a determination could result in forum shopping, the facts and circumstances of this action support a finding that the Brussels Convention, if applicable, is procedural in nature. United States law directs that Gijonesa deposit security that equals the value of the vessel plus pending freight. *See* Rule F(7); 46 U.S.C. § 183. The Court notes that this valuation is similarly defined by section 837 of the Commercial Code.

Furthermore, the Court notes that the parties agree that the official rate of gold has been eliminated by the IMF and Spain. Thus, even assuming *arguendo* that the substantive law of Spain is to be applied, it is disputed what calculation would govern. There is lack of proof in this area. Furthermore, the formula of the Brussels Convention has not been applied in Spain. The Commercial Code uses the same valuation as the federal rules. While Gijonesa seeks to employ the official rate of gold and values a poincare franc in Spain at 4.6434 pesetas, the Court declines to do so for the reasons asserted above. Because the rate of conversion employed in Spain has not been adequately established, the Court would have to assume that Spanish law is the same as United States law and would apply the same valuation for calculating the limitation of liability.

In conclusion, Gijonesa is directed to increase the security posted with the Court so that it equals $1,784,800.00.

Conclusion

Wah Yuen's motion to increase the security fund from $98,110.77 to $1,784,800.00 is granted. Fed. R. Civ. P., Supp. R. F(7).

Gijonesa is directed to post, within fourteen (14) days of this Memorandum and Order, additional security with the Court so that the total sum will equal $1,784,800.00.

The parties have sixty (60) days from the date of this Memorandum and Order to complete discovery.

So Ordered.

Other opinions about the nature of limitation conventions

In *Victrawl Pty Ltd v. AOTC Ltd; Sanko Steamship Co. Ltd v. Sumitomo Australia Ltd* (1995) 183 C.L.R. 595, the High Court of Australia held that the Convention on Limitation of Liability for Maritime Claims 1976 (the London Convention, or LLMC 1976, which superseded the Brussels Convention of 1957) was substantive in nature, not procedural.

CHAPTER 6 — GENERAL AVERAGE

Introductory Note

In *Empire Stevedoring Co. v. Oceanic Adjuster, Ltd.,* 315 F. Supp. 921, 927-28, 1971 AMC 795 (S.D.N.Y. 1970), the court described the concept of general average in the following way:

The law of general average, which derives from ancient usage dating back at least to the Rhodian law and to which all the principal maritime nations subscribe, rests on the principle that loss or expenditures incurred by one who partakes in a maritime venture for the benefit of all should be shared ratably by all who participate in the venture. *See generally,* Lowndes & Rudolph, at 3-25; Gilmore & Black, § 5-1, at 22023; *Barnard v. Adams,* 51 U.S. 270, 303, 10 How. 270, 13 L. Ed. 417 (1850). The right to general average has been said to rest both on an implied contract between the parties to the common adventure and upon the established law of the sea. *Ralli v. Troop,* 157 U.S. 386, 397, 15 S. Ct. 657, 39 L. Ed. 742 (1895). General average is conceived as a "measure of justice for a meritorious service, to distribute among all who were benefited [by the sacrifice or the incurring of extraordinary expenses] a due proportion of what was sacrificed or expended." *Hobson v. Lord,* 92 U.S. 397, 409, 23 L. Ed. 613 (1876).

The device was clearly conceived as one to equitably distribute extraordinary sacrifices and expenses among the partners to a common maritime adventure. It has been recognized, moreover, that in general average the interests of strangers to a maritime adventure "neither contribute nor are contributed for". *Ralli v. Troop,* 157 U.S. at 411, 15 S. Ct. at 667 (1895).... Lord Porter, writing for the House of Lords majority [in *Morrison Steamship Co., Ltd. v. Greystoke Castle,* [1947] A.C. 265, at 294, noted further that the cargo owner's' "liability was to reimburse the owner's of the Greystoke Castle who incurred the expense on their behalf and not to pay those who did the work necessary to enable that ship to proceed on her voyage." *Id.,* at 295. And that Court, in rejecting the contention that claims against outsiders for damage to an adventure as a whole be considered in fixing contributory values, noted:

The law of general average, when the contingency arises on which it can properly be invoked, is the partnership law of the adventure, and concerns itself, not with the claims for damage to the adventure by outsiders, but wholly with the equitable adjustment, under its rules, of the rights and liabilities inter se of the partners to the adventure. It governs the domestic relations of the adventure, and to import into it, for any purpose, claims against outsiders would be not only to distort it, but to involve it in such practical difficulties as would make the boldest adjuster tremble. *The Andree,* 41 F. 2d 812, 816-817 (S.D.N.Y. 1930), *rev'd on other grounds,* 47 F. 2d 874 (2d Cir. 1931).

So ... it might be said that the law of general average, the partnership law of the adventure, does not concern itself with claims that the shipowner who incurred debts for the benefit of the common adventure defaulted in payment on those debts. Any fiduciary relationship arising out of the law of general average runs solely in favor of the ship, freight and cargo interests, respectively. Those who render services which are treated as general average expenditures are not the intended beneficiaries.

The York-Antwerp Rules

Few, if any, modern disputes about general average are determined by reference to the general maritime law. In practice, general average losses and expenditures are now usually allocated by application of the York-Antwerp Rules. Those Rules began their life as the York Rules in 1864. They have been revised many times since then, the most recent revision being the York-Antwerp Rules 2016, which were adopted by the 42nd Conference of the Comité Maritime International (CMI) in New York in May 2016. The text of the 2016 version of the York-Antwerp Rules can be found at http://www.comitemaritime.org/Uploads/Work%20Product/York-Antwerp%20Rules%202016%20(Final).pdf.

The York-Antwerp Rules contain detailed provisions for the adjustment of general average, but they are not an international convention. They take effect only when expressly incorporated into a contract. So many maritime contracts incorporate a version of the York-Antwerp Rules that one noted commentator has observed: "It may safely be said that general average is the field of maritime law where the international unification effort has succeeded to the greatest degree". Selmer, *The Survival of General Average* (1958), p. 58.

It is always important to note which version of the Rules has been incorporated into the contract. The 2004 version of the Rules does not have automatic effect: it will only apply when (and if) parties to maritime contracts begin to incorporate it in preference to one of its predecessors.

Many maritime contracts continue to incorporate one of the previous two versions, the York-Antwerp Rules 1994 and the York-Antwerp Rules 1974 as amended 1990.

A. Underlying Theory and Codification of the York-Antwerp Rules: "Peril" or "Safe Prosecution of the Voyage"

EAGLE TERMINAL TANKERS v. INSURANCE CO. OF U.S.S.R.

637 F.2d 890, 1981 AMC 137 (2nd Cir. 1981)

FEINBERG, Chief Judge

This is an appeal from a grant of summary judgment in the United States District Court for the Southern District of New York, Whitman Knapp, J., to defendant appellee Insurance Company of U.S.S.R. (Ingosstrakh), Ltd. in an action brought by plaintiff-appellant Eagle Terminal Tankers, Inc. (Eagle). Plaintiff Eagle sued to recover a general average contribution from defendant, the cargo insurer, for Eagle's expenses in repairing damage to the propeller of its ship, the S.S. Eagle Courier. Because the district judge construed the applicable law and rules of general average too narrowly, we reverse the judgment of the district court and remand for further proceedings.

I.

According to the record now before us, Eagle's general average claim arose in the following manner. On December 30, 1975, the S.S. Eagle Courier left Port Arthur, Texas, bearing some 26,000 metric tons of grain destined for Leningrad. At 7:45 on the evening of January 13, 1976, as the ship was maneuvering off the English coast to pick up a pilot, the first assistant engineer advised the officer on watch that he had felt a bump. Visibility was good, with only light winds, but nothing could be seen in the water near the ship at the time. The ship continued sailing toward Rotterdam, its next scheduled port of call. By 3:00 P.M. the next day, metallic scraping noises could be heard coming from the stern. The ship successfully completed its voyage, however, reaching a mooring buoy at Rotterdam two and a half hours later. Shortly thereafter, divers hired by the ship's captain conducted an underwater examination of the ship. Their report disclosed extensive damage to the propeller; among other things, the propeller's blades were bent and the propeller itself appeared to have shifted aft from the tailshaft. When turned, the propeller produced a scouring noise. This damage was serious enough, as defendant has conceded, to make repairs necessary before the voyage could be resumed. Accordingly, after a portion of the cargo was unloaded and the ship placed in drydock, the propeller shaft was replaced and a spare propeller installed. The cargo was then reloaded and the ship continued on to Leningrad, discharging its cargo there between February 9 and February 23.

Eagle declared a general average, seeking contribution for expenses arising from the Rotterdam repairs from the ship's underwriters and from defendant as insurer of the cargo. The expenses covered by the statement of general average included the costs of unloading and reloading the cargo in connection with the drydocking, as well as the costs of maintaining the ship's crew and officers during the repair period. Defendant's assessed share of these expenses totalled $126,951.61. When defendant refused to pay, Eagle brought this suit in the district court.

In May 1980, Judge Knapp granted defendant's motion for summary judgment on the ground that no general average situation existed in the circumstances of this case. 489 F. Supp. 920 (S.D.N.Y. 1980). Specifically, Judge Knapp found that the ship had not been threatened by any "peril," as required under traditional principles of the law of general average and under the York-Antwerp Rules of 1950, which apply to this case in accordance with the terms of the voyage charter party.[1] Noting that the damage was discovered only after the ship was safely moored, Judge Knapp concluded that "[t]he vessel could have remained moored indefinitely at Rotterdam without incurring the slightest peril to itself or its cargo." *Id.* at 923. That the voyage could not have been completed without the repairs was deemed "irrelevant." *Id.* Eagle appeals from this judgment.

---

[1] Clause 2 of the voyage charter party, dated November 15, 1975, provided: General Average shall be payable according to York/Antwerp Rules, 1950, and to be settled in New York.

II.

Resolution of the issues posed by this appeal requires an understanding of the history and content of both the law of general average and the York-Antwerp Rules. We turn first to the former.

General Average

The central principle of the law of general average is that "[w]hat is given, or sacrificed, in time of danger, for the sake of all, is to be replaced by a general contribution on the part of all who have been thereby brought to safety." R. Lowndes & G. Rudolph, The Law of General Average and the York-Antwerp Rules ¶ 1 (10th ed. J. Donaldson, C. Staughton, D. Wilson 1975) (Vol. 7 of British Shipping Laws). In this country, the principle was defined in fuller terms in the early case of *Barnard v. Adams*, 51 U.S. (10 How.) 270, 303 13 L. Ed. 417 (1850):

In order to constitute a case for general average, three things must concur:—

1st. A common danger; a danger in which ship, cargo, and crew all participate; a danger imminent and apparently "inevitable," except by voluntarily incurring the loss of a portion of the whole to save the remainder. 2d. There must be a voluntary jettison, jactus, or casting away, of some portion of the joint concern for the purpose of avoiding this imminent peril, *pericula imminent is evident causa*, or, in other words, a transfer of the peril from the whole to a particular portion of the whole.

3d. This attempt to avoid the imminent common peril must be successful. This formula still describes the classic general average case, but it is too narrow to encompass the full range of such cases recognized today. Two ways in which the *Barnard* formula has been liberalized are of special relevance to this appeal.

First, general average is not limited to cases involving a literal "voluntary jettison" or "casting away"; other "sacrifices" made to save the common venture may also give rise to a right of contribution from the benefited parties. As the Supreme Court observed in another leading case, *The Star of Hope,* 76 U.S. (9 Wall.) 203, 228, 19 L. Ed. 638 (1869):

Losses which give a claim to general average are usually divided into two great classes: (1.) Those which arise from sacrifices of part of the ship or part of the cargo, purposely made in order to save the whole adventure from perishing. (2.) *Those which arise out of extraordinary expenses incurred for the joint benefit of ship and cargo.*

(Citation omitted; emphasis added.) This category of "extraordinary expenses" has long been recognized to include the costs incurred by a ship s interruption of its voyage to enter a port or similar shelter for repairs necessary for the safe completion of the venture. In *Hobson v. Lord,* 92 U.S. 397, 23 L. Ed. 613 (1876), for example, a ship had been badly damaged in a collision at sea, "and being in distress, and unable to prosecute her voyage by reason of such injuries, she proceeded to the port of Callao," her intended port of call. *Id.* at 400. Extensive repairs were made, requiring the discharge of the ship's cargo; "the repairs, though they were of a permanent character, were necessary to enable the ship to prosecute her voyage to its termination." *Id.* at 401. In holding the costs of these repairs to be subject to general average, the Court stated:

Where the disaster occurs in the course of the voyage, and the ship is disabled, the necessary expenses to refit her to go forward create an equity to support ... a claim [for proportionate contribution], just as strong as a sacrifice made to escape [an imminent sea] peril, if it appears that the cargo was saved, and that the expenses incurred enabled the master to prosecute the voyage to a successful termination.

Id. at 405. The recoverable expenditures included not only the cost of the repairs, but also wages and provisions "during the consequent and necessary *interruption* of the voyage, occasioned by the disaster." *Id.* at 407 (emphasis in original). These principles, as will be seen below, were subsequently codified in the York-Antwerp Rules.

·

The second direction of liberalization of *Barnard's* strict definition of general average acts has involved the degree of "peril" necessary to render sacrifice or extraordinary expenses recoverable. The early cases uniformly speak, as does *Barnard*, of "imminent" or "impending" peril threatening the ship. In *The Star of Hope*, for example, a fire aboard a ship carrying gunpowder and "large quantities of spirituous liquors" caused "[g]reat alarm," which "increased as the impending peril became more imminent." 76 U.S. (9 Wall.) at 225-26. The master decided to seek shelter in an unfamiliar bay, sailing in without a pilot and as a result grounding the ship on a reef. The grounding created a leak in the hull; the water that poured in extinguished the fire but made it necessary to return the ship to its previous port of call for repairs. The Supreme Court held that the expenses of the repairs could be recovered as general average costs. *See also Columbian Insurance Co. v. Ashby & Stribling*, 38 U.S. (13 Pet.) 331, 338, 10 L. Ed. 186 (1839) ("[T]he ship and cargo should be placed in a common imminent peril.... Hence, if there was no imminent danger or necessity for the sacrifice, as if the jettison was merely to lighten a ship too heavily laden, by the fault of the master, in a tranquil sea, no contribution was due."); E. Congdon, General Average 11 (1952) (citing cases).

It is clear that the law of general average continues to require a showing of peril.[2] But in this century, perils less than "imminent" have been recognized as sufficient to create a general average situation. Writing for this court in 1937, Judge Augustus Hand expressed this changing view:

> There must be fair reason to regard a vessel in peril in order to require a contribution in general average. While the courts in some cases have used expressions indicating that both in general average and in salvage cases it is essential that the property at risk be subject to an immediately impending danger, we think the "imminency" of the peril is not the critical test. *If the danger be real and substantial, a sacrifice or expenditure made in good faith for the common interest is justified, even though the advent of any catastrophe may be distant or indeed unlikely.*

Navigazione Generale Italiana v. Spencer Kellogg & Sons, 92 F.2d 41, 43 (2d Cir.), *cert. denied*, 302 U.S. 751 (1937) (emphasis added). *See also Shaver Transportation Co. v. Travelers Indemnity Co.*, 481 E Supp. 892, 897-98 (D. Ore. 1979); *Todd Shipyards Corp. v. United States*, 391 E Supp. 588, 590 (S.D.N.Y. 1975); *United States v. Wessel, Duval & Co.*, 123 F. Supp. 318, 328 (S.D.N.Y. 1954) (denying general average recovery in absence of evidence of "substantial peril, either present or probable in the future"). The concern underlying this more flexible view of "peril" is that the master should not be discouraged from taking timely action to avert a threat to the safety of the ship and its cargo.[3] The critical issue, then, in the modern law of general average is the seriousness of the danger created by an accident or peril at sea rather than its immediacy.

York-Antwerp Rules

Although the principles of the law of general average discussed above are relevant to this case, more immediately significant is their codification in the York-Antwerp Rules. As already indicated, *see* note 1 *supra*, these Rules were made applicable to the voyage of the Eagle Courier by the terms of the voyage charter party. A brief description of the development of the Rules will be helpful.

The movement to achieve some sort of international consensus on basic principles of general average began in Great Britain in 1860 as a response to concern over the costs, confusion, and abuses resulting from diverse national approaches to the question. The end result of many years of discussion and several conferences was the promulgation of the York-Antwerp Rules of 1890 by the Conference of the Association for the Reform and Codification of the Law of Nations (later the International Law Association). The Conference, attended by representatives of shipping

---

[2] *See, e.g., Aktieselskabet Cuzco v. The Sucarseco*, 294 U.S. 394, 401 (1935); G. Gilmore & C. Black, The Law of Admiralty § 5-6 at 254 (2d ed. 1975); L. Buglass, Marine Insurance And General Average In The United States, 122-23 (1973); E. Congdon, *supra*, at 11.

[3] *See* R, Lowndes & G. Rudolf, *Supra*, P51:

> Although the peril must be real. "it is not necessary that the ship should be actually in the grip, or even nearly in the grip, of the disaster that may arise from a danger. It would be a very bad thing if shipmasters had to wait until that state of things arose in order to justify them doing an act which would be a general average act." (Quoting from *Vlassopoulos v. British & Foreign Marine Ins. Co.* (The "Makis"), [1929] 1 K.B.187, 199).

and insurance interests in the United Kingdom, France, Germany, Belgium, Denmark, and the United States, adopted a set of eighteen rules designed to resolve specific, common problems of general average rather than to set out a comprehensive approach to the subject. The Rules came rapidly to be accepted as a standard code of practice by shippers in virtually all maritime states, although the original objective of uniformity through national legislation based on the Rules was not met. *See generally* R. LOWNDES & G.RUDOLF, *supra* ¶¶ 481-508; Felde, *General Average and the York-Antwerp Rules*, 27 TULANE L. REV. 406, 427-29 (1953).

Pressures for revision of some of the Rules and their expansion to deal with new problems led to the convening of another conference following World War I. This conference produced the York-Antwerp Rules of 1924, consisting of twenty-three "numbered" rules dealing with specific questions (mostly based on the Rules of 1890), as well as seven new "lettered" rules setting out more general definitions and principles of general average. The 1924 Rules met with general approval in the maritime states, including, it appears, the Soviet Union, *see* Felde, *supra*, 27 TULANE L. REV. at 432-33. However, several provisions of the new Rules were strenuously opposed by shippers, insurers, and other maritime interests in the United States, which devised contractual formulas providing for only selective application of the Rules. *See* R.LOWNDES & G.RUDOLF, *supra*, ¶ 510.

Following World War II, the International Law Association undertook a new effort to achieve universally acceptable Rules. Representatives from thirteen countries, including the United States, met in 1949 to consider further revisions. The results were the York-Antwerp Rules of 1950, the Rules of particular interest in the present case. The principal modification introduced in 1950 was the addition of the following "Rule of Interpretation" at the beginning of the Rules:

> In the adjustment of general average the following lettered and numbered Rules shall apply to the exclusion of any Law and Practice inconsistent therewith.
> *Except as provided by the numbered Rules, General Average shall be adjusted according to the lettered Rules.*

(Emphasis added.) The new Rule thus gave priority to the numbered Rules, making it clear that "if the facts support a claim in general average under the numbered rules, it matters not that there has been no general average act within the meaning of Rule A." R.LOWNDES & G.RUDOLF, *supra*, ¶ 548 at 256.

Added at the request of the British delegation, the new Rule was designed to overrule the interpretation of the 1924 Rules rendered in the case of *Vlassopoulos v. British & Foreign Marine Insurance Co.*, [1929] 1 K.B. 187. This decision, which "upset all preconceived ideas" on the relationship between the lettered and numbered Rules, *see* R.LOWNDES & G.RUDOLF, *supra*, ¶ 511 at 247, ¶ 545 at 255-56, held that the numbered Rules were merely specific examples of types of general average situations, subordinate to the principles set forth in the lettered Rules. To overcome the "embarrassment" this decision caused in commercial circles, *id.* ¶ 511 at 248, shippers began inserting a new contractual provision, known as the "Makis Agreement" (after the ship involved in *Vlassopoulos*), which made clear that recourse would be had to the lettered Rules only when none of the numbered Rules was applicable. The new Rule of Interpretation formalized this Agreement by incorporating its substance into the body of the Rules.

The 1950 Rules achieved the widespread acceptance sought by the sponsors of the 1949 Conference. In the United States, the Rules were approved by the Maritime Law Association in May 1950. See 1950 A.M.C. 895; L.BUGLASS, *supra*, at 119. In 1974, the Rules were further amended in respects not directly relevant here,[4] see R.LOWNDES & G.RUDOLF, *supra*, at ¶¶ 518-24.

We see no reason not to give the Rules full effect in this case, in accordance with the agreement between the parties. Although they have not been formally sanctioned on an intergovernmental basis, and thus lack the force of law, the Rules reflect an important consensus of the international shipping industry and merit "full judicial cognizance," *see* 2 BENEDICT ON ADMIRALTY § 183 at 13-14 (7th ed. 1975), at least insofar as they do not conflict with statutory or other policies of equal or greater importance. See *Sea-Land Service, Inc. v. Aetna Insurance Co.*, 545 F.2d 1313, 1315 n.* (2d Cir. 1976).

---

[4] *But see* note 7 *infra.*

III.

Against this background, we can now look more closely at the arguments made in this case. Appellant Eagle's central contention is that the district court erred by applying one of the lettered Rules, Rule A, to the facts presented here and by ignoring the numbered Rules. Rule A provides:

> There is a general average act when, and only when, any extraordinary sacrifice or expenditure is intentionally and reasonably made or incurred for the common safety for the purpose of preserving from peril the property involved in a common maritime adventure.

The district court concluded that no "purpose of preserving from peril" had been shown, since the ship was safely moored when the damage was discovered and "could forever have remained at its Rotterdam mooring without being subject to any dangers except those incident to old age." 490 F. Supp. at 923. The judge thus held that no general average act had occurred.

The district court's error, appellant contends, lay in its failure to consider the applicability of two of the numbered rules addressed to precisely the type of situation involved here. Specifically, appellant points to Rule X(b), which provides:

> (b) The cost of handling on board or discharging cargo, fuel or stores, whether at a port or place of loading, call or refuge, shall be admitted as general average when the handling or discharge was necessary for the common safety *or to enable damage to the ship caused by sacrifice or accident to be repaired, if the repairs were necessary for the safe prosecution of the voyage.*

(Emphasis added.) Appellant also cites Rule XI(b), a related provision:

> (b) When a ship shall have entered or been detained in any port or place in consequence of accident, sacrifice or other extraordinary circumstances which render that necessary for the common safety, *or to enable damage to the ship caused by sacrifice or accident to be repaired, if the repairs were necessary for the safe prosecution of the voyage*, the wages and maintenance of the master, officers and crew reasonably incurred during the extra period of detention in such port or place until the ship shall or should have been made ready to proceed on her original voyage, shall be admitted in general average....
>
> Fuel and stores consumed during the extra period of detention shall be admitted as general average, except such fuel and stores as are consumed in effecting repairs not allowable in general average.
>
> Port charges incurred during the extra period of detention shall likewise be admitted as general average except such charges as are incurred solely by reason of repairs not allowable in general average.

(Emphasis added.) If, as appellant contends, these two Rules govern on the facts of this case, then they must be given precedence over the language of Rule A in conformity with the Rule of Interpretation discussed above.

Rules X(b) and XI(b), which in substance date back to the original 1890 Rules, do appear to contemplate contribution in general average toward expenses that might not qualify under Rule A. This is particularly evident in the alternative basis of recovery set out in the numbered Rules: recovery of expenses incurred "to enable damage to the ship caused by sacrifice or accident to be repaired, if the repairs were necessary for the safe prosecution of the voyage..." (the safe prosecution clause). Under this clause, repairs necessary for the safe continuation of the voyage can be deemed general average acts, even if they would not be so regarded under Rule A alone. Buglass gives the following explanation:

> [T]he York/Antwerp Rules adopted and legalized the so-called "artificial general average" or "general average by agreement" in the numbered rules by admitting as general average port of refuge expenses incurred not only

consequent on putting into port "for the common safety," but also while detained at a port of loading or call undergoing repairs necessary for the safe prosecution of the voyage. [Knut] Selmer, a Norwegian authority, rationalizes this by reasoning that it is not the *actual* danger but rather the *eventual* danger that might arise during the subsequent part of the voyage which gave rise to the claim for general average contribution. In short, the principles laid down by Rule A are greatly modified; it is sufficient that a situation has arisen in which the further prosecution of the voyage might entail actual danger for vessel and cargo....

> It seems clear ... that under the York/Antwerp Rules, as long as a peril does exist, not only need it not be imminent, it is permissible that it be merely anticipated; and presumably, as in other general average matters, the opinion of the master will not be lightly challenged. In practice a situation of reasonable apprehension, although not of actual danger, is sufficient.

L. BUGLASS, *supra*, at 123-24. In effect, then, the safe prosecution clause is to be read not as eliminating the requirement of peril but as presuming its presence in cases where, because of accident or sacrifice, a voyage cannot safely be resumed without repairs. Such a presumption is entirely consistent with the modern interpretation of the peril requirement in *Navigazione General, supra,* which, as noted above, involves only a showing of "real and substantial" danger even though ultimate catastrophe "may be distant or indeed unlikely." Lowndes and Rudolf agree that the safe prosecution clause "is a notable example of the occasions where those who supported completion of the adventure as the basis of general average prevailed over those who supported the common safety." R. LOWNDES & G. RUDOLF, *supra,* ¶ 692. We believe that this interpretation of Rules X(b) and XI (b) gives proper effect to their language and purpose.

Under this view of the Rules, we are satisfied that this record establishes a prima facie general average claim. Although the ship here had not lost its propeller, *cf.* note 5 *supra,* the record shows that it has been seriously damaged and that its condition was deteriorating. As indicated above, the damage report revealed that the propeller "had backed down the taper of the tailshaft by about 250 mm and the top of the taper was clearly visible." As we read these facts, the ship's condition, allegedly as the result of an accident at sea, presented a "real and substantial" danger of loss or complete incapacitation of the propeller—and consequent peril—if the ship had still been at sea or if it returned to sea without repairs. Defendant implicitly recognized this threat by conceding the necessity of the repairs prior to the resumption of the voyage. Under these circumstances, we believe the requirements for a prima facie claim under Rules X(b) and XI(b) have been satisfied.[6]

We are aware of the different view of these Rules taken by the Fifth Circuit in *Orient Mid-East Lines v. A Shipment of Rice,* 496 F.2d 1032, 1038-39 (5th Cir. 1974), *cert. denied,* 420 U.S. 1005 (1975). But we respectfully disagree with the assumption in that case that "Rules X and XI are limited to actions taken 'for the common safety,'" *Id.* at 1039—an assumption that overlooks the alternative basis of recovery set forth in the safe prosecution clause. We note, in any event, that the primary basis of the court's decision was not the inapplicability of the Rules to the facts there but its finding that general average recovery was unavailable in any event because the damage had been incurred in the process of making the ship seaworthy. *Id.* at 1038.

---

[5] The authors do, however, play down to some extent the distinction between the common safety and safe prosecution clauses, asserting that "[t]he degree of *damage* to the ship necessary to meet the requirements of the expression is the same as—no less than—would be necessary to endanger the 'common safety' of the adventure if the vessel were at sea." As an example of the requisite "damage," the authors cite the loss of a propeller at sea, rendering a ship "unfit to encounter the ordinary perils of the sea." *Id.* ¶ 692 at 330. Under such circumstances, they note, "once within a port where repairs can be effected, safety will have been attained"; the safe prosecution clause "merely provides for a situation in port which, if the ship were at sea, would endanger the common safety." *Id.*

This interpretation appears to reflect a narrower reading of the safe prosecution clause than that contained in the previous edition of the same work, which asserted that the clause "contemplates repairs to avert a frustration of the adventure and is to be contrasted with repairs 'necessary for the common safety' which is concerned with physical safety." R. LOWNDES & G. RUDOLF, THE LAW OF GENERAL AVERAGE ¶ 708 at 350 (9th ed. J. Donaldson, C. Ellis, C. Staughton 1964). The earlier edition also specifically recognized that the safe prosecution clause would permit general average contribution under circumstances "which would not be a general average act either at common law or under Rule A unless incurred for the common safety or as a direct consequence of a general average act." *Id.* P671 at 336.

The change in emphasis in the 10th edition may reflect a recent trend toward tightened definition of general avarage acts. *See, e.g.,* R. LOWNDES & G. RUDOLF (10th edition), *supra,* ¶ 694 at 331, noting that at the 1974 Conference to amend the Rules "some effort was made to reduce the incidence of general average costs by increasing the stringency of the criteria by which it should be determined whether a general average situation exists." *But see* G. GILMORE & C. BLACK, *supra,* § 5-16 at 271.

Moreover, we see no basis here for the concern voiced in *Orient Mid-East Lines, id.* at 1039, over the possibility of conflict between the Rules and the Carriage of Goods by Sea Act (COGSA), 46 U.S.C. §§ 1300 *et seq.* In particular, we note that the record before us presents no issues of negligence or unseaworthiness, which might implicate COGSA policies with respect to limitations of liability, *see* 46 U.S.C. § 1308(8).

IV.

In light of these considerations, we conclude that the district court erred in relying solely on Rule A to the exclusion of Rules X(b) and XI(b). Giving the latter precedence, as required by the Rule of Interpretation, we are persuaded that Eagle presented a valid prima facie claim.

Of course, we are concerned here with the grant of summary judgment; our holding is merely that a claim has been stated, not that it has been proved. Eagle still bears the burden of showing that the requirements of the Rules have been satisfied. *See* Rule E of the 1950 Rules, providing that "[t]he onus of proof is upon the party claiming in general average to show that the loss or expense claimed is properly allowable as general average." *See also* L. Buglass, *supra,* at 130. Thus, for example, appellant must show that the damage requiring repair was the result of an "accident," rather than a latent defect attributable to the ship's unseaworthiness.[7] We express no views on this or any other factual issue that may arise at trial

The judgment is reversed and the case remanded for further proceedings.

———————

ROYAL INSURANCE CO. OF AMERICA v. CINERARIA SHIPPING CO.

894 F. Supp. 1557, 1996 AMC 2051 (M.D. Fla. 1995)

BUCKLEW, District Judge

* * *

Facts

On October 24, 1986, the M/V KALLIOPI II came into the Tampa Bay port under pilotage to load a shipment of scrap iron cargo bound for Korea (D-36, Stipulation ["Stip."] 1). The loading of the cargo was completed on October 29, 1986, and shortly thereafter, the crew prepared the vessel for sailing (D-36, Stip. 3, 4). The crew's preparation included testing all of the vessel's navigational equipment including the steering gear, radar and other items (D-36, Stip. 4).

Captain George McDonald, a Tampa Bay pilot, boarded the vessel at approximately 2125 hours and instructed the crew to secure the Tug ORANGE on the port bow and the Tug TAMPA on the port quarter. The crew complied with Captain McDonalds instructions (D-36, Stip. 5). At 2140 hours, the engines of the M/V KALLIOPI II were tested and placed on standby (D-36, Stip. 6). Shortly thereafter at 2145 hours, the vessel dropped her lines, and the two tugs backed the vessel out of her slip, berth 223, into the Cut D Channel, which runs perpendicular to the berth (D-36, Stip. 6, 7).[2] Not using the ships engines until 2159 hours in an attempt to line the vessel up with the channel, the Captain ordered "slow ahead" and then ordered the helm "hard to starboard" (D-36, Stip. 9). Until this point, all movement of the vessel was controlled by the Tug TAMPA and the Tug ORANGE (D-36, Stip. 9).

Upon hearing the "hard to starboard" order, the master noticed that the rudder angle indicator did not match the helm order. He thus switched the steering gear motors on bridge and thereafter observed problems in getting the helm orders to synchronize with the rudder indicator. Upon investigation by the chief engineer and second officer, it was discovered that the steering gear machinery was damaged (D-36, Stip. 10). It was further determined that the rudder damage was apparently caused by the pilot backing the vessel too far and striking the western bank of

---

[7] It is worth noting in this connection two amendments to the numbered Rules adopted in 1974 designed to make clear that damage must have been incurred as the result of accident during voyage. An amendment to Rule X(b) qualified the availability of contribution under that rule by excluding "cases where the damage to the ship is discovered at a port or place of loading or call without any accident or other extraordinary circumstance connected with such damage having taken place during the voyage." Rule XI (b) was similarly amended by the addition of a provision to the same effect. See R. LOWNDES & G. RUDOLF, *supra,* PP694, 729-30.

[2] Notably, the M/V KALLIOPI II was docked "bow in" while in berth 223 (D-36, Stip. 7). Captain McDonald intended to back the M/V KALLIOPI II out far enough so that he could swing the blow to starboard bringing the vessel into line with the Cut D channel in order to proceed down Tampa Bay (D-36, Stip. 8).

Channel D with the rudder (D-36, Stip. 11). Upon the masters determination that the M/V KALLIOPI II could not proceed on her own, the vessel was returned to berth 223 with tug assistance for further inspection (D-36, Stip. 12). At that point, it was determined that disabling damage to the rudder stock occurred (D-36, Stip. 12).

Throughout this entire incident, the vessel remained within the Tampa port with tug services readily available (D-36, Stip. 13). The damage did not affect the hull of the vessel, and there was no danger of entry of seawater into the vessel as a consequence of the incident (D-36, Stip. 11). No distress calls were made by the vessel during the incident (D-36, Stip. 13). Seas were calm with winds of Beaufort force 3 at departure and diminishing to force 1 upon the vessels return to berth (D-36, Stip. 14).

Once it was determined that the rudder was disabled and the vessel could not continue its voyage, the shipowners declared general average (D-36, Stip. 15). Following the declaration of general average, it was determined that the M/V KALLIOPI II could not be repaired with all of the cargo onboard (D-36, Stip. 21). A portion of the cargo was therefore discharged, placed on the dock, and then reloaded after the repairs were completed (D-36, Stip. 21). The repairs were performed at Tampa shipyard, and thereafter the cargo was reloaded, and the vessel completed its voyage delivering the cargo to its destination (D-36, Stip. 21).

Due to the general average declaration, all of the cargo interests were required to post security for the general average claim (D-36, Stip. 16). A general average statement was thus prepared setting forth both the general average and particular average items (D-36, Stip. 22). The statement calculates that the Plaintiff's contribution to general average would be $108,744.02 (D-36, Stip. 23). Royal Insurance Company ["Royal"], as insurer of the cargo, posted the requisite security, but contends that this is not a general average act and thus, contribution is not due on their part.

Plaintiff Royal now seeks a declaratory judgment requesting the Court find that: 1) the October 29, 1986 incident was not a proper general average event; 2) Defendant had no right to declare general average and seek contribution from cargo interests; 3) Defendants claim for contribution in general average is denied; 4) the general average guarantee issued in response to Defendant's demand is released; 5) denying Defendant's counterclaim for contribution in *toto;* and 6) granting Plaintiff such other, further, and/or different relief as this Court deems proper. In opposition, the Defendant seeks summary judgment in favor of its counterclaim for general average contribution in the amount of $108,744.02, as well as interest and costs from the time of the general average adjustment.

Based on the foregoing, the Court has before it two issues for consideration: 1) whether these facts establish a general average event; and 2) whether Plaintiff is required to contribute to general average under the provisions of the charter party.

General Average Act

General average is an equitable doctrine that is applicable "when, and only when, any extraordinary sacrifice or expenditure is intentionally and reasonably made or incurred for the common safety for the purpose of preserving from peril the property involved in a common maritime adventure." *Deutsche Shell Tanker Gesellschaft v. Placid Refining Co.,* 993 F.2d 466, 469 (5th Cir. 1993) (quoting York/Antwerp Rule A (1974)). In such circumstances, "the party suffering the loss has a right ... to claim contribution from all who participate in the venture," including the cargo interests. *Ceramic Corp. of Am. v. Inka Maritime Corp.,* 1 F.3d 947, 948 (9th Cir. 1993) (quoting Thomas J.Schoenbaum, Admiralty and Maritime Law § 16-1, at 522-23 (1987)).

A claim for general average requires a three prong analysis. *Deutsche Shell,* 993 F.2d at 468. First, the vessel owner must establish that a general average act occurred and that there was a separate cargo owner at the time of the act. *Id.* If the vessel owner meets this first requirement, the cargo owner may avoid liability by proving that the vessel was unseaworthy at the start of the voyage, and the unseaworthiness was the proximate cause of the general average act. *Id.* Lastly, if the cargo owner establishes unseaworthiness, the vessel owner may still succeed if it proves that it exercised "due diligence" to make the vessel seaworthy at the commencement of the voyage. *Id.*

* * *

Historically, courts throughout the jurisdictions have typically found that general average acts existed in situations involving "**imminent** peril." *See Barnard v. Adams,* 51 U.S. (10 How.) 270, 303, 13 L.Ed. 417 (1850);

The Star of Hope, 76 U.S. (9 Wall.) 203, 19 L.Ed. 638 (1869); *Hobson v. Lord,* 92 U.S. 397, 23 L.Ed. 613 (1876); *Aktieselskabet Cuzco v. The Sucarseco,* 294 U.S. 394, 401, 55 S. Ct. 467, 470, 79 L.Ed. 942 (1935). In more recent times, however, courts have varied slightly as to requisite degree of "peril" necessary to render sacrifice or extraordinary expenses recoverable under general average. Some courts have adhered to the stricter, more traditional, interpretation of "peril,"[6] while other courts have endorsed a looser interpretation of a "perilous situation."[7]

Plaintiff asserts that the instant case does not involve a general average act because the incident did not place the M/V KALLIOPI II or its cargo in "peril." In opposition, Defendant contends that the instant case qualifies as a proper general average event under the York/Antwerp Rules of 1974 and *Eagle Terminal Tankers, Inc. v. Insurance Co. of U.S.S.R, Ltd.,* 637 F.2d 890 (2d Cir. 1981), because the vessel could not continue its voyage without repairs, and as such, the vessel and its cargo were in peril until such time as the repairs were made. The Defendant therefore asserts that it is entitled to general average contribution.

Plaintiff contends that *Eagle Terminal,* as relied upon by the Defendant, is an aberration and creates an "artificial general average" that allows for general average contribution without a showing of actual danger or peril (D-42, pg. 4-5; D-43, pg. 5). The Plaintiff further asserts that the Second Circuit faithfully adhered to the peril requirement until its decision in *Eagle Terminal* (D-42, pg. 4). This Court notes that such statement is inaccurate[8] and that the Plaintiff has misconstrued *Eagle Terminal's,* interpretation of "peril." The *Eagle Terminal* court specifically held that:

It is clear that the law of general average continues to require a showing of peril. But in this century, perils less than "imminent" have been recognized as sufficient to create a general average situation.

Id. at 893. Moreover, the *Eagle Terminal* court further explained that under Rule XI(b) of the York/Antwerp Rules of 1974 the requirement of "peril" is not eliminated, but rather is presumed in cases where a voyage cannot continue without repairs due to accident or sacrifice. *Id.* at 896. This Court endorses the *Eagle Terminal's* interpretation of "peril." Thus, this Court does not limit "peril" to the risk of sinking or vast destruction aboard ship, but rather finds that it is a broader term wherein the prosecution of a voyage is severely threatened.

Defendant's reliance on *Eagle Terminal* is strongly rooted in its factual similarities to the present case.

* * *

As in *Eagle Terminal,* the M/V KALLIOPI II had left her place of loading and thereafter had an accident. As a consequence, she had to enter a "port or place of refuge," specifically she had to return to her place of loading due to the rudder damage. If M/V KALLIOPI II's steering mechanism had not been repaired, it is highly improbable that the ship would have been able to safely complete its voyage. It seems self-evident to this Court that the M/V KALLIOPI II could not proceed without steering gear, and repairs to a part of a ship as significant as the rudder must be made for the common safety of the ship and cargo. The vessels perilous situation was further demonstrated by the ship's request for tug assistance to return to the berth. If M/V KALLIOPI II had continued its voyage without the needed repairs, it is highly probable that immediate peril would have followed, or at least a "real and substantial" danger of loss. As in *Eagle Terminal,* this Court finds Rules X and XI of the York/Antwerp Rules, 1974, are applicable to the instant case wherein the M/V KALLIOPI II may not have been in "imminent" peril, but she could not complete the "safe prosecution" of her voyage if she had not returned to port for repairs.

The Fifth Circuit Court of Appeals took a different view of Rules X(b) and XI(b) than the Second Circuit in *Orient Mid-East Lines, Inc. v. A Shipment of Rice,* 496 F.2d 1032, 1039 (5th Cir. 1974), *cert. denied,* 420 U.S. 1005,

---

[6] *See Deutsche Shell Tanker,* 767 F. Supp. 762 (E.D. La. 1991), *aff'd,* 993 F.2d 466 (5th Cir. 1993); *Orient Mid-East Lines, Inc. v. A Shipment of Rice,* 496 F.2d 1032 (5th Cir. 1974).

[7] *See Eagle Terminal,* 637 F.2d 890 (2d Cir. 1981); *Navigazione Generale Italiana v. Spencer Kellogg & Sons, Inc.,* 92 F.2d 41 (2d. Cir.), *cert. denied,* 302 U.S. 751, 58 S. Ct. 271, 82 L. Ed. 580 (1937).

[8] Before the court's opinion in *Eagle Terminal,* the Second Circuit Court of Appeals in *Navigazione,* 92 F.2d 41, 43 (2d. Cir. 1937), also applied a broader interpretation of "peril" stating that contribution in general average requires an element of peril, however:

[T]he 'imminency' of the peril is not the critical test. If the danger be real and substantial, a sacrifice or expenditure made in good faith for the common interest is justified, even though the advent of any catastrophe may be distant or indeed unlikely.

95 S. Ct. 1447, 43 L. Ed. 2d 763 (1975), where the court denied general average contribution of the shipowner finding that the ship was never in "peril." In that case, the ship was intentionally anchored at sea to complete some repair work on its port boiler. *Id.* at 1036. Due to the soft silt at the point of anchorage, the repairs could not be completed, and it was decided that the ship should be towed back to berth. Id. With difficulty the vessel was removed from the mud and silt, and upon breaking free, it rapidly proceeded backward across the river barely avoiding a collision with a dock on the opposite side of the river. *Id.* Thereafter, the ship proceeded across the channel and once again was grounded. *Id.* Later in the voyage, further damage occurred to the propulsion system. Id. at 1037. The shipowner thus brought a claim for general average for the expenses incurred in the voyage from the combined incidents. Id.

The court in *Orient Mid-East* explained that Rules X and XI concern expenses incurred at a port of refuge and are limited to actions taken "for the common safety." Id. at 1039. The *Eagle Terminal* court disagreed with *Orient Mid-East* court's limitation of Rules X and XI to actions taken solely "for the common safety," noting that the *Orient Mid-East* court was ignoring recovery under the safe prosecution clause of Rule XI. *Eagle Terminal,* 637 F.2d at 897. The Orient Mid-East court further noted as explained by the district court that the requisite peril was not present where the ship was intentionally and safely anchored in the soft silt; the vessel was not in danger of colliding with another ship, and it was not causing any interference with navigation. 496 F.2d at 1039.

Unlike *Orient Mid-East,* where the requisite peril was not present for general average contribution, the instant case demonstrates a perilous situation warranting general average. If the M/V KALLIOPI II only had to be pulled from a soft silt grounding where it had been intentionally and safely anchored as in *Orient Mid-East,* the Court would follow the Orient *Mid-East* ruling and deny general average. However, the instant case is distinguishable from *Orient Mid-East.* Notably, the M/V KALLIOPI II was in navigation at the time of the accident and was not in a safe anchorage as the vessel was in *Orient Mid-East.* Because of the location of the accident in the present case, the M/V KALLIOPI II would have been a hazard to navigation if she proceeded with a damaged rudder unlike the situation in *Orient Mid-East.*

Moreover, in *Orient Mid-East* the court explained, in part, that Rules X and XI were not applicable because such rules "concern expenses incurred at a port of refuge entered as a general average act." *Orient Mid-East,* 496 F.2d at 1039. In *Orient Mid-East,* the initial damage caused by grounding the ship did not require her to return to a port or place of refuge for repairs as required under Rules X and XI of the York/Antwerp Rules, 1974.[10] In contrast however, the M/V KALLIOPI II had to return to her port as a "consequence of accident, sacrifice or other extraordinary circumstances" necessary for the common safety and to "enable damage to the ship caused by sacrifice or accident to be repaired." *See* Rule X(a), Lowndes & Rudolf, *supra* ¶ 676, at 319; Rule XI(b), Lowndes & Rudolf, *supra* ¶ 730, at 347. The Court therefore finds that Rules X and XI are applicable to the instant case, and thus, the broader interpretation of "peril" under the Rules is appropriate.

In addition to the *Orient Mid-East* court's denial of general average contribution due to the inapplicability of the York/Antwerp Rules, the court primarily denied contribution due to the shipowners lack of due diligence in making the vessel seaworthy. 496 F.2d at 1038. Similarly, in *Deutsche Shell,* 993 F.2d 466, 469 (5th Cir. 1993), the court denied general average contribution due to the shipowner's failure to exercise due diligence in maintaining the seaworthiness of the ship. In *Deutsche Shell,* a crude oil tanker ran aground in the Mississippi River, and thereafter the shipowner declared general average for the cost of degrounding the tanker. *Id.* at 468. Based solely on the vessel's unseaworthy condition, the Fifth Circuit upheld the district court's decision precluding general average and further commented that, "we need not decide whether the vessel was in peril nor whether the issue was raised properly."[11] *Id.* at 469.

In the instant case, there are no allegations of unseaworthiness. Because the Deutsche Shell court denied general average due to the unseaworthiness of the vessel, the Court does not find Deutsche Shell to be persuasive

---

[10] The ship did however have to return to a port for repairs to the high pressure turbine. However, general average for this incident was denied based on the unseaworthiness of the ship. *Orient Mid-East,* 496 F.2d at 1039-40.

[11] The Court notes however that the district court in *Deutsche Shell* did address the "peril" issue finding that the cost of degrounding the oil tanker did not constitute a general average event because the ship did not sustain severe damage nor was there an imminent or significant threat of an oil spill into the river. *Deutsche Shell,* 767 F. Supp. 762, 784 (E.D. La. 1991).

or applicable to the instant case. Moreover, it is important to note that there was no assertion in *Deutsche Shell* that Rule X or XI of the York/Antwerp Rules, 1974, applied to the case. The damage that occurred in *Deutsche Shell* did not require the vessel to return to a "port or place of refuge" as a consequence of the accident. The Court therefore finds that *Deutsche Shell* is not analogous to the instant case.

Based on the foregoing analysis, this Court adopts the court's reasoning in *Eagle Terminal* as well as its endorsement of Rules X and XI of the York/Antwerp Rules, 1974, and thus finds that the M/V KALLIOPI II's accident created a situation of "peril" such that the voyage could not be continued until necessary repairs were made. The Court therefore finds that a general average event occurred in the present case.

General Average Under the Charter Party

Having found that the M/V KALLIOPI II was involved in a general average act, the Court now addresses whether the Defendant has a contractual right to general average under the charter party (D-39, Ex. 2). This issue arises out of the alleged conflict between Paragraph twelve (12) of the charter party, the New Jason Clause,[12] and Paragraph fifty-one (51) of the rider to the charter party. Defendant asserts that it is entitled to contribution based on the following provisions of the charter party:

[¶12] General average to be settled according to York-Antwerp rules, 1974. Proprietors of cargo to pay the cargo's share in the general expenses even if same have been necessitated through neglect or default of the Owner's servants (see clause 2).

(D-39, Ex. 2).

New Jason Clause

In the event of accident, danger, damage or disaster before or after commencement of the voyage resulting from any cause whatsoever, whether due to negligence or not, for which, or for the consequences of which, the Carrier is not responsible by statute, contract or otherwise, the goods, shippers, consignees, or owner's of the goods shall contribute with the Carrier in general average to the payment of any sacrifices, losses or expenses of a general average nature that may be made or incurred, and shall pay salvage and special charges incurred in respect of the goods.

If a salving ship is owned or operated by the Carrier, salvage shall be paid for as fully as if such salving ship or ships belonged to strangers. Such deposit as the Carrier or his agents may deem sufficient to cover the estimate contribution of the goods and any salvage and special charges thereon shall, if required, be made by the goods, shippers, consignees or Owners of the goods to the Carrier before delivery.

(D-36, Stip. 20; D-39, Ex. 2).

In opposition, Plaintiff asserts that the following provision (¶51) of the rider to the charter party relieves it from any liability due to the pilot's negligence:

[¶51] The pilot, Master, officers, crew of the vessel and any towboat person or facility assisting the vessel excluding Charterers, Shippers or Receivers personnel or their servants shall not be agents or employees of the Charterers and Charterers shall not be liable for any loss damage or claims resulting from or arising out of negligence or error of any of them while vessel is proceeding to or lying at any place of loading and/or discharging.
(D-36, Stip. 19; D-39, Ex. 2).

The Court notes that the New Jason Clause and Paragraph 12 speak directly to the issue of general average. As such, this Court finds that these provisions are controlling as to general average contribution. While Paragraph

---

[12] Paragraph 40 of the charter party contained a provision incorporating the "New Jason Clause" into the charter party (D-39, Ex. 2).

51 and Paragraph 12, in combination with the New Jason Clause, may appear to be contradictory, the Court finds that they can be reconciled. The Court interprets Paragraph 51 as precluding the Defendant from bringing an independent lawsuit for damages against the Charterers caused in this case by the pilot's negligence. In the instant case, however, the Defendant is not suing the Charterer for the entire amount of damages due to the pilot's fault, but rather is asking for an equitable sharing of the accident's expenses.

A New Jason Clause is enforceable and provides for general average contribution even where the carrier is negligent, unless the carrier is responsible for damage under the Carriage of Goods by Sea Act (COGSA), 46 U.S.C. §§ 1300-1315. See *Deutsche Shell*, 993 F.2d at 468; *Louis Dreyfus Corp. v. 27,946 Long Tons of Corn*, 830 F.2d 1321, 1330 (5th Cir. 1987); *Atlantic Richfield Co. v. United States*, 640 F.2d 759, 761 (5th Cir. 1981). COGSA holds a carrier (or ship) at fault for damage to the cargo caused by unseaworthiness as a result of "want of due diligence on the part of the carrier to make the ship seaworthy." 46 U.S.C. § 1304; *Deutsche Shell*, 993 F.2d at 468; *Atlantic Richfield*, 640 F.2d at 761.

In the present case, there is no assertion of the vessel's unseaworthiness. Moreover, the stipulated facts indicate to the contrary. Specifically, the parties agree that shortly before the beginning of M/V KALLIOPI II's voyage, "the crew tested all of the vessel's navigational equipment including the steering gear, radar and other items" (D-36, Stip. 4). With no allegations of the carriers failure to exercise due diligence to make the vessel seaworthy, the Court finds that the Defendant is not precluded by COGSA from general average contributions under the New Jason Clause. Having found no limitation under COGSA for general average, the Court finds that the Defendant is entitled to general average contribution under Paragraph 12 and the New Jason Clause, even in light of the pilot's negligent acts.

Accordingly, it is Ordered and Adjudged that:

1) The Plaintiff's Motion for Summary Judgment (D-37) is DENIED.
2) The Defendant's Motion for Summary Judgment (D-40) is GRANTED.
3) The Plaintiff shall contribute to general average in the amount of $108,744.02, plus interest and costs from the time of the general average adjustment.

*   *   *

DONE AND ORDERED.

B. Causation-Damages: "Direct Consequences"

SEA-LAND SERVICE, INC. v. AETNA INSURANCE CO.

545 F.2d 1313, 1976 AMC 2164 (2nd Cir. 1976)

MULLIGAN, Circuit Judge

Sea-Land Service, Inc. (Sea Land), the charterer of the S.S. Beauregard (Beauregard), and its underwriters appeal from that portion of a judgment of the United States District Court for the Southern District of New York, denying them a general average contribution from the defendant marine insurance carriers which had insured cargo interests. The contribution sought was stipulated to be $478,816 representing bottom damage to the Beauregard incurred during a salvage operation at Rio Haina, Dominican Republic in May 1967. The opinion of the Honorable Whitman J. Kanpp, who conducted a bench trial on July 15, 16 and 17, 1975, was filed on February 10, 976. A consent judgment in favor of the plaintiffs was entered on May 19, 1976 awarding them the sum of $54,231.17 for certain costs of towing and salvage, plus interest. The only issue before this court is whether or not the trial court properly determined that the substantial bottom damage to the Beauregard was not a general average loss which should be ratably shared by cargo interests.

I.

The Beauregard was built in 1943 as a break-bulk cargo carrier and was converted in 1957 into a container carrier. In 1967 she was operated by Sea Land, sailing from New York on April 28, 1967 with cargo in containers bound for Rio Haina, Dominican Republic. While proceeding into the harbor of Rio Haina on May 5, 1967, the Beauregard encountered serious difficulties in approaching the entrance because of adverse weather and sea conditions. Her Master, Captain Boehm, was an experienced mariner who had held a Master's license for 23 years. He had been Captain of the vessel for about two years and had previous experience entering Rio Haina. The first approach to the harbor entrance was aborted because of heavy rain squalls and poor visibility. A second approach was attempted after the Dominican Government Harbor Pilot E. Torres had boarded the Beauregard from a small boat. Again the adverse weather conditions prevented the entry. When the weather appeared to have improved, a third effort was made at 1802 hours. However, freshening winds, and strong currents drove the ship into the rubble of the west breakwater of the harbor at 1813 hours, where she grounded at what the parties have termed Position A (bow pointed 357 degrees True, the bow being about 15 feet from and 20 feet inshore of the west breakwater). The vessel was then six feet onto the rocks on the port side. Captain Boehm ordered full astern in an unsuccessful effort to release the ship through its own power. She remained grounded with the port bow against a wrecked tanker. Pilot Torres blew a danger signal requesting assistance, and a tug was at the scene within ten minutes. The tug was directed to the starboard quarter and a manila hawser was attached to the tug which took up the slack and pulled while the ship's engines were kept full astern at the same time. After ten minutes of pulling, as the vessel was beginning to move out before she left the strand, the towline broke. After the line broke, the vessel was pushed sideways to port by the winds and the waves, sustaining the bottom damage which occasioned this litigation. The ship's bow now rested in Position B (vessel's bow was pointing 015° True, the bow being about 175 feet inshore of the end of the west breakwater.) At 2108 hours, on May 8, 1967, the Beauregard was eventually refloated. She remained underway at sea all night and at daybreak entered Rio Haina harbor with her cargo and crew safe and sound; a happy ending for mariners, but predictably the genesis of an acerbic dispute among underwriters and their counsel. 'Twas ever thus.

II.

The concept of general average contribution in maritime law is ancient, dating back to the Romans, surviving we are told the fall of the Roman Empire and recognized from the Middle Ages until the present time by all the principal maritime nations. G. GILMORE AND C. BLACK, THE LAW OF ADMIRALTY 244-45 (2d ed. 1975). The principle is simply stated—when one who partakes in a maritime venture incurs loss for the common benefit, it should be shared ratably by all who participate in the venture. *CIA. Atlantica Pacifica, S.A. v. Humble Oil & Refining Co.*, 274 F. Supp. 884, 891 (D. Md. 1967). Modern law and practice relating to the adjustment of general average is determined generally by the York-Antwerp Rules, 1950. The complaint in this action alleges in Par. 8 that the bills of lading issued for the cargo carried on board the Beauregard provide that "General Average shall be adjusted, stated and settled according to the York-Antwerp Rules 1950...."

Rule A of these Rules defines a general average act as "any extraordinary sacrifice or expenditure [which] is intentionally and reasonably made or incurred for the common safety for the purpose of preserving from peril the property involved in a common maritime adventure." There is no dispute here that the effort of the Master of the Beauregard to free the vessel from the strand by the use of the tow was an act of general average. The costs of the tow have already been determined and stipulated on that basis. The vessel, the crew and the cargo were in imminent peril, and the Captain acted promptly and reasonably for the common good. No negligence on the part of either the Master or the Pilot caused the stranding.

However, it does not follow that the damage to the bottom of the Beauregard is recoverable as general average. Rule C of the York-Antwerp Rules, 1950 provides: "Only such losses, damages or expenses which are the *direct consequence* of the general average act shall be allowed as general average...." (emphasis supplied). Moreover, Rule E provides: "The onus of proof is upon the party claiming in general average to show that the loss or expense claimed is properly allowable as general average." There was, however, no finding of fact that the damage incurred by the shift of the vessel from Position A to B was caused by the act of sacrifice, the towing. The only record reference made by the appellant's (Rec. at 405) is to a colloquy between Judge Knapp and counsel at the end of the trial where Judge Knapp stated: "Again, I don't know what I will conclude after reading the deposition which isn't the basis of what I heard on cross examination of various witnesses and what the gentlemen might have said about it in different parts of the trial, but it is my guess that I will conclude that the pulling off materially increased the possibility of the shift from A to B." The point is that Judge Knapp actually made no such finding. On the contrary, he found:

8. It is more likely than not that the ship would have shifted roughly to "position B", regardless of whether the tow had been attempted. This finding is based on the evidence of wind and current and the testimony of eyewitnesses.

9. In light of finding 8, had the tow not been attempted at least the damage actually suffered would have occurred.

In an effort to establish that the aborted towing did contribute to the sideward movement of the vessel after the towline break, appellant's argue that the Beauregard's bow was firmly embedded when she first ran aground, and that the tow had moved her out far enough to permit the bow to pivot and the stern to swing to port. While plaintiffs' proposed finding of fact No. 10 was "The vessel did not move or break free until the tug started to pull, when her bow was felt coming free," this finding was rejected by the court below. It is conceded moreover that after the towline broke, the Beauregard was still stranded. While there was testimony that the vessel had begun to move, there is no evidence that the vessel was in substantially any different position than when she originally grounded. Sea Land argues that the Beauregard could not have swung to port from Position A as she did until the tow had moved her out far enough to clear the wrecked tanker. We are referred to maps and photographs in support of this contention. There is no doubt but that the vessel was stranded with the wrecked tanker on her port bow. The court below so found. However, the court's finding that it was more probable that the vessel would have moved from Position A to B by the wind and current was based upon the eyewitness testimony of experienced mariners, Captain Boehm, Pilot Torres and the tug Captain Rojo, all of whom testified that the ship would have been so moved by the wind and the heavy seas. There is no eyewitness testimony that the towing operation had in any way caused the move from Position A to B. In fact, in Finding of Fact No. 12, which is not challenged on appeal, the court found: "The master's action in attempting the tow in no way increased the danger to the ship." We conclude that the plaintiffs did not shoulder the burden of proof of establishing that the towing so moved the vessel that she became more vulnerable to natural forces, thereby rendering the bottom damage general average.

* * *

Appellants warn us that an affirmance here will encourage refusals to share in general average losses and will open a new line of litigation in an area where general average adjusters' opinions have been dispositive in the past. It is true that Mr. Howard Myerson, the general average adjuster here employed, classified the bottom damage as general average. However, his testimony indicates that this was based on Mr. Ganly's opinion that the vessel was so firmly fixed by the bow that had the tow not been attempted, she would not have suffered further damage. It further appears that Mr. Myerson's conclusions would probably have been different had the facts been as found by the court. Judge Knapp, in questioning Myerson, commented:

The Court: I understand your position that if the towing operation substantially increased the probability of it going over that is general average?

The Witness: Yes.

The Court: If it didn't substantially increase the probability of it going over it is not general average?

The Witness: Yes.

The Court: If it didn't substantially increase the probability of it going over it is not general average?

The Witness: Yes.

III.

In an effort to avoid the "clearly erroneous" rule, appellant's urge that the court below applied an erroneous test in determining general average. We are told that we need not decide that the towage attempt caused the sideward movement to define it as general average. "The Court only needs to determine that the sideward movement was avoidable when the vessel first ran aground and that the method of salvage chosen by the Master, the General Average sacrifice, allowed it to occur." We agree that the Master did or should have anticipated that the towline might part. We further agree that if the breaking of the towline permitted a sideward movement that would not otherwise have occurred, the damage would be general average and cases such as *Australian Coastal Shipping Commission v. Green*, [1971] 1 Ll. Rep. 16 (C.A. 1970) and *Anglo-Grecian Steam Trading Co. v. T. Beynon & Co.*, [1926] 25 Ll. L. Rep. 122 (K.B. 1926) would be in point. In both cases the act of towing caused the damage. In *Green*, which involved two incidents of towing by tugs where the snapping of the towlines caused them to become ensnarled in the propellers of the tugs, the resulting damage to the tugs was properly found to be the direct consequence of the sacrifice. The subsequent accident, the parting of the towline, did not break the chain of causation. In *Benyon*, the vessel was in peril and was taken in tow. The intention was to beach the vessel in the center of a bay. On the way she grounded, the towlines parted and the ship was damaged on the rocks. Again, it was held to be general average damage directly caused by the act of sacrifice. However, the applicability of these cases here depends upon Sea Land's ability to establish that the tow had permitted the vessel to be pulled free enough to permit a sideward motion which otherwise would not have occurred. In sum, Sea Land cannot escape the issue of fact which, as we have already indicated, it has failed to do.

Appellants argue that the Master could have held the vessel fast in her initial position with the use of her engines alone. This is based on no testimony of eyewitnesses but again the testimony of Mr. Ganly which the court below obviously discredited. Finding of Fact No. 10 was:

> It was not open to the master to attempt to hold the ship in "position A" by using "full ahead" power and thus driving her further on the rocks.

Appellants urge that this finding was clearly erroneous and represents an improper judicial "second guessing" of the Master of the Beauregard. The argument is curious. The court did not second guess the Captain. It found that his action in seeking the tow to refloat the vessel was not negligent. It found she "could have been holed and broken where she was" (Plaintiff's Proposed Finding No. 6, accepted below) and that "The master's action in attempting to tow in no way increased the danger to the ship." (Finding No. 12). By raising the argument on appeal that in fact the Beauregard could have been held in Position A, thus avoiding the damage incurred by the move to Position B, it is the appellant's rather than the court who are in fact second guessing the Captain. If pressed to its ultimate conclusion, it might be argued that Boehm did not act reasonably and therefore no general average act occurred. Appellants naturally do not go this far. They are raising the point to establish that the act of towing was responsible for the lateral movement of the vessel. We repeat, there was no such proof. In any event, the only testimony that the vessel could have held her position by going ahead with a left rudder was Mr. Ganly's who was not present. Captain Boehm testified that he could not hold the vessel in Position A by using an anchor and tugs. Moreover, there is no proof as to how long her engines could operate because of the sand and water which were being sucked in due to the stranding. The court below had the opportunity to observe Mr. Ganly as he testified, and we cannot characterize its finding which rejected that testimony as clearly erroneous.

Appellants urge that an affirmance here will promote appeals from general average adjustments and will discourage Masters from saving cargo. We believe, on the contrary, that this case represents no departure at all from general average principles, and that appellant's have simply failed to sustain their burden of proof of direct damage as a result of the general average sacrifice as required by York-Antwerp Rules, 1950. We state emphatically that we have no ambition to encourage general average litigation. Here, the expert adjuster, a self-styled "desk man", accepted the version of the facts received from a naval architect who examined the Beauregard in Hoboken, New Jersey several weeks after the incident and whose opinion was ultimately rejected by the court below. There was no difference between the court and the adjuster as to the principles to be applied. We do not consider it realistic to assume that Masters of ships facing imminent peril on the high seas will base their professional maritime decisions upon what allocation of general or particular average an adjuster might make and what a trial or appellate court might thereafter decide. The time it would take to make such calculations could only result in the proliferation of maritime disasters. Decisions such as those made here will hopefully continue to be made by experienced and skilled mariners for the common good of the vessel, the cargo and the crew.

FRIENDLY, Circuit Judge (dissenting):

My disagreement with the majority is narrow. As I read my brother Mulligan's opinion, he does not dispute that if the vessel had sustained her burden of proving that the towing operation, with its hazard of a broken tow line, significantly enhanced the risk that the Beauregard would drift to port and scrape her bottom, the damage would have been a "direct consequence" of the general average act under Rule C of the York-Antwerp Rules. *Cf.* RESTATEMENT (SECOND) OF TORTS § 442B, Comment b at 470 (1965), *see also id.* § 432. The majority considers, however, that the district court found, and properly could find, that the maneuver did not significantly enhance the risk of what in fact occurred. I do not read the findings that way.

* * *

In my view the difficulty here has arisen because of the district court's shift from the standard it enunciated at the end of the trial, namely, whether the towing "materially increased the possibility of the shift from A to B" to the concept, implicit in finding 8, that general average would not lie if it was "more likely than not that the ship would have shifted roughly to 'Position B', regardless of whether the tow had been attempted." Since we all agree that the former is the correct standard, I would reverse and remand for explicit findings in regard to it.

C. The Interrelationship between General Average, COGSA, and "The New Jason Clause"

Introductory Note

In *The Irrawaddy*, 171 U.S. 187, 18 S.Ct. 831 (1898), the Supreme Court held that where a marine adventure has become imperiled due to the fault of the carrier, the carrier may not recover a claim in general average made against its cargo. To avoid this result, carriers began to insert a clause in their bills of lading which bound cargo to make general average contributions even where the carrier was at fault so long as the carrier's fault was not such as would make it liable for damage to cargo. The validity of such clauses was upheld by the Court in *The Jason*, 225 U.S. 32, 32 S.Ct. 560, 56 L.Ed. 969 (1912), and consequently such clauses are referred to as "Jason" or "New Jason Clauses." Today, most charter parties, bills of lading, and other contracts of affreightment include such a clause which generally provides the following:

> In the event of accident, danger, damage or disaster before or after commencement of the voyage resulting from any cause whatsoever, due to negligence or not, for which, or for the consequence of which, the carrier is not responsible, by statute, contract, or otherwise the goods, shipper, and consignees or owners of the goods shall contribute with the carrier in general average, to the payment of any sacrifices, losses, or expenses of a general average nature that may be made or incurred, and shall pay salvage and special charges incurred in respect of the goods.

A typical example of a negligent carrier's non-liability to damaged cargo is the errors in navigation and management defense provided by § 1304(2) of the Carriage of Goods by Sea Act (COGSA). Thus, if a vessel is imperiled because of an error in navigation by the master and as a consequence cargo is damaged and expenses are incurred to protect the vessel and the other cargo on board, the owner of the damaged cargo will not only be denied recovery for the damage to its cargo but will also be required to make its proportionate general average contribution if the bill of lading so provides and as under an applicable New Jason Clause.

CALIFORNIA & HAWAIIAN S. CO. v. COLUMBIA S.S. CO., INC.

391 F. Supp. 894, 1973 AMC 676 (E.D. La. 1972), *aff'd* 510 F.2d 542, 1975 AMC 1309 (5th Cir. 1975)

BOYLE, District Judge

California and Hawaiian Sugar Company, a non-profit agricultural cooperative association, brought this action in admiralty to recover for cargo loss and damage against Columbia Steamship Company and the SS COLUMBIA BREWER arising out of the stranding of the vessel in the shallow waters of Old Providence Island off the coast of Nicaragua in the early hours of June 25, 1970. Columbia Steamship Company, Inc. denied liability to cargo and asserted a counterclaim to recover cargos share in contribution to general average.

Since the issue have been severed, this opinion treats only the question of liability.

On May 18, 1970 California and Hawaiian Sugar Company (Plaintiff) entered into a charter party agreement[1] whereby it chartered the COLUMBIA BREWER[2] from Columbia Steamship Company, Inc. (Defendant) for the transporting of bulk sugar from a port in Hawaii to a port on the Gulf of Mexico. On or about June 7, 1970, plaintiff delivered to the defendant and to the COLUMBIA BREWER at the port of Nawiliwili, Kauai, a cargo of 11,941.395 short tons of bulk sugar. The sugar was received in apparent good order and condition for shipment and a bill of lading was accordingly issued. The COLUMBIA BREWER departed Nawiliwili, Kauai, and sailed to the Panama Canal Zone without incident. On June 24, 1970, the vessel completed its transit of the Panama Canal and set a course for New Orleans. On June 25 at approximately 0628 hours the vessel stranded just off Old Providence Island in the Caribbean Sea.

After the stranding of the vessel the master attempted to back off the strand with her main engine. His attempts were unsuccessful and on June 27 he signed a Lloyds open form salvage contract and declared General Average. In the course of the ensuing salvage operations approximately 1300 tons of sugar were transferred from the COLUMBIA BREWER to the M/V PASSAT in order to lighten the stranded vessel. On July 6 the transfer of sugar to the PASSAT was completed and the COLUMBIA BREWER was refloated with the assistance of the Salvage Tug RESCUE.

Plaintiff, in seeking damages for the cargo loss resulting from the stranding, its proportion of the salvage award, fees and expenses, takes the position that it is entitled to judgment as prayed for because the stranding of the COLUMBIA BREWER—which caused the cargo loss, the salvage and General Average Expenses—was due to the unseaworthiness of the vessel in the following respects: (1) the absence of Hydrographic Office (H.O.) Chart 1372; (2) the unavailability of H.O. Publication No. 20; (3) inadequate radar; (4) disconnected gyrocompass repeaters, and (5) a faulty fathometer. Defendant shipowner takes the position that the stranding was solely due to a neglect or error in navigation by the master which is an excepted peril under Section 4(2)(a) of the Carriage of Goods by Sea Act, 46 U.S.C. § 1304(2)(a). Shipowner also denies that its vessel was unseaworthy in any manner as alleged by the plaintiff and in the alternative argues that there is no causal connection between the stranding and the alleged unseaworthiness.

The Charter contained a "U.S.A. Clause Paramount"[6] under which the provisions of the Carriage of Goods by Sea Act (COGSA), 46 U.S.C. § 1301 *et seq.*, are incorporated in the charter party and the bill of lading issued subsequent thereto. The charter also included a "New Jason Clause"[7] which obligated the plaintiff, as shipper, to pay salvage costs attributable to cargo as well as expenses in the nature of General Average brought about by accident or damage for which the defendant, as shipowner, is not liable.

---

[1] Exhibit Webb #1.

[2] The charter agreement described the COLUMBIA BREWER as a U.S. Flag C-2 type vessel built in 1945 having two decks, five holds with five hatches, engines located amidship and a fully extent, but no further."

[6] "U.S.A. Clause Paramount. This Charter Party and any bill of lading issued hereunder shall have effect subject to the provisions of the Carriage of Goods by Sea Act of the United States, approved April 16, 1936, which shall be deemed to be incorporated herein, and nothing herein contained shall be deemed a surrender by the Owner of any of its rights or immunities or an increase of any of its responsibilities or liabilities under said Act. If any term of this Charter Party or any bill of lading issuer hereunder be repugnant to said Act to any extent, such term shall be void to that *Corp. v. United States, supra.*

[7] "New Jason Clause. In the event of accident, danger, damage or disaster before or after commencement of the voyage resulting from any cause whatsoever, whether due to negligence or not, for which, or for the consequence of which, the Owner is not responsible, by statute, contract, or otherwise, the goods, shippers, consignees, or owner's of the goods shall contribute with the Owner in general average to the payment of any sacrifices, losses, or expenses of a general average nature that may be made or incurred, and shall pay salvage and special charges incurred in respect of the goods.

"If a salving ship is owned or operated by the Owner, salvage shall be paid for as fully as if such salving ship or ships belonged to strangers. Such deposit as the Owner or his agents may deem sufficient to cover the estimated contribution of the goods and any salvage and special charges thereon shall, if required, be made by the goods, shippers, consignees or owner's of the goods to the Owner before delivery."

The bill of lading evidencing delivery of the cargo to the vessel in good order together with the stipulation to the partial cargo loss[8] demonstrate that the plaintiff has carried its initial burden of proof and made out a prima facie case on its main demand. Defendant concedes that it thus has the burden of proof in bringing itself within COGSA's 4(2) (a) exception by showing that the stranding resulted from an error of navigation or management. *Director General of India Supply Mission v. S.S. Maru,* 459 F.2d 1370 (2nd Cir. 1972); *Lekas & Drivas. Inc. v. Goulandris,* 306 F.2d 426 (2nd Cir. 1962); Gilmore & Black, The Law of Admiralty 162-63, § 3-43 (1957)....

* * *

Thus we shall proceed on the basis that the shipowner has the burden of bringing itself within the excepted peril of negligent navigation. Should the defendant shipowner sustain its burden, the burden would then shift to the plaintiff to establish unseaworthiness and that the unseaworthiness caused the stranding and the resulting damages. *Director General of India Supply Mission v. S.S. Maru, supra; Firestone Synthetic Fibers Co. v. M/S Black Heron,* 324 F.2d 835, 837 (2nd Cir. 1963); *Cia. Atlantica Pacifica, S.A. v. Humble Oil & Refining Co.,* 274 F. Supp. 884 (D.C. M.D. 1967). Should the plaintiff carry this burden, defendant could still escape liability by proving that the unseaworthiness occurred despite its exercise of due diligence to make the ship seaworthy and to see that the ship is properly manned, equipped and supplied. Section 4(1) COGSA, 46 U.S.C. § 1304(1).

On June 24, 1970 at approximately 1118 hours the COLUMBIA BREWER departed the Panama Canal northbound on a course of 335E. Captain Webb, master of the COLUMBIA BREWER at the time of the stranding, testified that it was his intention to steer a course which would carry the vessel through the Caribbean Sea past Old Providence Island, through the Yucatan Channel and from there into the Gulf of Mexico. At 1200 the vessels course was altered to 342 degrees and again at 2100 to 344E.

In navigating from the Panama Canal to Old Providence Island, Captain Webb consulted H.O. Chart 945 (Exhibit Webb #21). The master testified that he intended to follow a course from the Panama Canal which would position his vessel off the southwest tip of Old Providence Island and allow him to pass about four miles to the west of the Island. (*See* line A-B, drawn in pencil, on Exhibit Webb 21). Webb explained that though the course actually steered, when plotted on the chart (*see* line A-C, in red ink, on Exhibit Webb 21), would place the vessels approach to Old Providence Island on the southeast side, the westerly set of the waters in that area of the Caribbean would bring her to the desired position.

During the night of June 24 star sights were not available and the vessel proceeded by dead reckoning, calculating her position on the basis of her estimated speed and her direction of travel, allowing for an anticipated westerly current. On the morning of the 25th Captain Webb was on the bridge at 0330 hours, at which time a radio direction finder (RDF) bearing was taken from a station on St. Andrews Island (Line D-E on Exhibit Webb #21). Another RDF bearing from St. Andrews was taken one-half hour later, at 0400 hours (Line D-F on Exhibit Webb #21), and with the assumption that the vessel was maintaining a speed of 12 1/2 knots, the master was able to establish the ship's approximate position (Point G on Exhibit Webb #21). Before dawn starsights were made by the second officer who had not yet made a detailed calculation of the vessel's position though he found the approximate position of the vessel from the star sights to be in conformity with the position determined on the basis of the two RDF bearings.

At 0530 hours a radar fix was obtained on the island which was then found to be slightly on the port bow at a distance of approximately fifteen to sixteen miles (Point H on Exhibit Webb #21). The master testified that because the radar fix indicated that the vessel was too far to the east of the intended position, he began steering, or conning, to the left; three course changes from the 0530 course of 344 degrees brought the vessel to a course of 315 degrees at 0606 hours. By then it had become light enough to see fairly well and visibility was average for approximately seven to nine miles.

Old Providence Island was first visually sighted by Captain Webb at 0606 hours, at which time the distance off by radar was ascertained to be seven miles (Point J on Exhibit Webb #21). This distance was confirmed by the visual fix which the master took by laying tangent bearings to the outer extremities of the island. At 0606 hours Captain Webb changed course to 305 degrees and began coordinating his visual bearings with his fathometer in an attempt

---

[8] *See* paragraph 7e of the amended pre-trial order.

to locate the 100 fathom curve and navigate around the southwest end of the island. Between 0606 and 0620 hours Captain Webb frequently checked the fathometer recorder which was located in the chart room just a few paces from his position on the bridge.

At 0620 hours the master again took visual tangent bearings which placed his position just over three miles off the island (Position L on Exhibit Webb #22) due south of South Hill. At this time the fathometer, which had a maximum range of 200 fathoms, recorded soundings of 120 fathoms for about seven minutes and then went back off soundings which, according to the master's testimony, indicated that the 100 fathom curve had not been reached. Captain Webb testified that from this position he steered further left to a course of 295 degrees.

The master no longer consulted the fathometer but continued to navigate on a course of 295 degrees solely on the basis of visual contact with the island. At 0628 hours the COLUMBIA BREWER, while in the process of rounding the island, ventured into waters of less depth than her draft of approxmately [sic] 28 feet and gradually drove herself full ahead onto a shoal. Captain Webb testified that the vessel stranded at a position slightly over three miles off the southeast tip of Old Providence Island (Point K on Exhibit Webb #22).

When asked why he navigated the COLUMBIA BREWER to within three miles of Old Providence Island, Captain Webb replied that he intended to pass over the 100 fathom curve off the south-west corner of the island so that he might determine an exact point of departure which he considered essential for purposes of navigating the remaining portion of the voyage. Captain Webb stated that his navigational equipment functioned to his satisfaction and that his only explanation for the stranding was that a strong northerly current, of which he was unaware, caused his vessel to steam slightly over a mile closer to the island than he intended to pass.

Captain Webb had made the northbound run past Old Providence Island between six to eight times in the two years immediately prior to the stranding. It was his practice to pass four miles to the west of the island thereby keeping inside of southbound traffic which, according to the master, passed approximately five miles west of the island. The Hydrographic Office sailing directions (H.O. Publication 20) for a northbound course west of Old Providence Island suggest that vessels pass the island at a distance of about eleven miles. These sailing directions are not binding on mariners and both Captain Ducros[12] and Captain Boyle,[13] who testified as experts at the trial, stated that it is quite acceptable to pass closer than eleven miles west of the island. While Captain Boyle stated that he had often passed four miles west of the island, Captain Ducros testified that he has only come as close as six miles in passing the island.

The sailing directions, H.O. Publication 20,[14] warn that shoals extend up to two miles offshore at the southwestern end of Old Providence Island and caution that strong and irregular currents exist in the vicinity of the island. While the master admitted that he consulted this publication on the southbound leg of the voyage, he did not consult H.O. Publication 20 on the northbound approach to the island since he knew the publication's contents and was familiar with the island and its shoals. Apparently H.O. Publication 20 had been misplaced when the chart room was painted; but it was neither sought after nor finally located until after the stranding.

Both Captain Boyle and Captain Ducros were called upon to give their opinion as to the navigation and course changes made by the master in approaching Old Providence Island. Captain Ducros was of the opinion that the vessel was in no immediate danger at its 0606 position of six to seven miles south of the island but that a course change to 270 degrees, due west, would be required to pass seven miles west of the island. He considered that the course of 305 degrees, taken by Captain Webb at 0606, would be wholly inadequate in that it would take the vessel too close to the island and the shoal. Captain Ducros described the vessel's 0620 position of three miles due south of South Hill as one of imminent danger requiring such immediate action that if the man at the wheel hesitated, he would grab it himself and make a course alteration.

---

[12] Raoul V. Ducros presently sails as a master with Lykes Brothers Steamship Company. Captain Ducros received his license, "Master, Unlimited Oceans," fifth issue, in 1947 and has continuously sailed as master on that license since the spring of 1957. Captain Ducros has had several years experience on C-2 type vessels and for the last seven years his more or less permanent run as been in the Caribbean between the Canal Zone and the Gulf of Mexico.

[13] Captain Benjamin F. Boyle presently holds a master's license, "Unlimited Oceans," seventh issue. Captain Boyle has had approximately twenty-five years experience as master of oceangoing vessels and as such has navigated vessels between Panama and the Gulf of Mexico on more than fifty voyages in the general area of Old Providence Island. He last navigated past Old Providence Island in 1965.

[14] Exhibit Webb #24.

Captain Boyle agreed that the vessel was in no danger at the 0606 position of six to seven miles south of the island and that he too would have steered further left, perhaps 10 to 20 degrees further left, than the course steered by Captain Webb at 0606 hours. Captain Boyle testified that if using H.O. Chart 945 he would have come to a course of about 293° or 295°, and if using H.O. Chart 1372 he would have steered either 295° or 297°. He explained that the larger scale H.O. Chart 1372 would have given him a better fix of his position from which he could steer a few less degrees to the left in order to safely pass the island without sacrificing too much distance. Captain Boyle was of the opinion that the course changes he would have made at 0606, assuming no drift or current, would have kept him outside of the 100 fathom curve approximately three and a half miles south of the island which is closer than he had ever been to the southern portion of the island. Captain Boyle considered that the vessel was not in a position of safety just three miles off the island at 0620 hours and he stated that he would have then "hauled away" to a course of at least 270° in order to clear the 100 fathom curve. It was also his opinion that at 0620 hours the vessel was in a position in which she had no business being and that a greater course change than the 295° course steered by Captain Webb was required at that time.

Captain Webb testified that when the COLUMBIA BREWER stranded at 0628 hours on the morning of June 25 visibility was average and there were a few passing showers on the horizon beyond Old Providence Island. He stated, however, that the early morning light was not bright enough for him to see the changing color of the water which would have indicated the presence of shoals, reefs or shallow water. His only explanation for the stranding was that a strong current carried the vessel in closer to the island than he had intended to navigate. Captain Boyle stated that if the fixes calculated by Captain Webb at 0606 and 0620 were correct and the courses steered by Webb were made good, the vessel should have cleared the danger. However, Boyle explained, the ship may have been further north of the positions determined by Webb at 0606 and 0620 and then encountered currents which put her even further north, thus accounting for the vessel's position (Point K on Webb #22) at the time of the stranding.

Though passing near a chartered [*sic*] island in order to accurately fix a vessel's position for purposes of further navigation is a recognized practice of good seamanship, said practice does not justify the actions of Captain Webb in bringing his vessel just three miles off the southwestern tip of Old Providence Island in waters he admittedly knew contained reefs and shoals. It is obvious from the testimony of Captain Webb and from that of the experts that Captain Webb navigated his vessel so close to the island as to place her in a position of danger; and once having done so, he failed to sufficiently alter course so as to extricate the vessel from said danger. The inescapable conclusion is that the stranding of the COLUMBIA BREWER resulted from an error in navigation and management of the vessel on the part of her master, Captain Webb.

* * *

We conclude from the evidence presented that the stranding of the COLUMBIA BREWER off Old Providence Island was due, not to a failure to supply the vessel with appropriate charts or to the malfunction of any of the vessel's navigational equipment, but to the failure of the master, Captain Webb, to make proper use of the information available to him and to make reasonable course corrections when he discovered that his vessel was to the southeast of the island which he intended to pass on the southwest. His error in the navigation and management of the vessel relieves the defendant shipowner from liability to the plaintiff and, together with the New Jason Clause, entitles the defendant to recover on its general average counterclaim against the plaintiff. *Director General of India Supply Mission v. S.S. Maru, supra.*

Judgment shall be entered accordingly.

This opinion shall serve as our findings of fact and conclusions of law.

———————————

Notes

Unseaworthiness: Denial of General Average Claim

In *Louis Dreyfus Corp. v. 27,946 Long Tons of Corn*, 830 F.2d 1321, 1988 AMC 1053 (5th Cir. 1987), a shipment of grain was damaged during onloading due to the partial flooding of the engine room of the M/V ORIENT TRADER caused by an open valve in the vessel's seawater cooling system. The ORIENT TRADER had been chartered by Louis Dreyfus Corp. from KMTC, the shipowner. The charter party agreement included a U.S.A. Clause Paramount (incorporating COGSA) and a New Jason Clause.

On appeal, KMTC argued inter alia that because the parties were governed by a private charter agreement they were entitled to contract as they wished regarding general average obligations even though the loss was caused by failure to exercise due diligence to make the vessel seaworthy. The Court of Appeals for the Fifth Circuit, rejecting this argument and affirming the lower court's denial of general average to the vessel owner, stated:

> The district court denied KMTC's claim for general average because (1) the "New Jason Clause" does not apply if the carrier is responsible under COGSA, and (2) under COGSA, a carrier cannot claim general average if its failure to provide a seaworthy vessel causes the loss. *Id.* at 1330.

The General Average Adjuster

1. A general average adjuster acts as an agent of the shipowner in preparing the adjustment in general average embodied in a general average statement. *See* GILMORE & BLACK, § 5-3, at 224-26. The profession is said to enjoy "a very high reputation for fairness to ship and cargo alike." *Id.,* at 225. Yet, an adjuster is not an arbitrator and his statement is not an "account stated"; rather, it is "a provisional estimate and calculation which his principal, the owner, [is] free to adopt or to put aside." *United States v. Atlantic Mut. Ins. Co.,* 298 U.S. 483, 491, 56 S. Ct. 889, 891, 80 L. Ed. 1296 (1936). The Supreme Court has described the adjuster's function, absent any stipulation, as "that of aiding or assisting the owner in gathering and stating data and making appropriate calculations as a suggested basis for an adjustment to be made by the owner, or under the owner's direction." *Id.*

2. Absent any agreement to the contrary, a general average statement prepared by a professional average adjuster is without any legal effect whatsoever and is open to question in every particular. *Id.* The effect of agreements to pay expenses upon an adjustment, according to the provisions of the contract of affreightment and applicable laws and usages, is not clear. *Compare Corrado Societa Anonima Di Navagazione v. L. Mundet Sons,* 18 F. Supp. 37 (E.D. Pa. 1936), *aff'd,* 91 F.2d 726 (3d Cir. 1937), *cert. denied,* 302 U.S. 751, 58 S. Ct. 271, 82 L. Ed. 581 (1937), with *Navigazione Generale Italiana v. Spencer Kellogg & Sons,* 92 F.2d4l (2d Cir.), *cert. denied,* 302 U.S. 751, 58 S. Ct. 271, 82 L. Ed. 580 (1937); GILMORE & BLACK, § 5-4, at 227-228. It has recently been held that such agreements render the statement prima facie proof of the fact that expenses were the consequence of a general average act and of the amount of the expenses, *CIA. Atlantica Pacifica, S.A. v. Humble Oil & Refining Co.,* 274 E Supp. 884, 898 (D. Md. 1967). However, all the authorities agree that the statement is not conclusive on the question of whether cargo interests are liable at all in general average. *Corrado Societa Anonima Di Navagazione v. L. Mundet Sons, supra; Navigazione Generale Italiana v. Spencer Kellogg & Sons, supra; CIA. Atlantica Pacifica, S.A. v. Humble Oil & Refining Co., supra.* Nothing in the case authorities indicates the existence of a duty to hold a portion of the fund in trust for one named in the statement. *Empire Stevedoring Co. v. Oceanic Adjustors, Ltd.,* 315 E Supp. 921, 927, 1971 AMC 795 (S.D.N.Y. 1970).

Calculation of General Average

It is the duty of the master to make the general average adjustment. However, since the computation of general average is very complex, the master typically hires professional adjusters. In either case, the master is acting in the interests of cargo as well as the ship. It is well established that the shipowner may recover the costs of adjustment as part of the general average contribution from the other interests int he adventure. *See Master Shipping agency, Inc. v. M.S. Farida,* 571 F.2d 131, 1978 AMC 1267 (2d Cir. 1978).

In *The Farida*, the cargo interest claimed that the cost of adjustment was not recoverable since the shipowner had failed to exercise due diligence to make the vessel seaworthy. Cargo argued that when the shipowner discovered the cause of the loss, they should have realized that general average was not recoverable and therefore the adjustment should not have been completed. The court rejected this argument on the grounds that since the fault of the ship was "'not at all free from doubt'" the master was justified in proceeding with the adjustment. *Id.* at 135.

CHAPTER 7 — GOVERNMENTAL IMMUNITIES

A. The Federal Government—Waiver of Sovereign Immunity

1. Relevant Statutes

a. The Suits in Admiralty Act

46 U.S.C.A. §§ 30901-30918

§ 30901. Short title
This chapter may be cited as the 'Suits in Admiralty Act'.

§ 30902. Definition
In this chapter, the term "federally-owned corporation" means a corporation in which the United States owns all the outstanding capital stock.

§ 30903. Waiver of immunity
(a) In general—In a case in which, if a vessel were privately owned or operated, or if cargo were privately owned or possessed, or if a private person or property were involved, a civil action in admiralty could be maintained, a civil action in admiralty *in personam* may be brought against the United States or a federally-owned corporation. In a civil action in admiralty brought by the United States or a federally-owned corporation, an admiralty claim *in personam* may be filed or a setoff claimed against the United States or corporation.

(b) Non-jury—A claim against the United States or a federally-owned corporation under this section shall be tried without a jury.

§ 30904. Exclusive remedy
If a remedy is provided by this chapter, it shall be exclusive of any other action arising out of the same subject matter against the officer, employee, or agent of the United States or the federally-owned corporation whose act or omission gave rise to the claim.

§ 30905. Period for bringing action
A civil action under this chapter must be brought within 2 years after the cause of action arose.

§ 30906. Venue
(a) In general—A civil action under this chapter shall be brought in the district court of the United States for the district in which—
> (1) any plaintiff resides or has its principal place of business; or
> (2) the vessel or cargo is found.

(b) Transfer—On a motion by a party, the court may transfer the action to any other district court of the United States.

§ 30907. Procedure for hearing and determination

(a) In general—A civil action under this chapter shall proceed and be heard and determined according to the principles of law and the rules of practice applicable in like cases between private parties.

(b) *In rem*—

(1) Requirements—The action may proceed according to the principles of an action *in rem* if—

(A) the plaintiff elects in the complaint; and

(B) it appears that an action *in rem* could have been maintained had the vessel or cargo been privately owned and possessed.

(2) Effect on relief *in personam*—An election under paragraph (1) does not prevent the plaintiff from seeking relief *in personam* in the same action.

§ 30908. Exemption from arrest or seizure

The following are not subject to arrest or seizure by judicial process in the United States:

(1) A vessel owned by possessed by or operated by or for the United States or a federally-owned corporation.

(2) Cargo owned or possessed by the United States or a federally-owned corporation.

§ 30909. Security

Neither the United States nor a federally-owned corporation may be required to give a bond or admiralty stipulation in a civil action under this chapter.

§ 30910. Exoneration and limitation

The United States is entitled to the exemptions from and limitations of liability provided by law to an owner, charterer, operator, or agent of a vessel.

§ 30911. Costs and interest

(a) In general—A judgment against the United States or a federally-owned corporation under this chapter may include costs and interest at the rate of 4 percent per year until satisfied. Interest shall run as ordered by the court, except that interest is not allowable for the period before the action is filed.

(b) Contract providing for interest—Notwithstanding subsection (a),if the claim is based on a contract providing for interest, interest may be awarded at the rate and for the period provided in the contract.

§ 30912. Arbitration, compromise, or settlement

The Secretary of a department of the United States Government, or the board of trustees of a federally-owned corporation, may arbitrate, compromise, or settle a claim under this chapter.

§ 30913. Payment of judgment or settlement

(a) In general—The proper accounting officer of the United States shall pay a final judgment, arbitration award, or settlement under this chapter on presentation of an authenticated copy.

(b) Source of payment—Payment shall be made from an appropriation or fund available specifically for the purpose. If no appropriation or fund is specifically available, there is hereby appropriated, out of money in the Treasury not otherwise appropriated, an amount sufficient to pay the judgment, award, or settlement.

§ 30914. Release of privately owned vessel after arrest or attachment

If a privately owned vessel not in the possession of the United States ora federally-owned corporation is arrested or attached in a civil action arising or alleged to have arisen from prior ownership, possession, or operation by the United States or corporation, the vessel shall be released without bond or stipulation on a statement by the United States, through the Attorney General or other authorized law officer, that the United States is interested in the action, desires release of the vessel, and assumes liability for the satisfaction of any judgment obtained by the plaintiff. After the vessel is released, the action shall proceed against the United States in accordance with this chapter.

§ 30915. Seizures and other proceedings in foreign jurisdictions

(a) In general—If a vessel or cargo described in section 30908 or 30914 of this title is arrested, attached, or otherwise seized by judicial process in a foreign country, or if an action is brought in a court of a foreign country against the master of such a vessel for a claim arising from the ownership, possession or operation of the vessel, or the ownership, possession, or carriage of such cargo, the Secretary of State, on request of the Attorney General or another officer authorized by the Attorney General, may direct the United States consul residing at or nearest the place at which the action was brought—

(1) to claim the vessel or cargo as immune from arrest, attachment, or other seizure, and to execute an agreement, stipulation, bond, or undertaking, for the United States or federally-owned corporation, for the release of the vessel or cargo and the prosecution of any appeal; or

(2) if an action has been brought against the master of such a vessel, to enter the appearance of the United States or corporation and to pledge the credit of the United States or corporation to the payment of any judgment and costs in the action.

(b) Arranging bond or stipulation—The Attorney General may—

(1) arrange with a bank, surety company, or other person, whether in the United States or a foreign country, to execute a bond or stipulation; and

(2) pledge the credit of the United States to secure the bond or stipulation.

(c) Payment of judgment—The appropriate accounting officer of the United States or corporation may pay a judgment in an action described in subsection (a) on presentation of a copy of the judgment if certified by the clerk of the court and authenticated by—

(1) the certificate and seal of the United States consul claiming the vessel or cargo, or by the consul's successor; and

(2) the certificate of the Secretary as to the official capacity of the consul.

(d) Right to claim immunity not affected—This section does not affect the right of the United States to claim immunity of a vessel or cargo from foreign jurisdiction.

§ 30916. Recovery by the United States for salvage services

(a) Civil action—The United States, and the crew of a merchant vessel owned or operated by the United States, or a federally-owned corporation, may bring a civil action to recover for salvage services provided by the vessel and crew.

(b) Deposit of amounts recovered—Any amount recovered under this section by the United States for its own benefit, and not for the benefit of the crew, shall be deposited in the Treasury to the credit of the department of the United States Government, or the corporation, having control of the possession or operation of the vessel.

§ 30917. Disposition of amounts recovered by the United States

Amounts recovered in a civil action brought by the United States on a claim arising from the ownership, possession, or operation of a merchant vessel, or the ownership, possession, or carriage of cargo, shall be deposited in the Treasury to the credit of the department of the United States Government, or the federally-owned corporation, having control of the vessel or cargo, for reimbursement of the appropriation, insurance fund or other fund from which the compensation for which the judgment was recovered was or will be paid.

§ 30918. Reports

The Secretary of each department of the United States Government, and the board of trustees of each federally-owned corporation, shall report to Congress at each session thereof all arbitration awards and settlements agreed to under this chapter since the previous session, for which the time to appeal has expired or been waived.

46 app. U.S.C. §§ 741-752

(Superseded Version)

§741. Exemption of United States Vessels and Cargoes From Arrest or Seizure

No vessel owned by the United States or by any corporation in which the United States or its representatives shall own the entire outstanding capital stock or in the possession of the United States or of such corporation or operated by or for the United States or such corporation, and no cargo owned or possessed by the United States or by such corporation, shall after March 9, 1920, in view of the provision herein made for a libel in personam, be subject to arrest or seizure by judicial process in the United States or its possessions: *Provided*, That this chapter shall not apply to the Panama Canal Commission

§ 742. Libel in Personam

In cases where if such vessel were privately owned or operated, or if such cargo were privately owned or possessed, or if a private person or property were involved, a proceeding in admiralty could be maintained, any appropriate nonjury proceeding in personam may be brought against the United States or against any corporation mentioned in section 741 of this title. Such suits shall be brought in the district court of the United States for the district in which the parties so suing, or any of them, reside or have their principal place of business in the United States, or in which the vessel or cargo charged with liability is found. In case the United States or such corporation shall file a libel in rem or in personam in any district, a cross libel in personam may be filed or a set-off claimed against the United States or such corporation with the same force and effect as if the libel had been filed by a private party. Upon application of either party the cause may, in the discretion of the court, be transferred to any other district court of the United States.

§ 743. Procedure in Cases of Libel in Personam

Such suits shall proceed and shall be heard and determined according to the principles of law and to the rules of practice obtaining in like cases between private parties. A decree against the United States or a corporation mentioned in section 741 of this title may include costs of suit, and when the decree is for a money judgment, interest at the rate of 4 per centum per annum until satisfied, or at any higher rate which shall be stipulated in any contract upon which such decree shall be based. Interest shall run as ordered by the court. Decrees shall be subject to appeal and revision as provided in other cases of admiralty and maritime jurisdiction. If the libelant so elects in his libel, the suit may proceed in accordance with the principles of libels in rem wherever it shall appear that had the vessel or cargo been privately owned and possessed a libel in rem might have been maintained. Election so to proceed shall not preclude the libelant in any proper case from seeking relief in personam in the same suit. Neither the United States nor such corporation shall be required to give any bond or admiralty stipulation on any proceeding brought hereunder.

* * *

§ 745. Causes of Action for Which Suits May Be Brought; Limitations; Exceptions; Actions Which May Not Be Revived; Interest on Claims

Suits as authorized by this chapter may be brought only within two years after the cause of action arises: *Provided*, That where a remedy is provided by this chapter it shall hereafter be exclusive of any other action by reason of the same subject matter against the agent or employee of the United States or of any incorporated or unincorporated agency thereof whose act or omission gave rise to the claim: ... *And provided further*, That after June 30, 1932, no interest shall be allowed on any claim prior to the time when suit on such claim is brought as authorized by section 742 of this title unless upon a contract expressly stipulating for the payment of interest.

§ 746. Exemptions and Limitations of Liability

The United States or a corporation described in section 741 of this title shall be entitled to the benefits of all exemptions and of all limitations of liability accorded by law to the owner's, charterers, operators, or agents of vessels.

* * *

§ 750. Recovery for Salvage Services by Vessel or Crew

The United States, and the crew of any merchant vessel owned or operated by the United States, or a corporation mentioned in section 741 of this title, shall have the right to collect and sue for salvage services rendered by such vessel and crew, and any moneys recovered therefrom by the United States for its own benefit, and not for the benefit of the crew, shall be covered into the United States Treasury to the credit of the department of the Government of the United States, or of such corporation, having control of the possession or operation of such vessel.

———————

b. The Public Vessels Act

46 U.S.C. §§ 31101-31113

§ 31101. Short title

This chapter may be cited as the "Public Vessels Act".

§ 31102. Waiver of immunity

(a) In general—A civil action *in personam* in admiralty may be brought, or an impleader filed, against the United States for—

(1) damages caused by a public vessel of the United States; or

(2) compensation for towage and salvage services, including contract salvage, rendered to a public vessel of the United States.

(b) Counterclaim or setoff—If the United States brings a civil action in admiralty for damages caused by a privately owned vessel, the owner of the vessel, or the successor in interest, may file a counterclaim *in personam*, or claim a setoff, against the United States for damages arising out of the same subject matter.

§ 31103. Applicable procedure

A civil action under this chapter is subject to the provisions of chapter 309 of this title except to the extent inconsistent with this chapter.

§ 31104. Venue

(a) In general—A civil action under this chapter shall be brought in the district court of the United States for the district in which the vessel or cargo is found within the United States.

(b) Vessel or cargo outside territorial waters—If the vessel or cargo is outside the territorial waters of the United States—

(1) the action shall be brought in the district court of the United States for any district in which any plaintiff resides or has an office for the transaction of business; or

(2) if no plaintiff resides or has an office for the transaction of business in the United States, the action may be brought in the district court of the United States for any district.

§ 31105. Security when counterclaim filed

If a counterclaim is filed for a cause of action for which the original action is filed under this chapter, the respondent to the counterclaim shall give security in the usual amount and form to respond to the counterclaim, unless the court for cause shown orders otherwise. The proceedings in the original action shall be stayed until the security is given.

§ 31106. Exoneration and limitation

The United States is entitled to the exemptions from and limitations of liability provided by law to an owner, charterer, operator, or agent of a vessel.

§ 31107. Interest

A judgment in a civil action under this chapter may not include interest for the period before the judgment is issued unless the claim is based on a contract providing for interest.

§ 31108. Arbitration, compromise, or settlement

The Attorney General may arbitrate, compromise, or settle a claim under this chapter if a civil action based on the claim has been commenced.

§ 31109. Payment of judgment or settlement

The proper accounting officer of the United States shall pay a final judgment, arbitration award, or settlement under this chapter on presentation of an authenticated copy. Payment shall be made from any money in the Treasury appropriated for the purpose.

§ 31110. Subpoenas to officers or members of crew

An officer or member of the crew of a public vessel may not be subpoenaed in a civil action under this chapter without the consent of—

(1) the Secretary of the department or the head of the independent establishment having control of the vessel at the time the cause of action arose; or

(2) the master or commanding officer of the vessel at the time the subpoena is issued.

§ 31111. Claims by nationals of foreign countries

A national of a foreign country may not maintain a civil action under this chapter unless it appears to the satisfaction of the court in which the action is brought that the government of that country, in similar circumstances, allows nationals of the United States to sue in its courts.

§ 31112. Lien not recognized or created

This chapter shall not be construed as recognizing the existence of or as creating a lien against a public vessel of the United States.

§ 31113. Reports

The Attorney General shall report to Congress at each session thereof all claims settled under this chapter.

46 app. U.S.C. §§ 781-790

(Superseded Version)

§781. Libel in Admiralty Against or Impleader of United States

A libel in personam in admiralty may be brought against the United States, or a petition impleading the United State, for damages caused by a public vessel of the United States, and for compensation for towage and salvage services, including contract salvage, rendered to a public vessel of the United States....

§ 782. Venue of Suit; Application of Provisions of Chapter 20

Such suit shall be brought in the district court of the United States for the district in which the vessel or cargo charged with creating the liability is found within the United States, or if such vessel or cargo be outside the territorial waters of the United States, then in the district court of the United States for the district in which the parties so suing, or any of them, reside or have an office for the transaction of business in the United States; or in case none of such parties reside or have an office for the transaction of business in the United States, and such vessel or cargo be outside the territorial waters of the United States, then in any district court of the United States. Such suits shall be subject to and proceed in accordance with the provisions of chapter 20 of this title [the Suits in Admiralty Act] or any amendment thereof, insofar as the same are not inconsistent herewith, except that no interest shall be allowed on any claim up to the time of the rendition of judgment unless upon a contract expressly stipulating for the payment of interest.

§ 783. Cross Libel, Set-off, or Counterclaim

In the event of the United States filing a libel in rem or in personam in admiralty for damages caused by a privately owned vessel, the owner of such vessel, or his successors in interest, may file a cross libel in personam or claim a set-off or counterclaim against the United States in such suit for and on account of any damages arising out of the same subject matter or cause of action: *Provided*, That whenever a cross libel is filed for any cause of action for which the original libel is filed by authority of sections 781-790 of this title, the respondent in the cross libel shall give security in the usual amount and form to respond to the claim set forth in said cross libel unless the court, for cause shown, shall otherwise direct; and all proceedings on the original libel shall be stayed until such security shall be given.

* * *

§ 785. Suits by Nationals of Foreign Government's

No suit may be brought under this chapter by a national of any foreign government unless it shall appear to the satisfaction of the court in which suit is brought that said government, under similar circumstances, allows nationals of the United States to sue in its courts.

* * *

§ 788. Lien Not Created Against Public Vessels

Nothing contained in sections 781-790 of this title shall be construed to recognize the existence of or as creating a lien against any public vessel of the United States.

§ 789. Exemptions and Limitations of Liability

The United States shall be entitled to the benefits of all exemptions and of all limitations of liability accorded by law to the owner's, charterers, operators or agents of vessels.

* * *

c. The Federal Tort Claims Act

Federal Tort Claims Act[1]

28 U.S.C. § 1346. United States as Defendant

* * *

(b) Subject to the provisions of chapter 171 of this title [§§ 2671-2680, Tort Claims Procedure], the district courts, together with the United States District Court for the District of the Canal Zone and the District Court of the Virgin Islands, shall have exclusive jurisdiction of civil actions on claims against the United States, for money damages, accruing on and after January 1, 1945, for injury or loss of property, or personal injury or death caused by the negligent or wrongful act or omission of any employee of the Government while acting within the scope of his office or employment, under circumstances where the United States, if a private person, would be liable to the claimant in accordance with the law of the place where the act or omission occurred.

(c) The jurisdiction conferred by this section includes jurisdiction of any set-off, counterclaim, or other claim or demand whatever on the part of the United States against any plaintiff commencing an action under this section.

* * *

28 U.S.C. § 2674. Liability of United States

The United States shall be liable, respecting the provisions of this title relating to tort claims, in the same manner and to the same extent as a private individual under like circumstances, but shall not be liable for interest prior to judgment or for punitive damages.

* * *

28 U.S.C. § 2680. Exceptions

The provisions of this chapter and section 1346(b) of this title shall not apply to—

(a) Any claim based upon an act or omission of an employee of the Government, exercising due care, in the execution of a statute or regulation, whether or not such statute or regulation be valid, or based upon the exercise or performance or the failure to exercise or perform a discretionary function or duty on the part of a federal agency or an employee of the Government, whether or not the discretion involved be abused.

* * *

(d) Any claim for which a remedy is provided by sections 741-752 [the Suits in Admiralty Act], 781-790 [the Public Vessels Act] of Title 46, relating to claims or suits in admiralty against the United States.

* * *

(j) Any claim arising out of the combatant activities of the military or naval forces, or the Coast Guard, during time of war.

(k) Any claim arising in a foreign country.

* * *

Note: Jurisdiction based on the Admiralty Extension Act, 46 U.S.C. § 740 (1948)

The Act also provides as follows:

...Provided, That as to any suit against the United States for damage or injury done or consummated on land by a vessel on navigable waters, the Public Vesels Act or Suits in Admiralty Act, as appropriate, shall constitute the exclusive remedy for all causes of action

---

[1] Act of Aug. 2, 1946, ch. 753, tit. IV, 60 Stat. 842. The title "Federal Tort Claims Act" was enacted as § 401. § 1346(b) is codified in this chapter on district court jurisdiction; §§ 2671-2680 comprise the chapter on tort claims procedure.

arising after June 19, 1948, and for all causes of action where suit has not been hitherto filed under the Federal Tort Claims Act: Provided further, That no suit shall be filed against the United States until there shall have expired a period of six months after the claim has been presented in writing to the Federal agency owning or operating the vessel causing the injury or damage.

---

2. *Comparison: Public Vessels Act and Suits in Admiralty Act*

UNITED STATES v. UNITED CONTINENTAL TUNA

425 U.S. 164, 96 S. Ct. 1319, 47 L. Ed. 2d 653, 1976 AMC 258 (1975)

Mr. Justice MARSHALL delivered the opinion of the Court

Respondent, a Philippine corporation owned largely by Americans, brought this suit against the United States in the United States District Court for the Central District of California, alleging jurisdiction under the Suits in Admiralty Act, 41 Stat. 525, as amended, 46 U.S.C. § 741 *et seq.,* and the Public Vessels Act, 43 Stat. 1112, as amended, 46 U.S.C. § 781 *et seq.* It sought recovery for damages resulting from the sinking of its fishing vessel, the MV Orient, after a collision with the U.S.S. Parsons, a naval destroyer of the United States.

Upon the United States' motion for summary judgment, the District Court held that since the naval destroyer was a "public vessel of the United States," the suit was governed by the provisions of the Public Vessels Act. *See* 46 U.S.C. § 781. In particular, the court held that respondent was subject to the Act's reciprocity provision, which bars any suit by a foreign national under the Act unless it appears that his government, "under similar circumstances, allows nationals of the United States to sue in its courts." § 785. Finding no such reciprocity, the District Court dismissed the complaint.

The Court of Appeals for the Ninth Circuit reversed on the ground that respondent's action, although involving a public vessel, is maintainable under the Suits in Admiralty Act without reference to the reciprocity provision of the Public Vessels Act. 499 F. 2d 774 (1974). We granted certiorari, 420 U.S. 971 (1975), and we now reverse.

I.

It is undisputed that before 1960 suits involving public vessels could not be maintained under the Suits in Admiralty Act. The Act then authorized suits involving vessels owned by, possessed by, or operated by or for the United States as follows:

[I]n cases where if such vessel were privately owned or operated, or if such cargo were privately owned and possessed, a proceeding in admiralty could be maintained at the time of the commencement of the action herein provided for, a libel *in personam* may be brought against the United States ... *provided* that such vessel is employed as a merchant vessel.... 41 Stat. 525, 46 U.S.C. § 742 (1958 ed.) (emphasis added).[1]

In 1960, however, Congress amended this provision of the Suits in Admiralty Act by deleting the proviso, italicized above, that the vessel must be "employed as a merchant vessel." 74 Stat. 912. Reading the amended provision literally, the Court of Appeals held that suits involving public vessels could now be brought under the Suits in Admiralty Act, free from the restrictions imposed by the Public Vessels Act. The court reached this result in spite of its acknowledgment that "such a conclusion permits the [Public Vessels Act's] reciprocity provision to be circumvented in a manner neither explicitly authorized nor perhaps contemplated by Congress." 499 F.2d, at 778.

The Court of Appeals' result would permit circumvention of not only the reciprocity requirement, but also several other significant limitations imposed upon suits brought under the Public Vessels Act. Under 46 U.S.C. § 784, for example, officers and members of the crew of a public vessel may not be subpoenaed in connection with any suit authorized by the Public Vessels Act without the consent of the Secretary of the Department, the commanding

---

[1] We need not concern ourselves in this case with the definitions of the terms "merchant vessel" and "public vessel." It suffices to say that the terms are mutually exclusive, and that the naval destroyer in this case is beyond question a "public vessel."

officer, or certain other persons. In time of war, the Secretary of the Navy can obtain a stay of any suit brought under the Public Vessels Act when it appears that prosecution of the suit would tend to interfere with naval operations. 10 U.S.C. §§ 7721-7730. And under the Public Vessels Act, unlike under the Suits in Admiralty Act, interest on judgments does not accrue prior to the time of judgment. *Compare* 46 U.S.C. § 782 with 46 U.S.C. § 745.

Under the Court of Appeals' interpretation of the 1960 amendment to the Suits in Admiralty Act, circumvention of these restrictive provisions of the Public Vessels Act would not be limited to a handful of cases. Since there is virtually no reason for a litigant to prefer to have his suit governed by the provisions of the Public Vessels Act, the import of the Court of Appeals' interpretation is to render the restrictive provisions of the Public Vessels Act ineffectual in practically every case to which they would otherwise have application. If Congress had intended that result, it might just as well have repealed the Public Vessels Act altogether.

The Public Vessels Act was not amended in 1960, and, as the Court of Appeals recognized, the 1960 amendment to the Suits in Admiralty Act contains no language expressly permitting claims previously governed by the Public Vessels Act to be brought under the Suits in Admiralty Act, free from the restrictive provisions of the Public Vessels Act. What amounts to the effective repeal of those provisions is urged as a matter of implication. It is, of course, a cardinal principle of statutory construction that repeals by implication are not favored.

* * *

The ultimate question in this case is whether Congress intended, by the deletion of the "employed as a merchant vessel" proviso from the Suits in Admiralty Act, to authorize the wholesale evasion of the restrictions specifically imposed by the Public Vessels Act, on suits for damages caused by public vessels. An examination of the history of the Suits in Admiralty Act, the Public Vessels Act and, in particular, the 1960 amendment to the Suits in Admiralty Act, indicates quite clearly that Congress had no such intent.

II.

A.

The history of the Suits in Admiralty Act and the Public Vessels Act has been the subject of the Court's attention on several prior occasions. The history is quite clear and, for our purposes, can be stated briefly.

Prior to 1916, the doctrine of sovereign immunity barred any suit by a private owner whose vessel was damaged by a vessel owned or operated by the United States. Recognizing the inequities of denying recovery to private owner's and the difficulties inherent in attempting to grant relief to deserving private owner's through private Acts of Congress, Congress provided in the Shipping Act, 1916, that Shipping Board vessels employed as merchant vessels were subject to "all laws, regulations, and liabilities governing merchant vessels." 39 Stat. 730, 46 U.S.C. § 808. In *The Lake Monroe*, 250 U.S. 246 (1919), this Court held that the Shipping Act had subjected all Shipping Board merchant vessels to proceedings *in rem* in admiralty, including arrest and seizure. Congress, concerned that the arrest and seizure of Shipping Board merchant vessels would occasion unnecessary delay and expense, promptly responded to the *Lake Monroe* decision by enacting the Suits in Admiralty Act. The Act prohibited the arrest or seizure of any vessel owned by, possessed by, or operated by or for the United States. 46 U.S.C. § 741. In the place of an *in rem* proceeding, the Act authorized a libel *in personam* in cases involving such vessels, if such a proceeding could have been maintained had the vessel been a private vessel, and "provided that such vessel is employed as a merchant vessel." 41 Stat. 525, 46 U.S.C. § 742 (1958 ed.). Significantly, Congress was urged to include in the Suits in Admiralty Act authorization for suits against the United States for damages caused by public vessels, but the suggestion was rejected in committee as a "radical change" in policy that might "materially delay passage" of the Act.

Until 1925 the only recourse for the owner of a vessel or cargo damaged by a public vessel was to apply to Congress for a private bill. In that year, Congress enacted the Public Vessels Act, which authorized a libel *in personam* against the United States "for damages caused by a public vessel of the United States." 46 U.S.C. § 781. The Act provided that suits involving public vessels "shall be subject to and proceed in accordance with the provisions of [the Suits in Admiralty Act] or any amendment thereof, insofar as the same are not inconsistent here-with...." §

782. Some of the inconsistencies lay in the Public Vessels Act's provisions, referred to above, restricting subpoenas to officers and crew members of a public vessel, barring recovery of prejudgment interest, and imposing a requirement of reciprocity. Each of these provisions must be assumed to have reflected deliberate policy choices by Congress. In particular, the notion of reciprocity was central to the scheme enacted by Congress.

* * *

Because of serious uncertainties about the reach of the Suits in Admiralty and Public Vessels Acts on the one hand, and the Tucker Act on the other, the crucial determination of the appropriate forum for a claim was often a difficult one. The jurisdictional uncertainties under these Acts were illustrated in *Calmar S.S. Corp. v. United States*, 345 U.S. 446 (1953). In that case the private owner of a steamship under charter to the United States brought suit for additional charter hire for the loss of its vessel, which was bombed by enemy airplanes while carrying military supplies and equipment. The vessel was clearly not a "public vessel" under the Public Vessels Act, because it was privately owned and operated. The question was whether the vessel, "undoubtedly 'operated ... for the United States' was 'employed as a merchant vessel' within the meaning of the [Suits in Admiralty] Act while carrying military supplies and equipment for hire." *Id.*, at 447. The District Court held that it was a merchant vessel and assumed jurisdiction under the Suits in Admiralty Act. The Court of Appeals reversed on the ground that while the vessel could have been employed as a merchant vessel under its charter, it was not so employed while transporting war materiel. Having thus successfully argued to the Court of Appeals that the suit was not cognizable under either the Suits in Admiralty Act or the Public Vessels Act, the Government reversed its position in this Court. It argued, and the Court held, that the nature of the cargo was irrelevant and that the vessel was employed as a merchant vessel within the meaning of the Suits in Admiralty Act. The Court was clearly sensitive to the fact that a contrary ruling would have relegated the plaintiff to the Court of Claims, *id.*, at 455, but even after *Calmar* there remained the possibility that a particular vessel would be held to be neither a "public vessel" nor "employed as a merchant vessel."

The sharp reversals of position by the Government and the courts in the *Calmar* case were but illustrative of the jurisdictional uncertainties faced by potential litigants. In several instances, courts reached conflicting results as to whether certain types of claims should be brought in the district court under the Suits in Admiralty Act or the Public Vessels Act on the one hand, or in the Court of Claims under the Tucker Act on the other.

It was the difficulty in determining the appropriate forum for a maritime claim against the United States that moved Congress to amend the Suits in Admiralty Act in 1960. The amendment first passed by the House in 1959 was designed to ameliorate the harsh consequences of misfilings by authorizing the transfer of cases between the district courts and the Court of Claims. The transfer provision would "prevent dismissal of suits which would become time-barred when the appropriate forum had finally been determined." But the Senate Committee on the Judiciary found the House bill inadequate:

The transfer bill would operate to prevent ultimate loss of rights of litigants, but it did nothing to eliminate or correct the cause of original erroneous choices of forum while it could increase the existing delays.

Accordingly, the committee, while accepting the House amendment, proposed several additional amendments, whose purpose was stated succinctly as follows:

The purpose of the amendments is to make as certain as possible that suits brought against the United States for damages caused by vessels and employees of the United States through breach of contract or tort can be originally filed in the correct court so as to proceed to trial promptly on their merits.

Two amendments were designed to clarify the jurisdictional language of the Suits in Admiralty Act. First, the committee added language authorizing suits against the United States where a suit would be maintainable "if a private person or property were involved." The prior version of the Act had authorized suits against the United States only when suits would be maintainable if the "vessel" or "cargo" were privately owned, operated, or possessed, and that language had generated considerable confusion.[14]

Second, the committee made the change that concerns us in this case: it deleted the language in the jurisdictional section of the Suits in Admiralty Act requiring that a vessel be "employed as a merchant vessel." We have already noted the confusion evidenced by the Government and the courts in the *Calmar* case over whether the vessel in question was "employed as a merchant vessel." In addition, the Senate Report referred to other cases in which the "employed as a merchant vessel" language had caused jurisdictional difficulties.

* * *

It was to make clear that such cases could be brought on the admiralty side of the district courts that the committee recommended the deletion of the confusing "employed as a merchant vessel" proviso.

C.

Respondent contends that the deletion of the "employed as a merchant vessel" proviso was intended to abolish the distinction between a merchant vessel and a public vessel, and thereby enable suits previously cognizable under the Public Vessels Act to be brought under the Suits in Admiralty Act, free from the restrictive provisions of the Public Vessels Act. There is no indication that Congress had any such broad purpose. The legislative history contains no explicit suggestion that Congress intended to render nugatory the provisions of the Public Vessels Act. Nor does it express any broad intent to put an end to all litigation over whether a vessel is a public vessel.

The definitions of "merchant vessel" and "public vessel" were of interest to Congress only insofar as they related to Congress' basic purpose: to remove uncertainty over the proper forum for a claim against the United States. In this regard, it is quite clear that Congress' concern was not with uncertainty whether a suit should be brought under the Suits in Admiralty Act or under the Public Vessels Act, since in either event the proper forum was the admiralty side of the district court. *See Calmar S.S. Corp.*, 345 U.S., at 454-455. The Senate Report stated the concern precisely:

> The serious problem, and the one to which this bill is directed, arises in claims exceeding $10,000 where there is uncertainty as to whether a suit is properly brought under the Tucker Act [in the Court of Claims] on the one hand or the Suits in Admiralty or Public Vessels Act [on the admiralty side of the district court] on the other.

In short, Congress saw confusion between the category of suits cognizable under the Suits in Admiralty Act or Public Vessels Act on the one hand, and the category of suits cognizable under the Tucker Act on the other. It attempted to eliminate the confusion between these two categories by expanding the scope of the Suits in Admiralty Act at the expense of the Tucker Act—thereby virtually eliminating the quasi-admiralty jurisdiction of the Court of Claims under the Tucker Act.[18] But Congress did nothing to alter the distinction between the Suits in Admiralty Act and the Public Vessels Act, or expand the one at the expense of the other.

* * *

Congress' concern was that because of differences in the authorizational language of the Suits in Admiralty Act and the Public Vessels Act, some claims that would clearly have been within the jurisdiction of the district court if merchant vessels were involved had been held to be beyond the district court's jurisdiction when public vessels

---

[14] SENATE REPORT 5, *citing Ryan Stevedoring Co. v. United States,*175 F. 2d 490 (CA2), *cert. denied,* 338 U.S. 899 (1949). *Compare Lykes Bros. S.S. Co. v. United States, supra, with States Marine Corp. v. United States, supra.*

This amendment, which has no bearing on this case, has generally been held to require that those maritime tort claims that were previously cognizable only on the law side of the district courts under the Federal Tort Claims Act now be brought on the admiralty side of the district courts under the Suits in Admiralty Act. [Citations omitted. Eds.]

[18] The Court of Claims has not been completely deprived of jurisdiction over claims arising in a maritime context. *In Amell v. United States,* 384, U.S. 158 (1966), we held that wage claims exceeding $10,000 by Government employees working aboard Government vessels are still cognizable exclusively in the Court of Claims, where wage claims by Government employees have traditionally been cognizable.

were involved. Thus, some courts had held that contract claims other than those expressly authorized by the Public Vessels Act were generally not cognizable under the Act.[20] Litigants with certain types of contract claims therefore faced the possibility that the appropriate forum would depend on the type of vessel involved. Congress' deletion of the "employed as a merchant vessel" proviso was clearly intended to remove such uncertainty as to the proper forum by bringing within the Suits in Admiralty Act whatever category of claims involving public vessels was beyond the scope of the Public Vessels Act.[21] But claims like the instant one, that fell within the Public Vessels Act, presented none of the problems with which Congress was concerned in 1960, and there is therefore no reason to infer that Congress intended to affect them.

III.

In sum, the interpretation of the 1960 amendment advanced by the respondent and adopted by the Court of Appeals would effectively nullify specific policy judgments made by Congress when it enacted the Public Vessels Act, by enabling litigants to bring suits previously subject to the terms of the Public Vessels Act under the Suits in Admiralty Act. The language of the amendment does not explicitly authorize such a result, and the legislative history reflects a narrow congressional purpose that would not be advanced by that result. We therefore hold that claims within the scope of the Public Vessels Act remain subject to its terms after the 1960 amendment to the Suits in Admiralty Act. Since there is no dispute that respondent's claim falls within the embrace of the Public Vessels Act, the Court of Appeals erred in concluding that the reciprocity provision of the Public Vessels Act is inapplicable.

* * *

The judgment of the Court of Appeals is reversed, and the case remanded for further proceedings consistent with this opinion.

It is so ordered.

[A dissenting opinion by Mr. Justice Stewart is omitted.]

---

3. Comparison: Suits in Admiralty Act and Federal Tort Claims Act

KELLY v. UNITED STATES

531 F.2d 1144, 1976 AMC 284 (2nd Cir. 1975)

COFFRIN, District Judge

This case arises from the drowning death of Richard C. Kelly on September 4, 1970 near Sodus Point, New York, on Lake Ontario following the capsize of a 19-foot sailboat on which Mr. Kelly and three companions had embarked for a pleasure trip. The plaintiff, decedent's administrator, contends that the United States Coast Guard was negligent in failing to rescue Mr. Kelly and in causing other would-be rescuers not to come to his aid.

Plaintiff filed a claim for settlement with the Coast Guard on August 31, 1972, as provided by 28 U.S.C. § 2672, the administrative adjustment provision of the Federal Tort Claims Act (FTCA), but his claim was denied on October 30, 1972. Plaintiff then filed a timely complaint against the United States in the Northern District of New York on March 13, 1973, as provided by 28 U.S.C. § 1346 (b), which gives the District Courts exclusive jurisdiction of claims under the FTCA. The complaint was dismissed from the bench by Judge Port on April 14, 1975 on the grounds of lack of subject matter jurisdiction. Judge Port ruled that plaintiff's suit was not cognizable under the FTCA since it stated an admiralty claim against the Government which was cognizable exclusively under

---

[20] *See, e.g., Eastern S.S. Lines v. United States,* 187 F.2d, at 959; *Continental Cas. Co. v. United States,* 140 Ct. Cl. 500, 156 F. Supp. 942 (1957). Other than claims for "damages caused by a public vessel of the United States," the only claims expressly authorized by the Public Vessels Act are claims "for compensation for towage and salvage services, including contract salvage, rendered to a public vessel of the United States." 46 U.S.C. § 781.

[21] It is not to be assumed that contract claims other than those expressly authorized by the Public Vessels Act were necessarily beyond the scope of the Act. As in *Calmar S.S. Corp. v. United States,* 345 U.S. 446, 456 n.8 (1953), we intimate no view on the subject.

the Suits in Admiralty Act, 46 U.S.C. §§ 741-752 (SIAA).[1] Because the SIAA contains a strict two-year statute of limitations[2] which was not timely tolled by the plaintiff, the judgment of the District Court, if upheld, would leave the plaintiff without remedy.

The plaintiff contends on appeal that: (1) his complaint does not state a claim in admiralty; and (2) if the complaint does state an admiralty claim, it is nevertheless not the type for which a remedy is provided by the SIAA; and that (3) in either case, suit under the FTCA is proper. These contentions are discussed below.

[The court's discussion upholding admiralty jurisdiction is omitted. Eds.]

* * *

Having concluded that plaintiff's complaint states an admiralty claim, we must now decide whether it is the type of admiralty claim against the United States which must be brought exclusively under the SIAA within the two year limitation period. Prior to 1960, this case would not have been cognizable under the SIAA, since maritime tort proceedings against the government which did not involve either "vessels" or "cargoes" of the United States were not then covered by 46 U.S.C. § 742. Accordingly, wrongful death actions against the Coast Guard for allegedly negligent rescue operations occurring prior to 1960 were brought without objection under the FTCA, not under the SIAA. *United States v. DeVane*, 306 F.2d 182 (5th Cir. 1962); *United States v. Gavagan*, 280 F.2d 319 (5th Cir. 1960), *cert. denied*, 364 U.S. 933 (1961); *United States v. Lawter*, 219 F.2d 559 (5th Cir. 1955).

However, Section 742 was amended in 1960 to include the following emphasized language:

In cases where if such vessel were privately owned or operated, or if such cargo were privately owned or possessed, or *if a private person or property were involved*, a proceeding in admiralty could be maintained, any appropriate nonjury proceeding *in personam* may be brought against the United States....

Appellant argues that, in spite of the plain meaning of the emphasized language in the statute, the amendment was intended only to clarify certain unrelated ambiguities and was not designed to permit admiralty suits against the government where government cargoes or vessels are not involved.

We agree with appellant that the legislative history of the 1960 amendment (S.R. No. 1894, 1960 U.S. Code Cong. & Adm. News, 3583 *et seq.*) does not expressly or clearly state a congressional purpose to bring all maritime claims against the U.S. into the admiralty jurisdiction of the district courts.[6] Nevertheless, in the absence of clear legislative direction or persuasive reasons to the contrary, we are obliged to construe statutory language in a manner consistent with its plain and ordinary meaning. *Burns v. Alcala*, 420 U.S. 575, 580-581 (1975). With this axiom in mind, we must conclude that the 1960 amendment to 46 U.S.C. § 742 (Pub. L. 86-770) was intended to bring all admiralty claims against the United States within the ambit of the SIAA, whether or not involving government

---

[1] 28 U.S.C. § 2680(d) makes it clear that tort claims which can be brought against the United States under the SIAA, 46 U.S.C. §§ 741-752, cannot be brought against the government under the Federal Tort Claims Act. Section 2680(d) provides that the FTCA does not apply to "[any] claim for which a remedy is provided by §§ 741-752, 781-790 of Title 46, relating to claims or suits in admiralty against the United States."

[2] 46 U.S.C. § 745.

[6] Read narrowly, the Senate Report might actually indicate a purpose *not* to expand the then existing jurisdiction of the district courts under 46 U.S.C. § 742. The Report states that the main purpose of the 1960 Amendment was as follows:

... to prevent the repetition of misfilings [of suits in the wrong court] in the future. It *restates* in brief and simple language *the now existing exclusive jurisdiction* conferred on the district courts, both on their admiralty and law sides, over cases against the United States which could be sued on in admiralty if private vessels, persons, or property were involved." (emphasis added) 1960 U.S. Code Cong. & Adm. News, p. 3583.

However, there is language in the Senate Report which shows that Congress was aware that the language added to § 742 by the 1960 amendment would expand maritime jurisdiction under that Section to its limits:

With respect to the amendment to the [SIAA] ... the original... Act authorizes a suit against the United States whenever an admiralty proceeding could have been maintained if private vessels or cargo vessels were involved, but it does not mention private persons and property generally. 1960 U.S. Code Cong, and Admin. News, pp. 3585-3586.

Reading this observation against the actual wording changes that were made in the 1960 amendment, it would be illogical to conclude that Congress did not intend, as stated by the Fifth Circuit, "to assimilate the Government to the private person in relation to any or all transactions giving rise to liability in the Admiralty." *De Bardeleben Marine Corp. v. United States*, 451 F.2d 140, 145 (5th Cir. 1971).

cargoes or vessels. This conclusion is in full accord with the views expressed in the *Per Curiam* opinion in *Szyka v. United States Secretary of Defense*, 525 F.2d 62, 64, n.5, Docket No. 75-6003 (2d Cir. 1975), as well as with the weight of authority.... Further, our conclusion is not inconsistent with the broad interpretation of the 1960 amendment made by this Court in *Ira S. Bushey & Sons, Inc. v. United States*, 398 F.2d 167, 169 (2d Cir. 1968), where it was said that the purpose of the amendment was to avoid "fruitless jurisdictional controversies and [to bring] all maritime claims against United States vessels into the admiralty jurisdiction of the district courts."

For the reasons expressed above, we hold that decedents claim should have been brought under the Suits In Admiralty Act, 46 U.S.C. §§ 741-752, and it cannot be maintained under 28 U.S.C. § 1346(b) because of the express prohibition of 28 U.S.C. § 2680(d). The suit is therefore barred by the provisions of 46 U.S.C. § 745, as it was not commenced under the Suits In Admiralty Act within two years of the date that the cause of action accrued. Accordingly, the judgment of the district court is affirmed.

---

4. SIAA: "Exclusivity"

Note: Suits Against the Federal Government

In *McCormick v. United States*, 680 F.2d 345, 1984 AMC 1799 (11th Cir. 1982), the court decided to follow *Kelly* and the other Circuits after having previously followed the rule that some maritime actions were cognizable under the Federal Tort Claims Act (FTCA). Under the SIAA, suit must be brought within two years after the cause of action arises. 46 U.S.C.A. § 30905 (formerly 46 U.S.C. § 745). The PVA also contains a two-year statute of limitations. 46 U.S.C.A. § 31103 (formerly 46 U.S.C. § 782). In contrast, Congress has enacted a three-year statute of limitations for most maritime personal injury and death actions. 46 U.S.C.A. § 30106 (formerly 46 U.S.C. § 763(a)).

It is important to recognize when a claim is an admiralty action due to the exclusivity of the SIAA. Under the FTCA, a tort claim against the United States is barred unless presented in writing to the appropriate Federal agency within two years after the claim accrues or unless action is begun within six months after final denial of the claim by the agency to which it was presented. 28 U.S.C. § 2401(b). An attorney who incorrectly presses an admiralty claim under the FTCA risks the time bar of the SIAA. Since the Act's limitations period is not subject to tolling or waiver. *See McCormick, supra* at 351.

It should be emphasized that in a Suits in Admiralty Act case the applicable substantive law will be federal maritime law. In contrast to the SIAA, the FTCA incorporates state tort law. *See Patentas v. United States*, 687 F.2d 707, 711, 1987 AMC 1076 (3d Cir. 1982).

Seamen employed by the United States have their exclusive tort remedy under the Federal Employees' Compensation Act. 5 U.S.C. § 8116(c). *See Johanson v. United States*, 343 U.S. 427, 72 S.Ct. 849, 96 L.Ed. 1051 (1952) [public vessels] and *Patterson v. United States*, 359 U.S. 495, 79 S.Ct. 936, 3 L.Ed.2d 971 (1959) [merchant vessels]. This bar is not applicable to a third party indemnity suit against the United States. *See Lockheed Aircraft Corp. v. United States*, 460 U.S. 190, 103 S.Ct. 1033, 74 L.Ed.2d 911, 1983 AMC 913 (1983).

Under the Public Vessels Act, venue is provided for the district in which any of the plaintiff's reside, have their principal place of business, or in which the vessel or cargo charged with liability is found. 46 U.S.C.A. § 31104 (formerly 46 U.S.C. § 782). *See Sneed v. United States*, 1980 AMC 1685 (N.D. Cal. 1980).

The Suits in Admiralty Act formerly required the plaintiff to "forthwith serve a copy" of his or her complaint on the U.S. attorney for the district where the suit was brought. 46 U.S.C. § 742. In *Henderson v. U.S.*, 517 U.S. 654, 116 S.Ct. 1638, 134 L.Ed.2d 880, 1996 AMC 1521 (1996), the Supreme Court held that the "forthwith service" requirement had been superseded by the expandable 120-day time prescription for service of process in Fed. R. Civ. P. 4. The "forthwith service" requirement was subsequently removed by amendment in 1996.

PADRO v. VESSEL CHARTERS, INC.

731 F. Supp. 145, 1990 AMC 1664 (S.D.N.Y. 1990)

Peter K. LEISURE, United States District Judge

Defendant Vessel Charters, Inc. ("VCI"), owner of the SS SANTA ADELA, claims that it is not a proper party to this lawsuit brought by its employee, seaman Gumersindo Padro. VCI supports its claim by citing the Suits in Admiralty Act ("SIAA" or the "Act") which, under certain circumstances, holds the United States exclusively liable for admiralty claims arising under the SIAA. 46 U.S.C. App. § 745. VCI time-chartered the vessel SS SANTA ADELA to the United States, through the Military Sealift Command, an agency of the Department of the Navy.

Because VCI believes the SIAA applies here, it seeks dismissal of the lawsuit for lack of subject matter jurisdiction. Alternatively, VCI requests that summary judgment be granted. After careful review of the SIAA and case law interpreting it, the Court denies VCI's motion for dismissal for lack of subject matter jurisdiction. As a number of factual issues remain to be resolved, VCI's motion for summary judgment is also denied.

Background

The facts not in dispute will be briefly summarized. In 1984, VCI entered into a time-charter agreement with the Department of the Navy. Pursuant to the agreement, VCI was to provide the vessel SS SANTA ADELA for the Navy's use, with VCI retaining responsibility for manning the ship with officers and crew, as well as navigation, care and custody of the ship....The resulting relationship provided that the Navy designate the cargo to be carried and the ports to be visited, while VCI had day-to-day operational control of the SS SANTA ADELA.

On April 3, 1988, with the time-charter agreement operative, plaintiff sustained a severely broken left leg while assisting at docking the ship in Yakohoma, Japan. His injury allegedly resulted when one of the mooring lines snapped and wrapped around his leg. As a result of the injury, plaintiff has been unable to return to work as a merchant seaman.

On March 17, 1989, plaintiff brought this lawsuit alleging that his injury was caused by VCI's negligence in maintaining its mooring lines, or, alternatively, by the unseaworthiness of the SS SANTA ADELA. In its answer, VCI alleged, as its first affirmative defense, that plaintiff's exclusive remedy lies against the United States pursuant to the SIAA. This motion is grounded on that defense and requests that VCI be dismissed as defendant because the Court lacks jurisdiction over it.

Discussion

The Court will first consider the SIAA and case law interpreting it before discussing its application here.

A. Suits In Admiralty Act

VCI claims that the United States is the exclusive defendant in this lawsuit, pursuant to the SIAA. Sections 741 through 745 of the Act provide the statutory frame for VCI's claim, and the sections must be read together to understand their use.

Section 741 provides in relevant part:

> No Vessel owned by the United States ... or in the possession of the United States ... or operated by or for the United States ... shall hereafter, in view of the provision herein made for a libel *in personam* [Section 742], be subject to arrest or seizure by judicial process in the United States or it possessions....

The important passage for this lawsuit is "[Vessels] ... operated by or for the United States," which the Court finds includes a vessel such as the SS SANTA ADELA. A reasonable interpretation of the plain language of the statute requires its application to a privately owned ship operated for the benefit of the United States. *See J. W. Peterson Coal & Oil Co. v. United States*, 323 E Supp. 1198, 1205-06 (N.D. 111. 1970) (articulates the meaning of "operated by or for the United States," and concludes that a time-charter is encompassed by the "operated for" language); *see also A.H. Bull S.S. Co. v. United States*, 105 F. Supp. 474, 479 (S.D.N.Y. 1952), *aff'd*, 208 F.2d 888 (2d Cir. 1953).

The Court must also consider section 742 to determine whether the SS SANTA ADELA is within the jurisdiction of the SIAA. Section 742 provides that, "[in] cases where ... if a private person or property were involved, a proceeding in admiralty could be maintained, any appropriate nonjury proceeding *in personam* may be brought against the United States." Certainly, absent the time-charter agreement, plaintiff could have maintained an admiralty proceeding against VCI, as the owner of the SS SANTA ADELA, to recover damages for his injury. *See Cosmopolitan Shipping Co. v. McAllister*, 337 U.S. 783, 791 (1949). Thus, at this stage of the analysis, plaintiff's claim appears to be within the jurisdiction of the SIAA because the SS SANTA ADELA was being operated for the United States and plaintiff's claim is one to be heard in an admiralty proceeding.

Finally, section 745, providing the remaining element in the SIAA framework, states that, "where a remedy is provided by this Act, it shall hereafter be exclusive of any other action by reason of the same subject matter against the agent or employee of the United States ... whose acts or omission gave rise to the claim." VCI claims that this exclusivity provision precludes plaintiff from maintaining this action against it, as the United States is the proper, and exclusive, party to the action. Plaintiff argues, on the other hand, that exclusivity only attaches when the remedy sought is provided by the SIAA, but not when the United States is merely a time-charterer without operational control of the vessel.

In sum, VCI argues that it was operating the SS SANTA ADELA for the United States pursuant to the time charter within the purview of section 741. Further, the United States was amenable to an admiralty claim by section 742. Finally, VCI is absolved of direct liability by the exclusivity provision of section 745. Although VCI's position may be supported by a plain reading of the SIAA, the case law interpreting the SIAA prevents the Court from adopting VCIs interpretation of the statute. Further, the Court believes such a restrictive reading of the SIAA is inappropriate under these circumstances.

B. Case Law Applying the SIAA

In *Williams v. Central Gulf Lines,* 874 F.2d 1058 (5th Cir. 1989), *cert. denied,* 493 U.S. 1045, 110 S. Ct. 843, 107 L. Ed. 2d. 837, (1990), the Fifth Circuit, interpreting the SIAA on facts similar to those here, ruled that the Act itself provides no actual remedy against the United States, but only serves to waive sovereign immunity for the United States in admiralty actions. *Id.* at 1059 (*citing Trautman v. Buck Steber, Inc.,* 693 F.2d 440, 444 (5th Cir. 1982)). The court proposed a two-part test which must be met to absolve a private ship owner, time-chartering its ship to the United States, from maritime liability because of the SIAA's exclusivity provision. First, the United States must have consented to the lawsuit, providing a "jurisdictional hook" to include the United States as a defendant. Second, the defendant asserting the exclusivity defense must show that the United States is susceptible to a "traditional admiralty claim" under the particular circumstances present in the case. *Williams, supra,* 874 F.2d at 1061. Unless both parts of the test are satisfied, the private ship owner may not use the SIAAs exclusivity provision to avoid being a party to the lawsuit. *Id.* The Court will adopt the analysis of the Fifth Circuit in *Williams.*

Sections 741 and 742 of the SIAA establish the first part of the test—the United States's consent to the lawsuit under the present facts. *Williams, supra* 874 F.2d at 1062. The legislative intent of the SIAA discloses Congress's desire to free United States merchant vessels from the possibility of arrest or seizure. To do this, Congress waived sovereign immunity for admiralty claims arising from the operation of such vessels. *Schnell v. United States,* 166 F.2d 479, 481 (2d Cir.), *cert. denied,* 334 U.S. 833 (1948). VCI satisfies this prong of the test by showing that the United States consented to the present lawsuit by time-chartering the SS SANTA ADELA for operation as a United States merchant vessel.

However, the second part of the test, whether a traditional admiralty claim may be asserted against the United States, is not as readily satisfied. The Second Circuit's general rule on a time-charterer's liability, clearly in accord with the Fifth Circuits rule, is that, "'[a] time charterer assumes no liability flowing from the unseaworthiness of the vessel or the negligence of the crew unless it is shown that the parties to the charter intended otherwise.'"*Atlantic Richfield Co. v. Interstate Oil Transport Co.,* 784 F.2d 106, 113-114 (2d Cir.), *cert. denied,* 479 U.S. 817 (1986) (*quoting Klishewich v. Mediterranean Agencies. Inc.,* 302 F. Supp. 712, 713 (E.D.N.Y. 1969)); *see P&E Boat Rentals, Inc. v. Ennia General Ins. Co.,* 872 F.2d 642, 647 (5th Cir. 1989). Therefore, to succeed, VCI must show that the intent of its time-charter agreement with the United States was that the United States would be liable for injuries such as the one incurred by seaman Padro here.

C. The Time-Charter Agreement

The time-charter agreement between VCI and the United States contains two provisions deemed dispositive by the *Williams* court in finding jurisdiction over the private ship owner for the seaman's injuries. The persuasive provisions, articles numbered 22(a) and 31, are numbered identically to the time-charter agreement involved here.

The articles indicate to the Court that VCI retained liability for the negligence of its crew and the unseaworthiness of the SS SANTA ADELA, and thus cannot avail itself of the exclusivity provision in the SIAA.

Article 31, titled "CHARTER NOT A DEMISE," leaves no doubt that a time-charter, as opposed to a demise or a bare-boat charter, is intended. Article 22(a), titled "THE MASTERS, OFFICERS AND CREW," sets forth the parties' responsibilities for the seamen aboard the SS SANTA ADELA. It states in relevant part:

> The Master, Officers and crew of this Vessel shall be appointed or hired by the Owner and shall be deemed to be the servants and agents of the Owner at all times except as otherwise specified in this Charter. The Master of the Vessel shall be under the direction of the Charterer as regards the employment of the Vessel, but shall not be under Charterer's orders as regards navigation, care and custody of the Vessel and care of the cargo.

Additionally, article 21(a), in its last sentence, states that, "[the] Owner shall pay for all expenses incurred in the navigation and management of the Vessel, except as otherwise specifically provided herein."

Reading these articles together, the intent of the time-charter agreement leaves VCI with responsibility for the crew of the SS SANTA ADELA, and, presumably, for any personal injuries sustained by the crew while carrying out its duties. None of the articles of the time-charter agreement unambiguously articulate an intent to pass liability for a seaman's personal injury to the United States. Thus, VCI is required to defend against plaintiff's admiralty claim, which alleges his personal injury while a crewmember aboard the SS SANTA ADELA. Indeed, it would be anomalous to allow VCI, as a private ship owner and private employer, to relieve itself of any obligations to it screw by entering into a contract with a third-party, albeit the United States.

Conclusion

Defendant's motion to dismiss the action under the Suits in Admiralty Act, or, in the alternative, for summary judgment is denied.

So Ordered

---

5. SIAA: "Discretionary Functions" Exception

McMELLON v. UNITED STATES

387 F.3d 329, 2004 AMC 2553 (4th Cir. 2004)

TRAXLER, Circuit Judge

Plaintiffs Carrie A. McMellon, Lori Dawn White, Kathy D. Templeton, and Cheri Call seek damages under the Suits in Admiralty Act, 46 U.S.C.A.App. § § 741-52 (West Supp. 2003) (the "SIAA" or the "Act") for injuries they suffered when they went over the gates of the Robert C. Byrd Locks and Dam while riding jet skis. The district court granted summary judgment in favor of the government, and the plaintiff's appealed. A divided panel of this court concluded that prior precedent from this circuit foreclosed the government's argument that the Suits in Admiralty Act contained an implied discretionary function exception that barred the plaintiffs' claims. The panel also concluded that the government had a duty to warn about the existence of the dam, and the panel reversed the district court's grant of summary judgment and remanded for further proceedings. *See McMellon v. United States,* 338 F.3d 287 (4th Cir.2003) *("McMellon I ").*

The government filed a petition for rehearing *en banc* with regard to the discretionary function exception issue. Sitting *en banc,* we now conclude that the government's waiver of sovereign immunity reflected in the Suits in Admiralty Act is subject to an implied exception similar to the discretionary function exception contained within the Federal Tort Claims Act, 28 U.S.C.A. § § 2671-2680 (West 1994 & Supp. 2003). Accordingly, we vacate the district court's summary judgment order and remand to allow the district court to determine whether the facts of this case fall within that exception to the waiver of sovereign immunity and to conduct any other proceedings that might become necessary.

I.

The relevant facts are set out in detail in the panel's opinion, and we will only briefly recount them here. The plaintiff's were riding two jet skis on the Ohio River in the vicinity of the Robert C. Byrd Locks and Dam, a government-owned and operated facility on the Ohio River. The plaintiffs approached what they believed to be a bridge but which turned out to be the gates of the dam. Unable to stop or turn around, the plaintiffs were injured when they went over the gates and dropped approximately twenty-five feet to the water below. At the time of the accident, there were several warning signs on the upstream side of the dam, but the plaintiffs did not see them, and their evidence indicated that the signs were difficult to see from the river. The plaintiffs brought this action under the SIAA, alleging that the government had a duty to warn about the dangers of the dam and that the signs in place were inadequate to satisfy this duty.

The government moved to dismiss, arguing that it was protected by an implied discretionary function exception to the SIAAs waiver of sovereign immunity. The government also moved for summary judgment on the merits of the plaintiffs' claims on the grounds that it had no duty to warn about the dam and that the warnings it provided were, in any event, adequate.

Relying on prior authority from this court, the district court rejected the government's claim that it was protected by an implied discretionary function exception. The court, however, granted the government's motion for summary judgment, concluding that the government had no duty to warn about the dam. The panel in *McMellon I* agreed with the district judge on the first point, but reversed the grant of summary judgment, concluding that the government in fact had a duty to warn. As noted above, we granted rehearing *en banc* to consider whether the SIAA contains an implied discretionary function exception to its waiver of sovereign immunity.

II.

At the heart of the question presented to this *en banc* court is the continuing viability of *Lane v. United States*, 529 F.2d 175 (4th Cir. 1975). In *Lane*, this court flatly rejected the argument that a discretionary function exception should be read into the SIAA. After *Lane*, however, two cases from this circuit arguably applied some form of a discretionary function exception to cases arising under the SIAA. *See Tiffany v. United States*, 931 F.2d 271, 276-77 (4th Cir. 1991); *Faust v. South Carolina State Highway Dep't*, 721 F.2d 934, 939 (4th Cir. 1983).

Because we are sitting *en banc*, there is no doubt that we have the power to overrule *Lane* should we conclude it was wrongly decided. *See, e.g., United States v. Lancaster*, 96 F.3d 734, 742 n. 7 (4th Cir. 1996) (en banc). The panel opinions in this case, however, raised the question of whether a panel of this court may likewise overrule a decision issued by another panel. The question of the binding effect of a panel opinion on subsequent panels is of utmost importance to the operation of this court and the development of the law in this circuit. Accordingly, before considering the merits of the discretionary function question, we first address this important procedural issue.

[After considering this procedural issue at some length, the court stated its conclusion as follows. Because *Lane* was the panel case first decided, that meant that it should be followed in preference to *Tiffany* and *Faust* — unless overruled by the *en banc* court in the present case. Eds.]

While we recognize that a three-judge panel has the statutory and constitutional power to overrule the decision of another three-judge panel, we believe that, as a matter of prudence, a three-judge panel of this court should not exercise that power. Accordingly, we conclude that when there is an irreconcilable conflict between opinions issued by three-judge panels of this court, the first case to decide the issue is the one that must be followed, unless and until it is overruled by this court sitting *en banc* or by the Supreme Court.

III.

We now proceed to the question that we granted rehearing *en banc* to consider: Whether we should overrule *Lane* and read into the SIAA a discretionary function exception. To put this issue in the proper context, some historical background is necessary.

During the first part of this century, the United States government had yet to waive its sovereign immunity in admiralty actions. Thus, if a vessel owned or operated by the government caused damage to a private vessel, the private owner was without recourse, even though the government, of course, could seek damages from a private vessel owner who negligently damaged a government vessel. *See Canadian Aviator, Ltd. v. United States,* 324 U.S. 215, 219, 65 S.Ct. 639, 89 L.Ed. 901 (1945). Congress frequently passed private bills authorizing relief for particular vessel owner's damaged by the government s actions, a method that proved to be rather cumbersome and inefficient, *see id.,* particularly once the government, through the Shipping Board, became the owner of many merchant vessels. *See Marine Coatings of Alabama v. United States,* 71 F.3d 1558, 1560 (11th Cir.1996). In 1916, Congress passed the Shipping Act, 46 U.S.C.A.App. § 801, which provided that "Shipping Board vessels while employed as merchant vessels were subject to all laws, regulations, and liabilities governing merchant vessels regardless of the fact that the United States owned or had an interest in them." *Canadian Aviator,* 324 U.S. at 219, 65 S.Ct. 639 (internal quotation marks omitted).

The Supreme Court interpreted the Shipping Act to authorize *in rem* actions and attendant arrests and seizure of government vessels. *See The Lake Monroe,* 250 U.S. 246, 39 S.Ct. 460, 63 L.Ed. 962 (1919). Congress responded to that decision in 1920 by passing the Suits in Admiralty Act, which prohibited *in rem* actions but instead authorized *in personam* admiralty actions in cases involving government-owned or operated vessels that were "employed as a merchant vessel." SIAA § 2, 41 Stat. 525-26 (1920). The SIAA expressly granted the government the right to take advantage of all of the statutory limitations of liability available to private parties, *see* SIAA § 6, 41 Stat. 527 (1920), but the Act did not include any exceptions to its waiver of sovereign immunity for the cases that fell within its scope.

For purposes of the original SIAA, a public vessel (such as a naval vessel) was distinct from a government-owned or operated merchant vessel. Accordingly, "the Government's sovereign immunity still prevented a claimant from bringing an *in rem* or any other proceeding in admiralty against the United States for injury caused by a public vessel." *Marine Coatings,* 71 F.3d at 1560. Congress rectified that anomaly in 1925 by passing the Public Vessels Act (the "PVA"), which authorized *in personam* admiralty actions seeking recovery for "damages caused by a public vessel of the United States." 46 U.S.C.A. App. § 781 (West 1975). Like the SIAA, the PVA contained no exceptions to its waiver of sovereign immunity for any particular claims otherwise falling within its scope.

When PVA and SIAA were enacted, Congress had yet to implement a waiver of the government's sovereign immunity as to non-maritime torts. While Congress had long believed that "the Government should assume the obligation to pay damages for the misfeasance of employees in carrying out its work," *Dalehite v. United States,* 346 U.S. 15, 24, 73 S.Ct. 956, 97 L.Ed. 1427 (1953), it took Congress nearly thirty years to reach agreement on the form that the waiver of sovereign immunity should take, *see id.* Finally, in 1946, Congress passed the Federal Tort Claims Act ("FTCA"), 28 U.S.C.A. § § 2671-2680 (West 1994 & Supp. 2003), which waives sovereign immunity for most torts committed by government employees, subject to several statutory exceptions. *See* 28 U.S.C.A. § 2680.

The most important of these exceptions to the waiver of sovereign immunity is the discretionary function exception. In 1942, while Congress was working on what would ultimately become the FTCA, an assistant attorney general testified before the House Judiciary Committee and stated his view that courts probably would not impose liability on the government for discretionary actions, even if the act waiving sovereign immunity did not include a specific exception for such actions. *See Dalehite,* 346 U.S. at 27, 73 S.Ct. 956; *see also United States v. S.A. Empresa de Viacao Aerea Rio Grandense (Varig Airlines),* 467 U.S. 797, 810, 104 S.Ct. 2755, 81 L.Ed.2d 660 (1984). Apparently not content to rely on the courts to protect the government from unintended liability, Congress included an express discretionary function exception in the FTCA. The exception states that the FTCAs waiver of sovereign immunity does not apply to claims "based upon the exercise or performance or the failure to exercise or perform a discretionary function or duty on the part of a federal agency or an employee of the Government, whether or not the discretion involved be abused." 28 U.S.C.A. § 2680(a).

The FTCA excludes from its reach claims for which a remedy is provided by the SIAA or the PVA. *See* 28 U.S.C.A. § 2680(d). In 1946, when the FTCA was enacted, the SIAA and PVA waived sovereign immunity only in cases involving public or merchant vessels. Thus, admiralty tort actions not involving public or merchant vessels could be pursued against the government under the FTCA. *See United States v. United Cont'l Tuna Corp.*, 425 U.S. 164, 172, 96 S.Ct. 1319, 47 L.Ed.2d 653 (1976) (explaining that "[m]aritime tort claims deemed beyond the reach of [the SIAA and PVA] could be brought only on the law side of the district courts under the Federal Tort Claims Act"); *see also Somerset Seafood Co. v. United States*, 193 F.2d 631, 634 (4th Cir. 1951) (concluding that certain maritime claims fell within the jurisdictional scope of the FTCA rather than the SIAA). Of course, any such actions under the FTCA would be subject to the limitations of that act, including the discretionary function exception.

During this time, the practice of maritime law proved to be exceedingly complex. The distinction between public vessels (subject to suit under the PVA) and merchant vessels (subject to suit under the SIAA) was elusive, and, beyond noting that the categories were mutually exclusive, courts had difficulty precisely articulating the difference between the types of vessels. *See Continental Tuna*, 425 U.S. at 172 n. 1, 96 S.Ct. 1319; *see also Blanco v. United States*, 775 F.2d 53, 57 n. 4 (2nd Cir. 1985). To further complicate matters, the Tucker Act provided that general contract actions against the government fell either within the exclusive jurisdiction of the Court of Claims or the concurrent jurisdiction of the Court of Claims and the district court, depending on the amount in controversy. *See Blanco*, 775 F.2d at 57 n. 4. But once the SIAA was passed, most (but not all) maritime contract actions involving the government fell within the admiralty jurisdiction of the district courts and were not subject to the Tucker Act. *See Matson Navigation Co. v. United States*, 284 U.S. 352, 359-60, 52 S.Ct. 162, 76 L.Ed. 336 (1932) (holding that the Court of Claims lacked jurisdiction over a contract whose subject matter was covered by the Suits in Admiralty Act); *see also Continental Tuna*, 425 U.S. at 172, 96 S.Ct. 1319 (explaining that "contract claims not encompassed by [the PVA or the SIAA] fell within the Tucker Act, which lodged exclusive jurisdiction in the Court of Claims for claims exceeding $10,000"). If an admiralty practitioner guessed wrong and filed in the wrong court or under the wrong act, the consequences could be dire, because the statutes of limitations under the SIAA and the PVA were substantially shorter than that of the Tucker Act, and there was no procedure for transferring cases between the Court of Claims and the district courts. *See Continental Tuna*, 425 U.S. at 172-73, 96 S.Ct. 1319; *Blanco*, 775 F.2d at 57 n. 4.

Congress put an end to these problems in 1960. First, Congress authorized transfers between the Court of Claims and district courts for cases filed in the wrong court. *See* Pub.L. No. 86-770, § § 1-2, 74 Stat. 912 (1960). In addition, Congress amended the SIAA by eliminating the reference to "merchant vessel." *See id*, § 3, 74 Stat. 912 (1960). Thus, after the 1960 amendments, the SIAA authorized *in personam* admiralty actions against the United States "[i]n cases where if such vessel were privately owned or operated, or if such cargo were privately owned or possessed, or if a private person or property were involved, a proceeding in admiralty could be maintained." 46 U.S.C.AApp. § 742 (West Supp.2003). As is relevant to this case, the 1960 amendments worked no other substantive change to the SIAA. Specifically, no limitations on the waiver of sovereign immunity similar to those contained in the FTCA were added to the Act.

There is no indication in the legislative history that Congress intended the 1960 amendments to do anything other than correct the jurisdictional problems mentioned above. Nonetheless, courts have consistently concluded that the 1960 amendments greatly expanded the reach of the SIAA to include essentially all admiralty tort actions that could be asserted against the government. *See, e.g., Trautman v. Buck Steber, Inc.*, 693 F.2d 440, 444 (5th Cir. 1982); *Bearce v. United States*, 614 F.2d 556, 558 (7th Cir. 1980); *Kelly v. United States*, 531 F.2d 1144, 1148-49 (2nd Cir. 1976); *Lane*, 529 F.2d at 179. Thus, after the 1960 amendments, admiralty actions that previously would have been brought under the FTCA instead had to be brought under the SIAA—both the SIAA and the FTCA make it clear that the SIAA provides the exclusive remedy for cases falling within its scope. *See* 46 U.S.C.A. § 745 ("[W]here a remedy is provided by this chapter it shall hereafter be exclusive of any other action by reason of the same subject matter...."); 28 U.S.C.A. § 2680(d) (excluding from the FTCA "[a]ny claim for which a remedy is provided by sections 741-752, 781-790 of Title 46, relating to claims or suits in admiralty against the United States").

After the 1960 amendments to the SIAA, questions began to arise as to whether the SIAA should be read to include an implied discretionary function exception. After all, the admiralty claims that had previously fallen under the FTCA had been subject to that act's discretionary function exception. If the SIAA did not include a discretionary function exception at least as to those claims that previously would have been brought under the FTCA, then the government would suddenly be exposed to liability in areas where it had been protected.

The argument that the SIAA included an implied discretionary function exception initially was not very well received. In *De Bardeleben Marine Corp. v. United States*, 451 F.2d 140 (5th Cir. 1971), the Fifth Circuit concluded that a review of the language of the amended SIAA and its legislative history foreclosed the argument:

> It is true that the legislative history says nothing concerning a purpose to surrender immunity [as to claims previously within the scope of the FTCA]. It is equally true, though, that § 742 by its own terms disavows governmental immunity in admiralty actions against the United States. Had the sole purpose of the legislation been to clarify the confusing language of the old SIA this would have been better done by modifying the old § 742 to contain a clear definition of merchant, public, vessels and cargoes plus a delineation of contract claims growing out of Governmental shipping operations.
>
> More positively, the legislative history shows that almost on the eve of a probable enactment of a narrowly constructed solution to conflicts in jurisdiction between the Court of Claims and the District Courts, Congress ... set out to solve the underlying problems by eliminating the historic restriction of SIA-PVA liability to noncontractual claims relating to ships or cargo. It was to assimilate the Government to the private person in relation to any or all transactions giving rise to liability in the Admiralty. It would be incongruous to impute to Congress a purpose to perpetrate confusion, not by reason of choosing the wrong forum, but by importing substantive standards of liability and governmental defenses by a retrospective analysis of what would have been the case prior to 1960. Reimportation of FTCA provisions or exceptions produces obviously unintended and irrational distinctions.

Id. at 145-46 (footnotes omitted). This court in *Lane* likewise rejected the argument:

[The SIAA] contains no discretionary function exception, and the Tort Claims Act contains a specific exception of claims for which the Suits in Admiralty Act provides a remedy. Thus it is clear that this action could not have been brought under the Tort Claims Act, and it is properly maintainable under the Suits in Admiralty Act, which is an effective waiver of sovereign immunity.

There is no basis upon which we can import the many exceptions in the Tort Claims Act into the Suits in Admiralty Act, where the United States is to be held accountable in admiralty whenever a private person, in similar circumstances, would be.

Lane, 529 F.2d at 179 (footnotes omitted).

Shortly after *Lane* was decided, however, the tide turned, and courts began accepting the argument that the post-1960 SIAA included an implied discretionary function exception. Coincidentally, the First Circuit was the first circuit to explicitly so conclude. *See Gercey v. United States*, 540 F.2d 536, 539 (1st Cir. 1976). After *Gercey*, every circuit to consider the question likewise concluded that an implied discretionary function exception should be read in the SIAA. *See Tew v. United States*, 86 F.3d 1003, 1005 (10th Cir. 1996); *Earles v. United States*, 935 F.2d 1028, 1032 (9th Cir.1991); *Sea-Land Serv., Inc. v. United States*, 919 F.2d 888, 893 (3d Cir.1990); *Robinson v. United States (In re Joint E. & S. Dists. Asbestos Litig)*, 891 F.2d 31, 34-35 (2d Cir. 1989); *Williams v. United States,* 747 F.2d 700 (11th Cir.1984) (per curiam), *aff'g Williams ex rel. Sharpley v. United States*, 581 F.Supp. 847 (S.D.Ga.1983); *Gemp v. United States*, 684 F.2d 404, 408 (6th Cir. 1982); *Canadian Transp. Co. v. United States,* 663 F.2d 1081, 1085 (D.C.Cir. 1980); *Bearce v. United States*, 614 F.2d 556, 560 (7th Cir. 1980). Even the Fifth Circuit, describing the discussion of the issue in *De Bardeleben* as non-binding dictum, has concluded that the SIAA includes a discretionary function exception. *See Wiggins v. United States,* 799 F.2d 962, 964-66 (5th Cir. 1986).

The question, then, is whether this court should overrule *Lane,* and as a consequence join the other circuits in concluding that the SIAA contains an implied discretionary function exception. For reasons that we will explain below, we conclude that the SIAAs waiver of sovereign immunity should be read to include an implied discretionary function exception to that waiver. Accordingly, we hereby overrule *Lane* to the extent that it concludes the SIAA does not include an implied discretionary function exception.

IV.

In support of its view that the SIAA includes an implied discretionary function exception, the government makes two primary arguments. First, the government contends that Congress did not intend to waive immunity under the SIAA for discretionary actions, and that this court, therefore, should not interpret the SIAA in a manner inconsistent with Congressional intent. Second, the government contends that principles of separation-of-powers require us to exclude discretionary actions from the SIAAs waiver of sovereign immunity. We consider these arguments in turn.

A.

First, we consider the government's argument that we must give effect to what the government contends is a clear Congressional intent to exclude discretionary acts from the SIAAs waiver of sovereign immunity.

The Supreme Court has repeatedly explained that the plain language of a statute is the best evidence of Congressional intent. *See, e.g., Holloway v. United States,* 526 U.S. 1, 6, 119 S.Ct.966, 143L.Ed.2d 1 (1999).As noted above, the SIAA includes no list of exceptions to its waiver of sovereign immunity, but instead provides only that the government is entitled to the limitations of liability that are available in admiralty to private defendants. Thus, the plain language of the SIAA seems to reflect a Congressional intent that discretionary acts should *not* be excluded from the waiver of sovereign immunity. *See Barnhart v. Sigmon Coal Co.,* 534 U.S. 438, 450, 122 S.Ct. 941, 151 L.Ed.2d 908 (2002) (explaining that when construing a statute, "[t]he first step is to determine whether the language at issue has a plain and unambiguous meaning with regard to the particular dispute in the case. The inquiry ceases if the statutory language is unambiguous and the statutory scheme is coherent and consistent." (citations and internal quotation marks omitted)).

The government, however, makes the rather remarkable argument that the legislative history of the *FTCA* supports its view of what Congress intended when it amended the *SIAA* nearly twenty years later. According to the government, the legislative history of the FTCA shows that Congress believed that the courts would not hold the government liable for discretionary acts whether or not the FTCA included an express exception for such actions. *See Varig,* 467 U.S. at 810, 104 S.Ct. 2755; *Dalehite,* 346 U.S. at 27, 73 S.Ct. 956. Accordingly, the government suggests that there was no reason for Congress to include a discretionary function exception when it amended the SIAA in 1960, because Congress assumed that courts would imply such an exception.

This is a difficult argument to accept. First of all, we fail to see how a 1942 legal opinion of an assistant attorney general as to the probability that courts would carve out discretionary acts from a waiver of sovereign immunity is indicative of what Congress did or did not intend some twenty years later. But more importantly, Congress in fact included a discretionary function exception in the FTCA even in the face of a legal opinion that the exception was not necessary. Thus, the discretionary function exception was important enough to Congress in 1946 that Congress included an express exception in the FTCA, to resolve any doubt about whether courts would create such an exception on their own. If the exception remained as important to Congress in 1960 when it amended the SIAA as it was when the FTCA was enacted, then it stands to reason that Congress would have written the exception into the SIAA then, particularly since the 1960 SIAA amendments transferred jurisdiction over a number of claims from the FTCA to the SIAA. *Cf., e.g., Binder v. Long Island Lighting Co.,* 933 F.2d 187, 193 (2nd Cir. 1991) ("Congress enacted the ADEA in the wake of Title VII, and we believe that any omission in the text of the ADEA of a provision found in Title VII is likely to reflect a deliberate decision on Congress's part.").

Likewise, resort to familiar canons of statutory construction fails to support the interpretation urged by the government. For example, it is well established that waivers of sovereign immunity "must be construed strictly in favor of the sovereign and not enlarged beyond what the language requires." *United States v. Nordic Village, Inc.,* 503 U.S. 30, 34, 112 S.Ct. 1011, 117 L.Ed.2d 181 (1992) (citation, internal quotation marks, and alterations omitted); *see also United States v. White Mountain Apache Tribe,* 537 U.S. 465, 472, 123 S.Ct. 1126, 155 L.Ed.2d 40 (2003) ("Jurisdiction over any suit against the Government requires a clear statement from the United States waiving sovereign immunity.... The terms of consent to be sued may not be inferred, but must be unequivocally expressed." (internal quotation marks omitted)). The waiver of sovereign immunity contained within the SIAA, however, is clear and unequivocal, providing that an *in personam* admiralty action may be brought against the government if such an action could be maintained against a private person. Contrary to the government's suggestion, we simply cannot create an ambiguity in the *SIAA* by looking to the language and structure of the *FTCA. Cf. Lamie v. United States Trustee,* 540 U.S. 526, 124 S.Ct. 1023, 1030, 157 L.Ed.2d 1024 (2004) (rejecting argument that statute was ambiguous based on assumption that Congress intended an amended statute to reflect the parallelism of a prior version of the statute: "One determines ambiguity, under this contention, by relying on the grammatical soundness of the prior statute. That contention is wrong. The starting point in discerning congressional intent is the existing statutory text, and not the predecessor statutes." (citation omitted)).

Moreover, even if the maxim requiring narrow construction of waivers of sovereign immunity were applicable, the result urged by the government runs contrary to another maxim of statutory construction which cautions that courts cannot "assume the authority to narrow the waiver that Congress intended." *Smith v. United States,* 507 U.S. 197, 203, 113 S.Ct. 1178, 122 L.Ed.2d 548 (1993); *accord Rayonier Inc. v. United States,* 352 U.S. 315, 320, 77 S.Ct. 374, 1 L.Ed.2d 354 (1957) ("There is no justification for this Court to read exemptions into the [FTCA] beyond those provided by Congress. If the Act is to be altered that is a function for the same body that adopted it.").

Accordingly, we cannot conclude that Congress clearly intended for the SIAA's waiver of sovereign immunity to be subject to an exception for discretionary functions, nor can we reach that conclusion by resort to traditional tools of statutory construction. But as we will explain below, we reach that very result by consideration and application of separation-of-powers principles.

B.

"Even before the birth of this country, separation of powers was known to be a defense against tyranny." *Loving v. United States,* 517 U.S. 748, 756, 116 S.Ct. 1737, 135 L.Ed.2d 36 (1996) (citing Montesquieu, *The Spirit of the Laws* 151-152 (T. Nugent transl. 1949); 1 W. Blackstone, *Commentaries* * 146-*147, *269-*270). Thus,

[t]he Constitution sought to divide the delegated powers of the new Federal Government into three defined categories, Legislative, Executive and Judicial, to assure, as nearly as possible, that each branch of government would confine itself to its assigned responsibility. The hydraulic pressure inherent within each of the separate Branches to exceed the outer limits of its power, even to accomplish desirable objectives, must be resisted.

INS v. Chadha, 462 U.S. 919, 951, 103 S.Ct. 2764, 77 L.Ed.2d 317 (1983).

The "concept of separation of powers," then, is exemplified by "the very structure of the Constitution." *Miller v. French,* 530 U.S. 327, 341, 120 S.Ct. 2246, 147 L.Ed.2d 326 (2000) (internal quotation marks omitted). "The Framers regarded the checks and balances that they had built into the tripartite Federal Government as a self-executing safeguard against the encroachment or aggrandizement of one branch at the expense of the other." *Buckley v. Valeo,* 424 U.S. 1, 122, 96 S.Ct. 612, 46 L.Ed.2d 659 (1976). "While the boundaries between the three branches are not 'hermetically' sealed, the Constitution prohibits one branch from encroaching on the central prerogatives of another." *Miller,* 530 U.S. at 341, 120 S.Ct. 2246 (citation and internal quotation marks omitted).

Accordingly, the Supreme Court has "not hesitated to strike down provisions of law that either accrete to a single Branch powers more appropriately diffused among separate Branches or that undermine the authority and independence of one or another coordinate Branch." *Mistretta v. United States,* 488 U.S. 361, 382, 109 S.Ct. 647, 102 L.Ed.2d 714 (1989). With regard to the Executive Branch, separation-of-powers concerns are focused "on the extent to which [a statute] prevents the Executive Branch from accomplishing its constitutionally assigned functions." *Nixon v. Administrator of Gen. Servs.,* 433 U.S. 425, 443, 97 S.Ct. 2777, 53 L.Ed.2d 867 (1977). In cases involving the Judicial Branch, the Court has traditionally acted to ensure "that the Judicial Branch neither be assigned nor allowed tasks that are more properly accomplished by other branches," and "that no provision of law impermissibly threatens the institutional integrity of the Judicial Branch." *Mistretta,* 488 U.S. at 383, 109 S.Ct. 647 (citation, internal quotation marks and alteration omitted). "Even when a branch does not arrogate power to itself, ... the separation-of-powers doctrine requires that a branch not impair another in the performance of its constitutional duties." *Loving,* 517 U.S. at 757, 116 S.Ct. 1737.

The Supreme Court has made clear that the discretionary function exception contained in the FTCA is grounded in separation-of-powers concerns. As the Court has explained, the exception "marks the boundary between Congress' willingness to impose tort liability upon the United States and its desire to protect certain governmental activities from exposure to suit by private individuals." *Varig Airlines,* 467 U.S. at 808, 104 S.Ct. 2755. Although *Varig* does not use the phrase "separation of powers," the Court's explanation of the purpose behind the exception makes it clear that the exception is a statutory embodiment of separation-of-powers concerns:

Congress wished to prevent judicial 'second-guessing' of legislative and administrative decisions grounded in social, economic, and political policy through the medium of an action in tort. By fashioning an exception for discretionary governmental functions, including regulatory activities, Congress took steps to protect the Government from liability that would seriously handicap efficient government operations.

Id. at 814, 104 S.Ct. 2755 (internal quotation marks omitted); *see also Payton v. United States,* 636 F.2d 132, 143 (5th Cir. 1981) ("The crux of the concept embodied in the discretionary function exception is that of the separation of powers."); *Allen v. United States,* 527 F.Supp. 476, 485 (D.Utah 1981) ("[T]he words 'discretionary function' as used in the Tort Claims Act are really the correlative, the other side of the coin, of the exercise of executive power.").

When the purpose of the discretionary function exception in the FTCA is considered, it becomes apparent that the absence of such an exception in the SIAA is problematic, to say the least. For example, without a discretionary function exception, the government could be held liable for an initial decision to build a dam across a particular navigable waterway or to otherwise change the course of a navigable waterway. *See Coates v. United States,* 181 F.2d 816, 817 (8th Cir. 1950) (concluding that plaintiffs' claim for damage to property caused by the government's decision to change the course of the Missouri River was barred by the discretionary function exception). The government could be held liable for the Coast Guard's drug-interdiction activities. *See Mid-South Holding Co. v. United States,* 225 F.3d 1201, 1206-07 (11th Cir.2000) (concluding that discretionary function exception precluded claim against government for damages to a private vessel that occurred during Coast Guard's search for drugs). The government could perhaps even be held liable for an inaccurate weather forecast. *See Brown v. United States,* 790 F.2d 199, 203-04 (1st Cir. 1986) (concluding that discretionary function exception barred negligence claims brought by relatives of fishermen who drowned during a storm that the National Oceanic and Atmospheric Administration failed to predict).

As these examples illustrate, if the SIAA does not include a discretionary function exception, the executive branch's ability to "faithfully execute [ ]" the law, U.S. Const., art. II § 3, would be substantially impaired. As the Second Circuit has explained,

The wellspring of the discretionary function exception is the doctrine of separation of powers. Simply stated, principles of separation of powers mandate that the judiciary refrain from deciding questions consigned to the concurrent branches of the government....

The doctrine of separation of powers is a doctrine to which the courts must adhere even in the absence of an explicit statutory command. Were we to find the discretionary function exception not to be applicable to the SAA, we would subject all administrative and legislative decisions concerning the public interest in maritime matters to independent judicial review in the not unlikely event that the implementation of those policy judgments were to cause private injuries. Such an outcome is intolerable under our constitutional system of separation of powers.

In re Asbestos Litig., 891 F.2d at 35 (citations and internal quotation marks omitted); *see also Tiffany,* 931 F.2d at 276 ("It is plain that the discretionary function exception to tort liability serves separation of powers principles by preventing judicial second-guessing of legislative and administrative decisions grounded in social, economic, and political policy through the medium of an action in tort." (alteration and internal quotation marks omitted)).

Moreover, if all executive-branch actions taking place in the maritime arena were subject to judicial review, the judiciary would be called upon to decide issues it is not equipped to resolve. We do not mean to suggest, of course, that judicial review is not the core responsibility of the judiciary, or that judicial review of all executive actions would impair the executive's obligation to faithfully execute the laws. But where the executive's discretionary functions are at issue, interference from the judicial branch is inappropriate. The discretionary function exception

articulate[s] a policy of preventing tort actions from becoming a vehicle for judicial interference with decisionmaking that is properly exercised by other branches of government.... Statutes, regulations, and discretionary functions, the subject matter of § 2680(a), are, as a rule, manifestations of policy judgments made by the political branches. In our tripartite governmental structure, the courts generally have no substantive part to play in such decisions. Rather the judiciary confines itself ... to adjudication of facts based on discernible objective standards of law. In the context of tort actions, ... these objective standards are notably lacking when the question is not negligence but social wisdom, not due care but political practicability, not reasonableness but economic expediency. Tort law simply furnishes an inadequate crucible for testing the merits of social, political, or economic decisions.

Blessing v. United States, 447 F.Supp. 1160, 1170 (E.D.Pa. 1978) (Becker, J.) (footnote omitted).

Because our structural separation of powers is "a self-executing safeguard against the encroachment or aggrandizement of one branch at the expense of another," *Buckley,* 424 U.S. at 122, 96 S.Ct. 612, we must read the SIAA in a way that is consistent with those principles. *See Limar Shipping, Ltd. v. United States,* 324 F.3d 1, 7 (1st Cir.2003) (applying discretionary function exception to SIAA and explaining that the "[a]bsence of an express Congressional directive to the contrary will not be read as a green light for federal courts to assume power to review all administrative and legislative decisions concerning the public interest in maritime matters") (internal quotation marks omitted); *Sea-Land Serv.,* 919 F.2d at 891 ("We understand *Varig* to teach that, as a matter of judicial construction, we should not read a general waiver of sovereign immunity to include a waiver of immunity with respect to damage occasioned by policy decisions. Accordingly, we hold that the SAA, which explicitly contains only a general waiver, also implicitly contains a discretionary function exception to its waiver of sovereign immunity."); *In re Joint Asbestos Litig,* 891 F.2d at 35 ("[W]e find the SAA to be subject to the discretionary function exception. This result is compelled by our steadfast refusal to assume powers that are vested in the concurrent branches."); *Canadian Transport Co. v. United States,* 663 F.2d 1081, 1086 (D.C.Cir.1980) (explaining that the discretionary function exception is "derived from the doctrine of separation of powers, a doctrine to which the courts must adhere even in the absence of an explicit statutory command.... Our recognition of a discretionary function exception in the Suits in Admiralty Act, therefore, is not an attempt to rewrite the statute, but merely an acknowledgment of the limits of judicial power."). Accordingly, like the other circuits to have considered the question, we now conclude that separation-of-powers principles require us to read into the SIAAs waiver of sovereign immunity a discretionary function exception.

We pause to note, however, that this conclusion is not as obvious as the cursory analysis of some opinions from other circuits might suggest. We have just explained our belief that the discretionary function exception embodies separation-of-powers principles that are important enough to require courts to apply a discretionary function exception to statutes that are silent on the issue. Under that analysis, then, one would expect to find cases from the early days of the SIAA and PVA where the courts refused to impose liability on the government for its conduct of discretionary functions. After all, judicial recognition of the inherent constraints of our constitutional structure is hardly new. The early case law, however, is more equivocal on this score than might be expected.

Certainly there are some early cases where courts using separation-of-powers-like language have questioned the wisdom of holding the government liable for the actions at issue in those cases. For example, in *Mandel v. United States*, 191 F.2d 164 (3rd Cir. 1951), *aff'd sub nom. Johansen v. United States*, 343 U.S. 427, 72 S.Ct. 849, 96 L.Ed. 1051 (1952), the court considered a claim filed under the PVA by the estate of a civilian employee killed when the vessel to which he was assigned hit a mine in an Italian port during World War II. After concluding that the estates sole remedy was under the Federal Employees Compensation Act, *see id.* at 166, the court stated that

> it would not be in the public interest to have judicial review of the question of negligence in the conduct of military, or semi-military, operations. The operation of ships or land forces in the presence of the enemy is a matter where judgments frequently have to be made quickly and where judgments so made by commanding officers must have prompt and immediate response. It will not, we think, aid in the operation of the armed forces if the propriety of a commanders judgment is to be tested months or years afterwards by a court or a court and jury. What, in the light of subsequent events, may appear to be a lack of caution may have been the very thing necessary, or apparently necessary, at the time the action was taken.
>
> ...
>
> .... No judge has it as part of his task to act as an intelligence officer for the armed forces. He cannot tell how the facts developed out of one incident, seemingly isolated and unimportant, may fit into a larger picture worked upon by an active and skilled hostile espionage system. We do not think he should be called upon to pass upon such a question.

Id. at 167, 168.

The Third Circuit articulated a similar analysis in *P. Dougherty Co. v. United States*, 207 F.2d 626 (3rd Cir. 1953) (en banc). In *Dougherty*, a private barge was damaged in a collision, and a Coast Guard cutter was sent to tow the barge to a harbor. Problems arose as the cutter approached the harbor with the barge in tow, and the cutter was eventually forced to cut the towing hawser. Adrift, the barge pounded against a breakwater for almost an hour and suffered substantial damage. The Third Circuit determined, for several reasons, that while the Coast Guard was negligent, that negligence did not give rise to liability on the part of the government. The court went on to say that public policy prevents the government from being held liable under the PVA "for fault of the Coast Guard in the conduct of a rescue operation at sea." *Id.* at 634. The court explained:

> There are two arrows in the quiver of this public policy. The first may be directed to the inevitable consequence on the morale and effectiveness of the Coast Guard if the conduct of its officers and personnel in the field of rescue operations under the indescribable strains, hazards and crises which attend them, is to be scrutinized, weighed in delicate balance and adjudicated by Monday-morning judicial quarterbacks functioning in an atmosphere of Serenity and deliberation far from the madding crowd of tensions, immediacy and compulsions which confront the doers and not the reviewers.
>
> .... A judicial determination that officers or men of the Coast Guard have been negligent in rescue operations would inevitably have a concomitant effect upon their service records. Aware of that fact, the instinct of self-

preservation would inevitably function even under the pressures of life or death crises which so often arise in rescue operations when members of the Coast Guard are called upon to make decisions. If men are to be brought to an abrupt halt in the midst of crisis—to think first that if they err in their performance they may expose their Government to financial loss and themselves to disciplinary measures or loss of existing status, and then to pause and deliberate and weigh the chances of success or failure in alternate rescue procedures, the delay may often prove fatal to the distressed who urgently require their immediate aid. Thus would the point of the second arrow in the quiver of public policy be blunted the arrow which is directed to preserve in the public interest our merchant marine and that of other nations with which we trade.

History establishes that tragic losses in men and ships all too frequently attend disasters at sea, and too often is it impossible to give successful succor despite the most gallant and efficient of efforts. To expose the men in the Coast Guard to the double jeopardy of possible loss of their own lives, and loss of status in their chosen careers, because they failed, in coping with the intrinsic perils of navigation, to select the most desirable of available procedures, or their skill was not equal to the occasion, is unthinkable and against the public interest.

Id. at 634-35 (footnotes omitted).

Thus, both *Mandel* and *Dougherty* seem to apply what amounts to a discretionary function exception. However, there is little indication in these opinions that the courts were considering the broader question of whether it is ever appropriate for a court to hold the government liable for its discretionary functions.

On the other hand, there are cases decided under the pre-1960 SIAA or PVA where the governments potential liability was determined by a straightforward application of common law principles, without mention of a discretionary function exception, even though the circumstances of the cases would seem to at least warrant a discussion of the possibility of such an exception. For example, in *McAllister v. United States,* 348 U.S. 19, 75 S.Ct. 6, 99 L.Ed. 20 (1954), the Supreme Court concluded that the government was liable under the SIAA to a seaman who contracted polio while serving on a ship located in Chinese waters in the fall of 1945, shortly after the World-War-II surrender of Japan. The government knew that polio was then prevalent in Shanghai, and the Court concluded that the government's decision to allow Chinese soldiers and stevedores from Shanghai "to have the run of the ship and use of its facilities" supported the district courts determination that the government was negligent. *Id.* at 21, 75 S.Ct. 6. There was no consideration of the possibility that the governments actions might fall within a discretionary function exception to the SIAA's waiver of sovereign immunity.

Likewise, in *Canadian Aviator, Ltd. v. United States,* 324 U.S. 215, 65 S.Ct. 639, 89 L.Ed. 901 (1945), the crew of a Navy patrol boat during World War II instructed a private vessel that the patrol boat would escort it into the Delaware Bay. As the private vessel followed the patrol boat directly astern, as ordered by the Navy crew, the private vessel struck a submerged wreck and was damaged. The owner of the private vessel sued the government under the PVA, arguing that the collision was caused by the negligence of the Navy crew. The issue before the Supreme Court was whether the PVA extended to claims where the damage was caused by the crew of a public vessel rather than by the public vessel itself. The Supreme Court concluded that the PVA did extend to such claims, and the Court therefore vacated the decision of the appellate court and remanded for further proceedings. *See id.* at 224-25, 65 S.Ct. 639. The factual setting of *Canadian Aviator*—the actions of a Navy patrol boat during war—would seem to make the case a good candidate for consideration of a discretionary function exception. But there is no indication in the opinions of the district court, the court of appeals, or the Supreme Court that the possibility of such an exception was ever suggested by the government or considered by the courts.

Likewise, there are several older circuit-court cases where the factual setting would seem to warrant consideration of a discretionary function exception, yet the opinions are silent in that regard. *See United States v. The S.S. Washington,* 241 F.2d 819, 821 (4th Cir. 1957) (concluding that government and private vessel were both at fault for collision between private vessel and Navy destroyer that was returning to its position in a flotilla of Navy vessels after completing a mission to pick up soldiers; possibility of a discretionary function exception was not discussed);

Pacific-Atlantic S.S. Co. v. United States, 175 F.2d 632 (4th Cir. 1949) (concluding that government was not at fault in collision between private vessel and Navy battleship which, "[d]ue to war conditions," was zig-zagging and operating without lights; court did not consider the possibility of a discretionary function exception); *United States v. The Australia Star,* 172 F.2d 472, 476 (2nd Cir. 1949) (concluding that, with regard to 1944 collision between the S.S. Hindoo and the S.S. Australian Star, the United States naval vessel that was escorting the Hindoo was partially responsible for the collision; no discussion of a possible discretionary function exception even though duty of commander of Navy escort was "to do what ... would safeguard the Hindoo" and the commander "had authority to give an emergency war time order to any Allied merchant vessel").

The ambiguity of the pre-1960 cases with regard to a broad discretionary function exception to the SIAA or PVA could indicate that, at least in the view of early courts, the exception was not warranted in maritime cases. But since some admiralty actions were cognizable under the FTCA before the 1960 SIAA amendments, it is clear that a discretionary function exception is not *per se* inappropriate or unwarranted in the maritime arena. Alternatively, the relative silence of the pre-1960 cases with regard to a discretionary function exception under the SIAA or PVA could indicate that there is something about those particular claims that warrants different treatment. That is, it could be that the nature of claims that were never cognizable under the FTCA and have always been cognizable only under the SIAA or the PVA is such that it would rarely be appropriate to apply a discretionary function exception as to those cases. If that were the case, then perhaps the discretionary function exception that we believe must be read into the SIAA should be limited to those claims that, before the 1960 amendments, were cognizable only under the FTCA. Claims that could have been brought under the SIAA before it was amended would not be subject to the exception.

We cannot, however, conceive of a difference in the nature of the claims that were cognizable under the FTCA and those that were cognizable only under the SIAA or the PVA that is substantial enough to warrant such a result. Broadly speaking, the PVA and pre-1960 SIAA applied to claims involving government vessels, public or merchant. Thus, the cases that were cognizable under the FTCA were those cases where the injury was not caused by a government vessel or its crew yet still fell within the admiralty jurisdiction of the federal courts. If anything, it seems that cases involving public or merchant vessels are more likely to involve the executives discretionary functions into which the judiciary should not intrude.

More importantly, however, any such limitation on the application of the discretionary function exception would give too much effect to the ambiguity of pre-1960 case law. While it may be that the preamendments courts did not consider the possibility of some form of a discretionary function exception because such an exception was not viewed as appropriate, the failure to address the issue could just as easily be attributed to some other factor— for example, the government's failure to press the issue. In any event, we do not believe that we can subordinate compelling separation-of-powers concerns to the ambiguous silence of the early SIAA and PVA cases. Accordingly, we conclude that a discretionary function exception applies to all cases brought under the SIAA, without regard to whether the claims, prior to the 1960 amendments, would have been brought under the FTCA or the SIAA. We now turn to one final point with regard to the scope of the SIAA's discretionary function exception. At oral argument, counsel for the plaintiff's suggested that the exception as it has developed under the FTCA has strayed beyond that which is required by separation-of-powers principles. That is, counsel contends that courts have applied the exception to exonerate the government from cases where an imposition of liability would not have been inconsistent with separation-of-powers principles. Thus, counsel argues that this court should not read into the SIAA an exception that is co-extensive with the exception as applied under the FTCA, but that we should instead hold that the SIAA is subject to a discretionary function exception only and to the precise extent necessary to serve the principles of separation of powers. If imposition of liability in any given case would not be offensive to separation-of-powers principles, then the government's conduct should not be excused, even if case law developed under the FTCA would characterize the government s action as falling within the discretionary function exception.

At bottom, counsel's argument reflects a concern that the discretionary function exception has been applied too broadly under the FTCA and that it will likewise be applied too broadly under the SIAA. While it may be that courts have in some instances applied the FTCAs discretionary function exception more broadly than Congress intended or than might be strictly required under separation-of-powers principles, these occasional judicial errors do not warrant a wholesale retreat from a body of law that has been developed and refined over the course of almost fifty years. As we have explained, separation-of-powers principles require us to read a discretionary function exception into the SIAA, and it was those same separation-of-powers concerns that drove Congress to create the discretionary function exception to the FTCA. *See Varig Airlines,* 467 U.S. at 808, 104 S.Ct. 2755 (explaining that the discretionary function exception "marks the boundary between Congress' willingness to impose tort liability upon the United States and its desire to protect certain governmental activities from exposure to suit by private individuals"). In our view, the discretionary function exception as it has been developed and applied under the FTCA is the best embodiment of those separation-of-powers concerns, and we believe that it is therefore appropriate for FTCA cases to guide the application of the exception under the SIAA.

V.

To summarize, we adhere to the rule previously applied in this circuit that requires a panel of this court faced with conflicting panel opinions to follow the earlier case. On the merits of the issue raised by the government, we conclude that, although the statute is silent on the issue, the SIAA must be read to include a discretionary function exception to its waiver of sovereign immunity. We hereby overrule *Lane v. United States,* 529 F.2d 175 (4th Cir. 1975), to the extent that it concluded that a discretionary function exception does not apply to cases brought under the SIAA. Because the discretionary function exception under the FTCA and the exception that we apply today to the SIAA are both grounded in concerns of separation of powers, the scope of the discretionary function exception under the SIAA should mirror that of the FTCA, and discretionary function cases decided under the FTCA should guide decisions under the SIAA. The district court in this case concluded as a legal matter that a discretionary function exception was not available to the government in this case, and the court therefore did not consider whether the facts of the case warranted application of such an exception. Accordingly, we vacate the order of the district court and remand to give the district court the opportunity to decide in the first instance whether the discretionary function exception we recognize today precludes the plaintiffs' claims and to conduct any other proceedings that might become necessary.

VACATED AND REMANDED.

WILKINS, Chief Judge, and WILLIAMS, KING, SHEDD and DUNCAN, Circuit Judges, concurred in the opinion of the Court.

WILKINSON, Circuit Judge, wrote a separate concurring opinion.

NIEMEYER, Circuit Judge, wrote an opinion concurring in part and dissenting in part.

MOTZ, Circuit Judge, wrote an opinion concurring in part and dissenting in part; MICHAEL, Circuit Judge, joined in that opinion.

WIDENER, Circuit Judge, LUTTIG, Circuit Judge and GREGORY, Circuit Judge, wrote separate dissenting opinions.

Note

In *Eklof Marine Corp. v. U.S.,* 762 F.2d 200, 1985 AMC 2141 (2d Cir. 1985), the court held that because the U.S. Coast Guard had taken some action to mark an obstruction to navigation or maritime danger, a duty arose to do so in a way that did not create a new hazard. Because the court held that the precise manner of marking the obstruction was not a discretionary act, it found it unnecessary to address the question whether the "discretionary function exception" in the F.T.C.A. is also implied into the S.I.A.A. The court said:

> The decision, however, to place a navigational aid at a particular location or to employ only one such aid at that location, as opposed to the initial decision to mark the obstruction, is not an expression of any "policy" of which we are aware and does not constitute an executive branch decision at a level that would implicate the separation of powers concerns that appellee raises.

Eklof, 762 F.2d 200, 205. (2d Cir. 1985)

B. State and Municipal Governments

FLORIDA DEPT. OF STATE v. TREASURE SALVORS, INC.

458 U.S. 670, 102 S. Ct. 3304, 73 L. Ed. 2d 1057, 1983 AMC 144 (1982)

Justice STEVENS announced the judgment of the Court and delivered an opinion, in which The Chief Justice, Justice MARSHALL, and Justice BLACKMUN joined.

In this admiralty *in rem* action, a federal court attempted to arrest property held by two state officials and bring it within the jurisdiction of the court. The property—artifacts of the *Nuestra Senora de Atocha*, a 17th-century Spanish galleon—was discovered by respondents on the floor of the ocean in international waters. The question presented is whether the Eleventh Amendment immunized the property from the federal court's process.

* * *

Stripped of its procedural complexities and factual glamour, this case presents a narrow legal question. The District Court attempted to seize artifacts held by state officials and to bring the property within its admiralty *in rem* jurisdiction. Although the seizure in this case was extraterritorial, and thus involved an application of Supplemental Admiralty Rule C(5), the question presented for our decision would not be any different if the State merely resisted an attachment of property located within the district.

In response to the warrant of arrest, the State contended that it was immune from the federal process under the Eleventh Amendment.[17] It argued that the contracts executed with Treasure Salvors "alone determined the rights and obligations of the contracting parties...." The difficult question presented in this case is whether a federal court exercising admiralty *in rem* jurisdiction may seize property held by state officials under a claim that the property belongs to the State.[18]

A suit generally may not be maintained directly against the State itself, or against an agency or department of the State, unless the State has waived its sovereign immunity. *Alabama v. Pugh*, 438 U.S. 781. If the State is named directly in the complaint and has not consented to the suit, it must be dismissed from the action. *Id.*, at 782.[19] Of course, the fact that the State should have been dismissed from an action that has proceeded to judgment does not mean that the judgment may not stand against other parties who are not immune from suit.[20]

The Eleventh Amendment does not bar all claims against officers of the State, even when directed to actions taken in their official capacity and defended by the most senior legal officers in the executive branch of the state government. In *Ex parte Young*, 209 U.S. 123, the Court held that an action brought against a state official to enjoin the enforcement of an unconstitutional state statute is not a suit against a State barred by the Eleventh Amendment. In response to the argument that the official in such a case could act only as an officer of the State and that the suit therefore could be characterized only as an action against the State itself, the Court explained:

---

[17] The Eleventh Amendment provides:

> The Judicial power of the United States shall not be construed to extend to any suit in law or equity, commenced or prosecuted against one of the United States by Citizens of another State, or by Citizens or Subjects of any Foreign State.

> Although the Amendment does not literally apply to actions brought against a State by its own citizens, the Amendment long has been held to govern such actions. *Hans v. Louisiana*, 134 U.S. 1. *See Employees v. Missouri Public Health Dept*, 411 U.S. 279, 280; *Edelman v. Jordan*, 415 U.S. 651, 662. Nor does the Amendment literally apply to proceedings in admiralty. Again, however, the Court has found it to govern certain admiralty actions. *See In re New York*, 256 U.S. 490, 500.

[18] The fact that the State appeared and offered defenses on the merits does not foreclose consideration of the Eleventh Amendment issue; "the Eleventh Amendment defense sufficiently partakes of the nature of a jurisdictional bar" that it may be raised at any point of the proceedings. *Edelman v. Jordan, supra*, at 678; *see Ford Motor Co. v. Department of Treasury*, 323 U.S. 459, 467 ("The Eleventh Amendment declares a policy and sets forth an explicit limitation on federal judicial power of such compelling force that this Court will consider the issue arising under this Amendment in this case even though urged for the first time in this Court").

[19] *But see Fitzpatrick v. Bitzer*, 427 U.S. 445, 456 ("Congress may, in determining what is 'appropriate legislation for the purpose of enforcing the provisions of the Fourteenth Amendment, provide for private suits against States or state officials which are constitutionally impermissible in other contexts"); *see also Hutto v. Finney*, 437 U.S. 678; *Maher v. Gagne*, 448 U.S. 122.

[20] Thus, in *Alabama v. Pugh*, our holding that the State of Alabama and the Alabama Board of Corrections should have been dismissed as parties did not affect the substance of the relief granted against a number of Alabama officials responsible for the administration of its prison system.

The act to be enforced is alleged to be unconstitutional, and if it be so, the use of the name of the State to enforce an unconstitutional act to the injury of complainants is a proceeding without the authority of and one which does not affect the State in its sovereign or governmental capacity It is simply an illegal act upon the part of a state official in attempting by the use of the name of the State to enforce a legislative enactment which is void because unconstitutional. If the act which the state Attorney General seeks to enforce is a violation of the Federal Constitution, the officer in proceeding under such enactment comes into conflict with the superior authority of that Constitution, and he is in that case stripped of his official or representative character and is subjected in his person to the consequences of his individual conduct. The State has no power to impart to him any immunity from responsibility to the supreme authority of the United States. *Id.,* at 159-160.

There is a well-recognized irony in *Ex parte Young,* unconstitutional conduct by a state officer may be "state action" for purposes of the Fourteenth Amendment yet not attributable to the State for purposes of the Eleventh. Nevertheless, the rule of *Ex parte Young* is one of the cornerstones of the Courts Eleventh Amendment jurisprudence. *See Edelman v. Jordan,* 415 U.S. 651, 663-664; *Quern v. Jordan,* 440 U.S. 332, 337.

* * *

These cases make clear that the Eleventh Amendment does not bar an action against a state official that is based on a theory that the officer acted beyond the scope of his statutory authority or, if within that authority, that such authority is unconstitutional. In such an action, however, the Amendment places a limit on the relief that may be obtained by the plaintiff. If the action is allowed to proceed against the officer only because he acted without proper authority, the judgment may not compel the State to use its funds to compensate the plaintiff for the injury. In *Edelman v. Jordan,* 415 U.S. 651, the Court made clear that "a suit by private parties seeking to impose a liability which must be paid from public funds in the state treasury is barred by the Eleventh Amendment." *Id.,* at 663. *See Ford Motor Co. v. Department of Treasury,* 323 U.S. 459; *Quern v. Jordan,* 440 U.S., at 337. In determining the relief that may be granted if a state officer is found to have acted without valid statutory authority, the question is whether the relief "[constitutes] permissible prospective relief or a 'retroactive award which requires the payment of funds from the state treasury.'" *Quern v. Jordan, supra,* at 346-347.

III.

In light of the principles set forth above, the proper resolution of the Eleventh Amendment issue raised in this case requires an answer to each of three specific questions: (a) Is this action asserted against officials of the State or is it an action brought directly against the State of Florida itself? (b) Does the challenged conduct of state officials constitute an *ultra vires* or unconstitutional withholding of property or merely a tortious interference with property rights? (c) Is the relief sought by Treasure Salvors permissible prospective relief or is it analogous to a retroactive award that requires "the payment of funds from the state treasury"?

A.

Treasure Salvors filed this admiralty *in rem* action in federal court, seeking a declaration of title to an abandoned sailing vessel that had been discovered on the ocean floor. The State of Florida was not named as a party and was not compelled to appear. Some of the property at issue, however, was held by officials of the Florida Division of Archives. Asserting that it was the rightful owner of the property, Treasure Salvors filed a motion "for an Order commanding the United States Marshal to arrest and take custody of those portions of the Plaintiffs' vessel now being held by L. Ross Morrell or James McBeth or being held under their custody, care or control."[28] As requested, the District Court issued a warrant of arrest commanding the Marshal of the United States for the Southern District of Florida "to take into your possession the portions of said vessel which have been in the possession or are in the possession of L. Ross Morrell and/or James McBeth, or under their custody, care or control and to bring said portions of said vessel within

---

[28] The motion identified L. Ross Morrell as the Director of the Division of Archives and James McBeth as the Bureau Chief of the Historical Museum of the Division of Archives.

the jurisdiction of this Honorable Court and transfer possession of same to the substitute custodian appointed in this action." It is this process from which the State contends it is immune under the Eleventh Amendment.[29]

It is clear that the process at issue was directed only at state officials and not at the State itself or any agency of the State. Neither the fact that the State elected to defend on behalf of its agents, nor the fact that the District Court purported to adjudicate the rights of the State, deprived the federal court of jurisdiction that had been properly invoked over other parties. *See Alabama v. Pugh*, 438 U.S. 781; n.20, *supra*. The process thus is not barred by the Eleventh Amendment as a direct action against the State.

B.

The second question that must be considered is whether the state officials named in the warrant acted without legitimate authority in withholding the property at issue.

* * *

No statutory provision has been advanced that even arguably would authorize officials of the Division of Archives to retain the property at issue. Throughout this litigation, the State has relied solely on the contracts that it executed with Treasure Salvors as a defense to the federal court's process; those contracts were predicated entirely on a state statute that on its face is inapplicable in this case.[34] Actions of state officials in holding property on the assumption that it was found on state land and for that reason belongs to the State—when it is undisputed that the property was not found on state land—is beyond the authority of any reasonable reading of any statute that has been cited to us by the State.

* * *

If a statute of the State of Florida were to authorize state officials to hold artifacts in circumstances such as those presented in this case, a substantial constitutional question would be presented. In essence, the State would have authorized state officials to retain property regardless of the manner in which it was acquired, with no duty to provide compensation for a public taking. If the Constitution provided no protection against such unbridled authority, all property rights would exist only at the whim of the sovereign.

Thus, since the state officials do not have a colorable claim to possession of the artifacts, they may not invoke the Eleventh Amendment to block execution of the warrant of arrest. Of course, the warrant itself merely secures possession of the property; its execution does not finally adjudicate the States right to the artifacts.... In ruling that the Eleventh Amendment does not bar execution of the warrant, we need not decide the extent to which a federal district court exercising admiralty *in rem* jurisdiction over property before the court may adjudicate the rights of claimants to that property as against sovereigns that did not appear and voluntarily assert any claim that they had to the *res*.

C.

Finally, it is clear that the relief sought in this case is consistent with the principles of *Edelman v. Jordan*, 415 U.S. 651. The arrest warrant sought possession of specific property. It did not seek any attachment of state funds and would impose no burden on the state treasury.

* * *

---

[29] As noted, the State immediately filed a motion to quash the warrant. Although that effort failed, the State asserted an Eleventh Amendment defense in its attempt to defeat a transfer of the property—and thus ultimate execution of the warrant—to Treasure Salvors.

[34] The fact that the contracts were executed on the basis of a mistaken understanding concerning the ownership of the *Atocha* cannot, of course, provide Florida with a colorable claim of ownership. For if the mistake had not occurred, it would have been apparent from the outset that Treasure Salvors had no reason to enter into a contract with Florida or any other stranger to the transaction. The State of Florida has never contended that it would benefit from a reformation of the contracts; Treasure Salvors' position does not depend on any change in the terms of the contracts. The Eleventh Amendment analysis in this case does not require any consideration of the doctrine of mistake.

Justice BRENNAN, concurring in the judgment in part and dissenting in part

I agree with the plurality that the Eleventh Amendment prohibited neither an execution of the warrant nor a transfer to respondents of the artifacts at issue in this case.... My rationale for this conclusion differs from the plurality's, however. Both respondents are corporations organized under the laws of the State of Florida. Thus this suit is not "commenced or prosecuted against one of the United States by citizens of another State." U.S. Const., Amdt. 11 (emphasis added). The plurality asserts that this constitutional provision "long has been held to govern" "actions brought against a State by *its own* citizens." *Ante*, at 683, n.17 (emphasis added), *citing Hans v. Louisiana*, 134 U.S. 1 (1890). I have long taken the view that *Hans* did *not* rely upon the Eleventh Amendment, and that that Amendment does *not* bar federal court suits against a State when brought by its own citizens. *See Employees v. Missouri Public Health Dept.*, 411 U.S. 279, 309-322 (1973) (dissenting opinion); *Edelman v. Jordan*, 415 U.S. 651, 687 (1974) (dissenting opinion). I adhere to this view, and I therefore believe that the Eleventh Amendment is wholly inapplicable in the present case. To this extent, I am in agreement with the plurality's disposition.

* * *

Justice WHITE, with whom Justice POWELL, Justice REHNQUIST, and Justice O'CONNOR join, concurring in the judgment in part and dissenting in part

The essence of this litigation is a dispute between the State of Florida and one of its citizens over ownership of treasure. The Eleventh Amendment precludes federal courts from entertaining such suits unless the State agrees to waive its Eleventh Amendment immunity. Because it is the State itself which purports to own the controverted treasure, and because the very nature of this suit, as defined in the complaint and recognized by both the District Court and Court of Appeals, is to determine the State's title to such property, this is not a case subject to the doctrine of *Ex parte Young*, 209 U.S. 123 (1908). In short, this is a suit against the State of Florida, without its permission. Moreover, were the suit to be characterized as one against only state agents, I would find that contract with the State provided a colorable basis upon which the agents could hold the property.

* * *

JUSTICE STEVENS' plurality opinion rests precariously on two transparent fictions. First, it indulges in the fantasy that the enforcement of process by arrest of the *res* is somehow divorced from the action to determine the State's claim to the *res*—a position contradicted by our own most apposite precedents, the two *In re New York* cases, 256 U.S. 490 (1921), and 256 U.S. 503 (1921). That dubious proposition is parlayed by a second fiction—that Florida's Eleventh Amendment freedom from suit is meaningfully safeguarded by not formally rejecting the State's claim to the artifacts although federal agents may seize the contested property and federal courts may adjudicate its title. Neither of these novel propositions follows from *Ex parte Young, supra*. The rule of *Ex parte Young* is premised on the axiom that state officials cannot evade responsibility when their conduct "comes into conflict with the superior authority of [the] Constitution." *Id.*, at 159. Today, the plurality dilutes the probative force behind that cornerstone decision by extrapolating it to allow federal courts to decide a property dispute between a State and one of its citizens, without the State's consent.

* * *

Notes:

Treasure Salvors Cases

In *Treasure Salvors* note the narrowness of the grounds of the Supreme Court's 5-4 decision and that eight of the justices agreed that the holding did not finally dispose of the issue as to the states *right* to the artifacts.

On remand, the Fifth Circuit ordered the artifacts to be turned over to Treasure Salvors: "Unless the State elects voluntarily to appear and to litigate ownership, the court shall enter final judgment in the usual form for *in rem* actions, decreeing Treasure Salvors to be the owner ..., but declaring expressly: 'This judgment does not determine in any way whether the State of Florida is the owner of these artifacts.'" 689 F. 2d 1254, 1256 (5th Cir. 1982).

States' Eleventh Amendment Immunity

A state's immunity from suit in federal court under the Eleventh Amendment presents an obstacle to bringing an admiralty claim in federal court against the state absent express waiver and consent. The Supreme Court has employed a strict approach regarding state waivers of immunity. In *Welch v. State Dept, of Highways and Public Transportation*, 483 U.S. 468, 107 S. Ct. 2941, 97 L. Ed. 2d 389, 1987 AMC 2113 (1987), a Jones Act seaman who was employed by the state of Texas as a ferry-boat crewman brought suit against Texas in federal district court for personal injuries. The Supreme Court upheld the lower court's determinations that Texas had not expressly waived its Eleventh Amendment immunity and found that the language of the Jones Act did not unmistakably evidence congressional intent to allow states to be sued in federal court under the act.

In *Magnolia Marine Transport Co. v. Oklahoma*, 366 F.3d 1153, 2004 AMC 1249 (10th Cir. 2004), the state of Oklahoma moved to dismiss a limitation of liability proceeding brought by the owner of a tugboat that had caused the collapse of a highway bridge, claiming that the tugboat owner's petition was a suit commenced or prosecuted against the state and thus subject to the state's Eleventh Amendment immunity. The U.S. Court of Appeals for the Tenth Circuit dismissed the state's motion, holding that Eleventh Amendment immunity did not apply to limitation proceedings, because:

> The limitation proceeding merely provides a forum for establishing a shipowner's right to limitation of liability and managing disbursement of a limitation fund to claimants who prove Magnolia is liable to them. The limitation proceeding thus lacks the traditional characteristics of a suit against the State.

366 F.3d 1153, 1157 (11th Cir. 2004).

Suits Against Municipal Governments

As a general rule in most states, municipal governments are immune from liability for negligence in performing governmental functions, but not for negligence in performing proprietary functions. *Fenon v. City of Norfolk*, 203 Va. 551, 125 S.E. 2d 808 (1962); *Workman v. City of New York*, 179 U.S. 552, 21 S.Ct. 212, 45 L.Ed. 314 (1900). But how is governmental activity defined? In *Workman*, a divided court took a narrow view of immunity by allowing the City of New York to be sued in admiralty *in personam* in connection with a collision that occurred when the fire boat was engaged in fighting a fire. On the other hand, the court held that the fire boat was not subject to seizure *in rem* since it was owned by the city to provide a governmental function. *But compare The West Point*, 71 F. Supp. 206, 1946 A.M.C. 1532 (E.D. Va. 1946) [ferry boat owned jointly by city and county subject to *in rem* action].

C. Foreign Governments

1. Foreign Sovereign Immunities Act (FSIA)

28 U.S.C. §§1605-1610

§ 1605. General exceptions to the jurisdictional immunity of a foreign state

(a) A foreign state shall not be immune from the jurisdiction of courts of the United States or of the States in any case—

> (1) in which the foreign state has waived its immunity either explicitly or by implication, notwithstanding any withdrawal of the waiver which the foreign state may purport to effect except in accordance with the terms of the waiver;
>
> (2) in which the action is based upon a commercial activity carried on in the United States by the foreign state; or upon an act performed in the United States in connection with a commercial activity of the foreign state elsewhere; or upon an act outside the territory of the United States in connection with a commercial activity of the foreign state elsewhere and that act causes a direct effect in the United State;

(3) in which rights in property taken in violation of international law are in issue and that property or any property exchanged for such property is present in the United States in connection with a commercial activity carried on in the United States by the foreign state; or that property or any property exchanged for such property is owned or operated by an agency or instrumentality of the foreign state and that agency or instrumentality is engaged in a commercial activity in the United States;

(4) in which rights in property in the United States acquired by succession or gift or rights in immovable property situated in the United States are in issue;

(5) not otherwise encompassed in paragraph (2) above, in which money damages are sought against a foreign state for personal injury or death, or damage to or loss of property, occurring in the United States and caused by the tortious act or omission of that foreign state or of any official or employee of that foreign state while acting within the scope of his office or employment; except this paragraph shall not apply to—

(A) any claim based upon the exercise or performance or the failure to exercise or perform a discretionary function regardless of whether the discretion be abused, or

(B) any claim arising out of malicious prosecution, abuse of process, libel, slander, misrepresentation, deceit, or interference with contract rights; or

(6) in which the action is brought, either to enforce an agreement made by the foreign State with or for the benefit of a private party to submit to arbitration all or any differences which have arisen or which may arise between the parties with respect to a defined legal relationship, whether contractual or not, concerning a subject matter capable of settlement by arbitration under the laws of the United States, or to confirm an award made pursuant to such an agreement to arbitrate, if (A) the arbitration takes place or is intended to take place in the United States, (B) the agreement or award is or may be governed by a treaty or other international agreement in force for the United States calling for the recognition and enforcement of arbitral awards, (C) the underlying claim, save for the agreement to arbitrate, could have been brought in a United States court under this section or section 1607, or (D) paragraph (1) of this subsection is otherwise applicable.

(b) A foreign state shall not be immune form the jurisdiction of the courts of the United States in any casein which a suit in admiralty is brought to enforce a maritime lien against a vessel or cargo of the foreign state, which maritimelien is based upon a commercial activity of the foreign state: *Provided*, That—

(1) notice of the suit is given by delivery of a copy of the summons and of the complaint to the person, or his agent, having possession of the vessel or cargo against which the maritime lien is asserted; and if the vessel or cargo is arrested pursuant to process obtained on behalf of the party bringing the suit, the service of process of arrest shall be deemed to constitute valid delivery of such notice, but the party bringing the suit shall be liable for any damages sustained by the foreign state as a result of the arrest if the party bringing the suit had actual or constructive knowledge that the vessel or cargo of a foreign state was involved; and

(2) notice to the foreign state of the commencement of suit as provided in section 1608 of this title is initiated within ten days either of the delivery of notice as provided in paragraph (1) of this subsection or, in the case of a party who was unaware that the vessel or cargo of a foreign state was involved, of the date such party determined the existence of the foreign state's interest.

(c) Whenever notice is delivered under subsection (b)(1), the suit to enforce a maritime lien shall thereafter proceed and shall be heard and determined according to the principles of law and rules of practice of suits *in rem* whenever it appears that, had the vessel been privately owned and possessed, a suit *in rem* might have been maintained. A decree against the foreign state may include costs of the suit and, if the decree is for a money judgment, interest as ordered by the court, except that the court may not award judgment against the foreign state in an amount greater than the value of the vessel or cargo upon which the maritime lien arose. Such value shall be determined as of the time notice is served under subsection (b)(1). Decrees shall be subject to appeal and revision as provided in other cases of admiralty and maritime jurisdiction. Nothing shall preclude the plaintiff in any proper case form seeking relief *in personam* in the same action brought to enforce a maritime lien as provided in this section.

(d) A foreign state shall not be immune from the jurisdiction of the courts of the United States in any action brought to foreclose a preferred mortgage, as defined in the Ship Mortgage Act, 1920 (46 U.S.C. 911 and following). Such action shall be brought, heard, and determined in accordance with the provisions of that Act and in accordance with the principles of law and rules of practice of suits *in rem*, whenever it appears that had the vessel been privately owned and possessed a suit *in rem* might have been maintained.

* * *

§ 1609. Immunity from attachment and execution of property of a foreign state.

Subject to existing international agreements to which the United States is a party at the time of enactment of this Act the property in the United States of a foreign state shall be immune from attachment arrest and execution except as provided in sections 1610 and 1611 of this chapter.

§ 1610. Attachment or Execution

(e) The vessels of a foreign State shall not be immune from arrest *in rem*, interlocutory sale, and execution in actions brought to foreclose a preferred mortgage as provided in section 1605(d).

Note: sanction for suit not permitted by FSIA

The sanction for attempting to arrest or attach a vessel or cargo owned by a foreign state is liability for "any damages sustained by the foreign state as a result of the arrest if the party bringing the suit had actual or constructive knowledge that the vessel or cargo of a foreign state was involved". 28 U.S.C. § 1605(b)(1). In *Coastal Cargo Co. Inc. v. M/V Gustav Sule*, 942 F. Supp. 1082, 1997 AMC 193 (E.D.La. 1996), it was held that this provision did not entitle a foreign state to recover legal fees and expenses incurred in bringing a motion for release of the security it had posted to obtain release of its vessel, because the plaintiff had lacked actual or constructive knowledge of the foreign state s status as bareboat charterer of the vessel at the time of the arrest.

---

2. Jurisdiction

CHINA NAT., ETC. v. M/V LAGO HUALAIHUE

504 F. Supp. 684, 1981 AMC 405 (D. Md. 1981)

Opinion by: THOMSEN

Defendants' motion to dismiss this case for lack of jurisdiction over the subject matter and over the defendants turns upon the proper construction of the Foreign Sovereign Immunities Act of 1976 (hereinafter FSIA), 28 U.S.C. § 1602 *et seq.*, particularly § 1605(b), dealing with maritime claims against foreign states.

I.

Section 1605(b) provides:

1605. General exceptions to the jurisdictional immunity of a foreign state.

(b) A foreign state shall not be immune from the jurisdiction of the courts of the United States in any case in which a suit in admiralty is brought to enforce a maritime lien against a vessel or cargo of the foreign state, which maritime lien is based upon a commercial activity of the foreign state: *Provided,* That

(1) notice of the suit is given by delivery of a copy of the summons and of the complaint to the person, or his agent, having possession of the vessel or cargo against which the maritime lien is asserted; but such notice shall not be deemed to have been delivered, nor may it thereafter be delivered, if the vessel or cargo is arrested pursuant to process obtained on behalf of the party bringing the suit unless the party was unaware that the vessel or cargo of a foreign state was involved, in which event the service of process of arrest shall be deemed to constitute valid delivery of such notice; and

(2) notice to the foreign state of the commencement of suit as provided in section 1608 of this title is initiated within ten days either of the delivery of notice as provided in subsection (b)(1) of this section or, in the case of a party who was unaware that the vessel or cargo of a foreign state was involved, of the date such party determined the existence of the foreign state's interest.

Whenever notice is delivered under subsection (b)(1) of this section, the maritime lien shall thereafter be deemed to be an *in personam* claim against the foreign state which at that time owns the vessel or cargo involved: Provided, That a court may not award judgment against the foreign state in an amount greater than the value of the vessel or cargo upon which the maritime lien arose, such value to be determined as of the time notice is served under subsection (b)(1) of this section.

Added Pub. L. 94-538, § 4(a), Oct. 21, 1976, 90 Stat. 2892.

Section 1603(d), dealing with the definition of certain terms used in the FSIA, states:

A "commercial activity" means either a regular course of commercial conduct or a particular commercial transaction or act. The commercial character of an activity shall be determined by reference to the nature of the course of conduct or particular transaction or act, rather than by reference to its purpose.

II.

Plaintiffs are the owner and insurer of a cargo of chemical fertilizer which, on March 10, 1980, was being carried from the United States to China on the M/V Sapporo Olympics. Defendants are the M/V Lago Hualaihue, a general cargo vessel owned and operated by the other defendant, Empresa Maritima del Estado (Empresa), the Chilean Government Merchant Marine. On March 10, 1980, the defendant vessel, while carrying a commercial cargo of bulk nitrates from Chile to Pensacola, Florida, collided with the M/V Sapporo Olympics in international waters off Panama. Plaintiffs allege that the collision was caused in whole or in part by negligence chargeable to defendants, and by unseaworthiness of the M/V Lago Hualaihue, without any contributory negligence on the part of plaintiffs, and that the collision resulted in some $1,500,000 damage to the chemical fertilizer on the M/V Sapporo Olympics.

After her cargo was discharged in Florida, the M/V Lago Hualaihue came to Baltimore, putting in at Maryland Shipbuilding & Drydock Company for repairs necessitated by the collision and by an allision with a helicopter platform near Galveston, Texas.

Seeking to enforce their alleged maritime lien against the M/V Lago Hualaihue for the cargo damage, plaintiff's brought this action under the FSIA on May 29, 1980. As required by 28 U.S.C. § 1605(b)(1) and (2), appropriate notice of the suit was timely given to the captain of the vessel, who had possession of her, and timely notice, in Spanish as well as in English, was sent to the Presidente of Empresa and to the Chilean Ministro de Relaciones Exteriores, both in Santiago, Chile.

Venue is proper under 28 U.S.C. § 1391(f), as amended by the FSIA.

* * *

It is not disputed that the M/V Lago Hualaihue was at all material times owned and operated by an "agency or instrumentality of a foreign state," as defined in 28 U.S.C. § 1605(b); that said agency or instrumentality (the defendant Empresa) was engaged in the carriage of goods by sea, "a regular course of commercial conduct," as that term is used in § 1603(d), quoted above, and that Empresa's vessel, the M/V Lago Hualaihue was engaged at the time of the collision in carrying a commercial cargo (bulk nitrates) from Chile for delivery in the United States. If the M/V Lago Hualaihue had not been owned by an agency of the Chilean government, it could have been seized by the Marshal of this court under Supplemental Rule F, F. R. Civ. P., and such a case could have resulted in the sale of the vessel. The principal purpose of § 1605(b), quoted at the beginning of this opinion, was and is to provide a forum where the rights and liabilities of the respective parties can be litigated in an admiralty proceeding in which a foreign government is protected from the sale of its vessel to satisfy an adverse judgment. This is made clear by the following passage from the Legislative History, at p. 6620:

> (b) *Maritime liens.* Section 1605(b) denies immunity to a foreign state in cases where (i) a suit in admiralty is brought to enforce a maritime lien against a vessel or cargo of that foreign state, (ii) the maritime lien is based upon a commercial activity of the foreign state, and (iii) the conditions in paragraphs (1) and (2) of section 1605(b) have been complied with.

The purpose of this subsection is the (*sic,* really to) permit a plaintiff to bring suit in a U.S. district court arising out of a maritime lien involving a vessel or cargo of a foreign sovereign without arresting the vessel, by instituting an *in personam* action against the foreign state in a manner analogous to bringing such a suit against the United States. *Cf.* 46 U.S.C. 741, *et seq.* In view of section 1609 of the bill, section 1605(b) is designed to avoid arrests of vessels or cargo of a foreign state to commence a suit. Instead, as provided in paragraph (1), a copy of the summons and complaint must be delivered to the master or other person having possession of the vessel or cargo (such as the second in command of the ship).

If, however, the vessel or its cargo is arrested or attached, the plaintiff will lose his *in personam* remedy and the foreign state will be entitled to immunity except in the case where the plaintiff was unaware that the vessel or cargo of a foreign state was involved....

* * *

The crux of the dispute between the parties is the proper interpretation of the following clause in § 1605(b): "which maritime lien is based upon a commercial activity of the foreign state." Defendants argue that Congress did not intend to include all maritime torts within the coverage of § 1605(b), but only to include those tort claims where there is a commercial relationship between the plaintiff and the foreign state; and, therefore, that Congress used the words "based upon" rather than "arose out of" or "in connection with" so that only maritime liens which would be covered would be liens for supplies, repairs, necessaries, damage to cargo carried on the foreign states ship, breach of charter, crew wages, towage, wharfage, liens on cargo for freight and like liens that are commercial in nature. Plaintiffs reply that Congress did not intend to limit § 1605(b) to cases where there is a commercial relationship between the injured party and the foreign state; rather, that Congress intended to allow plaintiff's, alleging such claims as are alleged in the complaint herein, to bring an action under § 1605(b) where the alleged maritime tort lien arises out of a commercial activity of a foreign state; *e.g.,* the operation of a commercial cargo vessel as distinguished from the operation of a naval vessel.

This court concludes that plaintiffs' interpretation of the statute is correct. The legislative history of the FSIA indicates that § 1605(b) was designed to provide a substitute for the usual *in rem* proceeding and to include collision claims, such as the claim in this case, among those claims which may be asserted against a foreign state if the provisions specified in that subsection are complied with.

* * *

Defendants also argue that "(n)o where in the legislative history of the Act is there any reference to jurisdiction in this country for non-commercial torts or maritime liens based upon torts that a foreign state is alleged to have committed abroad." It is true that there is no specific reference to such a case as the one at bar. On the other hand, there is no language in the Act or in the legislative history which would exclude torts covered by § 1605(b) which a foreign state is alleged to have committed abroad. We are concerned in this case with a suit in admiralty, governed by § 1605(b), and not with a different kind of civil action not governed by that subsection.

This court is satisfied that the allegations of the complaint there in meet the requirements of § 1605(b), and that defendants' motion to dismiss should be denied.

It is so ordered.

CASTILLO v. SHIPPING CORP. OF INDIA

606 F. Supp. 497, 1985 AMC 2926 (S.D.N.Y. 1985)

Gerard L. GOETTEL, U.S.D.J.

The defendant, the Shipping Corp. of India ("SCI"), is a corporation wholly owned by the government of India and formed under the laws of that country. It is engaged in shipping activities in the United States and throughout the world. SCI owns and operates a fleet of vessels, including the State of Andhra Pradesh. That ship has not called at the Port of New York since 1980 and is presently assigned to an Asian route.

On October 14, 1981, Luis Castillo, a citizen and resident of the Dominican Republic, was injured in the Dominican Republic while working aboard the Andhra Pradesh. Castillo alleges that SCI committed numerous negligent acts that were the direct and proximate causes of his injuries. Castillo now brings this action seeking $300,000 in damages. SCI's New York agents and the Indian Embassy in Washington, D.C., have been served with a summons and complaint.

SCI moves to dismiss the action for lack of personal jurisdiction and *forum non conveniens*. SCI asserts that it is a "foreign state" under the Foreign Sovereign Immunities Act of 1976 (the "FSIA" or the "Act"), 28 U.S.C. §§ 1330, 1602-1611 (1982), entitled to immunity from the jurisdiction of the United States' federal and state courts. Both parties buttressed their arguments on this motion with affidavits. Consequently, we treat this as a motion for summary judgment pursuant to FED. R. CIV. P. 56. We may grant the motion only if the memoranda and supporting materials before us "disclose 'that there is no genuine issue as to any material fact and that the moving party is entitled to a judgment as a matter of law.'" C. WRIGHT, A. MILLER & M. KANE, FEDERAL PRACTICE AND PROCEDURE § 2725 (2d ed. 1983) (*quoting* Fed. R. Civ. P. 56(c)). For the reasons stated below, the Court is convinced that the defendant qualifies for the immunity provided by the FSIA. Therefore, its motion for summary judgment is granted.

I. Discussion

A. The Foreign Sovereign Immunities Act

The FSIA regulates the Court's jurisdiction in this case. This relatively new statute raises difficult interpretive questions, but provides little guidance in the resolution of those questions. *See Gibbons v. Udaras na Gaeltachta*, 549 F. Supp. 1094, 1106 (S.D.N.Y. 1982). A tangled web of provisions in the FSIA governs the central issues of subject matter jurisdiction,[1] personal jurisdiction, and sovereign immunity. These, in turn, determine a foreign state's amenability to suit. Section 1330(a) of the Act confers subject matter jurisdiction upon the district courts in certain actions against foreign states "not entitled to immunity." Personal jurisdiction exists when the district court has subject matter jurisdiction and process has been served in conformity with section 1608.[2] 28 U.S.C. § 1330(b)

---

[1] SCI does not argue that this Court lacks subject matter jurisdiction. However, if immunity is recognized under the FSIA, the Court possesses neither subject matter nor personal jurisdiction over the defendant. *Verlinden B. V v. Central Bank of Nigeria*, 461 U.S. 480,485 n.5 (1983). A court can raise the issue of subject matter jurisdiction on its own motion at any time. Fed. R. Civ. P. 12(h) (3).

[2] Section 1608 prescribes acceptable methods of service of process upon a foreign state or its instrumentality. For purposes of section 1605(a)(2), the plaintiff's service upon SCI's agents in New York was proper, 28 U.S.C. § 1608(b)(2) (1982); however, service upon the Indian embassy was improper and ineffective. House Reports 1976 U.S. Code Cong. & Ad. News 6604 at 6625.

(1982). Thus, the absence of sovereign immunity is essential for the existence of subject matter jurisdiction, which, in turn, is necessary for the attainment of personal jurisdiction.[3]

Section 1604 governs claims of sovereign immunity by foreign nations. It provides as follows:

Subject to existing international agreements to which the United States is a party at the time of enactment of this Act a foreign state shall be immune from the jurisdiction of the courts of the United States and of the States except as provided in sections 1605 to 1607 of this chapter.

28 U.S.C. § 1604 (1982). Although this section gives foreign countries a general grant of immunity, it limits the applicability of that immunity. First, the grant may be subject to international agreements. Second, the party seeking refuge under the Act must be a foreign state within the meaning of the FSIA. Finally, the immunity is subject to exceptions contained in other sections of the Act.

That the first two conditions are not germane is undisputed. Neither party alleges or attempts to prove the existence of any international agreement affecting section 1604's grant of immunity. Similarly, both the plaintiff and the defendant agree that SCI is a foreign state as section 1603(b) of the Act defines that term.[4] The sole dispute between the parties and the central issue in the case is whether any of the exceptions to immunity embodied in sections 1605 to 1607 remove the cloak of immunity from the defendant and render it subject to the jurisdiction of this Court. Specifically, the plaintiff asserts that the exception to immunity in the first clause of section 1605(a)(2) and the exception contained in section 1605(b) apply to the defendant and subject it to our jurisdiction.

1. Section 1605(a)(2)

The first clause of section 1605(a)(2) provides that a foreign nation is not immune in actions "based upon a commercial activity carried on in the United States by [that] foreign state." 28 U.S.C. § 1605(a)(2) (1982).[5] Plaintiff Castillo claims that this negligence action, which arose in the Dominican Republic on one of the defendant's vessels, is "based upon" SCI's United States shipping operations within the meaning of section 1605(a)(2). The defendant disputes this contention. Resolution of their dispute requires us to examine the FSIA's language and purposes as well as the cases interpreting the Act.

A commercial activity carried on in the United States is one having substantial contact with this country. 28 U.S.C. § 1603(e) (1982). Castillo alleges that SCI engages in shipping operations in the United States, that its ships call regularly at U.S. ports, and that it earns a large portion of its revenues here. In a supporting affidavit, the plaintiff claims that a spot check of Lloyd's listing revealed that two of SCI's vessels recently called at the Port of New York. Taking these allegations as true for purposes of this motion, we conclude that SCI carries on shipping activities having substantial contact with the United States. *See In re Rio Grande Transport, Inc.*, 516 F. Supp. 1155, 1161 & n.5 (S.D.N.Y. 1981) (citing similar activities as support for asserting jurisdiction under the Act). Moreover, the shipping activities involved in this case are commercial, not governmental, in nature. *See China National Chemical Import & Export Corp. v. M/V Lago Hualaihue*, 504 F. Supp. 684, 689 (D. Md. 1981) (the operation of commercial

---

[3] Confusion has arisen as to the relationship between the statutory provision relating to personal jurisdiction and the due process limitations of the fifth and fourteenth amendments. Some courts, relying on the legislative history of the Act, assert that the FSIAs immunity provisions should be interpreted to embody the due process requirements set forth in *International Shoe v. Washington*, 326 U.S. 310 (1945), and its progeny. *See, e.g., Alberti v. Empresa Nicaraguense de la Carne*, 705 F.2d 250 (7th Cir. 1983). However, the Second Circuit treats the statutory and constitutional questions separately. *See Texas Trading & Milling Corp. v. Federal Bank of Nigeria*, 647 F.2d 300, 308 (2d Cir. 1981), *cert. denied*, 454 U.S. 1148 (1982). The Second Circuits mode of analysis enhances the resolution of the interpretive questions raised by the Act and helps untie "the FSIAs Gordia knot." *Id.* at 307.

[4] Section 1603 defines a foreign state to include an instrumentality of a foreign nation

(1) which is a separate legal person, corporate or otherwise, and

(2) which is an organ of a foreign state ... or a majority of whose shares... is owned by a foreign state or a political subdivision thereof, and

(3) which is neither a citizen of a State of the United States... nor created under the laws of any third country. 28 U.S.C. § 1603(b) (1982). The defendant, a legally distinct corporation, wholly owned by the government of India and incorporated in that country, clearly fits within the definition of a foreign state set out in section 1603. *See, e.g., Sugarman v. Aeromexico, Inc.*, 626 F.2d 270 (3d Cir. 1980), (holding that a Mexican corporation that was wholly owned by the Mexican government was a "foreign state").

[5] The broad or classical theory of sovereign immunity shielded foreign states from any action against them in the court of another sovereign unless they consented to defend the action. *Sugarman v. Aeromexico, Inc., supra*, 626 F.2d at 274. The FSIA codified in large part a more restrictive theory of sovereign immunity. *See Verlinden B. V. v. Central Bank of Nigeria*, 461 U.S. 480, 487-88 (1983); *Sugarman v. Aeromexico, Inc., supra*, 626 F.2d at 274-75. This "restrictive" theory accords immunity only to a foreign state's governmental acts, not to its commercial or private activities. *Sugarman v. Aeromexico, Inc., supra*, 626 F.2d at 274.

cargo vessels is a commercial activity). The issue, then, is whether this action is "based upon" SCI's United States shipping activities within the meaning of section 1605(a)(2).

Courts, attempting to define the words "based upon," have employed a number of formulations to describe the specific connection required between the lawsuit and the United States activity relied upon for jurisdiction. In *Ministry of Supply, Cairo v. Universe Tankships, Inc.*, 708 F.2d 80, 84 (2d Cir. 1983), the Second Circuit stated that the acts sued upon must "comprise an integral part of the states" U.S. activities. The same court, in *Gemini Shipping, Inc. v. Foreign Trade Organization for Chemicals and Foodstuffs*, 647 F.2d 317, 319 (2d Cir. 1981), held that an action on a guarantee was "based upon" the United States activity because it was "part and parcel" of the United States activity. Finally, in *Sugarman v. Aeromexico, Inc.*, 626 F.2d 270, 272 (3d Cir. 1980), the Third Circuit required that a "nexus" exist between the grievance and the activity carried on in this country. In the case before us, jurisdiction would not lie under any of these formulations.

Neither the act complained of nor the injury sustained had any impact on or tie to SCI's commercial activities in this country.[6] The plaintiff's alleged injuries were caused by acts that occurred in the Dominican Republic on a foreign government-owned ship, on a voyage having no connection with the United States. This lawsuit's only link to SCI's shipping activities in the United States is that it occurred on one of the defendants 144 vessels, some of which occasionally call at United States ports. The mere happenstance of an accident on one of SCI's ships moored anywhere in the world cannot convert an ordinary negligence action into one "based upon" SCI's United States activities. To hold otherwise would rob the words "based upon" of all meaning and would convert a federal long arm act, *see* H.R. Rep No. 1487, 94th Cong., 2d Sess., 13, reprinted in 1976 U.S. Code Cong. & Ad. News 6604, 6612 [hereinafter cited as House Reports], into a "doing business" statute. *Vencedora Oceanica Navigacion, S.A. v. Compagnie Nationale Algerienne de Navigation*, 730 F.2d 195, 202-03 (5th Cir. 1984) (*per curiam*); *Harris v. VAO Intourist, supra*, 481 F. Supp. at 1059-63. The result would be to open our courts to suits against most of the world's governmentally-owned transport lines (air as well as sea), since most countries trade with the United States.

The plaintiff relies on *In re Rio Grande Transport, Inc.*, 516 F. Supp. 1155 (S.D.N.Y. 1981), for support. *Rio Grande* involved an action against a foreign instrumentality for wrongful death, personal injury and cargo loss arising out of a collision in the Mediterranean Sea between the foreign state's ship and an American-owned vessel. The court interpreted the phrase "commercial activity" to encompass the foreign states world-wide shipping operations, and held that the suit was "based upon" those activities within the meaning of section 1605(a)(2). *In re Rio Grande Transport, Inc., supra*, 516 F. Supp. at 1161-62.

Rio Grande's far-reaching interpretation has been the subject of much criticism, *see, e.g., Vencedora Oceanica Navigacion, S.A. v. Compagnie Nationale Algerienne de Navigation, supra*, 730 F.2d at 201-03, and is at odds with the overwhelming majority of cases[7] *See, e.g., Paterson, Zochonis (U.K.) Ltd. v. Compania United Arrow, S.A.*, 493 F. Supp. 621 (S.D.N.Y. 1980); *Harris v. VAO Intourist, supra*, 481 F. Supp. 1056. The court itself was sufficiently troubled by its novel interpretation that it also rested its decision upon the third clause of section 1605(a)(2). *See In re Rio Grande Transport, Inc., supra*, 516 F. Supp. at 1162. Although we do not disagree with the *Rio Grande* court's ultimate result, we find the reasoning relied upon by the plaintiff unpersuasive.

Surely, Congress did not intend the FSIA "to open the floodgates to any controversy around the world, against any foreign entity 'doing business' in the United States." *Vencedora Oceanica Navigacion, S.A. v. Campaignie Nationale Algerienne de Navigation, supra*, 730 F.2d at 202; see *also Jurisdiction of U.S. Courts in Suits Against Foreign States: Hearings Before the Subcomm. on Administrative Law and Governmental Relations of the House Comm. on the Judiciary on H.R. 11315*, 94th Cong., 2d Sess. 31 (1976) (statement of Brunon A. Ristau, Chief of the Foreign Litigation Section of the Civil Division of the Justice Department) (the bill was designed to confer jurisdiction only over those disputes having a relation to the United States). Rather, Congress sought to harmonize two competing principles.

---

[6] Of course, the acts giving rise to the cause of action need not take place in the United States, as long as the acts sued upon were performed in connection with the commercial activity carried on in the United States. *Gibbons v. Udaras na Gaeltachta*, 549 F. Supp. 1049, 1108 N.5 (S.D.N.Y. 1982). Nor does the plaintiff have to be a United States citizen to sue under the Act. *Verlinden B.V. v. Central Bank of Nigeria*, 461 U.S. 480 (1983). These factors merely contribute to the overall analysis.

[7] We have found no case decided in the four years since *Rio Grande* that has relied upon the reasoning advanced by the plaintiff.

On one hand, it wanted to further the very purpose of sovereign immunity—the fostering of harmonious relations between nations. On the other hand, Congress sought to provide a forum for persons aggrieved by foreign nations in ordinary legal disputes. HOUSE REPORTS at 6605. Congress struck the balance by conferring a general grant of immunity upon foreign states and then carving out specific exceptions to that immunity. HOUSE REPORTS at 6616. Thus, the FSIA limits the exercise of jurisdiction over foreign states, *Harris v. VAO Intourist,* 481 F. Supp. 1056, 1059 (E.D.N.Y. 1979), to those instances in which the propriety of asserting jurisdiction outweighs the possibility of a harmful impact upon foreign relations. This case is not such an instance. To conclude otherwise would be to strain the language of the Act, ignore its legislative history and frustrate Congressional intent. Accordingly, we hold that this action is not "based upon" the commercial shipping activities carried on in the United States by SCI.

2. Section 1605(b)

The plaintiff next argues that section 1605(b) provides a basis for exercising jurisdiction. That section states that immunity will not extend to admiralty actions brought to enforce maritime liens against vessels of foreign states where the lien is based upon the commercial activity of that foreign state. A further prerequisite to the assertion of jurisdiction under section 1605 is that service be made upon "the person, or his agent, having possession of the vessel," 28 U.S.C. § 1605(b)(1), and upon the foreign state or instrumentality, 28 U.S.C. § 1605(b)(2) (1982). Castillo contends that the service upon SCI's general agents in New York is sufficient under the section 1605(b)(1) and that section 1605(b) is applicable despite the vessels continued absence from this forum. These contentions are wholly without merit.

Section 1605(b) provides a substitute for the usual *in rem* proceeding to enforce a maritime lien. *China National Chemical Import & Export Corp. v. M/V Hualaihue, supra,* 504 F. Supp. at 689 & n.l. The notice requirements replace the conventional requirement that attachment of the foreign vessel precede the exercise of jurisdiction. *Jet Line Services, Inc. v. M/V El Harigo,* 462 F. Supp. 1165, 1174 (D. Md. 1978). Once service has been made, the suit is deemed an *in personam* claim limited to the value of the vessel. 28 U.S.C. § 1605(b) (1982).

Under this section, service must be made on the master of the ship or his second in command, House Reports at 6620. Service on the general agent of the corporate owner is insufficient. Moreover, although Congress has changed the procedures for obtaining jurisdiction, it has not altered the fundamental requirement that the ship be present in the forum when service is effected. The defective service and the vessel's absence from the forum defeat the plaintiff's claim under the Act. Thus, section 1605 (b) does not provide a basis for exercising jurisdiction over the defendant.

* * *

II. Forum Non Conveniens

Even if we were to conclude that the FSIA sanctions the exercise of jurisdiction in this case, we would decline to do so because of the doctrine of *forum non conveniens.* The FSIA has not altered that doctrine, *Verlinden B. V. v. Central Bank of Nigeria,* 461 U.S. 480, 490 n.15 (1983), under which courts have the discretionary power to decline to exercise jurisdiction when a suit would be more appropriately tried elsewhere. *Gulf Oil Corp. v. Gilbert,* 330 U.S. 501, 507 (1947). In applying the doctrine, courts weigh two factors, the parties' convenience and the forum's interests. *Id.* at 508. They consider the availability of compulsory process for unwilling witnesses, the cost of obtaining witnesses, the ease of access to sources of proof, the relation of the litigation to the forum, and the court's familiarity with the applicable laws. *Id.* at 508-09. That this is an action in admiralty does not alter those considerations. Nor does the fact that a plaintiff can expect a larger verdict in American courts. This would be true even if the plaintiff was an American citizen. *Alcoa S.S. Co. v. M/V Nordic Regent,* 654 F.2d 147 (2d Cir. 1981) (*en banc*).

Turning to the facts of this case, it is clear that New York is an inconvenient forum. SCI is a foreign corporation whose witnesses, the crewmen aboard the vessel, are Indian citizens. Castillo is a citizen of the Dominican Republic and his witnesses are located there. Not one witness for either side resides in the United States and all are outside the reach of this Court's compulsory process power. The laws of the Dominican Republic would, in all likelihood, govern this action. Moreover, not one act connected with this lawsuit occurred here. In sum, this litigation has no connection to New York and New York has no interest in this litigation. This action should be dismissed on grounds of *forum non conveniens.*

The plaintiff contends that this Court cannot dismiss the action on *forum non conveniens* grounds because New York is his only available forum. The plaintiff had a most convenient forum, the Dominican Republic. But, through his own inaction, he lost access to it. He let the Dominican Republic's six-month statute of limitations pass and has lost his remedy there, as well as in India, which presumably would follow the Dominican Republic's statute. It would be a strange world if a litigant could "bootstrap" himself into a New York court by missing the statute of limitations in the proper forum.

In re Air Crash Disaster Near Bombay, 531 F. Supp. 1175 (W.D. Wash. 1982), is inapposite. In that case, a number of Indian citizens brought wrongful death actions against United States manufacturers of component parts of an aircraft that had crashed in India. The plaintiffs had instituted their suit within the time limits prescribed by the Indian statute of limitations. By the time the court decided the *forum non conveniens* issue, the Indian statute of limitations had run. The court recognized that *forum non conveniens* would normally apply, even though the defendants were American citizens and the product had been manufactured in this country. Nevertheless, the court declined to dismiss the action because the plaintiffs no longer had an alternative forum for their claims since, under prevailing Indian law, the limitations period could not be waived by the defendant. Unlike the plaintiffs in *In re Air Crash Disaster Near Bombay,* Castillo did not file suit within the time limitations imposed by the Dominican Republic. Had he done so, dismissal here would be conditioned on the defendant not raising a limitations defense to a new action filed promptly in the Dominican Republic. Therefore, we conclude that the doctrine of *forum non conveniens* is both applicable and appropriate in this case. Were we possessed with jurisdiction, we would, nonetheless, dismiss this action.

III. Conclusion

The defendant's motion to dismiss this action is granted. The Clerk will enter judgment accordingly. So ORDERED.

Note: Dismissal Based Upon Forum Non Conveniens

In *Castillo, supra,* the Court stated that even if it possessed jurisdiction under the FSIA, the action would have been dismissed based upon the doctrine of *forum non conveniens.* Even where the FSIA sanctions the exercise of jurisdiction, courts may decline to do so when it would be more appropriate to try a suit elsewhere.

In *Piper Aircraft Co. v. Reyno,*[43] the Supreme Court dismissed an action brought in the United States based on an airplane crash which occurred in Scotland on the common law ground off forum non conveniens. The Court, citing favorably the balancing test set forth in Gulf Oil Corporation v. Gilbert,[44] held that it is within the discretion of the courts to decline jurisdiction over a controversy when the plaintiff's chosen forum is inconvenient or unduly burdensome.

a. Under the Gilbert test, the chosen forum must balance the strong presumption in favor of honoring the plaintiff's choice of forum with the public and private interest factors which point towards adjudication in an alternative forum.

i. Private factors which may be considered include:

— location of evidence
— authority to subpoena need witnesses
— convenience to the parties (resolution of dispute in one trial, ability to implead potential third party defendants)

---

[43] 454 U.S. 235, 102 S.Ct. 252, 70 L.Ed.2d 419, 1982 AMC 214 (1981).
[44] 330 U.S. 501, 67 S.Ct. 839, 91 L.Ed. 1055 (1947).

ii. Public factors to be considered include:

— choice of law
— Jury confusion
— comparative interest of each forum in the litigation
— convenience of the chosen forum (time and energy which may be expended in adjudicating the controversy

b. When the balance falls in favor of the alternative forum, the court may in its discretion dismiss the suit.

c. The fact that the law of the alternative forum may not be favorable to the plaintiff is not a relevant factor in the decision.

d. In *Piper*, the court found that adjudication in Scotland was more appropriate, and dismissed the action.

i. The important evidence and witnesses were all located in Scotland, as were several potential third party defendants.

ii. In addition, the court found that because the plaintiff's were Scottish citizens, that country had a greater interest in adjudicating the dispute.

iii. The court refused to consider evidence indicating that Scottish tort law was not as favorable towards the plaintiff's as was American law.

e. In *Piper*, the plaintiffs were foreign citizens attempting to take advantage of liberal American tort laws.

f. A particularly difficult problem is presented when a U.S. plaintiff is faced with dismissal on *forum non conveniens* grounds. Some courts have held that the plaintiff's special status limits the discretion of the court or precludes completely a dismissal of the action, but the modern trend is to apply the *Gilbert* balancing test without regard to the plaintiff's citizenship.[45] In the context of a diversity case, this analysis makes sense. But should this carry over to other types of cases?

* * *

Note: Suits Against Foreign Governments

Under the FSIA, personal jurisdiction must be obtained over the defendant to maintain suit. Was it a sound policy for Congress to have eliminated the right to proceed *in rem* against a vessel owned by a foreign sovereign or a public trading company? How can a preferred ship mortgage be enforced against a commercial vessel of a foreign state? In 1988, Congress addressed this problem by amending the FSIA. *See* 28 U.S.C. § 1610(e). For an in-depth analysis of this Act prior to the 1988 amendments, *see* Yiannopoulos, *Foreign Sovereign Immunity and the Arrest of State Owned Ships; The Need for an Admiralty FSIA,* 57 Tul. L. Rev. 1274 (1983). For an analysis of the 1988 FSIA amendments, *see* Dorsey, *Recent Admiralty Amendments to the Foreign Sovereign Immunities Act,* MLA Rep. 9260 (1989).

There is no right to a jury trial under the FSIA. However, is FSIA the only basis of jurisdiction in a suit against a foreign government or its instrumentalities? May a plaintiff also invoke "diversity" or "arising under" jurisdiction and claim the right to a jury trial? Demands for jury trials were struck in *Houston v. Murmansk Shipping Co.,* 667 F.2d 1151, 1982 AMC 609 (4th Cir. 1982); *Rex v. Cia Pervana de Vapores,* 660 F.2d 61, 1981 AMC 2900 (3d Cir. 1981); *Williams v. Shipping Corp. of India,* 653 F.2d 875, 1981 AMC 2924 (4th Cir. 1981). *But see Lonon v. Companhia de Navegacion Lloyd Basileiro,* 1980 AMC 1978 (E.D. Pa. 1979). In *Verlinden V.V. v. Central Bank of Nigeria,* 461 U.S. 480, 103 S.Ct. 1962, 76 L. Ed. 2d 81 (1983), the Supreme Court declared that "every action against a Foreign sovereign necessarily involves application of a body of substantive federal law, and accordingly, 'arises under' federal law."

Are the assets of a foreign government immune from attachment or garnishment after a judgment has been rendered against it? *See Birch Shipping v. Embassy of United Republic,* 507 F. Supp. 311, 1981 AMC 2666 (D.D.C. 1980) (garnishment of checking account in the U.S. allowed to enforce arbitration award). Can there be a post-judgment attachment of a vessel of a foreign government?

---

[45] *Compare Aloa S.S. Co., Inc. v. M/V Nordic Regent,* 654 F.2d 147, 1980 AMC 309 (2d Cir.) *cert. denied,* 449 U.S. 890 (1980) (dismissal appropriate if *Gilbert* test is satisfied) *with Mobile Tankers Co., S.A. v. Mene Grande Oil Co.,* 363 F.2d 611 (3rd Cir. 1966) (dismissal inappropriate absent a showing of manifest injustice to the defendant/petitioner) and *Bolden v. Jensen,* 70 F. 505 (1895).

CPSIA information can be obtained
at www.ICGtesting.com
Printed in the USA
BVHW051151271221
624766BV00007B/294